W9-BDD-498

New York City
5-Borough

streetguide

We want to hear from you!
Give us your feedback at:
http://go.randmcnally.com/comments

Help us keep your street guide more accurate than
online maps. If you find an error, report it here:
http://go.randmcnally.com/report

The paper used inside this
book is manufactured using
an elemental chlorine-free method
and is sourced from forests that
are managed responsibly through
forest certification programs such
as the Sustainable Forestry Initiative.®

randmcnally.com
If you have a comment, suggestion, or
even a compliment, please email us at
consumeraffairs@randmcnally.com,
Or write to:
Rand McNally Consumer Affairs
P.O. Box 7600
Chicago, IL 60680-9915

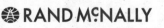

Contents
Contenidos

Introduction
Introducción

Legend   B
Leyenda

Using Your Street Guide   C
Como usar su Street Guide

PageFinder™ Maps   D
Mapas de Páginas

Maps
Mapas

Large Scale Maps   101-121
Mapas de escala grande

Street Guide Detail Maps   6048-7208
Mapas de calles

Lists and Indexes
Lista e índices

List of Abbreviations   1
Lista de abreviaciones

Cities & Communities   2
Indice de ciudades y comunidades

**Street Index and
Points of Interest Index**   4
Indice de calles y
puntos de interés

Legend
Leyenda

Interstate highway	Autopista Federal
Interstate (business) highway	Ruta Comerciál de Autopista Federal
U.S. highway	Carretera Federal
State/provincial highway	Carretera Estatal o Provincial
Secondary state/provincial highway/county highway	Carretera Secundaria Estatal, Provincial, o del Condado
Trans-Canada Highway	Carretera Trans-Canadá
Canadian autoroute	Carretera Trans-Canadá
Mexican highway	Carretera Mexicana
Other highway designation	Carretera de otra designación
Exit number	Número de salida
Free limited-access highway (with tunnel)	Autopista (con sección in túnel)
Toll highway, toll plaza	Autopista de cuota, caseta de cobro
Ramp	Acceso y salida
Highway	Carretera
Primary road	Ruta mayor
Secondary road	Ruta secundaria
Minor road, unpaved road	Calle menor, calle sin pavimentar
Walkway or trail	Camino peatonál
One-way road	Circulación

Railroad, station	Ferrocarril, estación
Transit line, station	Línea de Metro, estación
Trolley	Tranvía
Bus station	Estación del autobús
Park and ride	Estacionamiento de tránsito
Rest area	Baños
Service area	Gasolina y servicios
Airport	Aeropuerto
Ferry	Transbordador
Waterway	Vía marina navegable
Dam, breakwater	Presa, rompeolas
International boundary	Frontera Internacionál
State/provincial boundary	Frontera estatal o Provincial
County boundary	Límite del condado
Township/range boundary, section corner	Límite de terrenos públicos
Postal code boundary	Límite de código postál
12345 Postal code	Código postál
1200 Block number	Número de cuadra
45°33'30" 90°33'30" Latitude, longitude	Latitud, longitud

Border crossing/port of entry	Aduana
City/town/village hall or other government building	Ayúntamiento
Courthouse	Oficina de justicia
Fire station	Estación de bomberos
Golf course	Campo de golf
Hospital	Hospitál
Information/visitor center/ welcome center	Información turística
Library	Biblioteca
Museum	Muséo
Police/sheriff, etc.	Policía
Post office	Correo
School	Escuela
Theater/performing arts center	Teatro
University or college	Universidad o colegio
Other point of interest	Punto de interés

Using Your Street Guide

The PageFinder™ Map

> Turn to the PageFinder™ Map. Each of the small squares outlined on this map represents a different map page in the Street Guide.

> Locate the specific part of the Street Guide coverage area that you're interested in.

> Note the appropriate map page number. Turn to that map page.

The Index

> The Street Guide includes separate indexes for streets, schools, parks, shopping centers, golf courses, and other points of interest.

> In the street listings, information is presented in the following order: block number, city, map page number, and grid reference.

> A grid reference is a letter-number combination (B6 for example) that tells you precisely where to find a particular street or point of interest on a map.

STREET			
Block	City	Map#	Grid
BROADWAY DR			
4400	SCH	533	B6
6200	PLA	532	D2
7800	WCH	532	A3

The Maps

> Each map is divided into a grid formed by rows and columns. These rows and columns correspond to letters and numbers running horizontally and vertically along the edges of the map.

> To use a grid reference from the index, search horizontally within the appropriate row and vertically within the appropriate column. The destination can be found within the grid square where the row and column meet.

> Adjacent map pages are indicated by numbers that appear at the top, bottom, and sides of each map.

> The legend explains symbols that appear on the maps.

Como usar su Street Guide

El PageFinder™ Map

• Refiérese al PageFinder™ Map. Cada una de las cuadras enumeradas en este mapa representan una página de mapa distinta de este guía.

• Identifica el área del mapa PageFinder que le interesa.

• Hágase cuenta del número en la cuadra representada.

• Ese número es la página del guía donde se representa el mapa de esa área.

El Índice

• Esta guía incluye índices para calles, escuelas, parques, centros de comercio, campos de golf, y otros lugares de interés.

• En el índice de calles, información esta representada en forma de: nombre de la calle, número de la cuadra, página, y cuadrícula.

• La cuadrícula es una combinación de letra y números (por ejemplo "B6") que le indica precisamente donde se halla una calle o punto de interés en la página del mapa indicado.

Los Mapas

• Cada mapa está dividido en una cuadrícula de columnas y filas. Estas columnas y filas corresponden a las letras y números que se encuentran por las orillas del mapa.

• Para localizar una cuadrícula representada en el índice, busca la letra de la columna y el número de la fila por las orillas del mapa indicado y sigue la fila y la columna hasta que se encuentren. La calle o punto de interés que busca se encontrará en la cuadra donde la fila y la columna se encuentren.

• Los mapas de continuación se encontrarán en las páginas indicadas por las orillas de los mapas.

• La leyenda explica la mayoría de los símbolos representados en los mapas.

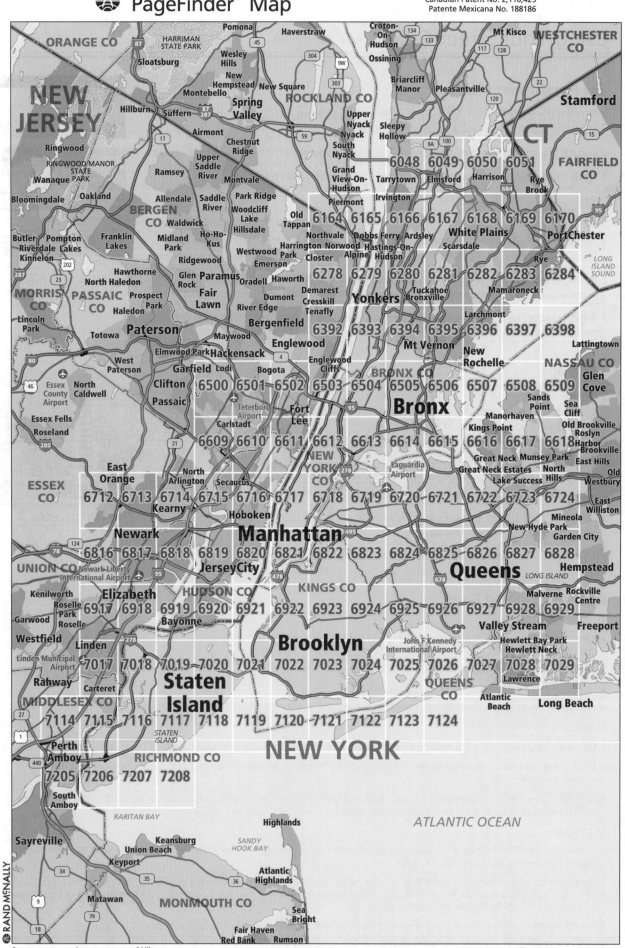

PageFinder™ Map

PageFinder™ Map
U.S. Patent No. 5,419,586
Canadian Patent No. 2,116,425
Patente Mexicana No. 188186

D

NEW JERSEY

ORANGE CO

HARRIMAN STATE PARK

Pomona Haverstraw

Croton-On-Hudson Mt Kisco WESTCHESTER CO

Sloatsburg Wesley Hills

New Hempstead Montebello Spring Valley

New Square New Square

ROCKLAND CO

Ossining Briarcliff Manor Pleasantville

Stamford

Hillburn Suffern Airmont

Chestnut Ridge

Upper Nyack Nyack Sleepy Hollow

CT

Ringwood

RINGWOOD MANOR STATE PARK

Ramsey Upper Saddle River Montvale

South Nyack

Grand View-On-Hudson Tarrytown Elmsford Harrison

FAIRFIELD CO

Rye Brook

Wanaque

Bloomingdale Oakland

BERGEN CO Allendale Saddle River Park Ridge Woodcliff Lake Hillsdale Old Tappan

Piermont Irvington

6048 **6049** **6050** **6051**

Waldwick

6164 **6165** **6166** **6167** **6168** **6169** **6170**

Butler Pompton Lakes Riverdale Kinnelon Franklin Lakes Midland Park Ho-Ho-Kus

Northvale Dobbs Ferry Ardsley White Plains Port Chester

Harrington Park Norwood Alpine Hastings-On-Hudson Scarsdale Rye

LONG ISLAND SOUND

Hawthorne North Haledon Glen Rock Paramus Ridgewood Westwood Emerson Closter

6278 **6279** **6280** **6281** **6282** **6283** **6284**

MORRIS CO PASSAIC CO Prospect Park Fair Lawn Oradell Haworth Demarest Cresskill Tenafly Yonkers Tuckahoe Bronxville Mamaroneck

Lincoln Park Haledon River Edge Bergenfield

6392 **6393** **6394** **6395** **6396** **6397** **6398**

Totowa Paterson Maywood Englewood Mt Vernon New Rochelle Larchmont Lattingtown

Elmwood Park Hackensack Englewood Cliffs

NASSAU CO

West Paterson Garfield Lodi Bogota

BRONX CO Glen Cove

Clifton **6500** **6501** **6502** **6503** **6504** **6505** **6506** **6507** **6508** **6509**

Passaic Teterboro Airport Fort Lee **Bronx** Sands Point Sea Cliff

Essex County Airport North Caldwell Carlstadt

Manorhaven Old Brookville Roslyn

Essex Fells Roseland

Kings Point Harbor Brookville

6609 **6610** **6611** **6612** **6613** **6614** **6615** **6616** **6617** **6618**

East Orange North Arlington Secaucus **NEW YORK CO** LaGuardia Airport Great Neck Munsey Park East Hills

ESSEX CO Great Neck Estates North Hills Old Westbury

6712 **6713** **6714** **6715** **6716** **6717** **6718** **6719** **6720** **6721** **6722** **6723** **6724**

Kearny Lake Success

East Williston

Hoboken Mineola

Newark **Manhattan** New Hyde Park Garden City

6816 **6817** **6818** **6819** **6820** **6821** **6822** **6823** **6824** **6825** **6826** **6827** **6828**

UNION CO Newark Liberty International Airport Jersey City **Queens** Hempstead

LONG ISLAND

Kenilworth Elizabeth HUDSON CO KINGS CO Malverne Rockville Centre

Roselle Park **6917** **6918** **6919** **6920** **6921** **6922** **6923** **6924** **6925** **6926** **6927** **6928** **6929**

Garwood Roselle Bayonne Valley Stream Freeport

Westfield Linden John F Kennedy International Airport Hewlett Bay Park Hewlett Neck

Linden Municipal Airport **Brooklyn**

7017 **7018** **7019** **7020** **7021** **7022** **7023** **7024** **7025** **7026** **7027** **7028** **7029**

Rahway Carteret **Staten Island** Lawrence

MIDDLESEX CO QUEENS CO Atlantic Beach Long Beach

7114 **7115** **7116** **7117** **7118** **7119** **7120** **7121** **7122** **7123** **7124**

Perth Amboy STATEN ISLAND **NEW YORK**

RICHMOND CO

7205 **7206** **7207** **7208**

South Amboy

RARITAN BAY Highlands *ATLANTIC OCEAN*

Sayreville Keansburg SANDY HOOK BAY

Union Beach

Keyport Atlantic Highlands

Matawan MONMOUTH CO Sea Bright

Fair Haven Red Bank Rumson

0   4   8 Miles

RAND McNALLY

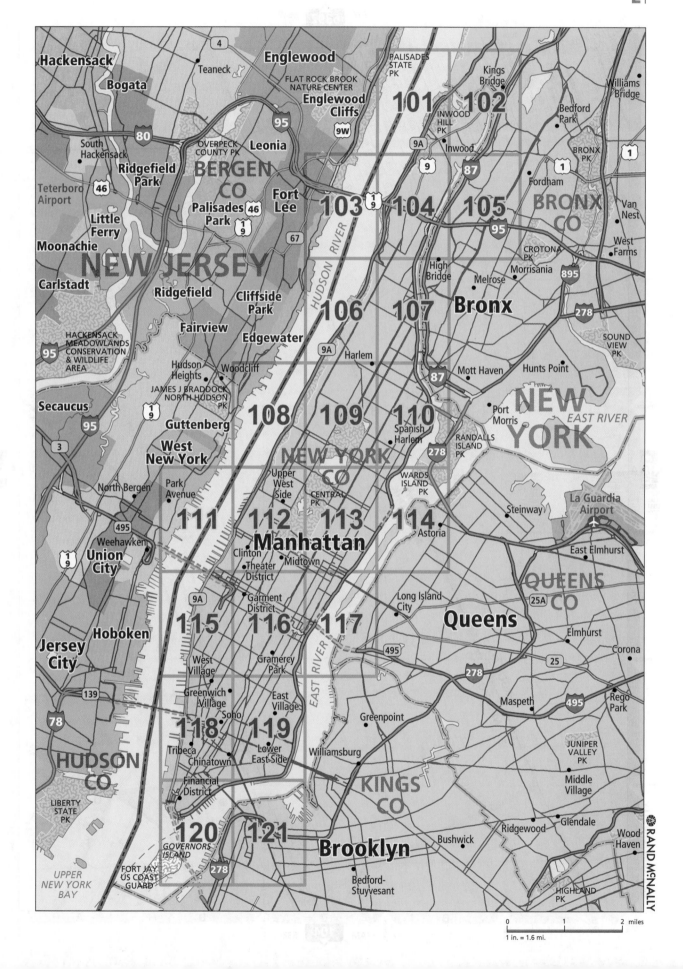

Hackensack
Bogata
Teaneck
Englewood
FLAT ROCK BROOK NATURE CENTER
Englewood Cliffs
PALISADES STATE PK
Kings Bridge
Williams Bridge
South Hackensack
OVERPECK COUNTY PK
Leonia
INWOOD HILL PK
Inwood
Bedford Park
BRONX PK
Ridgefield Park
BERGEN CO
Fort Lee
Fordham
BRONX CO
Teterboro Airport
Palisades Park
Van Nest
Little Ferry
Moonachie
NEW JERSEY
West Farms
Carlstadt
Ridgefield
Cliffside Park
High Bridge
CROTONA PK
Morrisania
Fairview
Edgewater
Harlem
Bronx
SOUND VIEW PK
HACKENSACK MEADOWLANDS CONSERVATION & WILDLIFE AREA
Hudson Heights
Woodcliff
Mott Haven
Hunts Point
Secaucus
JAMES J BRADDOCK NORTH HUDSON PK
Spanish Harlem
Port Morris
NEW YORK
EAST RIVER
Guttenberg
NEW YORK CO
RANDALLS ISLAND PK
West New York
Upper West Side
CENTRAL PK
WARDS ISLAND PK
North Bergen
Park Avenue
La Guardia Airport
Weehawken
Steinway
Manhattan
Astoria
East Elmhurst
Union City
Clinton
Theater District
Midtown
QUEENS CO
Jersey City
Hoboken
West Village
Garment District
Long Island City
Queens
Elmhurst
Corona
Gramercy Park
Greenwich Village
East Village
Maspeth
Rego Park
Soho
Greenpoint
HUDSON CO
Tribeca
Chinatown
Lower East Side
Williamsburg
JUNIPER VALLEY PK
Financial District
KINGS CO
Middle Village
LIBERTY STATE PK
Ridgewood
Glendale
Wood Haven
GOVERNORS ISLAND
Brooklyn
Bushwick
HIGHLAND PK
UPPER NEW YORK BAY
FORT JAY US COAST GUARD
Bedford-Stuyvesant

101 102
103 104 105
106 107
108 109 110
111 112 113 114
115 116 117
118 119
120 121

RAND McNALLY

0   1   2 miles
1 in. = 1.6 mi.

MAP
101

1:12,000
1 in. = 1000 ft.
0   0.125   0.25
miles

MAP
101

SEE 6392 MAP

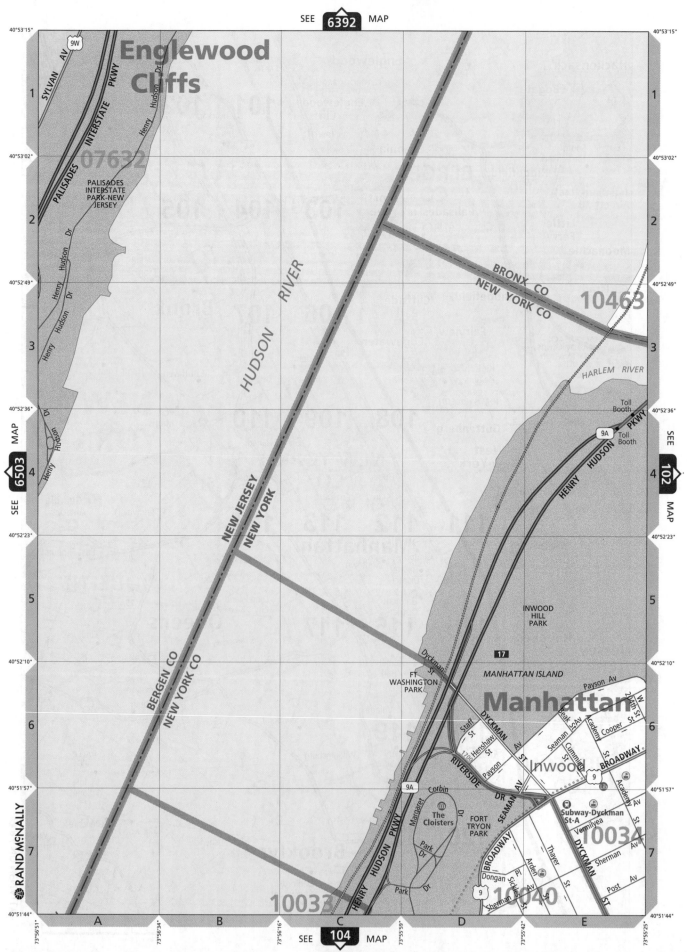

Englewood Cliffs

9W

SYLVAN AV

PALISADES INTERSTATE PKWY

Henry Hudson Dr

07632

PALISADES INTERSTATE PARK-NEW JERSEY

Hudson Dr

Henry Hudson Dr

Henry Hudson Dr

HUDSON RIVER

BRONX CO
NEW YORK CO

10463

HARLEM RIVER

Toll Booth

9A Toll Booth

HENRY HUDSON PKWY

MAP 6503

SEE 102 MAP

NEW JERSEY
NEW YORK

BERGEN CO
NEW YORK CO

INWOOD HILL PARK

17

MANHATTAN ISLAND

Dyckman St

FT WASHINGTON PARK

Payson Av

W 207th St

Manhattan

Beak St
Staff St
DYCKMAN
Henshaw St
170
Academy St
Seaman Av
Cummings St
Cooper St

RIVERSIDE
Payson Av

Inwood

9
BROADWAY

HENRY HUDSON PKWY

9A
Corbin

Margaret

The Cloisters

FORT TRYON PARK

Park Dr

Park Dr

SEAMAN AV

BROADWAY

DR

Subway-Dyckman St-A

Vermilyea

Academy Av

10034

DYCKMAN ST

Thayer St

Sherman Av

Dongan Pl

Sickle

Arden
St

Post Av

9
Sherman

10033

10040

SEE 104 MAP

MAP
102

MAP
102

1:12,000
1 in. = 1000 ft.

0   0.125   0.25
miles

SEE 6393 MAP

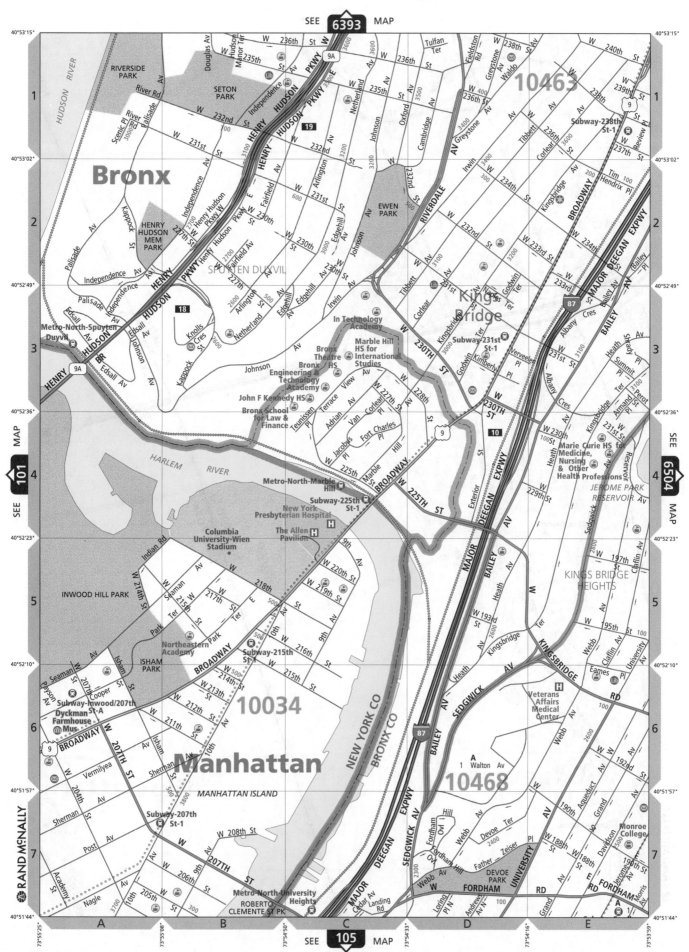

40°53'15"
40°53'15"

10463

Bronx

RIVERSIDE PARK

SETON PARK

HUDSON RIVER

Subway-238th St-1

40°53'02"
40°53'02"

HENRY HUDSON PKWY

EWEN PARK

RIVERDALE AV

BROADWAY

Kings Bridge

40°52'49"
40°52'49"

SPUYTEN DUYVIL

HENRY HUDSON MEM PARK

In Technology Academy

Marble Hill HS for International Studies

Bronx Theatre / Bronx HS

Engineering & Technology Academy

John F Kennedy HS

Bronx School for Law & Finance

Metro-North-Spuyten Duyvil

Subway-231st St-1

230TH ST

230TH ST

40°52'36"
40°52'36"

HARLEM RIVER

Marie Curie HS for Medicine, Nursing & Other Health Professions

JEROME PARK RESERVOIR

SEE 6504 MAP

Metro-North-Marble Hill

Subway-225th St-1

New York Presbyterian Hospital

The Allen Pavilion

40°52'23"
40°52'23"

Columbia University-Wien Stadium

KINGS BRIDGE HEIGHTS

SEE 101 MAP

INWOOD HILL PARK

Northeastern Academy

ISHAM PARK

Subway-215th St-1

BROADWAY

KINGSBRIDGE RD

40°52'10"
40°52'10"

10034

Subway-Inwood/207th St-A

Dyckman Farmhouse Mus

Broadway

207TH ST

Veterans Affairs Medical Center

Manhattan

1 Walton Av

10468

40°51'57"
40°51'57"

MANHATTAN ISLAND

NEW YORK CO
BRONX CO

Subway-207th St-1

Monroe College

207TH ST

MAJOR DEEGAN EXPWY

SEDGWICK AV

UNIVERSITY

DEVOE PARK

FORDHAM

FORDHAM RD

40°51'44"
40°51'44"

Metro-North-University Heights

ROBERTO CLEMENTE ST PK

A   B   C   D   E

MAP
103

MAP
103

1:12,000
1 in. = 1000 ft.
0   0.125   0.25
miles

Fort Lee

07024

PALISADES
INTERSTATE
PARK-NEW
JERSEY

Fort Lee
Historic
Park

SEE 6502 MAP

SEE 104 MAP

BERGEN CO
NEW YORK CO

GEORGE WASHINGTON BR

HUDSON RIVER

NEW JERSEY
NEW YORK

07020

Edgewater

Manhattan

MANHATTAN
ISLAND

FORT
WASHINGTON
PARK

10032

RAND M?NALLY

MAP 104

MAP 104

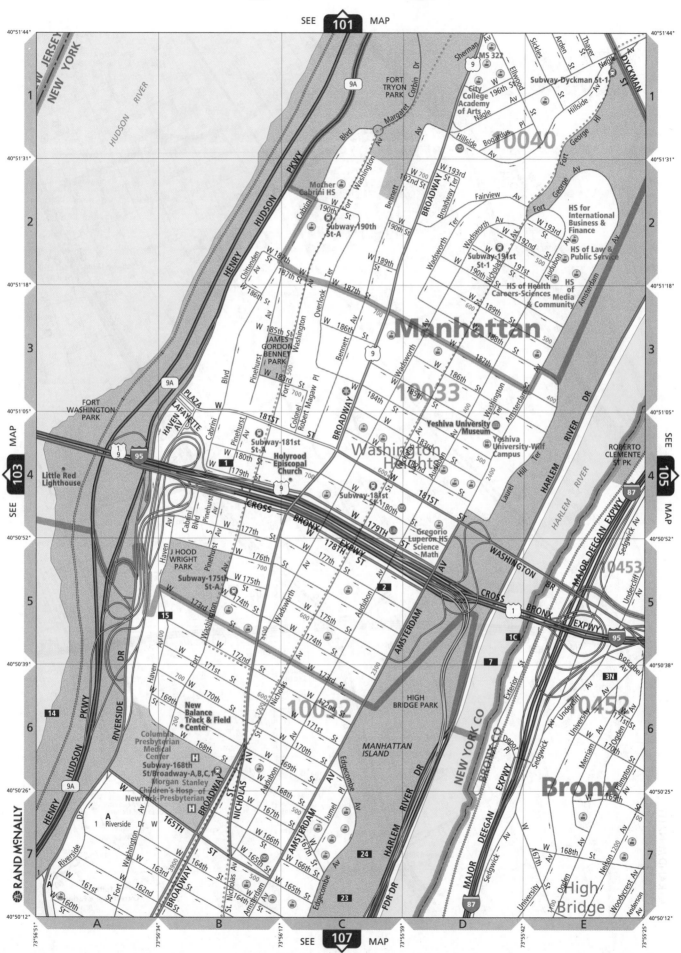

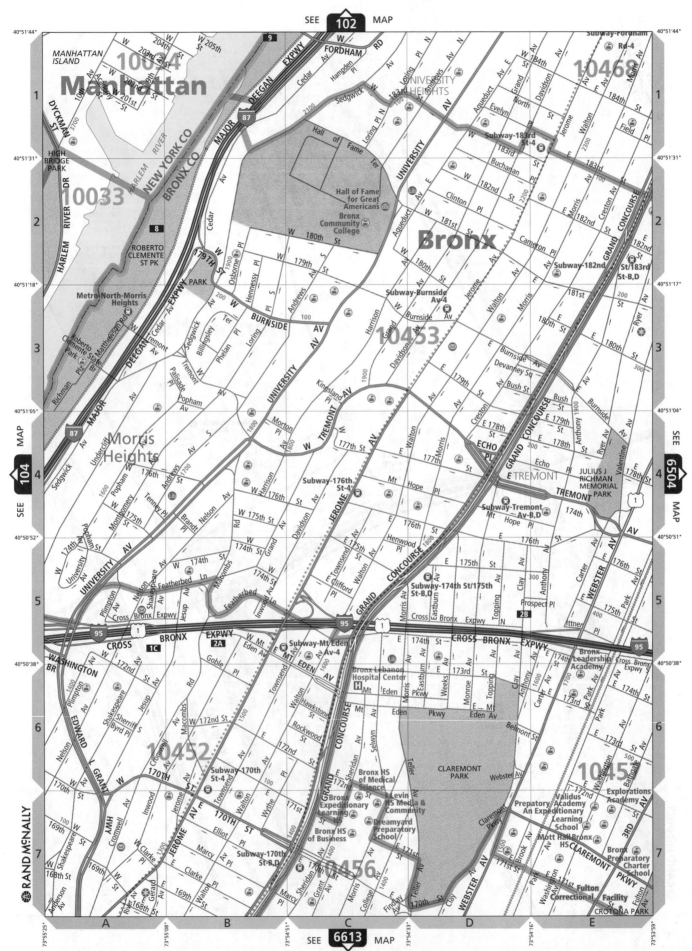

MAP
106

MAP
106

1:12,000
1 in. = 1000 ft.

0   0.125   0.25

miles

N

SEE **103** MAP

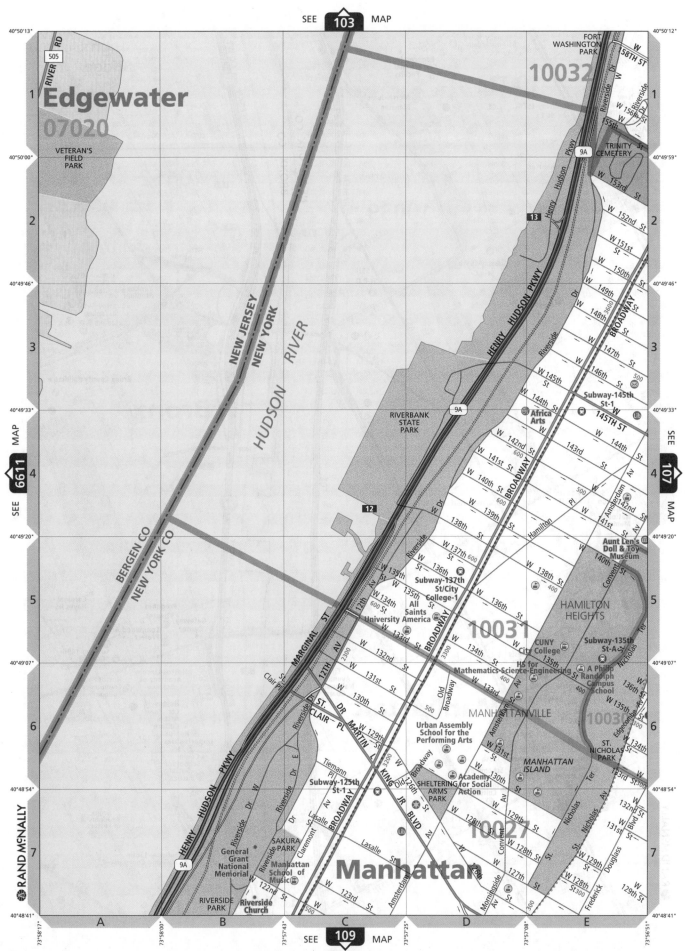

40°50'13"
40°50'12"

FORT
WASHINGTON
PARK

10032

W 58TH ST

Riverside Dr

W 156th St

155th

Edgewater

07020

TRINITY
CEMETERY

9A

VETERAN'S
FIELD
PARK

40°50'00"

W 153rd St

40°50'00"

Henry Hudson Pkwy

13

W 152nd St

1

NEW JERSEY

NEW YORK

HUDSON RIVER

W 151st St

W 150th St

40°49'46"

Dr

W 149th St

40°49'46"

W 148th St

3600

HENRY HUDSON PKWY

BROADWAY

2

Riverside

W 147th St

W 146th St

500

W 145th St

Subway-145th
St-1

3

W 144th St

Africa
Arts

145TH ST

40°49'33"

9A

40°49'33"

RIVERBANK
STATE
PARK

W 142nd St

143rd

W 144th

600

St

Av

SEE **6611** MAP

W 141st St

BROADWAY

Amsterdam

Pl

142nd

W 140th St

600

500

St

41st

4

12

W Dr

W 139th St

138th

St

Hamilton

40°49'20"

40°49'20"

Aunt Len's
Doll & Toy
Museum

4

SEE **107** MAP

W 137th St

600

140th

Riverside

W 136th St

138th St

400

Convent St

Subway-137th
St/City
College-1

W

5

W 135th St

136th

St

HAMILTON
HEIGHTS

12th

W 134th St

600 St

All
Saints

University America

10031

134th

CUNY

St

City College

Subway-135th
St-A-1

Nicholas Ter

W 133rd

St

HS for
Mathematics-Science-Engineering

135th

A Philip
Randolph
Campus
School

136th St

40°49'07"

AV

W 132nd

St

3300

133rd

400

40°49'07"

MARGINAL ST

12TH

2300

St

Old

Broadway

St

W 135th Av

W 131st St

130th

W

Edgecombe Av

6

St

500

MANHATTANVILLE

10030

ST. NICHOLAS
PARK

W 134th

Ter

Riverside Dr

ST.
CLAIR PL

W 129th

St

Urban Assembly
School for the
Performing Arts

Broadway

W 131st

St

MANHATTAN
ISLAND

133rd St

300

DR. MARTIN L

Tiemann

Pl

Dr E

3200

St

130th

Academy
for Social
Action

St

Nicholas Ter

Riverside Dr W

Subway-125th
St-1

126th

Old

SHELTERING
ARMS
PARK

129th

40°48'54"

KING

Lasalle

St

Broadway

W 128th

Av

Nicholas Av

132nd St

40°48'54"

7

9A

Claremont Av

JR. BLVD

St

Convent

St

131st St

General
Grant
National
Memorial

SAKURA
PARK

Manhattan

10027

128th

St

W 129th

St

W 129th

St

Manhattan
School of
Music

St

W 128th St

129th St

RIVERSIDE
PARK

Riverside
Church

122nd St

W 123rd

St

500

Amsterdam

127th

Morningside

300

Frederick Douglass

40°48'41"
40°48'41"

73°58'17"   73°58'00"   73°57'43"   73°57'25"   73°57'08"   73°56'51"

A   B   C   D   E

SEE **109** MAP

MAP
107

1:12,000
1 in. = 1000 ft.

0   0.125   0.25

miles

MAP
107

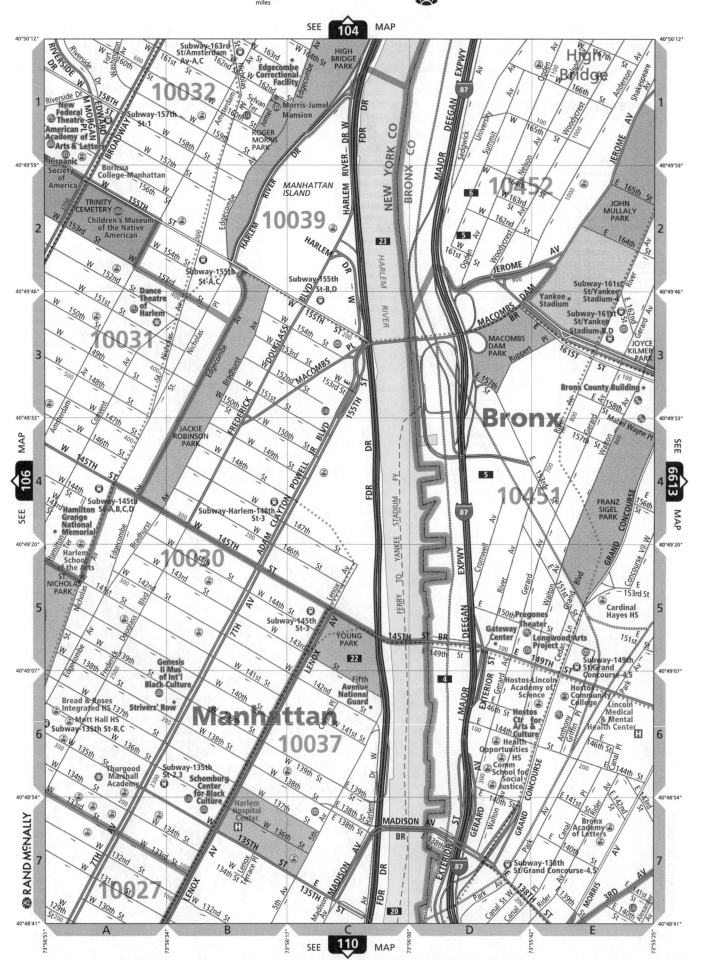

MAP
108

MAP
108

1:12,000
1 in. = 1000 ft.
0   0.125   0.25
miles

N

SEE 6611 MAP

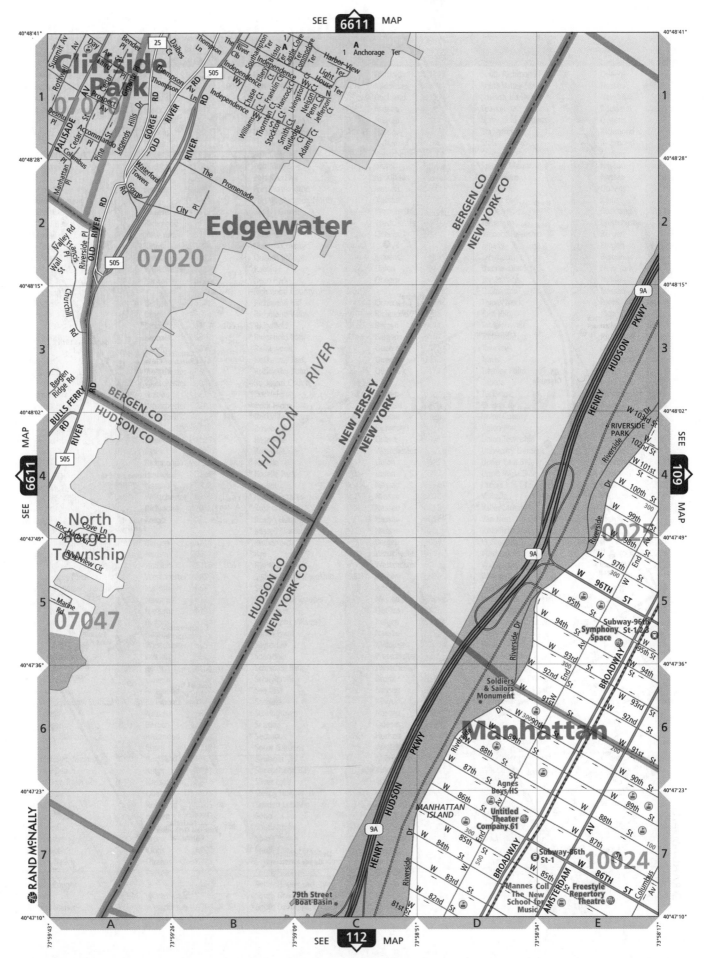

Cliffside Park
07010

PALISADE

Edgewater

07020

North Bergen Township

07047

Manhattan

10024

HUDSON RIVER

NEW JERSEY
NEW YORK

BERGEN CO
NEW YORK CO

HUDSON CO
NEW YORK CO

BERGEN CO
HUDSON CO

RIVERSIDE PARK

0025

Soldiers & Sailors Monument

Symphony Space

Subway-96th St-1,2,3

Subway-86th St-1

St. Agnes Boys HS

Untitled Theater Company 61

MANHATTAN ISLAND

Mannes Coll The New School for Music

Freestyle Repertory Theatre

79th Street Boat Basin

BROADWAY

AMSTERDAM AV

HENRY HUDSON PKWY

9A

SEE 6611 MAP

SEE 109 MAP

SEE 112 MAP

MAP
109

MAP
109

1:12,000
1 in. = 1000 ft.

0   0.125   0.25

miles

SEE 106 MAP

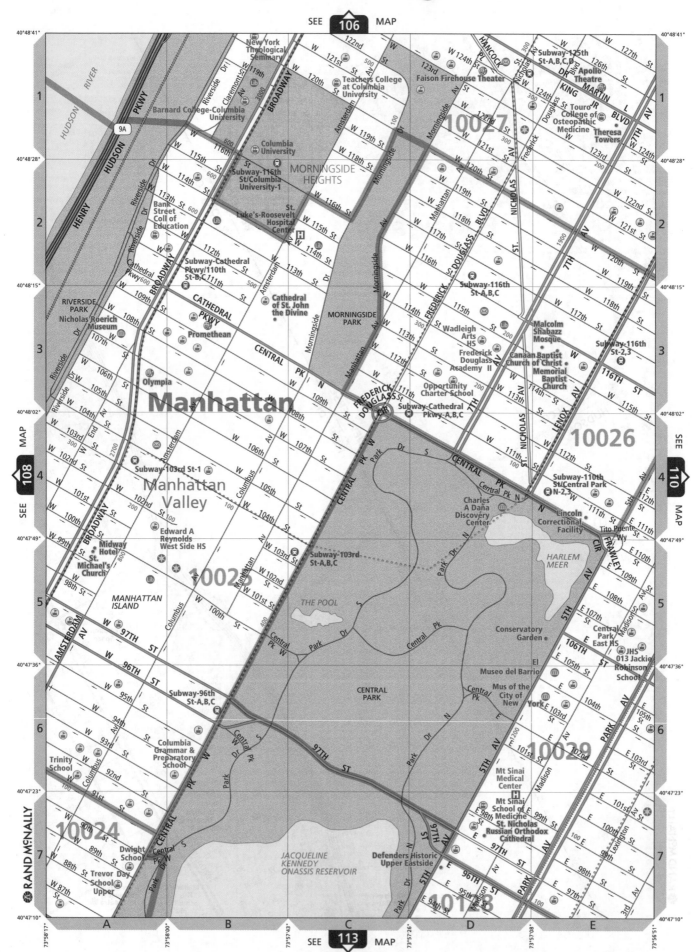

MAP 108

SEE 110 MAP

HUDSON RIVER

HENRY HUDSON PKWY

9A

RIVERSIDE PARK

New York Theological Seminary

Barnard College-Columbia University

Teachers College at Columbia University

Columbia University

Subway-116th St/Columbia University-1

MORNINGSIDE HEIGHTS

Bank Street Coll of Education

St. Luke's-Roosevelt Hospital Center

Subway-Cathedral Pkwy/110th St-B,C

Cathedral of St. John the Divine

Nicholas Roerich Museum

CATHEDRAL PKWY

MORNINGSIDE PARK

Promethean

CENTRAL PK N

Olympia

Manhattan

FREDERICK DOUGLASS CIR

Subway-Cathedral Pkwy-A,B,C

Subway-103rd St-1

Manhattan Valley

10025

CENTRAL PK W

Edward A Reynolds West Side HS

Subway-103rd St-A,B,C

THE POOL

MANHATTAN ISLAND

Midway Hotel

St. Michael's Church

Subway-96th St-A,B,C

CENTRAL PARK

Columbia Grammar & Preparatory School

Trinity School

10024

Dwight School

Trevor Day School Upper

JACQUELINE KENNEDY ONASSIS RESERVOIR

Faison Firehouse Theater

Subway-125th St-A,B,C,D

Apollo Theatre

KING

MARTIN L

Touro College of Osteopathic Medicine

Theresa Towers

7TH AV

10027

NICHOLAS AV

ST. NICHOLAS AV

FREDERICK DOUGLASS BLVD

Subway-116th St-A,B,C

Malcolm Shabazz Mosque

Subway-116th St-2,3

St Wadleigh Arts HS

Frederick Douglass Academy II

Canaan Baptist Church of Christ

Memorial Baptist Church

Opportunity Charter School

116TH ST

LENOX AV

7TH AV

Subway-Cathedral Pkwy-A,B,C

CENTRAL PK N

10026

Subway-110th St/Central Park N-2,3

Charles A Dana Discovery Center

Lincoln Correctional Facility

Tito Puente Wy

FRAWLEY CIR

HARLEM MEER

Central Park East HS

JHS 013 Jackie Robinson School

Conservatory Garden

El Museo del Barrio

Mus of the City of New York

5TH AV

106TH ST

PARK AV

MADISON AV

10029

Mt Sinai Medical Center

Mt Sinai School of Medicine

St. Nicholas Russian Orthodox Cathedral

Defenders Historic Upper Eastside

10128

40°48'41"
40°48'28"
40°48'15"
40°48'02"
40°47'49"
40°47'36"
40°47'23"
40°47'10"

A   B   C   D   E

1   2   3   4   5   6   7

73°58'17"   73°58'00"   73°57'43"   73°57'26"   73°57'08"   73°56'51"

SEE 113 MAP

MAP
110

MAP
110

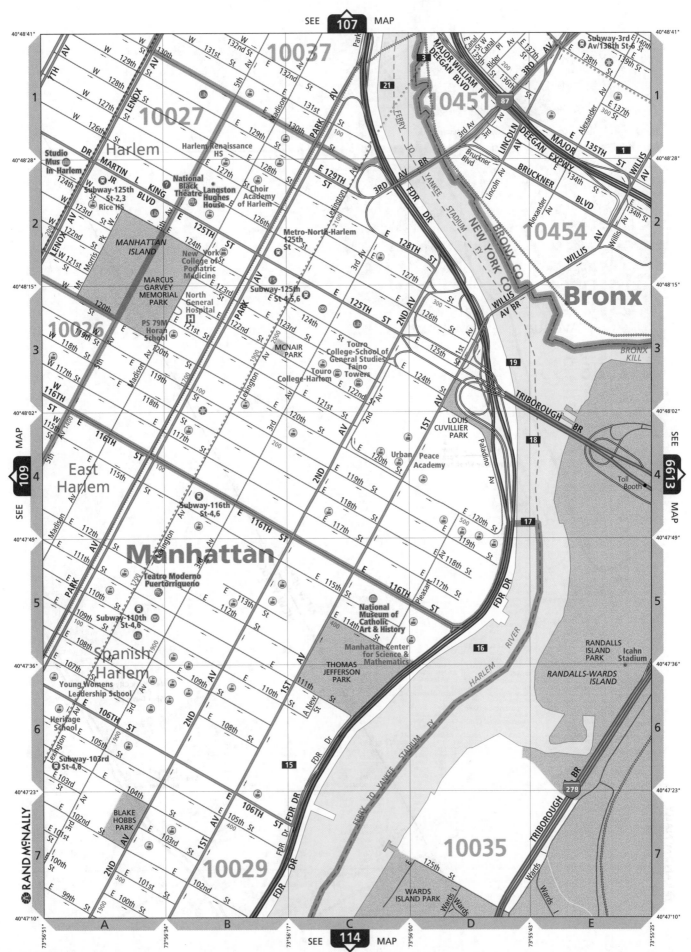

1:12,000
1 in. = 1000 ft.
0   0.125   0.25
miles

40°48'41"

10037

10451

10027

Harlem

Studio
Mus
in Harlem

Subway-125th
St-2,3
Rice HS

National
Black
Theatre

Langston
Hughes
House

Choir
Academy
of Harlem

Harlem Renaissance
HS

Metro-North-Harlem
125th
St

Bronx

10454

10026

MANHATTAN
ISLAND

MARCUS
GARVEY
MEMORIAL
PARK

New York
College of
Podiatric
Medicine

North
General
Hospital

PS 79M
Horan
School

Subway-125th
St-4,5,6

McNAIR
PARK

Touro
College-School of
General Studies

Touro
College-Harlem

Taino
Towers

BRONX
KILL

East
Harlem

LOUIS
CUVILLIER
PARK

Subway-116th
St-4,6

Urban Peace
Academy

SEE 6613 MAP

Manhattan

Toll
Booth

National
Museum of
Catholic
Art & History

Manhattan Center
for Science &
Mathematics

RANDALLS
ISLAND
PARK

Icahn
Stadium

Teatro Moderno
Puertorriqueno

Subway-110th
St-4,6

Spanish
Harlem

THOMAS
JEFFERSON
PARK

RANDALLS-WARDS
ISLAND

HARLEM RIVER

Young Womens
Leadership School

Heritage
School

Subway-103rd
St-4,6

FDR DR

10035

RAND McNALLY

BLAKE
HOBBS
PARK

10029

WARDS
ISLAND PARK

Bronx

MAP
111

MAP
111

1:12,000
1 in. = 1000 ft.

0   0.125   0.25

miles

N

07093

West
New
York

Union
City

07087

07086

Park Avenue

Weehawken
Township

NJ Transit-HBLR-Port
Imperial

New York
Waterway-Weehawken

HUDSON RIVER

HUDSON CO

NEW YORK CO

Pier 98

Pier 97

Pier 96

Pier 95

Pier 94

New York
City
Convention
Pier

Pier 92

10019

HUDSON
RIVER
PARK

DE WITT
CLINTON

Pier 90

NEW JERSEY

NEW YORK

New York City
Passenger
Ship Terminal

Pier 88

Manhattan

Pier 86

Intrepid
Sea-Air-Space
Museum

LINCOLN TUN

495

495

PORT IMPERIAL-PIER 11 FY

PORT IMPERIAL-PIER 23 FY

LINCOLN TUN

Pier 84

Pier 83

Pier 81

10018

10036

MANHATTAN
ISLAND

RAND McNALLY

MAP 112

MAP 112

1:12,000
1 in. = 1000 ft.

0   0.125   0.25

miles

SEE 111 MAP

SEE 113 MAP

MAP
113

1:12,000
1 in. = 1000 ft.
0   0.125   0.25
miles

N

MAP
113

SEE 109 MAP

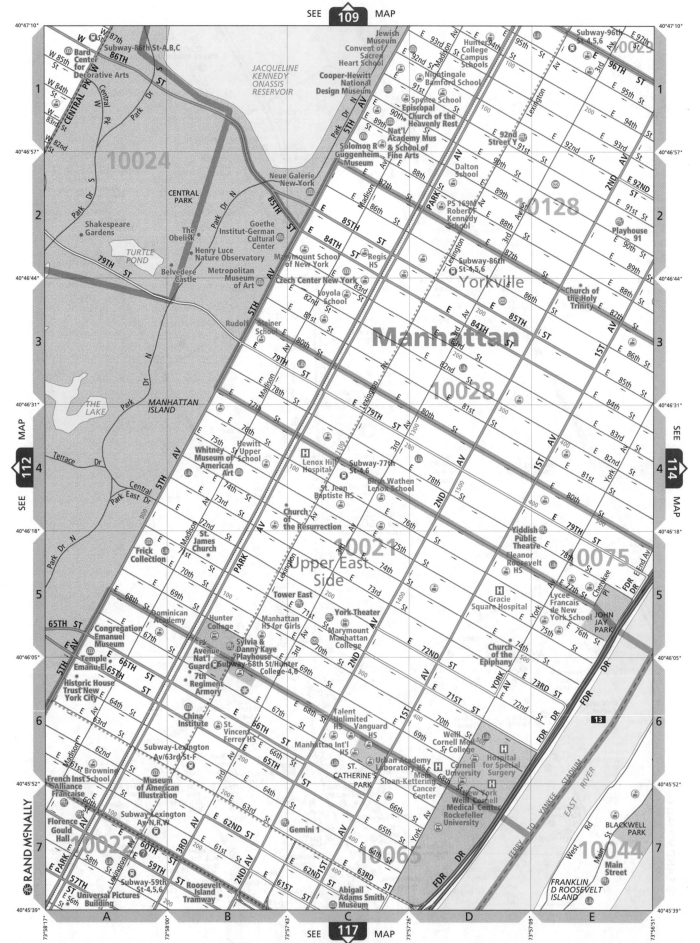

SEE 112 MAP

SEE 114 MAP

SEE 117 MAP

RAND McNALLY

MAP
114

1:12,000
1 in. = 1000 ft.

0   0.125   0.25

miles

MAP
114

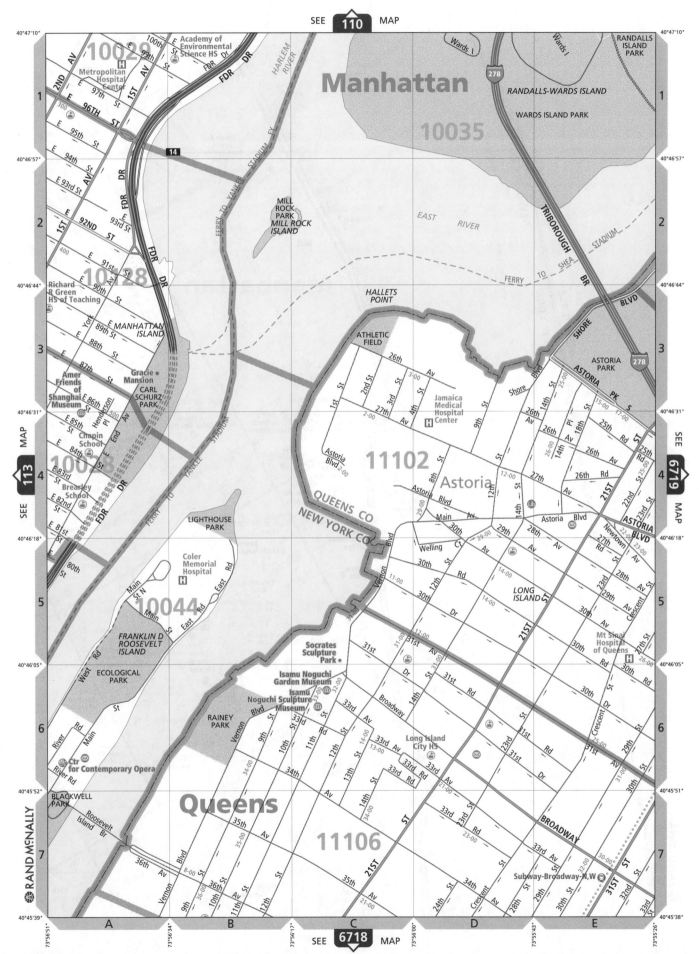

SEE 110 MAP

Manhattan

RANDALLS ISLAND PARK

278

RANDALLS-WARDS ISLAND

WARDS ISLAND PARK

Wards I

Wards I

10035

EAST RIVER

HARLEM RIVER

MILL ROCK PARK
MILL ROCK ISLAND

FERRY TO SHEA STADIUM

TRIBOROUGH BR

FERRY TO YANKEE STADIUM

FERRY TO SHEA STADIUM

SHORE BLVD

ASTORIA

278

ASTORIA PARK

ASTORIA PK S

10029

Metropolitan Hospital Center

100th
99th
E 97th St
E 96TH ST
E 95th St
E 94th St
E 93rd St
E 92ND St
E 91st St
E 90th St
E 89th St
E 88th St
E 87th St
E 86th St
E 85th St
E 84th St
E 83rd St
E 82nd St
E 81st St
80th St

2ND AV
1ST AV
1ST AV
2ND AV
York AV
Henderson
E End Av
East End Av

Academy of Environmental Science HS

FDR Dr

FDR DR

14

FDR DR

FDR DR

10128

Richard R Green HS of Teaching

E MANHATTAN ISLAND

Amer Friends of Shanghai Museum

Gracie Mansion

CARL SCHURZ PARK

Chapin School

10028

Brearley School

HALLETS POINT

ATHLETIC FIELD

26th St
27th St

1st St
2nd St
3rd St
4th St

3-00
2-00

Astoria Blvd 2-00

8th St

Astoria Blvd

Main Av

Welling Ct

30th Av

30th Rd

31st Av

Jamaica Medical Hospital Center
H

11102

Astoria

Shore Blvd

9th St

25-00

14th St
26th Av
26th
14th Pl
14th Av
18th St
24th

25-00
17-00

Newtown

26th Rd
26th Av
27th St
26th Rd

25th St
25th Rd

21ST ST

22nd
23rd
22nd St
28th St

ASTORIA BLVD

12th St

14th St

28th St

Newtown Rd
27th Av

LONG ISLAND ST

29th St

30th Av

30th Av

Mt Sinai Hospital of Queens
H

30th

26-00

LIGHTHOUSE PARK

Coler Memorial Hospital
H

10044

FRANKLIN D ROOSEVELT ISLAND

Main St N
East Rd
East Rd
East Rd
Main St

West Rd

ECOLOGICAL PARK

St

QUEENS CO
NEW YORK CO

Vernon Blvd

34th Av

Vernon Blvd

Socrates Sculpture Park

Isamu Noguchi Garden Museum

Isamu Noguchi Sculpture Museum

RAINEY PARK

31st

31st Dr

Broadway

31st Rd

14th St

Broadway

31st Av

31st Dr
31st Av

31st Rd

23rd Av

30th Dr

30th

Crescent St

30th Rd

Long Island City HS

33rd

33rd Av

33rd Rd

33rd Rd

21-00

33rd St

23rd St

30th Av

BLACKWELL PARK

River Rd
Main
River Rd

Ctr for Contemporary Opera

Roosevelt Island Br

Queens

9th St
10th St
11th St
12th St

35th Av

34th

35-00

8-00

36th Av

9th St
10th St
11th St
12th St

36th St
35-00
36-00

21-00

11106

33rd Rd
33rd Av
13th St
14th St

34th
34-00

35th Av
35th Av

21ST ST

34th St

23rd Av

33rd Av

30th Av

BROADWAY

33rd Av

22-00

30-00

Subway-Broadway-N,W

31ST ST
32nd St
33rd St

24th St
28th St
29th St
30th St

SEE 6718 MAP

SEE 113 MAP

SEE 6719 MAP

RAND M⸰NALLY

A   B   C   D   E

40°47'10"
40°46'57"
40°46'44"
40°46'31"
40°46'18"
40°46'05"
40°45'52"
40°45'39"

73°56'51" 73°56'34" 73°56'17" 73°56'00" 73°55'43" 73°55'26"

40°47'10"
40°46'57"
40°46'44"
40°46'31"
40°46'18"
40°45'51"

MAP
115

MAP
115

1:12,000
1 in. = 1000 ft.

0   0.125   0.25

miles

SEE 111 MAP

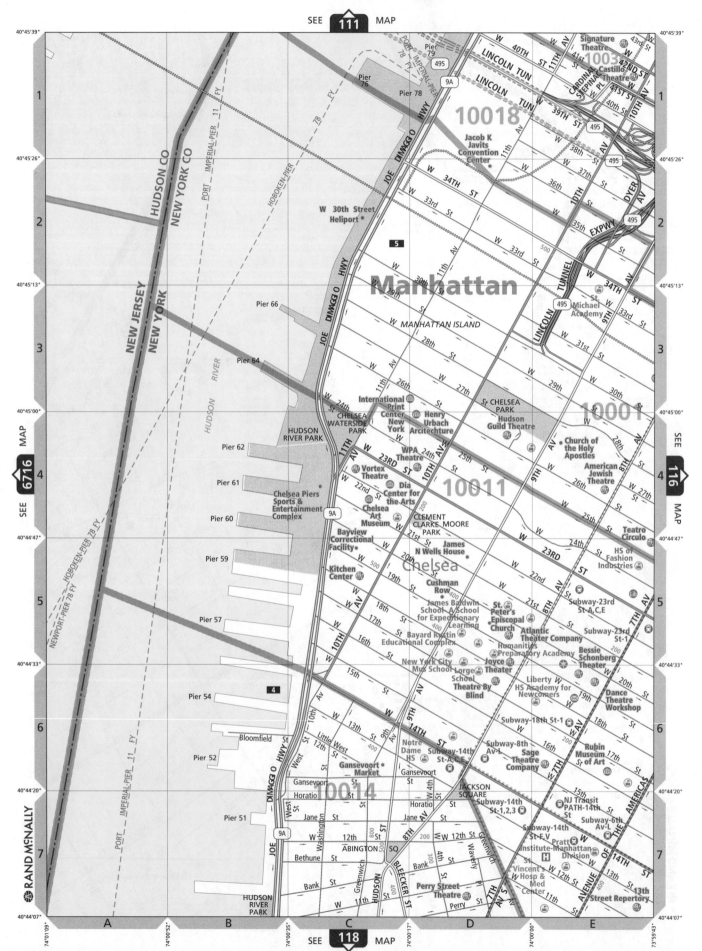

Manhattan

W MANHATTAN ISLAND

Chelsea

10018
10031
10001
10011
10014

SEE 6716 MAP

SEE 116 MAP

RAND M°NALLY

MAP
116

MAP
116

1:12,000
1 in. = 1000 ft.
0   0.125   0.25
miles

N

SEE [112] MAP

SEE [115] MAP

SEE [117] MAP

SEE [119] MAP

RAND MᶜNALLY

MAP
117

1:12,000
1 in. = 1000 ft.

0   0.125   0.25

miles

MAP
117

SEE 113 MAP

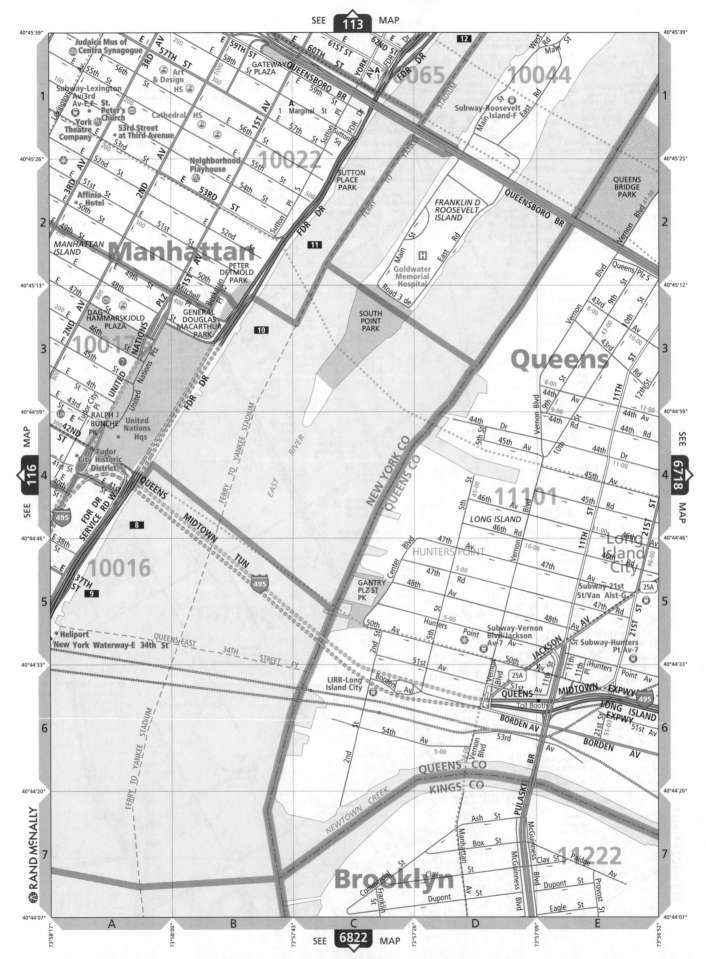

SEE 116 MAP

SEE 6718 MAP

SEE 6822 MAP

RAND McNALLY

MAP
118

MAP
118

1:12,000
1 in. = 1000 ft.

0   0.125   0.25

miles

SEE 115 MAP

SEE 6820 MAP

SEE 119 MAP

SEE 120 MAP

Manhattan

West Village

Greenwich Village

Soho

Tribeca

Chinatown

10011
10014
10012
10013
10282
10007
10281
10280
10038
10000

RAND McNALLY

MAP
119

MAP
119

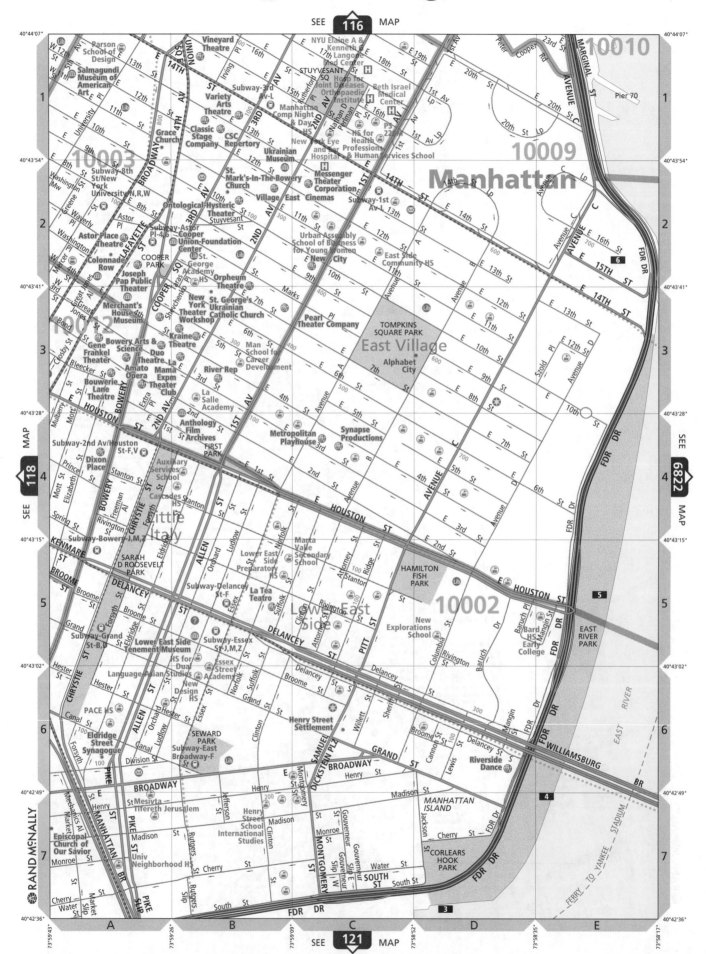

1:12,000
1 in. = 1000 ft.

0   0.125   0.25

miles

N

10010

Pier 70

Manhattan

10009

10003

East Village

Alphabet City

TOMPKINS SQUARE PARK

10002

Lower East Side

Little Italy

HAMILTON FISH PARK

EAST RIVER PARK

SARAH D ROOSEVELT PARK

SEWARD PARK

EAST RIVER

MANHATTAN ISLAND

CORLEARS HOOK PARK

FERRY TO YANKEE STADIUM

WILLIAMSBURG BR

SEE 118 MAP

SEE 6822 MAP

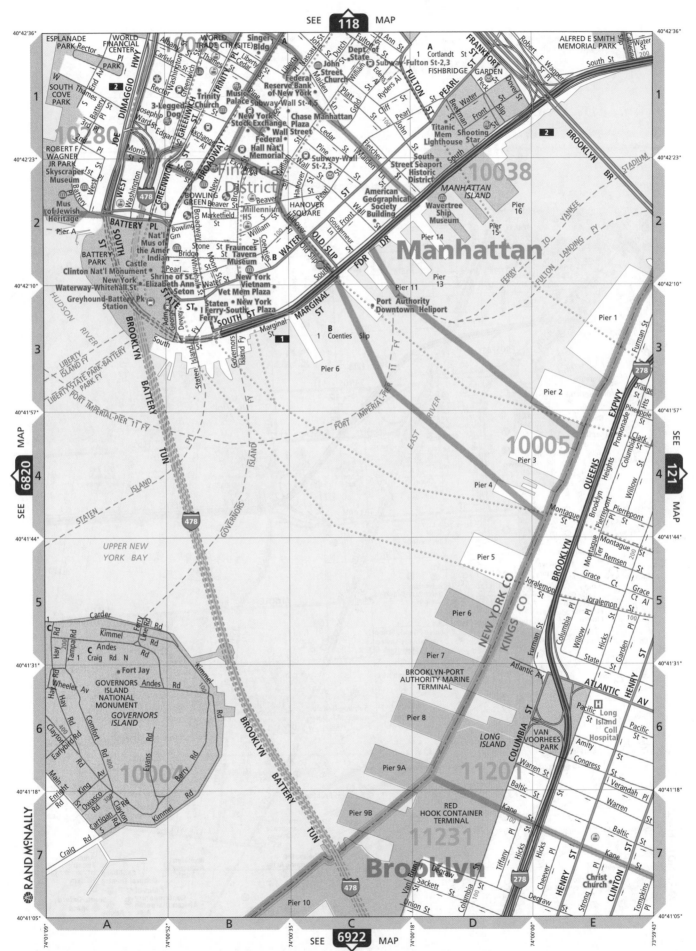

MAP
120

MAP
120

1:12,000
1 in. = 1000 ft.
0   0.125   0.25
miles

SEE 118 MAP

SEE 6820 MAP

SEE 121 MAP

SEE 6922 MAP

RAND McNALLY

MAP
121

1:12,000
1 in. = 1000 ft.

0   0.125   0.25
miles

MAP
121

SEE 119 MAP

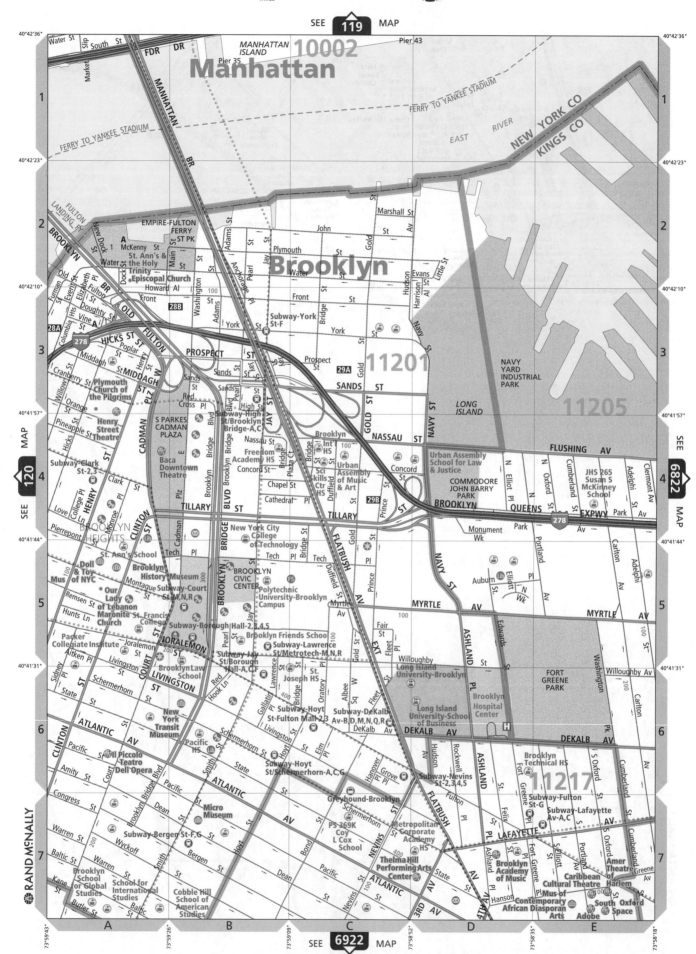

SEE 120 MAP

SEE 6822 MAP

SEE 6922 MAP

RAND McNALLY

MAP
6048

MAP
6048

1:24,000
1 in. = 2000 ft.

0   0.25   0.5

miles

N

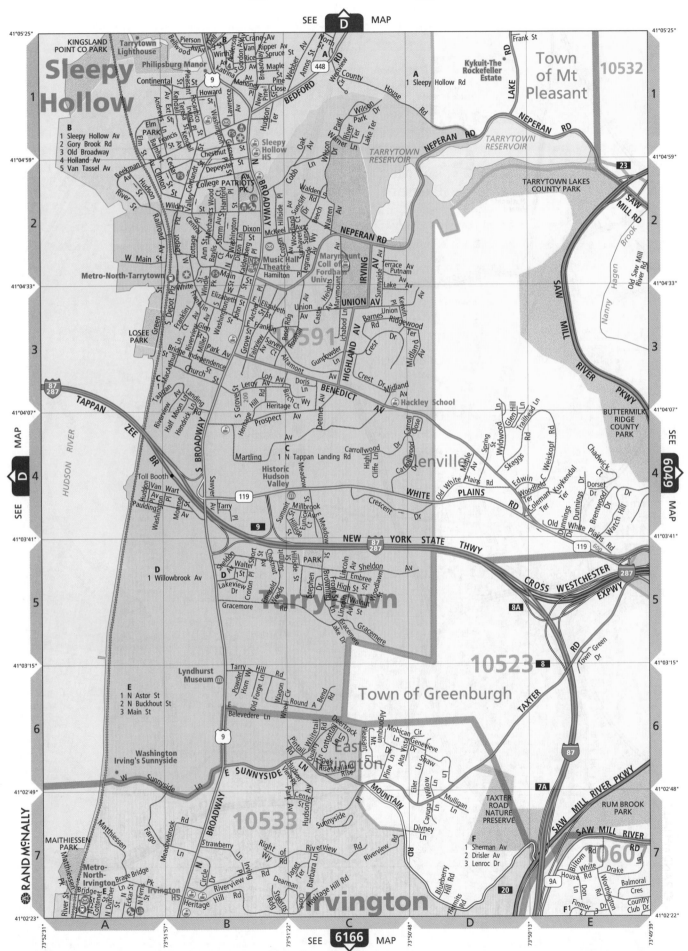

MAP
6049

MAP
6049

1:24,000
1 in. = 2000 ft.
0   0.25   0.5
miles

N

SEE D MAP

41°05'25"   41°05'25"

10532

Westchester County Medical Center
New York Medical College
Mt Pleasant-Blythedale School
Emergency Dr

MT EDEN CEMETERY
GATE OF HEAVEN CEMETERY
LAKEVIEW
KENSICO CEMETERY

Town of Mt Pleasant
10595

Valhalla National Guard

41°04'59"   41°04'58"

Hawthorne Country Day

GRASSLANDS RD
100C

Broadway Plz

41°04'33"   41°04'32"

Blythedale Children's Hospital

Town of Greenburgh

B
1 Nepperhan Av
2 Williams St
3 Frontage St
4 N Mortimer Av
5 Elm Pl

A
1 Wilson Av
2 Davis Av

Southern Westchester Races

GRASSLANDS RD
100

Westchester Community College

10523

41°04'07"   41°04'06"

C
1 Parkway Plz
2 Woodland Av
3 Putnam Av

SEE 6048 MAP

BUTTERMILK RIDGE CO PARK

10591

D
1 Heirloom Ct
2 Reunion Rd
3 Classic Ct
4 Reverie Ct
5 Friendship Ct
6 Tradition Rd
7 Limerick Ct
8 Allegra Ct
9 Legend Cir
10 Victory Ct
11 Camelot Ct

SEE 6050 MAP

PAYNE RD

41°03'41"   41°03'40"

KNOLLWOOD COUNTRY CLUB

MT CALVARY CEMETERY

E
1 Greenburgh Commons Wy

WESTCHESTER EXPWY
287

F
1 Old Knollwood Av
2 S Evarts Av
3 S Perkins Av
4 S French Av
5 Van Wart St

10603

41°03'15"   41°03'14"

New York School for the Deaf

G
1 Hampton Ter
2 Downing Dr E

H
1 Quintard Pl
2 Geyser Pl

Alexander Hamilton JHS

J
1 Shatterhand Close

TRAVIS HILL PARK

RUM BROOK PARK

YOSEMITE PARK

OLD TARRYTOWN RD

41°02'48"   41°02'48"

K
1 Surrey Wy

White Plains Social Security Administration

10607

DOBBS FERRY RD

CROSS WESTCHESTER EXPWY
287

ELMWOOD COUNTRY CLUB

RUM BROOK PARK EAST

METROPOLIS CC

41°02'22"   41°02'22"

A   B   C   D   E

SEE 6167 MAP

MAP 6050

MAP 6050

1:24,000
1 in. = 2000 ft.
0   0.25   0.5
miles

N

SEE **D** MAP

41°05'25" 41°05'24"

A
1 Highclere Ln
2 Colonial Ln

Valhalla Middle-HS

Town of Mt Pleasant

Westlake

COLUMBUS AV
LAKEVIEW AV
St
Ann
Locust St
Shelley St
Wall St
Beech St
E Maple St
Maple Av
Elm St
E Elm St
Westlake
Clinton St
E Clinton St
Waverly St
E Cambridge St
Oxford Pl
E Oxford St
Jefferson
Livingston Dr
Linden
Franklin Av
Ardena
Bela
Prospect
Sherwood
Elm Pl
Lakeside Dr
Lakeside
Prospect
Cedar

RYE LAKE-KENSICO RESERVOIR

B
1 Fountain Dr
2 Cambridge St
3 W Livingston St

C
1 Cedar St Ext
2 Madison Av
3 Hillside Av

Town of North Castle

22

QUARRY HGTS

GREAT ISLAND

10504

RYE LAKE-KENSICO RESERVOIR

CRANBERRY LAKE PARK

41°04'58" 41°04'58"

Kensico Dam
Westlake Dr

KENSICO CEM

KENSICO PLAZA PARK

Rye Lake School Campus

STRAUSS PARK

ORCHARD ST

Indian Hill Rd
Johnson Pl
Rockland Rd
Woodland Rd
Memorial Ln

PARK

Horton LN

Burns Rd

41°04'32" 41°04'32"

Legion
Howard Av
High
Metro-N Valhalla
Entrance Wy
Summit Av
Harding Av
Roosevelt Dr
Wilson Av
Davis Av
McKinley
Livingston
Overlook Dr
Kensico
Blvd

LEGION

COMMERCE

KENSICO DR

VIRGINIA RD

Lawrence
Carlisle Av

Quarry Heights

Jameson
Starkey
McClure St
Helena Av
Morningside
Valhalla
Rock
Cliff Pl

White Plains

Stonewall Ln
Jamison Ct
Shelley Ln
Quaker Ln
Stonewall Cir

Deer Ln
Oak Ridge Ct
Nicols Ct
White Ct
Mill Rd

41°04'06" 41°04'06"

D
1 Vintage Ct
2 Valimar Blvd
3 Legacy Cir
4 Eldorado Ct
5 Primrose Ct

Harrison

Stonewall
Cir

FOR LAKE

Forest
Lake Dr
Dawson Ct

BRONX RIVER PKWY

10603

Hillandale
Emmalon Av
Clove
Nethermont
Overlook
MT KISCO RD

Custis
Washington

Carriage Hill Rd
Buckout

41°03'40" 41°03'40"

E
1 Beal Pl

Lawrence Ct
Eden
Amity
Festival
Reunion

22

Washington's Headquarters Museum

McDougal
Shallwood
Heath Pl
Roberta
Freedom Rd
Pleasant Rd

TO KENSICO RD

Buckout Rd

Castle Rd
Brooke Rd
Golden Pond
Silver Stream Dr

LAKE ST
BARNES

10604

41°03'14" 41°03'14"

F
1 County Center Rd
2 Manitou Tr

G
1 Arborwood Ln

H
1 Taylor Sq

Olive
Augustine
North
Edgepark

Tompkins
Bond
Otis St
Seneca
Thompson

North White Plains

RESERVOIR

General

Lakeview Dr N

RES

OLD RD

Hall Av

SILVER LAKE PARK

SILVER LAKE

Story Hill Rd

41°02'48" 41°02'48"

Metro-North North White Plains

WHITE PLAINS RURAL CEMETERY

TRAVIS HILL PK

TARRYTOWN RD

287

6

CROSS WESTCHESTER EXPWY

22

GARDELLA ALBRO PARK

Westview
Wardman

Lenox Av
Crane Av

Pace Univ-White Plains

7

Glenn
Brookdale
Holland
Benedict
McBride
Hawthorne
Orchard
Archer
Fisher

ORCHARD ST
BEECH ST

Chadwick
Gilvert Pl
Garretson

Clinton
Grant
Mt Morris
Henry

BALDWIN FARM

TODD'S POND

Northminster
Abbey
Woodale
Birch St
Hilldale Av

Sunset
Hiway

DELFINO PARK

VETERANS MEMORIAL DR

HARRISON BLVD

GAINSBORG AV

WASHINGTON ST

10577

BRAE BURN GOLF CLUB

Augusta
Pinehurst

Dorado Dr
O'Shanter Dr
Cypress
Tam
Merion
Oakmont

CENTURY COUNTRY CLUB

UNDERHILL

41°02'48"

41°02'22" 41°02'21"

A   B   C   D   E

73°46'46" 73°46'12" 73°45'37" 73°45'03" 73°44'29" 73°43'54"

SEE 6168 MAP

SEE 6049 MAP

SEE 6051 MAP

MAP
6051

MAP
6051

1:24,000
1 in. = 2000 ft.
0   0.25   0.5
miles

N

SEE **D** MAP

41°05'24"

Town of
North
Castle
10504

120

KING ST

LOCUST RD

684

NEW KING ST

PURCHASE ST

135

2

BEDFORD RD

Whitney Dr

120A

KING ST

Audubon Ln

NATIONAL
AUDUBON
SOCIETY

Richmond Hill Rd

Quaker Ln

WILDFLOWER
SANCTUARY

RIVERSVILLE RD

Fairchild Ln

Town of
Greenwich

Heronvue Rd

Laub Pond Rd

Selden Ln

Corrigan Ln

Hardscrabble Rd

Quaker Ridge Rd

41°05'24"

1

41°04'58"

GRIFFITH E
HARRIS
GOLF
COURSE

CLIFFDALE RD

WOOLEY
POND

41°04'57"

2

RYE
LAKE-KENSICO
RESERVOIR

Loop
Taxi Ln

AIRPORT RD

RYE LAKE AV

KING ST

Byram River

NATURE
CONSERVANCY

41°04'32"   41°04'31"

3

Access Rd

County Rd

Airport Rd

Terminal

CONNECTICUT
NEW YORK
FAIRFIELD CO.
WESTCHESTER CO.

Convent of
Sacred
Heart School

FAIRVIEW
COUNTRY
CLUB

Hycliff Rd

New King St

Rye Lake Rd

LAKE ST

10604

Avery Ct

Old Mill Rd

Old Lake St

200

Kempner Ln

PURCHASE ST

Westchester
County
Airport

06831

SEE 6050 MAP

SEE **D** MAP

41°04'06"   41°04'05"

4

41°03'40"

Tower Ln

Wolfe Ln

Windsor Ct

Av

41°03'39"

5

PARK LN

Oak Valley Ln

Harrison

Katsura Dr

Sycamore Ct

Azalea Cir

Hickory Ct

Pine Ct

Magnolia

Laurel Ln

Fox Run

Wy Dr

Lincoln Av

Millenium Pl

Vintage Ct

Belle Fair Blvd

Legendary Cir

Legacy Fair Blvd

Milestone Rd

Reunion Rd

Heritage

High Ct

Belle Point

Heirloom

House Ct

Meeting Cir

Parade Ln

Fellowship Ln

Chieftans Rd

SHERWOOD AV

41°03'14"

BARNES LN

Legend Ct

Parkside Ct

Brae Burn Dr

Cedar Ln

Fairway Dr

Country Club Dr

White Oak Cir

West Rd

East Rd

Cottage Av

West Rd

SUNY PURCHASE

Lincoln Av

West Rd

East Rd

**Rye
Brook**
10573

International Dr

120A

Blind Brook

Willow Run Rd

41°03'13"

6

PURCHASE ST

GOLF CLUB OF PURCHASE

10577

Performing
Arts Center

DORAL
GOLF
CLUB

Doral Greens Dr

ArrowWood Cir

W Doral Green Dr

Doral Green E Ct

Alfred Green Ct

41°02'48"

BRAE BURN
GOLF CLUB

Pineview Cir

Sarosca
Farm Ln

Doran Rd

120

East Rd

Cottage Av

Pine Tree Dr

Doral Cir

41°02'47"

7

684

OLD OAKS COUNTRY CLUB

PURCHASE

Ponds Ln

CENTURY
COUNTRY
CLUB

ANDERSON
HILL RD

BLIND
BROOK
COUNTRY
CLUB

41°02'21"   41°02'21"

A   B   C   D   E

73°43'54"   73°43'20"   73°42'45"   73°42'11"   73°41'36"   73°41'02"

SEE 6169 MAP

MAP
6164

MAP
6164

1:24,000
1 in. = 2000 ft.

0   0.25   0.5
miles

SEE D MAP

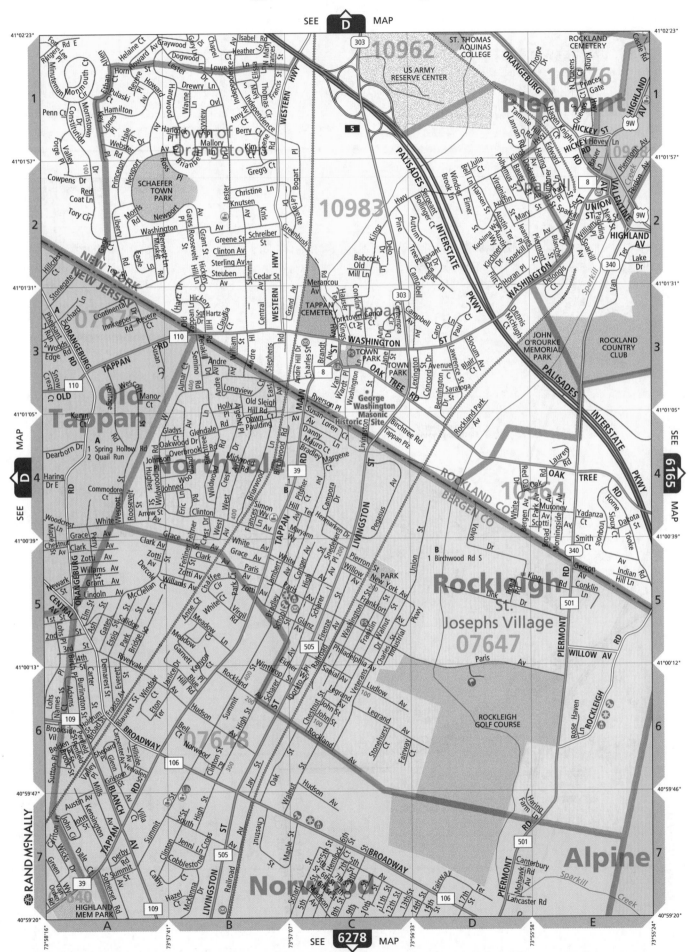

MAP
6165

MAP
6165

1:24,000
1 in. = 2000 ft.

0   0.25   0.5

miles

SEE **D** MAP

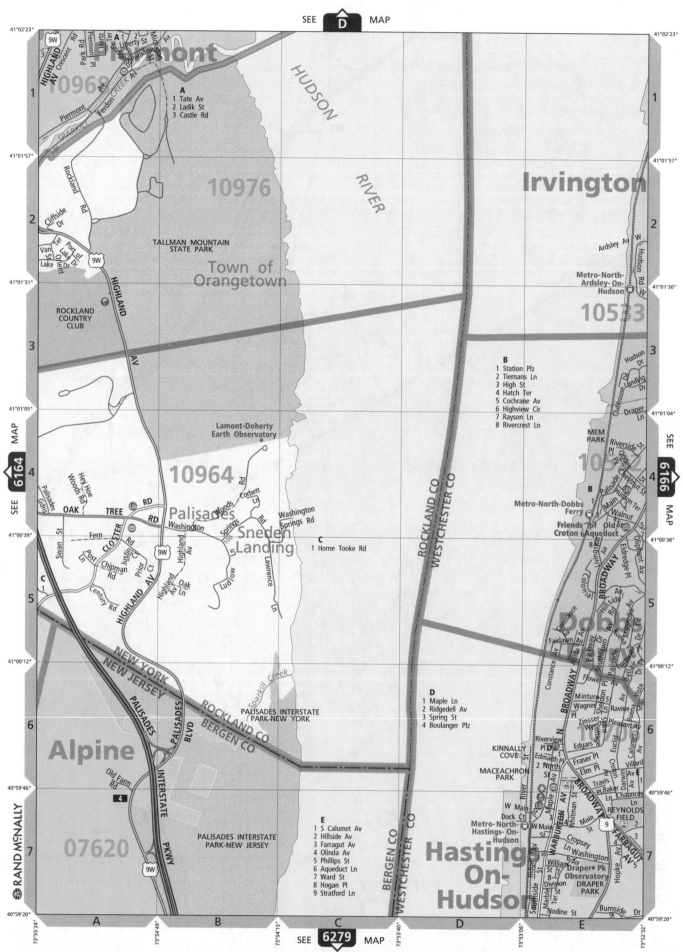

Piermont

10968

10976

Irvington

HUDSON

RIVER

TALLMAN MOUNTAIN
STATE PARK

Town of
Orangetown

Metro-North-
Ardsley- On-
Hudson

10533

ROCKLAND
COUNTRY
CLUB

A
1 Tate Av
2 Ladik St
3 Castle Rd

B
1 Station Plz
2 Tiernans Ln
3 High St
4 Hatch Ter
5 Cochrane Av
6 Highview Cir
7 Rayson Ln
8 Rivercrest Ln

Lamont-Doherty
Earth Observatory

MEM
PARK

10522

10964

Palisades

Metro-North-Dobbs
Ferry

OAK   TREE   RD

Friends of
Croton Aqueduct

Washington
Springs Rd

Sneden
Landing

C
1 Horne Tooke Rd

**Dobbs
Ferry**

NEW YORK
NEW JERSEY

PALISADES INTERSTATE
PARK-NEW YORK

D
1 Maple Ln
2 Ridgedell Av
3 Spring St
4 Boulanger Plz

10706

Alpine

KINNALLY
COVE

MACEACHRON
PARK

Old Farm
Rd

4

PALISADES INTERSTATE
PARK-NEW JERSEY

E
1 S Calumet Av
2 Hillside Av
3 Farragut Av
4 Olinda Av
5 Phillips St
6 Aqueduct Ln
7 Ward St
8 Hogan Pl
9 Stratford Ln

Metro-North-
Hastings-On-
Hudson

Draper Pk
Observatory

07620

REYNOLDS
FIELD

DRAPER
PARK

**Hastings-
On-
Hudson**

RAND McNALLY

A   B   C   D   E

MAP
6166

MAP
6166

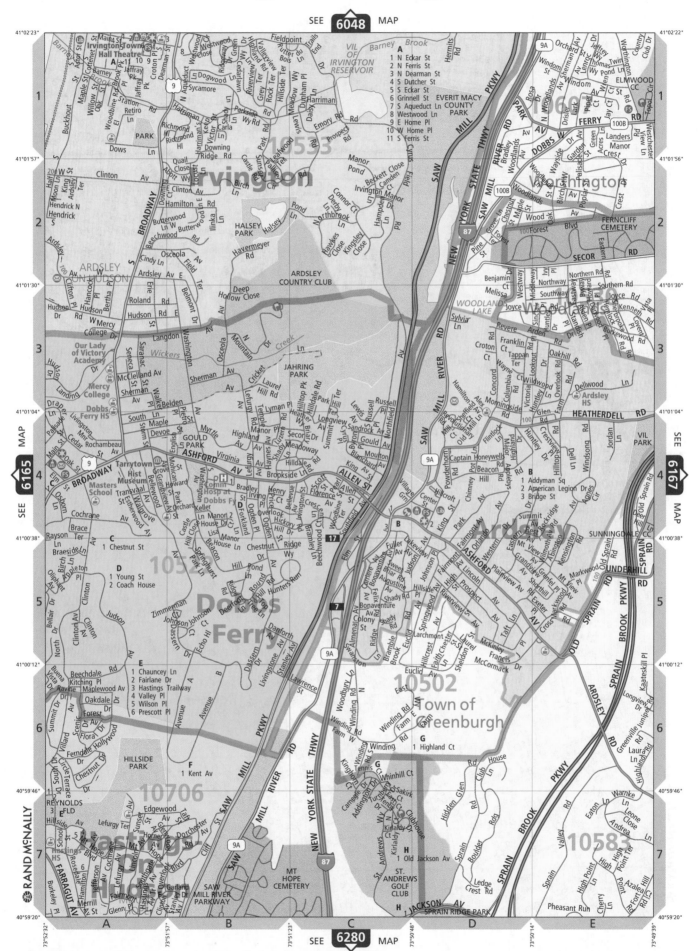

1:24,000
1 in. = 2000 ft.

0   0.25   0.5
miles

MAP 6167

MAP 6167

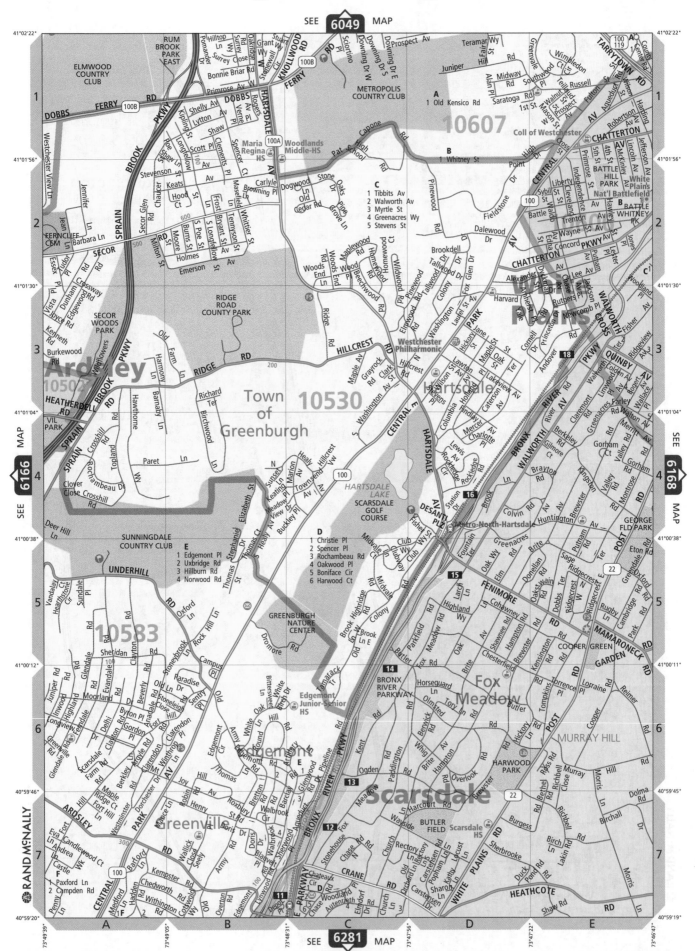

SEE 6049 MAP

SEE 6166 MAP

SEE 6168 MAP

SEE 6281 MAP

1:24,000
1 in. = 2000 ft.
0   0.25   0.5
miles

MAP
6168

MAP
6168

1:24,000
1 in. = 2000 ft.

0   0.25   0.5
miles

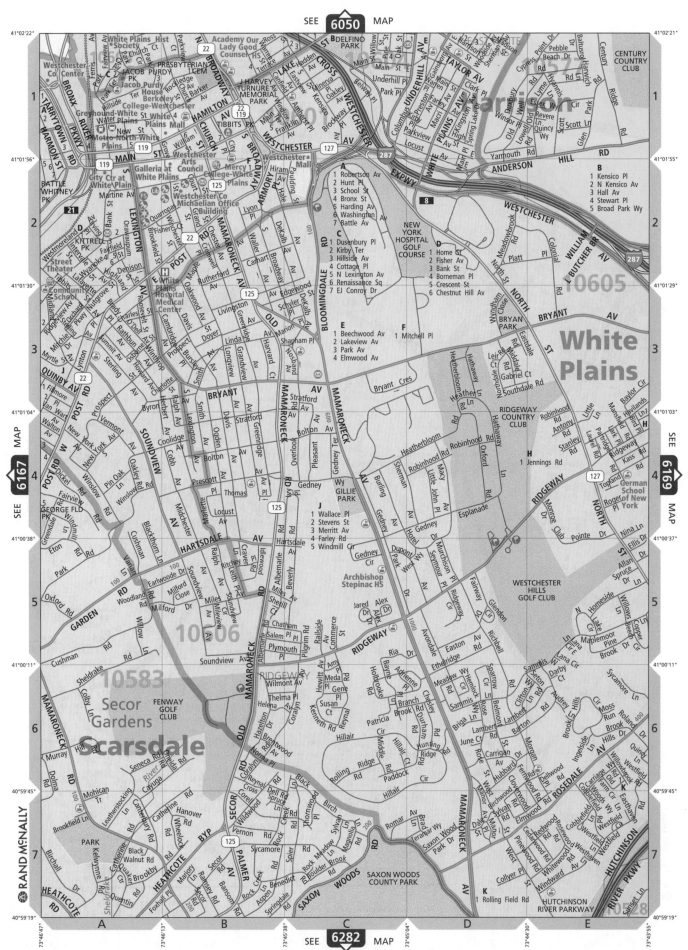

SEE 6050 MAP

SEE 6167 MAP

SEE 6169 MAP

SEE 6282 MAP

A
1 Robertson Av
2 Hunt Pl
3 School St
4 Bronx St
5 Harding Av
6 Washington
7 Battle Av

C
1 Dusenbury Pl
2 Kirby Ter
3 Hillside Av
4 Cottage Pl
5 N Lexington Av
6 Renaissance Sq
7 EJ Conroy Dr

D
1 Home St
2 Fisher Av
3 Bank St
4 Borneman Pl
5 Crescent St
6 Chestnut Hill Av

E
1 Beechwood Av
2 Lakeview Av
3 Park Av
4 Elmwood Av

F
1 Mitchell Pl

H
1 Jennings Rd

J
1 Wallace Pl
2 Stevens St
3 Merritt St
4 Farley Rd
5 Windmill Cir

1 Kensico Pl
2 N Kensico Av
3 Hall Av
4 Stewart Pl
5 Broad Park Wy

K
1 Rolling Field Rd

White
Plains

Scarsdale

Secor
Gardens

Harrison

NEW
YORK
HOSPITAL
GOLF
COURSE

CENTURY
COUNTRY
CLUB

RIDGEWAY
COUNTRY
CLUB

WESTCHESTER
HILLS
GOLF CLUB

FENWAY
GOLF
CLUB

SAXON WOODS
COUNTY PARK

HUTCHINSON
RIVER PARKWAY

10606

10583

10605

German
School
of New
York

RAND McNALLY

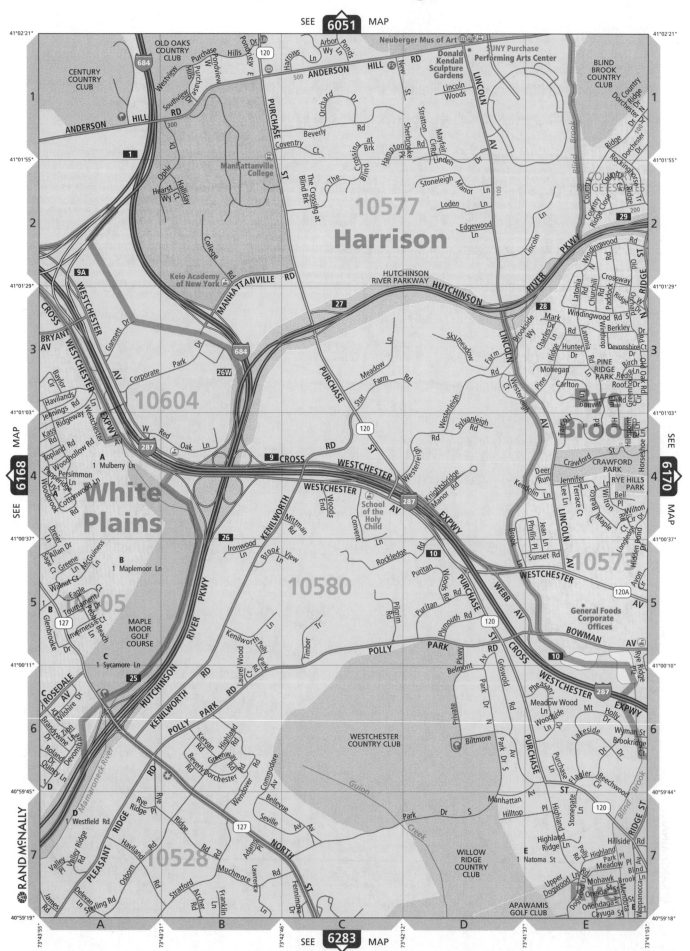

MAP 6169

MAP 6169

1:24,000
1 in. = 2000 ft.

0   0.25   0.5

miles

N

SEE 6051 MAP

41°02'21"
41°01'55"
41°01'29"
41°01'03"
41°00'37"
41°00'11"
40°59'45"
40°59'19"

SEE 6168 MAP

SEE 6170 MAP

41°02'21"
41°01'55"
41°01'29"
41°01'03"
41°00'37"
40°59'44"
40°59'18"

CENTURY COUNTRY CLUB

OLD OAKS COUNTRY CLUB

Neuberger Mus of Art

Donald Kendall Sculpture Gardens

SUNY Purchase Performing Arts Center

BLIND BROOK COUNTRY CLUB

ANDERSON HILL RD

Manhattanville College

10577

Harrison

Keio Academy of New York

HUTCHINSON RIVER PARKWAY

10604

White Plains

10605

MAPLE MOOR GOLF COURSE

10580

Rye Brook

PINE RIDGE PARK

CRAWFORD PARK

RYE HILLS PARK

10573

General Foods Corporate Offices

BOWMAN AV

School of the Holy Child

POLLY PARK

WESTCHESTER COUNTRY CLUB

Biltmore

10528

ROSEDALE AV

WILLOW RIDGE COUNTRY CLUB

APAWAMIS GOLF CLUB

SEE 6283 MAP

A   B   C   D   E

73°43'55"   73°43'21"   73°42'46"   73°42'12"   73°41'37"   73°41'03"

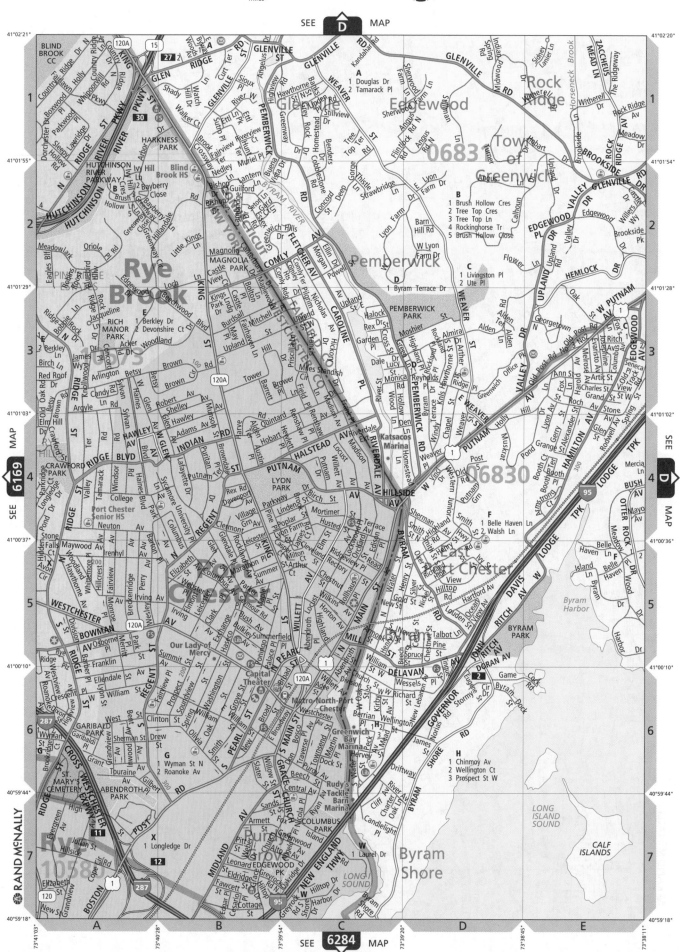

MAP 6278

1:24,000
1 in. = 2000 ft.
0   0.25   0.5
miles

N

MAP 6278

SEE 6164 MAP

BROADWAY RD

Harrington Park
07640

Norwood

07648

Closter
07624

Alpine
07620

Demarest

SEE MAP D

SEE 6279 MAP

HIGHLAND MEM PK

ORADELL RESERVOIR

MEM PARK

ALPINE PARK

WAKELEE FIELD

Old Church Cultural Ctr

A
1 Kohring Cir S

B
1 Mountain View Rd
2 Laurel Rd
3 Heather Hill Ct
4 Elmwood Ter

HARDENBURGH

Cresskill HS

ALPINE COUNTRY CLUB

07627

Demarest Brook

Cresskill Brook

CLOSTER DOCK RD

Academy of the Holy Angels

HILLSIDE AV

07626

Cresskill

1 Engle St

PALISADES INTERSTATE PARK-NEW JERSEY

9W

RAND McNALLY

A   B   C   D   E

MAP
6279

MAP
6279

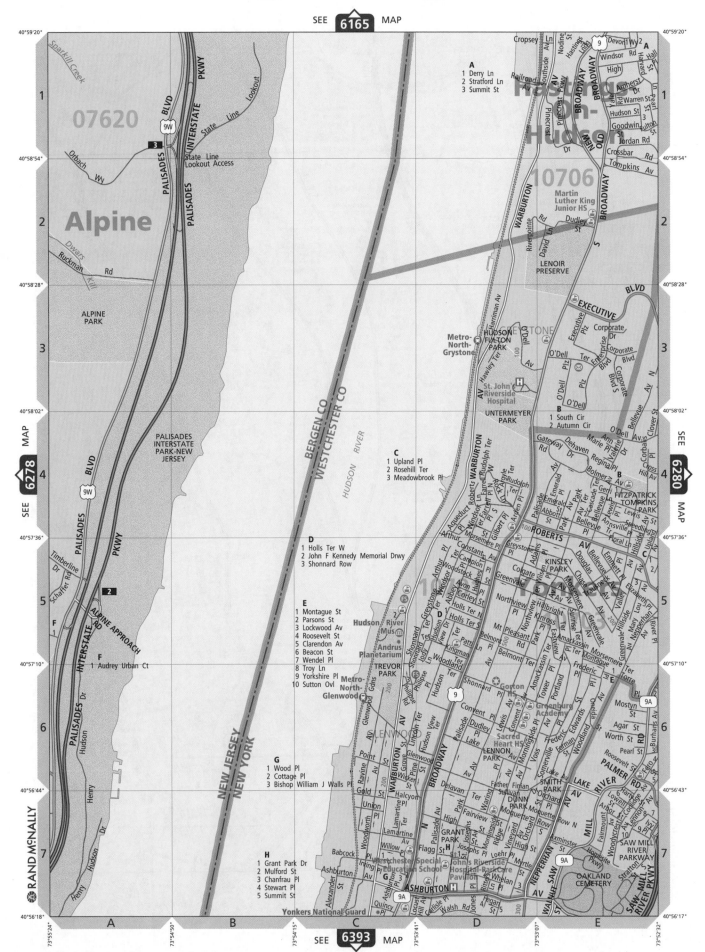

1:24,000
1 in. = 2000 ft.
0   0.25   0.5
miles

40°59'20"
40°58'54"
40°58'28"
40°58'02"
40°57'36"
40°57'10"
40°56'44"
40°56'18"

07620

Alpine

Sparkill Creek

Orbach Wy

State Line Lookout

State Line Lookout Access

INTERSTATE PALISADES PKWY

PALISADES BLVD

3

9W

Dwars Kill

Ruckman Rd

ALPINE PARK

PALISADES INTERSTATE PARK-NEW JERSEY

Timberline Dr

Schaffer Rd

2

ALPINE APPROACH RD

INTERSTATE

PALISADES PKWY

PALISADES Dr

F
1

F
1 Audrey Urban Ct

Hudson

Henry

Henry Dr

Hudson Dr

NEW JERSEY
NEW YORK

RAND McNALLY

BERGEN CO
WESTCHESTER CO

Hudson River

SEE 6278 MAP

SEE 6280 MAP

A
1 Derry Ln
2 Stratford Ln
3 Summit St

Cropsey Ln
Nodine Ln
Hastings
Laddin
Southside
Railroad Av
Pinecrest Dr
Pinecrest
Av

Devon Wy
Windsor Rd
High
Hall
Parkel St
Amherst Dr
Warren St
Hudson St
Goodwin St
Jordan Rd
Crossbar Rd
Tompkins Av

9

Hastings-On-Hudson

10706

BROADWAY
BROADWAY
NEW
OLD
BROADWAY

WARBURTON

Martin Luther King Junior HS

Riverpointe
Rd
David Ln
Dudley St

LENOIR PRESERVE

Harriman Av

EXECUTIVE BLVD

GREYSTONE

Metro-North-Grystone

HUDSON FULTON PARK

O'Dell
Hawley Av

St. John's Riverside Hospital

UNTERMEYER PARK

Executive Plz
Corporate Dr
Corporate
Enterprise Blvd
O'Dell Ter
O'Dell Plz
Corporate Blvd S
O'Dell

B
1 South Cir
2 Autumn Cir

Gateway Rd
Dehaven Dr
Marie Regina Pl
Ann

O'Dell Av
Bellevue
Corbalis
Cross
Hill Av

B

FITZPATRICK
TOMPKINS PARK

Clover St

C
1 Upland Pl
2 Rosehill Ter
3 Meadowbrook Pl

WARBURTON

Aqueduct
Roberts
Farrell
Rudolph Ter
Algrie
Rudolph
Emerald Av
Emerald
Abbott
Palisade

Ansville Av
Speeding
Lewis St
Floral
Bellevue
Upland

ROBERTS AV

KINSLEY PARK

Bellevue
Douglas
Emmett
Chase

C

D
1 Holls Ter W
2 John F Kennedy Memorial Drwy
3 Shonnard Row

Arthur
Constant Av
Campion
Morsemere Av
Woodstock
Avon Pl
Corley St
Abbey
Holls Ter S
Greystone

Greenvale
Colgate
Northview
Northview
Hillbright
Kinross

Yonkers

Valley
Many Lou
Hillside
Sunrise
Montague Ter

E
1 Montague St
2 Parsons St
3 Lockwood Av
4 Roosevelt St
5 Clarendon Av
6 Beacon St
7 Wendel Pl
8 Troy Ln
9 Yorkshire Pl
10 Sutton Ovl

Hudson River Mus

Andrus Planetarium

TREVOR PARK

Metro-North-Glenwood

D

Shonnard
Hudson
Holls Ter S
Patti
Kingman
Woodland Ter

Mt Pleasant Rd
Belmont
Belmont

Belmont Ter

Amackassin Ter
Morsemere Ter
Greenvale
Frederic
Frederic
Torre

E

9A

D

Shonnard
Philipse
Gorton HS

Convent Av
Lewis
Convent Av

Greenburg Academy

Sacred Heart HS

Tower
Portland
Edwards
Woodland

Mostyn
Agar St
Worth St
Pearl St
Roosevelt St

9A

F
1
G
1 Wood Pl
2 Cottage Pl
3 Bishop William J Walls Pl

Glenwood Gdns

GLENWOOD

Point
Ravine
Gold
Union
Woodnorth

WARBURTON AV

Grove
Wicker
Glenwood

BROADWAY

Delavan

Lincoln Ter
Hudson View Ter
Palisade
Lake

Father Finian
Sullivan

LENNON PARK

Morningside Pl
Voss
Forman

Somerville
Lake Av

PALMER PARK

Lake Av

RIVER
MILL
RD

Burhans

H
1 Grant Park Dr
2 Mulford St
3 Chanfrau Pl
4 Stewart Pl
5 Summit St

Babcock

Ashburton

Alexander St

Quincy
Pl

Woodworth
Lamartine
Lamartine Av
Willow
Flagg

Halcyon
High
Palisade Pl

GRANT PARK

Joseph's
Joseph's

Irving Av
Ashburton

ASHBURTON

9A

Yonkers National Guard

Westchester Special Hospital-Education School

H

St John's Riverside Hospital-ParkCare Pavilion

Locust
Hill Av
Carlisle Pl

Waring
Fairview

Maple

Vineyard

Orchard
Orchard

DUNN PARK

Moquette Row N
Moquette Row S

Morningside
Ridge
Loehr Pl
Myrtle
Whelan

SMITH PARK

Oneida

Axminster
Homeside

Lowell
Coolidge
9 Pl

Arbor
Woodhollow

Lodge
Fairmount

Stratton

OAKLAND CEMETERY

NEPPERHAN AV
WALNUT
SAW MILL

Fairmount

SAW MILL RIVER PARKWAY

SAW MILL RIVER PKWY

40°59'20"
40°58'54"
40°58'28"
40°58'02"
40°57'36"
40°57'10"
40°56'43"
40°56'17"

73°55'24"
73°54'50"
73°54'15"
73°53'41"
73°53'07"
73°52'32"

A   B   C   D   E

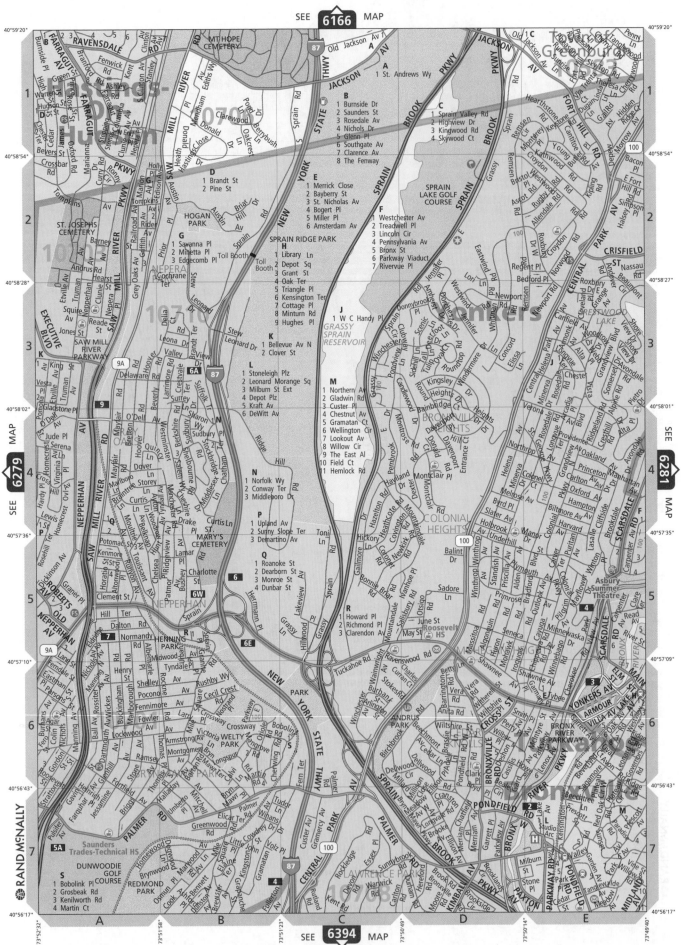

MAP 6280

MAP 6280

1:24,000
1 in. = 2000 ft.

0   0.25   0.5

miles

SEE 6166 MAP

SEE 6279 MAP

SEE 6281 MAP

SEE 6394 MAP

RAND McNALLY

A
1 St. Andrews Wy

B
1 Burnside Dr
2 Saunders St
3 Rosedale Av
4 Nichols Dr
5 Glenn Pl
6 Southgate Av
7 Clarence Av
8 The Fenway

C
1 Sprain Valley Rd
2 Highview Dr
3 Kingwood Rd
4 Skywood Ct

D
1 Brandt St
2 Pine St

E
1 Merrick Close
2 Bayberry St
3 St. Nicholas Av
4 Bogert Pl
5 Miller Pl
6 Amsterdam Av

F
1 Westchester Av
2 Treadwell Pl
3 Lincoln Cir
4 Pennsylvania Av
5 Bronx Rd
6 Parkway Viaduct
7 Rivervue Pl

G
1 Savanna Pl
2 Minetta Pl
3 Edgecomb Pl

H
1 Library Ln
2 Depot Sq
3 Grant St
4 Oak Ter
5 Triangle Pl
6 Kensington Ter
7 Cottage Pl
8 Minturn Rd
9 Hughes Pl

J
1 W C Handy Pl

K
1 Bellevue Av N
2 Clover St

L
1 Stoneleigh Plz
2 Leonard Morange Sq
3 Milburn St Ext
4 Depot Plz
5 Kraft Av
6 DeWitt Av

M
1 Northern Av
2 Gladwin Rd
3 Custer Pl
4 Chestnut Av
5 Gramatan Ct
6 Wellington Cir
7 Lookout Av
8 Willow Cir
9 The East Al
10 Field Ct
11 Hemlock Rd

N
1 Norfolk Wy
2 Conway Ter
3 Middleboro Dr

P
1 Upland Av
2 Sunny Slope Ter
3 Demartino Av

Q
1 Roanoke St
2 Dearborn St
3 Monroe St
4 Dunbar St

R
1 Howard Pl
2 Richmond Pl
3 Clarendon Av

S
1 Bobolink Pl
2 Grosbeak Rd
3 Kenilworth Rd
4 Martin Ct

MAP
6281

MAP
6281

SEE 6167 MAP

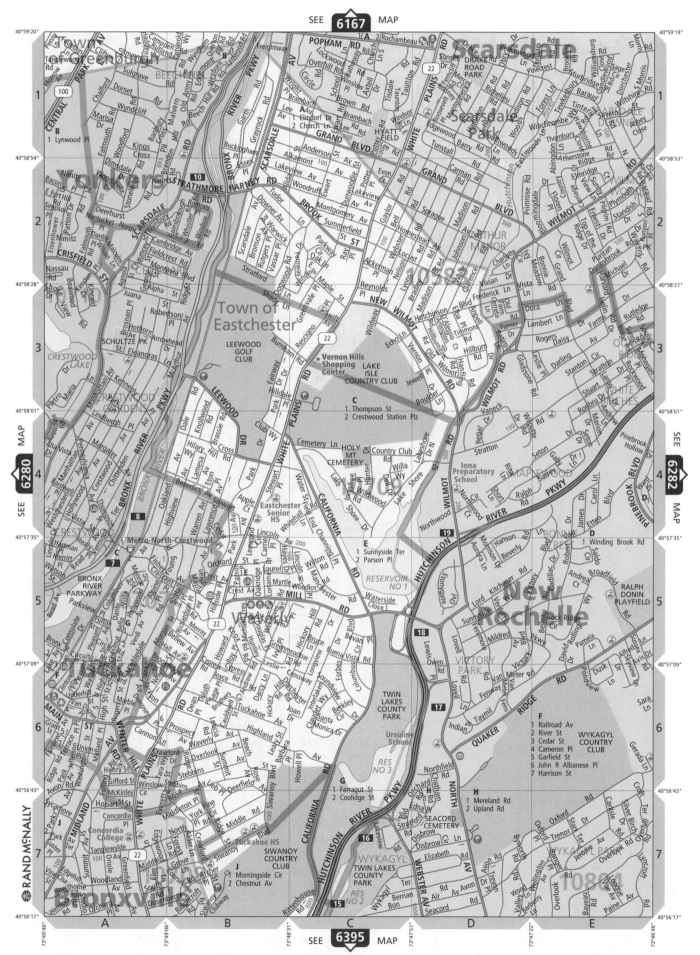

1:24,000
1 in. = 2000 ft.

0   0.25   0.5

miles

MAP 6280

SEE 6282 MAP

SEE 6395 MAP

RAND McNALLY

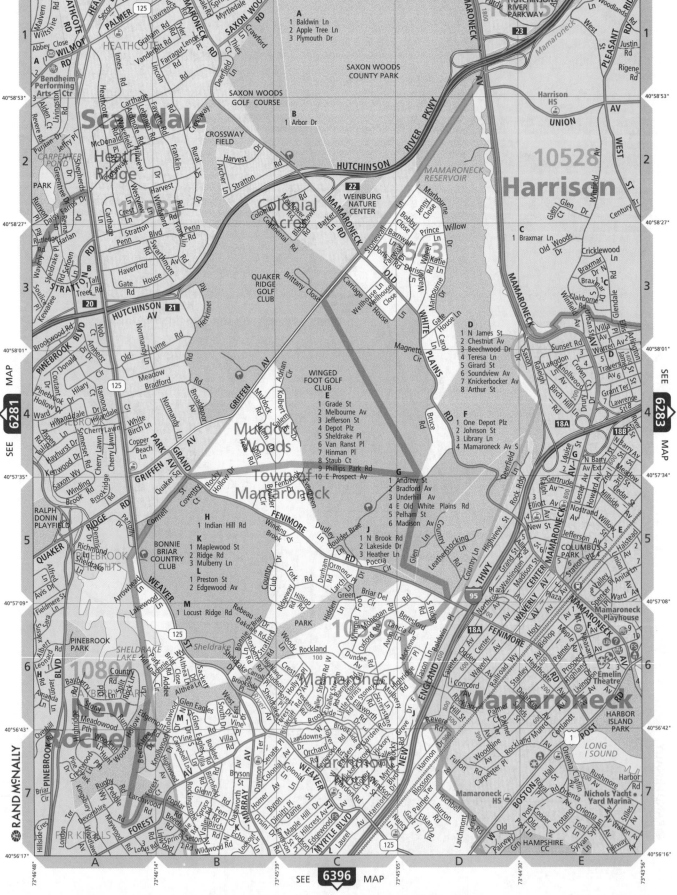

MAP
6283

MAP
6283

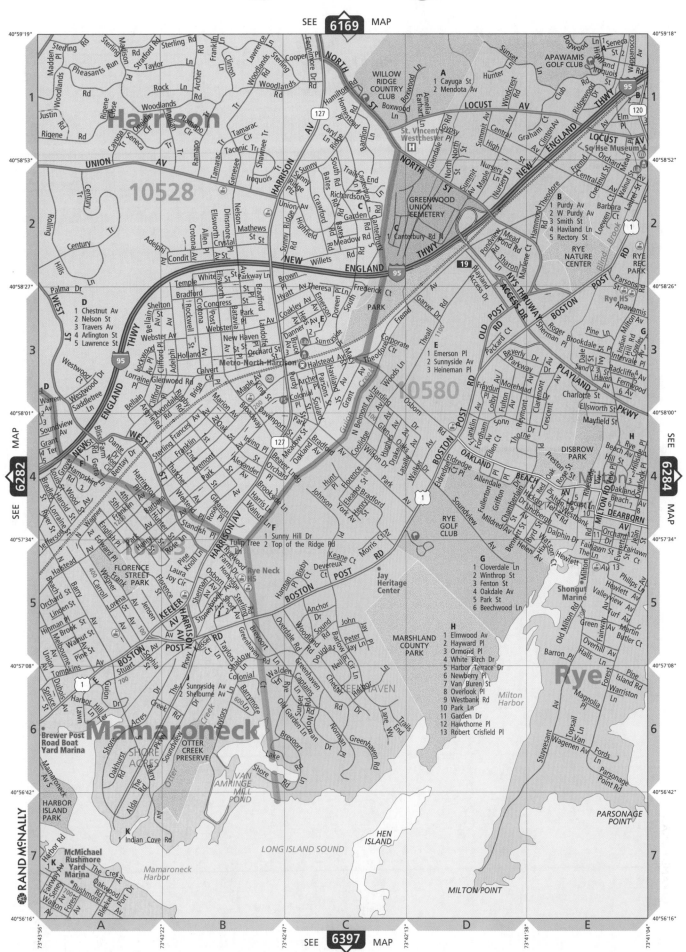

1:24,000
1 in. = 2000 ft.

0   0.25   0.5

miles

N

SEE 6282 MAP

SEE 6284 MAP

RAND McNALLY

MAP
6284

MAP
6284

1:24,000
1 in. = 2000 ft.

0   0.25   0.5
miles

N

SEE 6170 MAP

40°59'18"   40°59'18"

New
Cedar
20 St
95
21
NEW
ENGLAND
287
THWY
Greylock
Rd
Shore
Dr
Dr
BYRAM
SHORE RD

U.S. 1
Metro-North Rye
Avon
Plz
22
Guion Rd
Rye Rd
Sackett
Lndg
Port
Chester

Hidden
Spring Ln
Thistle
Larkspur Dr
Beck
Beaty
Ct
Kirby
Ln
N
St
Guion
Rd

1   1

Purdy
Av
Smith
St
Greenleaf
Howard
Lavender
Ln
Holly Ln
Rye
Church
Grace
Church

A
1 Grandview Av
2 Station Plz
3 2nd St
4 McCullough Pl
5 1st St
6 School St
7 Mistletoe Ln
8 Barberry Ln
9 Cazenove Pl
10 Loder St

N Island
Dr
Island
Dr

Ralston
St
Church
St
Grapal
Manursing
Av
B
1 Grapal Pl

KIRBY
POND

W Island
Dr

40°58'52"   40°58'52"

Rye Arts
Center
Milton
Rd
Rectory
Richard
Pl
Palisade
Palisades
Rd
Cedar St
B
Sylvan
Pl
Maple Dr
Pleasant St
Gramercy
Av
Davis
Drake
Av
Smith
Ln
Forest

Tide Mill
Yacht
Basin
Kirby
Manursing

2   2

RYE
RECREATION
PARK
Goldwin
St
Ellis Ct
Rockridge
Ann Ln
Stonecrest Rd
Manursing
Wy
Island Dr

Billington
Ct
Boulder Rd
Rd

40°58'26"   40°58'25"

C
Platt
Ln
George
Clark Ln
Eve
Fieldstone
Rd
Hook
Rd

MANURSING
LAKE

Manursing
Wy

Rensselaer
Rd

Cowles
Av
Lea
Langeloh
Pl
Apawamis
Av
Beary
Ct
Martin
Heritage
Rd
C
1 Greenacres Dr
2 Hillcrest Ln
3 Cloverdale Ln
4 Intervale Pl

Van

3   3

Lynden
Brown St
Sanford
Adelaide St
Rosemere St

Centre
Orchard Ln

D
1 Wards Pk E
2 Wards Pk W

WESTCHESTER
COUNTY
PLAYLAND
PARK

Wetmore
Pl
Cir
Horton
St
Wainwright St
Beck
Av
D

40°58'00"   40°57'59"

Bulkley
Ridgeland
Mnr

PLAYLAND
Ridgeland
Elmwood
PKWY
Ter
Redfield
St
Playland
Pkwy
Playland
Pkwy

SEE D MAP

Oakwood
Overlook
Pl
Rye
Beach Av
Playland Amusement Park

6283 MAP

4   4

Ormond
Pl
E
FOREST AV
E
1 Oakland Beach Av
2 Rickbern St
3 Stanley Keyes Ct

Halstead
Rye
Beach
RYE
TOWN
PARK

Dearborn
Av

40°57'34"   40°57'33"

Forest
Av
3rd
Cornell Pl
Bird
Oakland
Beach

Forest
Cove

Phillips
Ln

LONG   ISLAND   SOUND

5   5

40°57'08"   40°57'07"

Pine
Island
Rd

6   6

40°56'42"   40°56'41"

RAND MNALLY

7   7

40°56'16"   40°56'15"

A   B   C   D   E

73°41'04"   73°40'30"   73°39'55"   73°39'21"   73°38'46"   73°38'12"

SEE 6398 MAP

MAP
6392

MAP
6392

1:24,000
1 in. = 2000 ft.

0   0.25   0.5

miles

SEE 6278 MAP

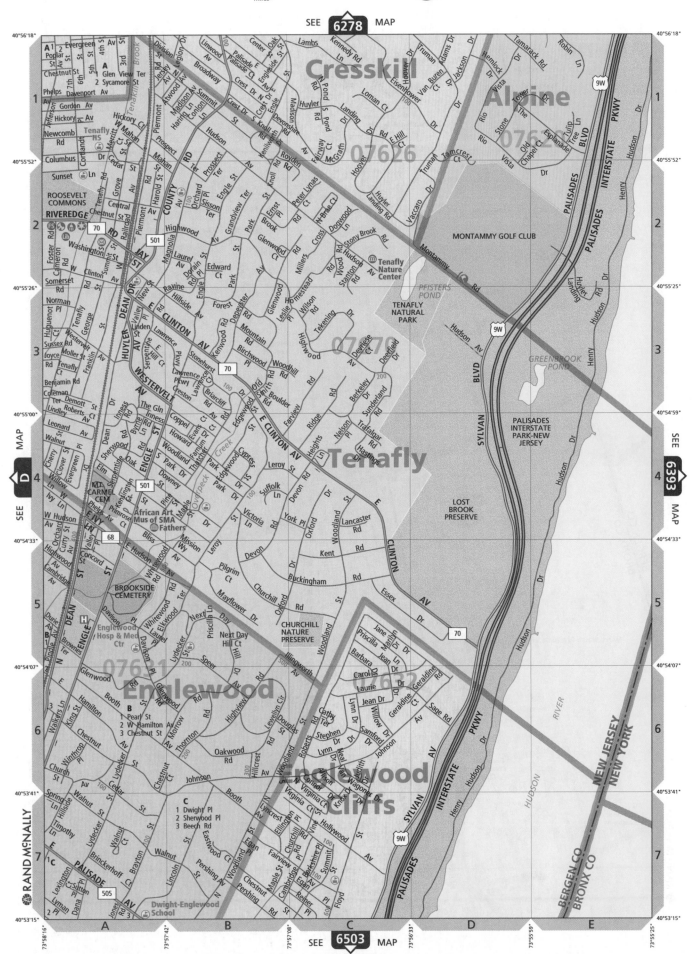

SEE 6393 MAP

SEE 6503 MAP

RAND MCNALLY

MAP 6393
MAP 6393

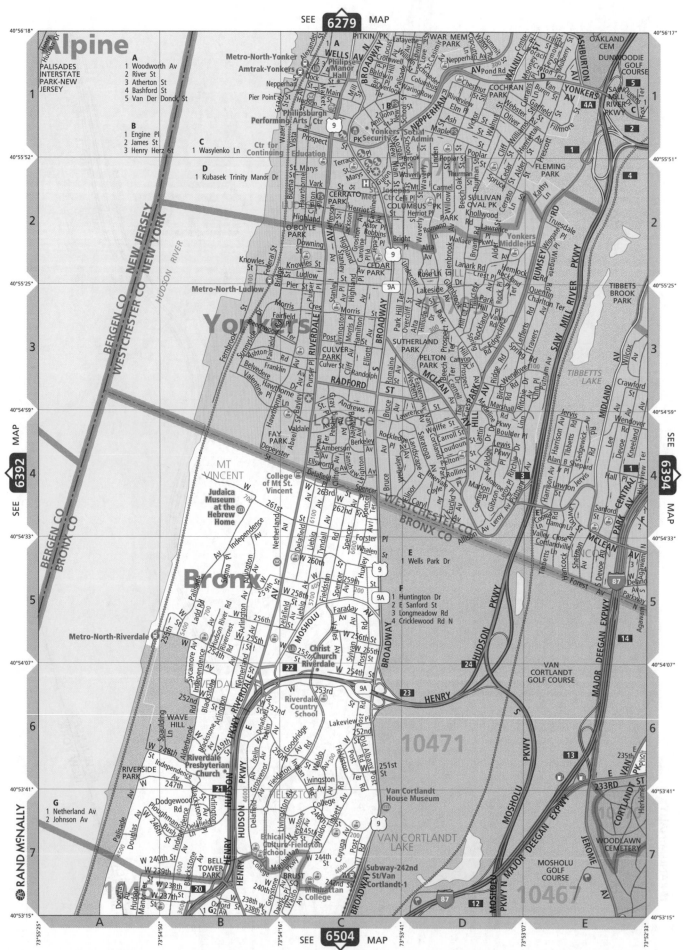

MAP
6394

1:24,000
1 in. = 2000 ft.
0   0.25   0.5
miles

MAP
6394

SEE 6280 MAP

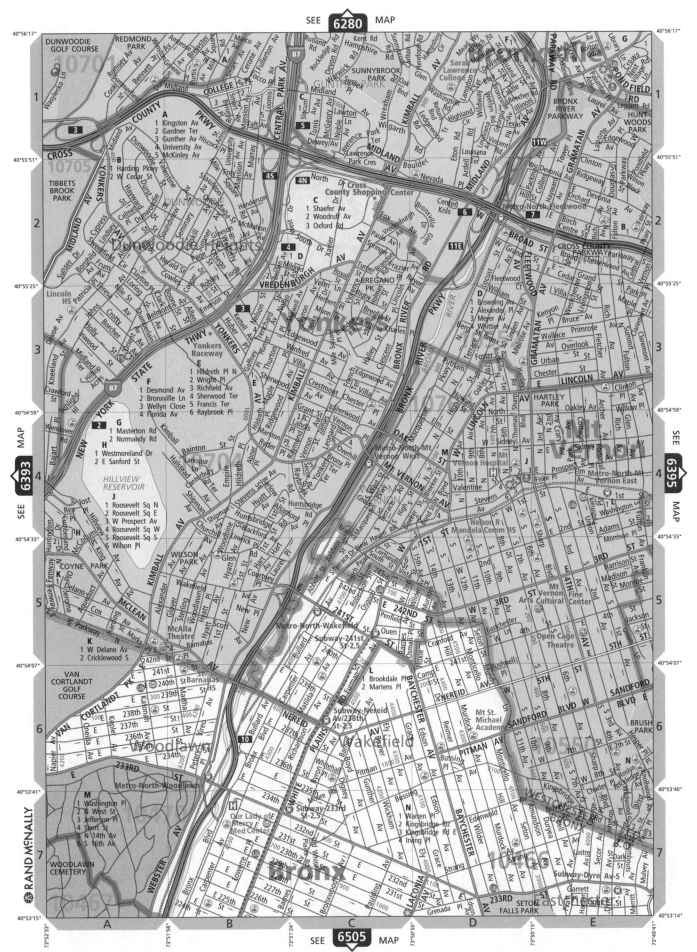

SEE 6393 MAP

SEE 6395 MAP

SEE 6505 MAP

MAP
6395

MAP
6395

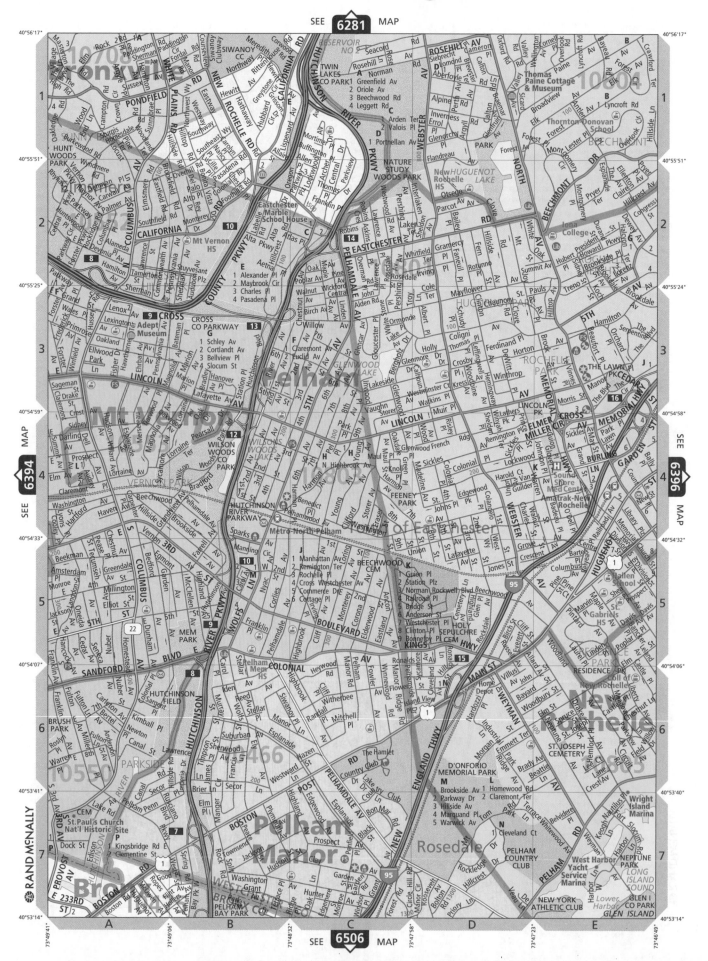

MAP
6396

MAP
6396

1:24,000
1 in. = 2000 ft.

0   0.25   0.5

miles

SEE 6282 MAP

SEE 6395 MAP

SEE 6397 MAP

SEE 6507 MAP

C
1 Pryer Pl
2 Beechmont Pl
3 Broadcast Plz

D
1 Linwood Rd
2 Rockingstone Av
3 Echo Ln
4 Emerson Rd
5 Edgewood Av
6 Thompson St
7 Cabot Rd
8 France Pl
9 Maple St
10 Maxwell Av

B
1 Ferndale Pl
2 Plymouth Rd
3 Harmony Dr
4 Railroad Wy
5 Franklin Av

E
1 The Serpentine

F
1 Glen Lake Dr
2 Rockhill Ter
3 Parkway St

G
1 Edgewater Pl
2 Doherty Pl

H
1 Frederic B Powers Sq
2 Pembroke St
3 Sherman St
4 Halligan St
5 Dearborn St
6 Homestead Pl
7 Commerce Dr
8 Radisson Plz

J
1 Fountain Pl
2 Harrison St
3 Lafayette St
4 Le Count Pl
5 Bayview Av
6 Alpha Pl
7 Bonnefoy Pl
8 S Division St

K
1 Chestnut Ln

LONG ISLAND
SOUND

RAND McNALLY

MAP
6397

1:24,000
1 in. = 2000 ft.
0   0.25   0.5
miles

N

MAP
6397

SEE 6283 MAP

40°56'16"

ORIENTA
Forest Av
Walton
Bleeker Av
Bloomingdale Av
Rushmore Av
Mamaroneck
Claflin Av
Westchester Day School
A
1 Seney Av
Greacen Point Rd
Orienta Av
Green Ln
Skibo Ln
Nine Acres Ln
Nautilus Ln
Seahaven Dr
Meadow Ln
Pirates Cove
1000
Seven Oaks Ln
Constable Dr N
Constable Dr S
Pirates Head
Bay
Orienta Dr
Flagler Dr
DELANCEY POINT

1

40°55'50"

2

40°55'24"

3

40°54'58"

MAP 6396 SEE

LONG ISLAND SOUND

4

40°54'32"

SEE 6398 MAP

40°54'31"

5

40°54'06"

40°54'05"

6

40°53'40"

40°53'39"

RAND MᶜNALLY

7

40°53'13"

40°53'13"

A   B   C   D   E

73°43'57"   73°43'23"   73°42'48"   73°42'14"   73°41'39"   73°41'05"

SEE 6508 MAP

40°56'16"

40°55'50"

40°55'23"

40°54'57"

40°54'05"

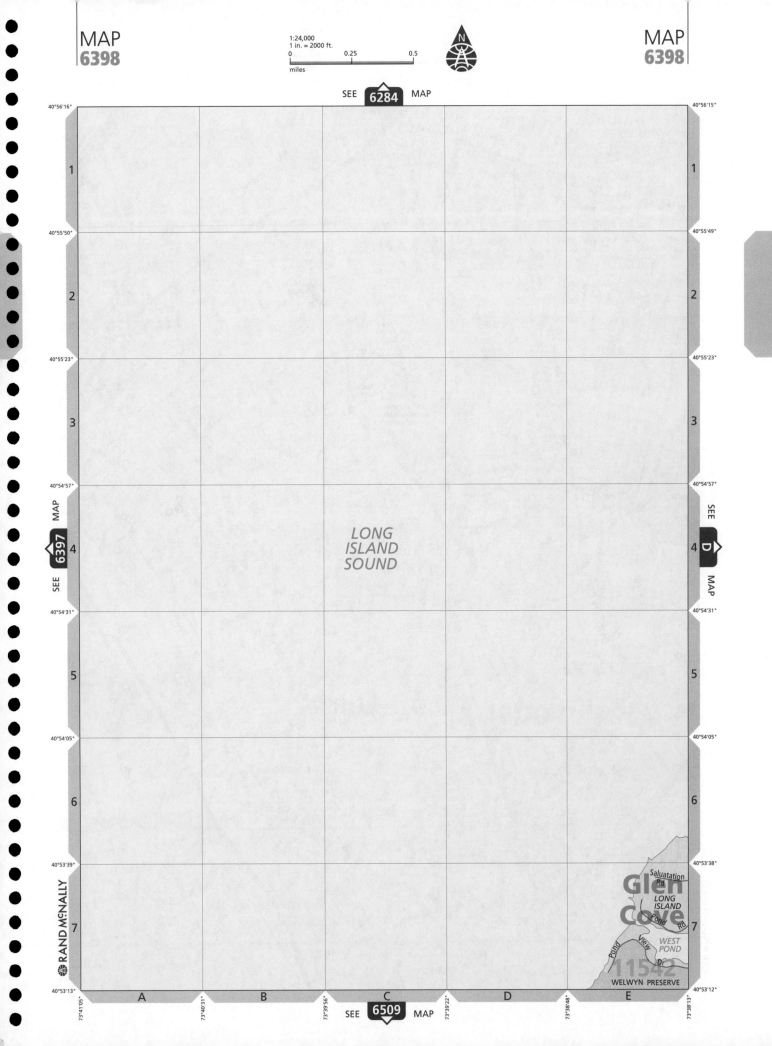

MAP
6398

MAP
6398

1:24,000
1 in. = 2000 ft.

0   0.25   0.5
miles

N

SEE 6284 MAP

40°56'16"
40°56'15"

1

40°55'50"
40°55'49"

2

40°55'23"
40°55'23"

3

40°54'57"
40°54'57"

SEE 6397 MAP

4

LONG
ISLAND
SOUND

SEE D MAP

40°54'31"
40°54'31"

5

40°54'05"
40°54'05"

6

40°53'39"
40°53'38"

Saluatation Rd

Glen
Cove

LONG
ISLAND
Pond
Rd

7

40°53'13"
40°53'12"

A   B   C   D   E

73°41'05"   73°40'31"   73°39'56"   73°39'22"   73°38'48"   73°38'13"

Pond View Dr

WEST
POND

11542

WELWYN PRESERVE

SEE 6509 MAP

MAP 6500
MAP 6500

1:24,000
1 in. = 2000 ft.
0   0.25   0.5
miles

SEE D MAP

SEE D MAP

SEE 6501 MAP

SEE 6609 MAP

A
1 Kensington Cross
2 Division Av

B
1 Front Row Rd
2 Spartan Row
3 Center Row
4 Rear Row
5 Top Row
6 Bergen Blvd

C
1 United Dr
2 Via Bagheria
3 Dress Ln

D
1 N Woodside Av

E
1 Washington Pl

F
1 Halstead Av

G
1 Hope St
2 Grant St
3 Chadwick St
4 Cottage Pl
5 Morton St

H
1 Helen Dr
2 Austin St
3 Charles Lindbergh Blvd

J
1 Vanderburgh Av
2 Wells Pl

K
1 Washington Pl
2 Lincoln Pl

Teterboro Airport

RAND MCNALLY

MAP 6501

MAP 6501

1:24,000
1 in. = 2000 ft.

0   0.25   0.5
miles

N

SEE D MAP

40°53'15"

40°52'49"

40°52'23"

40°51'57"

40°51'31"

40°51'05"

40°50'39"

40°50'13"

40°53'15"

40°52'49"

40°52'23"

40°51'57"

40°51'31"

40°51'05"

40°50'39"

40°50'13"

SEE 6500 MAP

SEE 6502 MAP

SEE 6610 MAP

Lodi

Teterboro

Moonachie

Hasbrouck Heights

Little Ferry

Ridgefield

07604

07608

07666

07601

07657

07663

07660 Teaneck Township

Bogota

Teaneck

FOSCHINI MEMORIAL PARK

BOGOTA PARK

Hackensack Univ Medical Center

Hackensack Univ Med HS

Bergen County Jail

USS Ling New Jersey Naval Museum

US Naval Museum

Social Security Administration

Bergen County Administration Building

Bergen County Plz

South Hackensack Township

Bergen County Technology HS-Teterboro

Aviation Hall of Fame & Museum

Teterboro Airport

Terminal

MAPLE GRV CEMETERY

INDIAN LAKE

WILLOW LAKE

CLAY PITS

NJ Transit-Teterboro

NJ Transit-Essex St

Church on 4th the Green

RAND M^{c}NALLY

NEW JERSEY TPK

B 1 Robinson Rd
2 Summit Ct

C 1 Railroad Pl
2 W Camden St
3 Midtown Bridge Pl

D 1 Henry C Luthin Pl
2 Oakdene Av
3 Hillside Av

E 1 Milano Ct
2 Tuve Ln

F 1 Demarest St
2 Warren St
3 Washington Pl
4 Church St
5 Court St

G 1 Charlton Av
2 Myers Av
3 Burton Av
4 Longworth Av
5 Stanley Av
6 Hasbrouck Av
7 Ottawa Av

H 1 Bonhomme St
2 Franklin St
3 Old Hoboken Rd
4 Blauvelt Pl
5 Williams Av

J 1 W Pleasant View Av
2 E Pleasant View Av
3 Longview Pl
4 Baldwin Ter

K 1 Webster Pl
2 Station Plz
3 Herbert St

L 1 W 3rd St
2 W 2nd St
3 E 3rd St
4 E 2nd St

MAP 6502

MAP 6502

1:24,000
1 in. = 2000 ft.
0   0.25   0.5
miles

N

SEE **D** MAP

A
1 Marjorie Ct
2 Myron Ct
3 Commonwealth Dr

B
1 Decatur Av

C
1 Azalea Ct
2 Tulip Cir

D
1 Sandburg Ct
2 Home St
3 Eliot Ct
4 Lowell Ct
5 Millay Ct
6 Wadsworth Ct
7 Sinclair Ct
8 Whitman St
9 Lawrence Ct
10 Carlyle Ct

E
1 Rock Creek Ter
2 Mallard Ct
3 Pheasant Run
4 Squire Ct

G
1 Edwin St
2 Barnes Dr W
3 Barnes Dr E
4 Barnes Dr

H
1 Village Cir Dr
2 Jacey Dr
3 Westgate Dr S

K
1 Veterans Plz
2 Ravenhill Av

L
1 Edgewood Ln
2 Cumbermeade Rd

M
1 Juanita Pl
2 Jassamine Wy

OVERPECK COUNTY GOLF COURSE

OVERPECK COUNTY PARK

American Hungarian Museum

CRYSTAL LAKE

TRUMBUL PARK

MADONNA CEMETERY

VETERANS PARK

Teaneck Township

Leonia

Fort Lee

Ridgefield Park

Palisades Park

Edgewater

Englewood

Ridgefield

07660   07031   07666   07024

NEW JERSEY TPK

FORT LEE RD

DEGRAW AV

CEDAR

SEE **6501** MAP
SEE **6503** MAP

RAND McNALLY

40°53'15" 40°52'49" 40°52'23" 40°51'57" 40°51'31" 40°51'05" 40°50'39" 40°50'13"

74°01'09" 74°00'34" 74°00'00" 73°59'25" 73°58'51" 73°58'17"

A B C D E

MAP
6503

MAP
6503

1:24,000
1 in. = 2000 ft.
0   0.25   0.5
miles

N

SEE 6392 MAP

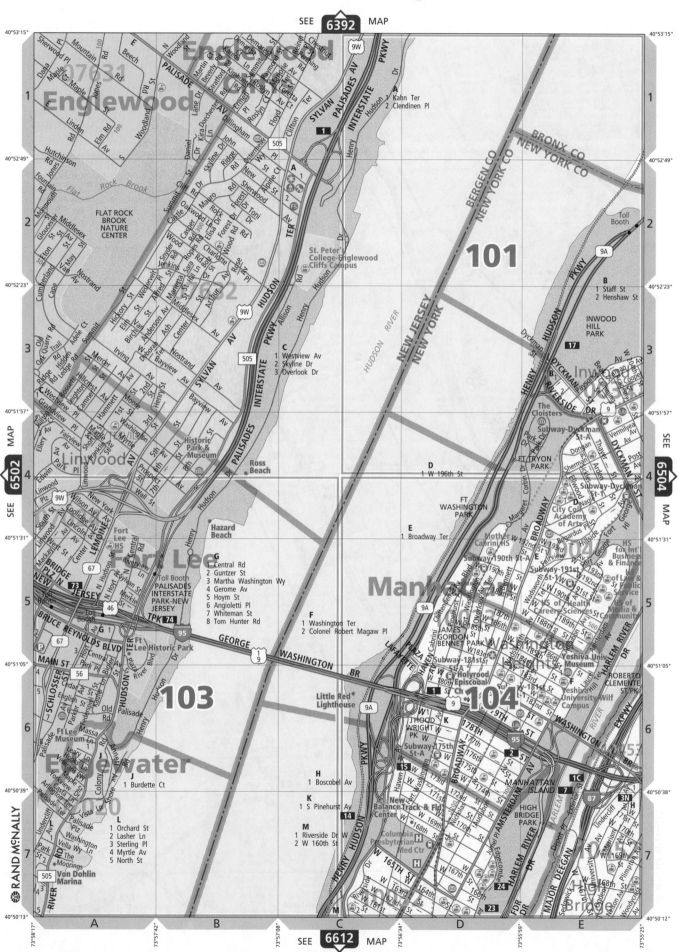

101

Manhattan

103

104

Englewood Cliffs

Englewood

07631

07632

Linwood

Fort Lee

Englewater

Edgewater

NEW JERSEY

FLAT ROCK BROOK NATURE CENTER

St. Peter's College-Englewood Cliffs Campus

HUDSON RIVER

NEW JERSEY / NEW YORK

BERGEN CO / NEW YORK CO

BRONX CO / NEW YORK CO

INWOOD HILL PARK

Inwood

The Cloisters

FT. TRYON PARK

FT. WASHINGTON PARK

Historic Park & Museum

Ross Beach

Hazard Beach

Fort Lee HS

Fort Lee Historic Park

Little Red Lighthouse

Columbia Presbyterian Med Ctr

MANHATTAN ISLAND

HIGH BRIDGE PARK

ROBERTO CLEMENTE ST/PK

Von Dohlin Marina

The Moorings

A
1 Kahn Ter
2 Clendinen Pl

B
1 Staff St
2 Henshaw St

C
1 Westview Av
2 Skyline Dr
3 Overlook Dr

D
1 W 196th St

E
1 Broadway Ter

F
1 Washington Ter
2 Colonel Robert Magaw Pl

G
1 Central Rd
2 Guntzer St
3 Martha Washington Wy
4 Gerome Av
5 Hoym St
6 Angioletti Pl
7 Whiteman St
8 Tom Hunter Rd

H
1 Boscobel Av

J
1 Burdette Ct

K
1 S Pinehurst Av

L
1 Orchard St
2 Lasher Ln
3 Sterling Pl
4 Myrtle Av
5 North St

M
1 Riverside Dr W
2 W 160th St

SEE 6502 MAP

SEE 6504 MAP

SEE 6612 MAP

MAP
6504

MAP
6504

1:24,000
1 in. = 2000 ft.
0   0.25   0.5
miles

N

SEE 6393 MAP
SEE 6503 MAP
SEE 6505 MAP
SEE 6613 MAP

RAND MCNALLY

MAP
6505

MAP
6505

1:24,000
1 in. = 2000 ft.

0.25   0.5

miles

N

SEE 6394 MAP

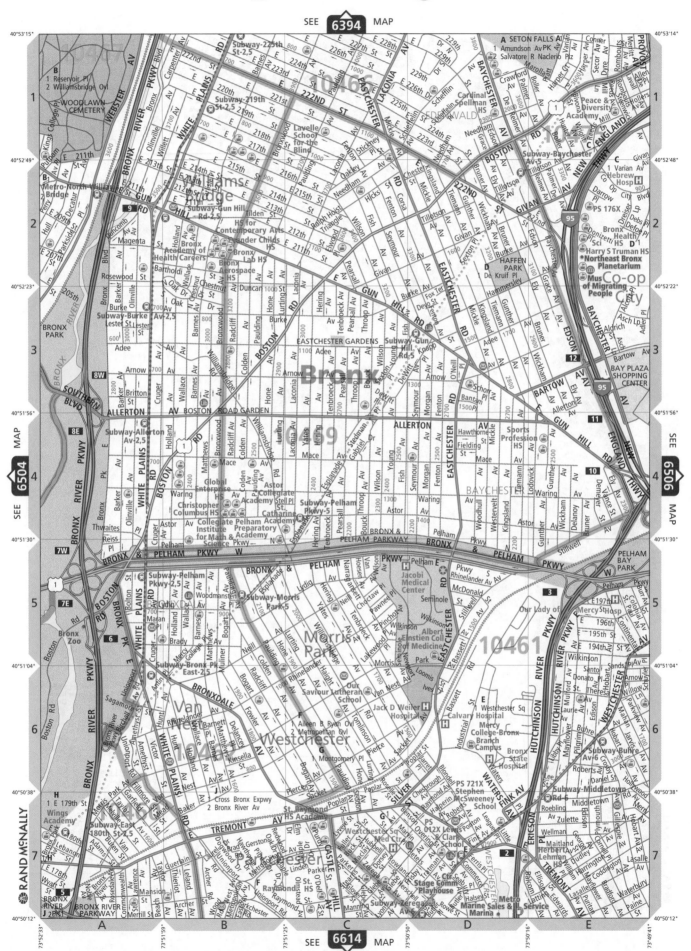

SEE 6614 MAP

MAP 6504

SEE

SEE 6506 MAP

MAP 6506

MAP 6506

1:24,000
1 in. = 2000 ft.

0   0.25   0.5
miles

N

SEE 6395 MAP

40°53'14"

A
1 Clementine St
2 Huguenot Av
3 McOwen Av
4 Pelham Bay Pk W
5 Peartree Av

Manor 10803 10805
Pelham
New Rochelle

NEW ENGLAND THWY
CONNER ST
95
14
6

HUTCHINSON RIVER PKWY

PELHAM-SPLIT ROCK GOLF COURSE

PELHAM BAY PARK

NEW YORK ATHLETIC CLUB

SHORE PARK

Bartow-Pell Mansion
Bartow-Pell Mansion Museum

WESTCHESTER CO
BRONX CO

GLEN I COUNTY PARK
GLEN ISLAND

Weyman Av

40°53'14"

1

40°52'48"

40°52'48"

10475

HUTCHINSON RIVER

2

2

40°52'22"

40°52'22"

800

ORCHARD BEACH RD

Orchard Beach Rd

Orchard Beach

SEE 6505 MAP
4
9

RIVER PKWY
5

SHORE RD

3

Bay Plaza Shopping Center

PELHAM BAY PARK

PARK DR

LONG ISLAND SOUND

3

40°51'56"

40°51'56"

HUTCHINSON RIVER
Einstein Lp N
Einstein Lp S
Einstein Elgar Pl

CITY ISLAND RD

B
1 Stillwell Av
2 Bassett Av
3 De Reimer Av

Rodmans Neck

North Wind Undersea Museum
Ann's Harbor Inn Marina

Stelter Boats & Motors Marina

SEE 6507 MAP

4

4

40°51'30"

8C

SHORE RD

10465

D
1 Leeward Ln
2 Deepwater Wy

City Island Br

Terrace St
Sutherland St
Kilroe St

40°51'30"

BRUCKNER EXPWY
8A

Subway-Pelham Bay Park-6
8B

C
1 Colonial Av
2 Sands Pl
3 Arnow Pl
4 Roberts Av

City Island Rd

PELHAM CEMETERY
Terminal-Fordham Dock
Hart I Fy

5

5

40°51'04"

I-95

Watt Av

Evers Seaplace Base & Marina

EASTCHESTER BAY

City Island

City I Museum

AMBROSINI FIELD
CITY ISLAND

40°51'04"

6

Bronx

Middletown Rd

E
1 Mahan Av
2 Dwight Pl
3 Jarvis Av
4 Siegfried Pl
5 Coddington Av
6 Lasalle Av
7 Crosby Av
8 Fairfax Av
9 Ellsworth Av
10 Dean Av

City Island Theatre Group

6

40°50'38"

40°50'37"

BRUCKNER EXPWY
695
7C
7B
7A

CHERRY TREE POINT

Belden St

BELDEN POINT

7

7

40°50'12"

40°50'11"

A   B   C   D   E

MAP
6507

MAP
6507

1:24,000
1 in. = 2000 ft.
0   0.25   0.5
miles

N

SEE 6396 MAP

40°53'14"

GLEN ISLAND
CO PARK

New
Rochelle
DAVIDS
ISLAND

10805

WHORTLEBERRY
ISLAND

40°53'14"

1

1

40°52'48"

WESTCHESTER CO
BRONX CO

COLUMBIA
ISLAND

PEA
ISLAND

Execution
Rocks
Lighthouse

40°52'47"

2

WESTCHESTER CO
NASSAU CO

2

40°52'22"

40°52'21"

3

3

40°51'56"

SEE 6506 MAP

LONG
ISLAND
SOUND

40°51'55"

SEE 6508 MAP

4

4

40°51'30"

POTTERS
FLD
CEMETERY

Bronx   HART
ISLAND

40°51'29"

5

5

Hart Island
Ferry
Terminal

HART ISLAND FY

10464

BRONX CO
NASSAU CO

40°51'04"

LONG
ISLAND

BARKER
POINT

11050

Sands
Point

40°51'03"

6

6

40°50'37"

40°50'37"

7

7

HEWLETT POINT

11024 Kings Point

40°50'11"

A   B   C   D   E

40°50'11"

73°46'50"   73°46'15"   73°45'41"   73°45'07"   73°44'32"   73°43'58"

SEE 6616 MAP

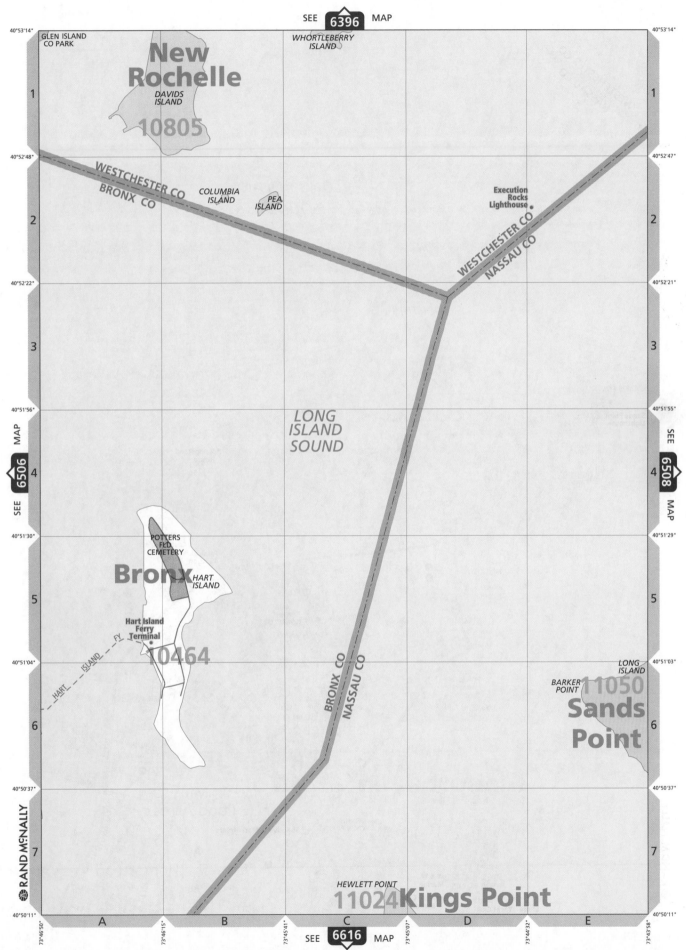

MAP
6508

MAP
6508

SEE 6397 MAP

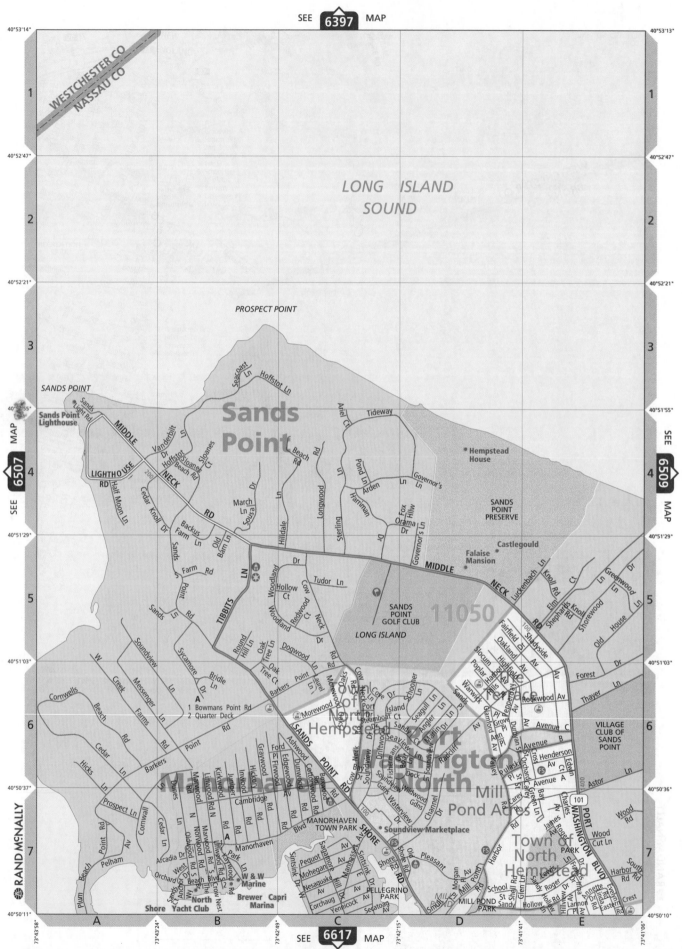

1:24,000
1 in. = 2000 ft.
0   0.25   0.5
miles

N

WESTCHESTER CO
NASSAU CO

LONG ISLAND
SOUND

PROSPECT POINT

SANDS POINT

Sands Point Lighthouse

Sands
Point

Seacoast Ln
Hoffstot Ln

Ariel Ct
Tideway

Hempstead House

MIDDLE

Vanderbilt Dr
Hoffstot
Sloanes Beach Rd
Sloanes Ct

Sands Light Rd

Beach Rd

Pond Ln
Arden

Governor's Ln

SANDS POINT PRESERVE

LIGHTHOUSE RD

Half Moon Ln

NECK

March Ln

Sousa Dr

Longwood
Sterling

Harriman
Dr

Fox Hllw

Orama Dr

Governor's Ln

Castlegould

Falaise Mansion

MIDDLE

NECK

Luckenbach Ln

Knoll Rd
Ct

Greenwood
Ln

Dr

Cedar Knoll Dr
Old Barn Ln
Backus Farm Ln

Sands Farm Rd

Sands Point Rd

Hilldale

Dr

Tudor Ln

Woodland

Hollow
Ct

Cow Neck Rd
Redwood Ct

Woodland

Elm Rd
Shephards Knoll
Shorewood

Old House Dr

TIBBITS LN

SANDS POINT GOLF CLUB

LONG ISLAND

11050

Fairfield Dr
Shadyside
Oakland Av
Slocum Highfield
Poplar Allis

RD

Soundview Ln

Messenger Ln

Sycamore Ln

Bridle Dr

A

Round Hill Ln
Oak Tree Ln
Oak Tree Ln

Dogwood

Laurel Ln

Barkers Point Rd

Cove Dr

Port

Island

Cow Neck Rd

Schooner

Wanwjk

Forest Ln

Thayer Ln

Cornwells

Creek
Farms

1 Bowmans Point Rd
2 Quarter Deck

A

Morewood

Town of
North
Hempstead

Steamboat Ct
Seaview

Seagull Ln

Marlin Ln

Sands Pl

Glamford
Grove

Rockwood Av

VILLAGE CLUB OF SANDS POINT

Cedar Rd

Beach Rd

Barkers

Point Rd

Ford Ln
Graywood

Hickory

Kirkwood

Inwood Rd

Edgewood

Firwood Pl

Dunwood

Cottonwood Rd

SANDS

Sounds

Port

Driftwood

Radcliff

Pl

Durham

Orchard Rd

Avenue C

Henderson

Avenue B

Manhaven

Marwood
Linwood Rd

Cambridge

Juniper

Dukes

POINT

Cow Neck

Bay

Wildwood

Gdns

Durham

Ann
Pl

Pulaski
St

Valley

Cross

Carey

Edwin
Av

Avenue A

Astor
Ln

Port
Washington
North

Mill Pond Acres

Hicks Ln

Cornwall

N Marwood Rd
Norwood Rd

Arcadia Dr

RD

SHORE

Manorhaven

Bvd

MANORHAVEN TOWN PARK

Soundview Marketplace

Seaview

Channel
Dr

Waterview

Gdns

Town of
North
Hempstead

PORT
WASHINGTON
BLVD

PARK

James
Rogers

Wood
Cut Ln

Wood Rd

Prospect Ln

Cedar Ln

West Shore Dr

Orchard Blvd

Crow Nest

Pelham

Pelham

Plum Beach Point Rd

North Shore Yacht Club

W & W Marine

Brewer Capri Marina

Manorhaven

A

Pequot Av

Simsink Dr

Mohegan

Nesaquake

Corchaug

Sagamore

Mattasauk

Yenticock

Simsink Dr

Segatoag Av

SHORE
RD

Shore Rd

Old Shore Rd

Pleasant

PELLEGRINO PARK

Harbor

Pleasant

Mill Pond Rd

Mill Pond Rd

Morgan

School St

Glen

Hollow

Sandy

101

Sandy Rd

Charles

Charles

Roger Av

Carey

Roger Ln

Hillview Rd

Annette

Lannon Rd

Harbor Rd

South
Harbor
Rd

Crest

Evelyn
Easter Rd

Town of
North
Hempstead

MILL POND PARK

SEE 6507 MAP

SEE 6509 MAP

SEE 6617 MAP

A   B   C   D   E

MAP
6509

1:24,000
1 in. = 2000 ft.
0   0.25   0.5
miles

N

MAP
6509

SEE 6398 MAP

40°53'13"   40°53'12"

WELWYN PRESERVE

Crescent

Cobble
Ct

Minden
Rd

Beach

1   1

40°52'47"   40°52'46"

RED SPRING
POINT

Cedar
Ln

Ridge Rd

Middle

Cross
Ln

Jackson

New Woods Rd

Reynolds Rd

Gold
Ct

Ct Coast

Holocaust
Memorial &
Education Center

Jodi

Murray
Ct

Soundside

Old
Estate Rd

Valley

Tower
Rd

Hickory

Pine
Low Rd

High

Pine Rd

Whitney

Tower
Cir

Glen Cove

LONG ISLAND

Seawart

2   2

40°52'21"   40°52'20"

Pembroke
Dr

Poppy

Woolsey

100 Av

A
1 Garden Pl

Fairview
Ln

Delapan

Gail
Ct

Tel Dr

Harwood

Westbury

Jefferson St

Lincoln

St

Sunview

Bluff

Willada Ln

Laurel Av

McKinley Pl

North   St

St

George
St

Miller

Cleveland Pl
Roosevelt Pl

3   3

Windward

Water's

Edge

Berry Ln

Barlow

Alvin St

St

Landing

Ellwood

Margaret

Rose

Rd

Charles

Woodland Rd

Soundview
Rd

Northfield

Dorser

Northfield
Rd

John

Gervais
Av

Av

St

St   St

Dickson St

Elizabeth
Pl

Terrace

Orchard

Sycamore Rd

Southfield

Rd

St Clement St

Valentine

Locust St

St

40°51'55"   40°51'54"

SEE 6508 MAP

MORGAN
MEMORIAL
PARK

Germaine

Jackson St

Gale

Mechanic

Coles   St

Carpenter

McLoughlin 100

Janet
St

The

SEE D MAP

Barry
St

Henry

Carol

Dr

Paula Rd

Dr

B
1 Harmony Ln
2 Mariners Wy
3 Daly Pl

Herbhill
Rd

Jerome

Daniel Dr

11542

4   4

Garvies Point
Museum &
Preserve

GARVIES
POINT
PRESERVE

Point

Rd

Garvies

CITY
STAD
PARK

Morris Av

40°51'29"   40°51'28"

Shepards Ln

Shorewood Dr

GLEN COVE CREEK

Jude Thaddeus
Glen Cove
Marina

SHORE

RD

B

Old
House

MOTT POINT

Dr

Forest Ct

Lillian Ct

Forest Ct

Mimosa Ln

Beverly

St

Whitman

Towle

Putnam Av

Hammond

2

100

Harbor

Altamont

Av

5   5

Wisteria
Pth

Shore Rd

ALBIN

AV

Conrad

Cromwell

Ironwell

1030

The

Blvd

PROSPECT

Winding

Dr

Daniel
Pl

Dubois

Harriet Ct

Locust

Irving Pl

Thayer
Ln

VILLAGE CLUB
OF SANDS
POINT

Cliff Wy

Foster Pl

Park
Wy

Summit
7th Av

Main

Carpenter

Sea

Dubois

Cliff

40°51'03"   40°51'02"

C
1 W 15th Av

Fairview
Pl

Sea
Cliff
Vil
Museum

10th Av

9th Av

Maple

12th
Av

14th Av

Glen

Tilley Pl

C

16th
Av

Central

16th

St

Brown

Franklin

Littleworth

6   6

Astor

Ln

Todd

Rd

Bay
Av

17th
Av

18th Av

17th Av

Adams

Resson

Hansen

Ln

Clinton St

Harbor Rd

East
Hill Rd

120th
Av

19th
Av

20th Av

Cedar

Franklin

Lafayette

Arlington Pl

Sands Point

Bridle Pth N

Southeast Rd

Sheridan

Ln

Brown

Dayton Av

Preston

Highland

Hawthorne

Horace
Pl

Glenlawn

Hillside
Av

Highland
Pl

Ransom

Leonard

40°50'36"   40°50'36"

Wood
Rd

Bridle Pth

Bridle Pth E

Hill Rd
Rd

100

Roslyn West Shore Dr

Laurel
Wy

Laurel
Av

Stenson
Av

Raymond
Av

Marble Ln

Barberry Ct

Dixon

Harbor

Middle

Rd

WEST

Woodridge

Circle

100

Richardson
Av

Florence
Av

Glenola

Town of
North
Hempstead

Bryant
Av

Willow

Orchard

Tanglewood
Ln

Park
Wy

Harbor
Wy

South

Dr

PROSPECT
AV

Shore
Rd

Littleworth

Gates

NORTH
SHORE
COUNTRY
CLUB

7   7

RAND McNALLY

LONG ISLAND
SOUND

Harbor

Hampton
Ct

Longview

Stratford
Rd

Hillcrest Rd

BEACON HILL RD

Summit

Roslyn

Downing

HEMPSTEAD
HBR COUNTY
PARK

40°50'10"   40°50'10"

A   B   C   D   E

73°41'06"   73°40'32"   73°39'57"   73°39'23"   73°38'49"   73°38'14"

SEE 6618 MAP

MAP 6609

1:24,000
1 in. = 2000 ft.

0   0.25   0.5
miles

N

MAP 6609

SEE 6500 MAP

SEE 6610 MAP

SEE 6715 MAP

Carlstadt

East Rutherford

Rutherford

Kingsland

Lyndhurst Township

North Arlington

Secaucus

07072
07070
07071
07094
07072

A
1 Beech St
2 Herman St
3 Springfield Av

B
1 Washington Pl
2 4th St
3 Small St
4 Joseph Pycior Jr Wy
5 Weir Wy

C
1 Summer St
2 Spring Dell Av
3 Passaic Av

D
1 Riverview Av
2 W Pierrepont Av

WALDEN SWAMP

Felician College-Rutherford

St. Mary HS

Rutherford HS

Williams Ctr for the Arts

NJ Transit-Rutherford

PRIGGIN MEM FIELD

HAROLD WALLS FIELDS

Meadowlands Museum

HILLSIDE CEMETERY

Becton Regional HS

Meadowlands Sports Complex
Giants Stadium
Meadowlands Racetrack
Izod Center
Meadowlands Connection

SERVICE RD
Meadowlands Plz
Toll Booth
Toll Booth

RICHARD DE KORTE PARK

Hackensack Meadowlands Development Commission Env Ctr & Mus

Libertyhealth-Meadowlands Hospital Medical Center

SNIPES BEACH PK

BERGEN CO
HUDSON CO

HACKENSACK RIVER

BERRYS CREEK

PATERSON PLANK RD

ERIE AV
UNION AV
PARK AV
MARGINAL RD
MEADOW RD
RIDGE RD
ORIENT WY
RUTHERFORD AV

95
17
3
120
130
32
30
55

MAP
6610

MAP
6610

1:24,000
1 in. = 2000 ft.
0   0.25   0.5
miles

N

SEE 6501 MAP

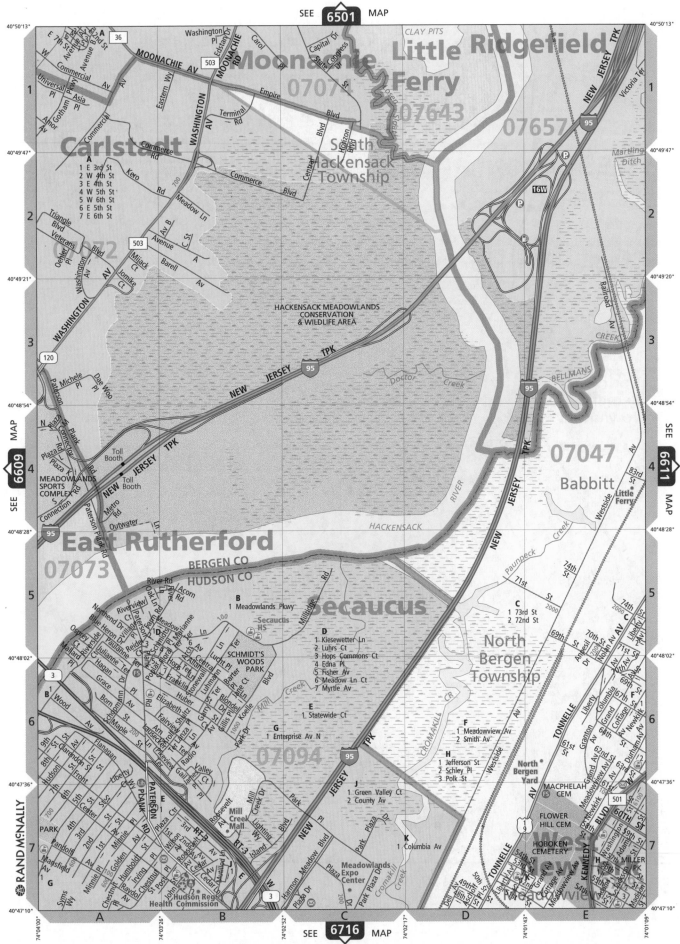

Carlstadt

A
1 E 3rd St
2 W 4th St
3 E 4th St
4 W 5th St
5 W 6th St
6 E 5th St
7 E 6th St

07072

Moonachie
07074

Little Ridgefield
Ferry
07643

07657

South
Hackensack
Township

CLAY PITS

HACKENSACK MEADOWLANDS
CONSERVATION
& WILDLIFE AREA

NEW JERSEY TPK
I-95

Doctor Creek

BELLMANS

07047

Babbitt
Little
Ferry

HACKENSACK

SEE 6609 MAP

SEE 6611 MAP

MEADOWLANDS
SPORTS
COMPLEX

Toll
Booth

Toll
Booth

East Rutherford
07073

BERGEN CO
HUDSON CO

Secaucus

B
1 Meadowlands Pkwy

Secaucus
HS

D
1 Kiesewetter Ln
2 Luhrs Ct
3 Hops Commons Ct
4 Edna Pl
5 Fisher Av
6 Meadow Ln Ct
7 Myrtle Av

E
1 Statewide Ct

G
1 Enterprise Av N

North
Bergen
Township

C
1 73rd St
2 72nd St

F
1 Meadowview Av
2 Smith Av

H
1 Jefferson St
2 Schley Pl
3 Polk St

J
1 Green Valley Ct
2 County Av

K
1 Columbia Av

North
Bergen
Yard

MACPHELAH
CEM

FLOWER
HILL CEM

HOBOKEN
CEMETERY

SCHMIDT'S
WOODS
PARK

07094

Mill
Creek
Mall

John F
Hudson Reg
Health Commission

Meadowlands
Expo Center

West
New
York

Meadowview

RAND McNALLY

SEE 6716 MAP

MAP
6611

MAP
6611

1:24,000
1 in. = 2000 ft.

0   0.25   0.5
miles

N

SEE 6502 MAP

07657

MARTLING
DITCH

A
1 Wilt Av
2 Bryant Pl

B
1 Shetland Ln
2 Grantwood Blvd
3 Grantview Blvd
4 Kingsland Ln
5 Jassamine Wy

C
1 Battaglia Ln

ENGLISH
NEIGHBORHOOD
PARK

VETERANS
MEMORIAL
PARK

Ridgefield

Fairview

**Ridgefield
Memorial HS**

All
Seasons
Theatre
Company

Cliffside
Park

Edgewater
Marina

MT MORIAH
CEMETERY

07022

D
1 Mayfair Ln
2 Adelaide Pl
3 Beverly Pl
4 Ascot Wy
5 Overview Ter
6 Panorama Dr

E
1 Duncan Rd
2 N. Glen Ln
3 Rockwood Pl
4 S. Glen Ln

North
Bergen
Township

FAIRVIEW
CEMETERY

COLUMBUS
PARK

VETERAN'S
PARK

Woodcliff

Hudson
Heights

High Tech
HS

North
Bergen

North
Bergen HS

Edgewater

NEW JERSEY
NEW YORK

BERGEN CO
YORK CO

F
1 Bristol Ter
2 The River Clb
3 Ellery Ct
4 Franklin Ct
5 Hancock Ct
6 Livingston Ct
7 Penn Ct
8 Jefferson Ct
9 Rutledge Ct

G
1 Thompson Av
2 Thompson Ln
3 Accommando Pl
4 Waterford Towers

H
1 Kamp Pl
2 Clement Pl

The Promenade

JAMES
J BRADDOCK
NORTH HUDSON
PARK

J
1 Meadowview Av

108

MANHATTAN
ISLAND

RIVERSIDE
PARK

Manhattan

HUDSON CO
NEW YORK CO

Guttenberg

07047

West
New York

Palisades
Medical
Center

Soldiers &
Sailors
Monument

Symphony
Space

Agnes
Boys HS

K
1 Brower Ct
2 Halfmoon Ct
3 Roslyn Ct
4 Buffalo Ct
5 Midland Ct
6 Oswego Ct
7 Albany Ct

79th Street
Boat Basin

Mannes
Coll
The New School
for Music

Subway-86th

RAND McNALLY

SEE 6717 MAP

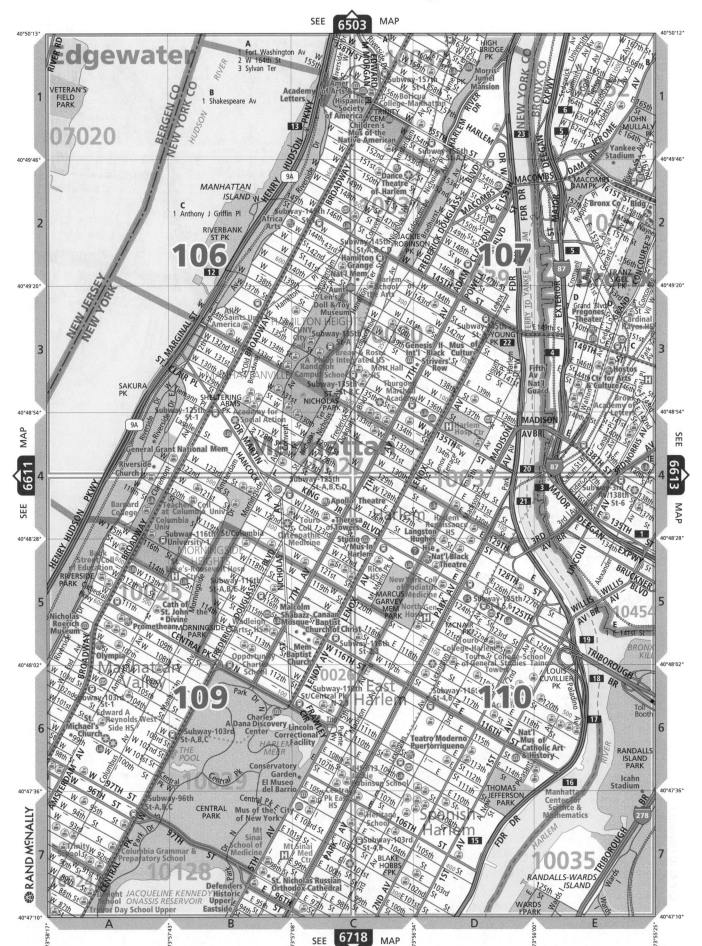

MAP 6612

MAP 6612

1:24,000
1 in. = 2000 ft.
0   0.25   0.5
miles

SEE 6503 MAP

40°50'13"
40°50'12"

A
1 Fort Washington Av
2 W 164th St
3 Sylvan Ter

B
1 Shakespeare Av

C
1 Anthony J Griffin Pl

Edgewater

VETERAN'S FIELD PARK

07020

MANHATTAN ISLAND

RIVERBANK ST PK

106

40°49'46"
40°49'46"

107

40°49'20"
40°49'20"

HAMILTON HEIGHTS

SAKURA PK

40°48'54"
40°48'54"

General Grant National Mem

Riverside Church

MORNINGSIDE HEIGHTS

40°48'28"
40°48'28"

Barnard College

Columbia Univ

MORNINGSIDE PARK

5

RIVERSIDE PARK

Nicholas Roerich Museum

40°48'02"
40°48'02"

East Harlem

109

110

Manhattan Valley

40°47'36"
40°47'36"

CENTRAL PARK

Spanish Harlem

RANDALLS ISLAND PARK

Icahn Stadium

10035

40°47'10"
40°47'10"

JACQUELINE KENNEDY ONASSIS RESERVOIR

RANDALLS-WARDS ISLAND

10128

A   B   C   D   E

73°58'17"   73°57'43"   73°57'08"   73°56'34"   73°56'00"   73°55'25"

SEE 6718 MAP

SEE 6611 MAP

SEE 6613 MAP

MAP
6613

1:24,000
1 in. = 2000 ft.

0   0.25   0.5
miles

N

MAP
6613

SEE 6504 MAP

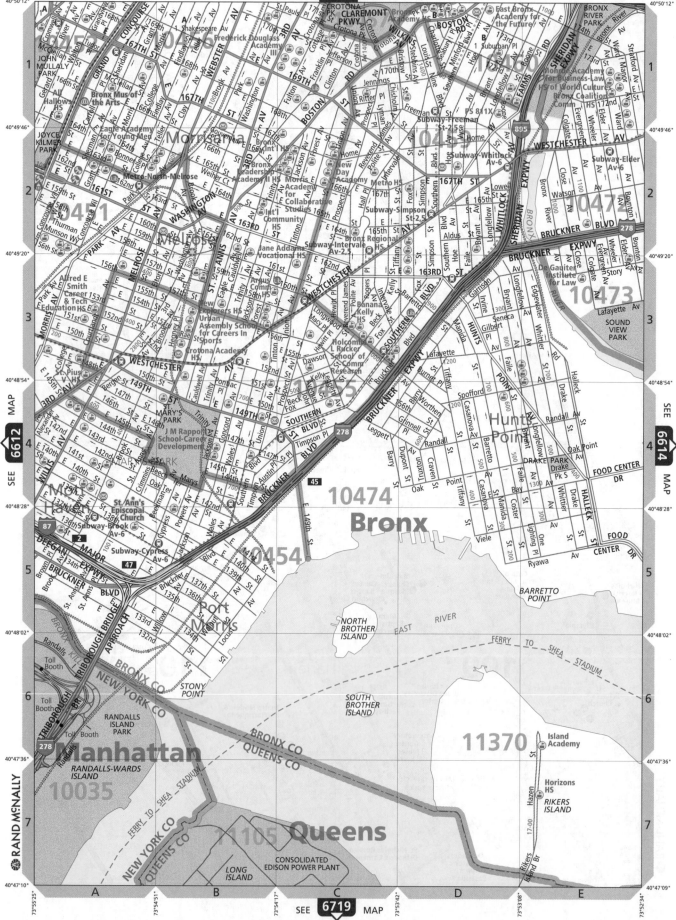

SEE 6612 MAP

SEE 6614 MAP

RAND MCNALLY

MAP
6614

MAP
6614

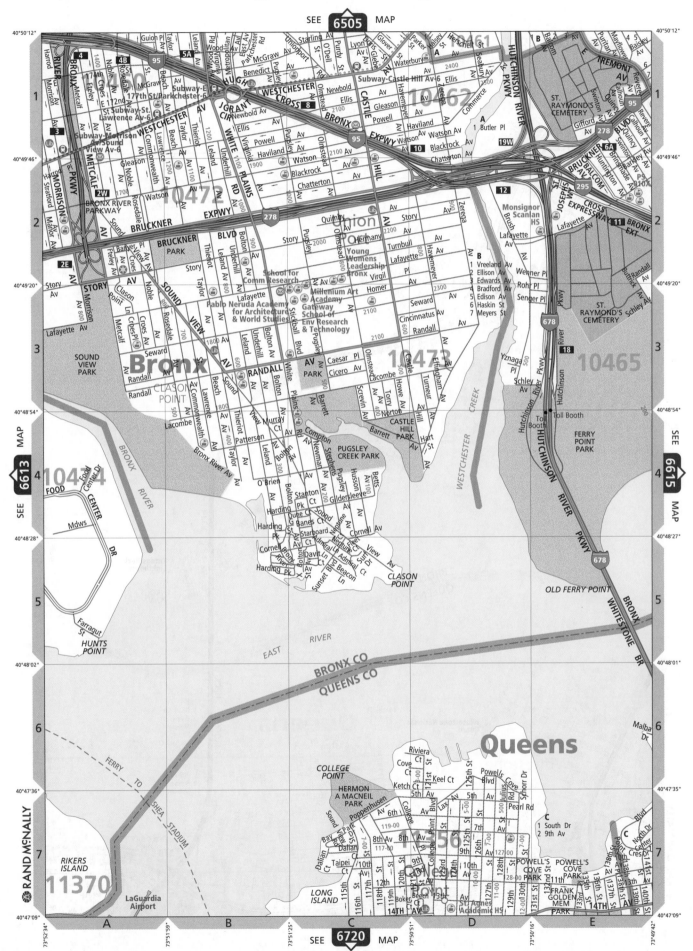

1:24,000
1 in. = 2000 ft.
0   0.25   0.5
miles

N

RAND M°NALLY

MAP
6615

MAP
6615

1:24,000
1 in. = 2000 ft.

0   0.25   0.5
miles

N

SEE 6506 MAP

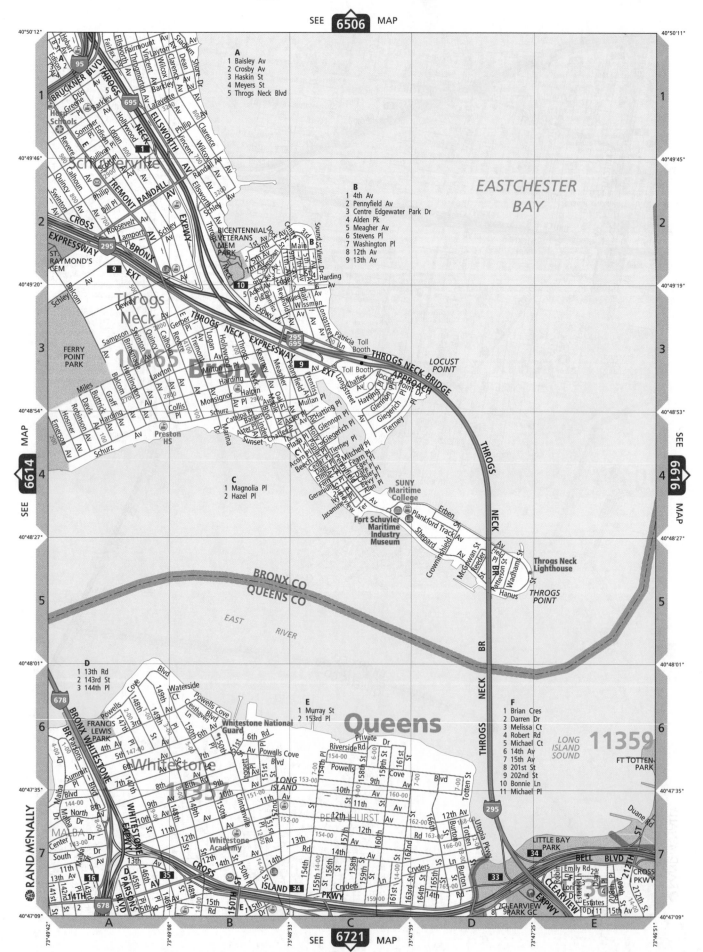

A
1 Baisley Av
2 Crosby Av
3 Haskin St
4 Meyers St
5 Throgs Neck Blvd

B
1 4th Av
2 Pennyfield Av
3 Centre Edgewater Park Dr
4 Alden Pk
5 Meagher Av
6 Stevens Pl
7 Washington Pl
8 12th Av
9 13th Av

C
1 Magnolia Pl
2 Hazel Pl

D
1 13th Rd
2 143rd St
3 144th Pl

E
1 Murray St
2 153rd Pl

F
1 Brian Cres
2 Darren Dr
3 Melissa Ct
4 Robert Rd
5 Michael Ct
6 14th Av
7 15th Av
8 201st St
9 202nd St
10 Bonnie Ln
11 Michael Pl

EASTCHESTER BAY

Throgs Neck Bronx

FERRY POINT PARK

11465

Preston HS

SUNY Maritime College

Fort Schuyler Maritime Industry Museum

THROGS NECK BRIDGE APPROACH

LOCUST POINT

THROGS NECK BR

Throgs Neck Lighthouse

THROGS POINT

BRONX CO
QUEENS CO

EAST RIVER

LONG ISLAND SOUND

11359

FT TOTTEN PARK

Queens

Whitestone

11357

FRANCIS LEWIS PARK

Whitestone National Guard

BELLHURST

Whitestone Academy

MALBA

LITTLE BAY PARK

BELL BLVD

CLEARVIEW

RAND MCNALLY

SEE 6614 MAP

SEE 6616 MAP

SEE 6721 MAP

MAP 6616

1:24,000
1 in. = 2000 ft.

0   0.25   0.5
miles

MAP 6616

SEE 6507 MAP

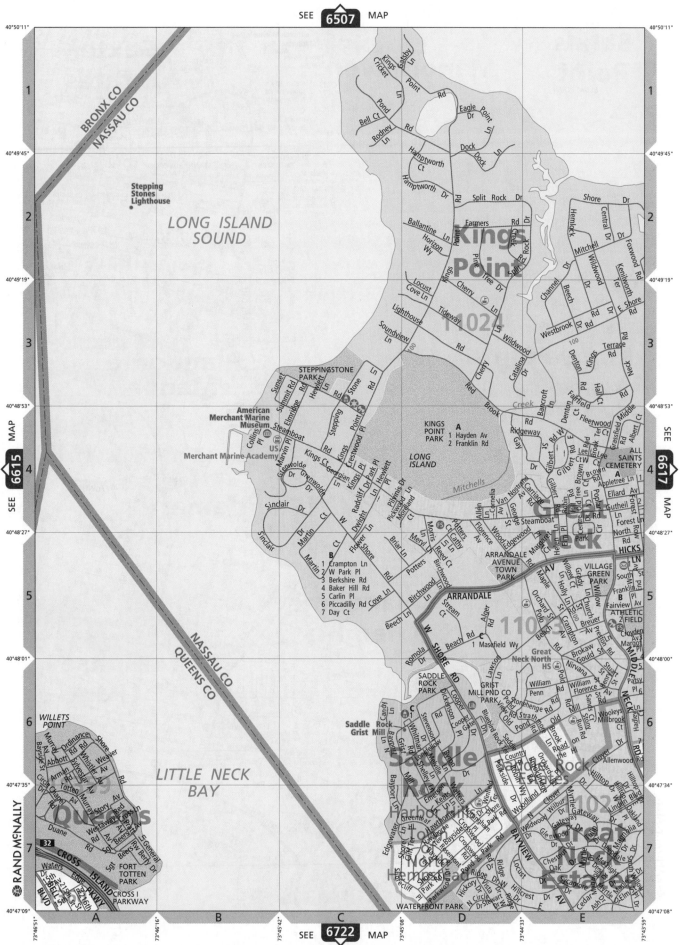

SEE 6615 MAP

SEE 6617 MAP

LONG ISLAND SOUND

Stepping Stones Lighthouse

Kings Point
11024

KINGS POINT PARK
A
1 Hayden Av
2 Franklin Rd

LONG ISLAND

STEPPINGSTONE PARK

American Merchant Marine Museum

Merchant Marine Academy
US

Great Neck

HICKS

ARRANDALE AVENUE TOWN PARK

ARRANDALE

B
1 Crampton Ln
2 W Park Pl
3 Berkshire Rd
4 Baker Hill Rd
5 Carlin Pl
6 Piccadilly Rd
7 Day Ct

ALL SAINTS CEMETERY

VILLAGE GREEN PARK

ATHLETIC FIELD

11023

C
1 Masefield Wy

Great Neck North HS

SADDLE ROCK PARK

GRIST MILL PND CO PARK

Saddle Rock Grist Mill

Saddle Rock

WILLETS POINT

LITTLE NECK BAY

Queens

BRONX CO
NASSAU CO

NASSAU CO
QUEENS CO

CROSS ISLAND PKWY
32

FORT TOTTEN PARK
CROSS I PARKWAY

Harbor
Town
Great Neck Estates
11021

RAND M^cNALLY

SEE 6722 MAP

40°50'11"
40°49'45"
40°49'19"
40°48'53"
40°48'27"
40°48'01"
40°47'35"
40°47'09"

73°46'51"
73°46'16"
73°45'42"
73°45'08"
73°44'33"
73°43'59"

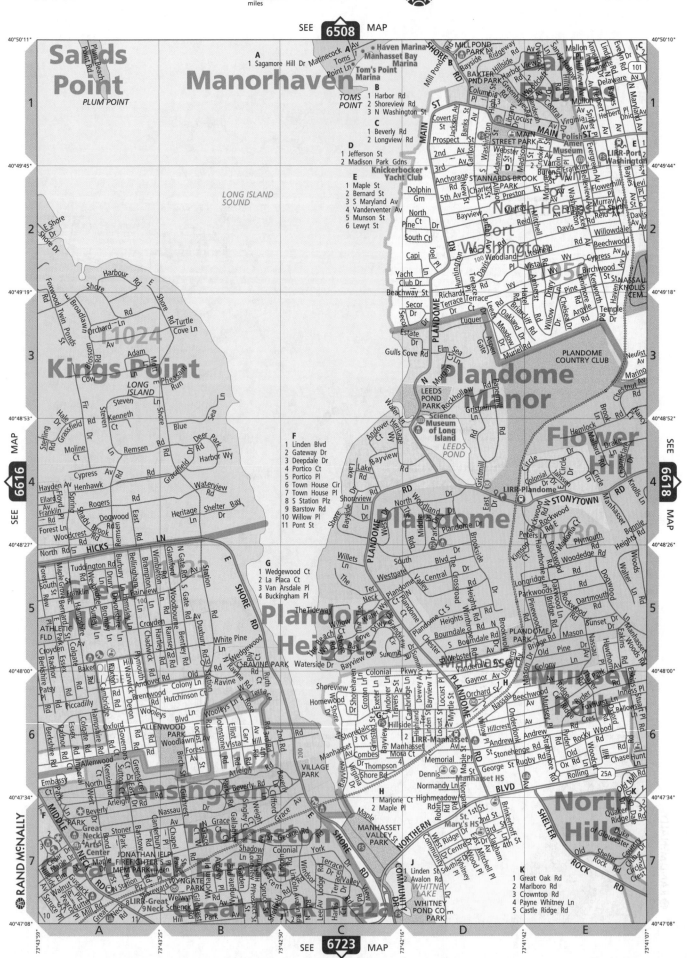

MAP 6618

MAP 6618

1:24,000
1 in. = 2000 ft.
0   0.25   0.5
miles

SEE 6509 MAP

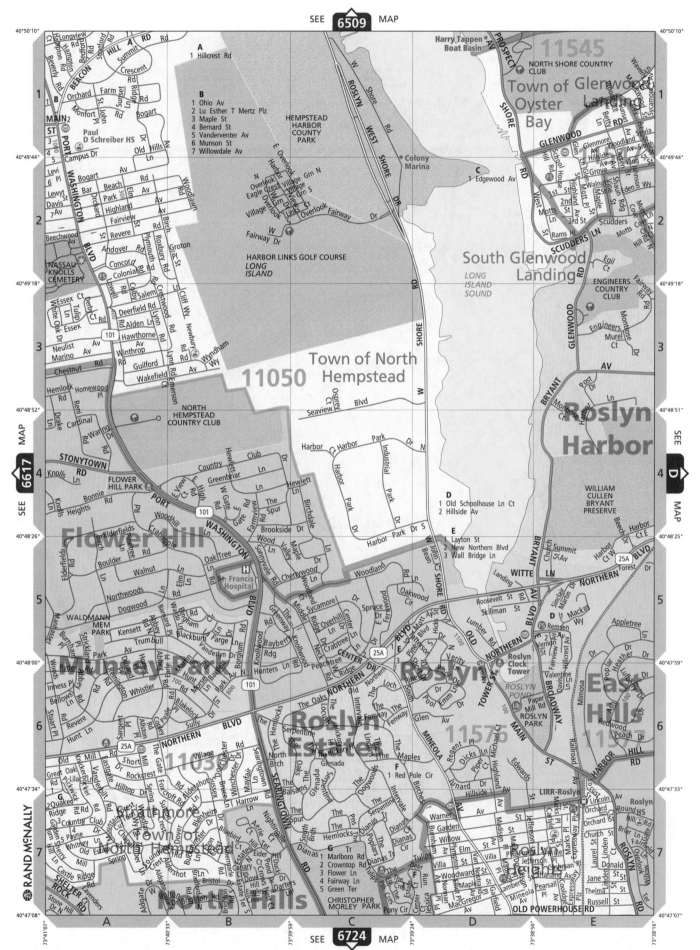

SEE 6617 MAP

SEE D MAP

SEE 6724 MAP

A
1 Hillcrest Rd

B
1 Ohio Av
2 Lu Esther T Mertz Plz
3 Maple St
4 Bernard St
5 Vanderventer Av
6 Munson St
7 Willowdale Av

C
1 Edgewood Av

D
1 Old Schoolhouse Ln Ct
2 Hillside Av

E
1 Layton St
2 New Northern Blvd
3 Wall Bridge Ln

F
1 Red Pole Cir

G
1 Marlboro Rd
2 Crowntop Rd
3 Flower Ln
4 Fairway Ln
5 Green Ter

Town of Glenwood
Oyster Bay

11545

NORTH SHORE COUNTRY CLUB

Harry Tappen Boat Basin

South Glenwood Landing

LONG ISLAND SOUND

ENGINEERS COUNTRY CLUB

Roslyn Harbor

WILLIAM CULLEN BRYANT PRESERVE

HEMPSTEAD HARBOR COUNTY PARK

Colony Marina

HARBOR LINKS GOLF COURSE
LONG ISLAND

Town of North Hempstead

11050

NORTH HEMPSTEAD COUNTRY CLUB

NASSAU KNOLLS CEMETERY

Paul D Schreiber HS

FLOWER HILL PARK

Flower Hill

St. Francis Hospital

WALDMANN MEM PARK

Muncy Park

Roslyn Estates

Roslyn

Roslyn Park

East Hills

11576

CHRISTOPHER MORLEY PARK

North Hills

Town of North Hempstead

OLD POWERHOUSE RD

LIRR-Roslyn

MAP **6712**

MAP **6712**

1:24,000
1 in. = 2000 ft.

0   0.25   0.5
miles

N

SEE **D** MAP

A
1 Gaston St
2 Municipal Plz
3 Old Northfield Av

B
1 Vosseler Ct
2 Vosseler Ter

City of Orange Twnshp

West Orange

West Orange Township

East Orange

South Orange Township

Newark

Irvington Township

Maplewood Township

Vailsburg

Edison National Historic Site

Rosedale Cemetery

Watsessing Park

Soverel Park

Seton Hall Preparatory School

Orange HS

Orange Park

Orange Comm Health Ctr

East Orange Social Security Administration

East Orange Gen Hosp

Memorial Park

Elmwood Park

Veteran's Hospital-East Orange

Marylawn of the Oranges HS

Meadowland Park

Seton Hall University Museum

Seton Hall University

Ivy Hill Park

Holy Sepulchre Cemetery

Vailsburg Park

Hebrew Cem

P
1 Washington Pl
2 Prospect Pl

J
1 Meadowbrook Pl
2 Comstock Pl
3 Academy St
4 Milligan Pl

L
1 Crescent Ct
2 Gifford Pl

N
1 Burr Rd
2 Hudson St

C
1 Cleveland Ter

E
1 Tony Galento Plz

F
1 N Arlington Av
2 City Hall Plz

H
1 Jack Jacobs Cir
2 Franklin Sigler Ln

K
1 Garfield Pl

M
1 Ferdinand St

Transit-Orange

Transit-Highland

Transit-Brick Church

Transit-East Orange

Transit-Mountain Station

07052

07050

07079

07018

07017

07106

07108

280
10
9
280
510
509
508
577
659
658
660
671
638
605
665
144
145
11
11B

RAND M^cNALLY

SEE **6816** MAP

SEE **D** MAP

SEE **6713** MAP

MAP
6713

1:24,000
1 in. = 2000 ft.

0   0.25   0.5
miles

MAP
6713

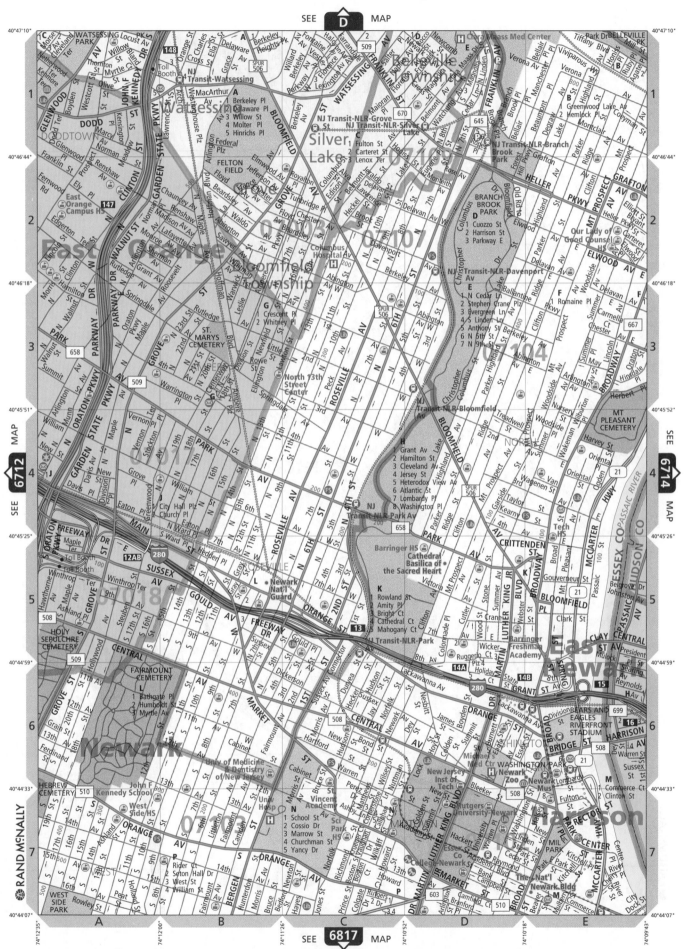

SEE 6712 MAP

SEE 6714 MAP

SEE 6817 MAP

RAND M℠NALLY

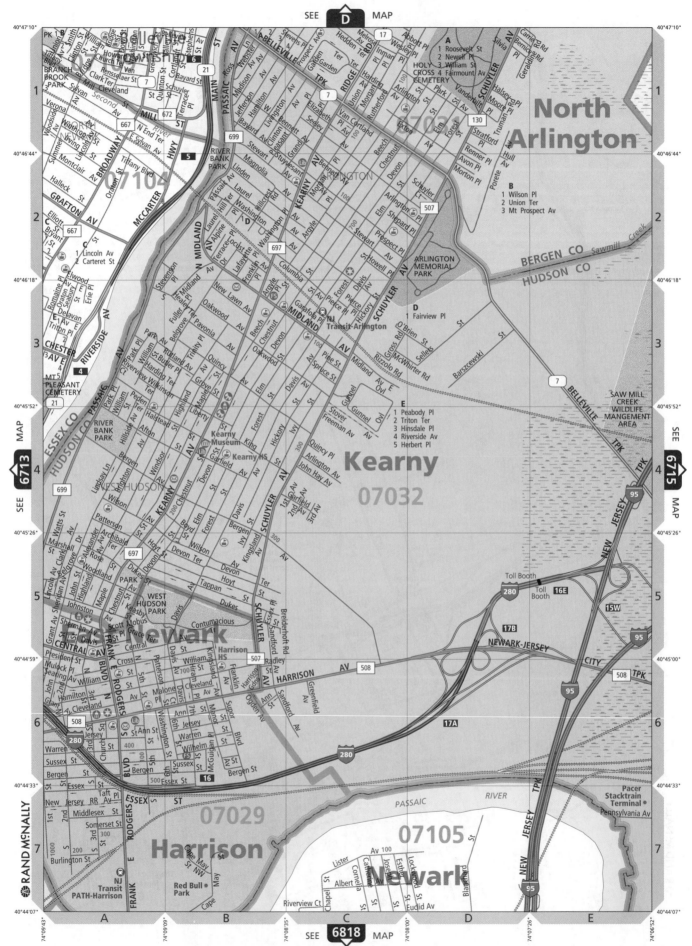

MAP 6714

MAP 6714

1:24,000
1 in. = 2000 ft.

0   0.25   0.5
miles

N

SEE D MAP
SEE 6713 MAP
SEE 6715 MAP
SEE 6818 MAP

North Arlington

07031

Kearny
07032

BERGEN CO
HUDSON CO
Sawmill Creek

ESSEX CO
HUDSON CO

RIVER BANK PARK

ARLINGTON MEMORIAL PARK

SAW MILL CREEK WILDLIFE MANGEMENT AREA

A
1 Roosevelt St
2 Newell Pl
3 William St
4 Fairmount Av

HOLY CROSS CEMETERY

B
1 Wilson Pl
2 Union Ter
3 Mt Prospect Av

C
1 Lincoln Av
2 Carteret St

D
1 Fairview Pl

E
1 Peabody Pl
2 Triton Ter
3 Hinsdale Pl
4 Riverside Av
5 Herbert Pl

Kearny Museum

Kearny HS

NJ Transit-Arlington

West Hudson Park

East Newark

Harrison
07029

Harrison HS

07105

Newark

NJ Transit PATH-Harrison

Red Bull Park

Pacer Stacktrain Terminal
Pennsylvania Av

PASSAIC RIVER

Toll Booth

Newark-Jersey City

MT PLEASANT CEMETERY

CHESTER AV E

BRANCH BROOK PARK

07104

RAND McNALLY

MAP
6715

MAP
6715

1:24,000
1 in. = 2000 ft.

0   0.25   0.5

miles

N

SEE 6609 MAP

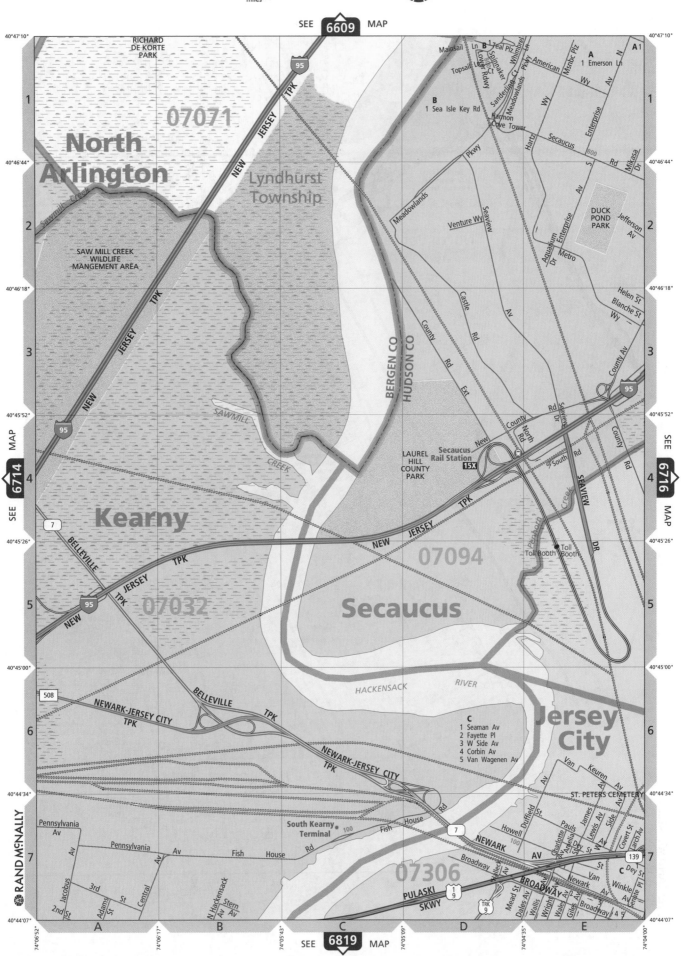

SEE 6714 MAP

SEE 6716 MAP

SEE 6819 MAP

RAND MCNALLY

North Arlington

Lyndhurst Township

07071

SAW MILL CREEK
WILDLIFE
MANGEMENT AREA

RICHARD
DE KORTE
PARK

Kearny

07032

Secaucus

07094

LAUREL
HILL
COUNTY
PARK

Secaucus
Rail Station

BERGEN CO
HUDSON CO

DUCK
POND
PARK

Jersey City

HACKENSACK RIVER

C
1 Seaman Av
2 Fayette Pl
3 W Side Av
4 Corbin Av
5 Van Wagenen Av

ST. PETERS CEMETERY

South Kearny
Terminal

NEWARK-JERSEY CITY TPK

BELLEVILLE TPK

NEWARK-JERSEY CITY TPK

07306

PULASKI SKWY

NEWARK AV

BROADWAY

A 1 Emerson Ln
B 1 Sea Isle Key Rd

40°47'10"
40°46'44"
40°46'18"
40°45'52"
40°45'26"
40°45'00"
40°44'34"
40°44'07"

74°06'52" 74°06'17" 74°05'43" 74°05'09" 74°04'35" 74°04'00"

A B C D E

MAP 6716

MAP 6716

1:24,000
1 in. = 2000 ft.

0   0.25   0.5
miles

N

SEE 6610 MAP

40°47'10"

Secaucus

New Jersey Turnpike

17

RT-3

PATERSON PLANK RD

West New York

North Bergen

GRV CHURCH CEMETERY

A
1 Park Plaza Dr

B
1 Newkirk Av
2 54th St
3 Madison St
4 55th St

C
1 Harrison Pl
2 Roosevelt St

40°46'44"

16E

Toll Booth

495

PENHORN AV

1

2

3

PALISADES CEMETERY

UNION TPK

WEEHAWKEN CEM

Pk Performing Arts Center

D
1 Roberts Pl
2 Givernaud Ter
3 Lincoln Ter

E
1 New Jersey Turnpike Bus Only Ln

95

Washington Av
Lincoln Av
Jefferson Av

North Bergen Township

F
1 Pleasant Av
2 Ridgley Pl
3 Baldwin Av

40°46'18"

NEW JERSEY TPK

Mesivta Sanz School

G
1 Parkview Av
2 Jefferson St
3 King Av
4 Sterling Av
5 Denning Pl
6 Bellevue St
7 Kingswood Rd

H
1 Clifton Ter
2 Liberty Pl

07047
Hudson City

07094

PATERSON PLANK

KENNEDY BLVD

TONNELLE AV

CHURCH SQUARE PK

HACKENSACK RESERVOIR NO 2

LINCOLN TUN

40°45'52"

MAP 6715

Land Bridge Terminal

501

St. Joseph & Michael the Archangel Church

16TH ST

Emerson HS

Transit-ABLR-Lincoln Harbor

NJ

Lincoln Harbor Yacht Club

SEE 6717 MAP

40°45'26"

Croxton Yard

07032
1 New Castle Rd

Jersey City

K
1 New Castle Rd

L
1 Skillman Av
2 Van Wagenen Av
3 Dey St
4 Berkeley Pl
5 Brooks Pl

SECAUCUS RD

Union City

Weehawken Township

07030

1 Riverview Dr

40°45'00"

659

BLVD

WASHINGTON PARK

501

681

PARK
COLUMBUS PARK

Maxwell's

Hoboken

ELYSIAN PARK

Stevens Inst of Technology

40°44'34"

GORDEN PARK

PULASKI SKWY

PERSHING FIELD

RES NO 2

RES NO 3

RIVER VIEW PARK

Sinatra's Birthplace

Hoboken

Hoboken Hist Museum
Constitution Ct
Independence Ct

Hudson School

Academy of Sacred Heart HS

CASTLE

Frank Sinatra Dr

M
1 Church Towers

FRANK SINATRA PARK

STEVENS St Park

HUDSON RIVER

RAND MCNALLY

139

St. Peters Cem

CROXTON

NEWARK AV

Jersey City Social Security Administration

OBSERVER HWY

NEWARK

677

637

681

Hoboken Univ Med Center

CHURCH SQ PARK

H

675

78 FY

40°44'07"

SEE 6820 MAP

A   B   C   D   E

MAP 6717

MAP 6717

1:24,000
1 in. = 2000 ft.

0   0.25   0.5
miles

N

SEE 6611 MAP

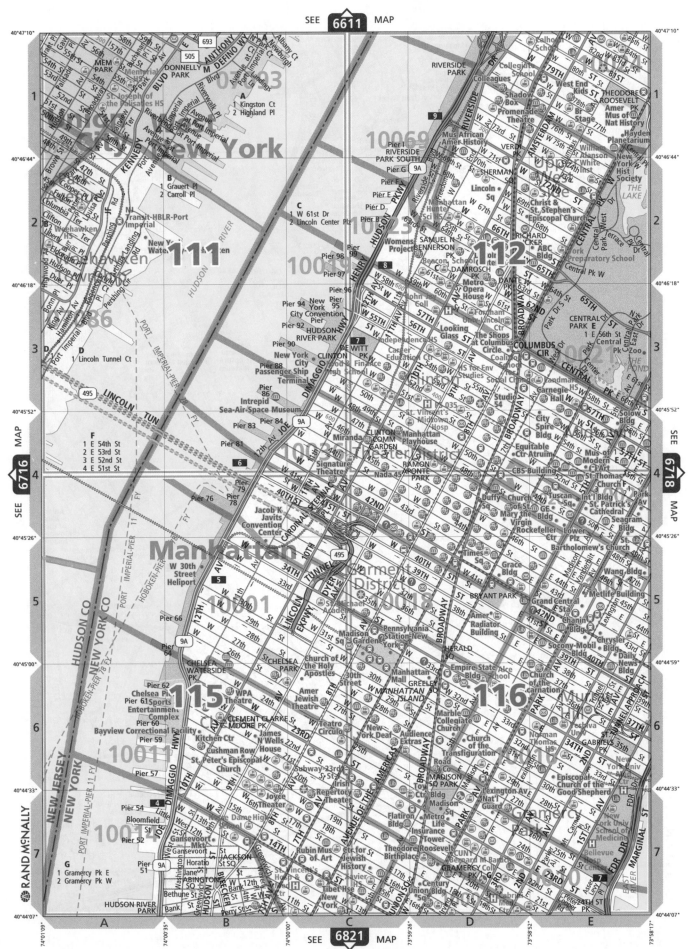

SEE 6716 MAP

SEE 6718 MAP

SEE 6821 MAP

MAP 6718

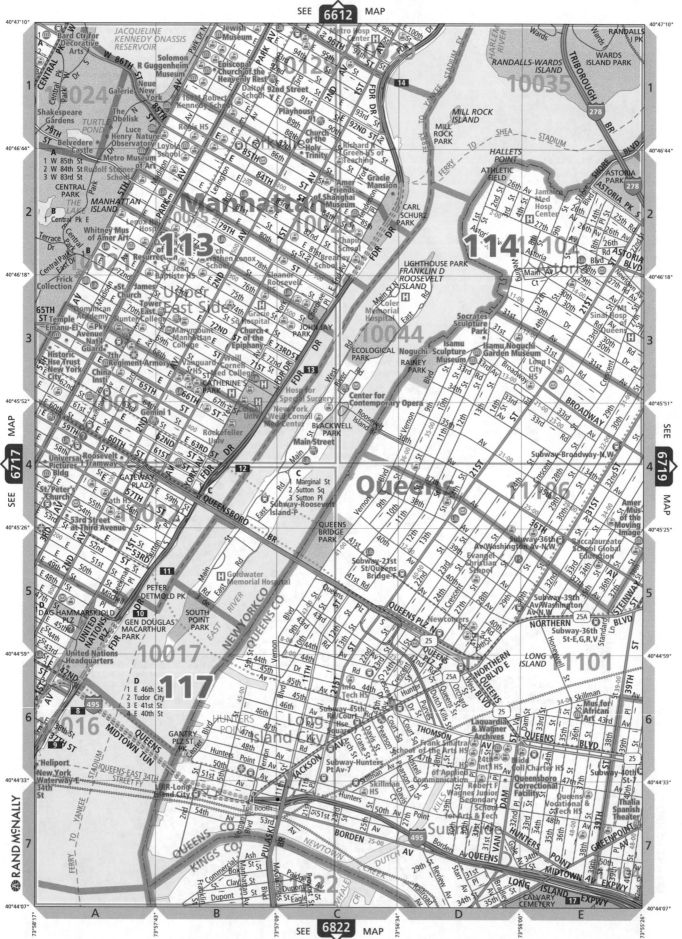

MAP 6718

SEE 6612 MAP

SEE 6717 MAP

SEE 6719 MAP

SEE 6822 MAP

1:24,000
1 in. = 2000 ft.

MAP
6719

MAP
6719

1:24,000
1 in. = 2000 ft.
0   0.25   0.5
miles

SEE 6613 MAP

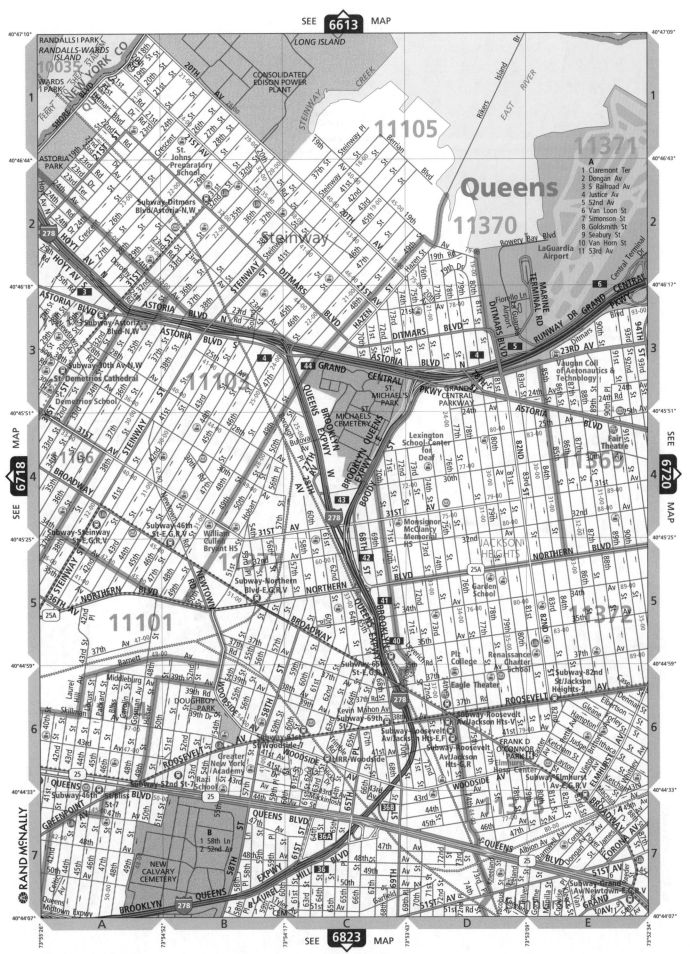

SEE 6718 MAP

SEE 6720 MAP

SEE 6823 MAP

MAP
6720

MAP
6720

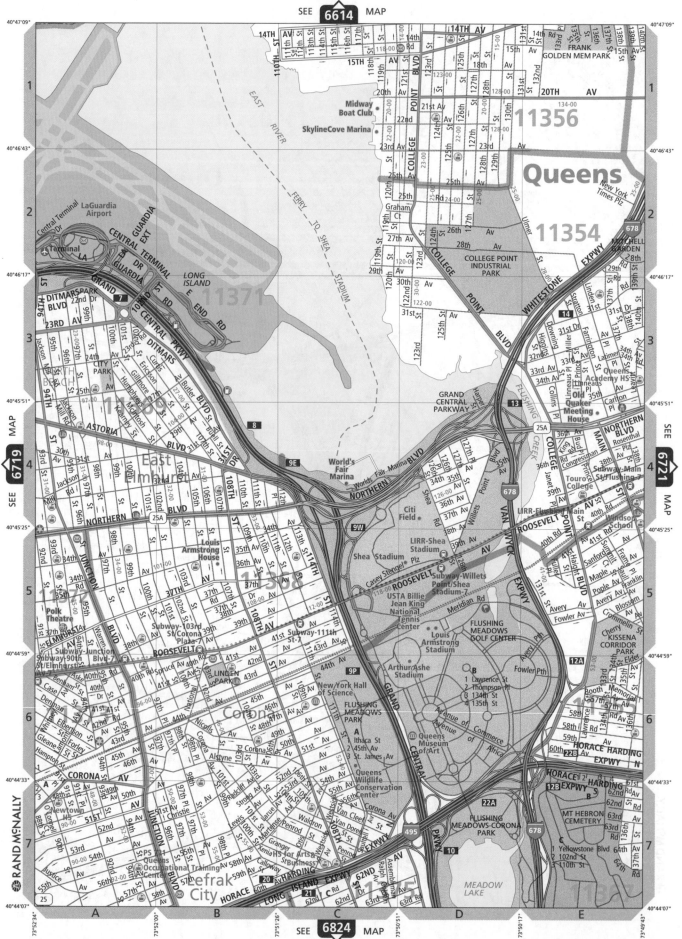

MAP
6721

MAP
6721

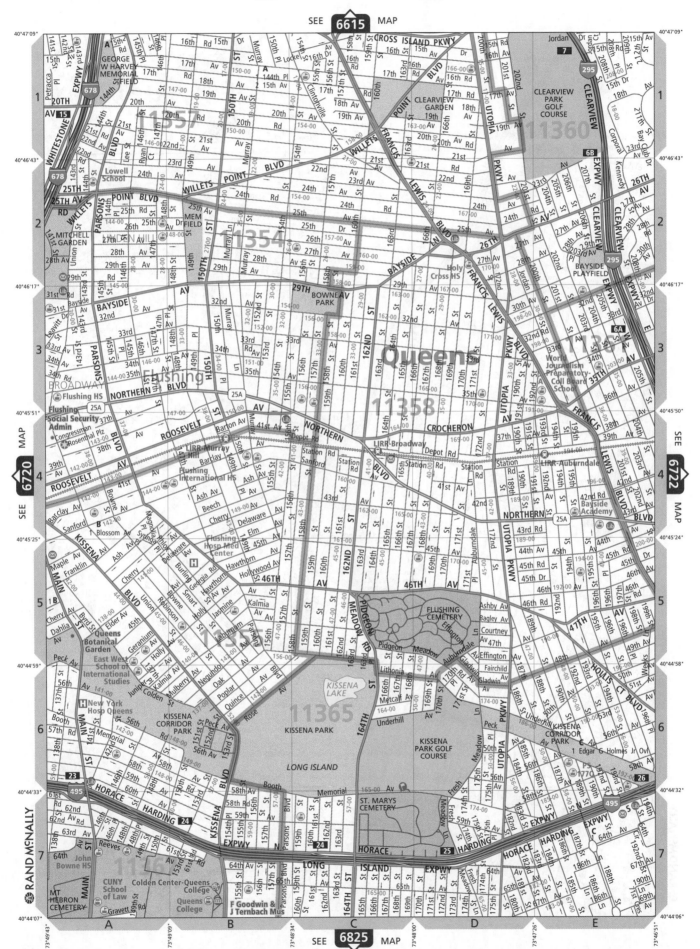

SEE 6720 MAP

SEE 6722 MAP

1:24,000
1 in. = 2000 ft.
0   0.25   0.5
miles

RAND McNALLY

MAP 6722

MAP 6722

1:24,000
1 in. = 2000 ft.

0   0.25   0.5
miles

N

SEE 6616 MAP

40°47'09"   40°47'08"

A
1 Prospect Pl
2 Chelsea Pl
3 Amherst Rd E
4 Gloucester Ct
5 Cutter Mill Rd
6 Old Cutter Mill Rd
7 Old Cutter Mill Ln

B
1 Pembroke Av
2 Van Nostrand Ct
3 W End Dr

C
1 Boyce Av

D
1 Weeks Ln

E
1 231st St
2 Country Pointe Cir
3 229th St

F
1 197th St
2 Underhill Av

SEE 6721 MAP

SEE 6723 MAP

Great Neck Estates
Town of North Hempstead
QUEENS CO.
NASSAU CO.
LITTLE NECK BAY
Bayside Marina
Bay Terrace Shop Ctr
JOHN GOLDEN PARK
CROCHERON PARK
RAYMOND M O'CONNOR FIELD
LIRR-Bayside
Oakland Gardens
Queensborough Comm College
Queensborough Comm College Art Gallery
OAKLAND LAKE
Alley Pond Environmental Center
FRANK TURNER INLET PARK
LIRR-Douglaston
LIRR-Little Neck
POND PARK
WATERFRONT PARK
LONG ISLAND
ALLEY CREEK
DOUGLASTON PARK GOLF COURSE
ALLEY POND PARK
CROSS ISLAND PARKWAY
CUNNINGHAM PARK
St. Francis Preparatory School
CCB School of Douglaston
Lifeline Ctr for Child Development
GRAND CENTRAL PARKWAY
UNION TPK

11020
11363
11362
11361
11364
11365
11004

RAND MCNALLY

SEE 6826 MAP

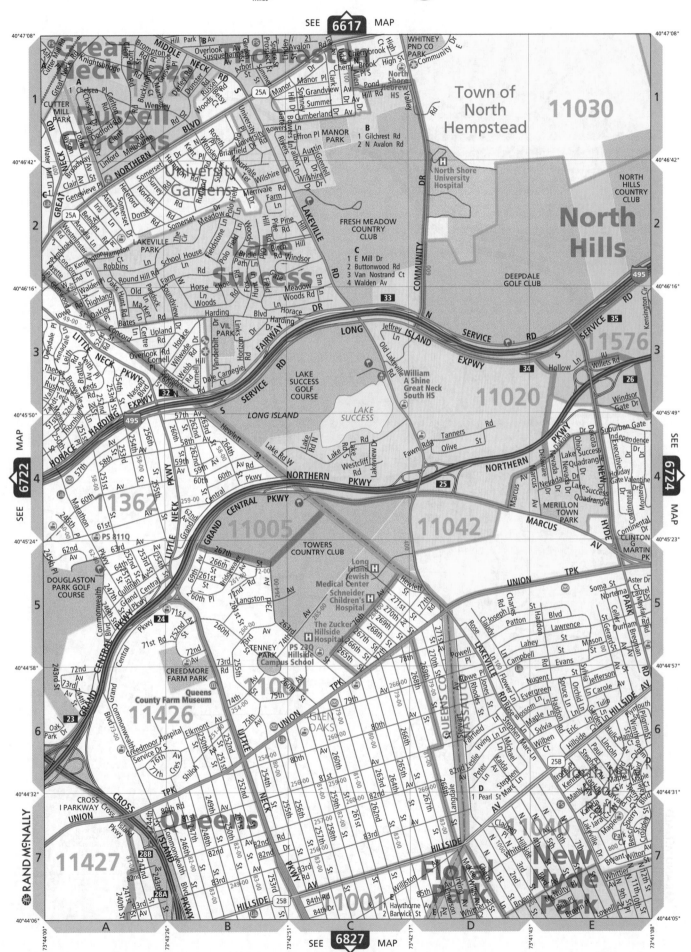

MAP
6723

MAP
6723

1:24,000
1 in. = 2000 ft.
0   0.25   0.5
miles

N

SEE 6617 MAP

SEE 6722 MAP

SEE 6724 MAP

SEE 6827 MAP

RAND McNALLY

11030

Town of
North
Hempstead

North
Hills

11576

11020

11005

11042

11362

11426

11427

11040

New
Hyde
Park

Floral
Park

11024

10010

MAP 6724

MAP 6724

SEE 6618 MAP

1:24,000
1 in. = 2000 ft.

0   0.25   0.5
miles

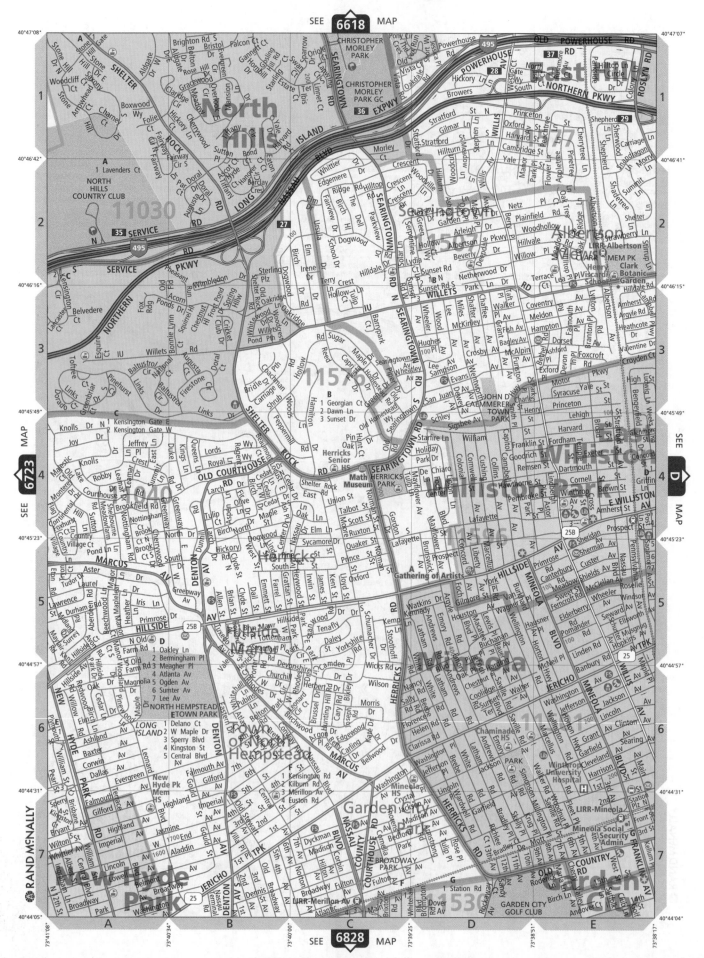

SEE 6723 MAP

SEE 6828 MAP

SEE 6723 MAP

RAND McNALLY

MAP
6816

MAP
6816

SEE 6712 MAP

1:24,000
1 in. = 2000 ft.
0   0.25   0.5
miles

SEE 6917 MAP

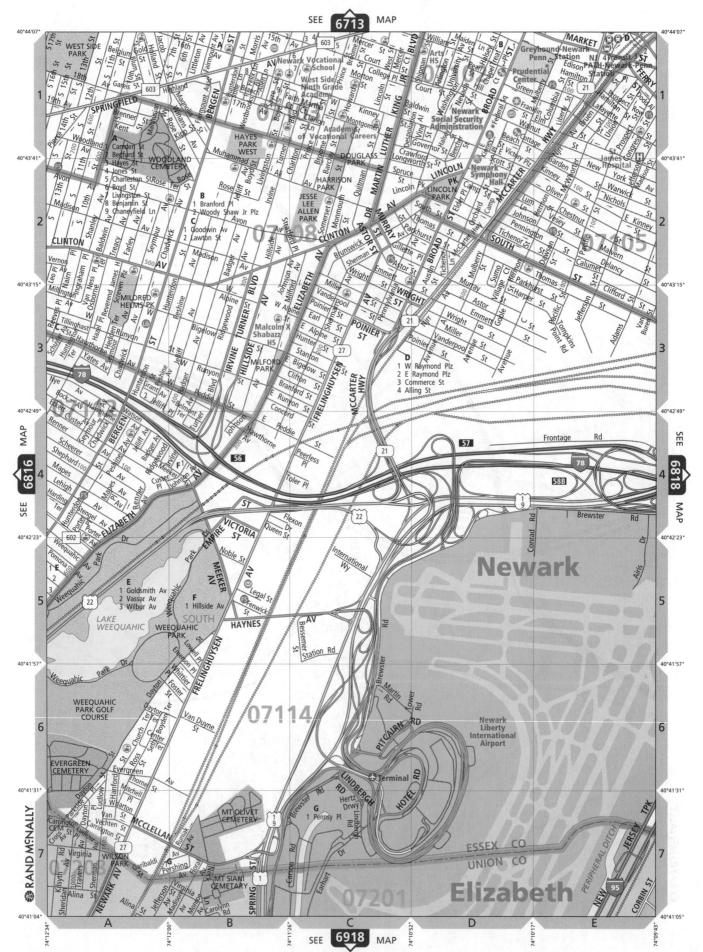

MAP 6818

1:24,000
1 in. = 2000 ft.
0   0.25   0.5
miles

N

MAP 6818

SEE 6714 MAP

40°44'07"

Commercial St
Cape May St
Riverview Ct
Chapel St
Euclid Av
1
A
2
PULASKI SKWY

FRANK E RODGERS BLVD S
Jersey St
RAYMOND BLVD
A
1 Lockwood St
2 Blanchard St
HAYES PARK
Wardell St
FERRY ST
95
I 95
TRK 9
LINCOLN HWY
1

40°43'41"

Prospect St
Congress St
Jefferson St
Downing St
RIVER BANK PARK
600
Fillmore St
Read St
Providence St
Mott St
Lexington St
Oxford St
Freeman St
Brill St
Schalk St
Richards St
Fleming St
Lentz Av
Vincent St
Cortland Pl
Manufacturers Pl
15E
Toll Booth
Toll Booth

MARKET ST
JACKSON St
Clove St
Buren St
Polk St
Merchant St
Chambers St
Somme St
Ferguson St
Christie St
Hawkins St
Cortland St
Horatio St
Roanoke St
Av
FERRY
Foundry St
Av
Roanoke

40°43'41"

Madison St
Monroe St
Adams St
Jackson St
Elm St
Lafayette St
FERRY
Alyea St
Wall St
Patterson St
Weccott St
Fillmore St
Magazine St
St George St
Main St
Franch St
Charles St
B
1 Warwick St
Rome St
BRILLS
NEW JERSEY TPK
Roanoke Av
Doremus Av
Roanoke Av

PASSAIC RIVER

Central Av

40°43'15"

Walnut St
New St
B
INDEPENDENCE PK
East Side HS
Warwick St
E Kinney St
Lang St
Ann St
Napoleon St
Garrison St
Kossuth St
Rome St
IRONBOUND
Ironbound Arena
Paris St
Marne St
Komorn St
Barbara St
Herbert St
Thornton St
Avenue P

07032
Kearny

WILSON AV
Kinney St
Oliver St
Chestnut St
Pulaski St
HENNESSY ST
Houston St
Garrison St
Gotthart St
Amsterdam St
Margaretta St
St Wilson Av
Marc St
K
C
1 Denbigh St
2 Ferdon St
3 Avenue I
Hyatt Av
Newark

40°43'15"

Vine St
Burns St
Malvern St
Hennessey St
Delancy St
Hanover St
Wheeler St
Point Rd
1C
2
3
Jabez St
Avenue I
Avenue L
Delancy St

HUDSON CO
ESSEX CO

40°42'49"

Clifford St
SOUTH ST
STOCKTON ST
1
9
95
I 95
Rutherford St
Wilson Av
Av
600
Av
Doremus Av

40°42'49"

Oak Island Terminal (Canadian Pacific)
OAK I JUNCTION
Bay Av
Delancy St
OAK ISLAND
07105

SEE 6819 MAP

40°42'23"

1
9
Frontage Rd
Frontage Rd
58B
Toll Booth
14
78
Toll Booth
E
Brewster St
PORT ST
07114

SEE 6817 MAP

Newark Liberty International Airport
Doremus Av
Doremus Avenue Auto Terminal
Firmench St

40°42'23"

40°41'57"

NEW JERSEY TURNPIKE EXT
Compass St
Kellogg St
Davit St
Distribution St
E Port St
Springline St
Martin St
Coastal St
God St
100
Doremus Av
78
NEWARK BAY

40°41'57"

NEW JERSEY TPK
Oak Island Terminal
NEWARK CHANNEL
Navy St
Dolphin St
Neptune St
Craneway

40°41'31"

NEW JERSEY TPK
CORBIN ST
Tyler St
Marsh St
Maritime St
Maritime St
PORT NEWARK
Marsh St

40°41'31"

I 95
Maritime St
Mohawk St
Coastwise St
Tyler St
Export St
Calcutta St
Calcutta St
STEPHEN R GREGG BAYONNE PARK

PORT NEWARK
ELIZABETH CHANNEL
ELIZABETH MARINE TERMINAL
07201
ESSEX CO
UNION CO
Panama St
Maracaibo St
Export St
Clipper St

40°41'05"

RAND McNALLY
N FLEET ST

SEE 6919 MAP

A   B   C   D   E

74°09'43"   74°09'09"   74°08'34"   74°08'00"   74°07'26"   74°06'52"

MAP
6819

MAP
6819

1:24,000
1 in. = 2000 ft.

0   0.25   0.5
miles

N

SEE 6715 MAP

07306

07304

07305

Kearny
07032

Jersey City

LINCOLN PARK

HACKENSACK RIVER

WEST SIDE

WEST BERGEN

NEWARK BAY

HUDSON CO
ESSEX CO

GREENVILLE

LIBERTY STATE PARK

LIBERTY NATIONAL GOLF CLUB

NEW YORK BAY

UPPER NEW YORK BAY

BAYVIEW CEMETERY

BAYSIDE PARK

BAY PARK SECTION CEM

COCHRANE PARK

COLUMBIA PARK

AUDUBON PARK

ARLINGTON PK

HOLY NAME CEMETERY

RICHARD A RUTKOWSKI PARK

STEPHEN R GREGG BAYONNE PARK

Marist HS

Snyder HS

Lincoln HS

Greenville Hospital

Afro-American Hist Society

Visual & Performing Arts HS

New Jersey City Univ

University Academy Charter HS

Create Charter School

A
1 Van Reipen Av
2 Magnolia Av
3 Academy St
4 Rocky Pope Pl
5 Tuers Av

B
(Cornelison Av area)

C
1 Stadium Ct
2 Alexander Ct
3 Tellicherry Ct
4 Surry Ct
5 Atlas Ct
6 Dempsey Ct
7 Carpenter Ct
8 Xavier Ct
9 Persimmon Ct
10 Mulberry St
11 Cypress St
12 Buttonwood St

D
1 New Hope Ln
2 New Heckman Dr
3 Liggons Ln

E
1 Summit Pl

NJ Transit-HBLR West Side Av

NJ Transit-Martin Luther King Dr

NJ Transit-HBLR-Garfield Av

NJ Transit-Richard St

NJ Transit-HBLR-Danforth Av

St. Peter's Coll

Hudson Catholic HS

St. Aloysius HS

Dominic Academy

Caritas Academy

BERGEN AV

COMMUNIPAW AV

GARFIELD AV

KENNEDY BLVD

DANFORTH AV

LINDEN AV

OCEAN AV

BAY VIEW AV

BIDWELL AV

JERSEY TURNPIKE EXT

NEW JERSEY TURNPIKE EXT

PULASKI SKWY

LINCOLN HWY

SEE 6818 MAP
SEE 6820 MAP
SEE 6920 MAP

Coordinates: 40°44'07", 40°43'41", 40°43'15", 40°42'49", 40°42'23", 40°41'57", 40°41'31", 40°41'05"

74°06'52", 74°06'17", 74°05'43", 74°05'09", 74°04'35", 74°04'00"

MAP
6820

MAP
6820

1:24,000
1 in. = 2000 ft.

0   0.25   0.5
miles

N

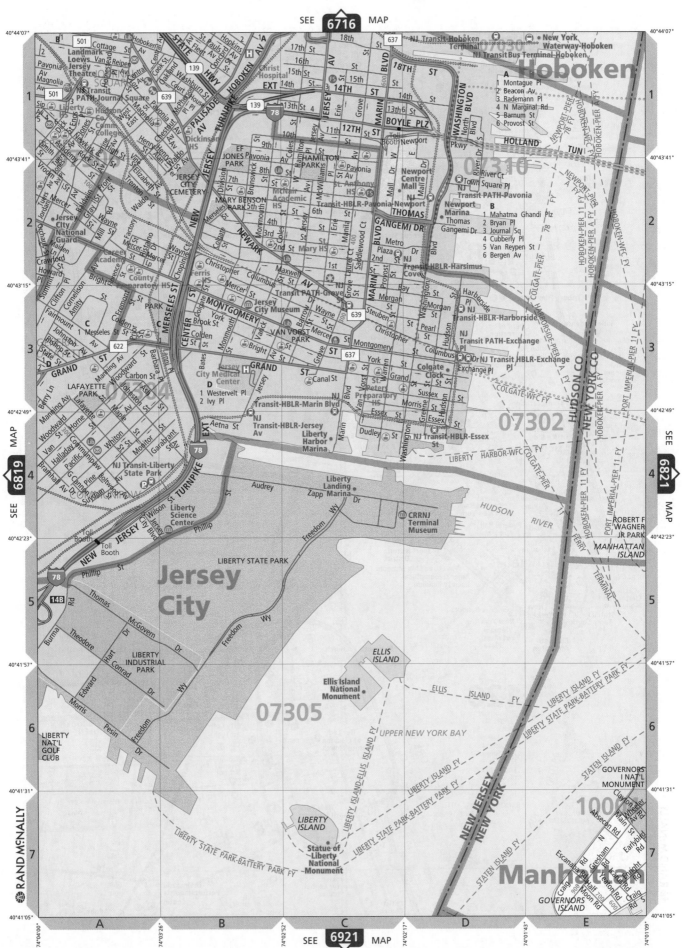

SEE 6716 MAP

SEE 6819 MAP

SEE 6821 MAP

SEE 6921 MAP

Hoboken

A
1 Montague Pl
2 Beacon Av
3 Rademann Pl
4 N Marginal Rd
5 Barnum St
6 Provost St

B
1 Mahatma Ghandi Plz
2 Bryan Pl
3 Journal Sq
4 Cubberly Pl
5 Van Reypen St
6 Bergen Av

C
1 Merseles Av

D
1 Westervelt Pl
2 Ivy Pl

Jersey
City

Manhattan

RAND McNALLY

MAP 6821

MAP 6821

SEE 6717 MAP

SEE 6820 MAP

SEE 6822 MAP

SEE 6922 MAP

MAP 6822

MAP 6822

1:24,000
1 in. = 2000 ft.
0   0.25   0.5
miles

N

SEE 6718 MAP

40°44'07"

BLISSVILLE

CALVARY CEMETERY

Queens

11101

Brooklyn

11378

QUEENS CO
KINGS CO

LONG ISLAND

NEWTOWN CREEK

KILLS
ENGLISH

40°43'41"

Greenpoint
Subway-Greenpoint Av-G
Greenpoint Monitor Museum

Greenpoint

11222

Automotive HS
Subway-Nassau Av-G

MCGOLDRICK PARK

MEEKER AV

KOSCIUSZKO BR

40°43'15"

MCCARREN PARK
Williamsburg Charter School

Subway-Bedford Av-L
El Puente Academy for Peace & Justice
Harry Van Arsdale HS

11211

COOPER PARK

METROPOLITAN AV

GRAND ST

40°42'49"

WILLIAMSBURG BR

Academy for Young Writers
Williamsburg

Subway-Graham Av-L
Subway-Metropolitan Av/Grand St-G
Subway-Grand

Grn School- An Academy for Env Careers
School for Legal Studies

A
1 Bushwick Ct
2 Thornton St
3 Sumner Pl

BROADWAY
Williamsburg Art & Hist Center

Yeshiva Ahavas Israel School
Beth Rachel School for Girls
Mesivta Yesode Hatorah-Boys

Subway-Hewes St-J,M
Subway-Montrose Av-L
Subway-Morgan Av-L

11237

Bushwick

FLUSHING AV

40°42'23"

LINDSAY PARK
Subway-Broadway-G

Juan Morel Campos Secondary School
Brooklyn Nat'l Guard

C

Bushwick Leaders HS
MARIA HERNANDEZ PARK

B
1 Dunham Pl
2 S 9th St
3 Harold W Cohn Memorial Sq

Bnos Yakov School for Girls
Yesh Mesivta Arugath Habosen

Subway-Flushing Av-G

NAVY YARD INDUSTRIAL PARK

11205

MYRTLE AV

40°41'57"

373 Brooklyn Transition Park Center
PS Martin King
Subway-Myrtle Av/Willoughby Av-G
Foundations Academy
Woodhull Medical-Mental Health Center

Subway-Myrtle Av-M,J,Z
Subway-Kosciuszko St-J

BROADWAY

Brooklyn Preparatory High School
JHS 117 Francis Scott Key School

FT GREENE
MYRTLE AV

11206

MYRTLE AV

DEKALB AV
LAFAYETTE AV

EBC HS for Public Service-Bush
Frederick Douglass Academy IV

40°41'31"

Pratt Institute
Walk Gate Hall
Pratt Activity Resource Center
St. Joseph's College

Delacorte Theater

TOMPKINS PARK
LAFAYETTE AV

Kosciuszko St-J

11221

Bedford

11216

Bishop Loughlin Mem HS
Paul Robeson Theatre
DEKALB AV

Subway-Clinton Av/Washington Av-G

11238

Bedford Academy HS
Brooklyn Academy HS

40°41'04"

SEE 6821 MAP
SEE 6823 MAP
SEE 6923 MAP

MAP
6823

MAP
6823

1:24,000
1 in. = 2000 ft.
0   0.25   0.5
miles

N

SEE 6719 MAP

SEE 6924 MAP

SEE 6822 MAP

SEE 6824 MAP

Queens

Brooklyn

Maspeth

Middle Village

Ridgewood

Grendale

Bushwick

Kings Co

Queens Co

Haberman

Bush Junction

Fresh Pond

11377
11378
11385
11379
11237
11221
11207
11208
11227

LONG ISLAND EXPWY
QUEENS MIDTOWN EXPWY
495
278

NEW CALVARY CEMETERY
MT ZION CEMETERY
MT OLIVET CEMETERY
MT NEBOH CEMETERY
NEW UNION FLD CEMETERY
MACHPELAH CEMETERY
MT CARMEL CEMETERY
HUNGARIAN CEMETERY
MT JUDAH CEMETERY
KNOLLWOOD PARK CEMETERY
EVERGREEN CEMETERY
THE MOST HOLY TRINITY CEMETERY
SHEARITH ISRAEL CEMETERY
SALEM FIELDS CEMETERY
CYPRESS HILLS NAT'L CEMETERY
CYPRESS HILLS CEMETERY
LUTHERAN CEMETERY
MT LEBANON CEMETERY
MT INDIANA CEMETERY
AHAWITH CHESED CEMETERY
LINDEN HILL CEMETERY
GROVER CLEVELAND PARK
JUNIPER VALLEY PARK
MASERA PARK
MARIA HERNANDEZ PARK
HIGHLAND PARK
RIDGEWOOD RESERVOIR

MASPETH CREEK
NEWTOWN CREEK
LONG ISLAND

METROPOLITAN AV
MYRTLE AV
COOPER AV
CYPRESS HILLS PKWY
ROBINSON
VERMONT
JACKIE
BATTISTA
JAMAICA
BROADWAY
FRESH POND RD
GRAND AV
PAGE PL
FLUSHING AV
CENTRAL AV
PUTNAM AV
BUSHWICK AV
CORNELIA ST

Subway-Metropolitan Av-M
Subway-Fresh Pond Rd-M
Subway-Forest Av-M
Subway-Seneca Av-M
Subway-DeKalb Av-L
Subway-Myrtle-Wyckoff Av-L
Subway-Knickerbocker Av-M
Subway-Halsey St-L
Subway-Wilson Av-L
Subway-Gates Av-J,Z
Subway-Halsey St-J

Metro Mall
Metro Plz
Christ the King Regional HS
Wyckoff Hts Med Center
All City Leadership Secondary School
Academy of Urban Planning HS
New York Harbor School
Robert E Peary School
Harman Street Playhouse
Bushwick Comm HS
Acorn HS for Social Justice
Bushwick

SARATOGA SQUARE PARK

RAND McNALLY

40°44'07"
40°43'41"
40°43'15"
40°42'49"
40°42'23"
40°41'57"
40°41'31"
40°41'05"

73°55'26"
73°54'52"
73°54'18"
73°53'43"
73°53'09"
73°52'35"

A   B   C   D   E
1   2   3   4   5   6   7

MAP
6824

MAP
6824

1:24,000
1 in. = 2000 ft.

0   0.25   0.5
miles

N

SEE 6720 MAP

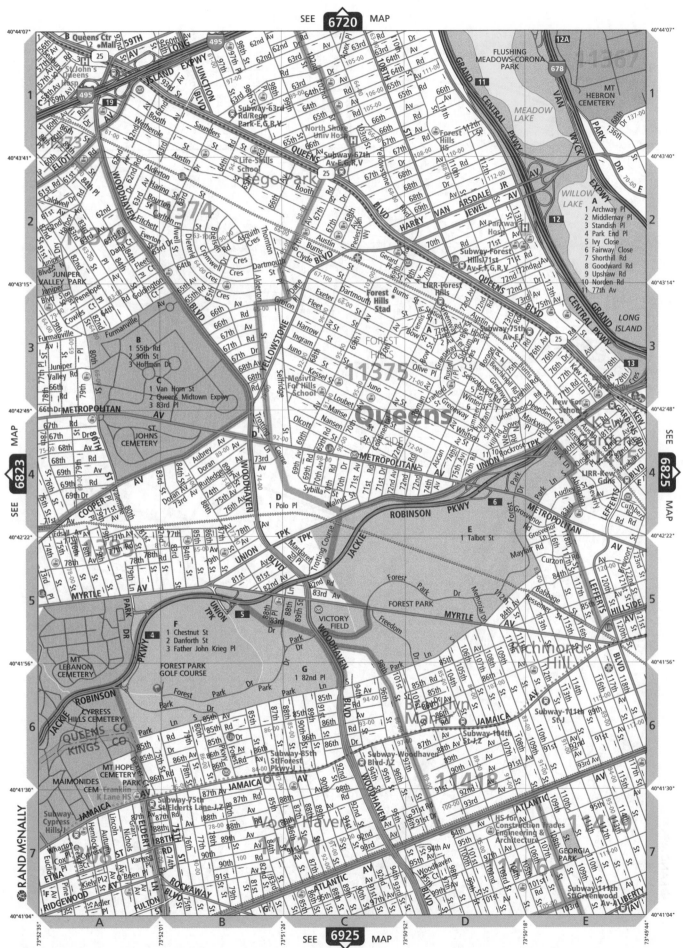

SEE 6823 MAP

SEE 6825 MAP

SEE 6925 MAP

MAP 6825   MAP 6825

1:24,000
1 in. = 2000 ft.
0   0.25   0.5
miles

N

SEE 6721 MAP

40°44'07"   40°44'06"

MT HEBRON CEMETERY

Townsend Harris HS

QUEENS COLLEGE

LONG ISLAND

SOUTH FLUSHING

Fresh Meadows

Bombay Theatre

JEWEL AV

Queens

11367

11365   11366

Utopia UNION

11432

KISSENA BLVD

Robert F Kennedy Comm HS

PS 255Q

Belson Soccer Stadium

St. John's University

Queens Ctr for Progress

UTOPIA PKWY

GRAND CENTRAL PKWY

MIDLAND PKWY

18

Thomas Edison Career & Tech AvHS

Queens Hosp Center

17

FLUSHING MEADOWS-CORONA PARK

678

UNION TPK

GRAND CENTRAL PKWY

Mary Louis Academy

Subway-179th St/Jamaica-F

TILLY PARK

Subway-169th St-F

HILLSIDE AV

The Afrikan Poetry Theatre

SEE 6824 MAP

SEE 6826 MAP

MAPLE GROVE CEMETERY

Archbishop Molloy HS

Queens Gateway to Health Sci Secondary School

Subway-Parsons Blvd-F

Subway-Sutphin Blvd-F

Mary Immaculate Hospital RUFUS KING PK

Rufus King Manor Museum

Jamaica Arts Center

Jamaica Nat'l Guard

LIBERTY PARK

METROPOLITAN AV

Subway-Jamaica/Van Wyck-E

Offsite Educational Services School

Ulman School

Jamaica Hospital

Subway-Jamaica Center-E,J,Z

Subway-Parsons/Archer AV-E,J,Z

York College

Queens HS for the Sci at York College

LIBERTY

MERRICK

11418   11419

Subway-121st St-J,Z

Subway-Sutphin Blvd/Archer AV-E,J,Z

LIRR-Jamaica

JAMAICA AV

94TH AV

LIBERTY AV

SOUTH AV

11433

ATLANTIC AV

Morris Park

VAN WYCK EXPWY

MARCONI MEM FLD

CEDAR MANOR

ST ALBANS MEM PK

South Richmond Hill

Jamaica

11435

SOUTH JAMAICA

LINDEN BLVD

BREWER BLVD

GUY R BREWER BLVD

LIBERTY BLVD

Subway-Lefferts Blvd-A

678 EXPWY

HS for Law Enforcement & Public Safety

11420   3   11436   11437

SEE 6926 MAP

A   B   C   D   E

MAP 6826

MAP 6826

1:24,000
1 in. = 2000 ft.
0   0.25   0.5
miles

N

SEE 6722 MAP

40°44'06"
40°43'40"
40°43'14"
40°42'48"
40°42'22"
40°41'56"
40°41'30"
40°41'03"

SEE 6825 MAP

SEE 6827 MAP

SEE 6927 MAP

1 2 3 4 5 6 7

A B C D E

CUNNINGHAM PARK

TERRACE HEIGHTS

Summit School

Yeshiva Univ HS-Girls

HILLSIDE AV

JAMAICA AV

BELLAIRE

Queens Village

JAMAICA

HEMPSTEAD AV

LIRR-Queens Village

LIRR-Hollis

Queens St Albans

Math Sci Research Magnet HS

Humanities & Arts Magnet HS

Law Government & Comm Service HS

Bethel Christian Learning Center

CAMBRIA HEIGHTS

LINDEN BLVD

ALBANS MEM PARK

LIRR-St Albans

ROY WILKENS PARK

MERRICK BLVD

MONTEFIORE CEMETERY

LONG ISLAND

GRAND CENTRAL PARKWAY

CLEARVIEW

SPRINGFIELD BLVD

BRADDOCK AV

FRANCIS LEWIS BLVD

FARMERS BLVD

HOLLIS AV

LIBERTY AV

11356 11427 11428 11429 11411 11412 11413 11434 11433 11432 11423

A 1 Oceana St
C 1 80th Dr 2 Troon Rd 3 Perth Rd 4 Haddon St
B 1 Country Pointe Cir
D 1 Marsden St 2 Smith St 3 Victoria Rd 4 119th Rd 5 Victoria Dr

MAP
6827

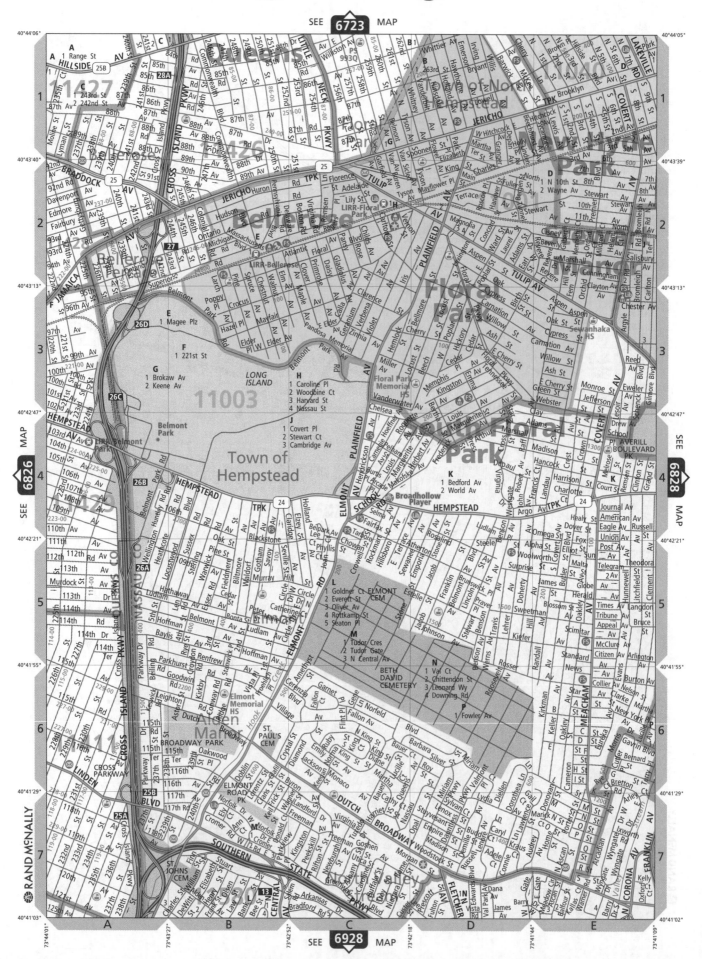

MAP
6827

SEE 6723 MAP

SEE 6826 MAP

SEE 6828 MAP

SEE 6928 MAP

MAP
6828

1:24,000
1 in. = 2000 ft.

0   0.25   0.5
miles

N

MAP
6828

SEE 6724 MAP

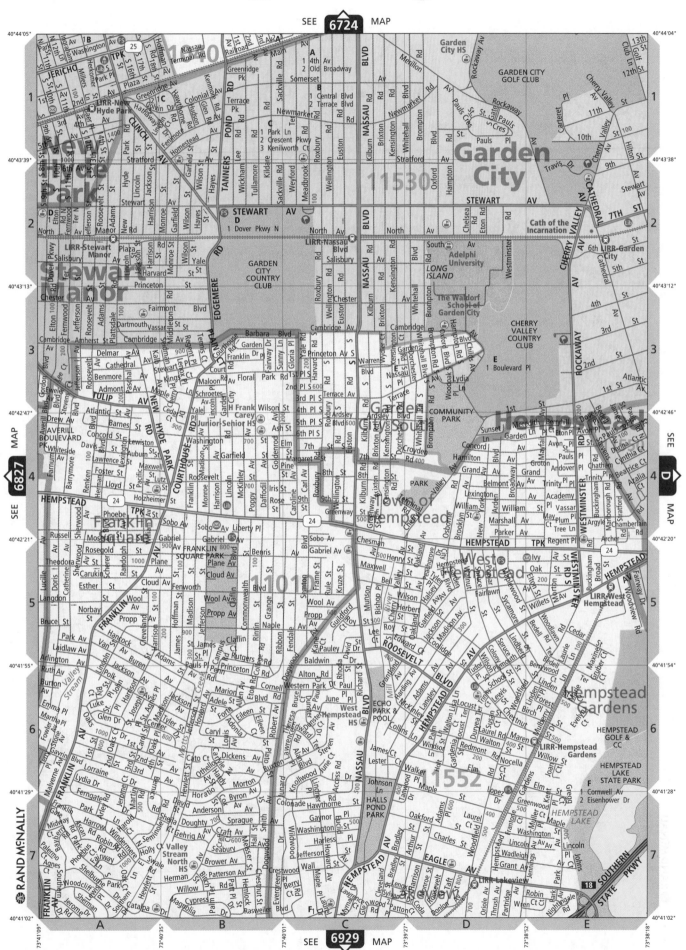

SEE 6827 MAP

SEE MAP 6828

RAND McNALLY

MAP
6917

MAP
6917

1:24,000
1 in. = 2000 ft.

0   0.25   0.5
miles

N

SEE 6816 MAP

40°41'04"
40°41'05"

A
1 Townley Av
2 Sherwood Rd
3 Huguenot Av
4 Dwight Ter

B
1 Union St
2 Harrison St
3 Julian Pl
4 Commerce Pl
5 William St
6 Lafayette St
7 Elizabethtown Plz
8 W Winfield Scott Plz
9 E Jersey St
10 Martin Luther King Jr Plz
11 Dickinson St
12 Morrell St

C
1 Home Ter
2 Fern St

D
1 Ely St
2 Eugenia Pl
3 Potiphar Ct
4 Dehart Pl
5 Montgomery Pl

E
1 Denton St
2 Morses Mill Rd
3 Fairbanks St
4 Fern Pl
5 Atlantic St

Union Township
07205
Kean University
Liberty Hall Museum
07083
KENNEDY RESERVATION
SUBURBAN GOLF CLUB
COLONIAL AV
SALEM RD
GALLOPING HILL RD
Elizabeth
07208
07202
07201
Roselle Pk
Roselle
07203
WARINANCO PARK
ELMORE RC PK
WESTFIELD AV
GRAND ST
WESTFIELD ST
GEORGES
07036
Linden
LINDEN OIL
BAYWAY
ROSEDALE CEMETERY
LINDEN PARK CEMETERY
MT CALVARY CEMETERY
SOUTH Mill RESERVOIR
ROSELLE
DR MARTIN LUTHER KING JR MEM PK
GEORGE T FAREWELL MEM
L RON HUBBARD PARK
FAIRMOUNT
Elizabeth River Park
ELIZABETH RIVER PARK
PHIL RIZZUTO PARK
Elizabeth Social Security Admin
NORTH AV
BROAD ST
NEWARK AV
MORRIS AV
RAILROAD AV
NJ Transit-Elizabeth
Union Co Admin Building
ELIZABETH
Ritz Theatre
Boxwood Hall ST Hist Site PARK
Elizabeth HS
CARTERET PARK
CALDWELL PK
VAN ARSDALE PARK
RAHWAY AV
WASHINGTON AV
Elizabeth HS-Halsey House
Trinitas Hosp
St. Mary of the Assumption HS
BAYWAY CIR
CARLTON ST
Elizabeth HS-Edison House
ELIZABETH RIVER PARK
WILLIAMS FIELD
MATTANO PARK
DROTAR FIELD
MCGILLVRAY PLACE PK
MILKOSKY PK
MACK PLACE PK
Toll Booth
Toll Booth
NEW JERSEY TPK
278

SEE 6918 MAP
SEE D MAP

RAND McNALLY

95

40°40'38"
40°40'12"
40°39'46"
40°39'20"
40°38'54"
40°38'28"
40°38'02"

74°15'25" 74°14'51" 74°14'17" 74°13'42" 74°13'08" 74°12'34"

MAP
6918

MAP
6918

1:24,000
1 in. = 2000 ft.

0   0.25   0.5

miles

N

SEE 6817 MAP

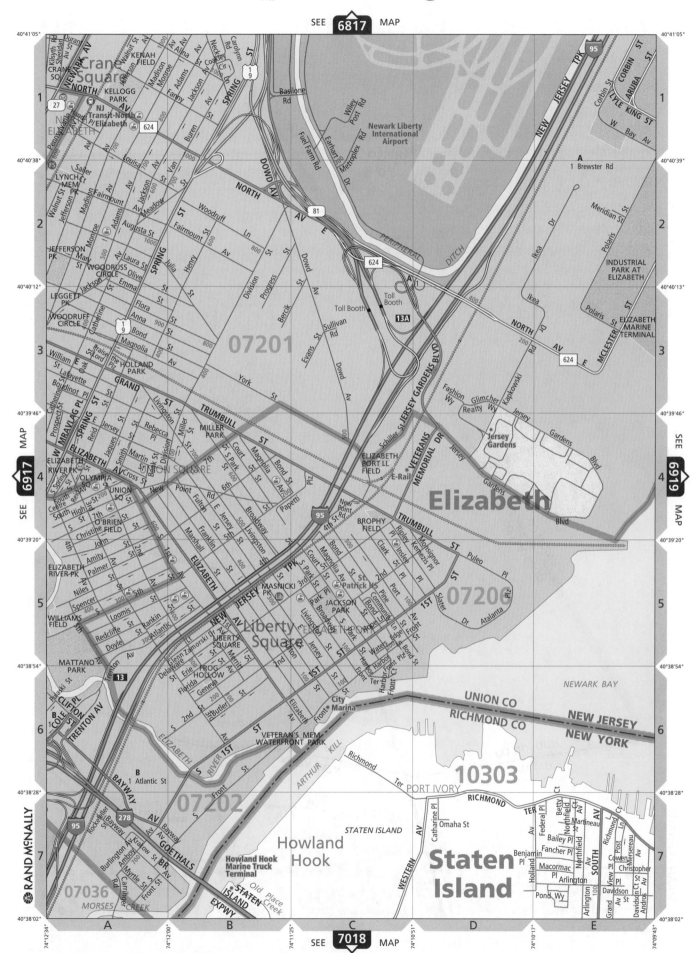

MAP 6917

SEE

SEE 6919 MAP

40°41'05"
40°40'38"
40°40'12"
40°39'46"
40°39'20"
40°38'54"
40°38'28"
40°38'02"

40°41'05"
40°40'39"
40°40'13"
40°39'46"
40°39'20"
40°38'54"
40°38'28"
40°38'02"

74°12'34"   74°12'00"   74°11'25"   74°10'51"   74°10'17"   74°09'43"

1   2   3   4   5   6   7

A   B   C   D   E

SEE 7018 MAP

RAND McNALLY

Crane Square
Newark Liberty International Airport
07201
Elizabeth
Liberty Square
07206
Staten Island
Howland Hook
10303
07202
07036
Newark Bay
Staten Island
Arthur Kill

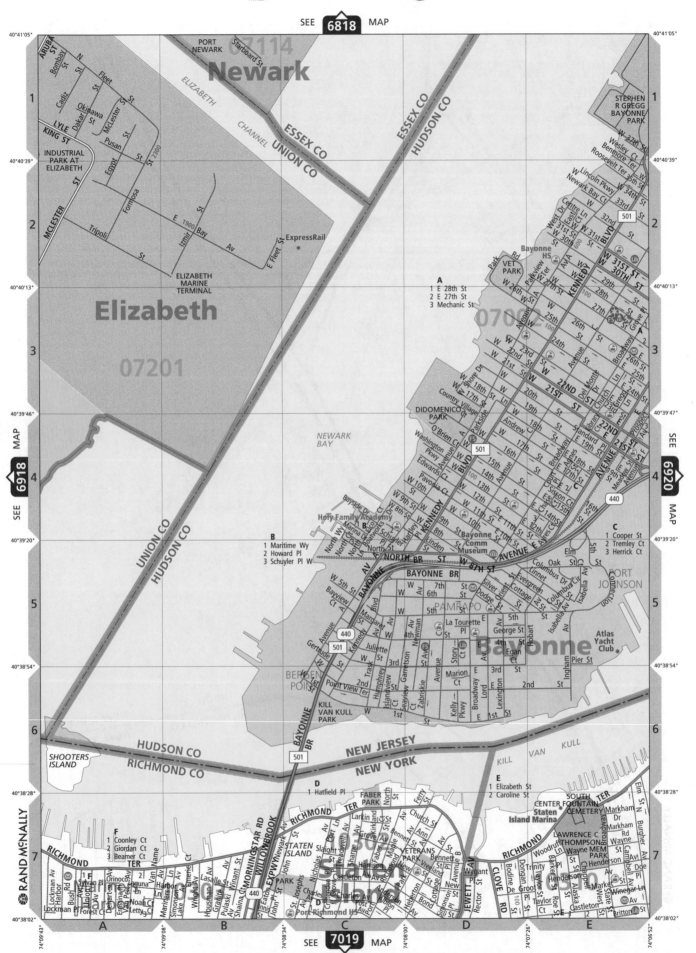

MAP
6919

MAP
6919

1:24,000
1 in. = 2000 ft.

0   0.25   0.5
miles

N

SEE 6818 MAP

PORT NEWARK

07114

Newark

Starboard St

ARUBA ST
Bombay St
N
Fleet St

Cadiz St
Okinawa St
McLester St
Dakar St

LYLE
KING ST

INDUSTRIAL PARK AT ELIZABETH

MCLESTER ST

Pusan St

Egypt St

Formosa St

Tripoli

St 2390

Izmir St

E 1900 Bay

E Bay Av

ELIZABETH MARINE TERMINAL

ExpressRail

ESSEX CO
UNION CO

ESSEX CO
HUDSON CO

ELIZABETH CHANNEL

Elizabeth

07201

NEWARK BAY

STEPHEN R GREGG BAYONNE PARK

W 37th St
Wesley Ct
Benmore Ter
Roosevelt Ter 35th St

W 34th St
Lincoln Pkwy
Newark Bay Ct
33rd St

501

Centre Ln
32nd St
BLVD

West Dr
Last W
W 31st St
W 31st St
W 30th
600

W 31ST ST
W 30TH ST

Bayonne HS

VET PARK

Park Rd
Parkway
Parkview Ter
W 27th St
AV A
KENNEDY WY

A
1 E 28th St
2 E 27th St
3 Mechanic St

W 28th W St
W 26th W St
W 25th Avenue St
W 24th
W 23rd

07002

26th St
27th St
28th
29th
100

Broadway
24th
Grove
26th St
25th St
E 24th

22ND ST

W 22nd St
W 21st St
W 20th Ln
W 19th
W 18th St
W 17th St

Del Monte
Church St
E
Av
E 23rd
Standard

22ND ST
E 21ST ST

DIDOMENICO PARK

Country Village Ct
Shore Rd
W 18th St
W 17th St

O'Brien Ct
Parkside
Washington Pkwy
Avenue
16th St
AVENUE C
AVENUE

Andrew
E 19th

501

W 15th St
Edwards Ct
Pavonia Ct

501
BLVD
100
14th St
13th St

440

Holy Family Academy

Bayside Dr
W 9th St
W 8th St
North Wy
North Ct
North St

Marina Del
Boardwalk
Barkley
Schuyler
KENNEDY
W 12th St
W 11th St
W 10th St

12th
9th St
10th St

E 14th St
E 13th St
E 12th St

B
1 Maritime Wy
2 Howard Pl
3 Schuyler Pl W

Linden
Bayonne Comm Museum

Andrew
E Aviles St
AVENUE E

8th St
AVENUE

C
1 Cooper St
2 Tremley Ct
3 Herrick Ct

NORTH BR ST
W 5th St
W 8TH ST

BAYONNE BR

Oak St
Elm St

PORT JOHNSON

W 5th St
Bayview Ct
BAYONNE BR

7th St
6th St
Dodge St
Silver St
Cottage

Columbus Dr Ct
Evergreen
Columbus Av
Linnet

Av
Margaret St
5th St
La Tourette Pl
Newman
4th St
Story Ct

5th
George St
Hobart
Isabella Av

PAMRAPO

Atlas Yacht Club

440
501
Avenue
Gertrude St

Juliette
3rd St
Trask
Humphrey
Zabriskie

Av
Garretson
Avenue
Marion Ct

Egan Ct
5th
3rd
2nd

Bayonne

BERGEN POINT

Point view Ter

2nd St
Beaview
1st
Avenue
Kelly Pkwy

Broadway
Lord
Lexington
E 1st St
Pier St
Ingham

KILL VAN KULL PARK

BAYONNE BR

501

HUDSON CO
RICHMOND CO

SHOOTERS ISLAND

HUDSON CO

NEW JERSEY
NEW YORK

KILL VAN KULL

D
1 Hatfield Pl

E
1 Elizabeth St
2 Caroline St

FABER PARK

RICHMOND TER

North St
Ferry St
Church St

Larkin St
Kirkland
Ann St

SOUTH CENTER
CEMETERY

FOUNTAIN
Staten Island Marina

TER
Markham Dr
Markham Rd
Wayne

F
1 Coonley Ct
2 Giordan Ct
3 Beamer Ct

RICHMOND TER

MORNINGSTAR RD
WILLOWBROOK
RICHMOND

Newark
Sharpe
Grove
Meple
Bennett

STATEN ISLAND

Nicholas
Charles
Post

VETERANS PARK
Vreeland
Pl

RICHMOND

Woodruff
THOMPSON

LAWRENCE C

Burger
Elm St
Wayne MEM PARK

R. McNALLY

RICHMOND TER

Lockman Av
Sylvan Pl
Bush
Union

EATON
440

Pulaski
Lasalle
Wright Av
Shaina Ct

St Josephs
John St

Port Richmond HS

Cottage
New

JEWETT
CLOVE RD

Bodine
De Groot
Rector

Trinity
Henderson
Alaska St
Market St
Taylor St
Roe St
Castleton

Campbell
Winegar Ln

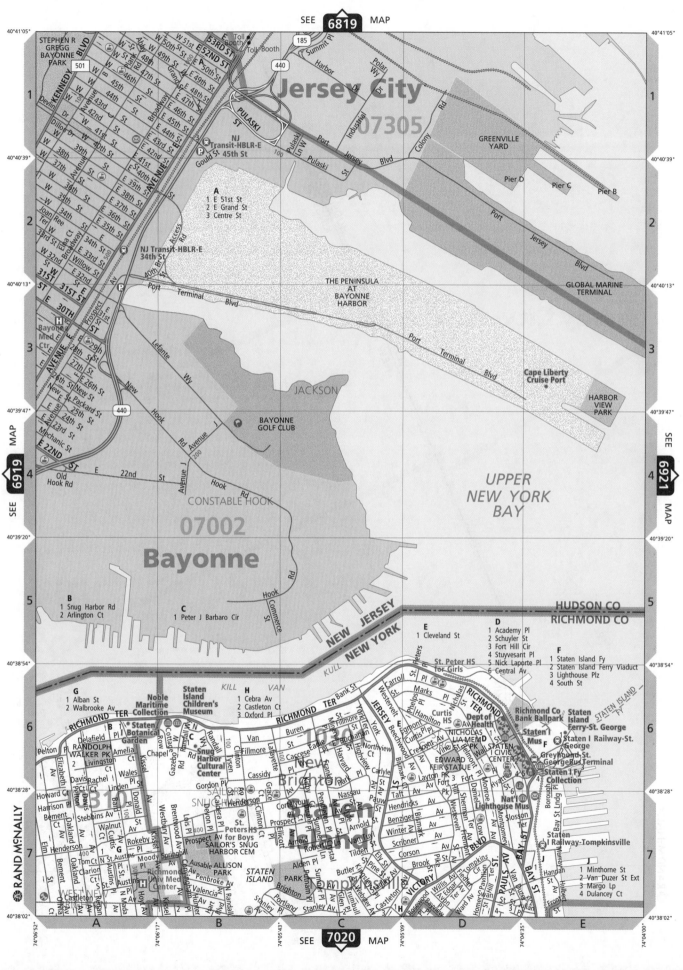

MAP
6921

MAP
6921

1:24,000
1 in. = 2000 ft.

0   0.25   0.5

miles

SEE **6820** MAP

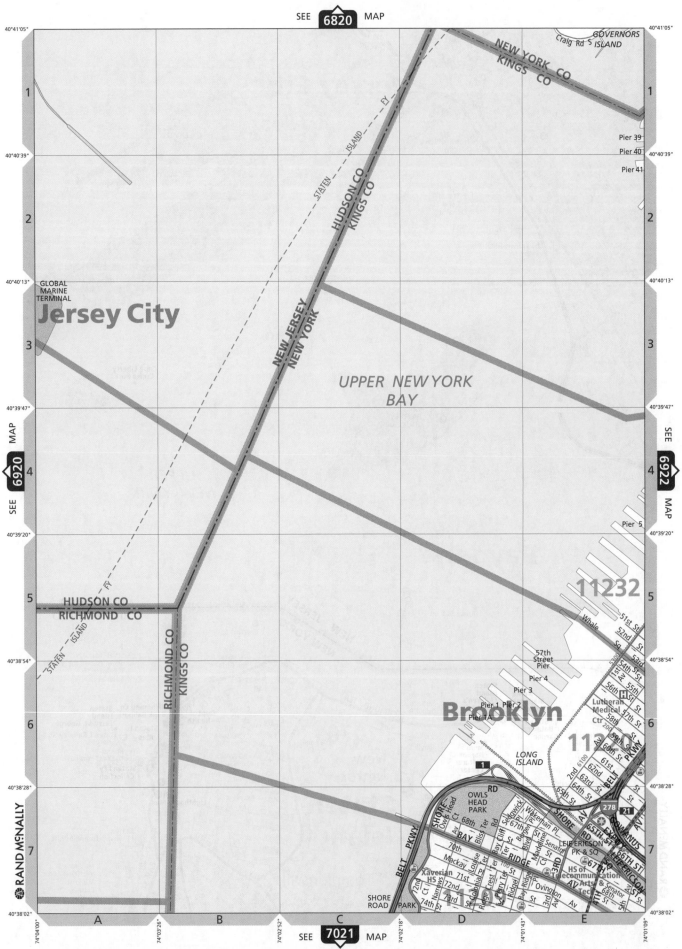

40°41'05"

GOVERNORS
Craig Rd S   ISLAND

NEW YORK CO
KINGS CO

Pier 39
40°40'39"
Pier 40
Pier 41

STATEN ISLAND EY

HUDSON CO
KINGS CO

40°40'13"

GLOBAL
MARINE
TERMINAL

Jersey City

NEW JERSEY
NEW YORK

UPPER NEW YORK
BAY

40°39'47"

SEE MAP **6920**

SEE **6922** MAP

Pier 5
40°39'20"

11232

HUDSON CO
RICHMOND CO

Whale
51st St
52nd St
53rd St

57th
Street
Pier
54th St
55th
56th St

40°38'54"

RICHMOND CO
KINGS CO

STATEN ISLAND FY

Pier 4
Pier 3

Lutheran
Medical
Ctr

57th St
58th St
59th St

Brooklyn

Pier 1 Pier 2
Pier 1A

11220

LONG
ISLAND

1

60th St

6100
2nd
61st
62nd

BELT PKWY

OWLS
HEAD
PARK

RD

63rd
64th St
65th St

40°38'28"

SHORE
Owl Head
Av Ct

Owl's Head
Av Ct
68th

Wakeman PL
Sedgwick
Cliff St
Ridge
67th St
Bigget Pl
Blvd

BAY
RIDGE

Bliss Ter
Bay
Madeline
Senator

SHORE
RD

278 21
66TH ST
67TH
AV
Senator

70th
Mackay
Louise
71st
Xaverian
HS
72nd
Narrows
73rd
74th
Colonial
Crest
Ter
Bay Ridge
Pkwy
Ridel
Ovington
3rd
Av

HS of
Telecommunication
Arts & Senator
Tech

2nd
4th

LEIF ERICSON
PK & SQ
67TH
65TH ST
66TH ST

40°38'02"

SHORE
ROAD
PARK

RAND MCNALLY

| A | B | C | D | E |

MAP
6922

MAP
6922

1:24,000
1 in. = 2000 ft.

N

SEE 6821 MAP

SEE 6921 MAP

SEE 6923 MAP

SEE 7022 MAP

RAND McNALLY

Brooklyn

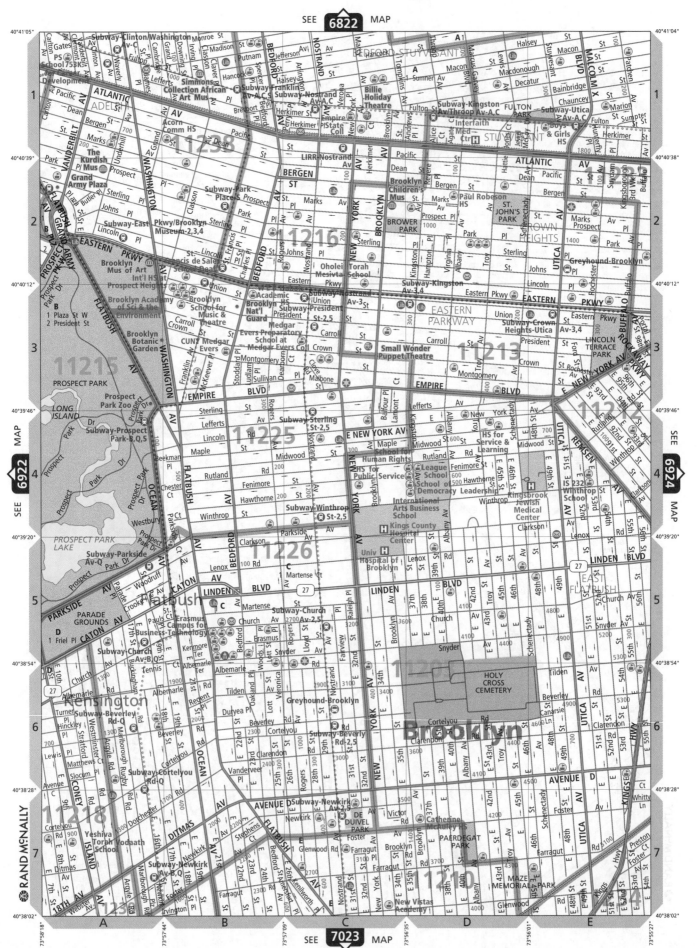

MAP
6923

MAP
6923

1:24,000
1 in. = 2000 ft.
0   0.25   0.5
miles

N

SEE 6822 MAP

MAP
6924

MAP
6924

1:24,000
1 in. = 2000 ft.

SEE 6823 MAP

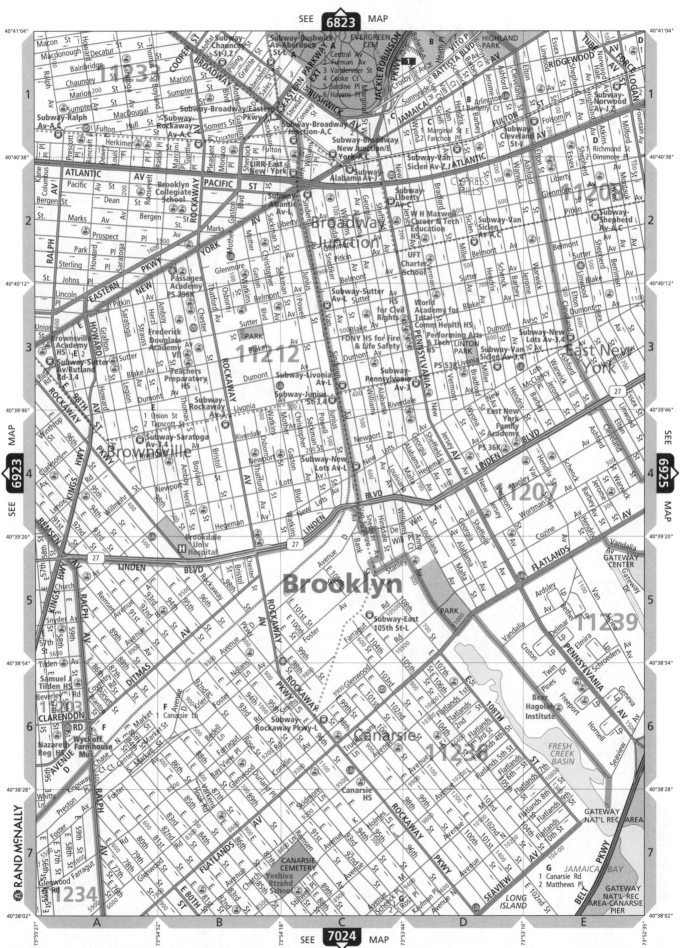

SEE 6923 MAP
SEE 6925 MAP
SEE 7024 MAP

MAP 6925

MAP 6925

1:24,000
1 in. = 2000 ft.
0   0.25   0.5
miles

N

SEE 6824 MAP

40°41'04"

B FULTON ST
Subway-Crescent St-J,Z
Chestnut St
Euclid
Pine St
Dinsmore Pl
Glen St
Sheridan Av
Grant
McKinley Av
Drew
Eldert
93rd Av
76th
78th
80th
81st
82nd
83rd
84th
85th
87th
88th
89th
91st
92nd
93rd
ATLANTIC AV
ROCKAWAY
BLVD
WOODHAVEN BLVD
103RD AV
Subway-104th St-J,Z
97th
98th
99th
100th
101st
103rd
Rd
Subway-Rockaway Blvd-A
104th
106th
107th
Subway-104th St Oxford Av-A
107th
109th
111th

1

Weldon St
McKinley Av
Lincoln
Autumn
Hemlock
Hill
101st
102nd
Rd
LIBERTY
AV
ROCKAWAY BLVD

Wells St
Transit Tech Career & Tech Education HS
EUCLID AV
Glenmore
Pitkin
Belmont
Subway-Grant Av-A
CONDUIT AV
Liberty
76th
78th
Old South
Subway-88th St/Boyd Av-A
Subway-80th St/Hudson St-A
BAYSIDE-ACACIA CEMETERY
Museum of Comedy
Liberty
86th
87th
88th
90th
91st
93rd
95th
97th
98th
109th
Clarke Pl
Plattwood Av
Rosita Rd
Sutter
Muriel
111th

40°40'38"

Ozone Pk

LOGAN ST
Doscher
Chestnut
Pitkin
Subway-Euclid Av-A,C
Crystal
Belmont
Hemlock
Autumn
Lincoln
Forbell
Ruby
S CONDUIT AV
N CONDUIT AV
CONDUIT AV
Sutter
82nd
84th
85th
133rd
Chicot Rd
Silver
Gold
89-00
Doxsey
Desarc
Peconic
Centreville St
105th St
106th
107th
108th

2

ROBERT VENABLE PARK
GRANT AV
Aqueduct Racecourse
A
1 Van Wicklen Rd
2 Jaegers Ln
11420

LOGAN ST
FOUNTAIN AV
Sutter
Blake
New Lot
EUCLID
PARK
PARK AV
Dumont
Linden
Ruby
Amber
Blake
LINDEN BLVD
OZONE PARK
TORING PARK
11420
Subway-Aqueduct/N Conduit Av-A
N CONDUIT AV

40°40'12"

LINDEN BLVD
11414
NASSAU
SHORE PARKWAY
27

LINDEN
BLVD
FOUNTAIN AV
Pine
Holy St
Crescent
Hemlock
Stanley
Drew
Emerald
Loring
149th
151st
153rd
84-00
155th
11208
BELT PKWY
SHORE PKWY EXPWY
27
19
CONDUIT AV
18A
JOHN F KENNEDY INTL AIRPORT

3

B
1 Father John Krieg Pl
2 Campus Pl
3 Nichols Av
4 74th Pl

Brooklyn
Stanley
Atkins
Shepherd
Wortman
Old Mill Rd
Flatlands Av
156th
157th
76th
80th
157th
158th
Shore Pkwy
82nd
84th
85th
86th
88th
89th
91st
92nd
Subway-Howard Beach/JFK Airport-A
SHELL BANK BASIN
Plaza Marina

40°39'46"

SEE 6924 MAP

KINGS CO
QUEENS CO
FLATLANDS
11207
FLATLANDS AV
Coane
Milford
Fountain
Queens
CROSS BAY BLVD
Howard Beach
HAWTREE BASIN
Church
Bayview
Broadway

SEE 6926 MAP

4

11239
Vandalia
Erskine
Seaview Av
BELT PKWY
15
LONG ISLAND
160th
161st
162nd
163rd
164th
165th
Lil Cricket Marina
FRANK M CHARLES MEM PARK

40°39'20"

5

Gateway Center
SPRING CREEK
Gateway
Plz
Site Dr
BELT PKWY
Dr

SPRING CREEK PARK
GATEWAY NATIONAL RECREATION AREA
164th St
165th

40°38'54"

6

STARRETT CITY
BELT PKWY

14
PENNSYLVANIA AV
Van Siclen Av

40°38'28"

JAMAICA BAY

7

RULERS BAR HASSOCK
CROSS BAY BLVD

GATEWAY NRA-JAMAICA BAY WILDLIFE REFUGE

40°38'01"

A   B   C   D   E

MAP
6926

MAP
6926

1:24,000
1 in. = 2000 ft.
0   0.25   0.5
miles

N

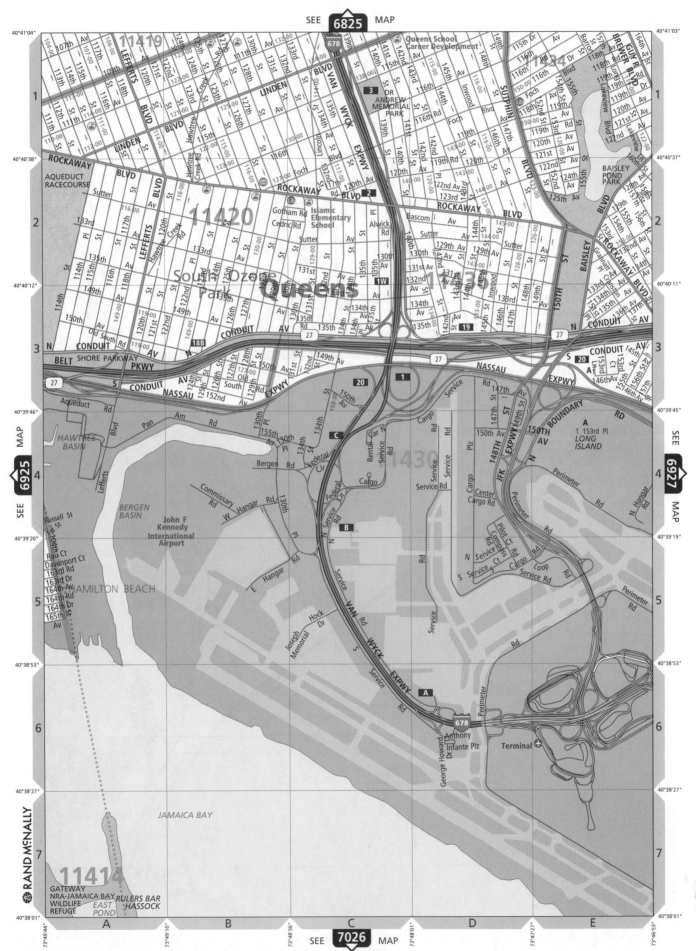

SEE 6825 MAP

SEE 6925 MAP

SEE 6927 MAP

SEE 7026 MAP

RAND McNALLY

MAP 6927

MAP 6927

1:24,000
1 in. = 2000 ft.

0   0.25   0.5

miles

N

SEE 6826 MAP

SEE 6926 MAP

SEE 6928 MAP

SEE 7027 MAP

40°41'03"
40°40'37"
40°40'11"
40°39'45"
40°39'19"
40°38'53"
40°38'27"
40°38'01"

40°41'03"
40°40'37"
40°40'11"
40°39'45"
40°39'19"
40°38'53"
40°38'26"
40°38'00"

73°46'53"   73°46'19"   73°45'44"   73°45'10"   73°44'36"   73°44'02"

1   2   3   4   5   6   7

A   B   C   D   E

Queens

Springfield Gardens

MONTEFIORE CEMETERY

ROCHDALE VILLAGE

A
1 121st Av
B
1 119th Rd
2 Victoria Dr
D
1 Mathewson Ct

LIRR-Locust Manor

11434

Springfield Gdns HS
George Washington Carver HS
Excelsior Preparatory
Queens Preparatory Academy
Excelsior Preparatory HS

ALBERT MEM PARK

LIRR-Laurelton

LIRR-Rosedale

Rosedale

SHORE PARKWAY

CONSELYEAS POND

BROOKVILLE PARK

11422

E
1 Southgate Dr
2 E Park Ct
3 Vandam St

HOOK CREEK

NORTH WOODMERE COUNTY PARK

NORTH WOODMERE PARK GC

QUEENS CO
NASSAU CO

Town of Hempstead

11516

11413

LONG ISLAND

International Airport Center

John F Kennedy International Airport

VAN WYCK EXPWY

JFK EXPWY

BELT PKWY

11430

Meadowmere Park

Bayview

JAMAICA BAY

MOTTS CREEK

11559

BELT PKWY

CONDUIT AV

S CONDUIT AV

SUNRISE HWY

ROCKAWAY BLVD

ROCKAWAY TPK

FARMERS BLVD

BREWER BLVD

GUY R BREWER BLVD

BAISLEY BLVD

SPRINGFIELD BLVD

MERRICK BLVD

FRANCIS LEWIS BLVD

CROSS ISLAND PKWY

BROOKVILLE BLVD

NASSAU EXPWY

ROCKAWAY BLVD

BOUNDARY RD

Old Rockaway Blvd

Perimeter Rd

RAND M?NALLY

MAP
6928

MAP
6928

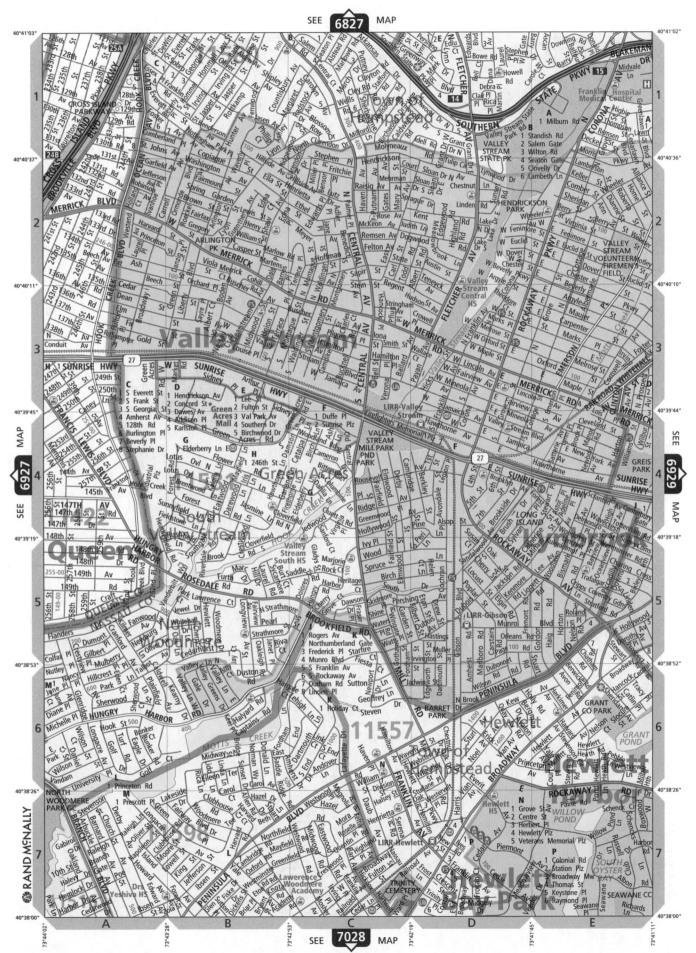

SEE 6827 MAP

1:24,000
1 in. = 2000 ft.
0   0.25   0.5
miles

SEE 6927 MAP

SEE 6929 MAP

RAND MCNALLY

SEE 7028 MAP

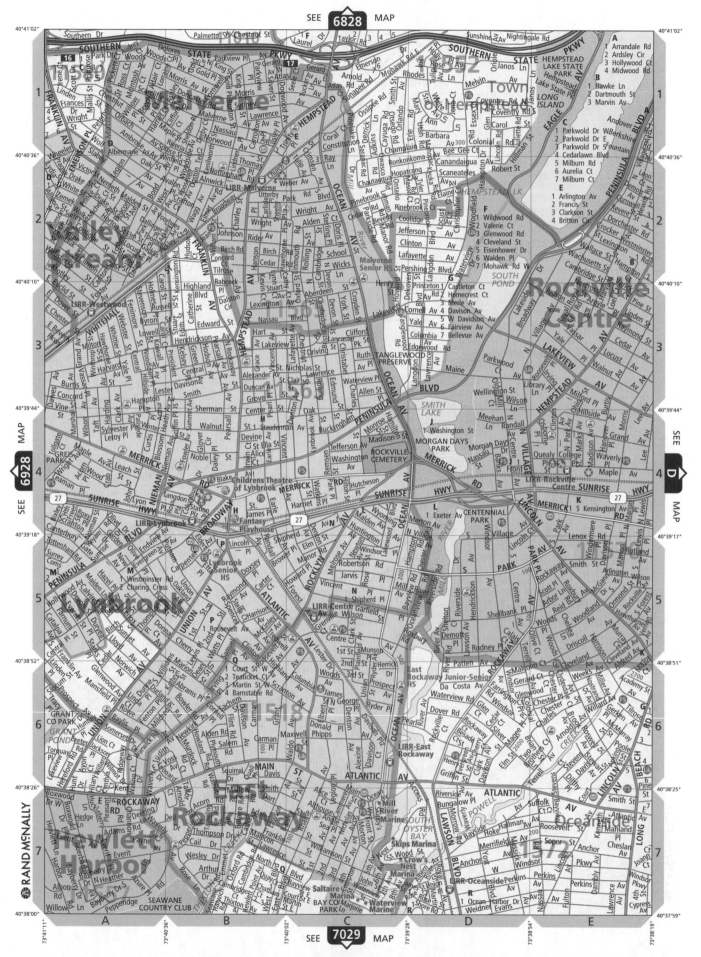

MAP
7017

MAP
7017

1:24,000
1 in. = 2000 ft.

0   0.25   0.5
miles

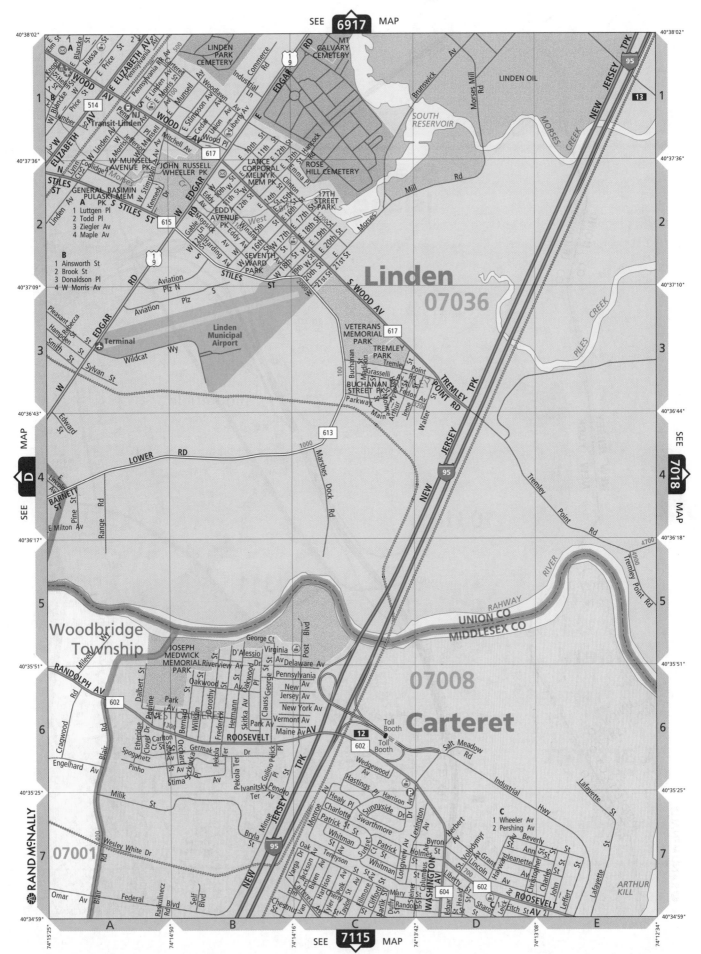

SEE **6917** MAP

40°38'02"
40°37'36"
40°37'09"
40°36'43"
40°36'17"
40°35'51"
40°35'25"
40°34'59"

40°38'02"
40°37'36"
40°37'10"
40°36'44"
40°36'18"
40°35'51"
40°35'25"
40°34'59"

Linden
07036

Carteret

Woodbridge Township

07008

07001

ARTHUR KILL

LINDEN OIL

SEE **7018** MAP

SEE **7115** MAP

74°15'25"
74°14'50"
74°14'16"
74°13'42"
74°13'08"
74°12'34"

A   B   C   D   E

1   2   3   4   5   6   7

RAND MCNALLY

MAP 7018

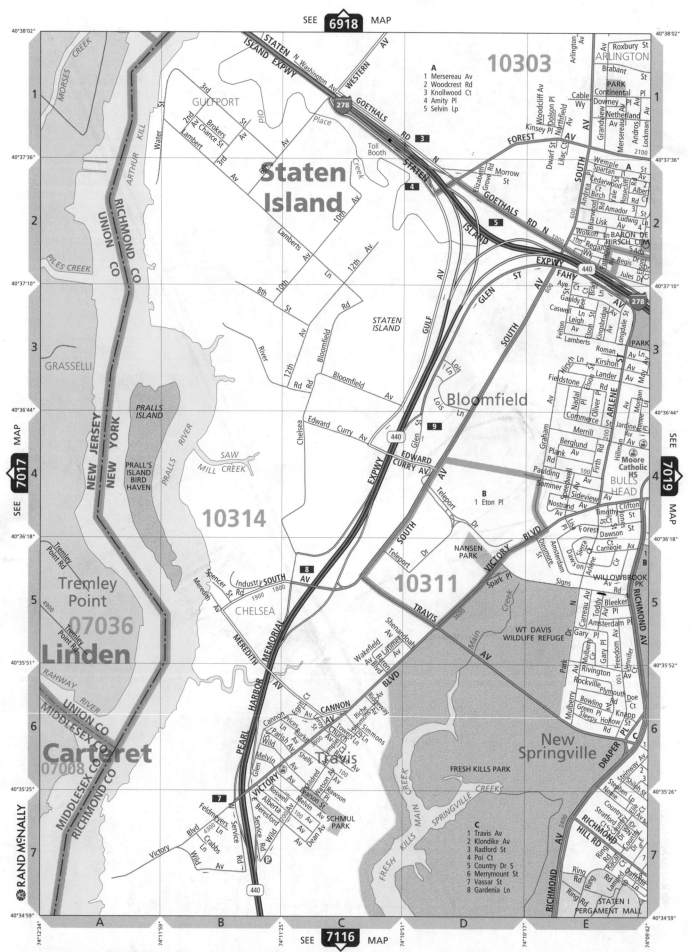

MAP 7018

1:24,000
1 in. = 2000 ft.
0   0.25   0.5
miles

SEE 6918 MAP

A
1 Mersereau Av
2 Woodcrest Rd
3 Knollwood Ct
4 Amity Pl
5 Selvin Lp

10303

ARLINGTON

Staten Island

10314

PRALL'S ISLAND BIRD HAVEN

NEW JERSEY
NEW YORK

PRALLS ISLAND

SAW MILL CREEK

GRASSELLI

PILES CREEK

RICHMOND CO
UNION CO

ARTHUR KILL

MORSES CREEK

GULFPORT

Bloomfield

B
1 Eton Pl

NANSEN PARK

10311

Moore Catholic HS

BULLS HEAD

WILLOWBROOK PK

Tremley Point
07036
Linden

CHELSEA

Carteret
07008

Travis

WT DAVIS WILDLIFE REFUGE

FRESH KILLS PARK

New Springville

SCHMUL PARK

C
1 Travis Av
2 Klondike Av
3 Radford St
4 Poi Ct
5 Country Dr S
6 Merrymount St
7 Vassar St
8 Gardenia Ln

RAND McNALLY

SEE 7116 MAP

SEE 7017 MAP

SEE 7019 MAP

STATEN I. PERGAMENT MALL

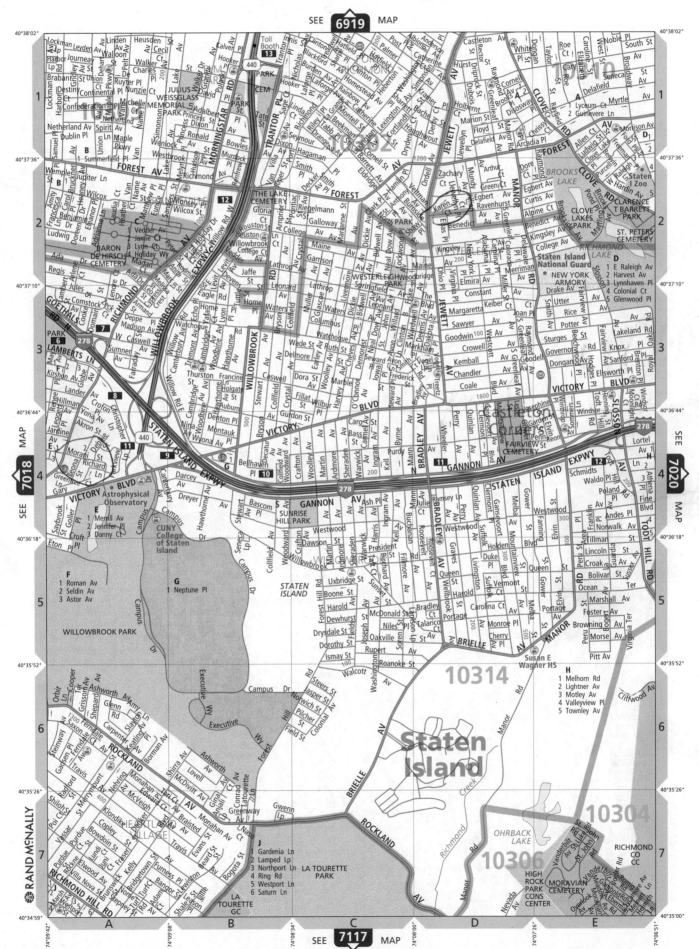

MAP 7019

MAP 7019

1:24,000
1 in. = 2000 ft.

0   0.25   0.5
miles

N

SEE 6919 MAP

SEE 7018 MAP

SEE 7020 MAP

SEE 7117 MAP

Staten Island

10314

10306

10304

RAND McNALLY

MAP
7020

MAP
7020

1:24,000
1 in. = 2000 ft.

0   0.25   0.5
miles

N

SEE 6920 MAP

40°38'02"

UPPER NEW YORK BAY

FOREST AV

SILVER LAKE PARK

SILVER LAKE RESERVOIR

SILVER LAKE GOLF COURSE

VICTORY

MARINE CEMETERY

SILVER MT CEMETERY

SILVER LK CEMETERY

WOODLAND CEMETERY

SILVER LAKE

Grymes Hill

Notre Dame Academy HS

HERO PARK

St. PAULS AV

A
1 Cross St
2 Thompson St
3 Dock St

B
1 Baring Pl
2 Wiederer Pl
3 Mickardan Ct

Staten I Railway-Stapleton

1 Merivale Ln
2 Amazon St
3 Memory Ct

D
1 Sylvaton Ter
2 Church Ln

PS 721 Staten I Occupational Training Center

Staten Island Railway-Clifton

CLOVE LAKES PARK

E
1 Glenwood Pl

CLOVE LAKE

SUNNYSIDE

VICTORY

G
1 Cattaraugus St
2 Otsego Av

St. John's University-Staten Island

Garibaldi-Meucci Museum

F
1 Cunard Av
2 Cornell Pl
3 Cliffside Av

FOOTHILLS

VANDERBILT AV

H
1 Rodeo Ln
2 Skyline Ln

Wagner College

NARROWS RD N

STATEN ISLAND EXPWY

278

CLOVE RD

Concord HS

HYLAN

SEE 7019 MAP

SEE 7021 MAP

Safety City

Michael J Petrides Staten HS

K
1 Silver Beach Rd

1 Hasbrouck Rd

DEER PARK

278

NARROWS RD

Staten I Railway-Grasmere

BRADY'S POND

BRADY'S PARK

15

St. Joseph Hill Academy HS

St. John Villa Academy HS

Todt Hill

REED'S BASKET WILLOW SWAMP PARK

RICHMOND

L
1 Dawson Pl
2 Dumont Av

TARGET ST

Staten Island

HYLAN

CAMERON POND

Staten I Railway-Old Town

St. MARY'S CEMETERY

M
1 Lake Side Av
2 Split Rail Dr
3 Grasmere Av

OLD TOWN RD

Old Town Station

St. MARY'S CEMETERY

Staten I Academy

N
1 Hillview Ln
2 Concord Ln

RICHMOND COUNTY COUNTRY CLUB

FOUR CORNERS RD

GARRETSON

SEAVIEW

Linden Park

South Beach

STATEN ISLAND

P
1 Clayton Av
2 Seth Lp
3 Cabot Pl
4 Wilton Ct
5 Wadsworth Ter
6 Meyer Ln
7 Garfield Av
8 Fillmore Pl
9 Harvey St

Q
1 Austin Av
2 Humbert St
3 Balfour St
4 Oceanside Av
5 Sunnymeade Vil

R
1 Maryland Ln
2 Kay Pl
3 Alta Vista Ct
4 Wagner St
5 Hillbrook Ct
6 Hilldale Ct
7 Hillridge Ct
8 Mendelsohn St

S
1 Nugent Av

GENERAL DOUGLAS A MACARTHUR PARK

T
1 Impala Ct
2 Cleveland Pl
3 Roderick Av
4 Columbia Av

Staten Island University Hospital-North

Staten I Railway-Dongan Hills

Staten I Railway-Jefferson Av

HYLAN BLVD

FATHER CAPODANNO BLVD

GATEWAY NATIONAL RECREATION AREA

LOWER NEW YORK BAY

40°35'00"

SEE 7118 MAP

A   B   C   D   E

MAP
7021

MAP
7021

1:24,000
1 in. = 2000 ft.

0   0.25   0.5
miles

SEE 6921 MAP

40°38'02"

40°37'36"

40°37'10"

40°36'44"

40°36'18"

40°35'52"

40°35'26"

40°35'00"

1

2

3

4

5

6

7

A
1 Church Ln
2 Sylva Ln

B
1 Abbott St
2 Anderson St
3 Seth Lp
4 Belair Ln
5 Hope Ln
6 Wilton Ct
7 Judith Ct
8 Bridge Ct
9 Garfield Av
10 Torricelli St

C
1 Hastings St
2 Pebble Ln
3 Waterford Ct
4 Galesville Ct
5 Railroad Av
6 Palisade St
7 Retner St
8 Seaside Ln
9 Ragazzi Ln
10 Seagate Ct
11 Oceanside Av
12 Sunnymeade Vil

UPPER
NEW YORK
BAY

LOWER
NEW YORK
BAY

Brooklyn

Staten
Island

Rosebank

SEE 7020 MAP

SEE 7022 MAP

SEE 7119 MAP

A   B   C   D   E

RAND McNALLY

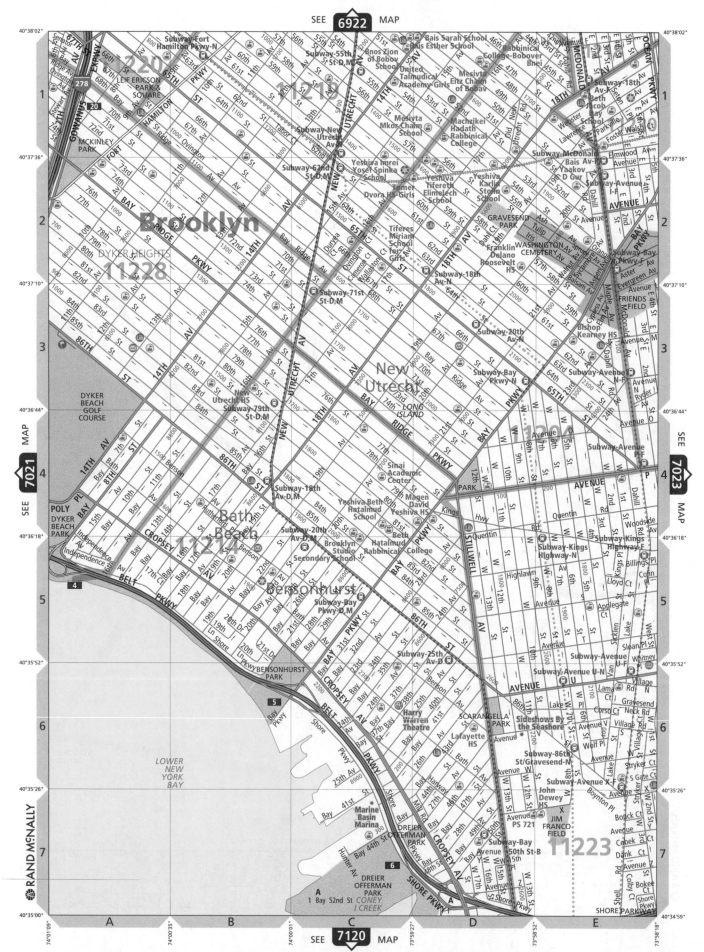

MAP
7023

MAP
7023

1:24,000
1 in. = 2000 ft.

0   0.25   0.5
miles

N

SEE 6923 MAP

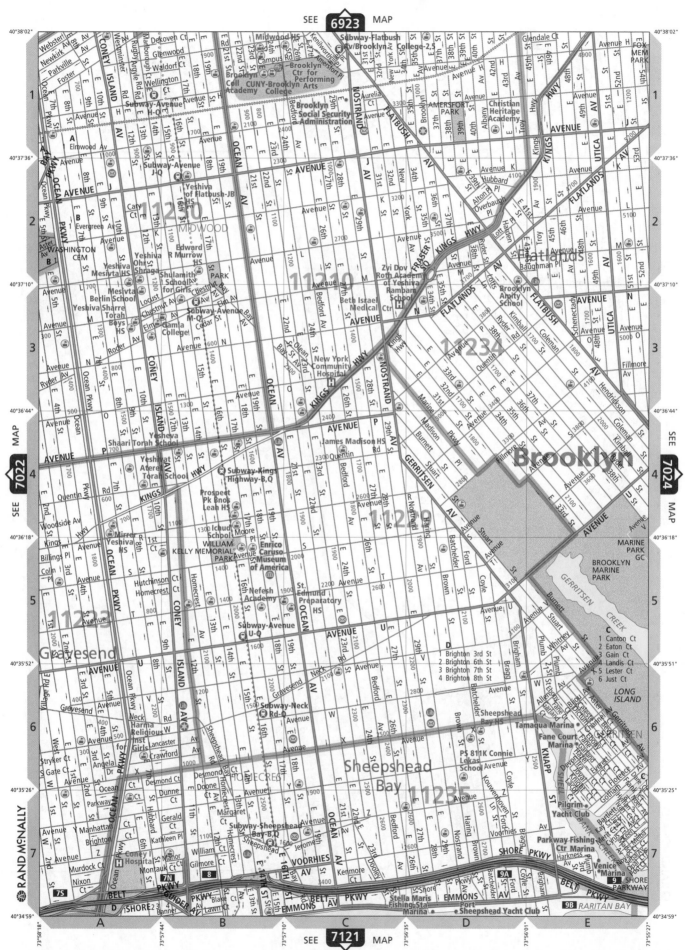

SEE 7022 MAP

SEE 7024 MAP

SEE 7121 MAP

RAND McNALLY

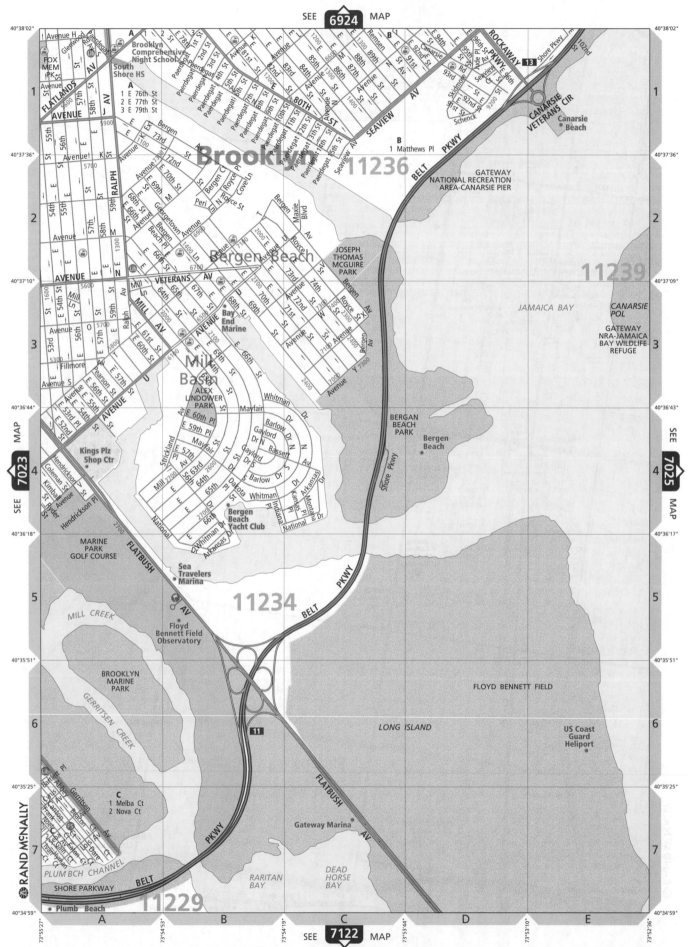

MAP 7024

MAP 7024

1:24,000
1 in. = 2000 ft.
0   0.25   0.5
miles

N

SEE 6924 MAP

40°38'02"

Brooklyn
Comprehensive
Night School
South Shore HS

A
1 E 76th St
2 E 77th St
3 E 79th St

FOX MEM PK

FLATLANDS AVENUE

B
1 Matthews Pl

40°37'36"

Brooklyn
11236

Bergen Beach

GATEWAY
NATIONAL RECREATION
AREA-CANARSIE PIER

CANARSIE
VETERANS CIR

Canarsie
Beach

ROCKAWAY PKWY

13

40°37'10"

JOSEPH
THOMAS
MCGUIRE
PARK

11239

JAMAICA BAY

CANARSIE POL

GATEWAY
NRA-JAMAICA
BAY WILDLIFE
REFUGE

40°37'09"

VETERANS AV

Mill Basin

Bay End Marine

ALEX
LINDOWER
PARK

40°36'44"

BERGAN
BEACH
PARK

Bergen
Beach

40°36'43"

Kings Plz
Shop Ctr

SEE 7023 MAP

Bergen
Beach
Yacht Club

Shore Pkwy

SEE 7025 MAP

40°36'18"

MARINE
PARK
GOLF COURSE

FLATBUSH

Sea
Travelers
Marina

11234

BELT PKWY

40°36'17"

40°35'51"

Floyd
Bennett Field
Observatory

MILL CREEK

BROOKLYN
MARINE
PARK

FLOYD BENNETT FIELD

40°35'51"

GERRITSEN CREEK

LONG ISLAND

11

US Coast
Guard
Heliport

40°35'25"

C
1 Melba Ct
2 Nova Ct

FLATBUSH AV

40°35'25"

RAND McNALLY

Gateway Marina

BELT PKWY

RARITAN
BAY

DEAD
HORSE
BAY

PLUM BCH CHANNEL

SHORE PARKWAY   BELT

11229

Plumb Beach

40°34'59"

40°34'59"

A   B   C   D   E

SEE 7122 MAP

MAP
7025

MAP
7025

1:24,000
1 in. = 2000 ft.

0   0.25   0.5

miles

N

SEE 6925 MAP

40°38'02"   40°38'01"

CROSS BAY BLVD

11414

1   1

40°37'36"   40°37'35"

11239

2   2

CANARSIE POL

40°37'09"   40°37'09"

Brooklyn

KINGS CO

QUEENS CO

WEST POND

3   3

RULERS BAR HASSOCK

40°36'43"   40°36'43"

MAP 7024

JAMAICA BAY

SEE 7026 MAP

4   4

SEE

40°36'17"   40°36'17"

GATEWAY
NRA-JAMAICA BAY
WILDLIFE
REFUGE

RUFFLE BAR

5   5

40°35'51"   40°35'51"

11693

6   6

Queens

40°35'25"   40°35'25"

7   7

FLOYD
BENNETT FIELD

BEACH 108TH ST

BEACH CHANNEL DR

LONG ISLAND

11694

40°34'59"   40°34'59"

A   B   C   D   E

73°52'36"   73°52'02"   73°51'28"   73°50'53"   73°50'19"   73°49'45"

RAND M°NALLY

SEE 7123 MAP

MAP
7026

MAP
7026

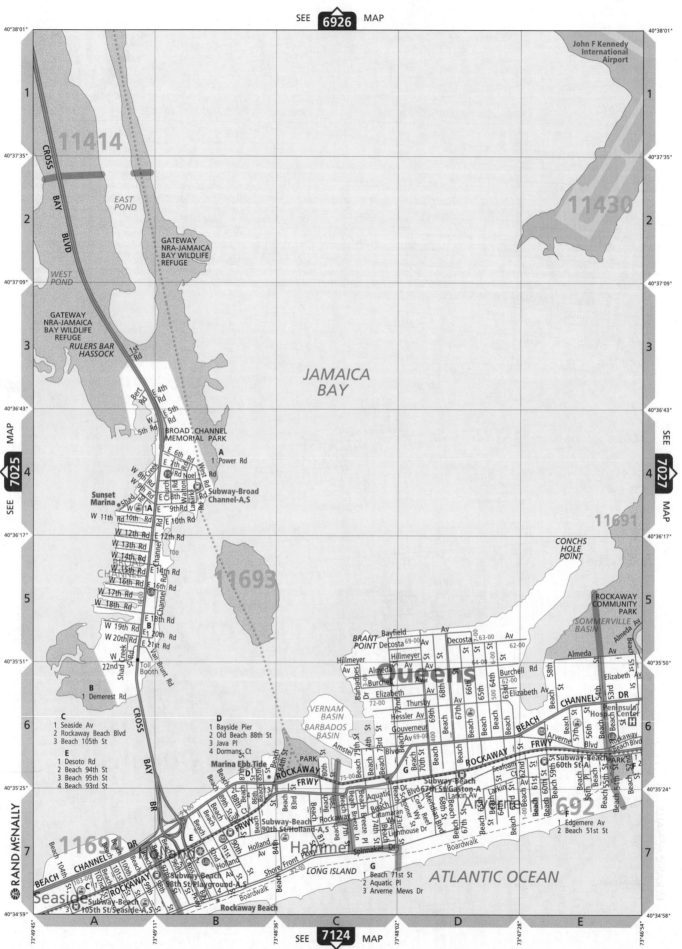

SEE 6926 MAP

1:24,000
1 in. = 2000 ft.
0   0.25   0.5
miles

N

11414

11430

EAST
POND

GATEWAY
NRA-JAMAICA
BAY WILDLIFE
REFUGE

WEST
POND

JOHN F Kennedy
International
Airport

GATEWAY
NRA-JAMAICA
BAY WILDLIFE
REFUGE
RULERS BAR
HASSOCK

JAMAICA
BAY

SEE 7025 MAP
SEE 7027 MAP

BROAD CHANNEL
MEMORIAL PARK

A
1 Power Rd

Sunset
Marina

Subway-Broad
Channel-A,S

11691

11693

CONCHS
HOLE
POINT

ROCKAWAY
COMMUNITY
PARK

SOMMERVILLE
BASIN

B
1 Demerest Rd

BRANT
POINT

Bayfield
Decosta   Av
Hillmeyer
Av

Decosta   Av

Barbadoes
Dr
Elizabeth

Almeda
Burchell

Almeda

Elizabeth

Queens

Channel
Dr

Peninsula
Hosp. Center

C
1 Seaside Av
2 Rockaway Beach Blvd
3 Beach 105th St

E
1 Desoto Rd
2 Beach 94th St
3 Beach 95th St
4 Beach 93rd St

D
1 Bayside Pier
2 Old Beach 88th St
3 Java Pl
4 Dormans Ct

VERNAM
BASIN
BARBADOS
BASIN

Thursby
Hessler Av
Gouverneur

PARK

ROCKAWAY
FRWY

ROCKAWAY   FRWY

Subway-Beach
60th St-A

Subway-Beach

G

Marina Ebb Tide

ROCKAWAY
FRWY

Subway-Beach
90th St/Holland-A,S

Subway-Beach
98th St/Playground-A,S

Arverne   692

F
1 Edgemere Av
2 Beach 51st St

Hammel

LONG ISLAND

G
1 Beach 71st St
2 Aquatic Pl
3 Arverne Mews Dr

ATLANTIC OCEAN

Boardwalk

RAND M°NALLY

11691

Seaside

Subway-Beach
105th St/Seaside-A,S

Rockaway Beach

SEE 7124 MAP

MAP
7027

MAP
7027

1:24,000
1 in. = 2000 ft.

0   0.25   0.5
miles

N

SEE 6927 MAP

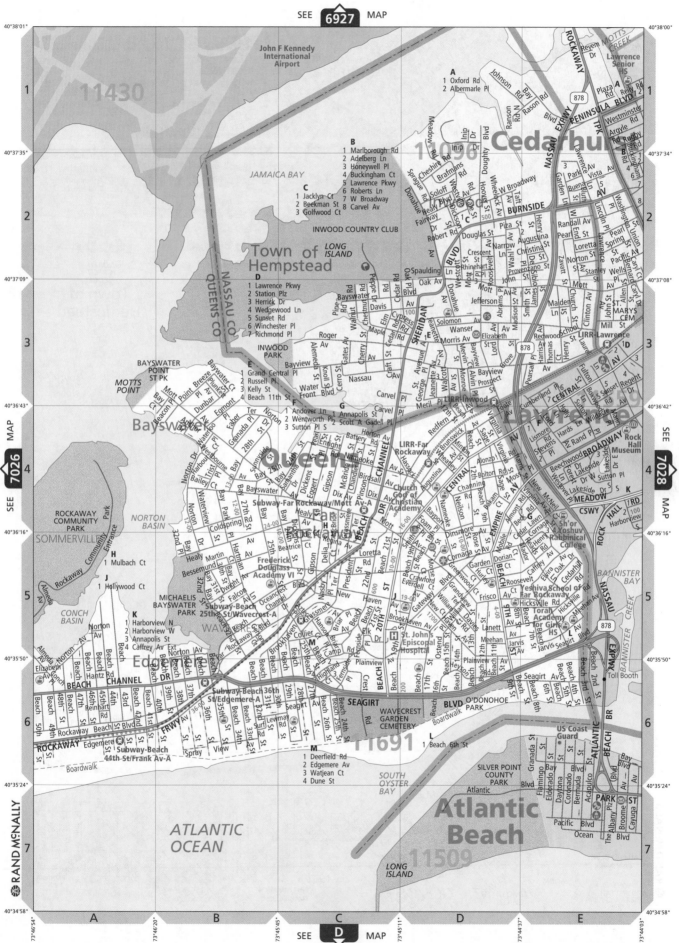

40°38'01"
40°37'35"
40°37'09"
40°36'43"
40°36'16"
40°35'50"
40°35'24"
40°34'58"

40°38'00"
40°37'34"
40°37'08"
40°36'42"
40°36'16"
40°35'50"
40°35'24"
40°34'58"

John F Kennedy
International
Airport

11430

JAMAICA BAY

Town of
Hempstead

LONG
ISLAND

INWOOD COUNTRY CLUB

11096

Cedarhu

BURNSIDE

SHERIDAN

NASSAU CO
QUEENS CO

INWOOD
PARK

BAYSWATER
POINT
ST PK

MOTTS
POINT

Bayswater

Queens

LIRR-Lawrence

LIRR-Inwood

Lawrence

Rock
Hall
Museum

BROADWAY

CENTRAL

ROCKAWAY
COMMUNITY
PARK

SOMMERVILLE

NORTON
BASIN

Far Rockaway

CONCH
BASIN

MICHAELIS
BAYSWATER
PARK

Edgemere

BANNISTER
BAY

Meadow

CSWY

ROCK HALL RD

St. John's
Episcopal
Hospital

Yeshiva School of
Far Rockaway
Torah
Academy
for Girls
HS

ATLANTIC BEACH BR

NASSAU

US Coast
Guard

SILVER POINT
COUNTY
PARK

SEAGIRT

WAVECREST
GARDEN
CEMETERY

11691

BEACH CHANNEL DR

ROCKAWAY

SOUTH
OYSTER
BAY

ATLANTIC
OCEAN

LONG
ISLAND

Atlantic
Beach
11509

A
1 Oxford Rd
2 Albermarle Pl

B
1 Marlborough Rd
2 Adelberg Ln
3 Honeywell Pl
4 Buckingham Ct
5 Lawrence Pkwy
6 Roberts Ln
7 W Broadway
8 Carvel Av

C
1 Jacklyn Ct
2 Beekman St
3 Golfwood Ct

D
1 Lawrence Pkwy
2 Station Plz
3 Herrick Dr
4 Wedgewood Ln
5 Sunset Rd
6 Winchester Pl
7 Richmond Pl

E
1 Grand Central Pl
2 Russell Pl
3 Kelly St
4 Beach 11th St

F
1 Andover Ln
2 Wentworth Pl
3 Sutton Pl S

G
1 Annapolis Rd
2 Scott A Gadell Pl

H
1 Mulbach Ct

J
1 Hollywood Ct

K
1 Harborview N
2 Harborview W
3 Annapolis St
4 Caffrey Av Ext

L
1 Beach 6th St

M
1 Deerfield Rd
2 Edgemere Av
3 Watjean Ct
4 Dune St

SEE 7026 MAP

SEE 7028 MAP

SEE D MAP

RAND McNALLY

A   B   C   D   E

40°34'58"

73°46'54"   73°46'20"   73°45'45"   73°45'11"   73°44'37"   73°44'03"

MAP
7028

MAP
7028

1:24,000
1 in. = 2000 ft.

0   0.25   0.5
miles

N

SEE 6928 MAP

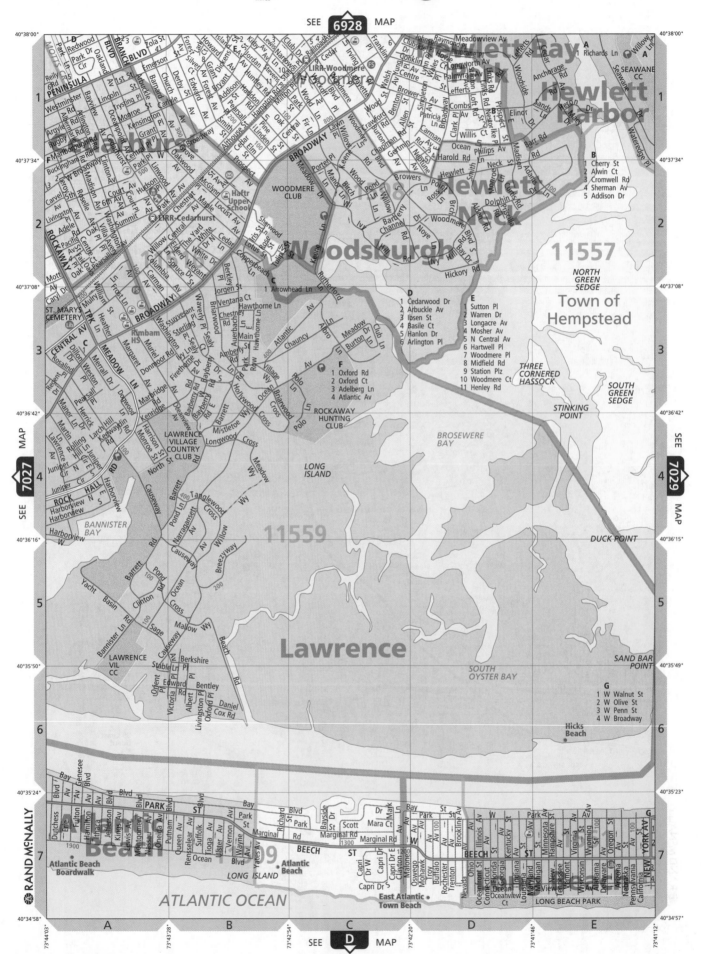

11557

Town of Hempstead

11559

Lawrence

Woodsburgh

The Hewlett Neck

Hewlett Harbor

SEAWANE CC

NORTH GREEN SEDGE

SOUTH GREEN SEDGE

THREE CORNERED HASSOCK

STINKING POINT

BROSEWERE BAY

LONG ISLAND

DUCK POINT

SOUTH OYSTER BAY

SAND BAR POINT

BANNISTER BAY

Hicks Beach

Cedarhurst

PENINSULA

ST. MARYS CEMETERY

ROCKAWAY HUNTING CLUB

LAWRENCE VILLAGE COUNTRY CLUB

ROCK HALL

LAWRENCE VIL CC

WOODMERE CLUB

B
1 Cherry St
2 Alwin Ct
4 Cromwell Rd
4 Sherman Av
5 Addison Dr

D
1 Cedarwood Dr
2 Arbuckle Av
3 Ibsen St
4 Basile Ct
5 Hanlon Dr
6 Arlington Pl

E
1 Sutton Pl
2 Warren Dr
3 Longacre Av
4 Mosher Av
5 N Central Av
6 Hartwell Pl
7 Woodmere Pl
8 Midfield Rd
9 Station Plz
10 Woodmere Ct
11 Henley Rd

F
1 Oxford Rd
2 Oxford Ct
3 Adelberg Ln
4 Atlantic Av

1 Arrowhead Ln

G
1 W Walnut St
2 W Olive St
3 W Penn St
4 W Broadway

Atlantic Beach Boardwalk

Atlantic Beach

East Atlantic Town Beach

LONG BEACH PARK

ATLANTIC OCEAN

SEE 7027 MAP

SEE 7029 MAP

SEE D MAP

RAND McNALLY

40°38'00"
40°37'34"
40°37'08"
40°36'42"
40°36'16"
40°35'50"
40°35'24"
40°34'58"

73°44'03"   73°43'28"   73°42'54"   73°42'20"   73°41'46"   73°41'12"

A   B   C   D   E

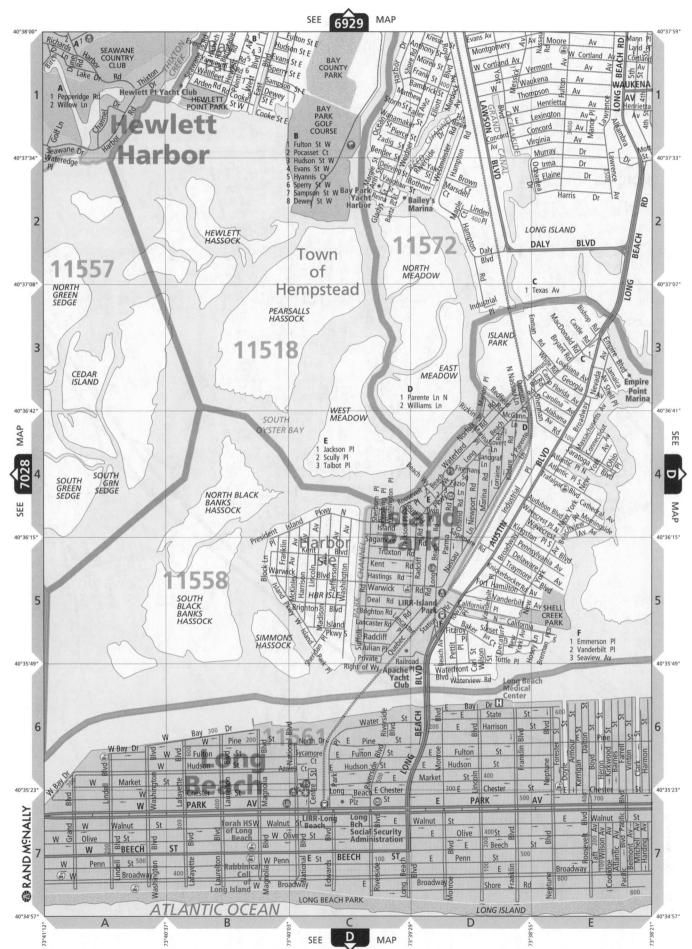

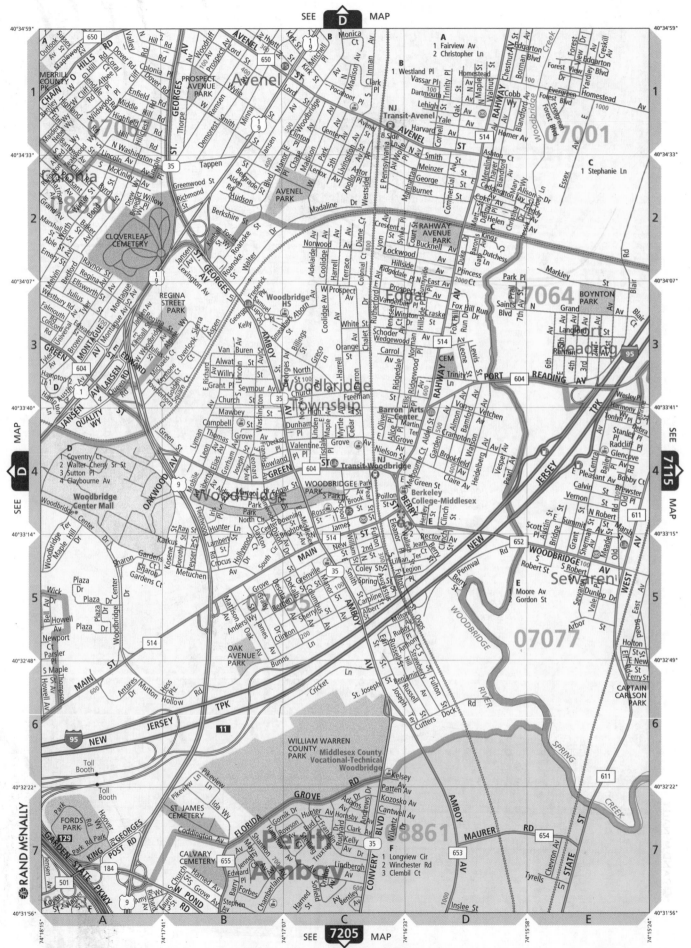

MAP 7115

MAP 7115

1:24,000
1 in. = 2000 ft.

0   0.25   0.5
miles

N

SEE 7017 MAP

40°34'59"   40°34'59"

A
1 Van Buren Av
2 Harrison Av
3 Steiner St

07001

07064

07008

Carteret

CHROME

Woodbridge
Township

07077

10314

MIDDLESEX CO
RICHMOND CO

NEW JERSEY
NEW YORK

ARTHUR KILL

SMITHS CREEK

ROSSVILLE

**Staten
Island**

B
1 Schindler Ct
2 Westfield Av
3 Larch Ct
4 Hemlock Ct

Arthur Kill
Correctional
Facility

**Cliffside
Marina**

**Boynton
Beach**

CAPTAIN
CARLSON
PARK

C
1 Prince Ln
2 Candon Ct
3 Wirt Ln
4 Phyllis Ct
5 Candon Av

STATEN
ISLAND

10309

D
1 Dunhill Ln

WOODROW

CLAY PIT

CLAY
PIT PONDS
STATE PARK

SPRING
CREEK

08861

**Perth
Amboy**

Charleston

SHARROTTS RD

BLOOMINGDALE PARK

SEE 7114 MAP

SEE 7116 MAP

40°34'33"
40°34'07"
40°33'41"
40°33'15"
40°32'49"
40°32'22"
40°31'56"

A   B   C   D   E

SEE 7206 MAP

74°15'24"   74°14'50"   74°14'16"   74°13'42"   74°13'07"   74°12'33"

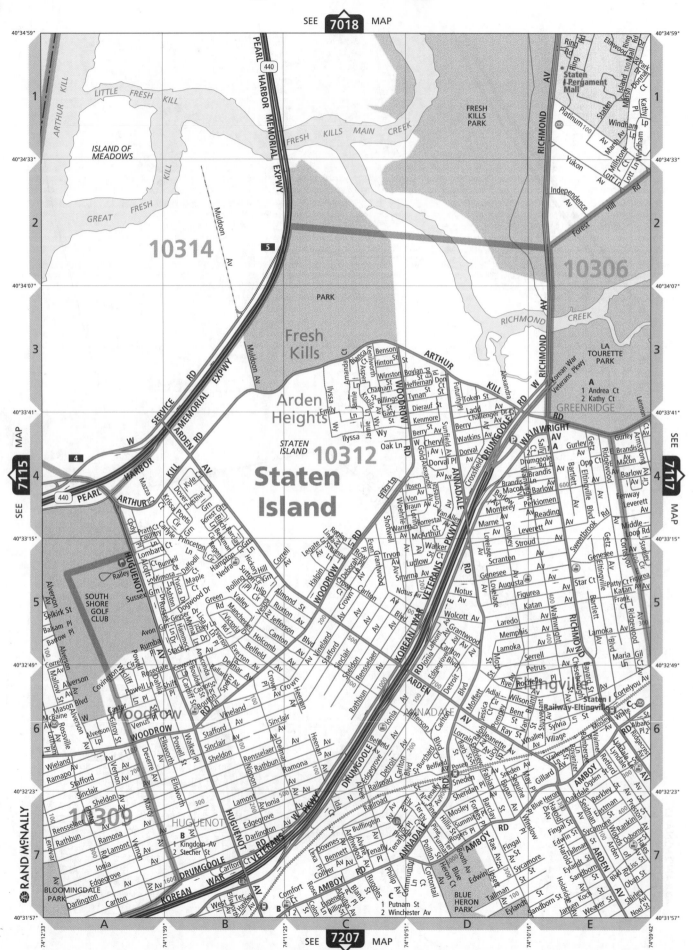

MAP
7116

MAP
7116

1:24,000
1 in. = 2000 ft.
0   0.25   0.5
miles

N

SEE 7018 MAP

ARTHUR KILL

LITTLE FRESH KILL

ISLAND OF MEADOWS

FRESH KILLS MAIN CREEK

FRESH KILLS PARK

RICHMOND AV

Staten I Pergament Mall

Ring Mall

Elmwood Rd

Platinum

Windham

Kathy Lp

Yukon Av

Millstone

Lott Ln Lott Rd

Independence Av

Forest Hill

GREAT FRESH KILL

10314

Muldoon Av

PEARL HARBOR MEMORIAL EXPWY

440

5

10306

PARK

RICHMOND CREEK

LA TOURETTE PARK

Fresh Kills

Arden Heights

ARTHUR KILL

WOODROW RD

RICHMOND AV

Korean War Veterans Pkwy

GREENRIDGE

A
1 Andrea Ct
2 Kathy Ct

STATEN ISLAND

10312

Staten
Island

SERVICE RD W

ARDEN RD

PEARL HARBOR MEMORIAL EXPWY

440

4

Muldoon Av

HUGUENOT

SOUTH SHORE GOLF CLUB

ARTHUR KILL AV

PEARL

ARTHUR

Railey

WOODROW RD

VETERANS WAR

KOREAN WAR RD

ARDEN AV

RICHMOND AV

WAINWRIGHT AV

ANNADALE

DRUMGOOLE RD

Eltingville

Staten I
Railway-Eltingville

Woodrow

WOODROW

DRUMGOOLE

ANNADALE

AMBOY RD

ARDEN AV

10309

HUGUENOT

HUGUENOT RD

W PKWY

VETERANS

DRUMGOOLE

KOREAN WAR

AMBOY RD

ANNADALE AV

AMBOY RD

BLOOMINGDALE PARK

BLUE HERON PARK

B
1 Kingdom Av
2 Stecher Ct

C
1 Putnam St
2 Winchester Av

SEE 7115 MAP
SEE 7117 MAP
SEE 7207 MAP

40°34'59"   40°34'33"   40°34'07"   40°33'41"   40°33'15"   40°32'49"   40°32'23"   40°31'57"

74°12'33"   74°11'59"   74°11'25"   74°10'51"   74°10'16"   74°09'42"

A   B   C   D   E

1   2   3   4   5   6   7

MAP
7117

MAP
7117

SEE 7019 MAP

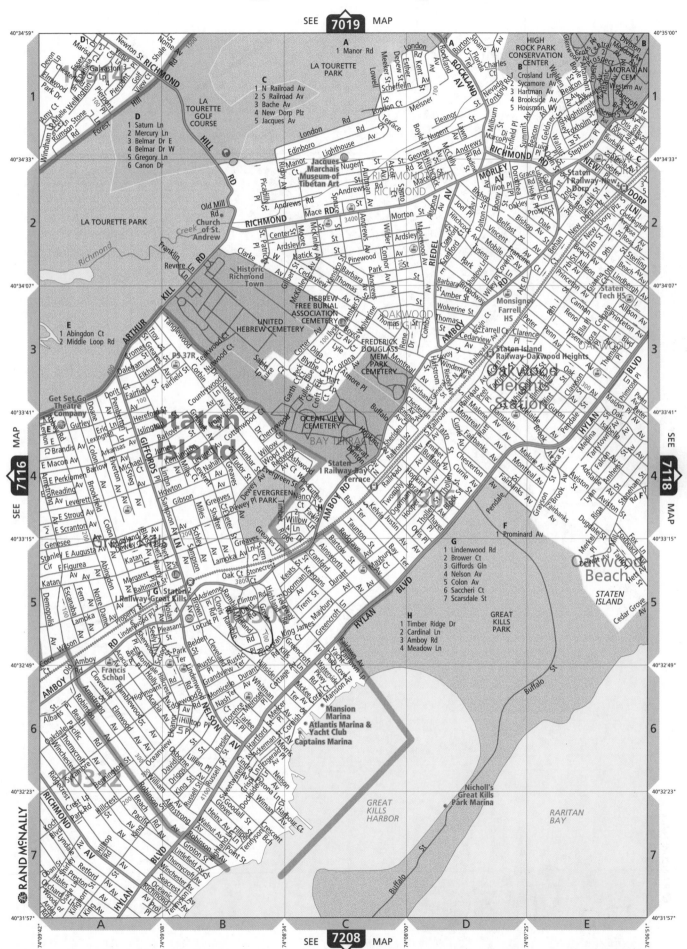

SEE 7116 MAP

SEE 7718 MAP

SEE 7208 MAP

MAP
7118

MAP
7118

1:24,000
1 in. = 2000 ft.

0   0.25   0.5

miles

SEE 7020 MAP

40°35'00"

MORAVIAN
CEM
HILL RD
RICHMOND RD
LODI AV
Grant City
MIDLAND
HYLAN BLVD
Staten I
Railway-Grant
City
LINCOLN AV
SEAVIEW AV
10305
LOWER
NEW YORK
BAY

40°34'33"

PARK
MIDLAND
LINCOLN AV
Midland
Beach
GATEWAY
NATIONAL
RECREATION
AREA
FATHER CAPODANNO BLVD

A
1 Flagg Pl
2 Barton Av
3 Zinzedorf Cir
4 Prospect Av
5 Kruser St

B
1 Iroquois St

DORP LN
NEW
HYLAN
New
Dorp HS

40°34'07"

STATEN ISLAND
MILLER FIELD

C
1 Lindbergh Av
2 Allison Av

10306
NEW DORP
BEACH

40°33'41"

Staten
Island

SEE 7117 MAP

SEE 7119 MAP

D
1 Riga St
2 Stoneham St

Cedar Grove
Beach Pl
GREAT
KILLS
PARK

40°33'15"

RARITAN   BAY

40°32'49"

40°32'23"

40°31'57"

A   B   C   D   E

SEE D MAP

74°06'51"   74°06'17"   74°05'43"   74°05'09"   74°04'35"   74°04'00"

MAP
7119

MAP
7119

1:24,000
1 in. = 2000 ft.

0   0.25   0.5

miles

N

SEE 7021 MAP

40°35'00"

1

10305

HOFFMAN
ISLAND

40°34'34"

40°34'33"

LOWER
NEW YORK
BAY

2

RICHMOND CO

KINGS CO

40°34'07"

40°34'07"

3

SWINBURNE
ISLAND

40°33'41"

40°33'41"

MAP 7118 SEE

4

SEE 7120 MAP

40°33'15"

40°33'15"

KINGS CO
QUEENS CO

5

RARITAN
BAY

RICHMOND CO
QUEENS CO

40°32'49"

40°32'49"

6

40°32'23"

40°32'23"

RAND M?NALLY

7

40°31'57"

40°31'57"

74°04'00"   74°03'26"   74°02'52"   74°02'18"   74°01'44"   74°01'09"

A   B   C   D   E

SEE D MAP

MAP
7120

MAP
7120

1:24,000
1 in. = 2000 ft.
0   0.25   0.5
miles

N

SEE 7022 MAP

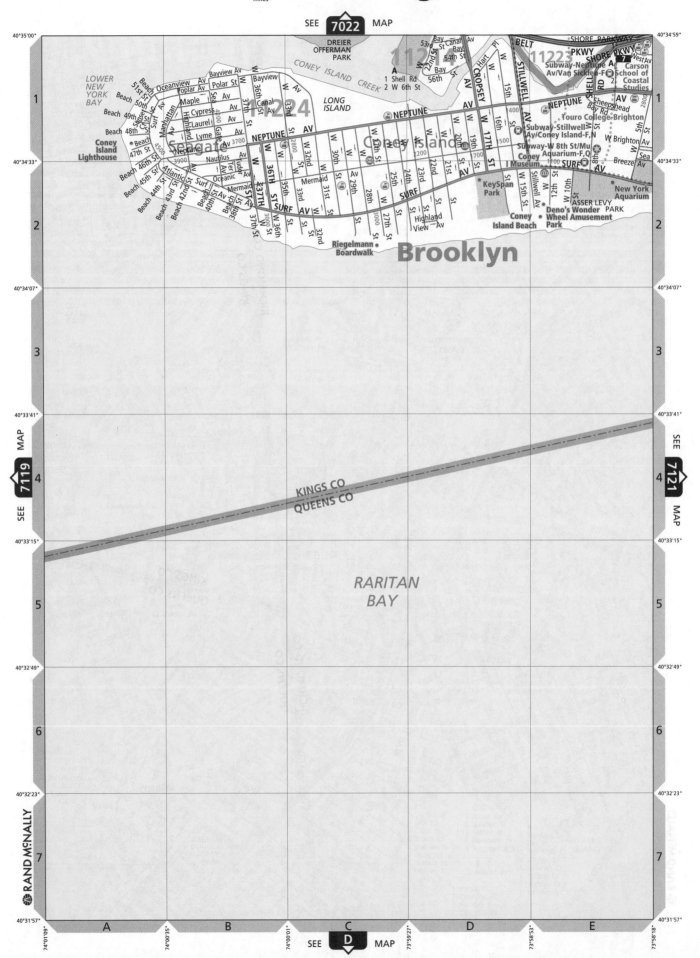

LOWER
NEW
YORK
BAY

DREIER
OFFERMAN
PARK

CONEY ISLAND CREEK

LONG
ISLAND

BELT
SHORE PARKWAY

PKWY
SHORE
PKWY

11223

Subway-Neptune
Av/Van Sickle-F

Carson
School of
Coastal
Studies

Bayview Av

Oceanview Av

Poplar Av

Polar St

Bayview
Av

Maple

Cypress

Laurel

Lyme

Nautilus

Manhattan

Highland

Gate

Sea   Av

Canal   Av

NEPTUNE   AV

Coney Island

NEPTUNE

Touro College-Brighton

Subway-Stillwell
Av/Coney Island-F,N

W Brighton Av

Subway-W 8th St/Mu
Aquarium-F,Q

Coney I Museum.

SURF AV

W Brighton

Sea Breeze Av

Coney
Island
Lighthouse

Beach

Seagate

Neptune

Atlantic

Oceanic

Mermaid

Judd

Surf

Mermaid

NEPTUNE AV

SURF AV

SURF

Mermaid

Highland
View Av

KeySpan
Park

ASSER LEVY PARK

New York
Aquarium

Deno's Wonder
Wheel Amusement
Park

Coney
Island Beach

Riegelmann
Boardwalk

Brooklyn

KINGS CO
QUEENS CO

RARITAN
BAY

MAP 7119
SEE

SEE 7121
MAP

40°35'00"

40°34'33"

40°34'07"

40°33'41"

40°33'15"

40°32'49"

40°32'23"

40°31'57"

40°34'59"

40°34'33"

40°34'07"

40°33'41"

40°33'15"

40°32'49"

40°32'23"

40°31'57"

1

2

3

4

5

6

7

A   B   C   D   E

SEE D MAP

MAP **7122**

MAP **7122**

1:24,000
1 in. = 2000 ft.
0   0.25   0.5
miles

N

SEE △ 7024 ▽ MAP

40°34'59"   40°34'59"

11229

DEAD
HORSE BAY

Brooklyn

FLOYD
BENNETT
FIELD

FLATBUSH AV

Aviation
Rd
Toll
Booth

1   1

11234

40°34'33"   40°34'33"

RARITAN BAY

JAMAICA
BAY

MARINE PARKWAY Gil
HODGES MEMORIAL BR

2   2

KINGS CO

QUEENS CO

40°34'07"   40°34'07"

US Coast
Guard
Station

BEACH
CHANNEL DR

Bayside
Av
Oceanview
Dr
Park End
Ter
Roxbury
Hillside
Av
Church
Boardwalk

11694

Roxbury
Rockaway
184th St
Beach
Boardwalk
Point Blvd
178th
Church
Beach
169th St

3   3

Bayside
Dr
Beach 201st St
Marshall Av
Beach
12th Av
Beach 204th St
Highland Pl
Beach 202nd
Market St
Market
Palmer Dr
Beach
209th St
Point Wk
12th
W
209-00
Seabreeze Dr
Beach 210th
10th Av
Beach 208th St
Beach 207th St
8th
Av
212th St
Beach
Arcadia
Beach
213th St
Oceanside
Av
7th Av
Beach
Breezy
Beach 300
204th St
Point
Beach 207th St
Blvd
Beach 214th St
Beach 215th St
Beach 100 St

A
1 Seabreeze Av

FORT TILDEN

JACOB
RIIS PARK

40°33'41"   40°33'41"

Rockaway Point Blvd
Beach 193rd St

LONG ISLAND

Rockaway Point

11697

Queens

SEE 7121 MAP

SEE 7123 MAP

4   4

40°33'15"   40°33'15"

BREEZY
POINT PARK

5   5

40°32'49"   40°32'49"

ATLANTIC OCEAN

6   6

40°32'23"   40°32'22"

7   7

RAND McNALLY

40°31'57"   40°31'56"

A   B   C   D   E

73°55'27"   73°54'53"   73°54'19"   73°53'45"   73°53'11"   73°52'36"

SEE △ D ▽ MAP

MAP
7123

MAP
7123

1:24,000
1 in. = 2000 ft.

0   0.25   0.5

miles

N

SEE 7025 MAP

40°34'59"

40°34'59"

MARINE PARK

Subway-Rockaway Park/116th St-A.S

ROCKAWAY FRWY

108TH ST

ROCKAWAY BLVD

KINGS CO
QUEENS CO

JAMAICA BAY

BEACH CHANNEL DR PARK

Rockaway Park

Queens

Croston

Newport

BLVD

DR

CHANNEL

Newport Av

Riis Av

146-00

ROCKAWAY BEACH

BLVD

Beach
Beach
Beach
Beach
Beach

500

500

500

5-00

4-00

Newport

Nepohsit

Beach Nepohsit

Beach 49th
Beach 47th
Beach 46th

Beach 300

148th St

144th St
142nd St
141st St
140th St
139th St
138th St
137th St
136th St
135th St
134th St
133rd
132nd
131st
130th
129th
128th
127th
126th
125th
124th
123rd
122nd
121st
120th
119th
118th
117th
116th
115th
114th
113th
112th
111th
110th
109th

ROCKAWAY BEACH St

145th St
149th St

St
St
St
St
St
St
St
St

1-00

100

7-00

Beach
Av
Av
Av
Av
Av
Av
Av

ROCKAWAY PARK

Belle Harbor

11694

Flight 587 Memorial

Boardwalk

A
1 Rockaway Beach Dr
2 Shore Front Pkwy

40°34'33"

40°34'33"

40°34'07"

40°34'06"

JACOB RIIS PARK

LONG ISLAND

ROCKAWAY BEACH BLVD

Rockaway Beach Blvd
Boardwalk

SEE 7122 MAP

SEE 7124 MAP

40°33'41"

40°33'40"

40°33'15"

40°33'14"

ATLANTIC OCEAN

40°32'49"

40°32'48"

40°32'22"

40°32'22"

40°31'56"

40°31'56"

RAND MCNALLY

A   B   C   D   E

SEE D MAP

73°52'36"
73°52'02"
73°51'28"
73°50'54"
73°50'20"
73°49'46"

MAP
7124

1:24,000
1 in. = 2000 ft.
0   0.25   0.5
miles

SEE 7026 MAP

N

MAP
7124

40°34'59"

A

7094

Rockaway
Beach Blvd

Beach 105th St
Beach 106th St

Shore
front

Boardwalk

Beach 101st St

Beach 102nd St

Beach 101st

Beach 99th

LONG
ISLAND

Beach 108th St

Queens

A

1   1 Beach 106th St

40°34'58"

1

40°34'33"   40°34'32"

2   2

40°34'06"   40°34'06"

3   3

40°33'40"   40°33'40"

MAP
7123
SEE

ATLANTIC
OCEAN

4   4

SEE
D
MAP

40°33'14"   40°33'14"

5   5

40°32'48"   40°32'48"

6   6

40°32'22"   40°32'22"

RAND M©NALLY

7   7

40°31'56"   40°31'56"

73°49'46"   A   73°49'11"   B   73°48'37"   C   73°48'03"   D   73°47'29"   E   73°46'55"

SEE D MAP

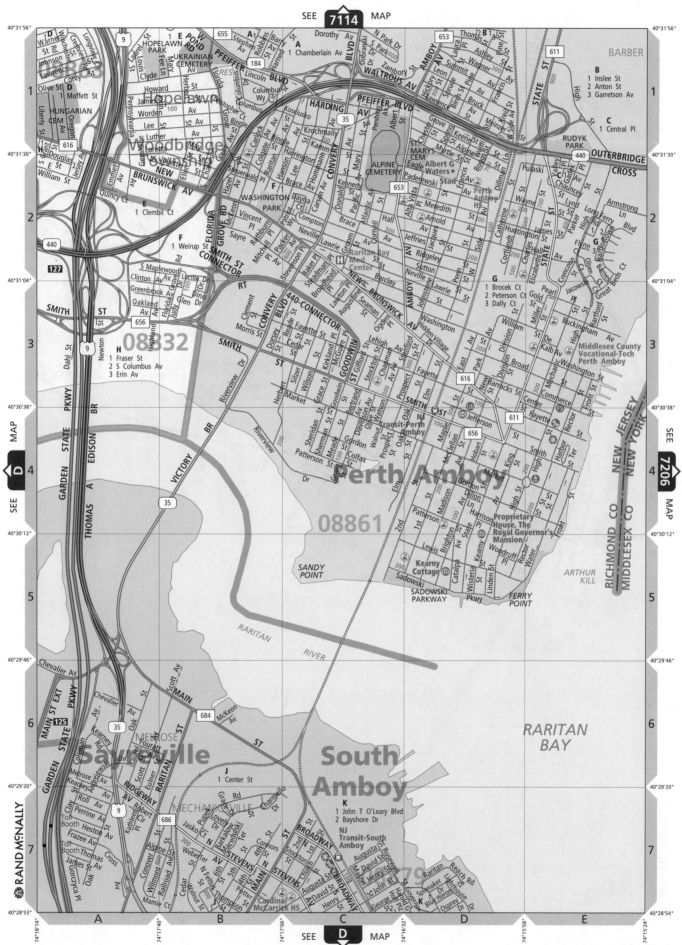

MAP
7206

MAP
7206

1:24,000
1 in. = 2000 ft.
0   0.25   0.5
miles

SEE **7115** MAP

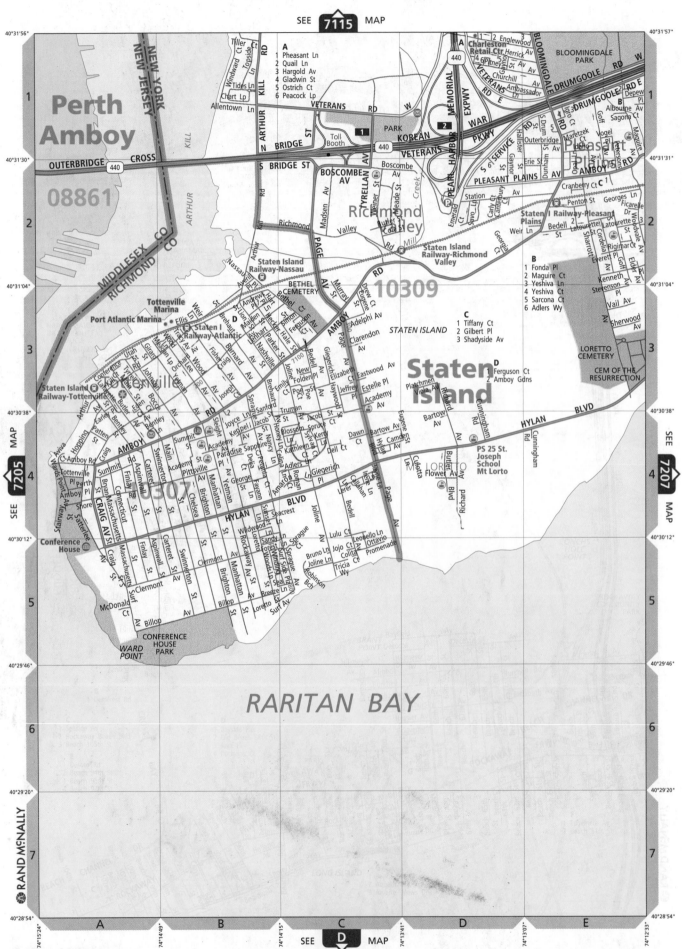

A
1 Pheasant Ln
2 Quail Ln
3 Hargold Av
4 Gladwin St
5 Ostrich Ct
6 Peacock Lp

B
1 Fonda Pl
2 Maguire Ct
3 Yeshiva Ln
4 Yeshiva Ct
5 Sarcona Ct
6 Adlers Wy

C
1 Tiffany Ct
2 Gilbert Pl
3 Shadyside Av

D
1 Ferguson Ct
2 Amboy Gdns

Perth Amboy

08861

Staten Island

10309

STATEN ISLAND

RARITAN BAY

SEE **7205** MAP

SEE **7207** MAP

SEE **D** MAP

MAP
7207

MAP
7207

1:24,000
1 in. = 2000 ft.
0   0.25   0.5
miles

N

SEE 7116 MAP

40°31'57"   40°31'57"

BLOOMINGDALE
PARK 1 2 3
B
DRUMGOOLE
Bradford
Ashland
Albourne
Minturn
Parkwood
Nathan
Foster
Queensland
Vernon
Ashland
Woodvill
Hawley Av
AMBOY
Prall
Androvette
RD
Algonkin
Billiou St
Comely St
Deisius St
Colon
Stephen
Arbutus
Arbutus
Louise
Jansen
Gentile

Denise
A
1   Ellsworth Av
Poillon

BLUE HERON
PARK

Jansen
St   Weaver   St
Shirley
Noel
Tyndale
Kinghorn
Ryan
Peare
Lipsett Av
Holdridge
Ravenna
Lenzie
Harold
Bennett
Sandgat
Embank
Bathgate

ARDEN

Staten
Island

STATEN
ISLAND

Newton St
Dole St
BLVD
Lynch
Lipsett Av
Oceanview
Ct
Bayview
Terrace Drwy
Ocean Pky

HYLAN
St Joseph
By the
Sea HS

ARBUTUS
LAKE

Kenwood
Nicolosi
Zephyr
Colony
Spanish
Boardwalk
Spanish

Nicolosi
Lp
Dr

1   Albourne
Vogel
Uncas
Av
Boynton
Terrace
Av
Wheeling
Av   O'Dell
Valdemar
Wheeling
Printewood
Madera
Hayes
Prall
Huguenot
AV
Eylandt
Capellan St
Tottenville
HS
Chisholm
1

PRINCES BAY

AMBOY
Waterbury
Utica St
Herbert
RD
Staten I Railway-Princes
Bay

B
1   Lenevar Av
2   Carlton Av
3   Parkwood Av

Edith Av
Colon St
Jarvis St

40°31'31"

10309
Lemon
Shadyside
Av
Excelsior
Av

Oswald
Percival
Elizabeth
MacGregor
Knox
Singleton St
Johanna
Siguine
Ln
Trenton
Direnzo
Ct
Seguine

WOLFE'S
POND
PARK
Holten
Corelia
Jansen St
Short Pl

Irving
Veith
Pl
Chester
Harriet   Av
Belle   Dr
Huguenot
Swaim
St
Chester   St
Yeomalt St

Irving
Av
Swann

Nicolosi
Av

2

Bayview
Finlay
Everett
Kenneth
Creston
St
Burton
Woodvale
Vail
Carol
Av
Bayview
Av
Hanover
Inez
St
BLVD
Keating
Ormsby
Armour
Case
Cooper
C
1   Kingsland St
Palmier
Carolyn
Ln
Woodvale
Admiralty
Commodore
Broken
Shell Rd
HYLAN
LEMON
CREEK
PARK
Memp
St
Melville St
Van Wyck
H   Staten
I Univ Hospital-South
Norman
C
WOLFE'S
POND

3

CEM
OF
THE
RESURRECTION
Marine
Edward
Bayside
Ln
Flagship
Cir
Johnston
Ter
Sandy's
Marina
Johnston
Marscher
Wilbur
Purdy Pl
Naygator
Ct
St

SEGUINE
POINT

40°30'38"

SEE 7206 MAP   MAP 7206   SEE 7208 MAP   4

RARITAN
BAY

5

6

7

SEE D MAP

A   B   C   D   E

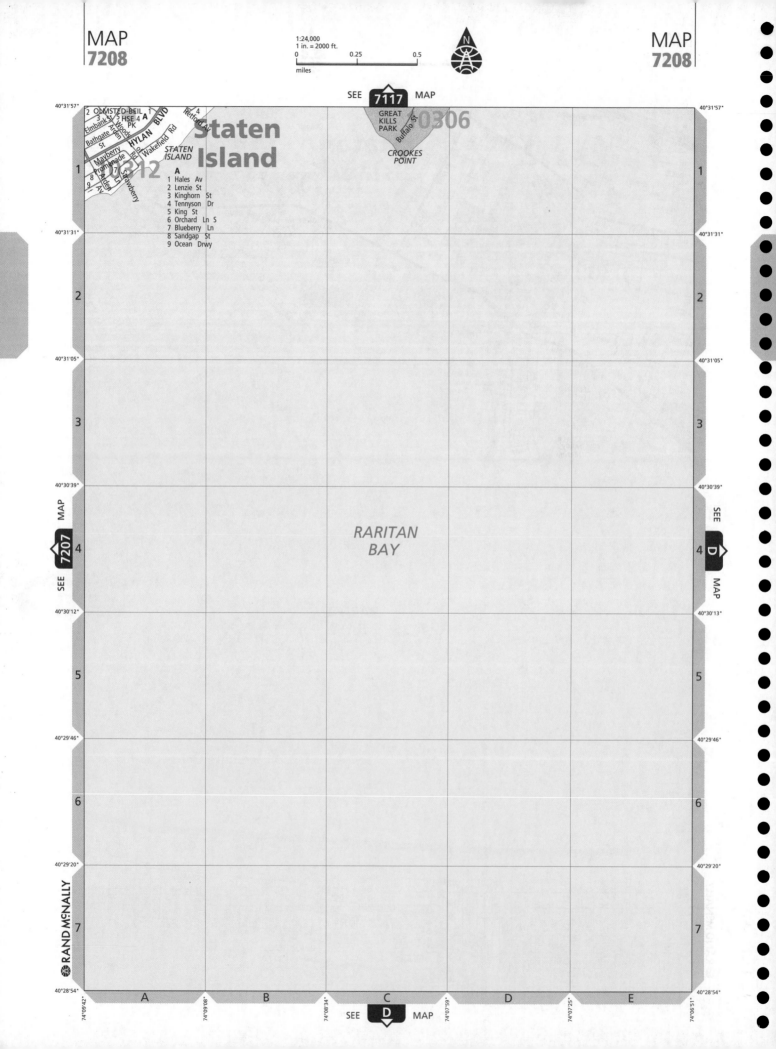

List of Abbreviations

Admin	Administration	Co	County	Jct	Junction	Reg	Regional
Agri	Agricultural	Ct	Court	Knl	Knoll	Res	Reservoir
Ag	Agriculture	Ct Hse	Court House	Lk	Lake	Rst	Rest
AFB	Air Force Base	Cv	Cove	Lndg	Landing	Rdg	Ridge
Arpt	Airport	Cr	Creek	Ln	Lane	Riv	River
Al	Alley	Cres	Crescent	Lib	Library	Rd	Road
Amer	American	Cross	Crossing	Ldg	Lodge	St.	Saint
Anx	Annex	Curv	Curve	Lp	Loop	Ste.	Sainte
Arc	Arcade	Cto	Cut Off	Mnr	Manor	Sci	Science/Scientific
Arch	Archaeological	Dept	Department	Mkt	Market	Shop Ctr	Shopping Center
Aud	Auditorium	Dev	Development	Mdw	Meadow	Shr	Shore
Avd	Avenida	Diag	Diagonal	Med	Medical	Skwy	Skyway
Av	Avenue	Div	Division	Mem	Memorial	S	South
Bfld	Battlefield	Dr	Drive	Metro	Metropolitan	Spr	Spring
Bch	Beach	Drwy	Driveway	Mw	Mews	Sq	Square
Bltwy	Beltway	E	East	Mil	Military	Stad	Stadium
Bnd	Bend	El	Elevation	Ml	Mill	St For, SF	State Forest
Bio	Biological	Env	Environmental	Mon	Monument	St Hist Site, SHS	State Historic Site
Blf	Bluff	Est	Estate	Mtwy	Motorway	St Nat Area, SNA	State Natural Area
Blvd	Boulevard	Exh	Exhibition	Mnd	Mound	St Pk, SP	State Park
Brch	Branch	Expm	Experimental	Mt	Mount	St Rec Area, SRA	State Recreation Area
Br	Bridge	Expo	Exposition	Mtn	Mountain	Sta	Station
Brk	Brook	Expwy	Expressway	Mun	Municipal	St	Street
Bldg	Building	Ext	Extension	Mus	Museum	Smt	Summit
Bur	Bureau	Fclt	Facility	Nat'l	National	Symph	Symphony
Bus	Business	Frgds	Fairgrounds	Nat'l For, NF	National Forest	Sys	Systems
Bswy	Busway	ft	Feet	Nat'l Hist Pk, NHP	National Historic Park	Tech	Technical/Technology
Byp	Bypass	Fy	Ferry	Nat'l Hist Site, NHS	National Historic Site	Ter	Terrace
Bywy	Byway	Fld	Field	Nat'l Mon, NM	National Monument	Terr	Territory
Cl	Calle	Flt	Flat	Nat'l Pk, NP	National Park	Thtr	Theater
Cljn	Callejon	For	Forest	Nat'l Rec Area, NRA	National Recreation Area	Theol	Theological
Cmto	Caminito	Fk	Fork	Nat'l Wld Ref, NWR	National Wildlife Refuge	Thwy	Throughway
Cm	Camino	Ft	Fort	Nat	Natural	Toll Fy	Toll Ferry
Cyn	Canyon	Found	Foundation	NAS	Naval Air Station	TIC	Tourist Information Center
Cap	Capitol	Frwy	Freeway	Nk	Nook	Twp	Township
Cath	Cathedral/Catholic	Gdn	Garden	N	North	Trc	Trace
Cswy	Causeway	Gen Hosp	General Hospital	Orch	Orchard	Trfwy	Trafficway
Cem	Cemetery	Gln	Glen	Ohwy	Outer Highway	Tr	Trail
Ctr	Center/Centre	GC	Golf Course	Ovl	Oval	Tran	Transit
Cent	Central	Gov't	Government	Ovlk	Overlook	Transp	Transportation
Cir	Circle	Grn	Green	Ovps	Overpass	Tun	Tunnel
Crlo	Circulo	Grds	Grounds	Pk	Park	Tpk	Turnpike
CH	City Hall	Grv	Grove	Pkwy	Parkway	Unps	Underpass
Civ	Civic	Hbr	Harbor/Harbour	Pas	Paseo	Univ	University
Clf	Cliff	Hvn	Haven	Psg	Passage	Vly	Valley
Clb	Club	HQs	Headquarters	Pass	Passenger	Vet	Veterans
Cltr	Cluster	Ht	Height	Pth	Path	Vw	View
Col	Coliseum	Hts	Heights	Pn	Pine	Vil	Village
Coll	College	HS	High School	Pl	Place	Vis Bur	Visitors Bureau
Com	Common	Hwy	Highway	Pln	Plain	Vis	Vista
Coms	Commons	Hl	Hill	Plgnd	Playground	Wk	Walk
Comm	Community	Hist	Historic/Historical	Plz	Plaza	Wy	Way
Co.	Company	Hllw	Hollow	Pt	Point	W	West
Cons	Conservation	Hosp	Hospital	Pnd	Pond	Wld	Wildlife
Cont HS	Continuation High School	Hse	House	Pres	Preserve	WMA	Wildlife Management Area
Conv & Vis Bur	Convention and Visitors Bureau	Ind Res	Indian Reservation	Prov	Provincial		
Conv Ctr	Convention Center	Info	Information	RR	Railroad		
Cor	Corner	Inst	Institute	Rwy	Railway		
Corp	Corporation	Int'l	International	Rch	Ranch		
Corr	Corridor	I	Island	Rcho	Rancho		
Cte	Corte	Is	Islands	Rec	Recreation		
CC	Country Club	Isl	Isle	Ref	Refuge		

Cities and Communities

Community Name	Abbr.	County	Map Page	Closeup Page	Community Name	Abbr.	County	Map Page	Closeup Page	Community Name	Abbr.	County	Map Page	Closeup Page
Albertson		Nassau	6724		East Harlem		New York	6612	110	Harlem		New York	6612	110
Alden Manor		Nassau	6827		* East Hills	EHLS	Nassau	6618		* Harrington Park	HRPK	Bergen	6278	
* Alpine	ALPN	Bergen	6278		East Irvington		Westchester	6048		* Harrison	HRSN	Westchester	6283	
Arden Heights		Richmond	7116		* East Newark	ENWK	Hudson	6714		* Harrison	HRSN	Hudson	6714	
* Ardsley	ARDY	Westchester	6166		East New York		Kings	6924		Hartsdale		Westchester	6167	
Arrochar		Richmond	7020		* East Orange	EORG	Essex	6712		* Hasbrouck Heights	HSBH	Bergen	6500	
Arverne		Queens	7026		East Port Chester		Fairfield	6170		* Hastings-On-Hudson	HAOH	Westchester	6165	
Astoria		Queens	6718	114	* East Rockaway	ERKY	Nassau	6929		Heath Ridge		Westchester	6282	
* Atlantic Beach	ATLB	Nassau	7027		* East Rutherford	ERTH	Bergen	6609		* Hempstead	HMPD	Nassau	6828	
Avenel		Middlesex	7114		East Village		New York	6821	119	Hempstead, Town of	HmpT	Nassau	6827	
Babbitt		Hudson	6610		* East Williston	EWLS	Nassau	6724		Hempstead Gardens		Nassau	6828	
Bath Beach		Kings	7022		Edgar		Middlesex	7114		Herricks		Nassau	6724	
* Baxter Estates	BXTE	Nassau	6617		Edgemere		Queens	7027		Hewlett		Nassau	6928	
* Bayonne	BAYN	Hudson	6919		Edgemont		Westchester	6167		* Hewlett Bay Park	HBPK	Nassau	6928	
Bay Park		Nassau	7029		* Edgewater	EDGW	Bergen	6611	108	* Hewlett Harbor	HWTH	Nassau	7029	
Bay Ridge		Kings	6922		Edgewood		Fairfield	6170		* Hewlett Neck	HWTN	Nassau	7028	
Bayside		Queens	6722		* Elizabeth	ELIZ	Union	6917		High Bridge		Bronx	6612	107
Bayswater		Queens	7027		Elmhurst		Queens	6719		Hillside		Union	6816	
Bedford		Kings	6822		Elmont		Nassau	6827		Hillside Manor		Nassau	6724	
Bedford Park		Bronx	6504		* Elmsford	EMFD	Westchester	6049		Hillside Township	HlsT	Union	6816	
Belle Harbor		Queens	7123		Elmsmere		Westchester	6395		* Hoboken	HBKN	Hudson	6716	
* Bellerose	BLRS	Nassau	6827		Eltingville		Richmond	7116		Holland		Queens	7026	
Bellerose		Queens	6827		* Englewood	EGLD	Bergen	6392		Hopelawn		Middlesex	7205	
Bellerose Terrace		Nassau	6827		* Englewood Cliffs	EGLC	Bergen	6503	101	Howard Beach		Queens	6925	
Belleville Township	BlvT	Essex	6714		--Essex County	EsxC				Howland Hook		Richmond	6918	
Bensonhurst		Kings	7022		--Fairfield County	FaiC				Hudson City		Hudson	6716	
Bergen Beach		Kings	7024		* Fairview	FRVW	Bergen	6611		--Hudson County	HdsC			
--Bergen County	BrgC				Fairview		Westchester	6049		Hudson Heights		Hudson	6611	
Bloomfield		Richmond	7018		Far Rockaway		Queens	7027		Hunts Point		Bronx	6613	
Bloomfield Township	BlmT	Essex	6713		Financial District		New York	6821	120	Hutton Park		Essex	6712	
* Bogota	BGTA	Bergen	6501		Flatbush		Kings	6923		Inwood		New York	6503	101
Borough Park		Kings	6922		Flatlands		Kings	7023		Inwood		Nassau	7027	
Boynton Beach		Middlesex	7115		* Floral Park	FLPK	Nassau	6827		Irvington		Essex	6816	
Breezy Point		Queens	7121		Floral Park		Queens	6827		* Irvington	IRVN	Westchester	6166	
Brighton Beach		Kings	7121		* Flower Hill	FLHL	Nassau	6618		Irvington Township	IrvT	Essex	6816	
Broadway Junction		Kings	6924		Flushing		Queens	6721		* Island Park	ISPK	Nassau	7029	
* Bronx	BRNX	Bronx	6613	105	Fordham		Bronx	6504		Jamaica		Queens	6825	
--Bronx County	BrxC				* Fort Lee	FTLE	Bergen	6502	103	* Jersey City	JSYC	Hudson	6820	
* Bronxville	BRXV	Westchester	6394		Fox Meadow		Westchester	6167		* Kearny	KRNY	Hudson	6714	
* Brooklyn	BKLN	Kings	6821	121	Franklin Square		Nassau	6828		Kensington		Kings	6923	
Brooklyn Manor		Queens	6824		Fresh Kills		Richmond	7116		* Kensington	KENS	Nassau	6617	
Brownsville		Kings	6924		Fresh Meadows		Queens	6825		Kew Gardens		Queens	6824	
Bushwick		Kings	6823		* Garden City	GDNC	Nassau	6828		Kings Bridge		Bronx	6504	102
Bushwick Junction		Queens	6823		Garden City Park		Nassau	6724		--Kings County	KngC			
Byram		Fairfield	6170		Garden City South		Nassau	6828		Kingsland		Bergen	6609	
Byram Shore		Fairfield	6170		* Garfield	GRFD	Bergen	6500		* Kings Point	KNGP	Nassau	6616	
Canarsie		Kings	6924		Garment District		New York	6717	116	* Lake Success	LKSU	Nassau	6723	
* Carlstadt	CARL	Bergen	6500		* Glen Cove	GLCV	Nassau	6509		Lakeview		Nassau	6828	
* Carteret	CART	Middlesex	7115		Glendale		Queens	6823		* Larchmont	LRMT	Westchester	6396	
Castleton Corners		Richmond	7019		Glen Ridge Township	GRdT	Essex	6712		Larchmont North		Westchester	6282	
* Cedarhurst	CDHT	Nassau	7028		Glenville		Westchester	6048		Laurelton		Queens	6927	
Charleston		Richmond	7115		Glenville		Fairfield	6170		* Lawrence	LWRN	Nassau	7027	
Chelsea		New York	6717	115	Glenwood Landing		Nassau	6618		Lefrak City		Queens	6720	
Chinatown		New York	6821	118	Gramercy Park		New York	6717	116	* Leonia	LEON	Bergen	6502	
City Island		Bronx	6506		Grant City		Richmond	7118		Liberty Square		Union	6918	
City of Orange Township	COrT	Essex	6712		Gravesend		Kings	7023		* Linden	LNDN	Union	7017	
* Cliffside Park	CLFP	Bergen	6611	108	Great Kills		Richmond	7117		Linden-Park		Richmond	7020	
Clifton		Richmond	7020		* Great Neck	GTNK	Nassau	6617		Linwood		Bergen	6503	
Clinton		New York	6717	112	* Great Neck Estates	GTNE	Nassau	6617		* Little Ferry	LFRY	Bergen	6501	
* Closter	CLST	Bergen	6278		* Great Neck Plaza	GTPZ	Nassau	6617		Little Italy		New York	6821	119
College Point		Queens	6614		Green Acres		Nassau	6928		Locust Manor		Queens	6927	
Colonia		Middlesex	7114		Greenburgh, Town of	GrbT	Westchester	6049		* Lodi	LODI	Bergen	6500	
Colonial Acres		Westchester	6282		Greenpoint		Kings	6822		* Long Beach	LBCH	Nassau	7029	
Coney Island		Kings	7120		Greenville		Westchester	6167		Long Island City		Queens	6718	117
Co-op City		Bronx	6505		Greenwich, Town of	GrwT	Fairfield	6051		Lower East Side		New York	6821	119
Corona		Queens	6720		Greenwich Village		New York	6821	118	Lowerre		Westchester	6393	
Crane Square		Union	6918		Grove		Essex	6713		* Lynbrook	LNBK	Nassau	6929	
* Cresskill	CRSK	Bergen	6278		Grymes Hill		Richmond	7020		Lyndhurst Township	LynT	Bergen	6609	
* Demarest	DMRT	Bergen	6278		* Guttenberg	GTBG	Hudson	6611		* Malverne	MLVN	Nassau	6929	
* Dobbs Ferry	DBSF	Westchester	6166		Haberman		Queens	6823		Mamaroneck		Westchester	6282	
Dunwoodie Heights		Westchester	6394		* Hackensack	HKSK	Bergen	6501		* Mamaroneck	MRNK	Westchester	6282	
Eastchester		Bronx	6394		Hammel		Queens	7026		Mamaroneck, Town of	MrnT	Westchester	6282	
Eastchester, Town of	EchT	Westchester	6281		Harbor Hills		Nassau	6616		Manhasset		Nassau	6617	
East Elmhurst		Queens	6720		Harbor Isle		Nassau	7029		* Manhattan	MHTN	New York	6821	118

*Indicates incorporated city

Cities and Communities

Community Name	Abbr.	County	Map Page	Closeup Page
Manhattan Beach		Kings	7121	
Manhattan Valley		New York	6612	109
* Manorhaven	MHVN	Nassau	6508	
Maplewood Township	MplT	Essex	6816	
Mariners Harbor		Richmond	6919	
Maspeth		Queens	6823	
* Maywood	MYWD	Bergen	6501	
Meadowmere Park		Queens	6927	
Meadowview		Hudson	6610	
Melrose		Bronx	6613	
Mews		Nassau	6724	
--Middlesex County	MidC			
Middle Village		Queens	6823	
Midland Beach		Richmond	7118	
Midtown		New York	6717	112
Mill Basin		Kings	7024	
Mill Pond Acres		Nassau	6508	
Milton		Westchester	6283	
* Mineola	MNLA	Nassau	6724	
--Monmouth County	MnhC			
* Moonachie	MNCH	Bergen	6501	
Morrisania		Bronx	6613	
Morris Heights		Bronx	6504	105
Morris Park		Bronx	6505	
Morris Park		Queens	6825	
Mott Haven		Bronx	6613	
* Mt Vernon	MTVN	Westchester	6394	
Mt Pleasant, Town of	MtPT	Westchester	6049	
* Munsey Park	MNPK	Nassau	6618	
Murdock Woods		Westchester	6282	
Murray Hill		New York	6717	116
--Nassau County	NasC			
Neponsit		Queens	7123	
* Newark	NWRK	Essex	6817	
New Brighton		Richmond	6920	
New Durham		Hudson	6716	
* New Hyde Park	NHPK	Nassau	6828	
* New Rochelle	NRCH	Westchester	6395	
New Springville		Richmond	7018	
New Utrecht		Kings	7022	
--New York County	NYkC			
* North Arlington	NARL	Bergen	6714	
North Bergen		Hudson	6611	
North Bergen Township	NBgT	Hudson	6716	108
North Castle, Town of	NoCT	Westchester	6050	
North Hempstead, Twn of	NHmT	Nassau	6617	
* North Hills	NHLS	Nassau	6724	
North New Hyde Park		Nassau	6723	
* Northvale	NVLE	Bergen	6164	
North Valley Stream		Nassau	6827	
North White Plains		Westchester	6050	
North Woodmere		Nassau	6928	
* Norwood	NRWD	Bergen	6164	
Oakland Gardens		Queens	6722	
Oakwood Beach		Richmond	7117	
Oakwood Heights Station		Richmond	7117	
Oceanside		Nassau	6929	
* Old Tappan	OLDT	Bergen	6164	
Old Town Station		Richmond	7020	
Orange		Essex	6712	
Orangetown, Town of	OrgT	Rockland	6165	
Oriental Beach		Kings	7121	
Oyster Bay, Town of	OybT	Nassau	6618	
Ozone Park		Queens	6925	
Palisades		Rockland	6165	
* Palisades Park	PALP	Bergen	6502	
Park Avenue		Hudson	6717	111
Parkchester		Bronx	6505	
Park Slope		Kings	6922	
Parsons Beach		Queens	6722	
* Passaic	PASC	Passaic	6500	
--Passaic County	PscC			
* Pelham	PLHM	Westchester	6395	
* Pelham Manor	PLMM	Westchester	6395	
Pemberwick		Fairfield	6170	
* Perth Amboy	PTHA	Middlesex	7205	
* Piermont	PRMT	Rockland	6165	
* Plandome	PLDM	Nassau	6617	
* Plandome Heights	PLNH	Nassau	6617	
* Plandome Manor	PLNM	Nassau	6617	
Pleasant Plains		Richmond	7206	
* Port Chester	PTCH	Westchester	6170	
Port Morris		Bronx	6613	
Port Reading		Middlesex	7114	
Port Washington		Nassau	6617	
* Port Washington North	PTWN	Nassau	6508	
Purdys Grove		Westchester	6170	
Quarry Heights		Westchester	6050	
* Queens	QENS	Queens	6824	114
--Queens County	QnsC			
Queens Village		Queens	6826	
* Rahway	RHWY	Union	7017	
Rego Park		Queens	6824	
--Richmond County	RchC			
Richmond Hill		Queens	6824	
Richmond Valley		Richmond	7206	
* Ridgefield	RDGF	Bergen	6611	
* Ridgefield Park	RDFP	Bergen	6501	
Ridgewood		Queens	6823	
Rockaway Park		Queens	7123	
Rockaway Point		Queens	7122	
--Rockland County	RkdC			
* Rockleigh	RCKL	Bergen	6164	
Rock Ridge		Fairfield	6170	
* Rockville Centre	RKVC	Nassau	6929	
Rosebank		Richmond	7021	
Rosedale		Queens	6927	
Rosedale		Westchester	6395	
* Roselle	ROSL	Union	6917	
* Roselle Park	ROSP	Union	6917	
* Roslyn	RSLN	Nassau	6618	
* Roslyn Estates	ROSE	Nassau	6618	
* Roslyn Harbor	ROSH	Nassau	6618	
Roslyn Heights		Nassau	6618	
* Russell Gardens	RSLG	Nassau	6723	
* Rutherford	RTFD	Bergen	6609	
* Rye	RYE	Westchester	6283	
* Rye Brook	RYEB	Westchester	6170	
Saddle Brook Township	SdBT	Bergen	6500	
* Saddle Rock	SDRK	Nassau	6616	
Saddle Rock Estates		Nassau	6616	
St. Albans		Queens	6826	
St. Josephs Village		Bergen	6164	
* Sands Point	SNPT	Nassau	6508	
* Sayreville	SRVL	Middlesex	7205	
* Scarsdale	SCDL	Westchester	6281	
Scarsdale Park		Westchester	6281	
Schuylerville		Bronx	6615	
* Sea Cliff	SCLF	Nassau	6509	
Seagate		Kings	7120	
Searingtown		Nassau	6724	
Seaside		Queens	7026	
* Secaucus	SECS	Hudson	6610	
Secor Gardens		Westchester	6168	
Sewaren		Middlesex	7114	
Sheepshead Bay		Kings	7023	
Silver Lake		Essex	6713	
* Sleepy Hollow	SYHW	Westchester	6048	
Sneden Landing		Rockland	6165	
Soho		New York	6821	118
* South Amboy	SAMB	Middlesex	7205	
South Beach		Richmond	7020	
* South Floral Park	SFPK	Nassau	6827	
South Glenwood Landing		Nassau	6618	
South Hackensack		Bergen	6501	
South Hackensack Twp	SHkT	Bergen	6501	
South Orange Township	SOrT	Essex	6712	
South Ozone Park		Queens	6926	
South Richmond Hill		Queens	6825	
South Valley Stream		Nassau	6928	
Spanish Harlem		New York	6612	110
Sparkill		Rockland	6164	
Springfield Gardens		Queens	6927	
Stapleton		Richmond	7020	
* Staten Island	STNL	Richmond	6920	
Steinway		Queens	6719	
* Stewart Manor	STMN	Nassau	6827	
Strathmore		Nassau	6618	
Sunnyside		Queens	6718	
Sunset Park		Kings	6922	
Tappan		Rockland	6164	
* Tarrytown	TYTN	Westchester	6048	
Teaneck Township	TnkT	Bergen	6502	
* Tenafly	TFLY	Bergen	6392	
* Teterboro	TETB	Bergen	6501	
Theater District		New York	6717	112
The Terrace		Nassau	6508	
* Thomaston	THSN	Nassau	6617	
Throgs Neck		Bronx	6615	
Todt Hill		Richmond	7020	
Tompkinsville		Richmond	6920	
Tottenville		Richmond	7206	
Townley		Union	6816	
Travis		Richmond	7018	
Tremley Point		Union	7018	
Tribeca		New York	6821	118
* Tuckahoe	TCKA	Westchester	6281	
* Union City	UNCT	Hudson	6716	111
--Union County	UnnC			
Union Port		Bronx	6614	
Union Township	UnnT	Union	6816	
University Gardens		Nassau	6723	
Upper East Side		New York	6718	113
Upper West Side		New York	6717	112
Utopia		Queens	6825	
Valhalla		Westchester	6050	
* Valley Stream	VLYS	Nassau	6928	
Van Nest		Bronx	6505	
Wakefield		Bronx	6394	
* Wallington	WLTN	Bergen	6500	
Washington Heights		New York	6503	104
Watsessing		Essex	6713	
Waverly		Westchester	6281	
Weehawken		Hudson	6716	
Weehawken Township	WhkT	Hudson	6716	111
Westchester		Bronx	6505	
--Westchester County	WesC			
West Farms		Bronx	6504	
West Hempstead		Nassau	6828	
* West New York	WNYK	Hudson	6611	111
West Orange		Essex	6712	
West Orange Township	WOrT	Essex	6712	
West Village		New York	6821	118
* White Plains	WHPL	Westchester	6168	
Whitestone		Queens	6615	
Williams Bridge		Bronx	6505	
Williamsburg		Kings	6822	
* Williston Park	WLPK	Nassau	6724	
Woodbridge		Middlesex	7114	
Woodbridge Township	WbgT	Middlesex	7114	
Woodcliff		Hudson	6611	
Wood Haven		Queens	6824	
Woodlands		Westchester	6166	
Woodlawn		Bronx	6394	
Woodmere		Nassau	7028	
* Wood-Ridge	WRDG	Bergen	6500	
Woodrow		Richmond	7116	
* Woodsburgh	WDBG	Nassau	7028	
Worthington		Westchester	6166	
* Yonkers	YNKR	Westchester	6393	
Yorkville		New York	6718	113

*Indicates incorporated city

New York City/5 Borough Street Index

STREET
Block City Map# Grid

HIGHWAYS

ALT - Alternate Route
BIA - Bureau of Indian Affairs
BUS - Business Route
CO - County Highway/ Road
FM - Farm to Market Road
HIST - Historic Highway
I - Interstate Highway
LP - State Loop
PK - Park & Recreation Road
PROV - Provincial Highway
RTE - Other Route
SPR - State Spur
SR - State Route/ Highway
TCH - Trans-Canada Highway
US - United States Highway

CO-8
- PRMT 6164 E2
10 NVLE 6164 C3
10 OrgT 6164 E2
CO-8 Main St
10 NVLE 6164 C3
10 OrgT 6164 C3
CO-8 Union St
10 OrgT 6164 E2
10 PRMT 6164 E2
CO-8 Washington St
- PRMT 6164 E2
100 OrgT 6164 C3
CO-16
400 FRVW 6611 B3
CO-16 Fairview Av
400 FRVW 6611 B3
CO-16 Tracy Av
700 FRVW 6611 B3
CO-21
10 DMRT 6278 C5
100 ALPN 6278 C5
100 CLST 6278 C5
CO-21 Anderson Av
10 DMRT 6278 C5
100 ALPN 6278 C5
100 CLST 6278 C5
CO-25
10 EDGW 108 A1
10 EDGW 6611 D3
200 CLFP 6611 D4
CO-25 Gorge Rd
10 EDGW 108 A1
10 EDGW 6611 D3
200 CLFP 6611 D4
CO-27
10 CLFP 108 A1
10 CLFP 6611 C5
10 NBgT 6611 C5
700 FTLE 6611 E2
CO-27 Palisade Av
10 CLFP 108 A1
10 CLFP 6611 C5
10 NBgT 6611 C5
700 FTLE 6611 E2
CO-29
10 FRVW 6611 C4
10 NBgT 6611 B4
200 CLFP 6611 D2
700 FTLE 6611 D1
1000 FTLE 6502 D7
CO-29 Anderson Av
10 FRVW 6611 C4
10 NBgT 6611 B4
200 CLFP 6611 D2
700 FTLE 6611 D1
1000 FTLE 6502 D7
CO-30
10 RTFD 6609 A2
CO-30 Park Av
10 RTFD 6609 A2
CO-31
10 PALP 6502 C7
10 RDGF 6502 C7
500 RDGF 6611 B1
CO-31 E Columbia Av
10 PALP 6502 C7
CO-31 Delia Blvd
10 PALP 6502 C7
10 RDGF 6502 C7
CO-31 Shaler Blvd
500 RDGF 6611 B1
700 RDGF 6502 C7
800 PALP 6502 C7
CO-32
- ERTH 6609 B2
10 RTFD 6609 A1
CO-32 E Erie Av
10 RTFD 6609 B2
CO-32 W Erie Av
10 ERTH 6609 B2
10 RTFD 6609 B2
CO-32 Park Av
- ERTH 6609 B2
- RTFD 6609 B2
CO-32 Union Av
10 ERTH 6609 B2
10 RTFD 6609 A1
CO-35
10 CLST 6278 B4
10 DMRT 6278 A5
CO-35 County Rd
10 CLST 6278 B4
10 DMRT 6278 A5
CO-36
10 CARL 6610 A1
10 MNCH 6500 D7
10 MNCH 6610 A1
100 MNCH 6501 A7
500 WRDG 6500 E7
CO-36 Moonachie Av
10 CARL 6610 A1
10 MNCH 6500 D7
10 MNCH 6610 A1
100 MNCH 6501 A7
500 WRDG 6500 E7

CO-38
10 LODI 6500 C4
10 SHKT 6500 C4
10 WRDG 6500 C4
200 HSBH 6500 D5
CO-38 Boulevard
100 HSBH 6500 D5
CO-38 Passaic Av
10 LODI 6500 C4
10 WRDG 6500 C4
200 HSBH 6500 D5
CO-38 Terhune Av
10 LODI 6500 C4
10 SHKT 6500 C4
10 WRDG 6500 C4
100 HSBH 6500 C4
CO-39
10 HRPK 6164 A7
10 NRWD 6164 A7
10 TnkT 6502 B1
100 RDFP 6501 E6
300 RDFP 6502 A5
400 NVLE 6164 C4
500 OrgT 6164 C3
CO-39 Tappan Rd
10 HRPK 6164 A7
10 NRWD 6164 A7
400 NVLE 6164 C4
500 OrgT 6164 C3
CO-39 Teaneck Rd
10 TnkT 6502 B1
100 RDFP 6501 E6
300 RDFP 6502 A5
CO-40
10 GRFD 6500 B3
10 LODI 6500 D2
100 HSBH 6500 E3
300 HSBH 6501 A3
CO-40 Passaic Av
300 GRFD 6500 B3
300 LODI 6500 C3
CO-40 Passaic St
10 GRFD 6500 B3
200 LODI 6500 B3
CO-40 Union St
10 LODI 6500 D2
200 HSBH 6500 E3
CO-40 Williams Av
100 HSBH 6500 E3
100 LODI 6500 E3
300 HSBH 6501 A3
CO-41
10 BGTA 6501 D1
10 RDFP 6501 D2
100 RDFP 6502 A5
200 CLST 6278 A3
500 TnkT 6501 D1
CO-41 Demarest Av
300 CLST 6278 B3
CO-41 Durie Av
200 CLST 6278 A3
CO-41 Mt Vernon St
10 RDFP 6501 E5
100 RDFP 6502 A5
CO-41 Railroad Av
10 RDFP 6501 D2
100 BGTA 6501 D3
CO-41 River Rd
10 BGTA 6501 D1
500 TnkT 6501 D1
CO-41 W Shore Av
10 BGTA 6501 D3
10 RDFP 6501 D3
CO-42
10 GRFD 6500 B1
100 LODI 6500 B1
100 SdBT 6500 B1
CO-42 Outwater Ln
10 GRFD 6500 A1
100 LODI 6500 C1
100 SdBT 6500 B1
CO-49
10 LFRY 6501 D5
500 HKSK 6501 D4
CO-49 River St
10 HKSK 6501 D4
10 LFRY 6501 D5
CO-49 S River St
500 HKSK 6501 D4
CO-50
10 RDFP 6501 E7
100 CLFP 6611 C3
100 RDFP 6502 A7
200 FRVW 6611 C3
400 RDGF 6611 A1
1100 RDGF 6502 A7
CO-50 Bergen Tpk
10 RDFP 6501 E7
100 RDFP 6502 A7
CO-50 Edgewater Av
500 CLFP 6611 C2
500 FRVW 6611 C2
500 RDGF 6611 C2
1100 RDFP 6502 A7
1100 RDGF 6502 A7
CO-50 Edgewater Rd
100 CLFP 6611 C3
200 FRVW 6611 C3
400 RDGF 6611 C2
CO-50 Hendricks Cswy
400 RDGF 6611 A1
1100 RDGF 6502 A7
CO-50 Remsen Pl
- RDGF 6611 A1
CO-50 Teaneck Rd
100 RDFP 6501 E6
CO-55
10 CARL 6500 C7
10 CARL 6609 C1
10 ERTH 6609 C1
10 HKSK 6501 B1
10 HSBH 6500 D6
10 RTFD 6609 B2
10 WRDG 6500 C7
200 HSBH 6501 A3
CO-55 1st St
10 HKSK 6501 B1
CO-55 Hackensack St
10 CARL 6500 C7
10 CARL 6609 C1
10 ERTH 6609 C1
10 WRDG 6500 C7
300 HSBH 6500 D6
300 RTFD 6609 B2
CO-55 Meadow Rd
10 ERTH 6609 B2

CO-55 Meadow Rd
10 RTFD 6609 B2
CO-55 Polifly Rd
10 HKSK 6501 B1
200 HSBH 6501 A3
CO-55 Terrace Av
10 HSBH 6500 D6
10 WRDG 6500 D6
400 HSBH 6501 A3
500 HKSK 6501 A3
CO-56
10 BGTA 6501 D2
10 FTLE 103 B4
10 FTLE 6503 A6
10 HKSK 6501 D2
10 LEON 6502 E5
10 TnkT 6502 A2
100 TnkT 6501 E2
200 FTLE 6502 E5
300 LODI 6501 A1
300 MYWD 6501 A1
CO-56 Degraw Av
10 TnkT 6502 A2
100 TnkT 6501 E2
300 BGTA 6501 E2
CO-56 E Degraw Av
10 LEON 6502 C3
10 TnkT 6502 C4
CO-56 Essex St
10 HKSK 6501 A1
300 LODI 6501 A1
300 MYWD 6501 A1
CO-56 Fort Lee Rd
10 LEON 6502 E5
10 TnkT 6502 C3
400 FTLE 6502 D5
CO-56 Main St
10 FTLE 103 B4
10 FTLE 6503 A6
200 FTLE 6503 A5
500 LEON 6502 E5
CO-56 E Main St
10 BGTA 6501 E2
100 TnkT 6501 E2
CO-56 W Main St
10 BGTA 6501 D2
CO-56 McCayan Memorial Br
- BGTA 6501 D1
- HKSK 6501 D1
CO-56 Midtown Bridge Appr St
10 HKSK 6501 C1
CO-56 E Salem St
10 HKSK 6501 D2
CO-56 E Salem St Ext
10 HKSK 6501 D1
CO-56 State St
10 HKSK 6501 C2
CO-57
10 HKSK 6501 A1
10 WRDG 6500 C6
100 HSBH 6500 D4
200 HSBH 6501 A2
300 CARL 6500 B7
300 ERTH 6500 B7
CO-57 4th St
10 WRDG 6500 C6
CO-57 Boulevard
10 WRDG 6500 D5
100 HSBH 6500 E3
500 HKSK 6501 A2
500 HSBH 6501 A2
CO-57 Monroe St
300 CARL 6500 B7
300 ERTH 6500 B7
600 WRDG 6500 C7
CO-57 Summit Av
10 HKSK 6501 A1
CO-57 S Summit Av
10 HKSK 6501 A1
200 HSBH 6501 A2
CO-57 Valley Blvd
100 WRDG 6500 C6
300 HSBH 6500 D5
CO-60
10 TnkT 6502 A1
CO-60 Cedar Ln
10 TnkT 6502 A1
CO-61
10 LODI 6500 C3
10 SHKT 6500 C4
10 WLTN 6500 B4
10 WRDG 6500 C4
CO-61 Hunter St
10 LODI 6500 C2
CO-61 Main Av
300 WLTN 6500 B4
500 SHKT 6500 B4
500 WRDG 6500 B4
CO-61 N Main St
100 LODI 6500 D2
CO-61 S Main St
10 LODI 6500 C3
10 SHKT 6500 B4
10 WLTN 6500 B4
10 WRDG 6500 C4
CO-61 Memorial Dr
10 LODI 6500 C3
CO-64
10 EGLD 6502 D1
CO-64 E Forest Av
10 EGLD 6502 E1
CO-64 W Forest Av
10 EGLD 6502 D1
CO-67
10 GRFD 6500 B2
200 SdBT 6500 B1
CO-67 Midland Av
10 GRFD 6500 B2
200 SdBT 6500 B1
CO-68
10 EGLD 6392 A4
CO-68 E Hudson Av
10 EGLD 6392 A4
CO-68 E Ivy Ln
10 EGLD 6392 A4
CO-70
10 TFLY 6392 D5
CO-70 E Clinton Av
10 TFLY 6392 D5
CO-70 Jay St
10 TFLY 6392 B2
CO-70 Riveredge Rd
10 TFLY 6392 A2

CO-74
10 CRSK 6278 C7
100 DMRT 6278 C7
200 ALPN 6278 C7
CO-74 Hillside Av
10 CRSK 6278 C7
100 DMRT 6278 C7
200 ALPN 6278 C7
CO-74 Madison Av
10 CRSK 6278 A7
CO-74 Union Av
10 CRSK 6278 A7
CO-80
10 DMRT 6278 C5
CO-80 Hardenburgh Av
10 DMRT 6278 A5
CO-104
400 CLST 6278 B3
CO-104 High St
400 CLST 6278 B3
CO-106
10 HRPK 6164 A5
10 NRWD 6164 B6
10 NRWD 6278 D1
10 OLDT 6164 A5
CO-106 Broadway
10 NRWD 6164 D7
10 NRWD 6278 D1
900 HRPK 6164 A5
1000 OLDT 6164 A5
CO-106 Central Av
10 HRPK 6164 A5
10 NRWD 6164 A5
10 OLDT 6164 A5
CO-110
10 NVLE 6164 B3
10 OLDT 6164 B3
10 OrgT 6164 B3
CO-110 Old Tappan Rd
10 NVLE 6164 B3
10 OLDT 6164 B3
10 OrgT 6164 B3
CO-110 Old Tappan Rd E
10 OLDT 6164 A3
CO-120
10 CARL 6609 C1
10 ERTH 6609 B1
100 ERTH 6500 A6
100 WLTN 6500 A6
400 CARL 6500 B7
CO-120 Paterson Av
10 CARL 6609 C1
10 ERTH 6609 B1
100 ERTH 6500 B7
100 WLTN 6500 B7
400 CARL 6500 B7
CO-124
10 HKSK 6501 C3
100 LFRY 6501 D5
CO-124 Bergen Tpk
100 LFRY 6501 D5
300 HKSK 6501 D4
CO-124 Hudson St
10 HKSK 6501 C3
400 LFRY 6501 D4
CO-130
10 KRNY 6714 D2
10 LynT 6609 A4
10 NARL 6714 D1
10 RTFD 6609 A4
CO-130 Orient Wy
10 LynT 6609 A4
10 RTFD 6609 A4
CO-130 Schuyler Av
10 KRNY 6714 D2
10 NARL 6714 D1
CO-135
- NoCT 6051 B2
CO-501
- FTLE 6611 C1
- PALP 6611 C1
- STNL 6919 C6
10 CLST 6278 C3
10 CRSK 6278 B7
10 CRSK 6392 B1
10 DMRT 6278 B7
10 EGLD 6392 A4
10 FRVW 6611 C3
10 JSYC 6820 A1
10 NBgT 6611 A5
10 NRWD 6164 D7
10 NRWD 6278 D1
10 OrgT 6164 E5
10 PALP 6502 D7
10 RCKL 6164 E5
10 TFLY 6392 A4
100 BAYN 6919 D4
100 EGLD 6502 E1
300 RDGF 6611 C1
500 FTLE 6502 D6
500 JSYC 6716 C5
500 NBgT 6716 D2
500 UNCT 6716 D2
500 WbgT 7114 A7
900 BAYN 6920 A1
1200 BAYN 6819 B7
1500 JSYC 6819 E1
4800 WNYK 6716 E1
5300 NBgT 6610 E7
5300 WNYK 6610 E7
6300 WNYK 6611 A5
6700 GTBG 6611 A6
CO-501 Bayonne Br
- BAYN 6919 C5
- STNL 6919 C6
CO-501 Bergen Blvd
- FTLE 6611 C1
- PALP 6611 C1
10 FRVW 6611 C3
10 NBgT 6611 A5
10 PALP 6502 D7
300 RDGF 6611 C1
500 FTLE 6502 D6
CO-501 E Central Blvd
10 PALP 6502 C6
CO-501 W Central Blvd
10 PALP 6502 C6
CO-501 E Clinton Av
10 TFLY 6392 A4
CO-501 County Rd
10 CRSK 6278 B7
10 CRSK 6392 B1
10 DMRT 6278 B7
10 TFLY 6392 A2

CO-501 Dean Dr
100 TFLY 6392 A3
CO-501 Engle St
10 EGLD 6392 A4
10 TFLY 6392 A4
CO-501 Grand Av
100 EGLD 6502 E1
CO-501 Huyler Av
10 TFLY 6392 A3
CO-501 John F Kennedy Blvd
10 JSYC 6820 A1
1500 BAYN 6819 B6
1600 JSYC 6819 D3
2900 JSYC 6716 C5
3700 NBgT 6716 C4
3700 UNCT 6716 C4
CO-501 Journal Square Plz
10 JSYC 6820 A1
CO-501 Kennedy Blvd
- JSYC 6819 B6
100 BAYN 6919 D4
900 BAYN 6920 A1
1100 BAYN 6819 B7
CO-501 Kennedy Blvd W
500 JSYC 6716 C4
500 NBgT 6716 D2
500 UNCT 6716 D2
4800 WNYK 6716 E1
5300 NBgT 6610 E7
5300 WNYK 6610 E7
6300 NBgT 6611 A5
6300 WNYK 6611 A5
6700 GTBG 6611 A6
CO-501 King Georges Post Rd
500 WbgT 7114 A7
CO-501 Piermont Rd
10 CLST 6278 C3
10 NRWD 6164 D7
10 NRWD 6278 D1
10 OrgT 6164 E5
10 RCKL 6164 E5
500 DMRT 6278 B5
CO-501 Westervelt Av
10 TFLY 6392 A3
CO-502
100 CLST 6278 C4
700 ALPN 6278 D5
1000 ALPN 6279 A6
CO-502 Closter Dock Rd
300 CLST 6278 C4
700 ALPN 6278 D5
1000 ALPN 6279 A6
CO-502 High St
100 CLST 6278 A3
CO-503
10 CARL 6610 B1
10 HKSK 6501 C3
10 LFRY 6501 C7
10 MNCH 6501 C7
100 MNCH 6610 B1
400 SHKT 6501 C4
CO-503 Liberty St
10 LFRY 6501 C7
400 SHKT 6501 C4
CO-503 Moonachie Rd
10 HKSK 6501 C4
10 MNCH 6501 C7
100 MNCH 6610 B1
200 CARL 6610 B1
400 LFRY 6501 C4
400 SHKT 6501 C4
CO-503 E Moonachie Rd
10 HKSK 6501 C3
CO-503 River St
10 HKSK 6501 C2
CO-503 S River St
10 HKSK 6501 C2
CO-503 Washington Av
600 CARL 6610 B1
800 MNCH 6610 B1
CO-505
10 EDGW 103 A7
10 EDGW 108 A4
10 EDGW 6503 B1
10 EDGW 6611 E3
10 EGLC 6503 B4
10 EGLD 6392 A7
10 FTLE 103 B4
10 FTLE 6503 A6
10 HRPK 6278 B1
10 NBgT 108 A4
10 NBgT 6611 C5
10 NRWD 6278 A1
10 WhkT 6716 E3
100 NRWD 6164 C5
100 NVLE 6164 B6
200 OrgT 6164 C4
300 EGLD 6503 A1
500 NBgT 6716 E2
500 UNCT 6716 E2
700 WhkT 111 A4
700 WhkT 6717 B1
1000 WNYK 111 B2
1000 WNYK 6717 A1
1100 EDGW 106 A1
1100 EDGW 6612 A1
6000 WNYK 6611 C6
6500 GTBG 6611 C7
CO-505 37th St
100 WhkT 6716 E2
500 NBgT 6716 E2
500 UNCT 6716 E2
CO-505 Anthony M Defino Wy
6000 WNYK 111 C1
6000 WNYK 6611 C6
6000 WNYK 6717 B1
CO-505 Highwood Ter
10 UNCT 6716 E2
10 WhkT 6716 E3
CO-505 Hudson Ter
10 EGLC 6503 B4
10 FTLE 6503 B4
2000 FTLE 103 B4
CO-505 JF Kennedy Blvd E
- WhkT 6716 E3
700 WhkT 111 A4
700 WhkT 6717 B1
1000 WNYK 111 B2

CO-505 JF Kennedy Blvd E
1000 WNYK 6717 A1
CO-505 Livingston St
10 HRPK 6278 B1
10 NRWD 6278 A1
100 NRWD 6164 B7
100 NVLE 6164 B6
200 OrgT 6164 C4
CO-505 Main St
10 EDGW 103 B4
10 EDGW 6503 A6
10 FTLE 103 B4
10 FTLE 6503 A6
CO-505 E Palisade Av
10 EGLD 6392 A7
300 EGLC 6503 B1
300 EGLD 6503 A1
CO-505 River Rd
10 EDGW 108 B1
10 EDGW 6611 D4
10 NBgT 108 A4
10 NBgT 6611 C5
1100 EDGW 103 A7
1100 EDGW 106 A1
1100 EDGW 6503 B1
1100 EDGW 6612 A1
1500 FTLE 103 B4
1500 FTLE 6503 A6
6500 GTBG 6611 C7
6500 WNYK 6611 C7
CO-506 SPUR
10 BlmT 6713 B1
10 BlvT 6713 C2
10 NWRK 6713 E5
CO-506 SPUR Bloomfield Av
10 BlmT 6713 C3
10 BlvT 6713 C2
10 NWRK 6713 E5
CO-507
10 GRFD 6500 A4
10 HRSN 6714 B6
10 KRNY 6714 B6
10 WLTN 6500 A5
10 WLTN 6500 A2
800 NARL 6714 D2
CO-507 Main Av
10 WLTN 6500 A5
CO-507 Midland Av
10 GRFD 6500 A4
10 WLTN 6500 A2
CO-507 River Dr
10 GRFD 6500 A4
CO-507 Schuyler Av
10 HRSN 6714 B6
10 KRNY 6714 B6
800 NARL 6714 D2
CO-508
10 COrT 6712 E5
10 EORG 6712 E5
10 EORG 6713 C6
10 HRSN 6713 E6
10 HRSN 6714 A6
10 NWRK 6713 E6
10 WOrT 6712 A2
500 KRNY 6715 A6
1800 KRNY 6714 E6
CO-508 Bridge St
- HRSN 6713 E6
10 NWRK 6713 E6
CO-508 Broad St
500 NWRK 6713 E7
CO-508 Center St
10 NWRK 6713 E7
CO-508 Central Av
10 COrT 6712 B3
10 EORG 6712 E5
10 EORG 6713 C6
10 NWRK 6713 A5
CO-508 Harrison Av
10 HRSN 6713 E6
10 HRSN 6714 A6
10 NWRK 6713 E6
100 KRNY 6714 C6
CO-508 Newark-Jersey City Tpk
500 KRNY 6715 A6
1800 KRNY 6714 E6
CO-508 Northfield Av
10 WOrT 6712 B2
CO-508 Park Pl
10 NWRK 6713 E7
CO-509
10 BlmT 6713 C1
10 EORG 6713 A3
200 IrvT 6816 D1
200 NWRK 6713 A5
300 HlsT 6816 C4
300 IrvT 6712 E6
300 NWRK 6712 E6
400 UnnT 6917 A1
400 UnnT 6816 B7
CO-509 Chestnut Av
1300 HlsT 6816 C5
1400 HlsT 6816 C4
CO-509 Coit St
200 IrvT 6816 D3
400 HlsT 6816 C4
CO-509 Franklin St
10 BlmT 6713 C1
CO-509 Grove St
10 BlmT 6713 C1
10 EORG 6713 B2
200 NWRK 6713 A5
300 IrvT 6712 E6
300 NWRK 6712 E6
600 IrvT 6816 D1
CO-509 N Grove St
10 EORG 6713 A4
600 BlmT 6713 B2
CO-509 S Grove St
10 EORG 6713 A3
200 NWRK 6713 A6
CO-509 Hillside Av
300 HlsT 6816 C4
CO-509 Liberty Av
- UnnT 6816 C7
900 HlsT 6816 C7
CO-509 Salem Rd
400 UnnT 6917 A1
800 UnnT 6816 B7
1100 HlsT 6816 C7
CO-509 Watsessing Av
200 BlmT 6713 C1
CO-510
10 NWRK 6713 A7

CO-510
100 SOrT 6712 A6
200 NWRK 6817 E1
500 NWRK 6712 E6
800 EORG 6712 D6
CO-510 Market St
10 NWRK 6713 D7
200 NWRK 6817 E1
CO-510 S Orange Av
10 NWRK 6713 A7
100 SOrT 6712 A6
500 NWRK 6712 E6
800 EORG 6712 D6
CO-510 Springfield Av
10 NWRK 6713 D7
CO-514
10 LNDN 7017 A1
10 WbgT 7114 D1
500 LNDN 6917 C5
700 ELIZ 6917 D5
CO-514 E Elizabeth Av
10 LNDN 7017 A1
500 LNDN 6917 C5
CO-514 W Elizabeth Av
10 LNDN 7017 A1
CO-514 Fay Av
700 ELIZ 6917 D5
700 LNDN 6917 C5
CO-514 Main St
10 WbgT 7114 D1
CO-514 Rahway Av
400 WbgT 7114 C4
CO-577
10 WOrT 6712 A1
CO-577 Gregory Av
10 WOrT 6712 A3
CO-577 Mt Pleasant Av
100 WOrT 6712 A1
CO-601
10 NWRK 6816 E5
400 IrvT 6816 E5
1000 MplT 6816 A2
CO-601 Chancellor Av
10 NWRK 6816 E5
400 IrvT 6816 E5
1000 MplT 6816 A2
CO-602
10 JSYC 6819 C6
10 NWRK 6816 E4
10 NWRK 6817 A5
10 WbgT 7017 A6
200 CART 7115 E1
400 IrvT 6816 C2
500 CART 7017 D7
CO-602 Danforth Av
10 JSYC 6819 C6
CO-602 Lyons Av
10 NWRK 6816 E4
10 NWRK 6817 A5
400 IrvT 6816 D3
CO-602 Randolph Av
10 WbgT 7017 A6
2500 CART 7017 A6
CO-602 Roosevelt Av
200 CART 7115 E1
500 CART 7017 A6
1400 WbgT 7017 A6
CO-603
10 NWRK 6713 D7
100 NWRK 6817 C1
600 NWRK 6816 E1
700 IrvT 6816 E1
CO-603 Springfield Av
10 NWRK 6713 D7
100 NWRK 6817 C1
600 NWRK 6816 E1
700 IrvT 6816 E1
CO-604
10 CART 7115 B2
10 WbgT 7114 C4
10 WbgT 7115 C2
200 CART 7017 D7
CO-604 Green St
10 WbgT 7114 C4
CO-604 Port Reading Av
10 WbgT 7114 D3
300 WbgT 7115 A3
900 CART 7115 C2
CO-604 Roosevelt Av
10 CART 7115 D2
10 WbgT 7115 C2
CO-604 Washington Av
10 CART 7115 B2
200 CART 7017 D7
CO-605
10 EORG 6712 D4
200 NWRK 6712 C7
800 IrvT 6816 B1
800 NWRK 6816 C1
CO-605 Sanford Av
200 EORG 6712 C5
200 NWRK 6712 C7
800 IrvT 6816 B2
800 NWRK 6816 C1
CO-605 Sanford St
10 EORG 6712 D4
200 NWRK 6712 C5
CO-607
10 JSYC 6819 D3
CO-607 Bergen Av
10 JSYC 6819 D3
CO-610
100 ELIZ 6917 D3
200 ROSL 6917 D3
CO-610 E 1st Av
200 ROSL 6917 D3
700 ELIZ 6917 B3
CO-610 W Grand St
100 ELIZ 6917 D3
900 ROSL 6917 B3
CO-611
10 PTHA 7114 E7
10 WbgT 7114 E6
600 WbgT 7115 A3
800 PTHA 7205 E1
CO-611 State St
10 PTHA 7114 E7
10 WbgT 7114 E6
800 PTHA 7205 E1
CO-611 West Av
300 WbgT 7114 E5
600 WbgT 7115 A3
CO-612
400 JSYC 6819 E3

CO-612 Communipaw Av
400 JSYC 6819 D2
CO-612 Grand St
700 JSYC 6819 E3
CO-613
100 LNDN 7017 C3
1800 RHWY 7017 C4
CO-613 Barnett St
2100 LNDN 7017 A4
2100 RHWY 7017 C4
CO-613 Lower Rd
100 LNDN 7017 C3
1800 RHWY 7017 A4
CO-614
100 ELIZ 6917 E4
CO-614 Pearl St
300 ELIZ 6917 E4
CO-614 S Pearl St
100 ELIZ 6917 E4
CO-615
10 LNDN 7017 A2
CO-615 N Stiles St
10 LNDN 7017 A2
CO-615 S Stiles St
10 LNDN 7017 A2
CO-616
10 ELIZ 6917 B3
10 LNDN 6917 C5
10 PTHA 7205 D3
10 ROSP 6917 A3
10 WbgT 7205 A1
400 UnnT 6917 A3
CO-616 Galloping Hill Rd
10 ELIZ 6917 B3
10 ROSP 6917 A3
400 UnnT 6917 A3
CO-616 New Brunswick Av
10 PTHA 7205 D3
10 WbgT 7205 A1
CO-616 N Park Av
10 LNDN 6917 C5
CO-616 S Park Av
10 LNDN 6917 C6
CO-616 E Westfield Av
400 ELIZ 6917 B3
400 ROSP 6917 A3
CO-617
10 LNDN 7017 C3
CO-617 Tremley Point Rd
3300 LNDN 7017 D3
CO-617 N Wood Av
10 LNDN 7017 C3
CO-617 S Wood Av
10 LNDN 7017 A1
CO-618
200 ELIZ 6917 C2
CO-618 Monmouth Rd
200 ELIZ 6917 C2
CO-619
100 LNDN 6917 A7
1000 IrvT 6816 A3
1100 UnnT 6816 A4
CO-619 Roselle St
100 LNDN 6917 A7
CO-619 Stuyvesant Av
1000 IrvT 6816 A3
1100 UnnT 6816 A4
CO-622
300 JSYC 6820 A3
CO-622 Grand St
300 JSYC 6820 A3
CO-623
500 ELIZ 6917 E1
800 ELIZ 6816 E7
900 HlsT 6816 E5
1500 NWRK 6816 E5
CO-623 N Broad St
500 ELIZ 6917 E1
800 ELIZ 6816 E7
900 HlsT 6816 E5
1500 NWRK 6816 E5
CO-623 S Broad St
10 ELIZ 6917 E5
CO-624
200 ELIZ 6918 C2
CO-624 North Av
1000 ELIZ 6918 A1
CO-624 North Av E
10 ELIZ 6918 E3
CO-628
10 HlsT 6816 D6
CO-628 Hillside Av
10 HlsT 6816 D6
CO-629
300 ELIZ 6917 D2
500 UnnT 6917 D2
CO-629 Morris Av
300 ELIZ 6917 D2
500 UnnT 6917 D2
CO-630
1000 UnnT 6816 A6
CO-630 Vauxhall Rd
1000 UnnT 6816 A6
CO-637
10 HBKN 6716 C7
10 JSYC 6716 C7
500 JSYC 6820 C1
CO-637 Henderson St
10 HBKN 6716 C7
10 JSYC 6716 C7
CO-637 Marin Blvd
200 JSYC 6820 C3
600 HBKN 6716 C7
600 JSYC 6716 C7
CO-638
10 COrT 6712 D1
10 SOrT 6712 A6
CO-638 High St
10 COrT 6712 D1
CO-638 Scotland Rd
10 COrT 6712 C2
10 SOrT 6712 A6
CO-639
100 JSYC 6820 B1
CO-639 Christopher Columbus Dr
10 JSYC 6820 C3
CO-639 Newark Av
100 JSYC 6820 B1

CO-645
800 NWRK 6713 D1
1000 BlvT 6713 D1
CO-645 Franklin Av
800 NWRK 6713 D1
1000 BlvT 6713 D1
CO-646
10 WbgT 7114 A5
CO-646 Woodbridge Center Dr
10 WbgT 7114 A5
CO-647
10 BlvT 6714 A1
CO-647 Union Av
10 BlvT 6714 A1
CO-650
10 WbgT 7114 B1
CO-650 Avenel St
10 WbgT 7114 B1
CO-650 Chain O Hills Rd
400 WbgT 7114 A1
CO-650 New Dover Rd
100 WbgT 7114 A1
CO-652
10 WbgT 7114 D5
CO-652 Berry St
300 WbgT 7114 D5
CO-652 Woodbridge Av
10 WbgT 7114 D4
CO-653
10 PTHA 7114 D7
10 WbgT 7114 D6
400 PTHA 7205 C2
CO-653 Amboy Av
10 PTHA 7114 D7
10 WbgT 7114 D6
400 PTHA 7205 C2
CO-654
10 PTHA 7114 E7
CO-654 Maurer Rd
10 PTHA 7114 E7
CO-655
- PTHA 7205 B1
- WbgT 7205 B1
400 PTHA 7114 B7
400 WbgT 7114 B7
CO-655 Florida Grove Rd
- PTHA 7205 B1
- WbgT 7205 B1
400 PTHA 7114 B7
400 WbgT 7114 B7
CO-656
10 WbgT 7205 A3
100 PTHA 7205 D4
400 ELIZ 6917 D5
700 LNDN 6917 D5
CO-656 Lidgerwood Av
400 ELIZ 6917 D5
700 LNDN 6917 D5
CO-656 E Linden Av
2000 LNDN 6917 D5
2500 ELIZ 6917 D5
CO-656 Smith St
10 WbgT 7205 A3
100 PTHA 7205 D4
CO-658
10 COrT 6712 C1
10 EORG 6713 A3
10 NWRK 6713 C4
10 WOrT 6712 C1
100 EORG 6712 E2
CO-658 Park Av
10 COrT 6712 C1
10 EORG 6713 A3
10 NWRK 6713 C4
10 WOrT 6712 C1
100 EORG 6712 E2
CO-659
10 COrT 6712 C2
10 JSYC 6716 B5
10 WOrT 6712 C1
100 NBgT 6716 B4
CO-659 Main St
10 COrT 6712 C2
10 WOrT 6712 C1
CO-659 Nelson Av
10 JSYC 6716 B5
100 NBgT 6716 B4
CO-660
10 WOrT 6712 B1
CO-660 Mt Pleasant Av
10 WOrT 6712 B1
CO-664
200 IrvT 6816 D3
CO-664 Coit St
200 IrvT 6816 D3
CO-665
10 SOrT 6712 A7
400 MplT 6712 A7
400 NWRK 6712 A7
500 MplT 6816 A1
500 NWRK 6816 A1
700 IrvT 6816 C1
CO-665 Clinton Av
1100 IrvT 6816 C1
CO-665 Irvington Av
10 SOrT 6712 A7
400 MplT 6712 A7
400 NWRK 6712 A7
500 MplT 6816 A1
500 NWRK 6816 A1
700 IrvT 6816 B1
CO-667
10 BlvT 6714 A1
10 NWRK 6713 E3
10 NWRK 6714 A2
CO-667 Broadway
10 NWRK 6713 E3
500 NWRK 6714 A1
900 BlvT 6714 A1
CO-667 Washington Av
10 BlvT 6714 A1
10 NWRK 6714 A1
CO-670
- UNCT 6716 D5
10 BlmT 6713 C1
10 BlvT 6713 C1
10 NWRK 6713 D1
100 HBKN 6716 E5
CO-670 14th St
- UNCT 6716 D5
100 HBKN 6716 D5

New York City/5 Borough Street Index

STREET
Block City Map# Grid

CO-670 Franklin St
10 BlmT 6713 C1
10 BlvT 6713 C1
10 NWRK 6713 D1
CO-670 Heller Pkwy
200 BlvT 6713 D1
200 NWRK 6713 D1
CO-671
10 COrT 6712 D1
10 WOrT 6712 D1
CO-671 Washington St
10 COrT 6712 D1
10 WOrT 6712 D1
CO-672
10 BlvT 6714 B1
CO-672 Mill St
10 BlvT 6714 A1
CO-674
300 UNCT 6716 D2
500 NBgT 6716 D2
CO-674 32nd St
300 UNCT 6716 D2
500 NBgT 6716 D2
CO-675
10 HBKN 6716 D7
CO-675 Willow Av
10 HBKN 6716 D7
CO-676
1400 NBgT 6716 D2
CO-676 Union Tpk
1400 NBgT 6716 D2
CO-677
- JSYC 6716 D7
300 WhkT 6716 E4
1400 HBKN 6716 E4
CO-677 JF Kennedy Blvd E
300 WhkT 6716 E4
CO-677 Newark Av
- JSYC 6716 D7
500 HBKN 6716 D7
CO-677 Park Av
1400 HBKN 6716 E4
1600 WhkT 6716 E4
CO-678
700 JSYC 6716 B4
700 NBgT 6716 B4
700 UNCT 6716 C5
CO-678 Secaucus Rd
700 JSYC 6716 B4
700 NBgT 6716 B4
700 UNCT 6716 C5
CO-679
10 HBKN 6716 E5
CO-679 Washington St
10 HBKN 6716 E5
CO-681
10 JSYC 6716 C6
100 HBKN 6716 D7
100 SECS 6716 C1
200 UNCT 6716 C6
800 NBgT 6716 C2
1000 SECS 6610 B7
CO-681 Observer Hwy
100 HBKN 6716 D7
CO-681 Paterson Av
10 HBKN 6716 C7
100 JSYC 6716 C7
CO-681 Paterson Plank Rd
10 JSYC 6716 C6
100 SECS 6716 C1
200 UNCT 6716 C6
800 NBgT 6716 C2
1000 SECS 6610 B7
CO-681 Paterson Plank Rd W
- SECS 6716 C1
3300 NBgT 6716 C1
CO-683
- JSYC 6716 C5
1300 UNCT 6716 D5
CO-683 Manhattan Av
1300 UNCT 6716 D4
CO-683 N Wing Viaduct
10 UNCT 6716 D5
CO-683 S Wing Viaduct
- JSYC 6716 C5
- UNCT 6716 D5
CO-684
10 SAMB 7205 B6
10 SRVL 7205 B6
CO-684 Main St
10 SAMB 7205 B6
10 SRVL 7205 B6
CO-686
10 SRVL 7205 B7
200 SAMB 7205 B7
CO-686 5th St
300 SAMB 7205 B7
CO-686 N Feltus St
200 SAMB 7205 B7
CO-686 Ridgeway Av
500 SAMB 7205 B7
500 SRVL 7205 B7
CO-686 Scott Av
10 SRVL 7205 A6
CO-686 N Stevens Av
200 SAMB 7205 B7
CO-691
- UNCT 6716 D2
3500 NBgT 6716 D1
CO-691 Bergen Tpk
- UNCT 6716 D2
3500 NBgT 6716 D1
CO-693
6000 WNYK 111 C1
6000 WNYK 6611 B7
6000 WNYK 6717 B1
6700 GTBG 6611 B5
7100 NBgT 6611 B5
CO-693 JF Kennedy Blvd E
6000 WNYK 111 C1
6000 WNYK 6611 B7
6000 WNYK 6717 B1
6700 GTBG 6611 B5
7100 NBgT 6611 B5
CO-693 Kennedy Blvd W
9100 NBgT 6611 B4
CO-697
10 ENWK 6714 A5
10 HRSN 6714 A5
10 KRNY 6714 B2
CO-697
800 NARL 6714 C1
CO-697 Frank E Rodgers Blvd N
10 HRSN 6714 A6
700 ENWK 6714 A5
700 KRNY 6714 A5
CO-697 Kearny Av
10 ENWK 6714 A5
10 HRSN 6714 A5
10 KRNY 6714 B2
800 NARL 6714 C1
CO-699
10 HRSN 6713 E6
10 KRNY 6713 E5
10 KRNY 6714 B1
200 ENWK 6713 E6
300 NWRK 6714 A3
900 NARL 6714 B1
CO-699 Passaic Av
10 HRSN 6713 E6
10 KRNY 6713 E5
10 KRNY 6714 B1
200 ENWK 6713 E6
300 NWRK 6714 A3
900 NARL 6714 B1
CO- 39 Tappan Rd
100 HRPK 6164 A7
CO- 39
100 HRPK 6164 A7
CO-S55
10 CARL 6609 C1
10 ERTH 6609 C1
200 CARL 6500 B7
200 ERTH 6500 B7
CO-S55 Hoboken Rd
10 CARL 6609 C1
10 ERTH 6609 C1
200 CARL 6500 B7
200 ERTH 6500 B7
FM-109
10 HRPK 6164 A6
10 NRWD 6164 A6
600 NRWD 6278 B1
FM-109 Blanch Av
10 HRPK 6164 A6
10 NRWD 6164 A6
600 NRWD 6278 A1
I-78
- BAYN 6818 E6
- BAYN 6819 E5
- HlsT 6816 C4
- IrvT 6816 D4
- JSYC 6819 B7
- JSYC 6820 B1
- NWRK 6816 E3
- NWRK 6817 C4
- NWRK 6818 E6
- UnnT 6816 C4
I-78 New Jersey Turnpike Ext
- BAYN 6818 E6
- BAYN 6819 E5
- JSYC 6819 B7
- JSYC 6820 B1
- NWRK 6818 A4
I-80
- BGTA 6501 E3
- HKSK 6501 A1
- LODI 6500 E1
- LODI 6501 A1
- RDFP 6501 E4
- RDFP 6502 A4
- SHkT 6501 D4
- TETB 6501 D3
- TnkT 6501 E3
- TnkT 6502 A4
I-87
- ARDY 6166 C5
- BRNX 102 D6
- BRNX 104 D7
- BRNX 105 A4
- BRNX 107 D7
- BRNX 110 D1
- BRNX 6393 D7
- BRNX 6503 E7
- BRNX 6504 B3
- BRNX 6612 E4
- BRNX 6613 A5
- GrbT 6048 E6
- GrbT 6166 C7
- GrbT 6280 C1
- IRVN 6048 E7
- TYTN 6048 C5
- YNKR 6280 B3
- YNKR 6393 E5
- YNKR 6394 A3
I-87 Major Deegan Expwy
- BRNX 102 D6
- BRNX 104 E4
- BRNX 105 A4
- BRNX 107 D7
- BRNX 110 D1
- BRNX 6393 D7
- BRNX 6503 E7
- BRNX 6504 B3
- BRNX 6612 E2
- BRNX 6613 A5
- YNKR 6393 E5
I-87 New York State Thwy
- ARDY 6166 C5
- BRNX 6393 E5
- GrbT 6048 E6
- GrbT 6166 C7
- GrbT 6280 C1
- IRVN 6048 E7
- TYTN 6048 B4
- YNKR 6280 B3
- YNKR 6393 E5
- YNKR 6394 A3
I-87 Tappan Zee Br
- TYTN 6048 C5
I-95
- BRNX 104 E5
- BRNX 105 E5
- BRNX 6503 E6
- BRNX 6504 A6
- BRNX 6505 E3
- BRNX 6506 A6
- BRNX 6613 E1
- BRNX 6614 A1
- BRNX 6615 A1
- CARL 6610 A5
- CART 7017 B7
- CART 7115 B1
I-95
- EGLD 6502 D2
- ELIZ 6817 E7
- ELIZ 6918 E1
- ERTH 6609 E5
- ERTH 6610 C3
- FTLE 103 C3
- FTLE 6502 E4
- FTLE 6503 B5
- GrwT 6170 E4
- HRSN 6283 C2
- KRNY 6714 E6
- KRNY 6715 A5
- LEON 6502 E3
- LNDN 6917 E7
- LNDN 6918 E1
- LNDN 7017 D4
- LRMT 6396 C1
- LynT 6609 C7
- LynT 6715 C1
- MHTN 103 E4
- MHTN 104 A4
- MHTN 6503 D6
- MRNK 6282 D5
- MRNK 6283 A3
- MrnT 6282 D5
- MrnT 6396 C1
- NBgT 6610 D5
- NRCH 6395 D6
- NRCH 6396 A3
- NWRK 6714 E5
- NWRK 6817 E7
- NWRK 6818 D1
- PLMM 6395 C7
- PLMM 6506 C1
- PTCH 6170 E4
- PTCH 6284 B1
- RDFP 6502 D2
- RDGF 6501 E7
- RDGF 6502 A7
- RDGF 6610 E1
- RTFD 6609 C7
- RYE 6283 E1
- RYE 6284 A1
- SECS 6610 C6
- SECS 6715 E3
- SECS 6716 A2
- TnkT 6502 E4
- WbgT 7114 A6
- WbgT 7115 A3
I-95 Bruckner Expwy
- BRNX 6506 A6
- BRNX 6614 E1
- BRNX 6615 A1
I-95 Cross Bronx Expwy
- BRNX 104 E5
- BRNX 105 C5
- BRNX 6503 E6
- BRNX 6504 D7
- BRNX 6613 E1
- BRNX 6614 A1
- MHTN 104 B4
- MHTN 6503 D6
I-95 George Washington Br
- FTLE 103 D3
- FTLE 6503 B5
- MHTN 103 E4
- MHTN 104 A4
- MHTN 6503 B5
I-95 Gov John Davis Lodge Tpk
- GrwT 6170 D6
- PTCH 6170 C7
I-95 New England Thwy
- BRNX 6505 E2
- BRNX 6506 B1
- GrwT 6170 C7
- HRSN 6283 B2
- LRMT 6396 C1
- MRNK 6282 D5
- MRNK 6283 A3
- MrnT 6282 D5
- MrnT 6396 C1
- NRCH 6395 E5
- NRCH 6396 A3
- PLMM 6395 C7
- PLMM 6506 C1
- PTCH 6170 E4
- PTCH 6284 B1
- RYE 6283 E2
- RYE 6284 A1
I-95 New Jersey Tpk
- CARL 6610 A5
- CART 7017 E1
- CART 7115 B1
- EGLD 6502 D1
- ELIZ 6817 E7
- ELIZ 6918 E1
- ERTH 6609 E5
- ERTH 6610 A5
- FTLE 103 A3
- FTLE 6502 E4
- FTLE 6503 B5
- KRNY 6714 D7
- KRNY 6715 E3
- LEON 6502 E3
- LNDN 6917 E7
- LNDN 6918 E1
- LNDN 7017 D4
- LynT 6609 C7
- LynT 6715 C1
- NBgT 6610 D4
- NWRK 6714 E5
- NWRK 6817 E7
- NWRK 6818 A7
- RDFP 6502 A5
- RDGF 6501 E7
- RDGF 6502 A7
- RDGF 6610 D4
- RTFD 6609 C7
- SECS 6610 C6
- SECS 6715 E4
- SECS 6716 A2
- TnkT 6502 E4
- WbgT 7114 C6
- WbgT 7115 A3
I-278
- BKLN 120 E3
- BKLN 121 A3
- BKLN 6821 C7
- BKLN 6822 A6
- BKLN 6921 E7
- BKLN 6922 B1
- BKLN 7021 E2
- BKLN 7022 A1
I-278
- BRNX 6613 C4
- BRNX 6614 B2
- ELIZ 6917 E6
- ELIZ 6918 A7
- LNDN 6917 E6
- MHTN 110 E7
- MHTN 114 D1
- MHTN 6612 E7
- MHTN 6613 A6
- MHTN 6718 E2
- QENS 114 E3
- QENS 6718 E2
- QENS 6719 C6
- QENS 6822 E1
- QENS 6823 A1
- STNL 6918 B7
- STNL 7018 E3
- STNL 7019 A3
- STNL 7020 E4
- STNL 7021 D4
I-278 TRK
29-00 QENS 6719 A3
I-278 TRK Astoria Blvd N
31-00 QENS 6719 A3
I-278 TRK Astoria Blvd S
33-00 QENS 6719 A3
I-278 Brooklyn Queens Expwy
- BKLN 120 E3
- BKLN 121 A3
- BKLN 6821 C7
- BKLN 6822 A6
- BKLN 6922 A6
- QENS 6719 A7
- QENS 6822 E1
- QENS 6823 A1
I-278 Brooklyn Queens Expwy W
- QENS 6719 C6
I-278 Bruckner Expwy
- BRNX 6613 E2
- BRNX 6614 B2
I-278 Goethals Br
- ELIZ 6918 A7
- STNL 6918 B7
I-278 Gowanus Expwy
- BKLN 6921 E7
- BKLN 6922 C2
- BKLN 7021 E2
- BKLN 7022 A1
I-278 TRK Hoyt Av N
29-00 QENS 6719 A3
I-278 TRK Hoyt Av S
29-00 QENS 6719 A3
I-278 Kosciuszko Br
- BKLN 6822 D2
- QENS 6822 E2
I-278 Staten Island Expwy
- STNL 6918 B7
- STNL 7018 C1
- STNL 7019 E4
- STNL 7020 C4
- STNL 7021 D4
I-278 Triborough Br
- MHTN 110 E7
- MHTN 114 D1
- MHTN 6612 E7
- MHTN 6613 A6
- MHTN 6718 E1
- QENS 114 E3
- QENS 6718 E2
- QENS 6719 A2
I-278 Triborough Br Approach
- BRNX 6613 A6
- MHTN 6613 A6
I-278 Verrazano-Narrows Br
- BKLN 7021 D4
- STNL 7021 A5
I-280
- COrT 6712 D3
- ENWK 6713 D6
- EORG 6712 E3
- EORG 6713 B5
- HRSN 6713 D6
- HRSN 6714 A6
- KRNY 6714 C6
- NWRK 6713 D6
- WOrT 6712 C3
I-287
- EMFD 6048 E5
- EMFD 6049 C6
- GrbT 6048 E5
- GrbT 6049 D7
- GrbT 6050 A7
- HRSN 6169 D4
- PTCH 6170 A7
- RYE 6170 B7
- RYE 6284 B1
- RYEB 6169 E6
- RYEB 6170 A7
- TYTN 6048 C5
- WHPL 6050 B7
- WHPL 6168 C1
- WHPL 6169 E6
I-287 Cross Westchester Expwy
- EMFD 6048 E5
- EMFD 6049 C6
- GrbT 6048 E5
- GrbT 6049 C7
- GrbT 6050 A7
- HRSN 6169 B4
- PTCH 6170 A7
- RYE 6170 A7
- RYE 6284 B1
- RYEB 6169 E6
- RYEB 6170 A7
- WHPL 6050 B7
- WHPL 6168 C1
- WHPL 6169 C4
I-287 New York State Thwy
- GrbT 6048 D5
- TYTN 6048 C5
I-287 Tappan Zee Br
- TYTN 6048 C5
I-295
- BRNX 6614 E2
- BRNX 6615 A2
- QENS 6615 D6
I-295
- QENS 6721 E1
- QENS 6722 A4
- QENS 6826 B1
I-295 Clearview Expwy
- QENS 6615 E7
- QENS 6721 E1
- QENS 6722 A4
- QENS 6826 B1
I-295 Cross Bronx Expwy Ext
- BRNX 6614 E2
- BRNX 6615 A2
I-295 Throgs Neck Br
- BRNX 6615 D4
- QENS 6615 D6
I-295 Throgs Neck Expwy
- BRNX 6615 B3
I-295 Throgs Neck Br Approach
- BRNX 6615 D7
I-478
- BKLN 120 C7
- BKLN 6821 B7
- BKLN 6922 B1
- MHTN 120 B4
- MHTN 6821 B7
I-478 Brooklyn Battery Tun
- BKLN 120 C7
- BKLN 6821 B7
- BKLN 6922 B1
- MHTN 120 B4
- MHTN 6821 B7
I-478 Gowanus Expwy
- BKLN 6922 B2
I-495
- EHLS 6724 E1
- LKSU 6723 C3
- MHTN 116 E5
- MHTN 117 B5
- MHTN 6717 E6
- MHTN 6718 A6
- NHLS 6723 E3
- NHLS 6724 A2
- NHmT 6724 C1
- QENS 117 E6
- QENS 6718 D7
- QENS 6719 A7
- QENS 6720 D7
- QENS 6721 A7
- QENS 6722 A6
- QENS 6723 A4
- QENS 6823 A1
- QENS 6824 B1
I-495 Long Island Expwy
- EHLS 6724 E1
- LKSU 6723 B3
- NHLS 6723 D3
- NHLS 6724 A2
- NHmT 6724 C1
- QENS 117 E6
- QENS 6718 D7
- QENS 6719 A7
- QENS 6720 D7
- QENS 6721 A7
- QENS 6722 A6
- QENS 6723 A4
- QENS 6823 A1
- QENS 6824 B1
I-495 Queens Midtown Expwy
- QENS 117 D6
- QENS 6718 D7
- QENS 6823 C2
I-495 Queens Midtown Tun
- MHTN 116 E5
- MHTN 117 A4
- MHTN 6717 E6
- MHTN 6718 A6
- QENS 117 D6
- QENS 6718 A6
I-495 Queens Midtown Tunnel
- QENS 117 E6
- QENS 6718 C7
I-678
- BRNX 6614 E3
- QENS 6614 E5
- QENS 6615 A6
- QENS 6720 E7
- QENS 6721 A1
- QENS 6824 E1
- QENS 6825 A3
- QENS 6926 C1
I-678 Bronx Whitestone Br
- BRNX 6614 E5
- QENS 6614 E5
- QENS 6615 A6
I-678 Hutchinson River Pkwy
- BRNX 6614 E5
I-678 Van Wyck Expwy
- QENS 6720 D4
- QENS 6824 E1
- QENS 6825 A3
- QENS 6926 C1
I-678 Whitestone Expwy
- QENS 6615 A7
- QENS 6720 E7
- QENS 6721 A1
I-684
- GrwT 6051 B1
- HRSN 6051 A7
- HRSN 6169 A1
- NoCT 6051 A7
I-695
- BRNX 6506 A7
- BRNX 6615 A1
I-695 Throgs Neck Expwy
- BRNX 6506 A7
- BRNX 6615 A1
I-895
- BRNX 6613 D2
I-895 Sheridan Expwy
- BRNX 6613 D2
SR-3
- ERTH 6609 E6
- ERTH 6610 A6
- NBgT 6716 C1
SR-3
- RTFD 6609 B4
- SECS 6609 E6
- SECS 6610 B7
- SECS 6716 C1
SR-3 Penhorn Av
- NBgT 6716 C1
- SECS 6716 C1
SR-4
- EGLD 6502 D2
- FTLE 6502 E3
- TnkT 6502 C1
SR-4 New Jersey Tpk
- FTLE 6502 E5
SR-5
- EDGW 6611 E1
- PALP 6502 C7
- RDGF 6502 C7
200 FTLE 6502 E7
400 FTLE 6611 D1
500 PALP 6611 D1
SR-5 Central Blvd
200 FTLE 6502 D7
SR-5 Columbia Av
400 FTLE 6611 D1
500 PALP 6611 C1
SR-5 Glen Rd
1000 FTLE 6502 D7
1000 FTLE 6611 D1
SR-5 Palisade Av
1000 FTLE 6611 E1
SR-7
10 BlvT 6714 A1
10 KRNY 6714 C1
10 NARL 6714 C1
800 KRNY 6715 A4
1000 JSYC 6715 D7
SR-7 Belleville Tpk
10 KRNY 6714 C1
10 NARL 6714 C1
800 KRNY 6715 A4
SR-7 Newark Av
1000 JSYC 6715 D7
SR-7 Newark-Jersey City Tpk
- JSYC 6715 D7
- KRNY 6715 D7
SR-7 Washington Av
10 BlvT 6714 A1
SR-9A
- BRNX 102 A3
- BRNX 6393 C6
- BRNX 6504 A1
- MHTN 101 E4
- MHTN 102 A3
- MHTN 103 E7
- MHTN 104 C1
- MHTN 106 E1
- MHTN 108 C7
- MHTN 109 A1
- MHTN 118 B1
- MHTN 6503 E2
- MHTN 6504 A2
- MHTN 6611 D7
- MHTN 6612 A4
- MHTN 6821 A2
10 EMFD 6049 B3
10 GrbT 6280 B1
10 HAOH 6280 B1
10 MHTN 115 C4
10 MHTN 6717 A7
10 MtPT 6049 A2
10 YNKR 6279 C7
10 YNKR 6393 C3
100 GrbT 6049 A6
300 GrbT 6166 C5
300 HAOH 6166 B7
400 YNKR 6280 A3
500 ARDY 6166 C5
600 MHTN 111 E6
700 MHTN 112 A5
1800 GrbT 6048 E7
SR-9A 12th Av
300 MHTN 115 D2
300 MHTN 6717 B5
SR-9A Ashburton Av
10 YNKR 6279 E7
SR-9A Broadway
6300 BRNX 6393 C5
6700 YNKR 6393 C4
SR-9A N Broadway
10 YNKR 6393 C1
100 YNKR 6279 C7
SR-9A S Broadway
10 YNKR 6393 C3
600 BRNX 6393 C4
SR-9A N Central Av
10 EMFD 6049 A5
SR-9A Henry Hudson Br
- BRNX 102 A3
- BRNX 6504 A2
- MHTN 102 A3
- MHTN 6504 A2
SR-9A Henry Hudson Pkwy
- BRNX 102 C1
- BRNX 6393 C6
- BRNX 6504 A1
- MHTN 101 E4
- MHTN 103 E7
- MHTN 104 A6
- MHTN 106 E3
- MHTN 108 D5
- MHTN 109 A1
- MHTN 112 A3
- MHTN 6503 E2
- MHTN 6611 D7
- MHTN 6612 A4
- MHTN 6717 D2
SR-9A Joe Dimaggio Hwy
10 MHTN 115 C5
100 MHTN 118 B5
100 MHTN 6717 A7
100 MHTN 6821 A3
400 MHTN 111 D7
700 MHTN 112 A5
SR-9A W Joe Dimaggio Hwy
- MHTN 111 E6
- MHTN 112 A5
- MHTN 115 C4
- MHTN 118 B1
- MHTN 6717 B6
- MHTN 6821 A2
SR-9A Manor House Sq
10 YNKR 6393 C1
SR-9A Prospect St
10 YNKR 6393 C1
SR-9A Riverdale Av
10 YNKR 6393 C1
SR-9A Saw Mill River Rd
10 EMFD 6049 A5
10 GrbT 6280 B1
10 HAOH 6280 B1
10 YNKR 6279 E6
100 GrbT 6049 A6
200 MtPT 6049 A2
300 GrbT 6166 C5
300 HAOH 6166 B7
400 YNKR 6280 A3
500 ARDY 6166 C5
1800 GrbT 6048 E7
SR-9A Saw Mill River Rd S
10 MtPT 6049 A2
SR-9A N Saw Mill River Rd
10 EMFD 6049 B3
100 GrbT 6049 B5
SR-9A W Side Hwy
- MHTN 111 E6
- MHTN 115 C1
- MHTN 6717 C3
SR-9A Warburton Av
10 YNKR 6393 C1
SR-9A Wells Av
10 YNKR 6393 C1
SR-9A West St
300 MHTN 118 B3
300 MHTN 6821 A2
SR-15
- GrwT 6170 A1
- RYEB 6170 A1
SR-15 Merritt Pkwy
- GrwT 6170 A1
- RYEB 6170 A1
SR-17
- CARL 6500 D7
- CARL 6609 C1
- ERTH 6609 C1
- HKSK 6501 A4
- HSBH 6500 E5
- HSBH 6501 A4
- LODI 6500 E1
- LODI 6501 A4
- RTFD 6609 D1
- WRDG 6500 E6
10 KRNY 6714 C1
10 LynT 6609 A4
10 NARL 6714 C1
SR-17 Ridge Rd
- RTFD 6609 A3
10 KRNY 6714 C1
10 LynT 6609 A4
10 NARL 6714 C1
SR-17 Rutherford Av
600 LynT 6609 A3
600 RTFD 6609 A3
SR-21
- BlvT 6714 B1
200 NWRK 6817 C4
800 NWRK 6713 E5
1500 NWRK 6714 A3
SR-21 McCarter Hwy
200 NWRK 6817 C4
800 NWRK 6713 E5
1500 NWRK 6714 A3
SR-22
10 BRXV 6281 D1
10 BRXV 6395 A5
10 EchT 6395 A1
10 MTVN 6395 A4
10 WHPL 6050 B7
10 WHPL 6168 B1
100 TCKA 6281 D1
200 EchT 6281 A6
300 SCDL 6168 A3
600 NoCT 6050 B7
700 BRNX 6395 A7
800 SCDL 6281 C2
1000 SCDL 6167 D7
2300 BRNX 6506 A1
3600 BRNX 6394 E7
3600 BRNX 6505 E1
SR-22 S 3rd Av
700 BRNX 6395 A7
700 MTVN 6395 A7
SR-22 Armory Pl
- WHPL 6168 B1
SR-22 N Broadway
10 WHPL 6050 B7
10 WHPL 6168 B1
600 NoCT 6050 B7
SR-22 S Broadway
10 WHPL 6168 B1
SR-22 N Columbus Av
10 MTVN 6395 A4
600 BRXV 6395 A1
600 EchT 6395 A1
SR-22 S Columbus Av
10 MTVN 6395 A4
SR-22 Mt Kisco Rd
- NoCT 6050 B3
SR-22 Post Rd
1000 SCDL 6167 D7
1200 SCDL 6168 A3
1200 WHPL 6168 A4
SR-22 E Post Rd
10 WHPL 6168 B2
SR-22 W Post Rd
10 WHPL 6168 A2
300 SCDL 6168 A4
SR-22 Provost Av
2300 BRNX 6506 A1
3600 BRNX 6394 E7
3600 BRNX 6505 E1
3900 BRNX 6395 A7
3900 MTVN 6395 A7
SR-22 Westchester Av
10 WHPL 6168 B1
SR-22 White Plains Rd
10 BRXV 6281 D1
10 BRXV 6395 A5
10 EchT 6395 A1
100 TCKA 6281 D1
200 EchT 6281 A6
800 SCDL 6281 C2
1000 SCDL 6167 D7
SR-24
10 HMPD 6828 E5
10 HmpT 6828 A4
88-00 QENS 6826 D3
100 HmpT 6827 B4
220-00 QENS 6827 B4
SR-24 212th St
88-00 QENS 6826 D2
SR-24 Fulton Av
10 HMPD 6828 E5
10 HmpT 6828 E5
SR-24 Hempstead Av
212-00 QENS 6826 D3
220-00 QENS 6827 B4
SR-24 Hempstead Tpk
- QENS 6827 A4
10 HMPD 6828 E5
10 HmpT 6828 A4
100 HmpT 6827 B4
SR-24 Hollis Ct Blvd
87-00 QENS 6826 C2
SR-24 Jamaica Av
211-30 QENS 6826 D3
SR-25
- HmpT 6827 C2
- QENS 6720 A7
10 FLPK 6827 C1
10 MNLA 6724 E5
10 NHmT 6827 E1
10 NHPK 6827 E1
29-00 QENS 6718 D5
40-01 QENS 6719 E7
120-00 QENS 6824 E3
121-00 QENS 6825 A4
181-00 QENS 6826 B3
224-01 QENS 6827 A2
246-32 BLRS 6827 B2
500 NHmT 6724 B7
1600 NHPK 6724 B7
SR-25 Braddock Av
- HmpT 6827 B2
220-00 QENS 6826 E1
224-01 QENS 6827 A2
SR-25 Hillside Av
138-36 QENS 6825 C4
181-00 QENS 6826 B3
SR-25 Jericho Tpk
10 FLPK 6827 C1
10 MNLA 6724 E5
10 NHmT 6827 E1
10 NHPK 6827 E1
10 QENS 6827 C2
244-00 HmpT 6827 C2
246-32 BLRS 6827 B2
500 NHmT 6724 B7
900 NHPK 6828 A1
1600 NHPK 6724 B7
SR-25 Queens Blvd
- QENS 6720 A7
32-01 QENS 6718 E6
40-01 QENS 6719 A6
120-00 QENS 6824 C2
121-00 QENS 6825 A4
SR-25A
- NasC 6618 D5
10 NHmT 6722 E2
10 NHmT 6723 A2
10-00 QENS 117 E5
10-00 QENS 6718 E5
39-00 QENS 6719 A5
132-01 QENS 6720 E4
137-63 QENS 6721 E4
200 RSLG 6723 A2
202-00 QENS 6722 A4
400 LKSU 6723 B1
500 THSN 6723 B1
900 NHmT 6617 E6
1000 FLHL 6618 C6
1000 MNPK 6618 C5
1000 NHmT 6618 C5
1000 ROSE 6618 C6
1000 RSLN 6618 C5
1600 MNPK 6617 E6
1600 ROSH 6618 E5
SR-25A Jackson Av
10-00 QENS 117 D6
10-00 QENS 6718 B7
SR-25A Northern Blvd
- NasC 6618 D5
10 NHmT 6722 E2
10 NHmT 6723 A2
29-39 QENS 6718 E5
39-00 QENS 6719 A5
91-00 QENS 6720 A4
137-63 QENS 6721 A3
200 RSLG 6723 A2
202-00 QENS 6722 A4
400 LKSU 6723 B1
500 THSN 6723 B1
900 NHmT 6617 E6
1000 FLHL 6618 C6
1000 MNPK 6618 C5
1000 NHmT 6618 C5
1000 ROSE 6618 C6
1000 RSLN 6618 C5
1600 MNPK 6617 E6
1600 ROSH 6618 E5
SR-25A Northern Blvd E
29-00 QENS 6718 D6
SR-25B
10 EWLS 6724 E4
10 QENS 6723 B7
10 WLPK 6724 E4
100 NHmT 6723 E6
229-01 QENS 6826 E1
235-30 QENS 6827 A1
300 MNLA 6724 D5
1600 NHmT 6724 B5
SR-25B Hillside Av
10 EWLS 6724 E4
10 WLPK 6724 E4
100 NHmT 6723 E6
229-01 QENS 6826 E1
235-30 QENS 6827 A1
247-00 QENS 6723 B7
300 MNLA 6724 D5
1500 NHmT 6724 B5
SR-25B E Williston Av
10 EWLS 6724 E4
10 WLPK 6724 E4
SR-27
- BKLN 6922 D4
- BKLN 6924 E3
- BKLN 6925 B2
10 BKLN 6923 A6
SR-27
10 ELIZ 6917 E3
10 LNBK 6929 A4
10 NWRK 6817 C3
10 RKVC 6929 D4
10 VLYS 6928 D4
87-01 QENS 6925 E3
113-01 QENS 6926 C3
155-00 QENS 6927 A3
200 LNBK 6928 E4
245-00 QENS 6928 A3
248-00 HmpT 6928 A3
700 ELIZ 6918 A1
700 LNDN 6917 B5
700 ROSL 6917 B5
900 ELIZ 6817 A7
SR-27 E 5th St
10 BKLN 6922 E6
SR-27 N Broad St
200 ELIZ 6917 E3
SR-27 Caton Av
500 BKLN 6922 E6
800 BKLN 6923 C5
SR-27 Cherry St
10 ELIZ 6917 D4
SR-27 Church Av
600 BKLN 6922 E6
SR-27 N Conduit Av
100-00 QENS 6925 E3
113-01 QENS 6926 C3
152-01 QENS 6927 C3
SR-27 S Conduit Av
- QENS 6925 D3
102-01 QENS 6926 A3
155-00 QENS 6927 A3
SR-27 Coney Island Av
300 BKLN 6923 A6
SR-27 Frelinghuysen Av
10 NWRK 6817 C3
900 ELIZ 6817 A7
SR-27 Linden Blvd
- BKLN 6925 B2
- QENS 6925 C2
10 BKLN 6923 B5
800 BKLN 6924 A5
SR-27 Nassau Expwy
- QENS 6925 D3
SR-27 Newark Av
500 ELIZ 6917 E2
700 ELIZ 6918 A1
900 ELIZ 6817 A7
1000 NWRK 6817 A7
SR-27 Poinier St
10 NWRK 6817 C3
SR-27 Prospect Expwy
- BKLN 6922 D4
SR-27 Rahway Av
100 ELIZ 6917 D4
700 LNDN 6917 C5
SR-27 E St. Georges Av
700 LNDN 6917 B5
700 ROSL 6917 B5
2100 ELIZ 6917 C5
SR-27 Sunrise Hwy
10 LNBK 6929 C4
10 RKVC 6929 D4
241-01 QENS 6927 E3
245-00 QENS 6928 A3
248-00 HmpT 6928 A3
248-00 VLYS 6928 A3
800 LNBK 6928 E4
SR-27 E Sunrise Hwy
10 VLYS 6928 D4
200 LNBK 6928 E4
SR-27 W Sunrise Hwy
10 VLYS 6928 D4
600 HmpT 6928 A3
700 QENS 6928 A3
SR-27 Westfield Av
10 ELIZ 6917 D3
SR-28
100 ELIZ 6917 D3
200 ROSP 6917 A3
SR-28 Westfield Av
100 ELIZ 6917 D3
900 ROSP 6917 B3
SR-28 E Westfield Av
200 ROSP 6917 A3
400 ELIZ 6917 A3
SR-35
- SAMB 7205 A7
10 PTHA 7114 C6
10 WbgT 7114 C6
200 PTHA 7205 B3
7000 SRVL 7205 A6
SR-35 Amboy Av
100 WbgT 7114 C6
SR-35 Convery Blvd
10 PTHA 7114 C5
10 WbgT 7114 C6
200 PTHA 7205 B3
SR-35 Main St
- SRVL 7205 A5
SR-35 St. Georges Av
700 WbgT 7114 B3
SR-35 Victory Br
- PTHA 7205 B4
- SRVL 7205 B4
SR-63
- FTLE 6611 C1
- PALP 6611 C1
10 FRVW 6611 C3
10 NBgT 6611 B4
10 PALP 6502 D6
300 RDGF 6611 C1
500 FTLE 6502 D6
SR-63 Bergen Blvd
- FTLE 6611 C1
- PALP 6611 C1
10 FRVW 6611 C3
10 NBgT 6611 B4
10 PALP 6502 D6
300 RDGF 6611 C1
500 FTLE 6502 D6
SR-67
1100 FTLE 6502 E7
1400 FTLE 103 A5
1400 FTLE 6503 A5
SR-67 Lemoine Av
1500 FTLE 103 B1
1500 FTLE 6503 A5
SR-67 Palisade Av
1100 FTLE 6502 E7
1400 FTLE 103 A5
1400 FTLE 6503 A6

New York City/5 Borough Street Index

STREET
Block City Map# Grid

SR-67 Schlosser St
1600 FTLE 103 A4
1600 FTLE 6503 A6
SR-81
- ELIZ 6918 C2
SR-82
600 UnnT 6917 C1
1100 UnnT 6816 C7
SR-82 Morris Av
600 UnnT 6917 C1
1100 UnnT 6816 C7
SR-93
10 LEON 6502 D2
10 PALP 6502 B6
400 EGLD 6502 D2
500 RDGF 6611 B1
600 RDGF 6502 B7
SR-93 Grand Av
10 LEON 6502 D2
10 PALP 6502 B6
400 EGLD 6502 D2
500 RDGF 6611 B1
600 RDGF 6502 B7
SR-100
10 GrbT 6049 E7
10 MtPT 6049 E5
10 WHPL 6167 E1
100 WHPL 6168 A1
400 GrbT 6167 A7
900 YNKR 6280 C7
900 YNKR 6394 C1
1000 GrbT 6281 A1
1100 YNKR 6281 A1
SR-100 Bradhurst Av
- GrbT 6049 C3
10 MtPT 6049 E5
SR-100 Central Av
100 WHPL 6167 E1
100 WHPL 6168 A1
500 GrbT 6167 D2
SR-100 Central Park Av
400 GrbT 6167 A7
900 YNKR 6280 C7
900 YNKR 6394 C1
1000 GrbT 6281 A1
1100 YNKR 6281 A1
SR-100 Grasslands Rd
10 GrbT 6049 E4
10 MtPT 6049 E4
SR-100 Hillside Av
10 GrbT 6049 D7
700 MtPT 6049 E4
SR-100 Hillside Av S
10 GrbT 6049 D7
SR-100 Tarrytown Rd
- WHPL 6168 A1
10 GrbT 6049 E7
10 GrbT 6167 E1
10 WHPL 6167 E1
SR-100A
10 GrbT 6167 B1
100 GrbT 6049 C7
300 EMFD 6049 C6
1100 MtPT 6049 C3
SR-100A W Hartsdale Av
10 GrbT 6167 B1
SR-100A Knollwood Rd
10 GrbT 6167 B1
100 GrbT 6049 C7
300 EMFD 6049 C6
1100 MtPT 6049 C3
SR-100B
10 GrbT 6049 D7
200 GrbT 6167 C1
800 GrbT 6166 E1
SR-100B Dobbs Ferry Rd
10 GrbT 6049 D7
200 GrbT 6167 C1
800 GrbT 6166 E1
SR-100B Tarrytown Rd
200 GrbT 6049 D7
SR-100C
10 GrbT 6049 B3
10 MtPT 6049 B3
SR-100C Grasslands Rd
10 GrbT 6049 B3
10 MtPT 6049 B3
SR-101
10 FLHL 6618 A3
10 MNPK 6618 B6
10 ROSE 6618 B6
300 NHmT 6618 A3
1200 NHmT 6617 E1
1300 NHmT 6508 E7
1300 SNPT 6508 E7
SR-101 Port Washington Blvd
10 FLHL 6618 A3
10 MNPK 6618 B6
10 ROSE 6618 B6
300 NHmT 6618 A3
1200 NHmT 6617 E1
1300 NHmT 6508 E7
1300 SNPT 6508 E7
SR-119
- EMFD 6048 E5
10 EMFD 6049 C6
10 GrbT 6049 E7
10 GrbT 6167 E1
10 TYTN 6048 E5
10 WHPL 6167 E1
10 WHPL 6168 A2
400 GrbT 6048 D4
SR-119 Armory Pl
- WHPL 6168 B1
SR-119 N Broadway
10 WHPL 6168 B1
SR-119 S Broadway
10 WHPL 6168 B1
SR-119 Hamilton Av
10 WHPL 6168 A1
SR-119 Main St
10 WHPL 6168 A2
SR-119 E Main St
- GrbT 6049 C7
10 EMFD 6049 C6
SR-119 W Main St
10 EMFD 6049 A5
SR-119 Tarrytown Rd
10 GrbT 6049 E7
10 GrbT 6167 E1
10 WHPL 6167 E1
10 WHPL 6168 A2
SR-119 Tarrytwn-White Plns Rd
- EMFD 6048 E5
- GrbT 6048 E5
SR-119 Westchester Av
10 WHPL 6168 B1
SR-119 White Plains Rd
10 TYTN 6048 E5
400 GrbT 6048 D4
SR-120
- CARL 6610 A3
- ERTH 6610 A3
10 CARL 6609 D1
10 ERTH 6609 D1
10 NoCT 6051 B1
10 RYE 6283 E1
10 RYE 6284 A1
100 RYE 6170 A7
200 HRSN 6169 D5
200 RYE 6169 E7
3000 HRSN 6051 B7
SR-120 King St
10 NoCT 6051 B1
SR-120 Paterson Plank Rd
10 CARL 6609 D1
10 ERTH 6609 D1
300 CARL 6610 A3
300 ERTH 6610 A3
SR-120 Purchase St
- NoCT 6051 B1
10 RYE 6283 E1
10 RYE 6284 A1
100 RYE 6170 A7
200 HRSN 6169 D5
200 RYE 6169 E7
3000 HRSN 6051 B7
SR-120 Westchester Av
- HRSN 6169 D5
SR-120A
- NoCT 6051 B1
10 PTCH 6170 C6
500 RYEB 6169 E5
500 RYEB 6170 A5
800 GrwT 6170 B3
1000 GrwT 6051 B1
1000 RYEB 6051 E6
3000 HRSN 6169 E5
SR-120A King St
- NoCT 6051 B1
10 PTCH 6170 C6
700 RYEB 6170 B3
800 GrwT 6170 B3
1000 GrwT 6051 E6
1000 RYEB 6051 E6
SR-120A N Pearl St
10 PTCH 6170 B6
SR-120A Westchester Av
10 PTCH 6170 C6
500 RYEB 6169 E5
500 RYEB 6170 A5
3000 HRSN 6169 E5
SR-124
1400 IrvT 6816 A2
1400 MplT 6816 A2
SR-124 Springfield Av
1400 IrvT 6816 A2
1400 MplT 6816 A2
SR-125
10 MrnT 6282 D7
10 MrnT 6396 D1
10 NRCH 6282 B6
10 SCDL 6168 B3
10 SCDL 6282 B6
10 WHPL 6168 B2
SR-125 Mamaroneck Av
10 WHPL 6168 B2
SR-125 Old Mamaroneck Rd
10 WHPL 6168 B3
300 SCDL 6168 B6
SR-125 Palmer Av
10 SCDL 6168 B7
10 SCDL 6282 A1
SR-125 Secor Rd
100 SCDL 6168 B3
200 WHPL 6168 B6
SR-125 Weaver St
10 MrnT 6282 D7
10 MrnT 6396 D1
10 NRCH 6282 B6
10 SCDL 6282 B6
SR-127
10 HRSN 6283 B4
10 MRNK 6283 B4
10 WHPL 6168 E4
200 HRSN 6169 C7
800 WHPL 6169 A5
SR-127 Harrison Av
10 HRSN 6283 B4
10 MRNK 6283 B4
SR-127 Keeler Av
900 MRNK 6283 A5
SR-127 North St
10 WHPL 6168 C2
200 HRSN 6169 C7
200 HRSN 6283 B4
800 WHPL 6169 A5
SR-127 Westchester Av
100 WHPL 6168 E4
SR-139
- JSYC 6715 E7
- JSYC 6820 B1
10 JSYC 6716 A7
SR-139 Hoboken Av
- JSYC 6820 B1
SR-139 Observer Hwy
10 JSYC 6716 A7
SR-139 State Hwy
- JSYC 6716 A7
- JSYC 6820 B1
SR-184
10 PTHA 7205 B1
10 WbgT 7114 A7
10 WbgT 7205 B1
SR-184 Pfeiffer Blvd
600 PTHA 7205 B1
700 WbgT 7205 B1
SR-184 W Pond Rd
10 PTHA 7205 B1
10 WbgT 7114 A7
10 WbgT 7205 B1
SR-185
- JSYC 6819 C7
- JSYC 6920 C1
SR-303
10 NVLE 6164 C4
10 OrgT 6164 C1
SR-340
10 OrgT 6164 E2
10 PRMT 6164 E2
800 RCKL 6164 E2
SR-340 Orangeburg Rd
100 OrgT 6164 D1
300 PRMT 6164 E2
SR-340 Piermont Av
10 OrgT 6164 E2
10 PRMT 6164 E2
SR-340 Valentine Av
400 OrgT 6164 E2
400 PRMT 6164 E2
SR-439
10 ELIZ 6917 D5
10 HlsT 6917 D2
10 UnnT 6917 D2
1300 ELIZ 6918 A1
SR-439 Bayway Av
500 ELIZ 6917 E6
SR-439 Elmora Av
10 ELIZ 6917 E1
400 UnnT 6917 C2
SR-439 S Elmora Av
900 ELIZ 6917 D5
SR-439 North Av
10 ELIZ 6917 E1
10 HlsT 6917 D2
10 UnnT 6917 D2
1300 ELIZ 6918 A1
SR-440
- BAYN 6819 A6
- BAYN 6919 E4
- BAYN 6920 A4
- JSYC 6920 C1
- PTHA 7205 E2
- PTHA 7206 A2
- STNL 6919 B7
- STNL 7018 E2
- STNL 7019 B1
- STNL 7115 D6
- STNL 7116 A4
- STNL 7206 D1
- WbgT 7205 A2
100 JSYC 6819 A6
SR-440 Bayonne Br
- BAYN 6919 C5
- STNL 6919 C6
SR-440 Korean War Vet Pkwy
- STNL 7206 C1
SR-440 Outerbridge Cross
- PTHA 7205 D1
- PTHA 7206 A2
- STNL 7206 B1
SR-440 Pearl Harbor Mem Expwy
- STNL 7018 B7
- STNL 7115 D6
- STNL 7116 A4
- STNL 7206 D1
SR-440 Staten Island Expwy
- STNL 7018 E2
- STNL 7019 A3
SR-440 Willowbrook Expwy
- STNL 6919 B7
- STNL 7019 A4
SR-448
10 SYHW 6048 C1
SR-448 Bedford Rd
10 SYHW 6048 C1
SR-495
- MHTN 111 B7
- MHTN 115 D1
- MHTN 116 A2
- MHTN 6717 C5
- NBgT 6716 E4
- UNCT 6716 D2
- WhkT 111 A6
- WhkT 6716 E3
- WhkT 6717 A3
SR-495 Dyer Av
- MHTN 115 E2
- MHTN 6717 C5
SR-495 Lincoln Tun
- MHTN 111 B7
- MHTN 115 E2
- MHTN 6717 C5
- WhkT 111 B7
- WhkT 6716 E3
- WhkT 6717 A3
SR-495 Lincoln Tunnel Expwy
- MHTN 115 E2
- MHTN 116 A2
- MHTN 6717 C5
SR-878
- HmpT 7027 E5
- LWRN 7027 E3
SR-878 Nassau Expwy
- HmpT 7027 D3
- LWRN 7027 D3
US-1
- BRNX 104 D5
- BRNX 105 A5
- BRNX 6503 E6
- FTLE 103 B3
- FTLE 6503 B5
- JSYC 6715 D7
- JSYC 6819 C1
- KRNY 6818 E1
- KRNY 6819 B1
- MHTN 103 E4
- MHTN 104 A4
- MHTN 6503 B5
- NWRK 6818 D1
- WbgT 7114 A3
10 FRVW 6611 B3
10 LNDN 7017 B1
10 MRNK 6283 D4
10 MrnT 6396 B3
10 NBgT 6611 A4
10 NRCH 6396 A4
10 PTCH 6170 C5
10 RYE 6283 E2
100 MRNK 6282 E7
200 GrwT 6170 D4
200 JSYC 6716 A7
300 BRNX 6504 C6
300 RDGF 6611 A2
400 NRCH 6395 E5
500 NBgT 6716 D1
600 RDGF 6502 B7
700 ELIZ 6917 E5
700 ELIZ 6918 B1
700 LNDN 6917 C7
900 PLMM 6395 D6
1000 ELIZ 6817 B7
1000 NWRK 6817 B7
1000 RYE 6284 A1
1200 MrnT 6282 E7
1200 RYE 6170 A7
1400 FTLE 6502 E5
1400 PALP 6502 D6
1500 LEON 6502 D5
2000 LRMT 6396 D1
2200 BRNX 6505 B4
4000 BRNX 6506 A1
4200 BRNX 6395 A7
4800 NBgT 6610 D7
US-1 Bergen Blvd
1400 FTLE 6502 E5
1500 LEON 6502 D5
US-1 Boston Rd
2200 BRNX 6505 A5
4000 BRNX 6506 A1
4200 BRNX 6395 A7
4300 PLMM 6395 A7
US-1 Boston Post Rd
10 MRNK 6283 B5
10 RYE 6283 E2
100 PTCH 6170 B6
1000 RYE 6284 A1
1200 MrnT 6282 D7
1200 MrnT 6396 D1
1200 RYE 6170 A7
2000 LRMT 6396 D1
4300 BRNX 6395 A7
4300 PLMM 6395 A7
4800 NRCH 6395 C6
US-1 E Boston Post Rd
- RYE 6283 B5
100 MRNK 6283 A6
US-1 W Boston Post Rd
100 MRNK 6282 E7
1200 MrnT 6282 E7
US-1 Broad Av
- RDGF 6611 B2
10 FRVW 6611 B3
10 NBgT 6611 A4
10 PALP 6502 B7
800 RDGF 6502 B7
US-1 Broad Av N
500 RDGF 6611 A1
600 RDGF 6502 B7
800 PALP 6502 B7
US-1 Broad Av S
300 FRVW 6611 B2
300 RDGF 6611 A2
US-1 Broadway
100 JSYC 6715 E7
US-1 Bronx & Pelham Pkwy E
- BRNX 6505 A5
US-1 Bronx & Pelham Pkwy W
- BRNX 6505 A5
US-1 Carlton St
700 ELIZ 6917 D5
700 LNDN 6917 D5
US-1 Cross Bronx Expwy
- BRNX 104 D5
- BRNX 105 C5
- BRNX 6503 E6
- BRNX 6504 A6
- MHTN 104 D5
- MHTN 6503 E6
US-1 E Edgar Rd
10 LNDN 7017 B1
800 LNDN 6917 C7
2500 ELIZ 6917 D5
US-1 W Edgar Rd
10 LNDN 7017 A2
US-1 E Fordham Rd
- BRNX 6505 B4
300 BRNX 6504 D4
US-1 George Washington Br
- FTLE 103 D3
- FTLE 6503 B5
- MHTN 103 E4
- MHTN 104 A4
- MHTN 6503 B5
US-1 Grand Av
500 RDGF 6611 B1
US-1 Hillside Av
10 GrwT 6170 C4
10 PTCH 6170 C4
US-1 Huguenot St
10 NRCH 6396 A4
100 NRCH 6395 E4
US-1 Jansen Av
- WbgT 7114 A4
US-1 Lincoln Hwy
- JSYC 6819 B2
- KRNY 6818 E1
- NWRK 6818 E1
100 KRNY 6819 A1
US-1 Main St
100 NRCH 6396 B3
400 NRCH 6395 E5
900 PLMM 6395 D6
US-1 E Main St
10 MrnT 6396 B3
10 NRCH 6396 B3
US-1 N Main St
10 PTCH 6170 C5
US-1 S Main St
10 PTCH 6170 C6
US-1 New Jersey Tpk
- FTLE 103 B3
- FTLE 6502 E5
- FTLE 6503 A5
US-1 Pulaski Skwy
- JSYC 6715 D7
- JSYC 6716 A7
- JSYC 6819 C1
- KRNY 6818 E1
- KRNY 6819 B1
- NWRK 6818 D1
US-1 Putnam Av
10 PTCH 6170 C4
US-1 W Putnam Av
200 GrwT 6170 D4
700 PTCH 6170 D4
US-1 Raymond Blvd
- KRNY 6818 E1
10 NWRK 6818 D1
US-1 Spring St
- ELIZ 6917 E5
100 ELIZ 6918 A3
1000 ELIZ 6817 B7
1000 NWRK 6817 B7
US-1 Tonnele Av
200 JSYC 6716 A7
800 NBgT 6716 B4
US-1 Tonnelle Av
- JSYC 6716 B4
500 NBgT 6716 D1
4800 NBgT 6610 D7
7500 NBgT 6611 A5
9100 FRVW 6611 A4
US-1 Wallis Av
100 JSYC 6715 E7
US-1 Webster Av
1700 BRNX 105 E4
1700 BRNX 6504 C6
US-9
- ELIZ 6817 B7
- FTLE 103 B3
- FTLE 6503 B5
- JSYC 6819 C2
- KRNY 6818 E1
- KRNY 6819 B1
- MHTN 103 E4
- MHTN 104 A4
- NWRK 6817 B7
- NWRK 6818 A4
- SAMB 7205 A7
- WbgT 7114 B4
- WbgT 7205 A1
10 DBSF 6165 E5
10 FRVW 6611 B3
10 HAOH 6165 E7
10 HAOH 6279 E1
10 IRVN 6048 B7
10 IRVN 6166 A4
10 LNDN 7017 A2
10 NBgT 6611 A4
10 PALP 6502 C6
10 TYTN 6048 B3
10 YNKR 6279 D6
10 YNKR 6393 C1
100 ELIZ 6918 A3
100 JSYC 6715 D7
100 SYHW 6048 B1
200 DBSF 6166 A3
200 JSYC 6716 A7
300 RDGF 6611 A2
500 NBgT 6716 D1
600 BRNX 6393 C5
600 RDGF 6502 B7
700 ELIZ 6917 E5
700 LNDN 6917 C7
700 MHTN 6503 E3
1400 FTLE 6502 E5
1500 LEON 6502 D5
4600 MHTN 101 D7
4800 MHTN 102 A6
4800 MHTN 6504 A3
4800 NBgT 6610 D7
5200 BRNX 102 E1
5800 BRNX 6504 C1
6000 SRVL 7205 A7
US-9 TRK
- JSYC 6716 A7
- JSYC 6819 C2
- KRNY 6818 E1
10 NWRK 6818 E1
100 JSYC 6715 D7
100 KRNY 6819 D1
US-9 W 178th St
700 MHTN 104 B4
700 MHTN 6503 D6
US-9 W 179th St
700 MHTN 104 C4
700 MHTN 6503 D6
US-9 Bergen Blvd
1400 FTLE 6502 E5
1500 LEON 6502 D5
US-9 Broad Av
- RDGF 6611 B2
10 FRVW 6611 B3
10 NBgT 6611 A4
10 PALP 6502 B7
800 RDGF 6502 B7
US-9 Broad Av N
500 RDGF 6611 A1
600 RDGF 6502 B7
800 PALP 6502 B7
US-9 Broad Av S
300 FRVW 6611 B2
300 RDGF 6611 A2
US-9 Broadway
10 DBSF 6165 E5
10 HAOH 6165 E5
100 JSYC 6715 E7
200 DBSF 6166 A4
600 IRVN 6166 A3
4200 MHTN 104 D1
4200 MHTN 6503 E3
4600 MHTN 101 E6
4800 MHTN 102 A6
4800 MHTN 6504 A3
5800 BRNX 102 E1
5800 BRNX 6504 C1
5900 BRNX 6393 C5
6700 YNKR 6393 C4
US-9 TRK Broadway
100 JSYC 6715 E7
US-9 N Broadway
- HAOH 6279 E2
10 IRVN 6048 B7
10 TYTN 6048 B2
10 YNKR 6393 C1
100 SYHW 6048 B1
100 YNKR 6279 D6
600 HAOH 6165 E7
US-9 S Broadway
10 HAOH 6279 E2
10 IRVN 6166 A4
10 TYTN 6048 B3
10 YNKR 6279 E2
10 YNKR 6393 C2
200 DBSF 6166 A3
600 BRNX 6393 C4
800 IRVN 6048 B6
US-9 Carlton St
700 ELIZ 6917 D5
700 LNDN 6917 D5
US-9 Cross Bronx Expwy
- MHTN 104 B4
- MHTN 6503 C6
US-9 E Edgar Rd
10 LNDN 7017 B1
1600 LNDN 6917 C7
2500 ELIZ 6917 D5
US-9 W Edgar Rd
10 LNDN 7017 A2
US-9 George Washington Br
- FTLE 103 D3
- FTLE 6503 B5
- MHTN 103 E4
- MHTN 104 A4
- MHTN 6503 B5
US-9 Grand Av
500 RDGF 6611 B1
US-9 Lincoln Hwy
- JSYC 6819 C2
- KRNY 6818 E1
- NWRK 6818 E1
100 KRNY 6819 D1
US-9 TRK Lincoln Hwy
- JSYC 6819 C2
- KRNY 6818 E1
- NWRK 6818 E1
100 KRNY 6819 D1
US-9 Manor House Sq
10 YNKR 6393 C1
US-9 New Broadway
10 HAOH 6279 E2
US-9 New Jersey Tpk
- FTLE 103 B3
- FTLE 6502 E5
- FTLE 6503 A5
US-9 Old Broadway
100 HAOH 6279 E1
US-9 Prospect St
10 YNKR 6393 C1
US-9 Pulaski Skwy
- JSYC 6715 D7
- JSYC 6716 A7
- JSYC 6819 C1
- KRNY 6818 E1
- KRNY 6819 B1
- NWRK 6818 D1
US-9 Raymond Blvd
- KRNY 6818 E1
10 NWRK 6818 E1
US-9 TRK Raymond Blvd
- KRNY 6818 E1
10 NWRK 6818 E1
US-9 Riverdale Av
10 YNKR 6393 C1
US-9 Spring St
- ELIZ 6917 E5
100 ELIZ 6918 A3
US-9 Thomas A Edison Br
- SRVL 7205 A4
- WbgT 7205 A4
US-9 Tonnele Av
200 JSYC 6716 A7
800 NBgT 6716 B4
US-9 Tonnelle Av
- JSYC 6716 B4
500 NBgT 6716 D1
4800 NBgT 6610 D7
7500 NBgT 6611 A5
9100 FRVW 6611 A4
US-9 Wallis Av
100 JSYC 6715 E7
US-9 TRK Wallis Av
100 JSYC 6715 E7
US-9 Warburton Av
10 YNKR 6393 C1
US-9 Wells Av
10 YNKR 6393 C1
US-9W
- ALPN 6278 E7
- ALPN 6279 A4
- ALPN 6392 E1
- OrgT 6164 E2
10 EGLC 6503 B4
10 PRMT 6164 E1
100 ALPN 6165 A7
100 OrgT 6165 A5
400 PRMT 6165 A1
500 EGLC 101 A1
500 EGLC 6392 C7
900 TFLY 6392 E1
2100 FTLE 103 A1
2100 FTLE 6502 E5
2100 FTLE 6503 A4
US-9W Fletcher Av
2100 FTLE 103 A1
2100 FTLE 6502 E5
2100 FTLE 6503 A4
US-9W Highland Av
10 PRMT 6164 E1
100 ALPN 6165 B6
100 OrgT 6165 A5
400 PRMT 6165 A1
US-9W Lemoine Av
- FTLE 103 B1
- FTLE 6503 B3
2400 EGLC 6503 B4
US-9W Palisades Blvd
- ALPN 6165 A7
- ALPN 6278 E7
- ALPN 6279 A1
- ALPN 6392 E2
- OrgT 6165 B6
- TFLY 6392 D3
US-9W Palisades InterSt Pkwy
- FTLE 103 A1
- FTLE 6503 A4
US-9W Sylvan Av
10 EGLC 6503 B4
10 FTLE 6503 B4
500 EGLC 101 A1
500 EGLC 6392 C7
900 TFLY 6392 D6
US-9W Sylvan Blvd
- ALPN 6392 E1
- EGLC 6392 D6
- TFLY 6392 E1
US-22
- NWRK 6817 A5
10 HlsT 6816 E5
10 NWRK 6816 E5
600 UnnT 6816 E6
US-46
- FTLE 103 A3
- FTLE 6503 A5
- HSBH 6500 E3
- HSBH 6501 B4
- RDFP 6502 B6
10 RDFP 6501 E6
10 RDGF 6502 B6
200 SHkT 6501 C5
300 LODI 6500 D1
300 SdBT 6500 D1
400 LFRY 6501 B5
500 TETB 6501 B5
1400 FTLE 6502 D5
1400 PALP 6502 D6
1500 LEON 6502 D5
US-46 Bergen Blvd
1400 FTLE 6502 E4
1500 LEON 6502 D5
US-46 New Jersey Tpk
- FTLE 103 A3
- FTLE 6502 E5
- FTLE 6503 A5
US-46 Sylvan Av
10 LFRY 6501 D5
US-46 Winant Av
10 LFRY 6501 D5
10 RDFP 6501 E6

A

A St
10 WbgT 7115 A3
1200 HmpT 6827 E6
Aaron Ln
10 STNL 7115 E5
Abbett St
10 JSYC 6716 B7
Abbey Ct
10 BKLN 7024 A7
Abbey Dr
10 WHPL 6050 C6
Abbey Pl
10 YNKR 6279 D5
Abbey Rd
10 MNPK 6618 A6
10 STNL 7117 A4
Abbey Rd N
400 MNPK 6618 A5
Abbey Close
10 NRCH 6281 E1
10 NRCH 6282 A1
Abbeyville Ln
10 GrbT 6049 B7
Abbi Rd
- CART 7115 D2
Abbie Ct
10 GTBG 6611 C7
Abbotsford Av
10 EORG 6712 C5
10 NWRK 6712 C5
Abbott Av
10 GrbT 6049 B4
10 PALP 6502 C7
10 RDGF 6502 C7
300 RDGF 6611 B2
Abbott Blvd
700 CLFP 6611 D1
800 FTLE 6611 D1
1100 FTLE 6502 E7
Abbott Pl
10 NARL 6714 C1
Abbott Rd
400 QENS 6616 A6
Abbott St
10 BRNX 6394 C5
10 MTVN 6394 C5
10 STNL 7021 B4
10 YNKR 6279 E4
Abby Pl
10 STNL 7020 B1
Abby St
10 BAYN 6920 A1
Abeel St
10 YNKR 6393 C4
Abend St
10 LFRY 6501 D7
Abendroth Av
10 PTCH 6170 C6
Abendroth Pl
10 PTCH 6170 C5
Aberdeen Rd
10 ELIZ 6917 E1
10 NHmT 6724 A5
180-00 QENS 6825 E2
186-00 QENS 6826 A2
Aberdeen St
10 BKLN 6924 B1
10 MLVN 6929 C3
Aberdeen Tower Wy
10 ALPN 6278 D4
Aberfoyle Rd
10 NRCH 6395 D1
Abigail Adams Av
159-00 QENS 6825 C3
Abingdon Av
10 STNL 7117 A5
Abingdon Ct
10 STNL 7117 A3
Abingdon Ln
10 NRCH 6281 E2
Abingdon Rd
82-00 QENS 6824 E4
85-00 QENS 6825 A5
Abinger Pl
10 NWRK 6712 C6
Abington Av
10 ARDY 6166 E5
300 BlmT 6713 B2
300 NWRK 6713 C2
400 EORG 6713 B2
Abington Av E
10 NWRK 6713 D3
Abington Av W
100 NWRK 6713 D3
300 BlmT 6713 C2
Able St
10 WbgT 7114 A2
Abner Pl
10 YNKR 6394 B4
Aborn Av
600 WbgT 7114 C3
Abott Wy
10 IRVN 6166 A2
Abrams Pl
10 ERKY 6929 B6
10 HmpT 6929 A6
10 HmpT 7027 D3
10 LNBK 6929 B6
Absecon Rd
800 MHTN 6820 E7
Acacia Av
100 STNL 7117 A5
Acacia Ter
10 NRCH 6396 A5
Academy Av
10 STNL 7206 B4
Academy Ln
10 CRSK 6278 C7
10 DMRT 6278 C7
Academy Pl
10 STNL 6920 D5
100 HmpT 6828 E4
Academy Rd
800 HmpT 6928 B7
Academy St
- STNL 7206 B4
10 JSYC 6820 A1
10 NWRK 6713 D7
10 SOrT 6712 A6
200 JSYC 6819 D1
400 MHTN 105 A1
400 MHTN 6504 A4
500 MHTN 101 E6
500 MHTN 102 A7
500 MHTN 6503 E3
2700 HmpT 6929 E6
Acapulco St
10 ATLB 7027 E7
Access Rd
- BAYN 6920 B2
500 HmpT 6828 C6
700 HlsT 6816 C4
1800 HmpT 6929 D6
Accommando Pl
10 CLFP 108 A1
10 CLFP 6611 D5
Achilles St
10 DMRT 6278 A5
Acker Dr
10 RYEB 6170 A3
Ackerman Pl
10 CRSK 6278 B7
10 EchT 6281 C2
10 PALP 6502 C5
Ackerman St
10 STNL 7117 B6
Ackerson St
10 HKSK 6501 B2
Ackley Av
10 HmpT 6929 A2
10 MLVN 6929 A2
Ackley Ct
10 HmpT 6929 A2
10 MLVN 6929 A2
Acme Pl
10 HlsT 6816 C6
Acme St
- ROSL 6917 C4
100 ELIZ 6917 C4
Acorn Ct
10 STNL 7115 E5
Acorn Ln
10 NRCH 6396 B1
Acorn Pl
10 BRNX 6615 C4
10 LNBK 6929 A4
Acorn Rd
10 ERKY 6929 B7
10 SECS 6610 B5
Acorn St
10 STNL 7117 D3
Acorn Ter
10 NRCH 6396 A3
Acorn Ponds Dr
10 NHLS 6724 B3
Ada Dr
10 STNL 7019 A2
100 STNL 7018 E2
Ada Pl
10 STNL 7020 C2
Adair Ct
10 MLVN 6929 A1
Adair St
125-00 QENS 6927 C1
Adam Ct
10 STNL 7019 A7
Adam Pl
2500 UNCT 6716 D3
Adam St
200 FRVW 6611 B2
Adam Clayton Powell Jr Blvd
2500 MHTN 107 B5
2500 MHTN 6612 D3
Adam Mott Ln
10 KNGP 6617 A3
Adams Av
10 PTCH 6170 B4
10 STNL 7020 A7
100 STNL 7118 B1
300 HmpT 6828 D6
400 ELIZ 6918 B1
600 PTHA 7114 C7
Adams Ct
100 EDGW 108 C1
100 EDGW 6611 D4
Adams Dr
10 CRSK 6278 C7
10 CRSK 6392 D1
Adams Ln
100 HWTN 7028 D2
200 HBPK 7028 D2
Adams Pl
10 GrbT 6049 E6
10 HRSN 6169 B7
10 LODI 6500 C3
10 YNKR 6279 D5
600 HmpT 6828 D7
2200 BRNX 6504 D5
Adams Rd
200 ERKY 6929 A7
200 HWTH 6929 A7
Adams St
10 BKLN 121 B2
10 BKLN 6821 D5
10 ERKY 6929 B7
10 FLPK 6827 D2
10 GDNC 6828 A3
10 HBKN 6716 D6
10 HRPK 6164 A6
10 IrvT 6816 C1
10 KRNY 6715 A7
10 KRNY 6819 A1
10 LFRY 6501 C7
10 LNDN 6917 C5
10 MNCH 6501 C7
10 MTVN 6394 E4
10 NHmT 6617 D2
10 NRCH 6396 A4
10 NRWD 6164 A6
10 NWRK 6818 A1
10 SCLF 6509 E6
100 NHPK 6828 A2
200 NWRK 6817 E3
600 ROSL 6917 C5
1300 HmpT 6827 D4
1500 SFPK 6827 D4
1600 BRNX 6505 A7
5400 WNYK 6610 E7
6000 WNYK 6611 A7
6700 GTBG 6611 A6
7100 NBgT 6611 A6
Adamson St
10 WLTN 6500 A5
Addee Cir
10 MrnT 6282 B6
Addington Dr
10 GrbT 6166 C7
Addison Av
10 RTFD 6609 A2
Addison Dr
700 HmpT 7028 E2
Addison Pl
10 VLYS 6928 B4
Addison St
10 LRMT 6396 C2
700 HmpT 7028 B1
Addyman Sq
400 ARDY 6166 D4
Adee Av
10 BRNX 6615 B3
600 BRNX 6505 C3
Adee St
10 PTCH 6170 C6
Adela Pl
10 MtPT 6050 A2
Adelaide Av
10 STNL 7117 D3
800 WbgT 7114 C2
Adelaide Pl
10 EDGW 6611 E3
Adelaide Rd
174-00 QENS 6826 A6
Adelaide St
10 FLPK 6827 C2
10 RYE 6284 A3
Adelberg Ln
300 CDHT 7028 C3
400 CDHT 7027 C2
Adele Av
10 CRSK 6278 A5
10 DMRT 6278 A5
Adele Ct
10 STNL 7020 D2
400 EGLD 6503 A3
1400 HmpT 6827 D7
Adele Ln
10 YNKR 6280 D6
Adele Rd
10 CDHT 7028 A2
10 HmpT 7028 A2
Adele St
10 STNL 7020 C6
700 HmpT 6828 B6
Adeline Pl
10 VLYS 6928 E4
Adelphi Av
10 HRSN 6283 B3
10 STNL 7206 C3
Adelphi St
10 BKLN 121 E5
10 BKLN 6821 E6
100 BKLN 6822 A7
100 ROSL 6917 A4
Adlai Cir
10 STNL 7116 D6
Adler Pl
- BRNX 6505 E3
- BRNX 6506 A3
10 BKLN 6824 A7
10 VLYS 6928 C2
Adlers Ln
10 STNL 7206 C4
Adlers Wy
2100 STNL 7206 E3
Adm George Dewey
- MHTN 120 B3
- MHTN 6821 B7
Admiral Av
64-00 QENS 6823 C4
Admiral Ct
10 BRNX 6614 C5
Admiral Ln
100 BRNX 6614 C5
Admiralty Lp
10 STNL 7207 A3
Admont Av
1000 HmpT 6828 A3
Adolphus Av
300 CLFP 6611 D4
Adonia St
600 HmpT 6828 B6
Adrian Av
10 MHTN 102 C4
10 MHTN 6504 B2
Adrian Cir
10 MrnT 6282 C4
Adrianne Ct
400 COrT 6712 C4
Adrianne Ln
10 STNL 7019 A2
Adrienne Pl
10 STNL 7117 B5
10 WHPL 6168 C6
Adult Dr
10 MNCH 6500 E7
10 MNCH 6501 A7

New York City/5 Borough Street Index

STREET
Block City Map# Grid

Aerie Ct
10 NHLS 6618 B7
Aetna Pl
10 MTVN 6395 B2
Aetna St
10 JSYC 6820 B4
Afton St
10 KRNY 6714 A4
Agar Av
10 NRCH 6396 B3
Agar Pl
10 SHKT 6501 C4
3200 BRNX 6506 A7
Agar St
- YNKR 6280 A6
10 YNKR 6279 E6
Agate Ct
10 BKLN 6923 D1
Agate Pl
10 NWRK 6713 E1
Agawam N
10 YNKR 6393 E5
Agawam S
10 YNKR 6393 E5
Agnes Cir
10 ARDY 6166 E4
Agnes Ct
1100 HmpT 6828 A7
Agnes Pl
10 STNL 7020 E7
Agnes St
10 BAYN 6919 E4
Agnew Pl
10 ERTH 6609 B1
10 RTFD 6609 B1
Agnola St
10 YNKR 6281 A2
Aguilar Av
155-00 QENS 6825 B1
Aida Ct
10 LODI 6500 E2
Aiken Wy
10 GrbT 6049 B7
Aileen B Ryan Ovl
10 BRNX 6505 C6
Ainslie St
10 BKLN 6822 C4
Ainsworth Av
10 STNL 7117 C5
Ainsworth St
300 LNDN 7017 A2
Airis Dr
- NWRK 6817 E5
Airport Rd
10 NoCT 6051 C2
100 RYEB 6051 C3
Aitken Pl
10 BKLN 121 A5
10 BKLN 6821 C6
Akron St
10 STNL 7019 A4
Alabama Av
10 BKLN 6924 C2
10 HmpT 7029 E4
Alabama Pl
10 STNL 7019 D2
Alabama St
10 LBCH 7028 E7
Aladdin Av
1600 NHmT 6724 B7
1600 NHPK 6724 A7
Alameda Av
240-00 QENS 6722 D3
Alameda Pl
10 MTVN 6395 A2
Alan Lp
10 STNL 7020 C5
Alan Pl
10 GrbT 6167 D1
500 HmpT 6828 C6
800 RDGF 6611 B1
3000 BRNX 6615 C4
Alan Ter
10 JSYC 6820 A1
Alan B Shepard Jr Pl
10 YNKR 6393 E4
Alaska St
10 GRFD 6500 A1
10 STNL 6919 E7
Alban St
10 STNL 6920 A6
Albany Av
10 BKLN 6923 D4
1500 BKLN 7023 D1
Albany Blvd
- CLST 6278 C2
10 ATLB 7027 E7
Albany Cres
3000 BRNX 102 E3
3000 BRNX 6504 C2
Albany Ct
400 WNYK 111 D1
400 WNYK 6611 C7
400 WNYK 6717 B1
Albany St
10 HmpT 6827 C7
10 MHTN 120 A1
10 MHTN 6821 A4
200 MHTN 118 A7
Albee Av
10 STNL 7116 C6
Albee Pl
10 WbgT 7114 A1
Albee Sq W
300 BKLN 121 C6
300 BKLN 6821 D7
Albemarle Pl
10 YNKR 6280 A5
Albemarle Rd
10 BKLN 6922 E6
200 WHPL 6168 B5
2100 BKLN 6923 B6
Albemarle Ter
2100 BKLN 6923 B6
Albermarle Av
10 NRCH 6396 A3
10 VLYS 6928 E3
100 VLYS 6929 A2
Albermarle Pl
500 CDHT 7027 D1
500 CDHT 7028 A1
Albermarle Rd
10 NHmT 6618 B7
400 CDHT 7028 A1

Albern Av
400 HmpT 6929 D7
Albert Av
10 NWRK 6714 C7
Albert Ct
10 KNGP 6616 E4
10 STNL 7018 E2
10 VLYS 6928 B3
Albert Pl
10 JSYC 6819 C6
10 NRCH 6395 D3
100 LWRN 7028 B6
Albert Rd
10 VLYS 6928 D3
93-00 QENS 6925 D2
Albert St
10 GRFD 6500 A1
10 MNCH 6501 B7
10 PTHA 7205 C1
10 STNL 7020 A3
10 WbgT 7114 C5
200 LODI 6500 D2
600 NHmT 6724 A7
600 NHPK 6724 A7
Alberta Av
10 STNL 7018 B7
2000 LNDN 6917 C5
2100 ELIZ 6917 C5
Albert Leonard Rd
10 NRCH 6282 A6
Albertson Av
10 NHmT 6724 E3
Albertson Pkwy
10 NHmT 6724 D2
Albin St
10 GLCV 6509 E5
10 SCLF 6509 E5
500 TnkT 6502 A2
Albion Av
7900 QENS 6719 D7
Albion Pl
10 STNL 6919 C7
10 STNL 7019 C1
Albon Rd
200 HWTH 6928 E7
200 HWTH 6929 A7
Albourne Av
400 STNL 7207 A1
500 STNL 7206 E1
Albourne Av E
10 STNL 7207 B1
Albright St
10 STNL 7020 C6
Albro Ln
10 LWRN 7028 C3
10 WHPL 6050 A7
Alcott Ct
10 TnkT 6502 B2
Alcott Pl
100 BRNX 6505 E3
Alcott St
10 STNL 7116 A5
Alda Rd
500 MRNK 6283 A7
Alden Av
10 HmpT 6827 B7
10 HmpT 6928 B1
10 YNKR 6280 D5
Alden Ct
10 MLVN 6929 C2
10 NRCH 6282 A2
Alden Ln
10 GrwT 6170 D3
10 NHmT 6618 A3
Alden Pk
- BRNX 6615 C2
Alden Pl
10 ARDY 6166 E3
10 BRXV 6394 E1
10 GrbT 6166 E3
10 MTVN 6394 B2
10 STNL 6920 C7
300 COrT 6712 D1
400 BRNX 6504 C6
Alden Rd
10 ERKY 6929 B6
10 GrwT 6170 D3
10 MrnT 6396 D1
100 HWTN 7028 D2
400 WbgT 7114 B2
Alden St
10 WLTN 6500 A5
300 COrT 6712 D1
400 WOrT 6712 D1
500 WbgT 7114 D4
Alden Ter
10 GrwT 6170 D3
10 PTCH 6170 B4
1300 UnnT 6816 B7
Alder Ln
10 BRXV 6281 B7
Alder St
10 JSYC 6819 B4
10 YNKR 6393 D2
Alderbrook Rd
10 BRNX 6393 B6
Aldershot Ln
100 NHmT 6618 A7
Alderton St
61-00 QENS 6824 B2
Alderwood Pl
10 STNL 7020 B5
Aldgate Dr E
10 NHLS 6618 A7
10 NHLS 6724 B1
Aldgate Dr W
10 NHLS 6618 A7
10 NHLS 6724 A1
Aldine St
- WbgT 7114 B4
10 NWRK 6816 E4
200 HlsT 6816 D4
Aldred Av
10 HmpT 6929 E6
10 RKVC 6929 E6
Aldrich St
10 YNKR 6394 D1
100 BRNX 6505 E3
Aldus St
900 BRNX 6613 D2
Alecia Av
219-00 QENS 6927 C2
Alemeda St
10 HmpT 7027 C3

Alex Cir
10 STNL 7021 A6
Alex Dr
10 WHPL 6168 C5
Alexander Av
10 BRNX 110 E1
10 BRNX 6612 E5
10 GrbT 6167 D2
10 HRSN 6283 B4
10 KRNY 6714 A5
10 LNBK 6929 B3
10 STNL 7116 D4
10 WHPL 6167 D2
10 YNKR 6394 A5
300 BRNX 107 E7
300 BRNX 6613 A4
400 LNDN 6917 C5
600 ROSL 6917 B5
1000 RDGF 6611 A1
Alexander Ct
10 JSYC 6819 A4
Alexander Pl
10 EchT 6395 B2
10 YNKR 6394 D3
Alexander St
10 EORG 6712 D6
10 GrwT 6170 E4
10 NWRK 6712 D7
10 YNKR 6279 C7
10 YNKR 6393 C1
Alexandra Ct
10 STNL 7116 D3
Alex Hamilton Av
10 ARDY 6166 D3
Alexine Av
10 ERKY 6929 C6
Alfred Av
300 EGLD 6502 C1
300 TnkT 6502 C1
Alfred Ct
10 RYEB 6051 E7
Alfred Ln
10 NRCH 6281 E5
10 NRCH 6282 A5
Alfred Pl
10 LFRY 6501 C5
Alfred St
200 EGLC 6503 B3
Alfred Wy
10 WbgT 7114 A2
Alger Av
10 HSBH 6500 E4
Alger Rd
10 KNGP 6616 D5
Algonkin St
10 STNL 7207 B1
Algonquin Dr
10 GrbT 6048 C6
Algonquin Pl
10 ELIZ 6917 E2
Algonquin Rd
10 YNKR 6280 D5
Alhambra Dr
10 HmpT 7029 E1
Alice Ct
10 BKLN 6923 D1
10 ERKY 6929 C7
10 LNBK 6929 B4
Alice Pl
500 WbgT 7114 C4
Alida St
- SCDL 6281 C4
10 EchT 6281 B2
10 YNKR 6394 A2
Alina St
1000 ELIZ 6918 B1
1200 ELIZ 6817 A7
1300 ELIZ 6816 E7
Alison Dr
10 WbgT 7114 D2
Alkamont Av
10 EchT 6281 B1
Allaire Av
300 LEON 6502 D4
Allaire St
10 EchT 6395 B1
Allan Dr
10 WHPL 6168 E5
10 WHPL 6169 A5
Allan Ter
10 SECS 6610 B6
Allard Av
10 NRCH 6395 D5
Allegra Ct
10 GrbT 6049 E5
Allegro St
10 STNL 7207 D1
Allen Av
10 BKLN 7023 E6
300 HmpT 6828 B6
Allen Ct
10 STNL 7019 E1
Allen Dr
10 NHmT 6723 C1
10 THSN 6723 C1
100 LKSU 6723 C1
Allen Ln
- NWRK 6817 B1
10 GTNK 6616 D4
Allen Pl
10 EchT 6395 C1
10 HRSN 6283 B2
10 STNL 7207 E1
2200 BRNX 6505 E1
Allen Rd
500 HmpT 6928 B7
Allen St
10 CRSK 6278 A7
10 DBSF 6166 C4
10 HmpT 6929 C3
10 IrvT 6816 C1
10 JSYC 6716 A6
10 LNBK 6929 C3
10 MHTN 119 B5
10 MHTN 6821 C3
10 MtPT 6049 E1
10 MtPT 6050 A1
10 NHmT 6724 B5
10 YNKR 6394 B3
200 HmpT 7027 E3
400 ELIZ 6917 E6
400 ELIZ 6918 A7
400 LNDN 6917 E6
900 HmpT 7028 C1

W Allen St
10 IrvT 6816 C1
100 NWRK 6816 C1
Allendale Dr
10 RYE 6283 D4
Allendale Rd
10 STNL 7020 D5
10 YNKR 6280 E2
Allendale St
95-00 QENS 6825 C6
Allentown Ln
2500 STNL 7206 B1
Allenwood Rd
10 GTNE 6616 E6
10 NHmT 6616 E6
10 NHmT 6617 A6
Allerton Av
600 BRNX 6505 A4
W Alley Rd
- QENS 6722 D5
Alliance St
10 VLYS 6928 E2
10 VLYS 6929 A2
Alling St
10 NWRK 6817 C3
700 MRNK 6282 D5
Alliotts Pl
10 PALP 6502 C6
Allison Av
10 YNKR 6393 D5
100 STNL 7117 E3
100 STNL 7118 A3
Allison Ct
100 EGLD 6502 E2
Allison Dr
10 EGLC 6392 C6
Allison Pl
10 STNL 7117 E1
Allison Rd
- EGLC 6503 C3
10 ALPN 6278 E6
Allison St
10 NHmT 6617 D2
Allston Pl
10 MNPK 6618 A6
Alma Pl
10 EMFD 6049 C6
Almar Ct
400 NVLE 6164 B3
Almeda Av
- QENS 7027 A5
62-00 QENS 7026 C6
Almena Av
500 ARDY 6166 C5
500 GrbT 6166 C5
Almira Dr
10 GrwT 6170 D3
Almon Av
500 WbgT 7114 D4
Almond St
10 STNL 7116 B5
Almont Rd
7-00 QENS 7027 D4
Alnwick Rd
10 MLVN 6929 B2
Alonzo Rd
10 LWRN 7027 D4
10 QENS 7027 D4
Alpha Pl
10 NRCH 6396 B5
Alpha St
10 YNKR 6281 A3
1400 HmpT 6827 D5
Alpine Av
10 STNL 7020 B3
Alpine Ct
10 DMRT 6278 C6
10 EGLC 6503 B2
10 RDFP 6501 E6
10 STNL 7019 D2
Alpine Dr
10 ALPN 6278 E6
10 CLST 6278 D3
800 TnkT 6502 B1
Alpine Pl
10 KRNY 6714 B2
100 TCKA 6281 A5
Alpine Rd
10 NRCH 6395 D1
10 YNKR 6280 E4
Alpine St
200 PTHA 7205 D1
300 SAMB 7205 A7
500 SRVL 7205 A7
E Alpine St
10 NWRK 6817 C3
W Alpine St
10 NWRK 6817 B3
Alpine Wy
200 WbgT 7114 B3
Alpine Approach Rd
- ALPN 6279 A5
Alsan Wy
10 LFRY 6501 C5
Alsop St
10 VLYS 6928 D4
Alstead Rd
10 HmpT 6827 C7
10 HmpT 6928 C1
Alston Pl
234-00 QENS 6722 C2
Alstyne Av
94-00 QENS 6720 B6
Alta Av
10 YNKR 6393 D3
Alta Dr
10 EchT 6395 B2
10 MTVN 6395 B2
Alta Pkwy
10 MTVN 6395 B2
Alta Pl
10 YNKR 6280 E4
Altamont Av
10 GLCV 6509 E5
10 SCLF 6509 E5
10 TYTN 6048 C3
Altamont Pl
10 YNKR 6394 B4
Altamont St
10 STNL 7117 E1
Alta Vista Cir
10 GrbT 6048 C6
Alta Vista Ct
10 STNL 7020 D7

Alta Vista Dr
10 YNKR 6280 E3
10 YNKR 6281 A4
Alta Vista Pl
600 PTHA 7205 D2
Alter Av
10 STNL 7020 B6
Althea Ln
- MrnT 6282 B6
Althouse Av
10 ERKY 6929 C7
Althouse St
700 CDHT 7028 B1
700 HmpT 7028 B1
Altman Dr
10 RTFD 6609 B3
Alto Av
10 PTCH 6170 B7
Alton Pl
10 BKLN 7023 D2
Alton Rd
600 HmpT 6828 C6
Alton St
100 ELIZ 6917 C4
Alton Ter
10 RYE 6283 E4
Altonwood Pl
10 YNKR 6280 A5
Altoona Av
- STNL 7117 D2
Alva St
10 BlmT 6713 C2
10 BlvT 6713 C2
Al Ventura Rd
4800 WLTN 6500 B4
Alverson Av
10 STNL 7115 E5
400 STNL 7116 A5
Alverson Lp
10 STNL 7116 A6
Alvin Pl
10 HmpT 7027 D3
Alvin St
10 GLCV 6509 E3
Alvine Av
10 STNL 7116 C7
Alwat St
10 WbgT 7114 B3
Alwick Rd
135-00 QENS 6926 C2
Alwin Ct
100 HmpT 7028 E2
Alwyn Ter
10 RTFD 6609 A1
Alyea St
10 NWRK 6818 A2
Alysia Ct
10 STNL 7115 E7
Amackassin Ter
100 YNKR 6279 E5
Amador St
10 STNL 7018 E2
Amanda Ct
10 STNL 7116 C3
Amanda Ln
10 NRCH 6282 A6
Amaron Ln
10 STNL 7206 C4
Amazon Ct
10 STNL 7020 E2
Ambassador Ln
10 STNL 7206 D1
Amber St
10 BKLN 6925 B2
10 QENS 6925 B2
10 STNL 7117 D3
Amberly Rd
10 LWRN 7028 B3
Amberson Av
10 YNKR 6393 C4
Amboy Av
10 PTHA 7114 D7
10 WbgT 7114 C5
400 PTHA 7205 D1
600 ELIZ 6918 A7
Amboy Av CO-653
10 PTHA 7114 D7
10 WbgT 7114 D6
400 PTHA 7205 D3
Amboy Av SR-35
100 WbgT 7114 C5
Amboy Gdns
7300 STNL 7206 D3
Amboy Ln
95-00 QENS 6826 E3
Amboy Rd
10 STNL 7117 C4
4400 STNL 7116 C7
5400 STNL 7207 A2
6000 STNL 7206 A4
Amboy St
10 BKLN 6924 B3
Ambrose Av
10 HmpT 6929 A1
10 MLVN 6929 A1
Ambrose Pl
10 YNKR 6394 B1
Amelia Ct
10 STNL 6920 A6
Amelia Rd
172-00 QENS 6927 A1
Amelia St
10 JSYC 6715 E7
Amelia Earhart Ln
10 HRSN 6283 D1
American Av
1300 HmpT 6827 E4
American Wy
10 SECS 6715 E1
American Legion Dr
10 ARDY 6166 D4
200 HKSK 6501 B1
600 TnkT 6501 E1
Amersfort Pl
10 BKLN 6923 B7
10 BKLN 7023 C1
Ames Av
10 LEON 6502 C5
10 RTFD 6609 B1
Ames St
100 HKSK 6501 A2
Amethyst St
10 HmpT 6827 C6
1900 BRNX 6505 A6

Amherst Av
10 STNL 7117 E4
1200 UnnT 6816 A5
2000 HmpT 6928 A4
2000 QENS 6928 A4
Amherst Dr
10 HAOH 6279 E1
10 NRCH 6282 A3
10 SCDL 6282 A3
10 YNKR 6280 D3
500 HmpT 6928 B6
Amherst Pl
10 GrbT 6167 D3
10 WHPL 6168 C1
Amherst Rd
10 GTNE 6722 E1
10 NHmT 6617 E2
10 NHmT 6722 E1
10 VLYS 6928 D6
Amherst Rd E
10 GTNE 6722 C1
Amherst St
10 BKLN 7121 C1
10 EORG 6712 D5
10 GDNC 6828 A3
10 HmpT 6828 A3
10 STMN 6828 A3
10 WLPK 6724 E4
Amity Ct
10 GrbT 6050 A5
Amity Pl
10 NWRK 6713 C5
10 STNL 7019 A2
100 STNL 7018 D1
Amity St
10 BKLN 120 E6
10 BKLN 6821 C7
10 ELIZ 6918 A5
10 JSYC 6820 A3
10 STNL 7020 E4
100 BKLN 121 A6
Amor Av
10 CARL 6609 E1
10 CARL 6610 A1
Amory Ct
21-00 QENS 6823 B4
Amos St
10 SYHW 6048 C1
Ampere Av
3100 BRNX 6506 A6
Ampere Pkwy
10 EORG 6713 B3
100 BlmT 6713 B2
Ampere Plz
10 EORG 6713 B3
Amstel Blvd
71-00 QENS 7026 C6
Amsterdam Av
10 MHTN 112 C3
10 MHTN 6717 E1
10 STNL 7018 E5
10 YNKR 6280 C2
400 MHTN 108 E7
400 MHTN 6611 E7
600 MHTN 109 A5
600 MHTN 6612 C3
1200 MHTN 106 D6
1700 MHTN 107 A4
2000 MHTN 104 C7
2000 MHTN 6503 E5
Amsterdam Pl
10 MTVN 6395 A5
10 STNL 7018 E5
Amsterdam St
10 NWRK 6818 B3
Amundson Av
10 BRNX 6394 D7
10 MTVN 6394 D7
3800 BRNX 6505 D1
Amy Ct
10 HmpT 6928 B6
10 OrgT 6164 B1
10 STNL 7117 A1
10 VLYS 6928 B6
Amy Ln
10 STNL 7019 A6
Amy Pl
10 WHPL 6168 C6
Amy Wy
10 WbgT 7114 A7
Anaconda St
10 STNL 7116 B5
Anadale Rd
10 GrbT 6167 A6
Anchor Av
100 HmpT 6929 D7
Anchor Dr
10 RYE 6283 C5
32-00 QENS 7027 B4
Anchor Pl
- STNL 7021 A4
Anchor Wy
10 MHVN 6508 B7
Anchorage Pl
10 BKLN 121 B2
10 BKLN 6821 D5
Anchorage Rd
10 HBPK 7028 E1
10 NHmT 6617 D2
Anchorage Ter
10 EDGW 108 C1
10 EDGW 6611 D4
Ancon Av
100 PLHM 6395 C5
200 PLMM 6395 C5
Anders Wy
200 WbgT 7114 B5
Anderson Av
10 ALPN 6278 D3
10 CLST 6278 D3
10 DMRT 6278 C6
10 EchT 6281 C1
10 EGLC 6503 A3
10 FRVW 6611 C4
10 MNCH 6500 E7
10 MTVN 6395 A6
10 NBgT 6611 B4
10 STNL 6919 C7
10 SYHW 6048 B1
10 WRDG 6500 D7
200 CLFP 6611 D1
600 HmpT 6828 B7
700 FTLE 6611 D1
900 BRNX 107 E1
900 BRNX 6612 E1

Anderson Av
1000 FTLE 6502 E6
1100 BRNX 104 E7
1100 BRNX 105 A7
1100 BRNX 6504 A7
Anderson Av CO-21
10 DMRT 6278 C6
100 ALPN 6278 C5
100 CLST 6278 C5
Anderson Av CO-29
10 NBgT 6611 B4
100 FRVW 6611 C3
200 CLFP 6611 D1
700 FTLE 6611 D1
1000 FTLE 6502 E6
Anderson Rd
178-00 QENS 6927 B1
179-00 QENS 6826 B7
Anderson St
10 NRCH 6395 C5
10 STNL 7020 E3
200 STNL 7021 B4
Anderson Hill Rd
- WHPL 6168 D2
10 HRSN 6168 D2
10 RYEB 6051 E7
100 HRSN 6169 A1
700 HRSN 6051 E7
Andes Pl
10 STNL 7019 E4
Andes Rd
100 MHTN 6821 A6
200 MHTN 120 A6
Andover Ct
10 GDNC 6724 E7
10 PLNM 6617 C4
Andover Ln
10 HmpT 6928 C6
10 LWRN 7027 C4
10 NHmT 6617 C6
Andover Pl
100 HmpT 6828 E4
Andover Rd
10 GrbT 6167 E3
10 GTNK 6617 A6
10 NHmT 6617 A6
10 NHmT 6618 A2
10 RKVC 6929 E1
10 YNKR 6280 E2
Andre Av
- NVLE 6164 B3
10 OrgT 6164 B3
Andre Hl
10 NVLE 6164 B3
10 OrgT 6164 B3
Andrea Ct
10 NRCH 6281 E5
10 STNL 7116 E3
Andrea Ln
10 GrbT 6166 E7
10 GrbT 6167 A7
Andrea Pl
10 STNL 7018 E2
Andrease St
10 STNL 7021 A3
Andre Hill Dr
10 OrgT 6164 C3
Andrejewski Dr
10 SRVL 7205 A7
Andrew Ln
10 NRCH 6281 E3
Andrew Rd
10 EchT 6281 B6
10 NHmT 6617 E6
Andrew St
10 BAYN 6919 D4
10 NHmT 6617 D6
100 MRNK 6282 D5
Andrews Av
10 STNL 7117 C2
54-00 QENS 6823 B3
Andrews Av N
2100 BRNX 105 C1
2100 BRNX 6504 B4
2200 BRNX 102 D7
Andrews Av S
1600 BRNX 105 C3
1600 BRNX 6504 A6
Andrews Dr
1000 PTHA 7114 C7
Andrews Ln
10 SYHW 6048 A1
Andrews Rd
100 MNLA 6724 D6
Andrews St
10 STNL 7020 E6
Andros Av
10 STNL 6918 E7
200 STNL 7018 E1
Androvette Av
10 STNL 7207 B1
Androvette St
10 STNL 7115 B7
Andrus Rd
10 YNKR 6280 A2
A New St
- MHTN 110 C6
- MHTN 6612 D7
Angela Dr
10 BKLN 7023 A6
Angelique St
100 UNCT 6716 E3
100 WhkT 6716 E3
Angelo Pl
10 PTCH 6170 B7
Angelus Dr
10 GrwT 6170 B1
Angioletti Pl
10 FTLE 103 A4
10 FTLE 6503 B5
Angler Ln
10 PTWN 6508 D6
Angle Sea Pl
10 ERKY 6929 C7
Angus Ln
10 GrwT 6170 D2
Angus Rd N
10 GrwT 6170 D1
Anita Ln
300 MRNK 6282 E5
Anita Rd
10 YNKR 6280 D6
Anita St
10 STNL 7019 B2

Anjali Lp
10 STNL 7019 B7
Ankener Av
79-00 QENS 6823 D1
Ann Ct
10 HmpT 6827 B7
10 WLTN 6500 B5
Ann Dr
10 OrgT 6164 C3
Ann Ln
10 RYE 6284 A2
Ann Pl
10 EchT 6281 B5
10 MtPT 6050 A1
10 NHmT 6508 D6
Ann St
10 ERTH 6609 B1
10 GrwT 6170 E3
10 HRSN 6050 C7
10 HRSN 6714 B6
10 JSYC 6716 A6
10 KRNY 6714 B6
10 LFRY 6501 B5
10 MHTN 118 C7
10 MHTN 120 C1
10 MHTN 6821 B4
10 NWRK 6818 A2
10 STNL 6919 D7
10 TYTN 6048 B2
10 VLYS 6928 E2
10 YNKR 6393 C1
1500 FTLE 6502 E5
3500 HmpT 7029 C2
Anna Ct
10 BKLN 6924 D5
Anna St
800 ELIZ 6918 A3
1100 ELIZ 6917 E2
Annadale Ln
49-00 QENS 6723 A3
Annadale Rd
10 STNL 7116 D4
Annapolis St
10-00 QENS 7027 C4
Ann Arbor Pl
10 CLST 6278 C2
Anne Ct
10 NRWD 6164 B5
Annett Av
10 EDGW 103 A6
10 EDGW 6503 A6
Annette Dr
10 NHmT 6508 E7
10 NHmT 6617 E1
Annfield Ct
10 STNL 7020 A5
Ann Marie Pl
10 YNKR 6279 E4
Annsville Tr
10 YNKR 6279 E4
Anpell Dr
10 EchT 6281 D3
Anpesil Dr
7000 NBgT 6610 E6
Antares Dr
- WbgT 7114 A6
Anthony Av
1600 BRNX 6504 B7
1700 BRNX 105 E4
Anthony Ct
10 WbgT 7114 C5
Anthony St
10 BKLN 6822 D2
10 NWRK 6713 D3
10 STNL 7115 E6
400 HmpT 7029 D1
Anthony Infante Plz
- QENS 6926 D6
Anthony J Griffin Pl
400 BRNX 107 E6
400 BRNX 6612 B2
Anthony M Defino Wy
6000 WNYK 111 C1
6000 WNYK 6611 B7
6000 WNYK 6717 B1
Anthony M Defino Wy CO-505
6000 WNYK 111 C1
6000 WNYK 6611 B7
6000 WNYK 6717 B1
Antin Pl
- BRNX 6505 A6
Antler Pl
10 NRCH 6395 E1
Anton St
10 PTHA 7205 E1
Antony Rd
10 WHPL 6168 E4
Apawamis Av
10 RYE 6283 E3
10 RYE 6284 A3
Apex Pl
62-00 QENS 6720 C7
62-00 QENS 6824 C1
Apking St
2800 HmpT 6929 E6
Apollo Av
10 WbgT 7114 C2
Apollo St
10 BKLN 6822 D2
10 JSYC 6819 D2
Appeal Av
1200 HmpT 6827 E5
Apple Ct
10 EchT 6281 B4
Appleby Av
10 STNL 7020 D6
Applegate Av
1000 ELIZ 6917 C4
Applegate Ct
10 BKLN 7022 E5
Appleton Pl
10 DBSF 6166 A5
Apple Tree Ln
10 NRCH 6282 C1
100 UnnT 6816 A5
Appletree Ln
10 ALPN 6278 D5
10 EHLS 6618 E5
10 GTNK 6616 E4
10 NHmT 6724 E2
Appletree Close
10 GrbT 6050 A5

Aquarium Dr
10 SECS 6715 E2
Aquatic Dr
74-00 QENS 7026 C7
Aquatic Pl
2-01 QENS 7026 C7
Aqueduct Av
10 YNKR 6394 A5
Aqueduct Av E
2100 BRNX 105 C2
2100 BRNX 6504 B5
Aqueduct Av W
2300 BRNX 102 E7
2300 BRNX 6504 C4
Aqueduct Dr
10 GrbT 6167 C7
Aqueduct Ln
10 HAOH 6165 C7
N Aqueduct Ln
10 IRVN 6166 B1
S Aqueduct Ln
10 IRVN 6166 C1
Aqueduct Pl
10 GrbT 6049 B4
10 YNKR 6279 D4
Aqueduct Rd
- QENS 6925 E3
- QENS 6926 A3
10 GrbT 6167 E1
10 WHPL 6167 E1
Arbor Ct
10 STNL 7020 A5
Arbor Dr
10 GrwT 6170 B1
10 NRCH 6282 C2
10 RYEB 6170 A1
Arbor Ln
- RKVC 6929 E5
Arbor St
10 NHmT 6723 B1
10 THSN 6723 B1
10 WbgT 7114 E5
10 YNKR 6279 E7
Arbor Wy
10 HRSN 6169 C1
Arborwood Ln
10 WHPL 6050 C6
Arbuckle Av
300 CDHT 7028 A1
500 HmpT 6928 A7
500 HmpT 7028 D3
Arbutus Av
10 STNL 7116 C7
10 STNL 7207 C1
Arbutus Ct
10 STNL 7207 C1
Arbutus Wy
10 STNL 7207 C1
Arc Pl
10 STNL 7117 D3
Arcade Av
183-00 QENS 6826 A5
Arcade Pl
10 HmpT 6827 C4
Arcadia Dr
10 MHVN 6508 B7
Arcadia Ln
4500 NHmT 6723 A2
Arcadia Pl
10 STNL 7019 D1
10 YNKR 6280 E4
Arcadia Rd
10 HKSK 6501 A1
10 LODI 6501 A1
Arcadia Wk
100 QENS 7122 B4
Arcadian Av
10 HmpT 6827 E7
Arcadian Wy
1000 FTLE 6611 E1
Arch Av
10 SECS 6610 B5
Arch Rd
200 EGLD 6502 E2
Arch St
- QENS 6718 C6
10 BlmT 6713 B1
Archer Av
10 MTVN 6394 E3
10 WHPL 6050 B6
137-00 QENS 6825 B5
179-00 QENS 6826 A4
Archer Dr
10 EchT 6395 C2
Archer Ln
10 SCDL 6282 B2
Archer Pl
10 BRXV 6281 B7
10 EchT 6281 B7
10 HRSN 6283 C3
10 TYTN 6048 B3
Archer Rd
10 HmpT 6828 E5
10 HRSN 6169 B7
10 HRSN 6283 B1
1500 BRNX 6505 B7
Archer St
10 EDGW 6611 D3
1800 BRNX 6505 B7
Archibald Ter
10 KRNY 6714 A5
Archway Pl
71-00 QENS 6824 E2
Archwood Av
10 STNL 7116 C7
Ardell Rd
10 YNKR 6394 D2
Arden Av
10 STNL 7116 B4
1500 STNL 7207 E1
1600 STNL 7208 A1
Arden Blvd
10 HmpT 6828 D4
100 GDNC 6828 D4
Arden Dr
10 GrbT 6166 E3
Arden Ln
10 SNPT 6508 C4
Arden Pl
10 MtPT 6050 A2
10 YNKR 6279 D4
Arden Rd
10 HmpT 7029 B1

New York City/5 Borough Street Index

STREET Block City Map# Grid

Arden St
10 MHTN 101 E7
10 MHTN 104 E1
10 MHTN 6503 E4
Arden Ter
10 MTVN 6395 C1
Ardmore Av
100 STNL 7019 C5
Ardmore Rd
10 SCDL 6282 A2
10 WOrT 6712 A2
Ardsley Av E
10 IRVN 6166 A2
Ardsley Av W
10 IRVN 6166 A2
100 IRVN 6165 E2
Ardsley Blvd
400 GDNC 6828 D4
400 HmpT 6828 C4
Ardsley Cir
10 RKVC 6929 E1
Ardsley Lp
10 BKLN 6924 E5
Ardsley Pl
10 GTPZ 6617 B7
10 THSN 6617 B7
Ardsley Rd
- SCDL 6167 B7
10 GrbT 6167 A7
37-00 QENS 6722 D2
400 GrbT 6166 E6
700 ARDY 6166 E5
Ardsley St
200 STNL 7117 B2
Ardsley Ter
10 IRVN 6166 A2
Area Pl
- STNL 7019 E5
Argenti Pl
400 NVLE 6164 B3
Argo Av
10 HmpT 6827 D4
Argon Pl
10 NHmT 6724 C6
Argonne St
10 STNL 7020 E6
Argyle Av
400 COrT 6712 A4
Argyle Pl
10 BRXV 6395 A1
10 KRNY 6714 C2
10 NARL 6714 C1
10 RKVC 6929 E3
Argyle Rd
10 BKLN 6923 A7
10 GrbT 6167 A6
10 HMPD 6828 E4
10 HmpT 6828 E4
10 HRSN 6283 A3
10 NHmT 6617 E3
10 PTCH 6170 A3
10 RYEB 6170 A3
10 STMN 6827 E3
100 HmpT 6827 E3
300 CDHT 7027 E1
300 CDHT 7028 A1
300 HmpT 7027 E1
400 MNLA 6724 D5
500 BKLN 7023 A1
500 NHmT 6724 D5
E Argyle St
10 VLYS 6928 E3
200 VLYS 6929 A3
W Argyle St
10 VLYS 6928 D2
Argyle Ter
10 IrvT 6816 D1
10 YNKR 6279 D4
Argyll Av
10 NRCH 6395 D1
Ariel Ct
10 SNPT 6508 C3
Arielle Ln
10 STNL 7117 A1
Arion Pl
10 BKLN 6822 D6
Arion Rd
88-00 QENS 6925 D2
Arizona Av
10 LBCH 7028 E7
Arizona Ln
- STNL 7021 A6
Arkansas Av
10 STNL 7117 A4
Arkansas Dr
- VLYS 6928 C1
10 BKLN 7024 C4
10 HmpT 6827 C7
100 HmpT 6928 C1
Arleigh Dr
10 NHmT 6724 D2
Arleigh Rd
10 KENS 6617 B6
234-00 QENS 6722 D2
Arlene Ct
10 STNL 7019 A2
Arlene St
10 STNL 7018 E4
Arley Ct
1200 HmpT 6827 E7
Arley Rd
600 HmpT 6828 A7
Arlington Av
10 BKLN 6924 D1
10 BlmT 6713 B2
10 JSYC 6819 E4
10 KRNY 6714 C4
10 MLVN 6929 E2
10 NARL 6714 C1
10 NWRK 6713 E3
10 RKVC 6929 E5
10 STNL 6918 E7
10 VLYS 6928 B2
100 STNL 7018 E1
500 EORG 6713 B2
1100 HmpT 6828 A5
1200 HmpT 6827 E5
2600 BRNX 102 B3
2600 BRNX 6504 A1
2600 BRNX 6393 B7
N Arlington Av
10 EORG 6712 D4
10 EORG 6713 A2
500 BlmT 6713 B2
S Arlington Av
10 EORG 6712 E5
Arlington Ct
10 STNL 6920 A5
Arlington Pl
10 BKLN 6923 C1
10 KRNY 6714 C2
10 RYEB 6170 A3
10 SCLF 6509 E6
10 STNL 6918 E7
500 CDHT 7028 D3
Arlington Rd
10 EchT 6281 D3
400 CDHT 7028 A1
500 HmpT 7028 A1
Arlington St
10 NWRK 6713 D7
10 NWRK 6817 D1
10 YNKR 6280 C6
1200 MRNK 6282 E4
1200 MRNK 6283 A3
Arlington Ter
10 EDGW 103 A6
10 EDGW 6503 A6
150-00 QENS 6825 D6
Arlo Rd
10 STNL 7020 B3
Arman Rd
- QENS 6616 A6
Armand Pl
10 BRNX 102 E4
10 BRNX 6504 C2
10 MtPT 6049 D2
Armand St
10 STNL 7019 A3
Armett St
10 PTCH 6170 B7
Armm Av
10 ERTH 6500 A6
10 WLTN 6500 A6
Armonk Av
10 YNKR 6280 E3
Armonk St
10 GrwT 6170 C5
Armory Pl
- WHPL 6168 B2
Armory Pl SR-22
- WHPL 6168 B2
Armory Pl SR-119
- WHPL 6168 B2
Armour Pl
10 STNL 7207 B2
Armour St
10 LBCH 7029 E6
Armour Villa Av
10 TCKA 6280 E6
Armstrong Av
10 JSYC 6819 D5
10 STNL 7117 A6
10 YNKR 6280 B6
900 STNL 7116 E4
Armstrong Ct
10 GrwT 6170 E4
Armstrong Ln
10 PTHA 7205 E2
Armstrong Rd
10 NHmT 6724 D7
Arn Ter
10 SECS 6610 A6
Arnet Av
800 UnnT 6816 B7
Arnett St
600 ELIZ 6917 E6
Arnold Av
10 CLST 6278 C3
54-00 QENS 6823 B3
200 PTHA 7205 D2
2800 HmpT 6929 E6
Arnold Ct
10 ERKY 6929 B7
Arnold Rd
500 HmpT 6929 C1
Arnold St
10 HlsT 6816 B5
10 STNL 6920 C7
Arnot Pl
100 WRDG 6500 B5
Arnot St
10 LODI 6500 C1
100 GRFD 6500 C1
Arnow Av
600 BRNX 6505 C3
Arnow Pl
3100 BRNX 6505 E6
3100 BRNX 6506 A5
Arnprior St
10 STNL 7019 B2
Arrandale Av
10 GTNK 6616 D5
10 KNGP 6616 D5
Arrandale Rd
10 RKVC 6929 E1
Arrow St
500 NVLE 6164 A4
Arrowhead Ct
10 NHLS 6724 A1
Arrowhead Dr
10 YNKR 6281 A3
Arrowhead Ln
10 LWRN 7028 B3
10 MrnT 6282 A5
Arrowood Ct
10 STNL 7115 E5
Arrowwood Cir
10 RYEB 6051 E6
Arsdale Pl
10 NWRK 6712 D6
Arsdale Ter
10 EORG 6712 D6
10 IrvT 6816 B4
10 NWRK 6712 D6
10 UnnT 6816 B4
Arsdale Ter N
10 IrvT 6816 A4
10 UnnT 6816 A4
Arsdale Ter S
1400 UnnT 6816 A4
Art Ln
500 RDGF 6611 C2
Arther St
10 GrwT 6170 D3
Arthur Av
10 CART 7115 C2
10 EGLC 6503 B3
10 HmpT 6827 D4
10 LNBK 6929 A4
10 SFPK 6827 D4
10 STNL 7020 E6
10 WbgT 7115 C2
2100 BRNX 6504 D5
Arthur Ct
10 CLST 6278 C4
10 DMRT 6278 B4
10 PTCH 6170 C5
10 STNL 7019 D2
Arthur Dr
10 ERKY 6929 B7
10 RTFD 6609 A4
Arthur Ln
10 GrbT 6049 C3
10 MtPT 6049 C3
Arthur Pl
10 VLYS 6928 B3
10 YNKR 6279 D5
Arthur St
10 RDFP 6501 E4
10 RDFP 6502 A4
10 YNKR 6279 D4
100 HlsT 6816 C6
100 LNDN 7017 C4
144-00 QENS 6927 C3
700 HmpT 6828 D7
1100 MRNK 6282 D4
Arthur Kill Rd
10 STNL 7117 A3
600 STNL 7116 D3
2100 STNL 7115 C7
4500 STNL 7206 B1
Arthurs Landing Rd
- WhkT 111 B4
- WhkT 6717 A2
Artic St
10 GrwT 6170 E3
Artillary Rd
- STNL 7021 A5
Artillery Ln
10 GrbT 6167 C6
Aruba St
1200 ELIZ 6918 E1
1200 ELIZ 6919 A1
Arverne Blvd
55-00 QENS 7026 E6
Arverne Ter
10 IrvT 6712 E7
Arverne Mews Dr
73-01 QENS 7026 C7
Ascan Av
98-00 QENS 6824 D4
Ascan Rd
600 HmpT 6828 A7
Ascan St
10 HmpT 6827 E7
800 HmpT 6928 E1
N Ascan St
700 HmpT 6827 E7
Asch Lp
10 BRNX 6505 E3
100 BRNX 6506 A3
Aschoff Pl
4700 NBgT 6610 D7
Ascot Av
- QENS 6720 C7
Ascot Ct
10 NHLS 6724 B2
Ascot Rd
10 YNKR 6280 D2
Ascot Rdg
- GTPZ 6722 E1
10 GTNE 6722 E1
10 NHmT 6722 E1
Ascot Wy
10 FTLE 6611 E3
Ash Av
- BKLN 7022 E2
149-00 QENS 6721 B4
Ash Dr
10 EHLS 6618 E6
10 GTNE 6616 E7
100 GTNE 6722 E1
Ash Ln
10 HmpT 6928 C4
Ash Pl
10 GTPZ 6723 A1
10 NHmT 6724 B4
10 STNL 7019 C4
Ash St
- NRWD 6164 A5
10 BKLN 117 D7
10 BKLN 6718 B7
10 CART 7115 C2
10 EGLC 6503 B3
10 FLPK 6827 D3
10 JSYC 6820 A3
10 VLYS 6928 A2
10 YNKR 6393 D1
100 QENS 6928 A2
700 HmpT 6828 B4
Ashburton Av
10 YNKR 6279 C7
300 YNKR 6393 E1
Ashburton Av SR-9A
10 YNKR 6279 C7
Ashburton Pl
10 YNKR 6279 C7
Ashby Av
171-00 QENS 6721 D5
Ashby Ln
10 NWRK 6713 C7
Ashford Av
10 DBSF 6166 D5
400 ARDY 6166 C4
700 GrbT 6166 E5
Ashford Pl
10 NHmT 6724 E3
10 YNKR 6280 B7
Ashford St
88-00 QENS 6826 E1
200 BKLN 6924 E2
Ashland Av
10 EORG 6712 E3
10 NHmT 6724 A6
10 WOrT 6712 C1
200 STNL 7207 A1
Ashland Av E
10 STNL 7207 B1
Ashland Pl
10 BKLN 121 D5
10 BKLN 6821 E7
10 EORG 6713 A5
Ashland St
10 NRCH 6396 A1
10 NWRK 6713 A7
Ashley Ct
10 NHmT 6724 D2
Ashley Dr
10 HmpT 6928 B1
1000 VLYS 6928 B1
Ashley Ln
10 STNL 7115 E5
Ashley Rd
10 HAOH 6280 A1
Ashley St
300 PTHA 7205 D1
Ashley Ter
10 MLVN 6929 B1
Ashton Av
300 LNDN 6917 D5
Ashton Ct
10 WbgT 7114 D2
Ashton Dr
10 STNL 7116 B5
Ashton Rd
10 YNKR 6393 B3
Ashwood Ct
10 STNL 7117 C4
Ashwood Rd
10 MHVN 6508 C6
Ashworth Av
10 STNL 7019 B6
Asia Pl
100 CARL 6610 A1
Aske St
40-00 QENS 6720 A6
Askins Pl
10 NRCH 6395 C2
Asmus Rd
10 CLST 6278 B2
Aspen Av
- BKLN 7022 E2
Aspen Ct
100 NRWD 6278 C1
Aspen Ln
10 NHmT 6724 B4
10 WbgT 7114 B3
Aspen Pl
10 GTNE 6722 D1
85-00 QENS 6825 D3
Aspen Rd
10 NRCH 6282 A4
10 SCDL 6168 B7
10 SCDL 6282 B1
Aspen St
10 FLPK 6827 D2
Aspen Gate
10 PLNM 6617 D3
Aspen Knolls Wy
10 STNL 7116 C3
Aspinwall St
10 STNL 7206 B5
Asquith Cres
62-00 QENS 6824 B2
Assemblyman Ralph Goldein Av
- QENS 6720 C7
Asser Levy Pl
300 MHTN 116 E7
300 MHTN 6717 E7
Aster Av
- BKLN 7022 E2
- BKLN 7023 A2
Aster Ct
10 BKLN 7023 E6
Aster Dr
10 NHmT 6724 A5
100 NHmT 6723 E5
Aster Ln
4500 NHmT 6723 A2
4500 RSLG 6723 A2
Aster Pl
10 BRNX 6615 B4
Aston Ter
1500 FTLE 6502 E6
Astor Av
10 STNL 7019 A5
700 BRNX 6505 D4
Astor Ln
10 NHmT 6508 E6
10 SNPT 6508 E6
10 SNPT 6509 A6
Astor Pl
10 JSYC 6819 E3
10 MHTN 119 A2
10 MHTN 6821 C1
10 NHmT 6508 E6
10 VLYS 6928 E4
10 WbgT 7114 C2
10 WLPK 6724 E4
10 YNKR 6393 C2
Astor St
10 NWRK 6817 C2
500 HmpT 6827 B6
N Astor St
10 IRVN 6048 A6
S Astor St
10 IRVN 6048 A7
10 IRVN 6166 A1
Astoria Blvd
4-00 QENS 114 E4
4-00 QENS 6718 E2
75-00 QENS 6719 D3
93-01 QENS 6720 A4
Astoria Blvd N
31-00 QENS 6719 A3
Astoria Blvd N I-278 TRK
31-00 QENS 6719 A3
Astoria Blvd S
32-00 QENS 6719 B3
Astoria Blvd S I-278 TRK
33-00 QENS 6719 A3
Astoria Pk S
12-00 QENS 114 E3
12-00 QENS 6718 E2
Atalanta Plz
10 ELIZ 6918 D5
Athena Pl
10 STNL 7019 E4
Atherstone Rd
10 NRCH 6281 E1
Atherton Av
1500 HmpT 6827 C5
Atherton St
- YNKR 6393 A1
Atilda Av
10 DBSF 6165 E5
10 HAOH 6165 E5
Atkins Av
10 BKLN 6924 E2
400 BKLN 6925 A3
Atkins Ter
10 ERTH 6500 A7
10 WLTN 6500 A7
Atlanta Av
10 EWLS 6724 A6
Atlantic Av
- GRFD 6500 A3
- STNL 7117 E1
10 BKLN 120 D6
10 BKLN 6821 B6
10 ERKY 6929 C6
10 FLPK 6827 B2
10 GDNC 6828 E3
10 HmpT 6929 C6
10 LNBK 6929 B5
10 NHmT 6724 C7
10 STNL 7020 B6
74-00 BKLN 6925 B1
74-00 QENS 6925 A1
78-86 QENS 6824 C7
100 BKLN 121 A6
100 LBCH 7029 E7
118-01 QENS 6825 A6
300 CDHT 7028 C3
300 HmpT 7028 A2
400 LWRN 7028 B3
500 BKLN 6922 E1
500 PTHA 7205 C2
700 BKLN 6923 D2
1900 BKLN 6924 A2
3600 BKLN 7120 A2
E Atlantic Av
10 HmpT 6929 E7
Atlantic Blvd
2000 ATLB 7027 D7
Atlantic Coms
10 BKLN 6922 C2
Atlantic Pl N
10 HmpT 7029 E4
Atlantic Pl S
10 HmpT 7029 E4
Atlantic St
- ELIZ 6917 E7
10 CART 7115 D2
10 ELIZ 6918 A5
10 GRFD 6500 A3
10 HKSK 6501 B1
10 JSYC 6819 D3
10 NWRK 6713 C4
1000 HmpT 6828 A4
E Atlantic St
10 HKSK 6501 C1
Atlantic Beach Br
- ATLB 7027 E6
- LWRN 7027 E6
Atlas Av
10 MLVN 6929 B1
Atlas Ct
10 HmpT 6929 C1
10 JSYC 6819 A4
10 MLVN 6929 C1
10 NHmT 6724 B6
Atlas Pl
10 MTVN 6395 B2
Atmore Pl
10 STNL 7117 C3
Attorney St
10 MHTN 6821 D3
100 MHTN 119 C5
Atwood Av
10 CRSK 6392 B1
10 TFLY 6392 B1
Aubrey Av
88-00 QENS 6824 B4
Auburn Av
10 STNL 7019 B3
Auburn Pl
10 BKLN 121 D5
10 BKLN 6821 E6
Auburn St
900 HmpT 6828 A4
Auburndale Ln
40-00 QENS 6721 D5
Audley St
10 QENS 6824 E4
Audrey Av
10 HmpT 6827 D7
10 MTVN 6395 A4
Audrey Ct
10 HmpT 6929 A1
10 MLVN 6929 A1
Audrey Ln
10 WHPL 6168 E6
Audrey Urban Ct
10 ALPN 6278 E5
10 ALPN 6279 A6
Audrey Zapp Dr
10 JSYC 6820 B4
Audubon Av
10 JSYC 6819 C4
10 MHTN 104 D4
10 MHTN 6503 D7
100 MTVN 6395 B3
Audubon Blvd
10 HmpT 7029 D4
Audubon Ln
10 GrwT 6051 C1
Audubon Rd
10 TnkT 6502 B1
200 EGLD 6502 E2
Auerbach Av
1200 HWTH 6929 A7
1300 HmpT 6929 A7
Auerbach Ln
10 CDHT 7028 B2
10 LWRN 7028 B3
August Ct
114-00 QENS 6825 D7
Augusta Av
10 STNL 7116 D5
E Augusta Av
10 STNL 7117 A5
Augusta Ct
10 HRSN 6050 E6
200 NHLS 6724 B3
Augusta Ln
10 NHLS 6724 B2
Augusta Pl
10 GrbT 6049 D5
Augusta St
- CLST 6278 C2
10 IrvT 6816 D2
100 SAMB 7205 C7
1000 ELIZ 6918 A2
Augustina Av
14-00 QENS 7027 D4
Augustina St
10 HmpT 7027 E2
Augustine Av
10 ARDY 6166 C5
Augustine Pl
400 PTHA 7205 C3
Augustine Rd
10 GrbT 6049 E5
100 GrbT 6050 A5
Augustus St
200 WbgT 7114 C5
Aultman Av
10 STNL 7117 C2
Aurelia Ct
10 BKLN 7023 C1
1100 HmpT 6929 E2
1100 VLYS 6929 E2
Aurora Av
300 CLFP 6611 D1
400 RDGF 6611 D1
Aurora Ln
10 NRCH 6281 D5
Auryansen Ct
10 CLST 6278 C3
Ausable Av
10 STNL 6920 B7
Austell Pl
47-00 QENS 6718 D6
Austin Av
10 NRWD 6164 A7
10 OrgT 6164 D2
10 STNL 7020 D7
10 STNL 7021 A6
10 WbgT 7114 A3
10 YNKR 6280 B2
Austin Blvd
- LBCH 7029 D6
10 ISPK 7029 D5
3800 HmpT 7029 D5
Austin Pl
10 HSBH 6500 D3
10 LKSU 6723 C1
10 PTCH 6170 B4
10 STNL 7020 C1
400 BRNX 6613 B4
400 COrT 6712 A3
Austin Rd
100 COrT 6712 C4
Austin St
10 MNCH 6500 E7
10 MNCH 6501 A7
10 NWRK 6817 D2
10 RDFP 6501 E4
10 VLYS 6928 D2
10 WbgT 7114 E5
67-00 QENS 6824 C2
83-00 QENS 6825 A4
Austin Ter
10 OrgT 6164 D2
Austin Wy
10 OrgT 6164 D2
Autenrieth Rd
10 SCDL 6167 C7
Autumn Av
10 BKLN 6824 A7
100 BKLN 6925 A1
Autumn Cir
10 YNKR 6279 E4
Autumn Dr
10 OrgT 6164 D2
Autumn St
10 LODI 6500 D3
Autumn Ter
10 ALPN 6278 D4
Ava Pl
86-00 QENS 6825 E3
Avalon Pl
10 MLVN 6929 A2
Avalon Rd
- THSN 6723 C1
10 HmpT 6928 D6
10 THSN 6617 D7
N Avalon Rd
10 THSN 6617 C7
10 THSN 6723 C1
Avenel St
100 WbgT 7114 C1
Avenel St CO-650
10 WbgT 7114 B1
Avenue A
- DBSF 6166 B6
- HAOH 6166 B6
10 BAYN 6919 D3
10 BKLN 6924 A5
10 CARL 6610 A2
10 HmpT 7027 D3
10 LODI 6500 D1
10 MHTN 119 C3
10 MHTN 6821 D2
10 MNCH 6501 A7
10 MNCH 6610 A1
10 NHmT 6508 E6
10 NWRK 6817 D3
10 PTWN 6508 D6
10 SNPT 6508 E6
Avenue at Port Imperial
- GTBG 6611 C7
- WNYK 6611 B7
10 WNYK 111 B2
10 WNYK 6717 A1
Avenue B
- DBSF 6166 B6
- HAOH 6166 B6
10 BAYN 6920 A1
10 BKLN 6924 A5
10 LODI 6500 D1
10 MHTN 119 C4
10 MHTN 6821 D2
10 MNCH 6610 A1
10 NHmT 6508 E6
10 NWRK 6817 D3
10 PTWN 6508 E6
10 SNPT 6508 E6
10 STNL 6919 D7
200 BAYN 6819 A7
200 CARL 6610 B2
Avenue C
- MHTN 116 E7
- MHTN 6717 E7
10 BKLN 6922 E7
10 LODI 6500 D1
10 MHTN 119 E2
10 MHTN 6821 E2
10 NHmT 6508 E6
10 NWRK 6817 D3
10 OrgT 6164 D3
10 PTWN 6508 E6
100 SNPT 6508 E6
200 BAYN 6919 D4
700 BAYN 6920 A2
700 BKLN 6923 A6
1000 BAYN 6819 B7
1100 JSYC 6819 B7
Avenue C Lp
- MHTN 119 E2
- MHTN 6821 E1
Avenue D
10 LODI 6500 D1
10 MHTN 119 E3
10 MHTN 6821 E2
2200 BKLN 6923 B7
5500 BKLN 6924 A6
Avenue E
10 BAYN 6919 D5
10 LODI 6500 D1
700 BAYN 6920 A2
800 JSYC 6920 B1
Avenue F
10 BAYN 6919 E4
10 BAYN 6920 A4
10 BKLN 7022 E1
10 LODI 6500 D1
Avenue H
- BKLN 7023 D1
5400 BKLN 7024 A1
Avenue I
10 BKLN 7022 E2
10 NWRK 6818 B3
1500 BKLN 7023 C1
5400 BKLN 7024 A1
Avenue J
10 BAYN 6920 B4
10 BKLN 7022 E2
500 BKLN 7023 A2
5300 BKLN 7024 A1
7500 BKLN 6924 B7
Avenue K
10 BKLN 7023 A2
10 NWRK 6818 B3
5300 BKLN 7024 A2
8300 BKLN 6924 D6
Avenue K Ext
- BKLN 7024 A2
Avenue L
10 BKLN 7022 E3
10 BKLN 7023 B2
10 NWRK 6818 B3
5300 BKLN 7024 A2
8600 BKLN 6924 C7
Avenue M
10 BKLN 7022 E3
4000 BKLN 7023 E2
7500 BKLN 7024 C1
9000 BKLN 6924 C7
Avenue N
10 BKLN 7022 E3
300 BKLN 7023 C3
5200 BKLN 7024 A3
9300 BKLN 6924 D7
Avenue O
10 BKLN 7022 D4
300 BKLN 7023 B3
5200 BKLN 7024 A3
Avenue of Africa
- QENS 6720 D6
Avenue of Commerce
- QENS 6720 D6
Avenue of the Americas
10 MHTN 118 C5
10 MHTN 6821 B2
400 MHTN 115 E7
400 MHTN 6717 C7
500 MHTN 116 B3
1200 MHTN 112 D7
Avenue of the Finest
10 MHTN 118 D7
10 MHTN 6821 B4
Avenue P
10 BKLN 7022 E4
10 NWRK 6818 C3
400 BKLN 7023 A4
Avenue R
10 BKLN 7023 A5
Avenue S
10 BKLN 7022 E5
300 BKLN 7023 B5
5200 BKLN 7024 A3
Avenue St. John
900 BRNX 6613 C4
Avenue T
10 BKLN 7022 E5
10 BKLN 7023 D5
5200 BKLN 7024 A3
Avenue U
10 BKLN 7022 D6
10 BKLN 7023 D5
5100 BKLN 7024 B3
Avenue V
10 BKLN 7022 D6
300 BKLN 7023 C6
3400 BKLN 7024 A4
Avenue W
10 BKLN 7022 E6
200 BKLN 7023 A6
3400 BKLN 7024 C3
Avenue X
10 BKLN 7022 E7
1600 BKLN 7023 C6
3400 BKLN 7024 C3
Avenue Y
10 BKLN 7022 D7
300 BKLN 7023 B6
3400 BKLN 7024 C3
Avenue Z
10 BKLN 7022 D7
500 BKLN 7023 A7
Averill Blvd
10 HmpT 6828 A4
200 STMN 6828 A3
Averill Pl
10 STNL 7206 B3
Avery Av
132-00 QENS 6720 E5
Avery Ct
10 HRSN 6051 A4
Avery Pl
200 CDHT 7028 A2
Avery Pth
- QENS 6720 E6
Aviation Plz N
- LNDN 7017 A2
Aviation Plz S
- LNDN 7017 A3
Aviation Rd
10 BKLN 7122 D1
Aviemore Dr
10 NRCH 6396 A1
Avis Dr
10 NRCH 6281 E5
10 NRCH 6282 A5
Aviston St
10 STNL 7117 E4
Aviva Ct
10 STNL 7206 A4
Avon Av
10 NWRK 6817 B2
400 NWRK 6816 E1
500 IrvT 6816 E1
W Avon Av
10 IrvT 6816 D1
Avon Cir
10 RYEB 6169 E5
10 RYEB 6170 A5
Avon Ct
200 HmpT 6929 A6
Avon Dr
10 NRCH 6281 D7
Avon Grn
- STNL 7116 A5
Avon Ln
10 STNL 7019 C3
Avon Pl
10 NARL 6714 D2
10 STNL 6920 D7
10 YNKR 6279 D5
100 HMPD 6828 E4
100 HmpT 6828 E4
Avon Plz
10 RYE 6284 B1
Avon Rd
10 BRXV 6280 E6
10 BRXV 6281 A7
10 HmpT 6928 E6
10 MrnT 6282 C6
10 NHmT 6724 A5
10 NRCH 6281 D7
182-00 QENS 6825 E2
184-00 QENS 6826 A2
Avon St
84-00 QENS 6825 E3
87-00 QENS 6826 A3
100 ROSP 6917 A3
Avondale Rd
10 HRSN 6283 A4
10 WHPL 6168 D5
10 YNKR 6280 E4
10 YNKR 6281 A4
Avondale St
10 VLYS 6928 D4
Avy St
1200 HlsT 6816 C6
Axminster St
10 YNKR 6279 E7
Axtell Dr
10 SCDL 6281 C1
Aye Ct
10 STNL 7018 E2
Ayer Pl
10 RTFD 6609 B1
Ayers Rd
- STNL 7021 A5
Aymar Av
10 STNL 7020 A4
Ayr St
10 EORG 6712 C5
10 NWRK 6712 C5
Ayres Ct
10 BAYN 6919 E5
Ayton Ln
10 YNKR 6280 A4
Azalea Cir
10 HRSN 6051 B5
Azalea Ct
10 GrbT 6166 E7
10 LBCH 7029 B6
10 STNL 7115 E5
10 TnkT 6502 D1
Azalea Dr
10 WLTN 6500 A6
Azalea Dr E
10 WLTN 6500 A6
Azalea Rd
1000 UnnT 6816 A7
Azalia Ct
10 HMPD 6828 E4
Aztec Pl
5-00 QENS 7027 C5
Azure Pl
1300 HWTH 6929 A7

B

B St
10 WbgT 7115 A3
1100 BRNX 6615 A1
1300 HmpT 6827 E6
Babbage St
113-00 QENS 6824 E5
Babbitt Ct
10 EMFD 6049 A6
10 GrbT 6049 A6
Babcock Ln
10 OrgT 6164 C2
Babcock Pl
10 HmpT 6929 B3
10 MLVN 6929 B3
10 WOrT 6712 C1
10 YNKR 6279 C7
Babylon Av
183-00 QENS 6826 A5
Bache Av
10 STNL 7117 B1
10 STNL 7118 A2
Bache St
10 STNL 7019 D1
Bacheller Av
400 LNDN 6917 D6
Bachman Pl
10 IrvT 6712 C7
10 IrvT 6816 A2
Backiel Av
10 LFRY 6501 D5
Backus St
10 NWRK 6818 A3
Backus Farm Ln
10 SNPT 6508 B4
Bacon Pl
10 YNKR 6280 E2
10 YNKR 6281 A2
Badeau Pl
10 NRCH 6395 E4
Baden Pl
10 STNL 7118 C1
Badger Av
10 NWRK 6817 B3
Baer Pl
300 NHPK 6828 A1
Bagley Av
10 NHmT 6724 D3
171-00 QENS 6721 D5
Bagley Pl
400 CLFP 6611 C1
400 RDGF 6611 C1
Bailey Av
10 HlsT 6816 E5
600 ELIZ 6917 C2
2400 BRNX 6504 C2
3300 BRNX 102 E3
Bailey Ct
29-00 QENS 7027 B4
Bailey Pl
10 NRCH 6395 D2
10 STNL 6918 E7
10 WbgT 7114 E4
3400 BRNX 102 E2
3400 BRNX 6504 C2
Bainbridge Av
- BRNX 6393 E7
2500 BRNX 6504 E1
Bainbridge Ct
10 YNKR 6280 D3
Bainbridge St
10 BKLN 6923 E1
200 BKLN 6924 A1
Bainton St
10 YNKR 6394 B4
Baisley Av
10 ERKY 6929 B7
100 HmpT 6929 B7
2800 BRNX 6614 E1
2900 BRNX 6615 B1
3100 BRNX 6506 A7
Baisley Blvd
151-00 QENS 6926 E2
161-00 QENS 6927 A1
174-00 QENS 6826 B7
Bajart Pl
10 YNKR 6394 A4
Bakam Ct
- QENS 7027 D4
Baker Av
10 HmpT 6927 D7
600 BRNX 6505 B7
Baker Ct
10 HmpT 7029 D5
10 ISPK 7029 D5
10 LFRY 6501 B5
Baker Ln
10 HAOH 6165 E6
Baker Pl
10 STNL 7020 A1
400 PTHA 7205 C2
600 ELIZ 6917 C3
Baker St
10 WbgT 7114 A2
1100 HlsT 6816 D6
Baker Hill Rd
10 GTNK 6616 C5
10 GTNK 6617 A5
10 NHmT 6617 A5
100 KNGP 6617 B5
Balcom Av
100 BRNX 6615 A3
1100 BRNX 6614 E1
1300 BRNX 6505 D7
Baldwin Av
10 HSBH 6500 E2
10 JSYC 6820 A2
10 LODI 6500 E2
10 MrnT 6396 C1
10 NWRK 6817 A2
10 WhkT 6716 B2
100 HSBH 6501 A3
400 JSYC 6716 B7
Baldwin Dr
10 HmpT 6828 C5
Baldwin Ln
10 NRCH 6282 C1
Baldwin Pl
10 ELIZ 6917 B3
10 YNKR 6393 C1
400 MRNK 6282 D6
Baldwin St
10 EORG 6712 D3
10 NWRK 6817 C1
4800 BRNX 6394 C5
4800 MTVN 6394 C5
Baldwin Ter
100 COrT 6712 C1
300 HSBH 6501 A5
Balfour Pl
10 BKLN 6923 C4
Balfour St
10 HmpT 6827 E7
10 STNL 7020 D7
800 HmpT 6928 E1
Balint Dr
10 YNKR 6280 D5
Ball Av
10 YNKR 6280 A6
Ball Pl
10 MplT 6816 A1
Ball St
10 IrvT 6816 D2
Ball Ter
10 MplT 6816 A1
Ballantine Ln
10 KNGP 6616 D2

New York City/5 Borough Street Index

STREET
Block City Map# Grid

Ballantine Pkwy
100 NWRK 6713 D3
Ballard Av
10 STNL 7116 B6
10 VLYS 6928 C3
Bally Pl
10 NRCH 6395 E4
Balmoral Cres
10 GrbT 6048 E7
10 GrbT 6049 A7
Balmoral Ln
10 GrbT 6049 A7
Balsam Av
- BKLN 7022 E2
Balsam Pl
10 BRNX 6615 B4
10 STNL 7115 E5
10 STNL 7116 A5
Balsam Wy N
900 UnnT 6816 A7
Balsam Wy S
700 UnnT 6816 A7
Baltic Av
10 STNL 7020 C4
Baltic St
10 STNL 7020 D1
100 BKLN 120 E7
100 BKLN 6821 B7
200 BKLN 121 A7
300 BKLN 6922 D1
Baltimore Av
10 HlsT 6816 C6
E Baltimore Av
10 LNDN 6917 B6
1100 ROSL 6917 A6
W Baltimore Av
10 LNDN 6917 B6
1200 ROSL 6917 A6
Baltimore St
10 STNL 7117 A5
Baltusrol Dr
10 HRSN 6050 E7
10 HRSN 6168 E1
Baltustrol Cir
300 NHLS 6724 A3
Bamberger Ln
10 STNL 7116 E6
Bambrick St
400 HmpT 7029 D1
Bamford Av
400 WbgT 7114 D4
Bamford Pl
10 IrvT 6816 C1
Banbury Cross
10 YNKR 6281 A1
Banbury Rd
100 MNLA 6724 E6
Bancker Pl
10 NRCH 6395 E5
Bancker St
10 EGLD 6502 D1
Bancroft Av
10 STNL 7117 E1
10 STNL 7118 A1
Bancroft Ln
10 KNGP 6616 E4
Bancroft Pl
10 BKLN 6924 A2
Bancroft St
10 CRSK 6278 A5
Banes Ct
10 BRNX 6614 C4
Bang Ter
10 STNL 7021 A4
Bangor St
10 STNL 7019 A7
Bank Pl
10 STNL 7020 C6
Bank St
10 BKLN 6924 C5
10 ELIZ 6918 A4
10 HmpT 6827 B7
10 HmpT 6928 B1
10 MHTN 115 D7
10 MHTN 6717 B7
10 NWRK 6713 D7
10 STNL 6920 C6
10 WHPL 6168 A2
1100 HlsT 6816 E7
Banker St
10 BKLN 6822 B2
Banks Av
10 RKVC 6929 D4
Banks St
10 BXTE 6617 D1
10 GrwT 6170 C1
10 NHmT 6617 D1
Banner Av
10 BKLN 7121 A2
800 BKLN 7023 A7
Banner 3rd Rd
10 BKLN 7121 A2
Banner 3rd Ter
10 BKLN 7121 A2
Bannister Ln
10 LWRN 7028 A5
Bansom Rd
10 SCDL 6168 B7
10 SCDL 6282 B1
Banta Av
100 GRFD 6500 A1
Banta Pl
10 HKSK 6501 C1
10 IrvT 6816 C4
700 RDGF 6611 B1
Bantam Pl
1500 BRNX 6505 D3
Banyer Pl
1600 BRNX 6614 A2
Bar Ct
10 STNL 7115 E5
Baraud Rd N
10 NRCH 6281 E1
Baraud Rd S
10 NRCH 6281 E2
Barb St
10 STNL 7116 D6
Barbadoes Dr
3-00 QENS 7026 C6
Barbara Blvd
600 HmpT 6828 B3
Barbara Ct
10 LODI 6500 E3
10 RYE 6283 E2
Barbara Dr
10 EGLC 6392 C5
700 TnkT 6502 C1
Barbara Ln
10 GrbT 6167 A2
10 IRVN 6048 C7
300 HmpT 6929 D1
1500 MRNK 6283 A4
Barbara Pl
10 EchT 6281 B6
10 JSYC 6820 A3
Barbara St
10 HmpT 6827 D6
10 NWRK 6818 B2
100 STNL 7117 C2
Bar Beach Rd
10 NHmT 6618 A2
Barber Pl
10 RYEB 6170 A5
Barberry Ct
10 BKLN 6924 D1
10 QENS 6924 D1
Barberry Ln
10 NRCH 6281 D7
10 RYE 6284 B2
10 SCLF 6509 E7
800 HWTN 7028 C2
800 WDBG 7028 C2
900 HmpT 7028 D2
Barbey St
200 BKLN 6924 D2
Barclay Av
10 STNL 7116 D7
142-00 QENS 6721 B4
300 STNL 7207 E1
Barclay Cir
10 STNL 7116 B4
Barclay Cres
10 NHLS 6724 B2
Barclay Rd
10 GrbT 6167 B7
Barclay St
10 MHTN 118 C7
10 MHTN 6821 A4
10 NWRK 6817 C2
200 PTHA 7205 C2
Bard Av
10 STNL 6920 A7
10 STNL 7020 A2
Bardion Ln
10 HRSN 6283 C1
Bardwell Av
208-00 QENS 6826 D4
Bardwell Pl
10 YNKR 6281 A4
Barell Av
400 CARL 6610 B2
Barford Ln
10 GrbT 6167 A7
Baring Pl
10 STNL 7020 E1
Barkalow St
10 SAMB 7205 B7
Barker Av
10 WHPL 6168 B1
2200 BRNX 6505 A4
Barker Ln
10 SCDL 6282 C3
Barker St
10 STNL 6919 E7
Barkers Point Rd
10 NHmT 6508 C6
10 PTWN 6508 C6
10 SNPT 6508 B6
Barkley Av
2700 BRNX 6614 E2
2800 BRNX 6615 A1
Barksdale Rd
10 GrbT 6049 B7
Barlik St
10 CART 7017 C7
10 CART 7115 C1
Barlow Av
10 GLCV 6509 E3
10 STNL 7117 A4
400 STNL 7116 E4
Barlow Dr N
10 BKLN 7024 B4
Barlow Dr S
10 BKLN 7024 B4
Barlow Ln
10 RYE 6283 C5
Barlow St
10 YNKR 6394 B4
Barnaby Ln
10 GrbT 6167 A3
Barnard Av
10 STNL 7206 B3
300 CDHT 7028 B1
300 HmpT 7028 A1
500 HmpT 6928 A7
Barnard Pl
10 ELIZ 6917 D2
10 MNPK 6618 A5
Barnard Rd
10 NRCH 6396 A1
200 MrnT 6396 B1
Barnell St
- BKLN 6922 A2
Barnes Av
2300 BRNX 6505 B3
3900 BRNX 6394 C6
4800 MTVN 6394 D5
Barnes Ct
10 PTHA 7205 E2
Barnes Dr
10 RDFP 6502 B4
Barnes Dr E
10 RDFP 6502 B4
Barnes Dr W
10 RDFP 6502 B4
Barnes Ln
10 HRSN 6050 E5
10 HRSN 6051 A6
Barnes Pl
10 VLYS 6928 B2
Barnes Rd
10 TYTN 6048 C3
Barnes St
10 LBCH 7029 E6
1000 HmpT 6828 A4
Barnett Av
43-00 QENS 6719 A6
Barnett Pl
10 BRNX 6505 B6
Barnett St
2100 LNDN 7017 A4
2100 RHWY 7017 A4
Barnett St CO-613
2100 LNDN 7017 A4
2100 RHWY 7017 A4
149-00 QENS 6721 B4
Barney Pk
10 IRVN 6166 A1
Barney St
10 EMFD 6049 B5
10 YNKR 6280 A2
Barnhart Av
10 SYHW 6048 A1
Barn Hill Rd
10 GrwT 6170 D2
Barnstable Rd
10 HmpT 6929 B7
10 HmpT 7029 B1
Barnum Rd
10 MrnT 6282 C6
Barnum St
- JSYC 6820 D1
Barnwall Ln
10 MrnT 6282 C3
Barnwell Av
79-00 QENS 6719 E7
Barnwell Dr
10 GrbT 6049 B7
Baron Blvd
10 STNL 7018 C5
Baron's Gate Av
1500 WbgT 7114 D2
Barr Av
200 HmpT 6928 C7
200 TnkT 6502 A1
Barr Pl
10 CLFP 6611 C5
10 NBgT 6611 C5
Barr Rd
10 HBPK 7028 D1
10 HWTN 7028 D1
Barracks St
100 PTHA 7205 D3
Barrett Av
10 MNCH 6500 E7
10 STNL 7019 C1
400 BRNX 6614 C3
Barrett Ln
10 PTCH 6170 B3
Barrett Rd
10 LWRN 7028 B4
Barretto St
200 BRNX 6613 D4
Barrington Rd
10 YNKR 6280 D6
Barrington St
87-00 QENS 6826 A3
Barron Av
400 WbgT 7114 C3
Barron Pl
10 RYE 6283 E5
Barron St
116-00 QENS 6825 E7
116-00 QENS 6926 E1
Barrow Pl
10 STNL 7115 E5
10 STNL 7116 A5
Barrow St
10 MHTN 118 D1
10 MHTN 6821 A1
200 JSYC 6820 C3
Barrows Av
10 RTFD 6609 A3
Barrows Ct
242-00 QENS 6722 E4
Barry Av
600 PTHA 7205 B1
700 PTHA 7114 B7
N Barry Av
100 MRNK 6283 A5
700 MRNK 6282 E4
S Barry Av
100 MRNK 6283 A6
Barry Ct
10 STNL 7118 A4
Barry Dr
10 GLCV 6509 D4
Barry Dr S
1100 HmpT 6827 E7
1100 HmpT 6928 E1
Barry Dr W
800 HmpT 6827 D7
800 HmpT 6928 E1
Barry Rd
10 MHTN 120 B6
10 MHTN 6821 A7
10 NRCH 6281 D1
10 SCDL 6281 D1
Barry St
10 STNL 7115 E5
700 BRNX 6613 C4
N Barry Av Ext
200 MRNK 6282 E4
Barrymore Blvd
10 HmpT 6828 A4
100 STMN 6828 A4
Barrymore Ln
600 MRNK 6283 B6
Barrypark Ct
10 NHmT 6724 C3
Barstow Rd
10 GTPZ 6617 A7
10 KENS 6617 A7
10 THSN 6617 C4
Barszczewski St
10 KRNY 6714 D3
Bartels Pl
10 NRCH 6395 E5
Barter Pl
10 SECS 6610 B6
Barthold St
10 GRFD 6500 A2
Bartholdi Av
10 JSYC 6819 B5
Bartholdi St
600 BRNX 6505 A2
Bartlett Av
10 STNL 7116 E5
Bartlett Dr
10 MNPK 6618 B6
Bartlett Pl
10 BKLN 7023 E7
Bartlett Pl
100 BKLN 7024 A6
Bartlett St
10 BKLN 6822 C5
Barton Av
10 STNL 7020 A7
10 STNL 7118 A2
Barton Pl
10 PTCH 6170 A4
Barton Rd
10 YNKR 6280 B6
100 WHPL 6168 D6
1500 UnnT 6816 A6
Bartow Av
10 STNL 7206 C4
10 WbgT 7114 A1
1600 BRNX 6505 E3
2000 BRNX 6506 A3
Bartow St
10 STNL 7117 C5
Bartz St
3500 HmpT 7029 C2
Baruch Dr
10 MHTN 119 D6
10 MHTN 6821 E3
Baruch Pl
10 MHTN 119 D5
10 MHTN 6821 E3
Barwick St
10 FLPK 6827 D1
10 NHmT 6827 D1
100 FLPK 6723 C7
100 NHmT 6723 C7
Bascom Av
140-00 QENS 6926 D2
Bascom Pl
10 STNL 7019 B4
Bashford St
10 YNKR 6393 A1
Basile Ct
10 HmpT 7028 D3
Basilone Rd
- ELIZ 6918 B1
Baskerville Av
400 UnnT 6917 B2
Bass St
10 STNL 7019 C4
Bassett Av
10 BKLN 7024 B4
1300 BRNX 6505 D5
2000 BRNX 6506 B5
Bassett Rd
10 BRNX 6505 D6
Bassford Av
2200 BRNX 6504 D5
Batavia Pl
10 HRSN 6283 B3
Batchelder St
10 BKLN 7023 D5
Bateman Pl
10 MTVN 6395 B3
Bates Rd
10 HRSN 6283 C2
10 LKSU 6723 A3
10 NHmT 6723 A3
10 QENS 6723 A3
Bates St
10 JSYC 6820 B3
Bath Av
10 STNL 7020 C6
1400 BKLN 7022 A4
Bathgate Av
1500 BRNX 105 E6
1900 BRNX 6504 C6
Bathgate Pl
10 NWRK 6713 A6
Bathgate St
10 STNL 7207 E1
10 STNL 7208 A1
Battaglia Ln
100 FRVW 6611 A2
Battery Av
10 BKLN 7021 E3
Battery Pl
10 MHTN 120 A2
10 MHTN 6821 A5
Battery Rd
10 STNL 7021 A5
22-00 QENS 7027 C4
Battle Av
10 WHPL 6167 E2
10 WHPL 6168 C2
Bauer Ct
500 HmpT 6827 C6
Bauer Ln
10 OrgT 6164 E2
10 PRMT 6164 E2
Bauer Pl
300 MNLA 6724 D5
Bauer St
10 OrgT 6164 D2
600 HmpT 6827 C7
Bauer Ter
10 HlsT 6917 D1
Baughman Pl
10 BKLN 7023 D2
Baur Ct
10 WLTN 6500 B4
Baxter Av
10 NHmT 6724 A6
80-00 QENS 6719 E6
Baxter St
10 MHTN 118 E5
10 MHTN 6821 B3
Bay Av
10 LRMT 6396 D3
10 NWRK 6818 A3
10 SCLF 6509 D6
2000 BKLN 7023 B3
E Bay Av
10 ELIZ 6919 B2
1200 BRNX 6613 D4
W Bay Av
100 ELIZ 6918 E1
100 ELIZ 6919 A1
Bay Blvd
10 CDHT 7027 E1
10 HmpT 7027 E1
1300 HmpT 7028 C7
1400 ATLB 7028 B7
2000 ATLB 7027 E6
Bay Ct
33-00 QENS 7027 B3
Bay Dr
10 NHmT 6508 C6
10 PTCH 6284 C1
10 PTWN 6508 C6
10 WDBG 7028 D2
E Bay Dr
300 LBCH 7029 D6
W Bay Dr
100 LBCH 7029 B6
Bay Drwy
10 PLNH 6617 C5
Bay Pkwy
10 BKLN 7022 C5
10 BKLN 7023 A2
Bay St
10 BKLN 6922 B2
10 BRNX 6506 D6
10 HmpT 7028 C7
10 JSYC 6820 C3
10 STNL 6920 E7
236-00 QENS 6722 D2
300 STNL 7020 D1
1100 STNL 7021 A4
Bay Ter
10 STNL 7117 C5
Bay 7th St
10 BKLN 7022 A4
Bay 8th St
10 BKLN 7022 A4
Bay 10th St
10 BKLN 7022 A4
Bay 11th St
10 BKLN 7022 A4
Bay 13th St
10 BKLN 7022 A5
Bay 14th St
10 BKLN 7022 A5
Bay 16th St
8100 BKLN 7022 A5
Bay 17th St
10 BKLN 7022 B5
Bay 19th St
100 BKLN 7022 B5
Bay 20th St
10 BKLN 7022 B5
Bay 22nd St
10 BKLN 7022 B5
Bay 23rd St
10 BKLN 7022 B5
Bay 24th St
13-00 QENS 7027 C4
Bay 25th St
6-00 QENS 7027 B4
10 BKLN 7022 B5
Bay 26th St
10 BKLN 7022 B5
Bay 27th St
11-00 QENS 7027 B4
Bay 28th St
10 BKLN 7022 C5
13-00 QENS 7027 B4
Bay 29th St
10 BKLN 7022 C5
Bay 30th St
10-00 QENS 7027 B5
Bay 31st St
10 BKLN 7022 C6
10-00 QENS 7027 B5
Bay 32nd Pl
11-00 QENS 7027 B5
Bay 32nd St
10 BKLN 7022 C6
10-00 QENS 7027 B5
Bay 34th St
10 BKLN 7022 C6
Bay 35th St
10 BKLN 7022 C6
Bay 37th St
10 BKLN 7022 C6
Bay 38th St
10 BKLN 7022 C6
Bay 40th St
10 BKLN 7022 C6
Bay 41st St
10 BKLN 7022 D6
Bay 43rd St
10 BKLN 7022 D6
Bay 44th St
10 BKLN 7022 C7
Bay 46th St
10 BKLN 7022 D7
Bay 47th St
10 BKLN 7022 D7
Bay 48th St
10 BKLN 7022 D7
Bay 49th St
10 BKLN 7022 D7
Bay 50th St
10 BKLN 7022 D7
Bay 52nd St
10 BKLN 7022 C7
Bay 53rd St
10 BKLN 7120 D1
Bay 54th St
10 BKLN 7120 D1
Bay 56th St
- BKLN 7120 D1
Bayard Av
10 KRNY 6714 B1
Bayard Pl
10 NWRK 6712 C7
Bayard St
10 BKLN 6822 C3
10 BlvT 6714 B1
10 LRMT 6396 C2
10 MHTN 118 E6
10 MHTN 6821 B4
10 NRCH 6395 D6
10 STNL 7116 E6
700 TnkT 6502 B1
Bayberry Ct
10 WbgT 7115 B2
Bayberry Dr
200 HWTH 6929 A7
Bayberry Dr N
200 HWTH 6929 A7
Bayberry Dr S
200 HWTH 6929 A7
Bayberry Ln
10 NRCH 6282 A6
10 RYEB 6170 A2
Bayberry Rd
10 GrbT 6049 C4
10 LWRN 7028 B3
Bayberry Rd
700 HmpT 6828 A7
Bayberry Rd E
- LWRN 7028 B4
Bayberry Rd W
- LWRN 7028 B4
Bayberry Rdg
- MNPK 6618 B5
10 FLHL 6618 B5
Bayberry St
10 YNKR 6280 C2
Bayberry Close
10 RYEB 6170 A2
Baychester Av
3200 BRNX 6505 D1
3800 BRNX 6394 C6
Bay Cliff Ter
6800 BKLN 6921 D7
Bay Club Dr
10 QENS 6721 E1
Bayeau Rd
10 NRCH 6281 E7
10 NRCH 6395 E1
Bayfield Av
65-00 QENS 7026 C5
Bay Green Ln
10 NHmT 6508 E7
Bay Head Dr
1000 MRNK 6397 A2
N Bayles Av
10 NHmT 6617 E1
S Bayles Av
10 NHmT 6617 E2
Bayley Av
10 YNKR 6393 C4
Baylis Av
2000 HmpT 6827 A5
Baylis Ct
10 TYTN 6048 B2
Baylis Pl
10 ERKY 6929 A6
10 HmpT 6929 A6
10 LNBK 6929 A6
Baylor Cir
10 WHPL 6168 E3
10 WHPL 6169 A3
Bayne Pl
10 WHPL 6168 C5
Bayonne Br
- BAYN 6919 C5
- STNL 6919 C6
Bayonne Br CO-501
- BAYN 6919 C6
- STNL 6919 C6
Bayonne Br SR-440
- BAYN 6919 C5
- STNL 6919 C6
Bay Park Dr
5-02 QENS 6614 C7
Bay Park Pl
11-00 QENS 7027 B4
Bayport Ln
10 SDRK 6616 C6
Bayport Ln N
10 SDRK 6616 C6
Bayport Pl
11-00 QENS 7027 D4
Bay Ridge Av
10 BKLN 6921 D7
400 BKLN 7021 E1
700 BKLN 7022 A1
Bay Ridge Pkwy
10 BKLN 7021 D1
600 BKLN 7022 C3
Bay Ridge Pl
10 BKLN 6921 E7
Bayshore Av
1400 BRNX 6506 B6
Bayshore Blvd
10 QENS 6722 D2
Bayshore Dr
10 SAMB 7205 C7
Bayside Av
10 BXTE 6617 D1
100 HmpT 6929 D7
142-00 QENS 6721 A3
Bayside Dr
10 BAYN 6919 D6
10 NHmT 6616 D7
10 PLDM 6617 C4
10 PLNM 6617 C4
100 HmpT 7028 C7
204-00 QENS 7122 B3
Bayside Ln
10 STNL 7207 A3
25-00 QENS 6721 C2
Bayside Pl
10 JSYC 6819 D5
Bayside St
600 QENS 6616 A6
Bayside Ter
10 JSYC 6819 D6
10 NHmT 6616 D7
Bayside Park Dr
10 JSYC 6819 D6
Bayside Pier
10 QENS 7026 B6
Bay St Lndg
100 STNL 6920 E7
Bayswater Av
23-00 QENS 7027 B4
Bayswater Blvd
10 HmpT 7027 C3
Bay View Av
10 JSYC 6819 D5
1500 BRNX 6506 B6
Bayview Av
- THSN 6617 C6
10 BKLN 7120 B1
10 EGLC 6503 B3
10 GTNE 6616 D7
10 GTNE 6722 E1
10 HlsT 6816 D4
10 HmpT 6927 D7
10 HmpT 7027 D3
10 NHmT 6616 D7
10 NHmT 6617 D2
10 NRCH 6396 B5
10 NWRK 6816 D5
10 QENS 6925 E4
10 STNL 7207 A2
10 VLYS 6928 E5
100 SDRK 6616 D6
155-00 QENS 6927 D7
235-00 QENS 6722 C1
Bayview Av
400 CDHT 7028 A1
500 HmpT 7028 A1
W Bayview Av
10 EGLC 6503 B3
Bayview Cir
- PLNH 6617 C5
Bayview Ct
10 BAYN 6919 C5
10 HmpT 7027 D3
10 NHmT 6617 C6
2900 HmpT 6929 E7
Bayview Ln
10 STNL 7207 A3
Bay View Pl
10 BKLN 6924 B6
Bayview Pl
10 STNL 6920 D7
10 STNL 7020 D1
Bayview Rd
10 ERKY 6929 D5
10 LNBK 6929 C5
10 PLDM 6617 C4
10 PLNM 6617 C4
Bayview St E
10 HmpT 6929 C7
Bayview Ter
10 NHmT 6617 D6
10 STNL 7207 E1
Baywater Ct
32-00 QENS 7027 B3
Bayway Av
10 ELIZ 6918 A7
500 ELIZ 6917 D5
Bayway Av SR-439
500 ELIZ 6917 D5
Bayway Cir
500 ELIZ 6917 D5
Beach Av
10 LRMT 6396 C3
10 STNL 7117 E2
100 MRNK 6283 A5
300 BRNX 6614 B3
300 STNL 7118 A3
1400 BRNX 6505 A7
4500 HmpT 7029 D5
4500 ISPK 7029 D6
S Beach Av
10 STNL 7020 E6
Beach Rd
- LWRN 7028 B5
10 GTNK 6616 E5
10 KNGP 6616 D5
10 SNPT 6508 C4
10 STNL 7117 A6
Beach St
10 BRNX 6394 C5
10 JSYC 6716 A6
10 MHTN 118 B5
10 MHTN 6821 A3
10 MTVN 6394 C5
10 NWRK 6817 D1
10 STNL 7020 D1
100 BRNX 6506 E5
Beach Wk
10 ISPK 7029 D4
Beach Wy
10 ISPK 7029 C4
Beach 2nd St
200 LWRN 7027 E5
Beach 3rd St
1-00 QENS 7027 E6
Beach 4th St
1-00 QENS 7027 E6
Beach 5th St
1-00 QENS 7027 E6
Beach 6th St
400 QENS 7027 D6
Beach 7th St
4-00 QENS 7027 E5
Beach 8th St
- QENS 7027 E5
Beach 9th St
10-00 QENS 7027 D4
Beach 11th St
15-00 HmpT 7027 B3
200 QENS 7027 D6
Beach 12th St
4-00 QENS 7027 D6
15-00 HmpT 7027 D4
Beach 13th St
200 QENS 7027 D6
Beach 14th St
2-00 QENS 7027 D6
Beach 15th St
200 QENS 7027 D6
Beach 16th St
2-00 QENS 7027 D6
Beach 17th St
100 QENS 7027 D6
Beach 18th St
16-00 QENS 7027 D5
Beach 19th St
100 QENS 7027 C6
Beach 20th St
2-00 QENS 7027 C6
Beach 21st St
10-00 QENS 7027 C5
Beach 22nd St
10-00 QENS 7027 C5
Beach 24th St
100 QENS 7027 C6
Beach 25th St
300 QENS 7027 C5
Beach 26th St
100 QENS 7027 C6
Beach 27th St
100 QENS 7027 C6
Beach 28th St
300 QENS 7027 C5
Beach 29th St
10 QENS 7027 C5
Beach 30th St
100 QENS 7027 B5
Beach 31st St
300 QENS 7027 B6
Beach 32nd St
10 QENS 7027 B6
Beach 33rd St
10 QENS 7027 B6
Beach 34th St
10 QENS 7027 B6
Beach 35th St
10 QENS 7027 B5
Beach 36th St
300 QENS 7027 B6
Beach 37th St
200 QENS 7027 B6
Beach 38th St
10 BKLN 7120 B2
10 QENS 7027 B6
Beach 39th St
3-00 QENS 7027 B5
Beach 40th St
10 BKLN 7120 B2
200 QENS 7027 A6
Beach 41st St
1-00 QENS 7027 A6
Beach 42nd St
10 BKLN 7120 B2
200 QENS 7027 A6
Beach 43rd St
10 BKLN 7120 A2
300 QENS 7027 A5
Beach 44th St
10 BKLN 7120 A2
300 QENS 7027 A5
Beach 45th St
10 BKLN 7120 A2
300 QENS 7027 A5
Beach 46th St
10 BKLN 7120 A2
10 QENS 7027 A5
Beach 47th St
10 BKLN 7120 A1
200 QENS 7027 A6
Beach 48th St
10 BKLN 7120 A1
10 QENS 7027 A6
Beach 49th St
10 BKLN 7120 A1
300 QENS 7027 A6
Beach 50th St
10 BKLN 7120 A1
300 QENS 7027 A6
Beach 51st St
- BKLN 7120 A1
10 QENS 7027 A6
300 QENS 7026 E5
Beach 52nd St
10 QENS 7026 E7
Beach 53rd St
300 QENS 7026 E6
Beach 54th St
100 QENS 7026 E7
Beach 55th St
100 QENS 7026 E7
Beach 56th Pl
- QENS 7026 E6
Beach 56th St
300 QENS 7026 E6
Beach 57th St
300 QENS 7026 E6
Beach 58th St
400 QENS 7026 E6
Beach 59th St
10 QENS 7026 E7
Beach 60th St
100 QENS 7026 E7
Beach 61st St
10 QENS 7026 E7
Beach 62nd St
1-01 QENS 7026 E7
Beach 63rd St
3-00 QENS 7026 D6
Beach 64th St
400 QENS 7026 D6
Beach 65th St
4-00 QENS 7026 D6
Beach 66th St
300 QENS 7026 D6
Beach 67th St
400 QENS 7026 D6
Beach 68th St
3-00 QENS 7026 D6
Beach 69th St
600 QENS 7026 D6
Beach 70th St
300 QENS 7026 D6
Beach 71st St
- QENS 7026 C7
Beach 72nd St
300 QENS 7026 D6
Beach 73rd St
1-01 QENS 7026 C6
Beach 74th St
1-00 QENS 7026 C7
Beach 75th St
3-00 QENS 7026 C6
Beach 77th St
1-00 QENS 7026 C7
Beach 79th St
2-00 QENS 7026 C7
Beach 80th St
2-00 QENS 7026 C7
Beach 81st St
1-00 QENS 7026 C7
Beach 83rd St
- QENS 7026 C7
Beach 84th St
4-00 QENS 7026 C6
Beach 85th St
300 QENS 7026 B7
Beach 86th St
200 QENS 7026 B7
Beach 87th St
2-00 QENS 7026 B7
Beach 88th St
2-00 QENS 7026 B6
Beach 89th St
300 QENS 7026 B6
Beach 90th St
1-00 QENS 7026 B7
Beach 91st St
1-00 QENS 7026 B7
Beach 92nd St
10 QENS 7026 B7
Beach 93rd St
100 QENS 7026 A7
Beach 94th St
2-00 QENS 7026 A6
Beach 95th St
2-01 QENS 7026 A6
Beach 96th St
2-00 QENS 7026 B7
Beach 97th St
2-00 QENS 7026 A7
Beach 98th St
3-00 QENS 7026 A7
Beach 99th St
100 QENS 7026 A7
100 QENS 7124 B1
Beach 100th St
100 QENS 7026 A7
Beach 101st St
- QENS 7124 A1
1-00 QENS 7026 A7
Beach 102nd St
1-00 QENS 7026 A7
1-00 QENS 7124 A1
Beach 104th St
300 QENS 7026 A7
Beach 105th St
1-00 QENS 7026 A6
1-00 QENS 7124 A1
Beach 106th St
2-00 QENS 7026 A7
2-00 QENS 7124 A1
Beach 108th St
2-01 QENS 7123 E1
3-00 QENS 7025 E7
100 QENS 7124 A1
Beach 109th St
2-00 QENS 7123 E1
Beach 110th St
100 QENS 7123 E1
Beach 111th St
100 QENS 7123 E1
Beach 112th St
100 QENS 7123 E1
Beach 113th St
100 QENS 7123 E1
Beach 114th St
100 QENS 7123 E1
Beach 115th St
100 QENS 7123 E1
Beach 116th St
100 QENS 7123 D1
Beach 117th St
100 QENS 7123 D1
Beach 118th St
100 QENS 7123 D1
Beach 119th St
100 QENS 7123 D1
Beach 120th St
100 QENS 7123 D1
Beach 121st St
100 QENS 7123 D1
Beach 122nd St
100 QENS 7123 D1
Beach 123rd St
100 QENS 7123 D1
Beach 124th St
100 QENS 7123 D1
Beach 125th St
100 QENS 7123 D1
Beach 126th St
100 QENS 7123 D1
Beach 127th St
100 QENS 7123 C1
Beach 128th St
100 QENS 7123 C1
Beach 129th St
100 QENS 7123 C1
Beach 130th St
100 QENS 7123 C1
Beach 131st St
100 QENS 7123 C1
Beach 132nd St
100 QENS 7123 C1
Beach 133rd St
1-00 QENS 7123 C1
Beach 134th St
1-00 QENS 7123 C1
Beach 135th St
5-00 QENS 7123 C1
Beach 136th St
100 QENS 7123 C1
Beach 137th St
1-00 QENS 7123 C1
Beach 138th St
1-00 QENS 7123 B1
Beach 139th St
100 QENS 7123 B1
Beach 140th St
100 QENS 7123 B1
Beach 141st St
100 QENS 7123 B2
Beach 142nd St
1-00 QENS 7123 B2
Beach 143rd St
100 QENS 7123 B2
Beach 144th St
400 QENS 7123 B2
Beach 145th St
100 QENS 7123 B2
Beach 146th St
- QENS 7123 B2
Beach 147th St
100 QENS 7123 B2
Beach 148th St
100 QENS 7123 B2
Beach 149th St
2-00 QENS 7123 B2
Beach 169th St
400 QENS 7122 E3
Beach 178th St
10 QENS 7122 D3
Beach 184th St
900 QENS 7122 D3
Beach 193rd St
10 QENS 7122 C3
Beach 201st St
100 QENS 7122 B4
Beach 202nd St
10 QENS 7122 B3
Beach 204th St
10 QENS 7122 B3
Beach 207th St
100 QENS 7122 A4
Beach 208th St
10 QENS 7122 A4
Beach 209th St
10 QENS 7122 A4
Beach 210th St
- QENS 7122 A3
Beach 212th St
10 QENS 7122 A4
Beach 213th St
10 QENS 7122 A4

New York City/5 Borough Street Index

Beach 214th St   Birch Hill Rd

STREET / Block	City	Map#	Grid
Beach 214th St			
10	QENS	7122	A4
Beach 215th St			
100	QENS	7122	E4
100	QENS	7122	E4
Beach 216th St			
-	QENS	7121	E3
Beach 217th St			
10	QENS	7121	E5
Beach 218th St			
-	QENS	7121	E4
Beach 219th St			
10	QENS	7121	E4
Beach 220th St			
10	QENS	7121	E4
Beach 221st St			
10	QENS	7121	E4
Beach 222nd St			
-	QENS	7121	E4
Beach 224th St			
9700	QENS	7121	E5
Beach Breeze Ln			
2-00	QENS	7026	C7
Beach Breeze Pl			
2-00	QENS	7026	C7
Beach Channel Dr			
10	QENS	7122	E3
10-01	QENS	7027	A6
14-88	HmpT	7027	C4
50-00	QENS	7026	E7
105-01	QENS	7025	E7
112-02	QENS	7123	C1
Beachfront Ln			
10	NRCH	6396	B4
Beachview Av			
10	STNL	7118	B1
4100	HmpT	7029	E6
Beachway St			
10	NHmT	6617	C3
Beach Wood			
200	COrT	6712	B5
Beacon Av			
10	JSYC	6716	A7
10	JSYC	6820	D1
10	STNL	7117	C1
Beacon Ct			
10	BKLN	7024	A7
Beacon Dr			
10	NHmT	6509	B7
Beacon Ln			
10	RYEB	6169	C4
100	BRNX	6614	C4
Beacon Pl			
10	STNL	7118	B3
14-00	QENS	7027	B4
Beacon St			
10	MLVN	6929	A2
10	NRCH	6396	A6
10	WbgT	7115	B3
10	YNKR	6279	C5
Beacon Hill Dr			
-	DBSF	6166	B6
Beacon Hill Rd			
10	ARDY	6166	D4
10	NHmT	6509	A7
10	NHmT	6618	A1
Beadel St			
10	BKLN	6822	D2
Beak St			
10	MHTN	101	E6
10	MHTN	6503	E3
Beal Pl			
10	BRNX	6615	C4
Beale Cir			
10	YNKR	6280	D6
Beamer Ct			
10	STNL	6919	A7
Bear St			
10	STNL	7020	B6
Beard St			
10	BKLN	6922	A2
10	STNL	7019	B7
Beardsley Av			
300	NWRK	6713	C2
400	BlmT	6713	B2
Beary Ct			
10	RYE	6284	A3
Beatrice Ct			
10	HMPD	6828	E4
Beattie Ln			
10	NRCH	6395	E6
Beaty Ct			
10	RYE	6284	A1
Beaufort Pl			
10	NRCH	6395	E3
Beaufort St			
10	BlmT	6049	B6
Beaumont Av			
2200	BRNX	6504	E5
Beaumont Cir			
10	YNKR	6280	C2
Beaumont Ct			
10	NHmT	6724	B4
Beaumont Pl			
10	IrvT	6816	B1
10	NWRK	6713	E1
Beaumont St			
10	BKLN	7121	C1
Beaumont Ter			
10	WOrT	6712	A2
Beaver Lndg			
10	HRSN	6283	B4
Beaver Rd			
150-00	QENS	6825	C6
Beaver St			
10	BKLN	6822	D5
10	MHTN	120	B2
10	MHTN	6821	A5
10	NWRK	6713	E4
Beaver Hill Rd			
10	BlmT	6049	B4
Beck Av			
10	RYE	6284	A4
Beck Rd			
700	QENS	7027	C4
Beck St			
500	BRNX	6613	C4
Becker Ter			
10	IrvT	6816	A4
Beckett Close			
10	DBSF	6166	C2
Beckwith Pl			
10	RTFD	6609	A1

STREET / Block	City	Map#	Grid
Bedell Av			
10	HMPD	6828	E4
10	HmpT	6828	E4
10	STNL	7206	C4
100	GDNC	6828	E4
Bedell Ln			
8700	BKLN	6924	B6
Bedell St			
112-00	QENS	6825	E7
126-00	QENS	6927	B1
Bedell Ter			
500	HmpT	6828	E5
Bedford Av			
10	BKLN	6822	A5
10	HmpT	6827	D4
10	NHmT	6724	C7
10	STNL	7118	A1
10	WbgT	7114	A3
200	MNLA	6724	D7
200	MTVN	6395	A5
1100	BKLN	6923	B5
2800	BKLN	7023	C1
Bedford Pl			
10	BKLN	6923	B1
10	YNKR	6280	D2
Bedford Rd			
10	GrwT	6051	C1
10	NHmT	6618	A1
10	SYHW	6048	C1
Bedford Rd SR-448			
10	SYHW	6048	C1
Bedford Ter			
10	IrvT	6816	C4
Bedford Park Blvd			
200	BRNX	6504	D3
Bedford Park Blvd E			
-	BRNX	6504	D3
Bedford Park Blvd W			
200	BRNX	6504	D2
Bedle Pl			
1600	LNDN	6917	D6
2500	ELIZ	6917	C2
Bee Ct			
10	STNL	7018	E3
Bee St			
800	HmpT	6827	B7
800	HmpT	6928	D1
Beebe Rd			
100	MNLA	6724	D4
Beebe St			
10	STNL	7020	A5
Beech Av			
140-00	QENS	6721	B4
Beech Ct			
10	MLVN	6929	A1
10	QENS	6614	D7
200	NRWD	6278	C1
Beech Dr			
-	ROSH	6618	E4
10	KNGP	6616	E3
Beech Ln			
10	KNGP	6616	C5
10	TYTN	6048	C2
Beech Pl			
10	BRNX	6615	C4
Beech Rd			
10	EGLD	6392	B7
10	EGLD	6503	A1
10	NRCH	6282	B7
Beech St			
10	EchT	6281	B6
10	EORG	6712	E4
10	ERTH	6500	A7
10	FLPK	6827	D3
10	GrbT	6049	D6
10	GRFD	6500	A2
10	GrwT	6170	D5
10	KRNY	6714	B3
10	LFRY	6501	C6
10	MtPT	6050	A1
10	NARL	6714	C1
10	PTCH	6170	C6
10	RTFD	6500	A7
10	RTFD	6609	C2
100	HKSS	6501	B1
100	HmpT	6827	C3
100	SFPK	6827	D3
100	VLYS	6928	A2
200	TnkT	6501	E3
200	TnkT	6502	A2
400	NHmT	6723	E7
500	COrT	6712	A4
600	WOrT	6712	A4
1200	HmpT	7028	C2
1400	ATLB	7028	C2
Beech St W			
10	WHPL	6050	B6
E Beech St			
10	LBCH	7029	D7
W Beech St			
10	LBCH	7029	A7
700	LBCH	7028	D7
1100	HmpT	7028	D7
Beech Ter			
10	YNKR	6393	B7
500	BRNX	6613	A4
Beech Av Ext			
-	QENS	6928	A2
-	VLYS	6928	A2
Beechdale Rd			
10	DBSF	6166	A6
Beecher Dr			
-	YNKR	6394	E7
Beecher St			
10	NWRK	6817	D1
Beech Hill Rd			
10	STNL	6281	D1
Beechhurst Av			
900	HmpT	6928	D1
Beech Knoll Av			
249-00	QENS	6722	D3
Beechknoll Rd			
74-00	QENS	6824	D3
Beechmont Av			
10	YNKR	6280	D7

STREET / Block	City	Map#	Grid
Beechmont Dr			
10	NRCH	6395	E2
200	NRCH	6396	A1
Beechmont Pl			
10	NRCH	6396	A1
Beech Spring Rd			
200	IrvT	6816	B4
200	UnnT	6816	B4
Beechtree Dr			
10	MrnT	6282	A7
10	NRCH	6282	A7
400	HmpT	6828	C5
Beech Tree Ln			
10	BRNX	6506	C1
10	PLMM	6506	C1
Beechtree Ln			
10	DBSF	6165	E6
10	DBSF	6166	A5
10	HAOH	6165	E6
Beechwood Av			
10	BGTA	6501	E3
10	HRSN	6050	A1
10	HRSN	6168	C3
10	MNPK	6617	D6
10	MTVN	6395	A4
10	NHmT	6617	A4
10	NHmT	6618	A2
10	NRCH	6395	D5
10	STNL	7020	C6
Beechwood Blvd			
10	PTCH	6170	B3
10	RYEB	6170	B3
Beechwood Cir			
10	HRSN	6169	E6
Beechwood Ct			
10	DBSF	6166	C5
Beechwood Dr			
10	LWRN	7027	E4
100	MRNK	6282	D4
Beechwood Ln			
10	NHmT	6724	A5
10	RYE	6283	D5
10	SCDL	6281	D1
Beechwood Pl			
10	ELIZ	6816	E7
10	HlsT	6816	E7
10	IrvT	6816	A3
10	STNL	7019	E3
300	LEON	6502	D4
Beechwood Rd			
10	BRXV	6281	A7
10	BRXV	6395	C1
10	GrbT	6167	C2
10	IRVN	6166	A2
10	YNKR	6393	B3
Beechwood Ter			
10	YNKR	6393	B3
Bee Gee Ct			
300	STNL	7116	B4
Beekman Cir			
10	STNL	7116	B4
Beekman Pl			
10	CRSK	6502	E6
10	MHTN	117	B3
10	MHTN	6718	A5
2000	BKLN	6923	A4
Beekman St			
10	HmpT	7027	C2
10	MHTN	118	C7
10	MHTN	6821	B4
10	STNL	7117	B5
100	MHTN	120	D1
Beethoven St			
10	STNL	7020	E4
Behan Ct			
10	STNL	7117	E2
Beiling Rd			
400	HmpT	6827	A6
Belair Ln			
10	STNL	7020	A4
10	STNL	7021	A4
Belair Rd			
10	STNL	7020	A4
10	STNL	7021	A4
Belden Av			
10	DBSF	6166	A3
10	YNKR	6394	B2
Belden Pl			
10	NRWD	6164	A6
Belden St			
10	BRNX	6506	E7
10	STNL	7117	B5
Belding Av			
10	GrbT	6049	E5
E Belevedere Ln			
10	TYTN	6048	E6
Belfast Av			
10	STNL	7117	D2
Belfield Av			
10	STNL	7116	B5
Belgium St			
10	NWRK	6817	A1
Belgrade St			
400	STNL	7114	B2
Belgrade Ter			
10	WOrT	6712	A2
Belgrove Dr			
10	KRNY	6713	E5
10	KRNY	6714	B3
Belknap Av			
10	FLPK	6827	D1
700	LBCH	7028	D7
1100	HmpT	7028	D7
Belknap St			
133-00	QENS	6927	C1
Bell Av			
10	MTVN	6394	E7
10	NRCH	6396	A3
100	HSBH	6500	E3
100	LODI	6500	E3
Bell Blvd			
13-00	QENS	6615	E7
13-38	QENS	6616	A7
16-00	QENS	6616	A7
80-00	QENS	6826	C1
Bell Ln			
-	NRWD	6164	B6
10	KNGP	6616	D7
900	HmpT	6928	D1
Bell Pl			
10	RYEB	6169	E4

STREET / Block	City	Map#	Grid
Bell Pl			
10	YNKR	6393	C1
Bell Rd			
10	EchT	6281	C2
100	SCDL	6281	C2
Bell St			
10	COrT	6712	C2
10	IrvT	6816	C1
10	STNL	7020	D4
400	HmpT	6828	C5
Bellain Av			
10	HRSN	6283	A1
Bellair Dr			
10	DBSF	6165	E6
10	DBSF	6166	A5
10	HAOH	6165	E6
Bellair Pl			
10	NWRK	6713	D1
Bellaire Pl			
99-00	QENS	6826	D4
Bellamy Lp			
100	BRNX	6506	A3
Bella Vista Av			
10	STNL	7020	E4
Bella Vista St			
10	TCKA	6281	C2
Belle Dr			
10	STNL	7207	C2
Belleau Av			
10	NRCH	6281	C6
Belle Fair Blvd			
-	GrwT	6051	D3
10	RYEB	6051	D3
Belle Haven Ln			
10	GrwT	6170	D4
Belle Haven Ln			
10	NHmT	6724	A5
10	RYE	6283	D5
10	SCDL	6281	D1
Belleview Av			
200	FTLE	6502	E7
Belleview Pl			
10	BXTE	6617	E1
10	NHmT	6617	E1
Belleview Ter			
200	HlsT	6816	D5
Belleville Av			
10	BlvT	6714	B1
Belleville Tpk			
10	KRNY	6714	B3
10	NARL	6714	B1
800	KRNY	6715	B6
Belleville Tpk SR-7			
10	KRNY	6714	B1
800	KRNY	6715	A5
Bellevue Av			
10	DBSF	6166	C4
10	HmpT	6929	D3
10	HRSN	6169	B7
200	YNKR	6279	E5
6800	GTBG	6611	B7
Bellevue Av N			
500	WHPL	6279	E4
Bellevue Pl			
10	YNKR	6279	E4
Bellevue St			
10	ELIZ	6917	C4
10	WhkT	6716	B3
Bellew Av			
10	EchT	6281	C6
Bellewood Av			
10	DBSF	6166	A4
Bellhaven Rd			
10	STNL	7019	B4
Bellingham Ln			
10	GTNK	6617	A5
Bellmore St			
10	FLPK	6827	D3
Bellows Ln			
10	MNPK	6617	E6
10	MNPK	6618	A6
Bellport Pl			
10	GRFD	6500	B1
Bellview Pl			
10	NRCH	6395	B3
Bellwood Av			
300	SYHW	6048	B1
Bellwood Dr			
10	MNLA	6724	C6
10	NHmT	6724	C6
Bellwood Pl			
10	ELIZ	6917	C3
Bellwood Rd			
10	GrbT	6049	D4
Belmar Dr E			
10	STNL	7117	D2
Belmar Dr W			
10	STNL	7117	A1
Belmar St			
10	DMRT	6278	A5
Belmont Av			
-	JSYC	6819	D2
-	QENS	6927	C1
10	BKLN	6924	B1
10	BlmT	6713	E5
10	BlvT	6713	C2
10	FLPK	6827	C1
10	GRFD	6500	A2
10	HRSN	6169	D6
10	NRCH	6396	B3
10	RYE	6283	D5
77-00	QENS	6925	B2
136-00	QENS	6927	C2
100	LBCH	7029	E7
200	HmpT	6828	D4
800	HmpT	6928	C4
1300	NHPK	6724	A7
1600	BKLN	6925	A7
2200	BRNX	6504	D5
N Belmont Av			
10	RYE	6283	C4
Belmont Blvd			
1400	BKLN	7022	A6
Belmont Dr			
10	DBSF	6166	B3
10	IRVN	6166	B3
Belmont Pl			
10	STNL	7020	E6
4500	NHmT	6723	A2

STREET / Block	City	Map#	Grid
Belmont St			
10	BRNX	105	D6
10	BRNX	6504	B7
10	WHPL	6168	D6
Belmont Ter			
10	NWRK	6817	B3
10	YNKR	6279	D5
Belmont Park Rd			
600	PTHA	7114	C7
Belpark Av			
10	HmpT	6827	C4
Belt Pkwy			
10	BKLN	6921	E6
10	BKLN	6922	A6
10	BKLN	6924	E7
10	BKLN	6925	A6
10	BKLN	7021	C1
10	BKLN	7022	C6
10	BKLN	7023	A7
10	BKLN	7024	A7
10	BKLN	7120	D1
10	HmpT	6827	A7
10	QENS	6827	A5
10	QENS	6925	E3
10	QENS	6926	A3
10	QENS	6927	A3
Belvedere Ct			
10	NHLS	6724	A3
Belvedere Dr			
10	NRCH	6393	B3
Belvidere Av			
100	JSYC	6819	D2
Belvidere Pl			
10	NRCH	6395	E7
Belvidere St			
10	BRNX	6822	D6
Bel Vista Ct			
10	LODI	6500	C2
Belway Pl			
10	WHPL	6168	C1
Bement Av			
400	STNL	7020	A1
800	STNL	6920	A2
1300	STNL	6920	B6
2000	BKLN	7024	B3
Bement Ct			
10	STNL	6920	A2
Benchley Pl			
10	BRNX	6506	A2
Bender Av			
10	ROSP	6917	A3
Bender Ct			
-	CLFP	108	A1
-	CLFP	6611	C4
Bender St			
400	HmpT	7029	C1
Benders Dr			
10	GrbT	6170	C1
Benedict Av			
10	EchT	6281	B4
10	STNL	7019	D2
10	TYTN	6048	C4
500	WHPL	6280	B3
Benedict Pl			
10	PLHM	6395	C4
Benedict Rd			
10	GrbT	6049	E7
10	SCDL	6168	B7
10	STNL	7020	A5
Benedict Wy			
10	WbgT	7114	A2
Bengeyfield Dr			
10	EWLS	6724	D4
Benham St			
40-00	QENS	6720	A4
Benjamin Av			
10	STNL	6166	D2
Benjamin Dr			
10	STNL	7019	A2
Benjamin Pl			
10	STNL	6918	D7
Benjamin Rd			
10	TFLY	6392	A4
Benjamin St			
-	NWRK	6817	A2
10	WbgT	7114	C6
Benmore Av			
1000	HmpT	6828	A3
Benmore Ter			
10	BAYN	6919	E1
Bennett Av			
10	KRNY	6714	C2
10	MHTN	104	C3
10	MHTN	6503	D5
10	NWRK	6713	B7
10	STNL	7116	C7
100	YNKR	6280	B7
Bennett Ct			
33-00	QENS	6927	C1
7100	BKLN	7021	E1
Bennett Ln			
10	CRSK	6278	A6
Bennett Pl			
10	BKLN	6924	B1
Bennett Rd			
10	STNL	7207	E1
Bennett St			
10	HRSN	6169	D6
10	NRCH	6396	B3
10	STNL	6919	D7
3500	NHmT	6713	D2
Bennington Dr			
10	STNL	6164	D3
Bennington St			
600	HmpT	6917	A3
Benris Av			
600	HmpT	6828	B2
Benson Av			
200	STNL	6827	D5
1400	BKLN	7022	A6
Benson Blvd			
10	DBSF	6166	B3
Benson Pl			
10	NWRK	6828	E3
Benson St			
5400	WNYK	111	A7
5400	WNYK	6611	A7
Bent Av			
9200	FRVW	6611	B4

STREET / Block	City	Map#	Grid
Bent St			
10	STNL	7116	D6
Bentay Dr			
10	HRSN	6283	A4
10	MRNK	6283	A4
Bentley Av			
10	JSYC	6819	D2
600	PTHA	7114	C7
Bentley Ln			
10	STNL	7206	A4
Bentley Rd			
10	GTNK	6617	B5
235-00	QENS	6927	D5
Bentley St			
10	STNL	7206	A4
Bentley Wy			
10	WbgT	7114	A1
Benton Av			
10	STNL	7020	C6
Benton Ct			
10	STNL	7117	C4
Benton St			
121-00	QENS	6826	C7
123-00	QENS	6927	C1
900	HmpT	7028	C1
Benziger Av			
10	STNL	6920	C7
Bercik St			
500	ELIZ	6918	B3
Beresford Av			
10	STNL	7018	B7
Beresford St			
10	MrnT	6282	D6
Berg St			
10	MTVN	6394	D3
Bergen Av			
10	JSYC	6819	C4
10	KRNY	6714	A4
10	OrgT	6164	D2
10	RDFP	6501	E3
10	TnkT	6501	E3
10	YNKR	6280	B7
Bergen Av CO-607			
10	JSYC	6819	C4
Bergen Blvd			
-	LEON	6502	E5
-	PALP	6502	E5
-	PALP	6611	C4
10	FRVW	6611	B4
10	LODI	6500	E2
10	NBgT	6611	B4
10	PALP	6502	C7
10	RDGF	6611	B3
500	FTLE	6502	D6
Bergen Blvd SR-63			
-	FTLE	6611	C1
10	GTNK	6617	A5
10	NBgT	6611	B4
10	PALP	6502	C7
300	RDGF	6611	B3
Bergen Blvd US-1			
1400	FTLE	6502	D5
1500	LEON	6502	D5
Bergen Blvd US-9			
1400	FTLE	6502	D5
1500	LEON	6502	D5
Bergen Blvd US-46			
1400	FTLE	6502	D5
1500	LEON	6502	D5
Bergen Ct			
10	BKLN	7024	B2
Bergen Pl			
6600	BKLN	6921	D7
Bergen Rd			
-	QENS	6926	B4
Bergen St			
10	BKLN	121	B7
10	BKLN	6821	D7
10	BKLN	6922	E1
10	CART	7115	D3
10	FLPK	6827	D2
10	GRFD	6500	A1
10	HKSS	6501	C4
10	HRSN	6714	A6
10	NWRK	6713	B7
10	PASC	6500	A4
100	BKLN	6922	E1
100	WbgT	7114	B5
1000	NWRK	6816	E5
1200	HlsT	6816	E5
1800	BKLN	6924	A2
Bergen Ter			
10	CRSK	6278	A6
Bergen Tpk			
10	UNCT	6716	D2
100	LFRY	6501	D5
100	RDFP	6501	D4
300	RDFP	6502	A7
Bergen Tpk CO-50			
10	RDFP	6501	D4
200	CARL	6501	D5
Bergen Tpk CO-124			
136-00	QENS	6927	C2
Bergen Tpk CO-691			
-	UNCT	6716	D2
3500	NHmT	6716	D2
Bergen Beach Pl			
-	BKLN	7024	A7
Bergen County Plz			
-	BKLN	7024	A2
Bergenline Av			
200	UNCT	6716	D2
5400	WNYK	6611	A7
5500	WNYK	6611	A7
6700	GTBG	6611	B5
9200	FRVW	6611	B4

STREET / Block	City	Map#	Grid
Bergen Ridge Rd			
10	NBgT	108	A3
10	NBgT	6611	C6
Bergenwood Av			
4300	NBgT	6716	E1
6400	WNYK	6611	A6
7900	NBgT	6611	B4
9200	FRVW	6611	B4
Bergenwood Rd			
10	FRVW	6611	B4
10	NBgT	6611	B4
Berger St			
10	MNCH	6500	D7
10	WRDG	6500	D7
Bergholz Dr			
10	YNKR	6395	C3
Berglund Av			
10	STNL	7018	E4
Bergman Dr			
10	HmpT	6928	D6
Berkeley Av			
10	BlmT	6713	C1
10	NWRK	6713	D3
10	YNKR	6393	C4
400	COrT	6712	B5
400	SOrT	6712	B5
Berkeley Dr			
10	TFLY	6392	C3
Berkeley Pl			
10	BKLN	6922	E2
10	BlmT	6713	B1
10	ELIZ	6917	B7
10	JSYC	6716	A5
Berkeley Rd			
10	SCDL	6167	E4
10	COrT	6712	B4
Berkeley Ter			
10	IrvT	6816	D1
Berkeley Heights Pk			
10	NBgT	6713	B1
Berkery Pl			
10	ALPN	6278	D5
Berkley Cir			
10	RYEB	6170	A3
Berkley Dr			
10	RYEB	6170	A3
Berkley Ln			
10	GrbT	6167	A6
Berkley Pl			
10	STNL	7117	A5
Berkley St			
800	FTLE	6611	D1
1000	FTLE	6502	D7
Berkshire Pl			
10	EGLC	6392	C7
10	IrvT	6816	C3
Berkshire Rd			
10	GTNK	6616	C5
10	GTNK	6617	A5
10	MplT	6816	A6
10	NHmT	6617	A6
10	RKVC	6929	E1
10	YNKR	6280	E5
Berkshire St			
10	WbgT	7114	B2
Bermingham Pl			
10	WLPK	6724	A5
Bermuda St			
10	ATLB	7028	E7
Bernard Av			
400	LNDN	6917	B5
500	ROSL	6917	B5
Bernard Pl			
300	RDGF	6611	B2
Bernard St			
10	CART	7017	B6
10	GTNK	6617	A5
10	HmpT	7027	E2
10	NHmT	6617	C2
10	NHmT	6618	A1
800	BKLN	6923	A6
5500	BKLN	6923	A6
Bernard Ter			
200	HlsT	6816	D5
Bernath St			
10	CART	7115	B1
Bernice Av			
10	LODI	6500	C2
Bernice Rd			
10	NARL	6714	D1
500	HmpT	6828	A6
Bernius Ct			
10	JSYC	6819	D4
Berrian Blvd			
40-00	QENS	6719	C1
Berrian Rd			
10	NRCH	6396	C2
Berriman St			
10	BKLN	6924	E2
500	BKLN	6925	A3
Berry Av			
10	STNL	7116	D4
200	CARL	6501	D5
Berry Av W			
10	STNL	7116	D4
Berry Ct			
10	ORgT	6164	B1
10	STNL	7115	E5
Berry Ln			
10	GrbT	6049	D6
Berry Pl			
10	BKLN	6822	A3
Berry St			
10	BKLN	6822	A3
10	HmpT	6929	C1
10	IrvT	6816	C4
Berry St CO-652			
-	FTLE	6502	E6
E Berry St			
10	HKSK	6501	D1

STREET / Block	City	Map#	Grid
Berrybush Ln			
10	STNL	6280	B1
Berryhill Ct			
100	HmpT	6828	E4
Berryman Pl			
300	COrT	6712	C1
Berrys Creek Rd			
-	ERTH	6609	D3
Berrywood Ct			
400	HmpT	6828	E6
Bert Av			
300	YNKR	7026	A3
Bertel Av			
10	MTVN	6395	A6
Bertha Pl			
10	IRVN	6166	D3
10	STNL	7020	C2
Bertha St			
10	HmpT	6827	D4
10	HmpT	6928	D6
Bertolotto Av			
10	LFRY	6501	C7
Bertram Av			
10	YNKR	7207	D1
Bertram Ter			
100	UnnT	6816	W
Bertrand Av			
200	PTHA	7205	C2
Berwick Pl			
10	STNL	7020	A2
Berwick Rd			
200	BRNX	6923	A2
Berwick St			
10	ELIZ	6917	C4
10	JSYC	6716	A5
Berwin Ln			
10	STNL	7019	C1
Berwyn St			
10	CORt	6712	D3
10	EORG	6712	D3
100	ROSP	6917	A3
Besade Pl			
2800	HmpT	6929	D6
Bessemer St			
10	ALPN	6278	D5
Bessemund Av			
25-00	QENS	7027	B5
Beth Ln			
10	UnnT	6816	A6
Beth Pl			
10	STNL	7117	A5
Bethel Av			
700	STNL	7206	C2
Bethel Lp			
10	BKLN	6924	C6
Bethel Rd			
10	NHmT	6724	A3
10	SCDL	6167	E7
Bethune St			
10	MHTN	115	C7
10	MHTN	6717	B7
Betsy Ct			
10	STNL	6823	B1
Betsy Brown Cir			
10	PTCH	6170	A3
Betsy Brown Rd			
100	RYEB	6170	B3
Betts Av			
100	BRNX	6614	C4
Betty Ct			
10	STNL	6918	C7
Betty Ln			
10	OybT	6618	E1
10	YNKR	6280	D6
Betty Rd			
10	HmpT	6724	C6
Bevan Pl			
10	EchT	6281	C5
Bevan St			
10	JSYC	6716	A7
Beverley Rd			
10	BKLN	6922	E6
800	BKLN	6923	A6
5500	BKLN	6924	A6
Beverly Av			
10	BKLN	6278	E5
10	MrnT	6282	B7
10	STNL	7018	E2
500	HmpT	6929	B2
Beverly Dr			
10	NHmT	6724	B4
10	RYE	6283	D3
Beverly Ln			
10	KENS	6617	B6
E Beverly Pkwy			
10	VLYS	6928	E3
W Beverly Pkwy			
200	VLYS	6928	D2
Beverly Pl			
10	EDGW	6611	E3
10	LRMT	6396	D1
10	VLYS	6928	A4
Beverly Rd			
10	GTNE	6617	A7
10	NHmT	6617	A7
10	WHPL	6050	C6
10	WOrT	6712	A3
700	HmpT	6828	B7
Birch St W			
10	DBSF	6166	C2

STREET / Block	City	Map#	Grid
Bevy Ct			
10	BKLN	7023	E6
Bevy Pl			
3000	BRNX	6615	C4
Bianca Ct			
10	STNL	7116	C3
Bidwell Av			
10	JSYC	7019	C3
E Bidwell Av			
100	JSYC	6819	D5
Biehn St			
10	NRCH	6396	B2
E Bigelow St			
10	NWRK	6817	C3
W Bigelow St			
10	NWRK	6817	B3
Bigler St			
1900	FTLE	103	B4
1900	FTLE	6503	A6
Bijou Av			
10	BKLN	7023	E6
Billings Pl			
10	BKLN	7022	E5
10	BKLN	7023	A5
Billings St			
10	STNL	7116	C3
Billingsley Ter			
1800	BRNX	105	B3
1800	BRNX	6504	A5
Billington Ct			
10	RYE	6284	A2
Billiou St			
10	STNL	7116	C7
200	STNL	7207	B1
Billop Av			
10	STNL	7206	A5
Bills Pl			
10	BKLN	6922	D6
Billy Diehl Rd			
2800	HmpT	6929	D6
Biltmore Av			
10	HmpT	6827	B5
10	HRSN	6169	B7
10	YNKR	6280	E4
Biltom Rd			
10	GrbT	6048	E7
Bingham Cir			
10	UnnT	6816	A6
Binghamton Wy			
-	EDGW	6611	E3
Bingle St			
700	PTHA	7205	B2
700	PTHA	7205	B1
Bionia Av			
10	STNL	7020	E6
Birch Av			
10	PLHM	6395	C3
10	STNL	7020	B2
900	UnnT	6917	B1
Birch Dr			
10	HWTH	7029	A1
10	NHmT	6724	B4
Birch Hl			
Birch Ln			
10	DBSF	6166	A5
10	FLHL	6618	A4
10	GDNC	6724	E7
10	HmpT	6928	C4
10	LRMT	6396	D1
10	NHmT	6724	A6
10	RYEB	6169	E3
10	RYEB	6170	A3
10	STNL	7116	B4
10	VLYS	6928	C5
10	WDBG	7028	C2
200	IRVN	6166	B2
400	LEON	6502	D3
Birch Pl			
10	NRWD	6164	C4
Birch Rd			
10	ALPN	6278	E5
10	MLVN	6929	B2
10	MrnT	6282	B7
10	STNL	7018	E2
500	HmpT	6929	B2
Birch St			
10	CART	7115	C2
10	EGLC	6503	A3
10	FLPK	6827	D3
10	HmpT	6929	A5
10	JSYC	6819	A4
10	KENS	6617	B6
10	LFRY	6501	C7
10	LNBK	6929	A5
10	NHmT	6617	B6
10	NRCH	6395	D5
10	PTCH	6170	C4
10	RDFP	6501	E6
Birch St W			
10	DBSF	6166	C2
E Birch St			
10	MTVN	6394	E2
Birch Wy			
10	TYTN	6048	B3
Birchall Av			
1900	BRNX	6505	A4
Birchall Dr			
10	SCDL	6167	C3
10	SCDL	6168	A7
Birchard Av			
10	STNL	7019	C5
Birchbrook Rd			
82-00	QENS	6824	E4
235-00	QENS	6927	C2
Birchdale Av			
10	YNKR	6280	C2
Birchdale Ln			
10	FLHL	6618	C4
Birchfield Rd			
10	MRNK	6282	B2
Birch Hill Ln			
1300	MRNK	6282	B2
Birch Hill Rd			
10	LKSU	6723	B2

New York City/5 Borough Street Index

STREET Block City Map# Grid

Birchtree Ln
400 NVLE 6164 B4
Birchtree Rd
10 OrgT 6164 C4
Birchwood Av
10 EORG 6712 E5
Birchwood Dr
10 HmpT 6928 B4
10 MNLA 6724 C6
10 NHmT 6724 B6
Birchwood Dr N
10 HmpT 6928 D1
Birchwood Dr S
10 HmpT 6928 C1
Birchwood Dr W
10 HmpT 6928 C1
10 VLYS 6928 C1
Birchwood Ln
10 GrbT 6167 B4
10 KNGP 6616 D5
Birchwood Pl
10 TFLY 6392 B3
Birchwood Rd
10 WHPL 6168 D7
400 NVLE 6164 B4
Birchwood Rd S
- NVLE 6164 D5
Birchwood St
10 NHmT 6617 E2
Bird Ln
10 RYE 6284 A5
Bird Pl
10 WHPL 6168 E4
Birdsall Av
21-00 QENS 7027 C4
Birks Pl
10 NWRK 6816 E3
Birmington Pkwy
222-00 QENS 6722 C4
Biscayne Blvd
1200 UnnT 6816 B6
Bishop Av
10 MRNK 6282 E6
Bishop Dr N
10 GrwT 6170 B2
10 RYEB 6170 B2
Bishop Dr S
10 GrwT 6170 B2
10 RYEB 6170 B2
Bishop Pl
10 HmpT 6828 C5
10 LRMT 6396 D2
Bishop Rd
10 HmpT 7029 E3
Bishop St
10 JSYC 6820 A3
100 STNL 7117 D2
200 UnnT 6917 C2
Bishop William J Walls Pl
10 YNKR 6279 B6
Bismark Av
10 STNL 6920 D7
10 VLYS 6928 E5
Bismark Ct
10 STNL 6920 C6
Bittersweet Ln
10 GrbT 6167 B6
10 HmpT 6928 C4
Bivona St
3400 BRNX 6505 E1
Bixby Ct
10 RYE 6283 C5
Bixley Dr
10 NHmT 6724 C6
Bixley Hth
10 LNBK 6928 E5
10 LNBK 6929 A4
Black St
10 PLMM 6395 C7
Black Birch Ln
10 SCDL 6168 C6
Blackburn Ln
10 MNPK 6618 B5
Blackburn Rd
10 HlsT 6816 C7
Blackford Av
10 STNL 7019 C1
10 YNKR 6394 B4
Blackhawk Rd
10 SCDL 6282 C3
Blackledge Ct
10 ALPN 6278 C4
10 CLST 6278 C4
Blackrock Av
1900 BRNX 6614 C2
Blackstone Av
3700 BRNX 6393 B7
Blackstone Pl
10 BRNX 6393 B7
Blackstone Rd
10 WbgT 7115 B2
Blackstone St
10 HmpT 6827 B5
Blackthorn Ln
10 WHPL 6168 A4
Black Walnut Rd
10 SCDL 6168 A7
Blaine Ct
10 STNL 7020 A2
Blair Av
200 BRNX 6615 C3
Blair Ct
10 OrgT 6164 D3
10 WbgT 7114 E3
Blair Rd
10 CART 7017 A7
10 WbgT 7017 A6
10 WbgT 7114 E3
200 WbgT 7115 A1
300 CART 7115 A1
Blair St
10 YNKR 6394 D1
Blaise Ct
10 STNL 7117 A4
Blake Av
10 BKLN 6924 D3
10 LNBK 6929 B4
75-00 BKLN 6925 B2
75-00 QENS 6925 B2
Blake Ct
10 BKLN 7023 B7
Blakeley Pl
10 GRFD 6500 A3

Blakelock Pl
10 MNPK 6618 B6
Blakeman Dr
- HmpT 6928 E1
- HmpT 6929 A1
Blanch Av
10 HRPK 6164 A6
10 NRWD 6164 A6
10 NRWD 6278 A1
200 CLST 6278 B1
Blanch Av FM-109
10 HRPK 6164 A6
10 NRWD 6164 A6
600 NRWD 6278 A1
Blanchard Av
10 DBSF 6166 C4
Blanchard St
10 CART 7115 D1
10 NWRK 6714 D7
10 NWRK 6818 C1
Blanche Av
10 CRSK 6278 A5
10 DMRT 6278 A5
Blanche St
10 OrgT 6164 E2
10 SECS 6715 E3
10 SECS 6716 A3
E Blancke St
10 LNDN 7017 A1
1100 LNDN 6917 B6
W Blancke St
10 LNDN 7017 A1
Bland Ct
10 BlmT 6713 A1
Bland Pl
10 STNL 7116 C7
Blandford Av
1000 WbgT 7114 D1
Blauvelt Pl
10 GrbT 6167 B7
10 HKSK 6501 D4
Blauvelt St
- NRWD 6164 A6
10 TnkT 6501 E3
10 TnkT 6502 A3
Bleecker St
10 BKLN 6823 A6
10 JSYC 6716 B5
10 MHTN 118 E3
10 MHTN 119 A3
10 MHTN 6821 B1
17-00 QENS 6823 B5
300 MHTN 115 C7
300 MHTN 6717 B7
Bleeker Av
400 MRNK 6283 A7
600 MRNK 6397 A1
Bleeker Pl
10 STNL 7018 E5
Bleeker St
10 NWRK 6713 D6
N Bleeker St
10 MTVN 6394 D4
S Bleeker St
10 MTVN 6394 C4
Blenheim Dr
10 NHmT 6618 B7
Blenis Pl
10 MtPT 6050 A4
Blind Brook Ln
10 RYE 6169 E7
10 RYE 6170 A7
Bliss Av
10 TFLY 6392 A4
Bliss St
39-00 QENS 6719 A6
Bliss Ter
6800 BKLN 6921 D7
Bliss Farm Rd
10 HRSN 6283 A4
Block Ln
100 HmpT 7029 B5
Block St
10 STNL 7117 D4
Blondel Dr
10 SECS 6610 B6
Blondell Av
1300 BRNX 6505 D6
Bloom St
100 HKSK 6501 C3
Bloomdale Av
600 MRNK 6283 A7
600 MRNK 6397 A1
Bloomfield Av
10 BlmT 6713 C2
10 BlvT 6713 D4
10 NWRK 6713 D4
10 STNL 7018 C3
Bloomfield Av CO-506 SPUR
10 BlmT 6713 C2
10 BlvT 6713 D4
10 NWRK 6713 D4
Bloomfield Pl
10 NWRK 6713 E5
Bloomfield Rd
- STNL 7018 C3
Bloomfield St
10 HBKN 6716 D7
10 MHTN 115 B6
10 MHTN 6717 A7
Bloomingdale Av
10 GRFD 6500 A3
Bloomingdale Dr
10 NRCH 6281 E2
Bloomingdale Rd
10 STNL 7206 E1
100 WHPL 6168 C3
300 STNL 7115 D6
Blossom Av
132-00 QENS 6720 E5
134-00 QENS 6721 A4
Blossom Ln
10 NHmT 6723 D6
10 STNL 7206 C4
Blossom Rd
10 KNGP 6617 A3
Blossom Row
10 HmpT 6928 C1
Blossom St
1300 HmpT 6827 E5
Blossom Ter
10 MrnT 6282 D7

Blossom Heath Av
10 LNBK 6929 A4
Bloy St
200 HlsT 6816 B5
Blueberry Ln
10 STNL 7208 A1
Blueberry Hill Rd
10 GrbT 6048 D7
10 IRVN 6048 D7
Bluebird Dr
300 EGLC 6503 B2
Bluebird Hllw
10 RYEB 6170 A2
Bluebird Hill Ct
10 NHLS 6618 B7
Blue Heron Ct
10 STNL 7116 D7
Blue Heron Dr
10 SAMB 7205 D7
10 STNL 7116 E7
100 SECS 6610 A5
Blue Hill Rd
10 NRWD 6164 B6
Blue Ridge Ct
4500 WLTN 6500 B4
Blue Sea Ln
10 KNGP 6617 B4
Bluff Rd
10 FTLE 6611 E1
10 GLCV 6509 D3
500 FTLE 6502 D7
500 PALP 6502 D7
Blum Blvd
10 WRDG 6500 D7
Blum St
10 NWRK 6817 A1
4400 WLTN 6500 B4
Bluth St
10 HmpT 7027 E2
Bly Ct
10 GTNK 6617 B5
10 NHmT 6723 E7
300 HmpT 6828 A6
Blythe Pl
10 STNL 7117 C3
Boa Pl
1400 HlsT 6816 D5
Boardwalk Av
10 STNL 7207 D1
Boat Ln
10 PTWN 6508 D6
Boatworks Dr
10 BAYN 6919 C5
Bobbie Ln
10 RYEB 6170 A3
Bobbink Ter
10 ERTH 6500 A7
10 WLTN 6500 A7
Bobby Ct
10 WbgT 7114 E4
Bobby Close
10 MrnT 6282 D2
Bobolink Pl
10 YNKR 6280 A7
Bobolink Rd
10 YNKR 6280 B6
Bocce Ct
10 STNL 7206 A3
Bock Av
10 NWRK 6817 A3
Boden Av
10 VLYS 6928 B3
Bodine St
10 STNL 6919 D7
Boelsen Cres
62-00 QENS 6824 B2
Boerum St
10 BKLN 6822 D5
Bogardus Pl
10 MHTN 104 D1
10 MHTN 6503 E5
Bogart Av
10 GRFD 6500 B4
10 NHmT 6618 A1
1600 BRNX 6505 B6
Bogart Pl
10 OrgT 6164 C2
Bogart St
100 BKLN 6822 D4
Bogert Av
10 STNL 7019 E5
10 WHPL 6167 E3
Bogert Ln
- BGTA 6501 D2
Bogert Pl
10 NWRK 6280 C2
Bogert Rd
10 DMRT 6278 B5
Bogert St
10 CLST 6278 B3
100 BGTA 6501 E3
Boggs St
700 PTHA 7205 D2
Bogota Gdns
100 BGTA 6501 D2
Bogota St
10 STNL 7019 B7
Boiling Springs Av
10 CARL 6609 C1
10 ERTH 6609 B1
Bokee Ct
10 BKLN 7022 E7
Boker Ct
120-00 QENS 6614 C7
Boland St
10 JSYC 6819 E2
Bolivar St
10 STNL 7019 E5
Boller Av
2100 BRNX 6506 A4
3500 BRNX 6505 E1
Bolmer Av
10 YNKR 6279 E4
Bolton Av
10 WHPL 6168 B4
800 BRNX 6614 B2
Bolton Dr
10 NHLS 6618 A7
10 NHLS 6724 B1
Bolton Gdns
10 BRXV 6394 E1
Bolton Pl
10 PTCH 6170 B3
10 RYEB 6170 B2

Bolton Rd
7-00 QENS 7027 D4
10 NHmT 6724 B6
1300 PLMM 6395 D7
Bolton St
2100 BRNX 6505 A5
Boltwood St
10 JSYC 6820 A4
Bolz St
300 EGLC 6503 B2
Bombay St
- ELIZ 6919 A1
10 STNL 7115 E6
Bon Air Av
10 NRCH 6281 C7
Bonaventure Av
10 ARDY 6166 C5
Bond Av
10 MLVN 6929 A2
Bond Ct
10 NHLS 6724 B1
Bond St
10 BKLN 121 C7
10 BKLN 6821 D7
10 ELIZ 6918 C5
10 GTPZ 6617 A7
10 FLPK 6827 C2
10 JSYC 6819 E1
10 KENS 6617 A7
10 MHTN 119 A3
10 MHTN 6821 C2
10 NWRK 6713 C6
10 STNL 6919 D7
10 WbgT 7114 A2
10 WHPL 6050 A6
10 WLTN 6500 A5
100 BKLN 6922 D1
1400 HlsT 6816 D5
N Bond St
10 MTVN 6394 D4
S Bond St
10 MTVN 6394 D4
Bonhomme St
100 HKSK 6501 D4
Boniface Cir
10 SCDL 6167 C5
Bonita Vista Dr
10 EchT 6395 B2
10 MTVN 6395 B2
Bon Mar Rd
10 PLMM 6395 C7
Bonn Pl
10 WhkT 111 A5
10 WhkT 6716 E3
10 WhkT 6717 A3
Bonnefoy Pl
10 NRCH 6395 C5
10 NRCH 6396 B5
Bonner Pl
200 BRNX 6613 A2
Bonnett Av
10 LRMT 6396 C1
Bonnett St
700 ELIZ 6917 E6
Bonnie Ln
14-00 QENS 6615 D6
Bonnie Wy
10 MrnT 6282 B6
Bonnie Briar Ln
10 MrnT 6282 B6
Bonnie Briar Rd
10 GrbT 6167 B1
10 YNKR 6280 C5
Bonnie Heights Rd
10 FLHL 6617 E4
10 FLHL 6618 A4
Bonnie Lynn Ct
10 NHLS 6724 B3
Bonnie Meadow Rd
10 NRCH 6281 E2
Bonta St
10 HmpT 6827 B5
Bonwit Rd
10 RYEB 6169 E3
Boody St
30-00 QENS 6719 C4
Boone Av
1400 BRNX 6613 E1
1700 BRNX 6504 E6
Boone St
10 STNL 7019 C5
10 YNKR 6394 B3
Booraem Av
10 JSYC 6716 B7
Booth Av
- STNL 7116 D7
10 EGLC 6392 B7
10 EGLD 6392 B7
Booth Ct
10 GrwT 6170 E4
Booth Pl
10 GrwT 6170 E4
Booth St
60-00 QENS 6824 A1
Booth Ter
10 GrwT 6170 E4
Booth Memorial Av
132-00 QENS 6720 E6
136-00 QENS 6721 A6
Borage Pl
107-00 QENS 6824 D3
Borcher Av
10 YNKR 6394 A3
Borden Av
2-00 QENS 117 E6
2-00 QENS 6718 D7
58-00 QENS 6823 B1
Borden Ter
10 MplT 6816 A2
Borghild Av
10 YNKR 6394 A2
Borglum Rd
10 MNPK 6618 B6
Borig Pl
10 LODI 6500 D1
Borinquen Pl
10 BKLN 6822 B4
Borkel Pl
90-00 QENS 6826 E1
Borman Av
10 STNL 7019 A6
10 WbgT 7114 D1
Born St
200 SECS 6610 A6

Borneman Pl
10 WHPL 6168 D2
Boro Pl
- LEON 6502 D4
Borough Ln
- RDGF 6611 C1
400 PALP 6502 C7
Borough Pl
- STNL 6920 E7
25-00 QENS 6719 B4
Borough St
10 RTFD 6609 B3
Boscobel Av
10 BRNX 104 E5
10 BRNX 6503 C6
Boscombe Av
10 STNL 7206 C2
Boss St
133-00 QENS 6925 E2
Boston Av
100 HlsT 6816 C6
Boston Ct
10 NWRK 6713 C7
Boston Rd
10 BLRS 6827 C2
10 FLPK 6827 C2
900 BRNX 6613 C1
1600 BRNX 6504 E7
2100 BRNX 6505 A5
4100 BRNX 6506 A1
4200 BRNX 6395 A7
4300 PLMM 6395 A7
Boston Rd US-1
2200 BRNX 6505 D2
4000 BRNX 6506 A1
4200 BRNX 6395 A7
4300 PLMM 6395 A7
Boston St
10 NWRK 6713 C7
Boston Post Rd
10 MRNK 6283 B5
10 RYE 6283 C5
100 PTCH 6170 B6
1000 RYE 6284 A1
1200 MrnT 6282 D7
1200 MrnT 6396 D1
1200 RYE 6170 A7
2000 LRMT 6396 B3
4300 BRNX 6395 A7
4300 PLMM 6395 B7
4800 NRCH 6395 C6
Boston Post Rd US-1
10 MRNK 6283 B5
10 RYE 6283 B5
100 PTCH 6170 B6
1000 RYE 6284 A1
1200 MrnT 6282 D7
1200 MrnT 6396 D1
1200 RYE 6170 A7
2000 LRMT 6396 B3
4300 BRNX 6395 A7
4300 PLMM 6395 B7
4800 NRCH 6395 C6
E Boston Post Rd
- RYE 6283 A6
900 MRNK 6283 A5
E Boston Post Rd US-1
- RYE 6283 A6
100 MRNK 6283 A6
W Boston Post Rd
100 MRNK 6282 D7
1200 MrnT 6282 D7
W Boston Post Rd US-1
100 MRNK 6282 D7
1200 MrnT 6282 D7
Bostwick Av
10 JSYC 6819 D4
Bosworth St
10 STNL 7020 A2
Botanical Sq S
400 BRNX 6504 E3
Botany St
10 GRFD 6500 A2
Bothner St
500 HmpT 7029 D2
Bouck Av
2700 BRNX 6505 C4
Bouck Ct
10 BKLN 7022 E7
Boudinot Pl
1000 ELIZ 6918 A3
Boulanger Plz
10 HAOH 6165 D6
Boulder Cir
10 MrnT 6282 B5
Boulder Ln
10 EchT 6281 D3
Boulder Pl
10 YNKR 6393 D4
Boulder Rd
10 FLHL 6618 A5
10 MrnT 6282 B7
10 RYE 6284 A2
10 TFLY 6392 B3
Boulder Rdg
10 GrbT 6166 D7
Boulder St
10 STNL 7116 B6
Boulder Tr
10 YNKR 6394 C2
Boulder Brae Ln
10 MrnT 6282 C5
Boulder Brook Rd
10 SCDL 6168 C7
Boulevard
10 HSBH 6500 E4
10 PLHM 6395 C5
10 QENS 6614 E7
10 QENS 6615 A7
10 WRDG 6500 D5
200 PLMM 6395 C5
500 HKSK 6501 A2
500 HSBH 6501 A2
Boulevard CO-38
100 HSBH 6500 D5
Boulevard CO-57
10 WRDG 6500 D5
100 HSBH 6500 E4
500 HKSK 6501 A2
500 HSBH 6501 A2
Boulevard W
- MTVN 6395 B5
600 PLHM 6395 B5
Boulevard Pl
400 HmpT 6828 D3

Boundary Av
10 STNL 7118 B1
N Boundary Rd
- QENS 6926 E4
- QENS 6927 A4
Bourndale Rd N
10 PLNH 6617 D5
S Bourndale Rd
10 PLNH 6617 D5
Bourton St
63-00 QENS 6824 A2
Bouton Ln
10 STNL 7116 B6
Bovanizer St
10 STNL 7116 E6
Bove Ter
500 JSYC 6716 B4
500 NBgT 6716 B4
Bow St
10 QENS 6824 D3
Bowbell Rd
10 GrbT 6049 B7
Bowden St
10 STNL 7118 B1
Bowdoin St
10 STNL 7019 A7
Bowe Rd
1500 HmpT 6928 D1
Bowen St
10 STNL 7020 D3
Bower Ct
10 STNL 7115 E5
Bower St
400 LNDN 6917 A7
Bowers Ln
10 ALPN 6278 D2
10 CLST 6278 D2
10 LKSU 6723 B1
Bowers St
10 JSYC 6716 B6
Bowers Ln Gate
10 LKSU 6723 C1
10 NHmT 6723 C1
Bowery
10 MHTN 118 E6
10 MHTN 119 A3
10 MHTN 6821 C2
Bowery Bay Blvd
- QENS 6719 D2
Bowler Rd
10 ERKY 6929 B6
Bowles Av
10 STNL 7019 B1
Bowling Grn
10 MHTN 120 B2
10 MHTN 6821 B6
Bowling Green Pl
10 STNL 7018 E6
Bowman Av
10 PTCH 6170 A5
10 RYEB 6170 A5
100 RYEB 6169 E5
200 HRSN 6169 E5
Bowmans Point Rd
- MHVN 6508 B6
Bowne St
10 BKLN 6922 B1
10 BRNX 6506 E5
41-53 QENS 6721 B5
Box St
10 BKLN 117 D7
10 BKLN 6718 B7
Boxwood Ct
300 ELIZ 6917 D4
Boxwood Dr
10 GTNE 6722 E1
Boxwood Dr E
1300 HWTH 6929 A7
Boxwood Dr W
1300 HWTH 6928 E7
1300 HWTH 6929 A7
Boxwood Ln
10 HRSN 6283 C1
10 LWRN 7027 E3
Boxwood Pl
10 RYEB 6170 A1
Boxwood Rd
10 MHVN 6508 C6
10 YNKR 6281 A2
Boxwood Wy
10 NHLS 6724 A1
Boyce Av
10 STNL 7117 C3
39-12 QENS 6722 A4
Boyd Av
100 JSYC 6819 C3
4100 BRNX 6394 C6
Boyd Ct
10 JSYC 6819 D3
Boyd Pl
10 YNKR 6280 D7
Boyd St
10 KRNY 6714 B4
10 LBCH 7029 E6
10 LODI 6500 D2
10 NWRK 6817 B1
10 STNL 7020 D2
Boyden Av
10 MplT 6816 A2
10 NWRK 6816 A3
400 IrvT 6816 A3
Boyden Pkwy
10 MplT 6816 A2
Boyden Pkwy S
10 MplT 6816 A2
Boyden St
10 BlmT 6713 A1
10 EORG 6713 A1
10 NWRK 6713 D6
Boylan St
10 EORG 6712 D6
10 NWRK 6712 D6
10 STNL 7116 D3
Boyle Pl
10 ELIZ 6917 D5
10 STNL 7117 D1
Boyle Plz
100 JSYC 6820 C1
Boyle St
10 STNL 7117 E1
Boynton Av
10 STNL 7207 A1
1000 BRNX 6613 E2

Boynton Pl
10 BKLN 7022 E7
Brabant St
10 STNL 7018 E1
10 STNL 7019 A1
Brace Av
300 PTHA 7205 C2
Brace Ter
10 DBSF 6166 A4
Brace Bridge Ln
10 IRVN 6048 A7
Brad Ln
10 STNL 7018 E3
10 WHPL 6168 D7
Braddock Av
- HmpT 6827 B2
87-00 QENS 6826 E1
226-00 QENS 6827 A2
Braddock Av SR-25
- HmpT 6827 B2
220-00 QENS 6826 E1
226-00 QENS 6827 A2
Bradford Av
10 GrbT 6050 A5
10 HRSN 6283 C4
10 RYE 6283 C4
10 STNL 7207 A1
10 WOrT 6712 A2
100 MRNK 6282 D5
1200 BRNX 6505 E7
1200 BRNX 6614 D3
Bradford Blvd
10 YNKR 6280 D5
Bradford Pl
10 HRSN 6283 B3
Bradford Rd
10 HmpT 6827 C7
10 HmpT 6928 C1
10 MTVN 6395 B4
10 NHLS 6618 B7
10 NRCH 6282 A4
10 SCDL 6282 A4
200 HlsT 6816 D7
Bradford St
10 BKLN 6924 D3
10 HRSN 6283 B3
300 COrT 6712 D1
Bradford Ter
1500 UnnT 6816 C5
Brad Gerston Rd
1500 BRNX 6505 B7
Bradhurst Av
- GrbT 6049 C3
10 MHTN 107 A5
10 MHTN 6612 D2
10 MtPT 6049 D1
Bradhurst Av SR-100
- GrbT 6049 C3
10 MtPT 6049 D1
Bradhurst Entrance South Rd
- MtPT 6049 C2
Bradley Av
10 GrbT 6166 D2
10 MTVN 6395 B3
10 STNL 7019 D4
31-00 QENS 6718 D7
36-00 QENS 6822 D1
100 NRWD 6164 B5
100 NVLE 6164 B5
Bradley Ct
10 MNLA 6724 D7
10 STNL 7019 D5
Bradley Pl
10 CLST 6278 D3
10 MNLA 6724 D7
Bradley Rd
10 EchT 6281 D3
100 SCDL 6281 D3
Bradley St
10 BRNX 6394 C4
10 DBSF 6166 B4
10 MTVN 6394 C4
700 MRNK 6283 A4
800 HmpT 6828 C7
Bradley Ter
10 WOrT 6712 A1
Brady Av
10 NRCH 6395 D6
600 BRNX 6505 B5
Brady Pl
10 WHPL 6168 A3
N Brae Ct
10 TFLY 6392 C2
Brae Burn Dr
10 HRSN 6050 E7
10 HRSN 6051 A6
Braemar Av
10 NRCH 6395 D1
Braeside Ln
10 DBSF 6166 A5
Brafmans Rd
10 HmpT 7027 D2
Bragaw Av
10 NWRK 6816 E3
Bragaw Pl
10 NWRK 6816 E3
Bragg St
10 BKLN 7023 D6
2800 BKLN 7121 E1
Braintree Ln
10 YNKR 6280 A4
Braisted Av
10 STNL 7019 B7
Brambach Av
10 EchT 6281 C1
Brambach Rd
10 EchT 6281 C1
10 SCDL 6281 C1
Bramble Brook Rd
10 ARDY 6166 C5
100 GrbT 6166 C5
Bramhall Av
100 JSYC 6820 A4
400 JSYC 6819 E3
Bramley Ln
10 DBSF 6166 C4
Brampton Ln
10 GTNK 6617 A5
10 KNGP 6617 A5
Branca Rd
10 ERTH 6609 C3
Branch Blvd
- HmpT 6927 E6
600 CDHT 7028 A1

Branch Blvd
600 HmpT 6928 A7
600 HmpT 7028 A1
Branch Ln
- NWRK 6817 B1
Branch Brook Pl
10 NWRK 6713 D1
Branch Brook Plz
10 NWRK 6713 D1
Branch Brook Rd
10 WHPL 6168 C6
Branch Gate
- HmpT 6928 A7
Brandis Av
10 STNL 7116 E4
E Brandis Av
10 STNL 7116 E4
10 STNL 7117 A4
Brandis Ln
10 STNL 7116 D4
Brandon Pl
500 CLFP 6611 D3
Brandon Rd
10 YNKR 6394 C3
Brandt Av
10 OrgT 6164 C3
Brandt Pl
10 BRNX 105 B4
10 BRNX 6504 A6
Brandt St
10 HAOH 6280 B2
10 LFRY 6501 C5
Brandt Ter
10 YNKR 6280 B3
Brandywine Dr
10 WHPL 6169 A6
Branford Pl
10 NWRK 6713 D7
10 NWRK 6817 B2
Branford Rd
10 HAOH 6280 A1
Branford St
10 NWRK 6817 B3
Branton Pl
10 NHmT 6724 E3
Branton St
10 BKLN 6924 A6
Brassie Ln
10 YNKR 6280 D6
Brassie Rd
10 EchT 6281 B4
Brattle Av
252-00 QENS 6723 A3
Braxmar Dr N
10 HRSN 6282 E3
Braxmar Dr S
10 HRSN 6282 E3
Braxmar Ln
10 HRSN 6282 E3
Brayton Rd
- SCDL 6167 E4
Brayton St
10 EGLD 6392 A7
Breckenridge Av
10 PTCH 6170 A5
Breckenridge Ter
10 IrvT 6712 E7
Breezy Point Blvd
211-00 QENS 7122 A4
215-14 QENS 7121 E4
Breezyway
200 LWRN 7028 B5
Breglia St
10 YNKR 6394 C3
Bregman Av
10 NHmT 6723 E5
Brehaut Av
10 STNL 7206 B3
Breiderhoft Rd
10 KRNY 6714 B5
Brendon Hill Rd
10 YNKR 6281 B2
Brengel Pl
- SCLF 6509 E6
Brennan Dr
- WOrT 6712 B2
Brennan Pl
4400 HmpT 7029 E5
Brenner Pl
10 ALPN 6278 D5
10 DMRT 6278 D5
Brenner St
10 NWRK 6817 A1
Brenton Pl
10 STNL 7019 E3
Brentwood Av
10 STNL 6920 B7
10 WHPL 6168 B6
Brentwood Dr
700 GrbT 6048 E4
Brentwood Ln
10 HmpT 6928 B4
Brentwood Rd
10 NHmT 6617 A6
Bretton Rd
10 GrbT 6167 B7
10 NHmT 6724 B6
10 YNKR 6280 A4
1200 HmpT 6827 E6
Breuer Av
10 GTNK 6616 E5
Brevoort Ln
10 MRNK 6283 B5
10 RYE 6283 B5
Brevoort Pl
10 BKLN 6923 B1
Brevoort St
82-00 QENS 6824 E5
Brewster Av
10 RDFP 6501 E5
10 YNKR 6394 B1
100 YNKR 6280 B7
Brewster Pl
10 WbgT 7114 E4
Brewster Rd
- ELIZ 6918 E2
- NWRK 6817 C7
- NWRK 6818 A4
10 SCDL 6167 D5
Brewster St
10 STNL 7020 D1
Brewster Ter
10 NRCH 6395 D1

Brian Cres
205-00 QENS 6615 D6
Brian St
10 NHmT 6724 B5
2700 HmpT 6929 D6
Brianbeth Pl
10 OrgT 6164 B1
Briar Cir
10 NRCH 6282 A7
Briar Ln
10 EHLS 6618 E7
10 KNGP 6616 C5
Briar Pl
300 QENS 7027 C5
800 HmpT 6928 B7
Briar Wy
1000 FTLE 6611 E1
1100 FTLE 6502 D7
Briarcliff Ct
10 MplT 6816 A1
Briarcliff Rd
10 MrnT 6282 C7
10 NHmT 6617 D3
10 STNL 7020 E5
10 TFLY 6392 B3
Briar Close Rd
10 MrnT 6282 B6
Briar Del Cir
10 MrnT 6282 C5
Briarfield Dr
10 LKSU 6723 B1
Briar Hill Dr
10 YNKR 6280 B2
Briarwood Av
10 NRWD 6278 D1
Briarwood Cross
100 LWRN 7028 B3
Briarwood Ln
10 CDHT 7028 B2
10 LWRN 7028 B3
400 NVLE 6164 B4
Briarwood Rd
10 JSYC 6819 A6
10 STNL 7018 E2
Briary Rd
10 DBSF 6166 C4
Brick Church Plz
10 EORG 6712 D3
Bridge Ct
10 STNL 7021 B4
Bridge Plz N
- FTLE 6502 E4
10 FTLE 103 A2
10 FTLE 6503 A5
Bridge Rd
10 FLHL 6617 E5
10 NHmT 6617 E5
10 PLDM 6617 E5
10 PLNH 6617 E5
Bridge St
- HRSN 6713 E6
- NRWD 6164 A5
- PRMT 6165 A1
10 ARDY 6166 D4
10 BlvT 6714 A1
10 ELIZ 6917 E4
10 HKSK 6501 C2
10 IRVN 6048 A7
10 MHTN 120 B2
10 MHTN 6821 B6
10 NRCH 6395 C5
10 NWRK 6713 E6
10 QENS 6925 E4
10 TYTN 6048 B3
10 WbgT 7114 E5
10 YNKR 6393 B2
100 BKLN 121 C4
200 BKLN 6821 D6
600 BRNX 6506 D5
600 HmpT 6928 B6
Bridge St CO-508
- HRSN 6713 E6
10 NWRK 6713 E6
N Bridge St
10 STNL 7206 C1
S Bridge St
10 STNL 7206 B2
Bridge Plaza Ct
- BKLN 121 B4
- BKLN 6821 D6
Bridgeton St
153-00 QENS 6925 E3
Bridgetown St
10 STNL 7019 A7
Bridgewater Av
260-00 QENS 6723 B5
Bridgewater St
10 BKLN 6822 D2
Bridle Ln
- SNPT 6508 B6
Bridle Pth
10 NHmT 6724 B3
10 SNPT 6509 A7
Bridle Pth E
10 SNPT 6509 A7
Bridle Pth N
10 SNPT 6509 A6
Bridle Wy
10 EDGW 6611 E1
10 FTLE 6611 E1
Bridle Path Ln
10 LKSU 6723 B2
Brielle Av
10 STNL 7019 D5
Brier Ln
10 PLMM 6395 B7
Briga Cir
10 HRSN 6283 B3
Briga Ln
10 WHPL 6168 D6
Briggs Av
10 YNKR 6280 A7
2500 BRNX 6504 D4
Brigham St
10 BKLN 7023 D5
Bright Ct
600 NWRK 6713 C5
Bright Pl
10 YNKR 6393 C2
Bright St
10 JSYC 6820 B3
1200 HlsT 6816 D6
S Bright St
1100 HlsT 6816 C6

New York City/5 Borough Street Index

STREET
Block City Map# Grid

Brighton Av
10 KRNY 6714 A4
10 PTHA 7205 D5
10 STNL 6920 B7
100 EORG 6712 E1
400 STNL 7020 B1
W Brighton Av
10 BKLN 7121 A3
300 BKLN 7120 E1
Brighton Blvd
10 HmpT 7029 C5
Brighton Ct
10 BKLN 7023 A7
Brighton Rd
10 ISPK 7029 C5
Brighton Rd N
10 NHLS 6618 B7
Brighton Rd S
10 NHLS 6618 B7
10 NHLS 6724 B1
Brighton St
10 STNL 7206 B5
100 WbgT 7114 C5
Brighton Ter
10 IrvT 6816 D1
Brighton 1st Pl
10 BKLN 7121 A1
Brighton 1st Rd
10 BKLN 7121 A2
Brighton 1st St
10 BKLN 7121 A1
Brighton 2nd Ln
10 BKLN 7121 B3
Brighton 2nd Pl
10 BKLN 7121 B2
Brighton 2nd Pth
10 BKLN 7121 B2
Brighton 2nd St
10 BKLN 7121 A1
Brighton 2nd Wk
10 BKLN 7121 B2
Brighton 3rd Ct
10 BKLN 7121 B2
Brighton 3rd Ln
10 BKLN 7121 B2
Brighton 3rd Pl
10 BKLN 7121 B3
Brighton 3rd Rd
10 BKLN 7121 A2
Brighton 3rd St
- BKLN 7023 D5
2900 BKLN 7121 A1
Brighton 4th Ct
10 BKLN 7121 B2
Brighton 4th Ln
10 BKLN 7121 B2
Brighton 4th Pl
10 BKLN 7121 B3
Brighton 4th Rd
10 BKLN 7121 A2
Brighton 4th St
10 BKLN 7121 A1
Brighton 4th Ter
10 BKLN 7121 A1
Brighton 5th Ct
10 BKLN 7121 B2
Brighton 5th Ln
10 BKLN 7121 B2
Brighton 5th Pl
10 BKLN 7121 B2
Brighton 5th St
10 BKLN 7121 A1
Brighton 6th Ct
10 BKLN 7121 B2
Brighton 6th St
10 BKLN 7023 D6
10 BKLN 7121 B1
Brighton 7th Ct
10 BKLN 7121 B2
Brighton 7th Ln
10 BKLN 7121 B2
Brighton 7th St
10 BKLN 7023 A7
10 BKLN 7121 A1
Brighton 8th Ct
10 BKLN 7121 A2
Brighton 8th Ln
800 BKLN 7121 B2
Brighton 8th Pl
10 BKLN 7121 B2
Brighton 8th St
10 BKLN 7023 D6
2900 BKLN 7121 B1
Brighton 10th Ct
10 BKLN 7121 B2
Brighton 10th Ln
10 BKLN 7121 B2
Brighton 10th Pth
10 BKLN 7121 B1
Brighton 10th St
10 BKLN 7121 B1
Brighton 10th Ter
10 BKLN 7121 B2
Brighton 11th St
10 BKLN 7121 B1
Brighton 12th St
10 BKLN 7121 B1
Brighton 13th St
10 BKLN 7121 B1
Brighton 14th St
- BKLN 7121 B2
Brighton 15th St
10 BKLN 7121 B1
Brighton Beach Av
10 BKLN 7121 A1
Brightwater Av
10 BKLN 7121 B2
Brightwater Ct
10 BKLN 7121 A2
Brill Pl
400 NHPK 6723 E7
Brill St
10 NWRK 6818 B1
Brinckerhoff Ct
100 EGLD 6392 A7
Brinkerhoff Av
10 TnkT 6501 E1
10 TnkT 6502 A1
150-00 QENS 6825 D7
183-00 QENS 6826 A5
400 FTLE 6502 D7
500 PALP 6502 D7
E Brinkerhoff Av
10 PALP 6502 C6
400 FTLE 6502 D7
Brinkerhoff Ln
10 NHmT 6617 D7
Brinkerhoff St
10 JSYC 6819 E3
10 RDFP 6501 E5
100 RDFP 6502 A6
Brinkerhoff Ter
10 PALP 6502 B6
Brinsmade Av
100 BRNX 6615 A3
900 BRNX 6614 E1
Brinsmaid Pl
10 NWRK 6818 C1
Brisbane St
10 NHmT 6724 A7
Brisbin St
95-00 QENS 6825 C6
Briscolina St
10 HKSK 6501 C2
Bristol Av
10 STNL 7020 A4
97-00 QENS 6925 E2
Bristol Ct
10 ALPN 6278 D5
Bristol Dr
10 NHLS 6618 B7
10 NHLS 6724 B1
Bristol Pl
10 YNKR 6280 D2
Bristol St
10 BKLN 6924 B4
10 LNBK 6929 C3
10 MLVN 6929 C3
Bristol Ter
10 EDGW 108 B1
10 EDGW 6611 E4
Bristow St
1300 BRNX 6613 C1
Brite Av
10 SCDL 6167 D6
Brittany Ln
10 LRMT 6396 D2
10 NRCH 6396 A7
Brittany Close
10 MrnT 6282 C3
10 SCDL 6282 C3
Britton Av
10 STNL 7020 C4
82-00 QENS 6719 E6
Britton Cir
10 MLVN 6929 E2
Britton St
10 JSYC 6819 E2
10 STNL 6919 E7
600 BRNX 6505 A3
600 ELIZ 6917 E5
Brixton Rd
10 GDNC 6828 C1
10 HmpT 6828 C4
200 GDNC 6724 C7
200 NHmT 6724 C7
Brixton Rd S
100 HmpT 6828 C4
300 GDNC 6828 C4
Broad Av
- RDGF 6611 B2
10 FRVW 6611 A4
10 NBgT 6611 A4
10 OrgT 6164 E5
10 PALP 6502 B7
10 RCKL 6164 E5
100 LEON 6502 C5
200 EGLD 6502 E1
800 RDGF 6502 B7
Broad Av US-1
- RDGF 6611 B2
10 FRVW 6611 A4
10 NBgT 6611 A4
10 PALP 6502 B7
800 RDGF 6502 B7
Broad Av US-9
- RDGF 6611 B2
10 FRVW 6611 A4
10 NBgT 6611 A4
10 PALP 6502 B7
800 RDGF 6502 B7
Broad Av N
500 RDGF 6611 B1
600 RDGF 6502 B7
800 PALP 6502 B7
Broad Av N US-1
500 RDGF 6611 B1
600 RDGF 6502 B7
800 PALP 6502 B7
Broad Av N US-9
500 RDGF 6611 B1
600 RDGF 6502 B7
800 PALP 6502 B7
Broad Av S
300 FRVW 6611 B2
300 RDGF 6611 A1
Broad Av S US-1
300 FRVW 6611 B2
300 RDGF 6611 A1
Broad Av S US-9
300 FRVW 6611 B2
300 RDGF 6611 A1
Broad St
10 CARL 6609 D1
10 CRSK 6278 B5
10 DMRT 6278 B5
10 ELIZ 6917 E3
10 GrbT 6050 A5
10 HmpT 6828 E5
10 LODI 6500 D2
10 MHTN 120 B2
10 MHTN 6821 A5
10 MNCH 6501 C7
10 NRWD 6164 A6
10 NWRK 6713 D7
10 PTCH 6170 C6
10 PTHA 7205 D3
10 STNL 7020 D2
10 WLPK 6724 E4
154-00 QENS 6927 D7
300 CARL 6500 C7
300 WbgT 7114 E6
300 WbgT 7115 A6
800 NWRK 6817 D2
800 TnkT 6502 B1
Broad St CO-508
500 NWRK 6713 E7
E Broad St
10 BGTA 6501 E2
10 MTVN 6394 E2
1100 ELIZ 6917 E3
N Broad St
200 ELIZ 6917 E1
800 ELIZ 6816 E7
900 HlsT 6816 E6
1500 NWRK 6816 E6
N Broad St CO-623
500 ELIZ 6917 E1
800 ELIZ 6816 E7
900 HlsT 6816 E6
1500 NWRK 6816 E6
N Broad St SR-27
200 ELIZ 6917 E2
S Broad St
10 ELIZ 6917 E5
700 LNDN 6917 D6
S Broad St CO-623
10 ELIZ 6917 E5
W Broad St
10 BGTA 6501 D2
10 MTVN 6394 D2
10 YNKR 6394 D2
Broadcast Plz
- SECS 6609 E6
10 NRCH 6396 A1
Broadfield Rd
10 NRCH 6281 E5
Broadhead Pl
400 PTHA 7205 C3
Broadlawn Av
10 KNGP 6617 A3
Broadman Pkwy
10 JSYC 6819 C4
Broadmoor Av
10 SCDL 6282 B4
Broad Park Wy
10 WHPL 6168 E2
Broadview Av
10 GrbT 6049 C7
100 NRCH 6395 E1
Broadway
- QENS 7027 E4
10 BAYN 6919 D6
10 CRSK 6278 A7
10 CRSK 6392 B1
10 DBSF 6165 E5
10 ELIZ 6918 C5
10 HKSK 6501 C2
10 HmpT 6828 D4
10 HRSN 6283 B3
10 JSYC 6715 E7
10 JSYC 6819 A3
10 LNBK 6929 A5
10 LWRN 7027 E4
10 MHTN 116 B3
10 MHTN 120 B2
10 MHTN 6821 B3
10 MLVN 6929 B2
10 MtPT 6050 A3
10 NHmT 6723 A2
10 NHmT 6724 C7
10 NRWD 6164 C7
10 NRWD 6278 D1
10 NWRK 6713 E5
10 QENS 6925 E4
10 RKVC 6929 D3
10 STNL 6919 E7
10 VLYS 6928 A3
11-00 QENS 114 E7
11-00 QENS 6718 D3
33-00 QENS 6719 E7
100 BKLN 6822 B4
100 MHTN 118 C6
144-69 QENS 6927 B3
200 DBSF 6166 A4
200 HAOH 6165 E6
200 LWRN 7028 A3
300 CDHT 7028 A3
300 HmpT 6929 A5
300 MNLA 6724 D7
300 STNL 7019 E1
500 HmpT 7028 C1
500 NWRK 6714 A2
600 BAYN 6920 A3
600 HmpT 6928 D6
600 IRVN 6166 A3
600 LNBK 6928 E6
600 MHTN 119 A2
600 STNL 7020 A2
700 WDBG 7028 C1
800 MHTN 6717 D6
900 BlvT 6714 A1
900 HRPK 6164 A5
1000 BAYN 6819 B7
1000 OLDT 6164 A5
1200 BKLN 6823 A7
1200 HlsT 6816 C6
1300 HBPK 6928 D6
1500 MHTN 112 C6
1600 BKLN 6924 B1
1600 NHPK 6724 A7
2200 MHTN 108 D7
2200 MHTN 6611 E7
2500 MHTN 109 B1
2500 MHTN 6612 A6
3000 MHTN 106 E3
3600 MHTN 107 A1
3800 MHTN 104 B7
3800 MHTN 6503 E4
3900 HmpT 7029 E4
4400 ISPK 7029 D5
4500 UNCT 111 B1
4500 UNCT 6717 A1
4500 WhkT 111 A3
4500 WhkT 6717 A2
4600 MHTN 101 E6
4800 MHTN 102 B6
4800 MHTN 6504 A3
4900 WNYK 111 B1
4900 WNYK 6717 A1
5000 BRNX 102 E2
5200 BRNX 6504 A3
5900 BRNX 6393 C7
5900 WNYK 6611 B6
6700 GTBG 6611 B6
6700 YNKR 6393 C4
7100 NBgT 6611 B6
Broadway CO-106
10 NRWD 6164 C7
10 NRWD 6278 D1
900 HRPK 6164 A5
1000 OLDT 6164 A5
Broadway CO-667
10 NWRK 6713 E5
Broadway CO-667
500 NWRK 6714 A2
900 BlvT 6714 A1
Broadway SR-9A
6300 BRNX 6393 C6
6700 YNKR 6393 C4
Broadway US-1
100 JSYC 6715 E7
Broadway US-9
10 DBSF 6165 E5
100 JSYC 6715 D7
200 DBSF 6166 A4
200 HAOH 6165 E6
600 IRVN 6166 A3
4200 MHTN 104 D2
4200 MHTN 6503 E5
4600 MHTN 101 D7
4800 MHTN 102 A6
4800 MHTN 6504 A3
5200 BRNX 102 E2
5200 BRNX 6504 A3
5900 BRNX 6393 C7
6700 YNKR 6393 C4
Broadway US-9 TRK
100 JSYC 6715 D7
Broadway N
100 SAMB 7205 C7
Broadway S
100 SAMB 7205 C7
E Broadway
10 HKSK 6501 D2
10 LBCH 7029 D7
10 MHTN 118 E7
10 MHTN 119 C6
10 MHTN 6821 D3
10 PTCH 6170 B6
10 RSLN 6618 E6
10 STNL 7117 D3
900 HmpT 7028 D1
900 HWTN 7028 D2
900 WDBG 7028 D2
1100 HmpT 6928 D7
N Broadway
- HAOH 6279 E2
- MtPT 6050 B3
10 IRVN 6048 B7
10 WHPL 6050 B7
10 WHPL 6168 B1
10 YNKR 6393 C1
100 SYHW 6048 B7
100 TYTN 6048 B6
100 YNKR 6279 D6
600 HAOH 6165 E6
600 NoCT 6050 B5
N Broadway SR-9A
10 YNKR 6393 C1
100 YNKR 6279 C7
N Broadway SR-22
10 WHPL 6050 B7
10 WHPL 6168 B1
600 NoCT 6050 B5
N Broadway SR-119
10 WHPL 6168 B1
N Broadway US-9
- HAOH 6279 E2
10 IRVN 6048 B7
10 YNKR 6393 C1
100 SYHW 6048 B2
100 TYTN 6048 B6
100 YNKR 6279 D6
600 HAOH 6165 E6
S Broadway
10 HAOH 6279 E2
10 IRVN 6166 A2
10 TYTN 6048 B4
10 WHPL 6168 B1
10 YNKR 6279 E2
10 YNKR 6393 C3
200 DBSF 6166 A3
600 BRNX 6393 C4
800 IRVN 6048 B6
S Broadway SR-9A
10 YNKR 6393 C3
600 BRNX 6393 C4
S Broadway SR-22
10 WHPL 6168 B1
S Broadway SR-119
10 WHPL 6168 B1
S Broadway US-9
10 HAOH 6279 E2
10 IRVN 6166 A2
10 TYTN 6048 B4
10 YNKR 6279 E2
10 YNKR 6393 C3
200 DBSF 6166 A3
600 BRNX 6393 C4
800 IRVN 6048 B6
W Broadway
- CDHT 7028 A2
10 LBCH 7029 B7
10 MHTN 118 B6
100 HmpT 7027 D2
200 MHTN 6821 B2
300 CDHT 7027 C2
600 HmpT 7028 B1
700 LBCH 7028 E6
800 HmpT 6928 C7
Broadway Mw
10 HmpT 6928 E7
Broadway Plz
10 GrbT 6049 B3
Broadway Ter
10 MHTN 104 D2
10 MHTN 6503 D5
Broadwell Av
300 UnnT 6816 A7
300 UnnT 6917 A1
Brocek Ct
10 PTHA 7205 D3
Brocher Rd
172-00 QENS 6927 A1
Brockway Pl
10 WHPL 6168 C1
Brodil Ct
10 CLST 6278 C4
Brokaw Av
10 FLPK 6827 A3
10 QENS 6827 A3
Brokaw Ln
10 GTNK 6616 E5
Broken Shell Rd
10 STNL 7207 A3
Brokers Chance St
10 STNL 7018 B1
Bromleigh Rd
10 STMN 6827 E3
Bromleigh Rd
200 HmpT 6827 E3
Bromleigh Rd N
10 STMN 6827 E2
Bromley Ln
10 GTNK 6617 A5
Brompton Rd
10 GDNC 6828 D1
10 GTPZ 6617 A7
10 GTPZ 6723 A1
10 THSN 6723 B1
100 GDNC 6724 D7
Brompton Rd S
100 GDNC 6828 D4
200 HmpT 6828 D3
Bronson Av
10 EchT 6281 B2
10 LRMT 6396 D2
Bronx Blvd
3200 BRNX 6505 A3
3900 BRNX 6394 B7
Bronx Pk E
2200 BRNX 6505 A4
Bronx Pk S
800 BRNX 6504 E6
Bronx St
- WHPL 6168 C2
10 MTVN 6394 D3
10 TCKA 6280 C2
10 TCKA 6281 A5
2000 BRNX 6504 E7
Bronx Ter
10 YNKR 6394 C4
Bronx & Pelham Pkwy E
- BRNX 6505 B5
- BRNX 6506 A5
Bronx & Pelham Pkwy E US-1
- BRNX 6505 A5
Bronx & Pelham Pkwy W
- BRNX 6505 D5
- BRNX 6506 A5
Bronx & Pelham Pkwy W US-1
- BRNX 6505 A5
Bronxdale Av
1500 BRNX 6505 B6
Bronx Park Av
300 BRNX 6504 E6
300 BRNX 6505 A7
Bronx Park Rd
- BRNX 6504 E5
Bronx Park Zoological
10 BRNX 6504 E6
Bronx River Av
400 BRNX 6614 B5
800 BRNX 6613 E2
1500 BRNX 6505 A7
Bronx River Pkwy
- BRNX 6394 C5
- BRNX 6505 A2
- BRNX 6614 A1
- EchT 6281 B3
- GrbT 6050 A6
- GrbT 6167 C7
- GrbT 6168 A1
- GrbT 6281 B2
- MtPT 6050 A4
- MTVN 6394 C3
- NoCT 6050 B3
- SCDL 6167 D4
- WHPL 6167 D7
- WHPL 6168 A1
- YNKR 6280 D7
- YNKR 6281 B2
- YNKR 6394 C4
Bronx River Rd
10 BRNX 6394 B6
10 YNKR 6394 C3
Bronx Science Blvd
10 BRNX 6504 D2
Bronxville Ln
10 YNKR 6394 A3
Bronxville Rd
10 YNKR 6394 D1
200 YNKR 6280 D6
Bronxville Glen Dr
10 YNKR 6394 D2
Bronx Whitestone Br
- BRNX 6614 E5
- QENS 6614 E5
- QENS 6615 A6
Bronx Whitestone Br I-678
- BRNX 6614 E5
- QENS 6614 E5
- QENS 6615 A6
Bronxwood Av
3300 BRNX 6505 B1
4000 BRNX 6394 C7
Brook Al
200 COrT 6712 D3
Brook Av
10 BRNX 6613 A4
10 STNL 7117 E4
10 WLTN 6500 B5
1500 BRNX 105 D7
1500 BRNX 6504 B7
2700 HmpT 6929 E6
Brook Ct N
10 NHmT 6724 A4
Brook Ct S
10 NHmT 6724 A5
Brook Dr
10 WOrT 6712 A2
N Brook Dr
10 HmpT 6928 D6
10 VLYS 6928 D6
Brook Ln
10 FLHL 6617 E3
10 GTNK 6616 E6
10 NHmT 6616 E6
10 RYEB 6169 D4
10 SCDL 6167 D4
10 WOrT 6712 B1
Brook Ln E
10 GrbT 6167 C5
Brook Ln W
10 GrbT 6167 C5
Brook Pl
10 IRVN 6166 A1
10 LRMT 6396 B2
10 VLYS 6928 E4
Brook Rd
10 HmpT 6928 B5
10 PTCH 6170 C4
10 TFLY 6392 B2
10 YNKR 6280 D7
N Brook Rd
10 MrnT 6282 C5
Brook St
10 BlvT 6713 C2
10 CLST 6278 A3
10 EchT 6281 C2
10 JSYC 6820 B3
10 LODI 6500 D1
10 MtPT 6049 E1
10 NRCH 6395 E3
10 NRWD 6164 A6
10 NWRK 6713 C2
10 STNL 6920 D7
10 WbgT 7114 C4
10 YNKR 6393 D2
300 LNDN 7017 A2
500 MRNK 6283 A5
Brook Ter
10 LEON 6502 D3
Brook Wy
- LRMT 6396 C2
10 CRSK 6278 B6
10 DMRT 6278 B6
Brookbridge Rd
10 GTNK 6616 E6
10 NHmT 6616 E6
Brookby Rd
10 SCDL 6168 A7
10 SCDL 6282 A1
Brook Crossway
10 GrwT 6170 B1
Brookdale Av
10 EORG 6712 D6
10 NRCH 6395 E3
10 NRCH 6396 A3
10 NWRK 6712 C7
10 WHPL 6050 A6
Brookdale Cir
10 NRCH 6396 A3
Brookdale Dr
10 YNKR 6280 E5
Brookdale Pl
10 MTVN 6394 C6
10 RYE 6283 E3
Brookdell Dr
10 GrbT 6167 D2
Brooke Av
10 YNKR 6280 D7
Brookfall Av
1300 UnnT 6816 B6
Brookfield Av
10 STNL 7117 A4
10 WbgT 7114 D4
Brookfield Ln
10 SCDL 6168 A7
Brookfield Rd
10 EchT 6395 A2
10 MTVN 6395 A2
10 NHmT 6724 A4
10 VLYS 6928 C5
Brookfield St
200 WHPL 6168 A2
Brookhaven Av
17-00 QENS 7027 C5
Brook Hills Cir
10 WHPL 6168 E6
Brook Hills Dr
10 WHPL 6168 E6
Brooklands Cir
10 YNKR 6280 D7
Brookline Av
10 HmpT 7028 D7
Brookline Rd
10 SCDL 6281 E1
Brooklyn Av
10 BKLN 6923 C1
10 HmpT 6828 D4
10 NHmT 6827 E1
10 NHPK 6827 E1
10 VLYS 6928 D4
1500 BKLN 7023 D1
Brooklyn Br
- BKLN 121 A2
- BKLN 6821 C4
- MHTN 118 D7
- MHTN 120 E1
- MHTN 121 A2
- MHTN 6821 B4
Brooklyn Rd
- BKLN 6923 C7
Brooklyn Battery Tun
- BKLN 120 A3
- BKLN 6821 B7
- BKLN 6922 B1
- MHTN 120 A3
- MHTN 6821 A6
Brooklyn Battery Tun I-478
- BKLN 120 A3
- BKLN 6821 B7
- BKLN 6922 B1
- MHTN 120 A3
- MHTN 6821 A6
Brooklyn Bridge Blvd
- BKLN 121 B5
- BKLN 6821 C7
Brooklyn Heights Promonade
- BKLN 120 E4
- BKLN 6821 C6
Brooklyn Queens Expwy
- BKLN 120 E5
- BKLN 121 D4
- BKLN 6821 C6
- BKLN 6822 A6
- BKLN 6922 B1
- QENS 6719 C5
- QENS 6822 E3
- QENS 6823 A1
Brooklyn Queens Expwy I-278
- BKLN 120 E5
- BKLN 121 D4
- BKLN 6821 E6
- BKLN 6822 A6
- BKLN 6922 B1
- QENS 6719 A7
- QENS 6822 E1
- QENS 6823 A1
Brooklyn Queens Expwy E
- QENS 6719 C4
Brooklyn Queens Expwy W
- QENS 6719 C4
Brooklyn Queens Expwy W I-278
- QENS 6719 C3
Brookridge Av
10 EchT 6281 A5
10 TCKA 6281 A5
Brookridge Ct
10 HRSN 6169 E6
10 RYEB 6169 E6
10 RYEB 6170 A6
Brookridge Rd
10 NRCH 6282 A5
Brooks Pl
10 JSYC 6716 A5
10 STNL 7019 D1
Brookside Av
- STNL 7117 D1
10 CRSK 6278 A5
10 DMRT 6278 A5
10 EGLD 6502 D2
10 IrvT 6816 D1
10 LODI 6500 D3
10 MTVN 6395 B4
10 PLHM 6395 D7
10 STNL 7019 E2
1200 UnnT 6816 B6
Brookside Cir
10 YNKR 6280 D7
Brookside Dr
10 FLHL 6618 B4
10 PLDM 6617 D4
100 GrwT 6170 E1
100 VLYS 6928 D4
1300 UnnT 6816 B7
E Brookside Dr
10 MrnT 6282 C6
W Brookside Dr
10 MrnT 6282 C6
Brookside Ln
10 DBSF 6166 B4
10 GrwT 6170 E1
10 HRSN 6283 B4
Brookside Lp
10 STNL 7115 E7
Brookside Pk
10 GrwT 6170 E2
Brookside Pl
10 MrnT 6282 B6
10 NRCH 6395 E2
Brookside Rd
10 WOrT 6712 B1
Brookside St
34-00 QENS 6722 D2
Brookside Vil
10 HRPK 6164 A6
Brookside Wy
10 HRSN 6169 D3
10 RYEB 6169 D3
Brooks Pond Pl
10 STNL 7019 E2
Brook View Ln
10 HRSN 6169 B5
Brookville Blvd
121-00 HmpT 6928 A1
121-00 QENS 6928 A2
134-00 QENS 6927 E7
Brookwold Dr
10 NHmT 6617 D5
10 PLNH 6617 D5
Brookwood Dr
10 MplT 6816 A2
Brookwood Rd
10 NRCH 6282 A3
Brookwood St
10 EORG 6712 D6
10 NWRK 6712 D6
Broome Av
10 ATLB 7027 E7
Broome St
- MHTN 6821 D3
10 BKLN 6822 C2
10 NWRK 6817 C1
300 MHTN 118 D4
300 MHTN 119 A5
Brosnan Pl
10 YNKR 6281 A3
Bross Pl
10 IrvT 6816 B2
Brothers Cir
10 EchT 6281 B6
Brother Stan Dr
- JSYC 6819 B5
Broun Pl
10 BRNX 6506 A2
Brower Av
10 HmpT 7028 C1
600 HmpT 6828 B7
Brower Ct
10 STNL 7117 D5
200 WNYK 6611 C7
Brower Pl
10 LNBK 6929 B5
10 PTCH 6170 B3
Browers Ln
10 NHmT 6724 D1
Browers Point Brch
900 HmpT 7028 C2
900 HWTN 7028 C2
900 WDBG 7028 C2
Brown Av
10 RYE 6284 A3
10 STNL 7117 B5
10 WbgT 7114 A3
Brown Ct
10 GTNK 6616 E4
400 HmpT 7029 D2
Brown Pl
10 HRSN 6283 C2
10 JSYC 6819 C7
10 STNL 7020 E4
57-00 QENS 6823 C2
100 BRNX 6613 A5
400 NHPK 6723 E7
400 NHPK 6827 E1
Brown Rd
10 GTNK 6616 E4
10 SCDL 6281 C1
Brown St
10 MplT 6816 A3
Brown St
10 SCLF 6509 D6
10 VLYS 6928 B2
10 WLPK 6724 E4
2600 BKLN 7023 D7
4500 UNCT 111 A3
4500 UNCT 6716 E2
4500 UNCT 6717 A2
Browndale Pl
10 PTCH 6170 B4
Brownell St
10 STNL 7020 E2
Brownes Ter
10 EGLD 6392 A5
Browning Av
10 STNL 7019 E5
10 YNKR 6394 D3
100 ELIZ 6917 A2
100 ROSP 6917 A2
100 UnnT 6917 B2
Browning Ln
10 GrbT 6167 B2
10 TYTN 6048 C5
Browns Blvd
500 QENS 7122 D3
Browns Ln
200 BRNX 6506 E6
Brownstone Wy
10 EGLD 6502 D1
Browvale Ln
45-00 QENS 6722 E3
46-00 QENS 6723 A3
Bruce Av
10 HRSN 6283 C3
10 MTVN 6394 E3
10 YNKR 6393 C4
Bruce Ct
10 LODI 6500 E3
10 SHkT 6501 B4
10 TETB 6501 B4
300 HmpT 6828 C6
Bruce Ln
10 EchT 6281 C5
10 NHmT 6618 B6
Bruce Rd
10 MrnT 6282 D4
Bruce St
10 NWRK 6713 C7
500 RDGF 6611 C1
1100 HmpT 6828 A5
1200 HmpT 6827 E5
Bruce Reynolds Blvd
10 FTLE 103 A3
10 FTLE 6503 A5
300 FTLE 6502 E5
Bruck Av
200 PTHA 7205 D1
Bruckner Av
10 STNL 7019 A2
Bruckner Blvd
- BRNX 6506 A7
10 BRNX 110 D2
10 BRNX 6612 E5
1000 BRNX 6613 E2
1500 BRNX 6614 A2
2800 BRNX 6615 A1
Bruckner Expwy
- BRNX 6506 A6
- BRNX 6613 D3
- BRNX 6614 A2
- BRNX 6615 A1
Bruckner Expwy I-95
- BRNX 6506 A7
- BRNX 6614 E1
- BRNX 6615 A1
Bruckner Expwy I-278
- BRNX 6613 C4
- BRNX 6614 A2
Bruen Av
10 IrvT 6816 D2
Bruen St
10 NWRK 6817 E1
Bruner Av
2700 BRNX 6505 E3
4000 BRNX 6394 C6
Bruno Ln
- STNL 7206 C5
Bruno St
10 MNCH 6501 C7
Brunswick Av
- LNDN 7017 D1
10 MNLA 6724 D5
10 NHmT 6724 D5
11-00 LWRN 7027 D4
12-00 QENS 7027 D4
500 ELIZ 6917 E7
700 LNDN 6917 D7
Brunswick Pl
1500 HmpT 6827 D5
Brunswick St
10 JSYC 6820 B2
10 NWRK 6817 C2
10 STNL 7019 A7
Brush Av
500 BRNX 6614 D2
S Brush Dr
10 VLYS 6928 D4
Brush Hollow Cres
10 RYEB 6170 D2
Brush Hollow Ln
10 RYEB 6170 A2
Brush Hollow Close
10 RYEB 6170 D2
Brussel Dr
10 NHmT 6724 C6
Bryan Pl
10 JSYC 6820 D2
Bryan St
10 STNL 7206 A4
Bryant Av
- HRSN 6169 A3
- NHPK 6724 A7
10 FLPK 6827 D1
10 GrbT 6049 C4
10 JSYC 6819 E1
10 NHmT 6723 E7
10 NHPK 6723 D7
10 QENS 6827 C1
10 ROSH 6618 E5
10 RSLN 6618 E5
10 SCLF 6509 D7
10 STNL 7117 E1
10 WHPL 6168 B3
100 STNL 7118 A2
300 BRNX 6613 D3
Bryant Av
300 NHmT 6827 D1
300 NHPK 6827 D1
300 WHPL 6169 A3
600 TnkT 6502 C2
900 NHmT 6724 A7
2100 BRNX 6504 E7
Bryant Cres
10 WHPL 6168 C3
Bryant Ct
10 IrvT 6816 C3
Bryant Pl
10 LODI 6500 C3
10 RDGF 6502 B7
10 RDGF 6611 B1
Bryant Rd
10 HmpT 7029 E3
10 YNKR 6393 D2
Bryant St
10 BKLN 6922 B3
10 GrbT 6167 B2
10 NWRK 6713 E2
10 NWRK 6714 A2
700 HmpT 7028 B1
800 HmpT 6928 B7
Bryla St
10 CART 7017 B7
Bryn Mawr Pkwy
10 YNKR 6280 C7
Bryn Mawr Pl
10 YNKR 6280 B7
300 NHmT 6724 B5
Bryn Mawr Ter
10 YNKR 6280 B6
Brynwood Rd
10 YNKR 6280 A7
Bryson Av
10 STNL 7019 B4
Bryson St
10 MrnT 6282 B7
Bucha Dr
- EORG 6712 C5
- SOrT 6712 C5
Buchanan Av
10 STNL 7019 C4
200 MNLA 6724 D5
Buchanan Pl
10 BRNX 105 D2
10 BRNX 6504 B4
5800 WNYK 111 B1
5800 WNYK 6717 A1
6000 WNYK 6611 A7
Buchanan St
10 CART 7115 C1
100 LNDN 7017 C3
500 HlsT 6816 B5
E Buchanan St
10 STNL 6920 C6
Buck St
2400 BRNX 6505 C7
N Buckhout St
10 IRVN 6048 A6
S Buckhout St
10 IRVN 6048 A7
10 IRVN 6166 A1
Buckingham Av
10 PTHA 7205 E3
Buckingham Ct
300 CDHT 7027 C2
Buckingham Dr
10 ALPN 6278 D3
10 CLST 6278 D3
Buckingham Pl
10 EchT 6281 B1
10 LNBK 6929 C4
10 NHmT 6617 B5
10 THSN 6723 A1
100 HmpT 6929 C3
Buckingham Rd
- BKLN 6923 A5
10 CRSK 6278 B7
10 HmpT 6828 E4
10 TFLY 6392 C5
10 YNKR 6280 A6
300 CDHT 7027 E1
300 CDHT 7028 A2
1000 FTLE 6611 E1
1100 FTLE 6502 E7
Buckley Pl
10 GrbT 6167 B4
Buckley St
10 BRNX 6506 E7
Buckminster Ln
10 NHmT 6618 B7
Bucknell Av
10 WbgT 7114 D2
Bucknell Rd
10 VLYS 6928 C3
Buckout Rd
10 HRSN 6050 D5
Bud Ct
10 PTHA 7114 C7
Bud Pl
36-00 QENS 6720 E4
Budd St
1500 HmpT 6827 D7
Buel Av
10 STNL 7020 B7
600 STNL 7118 D1
Buell Av N
1000 UnnT 6917 B1
Buell Av S
900 UnnT 6917 B2
Buell St
31-00 QENS 6720 B4
Buena Vista Av
10 CDHT 7027 E2
10 HmpT 7027 E2
10 YNKR 6393 C2
Buena Vista Dr
10 DBSF 6166 A6
10 GrbT 6049 C4
10 GrwT 6170 B2
10 HAOH 6165 E6
10 HAOH 6166 A6
100 DBSF 6165 E5
Buena Vista Rd
10 EchT 6281 C5
Buffalo Av
10 HmpT 7028 D7
100 BKLN 6923 E3
Buffalo Ct
400 WNYK 6611 C7
Buffalo St
10 HmpT 6827 C7

New York City/5 Borough Street Index

STREET Block City Map# Grid

Buffalo St
10 STNL 7117 E6
200 STNL 7208 C1
Buffington Av
10 STNL 7116 C7
Buffington Pl
10 EchT 6395 C1
Buffington St
10 IrvT 6816 D3
10 NWRK 6816 D3
Buhre Av
2800 BRNX 6505 E6
3100 BRNX 6506 A6
Bulaire Rd
10 ERKY 6929 B7
Bulkley Av
10 PTCH 6170 B5
Bulkley Mnr
10 RYE 6284 A3
Bullard Av
4400 BRNX 6394 C5
Bulls Ferry Rd
- NBgT 108 A4
8200 NBgT 6611 C6
Bulova Av
10 QENS 6719 C4
Bulwer Pl
10 BKLN 6924 D1
10 QENS 6924 D1
Bungalow Pl
10 HmpT 6929 D7
Bunker Ct
500 HmpT 6928 A6
Bunker Rd
700 HmpT 6928 A6
Bunnecke Ct
63-00 QENS 6823 C4
Bunnell Ct
10 STNL 7116 A5
Bunns Ln
10 WbgT 7114 B6
Burbank Av
10 STNL 7117 E1
100 STNL 7118 A2
Burbank St
10 YNKR 6280 C6
Burbury Ln
10 GTNK 6617 A5
10 KNGP 6617 A5
Burchard Av
10 EORG 6712 D2
Burchard Ct
10 STNL 7116 D6
Burchell Av
69-00 QENS 7026 C6
Burchell Rd
62-00 QENS 7026 D6
Burden Av
10 STNL 7019 C1
Burden Cres
140-00 QENS 6825 B4
Burdett Pl
10 FRVW 6611 B3
Burdette Ct
10 EDGW 103 A5
10 EDGW 6503 A6
Burdette Pl
88-00 QENS 6825 C4
Burdsall Dr
10 GrwT 6170 B3
10 PTCH 6170 B3
Burgener Ln
10 OrgT 6164 E2
Burgess Rd
10 SCDL 6167 D7
Burgher Av
10 STNL 7020 C6
N Burgher Av
10 STNL 6919 E7
200 STNL 7020 A1
Burhans Av
10 YNKR 6279 E6
10 YNKR 6280 A6
Burke Av
10 STNL 7018 C6
600 BRNX 6505 B3
Burke St
10 CART 7115 D1
Burkeley Pl
10 HAOH 6166 A7
Burkewood Rd
10 ARDY 6166 E3
10 GrbT 6166 E3
10 GrbT 6167 A3
10 MTVN 6395 A1
Burkhard Av
200 MNLA 6724 D5
300 WLPK 6724 D5
Burling Av
10 WHPL 6168 C4
Burling Ln
10 NRCH 6395 E4
Burling St
43-00 QENS 6721 B5
Burlington Av
600 ELIZ 6918 A7
Burlington Pl
1200 HmpT 6928 A4
1200 VLYS 6928 A4
Burlington St
10 CART 7115 D2
10 HRPK 6164 A6
10 NRWD 6164 A6
200 HRSN 6714 A7
Burma Rd
10 JSYC 6820 A5
Burnet Pl
100 WRDG 6500 B5
1100 BRNX 6613 D3
Burnet St
10 ELIZ 6917 E4
10 WbgT 7114 D2
Burnett St
10 BKLN 7023 D4
10 HlsT 6816 B5
10 NWRK 6713 D6
N Burnett St
10 EORG 6712 E4
S Burnett St
10 EORG 6712 E4
Burnham Av
10 NHLS 6618 D7
10 NHmT 6618 D7
10 ROSE 6618 D7
Burnham Pl
10 MNPK 6618 A5
Burnham Rd
10 EchT 6281 B3
500 ELIZ 6917 C4
Burns Av
10 LODI 6500 C2
Burns Rd
10 HRSN 6050 D3
Burns St
10 GrbT 6167 B2
66-00 QENS 6824 C2
Burnsdale Av
10 MtPT 6049 E1
Burnside Av
10 STNL 7019 C2
200 CDHT 7027 E2
200 HmpT 7027 D2
E Burnside Av
10 BRNX 6504 C6
100 BRNX 105 E3
W Burnside Av
100 BRNX 105 B3
100 BRNX 6504 A5
Burnside Dr
- HAOH 6280 C1
10 HAOH 6165 E7
10 HAOH 6166 A7
Burnside Pl
10 COrT 6712 D1
10 HAOH 6280 A1
Burnside St
400 COrT 6712 D1
Burr Av
2000 BRNX 6506 A5
2100 BRNX 6505 E5
Burr Pl
10 PALP 6502 C5
10 WhkT 111 A4
10 WhkT 6717 A2
100 HSBH 6500 E5
Burr Rd
10 MplT 6712 A7
10 SOrT 6712 A7
Burroughs Wy
10 MplT 6712 A7
10 MplT 6816 A1
Bursley Pl
10 WHPL 6168 B3
Burt Ct
10 HmpT 6928 B5
Burtis Av
10 RKVC 6929 E4
10 YNKR 6394 B1
Burtis Pl
10 HmpT 6827 C4
Burtis St
10 LNBK 6929 A3
Burton Av
10 HmpT 7028 C1
10 HSBH 6500 D5
10 STNL 7207 A2
10 WDBG 7028 C2
500 HSBH 6501 A3
1100 HmpT 6828 A6
1200 HmpT 6827 E6
Burton Ct
10 STNL 7117 D1
Burton Ln
10 LWRN 7028 C3
Burton Rd
10 MrnT 6282 D7
Burton St
10 MLVN 6929 B1
10-00 QENS 6615 D7
Buscher Av
100 VLYS 6928 B2
Bush Av
10 GrwT 6170 E4
10 PTCH 6170 B5
10 STNL 6919 A7
Bush St
100 BKLN 6922 B2
100 BRNX 6504 B5
200 BRNX 105 E3
Bushey Av
10 YNKR 6280 B5
Bushnell Pl
10 BRNX 6394 D6
10 MTVN 6394 D6
Bushwick Av
10 BKLN 6822 D4
900 BKLN 6823 A7
1300 BKLN 6924 C1
Bushwick Ct
10 BKLN 6822 E4
Bushwick Pl
10 BKLN 6822 D5
Bussing Av
1500 BRNX 6394 C7
2100 MTVN 6394 C7
Bussing Pl
10 BRNX 6394 D6
Butler Av
10 STNL 7206 A3
21-00 QENS 6823 B4
Butler Blvd
10 HmpT 6827 E5
10 STNL 7206 D4
Butler Pl
10 BKLN 6923 A2
10 KRNY 6714 A3
10 STNL 7020 E3
10 YNKR 6280 E2
2400 BRNX 6505 D7
2400 BRNX 6614 D1
Butler Rd
10 SCDL 6167 C5
Butler St
10 BKLN 121 A7
10 BKLN 6821 C7
10 ELIZ 6918 B6
10 STNL 7206 C2
24-00 QENS 6720 B3
100 BKLN 6922 D1
Butler Ter
10 STNL 6920 C7
Butterwood Ln E
10 IRVN 6166 B2
Butterwood Ln W
10 IRVN 6166 A2
Butterworth Av
10 STNL 7020 A5
Buttonwood Rd
10 STNL 7020 A6
4500 NHmT 6723 C2
Buttonwood St
10 JSYC 6819 A4
Buttrick Av
100 BRNX 6615 A3
600 BRNX 6614 E2
Buxton Av
500 HmpT 6828 B6
Buzzoni Dr
10 CLST 6278 D2
Bye St
10 QENS 6824 D3
Byram Dr
10 GrwT 6170 E5
Byram Rd
10 GrwT 6170 D4
Byram Dock St
10 GrwT 6170 D6
Byram Shore Rd
- GrwT 6284 C1
10 GrwT 6170 D7
Byram Terrace Dr
10 GrwT 6170 D3
Byrd Pl
10 YNKR 6280 D4
Byrd St
10 RYE 6283 E5
10 WbgT 7114 A2
43-00 QENS 6721 A5
Byrne Av
10 STNL 7019 C4
Byrne Ln
10 TFLY 6392 A4
Byrne Rd
10 WOrT 6712 A1
Byron Av
10 WHPL 6168 A3
10 YNKR 6394 C3
600 HmpT 6828 B7
900 ELIZ 6917 A2
1100 UnnT 6917 A2
1800 HmpT 6827 B6
4200 BRNX 6394 C6
Byron Ln
10 MrnT 6282 B7
10 SDRK 6616 D6
Byron Pl
10 DBSF 6166 C4
10 GrbT 6167 A6
10 MrnT 6396 B1
10 YNKR 6394 B1
Byron St
10 CART 7017 D7
10 LNBK 6929 A3
Byway
10 GrbT 6166 E3
E Byway
10 GrwT 6170 B1
Byworth Rd
10 NRCH 6281 D7

C

C St
- WbgT 7115 A3
200 CARL 6610 B2
1300 HmpT 6827 E6
Cabinet St
10 NWRK 6713 C6
Cable Wy
10 STNL 7018 E1
Cabot Av
10 EMFD 6049 B4
10 GrbT 6049 B5
900 UnnT 6917 B2
Cabot Pl
10 STNL 7020 D7
Cabot Rd
10 MrnT 6396 D3
57-00 QENS 6823 C6
Cabrini Blvd
10 MHTN 104 B4
10 MHTN 6503 D5
Caccese Wy
100 STNL 6920 C6
Cadillac Dr
10 NRCH 6281 E5
Cadiz St
- ELIZ 6919 A1
Cadman Plz E
100 BKLN 121 B5
100 BKLN 6821 D6
Cadman Plz W
100 BKLN 121 A4
100 BKLN 6821 C6
Caerleon Av
10 MrnT 6396 C1
Caesar Pl
10 MNCH 6501 A7
10 MNCH 6609 E1
2000 BRNX 6614 C3
Caffrey Av
9-00 QENS 7027 E5
Caffrey Av Ext
- QENS 7027 A5
Cail Dr
10 ERKY 6929 B7
Calais Ct
10 RKVC 6929 D5
Calamus Av
69-00 QENS 6823 D1
Calamus Cir
74-00 QENS 6823 D1
Calcutta St
10 NWRK 6818 B7
Calder Pl
10 BKLN 6922 D4
Caldera Pl
10 STNL 6920 B7
Caldwell Av
68-00 QENS 6823 E2
82-34 QENS 6824 A2
700 HmpT 6928 A6
Caldwell Pl
- NWRK 6712 D7
10 ELIZ 6917 E3
Caldwell Rd
10 HmpT 6928 C1
10 VLYS 6928 C1
Calhoun Av
10 NRCH 6395 D3
600 BRNX 6615 A2
1100 BRNX 6614 E1
Calhoun Dr
10 GrwT 6170 D2
Calicooneck Rd
10 SHKT 6501 C4
California Pl N
10 HmpT 7029 D5
10 ISPK 7029 D5
California Pl S
10 HmpT 7029 D5
10 ISPK 7029 D5
California Rd
10 MTVN 6395 A2
300 EchT 6395 B1
600 EchT 6281 C7
California St
10 LBCH 7028 E7
Calla Av
10 FLPK 6827 C3
Callahan Ct
10 NWRK 6713 C7
Callahan Ln
10 STNL 7206 C4
Callan Av
10 STNL 7020 A5
Calloway St
58-01 QENS 6720 B7
Calmet Pl
10 YNKR 6394 A2
Calton Ln
10 NRCH 6395 D1
Calton Rd
10 NRCH 6395 D1
Calumet Av
10 HAOH 6165 E6
S Calumet Av
10 HAOH 6165 C7
Calumet St
10 NWRK 6817 E2
Calvert St
10 HRSN 6283 B3
Calvi Ln
10 YNKR 6280 B6
Calvin Ct
10 GrbT 6049 C4
Calvin St
10 HmpT 6929 A5
10 LNBK 6929 A5
10 STNL 7020 D1
10 WbgT 7114 E4
Calyer St
10 BKLN 6822 B1
Cambreleng Av
2200 BRNX 6504 D5
Cambria Av
246-00 QENS 6722 E4
Cambria St
10 STNL 7020 E6
Cambridge Av
- HmpT 6827 E3
10 EGLD 6392 A5
10 GDNC 6828 A3
10 GRFD 6500 A3
10 MHVN 6508 B7
10 NHmT 6508 C6
10 STMN 6827 C4
10 STMN 6828 A3
10 WHPL 6168 B3
10 YNKR 6281 A2
100 HmpT 6828 A3
100 JSYC 6716 C6
100 STNL 7019 B4
3100 BRNX 102 D1
3100 BRNX 6504 B1
Cambridge Ct
10 HmpT 6929 B7
10 LRMT 6396 C1
Cambridge Dr
10 GrwT 6170 B2
Cambridge Ln
10 NHmT 6617 D6
Cambridge Pl
10 BKLN 6822 A7
10 BKLN 6923 A1
10 EGLC 6392 B7
Cambridge Rd
10 GTNK 6617 A6
10 HmpT 6929 B7
10 NHmT 6617 A6
10 SCDL 6167 E5
184-00 QENS 6826 A3
800 HmpT 6928 B7
Cambridge St
10 EORG 6712 D4
10 LNBK 6929 C3
10 MLVN 6929 C3
10 MtPT 6050 B2
10 NHmT 6724 D1
10 RKVC 6929 E2
10 VLYS 6928 C4
E Cambridge St
10 MtPT 6050 A2
N Cambridge St
10 MLVN 6929 C2
Cambridge Ter
10 HKSK 6501 A1
Cambridge Wy
10 ALPN 6278 D4
10 CLST 6278 D4
Camden Av
10 STNL 7206 C4
183-00 QENS 6826 A5
Camden Ct
10 IRVN 6166 C2
Camden Pl
10 NHmT 6724 C6
Camden St
10 NWRK 6713 B7
10 STNL 7020 E2
200 NWRK 6817 A1
E Camden St
10 HKSK 6501 C1
W Camden St
10 HKSK 6501 D2
Camdike St
10 VLYS 6928 C3
Camelot Ct
10 GrbT 6049 E5
Camelot Dr
100 WbgT 7115 B2
Cameron Av
10 STNL 7020 D6
Cameron Ct
10 BKLN 7022 C2
Cameron Ln
10 HmpT 6928 C4
Cameron Pl
10 BRNX 105 D2
10 BRNX 6504 E6
10 NRCH 6395 D1
10 TCKA 6281 E6
Cameron Rd
10 TFLY 6392 A2
500 SOrT 6712 B6
600 NWRK 6712 B6
Cameron St
400 HmpT 6827 E6
Camfield Ct
10 NWRK 6713 D7
Camille Ct
- LFRY 6501 B5
Cammerer Av
10 ERKY 6929 C7
Camner St
10 EGLC 6503 A3
10 FTLE 6503 A4
Camp Al
10 NWRK 6817 D2
Camp Rd
10 HmpT 7029 E3
21-00 QENS 7027 C5
Camp St
10 NWRK 6817 D2
2000 BRNX 6394 D6
Campbell Av
10 CLST 6278 B3
10 HKSK 6501 C2
10 OrgT 6164 C3
10 STNL 6919 E7
10 WLPK 6724 D4
Campbell Dr
3200 BRNX 6506 B7
Campbell Ln
10 MrnT 6282 B7
Campbell Pkwy
10 NHmT 6724 E3
Campbell St
10 NHmT 6723 D5
10 NWRK 6713 D7
300 WbgT 7114 B4
Campden Rd
10 GrbT 6167 A7
10 GrbT 6281 A1
Campfield St
10 IrvT 6816 C3
Campion Pl
10 YNKR 6279 D5
Campora Dr
10 NVLE 6164 C4
Camptown Rd
10 IrvT 6816 A3
10 MplT 6816 A3
Campus Dr
- STNL 7019 B6
10 NHmT 6618 A2
Campus Pl
10 BKLN 6925 B3
10 GrbT 6167 B5
Campus Rd
10 STNL 7020 B3
300 HmpT 6828 B5
2300 BKLN 7023 B1
Canaan Ct
10 WbgT 7115 B2
Canal Av
10 BKLN 7022 D7
10 BKLN 7120 D1
Canal Pl
10 BRNX 107 E7
10 BRNX 110 D1
10 BRNX 6612 E4
Canal Rd
10 PLMM 6395 A7
Canal St
10 JSYC 6820 C3
10 MHTN 119 A6
10 MHTN 6821 C3
10 MTVN 6395 A6
10 STNL 7020 D2
100 MHTN 118 D5
Canal St W
10 BRNX 107 D7
10 BRNX 110 D1
10 BRNX 6612 E4
Canandaigua Av
300 HmpT 6929 D2
Canarsie Ln
- BKLN 6923 E6
8700 BKLN 6924 B6
Canarsie Rd
10 BKLN 6924 E7
1600 BKLN 7024 D1
Canarsie Veterans Cir
- BKLN 7024 D1
Canary Cres
10 NHLS 6618 B7
Candlelight Pl
10 GrwT 6170 C7
Candlewood Ct
10 GrbT 6167 A7
Candlewood Dr
10 YNKR 6280 C3
Candlewood Rd
10 NRCH 6281 E1
Candon Av
200 STNL 7115 B6
Candon Ct
10 STNL 7115 B6
Candy Ln
10 PTCH 6170 A3
10 RYEB 6170 A3
10 SDRK 6616 C6
Cane St
10 BGTA 6501 E2
10 TnkT 6501 E2
Caney Ln
138-00 QENS 6928 A4
142-00 QENS 6927 E4
Caney Rd
240-00 QENS 6927 E4
Canfield Av
10 WHPL 6168 B1
10 YNKR 6280 E3
Canfield St
10 COrT 6712 D2
Cannon Av
10 STNL 7018 B6
Cannon Blvd
10 STNL 7117 E3
Cannon Ln
10 EchT 6281 A6
Cannon Pl
3800 BRNX 6504 C1
Cannon St
10 MHTN 119 D6
10 MHTN 6821 E3
Canon Dr
10 STNL 7117 A2
Cantello St
100 UNCT 6716 E3
100 WhkT 6716 E3
Canterbury Av
400 STNL 7019 A4
Canterbury Ct
10 ALPN 6278 D4
10 CLST 6278 D4
10 STNL 7206 D2
Canterbury Dr
10 GrwT 6170 B2
Canterbury Ln N
10 HRSN 6283 C2
Canterbury Rd
10 GTPZ 6617 A7
10 KENS 6617 A7
10 NRWD 6164 D7
10 SCDL 6168 A7
10 YNKR 6394 B4
100 GrbT 6049 A7
100 WLPK 6724 E5
Canterbury Rd N
10 HRSN 6283 C2
Canterbury Rd S
10 HRSN 6283 C2
Canterbury Gate
10 LNBK 6928 E4
10 LNBK 6929 A4
10 VLYS 6928 E4
Cantitoe Rd
10 YNKR 6280 E1
Canton Av
10 STNL 7116 B5
Canton Ct
10 BKLN 7024 A7
10 BKLN 7023 E5
Canton St
700 ELIZ 6917 C4
Cantwell Av
600 PTHA 7114 C7
Canyon Cir
10 YNKR 6393 D3
Capellan St
10 STNL 7207 C1
Cape May St
10 HRSN 6714 B7
300 EGLD 6503 A3
600 HRSN 6818 A1
Cape May St NW
- HRSN 6714 B7
Capi Ln
10 NHmT 6617 D2
Capital Dr
10 MNCH 6610 C1
Capitol Av
10 WLPK 6724 D4
Capitol Cir
- CLST 6278 C2
Capp St
10 CART 7115 B1
Capri Dr
- HmpT 7028 C7
10 NHmT 6724 C3
100 WbgT 7115 B2
Capri Dr E
- HmpT 7028 C7
Capri Dr S
- HmpT 7028 C7
Capri Dr W
- HmpT 7028 C7
Captain Honeywells Rd
10 ARDY 6166 D4
Captains Ln
10 RYE 6283 C6
Captains Rd
10 HmpT 6928 B6
10 VLYS 6928 B6
Carbon Pl
10 JSYC 6819 C3
Carbon St
200 JSYC 6820 A3
Carder Rd
100 MHTN 120 A5
100 MHTN 6821 A6
Cardiff St
10 STNL 7116 B6
Cardinal Ln
10 STNL 7117 D5
Cardinal Rd
10 FLHL 6618 A4
Cardinal Hayes Pl
10 MHTN 118 D7
10 MHTN 6821 E4
Cardinal Stepinac Pl
- MHTN 115 E1
- MHTN 6717 C5
Carey Pl
10 NHmT 6508 D7
10 PTWN 6508 D7
Carey St
10 NHmT 6508 E6
Cargo Plz
- QENS 6926 D4
S Cargo Rd
- QENS 6926 D5
Cargo Service Rd
- QENS 6926 C4
Carhart Av
10 WHPL 6168 B2
Carl Av
10 HmpT 6828 C4
Carl St
10 VLYS 6928 C2
4500 HmpT 7029 D6
Carla Ln
10 IRVN 6166 B1
Carlen Ct
10 FRVW 6611 B3
Carleton Av
10 MTVN 6395 A6
Carlin Pl
10 GTNK 6616 C5
10 GTNK 6617 A6
Carlin St
10 STNL 7115 C7
Carling Dr
10 NHmT 6724 C6
Carlisle Av
- GrbT 6050 A4
- MtPT 6050 A4
Carlisle Pl
10 MLVN 6929 B2
10 YNKR 6279 D7
3500 BRNX 6505 B2
Carlisle Rd
10 NRCH 6281 E7
Carlisle St
10 MHTN 120 A1
10 MHTN 6821 A4
Carlock Av
600 PTHA 7205 B1
Carlotta Wy
10 DMRT 6278 B6
Carlsen Dr
1400 UnnT 6816 A5
Carlson Ct
10 CLST 6278 B2
Carlson St
10 LFRY 6501 C6
Carlton Av
10 BKLN 121 E5
10 BKLN 6821 E6
10 BXTE 6617 D1
10 ERTH 6500 A7
10 JSYC 6716 A6
10 NHmT 6617 D1
10 RTFD 6500 A7
10 YNKR 6280 E4
300 BKLN 6822 A7
400 BKLN 6923 A1
500 BKLN 6922 E1
1600 STNL 7116 A7
1800 STNL 7207 B1
Carlton Blvd
700 STNL 7116 D6
Carlton Ct
10 STNL 7116 B7
Carlton Ln
10 HRPK 6164 A7
10 RYEB 6169 E3
Carlton Pl
10 ERTH 6500 A7
10 RTFD 6500 A7
10 STNL 7020 B4
136-00 QENS 6720 E4
Carlton Rd
10 RSLG 6723 A1
10 YNKR 6280 C7
10 YNKR 6394 C1
Carlton St
10 CART 7017 A6
10 EORG 6712 E3
10 FLPK 6827 C2
10 GrbT 6049 D7
10 MLVN 6929 A3
63-00 QENS 6824 A2
700 ELIZ 6917 D5
700 LNDN 6917 D5
Carlton St US-1
700 ELIZ 6917 D5
700 LNDN 6917 D5
Carlton St US-9
700 ELIZ 6917 D5
700 LNDN 6917 D5
Carlton Ter
10 STMN 6827 E3
200 HmpT 6827 E3
Carly Ct
10 STNL 7206 D2
Carlyle Av
600 HmpT 6828 B6
Carlyle Ct
10 CARL 6500 B6
10 TnkT 6502 C2
10 WhkT 111 A4
10 WhkT 6717 A2
Carlyle Grn
10 STNL 7116 A4
Carlyle Pl
10 GrbT 6167 B2
10 NHmT 6618 E7
10 RSLN 6618 E7
Carlyle St
10 STNL 6920 C6
600 CDHT 7028 A1
600 HmpT 7028 A1
Carman Av
10 CDHT 7028 A2
10 ERKY 6929 B6
10 HmpT 7028 D1
10 HWTN 7028 D1
10 LWRN 7028 A2
Carman Pl
10 ERKY 6929 B6
Carman Rd
10 SCDL 6281 D2
Carmel Av
10 STNL 7019 C4
Carmel Ct
10 STNL 7020 C6
Carmella Ct
10 NWRK 6713 E3
Carmine St
10 MHTN 118 D2
10 MHTN 6821 B1
Carmita Av
10 ERTH 6500 A7
10 RTFD 6500 A7
10 RTFD 6609 A1
Carnation Av
10 FLPK 6827 D3
Carnegie Av
10 EORG 6712 E4
10 HmpT 6827 C4
10 STNL 7018 E5
Carnegie Dr
10 GrbT 6166 C7
Carnegie St
10 LNDN 6917 B6
Caro St
10 STNL 7019 C4
Carol Av
200 PLHM 6395 B5
900 HmpT 6928 B6
Carol Ct
10 DMRT 6278 C5
10 LNBK 6929 A3
10 STNL 7207 A3
800 HmpT 6928 B7
Carol Dr
10 EGLC 6392 C6
Carol Ln
10 MrnT 6282 D3
10 NRCH 6281 E4
10 OrgT 6164 D3
Carol Pl
10 MNCH 6501 B7
10 MNCH 6610 B1
10 STNL 7019 A2
400 PLMM 6395 B5
Carol St
10 HmpT 6929 D1
10 LNBK 6929 A2
10 MLVN 6929 A2
400 HmpT 6828 A6
1800 LNDN 6917 C5
2100 ELIZ 6917 C5
Carole Av
10 NHmT 6723 E6
Carole Ct
10 VLYS 6928 D5
1300 HmpT 6928 D1
Carol Gate
- GLCV 6509 D4
Carolin St
39-00 QENS 6719 A6
Carolina Av
10 HmpT 7029 E3
10 NWRK 6712 D7
100 IrvT 6712 D7
Carolina Ct
10 STNL 7019 D5
Carolina Pl
10 STNL 7019 D2
Carolina Rd
240-00 QENS 6722 D4
Caroline Av
10 HmpT 6827 C7
10 HmpT 6828 C4
10 YNKR 6393 C2
1800 LNDN 6917 C5
2100 ELIZ 6917 C5
Caroline Ct
10 CLST 6278 C2
Caroline Pl
10 FLPK 6827 C3
10 GrwT 6170 C3
10 YNKR 6393 C2
Caroline St
10 STNL 6919 D7
10 STNL 7019 E1
10 WbgT 7114 C5
Carolyn Av
10 HmpT 6928 C1
Carolyn Ct
10 STNL 7207 A3
Carolyn Pl
10 EchT 6395 B1
Carolyn Ter
10 LNDN 6917 B5
10 ROSL 6917 B5
Carolynn Rd
10 ELIZ 6817 B7
10 ELIZ 6918 B1
Carpenter Av
10 GLCV 6509 E5
10 LNBK 6929 B5
10 NRWD 6164 A6
10 SCLF 6509 E6
10 STNL 7019 A6
10 YNKR 6280 E5
195-00 QENS 6826 C4
3800 BRNX 6505 B1
3900 BRNX 6394 B6
4800 MTVN 6394 C5
Carpenter Ct
10 JSYC 6819 A4
Carpenter Pl
10 MTVN 6395 A4
10 UnnT 6816 A7
500 RDGF 6611 C2
800 MRNK 6282 D7
Carpenter St
10 GLCV 6509 E4
E Carpenter St
10 VLYS 6928 E3
Carpenter Av Ext
10 GLCV 6509 E5
10 SCLF 6509 E5
Carreau Av
10 STNL 7018 E5
Carriage Ct
10 NRCH 6281 E2
Carriage Ln
10 HmpT 6724 E1
Carriage Rd
10 GTNK 6616 E4
10 NHLS 6724 B3
10 NHmT 6724 B3
Carriage Wy
10 WHPL 6168 E6
Carriage Hill Rd
10 HRSN 6050 D5
Carriage House Ln
10 MrnT 6282 C3
10 SCDL 6282 C3
Carrie Pl
10 EchT 6281 B5
Carrie Rd
10 NARL 6714 D1
Carriere Av
10 ARDY 6166 C5
Carrigan Av
10 WHPL 6168 D6
Carrihger Rd
- ELIZ 6918 A7
- LNDN 6918 A7
Carrington St
1300 ELIZ 6817 A7
1300 NWRK 6817 A7
Carrol Av
10 JSYC 6716 A5
100 WbgT 7114 C3
Carroll Av
10 VLYS 6928 A2
100 HmpT 6928 A2
100 MRNK 6283 A5
Carroll Pl
10 MrnT 6282 B6
10 STNL 6920 C6
10 WhkT 111 A4
10 WhkT 6717 B2
600 TnkT 6502 A1
1000 BRNX 6613 A1
Carroll St
10 YNKR 6393 D4
300 BKLN 6922 E2
900 BKLN 6923 C3
Carroll Close
200 TYTN 6048 D4
Carrollwood Dr
10 TYTN 6048 C4
Carrolton Pl
10 MLVN 6929 B1
Carson Av
500 PTHA 7205 C2
Carson Rd
- ELIZ 6817 C7
- NWRK 6817 C7
Carson St
137-00 QENS 6927 D2
Carstairs Rd
10 VLYS 6928 D5
Carstensen Dr
10 SCDL 6167 D7
Carstensen Rd
10 SCDL 6167 D7
Carter Av
1700 BRNX 105 E5
1700 BRNX 6504 C7
Carter Ct
10 LNBK 6929 B5
Carter Rd
10 WOrT 6712 A2
Carter St
10 NRWD 6164 A6
Carteret Av
10 CART 7115 C1
100 JSYC 6819 E4
300 CART 7017 C7
800 UnnT 6816 B7
Carteret Pl
10 GDNC 6828 E1
300 COrT 6712 B4
Carteret St
10 BlmT 6713 C1
10 LNDN 7017 A1
10 NWRK 6713 E2
10 NWRK 6714 A2
10 STNL 7206 B4
10 WbgT 7115 A2
600 ELIZ 6917 E6
Carteret Ter
200 COrT 6712 C4
Carthage Ln
10 SCDL 6282 A2
Carthage Rd
10 SCDL 6282 A2
Cartigan Rd
300 MHTN 120 A7
300 MHTN 6821 A7
Carukin St
1000 HmpT 6828 A5
Caruso St
- HKSK 6501 A2
Carvel Av
300 CDHT 7027 C2
300 CDHT 7028 A2
300 HmpT 7027 C2
Carvel Pl
- HmpT 7027 C3
Carver Lp
100 BRNX 6506 A2
Carver Ter
10 YNKR 6280 E5
Carwall Av
10 MTVN 6395 A2
Cary Av
10 STNL 7020 A1
300 STNL 7019 E1
Cary Ct
10 BKLN 7023 A2
Cary Rd
10 GTNK 6617 B6
10 NHmT 6617 B6
10 NHmT 6724 C6
Cary St
10 COrT 6712 B3
10 WOrT 6712 B3
Caryl Av
10 YNKR 6393 D4
Caryl Ct
200 HmpT 7027 E2
200 HmpT 7028 A2
1400 HmpT 6827 D7
Caryl Dr
200 HmpT 7027 E3
200 HmpT 7028 A3
Caryl Ln
10 HRSN 6283 C1
Caryl St
700 HmpT 6828 B6
Casals Pl
10 BRNX 6506 A2
Casanova St
300 BRNX 6613 D4
Casarella Wy
10 HRSN 6050 D7
Cascade St
10 STNL 7118 B1
Cascade Ter
10 YNKR 6279 E4
Case Av
10 STNL 7207 B3
Case St
40-00 QENS 6719 E6
40-17 QENS 6720 A6
Casey St
10 CART 7115 C2
Casey Stengel Plz
- QENS 6720 C5
Cashman Pl
10 NHmT 6618 E7
Casler Pl
3000 BRNX 6615 C4
Caspars Ln
10 FTLE 6502 E4
10 LEON 6502 E4
Casper Ct
10 JSYC 6819 C4
10 PTCH 6170 B5
Casper Rd
300 EGLC 6503 B2
Casper St
100 VLYS 6928 B2

New York City/5 Borough Street Index

STREET
Block City Map# Grid

Cass Pl
10 BKLN 7121 B1
Cassandra Dr
10 ALPN 6278 E5
Cassidy Pl
10 STNL 6920 B6
Cassilis Av
10 YNKR 6280 D6
Casta Ln
10 EDGW 103 A6
10 EDGW 6503 A6
Castle Dr
- GrwT 6170 E2
200 EGLC 6503 B2
Castle Lndg
10 PTCH 6170 B3
10 RYEB 6170 B3
Castle Pl
10 NRCH 6395 E5
W Castle Pl
10 NRCH 6395 E6
Castle Rd
10 HmpT 7029 E3
10 IRVN 6166 B2
10 OrgT 6164 E1
10 PRMT 6164 E1
10 PRMT 6165 B1
10 SECS 6715 D3
Castle St
10 YNKR 6394 D1
Castle Wk
10 GrbT 6167 A7
Castle Brooke Rd
10 HRSN 6050 E5
Castle Cove Ter
10 EDGW 108 B1
10 EDGW 6611 D4
Castle Heights Av
10 TYTN 6048 C3
Castle Heights Pl
10 NoCT 6050 B5
Castle Hill Av
10 BRNX 6614 C3
1500 BRNX 6505 C7
Castle Hill Close
10 DBSF 6166 B4
Castle Point Ter
900 HBKN 6716 E6
Castle Ridge Rd
10 NHmT 6617 D7
10 NHmT 6618 A7
Castleton Av
100 STNL 7020 B1
300 STNL 6920 A7
900 STNL 6919 E7
1200 STNL 7019 D1
Castleton Ct
10 HmpT 6929 D3
10 STNL 6920 B6
Castle View Ct
10 RYEB 6170 B2
Castor Pl
10 STNL 7116 B6
W Castor Pl
10 STNL 7116 A6
Caswell Av
10 STNL 7019 B3
W Caswell Av
500 STNL 7019 A3
Caswell Ln
10 STNL 7018 E3
Catalina Dr
10 KNGP 6616 D3
Catalpa Av
10 HmpT 6929 A5
10 LNBK 6928 E5
10 LNBK 6929 A5
10 PTHA 7205 D5
56-00 QENS 6823 D5
500 TnkT 6501 D1
Catalpa Dr
800 HmpT 6828 A7
Catalpa Ln
10 HmpT 6928 C4
Catalpa Pl
10 BRNX 6615 B4
Catamaran Wy
- QENS 7026 C7
Caterson Ter
10 GrbT 6167 D3
Catharine Pl
10 STNL 6918 D7
Cathay Rd
10 ERKY 6929 B7
Cathedral Av
10 GDNC 6828 E2
200 HmpT 7029 E4
900 HmpT 6828 A3
Cathedral Ct
200 NWRK 6713 C5
Cathedral Pkwy
500 MHTN 109 B3
500 MHTN 6612 A5
Cathedral Pl
10 BKLN 121 B4
10 BKLN 6821 D6
Catherine Av
10 HmpT 6828 A5
Catherine Ct
10 HmpT 6827 B5
10 JSYC 6819 B7
10 STNL 7019 D1
Catherine Ln
10 MHTN 118 D6
10 MHTN 6821 A2
Catherine Rd
10 SCDL 6168 A7
Catherine St
10 BKLN 6822 D4
10 CART 7115 C1
10 ELIZ 6918 A3
10 HmpT 6929 B3
10 LNBK 6929 B3
10 MHTN 118 E7
10 MHTN 6821 C4
10 NWRK 6714 C7
10 STNL 7019 C1
10 VLYS 6928 D5
400 FTLE 6502 E5
600 PTHA 7205 D2
Catherine Slip
- MHTN 118 E7
- MHTN 6821 C4
10 MHTN 120 E1
Cathrine St
10 WbgT 7114 E4
10 WbgT 7115 A4
Cathy Ct
10 MLVN 6929 B2
10 NRWD 6164 A7
700 HmpT 6827 C7
Cathy Ln
10 GTNK 6616 D5
Cathy Ter
10 EGLC 6392 C6
Catlin Av
10 STNL 7020 D1
Catlin Pl
10 HmpT 6928 E6
Cato Ct
500 HmpT 6828 B6
Caton Av
10 BKLN 6922 E6
900 BKLN 6923 A5
Caton Av SR-27
500 BKLN 6922 E6
900 BKLN 6923 A5
Caton Pl
10 BKLN 6922 D5
Cator Av
10 JSYC 6819 C6
Catskill Av
10 YNKR 6394 B2
Catskill Pl
10 GrbT 6049 B4
Cattaraugus St
10 STNL 7020 A3
Cauldwell Av
600 BRNX 6613 B3
Cauldwell St
10 EchT 6281 B6
Causeway
10 LWRN 7028 A5
Caven Point Av
10 JSYC 6819 E5
Caven Point Rd
10 JSYC 6819 D6
Cayuga Av
10 ATLB 7027 E7
10 STNL 7020 B3
4400 BRNX 6393 C7
Cayuga Ln
10 GrbT 6048 D7
Cayuga Rd
10 SCDL 6168 A6
10 YNKR 6280 E5
700 HmpT 6929 C1
Cayuga St
10 RYE 6169 E7
10 RYE 6283 D1
Cayuga Tr
10 HRSN 6283 A1
Cazenove Pl
10 RYE 6284 B2
Cebra Av
10 STNL 6920 B6
10 STNL 7020 D1
Cecelia Av
10 CLFP 6611 D3
Cecelia Pl
300 CLFP 6611 D3
Cecil Ct
10 STNL 7019 A1
Cecil Crest Rd
10 YNKR 6280 B6
Cedar Av
10 ELIZ 6917 C5
10 HBPK 6928 D7
10 LNDN 7017 B1
10 LRMT 6396 D3
10 NWRK 6712 D6
10 RKVC 6929 E3
10 STNL 7021 A6
100 EORG 6712 D6
100 HBPK 7028 E1
100 STNL 7020 E6
200 HWTN 7028 D1
400 MTVN 6395 A5
500 WbgT 7114 C4
700 LNDN 6917 C5
800 SECS 6610 B7
1800 BRNX 105 B2
1800 BRNX 6504 B4
2200 BRNX 102 C7
Cedar Ct
300 NRWD 6278 C1
900 HmpT 6828 B3
2600 HmpT 6929 D6
Cedar Dr
10 GTNE 6616 E7
10 GTNE 6617 A7
10 GTNE 6722 D1
10 GTPZ 6617 A7
10 KENS 6617 A7
Cedar Dr E
1000 NHmT 6724 B4
Cedar Dr N
1000 NHmT 6724 B4
Cedar Dr S
1000 NHmT 6724 B4
Cedar Dr W
1100 NHmT 6724 B4
Cedar Ln
10 CDHT 7028 B2
10 EGLD 6502 C2
10 GLCV 6509 D2
10 HRSN 6051 B6
10 LWRN 7028 B2
10 NHmT 6724 A6
10 SNPT 6508 B7
10 TnkT 6502 A1
10 YNKR 6280 D6
38-01 QENS 6722 D2
200 CLST 6278 A2
500 BRNX 107 E5
500 BRNX 6612 E3
700 HmpT 7028 B1
1000 HmpT 6928 C7
1100 SECS 6610 B7
Cedar Ln CO-60
10 TnkT 6502 A1
E Cedar Ln
10 TnkT 6502 B1
N Cedar Ln
10 NWRK 6713 D3
S Cedar Ln
10 NWRK 6713 D1
Cedar Pl
- TCKA 6281 B4
10 BRNX 6615 C4
10 EchT 6281 B4
10 FLPK 6827 D3
10 RYE 6284 A2
10 SCLF 6509 D6
10 SFPK 6827 D3
10 YNKR 6393 C2
Cedar Rd
10 HmpT 7027 C3
10 MLVN 6929 B2
500 HmpT 6929 C2
Cedar St
- WLTN 6500 B5
10 BKLN 6822 E6
10 BRXV 6280 E7
10 DBSF 6166 A4
10 FLPK 6827 D3
10 GRFD 6500 A2
10 GrwT 6170 D5
10 HAOH 6280 A1
10 HlsT 6816 D6
10 HmpT 6827 B5
10 HmpT 6929 A6
10 JSYC 6819 A5
10 LNBK 6929 A5
10 MHTN 120 C1
10 MHTN 6821 A4
10 MtPT 6050 A3
10 NRCH 6396 A4
10 NWRK 6713 D7
10 OrgT 6164 B2
10 PTHA 7205 C3
10 RDFP 6501 E5
10 RYE 6283 E1
10 RYE 6284 A1
10 STNL 7020 D2
10 SYHW 6048 B2
10 TCKA 6281 E6
10 TFLY 6392 A1
10 VLYS 6928 A3
10 YNKR 6393 D2
100 CLFP 108 A1
100 CLFP 6611 C4
100 EGLD 6392 A6
100 FTLE 103 A4
100 FTLE 6503 A6
100 MHTN 118 A7
100 NRCH 6395 E3
100 QENS 6928 A2
100 RDFP 6502 A5
300 SAMB 7205 B7
400 HmpT 6828 E5
600 MRNK 6282 E5
1600 BKLN 7023 B3
E Cedar St
10 MTVN 6394 E2
W Cedar St
10 MTVN 6394 A2
Cedar Ter
10 STNL 7020 C3
Cedar Cliff Rd
10 STNL 7020 C3
Cedarcroft Rd
170-00 QENS 6825 D4
Cedar Grove Av
- STNL 7117 E5
10 STNL 7118 B4
Cedar Grove Ct
10 STNL 7118 B3
Cedar Grove Beach Pl
10 STNL 7118 B4
Cedarhill Rd
5-00 QENS 7027 E5
Cedarhurst Av
10 CDHT 7028 A1
10 LWRN 7028 B2
500 HmpT 7028 A1
Cedarhurst St
800 HmpT 6928 B5
Cedar I
10 LRMT 6396 D2
10 WesC 6396 D2
Cedar Knoll Dr
10 SNPT 6508 A4
Cedar Lawn Av
6-00 QENS 7027 D5
10 LWRN 7027 D5
Cedarlawn Blvd
10 HmpT 6928 E1
10 VLYS 6928 E1
100 HmpT 6929 E2
Cedarlawn Rd
10 IRVN 6166 B1
Cedar St Ext
- MtPT 6050 B2
Cedarview Av
10 STNL 7117 D3
W Cedarview Av
10 STNL 7117 C2
Cedarwood Ct
10 STNL 7018 E2
Cedarwood Dr
400 HmpT 6928 A7
400 HmpT 7028 D3
Cedarwood Rd
10 WHPL 6168 D7
Cedric Rd
128-00 QENS 6926 B2
Celebration Ln
10 STNL 7020 D4
Celeste Ct
10 BKLN 7023 E6
Celina Ln
- STNL 7206 B4
Celler Av
10 NHmT 6723 E5
Celli Pl
10 YNKR 6393 C2
Celtic Av
50-00 QENS 6719 A7
Celtic Pl
10 STNL 7118 A3
Cemetery Ln
10 EchT 6281 C4
10 NRCH 6395 D5
Cemetery Rd
- GrbT 6050 A7
- WHPL 6050 A7
10 ALPN 6278 E6
Center Al
- COrT 6712 D3
Center Av
10 LRMT 6396 C2
10 SECS 6610 A7
300 MRNK 6282 D6
300 SECS 6609 E6
1400 FTLE 6502 E6
2000 FTLE 103 A2
2000 FTLE 6503 A5
Center Blvd
47-00 QENS 117 C5
47-00 QENS 6718 B6
Center Cir
10 WbgT 7114 B4
Center Ct
10 NHLS 6618 D7
Center Dr
- MHTN 112 D6
- MHTN 6717 E3
- ROSE 6618 C5
- RSLN 6618 C5
10 FLHL 6618 D5
10 NHmT 6724 B5
10 QENS 6614 E7
10 QENS 6615 A7
29-00 QENS 6722 D2
800 HmpT 6828 A6
Center Knls
10 YNKR 6394 D2
Center Pl
10 STNL 7118 B3
400 TnkT 6501 D1
Center Row
10 LODI 6500 E1
Center St
- NRWD 6278 B1
10 ARDY 6166 D4
10 CRSK 6278 B7
10 CRSK 6392 B1
10 EGLC 6503 B3
10 IRVN 6048 C7
10 JSYC 6820 B3
10 NWRK 6713 E7
10 PTHA 7205 E3
10 STNL 7117 B2
10 WLPK 6724 D4
100 NHmT 6724 D4
100 WbgT 7114 C1
300 CARL 6500 C6
300 WRDG 6500 C6
400 FTLE 6502 E5
400 SAMB 7205 B6
600 RDGF 6611 C1
1400 HlsT 6816 D5
Center St CO-508
10 NWRK 6713 E7
N Center St
100 COrT 6712 D2
S Center St
10 COrT 6712 C5
700 EORG 6712 C5
700 SOrT 6712 C5
Center Ter
100 NWRK 6817 A6
Center Cargo Rd
- QENS 6926 D4
Center Market St
10 BKLN 6924 A6
Centerway
10 EORG 6713 B3
Central Av
- JSYC 6820 A1
- NWRK 6713 E5
- STNL 7019 E7
- STNL 7117 E1
10 BKLN 6822 E5
10 COrT 6712 B3
10 DMRT 6278 B5
10 ENWK 6713 E5
10 ENWK 6714 A5
10 EORG 6712 D4
10 EORG 6713 C6
10 HKSK 6501 C1
10 HlsT 6816 D6
10 HRPK 6164 A5
10 HSBH 6500 D3
10 JSYC 6716 B6
10 KRNY 6818 E2
10 KRNY 6819 A2
10 LODI 6500 D3
10 LWRN 7027 E3
10 NHmT 6724 B7
10 NRCH 6395 C3
10 NRWD 6164 A5
10 OLDT 6164 A5
10 OrgT 6164 B3
10 PLHM 6395 C3
10 PTCH 6170 C6
10 RDFP 6501 E4
10 RYE 6283 D1
10 SCLF 6509 D6
10 STNL 6920 D6
10 TETB 6501 B4
10 TFLY 6392 A2
10 TYTN 6048 B2
10 WbgT 7114 E4
10 WOrT 6712 B3
12-00 QENS 7027 D4
61-00 QENS 6823 D5
100 BGTA 6501 E2
100 FTLE 103 B3
100 FTLE 6503 A5
100 LNBK 6929 A3
100 SYHW 6048 B2
100 WHPL 6167 E2
100 WHPL 6168 A1
200 BKLN 6823 B7
200 KRNY 6715 A7
200 LWRN 7028 B1
300 CDHT 7028 A2
300 ERTH 6500 A7
300 HRSN 6714 A5
400 CARL 6500 C7
400 UNCT 6716 C4
500 GrbT 6167 D2
600 HmpT 7028 B2
700 BKLN 6924 C1
Central Av CO-106
10 HRPK 6164 A5
10 NRWD 6164 A5
10 OLDT 6164 A5
Central Av CO-508
10 COrT 6712 C3
10 EORG 6712 D4
10 EORG 6713 C6
10 NWRK 6713 A5
Central Av SR-100
100 WHPL 6167 E2
100 WHPL 6168 A1
500 GrbT 6167 D2
N Central Av
10 EMFD 6049 A5
10 VLYS 6928 C2
300 HmpT 6928 C2
900 HmpT 7028 D3
1800 HmpT 6827 B7
N Central Av SR-9A
10 EMFD 6049 A5
S Central Av
10 VLYS 6928 C3
Central Blvd
10 MNCH 6610 C2
10 NHPK 6828 C1
10 SHkT 6610 C2
200 FTLE 6502 D7
200 NHPK 6724 A7
400 PALP 6502 D7
600 NHmT 6724 B6
700 CARL 6610 C2
Central Blvd SR-5
200 FTLE 6502 E7
E Central Blvd
10 PALP 6502 D7
400 FTLE 6502 D7
E Central Blvd CO-501
10 PALP 6502 C6
W Central Blvd
10 PALP 6502 B6
W Central Blvd CO-501
10 PALP 6502 B6
Central Ct
10 HmpT 6928 C1
Central Dr
10 BXTE 6617 E1
10 EchT 6395 C2
10 KNGP 6616 E2
10 NHmT 6617 E1
10 NRCH 6396 B3
10 PLDM 6617 D5
Central Ln
10 SECS 6610 B6
Central Pk
- MHTN 109 D5
- MHTN 112 E4
- MHTN 6612 B6
- MHTN 6717 E2
Central Pk E
- MHTN 109 D6
- MHTN 6612 B7
Central Pk N
10 MHTN 109 B3
10 MHTN 6612 B5
Central Pk S
10 MHTN 112 D6
10 MHTN 6717 E3
Central Pk W
10 MHTN 112 D4
10 MHTN 6717 E2
200 MHTN 109 A7
200 MHTN 113 A1
200 MHTN 6612 A6
200 MHTN 6718 A1
Central Pkwy
10 MTVN 6394 E2
10 MTVN 6395 A2
300 BRXV 6395 A1
Central Pl
10 HmpT 6928 E6
10 HmpT 6929 A5
10 WOrT 6712 A4
100 COrT 6712 D3
500 CDHT 7028 A1
700 PTHA 7205 E1
Central Rd
2000 FTLE 103 B4
2000 FTLE 6503 B5
N Central Rd
2100 FTLE 103 B2
2100 FTLE 6503 A5
Central Park Av
10 BRNX 6393 E4
10 YNKR 6393 E4
100 YNKR 6394 B1
400 GrbT 6167 C4
1000 GrbT 6281 A1
1000 YNKR 6280 C7
1200 YNKR 6281 A1
Central Park Av SR-100
400 GrbT 6167 A7
900 YNKR 6280 E3
900 YNKR 6394 C1
1000 GrbT 6281 A1
1200 YNKR 6281 A1
Central Park St
10 SCLF 6509 D6
Central Park East Dr
- MHTN 112 E6
- MHTN 113 A4
- MHTN 6717 E3
- MHTN 6718 A2
Central Park West Dr
- MHTN 112 E3
- MHTN 6717 E2
Central Terminal Dr
- QENS 6719 E2
- QENS 6720 A2
Central Westchester Pkwy
- NoCT 6050 B5
- WHPL 6050 B5
Centre Av
10 ERKY 6929 C5
10 NRCH 6395 E5
10 STNL 7020 C3
100 HmpT 6929 C5
200 NRCH 6396 A6
N Centre Av
10 RKVC 6929 D4
S Centre Av
10 RKVC 6929 D5
Centre Dr
10 GTNK 6616 E4
10 NHmT 6617 D7
Centre Ln
- LKSU 6723 A3
- NHmT 6723 A3
10 BAYN 6919 E2
Centre Pl
10 NWRK 6713 E7
10 PALP 6502 B6
10 YNKR 6393 D1
Centre St
- HmpT 6928 D7
10 BKLN 6922 B2
10 BRNX 6506 E7
10 BRNX 6615 B2
10 ELIZ 6918 A4
10 HmpT 7028 C1
10 LFRY 6501 C6
10 LNBK 6929 B4
10 MHTN 118 C7
10 MHTN 6821 C3
10 MTVN 6394 E2
10 RYE 6284 A3
16-00 BKLN 6823 B6
16-00 QENS 6823 C6
100 BAYN 6920 B2
200 CDHT 7028 A2
300 SOrT 6712 B6
400 LBCH 7029 C7
500 COrT 6712 C5
500 EORG 6712 C5
S Centre St
10 SOrT 6712 B6
Centre Edgewater Park Dr
10 BRNX 6615 C2
Centre Market Pl
10 MHTN 118 E5
10 MHTN 6821 A2
Centreville St
109-00 QENS 6925 E2
Century Rd
10 OrgT 6165 A5
Century Tr
10 HRSN 6282 E2
10 HRSN 6283 A2
Century Ridge Rd
10 HRSN 6050 E7
10 HRSN 6168 E1
Cerenzia Blvd
10 HmpT 6827 B6
Cerone Av
10 YNKR 6394 B1
Cerrato Ln
10 YNKR 6393 D2
Cerreta Ln
10 EchT 6281 D3
10 NRCH 6281 D3
Cerro St
10 HmpT 7027 C3
Cesario Pl
10 PTCH 6170 B7
Cespino-Russo Memorial Cir
- STNL 7021 A7
Chadwick Av
300 NWRK 6817 A4
Chadwick Ct
1400 GrbT 6048 E4
Chadwick Rd
10 GTNK 6617 A5
10 NHmT 6617 A6
10 TnkT 6502 A1
10 WHPL 6050 B6
Chadwick St
10 ERTH 6500 B6
Chaffee Av
10 BRNX 6615 B4
10 NHmT 6724 D3
Chaffee Cir
10 NRWD 6164 B5
Chain O Hills Rd
200 WbgT 7114 A1
Chain O Hills Rd CO-650
400 WbgT 7114 A1
Chalet Dr
600 WbgT 7114 C3
Chalford Ln
10 GrbT 6167 A7
10 GrbT 6281 A1
10 YNKR 6281 A1
Challenger Dr
10 STNL 7116 D4
Challenger Rd
10 RDFP 6502 A6
Chamberlain Av
10 LFRY 6501 C6
10 YNKR 6394 A3
500 PTHA 7114 B7
700 PTHA 7205 C1
Chamberlain Rd
10 HmpT 6828 E4
Chamberlain St
10 RYE 6283 D4
Chambers St
10 MHTN 118 B6
10 MHTN 6821 A3
10 NWRK 6818 A1
Champlain Av
10 STNL 7117 D3
300 HmpT 6929 C1
Chancellor Av
10 NWRK 6816 D4
400 IrvT 6816 B3
1000 MplT 6816 A2
Chancellor Av CO-601
10 NWRK 6816 D4
400 IrvT 6816 B3
1000 MplT 6816 A2
Chancellor St
700 ELIZ 6917 B4
Chandler Av
10 STNL 7019 D3
100 LNDN 6917 B6
100 ROSL 6917 A5
Chandler St
13-00 QENS 7027 C4
W C Handy Pl
10 YNKR 6280 C3
Chaneyfield Ln
- NWRK 6817 A2
Chanfrau Pl
10 YNKR 6279 B7
Channel Av
10 BKLN 7023 E6
Channel Dr
10 HWTN 7028 D2
10 KNGP 6616 E3
10 MHVN 6508 D7
10 PTWN 6508 D7
10 WDBG 7028 C2
1000 HWTH 7029 A1
Channel Rd
16-00 QENS 7026 B5
Channing Pl
- EchT 6281 C4
Channing Rd
11-00 QENS 7027 D4
Channon Rd
200 ERKY 6929 A7
200 HmpT 6929 A7
200 HWTH 6929 A7
Chanticlare Dr
10 FLHL 6617 E4
Chapel Av
10 JSYC 6819 D6
Chapel Ct
- SOrT 6712 A7
10 NWRK 6817 D1
10 OrgT 6164 B1
Chapel Pl
10 GTPZ 6617 B7
10 KENS 6617 B7
Chapel Rd
- STNL 6920 A6
10 NHmT 6618 A7
600 QENS 6616 A7
Chapel St
10 BKLN 121 B4
10 BKLN 6821 D6
10 GrwT 6170 D4
10 NWRK 6714 C7
10 NWRK 6818 C1
100 COrT 6712 C2
Chapin Av
10 STNL 7020 B6
Chapin Ct
165-00 QENS 6825 D3
Chapin Pkwy
84-00 QENS 6825 C3
Chapman Av
10 PTHA 7205 C3
Chapman Dr
10 LFRY 6501 C7
Chapman Pl
10 IrvT 6816 B2
Chapman Rd
- HmpT 7028 C1
- WDBG 7028 C1
Chapman St
100 COrT 6712 C3
200 NWRK 6712 C7
200 NWRK 6816 C1
300 IrvT 6816 C1
500 HlsT 6816 B6
Chappell St
10 STNL 6919 E7
Charing Cross
10 LNBK 6928 E5
10 VLYS 6928 E5
100 LNBK 6929 A5
Charlecote Rdg
83-00 QENS 6825 E3
Charles Av
10 NHmT 6508 E7
200 STNL 6919 C7
Charles Ct
10 LODI 6500 E2
10 STNL 7117 D1
10 VLYS 6928 C3
700 FTLE 6502 D6
3500 NBgT 6716 D2
Charles Ln
10 MHTN 118 B1
10 MHTN 6821 B1
10 RYEB 6169 E3
Charles Pl
10 BKLN 6822 E6
10 EchT 6395 B3
10 MTVN 6394 E7
10 STNL 7019 A1
10 YNKR 6394 C3
400 LEON 6502 D5
Charles Rd
10 NHmT 6723 D5
Charles St
10 BlmT 6713 B1
10 CART 7017 E7
10 CLST 6278 A2
10 EORG 6712 E1
10 FLPK 6827 D2
10 GLCV 6509 E3
10 GRFD 6500 B2
10 GrwT 6170 E3
10 JSYC 6716 B6
10 LFRY 6501 C5
10 LNBK 6929 C3
10 LODI 6500 B2
10 MHTN 118 C1
10 MHTN 6821 B1
10 MLVN 6929 B2
10 MNCH 6501 C7
10 NHmT 6617 D2
10 NHPK 6827 E1
10 NRCH 6395 D4
10 NVLE 6164 C5
10 OrgT 6164 C3
10 WHPL 6168 A3
10 WLPK 6724 D3
10 WOrT 6712 C1
100 HKSK 6501 A2
100 SECS 6716 A2
200 HmpT 6828 D7
500 PTHA 7205 E2
900 HmpT 6827 A7
1000 HmpT 6828 A1
1000 LNDN 6917 A6
1100 ROSL 6917 A6
2800 HmpT 6929 E6
S Charles St
10 WbgT 7205 B2
Charles Curran Ct
10 YNKR 6280 D6
Charles J Cimi Pl
- BRNX 6506 A6
Charles Lindbergh Blvd
10 MNCH 6500 E7
Charleston Av
10 STNL 7115 E5
Charleston St
- NWRK 6817 A2
Charlotte Av
10 JSYC 6715 E7
Charlotte Ct
1400 HmpT 6827 E4
Charlotte Ln
10 NRCH 6281 D2
Charlotte Pl
10 EGLC 6503 B2
10 GrbT 6167 D4
100 EGLD 6503 B2
Charlotte St
10 CART 7017 C7
10 QENS 6823 A4
10 RYE 6283 E3
10 WHPL 6168 A3
10 YNKR 6280 B5
1400 BRNX 6613 D1
Charlotte Ter
100 ROSP 6917 A3
700 RDGF 6611 A2
Charlton Av
10 LODI 6500 E2
100 HSBH 6500 E2
100 SOrT 6712 A6
300 HSBH 6501 A4
Charlton St
10 MHTN 118 C3
10 MHTN 6821 B2
10 NWRK 6817 C2
Charmello Dr
10 SAMB 7205 B7
Charney Ct
10 NHLS 6724 A1
Charney Pl
10 ALPN 6278 D4
Chart Lp
10 STNL 7206 B1
Charter Rd
144-00 QENS 6825 B3
Charter Oak Ln
10 GrwT 6170 C7
Charter Oak Rd
10 STNL 7020 A7
Charter Oak St
10 CARL 6500 C7
10 WRDG 6500 C7
Chase Av
10 WbgT 7114 C2
10 WHPL 6167 E2
10 YNKR 6279 E5
Chase Ct
10 BAYN 6919 E4
300 EDGW 108 B1
300 EDGW 6611 D4
8000 BKLN 6924 A6
Chase Rd
10 NHmT 6617 E6
10 SCDL 6167 C7
10 SCDL 6281 C1
Chase Rd N
10 SCDL 6167 C7
Chateaux Cir
10 SCDL 6167 C7
Chatfield Rd
10 YNKR 6280 D7
Chatham Ct
10 HmpT 6929 B7
Chatham Pl
10 HMPD 6828 E4
10 HmpT 6828 E4
10 WHPL 6168 B5
Chatham Rd
10 HmpT 6928 E5
10 NRCH 6281 D6
Chatham Sq
10 MHTN 118 E7
10 MHTN 6821 C4
Chatham St
10 STNL 7116 C3
Chatham Ter
10 YNKR 6280 B4
Chatsworth Av
- MrnT 6396 C1
10 LRMT 6396 C1
N Chatsworth Av
10 LRMT 6396 C1
10 MrnT 6282 B7
10 MrnT 6396 B1
Chatsworth Pl
10 NRCH 6396 A1
Chatterton Av
10 WHPL 6167 E1
10 WHPL 6168 A1
1900 BRNX 6614 C2
Chatterton Pkwy
10 WHPL 6167 D2
10 WHPL 6168 A2
200 GrbT 6167 E2
Chaucer St
10 GrbT 6167 A2
Chauncey Av
10 EORG 6713 B2
10 NRCH 6395 D3
Chauncey Ln
10 HAOH 6165 E7
10 HAOH 6166 A6
Chauncey St
10 BKLN 6923 E1
10 YNKR 6281 A2
100 PTHA 7205 E2
200 BKLN 6924 A1
600 BKLN 6823 B7
Chauncy Ln
10 LWRN 7028 C3
Chautauqua Av
500 HmpT 6929 C2
Chedworth Rd
10 GrbT 6167 A7
Cheever Pl
10 BKLN 120 E7
10 BKLN 6821 C7
Chelsea Av
10 EORG 6712 E6
10 NWRK 6712 E6
Chelsea Dr
10 NHmT 6617 E3
Chelsea Ln
10 RKVC 6929 E5
Chelsea Pl
10 EORG 6712 E2
10 GTPZ 6722 C1
10 GTPZ 6723 A1
10 YNKR 6280 B5
Chelsea Rd
10 GDNC 6828 D2
10 GrbT 6049 D3
10 MtPT 6049 D3
10 NRCH 6396 A5
10 STNL 7018 C4
S Chelsea Rd
400 GrbT 6049 D5
Chelsea St
10 HmpT 6827 C3
10 SFPK 6827 C3
10 STNL 7206 B4
85-00 QENS 6826 A3
Chemical Ln
- STNL 7115 D5
Cheney St
134-00 QENS 6927 B2
Cherokee Pl
10 MHTN 113 E5
10 MHTN 6718 C3
Cherokee Rd
10 YNKR 6280 E6
Cherokee St
10 STNL 7118 C1
Cherry Av
10 LRMT 6396 D2
10 NRCH 6396 B3
133-00 QENS 6720 E5
140-00 QENS 6721 A5
Cherry Ct
2800 HmpT 6929 D6
Cherry Ln
10 ERKY 6929 B5
10 GrbT 6166 E7
10 GrbT 6280 E1
10 KNGP 6616 D3
10 LNBK 6929 B5
10 NHmT 6827 D1
10 NHPK 6827 D1
10 TnkT 6502 B1
100 NHmT 6723 D7
100 NHPK 6723 D7
200 QENS 6723 D7
800 HmpT 6928 B5
900 HmpT 6828 B3
Cherry Pl
10 MplT 6816 B1
10 STNL 7019 D5
Cherry St
10 BKLN 6822 D2
10 ELIZ 6917 D3
10 FLPK 6827 C3
10 GRFD 6500 A1
10 HmpT 7027 C3
10 JSYC 6819 A5
10 MHTN 118 E7
10 MHTN 6821 D4
10 NWRK 6713 E7
10 TFLY 6392 A4
10 VLYS 6928 D5
100 HmpT 7028 E2
236-00 QENS 6722 D3
400 MHTN 119 D7
Cherry St SR-27
10 ELIZ 6917 D3
E Cherry St
100 CART 7017 C7
100 FLPK 6827 E3
Cherrybrook N
10 NHmT 6723 C1
Cherry Brook Pl S
10 NHmT 6723 C1
Cherry Grove Ct
10 HmpT 6928 C5
10 VLYS 6928 C5
Cherry Lawn
- NRCH 6282 A4
- SCDL 6282 A4
Cherrytree Ln
10 NHmT 6724 E1
Cherry Valley Av
10 GDNC 6828 D4
10 HmpT 6828 D4
200 GDNC 6724 E7
200 MNLA 6724 E7
S Cherry Valley Av
10 HmpT 6828 C5
Cherrywood Ct
10 STNL 7117 B4
Cherrywood Dr
10 NHmT 6724 A4
Cherrywood Ln
10 FLHL 6618 B5
10 NHLS 6724 B1
Cherrywood Rd
10 GrbT 6280 E1
10 YNKR 6280 E1
Cherwing Rd
10 YNKR 6280 B6
Cheryl Av
10 STNL 7116 D4
Cheryl Dr
200 WbgT 7114 A4
Chesbrough Av
2600 BRNX 6505 D7
Chesebrough St
10 STNL 7116 E5
Cheshire Ln
10 YNKR 6280 B4
Cheshire Pl
10 STNL 7020 A3
E Cheshire Pl
10 STNL 7020 B2
Cheshire Rd
10 HmpT 7027 D2
Cheslan Ct
10 HmpT 6929 E7
Chesley Rd
10 WHPL 6168 D6
Chesman St
400 HmpT 6828 C5
Chester Av
10 BKLN 6922 D6
10 BlmT 6713 C2
10 BlvT 6713 C2
10 EMFD 6049 B6
10 FLPK 6827 E3
10 IrvT 6816 C3
10 STMN 6827 E3
10 STMN 6828 A3
10 STNL 7207 C2
10 WHPL 6168 B2
100 GDNC 6828 C3
Chester Av E
10 NWRK 6713 E3
10 NWRK 6714 A3
Chester Ct
10 BKLN 6923 B4
2600 HmpT 6929 E6
Chester Dr
10 NHmT 6617 D5
10 PLNH 6617 D5
10 RSLG 6723 A1
10 RYE 6283 C6
10 YNKR 6280 E3
Chester Pl
10 EchT 6395 B2
10 GrbT 6049 D6

New York City/5 Borough Street Index

STREET Block City Map# Grid

Chester Pl
10 MrnT 6396 B3
10 NRCH 6396 B3
10 STNL 7020 C1
10 YNKR 6394 C3
2900 HmpT 6929 E6
Chester Rd
10 ERKY 6929 D5
10 LNBK 6929 D5
10 RKVC 6929 D5
Chester St
10 BKLN 6924 B3
10 GrbT 6166 D5
10 MTVN 6394 E3
700 PTHA 7205 D1
1000 HlsT 6816 C7
1500 BRNX 6505 D2
2800 HmpT 6929 E6
E Chester St
10 VLYS 6928 E2
200 LBCH 7029 D7
200 VLYS 6929 A3
W Chester St
10 LBCH 7029 B7
10 VLYS 6928 D2
Chester Ter
10 HAOH 6280 A1
Chesterfield Ln
10 STNL 7117 A1
Chesterfield Rd
10 SCDL 6167 D5
Chesterton Av
100 STNL 7117 D4
Chesterwood Av
10 MTVN 6394 E2
Chestney Rd
10 LWRN 7028 B3
Chestnut Av
10 BGTA 6501 D3
10 BKLN 7023 A3
10 BRXV 6280 C4
10 BRXV 6281 B7
10 CLST 6278 B4
10 FLPK 6827 B2
10 IrvT 6816 C5
10 JSYC 6820 B1
10 LRMT 6396 C2
10 OLDT 6164 A5
10 PLHM 6395 C3
10 STNL 7020 E3
10 TYTN 6048 B5
100 HlsT 6816 C5
300 HKSK 6501 C4
300 MRNK 6282 D3
300 SHKT 6501 C3
400 HRSN 6283 A3
400 MRNK 6283 A3
500 TnkT 6501 E1
Chestnut Av CO-509
1300 HlsT 6816 C5
1400 IrvT 6816 C5
Chestnut Cir
10 STNL 7116 B4
Chestnut Ct
10 BKLN 6925 A1
10 EGLD 6392 A6
Chestnut Dr
10 GTNE 6616 E7
10 HAOH 6166 A6
10 HmpT 6928 D6
N Chestnut Dr
3200 BRNX 6505 B3
Chestnut Hl
10 NHLS 6724 B3
Chestnut Ln
10 NRCH 6395 E6
10 NRCH 6396 A7
10 VLYS 6928 D2
Chestnut Pl
10 MTVN 6395 A4
300 MNLA 6724 D6
500 TnkT 6501 E1
600 SECS 6610 A7
600 SECS 6716 A1
Chestnut Rd
10 FLHL 6617 E3
10 FLHL 6618 A3
10 HmpT 7027 C3
10 NHmT 6618 A3
Chestnut St
10 BKLN 6823 E7
10 BKLN 6824 B5
10 CART 7017 B7
10 CART 7115 B1
10 CRSK 6392 A1
10 DBSF 6165 E4
10 DBSF 6166 A5
10 EGLC 6503 C1
10 EGLD 6392 A6
10 EORG 6712 E4
10 ERTH 6609 B1
10 GrbT 6166 D2
10 GRFD 6500 A1
10 GrwT 6170 D5
10 KRNY 6714 B4
10 LNBK 6929 C3
10 LODI 6500 C3
10 MLVN 6929 A1
10 NARL 6714 D1
10 NRWD 6164 B7
10 NWRK 6817 E2
10 PTCH 6170 C5
10 RDFP 6501 E6
10 RTFD 6609 A2
10 RYE 6283 E2
10 STNL 7020 D2
10 SYHW 6048 B1
10 TCKA 6281 A5
10 TFLY 6392 A2
10 WbgT 7114 D1
10 WhkT 6716 D4
10 WLTN 6500 B5
10 YNKR 6393 D1
100 BKLN 6925 A1
100 EGLC 6392 B7
100 LEON 6502 D4
100 NVLE 6164 C6
200 FRVW 6611 B2
200 HmpT 6828 D6
300 NWRK 6818 A2
300 RDGF 6611 B2
400 CDHT 7028 B2
500 COrT 6712 A4
600 HmpT 7028 B1
600 SECS 6610 A7
600 WOrT 6712 A4
700 BRNX 6505 B2
800 HmpT 6929 B1
1100 ELIZ 6917 E3
Chestnut Hill Av
10 WHPL 6168 D3
Chestnut Ridge Wy
10 DBSF 6166 B5
Chetwood St
600 ELIZ 6917 E6
Chevalier Av
10 SRVL 7205 A6
Cheves Av
10 STNL 7019 C3
Chevron Av
- PTHA 7114 E7
Chevy Chase St
80-00 QENS 6825 E2
85-00 QENS 6826 A3
Chicago Av
10 STNL 7020 E5
Chicot Rd
91-00 QENS 6925 D2
Chieftans Rd
10 GrwT 6051 E5
Childs Av
10 FLPK 6827 C2
300 GDNC 6828 D3
300 HmpT 6828 D3
Chilton St
10 ELIZ 6917 D3
Chimney Pot Ln
10 ARDY 6166 D4
Chinmoy Av
10 GrwT 6170 D6
Chipman Rd
10 OrgT 6165 A5
Chipperfield Ct
10 STNL 7020 A4
Chippewa Rd
10 YNKR 6280 E6
Chippewa St
10 SHKT 6501 B4
10 TETB 6501 B4
Chisholm St
- STNL 7207 B1
1200 BRNX 6613 C1
Chisum Pl
10 MHTN 107 C6
10 MHTN 6612 D3
Chittenden Av
10 MHTN 104 B2
10 MHTN 6503 D5
10 YNKR 6281 A4
Chittendon St
10 HmpT 6827 D6
Choctaw Pl
1200 BRNX 6505 C5
Chopin Ct
10 JSYC 6820 B2
Chowan St
1800 HmpT 6827 C5
Chrissy Ct
10 STNL 7019 E1
Christabel St
10 LNBK 6929 C3
Christie Av
95-00 QENS 6720 B7
Christie Ln
400 FTLE 6502 D5
400 LEON 6502 D5
Christie Pl
10 SCDL 6167 C5
Christie St
10 DMRT 6278 A5
10 LEON 6502 C4
10 LODI 6500 D2
10 NWRK 6818 C1
10 RDFP 6501 E5
100 RDFP 6502 A5
Christie Heights St
100 LEON 6502 D4
Christie Heigths St
10 LEON 6502 D3
Christina Dr
10 WbgT 7114 D2
10 WbgT 7115 A3
Christina St
10 HmpT 7027 D2
10 LFRY 6501 C6
Christine Ct
10 STNL 7207 C1
Christine Ln
10 OrgT 6164 B2
Christine St
10 ELIZ 6918 A4
Christopher Av
10 BKLN 6924 B2
Christopher Ct
10 LODI 6500 E2
700 PTHA 7205 B1
1000 HmpT 6929 D2
Christopher Ln
10 STNL 7019 A3
10 WbgT 7114 D1
Christopher St
10 CART 7017 D7
10 LODI 6500 E2
10 MHTN 118 C1
10 MHTN 6821 A1
10 SHKT 6501 B3
10 STNL 6918 E7
500 COrT 6712 A4
W Christopher St
600 COrT 6712 A4
Christopher Columbus Dr
- NWRK 6713 D2
10 JSYC 6820 C3
Christopher Columbus Dr CO-639
10 JSYC 6820 C3
Chrome Av
10 CART 7115 D3
Chrystie St
10 MHTN 119 A6
10 MHTN 6821 C3
Chubb Av
10 LynT 6609 B6
Church Av
10 BKLN 6922 E6
10 QENS 7122 E3
10 STNL 7018 C6
300 CDHT 7028 B1
300 HmpT 7028 A1
500 HmpT 6928 A7
900 BKLN 6923 A6
5600 BKLN 6924 A5
Church Av SR-27
600 BKLN 6922 E6
Church Ct
10 CLST 6278 D3
10 WHPL 6168 A1
Church Ln
10 BAYN 6919 E3
10 SCDL 6167 C7
10 SCDL 6281 C1
10 STNL 7020 E2
10 STNL 7021 A3
8500 BKLN 6924 B7
Church Ln S
10 SCDL 6281 C1
Church Pl
10 EORG 6713 B4
Church Rd
600 QENS 7026 B4
Church Sq
10 HRSN 6714 A6
Church St
- COrT 6712 A4
- NoCT 6050 B5
10 ALPN 6278 D7
10 EGLD 6392 A6
10 EHLS 6618 E7
10 GTNK 6616 E5
10 HKSK 6501 B4
10 HmpT 7027 E3
10 LODI 6500 E2
10 MHTN 118 B7
10 MHTN 120 B1
10 MHTN 6821 B3
10 MLVN 6929 B2
10 NHmT 6618 E7
10 NRCH 6395 E6
10 NRCH 6396 A5
10 QENS 6925 E4
10 ROSH 6618 E5
10 RSLN 6618 E5
10 STNL 6919 D7
10 TYTN 6048 B3
10 WHPL 6168 B1
100 SAMB 7205 C7
100 WbgT 7114 B3
200 WHPL 6050 A7
300 HSBH 6500 E3
400 RDGF 6611 A1
1100 HlsT 6816 E7
Church St W
10 GrwT 6170 C6
S Church St
10 WbgT 7114 B7
Church Ter
10 BlvT 6714 A1
100 NWRK 6817 A6
Churchill Av
10 STNL 7206 D1
10 YNKR 6394 B4
Churchill Dr
10 NHmT 6724 B6
1900 UnnT 6816 A6
Churchill Rd
- EDGW 108 A3
- EDGW 6611 C5
- NBgT 108 A3
- NBgT 6611 C5
10 CRSK 6278 B7
10 EGLC 6392 C7
10 RYEB 6169 E3
10 TFLY 6392 B5
Churchman St
- NWRK 6713 C7
Church Towers
10 HBKN 6716 E7
Cicero Av
2000 BRNX 6614 C3
Cincinnatus Av
2200 BRNX 6614 C3
Cindra Av
10 STNL 7117 B6
Cindy Ln
10 IRVN 6166 A2
Circle Av
10 LRMT 6396 D3
Circle Dr
10 HAOH 6166 A6
10 IRVN 6048 B7
10 NHmT 6724 E1
10 PLDM 6617 E4
10 PLNM 6617 E4
600 QENS 6616 A6
Circle Dr E
100 HmpT 6827 B5
Circle Dr N
10 HmpT 6827 C5
Circle Dr W
10 HmpT 6827 B5
E Circle Dr
- PLNM 6617 E4
N Circle Dr
10 GTNE 6616 D7
S Circle Dr
10 GTNE 6722 D1
Circle Ln
10 PLNM 6617 E4
10 RTFD 6609 A1
Circle Lp
10 STNL 7020 D3
Circle Rd
10 SCDL 6281 C1
10 STNL 7020 A5
10 TCKA 6281 A5
38-00 QENS 6722 D2
Circle Wy
10 SCLF 6509 D7
Circle Crest
10 NHmT 6617 E7
Circle Hill Rd
10 PLMM 6395 D7
Circuit Av
10 TCKA 6281 A5
Circuit Rd
10 NRCH 6395 E6
Cisney Av
10 FLPK 6827 E2
10 STMN 6827 E2
Citizen Av
1300 HmpT 6827 E5
City Blvd
10 STNL 7020 B1
City Pl
10 EDGW 108 B2
10 EDGW 6611 D5
10 WHPL 6168 B1
City Dock St
10 NWRK 6713 E7
10 NWRK 6817 E1
City Hall Plz
10 EORG 6712 D4
10 EORG 6713 B4
City Island Av
10 BRNX 6506 E5
City Island Br
- BRNX 6506 D5
City Island Rd
- BRNX 6506 C4
City Park Rd
- NRCH 6396 A2
Civic Sq
10 IrvT 6816 C2
Civic Sq W
10 IrvT 6816 C2
Claflin Av
300 MRNK 6282 E7
600 MRNK 6396 E1
600 MRNK 6397 A1
2700 BRNX 102 E5
2700 BRNX 6504 C3
Claflin Blvd
10 HmpT 6828 B5
Claflin Ct
200 HmpT 6828 B5
Clair Pl
1500 HmpT 6928 D1
Clair St
10 NHmT 6723 A2
Clairborne Rd
10 HRSN 6282 E3
Claire Av
10 NRCH 6395 E2
10 WbgT 7114 D4
Claire Ct
10 STNL 7020 C3
Clairmont Ter
100 COrT 6712 C5
Clapham Av
10 NHmT 6617 D7
Clara St
10 BKLN 6922 D6
Claradon Ln
10 STNL 7020 E5
Clara Maass Dr
10 BlvT 6713 D1
10 NWRK 6713 D1
Claran Ct
65-00 QENS 6823 C1
Clare Ter
10 YNKR 6280 E5
Claremont Av
10 CLFP 6611 D3
10 LFRY 6501 B5
10 MHTN 106 C7
10 MHTN 109 B1
10 MHTN 6612 A4
10 MTVN 6395 A3
10 RYE 6283 E3
300 JSYC 6819 C3
300 MTVN 6394 E3
Claremont Pkwy
400 BRNX 105 E7
400 BRNX 6504 C7
500 BRNX 6613 C1
Claremont Pl
10 MTVN 6395 A4
Claremont Rd
10 EDGW 6611 E1
10 FTLE 6611 E1
10 SCDL 6167 E4
Claremont Ter
- MTVN 6395 D7
10 ELIZ 6917 C4
10 QENS 6719 E2
Clarence Av
10 HAOH 6280 C2
600 BRNX 6615 B1
Clarence Pl
10 STNL 7117 D3
Clarence Rd
10 EchT 6281 D3
100 SCDL 6281 D2
Clarence St
10 FLPK 6827 C3
Clarendon Av
10 STNL 7206 C3
10 YNKR 6279 C5
10 YNKR 6280 C5
Clarendon Dr
10 HmpT 6928 C1
10 VLYS 6928 C1
Clarendon Pl
10 GrbT 6167 B6
300 COrT 6712 B3
Clarendon Rd
10 GrbT 6167 A6
2100 BKLN 6923 B6
5500 BKLN 6924 A6
Clarendon St
200 SECS 6610 A6
Clarewood Dr
10 GrbT 6280 B1
Claridge Av
10 HmpT 6827 B4
Claridge Cir
10 NHLS 6724 A1
Clarion Ct
10 STNL 6920 A7
Clarion Ln
10 STMN 6827 E2
Clarissa Rd
400 MNLA 6724 D6
400 NHmT 6724 C6
Clark Av
- NRWD 6164 A5
- NVLE 6164 B5
10 KRNY 6714 A5
10 LNBK 6929 A4
10 OLDT 6164 A5
600 PTHA 7114 C7
600 RDGF 6611 B2
2800 HmpT 6929 D6
E Clark Av
700 COrT 6712 A4
Clark Ct
10 HSBH 6500 E2
10 LODI 6500 E2
10 LRMT 6396 D2
Clark Dr
10 LKSU 6723 C1
10 NHmT 6723 C1
10 THSN 6723 C1
Clark Ln
10 RYE 6284 A3
10 STNL 7020 D1
Clark Pl
10 HRSN 6168 D1
10 PTCH 6170 B5
10 STNL 7019 C2
10 UnnT 6816 A7
10 WbgT 7114 C1
10 YNKR 6280 D6
100 ELIZ 6918 C5
900 HmpT 7028 D1
900 HWTN 7028 D1
E Clark Pl
10 COrT 6712 A5
10 SOrT 6712 A5
Clark St
10 BKLN 120 E4
10 BKLN 121 A4
10 BKLN 6821 C6
10 CRSK 6278 A6
10 DMRT 6278 A6
10 ERKY 6929 C5
10 GrbT 6167 C3
10 GRFD 6500 B3
10 HlsT 6816 D5
10 LBCH 7029 E6
10 LODI 6500 E3
10 NWRK 6713 E5
10 YNKR 6394 A3
200 HKSK 6501 A2
200 SOrT 6712 A5
500 COrT 6712 A5
600 LNDN 6917 A7
Clark Ter
10 BlvT 6714 A1
200 CLFP 6611 C3
200 FRVW 6611 C3
Clarke Av
10 JSYC 6819 C3
10 STNL 7117 B2
E Clarke Pl
10 BRNX 105 B7
10 BRNX 6504 A7
W Clarke Pl
10 BRNX 105 A7
10 BRNX 6504 D7
Clarke St
10 CLST 6278 B4
1200 HmpT 6827 E6
Clarkson Av
10 BKLN 6923 D4
400 ELIZ 6917 E5
1000 BKLN 6924 A4
Clarkson St
10 MHTN 118 B2
10 MHTN 6821 A1
10 MLVN 6929 E2
Clason Point Ln
10 BRNX 6614 A3
Classic Ct
10 GrbT 6049 E4
Classon Av
10 BKLN 6822 B6
10 BKLN 6923 B2
Claude Av
160-00 QENS 6825 E7
Claudet Wy
10 EchT 6281 C6
Claudia Ct
10 OrgT 6164 B3
10 STNL 7019 A2
Claudy Ln
100 NHmT 6723 D5
Clausen Pl
10 NHmT 6723 D7
Clauss St
10 CART 7017 B6
Claver Pl
10 BKLN 6923 B1
Clawson St
10 STNL 7118 A2
400 STNL 7117 E3
Clay Av
200 LynT 6609 B5
900 BRNX 6613 B1
1000 PLMM 6395 C7
1200 BRNX 105 D5
1200 BRNX 6504 B7
E Clay Av
300 ROSP 6917 A3
500 ELIZ 6917 A3
Clay St
10 BKLN 117 D7
10 BKLN 6718 B7
10 COrT 6712 C4
10 EORG 6712 C4
10 HKSK 6501 C1
10 NWRK 6713 E5
10 SRVL 7205 A7
100 ENWK 6713 E5
1300 HmpT 6827 D3
Clayboard St
10 STNL 7118 A3
Claybourne Av
10 WbgT 7114 A4
Clay Pit Rd
10 STNL 7115 D6
Clayton Av
10 FLPK 6827 E3
10 HmpT 7028 C7
10 STMN 6827 E2
Clayton Ct
10 WbgT 7114 B4
Clayton Pl
10 YNKR 6394 A2
Clayton Rd
10 GrbT 6167 A6
300 MHTN 120 A6
300 MHTN 6821 A7
400 MHTN 6820 E6
1000 HmpT 6928 C1
Clayton St
10 STNL 7020 D7
Clearbrook Rd
10 GrbT 6049 B3
10 MtPT 6049 B3
Clearmont Av
10 STNL 7207 A1
Clearstream Av
10 VLYS 6928 B3
Clearview Expwy
- QENS 6615 E7
- QENS 6721 E1
- QENS 6722 B7
- QENS 6826 C1
Clearview Expwy I-295
- QENS 6615 E7
- QENS 6721 E1
- QENS 6722 B7
- QENS 6826 C1
Clearview Expwy E
26-01 QENS 6721 E2
Clearview Expwy W
26-00 QENS 6721 E2
Clearview Ter
10 WOrT 6712 A1
Clembil Ct
10 WbgT 7114 A2
10 WbgT 7205 A2
Clement Av
10 HmpT 6827 E5
Clement Pl
9000 NBgT 6611 C5
Clement St
- PTHA 7205 B3
10 GLCV 6509 E3
10 YNKR 6280 A5
Clementine St
2300 BRNX 6395 A7
2300 BRNX 6506 B1
Clements Pl
10 GrbT 6167 B1
10 IrvT 6816 B1
Clendenny Av
10 JSYC 6819 D3
Clendinen Pl
10 EGLC 6503 C1
Clent Rd
10 GTPZ 6723 A1
10 RSLG 6723 A1
10 THSN 6723 A1
Cleremont Av
10 IrvT 6816 C3
Clerk St
10 JSYC 6819 D4
Clermont Av
10 BKLN 121 E4
10 BKLN 6821 E5
10 BKLN 6822 A6
10 PTCH 6170 B4
10 STNL 7206 B5
400 BKLN 6923 A1
Clermont Pl
100 STNL 7019 D4
Clermont Ter
200 ELIZ 6917 A2
200 UnnT 6917 A2
Cletus St
10 STNL 7020 B7
Cleveland Av
10 HmpT 6929 E6
10 HRSN 6713 C4
10 HRSN 6714 A6
10 NRCH 6395 D6
10 NWRK 6712 C7
10 RKVC 6929 E6
10 STNL 7117 B5
100 MNLA 6724 E6
300 HSBH 6500 D5
500 LNDN 6917 A7
600 ELIZ 6917 C2
Cleveland Ct
10 NRCH 6395 D7
Cleveland Pl
10 GLCV 6509 E3
10 MHTN 118 E4
10 MHTN 6821 C2
10 PALP 6502 C6
10 STNL 7020 D7
10 YNKR 6280 E3
Cleveland Rd
10 UnnT 6816 A5
Cleveland St
10 BKLN 6924 D1
10 BlvT 6714 A1
10 HKSK 6501 B2
10 LNBK 6928 E4
10 MtPT 6050 A3
10 STNL 6920 D5
10 VLYS 6928 E4
10 WHPL 6167 E2
100 CLST 6278 B3
100 COrT 6712 D2
100 HmpT 6828 A5
200 PTCH 6170 C5
900 HmpT 6929 D2
Cleveland Ter
10 BlmT 6713 A1
10 EORG 6712 E1
10 EORG 6713 A1
Cley Rd
1000 HmpT 6928 C1
Cliff Av
10 GrwT 6170 C7
10 PLHM 6395 C5
10 YNKR 6393 C3
300 PLMM 6395 C5
Cliff Ct
10 STNL 7021 A4
Cliff Dr
10 EGLD 6502 E3
Cliff Ln
300 CLFP 6611 C4
Cliff Pl
10 PLMM 6395 C6
Cliff Rd
10 EGLC 6503 B2
10 EGLD 6503 B2
300 WbgT 7115 A4
E Cliff Rd
10 WbgT 7114 A1
S Cliff Rd
10 WbgT 7114 A2
W Cliff Rd
10 WbgT 7114 A1
Cliff St
10 HAOH 6166 B7
10 JSYC 6716 A6
10 MHTN 120 C1
10 MHTN 6821 B6
10 NRCH 6395 D5
10 NWRK 6712 C6
10 STNL 7021 A4
10 YNKR 6393 D1
100 CLFP 6611 C3
200 FRVW 6611 C3
200 WRDG 6500 D6
1700 UNCT 6716 D4
Cliff Wy
10 LRMT 6396 B2
10 NHmT 6618 B3
10 SCLF 6509 D6
Cliffdale Rd
10 GrwT 6051 D2
Cliff Hill Pl
10 NWRK 6712 C7
Clifford Av
- NRCH 6395 C4
10 PLHM 6395 C4
Clifford Ct
10 MLVN 6929 B1
Clifford Ln
- KENS 6617 B6
Clifford Pl
10 BKLN 6822 B2
10 HRSN 6283 B3
E Clifford Pl
10 BRNX 105 C5
10 BRNX 6504 B6
Clifford St
10 CART 7017 C7
10 CART 7115 C1
10 EORG 6712 D4
10 HmpT 6929 C3
10 LNBK 6929 C3
10 NWRK 6817 E3
100 HlsT 6816 C7
100 NWRK 6818 A3
Cliffside Av
10 STNL 7020 C3
800 HmpT 6927 E5
800 HmpT 6928 A6
Cliffside Dr
10 OrgT 6165 A2
10 YNKR 6280 E4
Cliffwood Av
10 STNL 7019 E6
10 STNL 7020 A6
Cliffwood Ter
10 ERTH 6500 A6
Clifton Av
10 BRNX 6393 C4
10 NWRK 6713 E3
10 STNL 7020 E4
10 STNL 7021 A3
10 YNKR 6393 C4
Clifton Ln
10 WHPL 6168 D6
Clifton Pl
10 BKLN 6822 B7
10 IRVN 6166 A2
10 JSYC 6819 E3
10 JSYC 6820 A3
Clifton Rd
10 GrbT 6281 A1
Clifton St
10 NWRK 6817 C3
10 STNL 7018 E4
400 ELIZ 6918 A6
500 ELIZ 6917 E6
Clifton Ter
10 EGLC 6503 C1
10 UNCT 6716 B3
10 WhkT 111 A4
10 WhkT 6716 B3
10 WhkT 6717 A2
1200 UnnT 6816 B7
Clinch Av
10 GDNC 6828 A1
100 NHPK 6828 A1
Clinch St
10 WbgT 7114 D5
Clinton Av
10 BKLN 6822 A6
10 ERKY 6929 B5
10 HAOH 6280 A1
10 HmpT 7027 E3
10 JSYC 6819 E3
10 KRNY 6714 B1
10 LNBK 6928 E4
10 LNBK 6929 B5
10 MNLA 6724 E6
10 NARL 6714 C1
10 NRCH 6395 D3
10 NWRK 6817 C2
10 OrgT 6164 B2
10 RKVC 6929 E4
10 RYE 6283 E1
10 STNL 6920 B6
10 VLYS 6928 E4
10 WbgT 7205 A2
66-00 QENS 6823 C2
200 CDHT 7028 A1
200 DBSF 6166 A5
300 HAOH 6166 A5
300 HmpT 6929 C2
400 BKLN 6923 A1
400 NVLE 6164 B4
700 NWRK 6816 B1
800 IrvT 6816 E2
1300 BRNX 6613 C1
1500 BRNX 6504 D7
Clinton Av CO-665
1100 IrvT 6816 C2
E Clinton Av
10 IRVN 6166 B2
10 TFLY 6392 C5
E Clinton Av CO-70
10 TFLY 6392 C4
E Clinton Av CO-501
10 TFLY 6392 A3
S Clinton Av
10 HAOH 6280 A1
W Clinton Av
10 IRVN 6166 A2
10 TFLY 6392 A2
Clinton Ct
10 STNL 6920 B7
Clinton Dr
10 WHPL 6050 B7
Clinton Ln
10 HRSN 6283 B1
Clinton Pl
10 BRNX 105 D2
10 BRNX 6504 B5
10 ERTH 6500 B7
10 ERTH 6609 B1
10 MTVN 6394 E3
10 MTVN 6395 A3
10 NRCH 6395 C5
10 NRCH 6396 A5
10 STNL 7019 C1
10 TCKA 6281 A6
10 WbgT 7114 C1
10 YNKR 6393 C2
165-00 QENS 6825 D4
500 NWRK 6816 D5
600 RDGF 6611 C1
1200 ELIZ 6917 E1
1400 HlsT 6816 D5
Clinton Rd
10 STNL 7117 B5
100 LWRN 7028 A5
Clinton St
10 BKLN 121 A6
10 BKLN 6821 C7
10 BlvT 6714 A1
10 HBKN 6716 D5
10 HmpT 6827 E4
10 LNDN 7017 B2
10 MHTN 6821 D3
10 MLVN 6929 A2
10 MtPT 6049 E2
10 MtPT 6050 A2
10 MTVN 6394 E1
10 NRWD 6164 A7
10 NWRK 6713 E7
10 PTCH 6170 A6
10 SCLF 6509 E6
10 STNL 7020 D1
10 SYHW 6048 A2
10 VLYS 6929 A2
10 WHPL 6050 B7
100 MHTN 119 B6
100 WbgT 7114 B5
200 BKLN 120 E7
500 BKLN 6922 B3
E Clinton St
10 MtPT 6050 A2
N Clinton St
10 EORG 6712 E3
400 EORG 6713 A2
500 BlmT 6713 A1
S Clinton St
10 EORG 6712 D5
500 NWRK 6712 D6
Clinton Ter
10 IrvT 6816 B1
Clinton B Fiske Av
10 STNL 7019 C3
Clintonville St
6-00 QENS 6615 B7
15-00 QENS 6721 C1
Clio St
86-00 QENS 6826 B3
Clipper St
10 NWRK 6818 B7
Cloister Pl
10 STNL 7117 E2
Clonover Rd
10 WOrT 6712 A4
Close Av
900 BRNX 6613 E2
Closter Rd
10 OrgT 6165 A5
Closter Dock Rd
10 CLST 6278 A2
700 ALPN 6278 D5
1000 ALPN 6279 A6
Closter Dock Rd CO-502
300 CLST 6278 B3
700 ALPN 6278 D5
1000 ALPN 6279 A6
Cloud Av
- HmpT 6828 B5
Clove Rd
10 BKLN 6923 C3
10 NoCT 6050 B4
10 NRCH 6395 D3
10 STNL 6919 D7
200 STNL 7019 D1
700 STNL 7020 B3
Clove Wy
10 STNL 7020 A2
Clove Lake Pl
10 STNL 7019 E2
Clovelly Dr
10 HmpT 6928 E2
Clover Av
10 FLPK 6827 C2
Clover Ct
10 CART 7017 A6
Clover Dr
10 GTNE 6616 E6
10 GTNK 6616 E6
N Clover Dr
10 GTNE 6616 E7
Clover Pl
10 NRCH 6396 A6
56-00 QENS 6823 C7
87-00 QENS 6826 B3
Clover Rd
10 MrnT 6282 C7
Clover St
10 ELIZ 6917 C4
10 NWRK 6818 A1
10 TFLY 6392 A4
10 YNKR 6279 E4
10 YNKR 6280 A3
Clover Close
- GrbT 6167 A4
Cloverdale Av
10 NoCT 6050 B5
10 STNL 7117 A6
10 WHPL 6050 B5
Cloverdale Blvd
49-00 QENS 6722 C4
Cloverdale Ln
10 RYE 6283 D5
10 RYE 6284 B3
67-01 QENS 6722 D6
Cloverfield Rd N
10 HmpT 6928 B4
Cloverfield Rd S
10 HmpT 6928 B5
Clover Hill Rd
87-00 QENS 6826 B3
Cloverwood Rd
10 WHPL 6168 D6
Clovis Rd
10 STNL 7117 B5
Club Blvd
10 WOrT 6712 A3
Club Dr
10 HmpT 7028 B1
1200 HWTH 6928 E7
Club Ln
10 EMFD 6049 C5
10 LWRN 7028 C3
Club Rd
10 RYE 6283 E1
800 TnkT 6502 B1
Club Wy
10 EchT 6281 B4
10 GrbT 6167 C5
Clubhouse Dr
- DBSF 6165 E4
- GrbT 6166 C7
Club House Ln
10 GrbT 6166 D6
Clubhouse Rd
500 HmpT 6928 B7
Club Pointe Dr
10 WHPL 6168 E4
Clubside Dr
10 HmpT 7028 C1
Clubway Cir
10 YNKR 6280 C3
Clubway Ln
10 GrbT 6167 C5
Cluett Rd
10 HmpT 6928 C4
10 VLYS 6928 C4
Clunie Av
10 HAOH 6280 A1
10 YNKR 6280 A3
Clyde Av
10 PTHA 7205 B1
10 WbgT 7205 A1
Clyde Pl
10 STNL 6920 C7
Clyde St
10 NHmT 6724 B5
66-00 QENS 6824 C2
Clyde St N
- NHmT 6724 B5
Clydesdale Ct
2600 HmpT 6929 E6
Clymer St
10 BKLN 6822 A5
Coach House
10 DBSF 6166 A5
Coachman Dr
10 NHLS 6724 B3
10 NHmT 6724 B3
Coakley Av
10 HRSN 6283 C3
Coakley Cir
10 ELIZ 6918 B1
Coale Av
10 STNL 7019 D3
Coastal St
10 NWRK 6818 C6
Coast Guard Dr
10 STNL 7021 A5
Coastwise St
10 NWRK 6818 B7
Cobane Ter
10 WOrT 6712 A2
N Cobane Ter
10 WOrT 6712 A2
Cobb Av
10 EMFD 6049 A6
10 WHPL 6168 B4
Cobb Ln
10 TYTN 6048 C2
Cobb Wy
300 WbgT 7114 D1
Cobble Ct
10 GLCV 6509 D1
Cobblefield Ln
10 WHPL 6168 E7
Cobblefield Rd
10 WHPL 6168 E6
Cobblers Ln
10 STNL 7020 C5
Cobblestone Cross
10 NRWD 6164 B7
Cobblestone Rd
10 GrwT 6170 C1
Cobek Ct
10 BKLN 7022 E7
Cochran Pl
10 VLYS 6928 D5
Cochrane Av
10 DBSF 6165 D3
10 DBSF 6166 A4
10 HAOH 6166 A7
Cochrane Ter
10 YNKR 6280 B2
Coco Ct
10 STNL 7117 A6
Coda Ct
900 HmpT 6828 D7
Coddington Av
10 PTHA 7114 B7
10 STNL 7117 E2
10 STNL 7118 A2
10 WbgT 7114 B7
2800 BRNX 6505 E7
3000 BRNX 6506 B7
E Coddington Av
10 WbgT 7114 D2
Codner St
400 COrT 6712 B3
Codwise Pl
51-00 QENS 6719 E7
51-18 QENS 6823 E1
Cody Av
10 OybT 6618 E1
16-00 QENS 6823 C6
Cody Pl
10 STNL 7116 A4
Coe Av
10 HlsT 6816 D7
Coenties Al
10 MHTN 120 B2
10 MHTN 6821 B6
Coenties Slip
10 MHTN 120 C3
10 MHTN 6821 B6
Coeyman St
10 NWRK 6713 E1
10 NWRK 6714 A1

New York City/5 Borough Street Index

STREET
Block City Map# Grid

Coffey St
10 BKLN 6922 A1
Cohancy St
150-00 QENS 6925 E3
Cohawney Rd
10 SCDL 6167 D5
Cohill Rd
10 VLYS 6928 B2
Coit St
10 IrvT 6816 C4
400 HlsT 6816 C4
Coit St CO-509
200 IrvT 6816 C4
400 HlsT 6816 C4
Coit St CO-664
200 IrvT 6816 D3
Coke Av
10 WbgT 7114 D2
Coke Pl
500 LNDN 6917 A7
Colangelo Pl
10 NRCH 6395 D4
Colby Av
10 RYE 6283 D3
Colby Ct
10 BKLN 7022 E7
Colby Ln
10 SCDL 6168 A6
Colby Rd
10 NHmT 6618 A3
Colden Av
10 SCDL 6167 E3
10 WHPL 6167 E3
2500 BRNX 6505 B3
Colden St
10 NWRK 6713 D7
42-00 QENS 6721 A6
100 JSYC 6820 A3
Coldspring Ct
10 STNL 7020 A6
Coldspring Rd
27-00 QENS 7027 B4
Cole Pl
400 ELIZ 6918 A6
Cole St
10 STNL 7206 C2
Cole Ter
10 NRCH 6395 D3
Coleman Av
10 SRVL 7205 A6
Coleman Sq
10 QENS 6925 E4
Coleman St
10 BKLN 7023 E4
2100 BKLN 7024 A4
Coleman Ter
10 GrbT 6048 E4
10 TFLY 6392 A3
Coleridge St
10 BKLN 7121 C1
Coles Ln
200 BRNX 6504 D4
Coles St
10 BKLN 6922 B1
10 GLCV 6509 D4
10 JSYC 6820 C1
300 JSYC 6716 C7
Coley St
10 WbgT 7114 C5
Colfax Av
10 STNL 7118 A1
E Colfax Av
300 ROSP 6917 A2
400 UnnT 6917 A2
Colfax Pl
600 HmpT 6927 E5
600 HmpT 6928 A5
Colfax St
109-00 QENS 6826 D4
300 PTHA 7205 C4
Colgan Av
10 CART 7115 C1
Colgate Av
10 YNKR 6279 D5
500 PTHA 7205 B2
1000 BRNX 6613 E1
Colgate Dr
10 NWRK 6713 C7
Colgate Pl
10 STNL 7117 E3
1700 UnnT 6816 A5
Colgate Rd
10 GTNK 6617 A6
10 NHmT 6617 A6
Colgate St
10 CLST 6278 D2
10 JSYC 6820 B3
Coligni Av
10 NRCH 6395 D3
Colin Pl
10 BKLN 7022 E5
10 BKLN 7023 A5
Colin St
10 YNKR 6280 A6
Colita Ct
10 STNL 7206 C5
Collard St
10 JSYC 6716 A7
Colleen St
10 NWRK 6712 C7
College Av
10 PTCH 6170 A4
10 RYEB 6170 A4
10 STNL 7019 B2
10 SYHW 6048 B2
400 BRNX 6613 A3
1200 BRNX 105 C7
1200 BRNX 6504 D7
College Ct
10 STNL 7019 B2
College Dr
10 JSYC 6819 C4
College Pl
5-00 QENS 6614 C7
10 BKLN 121 A4
10 BKLN 6821 C6
10 NWRK 6817 C1
10 RDFP 6501 E6
10 RKVC 6929 E4
10 STNL 7020 A6
10 YNKR 6394 B1
100 SOrT 6712 A7
College Rd
10 HRSN 6169 B2

College Rd
200 BRNX 6393 C7
300 HmpT 6828 B6
College St
10 JSYC 6819 C4
College Point Blvd
5-00 QENS 6614 D7
50-22 QENS 6720 E4
Collfield Av
500 STNL 7019 B4
Collier Av
22-00 QENS 7027 C5
1300 HmpT 6827 E6
Collins Av
10 CLST 6278 C3
10 WLPK 6724 D4
200 MTVN 6394 E2
200 NHmT 6724 D4
400 HSBH 6500 E3
500 HSBH 6501 A3
Collins Ln
300 HmpT 6828 C6
Collins Pl
- KNGP 6616 B4
34-00 QENS 6720 E3
Collis Pl
2800 BRNX 6615 B3
Collister St
10 MHTN 118 C5
10 MHTN 6821 B3
Collyer Av
10 STNL 7116 C7
Collyer Pl
10 WHPL 6168 D7
Colon Av
10 STNL 7117 A4
Colon St
10 STNL 7116 C7
300 STNL 7207 C2
Colonade Rd
500 HmpT 6828 B7
Colonel Ct
10 YNKR 6280 E4
Colonel Robert Magaw Pl
10 MHTN 104 C4
10 MHTN 6503 C5
Colonia Pl
10 WbgT 7114 A1
Colonia Rd
800 ELIZ 6917 B3
900 ROSP 6917 B3
Colonial Av
- MTVN 6395 B5
10 DBSF 6165 E5
10 DBSF 6166 A5
10 GDNC 6828 B1
10 MrnT 6282 B7
10 STNL 7019 C6
10 WLPK 6724 D4
400 UnnT 6917 A1
500 PLHM 6395 B6
500 PLMM 6395 B6
500 UnnT 6816 A7
800 NRCH 6395 C5
2000 BRNX 6505 E5
2000 BRNX 6506 A5
Colonial Ct
10 BKLN 7021 C1
10 STNL 7019 E2
10 STNL 7020 A2
10 WbgT 7114 C3
1300 MRNK 6283 B6
Colonial Dr
10 BAYN 6819 A6
10 JSYC 6819 A6
100 PLNM 6617 E4
Colonial Ln
10 MrnT 6282 C7
10 MtPT 6050 A1
Colonial Pkwy
10 NHmT 6617 C6
10 YNKR 6280 E5
Colonial Pkwy N
10 YNKR 6280 E5
Colonial Pl
10 HRSN 6283 C3
10 MTVN 6395 A6
10 NRCH 6395 D4
2600 HmpT 6929 D6
Colonial Rd
10 BLRS 6827 B2
10 EchT 6395 B2
10 FLPK 6827 B2
10 HmpT 6827 B2
10 HmpT 6929 D1
10 NHmT 6618 A2
10 QENS 6827 B2
10 SCDL 6282 B2
10 WHPL 6168 E2
100 NHmT 6617 C7
100 THSN 6617 B7
400 ELIZ 6917 A3
400 ROSP 6917 A3
1200 HBPK 6928 E7
1200 HmpT 6928 E7
6600 BKLN 6921 D7
7300 BKLN 7021 D2
Colonial Ter
10 EORG 6712 E1
Colonial Arms Rd
600 UnnT 6917 A1
Colonnade Pl
10 NWRK 6713 D5
Colony Av
100 STNL 7118 B2
Colony Ct
10 WOrT 6712 A2
Colony Dr
500 GrbT 6167 D3
Colony Dr E
10 WOrT 6712 A2
Colony Dr W
10 WOrT 6712 A2
Colony Ln
10 FLHL 6617 E5
10 NHmT 6724 E1
Colony Rd
10 EDGW 103 B5
10 EDGW 6503 A7
10 JSYC 6920 D1
Colony St
10 ARDY 6166 C5
200 HmpT 6828 D5

Colorado Av
10 GrbT 6049 C7
Colorado St
10 STNL 7019 D2
Colton St
10 STNL 7020 D4
Columbia Av
- PALP 6611 C1
10 CDHT 7028 A2
10 CLFP 6611 C1
10 EDGW 6611 E2
10 ERKY 6929 C6
10 GrbT 6167 D4
10 HAOH 6280 A1
10 JSYC 6716 B5
10 KRNY 6714 B2
10 LODI 6500 E2
10 LWRN 7028 A2
10 NWRK 6712 D6
10 STNL 7020 D7
100 IrvT 6712 D7
200 IrvT 6816 A2
400 HmpT 6929 D3
400 RDGF 6611 C1
400 RKVC 6929 D3
500 FTLE 6611 C1
500 HlsT 6816 B6
3100 NBgT 6716 D2
5000 NBgT 6610 D7
8400 NBgT 6611 A4
9100 FRVW 6611 A4
Columbia Av SR-5
400 FTLE 6611 D1
500 PALP 6611 C1
E Columbia Av
10 PALP 6502 C7
E Columbia Av CO-31
10 PALP 6502 C7
W Columbia Av
10 PALP 6502 B6
Columbia Blvd
300 WRDG 6500 C6
Columbia Hts
10 BKLN 120 E4
10 BKLN 121 A3
10 BKLN 6821 C6
Columbia Ln
10 LODI 6500 D1
Columbia Pl
10 BKLN 120 E5
10 BKLN 6821 C6
10 BXTE 6617 D1
10 MTVN 6395 A2
1100 HlsT 6816 C6
Columbia Rd
10 ARDY 6166 D3
Columbia St
10 BKLN 120 D7
10 BKLN 6821 B7
10 CARL 6500 D7
10 MHTN 119 D5
10 MHTN 6821 E3
10 NWRK 6817 E1
10 WOrT 6712 C1
10 WRDG 6500 D7
300 BKLN 6922 B2
300 COrT 6712 C3
Columbia Ter
10 EDGW 6611 E2
10 WhkT 111 A3
10 WhkT 6717 A2
1700 UnnT 6816 A5
Columbine Ln
10 HmpT 6928 C4
Columbus Av
- WHPL 6168 C1
10 CART 7017 D7
10 CLST 6278 A3
10 EGLD 6502 D1
10 GrwT 6170 E3
10 HRSN 6168 C1
10 HSBH 6500 D5
10 LFRY 6501 C7
10 MHTN 112 C5
10 MHTN 6717 E2
10 MtPT 6050 A1
10 NRCH 6395 E5
10 PTCH 6170 B4
10 STNL 7020 C5
10 TCKA 6281 A5
100 DMRT 6278 A3
100 HRSN 6050 D7
100 PALP 6502 B6
200 ROSL 6917 A6
200 WbgT 7114 C5
300 EchT 6281 A4
500 MHTN 108 E7
500 MHTN 109 B4
500 MHTN 6611 E7
500 MHTN 6612 A7
N Columbus Av
10 MTVN 6395 A2
600 BRXV 6395 A1
600 EchT 6395 A1
N Columbus Av SR-22
10 MTVN 6395 A2
600 BRXV 6395 A1
600 EchT 6395 A1
S Columbus Av
10 MTVN 6395 A5
10 WbgT 7205 A3
S Columbus Av SR-22
10 MTVN 6395 A5
Columbus Cir
10 BAYN 6919 E5
10 EchT 6281 C6
10 MHTN 112 C6
10 MHTN 6717 D3
600 PTHA 7205 B1
Columbus Dr
10 BAYN 6919 E5
10 LNBK 6929 B4
10 TFLY 6392 A2
700 PTHA 7205 B1
700 TnkT 6502 C1
Columbus Pl
- FRVW 6611 C4
10 BKLN 6924 A2
10 CLFP 108 A1
10 CLFP 6611 C4
10 STNL 7019 C3
10 YNKR 6393 D1
Columbus Rd
10 DMRT 6278 A4
100 CLST 6278 A4
Columbus St
10 BlmT 6713 C2

Columbus Wy
- PTHA 7205 B1
Colvin Dr
10 GDNC 6828 A1
Colvin Rd
10 SCDL 6167 D4
Comber St
10 VLYS 6928 E2
Combes Dr
10 NHmT 6617 C6
Combs Av
10 STNL 7117 D3
100 HBPK 7028 D1
100 HmpT 7028 D1
Comely St
10 STNL 7207 C1
Comet Wy
10 HKSK 6501 B1
Comfort Ct
10 STNL 7116 B7
Comfort Rd
300 MHTN 120 A6
300 MHTN 6821 A7
Comley Hts
10 GrwT 6170 C2
Comly Av
10 GrwT 6170 B2
10 RYEB 6170 B2
Comly Rdg
10 GrwT 6170 B2
Comly Ter
- GrwT 6170 C2
Commerce Av
1000 BRNX 6614 D1
1300 BRNX 6505 D7
Commerce Blvd
200 CARL 6610 B2
Commerce Ct
10 NWRK 6713 E7
Commerce Dr
10 NRCH 6395 C5
10 NRCH 6396 C4
Commerce Pl
200 ELIZ 6917 B4
Commerce Rd
10 CARL 6610 A1
300 LNDN 7017 B1
Commerce St
- MtPT 6050 A3
10 BAYN 6920 B5
10 BKLN 6922 A1
10 GRFD 6500 A3
10 MHTN 118 C2
10 MHTN 6821 B1
10 MtPT 6049 D1
10 NWRK 6713 E7
10 PTHA 7205 E3
10 STNL 7018 E4
10 WHPL 6168 C5
100 NWRK 6817 C3
Commercial Av
10 CARL 6610 A1
10 FRVW 6611 B3
10 MNCH 6610 A1
10 WbgT 7114 D2
100 PALP 6502 B5
300 CLFP 6611 C3
W Commercial Av
10 CARL 6610 A1
10 MNCH 6610 A1
100 MNCH 6609 E1
200 MNCH 6500 E7
Commercial St
10 BKLN 117 C7
10 BKLN 6718 B7
10 NWRK 6818 A1
Commissary Rd
- QENS 6926 B4
Commodore Av
10 HRSN 6169 B6
Commodore Ct
10 OLDT 6164 A4
Commodore Dr
10 STNL 7207 A3
Commodore Ter
10 EDGW 108 C1
10 EDGW 6611 D4
Commonwealth Av
10 NWRK 6712 C7
100 MTVN 6395 A3
400 BRNX 6614 B3
1400 BRNX 6505 A7
Commonwealth Blvd
10 BLRS 6827 B2
10 FLPK 6827 B2
10 QENS 6827 B1
72-00 QENS 6723 A7
Commonwealth Dr
800 TnkT 6502 C1
Commonwealth St
10 HmpT 6828 B5
Communipaw Av
10 JSYC 6820 A4
400 JSYC 6819 D2
Communipaw Av CO-612
400 JSYC 6819 D2
Community Dr
10 NHmT 6617 C7
10 NHmT 6723 D3
100 LKSU 6723 D2
400 NHLS 6723 D2
Community Dr E
- NHmT 6617 D7
- NHmT 6723 D1
Community Ln
- ELIZ 6918 C5
200 STNL 7116 D7
Commuter Bus Rd
- ERTH 6609 D4
Como Av
196-00 QENS 6826 B2
Compass Rd
- QENS 6926 D4
Compass St
- NWRK 6818 B5
Compton Av
100 BRNX 6614 C4
300 PTHA 7205 C2
Compton Pl
1500 HlsT 6816 D5
1500 NWRK 6816 D5
Compton St
10 HmpT 6929 C7

Compton Ter
1400 HlsT 6816 D5
Comstock Av
10 STNL 7019 A3
Comstock Pl
- SOrT 6712 A6
Conant Av
- UnnT 6917 B1
400 ELIZ 6917 B2
Conant St
100 HlsT 6816 C7
Conch Pl
- QENS 7027 A6
Concord Av
10 HmpT 7029 E1
10 LRMT 6396 C1
10 WHPL 6167 E2
50-00 NHmT 6723 A2
50-00 QENS 6723 A2
100 GrbT 6167 E2
200 HmpT 6828 D4
300 BRNX 6613 B4
300 GDNC 6828 D4
500 MRNK 6282 D6
500 WLPK 6724 D5
600 NHmT 6724 D5
Concord Ct
10 HmpT 6929 B2
Concord Dr
10 OrgT 6164 D3
Concord Ln
10 STNL 7020 A6
Concord Pl
10 RYEB 6170 A3
10 STNL 7020 C4
1400 ELIZ 6816 E7
1400 HlsT 6816 E7
Concord Rd
10 ARDY 6166 D3
10 NHmT 6618 A2
10 WbgT 7114 A3
100 YNKR 6280 D3
Concord St
10 BKLN 121 B4
10 EGLD 6392 A5
10 FLPK 6827 D2
10 GrwT 6170 C2
10 JSYC 6820 B1
10 LNBK 6928 B3
10 LNBK 6929 A3
10 MNCH 6500 D7
10 NWRK 6817 B3
10 WRDG 6500 D7
52-00 QENS 6723 A3
100 BKLN 6821 D6
100 EWLS 6724 E4
1000 HmpT 6828 A4
Concordia Pl
10 BRXV 6281 A7
Concourse Vil E
700 BRNX 6613 A2
Concourse Vil W
600 BRNX 107 E5
600 BRNX 6612 E3
600 BRNX 6613 A2
Condict St
10 JSYC 6819 D2
Condit St
10 HRSN 6283 B2
Condit Ter
10 WOrT 6712 B1
N Conduit Av
75-01 BKLN 6925 A1
93-00 QENS 6925 E3
113-01 QENS 6926 B3
152-01 QENS 6927 A3
244-00 QENS 6928 A3
N Conduit Av SR-27
100-00 QENS 6925 E3
113-01 QENS 6926 A3
152-01 QENS 6927 A3
S Conduit Av
75-00 BKLN 6925 B2
79-00 QENS 6925 C2
102-01 QENS 6926 E3
155-00 QENS 6927 B3
S Conduit Av SR-27
- QENS 6925 D3
102-01 QENS 6926 E3
155-00 QENS 6927 B3
Coney Island Av
10 BKLN 6922 E5
300 BKLN 6923 A6
900 BKLN 7023 A1
3000 BKLN 7121 B2
Coney Island Av SR-27
300 BKLN 6923 A6
Confederation Pl
10 STNL 7019 A1
Conference Ct
10 STNL 7206 A3
Conger Av
300 NVLE 6164 C5
Conger St
10 STNL 7021 A5
Congress Dr
10 MNCH 6610 C1
Congress St
10 BKLN 120 E6
10 BKLN 6821 B7
10 HRSN 6283 B3
10 JSYC 6716 C5
10 NRCH 6395 E2
10 NRCH 6396 A2
10 NWRK 6817 E2
10 NWRK 6818 A1
10 STNL 7020 D1
100 BKLN 121 A7
Congressman Rosenthal Plz
133-00 QENS 6720 E4
136-39 QENS 6721 A4
Conklin Av
10 BKLN 6924 B6
10 HmpT 7028 C1
10 OrgT 6164 C3
200 HlsT 6816 D5
Conklin Ln
10 RCKL 6164 E5
Conklin Pl
500 LNDN 6917 A7
Conlon Ln
10 TFLY 6392 B1
Connecticut Av
10 LBCH 7028 D7

Connecticut Av
4000 HmpT 7029 E4
Connecticut St
10 STNL 7206 A4
S Connection Rd
- ERTH 6609 E4
- ERTH 6610 A4
N Connector Rd
- ERTH 6609 E4
- ERTH 6610 A4
Connell Pl
3100 BRNX 6506 A7
Connell St
10 MrnT 6282 A5
10 NRCH 6282 A5
10 SCDL 6282 A5
Conner St
2100 BRNX 6505 E1
3200 BRNX 6506 A1
Connett Pl
100 SOrT 6712 A6
Connie Ln
700 HmpT 6827 D7
Connor Av
10 STNL 7117 C2
Connor Ct
10 IRVN 6166 C2
Connor Dr
10 EGLC 6392 C6
Connors St
200 SAMB 7205 B7
Conor Ct
10 OrgT 6164 C3
Conover St
10 BKLN 6922 A1
200 SAMB 7205 A7
Conover Ter
400 COrT 6712 B3
Conrad Av
10 STNL 7019 B7
Conrad Pl
10 GLCV 6509 E5
10 SCLF 6509 E5
Conrad Rd
10 NWRK 6817 E5
Conselyea St
10 BKLN 6822 C3
Constable Dr N
1000 MRNK 6397 A2
Constable Dr S
1000 MRNK 6397 A2
Constance Av
10 DBSF 6165 D5
10 HAOH 6165 E6
Constant Av
10 STNL 7019 D3
10 YNKR 6279 D5
Constitution Ct
10 HBKN 6716 E5
Constitution Dr
- LODI 6500 C2
10 OrgT 6164 A1
Constitution Ln
- MLVN 6929 C1
Consulate Dr
10 TCKA 6281 A5
Contant Av
10 LODI 6500 C1
Contempra Cir
- OrgT 6164 C3
Continental Av
10 QENS 6824 C4
2000 BRNX 6505 E5
Continental Dr
10 NHmT 6724 A4
10 OLDT 6164 A3
200 NHmT 6723 E4
Continental Pl
10 STNL 7019 A1
100 STNL 7018 E1
Continental Rd
10 SCDL 6282 B2
Continental St
10 SYHW 6048 A1
Contumacious Tr
- HRSN 6714 B5
- KRNY 6714 B5
Convent Av
10 MHTN 106 D7
10 MHTN 6612 C2
10 STNL 7115 E7
10 YNKR 6279 D6
200 MHTN 107 A4
Convent Ln
10 HRSN 6169 C4
Convent Pl
10 YNKR 6279 D6
Convent Garden Av
1000 HlsT 6816 C7
Convery Blvd
10 PTHA 7114 C7
10 WbgT 7114 C6
200 PTHA 7205 B3
Convery Blvd SR-35
10 PTHA 7114 C7
10 WbgT 7114 C6
200 PTHA 7205 B3
Conway Rd
10 NHmT 6724 B6
500 HmpT 6827 B6
Conway St
10 BKLN 6924 C1
Conway Ter
10 YNKR 6280 B4
Conyingham Av
10 STNL 6920 B7
Cook Av
10 YNKR 6280 B7
10 YNKR 6394 A1
73-00 QENS 6823 E4
Cook St
10 JSYC 6820 B1
100 BKLN 6822 D5
Cooke Av
10 CART 7115 D1
Cooke Ct
- BKLN 6924 C1
Cooke St
10 STNL 7019 A3
Cooke St E
10 HmpT 7029 B1
Cooke St W
10 HmpT 7029 B1

Cooley Pl
10 MTVN 6395 A4
Coolidge Av
10 CART 7115 C1
10 NHmT 6618 E7
10 RYE 6283 C4
10 WHPL 6168 A4
10 YNKR 6279 E7
100 EGLD 6502 D1
100 LBCH 7029 E7
100 MNLA 6724 D6
135-00 QENS 6825 A3
200 FTLE 103 A1
200 FTLE 6503 A4
200 HSBH 6501 A2
400 HmpT 6929 C2
700 WbgT 7114 C2
Coolidge Rd
10 MplT 6816 A1
900 ELIZ 6917 A2
1100 UnnT 6917 A2
Coolidge St
10 IrvT 6816 A3
10 LRMT 6396 B2
10 MLVN 6929 A2
10 MrnT 6396 B2
10 TCKA 6281 C7
10 VLYS 6929 A2
100 LNDN 7017 A2
300 HmpT 6828 D5
Coombs St
140-00 QENS 6927 C2
Coonley Ct
10 STNL 6919 A7
Co Op City Blvd
10 BRNX 6506 A3
900 BRNX 6505 E2
Cooper Av
10 STNL 7020 C6
15-00 BKLN 6823 C6
15-00 QENS 6823 C6
74-00 QENS 6824 A4
300 MRNK 6282 E7
Cooper Dr
10 NRCH 6396 B3
10 SDRK 6616 D6
Cooper Ln
10 MrnT 6282 C7
Cooper Pl
- BRNX 6506 A2
10 HRSN 6283 C1
10 STNL 7207 B2
10 UNCT 111 A3
10 UNCT 6717 A2
10 WhkT 111 A3
10 WhkT 6717 A2
Cooper Rd
10 GrbT 6049 E7
10 SCDL 6167 E6
Cooper Sq
10 MHTN 119 A3
10 MHTN 6821 C2
Cooper St
10 BAYN 6919 E4
10 BKLN 6823 B7
10 BKLN 6924 B1
10 MHTN 101 E6
10 MHTN 102 A6
10 MHTN 6503 E3
10 MHTN 6504 A3
10 YNKR 6394 B3
300 QENS 6823 B7
Cooper Ter
10 STNL 7019 A6
Cooper Gate
- SDRK 6616 D6
Coover St
100 LEON 6502 D4
Copcutt Ln
10 YNKR 6393 D1
Cope Cir
10 RYE 6170 A7
Copiague St
10 VLYS 6928 B1
Copley Av
10 TnkT 6502 A2
Copley Blvd
- HRPK 6278 A1
Copley Rd
10 MNPK 6618 A6
10 MrnT 6396 D1
10 NHmT 6618 A6
Copley St
10 STNL 7019 A7
Coppel Dr
10 TFLY 6392 B4
Copper Beach Ln
10 NRCH 6282 A4
10 SCDL 6282 A4
Copperbeach Ln
10 CDHT 7028 B2
10 LWRN 7028 B2
Copper Beech Cir
10 WHPL 6168 E5
Copperflagg Ln
10 STNL 7020 A7
Copperleaf Ter
10 STNL 7020 A7
Corabelle Av
10 LODI 6500 C2
S Corabelle Av
10 LODI 6500 C2
Coral Ct
10 MLVN 6929 C1
10 STNL 7117 C6
10 WbgT 7114 A1
Coral Reef Wy
- QENS 7026 D7
Coralyn Av
10 SCDL 6168 B6
10 WHPL 6168 C6
Coralyn Rd
10 SCDL 6168 B6
10 WHPL 6168 B6
Corbalis Pl
10 YNKR 6279 E4
Corbett Ln
10 OrgT 6165 B4
Corbett Rd
215-00 QENS 6722 B3
Corbin Av
10 JSYC 6819 E1
10 NHmT 6724 C7
10 STNL 7117 B3
100 JSYC 6715 D6

Corbin Pl
10 BKLN 7121 B1
Corbin St
- ELIZ 6918 E1
10 NWRK 6818 A6
100 ELIZ 6817 E7
100 ELIZ 6818 A7
Corchaug Av
10 MHVN 6508 C7
Corcoran St
10 JSYC 6819 D5
Cordelia Av
10 STNL 7206 E2
Cordier St
10 IrvT 6816 D4
Corell Rd
10 SCDL 6168 B7
Corey St
10 WbgT 7205 A1
Corlear Av
3000 BRNX 102 D3
3000 BRNX 6504 B1
Corley St
10 YNKR 6279 D5
Corlies Av
100 PLHM 6395 B5
300 PLMM 6395 B5
Cornaga Av
7-69 QENS 7027 D5
Cornaga Ct
7-00 QENS 7027 E5
Cornelia Av
10 GTNK 6616 D4
10 NHmT 6724 C7
200 STNL 7207 B2
Cornelia St
10 BKLN 6823 A7
10 MHTN 118 D2
10 MHTN 6821 A1
10 NWRK 6714 C7
10 STNL 7020 C6
16-00 QENS 6823 B5
100 ERTH 6609 B1
Cornelison Av
10 JSYC 6819 E4
10 JSYC 6820 A3
Cornell Av
10 STNL 7019 D1
10 YNKR 6393 D3
400 HmpT 6929 C3
400 RKVC 6929 D3
700 BRNX 6614 B5
Cornell Dr
10 GrbT 6167 D3
10 NHmT 6723 B3
Cornell Ln
43-00 QENS 6722 E3
Cornell Pl
10 ERKY 6929 B6
10 NHmT 6723 A3
10 NRCH 6395 E1
10 RYE 6284 A5
10 STNL 7020 C3
300 HlsT 6816 B5
1300 UnnT 6816 B6
1400 BRNX 6505 E7
Cornell Rd
600 HmpT 6828 B6
Cornell St
10 IrvT 6816 B3
10 STNL 7019 C1
10 WbgT 7114 D1
10 WLPK 6724 E4
400 PTHA 7205 C2
Cornerstone Ln
10 NWRK 6713 C7
Cornish Av
80-00 QENS 6719 E7
Cornish St
10 STNL 7117 C6
Cornwall Ln
10 MHVN 6508 A7
10 SNPT 6508 A7
Cornwell Av
10 MLVN 6929 B1
10 VLYS 6928 E3
10 VLYS 6929 A3
10 WLPK 6724 D4
200 HmpT 6828 E7
700 HmpT 6929 C1
Cornwell St
10 RKVC 6929 E2
Cornwells Beach Rd
10 SNPT 6508 A6
Corona Av
10 PLHM 6395 C5
10 STNL 7117 C3
47-00 QENS 6720 B6
84-00 QENS 6719 E7
300 PLMM 6395 C5
N Corona Av
10 VLYS 6928 D3
400 HmpT 6928 E1
700 HmpT 6827 E7
S Corona Av
10 VLYS 6928 D4
Coronado St
10 ATLB 7027 E7
Coronet Rd
10 YNKR 6280 C5
Corporal Kennedy St
18-00 QENS 6721 E1
30-00 QENS 6722 A3
Corporal Stone St
35-00 QENS 6722 A3
Corporate Blvd
- YNKR 6279 E3
Corporate Blvd S
200 YNKR 6279 E3
Corporate Ctr
10 HRSN 6283 C3
10 RYE 6283 C3
Corporate Dr
100 YNKR 6279 E3
Corporate Park Dr
- WHPL 6169 A3
100 HRSN 6169 A3
Correll Av
10 STNL 7116 B5
500 STNL 7115 E6
Corrigan Ln
10 GrwT 6051 E2
Corsa Av
3200 BRNX 6505 C2

Corso Ct
10 BKLN 7022 E6
Corson Av
10 STNL 6920 D7
Cortelyou Av
10 STNL 7116 E5
400 STNL 7117 A5
Cortelyou Pl
10 STNL 6920 B7
Cortelyou Rd
10 BKLN 6922 E7
700 BKLN 6923 A7
E Cortland Av
10 HmpT 7029 E1
W Cortland Av
10 HmpT 7029 E1
Cortland Pl
10 CLFP 6611 D3
10 NWRK 6818 C1
Cortland St
10 NWRK 6818 C1
Cortlandt Al
10 MHTN 118 D6
10 MHTN 6821 A2
Cortlandt Av
10 NRCH 6395 B3
10 NRCH 6396 A2
300 MRNK 6282 E7
Cortlandt Pl
10 CRSK 6392 A2
10 TFLY 6392 A2
Cortlandt St
10 BlvT 6714 B1
10 MHTN 118 B7
10 MHTN 120 D1
10 MHTN 6821 A4
10 MTVN 6394 C5
10 STNL 7019 C1
10 SYHW 6048 B2
10 TYTN 6048 B2
500 PTHA 7205 D2
Cortlandville Ln
10 YNKR 6393 E5
Corwin Av
10 NHmT 6724 A6
Corwood Rd
10 EchT 6395 B1
Cosma Ln
- YNKR 6393 E4
Cossio Dr
10 NWRK 6713 C7
Costa Trailer Ct
- LODI 6500 D2
Coster St
200 BRNX 6613 D4
Cotswold Wy
10 GrbT 6167 B7
10 GrbT 6281 B1
10 YNKR 6281 B1
Cottage Av
10 HRSN 6051 C6
10 MTVN 6394 E4
10 STNL 7117 B6
4600 NBgT 6716 D1
6400 NBgT 6610 E6
7000 NBgT 6611 A6
Cottage Cir
10 MrnT 6396 B2
Cottage Ln
100 CLFP 6611 C3
2600 NBgT 6716 C2
Cottage Pl
10 CRSK 6278 A7
10 EORG 6712 E1
10 ERTH 6500 B6
10 IrvT 6816 C1
10 LEON 6502 D3
10 NRCH 6395 C5
10 STNL 6919 D7
10 TCKA 6280 C3
10 TYTN 6048 B2
10 WHPL 6168 C2
10 YNKR 6279 B6
100 FRVW 6611 B3
1000 BRNX 6613 C1
4500 UNCT 6716 E1
Cottage Row
10 STNL 6920 B6
Cottage St
10 BAYN 6919 D5
10 JSYC 6820 A1
10 NWRK 6817 D1
10 PTCH 6170 B7
10 RYE 6170 B7
10 SOrT 6712 A6
N Cottage St
100 VLYS 6928 E2
S Cottage St
10 VLYS 6928 E4
N Cottenet St
10 IRVN 6048 A7
S Cottenet St
10 IRVN 6166 A1
Cotter Av
10 STNL 7117 C3
Cottontail Ct
10 STNL 7116 D7
Cottontail Ln
10 TYTN 6048 C6
Cottonwood Ct
10 STNL 7117 B4
Cottonwood Ln
10 WHPL 6169 A4
Cottonwood Rd
10 MHVN 6508 C6
Cottonwood St
10 JSYC 6819 A5
Couchon Dr
10 LFRY 6501 B5
Coudert Pl
100 SOrT 6712 A7
Coughlan Av
10 STNL 7020 A2
Countisbury Av
10 HmpT 6928 B1
Country Dr E
10 STNL 7018 E7
Country Dr N
10 STNL 7018 E7
Country Dr S
10 STNL 7018 D7
Country Dr W
10 STNL 7018 E7
Country Ln
10 MrnT 6282 D5

New York City/5 Borough Street Index

STREET / Block City Map# Grid

Country Ln
10 STNL 7116 A5
Country Pl
10 NHmT 6616 D6
Country Rd
10 MrnT 6282 D5
Country Club Dr
- PLMM 6395 C6
10 FLHL 6618 B4
10 GrbT 6048 E7
10 GrbT 6166 E1
10 HRSN 6051 B6
10 MrnT 6282 B5
10 NHLS 6617 E7
10 NHmT 6617 E7
10 NHmT 6618 A7
700 TnkT 6502 B1
Country Club Ln
10 ELIZ 6816 E7
10 PLMM 6395 C7
Country Club Rd
10 EchT 6281 C4
3100 BRNX 6506 A7
Country Club Wy
10 DMRT 6278 C6
Country House Rd
10 MtPT 6048 D1
10 SYHW 6048 D1
10 TYTN 6048 D1
Country Pointe Cir
82-01 QENS 6722 D6
82-01 QENS 6826 D1
Country Ridge Cir
10 RYEB 6169 E2
Country Ridge Dr
10 RYEB 6170 A1
100 RYEB 6169 E2
Country Ridge Dr N
10 RYEB 6169 E1
10 RYEB 6170 A1
Country Ridge Rd
10 NRCH 6281 E2
Country Ridge Close
10 RYEB 6169 E2
Country Village Ct
10 BAYN 6919 D3
10 NHmT 6724 A5
Country Village Ln
10 NHmT 6724 A4
Country Village Rd
10 JSYC 6819 A6
Countrywood Ln
10 STNL 7117 B3
County Av
10 SECS 6715 E3
100 SECS 6716 A2
700 SECS 6610 C7
County Rd
- JSYC 6716 A6
10 CLST 6278 B4
10 CRSK 6278 B7
10 CRSK 6392 B2
10 DMRT 6278 B7
10 JSYC 6715 E4
10 SECS 6715 E4
10 TFLY 6392 A2
County Rd CO-35
10 CLST 6278 B4
10 DMRT 6278 B4
County Rd CO-501
10 CRSK 6278 B7
10 CRSK 6392 B2
10 DMRT 6278 B7
10 TFLY 6392 B1
County Airport Access Rd
- RYEB 6051 C3
County Center Rd
10 GrbT 6049 E7
10 GrbT 6167 E1
10 WHPL 6167 E1
300 GrbT 6050 C6
County Courthouse Rd
10 NHmT 6724 C7
County House Rd
10 MtPT 6048 D1
10 SYHW 6048 C1
10 TYTN 6048 C1
County Rd Ext
1000 SECS 6715 D3
Courrier Pl
10 ERTH 6500 A7
10 RTFD 6500 A7
Coursen Ct
10 STNL 7020 D2
Coursen Pl
10 STNL 7020 D3
Courseview Rd
10 BRXV 6281 B7
10 BRXV 6395 B1
Court Av
- WbgT 7205 B2
400 CDHT 7028 A2
600 PTHA 7205 B1
Court Pl
10 BAYN 6919 E4
200 CDHT 7028 A2
1400 HmpT 6928 E6
Court Rd
800 HmpT 6828 B3
Court Sq
45-00 QENS 6718 D6
Court St
10 BKLN 121 A6
10 BKLN 6821 C7
10 ELIZ 6918 C5
10 HBKN 6716 D7
10 HKSK 6501 B4
10 HmpT 6827 E4
10 NWRK 6817 C1
10 STNL 7020 D1
10 VLYS 6928 C2
10 WHPL 6168 B2
200 BKLN 6922 C2
800 WbgT 7114 D2
2800 HmpT 6929 E7
Court St E
10 HmpT 6929 B7
Court St W
10 HmpT 6929 B6
Courter Av
10 YNKR 6393 D4
Court House Pl
10 JSYC 6820 B1
Courthouse Rd
10 HmpT 6828 B3
Courtlandt Av
400 BRNX 6613 A3
Courtney Av
171-00 QENS 6721 D5
Courtney Lp
- STNL 7021 A4
Courtney Pl
10 YNKR 6394 B5
Coutant Dr
10 NRCH 6282 A4
Cove Ct
- SECS 6609 E7
120-00 QENS 6614 C6
Cove Dr
10 PLNH 6617 C5
Cove Ln
10 BKLN 7024 B2
10 KNGP 6616 C5
10 PTWN 6508 C6
Cove Ln N
10 NBgT 108 A4
10 NBgT 6611 C6
Cove Rd
700 MRNK 6396 E1
Cove I
10 MRNK 6396 E1
Covent Pl
10 GrbT 6166 E3
Coventry Av
10 NHmT 6724 D3
Coventry Ct
- WbgT 7114 A4
10 HRSN 6169 B1
10 MrnT 6282 B5
Coventry Gdns
10 LNBK 6928 E5
10 VLYS 6928 E5
Coventry Ln
10 NRCH 6396 A5
Coventry Lp
10 STNL 7116 B6
Coventry Rd
10 BKLN 6924 A6
10 STNL 7020 A7
Coventry Rd N
200 HmpT 6929 D1
Coventry Rd S
200 HmpT 6929 D1
Coverly Av
10 STNL 7020 B5
Coverly Av N
10 STNL 7020 A5
Coverly St
10 STNL 7117 D2
Covert Av
10 FLPK 6827 E4
10 HmpT 6827 E4
10 NHPK 6827 E1
10 STMN 6827 E4
S Covert Av
10 HmpT 6827 E5
Covert Ln
- ISPK 7029 D4
Covert Pl
10 FLPK 6827 C4
10 STMN 6827 C4
Covert St
- DMRT 6278 B5
10 BKLN 6823 B7
10 JSYC 6715 E7
10 NHmT 6617 D1
15-00 QENS 6823 C6
Covington Cir
10 STNL 7116 A6
Covington Rd
10 YNKR 6280 C5
Cow Ln
10 KNGP 6617 A3
Cowdrey St
10 YNKR 6280 B7
Cowen Pl
10 STNL 6918 E7
Cowles Av
10 RYE 6283 E3
10 RYE 6284 A3
10 YNKR 6394 A2
Cowles Ct
80-00 QENS 6824 A3
Cow Neck Rd
10 NHmT 6508 C6
10 PTWN 6508 C6
10 SNPT 6508 C5
Cow Neck Rd S
10 MHVN 6508 C6
10 NHmT 6508 C6
10 PTWN 6508 C6
100 SNPT 6508 C6
Cowpens Dr
100 OrgT 6164 A2
Cox Av
10 YNKR 6394 A5
Cox Pl
10 BKLN 6824 A7
Cox St
500 HmpT 6828 B7
Coyle Pl
10 YNKR 6393 D4
Coyle St
2400 BKLN 7023 D6
Cozine Av
10 BKLN 6924 E5
400 BKLN 6925 A4
Crab Av
10 LNBK 6929 A4
Crabapple Ct
10 JSYC 6819 A4
Crabapple Rd
10 FLHL 6618 A4
Crabbs Ln
10 STNL 7018 B7
Crabtree Av
10 STNL 7115 D6
Crabtree Ln
10 FLHL 6618 C5
10 STNL 7115 D6
Craft Av
253-00 QENS 6927 E5
256-00 QENS 6928 A5
600 HmpT 6828 B7
Craft Ct
700 HmpT 6828 B7
Craft St
10 HmpT 7027 C3
Crafton Av
10 STNL 7019 C4
Crafton Ct
10 MLVN 6929 B2
Cragwood Rd
10 WbgT 7017 A6
Craig Av
600 STNL 7206 A5
Craig Rd N
300 MHTN 120 A5
300 MHTN 6820 E7
300 MHTN 6821 A7
800 MHTN 6921 E1
Craig Rd S
300 MHTN 120 A7
300 MHTN 6821 A7
400 MHTN 6820 E7
800 MHTN 6921 E1
Crampton Av
10 GTNK 6616 E5
10 WbgT 7114 D4
Crampton Ln
10 GTNK 6616 C5
Crampton Rd
10 BRXV 6395 A1
Cranberry Ct
10 STNL 7206 E2
Cranberry St
10 BKLN 121 A3
10 BKLN 6821 C5
Cranbrook Rd
1000 UnnT 6816 A6
Cranbury Rd
1100 UnnT 6917 A1
Crandall Av
178-00 QENS 6927 C2
Crane Av
10 RTFD 6609 A3
10 SYHW 6048 B1
10 WHPL 6050 B7
Crane Rd
10 SCDL 6167 C7
Crane St
10 ELIZ 6917 D3
10 NWRK 6713 D5
46-00 QENS 6718 C6
300 COrT 6712 C3
Craneway St
10 NWRK 6818 C6
Cranford Av
10 LNDN 6917 B6
10 STNL 7117 D2
700 BRNX 6394 D5
800 HmpT 6928 A5
900 MTVN 6394 D5
1000 RVSL 6917 B6
Cranford Ct
10 STNL 7117 D2
Cranford St
10 STNL 7117 C5
104-00 QENS 6824 D3
Crann St
100 HlsT 6816 C6
Crans St
600 HmpT 6827 B7
Cranston Pl
10 YNKR 6280 D7
Cranston St
133-00 QENS 6926 E2
Crary Av
100 MTVN 6394 E4
Craske St
10 WbgT 7114 D3
Craven Ln
10 WHPL 6168 B5
Craven St
500 BRNX 6613 D4
Crawford Av
10 BKLN 7023 A6
2000 BRNX 6505 D1
Crawford Ct
10 QENS 7027 D5
Crawford Dr
10 EchT 6281 A6
10 TCKA 6281 A6
Crawford Ln
10 SCDL 6282 B1
Crawford Pl
200 ELIZ 6917 C3
Crawford Rd
10 HRSN 6283 C2
900 HmpT 7028 C1
900 WDBG 7028 C1
Crawford St
- RYEB 6169 E4
- RYEB 6170 A4
10 BRXV 6281 B7
10 EchT 6281 B7
10 EORG 6712 D5
10 JSYC 6820 A2
10 NWRK 6817 C1
10 YNKR 6393 E3
10 YNKR 6394 A3
100 NWRK 6712 D5
Crawford Ter
10 NRCH 6395 E1
Creamer St
100 BKLN 6922 B2
Creedmoor Hosp Service Dr S
- QENS 6723 A6
Creek Rd
10 KNGP 6616 D2
300 MRNK 6283 A6
W Creek Farms Rd
10 SNPT 6508 A6
Creekside Av
500 QENS 7122 D3
Crencoun St
200 PTHA 7205 E3
Crescent Av
10 CLFP 6611 D2
10 HlsT 6816 D4
10 JSYC 6819 E3
10 LEON 6502 C4
10 NRCH 6395 D5
10 NWRK 6816 D4
10 RYE 6283 E4
10 STNL 6920 D6
600 BRNX 6504 D5
Crescent Bch
10 STNL 7117 B7
Crescent Ct
- FTLE 6611 E1
10 NWRK 6712 B7
Crescent Dr
- QENS 6718 C6
10 NHmT 6724 C2
1100 TYTN 6048 C4
Crescent Dr S
10 EMFD 6049 C6
Crescent Ln
10 DBSF 6166 C4
10 IrvT 6816 C2
10 NHmT 6724 C2
200 CLFP 6611 D2
Crescent Pkwy
- GDNC 6828 B1
Crescent Pl
- EORG 6713 B3
10 RYEB 6170 A6
10 TCKA 6281 A5
10 YNKR 6394 C3
Crescent Rd
- PRMT 6165 A1
10 EORG 6712 E2
10 MrnT 6282 C6
10 NHmT 6618 A1
10 THSN 6617 B7
10 WLTN 6500 B4
Crescent St
10 BKLN 6824 A7
10 HmpT 6928 D7
10 HmpT 7027 D2
10 LFRY 6501 D7
10 WHPL 6168 D3
20-00 QENS 6719 A1
27-00 QENS 114 E6
28-00 QENS 6718 E3
100 WbgT 7114 C2
400 BKLN 6925 A3
Crescent Wy
10 FTLE 6611 E1
Crescent Beach Rd
10 GLCV 6509 E1
Creskill Av
10 WbgT 7114 E1
Cresskill Av
10 CRSK 6278 A7
Cresskill Pl
95-00 QENS 6825 B6
Crest Av
10 EchT 6281 B5
10 HmpT 6827 E4
10 MrnT 6282 C6
10 MTVN 6395 A4
10 TCKA 6281 B5
Crest Dr
10 GrbT 6166 E1
10 TYTN 6048 C3
400 NVLE 6164 B4
Crest Dr E
- CRSK 6392 B1
Crest Dr N
10 CRSK 6392 B1
Crest Dr S
10 CRSK 6392 B1
Crest Ln
10 SCDL 6282 A2
3000 FTLE 6502 E4
3000 FTLE 6503 A4
Crest Lp
10 STNL 7117 A7
Crest Pl
10 EMFD 6049 B6
10 YNKR 6393 D2
Crest Rd
10 NHmT 6724 A4
20-00 QENS 7027 C6
Cresthaven Ln
3-00 QENS 6615 B6
Cresthill Rd
10 YNKR 6280 E4
Crest Hollow Ln
10 NHmT 6724 C2
Crestmont Av
10 YNKR 6394 C3
Creston Av
10 TFLY 6392 B3
1900 BRNX 105 D4
1900 BRNX 6504 C5
Creston Pl
10 STNL 7020 D1
Creston St
10 STNL 7207 A2
Crestvale Ter
10 YNKR 6280 B3
Crestview Av
800 HmpT 6928 A5
Crestview Dr
10 WHPL 6050 C7
Crestview Pl
10 ARDY 6166 E4
10 NRCH 6396 A2
200 BGTA 6501 E2
200 TnkT 6501 E2
Crestview Rd
10 WbgT 7205 A1
Crestwater Ct
10 STNL 7020 E7
Crestwood Av
10 YNKR 6281 A4
Crestwood Ln
10 HmpT 6928 B5
10 NRCH 6282 A7
Crestwood Pl
10 GTNK 6616 C4
700 HmpT 6828 B7
Crestwood Rd
10 NHmT 6618 A3
1000 HmpT 6928 C7
Crestwood Station Plz
10 TCKA 6281 C4
Cricket Ln
10 DBSF 6166 B3
10 KNGP 6616 C1
10 WbgT 7114 C6
Cricket Club Dr
10 NHLS 6724 B3
Cricklewood S
10 YNKR 6394 A5
Cricklewood Ln
10 HRSN 6282 E3
Cricklewood Rd N
10 YNKR 6393 D5
10 YNKR 6394 A5
Crimmins Av
300 BRNX 6613 A4
Crimson Av
10 MLVN 6929 C1
Crimson Av S
10 MLVN 6929 C2
Cripps Ln
10 VLYS 6928 E5
Crisfield St
10 YNKR 6280 E2
10 YNKR 6281 A2
Crispi Ln
10 STNL 7117 B6
Crist St
10 STNL 7020 D5
Crittenden Pl
10 STNL 6919 C7
Crittenden St
10 NWRK 6713 D5
Croak Av
10 STNL 7019 E5
Crocheron Av
161-01 QENS 6721 D4
Crocker St
10 RKVC 6929 E2
Crocus Av
10 FLPK 6827 B3
Crocus Hl
300 NRWD 6278 E1
Crocus St
10 WbgT 7114 B5
Croes Av
700 BRNX 6614 A3
Croes Pl
1600 BRNX 6614 A3
Croft Ct
10 STNL 7117 C3
Croft Pl
10 STNL 7019 A4
Croft Ter
10 NRCH 6281 E6
Cromer Rd E
10 HmpT 6827 B7
Cromer Rd W
10 HmpT 6827 B7
Cromer St
10 STNL 7117 A3
Crommelin St
42-00 QENS 6720 E5
43-00 QENS 6721 A5
Cromwell Av
10 STNL 7020 C7
10 STNL 7117 D1
200 BRNX 107 D5
200 BRNX 6612 E2
800 BRNX 6613 A1
1200 BRNX 105 A6
1200 BRNX 6504 A7
Cromwell Cir
10 STNL 7020 A6
Cromwell Cres
62-00 QENS 6824 B2
Cromwell Pl
10 SCLF 6509 E5
10 WHPL 6168 B2
10 YNKR 6393 C1
Cromwell Rd
10 HmpT 7028 E2
Cronston Av
123-00 QENS 7123 C1
Crooke Av
10 BKLN 6923 A5
Crooker Pl
10 NHmT 6617 E1
Crooks St
10 EMFD 6049 B5
Cropsey Av
1400 BKLN 7022 A4
3000 BKLN 7120 D1
Cropsey Ln
- HAOH 6165 E7
10 HAOH 6279 D1
Crosby Av
10 BKLN 6924 C1
10 NHmT 6724 D3
1100 BRNX 6615 B1
1200 BRNX 6505 E6
1200 BRNX 6506 B7
Crosby Pl
10 NRCH 6395 D3
Crosby St
10 MHTN 118 D5
10 MHTN 6821 C2
100 MHTN 119 A3
Crosland Ln
- STNL 7019 E7
- STNL 7117 D1
Cross Av
- NRCH 6395 E4
- STNL 7019 E7
- STNL 7117 E1
10 SAMB 7205 A7
10 SRVL 7205 A7
800 ELIZ 6917 E1
900 ELIZ 6816 E7
1000 ELIZ 6817 A7
1100 NWRK 6817 A7
Cross Rd
10 ARDY 6166 E5
10 GrbT 6166 E5
Cross St
- WLTN 6500 B5
10 BGTA 6501 D3
10 BlmT 6713 B1
10 BlvT 6713 D1
10 COrT 6712 A3
10 GrbT 6167 E1
10 GrwT 6170 C3
10 HmpT 6827 D4
10 NHmT 6508 E6
10 PTWN 6508 E6
10 STNL 7020 E1
10 WHPL 6167 E1
10 WLPK 6724 E4
10 WOrT 6712 A3
10 YNKR 6280 D6
100 BRNX 6506 D5
100 DMRT 6278 A5
100 ENWK 6714 A6
100 HRSN 6714 A6
800 ELIZ 6918 A4
Crossbar Rd
10 HAOH 6279 E1
10 HAOH 6280 A2
Cross Bay Blvd
- QENS 7025 E1
- QENS 7026 A1
105-16 QENS 6925 D1
Cross Bay Br
- QENS 7026 A6
Cross Bay Pkwy
- QENS 7026 B7
Cross Bronx Expwy
- BRNX 104 E5
- BRNX 105 D5
- BRNX 6503 E6
- BRNX 6504 D7
- BRNX 6505 B7
- BRNX 6613 E1
- BRNX 6614 B1
- MHTN 104 B4
- MHTN 6503 C6
Cross Bronx Expwy I-95
- BRNX 104 E5
- BRNX 105 D5
- BRNX 6503 E6
- BRNX 6504 D7
- BRNX 6613 E1
- BRNX 6614 B1
- MHTN 104 B4
- MHTN 6503 E6
Cross Bronx Expwy US-1
- BRNX 104 E5
- BRNX 105 D5
- BRNX 6503 E6
- BRNX 6504 A6
- MHTN 104 B4
- MHTN 6503 E6
Cross Bronx Expwy US-9
- MHTN 104 A4
- MHTN 6503 D6
Cross Bronx Expwy N
100 BRNX 105 E5
100 BRNX 6504 B6
Cross Bronx Expwy S
400 BRNX 105 E5
400 BRNX 6504 C6
Cross Bronx Expressway Ext
- BRNX 6615 A2
2500 BRNX 6614 E2
Cross Bronx Expwy Ext I-295
- BRNX 6614 E2
- BRNX 6615 A2
Cross County Pkwy
- EchT 6281 C7
- EchT 6395 C1
- MTVN 6394 A1
- MTVN 6395 A3
- YNKR 6393 E1
- YNKR 6394 B1
Cross Creek Dr
10 EGLD 6502 E3
Crossfield Av
10 STNL 7116 D4
Crossgate Rd
10 JSYC 6819 B6
Cross Hill Av
10 YNKR 6279 E4
10 YNKR 6280 A4
Cross Hill Rd
10 EchT 6281 B4
Crosshill Rd
10 GrbT 6167 A4
Crosshill St
10 STNL 7020 B1
Cross Island Pkwy
- HmpT 6827 A6
- HmpT 6928 A2
- QENS 6616 A7
- QENS 6723 A7
- QENS 6827 B2
- QENS 6927 E3
- QENS 6928 A2
10-01 QENS 6615 B7
28-00 QENS 6722 D5
160-00 QENS 6721 C1
Crossway
10 EchT 6281 C6
10 NRCH 6282 A2
10 RYEB 6169 E2
10 SCDL 6282 B2
10 YNKR 6280 B6
Crossway Rd
- GrbT 6167 A2
Cross Westchester Av
- NRCH 6395 C5
Cross Westchester Expwy
- EMFD 6048 E5
- EMFD 6049 A5
- GrbT 6048 D5
- GrbT 6049 D7
- GrbT 6050 A7
- HRSN 6169 D5
- PTCH 6170 A6
- RYE 6170 A7
- RYE 6284 B1
- RYEB 6169 E6
- RYEB 6170 A6
- WHPL 6050 A7
- WHPL 6168 C1
- WHPL 6169 A3
Cross Westchester Expwy I-287
- EMFD 6048 E5
- EMFD 6049 A5
- GrbT 6048 D5
- GrbT 6049 D7
- GrbT 6050 A7
- HRSN 6169 B4
- PTCH 6170 A6
- RYE 6170 A7
- RYE 6284 B1
- RYEB 6169 E6
- RYEB 6170 A6
- WHPL 6050 A7
- WHPL 6168 C1
- WHPL 6169 A3
Crosswood Rd
10 NHmT 6616 D7
10 SDRK 6616 D7
Croton Av
10 HAOH 6165 E6
10 STNL 7020 B2
10 TYTN 6048 C2
Croton Ct
10 ARDY 6166 D3
Croton Lp
10 BKLN 6924 D5
Croton Pl
- STNL 7019 A3
10 IRVN 6166 A1
10 TYTN 6048 B5
Croton Ter
10 YNKR 6393 E1
Crotona Av
100 HRSN 6283 B2
1300 BRNX 6613 C1
1500 BRNX 6504 D7
Crotona Pk E
1400 BRNX 6613 C1
1500 BRNX 6504 D7
Crotona Pk N
600 BRNX 6504 C7
Crotona Pk S
500 BRNX 6613 C1
Crotona Pkwy
1800 BRNX 6504 E6
Crotona Pl
1400 BRNX 105 E7
1400 BRNX 6504 C7
1400 BRNX 6613 C1
Crotty Av
10 YNKR 6394 A3
Crowell Av
10 STNL 7019 D3
Crowell Pl
10 VLYS 6928 D3
Crowell St
10 HmpT 6827 C5
Crown Av
10 HmpT 6827 E4
10 STNL 7116 B6
Crown Cir
10 BRXV 6395 A1
Crown Ct
10 STNL 7116 C5
100 EDGW 6611 E2
1300 MRNK 6282 E4
Crown Pl
10 STNL 7116 B6
Crown St
10 BKLN 6923 B3
10 NWRK 6712 D7
Crow Nest
10 MHVN 6508 B7
Crowninshield St
- BRNX 6615 D5
Crowntop Rd
10 NHmT 6617 D7
10 NHmT 6618 C7
Crows Nest Ct
10 NHLS 6618 B7
Crows Nest Rd
10 BRXV 6394 E1
Croyden Av
10 GTNK 6616 E5
10 GTNK 6617 A5
Croyden Ct
10 NHmT 6724 E3
Croyden Rd
400 GDNC 6828 D4
400 HmpT 6828 D4
Croyden St
10 LNBK 6929 C3
10 MLVN 6929 C3
10 NHmT 6723 E7
Croydon Rd
10 YNKR 6280 E2
173-00 QENS 6825 E3
500 HmpT 6827 B6
Cruger Av
2400 BRNX 6505 A3
Cryders Ln
154-00 QENS 6615 C7
Crystal Av
10 STNL 7019 C2
Crystal Ct
10 HmpT 6928 D7
Crystal Dr
10 GTNE 6722 E2
Crystal Ln
- STNL 6920 C7
Crystal Pl
10 MNLA 6724 C7
10 NHmT 6724 C7
Crystal St
10 BKLN 6925 A2
10 HmpT 6827 B6
10 HRSN 6283 B2
Crystal Ter
200 HlsT 6917 D2
Cuba Av
10 STNL 7118 A3
Cubberly Pl
10 JSYC 6820 D2
10 STNL 7117 E2
Cullman Av
246-00 QENS 6723 A5
Culloden Pl
95-00 QENS 6925 B1
Culotta Ln
10 STNL 7206 D4
Culver Av
10 JSYC 6819 C4
Culver St
10 YNKR 6393 C3
Cumberland Av
10 LKSU 6723 C1
10 NHmT 6723 C1
Cumberland Dr
10 YNKR 6394 A4
Cumberland Pl
10 HmpT 6928 A1
10 QENS 6928 A1
10 VLYS 6928 A1
100 LWRN 7027 E4
Cumberland St
10 BKLN 6821 E7
300 BKLN 121 E7
300 BKLN 6922 C2
300 EGLD 6503 A3
Cumbermeade Rd
10 FTLE 6611 E1
1100 FTLE 6502 D6
Cumley Ter
200 LEON 6502 D4
Cumming St
10 MHTN 101 E6
10 MHTN 6503 E3
Cummings Av
10 WHPL 6050 B6
Cummings Av N
10 GrbT 6049 E5
Cummings St
10 IrvT 6816 C1
Cunard Av
10 STNL 7020 C3
Cunard Pl
10 STNL 7020 C3
Cuneo Pl
10 JSYC 6716 C7
Cunningham Av
10 FLPK 6827 E2
10 STMN 6827 E2
Cunningham Rd
- STNL 7206 D3
Cuozzo St
10 BlvT 6713 D2
Curie Av
10 ERTH 6500 B7
10 WLTN 6500 B7
Currans Ln
10 YNKR 6393 E1
Currie Av
10 STNL 7117 D4
Curry Av
300 EGLD 6392 A5
Curry Rd
10 HAOH 6280 A2
10 YNKR 6280 A2
Curt Ter
10 GrwT 6170 B1
Curtis Av
10 STNL 7019 D2
Curtis Ct
10 STNL 6920 A7
Curtis Ln
10 YNKR 6280 A4
Curtis Pl
- CLST 6278 A2
10 LNBK 6929 A4
10 STNL 6920 D6
Curtis Rd
100 HWTN 7028 D2
Curtis St
24-00 QENS 6720 A3
E Curtis St
200 LNDN 6917 A6
Curzon Rd
115-00 QENS 6824 E5
Cushing Av
10 WLPK 6724 D4
Cushman Rd
10 SCDL 6168 A6
10 WHPL 6168 A4
Custer Av
10 NWRK 6817 A4
10 WLPK 6724 E5
10 YNKR 6280 C7
100 JSYC 6819 B6
Custer Pl
10 BRXV 6280 C4
10 BRXV 6281 A7
10 NWRK 6817 A4
Custer St
800 HmpT 6827 C7
900 HmpT 6928 C1
Custis Av
10 NoCT 6050 B4
Cuthbert Rd
84-00 QENS 6824 E4
85-00 QENS 6825 A4
Cutler Pl
500 HmpT 6827 E6
Cutler St
10 NWRK 6713 D5
Cutter Av
- NHmT 6722 E2
- QENS 6722 E2
Cutter St
10 RDFP 6501 E4
Cutter Mill Rd
10 GTPZ 6617 A7
10 GTPZ 6722 E1
10 GTPZ 6723 A1
100 GTNE 6722 E1
Cutters Dock Rd
10 WbgT 7114 D6
Cynthia Ct
10 HMPD 6828 E4
1600 HmpT 6929 A7
1600 HWTH 6929 A7
Cypress Av
- BKLN 7022 E3
1-01 BKLN 6823 A4
1-01 QENS 6823 D7
10 BGTA 6501 E3
10 HmpT 6929 E7
10 KNGP 6617 A4
10 NHmT 6617 E2
10 STNL 7020 A3
100 BRNX 6613 B5
3700 BKLN 7120 B1
Cypress Ct
10 BKLN 6824 A7
Cypress Dr
600 HmpT 6828 B7
Cypress Lp
10 STNL 7115 E5
Cypress Pl
10 DMRT 6278 C7
Cypress Rd
10 EchT 6281 B5
10 HmpT 7027 C3
Cypress St
10 CART 7115 C1
10 FLPK 6827 D3
10 JSYC 6819 A4
10 MtPT 6050 A2
10 NWRK 6816 E2
10 TFLY 6392 B4
10 YNKR 6394 A2
200 HmpT 6827 E3
Cypress Crest Ln
- STNL 7019 A3
Cypress Hills St
10 QENS 6823 B6
200 BKLN 6823 E7
4700 BKLN 6824 A7
Cypress Point Dr
10 HRSN 6050 E7
10 HRSN 6168 D1
Cyrus Av
10 BKLN 7023 E7
10 BKLN 7024 A7
Cyrus Pl
10 DBSF 6166 C4
400 BRNX 6504 B3
Cyrus Field Rd
10 DBSF 6166 C3
10 IRVN 6166 C1

D

D St
1300 HmpT 6827 E6
Da Costa Av
500 HmpT 6929 D6
Dae Woo Pl
10 CARL 6610 A3
Daffodil Av
10 HmpT 6828 B4
Daffodil Ct
10 STNL 7116 B5
Daffodil Dr
300 NRWD 6278 E1
Daffodil Ln
10 STNL 7018 E7
10 STNL 7019 A7
Daffys Wy
10 SECS 6716 B1
Dahill Rd
10 BKLN 6922 E6
1200 BKLN 7022 E3
Dahl Ct
10 BKLN 7022 D2
Dahl St
10 WbgT 7205 A3
Dahlgren Pl
10 BKLN 7021 E3
Dahlia Av
134-00 QENS 6721 A5
Dahlia Ln
10 HmpT 6928 C4
Dahlia St
10 STNL 7116 A6
Dahnerts Park Ln
10 GRFD 6500 B1
Daibes Ct
100 EDGW 108 B1
100 EDGW 6611 D4
Dail St
10 NHmT 6724 B5
Daisy Av
10 FLPK 6827 C2
Daisy Ln
10 IRVN 6166 C1
Daisy Pl
10 BRNX 6615 C4
Daisy Farms Dr
10 NRCH 6281 E3
300 NRCH 6282 A2
300 SCDL 6282 A2
Dakar St
1300 ELIZ 6919 A1
Dakota Av
- GrbT 6049 C7
Dakota Dr
10 LKSU 6723 E4
10 NHmT 6723 E4
Dakota Pl
10 BKLN 7024 B4
10 STNL 7019 D3
Dakota St
10 OrgT 6164 E4
Dalbert St
10 CART 7017 A6
Dale Av
10 STNL 7117 E2
Dale Ct
10 HRPK 6164 A7
10 NRWD 6164 A7
Dale Dr
10 GrwT 6170 C3
Dale Pl
10 VLYS 6928 B2
Dale Rd
10 EchT 6281 B4
10 TCKA 6281 B4
Dale St
10 RYE 6283 E3
10 WHPL 6168 D7
Dale Carnegie Ct
10 LKSU 6723 B3
Daleham St
10 STNL 7117 A3
Dalemere Rd
10 STNL 7020 B6
Dales Av
10 JSYC 6715 D7
10 JSYC 6819 D1
D'Alessio Ct
10 EchT 6281 D3
D'Alessio Dr
10 CART 7017 B5
Dalewood Dr
10 GrbT 6167 D2
Daley Pl
10 LNBK 6929 B4
Daley St
10 NHmT 6724 C5
Dalian Ct
114-00 QENS 6614 C7
Dallas Av
10 NHmT 6724 A6
Dallas St
10 STNL 7020 A2
Dallinger Pl
10 MLVN 6929 A2
Dally Ct
10 PTHA 7205 D3
Dalny Rd
87-00 QENS 6826 A3
175-00 QENS 6825 E3
Dalphin Dr
10 RYE 6283 E4
Dalston Cir
10 HmpT 6929 B3
Dalton Av
10 STNL 7117 D2
Dalton Rd
10 YNKR 6280 A5
Dalton St
10 LBCH 7029 E6

STREET Block City	Map# Grid

Daly Av
1800 BRNX 6504 E7
Daly Blvd
10 HmpT 7029 E2
Daly Pl
10 GLCV 6509 E4
Damato Dr
10 ISPK 7029 D3
Dambly Av
3100 HmpT 6929 E7
Damon Ln
10 YNKR 6393 A2
Damson Ln
10 HmpT 6928 B4
Dana Av
800 HmpT 6827 D2
900 HmpT 6928 D1
Dana Ct
84-00 QENS 6824 A2
Dana Pl
10 EGLD 6392 A7
10 EGLD 6503 A1
100 EGLD 6502 E1
Dana Rd
10 MtPT 6049 B2
Dana St
10 STNL 7020 E4
Danby Pl
10 YNKR 6281 D1
Dane Ct
- NBgT 6611 A5
Dane Pl
72-00 QENS 6824 C3
Danforth Av
10 DBSF 6166 B5
10 JSYC 6819 C6
Danforth Av CO-602
10 JSYC 6819 C2
Danforth St
10 BKLN 6824 B5
Daniel Av
10 RTFD 6609 A2
Daniel Dr
10 EGLC 6503 B1
10 EGLD 6503 B2
10 GLCV 6509 D4
Daniel Pl
10 SCLF 6509 E5
Daniel St
10 CART 7115 C2
10 HRSN 6050 D7
10 LFRY 6501 C7
10 MNCH 6501 C7
10 WbgT 7115 C2
100 HKSK 6501 A2
700 HmpT 6928 A6
2900 BRNX 6505 E6
Daniela Ct
10 STNL 7117 A1
Daniel Cox Rd
10 LWRN 7028 B6
10 STNL 6920 E2
Daniels Pl
10 WHPL 6050 A7
Daniels St
83-00 QENS 6825 B3
Dank Ct
10 BKLN 7022 E7
Dankoff Av
10 WLTN 6500 A5
Danner Av
10 HRSN 6283 C3
Danny Ct
10 STNL 7019 A4
Danny Ln
300 NVLE 6164 C4
Danny Pl
10 WbgT 7114 D2
Dante Av
100 TCKA 6281 A5
Dante Dr
10 HRSN 6283 A4
Dante St
10 MrnT 6282 C4
Danzig Ct
10 VLYS 6928 B2
Darby Ct
10 WHPL 6168 E6
Darby Ln
1100 UnnT 6917 C2
Darcey Av
10 STNL 7019 B4
Darcy Ln
10 EchT 6281 C4
Darcy St
10 NWRK 6818 D1
Dare Ct
10 BKLN 7024 A7
100 BKLN 7023 E6
Dare Pl
3000 BRNX 6615 C4
Darewood Ln
10 HmpT 6928 B4
Darien Ter
900 STNL 6502 B1
Darina Ct
10 HMPD 6828 E4
Dark St
2300 BRNX 6394 E7
Darley Rd
10 RSLG 6723 B2
10 THSN 6723 B1
Darling Av
10 MTVN 6395 A4
10 NRCH 6281 E3
Darlington Av
10 STNL 7116 A4
Darnell Ln
10 STNL 7115 D7
Darren Dr
207-00 QENS 6615 D6
Darrow Pl
100 BRNX 6505 C2
Dart St
10 EGLC 6929 E6
Darters Ln
100 NHLS 6618 B4
Dartmouth Av
10 WbgT 7114 C7
10 YNKR 6280 A6
Dartmouth Ln
900 HmpT 6928 C6

Dartmouth Rd
10 FLHL 6617 E5
10 WOrT 6712 A3
Dartmouth St
10 GDNC 6828 A3
10 RKVC 6929 E1
10 VLYS 6928 A1
10 WLPK 6724 E4
Dartmouth Ter
10 GrbT 6049 B7
1200 UnnT 6816 A5
Darwin Av
10 HAOH 6165 E6
Darwood Pl
- ARDY 6166 E3
10 GrbT 6166 E3
10 MTVN 6395 A4
Dash Pl
10 BRNX 6393 B7
Dassern Dr
10 DBSF 6166 B6
Dassing Av
10 IrvT 6712 E7
10 NWRK 6712 E7
Daub Pl
300 HAOH 6928 C7
Dauntless Pkwy
600 HmpT 6827 D7
Davenport Av
10 CRSK 6392 A1
10 NRCH 6396 A6
10 NWRK 6713 C2
10 PTCH 6170 B4
10 TFLY 6392 A1
10 BlvT 6713 C2
219-00 QENS 6826 E2
223-00 QENS 6827 A2
Davenport Ct
99-00 QENS 6925 E5
102-00 QENS 6926 A5
Davenport Pl
- YNKR 6280 D4
10 YNKR 6280 D4
Davenport Rd
10 YNKR 6280 D4
Davenport St
10 HRSN 6283 B4
David Dr
10 NRCH 6281 E5
David Ln
10 HAOH 6279 E2
10 YNKR 6279 E2
David Pl
10 STNL 7019 B1
David St
10 STNL 7117 B6
100 SAMB 7205 C7
David Ter
10 WHPL 6050 A7
Davidson Av
1900 BRNX 105 C3
1900 BRNX 6504 C4
2300 BRNX 102 E7
W Davidson Av
10 HmpT 6929 D3
Davidson Ct
10 BKLN 6918 E7
Davidson St
10 BKLN 6918 E7
Davies Rd
13-00 QENS 7027 D5
Davis Ct
10 NoCT 6050 B3
10 EORG 6713 A7
10 HmpT 7027 C3
10 KRNY 6714 C3
10 MtPT 6049 B3
10 MtPT 6050 A3
10 NHmT 6617 E2
10 NHmT 6618 A4
10 NRCH 6395 E5
10 RYE 6284 A2
10 RYE 6284 A7
10 WHPL 6168 B3
100 BRNX 6615 A3
500 STNL 7020 A1
600 HRSN 6714 B5
Davis Ct
10 HRSN 6714 B6
10 BKLN 6922 E1
47-00 QENS 6718 C7
Davis Dr
10 LODI 6500 E3
Davis Ln
10 RSLN 6618 E6
Davis Rd
10 EORG 6713 A4
Davis St
10 ENWK 6714 A5
10 ERKY 6714 B6
10 HRSN 6714 A5
45-00 QENS 6718 C6
1000 HmpT 6828 A4
2800 HmpT 6929 E6
Davison Av
10 ERKY 6929 B6
10 HmpT 6929 D3
10 LNBK 6929 A3
Davison Ct
10 ERKY 6929 C4
Davison Pl
10 EGLD 6392 A4
10 RKVC 6929 E5
Davison Plz
10 ERKY 6929 C4
Davison St
2700 HmpT 6929 D6
Davit Ct
10 BRNX 6614 C4
Davit St
- NWRK 6818 D5
Dawes Pl
10 LNBK 6929 B4
10 LNBK 6929 A3
Dawn Ct
10 STNL 7206 C4
300 NVLE 6164 D4

Dawn Dr
10 WbgT 7115 B2
Dawn Ln
10 NHmT 6724 C4
Dawson Cir
10 STNL 7018 E5
Dawson Ct
10 HRSN 6050 A4
10 STNL 7018 E5
Dawson Dr
10 HmpT 7020 B5
Dawson Pl
100 WbgT 7114 B4
Dawson St
10 NWRK 6714 A4
10 STNL 7019 C5
600 BRNX 6613 C3
Day Av
200 CLFP 108 A1
200 CLFP 6611 C4
200 FRVW 6611 C4
500 RDGF 6611 B1
Day Ct
10 NHmT 6616 C5
N Day St
10 CORT 6712 D2
S Day St
10 CORT 6712 C3
Day Ter
1500 UnnT 6816 C5
Daymon Ter
10 MrnT 6282 B7
Dayna Ct
10 PTHA 7205 C2
Dayna Dr
10 STNL 7020 E4
Dayton Pl
100 NWRK 6817 A7
Dayton St
10 ELIZ 6917 C2
10 SCLF 6509 D6
300 ELIZ 6817 A7
Dayton Ter
10 ELIZ 6917 C2
Daytona St
10 NHLS 6618 D7
10 RYEB 6169 E4
Deacon Pl
10 CRSK 6278 A6
Deal Ct
10 STNL 7020 E4
Deal Rd
10 ISPK 7029 C5
Dean Av
10 STNL 7018 C7
Dean Dr
10 EGLD 6392 A4
10 TFLY 6392 A3
Dean Dr CO-501
10 TFLY 6392 A3
Dean Pl
10 EchT 6281 B6
Dean St
10 BKLN 121 A7
10 BKLN 6821 D7
10 ERKY 6929 B6
10 HKSK 6501 B2
10 WOrT 6712 B3
100 QENS 6928 A3
10 VLYS 6928 A3
200 BKLN 6922 E1
400 BKLN 6923 D2
1800 BKLN 6924 A2
N Dean St
100 TFLY 6392 A5
500 TFLY 6392 A4
S Dean St
10 EGLD 6502 D2
Dean Ter
10 UnnT 6816 A6
Deane Pl
10 LRMT 6396 C3
10 LRMT 6396 B3
Dearborn Av
10 RYE 6283 E4
100 RYE 6284 A4
300 BGTA 6501 C2
600 NWRK 6713 E1
Dearborn Ct
10 BKLN 6923 C2
100 TnkT 6502 A2
300 BGTA 6501 C1
Dearborn Dr
10 EGLD 6164 A4
Dearborn Rd
10 NRWD 6278 D1
1000 FTLE 6611 D1
Dearborn St
10 NRCH 6396 C4
10 YNKR 6280 B5
N Dearborn St
10 IRVN 6166 C1
S Dearborn St
10 IRVN 6166 A1
Dearman Close
10 NHmT 6048 B7
Debbie St
10 STNL 7019 A4
Debevoise Av
10 BKLN 6822 D3
Debevoise St
10 BKLN 6822 D5
Deborah Lp
10 STNL 7116 C5
Deborah Ter
10 EGLC 6503 A3
Debra Pl
10 WbgT 7114 E4
10 WbgT 7115 A4
1500 HmpT 6928 D1
Debs Pl
10 BRNX 6505 E2
Decatur Av
10 BKLN 7121 D1
1000 BRNX 6504 D1
2500 BRNX 6504 D4
3100 BRNX 6505 A2
Decatur Pl
4500 HmpT 7029 D5
Decatur Rd
10 NRCH 6396 A4

Decatur St
10 BKLN 6923 A1
15-00 BKLN 6823 B7
16-00 BKLN 6823 C6
400 BKLN 6924 A1
De Chiaro Ln
10 NHmT 6724 D4
Decker Av
10 ELIZ 6917 C2
10 STNL 7019 C2
10 UnnT 6917 C2
Decker Pl
100 WbgT 7114 B4
Decker St
100 HmpT 6928 E1
10 VLYS 6928 E1
Decosta Av
62-00 QENS 7026 D5
Dederer Av
10 GLCV 6509 D3
Deems Av
10 STNL 7019 C3
Deepdale Av
248-00 QENS 6722 E4
Deep Dale Dr
10 NHmT 6617 E6
Deepdale Dr
10 GTNE 6616 E7
10 GTNE 6617 C4
Deepdale Pkwy
10 NHmT 6724 D2
Deepdale Pl
50-00 QENS 6722 E3
50-00 QENS 6723 A3
Deepdene Rd
10 YNKR 6394 A5
Deep Gorge Rd
10 GrbT 6170 C2
Deep Hollow Close
10 IRVN 6166 B3
Deepwater Wy
10 BRNX 6506 C5
Deer Run
10 NHLS 6618 D7
10 RYEB 6169 E4
Deere Park Pl
10 STNL 7020 B6
Deerfield Av
10 EchT 6281 B7
Deerfield Dr
100 TFLY 6392 C3
Deerfield Ln
10 MRNK 6282 D4
10 MrnT 6282 D5
10 SCDL 6282 B1
Deerfield Rd
10 NHmT 6618 A3
Deerfoot Ln
10 DBSF 6166 E4
10 YNKR 6280 D3
Deer Hill Ln
10 GrbT 6166 E4
10 GrbT 6167 A4
Deer Hill Rd
10 ALPN 6278 C6
10 DMRT 6278 C6
Deerhurst Rd
10 YNKR 6281 A2
Deering Ln
10 ERKY 6929 C1
Deer Park Rd
10 KNGP 6617 B4
Deertrack Ln
- IRVN 6048 C6
10 TYTN 6048 C6
Deerwood Rd
300 FTLE 6611 D1
400 FTLE 6502 D7
500 PALP 6502 D7
Defoe Pl
10 BRNX 6505 E2
Defoe St
125-00 QENS 6927 C1
Degraw Av
10 TnkT 6502 A2
100 TnkT 6501 C4
300 BGTA 6501 C1
600 NWRK 6713 E1
Degraw Av CO-56
100 TnkT 6502 A2
300 BGTA 6501 C1
E Degraw Av
- LEON 6502 C3
E Degraw Av CO-56
- LEON 6502 C3
Degraw St
10 BKLN 120 D7
10 BKLN 6821 B7
10 BKLN 6922 C1
100 BKLN 6922 B2
N Degraw St
10 DMRT 6278 C6
S Degraw St
10 IRVN 6166 A1
Dehart Av
10 ELIZ 6919 A7
Dehart Pl
10 STNL 7019 A4
Dehaven Dr
10 YNKR 6279 E4
Deidre Ct
10 STNL 7020 C4
Deirving St
400 HmpT 7029 A3
Deisius St
10 STNL 7207 C1
De Kalb Av
10 PTHA 7205 D2
DeKalb Av
10 BKLN 121 C6
10 BKLN 6822 A7
17-01 BKLN 6823 D1
1000 BRNX 6504 C1
2500 BRNX 6504 C4
3100 BRNX 6505 A2
3400 BRNX 6504 D4
Dekay St
10 STNL 7020 A1

Dekoven Ct
10 BKLN 7023 A1
Dekoven St
1200 HmpT 6929 D3
De Kruif Pl
100 BRNX 6505 D2
Delafield Av
10 STNL 7019 E1
400 STNL 7019 E1
5000 BRNX 6393 B6
Delafield Ln
10 BRNX 6393 B7
Delafield Pl
10 STNL 6822 C6
400 BRNX 6393 C4
De Lalla Ter
700 RDGF 6611 B2
Delamar Ct
62-00 QENS 7026 D5
Delamar Av
10 GLCV 6509 D3
Delancey Av
100 MRNK 6282 D6
Delancey St
100 BRNX 6505 B6
10 MHTN 119 B5
10 MHTN 6821 D3
Delancey St S
10 MHTN 6816 E6
10 MHTN 6821 D3
Delancy St
10 NWRK 6817 E2
10 NWRK 6818 A3
Delano Av
10 CLFP 6611 C3
200 FRVW 6611 C3
2200 BRNX 6505 E4
De Lavall Av
3300 BRNX 6506 A1
3400 BRNX 6505 E1
Delavan Av
10 GrwT 6170 C3
Delavan Av E
20-00 QENS 7026 A6
Delavan Av W
10 HmpT 6827 D7
Delavan Pl
10 BlvT 6713 D2
Delavan St
10 BKLN 6922 B1
Delavan Ter
10 YNKR 6280 D3
Delaware Av
10 BlmT 6713 B1
10 STNL 7019 D3
Delaware Dr
10 LKSU 6723 E4
Delaware Ln
10 HRSN 6169 A7
Delaware Rd
10 BLRS 6827 B2
10 FLPK 6827 B2
10 YNKR 6828 B3
Delaware St
10 ELIZ 6918 A6
10 YNKR 7020 B6
Delevan Ln
10 HRSN 6169 A7
Delevan St
111-00 QENS 6826 E5
Delford St
10 STNL 7020 C3
Delhi Rd
10 GrbT 6167 A6
Delia Blvd
10 PALP 6502 C7
Delia Blvd CO-31
10 PALP 6502 C7
10 RDGF 6502 C7
Delia Ct
10 STNL 7206 B4
10 YNKR 6922 C2
Delia St
10-01 QENS 7027 C5
Dell Av
200 CLFP 6611 D2
Dell Ct
10 NHmT 6617 D6
10 NHmT 6724 D7
Dell Dr
10 EchT 6929 B7
Dell Ln
10 ARDY 6166 E4
Dell Rd
10 SCDL 6168 B7
500 CARL 6609 A4
Dell St
10 SYHW 6048 B1
Dell Wy
10 NHmT 6724 D6
Dell Glen Av
10 BKLN 6500 E7
Dellwood Cir
10 STNL 7206 B4
Dellwood Ln
10 STNL 7206 B4
Dellwood Rd
10 STNL 7019 E6
10 WHPL 6168 E6
10 YNKR 6280 D6

Delmar Av
10 BKLN 6924 E5
Delmar Fl
10 IrvT 6712 D7
10 STNL 6816 D1
Delmar Rd
10 STNL 6819 B6
Delmonico Pl
10 BKLN 6822 C6
10 VLYS 6928 E4
Del Monte Dr
10 BAYN 6919 E2
Delmore St
10 STNL 7019 B3
Delo Dr
10 OrgT 6164 C7
Delongis Ct
10 OrgT 6164 C7
Delphine Ter
10 STNL 7020 D6
Del Ray Ct
10 STNL 7020 D2
Del Rey Dr
10 MTVN 6395 B2
Delwitt Av
10 STNL 7117 E5
Demarest Av
10 DMRT 6278 B5
10 EGLC 6503 B1
200 CLST 6278 A3
Demarest Av CO-41
300 CLST 6278 A3
E Demarest Av
10 EGLD 6392 A6
Demarest Rd
10 TnkT 6502 A2
Demarest St
10 HKSK 6501 B1
10 NRWD 6164 A5
10 NWRK 6816 E3
Demartino Av
10 YNKR 6280 B5
Demeres Rd
20-00 QENS 7026 A6
Demeyer St
2300 BRNX 6505 E4
Demille Av
10 HmpT 6827 D7
Demopolis Av
10 STNL 7117 A5
Demorest Av
2100 BRNX 6506 B5
3300 BRNX 6505 E2
3800 BRNX 6506 D6
Demott Av
10 STNL 7116 A6
10 WbgT 7114 B1
Demott Pl
10 RKVC 6929 D5
De Mott St
200 MNLA 6724 D7
Demott St
10 TFLY 6392 A3
Dempsey Av
10 EDGW 6611 E2
Dempsey Ct
10 JSYC 6819 A4
Dempsey Dr
10 EchT 6281 C4
Den Ln
400 GrwT 6170 D4
Denbigh St
10 STNL 6918 B3
Denim Pl
10 NoCT 6050 B4
Denis St
134-00 QENS 6927 B1
Denise Ct
10 STNL 7207 C1
Denison St
10 WHPL 6168 A2
Denker Av
10 STNL 7019 A7
Denman Pl
10 ELIZ 6917 D1
10 HlsT 6917 D2
10 IrvT 6816 D3
10 MTVN 6395 A2
W Denman Av
10 IrvT 6816 D3
40-00 QENS 6719 E6
40-39 QENS 6720 A6
Dennett Pl
10 BKLN 6922 C2
Denning Pl
10 WhkT 6716 B3
Dennis McHugh Ct
10 EGLC 6164 D2
Dennis Pl
10 NRCH 6282 A5
Dennis St
600 LNDN 6917 D6
10 NHmT 6617 D6
10 NHmT 6724 D7
Denton Av
10 ERKY 6929 A1
10 LNBK 6929 A1
10 NHmT 6724 D6
Denton Av S
- GDNC 6828 B3
Denton Rd
10 KNGP 6616 E3
Denton St
10 ELIZ 6917 E7

Depan Av
10 FLPK 6827 D1
Depaul St
1500 HmpT 6827 D4
Depew Av
10 YNKR 6280 E2
Depew Pl
10 STNL 7206 E1
Depeyster Av
10 TFLY 6392 B3
Depeyster St
10 SYHW 6048 B2
10 YNKR 6393 B4
Depot Pl
10 BRNX 104 D6
10 BRNX 6503 D7
10 PALP 6608 B7
10 SCDL 6167 B7
Depot Plz
10 SYHW 6048 B2
10 BRXV 6280 D4
10 MLVN 6929 C2
10 TYTN 6048 B2
S Depot Plz
10 TYTN 6048 B3
Depot Rd
162-00 QENS 6721 D4
Depot Sq
10 OrgT 6164 C2
10 TCKA 6280 C2
10 TCKA 6281 A6
Depot Wy E
10 LRMT 6396 C1
Depot Wy W
10 LRMT 6396 C1
Deppe Pl
10 STNL 7019 A3
Derby Av
10 CDHT 7028 B1
10 HmpT 7028 B1
500 HmpT 6928 A7
Derby Ct
10 MLVN 6929 B1
10 STNL 7019 D1
Derby Ln
10 IRVN 6166 C2
Derby Rd
10 NHmT 6618 A3
10 NRWD 6164 A7
Derby St
10 EORG 6712 C5
10 NWRK 6712 C5
500 CLFP 6928 C4
Dercole Ct
400 NRWD 6164 A5
De Reimer Av
2100 BRNX 6506 B5
3300 BRNX 6505 E2
3800 BRNX 6506 D6
Derrick Adkins Ln
800 HmpT 6929 C1
Derry Ln
10 HAOH 6279 D1
De Ruyter Pl
10 STNL 7019 A1
De Sales Pl
10 BKLN 6924 B1
Desanti Plz
10 GrbT 6167 D4
Desar Rd
89-00 QENS 6925 D2
Desbrosses St
10 MHTN 118 B4
10 MHTN 6821 B4
Deserre Av
10 STNL 7116 A6
Deshon Av
10 YNKR 6280 D6
De Sibio Pl
10 HmpT 7027 E2
Desmond Av
10 YNKR 6394 A3
Desmond Ct
10 BKLN 7023 B6
Desota Av
200 WbgT 7114 B5
Desoto Ct
92-00 QENS 7026 A6
Desoto Pl
10 CLFP 108 A7
200 FRVW 6611 C4
Despoilation Al
- NWRK 6817 D1
Destiny Ct
10 STNL 7019 A1
Detmer Av
10 TYTN 6048 C4
Detroit Av
200 STNL 7116 C6
Devanney Sq
1400 BRNX 6505 D3
Devens St
10 BKLN 7023 B6
Devereux Ct
10 RYE 6283 C5
Devine Av
600 ELIZ 6917 E4
Devine St
10 LNBK 6929 B4
S Devine St
10 NWRK 6712 E7
Devlin Pl
- BAYN 6920 A1
Devoe Av
12-00 QENS 6615 E7
Devoe Pl
10 YNKR 6393 E4
Devoe St
10 BKLN 6822 C4
10 DBSF 6166 A4
Devoe Ter
2400 BRNX 6504 D7
2400 BRNX 6504 B4
Devon Av
10 SCDL 6168 A4

Devon Lp
10 STNL 7117 A1
Devon Pl
10 CRSK 6278 C7
10 DMRT 6278 C7
10 STNL 6920 B7
Devon Rd
10 GTNK 6617 A5
10 LRMT 6396 C1
10 MtPT 6049 A1
10 NHmT 6617 A6
10 NHmT 6724 E3
10 TFLY 6392 B5
10 YNKR 6280 C7
10 YNKR 6394 C1
Devon St
10 HRSN 6714 A5
10 KRNY 6714 A5
10 LNBK 6929 A5
10 MLVN 6929 C3
10 NARL 6714 B3
N Devon St
10 MLVN 6929 C2
Devon Ter
10 KRNY 6714 B5
Devon Wy
10 HAOH 6279 E1
E Devonia Av
10 MTVN 6394 B2
10 MTVN 6395 A2
W Devonia Av
62-00 QENS 6824 B2
Devonshire Ct
10 RYEB 6169 E3
10 RYEB 6170 A3
Devonshire Dr
10 NHmT 6724 B6
10 WHPL 6169 A6
Devonshire Ln
10 BKLN 6922 A2
Devonshire Rd
10 CRSK 6392 B1
10 NRCH 6282 A3
Dewey Pl
10 NHmT 6617 A6
10 NHmT 6724 D3
10 NRCH 6395 E2
10 STNL 7117 B4
Dewey St
10 GRFD 6500 A1
10 NWRK 6816 E3
Dewey St E
10 HmpT 7029 B1
Dewey St W
10 HmpT 7029 C2
Dewhurst St
10 STNL 7019 C5
De Witt Av
10 BKLN 6924 C4
DeWitt Av
10 ELIZ 6917 E1
DeWitt Rd
10 ELIZ 6917 E1
DeWitt St
10 GRFD 6500 A2
10 HmpT 6827 B7
10 HmpT 6928 A1
Dexter Av
10 STNL 7115 C7
Dexter Ct
85-00 BKLN 6824 A6
85-00 BKLN 6824 A6
Dexter Rd
10 YNKR 6280 D4
Dey St
10 HRSN 6050 C7
10 HRSN 6713 E6
10 JSYC 6715 E7
10 JSYC 6716 A1
10 MHTN 118 B7
10 NWRK 6713 D6
Deyo St
200 STNL 7116 C6
Diamond St
10 MNCH 6501 B7
Dianas Cir
10 ROSE 6618 C7
Dianas Tr
10 ROSE 6618 C7
Diane Av
800 WbgT 7114 C2
Diane Pl
12-00 QENS 6615 E7
500 HmpT 6927 E6
500 HmpT 6928 A6
Dianne St
10 VLYS 6928 E2
Diaz Ct
10 STNL 7118 A3
Diaz St
10 STNL 7020 E6
Dicarolis St
10 HKSK 6501 B1
Dick St
10 JSYC 6820 A1
Dickel Rd
10 SCDL 6168 A4

Dickens Av
600 HmpT 6828 B6
Dickens St
10-00 QENS 7027 C4
800 HmpT 6928 B7
800 HmpT 7028 B1
Dickenson Pl
10 SDRK 6616 D6
Dickerson Av
10 NWRK 6713 B6
Dickie Av
10 STNL 7019 C2
Dickinson Av
- BRNX 6504 D1
10 BRNX 6280 A5
Dickinson St
1100 HmpT 6917 B6
Dickson St
10 GLCV 6509 E3
10 HmpT 7027 D2
Dictum Ct
10 BKLN 7023 E6
Diellen Ln
600 HmpT 6827 D7
Dierauf St
10 STNL 7116 D3
Dieterle Cres
62-00 QENS 6824 B2
Dietrichs St
10 LFRY 6501 D7
Dietz Pl
2200 NBgT 6716 C3
Digby Ct
96-00 QENS 6925 C1
Digney Av
4100 BRNX 6394 C6
Dikeman St
10 BKLN 6922 A2
Dill Av
1100 LNDN 6917 B6
2100 ELIZ 6917 C5
Dill Pl
2800 BRNX 6615 A2
Dillingham Pl
10 EGLC 6503 B1
10 EGLD 6503 B1
Dillman Dr
10 PTHA 7205 D2
Dillon Dr
- BAYN 6920 A1
10 LWRN 7028 A3
Dillon Ln
10 PTHA 7205 D4
Dillon Rd
10 MrnT 6396 B3
Dillon St
112-00 QENS 6825 E7
Dilthy Pl
- HmpT 6929 E6
Di Marco Pl
10 STNL 7117 D1
Dimitri Pl
10 MrnT 6282 B7
Dimsdale Dr
10 YNKR 6281 A2
Dina Ct
10 STNL 7117 C3
Dinallo St
10 SHkT 6501 B3
Dino Dr
10 STNL 7019 D1
Dinsmore Av
12-00 QENS 7027 D5
Dinsmore Pl
10 BKLN 6925 A1
10 BKLN 6925 A2
2600 BRNX 6505 C3
Dinsmore St
10 STNL 7018 C3
Direnzo Ct
10 NRCH 6281 D7
Disbrow Cir
10 NRCH 6281 D7
Disbrow Ln
10 NRCH 6281 D7
Disosway Pl
10 STNL 7019 D1
Distribution St
10 STNL 6818 B5
Ditmars Blvd
18-00 QENS 6719 C3
93-72 QENS 6720 A3
Ditmars St
10 BKLN 6822 E6
10 BRNX 6506 B6
Ditmars Blvd Sq
10 QENS 6720 A3
Ditmas Av
10 BKLN 6922 B7
1000 BKLN 6923 B7
5700 BKLN 6924 B6
Ditson St
10 STNL 7020 E3
Divine St
10 STNL 7020 E4
Division Av
- STNL 7117 E1
10 BKLN 6822 A4
10 HSBH 6500 D6
100 GRFD 6500 D1
200 CARL 6609 C1
300 CARL 6500 B7
Division St
10 BKLN 6822 D3
10 EORG 6713 A4
10 CLST 6392 A1
10 EGLC 6918 B3
10 EORG 6713 D3
10 FRVW 6611 C4
10 HAOH 6165 E7
10 JSYC 6820 B2
10 LODI 6500 E2
10 MHTN 119 A6
10 MHTN 6821 C3
10 NRCH 6395 E4
10 NWRK 6713 E6
10 RYEB 6170 A5
10 SHkT 6501 B2

New York City/5 Borough Street Index

STREET Block City Map# Grid

Division St
10 WbgT 7115 B2
100 CART 7115 B2
100 HKSK 6501 B3
200 CLFP 6611 D2
300 PTHA 7205 D3
1100 HmpT 6928 C7
Division St W
10 GrwT 6170 C6
S Division St
10 NRCH 6395 E5
10 NRCH 6396 B5
Divney Ln
10 GrbT 6048 D7
10 IRVN 6048 D7
Dix Av
21-00 QENS 7027 C4
Dix Pl
10 STNL 7020 D2
Dixon Av
10 STNL 7019 B1
Dixon Ct
10 SCLF 6509 E7
Dixon Dr
10 WbgT 7114 B4
Dixon Ln
10 TYTN 6048 B2
Dixon St
10 RYEB 6170 A6
10 TYTN 6048 B2
Doane Av
10 STNL 7117 A3
Dobbin St
10 BKLN 6822 B2
Dobbs Pl
10 STNL 7020 A3
Dobbs Ter
10 SCDL 6167 E5
Dobbs Ferry Rd
10 GrbT 6049 C7
200 GrbT 6167 B1
800 GrbT 6166 E1
Dobbs Ferry Rd SR-100B
10 GrbT 6049 C7
200 GrbT 6167 B1
800 GrbT 6166 E1
Doblin St
600 HmpT 6827 B6
Dobranski Dr
10 PTHA 7205 C1
Dock Ct
- HAOH 6165 D7
Dock Ln
10 KNGP 6616 D2
10 PTWN 6508 D6
Dock Rd
- STNL 7021 B4
Dock St
- BRNX 6615 B2
10 BKLN 121 A2
10 BKLN 6821 D4
10 MTVN 6395 A7
10 PTCH 6170 C6
10 STNL 7020 E1
10 YNKR 6393 C1
Dock Pathway St
10 NRCH 6396 B3
Dockside Ln
10 STNL 7117 B7
Dod Ct
10 ELIZ 6917 E2
Dod Pl
10 HlsT 6816 D6
Dodd Al
10 NWRK 6817 E1
Dodd St
10 BlmT 6713 A1
10 EORG 6713 A1
100 EORG 6712 E1
100 UNCT 6716 D3
100 WhkT 6716 D3
200 COrT 6712 E1
Dodd Ter
10 EORG 6713 A1
Dodford Rd
10 RSLG 6723 A1
Dodge St
10 BAYN 6919 D5
Dodgewood Rd
4600 BRNX 6393 A7
Dodworth St
10 BKLN 6822 C5
Doe Ct
10 STNL 7018 E6
Doe Pl
10 STNL 6919 E7
Dogwood Av
10 HmpT 6828 B7
10 HmpT 6929 B1
10 MLVN 6929 B1
Dogwood Ct
400 LEON 6502 D4
400 NRWD 6278 C1
Dogwood Dr
- BRNX 6505 B7
10 EchT 6281 B3
10 STNL 7116 B5
Dogwood Ln
10 ALPN 6278 E5
10 CRSK 6278 B7
10 DMRT 6278 A5
10 FLHL 6618 A5
10 GrbT 6167 C2
10 IRVN 6166 B1
10 LWRN 7028 A3
10 MrnT 6396 C3
10 NHmT 6724 B5
10 NRCH 6396 C3
10 OrgT 6164 B1
10 RYE 6169 E7
10 RYE 6283 E1
10 SNPT 6508 C5
10 STNL 7020 E5
10 TFLY 6392 C2
10 TnkT 6502 C1
10 YNKR 6280 B7
300 FLHL 6617 E5
400 PLDM 6617 E5
Dogwood Rd
10 KNGP 6617 A4
10 NHmT 6724 C2
100 VLYS 6928 C2
Dogwood St
10 JSYC 6819 B5
Doherty Av
10 HmpT 6827 D5
Doherty Pl
10 MrnT 6396 C4
Dohrmann Av
10 TnkT 6502 A2
Dole St
10 STNL 7207 D1
Dolma Rd
10 SCDL 6167 E7
10 SCDL 6168 A6
Dolores Dr
10 HmpT 6928 C5
10 VLYS 6928 C5
Dolores Pl
10 MLVN 6929 A1
Dolphin Dr
100 HWTN 7028 D2
100 WDBG 7028 D2
Dolphin Grn
10 NHmT 6617 D2
Dolphin St
10 NWRK 6818 C6
Dolson Pl
10 STNL 7018 E1
Domain St
10 STNL 7019 A3
Dominick St
10 MHTN 118 C3
10 MHTN 6821 A1
Don Ct
10 STNL 7116 D3
Don Ln
10 GrbT 6048 E7
Donahue Av
100 HmpT 7027 D2
Donald Av
500 PTHA 7205 C2
Donald Ct
10 HmpT 6827 B7
10 YNKR 6280 D4
Donald Dr
10 GrbT 6280 B1
10 HAOH 6280 B1
10 NRCH 6282 A4
Donald Ln
500 HmpT 6928 B6
Donald Pl
10 ELIZ 6917 C2
10 ERKY 6929 C6
10 STNL 6920 A7
10 UnnT 6917 C2
900 HmpT 6928 E1
Donald St
10 EHLS 6618 E7
10 NHmT 6618 E7
Donaldson Av
10 RTFD 6609 A2
Donaldson Pl
10 LNDN 7017 A2
10 NHmT 6618 D7
Don Bosco Pl
10 PTCH 6170 C6
Doncaster Pl
82-00 QENS 6825 E2
Doncaster Rd
10 MLVN 6929 B1
Donellan Rd
10 SCDL 6167 D5
Dongan Av
10 STNL 7019 E3
81-00 QENS 6719 E7
Dongan Pl
10 MHTN 101 D7
10 MHTN 6503 E4
Dongan St
10 STNL 6919 D7
100 STNL 7019 D1
Dongan Hills Av
100 STNL 7020 C7
300 STNL 7118 C1
Donizetti Pl
100 BRNX 6505 E2
Donley Av
10 STNL 7020 D4
Donlon Av
700 HmpT 6828 D7
Donmoor Rd
300 LWRN 7028 A3
Donna Ct
10 STNL 7116 E1
100 LNBK 6929 A5
Donnybrook Dr
10 DMRT 6278 A4
Donnybrook Pl
10 YNKR 6280 D3
Donnybrook Rd
10 NRCH 6281 E2
Donovan Av
10 CART 7115 B1
Donovan St
600 HmpT 6827 E7
Dooley St
10 BKLN 7023 C7
Doone Ct
10 BKLN 7023 B6
Dora Ln
10 NRCH 6281 D3
Dora St
10 STNL 7019 C3
Dorado Ct
500 NHLS 6724 A3
Dorado Dr
10 HRSN 6050 E7
Dorain Pl
10 TFLY 6392 B2
Doral Ct
100 NHLS 6724 B3
Doral Dr
10 NHLS 6724 B2
Doral Green Dr
- RYEB 6051 E7
Doral Green Dr E
10 RYEB 6051 E6
Doral Greens Dr W
10 RYEB 6051 E7
Doran Av
10 GrwT 6170 D5
83-00 QENS 6824 B4
Doran Rd
10 HRSN 6051 B7
Dorato Pl
100 NVLE 6164 C6
Dorchester Av
10 HAOH 6166 B7
Dorchester Dr
10 GrbT 6167 A7
10 NHmT 6618 B6
10 RYEB 6169 E1
10 RYEB 6170 A1
10 YNKR 6280 D3
Dorchester Rd
10 EchT 6281 B6
10 EGLC 6503 B1
10 EGLD 6503 B1
10 HRSN 6169 B6
10 NRCH 6281 E1
10 RKVC 6929 E2
100 HmpT 6828 C4
100 NRCH 6282 A1
1000 BKLN 6923 A7
Dorchester Rd S
200 HmpT 6828 D3
Dore Ct
10 STNL 7019 D2
Doreen Dr
10 STNL 7019 A2
Doreen Pl
10 HRSN 6283 C3
Doremus Av
10 NWRK 6818 D4
Doremus Pl
1300 HlsT 6816 D6
Dorer Av
200 HlsT 6816 D5
Dorian Ct
8-00 QENS 7027 D5
Dorigo Ln
10 SECS 6716 B1
Dorin Ct Rd
200 FTLE 6611 D1
Doris Av
10 HmpT 6828 A5
Doris Dr
10 GrbT 6167 B7
Doris Ln
10 MrnT 6282 D3
10 TYTN 6048 C3
Doris Pl
10 MLVN 6929 C2
Doris Rd
10 MrnT 6282 C3
Doris St
1400 BRNX 6614 C1
Dorit Ct
10 STNL 7117 A3
Dormans Ct
87-00 QENS 7026 B6
Dormans Rd
186-00 QENS 6826 B6
Dorothea Ln
600 HmpT 6827 D7
Dorothea Pl
10 BRNX 6504 D4
10 STNL 7117 D2
Dorothy Av
600 PTHA 7205 C1
Dorothy Pl
10 HmpT 6928 E5
10 LNBK 6928 E5
29-00 QENS 6719 A2
Dorothy St
10 CART 7017 B6
10 STNL 7019 C5
10 WbgT 7114 B5
Dorset Av
10 NHmT 6724 E3
Dorset Dr
1300 GrbT 6048 E4
Dorset Rd
10 NHmT 6723 A2
10 YNKR 6281 A1
Dorset St
10 BKLN 6924 A6
Dorset Wy
10 IRVN 6166 A1
Dorsey Ct
10 GLCV 6509 D3
Dorsey St
300 PTHA 7205 B3
2400 BRNX 6505 C7
Dorval Av
10 STNL 7116 D4
Dorval Pl
10 STNL 7116 D4
Doscher St
10 BKLN 6925 A2
Dottino Ln
10 FRVW 6611 C4
10 NBgT 6611 B4
Doty Av
10 STNL 7021 A6
Doubleday Cir
200 BKLN 6922 D3
Doughty Av
700 HmpT 6828 B7
Doughty Blvd
10 HmpT 7027 D2
10 LWRN 7027 D4
Doughty St
10 BKLN 121 A3
10 BKLN 6821 C5
Douglas Av
10 STNL 7020 A2
10 YNKR 6279 E5
168-00 QENS 6825 E5
3100 BRNX 102 B1
3100 BRNX 6504 A1
4400 BRNX 6393 A7
Douglas Cir
10 RYE 6283 C5
Douglas Ct
10 STNL 7020 C4
Douglas Dr
10 CRSK 6278 A6
10 GrwT 6170 C1
Douglas Ln
10 LRMT 6396 D2
Douglas Pl
10 EchT 6281 B5
10 MTVN 6394 E2
200 MTVN 6395 A1
Douglas Rd
10 STNL 7020 C4
32-00 QENS 6722 D2
Douglas St
10 HmpT 7027 D2
10 WbgT 7205 A2
400 EGLD 6392 B6
Douglas Rd Ext
- STNL 7020 B4
Douglass St
10 BKLN 6922 D1
Douglaston Pkwy
45-00 QENS 6722 D4
Dove Hill Dr
10 NHLS 6618 B7
Dover Av
10 GDNC 6724 D7
Dover Grn
10 STNL 7116 B4
Dover Ln
- UnnT 6917 A1
10 YNKR 6280 A4
Dover Pkwy
10 STMN 6828 A2
200 HmpT 6828 A3
Dover Pkwy N
10 STMN 6828 B2
Dover Pl
10 GDNC 6828 E4
10 HMPD 6828 E4
10 HmpT 6828 E4
Dover Rd
10 NHmT 6618 B7
10 WbgT 7114 A1
500 HmpT 6929 D6
Dover St
10 BKLN 7121 C1
10 MHTN 120 D1
10 MHTN 6821 C5
10 NWRK 6712 C6
1300 HmpT 6827 E4
E Dover St
10 VLYS 6928 E2
200 MLVN 6929 A3
200 VLYS 6929 A3
W Dover St
10 VLYS 6928 D2
Dow Pl
500 EGLD 6502 D2
Dow St
10 BlvT 6714 A1
Dowd Av
100 ELIZ 6918 C3
Downer Av
10 EchT 6281 B2
Downes Av
10 STNL 7116 C7
Downey Dr
10 TFLY 6392 A4
Downey Pl
10 STNL 7018 E1
Downing Av
10 SCLF 6509 D7
Downing Ct
10 IRVN 6166 A2
Downing Dr E
10 GrbT 6049 D6
10 GrbT 6167 C1
Downing Dr S
10 GrbT 6167 C1
Downing Dr W
10 GrbT 6049 C7
10 GrbT 6167 C1
Downing Rd
800 HmpT 6827 D6
800 HmpT 6928 E1
Downing St
10 BKLN 6822 B7
10 BKLN 6923 B1
10 MHTN 118 D2
10 MHTN 6821 B1
10 NWRK 6818 A1
10 YNKR 6393 C2
31-00 QENS 6720 E3
100 WbgT 7114 B4
Downing Ridge Rd
10 IRVN 6166 B1
Dows Ln
10 IRVN 6166 A1
Doxsey Pl
10 LNBK 6929 B5
10 QENS 6925 D2
Doyer Av
10 WHPL 6168 B3
Doyers St
10 MHTN 118 E6
10 MHTN 6821 E4
Doyle St
10 LBCH 7029 E6
300 ELIZ 6918 A5
Drahos Av
800 PTHA 7114 C7
Drake Av
10 NRCH 6395 E6
10 RYE 6283 C4
10 STNL 7019 E3
100 ROSL 6917 A4
1100 LNDN 6917 B5
Drake Ln
10 FLHL 6617 E4
10 FLHL 6618 A4
10 GrbT 6048 E7
Drake Pk S
1300 BRNX 6613 E4
Drake Pl
10 YNKR 6280 B4
Drake Rd
10 NRCH 6281 E1
10 SCDL 6167 D7
10 SCDL 6281 D1
Drake St
10 MLVN 6929 A2
10 MTVN 6395 A3
10 VLYS 6929 A2
400 BRNX 6613 E4
Drakes Ln
10 IrvT 6816 C1
Drake Smith Ln
10 RYE 6284 B2
Draper Ln
100 DBSF 6165 E4
100 DBSF 6166 A3
Draper Pl
10 STNL 7018 E6
Dreier Ln
10 WHPL 6169 A4
Dreiser Lp
100 BRNX 6505 E2
Dresden Pl
10 STNL 7020 A5
Dress Ln
- LODI 6500 B2
Drew Av
1100 HmpT 6828 A4
1300 HmpT 6827 E4
Drew Ct
10 STNL 7206 C3
Drew St
10 PTCH 6170 A6
10 QENS 6925 B1
10 VLYS 6928 D5
600 BKLN 6925 B3
Drew Wy
10 WbgT 7114 A2
Drewry Ln
10 OrgT 6164 B1
Dreyer Av
10 STNL 7019 B4
Driftway
10 GrwT 6170 C6
Driftwood Dr
10 PTWN 6508 C6
Driggs Av
10 BKLN 6822 A4
Driggs St
10 STNL 7117 B6
Driprock St
10 STNL 7019 D1
Driscoll Av
10 RKVC 6929 E5
Drisler Av
10 GrbT 6166 E1
100 GrbT 6048 D7
Driving Pk
10 HmpT 6929 C3
10 LNBK 6929 C3
Dr Martin L King Jr Blvd
10 MHTN 110 A1
10 MHTN 6612 B4
200 MHTN 109 E1
400 MHTN 106 C6
Dr Martin Luther King Jr Blvd
10 NWRK 6713 D7
500 NWRK 6817 C2
Dromore Rd
10 GrbT 6167 B5
Droyers Point Blvd
10 JSYC 6819 A4
Drum Av
10 STNL 7021 A5
S Drum St
10 STNL 7206 E1
Drumgoole Rd E
100 STNL 7116 C6
1200 STNL 7207 A1
1600 STNL 7206 E1
Drumgoole Rd W
10 STNL 7116 B7
1700 STNL 7207 A1
1800 STNL 7206 E1
Drury Av
10 STNL 7021 A6
Drury Dr
10 MRNK 6282 E4
Drury Ln
10 DMRT 6278 A5
10 FTLE 6502 D7
10 GTNK 6617 A5
10 NHmT 6617 E3
Dryden Ct
10 STNL 7019 C1
Dry Harbor Rd
61-00 QENS 6824 A2
Drysdale St
10 STNL 7019 C5
Duane Ct
10 STNL 6920 C7
Duane Ln
10 DMRT 6278 C5
Duane Rd
- QENS 6615 E7
10 QENS 6616 A7
Duane St
10 MHTN 118 C6
10 MHTN 6821 B3
100 COrT 6712 D2
Dublin Pl
10 STNL 7019 A1
Du Bois Av
10 ALPN 6278 E6
Dubois Av
10 SCLF 6509 E6
10 STNL 7019 D1
100 MRNK 6283 A6
200 VLYS 6928 D5
600 HmpT 6928 C5
Dubois Ct
10 SCLF 6509 E5
Dubois St
10 ERTH 6609 B2
Dubonnet Rd
10 VLYS 6928 D6
Duck Pond Dr
10 NHLS 6618 B7
Duck Pond Rd
10 ALPN 6278 D7
10 DMRT 6278 D7
10 SCDL 6167 D7
Dudley Av
10 STNL 7020 B3
2800 BRNX 6505 E7
Dudley Ln
10 MrnT 6282 C5
Dudley Pl
10 YNKR 6279 D6
Dudley St
10 HAOH 6165 E7
10 JSYC 6820 C4
10 YNKR 6279 E2
Duell Rd
10 GrbT 6049 E7
10 GrbT 6050 A7
Duer Av
10 STNL 7021 A5
Duer Ln
10 STNL 7020 C1
Duer Pl
10 WhkT 111 A4
10 WhkT 6716 E3
10 WhkT 6717 A2
Duffe Pl
10 VLYS 6928 C4
Duffield Av
10 JSYC 6715 E7
Duffield St
- BKLN 121 C5
- BKLN 6821 D6
Duffy St
10 CART 7017 C7
Dugan Ln
10 YNKR 6280 E1
Dugdale St
10 STNL 7117 E4
Duke Dr
10 NHmT 6724 A4
600 WbgT 7114 D2
Duke Pl
10 STNL 7019 D5
Duke of Gloucester
10 NHLS 6617 E7
10 NHmT 6617 E7
Dukes St
10 HRSN 6714 A5
10 KRNY 6714 A5
Dulancey Ct
10 STNL 6920 E7
Duluth Pl
10 EchT 6281 B6
Dumfries Pl
80-00 QENS 6825 E2
Dumont Av
10 STNL 7020 B5
83-00 QENS 6925 C2
400 BKLN 6924 D3
1100 BKLN 6925 A3
Dumont Pl
700 HmpT 6928 A5
Dunbar St
10 STNL 7117 B4
10 YNKR 6280 B5
14-00 QENS 7027 B4
Duncan Av
10 JSYC 6819 C1
10 LNBK 6929 B3
Duncan Ct
10 JSYC 6819 E2
Duncan Rd
10 STNL 7020 C2
1200 FTLE 6502 E7
1200 FTLE 6611 E3
Duncan St
10 STNL 7020 B5
900 BRNX 6505 B3
Duncomb Av
3400 BRNX 6505 A2
Dundee Rd
10 MrnT 6282 C6
Dunderave Rd
10 GrbT 6049 E6
10 GrbT 6050 A6
Dune Ct
10 BRNX 6614 C4
Dune Rd
10 HWTH 7029 A1
Dune St
10 QENS 7027 C6
Dunes Ln
10 MHVN 6508 B6
10 SNPT 6508 B6
Dunham Av
400 MTVN 6395 A5
Dunham Pl
10 BKLN 6822 A5
10 IRVN 6166 C1
100 WbgT 7114 C4
Dunham Rd
10 GrbT 6167 A3
10 SCDL 6281 E1
Dunham St
10 STNL 7206 E2
Dunhill Ln
10 STNL 7115 D6
Dunhill Rd
10 NHmT 6724 B5
Dunkirk Dr
187-00 QENS 6826 B6
Dunkirk St
104-00 QENS 6826 A5
Dunlap Wy
10 NoCT 6050 B5
Dunlin Plz
400 SECS 6609 D7
Dunlop Av
183-00 QENS 6826 A5
Dunlop Dr
10 WbgT 7114 E5
Dunn Av
10 BGTA 6501 E3
Dunne Ct
10 BKLN 7023 B7
Dunne Pl
10 ERKY 6929 A6
10 LNBK 6929 A6
Dunnings Dr
- GrbT 6048 E4
Dunster Ct
400 HmpT 6828 C6
Dunster Dr
400 HmpT 6828 C6
Dunster Rd
10 RSLG 6723 B1
10 THSN 6723 B1
Dunster St
10 CART 7115 B1
Dunston Av
10 YNKR 6280 B7
10 YNKR 6394 A1
Dunton Av
194-00 QENS 6826 B3
Dunton St
86-00 QENS 6826 B2
Dunwood Rd
10 MHVN 6508 C6
Dunwoodie St
10 EchT 6281 C2
10 YNKR 6394 A2
Dupont Av
10 WHPL 6168 C5
Dupont Pl
10 IrvT 6816 C4
Dupont St
10 BKLN 117 D7
10 BKLN 6718 B7
500 BRNX 6613 D4
Duquesne Ter
500 UnnT 6917 A1
Durand Pl
10 IrvT 6816 B2
10 MNPK 6618 A5
S Durand Pl
10 IrvT 6816 B3
Durand St
10 NRCH 6395 E2
Durant Av
10 STNL 7117 C5
Durant Ln
10 CLST 6278 B2
Durant St
1200 ELIZ 6918 A1
1300 ELIZ 6917 E1
Durbyan St
10 NHmT 6508 D6
10 PTWN 6508 D6
Durges St
10 STNL 7020 C5
Durham Av
4300 NBgT 6716 D1
6100 NBgT 6610 E6
8900 NBgT 6611 B4
9100 FRVW 6611 B4
Durham Rd
10 GrbT 6049 A7
10 HmpT 6928 C6
10 MrnT 6282 C5
10 NHmT 6723 E5
10 NHmT 6724 A5
10 WHPL 6168 D6
10 YNKR 6280 D7
Durie Av
10 EGLD 6392 A5
200 CLST 6278 A3
Durie Av CO-41
200 CLST 6278 A3
Durland Pl
10 BKLN 6924 B6
Durland Rd
10 ERKY 6929 A6
10 HmpT 6929 A6
10 LNBK 6929 A6
Durling Rd
400 ELIZ 6917 B2
400 UnnT 6917 B2
Durst Pl
10 YNKR 6394 A2
Duryea Av
10 BRNX 6394 E7
10 MTVN 6394 E7
Duryea Ct
6600 BKLN 7022 C2
Duryea Pl
10 BKLN 6923 B6
10 LNBK 6929 A5
Duryea St
10 NWRK 6713 C6
Duryea Ter
400 HmpT 6828 D6
Dusenberry Rd
10 BRXV 6281 A7
10 EchT 6281 B7
Dusenbury Pl
10 WHPL 6168 C2
Dusk Dr
10 NRCH 6281 E6
Dustan St
10 STNL 7118 B3
Duston Rd
1000 HmpT 6928 B6
Dutch St
10 MHTN 120 C1
10 MHTN 6821 B6
Dutch Broadway
- QENS 6827 B6
10 HmpT 6827 C7
1100 HmpT 6828 A7
N Dutcher St
10 IRVN 6048 A7
S Dutcher St
10 IRVN 6166 C1
Dutchess Av
10 STNL 7020 B6
Dutchess Blvd
10 ATLB 7028 A7
Dutchess Ln
800 WbgT 7114 D2
Dutch Kills St
43-00 QENS 6718 D6
Duxbury Rd
10 GTNK 6617 B5
10 HRSN 6168 D1
10 KNGP 6617 B5
Dwarf St
10 STNL 7018 E2
Dwars Kill Ln
10 NRWD 6278 D2
Dwight Av
29-00 QENS 7027 B5
Dwight Ln
10 GTNK 6616 C4
10 KNGP 6616 C5
Dwight Pl
10 EGLD 6392 B7
10 EGLD 6502 E1
300 RDGF 6611 B2
1400 BRNX 6506 B7
S Dwight Pl
100 EGLD 6502 E1
Dwight St
10 BKLN 6922 B2
10 JSYC 6819 D5
Dwight Ter
600 UnnT 6917 C1
Dyckman Av
10 NHmT 6724 C7
Dyckman St
- GrbT 6167 E2
10 MHTN 104 E1
10 MHTN 105 A1
10 MHTN 6503 E3
10 MHTN 6504 A4
100 MHTN 101 D5
Dyer Av
- MHTN 115 E2
- MHTN 116 A1
- MHTN 6717 C5
10 SHKT 6501 C3
Dyer Av SR-495
- MHTN 115 E2
- MHTN 6717 C5
Dyer Ct
10 NRWD 6278 C1
Dyker Pl
8200 BKLN 7021 E2
Dyre Av
3600 BRNX 6505 E1
3700 BRNX 6394 E7
4000 MTVN 6394 E7
Dyson St
10 STNL 7020 D1

E

E St
1300 HmpT 6827 E6
Eadie Pl
10 STNL 6920 C6
Eagan Av
10 STNL 7116 D6
Eagle Av
- HmpT 6929 E1
- RKVC 6929 E1
200 HmpT 6828 D7
200 PTHA 7205 D2
500 BRNX 6613 B3
1300 HmpT 6827 E4
Eagle Ct
10 WHPL 6169 A5
Eagle Dr
700 HmpT 6928 A6
Eagle Ln
10 OrgT 6164 A2
Eagle Rd
10 STNL 7019 B3
Eagle St
10 BKLN 6822 B1
10 NWRK 6713 D6
100 BKLN 117 E7
100 BKLN 6718 C7
Eagle Crest
10 RTFD 6609 B3
100 NHmT 6618 B2
Eagle Knolls Rd
500 MRNK 6396 D1
500 MrnT 6396 D1
Eagle Point Dr
10 KNGP 6616 D1
Eagles Blf
10 RYEB 6170 A2
Eagles Cres
100 NHLS 6618 B7
Eagles Notch Dr
10 EGLD 6502 E3
Eakins Rd
10 MNPK 6617 E5
200 FLHL 6617 E5
Eames Pl
100 BRNX 102 E6
100 BRNX 6504 D2
Earhart Dr
- ELIZ 6817 C7
- ELIZ 6918 C1
- NWRK 6817 C7
Earhart Ln
10 BRNX 6506 A4
Earl St
10 FLPK 6827 D2
10 NWRK 6817 C3
100 WbgT 7114 C5
1600 UnnT 6816 A5
Earle Av
10 ERKY 6929 C5
10 LNBK 6929 B4
Earle Pl
10 MNPK 6618 B6
10 NRCH 6396 A2
Earley Av
10 STNL 7019 C3
Earley Pl
- STNL 7206 A4
Earley St
10 BRNX 6506 E7
Earlwoode Dr
10 SCDL 6168 A5
10 WHPL 6168 A5
Earlybird Rd
300 MHTN 120 A6
300 MHTN 6820 E7
300 MHTN 6821 A7
East Av
10 HmpT 6927 E7
10 LRMT 6396 C1
10 VLYS 6928 C2
300 PTHA 7205 D3
300 WbgT 7114 E5
400 NVLE 6164 B3
400 OrgT 6164 B3
400 WbgT 7115 A5
1400 BRNX 6505 B7
1400 BRNX 6614 B1
N East Av
10 WbgT 7114 D3
East Blvd
10 HmpT 6929 B7
10 HmpT 7029 B1
East Ct
10 BAYN 6919 E2
10 GrbT 6166 C7
10 NHmT 6724 E1
East Dr
- NRCH 6396 C4
10 GTPZ 6617 A6
10 KENS 6617 A6
10 MrnT 6282 B6
10 NHmT 6617 D7
10 PLDM 6617 D4
27-00 QENS 6722 D1
East Ln
10 NHmT 6724 A4
East Pl
10 LODI 6500 D2
10 NRCH 6396 A2
East Rd
- HRSN 6051 D5
- MHTN 114 B5
- MHTN 117 D2
- MHTN 6718 B5
- MHTN 6719 A4
10 GTNK 6617 A4
10 KNGP 6617 A4
10 SNPT 6509 A6
East Row
10 LODI 6500 D2
East St
10 JSYC 6820 A1
10 NHmT 6724 C4
East Wy
- GrbT 6166 C6
Eastburn Av
1600 BRNX 105 D6
1600 BRNX 6504 B7
Eastchester Ln
10 BRNX 6394 D5
10 MTVN 6394 D5
Eastchester Pl
2500 BRNX 6506 A1
Eastchester Rd
10 NRCH 6395 C2
300 PLHM 6395 C2
1600 BRNX 6505 D4
Eastdale Rd
10 WHPL 6168 D3
East End
900 HmpT 6928 B6
Eastentry Rd
10 STNL 7020 B7
Eastern Av
- YNKR 6393 D3
Eastern Dr
10 ARDY 6166 D5
10 NHmT 6724 B6
Eastern Pkwy
10 BKLN 6923 D3
10 HlsT 6816 A5
10 IrvT 6712 E7
10 JSYC 6819 C5
10 NWRK 6712 E7
100 NWRK 6816 B1
200 IrvT 6816 D2
300 MplT 6816 B1
1300 BKLN 6924 A3
Eastern Rd
- QENS 6927 B5
10 GrbT 6166 E2
Eastern Wy
10 RTFD 6609 B3
800 CARL 6610 B1
800 MNCH 6610 B1
Eastern Crest Rd
10 NHmT 6508 E7
10 SNPT 6508 E7
Eastern Loop Rd
10 STNL 7020 B7
Eastern Parkway Ext
2000 BKLN 6924 C1
Eastfield Rd
10 MTVN 6395 A2
East Gate
10 LFRY 6501 C5
Eastgate
10 MNPK 6618 A6
10 NHmT 6618 A6
Eastgate Plz
137-00 QENS 6927 C1
Easthaven Ln
10 WHPL 6168 E7
Eastland Av
200 PLHM 6395 C5
Eastlawn Ct
1000 TnkT 6502 C1
Eastlawn Dr
700 TnkT 6502 B1
Eastman Pl
10 YNKR 6280 A6
Eastman St
10 STNL 7116 E7
Easton Av
10 WHPL 6168 D5
Eastview Av
10 LEON 6502 D3
10 WHPL 6168 C1
10 YNKR 6279 E5
Eastview Ter
10 DMRT 6278 B4
Eastward Pl
10 GrbT 6049 B4
Eastway
10 BRXV 6395 B1
10 EchT 6395 B1
10 GrbT 6166 E3
Eastwind Rd
10 YNKR 6280 D2
Eastwood Av
- QENS 6823 E4
10 STNL 7206 C3
Eastwood Ct
300 EGLD 6392 B7
Eastwood Ln
10 HmpT 6928 B4
Eastwood Rd
300 HmpT 6928 C7
Eastwood St
10 EORG 6712 E2
Eastwoods Ln
10 SCDL 6281 D2
Easy St
8700 NBgT 6611 A4
Eaton Ct
10 BKLN 7024 A7
10 NHLS 6724 B1
100 BKLN 7023 E5
Eaton Ln
10 GrbT 6166 E7
Eaton Pl
10 EORG 6713 A4
10 NWRK 6713 B4
10 STNL 6919 B7
Eaton St
700 ELIZ 6917 C4
Ebbitts St
10 STNL 7118 A3
Eberhard Ln
10 GRFD 6500 B1
Eberhardt Pl
10 IrvT 6712 D7
Eberman Rd
- STNL 7019 E7
- STNL 7117 E1
Ebey Ln
10 STNL 7116 B5
Ebony Ct
10 BKLN 7023 E6
Ebony St
10 STNL 7117 D2
Echo Av
10 NRCH 6396 A4
Echo Hl
10 DBSF 6166 B5
Echo Ln
10 EchT 6281 C3
10 MrnT 6282 B7
10 MrnT 6396 D2

New York City/5 Borough Street Index

Echo Pl — S End Dr

STREET / Block	City	Map#	Grid

Echo Pl
10 STNL 7019 B3
200 BRNX 105 E4
200 BRNX 6504 B6
Echo Bay Dr
10 NRCH 6396 B5
Echo Bay Pl
10 NRCH 6396 B5
Eck Pl
10 NRCH 6396 A1
N Eckar St
10 IRVN 6048 A7
10 IRVN 6166 C1
S Eckar St
10 IRVN 6166 C1
Eckel Rd
10 LFRY 6501 C7
Eckerson Av
10 CLST 6278 A3
Eckert Av
10 NWRK 6816 E3
10 NWRK 6817 A3
Eckford Av
97-00 QENS 6925 E2
Eckford St
10 STNL 6822 C2
Eddy Av
1100 LNDN 7017 B2
Eddy St
10 STNL 7020 C2
Eden Ct
10 HmpT 6928 A6
10 STNL 7206 A3
100 DBSF 6050 A1
Eden Wy
10 ROSH 6618 E2
Edens Al
10 MHTN 120 C1
10 MHTN 6821 B6
Edenwald Av
100 BRNX 6394 D7
100 BRNX 6394 D7
Eder Ter
10 MplT 6712 A7
10 SOrT 6712 A7
Edgar Pl
10 PTCH 6170 B7
10 STNL 7020 C4
200 ELIZ 6917 D3
Edgar Rd
400 ELIZ 6917 D5
700 LNDN 6917 D5
E Edgar Rd
10 LNDN 7017 B1
700 LNDN 6917 C7
2500 ELIZ 6917 D5
E Edgar Rd US-1
10 LNDN 7017 B1
700 LNDN 6917 C7
2500 ELIZ 6917 D5
E Edgar Rd US-9
10 LNDN 7017 B1
700 LNDN 6917 C7
2500 ELIZ 6917 D5
W Edgar Rd
10 LNDN 7017 A3
W Edgar Rd US-1
10 LNDN 7017 A3
W Edgar Rd US-9
10 LNDN 7017 A3
Edgar St
10 CLST 6278 B2
10 CART 6017 D7
10 CART 7115 D1
10 EORG 6712 D5
10 MHTN 120 A1
10 WbgT 7114 B4
100 WhkT 6716 E4
Edgar Ter
10 STNL 6920 D7
Edgar G Holmes Jr Ovl
- QENS 6721 E6
Edgars Ln
10 HAOH 6165 E4
100 DBSF 6165 E4
Edgarton Blvd
10 WbgT 7114 D1
Edge St
10 BRNX 6615 B3
Edgecliff Ter
10 YNKR 6393 D3
Edgecomb Pl
10 YNKR 6280 D7
Edgecombe Av
10 MHTN 106 D4
10 MHTN 107 A6
10 MHTN 6612 D2
600 MHTN 104 C6
600 MHTN 6503 D7
Edgegrove Av
10 STNL 7116 C6
Edgehill Av
10 WOrT 6712 C1
3000 BRNX 102 C2
3000 BRNX 6504 B1
Edgehill Cir
10 WOrT 6712 C1
Edgehill Clse
10 BRXV 6281 A7
Edgemere Av
32-01 QENS 7027 A6
50-00 QENS 7026 E7
Edgemere Dr
10 NHLS 6724 C2
10 NHmT 6724 C2
Edgemere Rd
10 GDNC 6828 D2
10 HmpT 6828 B3
Edgemere St
10 BRNX 6506 C6
10 PLMM 6395 D7
10 PLMM 6506 C1
Edgemont Cir
10 GrbT 6167 B5
Edgemont Pl
10 MHTN 107 B6
10 MrnT 6282 B6
10 NRCH 6282 A6
10 YNKR 6281 B1
Edgemont Rd
10 GrbT 6167 B2
10 MrnT 6282 A6
10 NRCH 6282 A6
10 YNKR 6281 B1
Edgepark Rd
10 GrbT 6050 A5

Edgerton Blvd
83-00 QENS 6825 E3
Edgerton Rd
177-00 QENS 6825 E2
Edgerton Ter
10 EORG 6713 A2
Edgewater Av
500 CLFP 6611 C2
500 FRVW 6611 C2
500 RDGF 6611 B1
1100 RDFP 6502 A7
1100 RDGF 6502 A7
Edgewater Av CO-50
500 CLFP 6611 C2
500 FRVW 6611 C2
500 RDGF 6611 B1
1100 RDFP 6502 A7
1100 RDGF 6502 A7
Edgewater Av W
1100 RDGF 6611 A1
1100 RDGF 6502 A1
Edgewater Ln
10 SDRK 6616 C7
Edgewater Pl
10 EDGW 6611 E2
10 MrnT 6396 C4
Edgewater Rd
10 EDGW 6611 D3
10 CLFP 6611 C2
200 FRVW 6611 C2
400 RDGF 6611 C2
700 BRNX 6613 E3
Edgewater Rd CO-50
100 CLFP 6611 C2
200 FRVW 6611 C2
400 RDGF 6611 C2
Edgewater St
10 STNL 7020 E3
100 STNL 7021 A3
Edgewater Towne Ctr
10 EDGW 6611 E2
Edgewold Rd
10 GrbT 6049 A7
Edgewood Av
10 GrwT 6170 E3
10 HAOH 6166 A4
Edgewood Ct
10 CRSK 6278 A5
10 DMRT 6278 A5
Edgewood Dr
10 EORG 6170 E2
10 NHmT 6724 C6
10 OrgT 6164 E1
10 WbgT 7114 A3
Edgewood Ln
10 BRXV 6281 A7
10 HRSN 6169 D2
700 CLFP 6611 D1
10 FTLE 6611 B1
1000 FTLE 6502 D6
Edgewood Pk
10 NRCH 6395 D4
Edgewood Pkwy
10 UnnT 6917 A2
1000 ELIZ 6917 A2
Edgewood Pl
10 GrwT 6170 E2
10 GTNE 6616 D5
- FTLE 6502 E3
10 EORG 6712 C1
10 GrbT 6167 A3
10 HmpT 6929 B3
10 HRPK 6278 A1
10 MHVN 6168 A5
10 RKVC 6929 D3
10 SCDL 6168 A5
10 STNL 7117 B6
10 VLYS 6928 D2
500 LEON 6502 E3
900 FTLE 6502 E4
Edgewood St
10 TFLY 6392 B4
10 WHPL 6168 D7
146-00 QENS 6927 E4
Edgeworth St
10 HmpT 6928 B5
10 VLYS 6928 D6
Edinboro Rd
10 STNL 7117 C1
Edison Av
10 BRNX 6395 A7
10 HAOH 6166 A4
10 MTVN 6395 A7
10 YNKR 6306 C5
500 BRNX 6615 A1
1000 BRNX 6505 E3
1200 BRNX 6505 D3
Edison Pl
10 ERTH 6609 B1
10 NWRK 6817 A4
10 PTCH 6170 C5
Edison St
10 BlmT 6713 C2
10 BlvT 6713 C2
10 RDFP 6501 E6
500 RDGF 6611 B1
Edisonia Ter
10 WOrT 6712 C1
Edith Av
10 STNL 7207 C2
Edith Pl
300 STNL 7207 D2
Edith St
10 HmpT 6929 B3
10 LNBK 6929 B3
Ediths Wy
10 STNL 6280 B7
Edlu Ct
800 HmpT 7029 D1
Edmarth Pl
10 EGLC 6392 E6
Edmonds Pl
10 NWRK 6816 D4
Edmore Av
221-00 QENS 6826 D2
222-00 QENS 6827 A2

Edmund Pl
10 IrvT 6816 B2
Edmund St
10 LNBK 6929 C3
Edna Ct
10 VLYS 6928 B2
Edna Pl
10 NRCH 6281 D7
10 SECS 6610 C6
500 VLYS 6928 B2
Edna St
10 WHPL 6167 E2
N Edo Ct
10 STNL 7115 E5
S Edo Ct
10 STNL 7115 E6
Edsall Av
71-00 QENS 6823 E5
74-00 QENS 6824 A5
2200 BRNX 102 A3
2200 BRNX 6504 A2
E Edsall Av
10 PALP 6502 C7
W Edsall Av
10 PALP 6502 B6
Edsall Blvd
400 FTLE 6502 E6
- FTLE 6502 D6
10 PALP 6502 D7
W Edsall Blvd
10 PALP 6502 C5
Edson Av
2300 BRNX 6505 E3
4000 BRNX 6394 D6
Edstan Dr
10 MNCH 6501 B7
Edstone Dr
10 STNL 7020 B2
Edward Av
10 GrbT 6049 A7
10 HmpT 7028 B1
500 HmpT 6928 A1
Edward Ct
10 LODI 6500 E2
10 STNL 7019 A7
10 TFLY 6392 B2
100 STNL 6828 C5
Edward Pl
10 PTHA 7114 B7
10 WbgT 7114 B7
400 MRNK 6283 A5
Edward St
10 DMRT 6278 B6
10 HRSN 6050 C7
10 OrgT 6164 E1
10 WbgT 7114 A3
1000 LNDN 7017 A4
4200 NBgT 6716 D1
E Edward St
10 WbgT 7114 A3
Edward Ter
10 STNL 6828 C6
Edward Bentley Rd
10 LWRN 7028 A6
Edward Curry Av
10 STNL 7018 D4
Edward Hart Dr
10 JSYC 6820 A6
Edward L Grant Hwy
1200 BRNX 105 A6
1200 BRNX 6504 A7
1200 BRNX 6613 A1
Edward M Morgan Pl
10 MHTN 107 A1
10 MHTN 6612 C1
Edwards Av
1300 BRNX 6505 E2
1300 BRNX 6614 D2
Edwards Blvd
10 LBCH 7029 C7
800 HmpT 6827 D7
800 HmpT 6928 D1
Edwards Ct
10 BAYN 6919 D4
Edwards Pl
10 VLYS 6928 B2
200 YNKR 6279 E6
Edwards St
10 NHmT 6618 D6
10 RSLN 6618 D6
300 RDGF 6611 B2
Edwin Av
2100 FTLE 103 A3
2100 FTLE 6502 E4
2100 FTLE 6503 A4
Edwin Ct
10 NHmT 6508 E6
Edwin Pl
10 NWRK 6816 B3
Edwin St
10 CART 7115 D2
10 RDFP 6501 B4
10 RDFP 6502 B4
10 STNL 7115 C2
Edwin C Weiskopf Pl
- GrbT 6048 D4
Edwin Love St
10 YNKR 6393 D1
Edwin L Ward Sr Memorial Hwy
700 LNBK 6929 B4
700 RTFD 6609 B4
Effingham Av
400 BRNX 6614 D3
Effington Av
172-00 QENS 6721 D7
Effron Pl
10 LKSU 6723 C1
Egan Ct
10 BAYN 6919 D5
Egan Pl
10 WhkT 111 A4
10 WhkT 6717 A2
Egbert Av
10 ATLB 7027 E7
Egbert Pl
10 STNL 7020 A4
10 STNL 7021 A4

Ege Av
10 JSYC 6819 D4
Eger St
3000 BRNX 6615 C4
Eggert Pl
13-00 QENS 7027 C4
Egil Ct
10 ROSH 6618 E2
Egmont Av
200 MTVN 6395 A5
Egmont Pl
10 STNL 6920 D6
14-00 QENS 7027 B4
Egret Ln
400 SECS 6609 D7
Egret Ct
10 STNL 7017 D1
Egrit Ct
10 STNL 7018 C6
Egypt St
2200 ELIZ 6919 A2
Ehler Ct
10 RDFP 6501 E4
Ehrbar Av
10 MTVN 6395 A3
Eider Hill Ct
10 STNL 6618 B7
Eidner Wy
10 NVLE 6164 B5
Eileen Ct
600 HmpT 6828 B6
Eileen St
10 HmpT 6828 B6
Eileen Ter
900 HmpT 6928 B6
Eiler Ln
10 GrbT 6048 D7
Eimer Av
10 MLVN 6929 B2
Eimer St
10 OrgT 6164 D2
Einstein Lp E
60-00 QENS 6823 C4
82-42 QENS 6824 A2
Einstein Lp N
100 BRNX 6506 A4
Einstein Lp S
10 BRNX 6506 A4
Eirik Pl
- BKLN 6922 A2
- BKLN 7022 A1
Eisenhower Dr
10 CRSK 6392 C1
10 YNKR 6281 D4
10 WbgT 7114 B7
Eisenhower Rd
10 CLST 6278 C2
EJ Conroy Dr
49-00 QENS 7027 C4
62-00 QENS 7026 D6
Elaine Ct
10 NWRK 6395 E6
1000 ELIZ 6917 E4
Elaine Dr
10 STNL 7029 E2
Elaine Ter
10 YNKR 6280 B7
Elaine Ter N
1400 HmpT 6816 A4
Elaine Ter S
1300 HmpT 6816 A4
Elba St
10 EchT 6281 D3
Elbe Av
10 STNL 7020 D4
1200 BRNX 105 A6
1200 BRNX 6504 A7
1200 BRNX 6613 A1
Elberson Ct
10 STNL 6816 B6
Elberta Rd
10 MplT 6816 A1
Elbertson St
40-00 QENS 6719 E6
41-00 QENS 6720 A6
El Camino Lp
10 STNL 7115 E7
Elco Ct
10 GrbT 6167 B4
Elder Av
10 BAYN 6919 C4
Elder Pl
10 VLYS 6928 B2
134-00 QENS 6720 E6
137-00 QENS 6721 A5
1000 BRNX 6613 E1
E Elder Av
10 FLPK 6827 C3
W Elder Av
10 FLPK 6827 B3
Elderberry Ln
10 STNL 7115 E7
Elderberry Ln E
10 STNL 6928 B4
Elderberry Rd
100 MNLA 6724 C5
Elderd Ln
10 CDHT 7028 B2
Elderfields Rd
10 STNL 6618 A5
Eldert Ln
10 BKLN 6824 A7
10 BKLN 6824 A7
10 BKLN 6925 B1
100 BKLN 6925 B2
200 QENS 6925 B1
Eldert St
10 LNBK 6929 B3
1500 BKLN 6823 B6
1500 QENS 6823 B6
Elderts Ln
1100 BKLN 6925 B3
Elderwood Av
20-00 QENS 7027 C6
300 PLHM 6395 C5
Eldorado Ct
10 STNL 6050 B4
Eldorado Pl
10 MHTN 111 A4
10 WhkT 6717 A2
Eldredge Ct
10 RYE 6283 D4
Eldredge Pl
10 DBSF 6165 E1
10 RYE 6283 D1

Eldridge Av
10 STNL 7019 D4
10 YNKR 6280 A5
Eldridge St
10 MHTN 119 A5
10 MHTN 6821 D2
10 PTCH 6170 B7
Eleanor Ln
10 STNL 7117 B6
Eleanor Pl
10 STNL 7019 A2
10 WbgT 7114 C4
Eleanor St
10 RYE 6283 C4
10 STNL 7117 D1
Elf Rd
300 WbgT 7114 E5
Elgar Pl
10 BRNX 6506 A4
Elgin Rd
10 VLYS 6928 D5
Elias Av
400 WbgT 7114 B4
Elias Pl
10 STNL 7019 D2
Elicar Ter
10 YNKR 6280 B7
Elie Ct
10 STNL 7018 E7
Elinor Av
400 ELIZ 6917 A3
400 ROSP 6917 A3
Elinor Pl
10 NWRK 6816 B1
Elinor Rd
1100 HBPK 6028 D1
1100 HmpT 7028 D1
Ellery Ct
300 EDGW 108 B1
300 EDGW 6611 E5
Ellery St
2400 BRNX 6506 A7
Eliot Av
60-00 QENS 6823 C4
82-42 QENS 6824 A2
Eliot Ct
10 TnkT 6502 C2
Elisa Dr
300 EGLC 6503 B2
Elise Ct
10 STNL 7117 C3
Elissa Ln
10 OrgT 6164 B1
10 YNKR 6280 D3
Elite Ct
600 RDGF 6611 B2
Elizabeth Av
- HIsT 6816 E5
10 ELIZ 6918 B6
10 KRNY 6714 C1
10 NWRK 6713 C1
10 STNL 6920 A6
N Elliott St
49-00 QENS 6727 B6
62-00 QENS 7026 D6
700 NWRK 6395 E6
1000 ELIZ 6917 E4
E Elizabeth Av
10 LNDN 7017 A1
400 LNDN 6917 B7
E Elizabeth Av CO-514
400 LNDN 7017 A1
1300 HmpT 6827 E5
W Elizabeth Av
10 LNDN 7017 A2
W Elizabeth Av CO-514
3200 HmpT 7029 D1
Elizabeth Ct
10 RTFD 6609 A1
10 WOrT 6712 A3
Elizabeth Rd
10 NRCH 6281 D7
Elizabeth St
10 FLPK 6827 D2
10 GLCV 6509 E3
10 GrbT 6167 B4
10 HKSK 6501 B2
10 HmpT 6827 B7
100 MHTN 118 E5
100 MHTN 119 C7
200 HmpT 7027 D3
200 CorT 6712 E2
300 FTLE 6502 E5
300 PTHA 7205 E3
E Elizabeth St
10 TYTN 6048 A3
W Elizabeth St
10 BlmT 6713 C2
10 BlmT 6713 C2
Elizabeth Ter
10 LEON 6502 C4
Elizabeth Grove Rd
10 STNL 7207 B1
Elizabethtown Plz
10 ELIZ 6917 E3
10 UnnT 6917 C1
Elk Av
10 STNL 6395 D1
Elk Ct
10 STNL 7117 E3
Elk Pth
100 NHLS 6618 C7
Elk St
10 MHTN 118 D6
10 MHTN 6821 C1
Elkan Rd
10 MrnT 6282 D7
Elkhart St
10 STNL 7117 A4
Elkmont Av
249-00 QENS 6723 B6
Elks Pl
10 FLPK 6827 B2
10 RYE 7115 E6
10 RYE 6283 D1

Elks Rd
79-00 QENS 6823 D1
Elkwood Ter
10 EGLD 6392 A5
10 TFLY 6392 B5
Ella Pl
10 STNL 7117 E3
Ella St
10 BlmT 6713 B1
10 LNBK 6929 B4
10 VLYS 6928 B2
Ellard Av
10 GTNK 6616 E4
10 GTNK 6617 A4
10 SNPT 6508 E5
10 SOrT 6712 B6
200 ELIZ 6917 D3
500 NRWD 6278 C1
Ellen Ct
10 RYE 6283 D1
Ellen Pl
500 HmpT 6927 E6
Ellen St
100 WbgT 7205 B2
Ellendale Av
10 PTCH 6170 A6
400 RYEB 6170 A6
Ellens Wy
10 ALPN 6278 E7
Ellenton Av
10 NRCH 6395 E2
Ellery Av
- FTLE 6502 E4
- FTLE 6503 A4
900 HAOH 6165 E4
Elinor Rd
10 IrvT 6816 B2
200 NWRK 6816 B7
Elliot Rd
10 GTNK 6617 B6
10 NHmT 6617 B6
Elliott Av
10 YNKR 6393 C3
10 STNL 6282 E5
Elliott Blvd
3200 HmpT 7029 D1
Elliott St
10 NWRK 6713 C1
10 NWRK 6714 A2
10 STNL 6919 E6
S Elliott St
10 BKLN 121 E7
10 BKLN 6821 E6
N Elliott Wk
10 BKLN 121 D5
10 BKLN 6821 D5
Ellis Av
10 FLPK 6827 D2
10 GLCV 6509 E3
1900 BRNX 6614 B1
Ellis Ct
10 GrbT 6167 B4
Ellis Dr
10 WHPL 6168 D7
Ellis Pl
10 BRNX 6506 A7
10 WbgT 7114 D3
500 BRNX 6614 B2
1600 HRSN 6282 E3
1600 MRNK 6282 E3
Ellis Rd
10 STNL 7115 B6
Ellison Av
10 YNKR 6280 D7
1300 BRNX 6505 E2
1300 BRNX 6614 C2
Ellison Pl
10 YNKR 6280 D7
Ellsworth Av
10 STNL 7116 B6
10 YNKR 6393 C4
100 MNLA 6724 C5
400 STNL 7207 B1
Ellsworth Pl
10 UnnT 6917 C1
Ellsworth Rd
10 STNL 7207 B1
Ellsworth St
10 QENS 6925 B2
Ellwell Cres
10 STNL 6824 B2
Ellwood Av
10 MTVN 6395 A4
Ellwood St
10 GLCV 6509 E3
Ellwood St
10 MHTN 118 A1
10 MHTN 119 A6
100 MHTN 104 D7
100 MHTN 6503 D7

Elm Av
10 LRMT 6396 C2
10 MTVN 6394 E4
10 MTVN 6395 A4
100 TnkT 6501 E1
146-49 QENS 6721 B4
500 RDGF 6611 C2
600 RDGF 6502 B7
Elm Ct
10 BAYN 6919 E5
10 NHmT 6508 E5
10 NHmT 6508 E5
10 SNPT 6508 E5
10 SOrT 6712 B6
200 ELIZ 6917 D3
500 NRWD 6278 C1
Elm Dr
300 NHmT 6724 C2
2100 BRNX 6505 C7
Elm Ln
10 BRXV 6281 A7
10 FLHL 6618 B5
10 LKSU 6723 C2
10 NHmT 6724 C4
Elm Pl
10 BKLN 121 C6
10 BKLN 6821 D7
10 BRNX 6615 C1
10 CRSK 6278 B7
10 DMRT 6278 B7
10 EMFD 6049 A3
10 EORG 6712 C5
10 GTNK 6616 E5
10 HAOH 6165 E4
10 HRSN 6168 C3
10 IrvT 6816 B2
10 PLMM 6395 D7
10 RYE 6283 D5
10 SCLF 6509 D2
10 STNL 7020 B3
10 MtpT 6050 A2
Elm Rd
10 NWRK 6818 A2
10 SCDL 6167 D5
10 EGLD 6503 A1
100 HmpT 7027 C3
Elm St
10 NRWD 6164 A5
10 ARDY 6166 A4
10 CART 7115 C1
10 CorT 6712 D2
10 DBSF 6166 A4
10 EGLC 6503 A3
10 ELIZ 6917 D3
10 EORG 6712 C5
10 ERTH 6609 A6
10 ERTH 6609 A1
10 GrbT 6049 C6
10 GTNE 6616 E1
10 GTNE 6617 A2
10 GTPZ 6617 A7
10 HmpT 7028 B1
10 JSYC 6716 A7
10 KRNY 6714 A1
10 LNBK 6929 C5
10 LODI 6500 D2
10 MLVN 6929 A2
10 MtpT 6050 A2
10 MTVN 6394 D4
10 NARL 6714 A1
10 NHLS 6618 D7
10 NHmT 6618 D7
10 NRCH 6395 E6
10 NWRK 6816 E1
10 NWRK 6817 E1
10 RDFP 6501 E6
10 ROSE 6618 D7
10 RTFD 6609 A1
10 STNL 6919 E6
10 SYHW 6048 A1
10 TCKA 6280 E6
10 TFLY 6392 A4
10 VLYS 6928 A3
10 WbgT 7114 A5
10 WLTN 6500 A6
10 YNKR 6393 D1
100 NWRK 6818 A2
100 QENS 6925 B2
200 CART 7017 B7
200 PTHA 7205 D3
300 SAMB 7205 D2
400 PTCH 6170 C5
500 HmpT 6828 E6
500 ROSL 6618 D7
2700 QENS 6929 D6
E Elm St
10 LNDN 6917 A7
10 LNDN 7017 B1
10 MpIT 6050 A2
Elmbank St
10 QENS 7207 E1
10 QENS 7208 A1
Elmdorf Dr
10 SCDL 6167 C7
Elmer Pl
1000 HIsT 6816 E7
Elmer Miller Pl
- NRCH 6395 E4
Elm Hill Dr
10 RYEB 6169 E3
Elmhurst Av
10 STNL 7020 A6
84-00 QENS 6719 E6
90-00 QENS 6824 A1
Elmira Av
10 STNL 7019 D3
183-00 QENS 6826 A5
Elmira Lp
10 BKLN 6924 E3
Elmira St
10 STNL 7117 D3
Elmont Av
10 HmpT 6827 C4
10 PTCH 6170 C5
Elmont Rd
10 HmpT 6827 C5
Elmora Av
10 ELIZ 6917 C4
400 ELIZ 6917 C4

S Elmora Av
900 ELIZ 6917 D5
S Elmora Av SR-439
900 ELIZ 6917 D5
Elmore Pl
10 CRSK 6278 B7
1300 FTLE 6502 E7
Elmridge Ct
10 STNL 6281 E2
Elmridge Rd
10 KNGP 6616 C4
100 FLPK 6723 D7
600 ELIZ 6917 C2
Elm Rock Rd
10 BRXV 6395 A1
Elm Sea Ln
10 NHmT 6618 B3
10 STNL 7020 B5
Elmsmere Rd
10 MTVN 6395 A2
Elmtree Av
10 STNL 7118 A3
Elm Tree Ln
10 BRNX 6506 C5
Elmwood Av
10 BGTA 6501 D3
10 BKLN 7022 E1
10 BlmT 6713 B2
10 CART 7115 C1
10 EMFD 6049 B6
10 EORG 6712 E5
10 HRSN 6168 C3
10 IrvT 6816 B2
10 RYE 6283 D5
10 RYE 6284 A4
200 MpIT 6816 A1
300 WbgT 7114 B4
500 BKLN 7023 A1
Elmwood Ct
10 ELIZ 6917 C2
Elmwood Rd
10 GrbT 6167 C3
10 YNKR 6394 B3
Elmwood Ter
10 CRSK 6278 A4
10 IrvT 6816 B2
Elmwood Park Dr
10 STNL 7116 E1
10 STNL 7117 A1
Elmwynd Dr
10 EORG 6712 B4
Elna Ct
10 BAYN 6920 A2
El Retiro Ln
10 IRVN 6166 A1
Elsman Ter
10 NWRK 6816 B1
Elsmere Pl
200 FTLE 6502 E6
700 BRNX 6504 D7
Elson Ct
10 STNL 7018 E2
Elson St
10 STNL 7018 E3
Eltinge St
10 STNL 7020 B5
Eltingville Blvd
10 STNL 7116 E1
Elton Av
400 BRNX 6613 B3
Elton Rd
10 STMN 6828 A3
10 STMN 6828 A3
Elton Rd N
10 STMN 6828 A3
Elton St
10 NHmT 6724 E7
200 BKLN 6924 E3
300 BKLN 6925 A4
Elverton Av
10 STNL 7117 A6
Elvin St
10 STNL 7019 E6
Elvira Av
10 STNL 7027 E5
Elwood Av
6-00 QENS 7027 D5
Elwood Pl
10 BKLN 6923 B3
10 CARL 6929 B1
10 HmpT 7029 B1
10 MNCH 6610 B1
10 SHkT 6610 B1
Emerald Ct
10 YNKR 6279 E4
Emerald Pl
10 YNKR 6279 E4
Emerald St
10 QENS 6925 B2
400 MHTN 108 E5
800 MHTN 109 A4
Emerald Woods
1600 NHmT 6724 B7
Emergency Dr
- MtpT 6049 C1
S End Ct
10 HmpT 6827 D5
S End Dr
900 HmpT 6928 C6

Emeric Ct
10 STNL 6919 B7
Emerson Av
10 CRSK 6723 D7
10 GrbT 6167 B2
10 HRSN 6283 C3
10 JSYC 6819 B5
10 NRCH 6396 B3
10 STNL 7020 B6
10 BRXV 6395 A1
Emerson Dr
10 NHmT 6618 D6
10 NRCH 6396 B3
10 SDRK 6616 D7
10 STNL 7020 C4
400 HmpT 6929 C1
Emerson Ln
- HIsT 6816 C5
10 SECS 6715 E1
10 SECS 6716 A1
Emerson Pl
10 BKLN 6822 A6
10 HRSN 6283 D3
10 NWRK 6817 A5
300 VLYS 6928 E3
S Emerson Pl
10 VLYS 6928 E4
Emerson Rd
10 MrnT 6282 C7
10 NRCH 6396 D2
200 MplT 6816 A1
300 WbgT 7114 B4
500 BKLN 7023 A1
Emery Rd
10 IRVN 6166 C1
200 MNLA 6724 D5
Emery St
10 JSYC 6819 D1
Emily Av
10 STNL 6827 C6
Emily Ct
10 DMRT 6278 C5
10 STNL 7206 C3
Emily Ln
10 STNL 7116 C4
Emily Rd
206-01 QENS 6615 E7
Emm Ln
10 RSLN 6618 D6
Emma Ln
1100 HmpT 6827 B4
1300 LNDN 7017 C2
Emma St
- HmpT 6827 D4
- SFPK 6827 D4
800 ELIZ 6918 A2
Emmalon Av
10 NoCT 6050 B4
Emmalon Cir
10 NoCT 6050 B4
Emmerson Pl
- ISPK 7029 E5
Emmet Av
10 ERKY 6929 B7
10 STNL 7117 D4
10 WbgT 7205 A2
Emmett Pl
10 YNKR 6279 E5
Emmett St
10 NHmT 6724 E7
200 BKLN 6924 E3
300 BKLN 6925 A4
Emmett Ter
10 NRCH 6395 D6
Emmons Av
10 BKLN 7023 C7
10 BKLN 7121 B1
Emory Rd
10 IRVN 6166 C1
200 MNLA 6724 D5
Emory St
10 JSYC 6819 D1
Empire Av
10 LWRN 7027 D5
6-00 QENS 7027 D5
Empire Blvd
10 BKLN 6923 B3
10 HmpT 7029 B1
10 MNCH 6610 B1
10 SHkT 6610 B1
Empire St
10 BKLN 6817 D3
1500 HmpT 6827 D7
Emporia Av
10 HmpT 6827 D5
E End Av
10 MHTN 113 E5
10 MHTN 6718 C3
N End Av
10 MHTN 118 A6
10 MHTN 6821 A3
S End Av
10 MHTN 120 A1
10 MHTN 6821 A4
W End Av
10 BGTA 6501 C2
10 BKLN 7121 B1
10 BKLN 7121 A1

New York City/5 Borough Street Index

STREET
Block City Map# Grid

W End Dr
253-00 QENS 6722 C2
255-00 NHmT 6723 A2
255-00 QENS 6723 A2
End Pl
10 EchT 6281 D3
10 STNL 7116 D3
N End Pl
- HAOH 6280 A1
W End Pl
10 ELIZ 6917 D4
E End Rd
- QENS 6720 B3
N End Ter
10 NWRK 6714 A1
Endicott Av
100 GrbT 6049 B4
Endor Av
10 STNL 7020 B4
Endres St
10 CLST 6278 B3
Endview Av
10 LNBK 6929 A5
Endview St
10 STNL 7116 D6
Enfield Pl
10 STNL 7117 D1
49-00 QENS 6722 C4
Enfield Rd
10 WbgT 7114 A1
Engelhard Av
10 CART 7017 A6
10 WbgT 7017 A6
Engert Av
100 BKLN 6822 C2
Engert St
10 STNL 7115 E4
Engine Pl
10 YNKR 6393 A1
Engineers Rd
10 ROSH 6618 E3
Engle St
10 CRSK 6392 B1
10 EGLD 6392 A4
10 TFLY 6392 A4
100 CRSK 6278 B7
Engle St CO-501
10 EGLD 6392 A4
10 TFLY 6392 A4
Englehardt Ter
500 RDGF 6611 B1
Engleside St
10 CRSK 6392 B1
Englewood Av
- STNL 7115 D7
400 STNL 7206 D1
English Ln
10 DBSF 6166 B4
English Pl
400 MRNK 6283 A4
English St
100 FTLE 103 A4
100 FTLE 6503 A6
100 HKSK 6501 B2
Enman Rd
10 HmpT 7029 D3
Enoch St
10 CARL 6609 C1
10 ERTH 6609 C1
Enos Pl
10 JSYC 6820 A1
Enright Rd
23-00 QENS 7027 C4
700 MHTN 120 A7
700 MHTN 6820 E7
700 MHTN 6821 A7
Ens Pl
10 IrvT 6816 C4
Enterprise Av N
10 SECS 6609 E7
10 SECS 6610 B6
10 SECS 6715 E1
Enterprise Av S
10 SECS 6715 E2
Enterprise Blvd
10 YNKR 6279 E3
Entrance Ct
10 YNKR 6280 D4
Entrance Wy
10 MtPT 6050 A3
Eppirt St
10 EORG 6712 D5
Epsom Course
198-00 QENS 6826 B2
Erasmus St
10 BKLN 6923 B5
Erastina Pl
10 STNL 6919 A7
Erben Av
- BRNX 6615 D4
Erdman Pl
100 BRNX 6506 A4
Erhardt St
1200 UnnT 6816 A6
Eric Ln
10 NHmT 6723 E6
10 STNL 7117 A4
400 NVLE 6164 B4
Eric Pl
10 DMRT 6278 B6
Erick Av
10 HmpT 6928 D6
Erico Av
400 ELIZ 6917 D5
Ericson Pl
1400 BRNX 6505 E7
Ericsson St
24-00 QENS 6720 A3
Erie Av
10 ATLB 7028 A7
E Erie Av
10 RTFD 6609 B2
E Erie Av CO-32
10 RTFD 6609 B2
W Erie Av
10 ERTH 6500 A7
10 ERTH 6609 B2
10 RTFD 6500 A7
10 RTFD 6609 B1
W Erie Av CO-32
10 ERTH 6609 B2
10 RTFD 6609 B2
Erie Pl
10 NWRK 6714 A3

Erie Rd
200 HmpT 6929 D1
Erie St
10 DBSF 6166 A3
10 ELIZ 6918 B6
10 GRFD 6500 A2
10 IRVN 6166 A2
10 JSYC 6820 C2
10 STNL 7206 E2
Erika Lp
10 STNL 7116 C4
Erin Av
10 WbgT 7205 A3
Ermeti Pl
10 EGLC 6503 B1
Ernest Dr
10 NRCH 6281 E2
Ernst Pl
10 TFLY 6392 B2
Errington Pl
10 STNL 7020 E2
Errol Pl
10 NRCH 6395 D1
Erskine Pl
100 BRNX 6506 A4
Erskine St
800 BKLN 6925 A4
Ervilla Dr
10 LRMT 6396 D2
Erwin Ct
10 STNL 7117 D3
Escanaba Av
10 STNL 7117 A5
Escanaba Rd
800 MHTN 6820 E7
Esmac Ct N
10 STNL 7020 A6
Esmac Ct W
10 STNL 7020 A6
Esplanade
10 MTVN 6395 A4
400 PLMM 6395 C7
1000 BRNX 6505 B5
Esplanade Pl
300 CLFP 6611 D4
Esquire Ct
10 NHLS 6724 A3
Essex Av
10 MplT 6712 A7
10 NWRK 6712 A7
1100 LNDN 6917 B6
Essex Av E
10 WbgT 7114 E2
N Essex Av
10 COrT 6712 C2
S Essex Av
10 COrT 6712 C3
Essex Ct
10 NHmT 6618 A3
900 HmpT 6929 D1
Essex Dr
10 STNL 7117 A1
10 TFLY 6392 C5
Essex Pl
10 EchT 6281 B2
10 GrbT 6167 A2
10 HmpT 6928 A1
10 KRNY 6714 B5
10 QENS 6928 A1
10 YNKR 6280 C7
Essex Rd
10 GrwT 6170 B2
10 GTNK 6617 A5
10 HmpT 6827 B5
10 MplT 6816 A1
10 NHmT 6617 A6
Essex St
- HKSK 6501 B2
10 BKLN 6823 E7
10 BKLN 6924 E1
10 CART 7115 D2
10 COrT 6712 D3
10 EORG 6712 D3
10 IrvT 6816 B3
10 JSYC 6820 D4
10 MHTN 119 B6
10 MHTN 6821 D3
10 NWRK 6713 D6
10 PASC 6500 A4
300 LODI 6501 A1
300 MYWD 6501 A1
400 HRSN 6714 A7
800 BKLN 6925 A4
Essex St CO-56
10 HKSK 6501 A1
300 LODI 6501 A1
300 MYWD 6501 A1
Essex Wy
10 HRSN 6168 E1
Essig St
- NRWD 6164 A5
Estate Ct
100 NHLS 6618 C7
Estate Dr
10 PLNM 6617 D3
Estate Pl
10 RTFD 6609 A1
Estate Ter S
10 NHLS 6724 B1
100 NHLS 6618 B7
Estates Dr
207-00 QENS 6615 E7
Estates Ln
12-00 QENS 6615 E7
Estates Ter N
- ROSE 6618 B7
10 NHLS 6618 B7
Estelle Av
1500 HmpT 6827 C5
Estelle Pl
10 STNL 7206 C3
Esther St
10 NWRK 6714 C7
1000 HmpT 6828 A5
Esther Depew St
10 STNL 7117 C1
Estherwood Av
10 DBSF 6166 A4
Ethan Allen Ct
10 OrgT 6164 A1
Ethel Blvd
10 WRDG 6500 D7
Ethel St
10 VLYS 6928 C2

Ethelridge Rd
10 WHPL 6168 D6
Ethelton Rd
10 GrbT 6049 E5
10 GrbT 6050 A5
Etheridge Dr
10 CART 7017 A6
Etna St
10 BKLN 6823 E7
100 BKLN 6824 A7
400 QENS 6824 A7
Eton Pl
- STNL 7018 D4
- TCKA 6281 B4
10 EchT 6281 B4
10 STNL 7019 A5
100 HmpT 6828 E4
Eton Rd
10 GDNC 6828 D2
10 MrnT 6282 C6
10 NHmT 6724 A5
10 SCDL 6167 E5
10 SCDL 6168 A5
10 YNKR 6394 D1
300 HmpT 6828 B6
800 HmpT 6928 B7
Eton St
10 VLYS 6928 D5
85-00 QENS 6826 A3
300 EGLD 6503 A2
Eton Ter
10 NRWD 6164 A6
Eton Crest
10 NHmT 6618 B7
Etta Pl
10 LNBK 6929 B5
Ettl Ln
10 GrwT 6170 B1
Ettl Pk
10 GrwT 6170 B1
Ettrick Ter
10 RTFD 6609 B2
Etville Av
10 YNKR 6280 A3
Eucker St
10 RDFP 6501 E7
Euclid Av
10 ARDY 6166 C5
10 BKLN 6824 A7
10 GrbT 6166 D5
10 HAOH 6165 E6
10 MTVN 6395 C3
10 NWRK 6714 D7
10 NWRK 6818 C1
10 RDFP 6501 E5
10 YNKR 6393 D4
200 BKLN 6925 A1
400 UnnT 6816 A7
500 HmpT 6828 C7
Euclid Pl
10 NRCH 6396 A5
Euclid Rd
10 FTLE 6502 E7
10 FTLE 6611 E1
E Euclid St
10 VLYS 6928 E2
200 MLVN 6929 A3
200 VLYS 6929 A3
W Euclid St
10 VLYS 6928 D2
Eugene Pl
10 BlvT 6713 D2
10 STNL 7116 C7
Eugene St
10 GrwT 6170 D6
10 STNL 7206 C3
Eugenia Pl
700 ELIZ 6917 C6
Eugenio Maria de Hostos Blvd
- BRNX 6613 A3
Eulner St
10 SRVL 7205 A7
Eunice Ct
10 TYTN 6048 C4
Eunice Pl
10 STNL 7019 A2
Eureka Av
400 HmpT 6827 E6
Euston Rd
- NHmT 6724 C7
10 GDNC 6828 C1
10 HmpT 6828 C3
100 GDNC 6724 C7
Euston Rd S
10 HmpT 6828 C4
300 GDNC 6828 C3
Eva Av
10 STNL 7118 A4
Eva Ln
10 GrbT 6167 A7
Evan Pl
10 STNL 7116 C5
Evandale Rd
10 GrbT 6167 A6
Evans Av
10 HmpT 6827 E6
10 HmpT 6929 D7
10 NHmT 6724 D3
10 RTFD 6609 A3
300 HmpT 7029 D1
Evans Ct
10 TFLY 6392 B4
Evans Rd
- MHTN 120 A6
10 CRSK 6278 A6
10 MHTN 6821 A7
158-00 QENS 6825 D5
Evans St
10 BKLN 121 D2
10 BKLN 6821 D5
10 NHmT 6723 E5
10 NRCH 6396 A4
10 STNL 7019 B7
600 ELIZ 6918 C3
Evans St E
10 HmpT 7029 B1
Evans St W
10 HmpT 7029 C2
Evans Terminal Rd
10 HlsT 6816 E6
Evarts Av
10 GrbT 6049 B6
N Evarts Av
10 EMFD 6049 B5

N Evarts Av
100 GrbT 6049 B5
S Evarts Av
10 EMFD 6049 C5
Eve Ln
10 RYE 6284 A3
Eveleth Rd
178-00 QENS 6927 B1
Evelyn Ct
10 IrvT 6816 A3
10 MplT 6816 A3
200 HmpT 6828 E6
Evelyn Pl
10 BRNX 105 D1
10 BRNX 6504 B4
10 STNL 7021 A4
Evelyn Rd
10 NHmT 6508 E7
10 NHmT 6617 E1
Everdell Av
18-00 QENS 7027 D5
Everdell Rd
10 HmpT 7029 B1
Everett Av
10 BKLN 7023 E6
10 STNL 7207 A2
Everett Pl
10 CLFP 6611 D3
10 ERTH 6609 B1
10 STNL 7206 E2
Everett Rd
10 DMRT 6278 B4
Everett St
10 CLST 6278 A3
10 EORG 6712 E1
10 HmpT 6827 B7
10 HmpT 6928 B1
10 JSYC 6819 C3
10 LNBK 6929 A5
10 NRCH 6395 D5
10 NRWD 6164 A6
10 RYE 6283 E5
10 TCKA 6281 A7
S Everett St
1100 HmpT 6928 A3
Evergreen Av
- BKLN 7022 E3
- BKLN 7023 A2
- RYEB 6170 A7
10 BKLN 6822 E5
10 BXTE 6617 E1
10 CRSK 6392 A1
10 LNBK 6929 A5
10 NHmT 6617 E1
10 NHmT 6724 A6
10 NRCH 6396 B3
10 NWRK 6817 A6
10 RYE 6170 A7
10 STNL 7020 C6
300 BKLN 6823 A6
1000 BRNX 6613 E1
2800 HmpT 6929 D6
Evergreen Cir
10 NHLS 6724 B1
Evergreen Dr
600 HmpT 6828 B7
Evergreen Ln
10 MrnT 6282 C5
10 NHmT 6723 D6
10 NWRK 6713 D3
Evergreen Pl
10 DMRT 6278 B6
10 EORG 6712 D4
10 TFLY 6392 A4
Evergreen St
10 BAYN 6919 D5
10 STNL 7117 B4
Evergreen Forest Blvd
300 WbgT 7114 E1
Everit Av
10 HBPK 6928 D6
10 HmpT 6928 D6
100 HWTH 6928 E7
200 HWTH 6929 A7
400 ERKY 6929 A7
Everit Pl
- QENS 6826 B7
1300 HWTH 6929 A7
Everit St
10 BKLN 121 A3
10 BKLN 6821 D4
Everton Av
10 STNL 7116 B5
Everton Pl
10 STNL 7116 B5
Everton St
63-00 QENS 6824 A2
Evon Ct
10 SCDL 6281 C2
Ewart Rd
10 SCDL 6281 C1
Ewart St
10 EchT 6281 C2
10 SCDL 6281 C1
Eweler Av
10 HmpT 6827 E3
10 HmpT 6828 A3
Excelsior Av
10 STNL 7207 A2
Exchange Al
10 MHTN 120 B1
10 MHTN 6821 B6
Exchange Pl
10 JSYC 6820 D3
10 MHTN 120 B1
10 MHTN 6821 B5
10 PTCH 6170 B5
Executive Blvd
10 GrbT 6049 B3
10 YNKR 6279 E3
10 YNKR 6280 A3
Executive Dr
10 FTLE 6502 E4
10 NHmT 6723 E4
100 NHmT 6724 A4
Executive Plz
10 YNKR 6279 E3
Executive Wy
10 STNL 7019 B6
Exeter Av
10 LNBK 6929 D4
Exeter Ln
10 NHmT 6617 C6
Exeter Pl
10 ARDY 6166 E5

Exeter Rd
10 JSYC 6819 B6
1700 HmpT 6929 A6
Exeter St
10 BKLN 7121 C1
10 STNL 7117 B4
10 WLPK 6724 E4
67-00 QENS 6824 C3
Exeter Wy
100 HlsT 6917 D1
Exford Pl
10 NHmT 6724 E3
Export St
10 NWRK 6818 B7
Expressway Plz
10 NHmT 6618 E7
Exterior St
- BRNX 104 D6
- BRNX 6503 E7
10 BRNX 6612 E3
300 BRNX 107 D6
2800 BRNX 102 D4
2800 BRNX 6504 B2
Exton Av
10 NARL 6714 C1
Extra Pl
10 MHTN 119 A3
10 MHTN 6821 C2
Eylandt St
100 STNL 7116 D7
700 STNL 7207 B1

F

F St
1300 HmpT 6827 E6
Faber Pl
10 GRFD 6500 A3
Faber St
10 STNL 6919 C7
Faber Ter
28-00 QENS 7027 B4
Fabian St
10 STNL 7116 D6
Fabry Ter
200 TnkT 6502 B3
Fabyan Br
- NWRK 6816 D3
Fabyan Pl
10 NWRK 6816 E3
300 IrvT 6816 D4
400 HlsT 6816 D4
Factory St
300 JSYC 6820 A2
Fahy Av
10 STNL 7018 E2
Faile St
200 BRNX 6613 D3
Fair St
10 BKLN 121 C5
10 BKLN 6821 D6
10 EORG 6712 E1
10 GrbT 6049 D7
10 GrbT 6167 D1
10 HKSK 6501 C2
100 PALP 6502 B5
Fairbanks Av
100 STNL 7117 D4
Fairbanks St
10 HlsT 6816 E7
700 ELIZ 6917 E7
700 LNDN 6917 E7
Fairbury Av
221-00 QENS 6826 E2
222-00 QENS 6827 A2
Fairchild Av
173-00 QENS 6721 D6
Fairchild Ln
10 GrwT 6051 E1
Fairchild Pl
10 HlsT 6816 B4
10 IrvT 6816 B4
Fairfax Av
1000 BRNX 6615 A1
1100 BRNX 6506 B7
Fairfax St
10 VLYS 6928 B2
1700 HmpT 6827 C4
Fairfield Av
10 NHmT 6508 D5
2700 BRNX 6504 A2
3000 BRNX 102 B2
Fairfield Ct
10 CRSK 6278 B6
10 DMRT 6278 B6
Fairfield Ln
10 EHLS 6618 E7
10 NHmT 6723 D6
10 QENS 6723 D6
Fairfield Pl
10 YNKR 6393 B3
Fairfield Rd
- EMFD 6049 B7
- GrbT 6049 B7
10 KNGP 6616 E3
10 YNKR 6393 B3
Fairfield St
10 STNL 7117 A3
10 VLYS 6928 C4
10 WHPL 6168 A2
Fairfield Wy
600 UnnT 6917 A1
Fairhaven Ln
10 PTCH 6170 B3
Fairlane Dr
10 HAOH 6166 A6
Fairlawn Av
10 DBSF 6165 E5
10 HAOH 6165 E5
10 STNL 7117 C5
100 HmpT 6828 D5
Fairlawn Ct
10 RYE 6283 E5
Fairlawn Lp
10 STNL 7117 C5
Fairlawn Pkwy
10 RYEB 6170 A1
Fairlawn St
10 RYE 6283 E5
Fairmont Av
10 ARDY 6166 D5
10 HAOH 6166 A7
Fairmont Blvd
10 GDNC 6828 A3

Fairmont St
10 EMFD 6049 B6
Fairmount Av
10 JSYC 6820 A3
10 KRNY 6714 B1
10 NARL 6714 D1
10 NWRK 6713 B6
10 YNKR 6279 E7
200 JSYC 6819 E2
400 NWRK 6817 B1
800 ELIZ 6918 A2
1100 ELIZ 6917 E2
3100 BRNX 6615 A1
3200 BRNX 6506 B7
Fairmount Pl
700 BRNX 6504 D7
1200 FTLE 6502 E7
Fairmount St
10 VLYS 6928 B2
Fairmount Ter
10 EORG 6712 D6
10 JSYC 6819 E2
10 NWRK 6712 D6
Fair Oaks Pl
200 CDHT 7028 A2
Fairview Av
4-00 QENS 6823 B4
10 BGTA 6501 D3
10 CLST 6278 A2
10 GTNK 6616 E5
10 GTNK 6617 A5
10 HmpT 6928 B5
10 HmpT 6929 D3
10 JSYC 6819 E2
10 MHTN 104 D2
10 MHTN 6503 E5
10 NHmT 6618 A2
10 RSLN 6618 E6
10 RTFD 6609 A1
10 SECS 6610 A6
10 SOrT 6712 A7
10 TCKA 6281 A6
10 TYTN 6048 B3
10 WHPL 6050 A7
10 WHPL 6168 A1
100 EGLC 6392 B7
100 KNGP 6617 B5
100 PTCH 6170 A5
100 STNL 7019 E3
300 COrT 6712 B4
300 FRVW 6611 A3
300 NBgT 6611 A3
300 WbgT 7114 D1
400 EGLD 6392 B7
400 FTLE 6503 A4
Fairview Av CO-16
400 FRVW 6611 B3
E Fairview Av
10 VLYS 6928 D3
W Fairview Av
10 VLYS 6928 D3
100 SOrT 6712 A7
Fairview Dr
10 NHmT 6724 C2
Fairview Ln
10 GLCV 6509 D3
700 CLFP 6611 D1
700 FTLE 6611 D1
1000 FTLE 6502 D7
Fairview Pl
10 BKLN 6923 C5
10 KRNY 6714 D3
10 NRCH 6396 A5
10 PTCH 6170 B6
10 SCLF 6509 D6
10 STNL 7020 A6
1000 HlsT 6816 D7
Fairview Rd
10 SCDL 6168 A4
Fairview St
10 PALP 6502 B6
10 YNKR 6279 D7
Fairview Ter
10 GrwT 6170 B1
10 RYEB 6170 B2
400 FRVW 6611 C2
400 RDGF 6611 C2
5100 WhkT 111 B2
5100 WhkT 6717 A1
5100 WNYK 111 B2
5100 WNYK 6717 A1
Fairview Park Dr
10 GrbT 6049 A3
Fairway Av
10 RYE 6283 E5
10 STNL 7020 D3
600 MRNK 6283 A7
800 MRNK 6282 E7
Fairway Cir N
10 NHLS 6724 A1
Fairway Cir S
10 NHLS 6724 B2
Fairway Ct
10 CRSK 6392 C2
10 NVLE 6164 C6
Fairway Dr
10 EchT 6281 B3
10 HMPD 6828 E5
10 HmpT 7027 D2
10 HRSN 6051 B6
10 LKSU 6723 B3
10 MrnT 6282 C3
10 NHLS 6724 A1
10 NHmT 6618 C2
10 NHmT 6723 B3
10 WHPL 6168 D5
10 WOrT 6712 B1
300 HmpT 6828 B3
400 LEON 6502 D4
500 HmpT 6928 B7
W Fairway Dr
10 NHmT 6618 B2
Fairway Grn
100 MRNK 6282 D7
900 MRNK 6396 D1
1000 MrnT 6396 D1
Fairway Ln
10 NHmT 6618 C7
10 STNL 7020 A3
900 MRNK 6396 E1
Fairway Pl
- MRNK 6282 E7
Fairway Rd
10 ROSH 6618 E2
900 HmpT 6828 A7

Fairway St
10 MTVN 6394 E2
Fairway Ter
10 NRWD 6164 D7
Fairway Close
10 QENS 6824 E2
Faith Ct
10 NWRK 6817 B1
Faith Ln
10 GrbT 6166 D6
Faitoute Av
1200 UnnT 6816 B6
Falcon Av
10 STNL 7117 E4
29-00 QENS 7027 B5
Falcon Ct
100 NHLS 6724 B1
Faller St
400 HmpT 7029 C1
Fallon Av
10 HmpT 6827 C6
Fallon Ct
10 HmpT 6827 C6
Falls Rd
10 MrnT 6282 C7
Falmouth Av
1400 NHmT 6724 A7
1400 NHPK 6724 A7
Falmouth Pl
10 NHmT 6724 E3
Falmouth Rd
10 WbgT 7114 A3
10 YNKR 6281 A2
Falmouth St
10 BKLN 7121 C1
Fancher Pl
10 STNL 6918 E7
Fanchon Pl
10 BKLN 6924 D1
Fane Ct
10 BKLN 7023 E6
Faneuil Pl
10 NRCH 6395 D2
Fanning St
10 STNL 7019 E4
Fanny St
1000 ELIZ 6918 B1
Fanshaw Av
10 YNKR 6393 C4
Fanwood Av
800 HmpT 6928 A5
Faraday Av
5600 BRNX 6393 C5
Fargo Ln
10 IRVN 6048 A7
10 TYTN 6048 B7
Farley Av
10 HRSN 6168 D1
10 NWRK 6817 A2
Farley Rd
10 SCDL 6167 E3
10 SCDL 6168 C5
10 WHPL 6167 E3
Farm Ln
10 LKSU 6723 B2
Farm Rd
10 ARDY 6166 E3
1000 SECS 6610 A5
S Farm Rd
10 SNPT 6508 B5
Farmers Blvd
99-00 QENS 6826 B5
122-01 QENS 6927 B3
Farmers Rd
10 KNGP 6616 D2
W Farms Rd
1000 BRNX 6613 E1
1700 BRNX 6504 E7
Farmview Rd
10 FLHL 6618 B4
Farnham Av
10 GRFD 6500 B3
100 LODI 6500 B2
Farnum Blvd
10 HmpT 6828 A4
100 STMN 6828 A3
Farnum Ct
10 TFLY 6392 B4
Farnum St
10 LNBK 6929 A5
Farquhar Av
10 YNKR 6280 A7
Farraday St
10 STNL 7019 A3
Farragut Av
- GrbT 6280 B1
10 HAOH 6165 C7
10 HAOH 6166 A7
10 STNL 7018 E2
200 HAOH 6280 A1
Farragut Cir
10 NRCH 6396 A4
Farragut Ct
200 TnkT 6502 C1
Farragut Dr
900 TnkT 6502 C1
Farragut Pkwy
500 HAOH 6280 A1
Farragut Pl
700 GTBG 6611 B7
700 WNYK 6611 B7
3100 BKLN 6923 C7
Farragut Rd
10 BKLN 6923 B7
10 SCDL 6282 B1
5600 BKLN 6924 B6
Farragut St
- BRNX 6614 A5
10 TCKA 6281 C7
Farrandale Av
10 BlmT 6713 C1
Farrant Ter
200 TnkT 6501 E2
Farrel St
10 NHmT 6724 B5
Farrell Av
10 MTVN 6395 B5
Farrell Ct
10 STNL 7117 D3
Farrell Pl N
10 YNKR 6279 D4
Farrell Pl S
10 YNKR 6279 D4

Farrell St
10 LBCH 7029 E6
Farrington Rd
400 HmpT 6929 D6
Farrington St
30-00 QENS 6720 E3
Far Rockaway Blvd
25-00 QENS 7027 B5
Farview Rd
10 TFLY 6392 C4
Fashion Wy
- ELIZ 6918 D3
Father Capodanno Blvd
10 STNL 7021 A7
200 STNL 7020 E7
400 STNL 7118 C3
Father Finian Sullivan Dr
10 YNKR 6279 D6
Father John Krieg Pl
10 BKLN 6824 B5
10 BKLN 6925 B3
Father Zeiser Pl
100 BRNX 102 D7
100 BRNX 6504 B4
Fawcett St
10 PTCH 6170 B7
Fawn Ln
10 STNL 7117 C4
Fawn Rdg
- LKSU 6723 C4
Fay Av
300 ELIZ 6917 D5
700 LNDN 6917 C5
Fay Av CO-514
700 ELIZ 6917 C5
700 LNDN 6917 C5
Fay Pl
10 WHPL 6050 B6
Fayann Ln
10 STNL 7206 B4
Fayette Av
10 STNL 7020 C5
300 MRNK 6282 D6
Fayette Pl
10 JSYC 6715 D6
4600 NHmT 6723 A2
Fayette Rd
10 SCDL 6282 A4
Fayette St
10 BKLN 6822 D5
10 PTHA 7205 E4
Fazio Ln
- ISPK 7029 D4
FDR Dr
- MHTN 104 C7
- MHTN 107 C4
- MHTN 110 D5
- MHTN 113 D7
- MHTN 114 B1
- MHTN 116 E7
- MHTN 117 C1
- MHTN 120 C2
- MHTN 121 A1
- MHTN 6503 E7
- MHTN 6612 D2
- MHTN 6717 E7
- MHTN 6718 B4
- MHTN 6821 B5
400 MHTN 119 D6
FDR Dr Service Rd E
- MHTN 116 E6
- MHTN 6717 E6
FDR Dr Service Rd W
- MHTN 116 E5
- MHTN 117 A4
- MHTN 6717 E6
- MHTN 6718 A6
Fearn Pl
3000 BRNX 6615 C4
Featherbed Ln
10 BRNX 105 B5
10 BRNX 6504 A6
Federal Blvd
200 CART 7017 A7
200 WbgT 7017 A7
Federal Cir
100 QENS 6926 C4
Federal Pl
10 STNL 6918 E7
Federal Plz
10 BlmT 6713 B1
Federal Sq
10 NWRK 6817 D1
Federal St
10 YNKR 6393 B2
Federspiel St
1600 FTLE 103 B4
1600 FTLE 6503 A6
Fedor Av
3000 LNDN 7017 C3
Fegan St
10 YNKR 6279 D7
Feiner Pl
10 IrvT 6816 B3
Feitiner St
- NRWD 6164 B5
- NVLE 6164 B5
Feitner St
- NRWD 6164 B4
- NVLE 6164 B5
Feldmeyers Ln
10 STNL 7018 B7
Felix Av
10 ARDY 6166 C5
Felix Ln
- NWRK 6817 B1
Feller Pl
400 BGTA 6501 D1
Fellowship Ln
10 RYEB 6051 D6
Felter Av
300 HmpT 6928 C7
Felton Av
10 VLYS 6928 C2
Felton St
10 STNL 7018 E3
N Feltus St
200 SAMB 7205 B7
N Feltus St CO-686
200 SAMB 7205 B7
Fenbrook Dr
10 MrnT 6282 C5

Fendale St
10 HmpT 6828 C5
Fenimore Av
10 GDNC 6828 B1
Fenimore Rd
- GrbT 6167 D5
10 MRNK 6282 D6
10 NHmT 6617 E2
10 NRCH 6281 D5
10 SCDL 6167 D5
10 TnkT 6502 A2
800 MrnT 6282 B5
1000 SCDL 6282 B4
1600 HmpT 6928 E6
Fenimore St
10 BKLN 6923 B4
10 LNBK 6929 A3
10 MLVN 6929 A3
E Fenimore St
10 VLYS 6928 E2
W Fenimore St
10 VLYS 6928 D2
Fennimore Av
10 YNKR 6280 A6
Fennimore Dr
10 HRSN 6169 C7
10 HRSN 6283 C1
Fenton Av
2200 BRNX 6505 D4
Fenton Pl
10 ERKY 6929 A6
10 LNBK 6929 A6
Fenton St
10 RYE 6283 D5
Fenway N
10 YNKR 6394 A5
Fenway S
10 YNKR 6394 A5
Fenway Cir
10 STNL 7116 E4
Fenway Ct
10 CRSK 6278 A6
Fenwick Rd
10 HAOH 6280 A1
Fenwick St
10 NWRK 6817 B5
Fenwood Dr
900 HmpT 6928 B1
1000 VLYS 6928 B1
Fenworth Blvd
500 HmpT 6828 B5
Ferdinand Pl
10 NRCH 6395 D3
Ferdinand St
10 NWRK 6712 E6
10 NWRK 6713 A6
Ferdon Av
10 OrgT 6164 E2
10 OrgT 6165 A2
10 PRMT 6164 E2
10 PRMT 6165 A1
Ferdon St
10 NWRK 6818 B3
Ferguson Ct
- STNL 7206 C3
Ferguson St
10 NWRK 6818 A1
Fern Av
10 IrvT 6816 C3
10 STNL 7117 A5
Fern Pl
10 BRNX 6615 C4
107-00 QENS 6825 E5
107-00 QENS 6826 A5
400 ELIZ 6917 E7
Fern Rd
10 MrnT 6282 B7
10 OrgT 6165 A5
Fern St
10 FLPK 6827 E3
10 LNDN 6917 B5
10 NRCH 6395 D2
10 ROSL 6917 B5
Fern Ter
10 YNKR 6280 C6
Fernbrook St
10 YNKR 6393 B3
Ferncliff Rd
10 JSYC 6819 B6
10 SCDL 6281 D1
Ferncroft Rd
100 MNLA 6724 E5
Ferndale Av
10 STNL 7019 A6
143-00 QENS 6825 C7
Ferndale Ct
10 STNL 7019 A6
Ferndale Dr
10 HAOH 6166 A6
Ferndale Pl
10 MrnT 6396 D1
Ferndale Rd
10 GrbT 6167 A6
Ferndale St
- MrnT 6396 D1
10 YNKR 6280 A6
Ferngate Dr
900 HmpT 6828 A7
Fernside Pl
2-00 QENS 7027 C6
Fernway
10 EchT 6281 C2
Fernwood Av
10 RYE 6283 E3
Fernwood Ln
10 FLHL 6618 C5
10 RSLN 6618 C5
Fernwood Rd
10 EORG 6712 E2
10 EORG 6713 A2
10 MplT 6816 A1
10 MrnT 6282 C7
10 WHPL 6168 D6
Fernwood Ter
10 ELIZ 6917 B3
10 ROSP 6917 A3
10 STMN 6828 A3
Fernwood Ter N
10 STMN 6828 A2
Fero St
10 YNKR 6279 E6
10 YNKR 6280 A6
Feronia Wy
10 RTFD 6609 B3

New York City/5 Borough Street Index

STREET Block	City	Map#	Grid
Ferris Av			
10	WHPL	6050	A7
10	WHPL	6168	A1
Ferris Pl			
1400	BRNX	6505	D7
Ferris St			
10	BKLN	6922	A1
N Ferris St			
10	IRVN	6048	A7
10	IRVN	6166	C1
S Ferris St			
10	IRVN	6166	C1
Ferry Rd			
-	GTBG	6611	B7
-	WNYK	6611	B7
Ferry St			
10	JSYC	6716	B7
10	NWRK	6817	E1
10	STNL	6919	D7
10	WbgT	7114	E6
10	WbgT	7115	A6
200	NWRK	6818	C1
Ferry Line Rd			
-	MHTN	120	A5
-	MHTN	6821	A6
Fessenden Pl			
10	NWRK	6816	E3
Festival Ct			
10	GrbT	6050	A5
Ficarelle Dr			
10	STNL	7206	E2
Fiedler Av			
10	STNL	6920	D7
Field Av			
10	HSBH	6500	E5
10	JSYC	6819	D1
10	NRCH	6395	E6
Field Ct			
10	BRXV	6280	C4
Field Pl			
-	BRNX	6615	D5
10	BRNX	105	E1
10	BRNX	6504	C4
10	HlsT	6816	D4
10	IrvT	6816	D4
10	NWRK	6816	D4
10	PTCH	6170	C3
Field Rd			
1000	UnnT	6816	A6
Field St			
10	STNL	7019	B6
Field Ter			
10	IRVN	6166	B2
Field Crest Dr			
400	GrbT	6049	A3
Fieldcrest Rd			
10	YNKR	6281	A2
Field End Ln			
10	EchT	6281	C4
Fielding Ct			
10	SOrT	6712	A6
Fielding St			
1500	BRNX	6505	D4
Fieldmere St			
10	HmpT	6827	B5
10	NRCH	6282	A6
Fieldpoint Dr			
10	IRVN	6166	B1
Fields Av			
10	STNL	7019	C5
Fieldston Rd			
3600	BRNX	102	D1
3600	BRNX	6504	A1
4600	BRNX	6393	B6
Fieldston Ter			
200	BRNX	6393	C6
Fieldstone Dr			
10	GrbT	6167	D2
Fieldstone Ln			
10	HmpT	6928	A4
10	LKSU	6723	B2
Fieldstone Rd			
10	RYE	6284	A3
10	STNL	7018	E3
Fieldway Av			
10	STNL	7117	B5
Fiesta Ct			
10	HmpT	6928	C5
Fiesta Dr			
10	NHmT	6724	C3
Figurea Av			
10	STNL	7116	D5
E Figurea Av			
10	STNL	7117	A5
100	STNL	7116	E5
Filbert St			
10	VLYS	6928	C5
Filipe Ln			
10	STNL	7117	B7
Fillat St			
10	STNL	7019	C3
Fillmore Av			
10	CART	7017	C7
10	CART	7115	C1
10	STNL	7019	C5
4800	BKLN	7023	E3
5200	BKLN	7024	A3
Fillmore Pl			
10	BKLN	6822	B3
10	STNL	7020	D7
10	STNL	7021	A4
10	WHPL	6168	A3
6000	WNYK	6611	A7
Fillmore St			
10	NWRK	6818	B1
10	STNL	6920	B6
10	YNKR	6393	E1
600	ELIZ	6917	E5
1700	BRNX	6505	A6
Findlay Av			
10	GrbT	6167	D3
900	BRNX	6613	B1
1200	BRNX	105	C7
1200	BRNX	6504	B7
Fine Blvd			
10	STNL	7020	A4
100	STNL	7019	E4
Fingal St			
10	STNL	7116	E7
Fingerboard Rd			
10	STNL	7021	A4
100	STNL	7020	E4
W Fingerboard Rd			
500	STNL	7020	D5
Fink Av			
-	BRNX	6505	D7
Finlay Av			
10	STNL	7207	A2
Finlay Pl			
10	NWRK	6712	C5
10	SOrT	6712	C5
Finlay St			
10	STNL	7206	A5
Finley Av			
200	STNL	7118	A4
Finmor Dr			
100	GrbT	6048	E7
Finn St			
10	HmpT	6827	B7
Finucane Pl			
100	HBPK	7028	D1
100	HmpT	7028	D1
Fiorello Ln			
-	QENS	6719	D3
Fir Ct			
600	NRWD	6278	C1
Fir Dr			
10	KNGP	6617	A3
10	NHmT	6724	B4
Fir Ln			
10	HmpT	7028	C1
10	WDBG	7028	C1
Fir Pl			
10	NRCH	6396	A3
Fir Rd			
10	JSYC	6819	B4
Fir St			
10	VLYS	6928	A3
200	QENS	6928	A3
Firefighters Memorial Plz			
10	VLYS	6928	C4
Firemans Sq			
-	ISPK	7029	D4
Firenze St			
100	NVLE	6164	C5
Firestone Cir			
10	NHLS	6724	B3
Firethorne Dr			
10	LWRN	7028	B3
Firethorne Ln			
10	HmpT	6928	B4
Firmench Wy			
10	NWRK	6818	C5
Firth Rd			
10	STNL	7018	E4
Firwood Pl			
109-00	QENS	6826	B5
Firwood Rd			
10	MHVN	6508	B6
Fish Av			
10	NHmT	6724	D3
2200	BRNX	6505	C4
Fisher Av			
10	BGTA	6501	E3
10	EchT	6281	B5
10	SECS	6610	C6
10	STNL	7206	B3
10	TCKA	6281	A5
10	WHPL	6168	D2
200	WHPL	6167	E3
Fisher Ct			
10	WHPL	6168	A2
Fisher Dr			
10	MTVN	6395	A3
Fisher Ln			
10	GrbT	6050	A5
10	WHPL	6050	A5
Fisher St			
-	GrbT	6167	D4
-	SCDL	6167	D5
Fishermans Dr			
10	PTWN	6508	C6
Fish House Rd			
100	KRNY	6715	B7
Fisk St			
10	JSYC	6819	C3
Fiske Dr			
800	HmpT	6928	B7
Fiske Pl			
10	BKLN	6922	E2
10	MTVN	6394	E4
Fitch St			
10	CART	7017	D7
10	CART	7115	E1
Fitchett St			
63-00	QENS	6824	A2
Fitzgerald Av			
10	STNL	7117	B6
Fitzpatrick St			
100	HlsT	6816	C6
Fitzroy Pl			
10	HmpT	7029	D5
Flag Ln			
10	NHmT	6724	A4
Flagg Ct			
10	STNL	7020	A7
Flagg Pl			
10	STNL	7020	A7
400	STNL	7118	A2
Flagg St			
10	YNKR	6279	D7
400	COrT	6712	A3
Flagler Dr			
10	HRSN	6169	E6
1100	MRNK	6396	E3
1100	MRNK	6397	A2
Flagship Cir			
10	STNL	7207	A3
Flagstone Dr			
10	WbgT	7115	B1
Flamingo St			
10	ATLB	7027	E7
Flamm Brook Rd			
10	CLST	6278	C4
Flanagan Wy			
10	SECS	6610	A6
Flanders Dr			
500	HmpT	6927	E5
600	HmpT	6928	A5
Flandreau Av			
10	NRCH	6395	D2
Flatbush Av			
10	BKLN	121	D7
10	BKLN	6821	D7
100	BKLN	6922	E1
300	BKLN	6923	A2
1500	BKLN	7023	C1
3000	BKLN	7024	C6
3300	BKLN	7122	D1
Flatbush Av Ext			
10	BKLN	121	C4
10	BKLN	6821	D6
Flatlands Av			
10	BKLN	7023	D3
5300	BKLN	7024	A1
10300	BKLN	6924	E5
12300	BKLN	6925	A4
Flatlands 1st St			
10	BKLN	6924	D6
Flatlands 2nd St			
10	BKLN	6924	D6
Flatlands 3rd St			
10	BKLN	6924	D6
Flatlands 4th St			
10	BKLN	6924	D6
Flatlands 5th St			
10	BKLN	6924	D6
Flatlands 6th St			
10	BKLN	6924	D6
Flatlands 7th St			
10	BKLN	6924	D7
Flatlands 8th St			
10	BKLN	6924	E7
Flatlands 9th St			
10	BKLN	6924	E7
Flatlands 10th St			
10	BKLN	6924	E7
Fleet Ct			
84-00	QENS	6824	A2
100	BRNX	6614	C5
Fleet Pl			
10	MNLA	6724	E7
100	BKLN	121	C5
100	BKLN	6821	D7
Fleet St			
-	BKLN	121	C6
-	BKLN	6821	D7
10	JSYC	6716	B7
10	JSYC	6820	B1
65-00	QENS	6824	C3
E Fleet St			
3000	ELIZ	6919	B2
N Fleet St			
1000	ELIZ	6818	A7
1200	ELIZ	6919	A1
Fleetwood Av			
10	MTVN	6394	D2
Fleetwood Ct			
10	KNGP	6616	E4
10	MTVN	6394	D2
Fleetwood Pl			
10	IrvT	6816	A3
10	NWRK	6816	B1
Fleetwood Rd			
10	WbgT	7114	B4
Fleming Av			
10	NWRK	6818	B1
Fleming Ter			
10	MplT	6816	A1
Fletcher Av			
10	GrwT	6170	C2
10	MTVN	6394	E3
10	VLYS	6928	D3
300	HmpT	6928	D2
2000	FTLE	6502	E5
2100	FTLE	103	A1
2100	FTLE	6503	A4
Fletcher Av US-9W			
2100	FTLE	103	A1
2100	FTLE	6502	E4
2100	FTLE	6503	A4
N Fletcher Av			
10	HmpT	6928	D1
10	VLYS	6928	D2
800	HmpT	6827	D7
Fletcher Pl			
400	BRNX	6504	B3
Fletcher St			
10	MHTN	120	C1
10	MHTN	6821	B5
10	STNL	7020	D4
Flexon Dr			
10	NWRK	6817	B4
Flint Av			
10	LRMT	6396	D2
2500	BRNX	6395	A7
Flint Pl			
10	HmpT	6827	C6
10	LRMT	6396	D2
Flint Rd			
10	ERKY	6929	B6
Flint St			
10	STNL	7117	E3
Flintlock Ln			
10	ARDY	6166	D4
Flintlock Rd			
10	GrwT	6170	C1
Flitt St			
10	OrgT	6164	D2
Flora St			
800	ELIZ	6918	A3
Floral Av			
10	ELIZ	6817	B7
10	NWRK	6817	B7
600	ELIZ	6917	C2
Floral Av N			
1000	UnnT	6917	B1
Floral Av S			
600	ELIZ	6917	C2
800	UnnT	6917	B2
Floral Blvd			
10	FLPK	6827	C2
Floral Dr			
10	HAOH	6166	A6
Floral Ln			
10	YNKR	6279	E5
200	CARL	6500	B6
200	WRDG	6500	B6
Floral Pkwy			
10	FLPK	6827	D2
Floral Ter			
1000	SECS	6610	B6
Floral Park Rd			
600	HmpT	6828	B3
Floren Pl			
10	NRCH	6281	E2
Florence Av			
10	BKLN	7023	E6
10	BlmT	6713	C1
10	BlvT	6713	C1
10	DBSF	6166	C4
10	GrbT	6049	D7
10	GTNK	6616	D4
10	IrvT	6816	B2
10	RYE	6283	C4
10	SCLF	6509	E7
100	NWRK	6816	B2
200	HlsT	6816	C5
Florence Dr			
10	UnnT	6816	A4
Florence Pl			
10	NWRK	6712	C7
10	STNL	7207	A2
700	CLFP	6611	D1
Florence Rd			
400	MNLA	6724	C6
400	NHmT	6724	C6
Florence St			
-	RDGF	6611	C1
10	BLRS	6827	C2
10	EGLD	6502	E1
10	FLPK	6827	C2
10	GTNK	6616	E6
10	SHkT	6501	C4
10	STNL	7117	B6
10	YNKR	6394	C3
100	MRNK	6283	A5
300	JSYC	6820	A2
Florida Av			
10	HmpT	7029	E3
10	STNL	7021	A5
10	YNKR	6394	A4
Florida Ct			
10	STNL	7021	A5
Florida St			
-	SHkT	6501	B3
-	TETB	6501	B3
10	ELIZ	6918	B6
10	LBCH	7028	D7
Florida Ter			
10	STNL	7117	D1
Florida Grove Rd			
100	PTHA	7205	B2
300	WbgT	7205	B1
400	PTHA	7114	B7
400	WbgT	7114	B7
Florida Grove Rd CO-655			
400	PTHA	7114	B7
400	WbgT	7114	B7
Flower Av			
10	DBSF	6165	E6
10	FLPK	6827	D1
10	HAOH	6165	E6
10	STNL	7206	D4
Flower Ln			
10	GrwT	6170	D2
10	KNGP	6616	C5
10	NHmT	6618	C7
10	NHmT	6723	D6
10	NHmT	6724	E2
Flower Rd			
10	HmpT	6928	B4
Flower St			
10	NRCH	6395	C6
Flowerhill Pl			
10	NHmT	6617	E2
Floyd Av			
10	BlmT	6713	B2
Floyd Pl			
10	GTNK	6617	A4
Floyd St			
10	JSYC	6716	A7
10	STNL	7019	D1
400	EGLC	6503	B1
600	EGLC	6392	C7
Flushing Av			
10	BKLN	121	E4
10	BKLN	6821	E6
17-00	BKLN	6823	A4
17-00	QENS	6823	A4
100	BKLN	6822	E5
Flynn Ct			
10	PTHA	7205	E2
Foam Pl			
11-00	QENS	7027	D4
Foch Av			
10	STNL	7020	E6
Foch Blvd			
-	WLPK	6724	D4
126-00	QENS	6926	E1
163-00	QENS	6825	E7
165-00	QENS	6826	A7
400	MNLA	6724	D5
500	NHmT	6724	D4
Folie Ct			
10	NHLS	6724	A1
Folin St			
2100	BRNX	6504	C5
Folsom Pl			
10	BKLN	6924	E1
Fonda Av			
183-00	QENS	6826	A5
Fonda Pl			
10	STNL	7206	E2
Fontaine Av			
10	BlmT	6713	C1
Food Center Dr			
100	BRNX	6613	E4
200	BRNX	6614	A4
Foote Av			
10	LWRN	7027	D4
10	QENS	7027	D4
10	STNL	7020	B3
Foothill Av			
196-00	QENS	6826	B3
Foothill Ct			
10	STNL	7115	E7
Foothill Rd			
10	EchT	6395	B2
10	MTVN	6395	B2
Forbell St			
10	QENS	6925	B1
600	BKLN	6925	B3
Forbes Av			
700	PTHA	7114	B7
Forbes Blvd			
10	EchT	6281	C6
Force Tube Av			
10	BKLN	6823	E7
100	BKLN	6924	E1
Ford Pl			
10	MHVN	6508	B6
10	STNL	7019	E1
Ford St			
-	DMRT	6278	A5
10	BKLN	6923	E3
10	BKLN	7023	D5
10	LODI	6500	E3
300	BRNX	6504	C5
Fordal Rd			
10	BRXV	6395	B1
Fordham Av			
10	RYE	6283	D4
Fordham Ln			
1000	HmpT	6928	B6
Fordham Pl			
300	BRNX	6506	E6
E Fordham Rd			
-	BRNX	6505	A5
10	BRNX	102	E7
300	BRNX	6504	E5
E Fordham Rd US-1			
-	BRNX	6505	A5
300	BRNX	6504	E5
W Fordham Rd			
-	MHTN	102	B7
-	MHTN	6504	A4
10	BRNX	102	D7
10	BRNX	6504	B4
200	BRNX	105	C1
Fordham St			
10	BRNX	6506	E6
10	VLYS	6928	C6
10	WLPK	6724	E4
Fordham Hill Ovl			
10	BRNX	102	D7
10	BRNX	6504	B4
Fords Ln			
10	RYE	6283	E6
Forest Av			
-	STNL	7117	E1
10	HAOH	6166	A6
10	LNBK	6929	C5
10	NHmT	6617	B6
10	NRCH	6395	E1
10	RYE	6284	A4
10	VLYS	6928	E4
62-00	QENS	6823	C5
100	STNL	7020	B1
100	YNKR	6393	E5
200	ERKY	6929	C5
200	HmpT	7028	B1
300	HmpT	6928	B7
300	NRCH	6396	A1
400	NRCH	6282	A7
600	MRNK	6283	A7
600	MrnT	6282	C6
700	BRNX	6613	B3
700	MRNK	6397	A1
700	RYE	6283	E6
700	STNL	7019	E1
2100	STNL	7018	D1
E Forest Av			
10	EGLD	6502	E1
E Forest Av CO-64			
10	EGLD	6502	E1
S Forest Av			
100	RKVC	6929	E5
W Forest Av			
10	EGLD	6502	D1
W Forest Av CO-64			
10	EGLD	6502	D1
Forest Blvd			
10	GrbT	6166	E2
Forest Cir			
10	NRCH	6395	E1
Forest Ct			
10	NRCH	6282	A7
10	STNL	6919	A7
Forest Dr			
10	EHLS	6618	E5
10	NHmT	6508	A6
10	SNPT	6508	E6
10	SNPT	6509	A5
300	EGLC	6503	B2
Forest Grn			
10	STNL	7116	B4
Forest Ln			
10	BRXV	6281	B7
10	GTNK	6616	E4
10	GTNK	6617	A4
10	LWRN	7027	E4
10	SCDL	6281	E1
10	STNL	7206	B5
Forest Pkwy			
84-00	QENS	6824	B6
Forest Pl			
10	BKLN	7021	D2
10	MrnT	6282	C6
10	NRCH	6395	D1
10	NWRK	6816	E4
300	HmpT	6828	E6
Forest Rd			
10	BRNX	6506	C1
10	DMRT	6278	B5
10	HmpT	6928	B4
10	PLMM	6395	C7
10	PLMM	6506	C1
10	STNL	7020	A6
10	TFLY	6392	B3
200	FTLE	6502	E7
237-00	QENS	6722	D2
Forest Row			
10	GTNK	6616	E4
10	GTNK	6617	A5
Forest St			
10	ALPN	6278	E6
10	BKLN	6822	D5
10	NARL	6714	D1
10	NHmT	6618	D7
10	STNL	7018	E4
200	KRNY	6714	B4
500	COrT	6712	A3
600	WOrT	6712	A3
Forest Ter			
10	GrbT	6166	D2
Forest Wy			
10	WOrT	6712	B1
Forest Cove			
10	RYE	6284	A5
Forester St			
10	LBCH	7029	E6
Forest Hill Pkwy			
10	NWRK	6713	D2
Forest Hill Rd			
-	STNL	7116	E2
10	STNL	7019	B6
10	WOrT	6712	A3
1500	STNL	7117	A1
Forest Lake Dr			
10	HRSN	6050	E4
10	HRSN	6051	A5
Forest Park Av			
10	LRMT	6396	C1
Forest Park Dr			
-	QENS	6824	D4
Forest Turn			
10	NHmT	6618	A7
Forest View Dr			
1500	WbgT	7114	E1
Forkland Ln			
10	DBSF	6166	B4
Forley St			
40-00	QENS	6719	E6
41-55	QENS	6720	A6
Forman St			
100	YNKR	6279	E6
Formosa St			
100	ELIZ	6919	A2
Fornes Pl			
10	STNL	7116	D7
Forrest St			
10	BKLN	6822	E5
10	JSYC	6819	E4
Forrestal Av			
10	STNL	7116	D4
Forrestal Ct			
10	STNL	7116	D4
Forster Av			
10	MTVN	6395	A3
Forster Pkwy			
10	MTVN	6395	A2
Forster Pl			
200	BRNX	6393	C5
Forsyth St			
10	MHTN	119	A4
10	MHTN	6821	C3
Fort Pl			
10	STNL	6920	D6
Fort Charles Pl			
10	MHTN	102	C4
10	MHTN	6504	B2
Forte Blvd			
600	HmpT	6828	B6
Fteley Av			
1100	BRNX	6614	A1
Fortfield Av			
10	YNKR	6280	A6
Fort George Av			
10	MHTN	104	E2
10	MHTN	6503	E5
Fort George Hl			
10	MHTN	104	E2
10	MHTN	6503	E4
Fort Greene Pl			
10	BKLN	121	D7
10	BKLN	6821	E7
100	BKLN	6922	C2
Fort Hamilton Av			
10	HmpT	7029	D5
Fort Hamilton Mnr			
10	BKLN	7021	E4
Fort Hamilton Pkwy			
2700	BKLN	6922	D6
5900	BKLN	7022	A2
8100	BKLN	7021	E2
Fort Hill Cir			
10	STNL	6920	D5
Fort Hill Ln			
10	GrbT	6167	A7
Fort Hill Pk			
10	STNL	6920	D6
Fort Hill Pl			
500	BKLN	7021	E3
Fort Hill Rd			
10	GrbT	6280	E1
10	YNKR	6280	E1
100	GrbT	6166	E7
200	GrbT	6167	A6
E Fort Hill Rd			
10	YNKR	6280	E2
10	YNKR	6281	A2
Fort Independence St			
3300	BRNX	6504	C2
Fort Lee Pl			
200	OrgT	6164	A1
Fort Lee Rd			
10	LEON	6502	C3
100	BGTA	6501	E3
100	TnkT	6501	E3
100	TnkT	6502	A3
400	FTLE	6502	D5
Fort Lee Rd CO-56			
10	LEON	6502	C3
10	TnkT	6502	C3
400	FTLE	6502	D5
E Fort Lee Rd			
10	BGTA	6501	E2
10	TnkT	6501	E2
E Fortlee Rd			
-	BGTA	6501	D2
W Fort Lee Rd			
10	BGTA	6501	D2
100	HKSK	6501	C2
W Fortlee Rd			
10	BGTA	6501	D2
Fort Slocum Rd			
10	NRCH	6395	E7
Fortuna St			
10	NWRK	6712	C6
Fort Washington Av			
10	MHTN	104	B6
10	MHTN	107	A1
10	MHTN	6503	D5
10	MHTN	6612	B1
Foschini Rd			
-	HKSK	6501	D1
Foster Av			
10	BKLN	7022	E1
10	HmpT	6928	A1
10	MLVN	6929	A2
10	QENS	6928	A1
10	STNL	7019	E5
10	VLYS	6928	E3
100	VLYS	6929	A3
600	BKLN	7023	A1
5400	BKLN	6923	E7
5400	BKLN	6924	A7
Foster Pl			
-	MTVN	6394	D3
10	SCLF	6509	D6
Foster Rd			
10	STNL	7207	A1
10	TFLY	6392	A2
100	STNL	7116	A7
Foster St			
10	NWRK	6817	B6
1000	HmpT	6828	A4
Foster Wy			
10	WbgT	7114	B2
Foundry St			
10	NWRK	6818	D1
Fountain Av			
10	BKLN	6924	E1
10	BKLN	6925	A1
10	RKVC	6929	E1
900	QENS	6925	B5
Fountain Dr			
10	MtPT	6050	B2
Fountain Ln			
10	GrbT	6281	A1
Fountain Pl			
10	NRCH	6396	B5
Fountain Rd			
200	EGLD	6502	E2
200	EGLD	6503	A2
Fountain Sq			
10	LRMT	6396	D3
Fountain Ter			
10	SCDL	6167	D5
Fouratt Av			
10	SRVL	7205	A6
Four Corners Rd			
10	STNL	7020	A6
Fowler Av			
10	JSYC	6819	C5
10	LNBK	6929	B4
10	YNKR	6280	A6
131-00	QENS	6720	E5
400	PLHM	6395	C6
400	PLMM	6395	C6
500	HmpT	6827	D6
500	HmpT	6828	A6
1600	BRNX	6505	B6
Fowler Pth			
-	QENS	6720	D6
Fox Av			
10	YNKR	6394	C2
Fox Hllw			
10	SNPT	6508	D4
Fox Ln			
10	GrwT	6170	E3
10	STNL	7118	A5
100	STNL	7117	E5
Fox Pl			
10	JSYC	6819	E1
Fox Rdg			
10	NHLS	6724	A3
Fox Run			
10	HRSN	6051	B5
10	NHLS	6724	D1
Fox St			
500	BRNX	6613	D2
1300	HmpT	6827	E5
Fox Ter			
10	BRNX	6505	D3
10	CLFP	6611	D3
10	YNKR	6393	E1
Foxbeach Av			
10	STNL	7117	E4
10	STNL	7118	A5
Foxcroft Rd			
10	NHmT	6618	A6
10	NHmT	6724	E3
Fox Glen Dr			
1300	GrbT	6167	D3
Foxhall Pl			
10	SCDL	6168	A7
Foxhall Rd			
10	SCDL	6168	B7
10	SCDL	6282	B1
Fox Hill Ter			
10	STNL	7020	E4
Fox Hill Run Dr			
10	WbgT	7114	D3
Foxholm St			
10	STNL	7117	E1
Foxhound Ct			
10	JSYC	6819	B4
Fox Hunt Ct			
10	STNL	7020	B3
Fox Hunt Ln			
10	LKSU	6723	B3
Foxhurst Ct			
10	NHmT	6724	A4
Foxhurst Ln			
10	NHmT	6617	E6
Fox Island Rd			
10	PTCH	6170	C7
Fox Meadow Rd			
10	SCDL	6167	C7
Fox Run Dr			
10	EGLD	6502	E3
Fox's Ln			
10	GrwT	6170	E3
Foxwood Rd			
10	KNGP	6616	E2
10	KNGP	6617	A2
Fradkin St			
10	WLTN	6500	B6
Frame Pl			
41-00	QENS	6720	E5
Frame St			
100	HmpT	6828	C5
France Pl			
10	MrnT	6396	D3
Frances Av			
10	HRSN	6283	B4
Frances Ct			
10	JSYC	6819	B4
Frances Dr			
1000	HmpT	6929	A1
Frances Ln			
400	NVLE	6164	B4
Frances Pl			
100	HlsT	6816	D6
Frances St			
10	MNCH	6501	C7
200	TnkT	6502	A1
Francesca Ln			
10	STNL	7019	A2
Francine Ct			
10	GrbT	6049	C7
10	STNL	7117	D2
Francine Ln			
10	STNL	7019	B3
Francis Av			
500	WbgT	7114	B4
Francis Ct			
10	HmpT	6827	E4
Francis Dr			
10	NHmT	6508	E7
Francis Ln			
10	GrwT	6170	C3
10	PTCH	6170	C3
Francis Pl			
10	STNL	7020	B5
8900	NBgT	108	A2
8900	NBgT	6611	C5
Francis St			
-	MLVN	6929	E2
10	SYHW	6048	B1
600	PLMM	6395	B6
700	PTHA	7205	D2
Francis Ter			
10	YNKR	6394	B3
Francis J McCormack Dr			
-	ARDY	6166	D5
-	GrbT	6166	D5
Francis Lewis Blvd			
-	QENS	6615	C7
16-01	QENS	6721	C1
46-23	QENS	6722	A6
73-23	QENS	6826	D6
130-00	QENS	6927	E2
147-00	QENS	6928	A3
Frank Av			
100	MRNK	6283	A5
Frank Ct			
-	STNL	7116	E5
10	BKLN	7023	E6
10	BKLN	7024	A7
Frank Pl			
10	PTCH	6170	C3
Frank St			
-	MtPT	6048	D1
10	HmpT	6827	B7
10	HmpT	6928	B1
400	HmpT	7029	D1
900	ROSL	6917	A5
1200	LNDN	6917	A6
S Frank St			
10	HmpT	6928	A3
Frank E Rodgers Blvd N			
10	HRSN	6714	A5
700	ENWK	6714	A5
700	KRNY	6714	A5
Frank E Rodgers Blvd N CO-697			
10	HRSN	6714	A5
700	ENWK	6714	A5
700	KRNY	6714	A5
Frank E Rodgers Blvd S			
10	HRSN	6714	A7
800	HRSN	6818	A1
1100	NWRK	6818	A1
Frankfort Av			
200	NVLE	6164	C5
Frankfort St			
10	MHTN	118	C7
10	MHTN	120	D1
10	MHTN	6821	B4
300	COrT	6712	C3
Franklin Av			
-	TETB	6500	E5
10	BKLN	6822	B6
10	FRVW	6611	B2
10	HmpT	6828	A7
10	HmpT	6928	C6
10	HmpT	6929	A1
10	HRSN	6283	A4
10	HRSN	6714	B6
10	HSBH	6500	D4
10	LNBK	6929	B3
10	LODI	6500	D4
10	LRMT	6396	D1
10	MLVN	6929	B2
10	MRNK	6283	A4
10	MtPT	6050	A2
10	MTVN	6394	E5
10	NHmT	6617	E2
10	NHmT	6723	E6
10	NRCH	6396	A4
10	RYE	6283	D4
10	SCLF	6509	E6
10	STNL	6920	C6
10	VLYS	6929	A2
10	WHPL	6168	B1
10	WLTN	6500	B5
10	YNKR	6393	B3
100	HmpT	7029	B5
134-01	QENS	6720	E5
134-01	QENS	6721	A5
200	CLFP	6611	D1
400	BKLN	6923	B3
400	MTVN	6395	A6
700	HmpT	6827	E7
800	NWRK	6713	D1
1000	BlvT	6713	D1
1000	BRNX	6613	C1
1400	GDNC	6724	E7
1500	MNLA	6724	E7
Franklin Av CO-645			
800	NWRK	6713	D1
1000	BlvT	6713	D1
N Franklin Av			
10	VLYS	6928	D3
S Franklin Av			
10	HmpT	6929	A5
10	LNBK	6929	A5
10	VLYS	6928	D4
100	LNBK	6928	C6
Franklin Blvd			
10	LBCH	7029	D6
Franklin Ct			
10	ARDY	6166	D3
10	TYTN	6048	B3
300	EDGW	108	B1
300	EDGW	6611	E5
Franklin Dr			
600	PTHA	7114	C7
700	WbgT	7114	C7
2000	LNDN	6917	C5
Franklin Ln			
10	HRSN	6169	B7
10	HRSN	6283	B1
10	STNL	7117	A2
Franklin Pl			
10	EchT	6395	C2
10	ERTH	6500	A6
10	GTNK	6616	E5
10	GTNK	6617	A5
10	HmpT	6928	C7
10	HmpT	7028	C1
10	KRNY	6714	B3
10	MHTN	118	D5
10	MHTN	6821	A2
10	PLHM	6395	B5
10	RTFD	6609	A2
10	STNL	7019	E4
10	WLTN	6500	A6
700	HmpT	6828	B3
Franklin Rd			
10	GTNK	6616	D4
10	GTNK	6617	A4
10	KNGP	6617	A4
10	SCDL	6282	B2
1900	HmpT	6928	B1
Franklin St			
10	BKLN	6822	B1
10	BlmT	6713	C1
10	BlvT	6713	C1
10	EchT	6281	A6
10	EGLD	6502	E1
10	EORG	6712	E1
10	EORG	6713	A1
10	ERKY	6929	B7
10	HKSK	6501	D4
10	HmpT	6827	D5
10	HmpT	6828	B4
10	JSYC	6716	B6
10	LFRY	6501	B5
10	MHTN	118	C5
10	MHTN	6821	B3
10	NWRK	6713	D1
10	NWRK	6817	D1
10	SECS	6610	B6
10	SHkT	6501	B4
10	TCKA	6281	A6
10	TFLY	6392	A3
10	WLPK	6724	D4
100	ELIZ	6918	B4
100	NVLE	6164	C5
200	BKLN	117	C7
200	BKLN	6718	B7
400	PTCH	6170	A5
400	RYEB	6170	A6
1400	HlsT	6816	D5
2300	FTLE	6503	A4
Franklin St CO-509			
10	BlmT	6713	C1
Franklin St CO-670			
10	BlmT	6713	C1
10	BlvT	6713	C1
10	NWRK	6713	D1
E Franklin St			
10	TYTN	6048	B3
W Franklin St			
10	HKSK	6501	C3
10	SHkT	6501	C3
10	TYTN	6048	B3
Franklin Ter			
10	IrvT	6816	B2
10	MplT	6816	B2
Franklin Gate			
1100	HmpT	6828	A7
Franklin Sigler Ln			
-	EORG	6712	D5
-	SOrT	6712	D5
Frank Simeone Sq			
600	BRNX	6504	B3
Frank Sinatra Dr			
-	HBKN	6716	E6
Frankton St			
137-00	HmpT	6928	A4
137-00	QENS	6928	A4
Frank W Burr Blvd			
100	TnkT	6502	B2
Frantone Ct			
10	HmpT	6828	D7
Frasco Av			
10	NRWD	6164	A6
Frasco Ln			
10	NRWD	6278	D2
Fraser Pl			
10	HAOH	6165	E6
10	HmpT	6928	C5
10	VLYS	6928	C5
Fraser Sq			
-	BKLN	7023	D2
Fraser St			
10	NRCH	6395	C4
10	PLHM	6395	C4
10	STNL	7019	A7
10	WbgT	7205	A3
Frawley Cir			
-	MHTN	109	E5
-	MHTN	6612	C6
Fraydun Pl			
10	RYE	6283	D3
Frazee Av			
10	SRVL	7205	A7
Frazier Pl			
10	YNKR	6394	C2
Frean St			
10	STNL	7020	D2
Freddy Av			
10	WbgT	7114	D2
Frederic Pl			
10	YNKR	6279	E6
Frederic St			
10	YNKR	6279	E6
Frederic B Powers Sq			
10	NRCH	6396	C4
Frederick Av			
10	HmpT	6827	D4
10	SFPK	6827	D4
200	FLPK	6827	D3
Frederick Ct			
10	HRSN	6283	C2
10	RYE	6283	C2
Frederick Ln			
10	EchT	6281	D3
10	NRCH	6281	D3
Frederick Pl			
10	MTVN	6395	A3
10	VLYS	6928	C5
Frederick St			
10	BlvT	6713	D1
10	CART	7017	B6
10	GRFD	6500	B2
10	HKSK	6501	C3
10	LFRY	6501	D5
10	LODI	6500	B3
10	MNCH	6501	C7

New York City/5 Borough Street Index

STREET
Block City Map# Grid

Frederick St
10 STNL 7019 C3
Frederick Ter
10 IrvT 6816 A2
Frederick Douglass Blvd
2000 MHTN 109 D1
2000 MHTN 6612 C4
2300 MHTN 106 E7
2400 MHTN 107 B4
Frederick Douglass Cir
- MHTN 109 C3
- MHTN 6612 B6
Fred Wehran Dr
100 LFRY 6501 B5
100 MNCH 6501 B5
100 SHkT 6501 B5
100 TETB 6501 B5
Freeborn St
10 STNL 7118 B2
Freedom Av
10 STNL 7018 E5
Freedom Dr
- QENS 6824 C5
Freedom Pl
10 JSYC 6819 D5
10 MHTN 112 B3
10 MHTN 6717 D2
Freedom Rd
10 NoCT 6050 B5
Freedom Rd S
10 NoCT 6050 B5
Freedom Wy
- JSYC 6820 B5
Freeman Al
10 MHTN 119 A4
10 MHTN 6821 C2
Freeman Av
10 EORG 6712 E5
10 HmpT 6827 C7
10 KRNY 6714 C4
100 NWRK 6712 E6
300 JSYC 6819 D1
Freeman Pl
10 STNL 7019 E1
10 WOrT 6712 A4
Freeman St
10 BKLN 6822 B1
10 COrT 6712 A3
10 NWRK 6818 B1
10 WbgT 7114 C3
10 WOrT 6712 A3
800 BRNX 6613 D1
Freeport Lp
10 BKLN 6924 E6
Freer St
10 LNBK 6929 A4
Freeway Dr
- NWRK 6713 B5
Freeway Dr E
- COrT 6712 D3
10 EORG 6713 A4
200 EORG 6712 D3
Freeway Dr W
10 COrT 6712 D3
10 EORG 6712 D3
Freightway
10 SCDL 6281 B1
Frelinghuysen Av
10 NWRK 6817 C4
900 ELIZ 6817 A7
Frelinghuysen Av SR-27
10 NWRK 6817 B6
900 ELIZ 6817 A7
Fremont Av
100 STNL 7118 A1
Fremont Pl
1300 ELIZ 6816 E7
Fremont Rd
10 VLYS 6928 D5
Fremont St
10 HRSN 6283 B4
10 JSYC 6820 A3
100 STNL 6920 D7
N French Av
10 EMFD 6049 B6
S French Av
10 EMFD 6049 C6
French Ct
300 TnkT 6502 C2
French Rdg
10 NRCH 6395 D4
French Ter
10 YNKR 6394 C3
Fresh Meadow Ln
47-00 QENS 6721 D7
67-00 QENS 6825 D1
Fresh Pond Rd
58-00 QENS 6823 C4
Frey Av
10 YNKR 6394 B2
Frick St
10 HmpT 6827 B7
Friel Pl
700 BKLN 6922 E6
800 BKLN 6923 A5
Friend St
10 WbgT 7115 B2
Friendship Ct
100 GrbT 6049 E5
Frisby Av
2400 BRNX 6505 D7
Frisco Av
12-00 QENS 7027 D5
Fritchie Pl
10 VLYS 6928 C2
Fritsch Av
400 CARL 6500 C6
400 WRDG 6500 C6
Frocan Ct
1100 HmpT 6928 D7
Froehlich Pl
400 HmpT 6827 B6
Front Row
10 LODI 6500 E1
Front St
10 BKLN 121 A3
10 BKLN 6821 C5
10 ELIZ 6918 C5
10 ERKY 6929 C7
10 JSYC 6820 A2
10 MHTN 120 C2
10 MHTN 6821 B5

Front St
10 RKVC 6929 D4
10 STNL 6920 E7
10 STNL 7020 E1
10 TYTN 6048 C5
100 MNLA 6724 E7
100 PTHA 7205 E5
100 SECS 6610 A6
300 SECS 6609 E6
S Front St
10 ELIZ 6918 B7
700 LNDN 6918 A7
Frontage Rd
10 NWRK 6817 E4
10 NWRK 6818 A4
Frontage St
10 EMFD 6049 A3
Frost Ln
10 GrbT 6167 B2
10 HmpT 6928 D7
10 LWRN 7028 A3
Frost St
10 BKLN 6822 C3
Frost Pond Dr
10 NHLS 6724 B3
Frum Av
10 YNKR 6394 A2
Fuel Farm Rd
- ELIZ 6918 C1
Fuller Av
10 ARDY 6166 C5
10 FLPK 6827 D2
Fuller Ct
10 STNL 7117 C3
Fuller Pl
10 BKLN 6922 E4
10 IrvT 6816 D1
10 KRNY 6714 B3
41-00 QENS 6720 E5
Fuller St
2400 BRNX 6505 C7
Fuller Ter
200 COrT 6712 C4
Fullerton Av
10 YNKR 6280 B7
10 YNKR 6394 B1
Fullerton Pl
10 RYE 6283 D4
Fulling Av
10 BRXV 6281 A7
10 TCKA 6281 A7
Fulton Av
10 ATLB 7028 A7
10 FRVW 6611 C4
10 HMPD 6828 E5
10 HmpT 6828 E5
10 NHmT 6724 C7
10 RYE 6283 D3
200 JSYC 6819 C4
1000 BRNX 6613 C1
1500 BRNX 105 E7
1500 BRNX 6504 C7
3000 HmpT 6929 E7
3200 HmpT 7029 E1
9000 NBgT 6611 C4
Fulton Av SR-24
10 HMPD 6828 E5
10 HmpT 6828 E5
N Fulton Av
10 MTVN 6394 E3
S Fulton Av
- PLMM 6395 A7
10 MTVN 6394 E4
200 MTVN 6395 A6
Fulton Ct
400 WNYK 6611 C7
Fulton Ln
100 MTVN 6395 A6
Fulton Pl
10 VLYS 6928 A3
400 RDGF 6611 A1
Fulton Rd
100 MRNK 6282 D7
Fulton St
- HAOH 6280 A1
10 BlmT 6712 E1
10 BlmT 6713 C1
10 ELIZ 6918 B5
10 EORG 6712 E1
10 HAOH 6279 E1
10 LFRY 6501 C5
10 MHTN 120 C1
10 MHTN 6821 B4
10 NWRK 6713 E7
10 STNL 7020 D2
10 TCKA 6281 A5
10 UNCT 111 A3
10 UNCT 6717 A2
10 WhkT 111 A3
10 WhkT 6717 A2
10 WHPL 6167 E1
100 GrbT 6167 E1
100 LWRN 7027 E3
100 MHTN 118 C7
200 WbgT 7114 C4
500 BKLN 121 D7
500 BKLN 6821 E7
700 BKLN 6822 A7
700 BKLN 6923 A1
800 HmpT 6827 D7
800 HmpT 6928 B3
2400 BKLN 6924 D1
3100 BKLN 6925 A1
3400 BKLN 6824 A7
3400 QENS 6824 B7
Fulton St E
10 HmpT 7029 C1
Fulton St W
10 HmpT 7029 C1
E Fulton St
10 LBCH 7029 D6
S Fulton St
10 WbgT 7114 D6
W Fulton St
100 LBCH 7029 B6
Fulton Ter
200 CLFP 6611 D3
200 FRVW 6611 C3
S Fulton St Ovps
- WbgT 7114 C5
Funston Av
10 NHmT 6724 D3
Furman Av
10 BKLN 6924 C1
4300 BRNX 6394 C6

Furman St
10 BKLN 120 E3
10 BKLN 121 A3
10 BKLN 6821 C5
10 STNL 7116 D7
Furmanville Av
75-00 QENS 6823 E3
80-00 QENS 6824 A3
Furness Pl
10 STNL 7019 A7
Furth Rd
1000 HmpT 6928 B5
Futurity Pl
10 STNL 7116 D3
Fycke Ln
10 TnkT 6502 B2

G

G St
- BRNX 6614 C4
1200 HmpT 6827 E6
Gabirol Dr
- HmpT 6928 A7
Gable Ln
300 LNDN 7017 B2
Gabriel Av
900 HmpT 6828 B5
Gabriel Ct
10 WHPL 6168 D3
Gabriel Dr
10 BRNX 6505 C4
Gaby Ln
10 NRCH 6281 E4
Gaddis Pl
10 MLVN 6929 A2
Gadek Pl
700 PTHA 7205 E2
Gadsen Pl
10 STNL 7019 A6
Gaffney Pl
10 YNKR 6394 B3
Gaffney Wy
10 WbgT 7115 B2
Gage Ct
10 OrgT 6164 A2
Gail Ct
10 STNL 7117 E2
500 TnkT 6502 A2
600 HmpT 6827 D7
Gail Dr
10 NRCH 6396 A6
Gail Pl
10 SECS 6610 B6
Gail Rd
10 YNKR 6280 E1
Gail Ter
10 GLCV 6509 D3
Gaillard Pl
10 MrnT 6396 B3
10 NRCH 6396 B3
Gailmore Dr
100 YNKR 6280 C5
Gain Ct
10 BKLN 7024 A7
100 BKLN 7023 E5
Gainsborg Av E
10 HRSN 6050 D7
10 HRSN 6168 D1
Gainsborough Rd
10 YNKR 6281 B2
Gair St
- PRMT 6165 A1
Gala Ct
10 GrbT 6049 E5
Gale Av
32-00 QENS 6718 D7
Gale Dr
10 HmpT 6928 B6
10 VLYS 6928 B6
Gale Pl
100 BRNX 6504 D1
Galesville Ct
10 STNL 7021 B5
Gallagher Ct
10 THSN 6617 B7
Gallatin Pl
10 BKLN 121 B6
10 BKLN 6821 D7
Galloping Hill Rd
10 ELIZ 6917 A2
10 ROSP 6917 A2
400 UnnT 6917 A2
Galloping Hill Rd CO-616
10 ELIZ 6917 A2
10 ROSP 6917 A2
400 UnnT 6917 A2
Galloway Av
10 STNL 7019 C2
Galloway Ln
10 MtPT 6049 E1
Galvaston Lp
10 STNL 7117 A1
Galvin Av
600 ROSL 6917 A4
Galway Av
184-00 QENS 6826 B5
Gambold Rd
- STNL 7019 E7
Game Cock Rd
10 GrwT 6170 D6
Gamewell St
10 HKSK 6501 B1
Gannett Ct
100 NHLS 6724 B1
Gannett Dr
10 HRSN 6169 A3
N Gannon Av
10 STNL 7019 D4
S Gannon Av
10 STNL 7019 C4
Gansevoort Blvd
100 STNL 7019 D4
Gansevoort St
10 MHTN 115 C6
10 MHTN 6717 B7
Garabrant St
10 JSYC 6820 A4
Garafola Pl
- KRNY 6714 C3
Gard Av
10 YNKR 6280 D7

Gard Ct
10 GrwT 6170 B2
Garden Av
10 BRXV 6280 E7
200 MTVN 6395 A5
400 WbgT 7114 D4
Garden Blvd
300 GDNC 6828 D3
300 HmpT 6828 C3
Garden Ct
10 NHmT 6723 E6
10 QENS 7027 D5
10 STNL 7020 A6
Garden Ct E
10 GRFD 6500 A1
Garden Ct N
10 GRFD 6500 A2
Garden Ct S
10 GRFD 6500 A2
Garden Dr
10 LNBK 6929 A4
10 LNDN 6917 B5
10 NHmT 6724 D2
10 ROSL 6917 B5
10 RYE 6283 D6
700 HmpT 6828 B3
Garden Ln
10 HmpT 7027 E2
Garden Pl
10 BKLN 120 E5
10 BKLN 6821 C7
10 EDGW 6611 E2
10 GLCV 6509 D3
10 GrwT 6170 C3
10 PLMM 6395 C7
100 HmpT 6828 D4
Garden Rd
10 HRSN 6283 C2
10 PLMM 6395 C7
10 SCDL 6167 E6
10 SCDL 6168 A5
100 WHPL 6168 A5
E Garden Rd
100 MrnT 6282 C7
W Garden Rd
10 MrnT 6282 C7
Garden St
- RSLN 6618 D7
- STNL 7019 D4
10 BKLN 6822 D5
10 GrbT 6166 E2
10 GTPZ 6617 B7
10 HBKN 6716 E5
10 LFRY 6501 C5
10 LODI 6500 D1
10 MNCH 6501 B7
10 NHmT 6618 D7
10 NRCH 6395 E4
10 NWRK 6817 E2
10 RDFP 6501 E6
10 THSN 6617 B7
10 VLYS 6928 C5
10 WRDG 6500 B7
100 ERTH 6609 B1
100 THSN 6723 B1
300 CARL 6500 B7
300 ERTH 6500 B7
600 BRNX 6504 D6
900 ELIZ 6917 D5
Garden Ter
10 JSYC 6819 B7
10 KRNY 6714 C1
10 NARL 6714 C1
Garden City Blvd
10 HmpT 6828 D5
Garden City Rd
200 HmpT 6828 B3
Gardenia Dr
10 WLTN 6500 A6
Gardenia Ln
10 STNL 7018 D7
10 STNL 7019 B7
Gardenia St
500 HmpT 6828 D6
Garden State Pkwy
- BlmT 6713 A2
- EORG 6712 E6
- EORG 6713 A4
- HlsT 6816 A5
- IrvT 6712 E7
- IrvT 6816 A5
- NWRK 6712 E6
- SRVL 7205 A7
- UnnT 6816 A5
- WbgT 7114 A7
- WbgT 7205 A4
Garden State Pkwy Express Ln
- SRVL 7205 A7
Garden Turn
10 NHmT 6617 E7
10 NHmT 6618 A7
Gardner Av
10 BKLN 6823 A4
10 JSYC 6819 E3
100 BKLN 6822 E4
200 SOrT 6712 A6
Gardner Pl
400 HKSK 6501 D4
Gardner St
400 HlsT 6816 B6
Gardner Ter
- YNKR 6394 B1
Gareis St
- NWRK 6817 A1
Garfield Av
10 BAYN 6819 B7
10 FLPK 6827 C1
10 GRFD 6500 B3
10 JSYC 6819 E5
10 LODI 6500 C3
10 QENS 6928 A2
10 STNL 7020 D7
10 STNL 7021 B4
10 VLYS 6928 A2
66-00 QENS 6719 C7
100 KRNY 6714 C4
100 MNLA 6724 E6
300 HmpT 6828 D5
400 NHmT 6724 D7
1000 JSYC 6820 A3
Garfield Pl
10 BKLN 6922 E2
10 EORG 6712 E6
10 ERKY 6929 C5
10 LFRY 6501 C5

Garfield Pl
10 LNBK 6929 C5
10 MplT 6712 A7
10 MplT 6816 A1
10 NHmT 6618 D7
10 RTFD 6609 A3
10 SHkT 6500 B4
10 SOrT 6712 A7
1300 ELIZ 6816 E7
Garfield St
10 GDNC 6828 B2
10 LFRY 6501 B5
10 LNDN 6917 C5
10 TCKA 6281 E6
10 YNKR 6393 E1
300 FRVW 6611 B4
500 ROSL 6917 B5
700 HmpT 6828 B4
1600 BRNX 6505 A7
Garibaldi Av
10 LODI 6500 D1
10 NWRK 6817 A7
10 STNL 7118 B3
300 HKSK 6500 E2
Garibaldi Pl
10 PTCH 6170 A6
10 RYEB 6170 A6
Garit Ln
10 MrnT 6282 D7
Garland Ct
10 BKLN 7023 E6
Garland Dr
10 HAOH 6166 B7
221-00 QENS 6722 C4
Garland Ln
10 HmpT 6928 B4
Garland Wy
10 LynT 6609 B5
10 RTFD 6609 B5
Garmany Pl
10 YNKR 6280 E6
Garnet Pl
10 HmpT 6827 C6
Garnet St
10 BKLN 6922 C2
Garnett Pl
10 NRWD 6164 B5
Garretson Av
10 BAYN 6919 D6
10 STNL 7020 B6
300 PTHA 7205 E1
Garretson Ln
10 STNL 7020 C5
Garretson Rd
10 WHPL 6050 B6
Garrett Av
10 TCKA 6280 E6
Garrett Pl
10 YNKR 6280 D7
2100 BRNX 6394 E7
Garrett St
133-00 QENS 6927 B2
Garrison Av
10 HSBH 6500 E4
10 JSYC 6819 E1
10 STNL 7019 C2
700 BRNX 6613 D3
Garrison St
10 NWRK 6818 A2
Garry Rd
10 CLST 6278 C2
Garry Ter
1000 SECS 6610 B6
Garside St
10 NWRK 6713 D4
Garth Ct
10 STNL 7117 C3
Garth Rd
10 EchT 6281 B1
10 SCDL 6167 B7
10 SCDL 6281 B1
Garver Dr
10 RYE 6283 D3
Garvies Point Rd
10 GLCV 6509 D4
Garwood Pl
10 IrvT 6816 D1
Gary Ct
10 STNL 7019 A4
Gary Ln
10 OrgT 6164 B1
Gary Pl
10 STNL 7018 E5
Gary Rd
10 UnnT 6816 A6
Gary St
10 STNL 7116 C4
Gaskell Rd
250-00 QENS 6722 E3
251-00 QENS 6723 A3
Gaston Av
10 GRFD 6500 B2
Gaston St
10 WOrT 6712 A1
E Gate
700 HmpT 6827 E7
S Gate
10 GDNC 6828 D1
W Gate
700 HmpT 6827 D7
800 HmpT 6928 D1
E Gate Ct
10 LODI 6500 D2
S Gate Ct
10 BKLN 7022 E6
10 BKLN 7023 A6
E Gate Rd
10 FLHL 6618 B4
N Gate Rd
10 GTNK 6617 B5
10 KNGP 6617 B5
S Gate Rd
10 GTNK 6617 B5
W Gate Rd
10 FLHL 6618 B4
Gate Wy
10 NHmT 6724 D1
Gate House Ln
10 MrnT 6282 D3
Gate House Rd
10 SCDL 6282 A3
Gates Av
10 BKLN 6822 C7
10 BKLN 6923 A1

Gates Av
10 HmpT 7027 C3
10 MLVN 6929 A2
10 VLYS 6928 C2
15-76 BKLN 6823 B5
59-00 QENS 6823 C4
100 JSYC 6819 B6
Gates Pl
10 OrgT 6164 B2
3400 BRNX 6504 E1
Gates Rd
200 LFRY 6501 D7
Gates St
- NRWD 6164 A5
Gates Ter
600 UnnT 6917 A2
700 ROSP 6917 A2
Gates Wy
10 SCLF 6509 E7
Gateway Blvd
12-00 QENS 7027 D5
Gateway Dr
- BKLN 6924 E5
- BKLN 6925 A5
10 GTNE 6616 E7
10 GTNE 6617 C4
10 STNL 7020 C5
Gateway Plz
10 BKLN 6925 A5
Gateway Rd
10 YNKR 6279 E4
Gateway St
800 HlsT 6917 D1
Gatling Pl
10 BKLN 7021 E3
Gaton St
10 STNL 7115 C7
Gatsby Ln
10 KNGP 6616 D1
Gauldy Av
10 STNL 7018 E3
Gautier Av
10 JSYC 6819 D2
Gavin St
10 YNKR 6280 A7
Gavrin Blvd
1100 HmpT 6827 E6
1100 HmpT 6828 A6
Gaw Pl
5500 WNYK 111 A1
5500 WNYK 6717 A1
Gay Dr
10 KNGP 6616 D4
Gay St
10 MHTN 118 D1
10 MHTN 6821 B1
Gaylor Rd
10 EchT 6281 C2
100 SCDL 6281 C2
Gaylord Dr N
10 BKLN 7024 B4
Gaylord Dr S
10 BKLN 7024 B4
Gaynor Av
10 NHmT 6617 D6
Gaynor Pl
600 HmpT 6828 C7
Gaynor St
10 STNL 7206 D1
Gazebo Rd
- STNL 6920 B6
G Cannon Dr
10 JSYC 6820 A4
Gebhardt Av
800 ELIZ 6917 C2
800 UnnT 6917 C2
Gedney Cir
10 WHPL 6168 C5
Gedney Ter
10 WHPL 6168 C4
Gedney Wy
10 WHPL 6168 C4
Gedney Esplanade
10 WHPL 6168 D4
Gedney Park Dr
10 WHPL 6168 C4
Gehrig Av
700 HmpT 6828 B7
Gehrs Pl
1400 NBgT 6716 D1
Geldner Av
10 STNL 7117 E1
Gelston Av
10 BKLN 7021 D3
Gem St
10 BKLN 6822 B2
Gene Ln
400 HmpT 6827 C6
Gene Pl
10 WHPL 6168 C6
General St
10 STNL 7117 D3
General Heath Av
10 NoCT 6050 B5
General Karge Ct
10 ELIZ 6917 E5
General Lee Av
10 BKLN 7021 D4
General Rw Berry Dr
100 QENS 6616 A7
Genesee Av
10 STNL 7117 A5
100 STNL 7116 E5
Genesee Blvd
10 ATLB 7028 A6
Genesee St
10 STNL 7020 B3
Genesee Tr
10 HRSN 6283 B2
Geneva Lp
10 BKLN 6924 E6
Geneva St
10 ELIZ 6918 B6
Genevieve Dr
10 GrbT 6048 D6
Genevieve Pl
10 NHmT 6723 A2
Gentile Ct
10 STNL 7207 C1
Gentry Dr
10 EGLD 6502 E2
Geo Ct
10 STNL 7020 D3

Geoffrey Ln
10 HmpT 6928 C6
George Ct
10 CART 7017 B5
10 HSBH 6500 E2
George Pl
10 BRNX 6394 E7
10 ERKY 6929 C6
10 MTVN 6394 E7
George St
10 BAYN 6919 D5
10 BKLN 6822 E5
10 CART 7017 B6
10 ERTH 6609 C1
10 GLCV 6509 E3
10 GTNK 6616 D4
10 HKSK 6501 B2
10 NHmT 6617 D6
10 NWRK 6818 B1
10 SAMB 7205 C7
10 STNL 7206 B4
10 TFLY 6392 A3
10 WbgT 7114 D2
10 WHPL 6050 C7
10 YNKR 6281 A3
16-00 BKLN 6823 C6
16-00 QENS 6823 C6
600 TnkT 6502 B2
1400 BRNX 6505 E7
George Frederick Plz
10 WbgT 7114 B3
George Howard Dr
- QENS 6926 D6
George Langeloh Ct
10 RYE 6284 A3
Georges Ln
10 STNL 7206 E2
Georges Pl
400 ROSL 6917 A5
Georgetown N
- GrwT 6170 E3
Georgetown Ln
10 BKLN 7024 A2
George Washington Br
- FTLE 103 D3
- FTLE 6503 B5
- MHTN 103 D3
- MHTN 104 A4
- MHTN 6503 B5
George Washington Br I-95
- FTLE 103 D3
- FTLE 6503 B5
- MHTN 103 D3
- MHTN 104 A4
- MHTN 6503 B5
George Washington Br US-1
- FTLE 103 D3
- FTLE 6503 B5
- MHTN 103 D3
- MHTN 104 A4
- MHTN 6503 B5
George Washington Br US-9
- FTLE 103 D3
- FTLE 6503 B5
- MHTN 103 D3
- MHTN 104 A4
- MHTN 6503 B5
Georgia Av
10 BKLN 6924 C2
10 HmpT 7029 E3
10 LBCH 7028 D7
10 YNKR 6394 D1
Georgia Ct
10 STNL 7206 D2
Georgia Rd
146-00 QENS 6721 B5
Georgia St
10 HmpT 6928 B1
S Georgia St
10 HmpT 6928 A3
Georgian Ct
10 ELIZ 6917 E1
10 HlsT 6917 E1
10 NHmT 6724 C3
Georgian Ln
10 GTNK 6616 C4
10 KNGP 6616 C4
Gerada Ln
10 NRCH 6281 E6
Gerald Ct
10 BKLN 7023 B7
Gerald H Chambers Sq
10 BKLN 7121 B1
Geraldine Ct
10 EGLC 6392 C6
Geraldine Rd
10 EGLC 6392 D6
10 NARL 6714 D1
Geraldine St
- WbgT 7205 A2
Geranium Av
10 FLPK 6827 C3
137-00 QENS 6721 A5
Geranium Pl
10 BRNX 6615 C4
10 WLTN 6500 A6
Gerard Av
10 NHmT 6723 E5
200 BRNX 107 E3
200 BRNX 6612 E2
900 BRNX 6613 A1
1200 BRNX 105 A7
1200 BRNX 6504 A7
Gerard Av E
10 HmpT 6929 C1
10 MLVN 6929 C1
Gerard Av W
10 HmpT 6929 B1
10 MLVN 6929 B1
Gerard Ct
2900 HmpT 6929 D6
Gerard Pl
105-00 QENS 6824 C2
Gerber Pl
2900 BRNX 6615 B3
Gerken Pl
2700 HmpT 6929 E6
Gerlach Pl
10 LRMT 6396 C2
Germaine St
10 GLCV 6509 D4

Germak Dr
10 CART 7017 B6
Gerome Av
1500 FTLE 103 A3
1500 FTLE 6502 E6
1500 FTLE 6503 B5
Gerri Ln
10 YNKR 6279 E4
Gerritsen Av
10 BKLN 7023 D4
2700 BKLN 7024 A7
Gerry St
10 BKLN 6822 C5
10 GrwT 6170 E4
Gerson Av
- OrgT 6164 E5
- RCKL 6164 E5
Gerson Ct
29-00 QENS 7027 B5
Gerta Ln
10 HRSN 6283 A4
10 MRNK 6283 A4
Gertmin Rd
10 HmpT 7028 C1
Gertrude Av
100 MRNK 6282 E5
Gertrude St
10 BAYN 6919 C5
200 HlsT 6816 C6
Gertz Av
10 LFRY 6501 C7
Gervais St
10 GLCV 6509 E3
Gervil St
10 STNL 7115 E5
Gesner Pl
10 SYHW 6048 B1
Gettysburg St
88-00 QENS 6827 A2
Getz Av
200 STNL 7116 E4
Geyser Dr
10 STNL 7116 B5
Geyser Pl
10 GrbT 6049 C6
Gianna Ct
10 STNL 7117 E3
Gibbons Ct
800 ELIZ 6917 D5
Gibson Av
10 GrbT 6049 D7
10 STNL 7117 B4
Gibson Blvd
10 VLYS 6928 D5
200 HmpT 6928 D5
Gibson Pl
10 ELIZ 6917 C3
10 YNKR 6393 D4
Giegerich Av
- STNL 7206 C3
Giegerich Pl
10 STNL 7206 C4
3000 BRNX 6615 C4
Gifford Av
10 JSYC 6819 D2
2700 BRNX 6614 E1
Gifford Ct
10 MplT 6816 A3
Gifford Pl
10 IrvT 6712 B7
10 IrvT 6816 C1
10 NWRK 6712 B7
200 TnkT 6502 A3
Gifford St
10 TCKA 6281 A6
300 PTHA 7205 C3
Giffords Gln
10 STNL 7117 D5
Giffords Ln
10 STNL 7117 A4
Gigante Pl
10 CLFP 108 A1
10 CLFP 6611 C4
Gil Ct
10 STNL 7116 E5
Gilbert Ct
10 FLPK 6827 E2
Gilbert Pl
10 PTCH 6170 A6
10 STNL 7206 D3
10 WHPL 6050 B6
10 WOrT 6712 A2
10 YNKR 6279 D5
700 HmpT 6928 A5
1200 BRNX 6613 D3
Gilbert Rd
10 GTNK 6616 E4
10 KNGP 6616 E4
Gilbert Rd E
10 KNGP 6616 E4
Gilbert Rd W
10 KNGP 6616 E4
Gilbert St
10 STNL 7117 C3
Gilchrest Rd
10 GTPZ 6617 B7
10 GTPZ 6723 C1
10 KENS 6617 B6
10 NHmT 6617 B6
10 THSN 6617 B7
10 THSN 6723 C1
Gilchrist Av
600 LNDN 6917 D6
Gilder St
10 LRMT 6396 C2
Gildersleeve Av
1900 BRNX 6614 C4
Giles Av
10 JSYC 6715 E7
10 JSYC 6819 E1
Giles Pl
10 STNL 7020 D5
3300 BRNX 6504 C2
Giletta Ct
10 ALPN 6278 D4
10 CLST 6278 D4
Gilford Av
1500 NHmT 6724 A7
1500 NHPK 6724 A7
Gillard Av
10 STNL 7116 E6
Gillespie Av
1300 BRNX 6505 E7

Gillette Pl
10 NWRK 6817 C2
Gillis Pl
1000 SECS 6610 B6
Gillmore St
24-00 QENS 6720 A3
Gilmar Ln
10 NHmT 6724 D1
Gilmore Av
10 CRSK 6278 A6
Gilmore Blvd
10 HmpT 6827 E3
10 STMN 6827 E3
Gilmore Ct
10 BKLN 7023 B7
10 SCDL 6167 E4
Gilmore St
200 WLPK 6724 D5
300 MNLA 6724 D5
Gilroy St
10 STNL 7116 A6
Gina Ct
10 STNL 7019 B7
Ginda Av
10 CART 7115 B1
Giordan Ct
10 STNL 6919 A7
Gipson St
13-00 QENS 7027 C4
Girard Av
10 EORG 6712 E1
Girard Pl
10 NWRK 6816 E2
Girard St
10 BKLN 7121 C1
10 STNL 7206 A3
1400 MRNK 6282 D4
Gist Pl
200 COrT 6712 D1
Givan Av
1200 BRNX 6505 C2
2200 BRNX 6506 A1
Givernaud Ter
3400 NBgT 6716 B2
Gladiolus Av
10 FLPK 6827 C2
Gladstone Av
10 NWRK 6712 E7
Gladstone Pl
10 YNKR 6280 A4
Gladstone Rd
10 NRCH 6281 D3
Gladwin Av
10 LEON 6502 C4
171-00 QENS 6721 D5
Gladwin Rd
10 BRXV 6280 C3
Gladwin St
- STNL 7115 D6
100 STNL 7206 C1
Gladys Ct
600 NVLE 6164 B4
Gladys St
10 HmpT 6928 C5
3500 HmpT 7029 C2
Glafil St
600 HmpT 6827 B6
Glamford Av
10 NHmT 6508 D6
10 PTWN 6508 D6
Glamford Rd
10 GTNK 6617 B5
10 KNGP 6617 B5
Glandstone Park Dr
- FTLE 103 A3
- FTLE 6503 A5
Glanz Av
100 NVLE 6164 C5
Glascoe Av
10 STNL 7019 C3
Glassboro Av
139-00 QENS 6825 C7
Gleane St
40-00 QENS 6719 E6
42-00 QENS 6720 A6
Gleason Av
1600 BRNX 6614 A2
Gleason Pl
10 HRSN 6283 B4
Glebe Av
2100 BRNX 6505 C7
2100 BRNX 6614 C1
Glebe St
400 COrT 6712 B2
500 WOrT 6712 B2
Gleeson Pl
10 YNKR 6394 B2
Glen Av
10 MTVN 6394 E4
10 PTCH 6170 B5
10 ROSE 6618 D6
10 RSLN 6618 D6
10 SCLF 6509 E6
10 STNL 6920 C7
100 WOrT 6712 B1
200 PALP 6502 C6
200 STNL 7020 C1
500 CLFP 6611 D2
500 LEON 6502 D6
W Glen Av
10 PTCH 6170 A3
10 RYEB 6170 A3
Glen Ct
10 HRSN 6282 E2
200 TnkT 6502 C1
500 HmpT 6929 D6
Glen Dr
10 HRSN 6282 E2
10 WbgT 7205 B3
800 HmpT 6928 B7
900 HmpT 6928 A6
Glen Ln
10 BXTE 6508 E7
10 MrnT 6282 D5
10 NHmT 6508 E7
10 OybT 6618 E1
N Glen Ln
- EDGW 103 A7
- EDGW 6503 A7
- EDGW 6611 E3
S Glen Ln
- EDGW 6611 E4
Glen Pl
10 NRCH 6395 D5

New York City/5 Borough Street Index

Column header (repeated for each of 8 columns): **STREET / Block City / Map# Grid**

Glen Rd
10 TCKA 6281 B5
10 ARDY 6166 E4
10 EchT 6281 B5
10 GDNC 6828 B1
10 HmpT 6929 D1
10 RTFD 6609 B2
10 WOrT 6712 A3
10 YNKR 6394 B5
700 CLFP 6611 D1
700 FTLE 6611 B1
1000 FTLE 6502 D7

Glen Rd SR-5
1000 FTLE 6502 D7
1000 FTLE 6611 D1

Glen St
10 BKLN 6925 A1
10 CLFP 6611 D2
10 GrwT 6170 E4
10 OybT 6618 E2
10 STNL 7018 B6
10 TYTN 6048 B3

Glenbrook Av
100 YNKR 6393 D2

Glenbrook Rd
10 NRCH 6396 A1

Glenbrooke Dr
10 WHPL 6169 A5

Glencar Av
10 NRCH 6395 C3

Glencove Av
10 WbgT 7114 E4

Glendale Av
10 STNL 7020 C5

Glendale Ct
10 BKLN 7023 D1

Glendale Pl
10 PTCH 6170 B4

Glendale Rd
10 HRSN 6167 A6
10 HRSN 6282 E3
10 RYE 6283 D2
10 WbgT 7114 A1
400 NVLE 6164 B4

Glendon Cir
10 WHPL 6168 D5

Glen Eagles Dr
10 MrnT 6282 B6

Glen Eagles Dr S
10 MrnT 6282 B6

Glenfruin Av
10 NRCH 6395 D1

Glen Goin Dr
10 ALPN 6278 E7
10 ALPN 6279 E7

Glenhill Av
10 YNKR 6280 A6

Glen Hill Ln
10 NRCH 6395 E4

Glen Lake Dr
10 LRMT 6396 B4

Glenlawn Av
10 SCLF 6509 E6

Glenlawn Ct
10 SCLF 6509 E7

Glenmore Av
10 BKLN 6924 E2
10 OybT 6618 E1
75-00 BKLN 6925 B1
75-00 QENS 6925 B1

Glenmore Dr
10 NRCH 6395 C3

Glenmore St
100 EWLS 6724 E4

Glenn Av
10 NRWD 6164 A6

Glenn Ct
10 ERTH 6500 A7

Glenn Ln
- JSYC 6819 C5

Glenn Pl
10 HAOH 6166 A4
10 HAOH 6280 C1

Glenn Rd
10 MrnT 6282 B7
10 STNL 7019 A6

Glenn St
10 WHPL 6050 A6

Glennon Pl
3000 BRNX 6615 C4

Glen Oaks Dr
10 RYE 6283 C4

Glenola Av
10 SCLF 6509 E7

Glenorchy Ct
10 NRCH 6395 D1

Glen Park Rd
10 HRSN 6168 E1

Glenridge Av
800 HmpT 6928 A6

Glen Ridge Rd
10 GrwT 6170 E4

Glenside Dr
10 WOrT 6712 A4

Glen View Ter
10 CRSK 6392 A4

Glenville Rd
10 GrwT 6170 D1

Glenville St
10 GrwT 6170 E1
10 RYEB 6170 B1

Glen Washington Rd
10 NRCH 6394 D1

Glenwood Av
- STNL 7117 E1
10 Blmt 6713 A1
10 COrT 6712 D3
10 DMRT 6278 B6
10 EDGW 6611 E2
10 EORG 6712 E2
10 EORG 6713 A1
10 HAOH 6166 A4
10 JSYC 6819 C5
10 LEON 6502 D5
10 LNBK 6929 A6
10 NRCH 6395 D1
10 PALP 6502 C5
10 STNL 7020 B1
10 YNKR 6502 B2
300 TnkT 6502 B2

Glenwood Ct
10 TFLY 6392 B2

Glenwood Ct
2900 HWTH 7029 D6

Glenwood Dr
10 GTNE 6616 E7

Glenwood Gdns
10 YNKR 6279 C6

Glenwood Pl
10 EORG 6713 A1
10 NRCH 6395 C4
10 STNL 7019 E2
10 STNL 7020 A3

Glenwood Rd
10 EGLD 6392 A6
10 GrbT 6167 C6
10 HRSN 6283 A3
10 OybT 6618 E1
10 ROSH 6618 A1
10 TFLY 6392 A3
100 ELIZ 6917 B2
100 UnnT 6917 B2
900 HmpT 6828 C7
900 HmpT 6929 D2
1600 BKLN 7023 A1
2900 BKLN 6923 D7
5600 BKLN 6924 A7
5600 BKLN 7024 A1

Glenwood St
10 WLPK 6724 D4
10 QENS 6722 E2

Glimcher Realty Wy
10 ELIZ 6918 D3

Globe Av
10 STNL 7019 A3
1200 HmpT 6827 E5

Gloria Ct
10 STNL 7019 E3

Gloria Pl
300 HmpT 6828 C3

Glorieux St
10 IrvT 6816 B3

Gloucester Ct
10 CLST 6278 C2

Gloucester Pl
10 BKLN 6822 E6
10 BKLN 6823 A7

Gloucester Rd
800 UnnT 6917 A1

Gloucester St
300 EGLD 6503 A2

Glover Cir
10 YNKR 6394 B7

Glover Ct
10 LNBK 6929 B4

Glover St
10 STNL 7117 B7
1400 BRNX 6614 C1
1500 BRNX 6505 C7

Glover Johnson St
10 NRCH 6395 E4

Goble Pl
10 BRNX 105 B5

Goble St
10 NWRK 6817 D3

God Wy
- NWRK 6818 C5

Godfrey Pl
10 CRSK 6278 A6

Godwin Ter
3000 BRNX 6504 B2
3100 BRNX 102 D3

Goethals Av
158-00 QENS 6825 C3

Goethals Br
- ELIZ 6918 A7
10 STNL 6918 A7

Goethals Br I-278
- ELIZ 6918 A7
10 STNL 6918 A7

Goethals Rd N
10 STNL 7019 A3
800 STNL 7018 C1

Goff Av
10 STNL 7206 E1

S Goff Av
10 STNL 7206 E2

Gold Av
10 STNL 7116 C4

Gold Cir
10 MLVN 6929 B7

Gold Pl
10 MLVN 6929 B7

Gold Rd
89-00 QENS 6925 D2

Gold St
10 BKLN 121 C2
10 BKLN 6821 D6
10 GrwT 6170 D1
10 MHTN 120 C1
10 NWRK 6817 A1
10 QENS 6928 A3
10 VLYS 6928 A3
10 YNKR 6279 D7
500 PTHA 7205 D2

Gold Coast Ct
10 GLCV 6509 E2

Golden Av
600 SECS 6610 C4
300 ERTH 6609 E2

Golden Ln
400 UNCT 6610 A1

Golden Pond Rd
10 HRSN 6050 D3

Goldenrod Av
10 STNL 7117 E1

Golden Square Ct
10 WbgT 7114 D2

Goldington Ct
166-00 QENS 6825 D4

Goldner Ct
84-00 QENS 6826 A3

Goldsmith Av
10 NWRK 6818 A3

Goldsmith St
51-00 QENS 6719 E6

Goldwin St
10 RYE 6284 A2

Golf Ct
10 TnkT 6502 B1

Golf Dr
500 HmpT 6928 A6

Golf Ln
200 HWTH 7029 A1

Golf Pl
10 EGLD 6502 E2

Golf Club Ln
10 GDNC 6724 E1
10 GDNC 6828 E1

Golf Course Dr
400 LEON 6502 D3

Golf View Ct
10 STNL 7117 A1

Golfwood Ct
10 STNL 7020 C5

Goller Pl
10 STNL 7019 A4

Good Pl
10 PLMM 6395 A7

Goodall St
10 STNL 7117 B7

Goodell St
10 STNL 7019 D3

Goodfellow Dr
10 WbgT 7115 B2

Goodrich St
10 WLPK 6724 D4

Goodridge Av
46-00 BRNX 6393 C6

Goodward Rd
10 STNL 6824 E7

Goodwin Av
10 EORG 6049 A6
10 NWRK 6816 B2
10 NWRK 6817 B2
10 STNL 7019 D3

N Goodwin Av
10 EMFD 6049 B5

S Goodwin Av
10 EMFD 6049 A6

Goodwin Ct
10 CLST 6278 C2

Goodwin Pl
10 BKLN 6822 E6
10 BKLN 6823 A7

Goodwin Rd
2200 HmpT 6827 B6

Goodwin St
10 HAOH 6279 E1
200 PTHA 7205 C3

Gorczyca Pl
10 SRVL 7205 A2

Gordon Av
10 SYHW 6048 B1
10 TFLY 6392 A1

Gordon Blvd
10 HmpT 6827 E3
100 HmpT 6827 E3
100 STMN 6828 A3

Gordon Dr
10 GTPZ 6617 A2
10 HmpT 6929 B3
10 KENS 6617 B7

Gordon Pl
10 GrbT 6167 A6
10 STNL 6920 B6

Gordon Rd
10 VLYS 6928 E3
100 HmpT 6928 E6

Gordon St
10 PTHA 7205 D4
10 RDFP 6502 A4
10 STNL 7020 D2
10 WbgT 7114 D5
200 HmpT 6828 A6

Gore Ct
10 BKLN 120 E5
10 BKLN 6821 C6
10 STNL 6920 B6

Gore Ct W
10 THSN 6617 B7

N Grace St
10 WbgT 7114 A7

Gorge Rd
10 EDGW 108 A1
10 EDGW 6611 C5
200 CLFP 6611 D2

Gorge Rd CO-25
10 EDGW 108 A1
10 EDGW 6611 C5
200 CLFP 6611 D2

Gorham Av
400 WbgT 7114 B4

Gorham Ct
10 SCDL 6167 E4

Gorham Rd
10 SCDL 6167 E4
10 SCDL 6168 A4

Gornik Dr
700 PTHA 7114 B7
700 WbgT 7114 B7

Gorsline St
51-00 QENS 6719 E7

Gory Brook Rd
10 SYHW 6048 A1

Goshen St
10 HmpT 6827 C7

Gosling Hill Rd
200 NHLS 6724 B7

Gosman Dr
39-00 QENS 6719 A6

Gotham Av
10 BKLN 7023 E7
10 BKLN 7024 A6

Gotham Pkwy
300 CARL 6609 E2
300 ERTH 6609 E2
600 CARL 6610 A1
700 MNCH 6610 A1

Gotham Rd
128-00 QENS 6926 B2

Gotham St
10 STNL 6920 C6
10 VLYS 6928 E3

Gothic Dr
166-00 QENS 6825 D4

Gotthart St
10 NWRK 6818 A3

Gould Av
10 DBSF 6166 C4
10 EORG 6713 A6
10 NWRK 6713 B5

Gould Pl
10 NWRK 6713 C4

Gould St
10 BAYN 6920 B2

Goulden Av
2800 BRNX 6504 D2

Gouverneur Av
69-00 QENS 7026 C6
3900 BRNX 6504 D1

Gouverneur Ln
10 MHTN 120 C2
10 MHTN 6821 A6

Gouverneur Pl
10 BRNX 6613 B2

Gouverneur St
10 MHTN 119 C7
10 MHTN 6821 D4

Gouverneur Slip E
100 MHTN 119 C7
100 MHTN 6821 D4

Gouverneur Slip W
100 MHTN 119 C7
100 MHTN 6821 D4

Governor Rd
10 STNL 7019 E3

Governor St
10 STNL 7019 D3

Governor Harold G Hoff Plz
- SAMB 7205 D7

Governor John Davis Lodge Tpk
- GrwT 6170 D6
- PTCH 6170 D6

Gov John Davis Lodge Tpk I-95
- GrwT 6170 D6
- PTCH 6170 D6

Governors Ct
10 NHmT 6617 A6

Governor's Ln
10 SNPT 6508 D5

Governors Rd
10 BRXV 6280 E6
10 TCKA 6280 E6
10 TCKA 6281 A6

Governors Island Fy
- MHTN 120 B3
- MHTN 6821 B6

Gowanus Expwy
10 BKLN 6921 E7
10 BKLN 6922 B2
85-01 QENS 6719 E7
10 EGLD 6502 B7
10 RDFP 6502 A4
10 BKLN 6923 B1
10 BKLN 6922 A1

Gowanus Expwy I-278
10 BKLN 6921 E7
10 BKLN 6922 A2
10 BKLN 7021 E3
10 BKLN 7022 A1

Gowanus Expwy I-478
10 BKLN 6921 B1
10 BKLN 6922 B1

Gower St
2300 BRNX 105 A7
4200 NBgT 6716 D1
6100 NBgT 6610 E6
7600 NBgT 6611 A5
9100 FRVW 6611 B4

Grace Av
10 GTPZ 6617 A2
10 HmpT 6929 B3
10 KENS 6617 B7
10 LNBK 6929 B3
100 NBgT 6610 E6

Grace Ct
10 BKLN 120 E5
10 BKLN 6821 C6
10 STNL 6920 B6
90-00 QENS 6825 C5

Grace Ct W
10 THSN 6617 B7

Grace Dr
10 SAMB 7205 B7

Grace St
10 BlmT 6713 B1
10 IrvT 6816 B2
10 JSYC 6716 B5
200 PTHA 7205 C3

Grace Ter
10 HRSN 6714 A5

Grace Church St
10 PTCH 6170 B6
10 RYE 6284 B2
400 PTCH 6284 A1

Grace Ct Al
10 BKLN 120 E5
10 BKLN 6821 C6

Gracefield Dr
10 KNGP 6617 B4

Gracemere
10 STNL 6048 C5

Gracemere Lake Dr
10 TYTN 6048 B5

Gracemore Rd
10 STNL 6048 B5

Gracewood Dr
10 NHLS 6724 B1

Gracie Ct
10 HKSK 6501 C3

Grade St
500 MRNK 6282 C4

Grady Ct
10 STNL 6616 E5

Grady Dr
200 WbgT 7114 B5

Grafe Ct
10 STNL 7115 E5

Graff Av
300 BRNX 6615 A3

Grafton Av
100 NWRK 6713 D2

Grafton St
10 BKLN 6924 A5

Graham Av
10 BKLN 6822 C5

Graham Blvd
10 STNL 7018 E4

Graham Ct
119-00 QENS 6720 C2

Graham Ln
10 LODI 6500 C2

Graham Rd
10 SCDL 6282 A1

Graham St
10 ALPN 6723 A6
10 JSYC 6716 B5

Grain Ct
10 NWRK 6713 A6

Gramatan Av
10 BRXV 6394 E1
10 MTVN 6394 E2

Gramatan Ct
10 BRXV 6280 C4

Gramatan Dr
10 YNKR 6280 B7

Gramercy Av
10 YNKR 6280 C7

Gramercy Pk E
10 MHTN 116 C7
10 MHTN 6717 A7

Gramercy Pk W
10 MHTN 116 B7
10 MHTN 6717 A7

Gramercy Pl
10 NRCH 6395 D2

Granada Cres
10 GrbT 6049 D6

Granada Pl
10 EGLD 6503 A3
14-00 QENS 7027 B4

Granada St
100 ATLB 7027 E6

Grand Av
- BKLN 6823 A3
- GDNC 6828 D4
10 LKSU 6723 C1
10 LEON 6502 C5
10 LNBK 6929 A3
10 MLVN 6929 A3
10 NHmT 6723 C1
10 PTCH 6170 A6
10 RYE 6170 A7
10 RYE 6284 B1
10 RYEB 6170 A7
10 WHPL 6168 A7
200 STNL 7018 E1

Grand Av CO-501
10 EGLD 6502 C5

Grand Av SR-93
10 LEON 6502 C5
10 PALP 6502 C5
500 RDGF 6502 B1
500 RDGF 6611 B1

Grand Av US-1
500 RDGF 6611 A5

Grand Av US-9
90-00 QENS 6825 C5

E Grand Av
10 RDFP 6502 A4

N Grand Av
10 WbgT 7114 A7

Grand Blvd
10 EchT 6281 B1
10 LBCH 7029 A4
10 MtpT 6049 A1
100 SCDL 6281 C1
600 BRNX 107 E5
600 BRNX 6504 D1

Grand Pl
10 KRNY 6714 C2
10 NARL 6714 C1

Grand St
10 GRFD 6500 A3
10 GrwT 6170 E1
10 HBKN 6716 D7
10 HmpT 6827 E4
10 JSYC 6820 A6
10 LFRY 6501 C5
10 MHTN 120 D4
10 RYEB 6170 A6
10 WHPL 6050 B7
300 HmpT 7028 B7
400 CARL 6609 E1
500 BKLN 6822 C5
500 BKLN 6925 B7
2200 BRNX 105 C7

W Grand St
10 BAYN 6920 B2
10 ELIZ 6918 A3

W Grand St CO-610
10 ELIZ 6918 A3

Grand Army Plz
10 BKLN 6923 B1

Grand Central Pkwy
10 QENS 6719 C2

Grand Central Pkwy
10 QENS 6720 C6
10 QENS 6722 E7
10 QENS 6723 A6
10 QENS 6825 E3
10 QENS 6826 A2
265-01 LKSU 6723 B4
65-00 QENS 6824 D1

Grand Central Pl
300 HmpT 7027 B3

Grand Concourse
10 BRNX 6613 A1
200 BRNX 6612 E3
600 BRNX 107 E5
1200 BRNX 105 D4
3100 BRNX 6504 D3

Grand Cove Wy
10 EDGW 6611 E2

Grand Park Av
10 MHTN 116 C7

Grand Ridge Dr
100 RDGF 6611 C2

Grand View Av
10 STNL 6918 E7
10 WbgT 6712 A2

Grandview Av
400 HmpT 6828 C6

Grandview Blvd
10 QENS 7027 D5
10 STNL 7117 D7

Grandview Cir
10 PLNH 6617 C5

Grandview Pl
400 EGLD 6503 A3
400 FTLE 6503 A3
1200 BRNX 6504 D3

Grandview Ter
10 QENS 7027 D5
10 STNL 7117 B6
10 TFLY 6392 B2
200 FTLE 6502 E4

Graner Pl
1600 BRNX 6504 A6
2300 BRNX 105 A7

Grange Av
10 NBgT 6716 D1
10 YNKR 6280 E3

Grange Ct
10 TnkT 6502 A1

Grange Rd
600 TnkT 6502 A1

Grange St
10 GrwT 6170 D1
10 HmpT 6828 B5

Granger Av
10 FLPK 6827 D1

Granger St
57-00 QENS 6720 B7

Granite Av
10 STNL 6919 B7
10 STNL 7019 B1

Granite Pl
10 RDFP 6502 A4

Granite St
10 BKLN 6924 B1

Grannatt Pl
132-00 QENS 6926 E2

Grant Av
- NRWD 6164 A5
10 BKLN 6824 A7
10 CART 7017 D7
10 CLFP 6611 D2
10 CRSK 6278 A6
10 EORG 6713 D4
10 ERKY 6929 B6
10 HRSN 6283 C3
10 HRSN 6714 A6
10 JSYC 6819 D4
10 KRNY 6714 A5
10 NWRK 6724 D3
10 OLDT 6164 A5
10 RYEB 6170 A6
10 WHPL 6050 A7
66-00 QENS 6823 A5
300 COrT 6712 D3

Grant Ct
10 ALPN 6278 C7

Grant Dr E
10 HmpT 6928 D1
10 VLYS 6928 D1

Grant Dr N
10 HmpT 6928 D2

Grant Dr W
10 HmpT 6928 D2

Grant Pl
10 IrvT 6816 C2
10 NWRK 6816 D1

Grant St
10 FRVW 6611 B4
10 HRSN 6050 D7
10 LFRY 6501 B5
10 LODI 6500 D1
10 NRCH 6396 A3
10 NWRK 6713 D6
10 OrgT 6164 B2
10 STNL 6920 D7
10 TCKA 6280 E6
10 TCKA 6281 A6
10 WbgT 7114 E5
10 WLTN 6500 B6
10 YNKR 6394 C3
100 PTHA 7205 C4
400 LNDN 6917 B5
500 ROSL 6917 B2

S Grant St
10 WbgT 7205 A2

Grant Ter
200 MRNK 6282 E4
300 MRNK 6283 A4
500 TnkT 6502 D2

Grant Wy
10 STNL 6167 B1

Grantland Av
400 HmpT 6828 C6

Granton Av
6100 NBgT 6610 E6

Grant Park Dr
3-00 QENS 6823 B7

Grantview Blvd
400 PALP 6611 A2

Grantwood Av
100 STNL 7116 C5

Grant Wood Blvd
10 PALP 6502 C7

Grantwood Blvd
- PALP 6611 A2
100 PALP 6502 C7

Grapal Pl
10 RYE 6284 A2

Grapal St
10 RYE 6284 A2

Grapanche St
10 YNKR 6280 D7

Graphic Pl
10 MNCH 6501 C7

Grasmere Av
1200 STNL 7020 D6

Grasmere Ct
10 STNL 7020 D5

Grasmere Dr
10 STNL 7020 E5

Grasselli Av
2600 LNDN 7017 C3

Grassfield Rd
- GTNK 6616 E4
10 KNGP 6616 E4
10 KNGP 6617 A4

Grasslands Rd
10 STNL 6049 B2

Grasslands Rd SR-100
10 STNL 6049 B2
10 MtpT 6049 D3

Grasslands Rd SR-100C
10 STNL 6049 B2
10 MtpT 6049 D3

Grassmere Ter
10-00 QENS 7027 C5

Grassy Ln
10 STNL 7117 B4

Grassy Sprain Rd
10 YNKR 6280 C5
900 YNKR 6280 D1

E Grassy Sprain Rd
10 STNL 6280 D2

Grattan St
10 BKLN 6822 E6

Grauert Pl
10 WhkT 111 A4
10 WhkT 6717 B2

Graves Av
10 STNL 7019 D5

Gravesend Neck Rd
10 BKLN 7022 E6
600 BKLN 7023 A6

Gravett Rd
- QENS 6825 A5
144-00 QENS 6721 A7

Gray Av
1200 UnnT 6816 B6

Gray Pl
10 YNKR 6393 C3

Gray St
10 BGTA 6501 E2
10 JSYC 6820 A7
10 NWRK 6713 B6

Grayrock Rd
10 EchT 6281 D7

Grayson St
121-00 QENS 7028 C7
121-00 QENS 6927 C1

Graywood Dr
10 STNL 7020 B1

Graywood Rd
10 MHVN 6508 B6

Greacen Ln
10 STNL 7117 C5

Greacen Point Rd
900 MRNK 6396 E1
900 MRNK 6397 A1

Great Beds Ct
300 PTHA 7205 D4

Great Jones Al
10 MHTN 119 A3
10 MHTN 6821 C1

Great Jones St
10 MHTN 119 A3
10 MHTN 6821 C1

Great Kills Rd
10 STNL 7117 B5

Great Neck Rd
10 NHmT 6723 B4
100 RSLG 6723 A1

Great Oak Ln
10 NHmT 6617 D7
10 NHmT 6618 A6

Greaves Av
10 STNL 7117 B4

Greaves Ct
10 STNL 7117 B4

Greaves Ln
10 STNL 7117 B5

Greco Ln
10 WbgT 7114 C2

Greeley Av
10 STNL 7118 B2
600 FRVW 6611 B2

Green Av
10 BKLN 6822 D1
30-00 BKLN 6822 D1
32-00 QENS 6718 E7
41-00 QENS 6719 A7

Green Ct
10 STNL 7019 D2
10 LODI 6500 D2

Green Dr
10 QENS 6724 C2

Green Ln
10 ELIZ 6917 B2
10 GrwT 6170 C2
500 FRVW 6611 B2

Green Pl
10 NRCH 6395 C4
500 HmpT 6928 A7

Green St
10 TYTN 6048 A3
10 BKLN 6822 C5
10 FLPK 6827 E1
10 HAOH 6280 B2
10 HKSK 6501 B2
10 NWRK 6817 B3
10 STNL 7020 A1
10 TETB 6501 A4
10 VLYS 6928 B3
10 WbgT 7114 A1
100 SHkT 6501 A4
500 ELIZ 6917 E6

Green Wy
10 HRPK 6164 A4
10 HKSK 6724 D2

Greenacre Rd
10 KENS 6617 A6

Greenacres Av
10 GrbT 6167 D4
10 SCDL 6167 D4
100 WHPL 6167 E3

Greenacres Dr
10 RYE 6284 B3

Greenbriar Ct
10 NHmT 6724 A4
400 NHLS 6724 A4

Greenbriar Ln
10 FLHL 6618 B4
10 RYEB 6169 A4

Greenbrook Rd
10 WbgT 7205 A3

Greenburgh Commons Wy
10 STNL 6049 D5

Greenbush Rd
10 OrgT 6164 B2

Greencroft Av
10 STNL 7117 C5

Greencroft Ln
10 STNL 7117 C5

Greendale Av
10 MTVN 6395 A5

Greendale Ln
10 SCDL 6167 E5

Greene Av
10 MHTN 115 D7
10 MHTN 118 C1
10 MHTN 6717 B7
10 MHTN 6821 A1
200 BKLN 6822 D7
700 BKLN 6823 A7

Greene Ln
10 WHPL 6169 A5

Greene Pl
10 YNKR 6394 B1
2900 BRNX 6615 B4

Greene Rd
10 STNL 6164 D2

Greene St
10 JSYC 6820 A7
121-00 QENS 7028 C7
10 MHTN 118 D4
10 OrgT 6164 B2
200 MHTN 119 A2

Greene Ter
71-00 QENS 6824 D3

Greenfield Av
10 BRXV 6394 B1
10 BRXV 6395 A1
10 KRNY 6714 D2
10 TnkT 7020 D2

Greenfield Ct
900 HmpT 6928 D1

Greenhaven Rd
10 RYE 6283 D1

Greenhayes Rd
10 RYEB 6169 E2

Greenhouse Cir
10 RYEB 6169 E2

Greenlawn Blvd
10 VLYS 6928 E1

Greenlawn Rd
10 CLST 6278 A2

Greenleaf Av
10 STNL 7019 D1

S Greenleaf Av
100 STNL 7019 D1

Greenleaf Hl
10 NHmT 6616 D7
10 SDRK 6616 D7

Greenleaf St
10 RYE 6284 A1

Green Meadow Ln
900 MRNK 6397 A4

Greenmeadow Rd
10 EchT 6281 B5

Greenmount Av
200 FTLE 6611 C2
400 FRVW 6611 C2

Greenpoint Av
10 BKLN 6822 D1
10 QENS 6822 D1
41-00 QENS 6719 A7

Greenport St
10 STNL 7020 B6

Greenridge Av
10 NHPK 6828 B3
10 GDNC 6828 B3
10 WHPL 6168 B3

Greenridge Pk
10 GDNC 6828 B3

Greentree Dr
10 NRCH 6282 A2

Greentree Ln
10 STNL 7019 A4

Greentree Rd
10 WOrT 6712 A1

Greenvale Av
10 YNKR 6279 E5

Greenvale Cir
10 GrbT 6049 E7
10 GrbT 6167 E1

Greenvale Pl
10 EchT 6281 C2

Green Valley Ct
10 SECS 6610 C2

Green Valley Rd
10 STNL 7116 B5

Greenville Av
10 JSYC 6819 C6

Greenville Rd
10 HRPK 6164 E6
10 GrbT 6167 A6

Greenway E
10 NHmT 6724 D7

Greenway N
10 QENS 6824 D3

Greenway S
72-00 QENS 6824 D3

Greenway W
10 NHmT 6724 D7

Greenway Blvd
1500 HmpT 6928 C1

Greenway Cir
10 CLST 6278 B2

Greenway Ct
10 CLST 6278 B2

Greenway Dr
10 GrwT 6170 B1
10 STNL 7020 A2
400 LEON 6502 E4

Greenway Ln
10 FLHL 6618 B4

Greenway Rd
10 HRSN 6169 B6

Greenway St E
500 HmpT 6828 C2

Greenway St S
500 HmpT 6828 C2

Greenway Ter
71-00 QENS 6824 D3

Greenway Close
10 RYEB 6170 A2

Greenwich Av
10 MHTN 115 D7
10 MHTN 118 D1
10 MHTN 6717 B7
10 MHTN 6821 A1

Greenwich Ln
10 MHTN 115 D7

Greenwich Mw
10 MHTN 118 C1

Greenwich St
10 BlvT 6714 A1
10 MHTN 120 A2
200 MHTN 118 D1
10 MHTN 6821 A3
700 MHTN 6821 C1
700 MHTN 6717 B7

Greenwich Hills Dr
10 GrwT 6170 B2

Greenwich Office Pk
10 GrwT 6170 B2

Greenwood Av
10 EORG 6713 A4
10 PTCH 6170 B7
10 STNL 7020 B1

Greenwood Ct
10 NHmT 6724 A5

Greenwood Pl
10 EMFD 6049 A6
10 SNPT 6508 E5

Greenwood Rd
10 YNKR 6280 D2

Greenwood Rd N
900 UnnT 6816 A7

Greenwood Rd S
600 UnnT 6816 A7

New York City/5 Borough Street Index

STREET Block City	Map#	Grid
Greenwood St 10 WbgT	7114	B2
Greenwood Ter 200 HlsT	6917	D2
Greenwood Lake Av 10 YNKR	6713	E1
Green Wy Dr 10 IRVN	6166	B1
Gregg Ct 10 OrgT	6164	B2
400 HmpT	6828	E6
Gregg Ln 10 BAYN	6919	E3
Gregg Pl 10 STNL	7020	B1
Gregg St 10 LODI	6500	E1
Gregory Av 10 WOrT	6712	A1
400 UNCT	6716	A4
400 WhkT	6716	E3
1400 UNCT	6816	A5
Gregory Av CO-577 10 WOrT	6712	A1
Gregory Ln 10 STNL	7117	A2
Gregory Pl 100 WOrT	6712	A2
Gregory St 10 VLYS	6928	B2
Grenada Pl 1100 BRNX	6394	D7
Grenfel Pl 10 ARDY	6166	E5
Grenfell Dr 10 LKSU	6723	C1
Grenfell St 80-00 QENS	6824	E4
Grenville Ct 10 ERKY	6929	C5
Grenville St 100 WhkT	7114	C5
Grenwolde Dr 10 KNGP	6616	C4
Gresham Rd 800 MHTN	6820	E7
Greta Pl 10 STNL	7020	C2
Grey Oaks Av 10 YNKR	6280	A3
Grey Rock Dr 10 PTCH	6170	C1
Greyrock Rd N 10 PTCH	6170	B7
Greyrock Rd S 10 PTCH	6284	B1
Grey Rock Ter 10 IRVN	6166	B1
Greystone Av 3400 BRNX	102	D1
3400 BRNX	6504	D7
3900 BRNX	6393	C7
Greystone Cir 10 EchT	6395	B1
Greystone Rd 10 YNKR	6279	D5
Greystone Rd 10 MrnT	6282	C6
Greystone Ter 10 YNKR	6279	D5
Gridley Av 10 STNL	7019	A1
Grieco Dr 10 JSYC	6819	B5
Grier Av 300 ELIZ	6917	E4
700 LNDN	6917	C5
Griffen Av 10 MrnT	6282	B4
10 NRCH	6282	A4
10 SCDL	6282	A4
Griffin Dr 10 LRMT	6396	D1
Griffin Ln 10 EWLS	6724	E4
Griffin Pl 10 LNBK	6929	B4
10 WHPL	6050	B7
Griffin St 400 HmpT	6929	D6
Griffith Av 10 YNKR	6280	A2
Griffith St 100 JSYC	6716	B6
Griffon Pl 10 RYE	6283	D4
Griffon St 10 NRCH	6396	A3
Griggs Av 200 TnkT	6501	E1
200 TnkT	6502	A1
Grille Ct 10 STNL	7115	C6
Grimes Rd N 10 STNL	7021	E4
Grimsby St 10 STNL	7118	B2
Grinnell Pl 1100 BRNX	6613	D4
Grinnell St 10 IRVN	6166	C1
Grinsted St 10 NHmT	6617	C6
Grissom Av 10 STNL	7019	A6
Grissom Dr 10 EchT	6395	D1
Grissom St 10 BRNX	6164	A6
Grist Mill Ln 10 NHmT	6616	C4
10 SDRK	6616	A4
Gristmill Ln 10 PLNM	6617	D3
Gristmill Rd 10 PLDM	6617	D4
Griswold Av 3100 BRNX	6506	A6
Griswold Ct 10 STNL	7020	B2

STREET Block City	Map#	Grid
Griswold Rd 10 HRSN	6169	D5
Groom Ct 400 PTHA	7205	C2
Grosbeak Rd 10 NWRK	6280	A7
Groshon Av 10 YNKR	6393	C2
Gross Rd 10 KRNY	6714	C3
Grosvenor Av 4600 BRNX	6393	B2
Grosvenor Ln 116-00 QENS	6824	C5
Grosvenor Pl 10 THSN	6723	A1
Grosvenor Rd 115-00 QENS	6824	D4
Grosvenor St 235-00 QENS	6722	C2
Grote St 600 BRNX	6504	C6
Groton Ln 10 NHmT	6617	C6
Groton Pl 10 NHmT	6618	B2
100 HmpT	6828	E4
Groton St 10 QENS	6824	B3
10 STNL	7117	B7
Grove Av 10 CDHT	7028	B3
10 HmpT	7028	B2
10 LRMT	6396	C3
10 NRCH	6395	D5
10 STNL	6919	C1
10 WbgT	7114	C4
E Grove Av 10 WhkT	7114	C4
S Grove Av 10 PTHA	7114	B7
10 WbgT	7114	B7
Grove Ln 10 BRXV	6281	D7
10 GrbT	6166	D2
Grove Pl 10 BAYN	6919	E2
10 BKLN	121	C6
10 BKLN	6821	D7
10 EORG	6713	A4
10 NHmT	6508	D6
10 STNL	6919	C7
Grove Rd 10 NoCT	6050	B5
10 SOrT	6712	A6
10 WHPL	6050	B5
Grove St 10 HmpT	6928	D7
10 BKLN	6823	A6
10 BlmT	6713	C6
10 CLST	6278	A3
10 DBSF	6166	A4
10 DMRT	6278	B2
10 EORG	6713	B2
10 HKSK	6501	C2
10 HmpT	7027	D3
10 HRSN	6283	A4
10 KRNY	6714	B3
10 LFRY	6501	C4
10 LNBK	6929	B3
10 LODI	6500	C4
10 MHTN	118	C1
10 MHTN	6821	A5
10 MTVN	6394	C4
10 NHmT	6618	A5
10 OybT	6618	B7
10 PTCH	6170	B6
10 RDFP	6501	E5
10 ROSH	6618	A2
10 RTFD	6609	A1
10 SHkT	6501	B4
10 STNL	7020	D2
10 TETB	6501	B4
10 TFLY	6392	A4
10 TYTN	6048	B3
10 WHPL	6050	C6
10 YNKR	6279	C6
16-00 QENS	6823	B5
100 WbgT	7114	B5
200 ERTH	6609	B1
200 JSYC	6820	C1
200 NWRK	6713	A4
200 PTHA	7205	D1
300 ERTH	6500	B7
300 NWRK	6712	E7
600 ELIZ	6917	E5
600 HBKN	6716	C7
600 JSYC	6716	C7
700 MRNK	6283	A4
Grove St CO-509 10 BlmT	6713	B2
10 EORG	6713	A4
200 NWRK	6713	A6
300 IrvT	6712	A6
300 IrvT	6712	E6
600 IrvT	6816	D1
E Grove St 10 BGTA	6501	E2
10 TnkT	6502	A2
100 LFRY	6501	C4
300 SHkT	6501	C4
N Grove St 10 EORG	6713	A3
10 VLYS	6928	E3
400 HmpT	6928	E1
N Grove St CO-509 10 EORG	6713	A3
600 BlmT	6713	A3
S Grove St 10 EORG	6713	A5
200 NWRK	6713	A6
S Grove St CO-509 10 EORG	6713	A5
200 NWRK	6713	A6
W Grove St 10 BGTA	6501	D2
Grove Ter 10 IrvT	6712	D7
10 NWRK	6712	E7
500 SOrT	6712	B5

STREET Block City	Map#	Grid
W Grove Ter 10 IrvT	6712	D7
100 NWRK	6712	D7
Gruber Ct 200 HmpT	6828	E6
Grumman Av 10 NWRK	6816	E5
Grymes Hill Rd 100 STNL	7028	C2
Guelisten Pl 10 GTNK	6616	E6
Guenther Av 10 VLYS	6928	B2
Guerlain St 1800 BRNX	6505	B7
Guernsey St 10 BKLN	6822	B2
Guider Av 10 BKLN	7121	B1
10 BKLN	7023	B7
Guildford Ct 100 HmpT	6828	C5
Guilford Ln 10 GrwT	6170	D7
Guilford Rd 10 NHmT	6618	A3
Guilford St 10 STNL	7021	A6
Guinevere Ln 10 STNL	7019	E1
Guinzburg Rd 150-00 QENS	6825	C6
Guion Dr 200 MRNK	6283	A6
Guion Ln 10 LRMT	6396	C3
Guion Pl 10 NRCH	6395	C5
1700 BRNX	6614	A1
Guion Rd 10 RYE	6284	A2
Guion St 10 YNKR	6393	C2
Gulf Av 10 STNL	7018	D3
Gulino Pl 10 CART	7017	B6
Gulf Ct 88-00 QENS	7026	B7
Gulls Cove Rd 10 PLNM	6617	C3
E Gun Hill Rd 10 BRNX	6504	E1
200 BRNX	6505	C3
W Gun Hill Rd 10 BRNX	6504	E1
Gunnel Ovl 10 KRNY	6714	C3
Gunpowder Ln 100 TYTN	6048	C3
Gunther Av 10 YNKR	6284	A3
2200 BRNX	6505	E5
4000 BRNX	6394	C6
Gunther Pl 10 BKLN	6924	B2
Gunton Pl 10 STNL	7115	A6
10 STNL	7116	A5
Guntzer St 10 STNL	7115	E5
200 FTLE	103	A3
200 FTLE	6502	E5
200 FTLE	6503	B5
Gurd Av 1200 HlsT	6816	C6
Gurdon St 10 STNL	7019	B4
Gurley Av 10 STNL	7117	A4
10 STNL	7116	E4
Gussack Plz 10 GTPZ	6617	A7
Gustav Av 1300 UNnT	6816	B6
Gutheil Ln 10 GTNK	6616	E4
Guyon Av 10 STNL	7117	E3
Guy R Brewer Blvd 92-00 QENS	6825	D1
116-00 QENS	6926	E1
119-55 QENS	6927	A2
Gwenn Lp 10 STNL	7119	B7
Gypsum St 10 KRNY	6819	A1
Gypsy Pl 10 HRSN	6283	D1
10 RYE	6283	D1
H		
H St 1300 HmpT	6827	E6
Haarlem Av 10 WHPL	6050	A6
Hackensack Av 10 RDFP	6501	D4
N Hackensack Av 10 KRNY	6715	B7
100 LFRY	6501	C4
S Hackensack Av 10 KRNY	6819	A1
Hackensack St 10 CARL	6500	C7
10 CARL	6609	B1
10 ERTH	6609	B2
10 WRDG	6500	D6
300 HSBR	6500	D6
Hackensack St CO-55 10 CARL	6500	C7
10 CARL	6609	C1
200 NWRK	6713	C1
300 RTFD	6609	D6
Hackensack Plank Rd 10 UNCT	6716	C5
Hackett Pl 10 RTFD	6609	A1
Hackett St 10 NWRK	6713	D7

STREET Block City	Map#	Grid
Hadden Av 10 WHPL	6168	C1
Hadden Ct 10 GrbT	6167	A7
10 GrbT	6281	A1
10 YNKR	6281	A1
Haddon Rd 100 NHmT	6723	E5
200 HmpT	7028	B1
Haddon St 80-00 QENS	6825	E1
81-24 QENS	6826	B2
Hadley Ct 10 GTNK	6616	E6
Hafstrom St 10 STNL	7117	D3
Hagaman Pl 10 STNL	7019	C1
Hagaman St 10 CART	7115	C2
10 WbgT	7115	C2
Hagan Ct 200 SECS	6610	A6
Hagel Av 200 LNDN	6917	C5
600 ROSL	6917	C5
Hagen Ct 10 STNL	7021	A6
Hague St 10 JSYC	6716	B4
10 UNCT	6716	C5
Haig Rd 10 HmpT	6928	E5
Haight Av 1500 BRNX	6505	C6
Haight Pl 10 CRSK	6278	A5
Haight St 41-00 QENS	6720	E5
Haines Blvd 10 PTCH	6170	A5
10 RYEB	6170	A3
Halcyon Pl 10 BlmT	6713	C1
10 YNKR	6279	C7
100 ROSL	6917	B4
Halcyon Ter 10 NRCH	6395	C7
Hale Av 10 BKLN	6823	E7
10 BKLN	6924	E1
10 WHPL	6168	B2
Hale Dr 10 KNGP	6617	A3
Hale Pl 10 OrgT	6164	A1
Hale St 10 STNL	7206	C3
Hales Av 10 STNL	7116	E7
10 STNL	7117	A7
10 STNL	7208	A1
Halevy Dr 500 HmpT	6928	D7
Haley Dr 10 HKSK	6501	B1
Halfmoon Ct 10 WNYK	6611	C7
Half Moon Isl 10 JSYC	6819	C7
Half Moon Ln 10 IRVN	6166	A2
10 SNPT	6508	A4
10 TYTN	6048	B4
200 MHTN	6820	E7
Hall Av 10 EchT	6281	A5
10 LRMT	6396	C1
10 TCKA	6281	A5
10 WHPL	6050	C6
10 WHPL	6168	B2
Hall Ct 10 HlsT	6816	C7
100 HmpT	6616	E3
300 SOrT	6712	B6
Hall Pl 10 EchT	6281	B6
10 HAOH	6279	D5
10 TCKA	6281	B6
10 YNKR	6393	E4
10 YNKR	6394	A4
Hall St 10 BKLN	6822	A4
10 EORG	6713	A3
600 HmpT	6828	D4
600 MRNK	6282	E7
Halladay Av 10 STNL	6280	A7
Halladay St 10 JSYC	6819	C5
100 JSYC	6820	A4
Halleck Av 10 STNL	6715	D7
Halleck St 10 BKLN	6922	E4
10 BRNX	6613	E4
10 NWRK	6714	A2
Halley St 10 YNKR	6394	A4
Halliday Ct 10 HRSN	6169	D3
Halligan St 10 NRCH	6396	C4
Hallister St 10 STNL	7206	D1
Hallman Av 200 HmpT	6929	D7
Hall of Fame Ter 10 BRNX	105	C1
10 BRNX	6504	B4
Halls Ln 10 RYE	6283	E5
Halock Dr 10 UNCT	6716	C5
Halperin Av 2600 BRNX	105	C4
2600 BRNX	6504	E4
Halpin Av 10 STNL	7116	C5

STREET Block City	Map#	Grid
Halsey Av 200 UnnT	6917	A1
300 UnnT	6828	D5
Halsey Ln 10 CLST	6278	C3
Halsey Pl 10 NARL	6714	D1
10 SOrT	6712	A5
Halsey Rd 100 YNKR	6280	E2
Halsey St 10 BKLN	6923	D1
10 NWRK	6713	E7
10 NWRK	6817	D1
600 BKLN	6822	E7
600 BKLN	6823	A7
1100 HmpT	6928	C7
1300 QENS	6928	C7
2400 BRNX	6614	D1
2500 BRNX	6505	D7
Halsey Pond Ln 10 RYE	6166	B2
Halstead Av 10 GrbT	6049	D5
10 HRSN	6283	A4
10 MRNK	6283	A5
10 PTCH	6170	A5
10 WLTN	6500	A7
10 YNKR	6394	B4
Halstead Pl 10 RYE	6284	A4
Halstead St 10 JSYC	6819	C4
10 VLYS	6928	E5
10 KRNY	6714	A4
Halsted Pl 10 ERKY	6929	D2
10 EORG	6712	D4
Halsted Rd 10 ELIZ	6917	B2
Halsted St 10 ELIZ	6917	B2
41-00 QENS	6917	E3
Halsted St 10 EORG	6712	D5
10 NWRK	6712	C6
Halyard Rd 10 HmpT	6928	B6
10 VLYS	6928	B6
Hamden Av 300 STNL	7118	B1
Hamden Av 10 STNL	7118	B1
Hamilton Av 10 ATLB	7028	A7
40-00 QENS	6719	E6
42-47 QENS	6720	A4
10 BRXV	6395	A1
10 FRVW	6611	C4
10 GrwT	6170	E4
10 HAOH	6166	A7
10 KRNY	6714	B1
10 MTVN	6395	A5
10 NBgT	6611	B4
10 OrgT	6164	A1
200 TnkT	6502	C1
400 MTVN	6395	A5
1000 HmpT	7029	A3
1000 HWTH	7029	A1
1300 HWTH	6928	E7
1300 HWTH	6929	A7
Hamilton Av SR-119 10 WHPL	6168	A1
E Hamilton Av 10 EGLD	6392	A6
W Hamilton Av 10 EGLD	6392	A6
Hamilton Dr 10 NHmT	6724	C3
Hamilton Pl 10 BKLN	6922	C2
10 HRSN	6050	D5
10 MHTN	106	E5
10 MHTN	6612	B3
10 TFLY	6392	A3
10 VLYS	6928	D2
55-00 QENS	6823	C2
Hamilton Rd 10 HRSN	6283	C1
10 IRVN	6166	A6
10 SCDL	6281	D1
10 YNKR	6393	E4
10 YNKR	6394	A4
Hamilton Ter 10 MHTN	107	A5
10 MHTN	6612	C2
Hanlon Dr 10 CDHT	7028	C3
Hamlin Pl 10 STNL	7019	C2
Hammersley Av 1400 BRNX	6505	D3
Hammett Av 10 EGLC	6503	A4
10 FTLE	6503	A4
Hammock Ln 10 STNL	7116	B5
Hammond Av 10 GLCV	6283	C2
10 RYE	6283	C2
Hammond House Rd 10 MpfT	6049	B7
10 GrbT	6049	E7
Hampden Ct 10 IRVN	6166	C2
Hampden St 800 LNDN	7017	A3

STREET Block City	Map#	Grid
Hampshire Cir 10 YNKR	6394	D1
Hampshire Rd 10 GTNK	6616	D1
10 NHmT	6617	A6
10 YNKR	6280	D7
Hampton Av 10 BKLN	7121	C1
10 NHmT	6724	E3
10 SOrT	6712	A5
600 MRNK	6283	A4
E Hampton Blvd 50-00 QENS	6722	D5
Hampton Ct 10 LKSU	6828	D2
10 NHmT	6509	A7
10 RKVC	6929	E2
Hampton Dr 900 HmpT	6929	D2
N Hampton Dr 10 GrbT	6049	D5
Hampton Grn 10 STNL	7116	B5
Hampton Ln 10 NRCH	6396	B6
Hampton Ovl 10 BKLN	6923	D2
10 LNBK	6929	D2
10 STNL	7115	E5
Hampton Pl 10 ERKY	6712	D4
10 GDNC	6828	D2
10 HRSN	6169	C2
10 LNBK	6929	D5
10 ELIZ	6917	B2
10 UnnT	6917	B2
Hampton Rd 10 ERKY	6929	D2
10 SCDL	6167	D5
10 YNKR	6279	D4
Hampton Rd S 300 GDNC	6828	D2
Hampton St 10 UnnT	6917	B1
Hampton Ter 10 COrT	6712	D4
10 EORG	6712	D3
Hamptworth Ct 300 EDGW	108	D7
300 EDGW	6611	E5
Hamptworth Dr 10 KNGP	6616	D1
Hancock Av 10 JSYC	6716	B6
10 YNKR	6393	E5
200 TnkT	6502	C1
400 MTVN	6395	A5
Hancock Ct 300 EDGW	108	E5
300 EDGW	6611	E5
Hancock Rd 10 STNL	7017	C1
Hancock St 10 BKLN	6923	B1
10 HRSN	6827	E4
10 HRSN	6050	D7
10 LODI	6500	D1
10 STNL	7020	C7
10 BKLN	6822	E7
700 BKLN	6823	A7
1600 QENS	6823	B3
1700 HmpT	6929	E7
Hand Pl 1100 ELIZ	6918	A1
Hand Rd 251-00 QENS	6722	E3
Hanfling Pl 10 EchT	6281	D3
Hanford Av 10 NRCH	6396	C2
Hanford Pl 10 TYTN	6048	B2
Hanford St 10 NWRK	6817	A7
46-00 QENS	6722	D4
E Hangar Rd - QENS	6926	E4
N Hangar Rd - QENS	6926	E4
- QENS	6927	A4
W Hangar Rd - QENS	6926	E4
Hank Pl 10 STNL	7207	B3
Hanlon Dr 10 CDHT	7028	C3
Hannah St 10 BKLN	6920	E7
Hannan Pl 10 RYE	6283	E3
Hannibal Pl 107-00 QENS	6826	B5
Hanover Av 10 STNL	7020	D4
Hanover Rd 10 NHLS	6724	B2
Hanover Sq 14-00 QENS	7027	A6
Hanover St 10 FLPK	6827	D2

STREET Block City	Map#	Grid
Hanover St 10 MHTN	120	C2
10 MHTN	6821	B6
10 BKLN	6818	A3
Hansbury Av 10 NWRK	6816	D4
Hansen Pl 10 SCLF	6509	E6
Hansen St 10 IrvT	6816	B3
Hanson Av 600 PTHA	7205	C2
Hanson Ln 10 NRCH	6281	D5
Hanson Pl 10 BKLN	121	D7
10 BKLN	6821	E7
10 RVRE	6929	B2
Hantz Rd 44-00 QENS	7027	A6
Hanus St 200 TnkT	6502	B7
Harbor Blvd - HBKN	6716	E5
500 WhkT	6716	E4
Harbor Ct 10 NHmT	6618	E4
200 BKLN	7021	D3
Harbor Ct E 10 ROSH	6618	E4
Harbor Ct W 10 ROSH	6618	E5
Harbor Dr 10 GrwT	6170	E5
10 JSYC	6920	C2
10 PTCH	6170	C7
400 HmpT	6928	A7
Harbor Ln 10 BKLN	7021	C1
10 NRCH	6395	E7
10 ROSH	6618	E4
10 RYE	6283	C6
10 STNL	6919	A7
Harbor Ln N 10 NRCH	6395	E7
Harbor Lp 10 STNL	7019	A1
Harbor Pl 500 WNYK	6611	C7
Harbor Rd 10 MRNK	6282	C7
10 MRNK	6283	A7
10 BXTE	6508	D7
10 BXTE	6508	E7
10 NHmT	6508	D7
10 PTWN	6508	D7
10 PTWN	6617	C1
10 SNPT	6508	E7
Harbor Ter 10 PTHA	7205	E4
Harbor Wy 10 KNGP	6616	D1
10 SCLF	6509	E7
Harbor Front Ct 10 ELIZ	6918	C6
Harbor Front Plz 10 ELIZ	6918	C6
Harbor Front Ter 10 ELIZ	6918	C6
Harbor Hill Ln 200 MRNK	6283	A6
Harbor Hill Rd 10 NHmT	6618	A4
10 GLCV	6509	D5
200 EHLS	6618	E6
Harbor Hills Dr 10 NHmT	6618	A4
Harbor Key Rd 10 SECS	6609	D7
Harbor Park Dr 10 NHmT	6618	A4
Harbor Park Dr N 10 NHmT	6618	D1
Harbor Park Dr S 10 NHmT	6618	D1
Harborside Pl 10 JSYC	6820	D3
Harbor Terrace Dr 17-00 BKLN	6823	A6
Harbortown Blvd 700 PTHA	7205	E4
Harborview E 100 LWRN	7028	A4
Harborview N 100 NRCH	6395	C4
100 LWRN	7028	A4
Harborview S 100 LWRN	7027	B5
Harborview W 100 LWRN	7028	A4
100 LWRN	7028	A4
Harbor View Ct 10 STNL	7020	C1
Harbor View Ln 10 NHmT	6618	A4
Harbor View Pl 10 LBCH	7029	E6
10 WHPL	6168	A1
Harborview Pl S 10 SECS	6715	D1
S Harbor View Pl 10 SECS	6609	E6
Harbour Ct 10 BXTE	6617	D1
10 EDGW	108	A7
Harbour Rd 600 QENS	7122	D3
14-00 QENS	7027	A6

STREET Block City	Map#	Grid
Harned Av 10 WHPL	7114	B7
Harned St 700 PTHA	7205	B1
800 PTHA	7114	C7
Harney Rd 10 YNKR	6281	B2
Harold Av 10 EGLD	6502	C1
10 GrwT	6170	A4
300 LEON	6502	D3
300 STNL	7207	E1
Harold Pl 10 NRCH	6395	D4
900 HmpT	6828	D4
Harold Rd 10 STNL	7028	D2
10 HWTN	7028	D2
Harold St 10 TFLY	6392	A2
200 MNLA	6724	D6
400 HmpT	6828	C6
Harold W Cohn Memorial Sq 10 BKLN	6822	A5
Harper Av 10 IrvT	6816	B3
3600 BRNX	6394	E7
3600 BRNX	6505	E7
3900 MTVN	6394	E7
Harper Ct 10 BRNX	6505	E1
Harper St 1200 BRNX	6614	B4
Harrell Av 10 WbgT	7114	C3
Harriet Av 10 STNL	7207	C3
E Harriet Av 10 PALP	6502	B7
W Harriet Av 10 PALP	6502	B7
Harriet Ct 10 KRNY	6714	A3
Harriet Pl 10 LNBK	6929	C4
Harriet St 1700 HmpT	6827	C7
Harriman Av 10 YNKR	6279	D3
Harriman Dr 10 SNPT	6508	C7
Harriman Rd 10 IRVN	6166	B1
Harriman's Keep 10 IRVN	6166	B1
Harrington Ct 10 CLST	6278	A2
2800 BRNX	6505	E7
Harrington Pl 10 HRSN	6283	A4
Harrington St 500 PTHA	7205	C1
Harris Av 10 STNL	6928	D7
10 HmpT	7027	D3
Harris Ct 10 THSN	6617	C7
Harris Dr 10 HmpT	7029	E2
Harris Ln 10 HRSN	6283	A4
10 STNL	7115	D6
Harris St 10 CART	7115	D1
11-00 QENS	7027	D4
Harrison Al 10 BRNX	121	D3
10 BRNX	6821	E5
Harrison Av 10 BKLN	6822	C5
10 CART	7017	C7
10 CART	7115	A1
10 GRFD	6500	D3
10 HmpT	6828	B4
10 HRSN	6283	B5
10 IrvT	7029	C5
10 NRCH	6283	B5
10 STNL	7019	C5
10 YNKR	6393	E4
10 KRNY	6714	C6
100 LODI	6500	B3
600 ROSL	6917	E6
600 SECS	6609	E6
Harrison Av CO-508 10 HRSN	6713	E6
10 HRSN	6714	B6
10 KRNY	6714	C6
Harrison Av SR-127 10 HRSN	6283	B5
S Harrison Av 10 WbgT	7114	A2
Harrison Blvd 10 STNL	6050	D7
Harrison Ct 10 SOrT	6712	A5
Harrison Dr 10 LRMT	6396	C1
10 MrnT	6396	C1
Harrison Gdns 600 QENS	6714	E6
Harrison Pl 10 BKLN	6822	C4
10 GrbT	6049	E5

New York City/5 Borough Street Index

STREET
Block City Map# Grid

Harrison Pl
10 IrvT 6816 D2
10 PTHA 7205 D4
10 STNL 6920 A7
500 LNDN 6917 A7
4500 UNCT 6716 B1
6000 WNYK 6611 A7
Harrison St
- HBKN 6716 C6
10 BlmT 6713 D2
10 GDNC 6828 A2
10 HRSN 6050 C7
10 LEON 6502 D3
10 MHTN 118 B5
10 MHTN 6821 A3
10 MTVN 6394 E5
10 NRCH 6396 B5
10 STNL 7020 D2
10 TCKA 6281 E6
100 HRSN 6168 D1
100 LWRN 7028 A4
200 ELIZ 6917 B4
700 HmpT 6828 D7
1300 HmpT 6827 E4
E Harrison St
200 LBCH 7029 D6
N Harrison St
10 EORG 6712 E3
S Harrison St
10 EORG 6712 D4
400 COrT 6712 C5
Harrod Av
1200 BRNX 6614 A1
Harrod Pl
1600 BRNX 6614 A2
Harrow Ln
- ROSE 6618 B7
10 NHmT 6618 B7
Harrow Rd
1000 HmpT 6828 A7
Harrow St
67-00 QENS 6824 C3
Harrows Ln
10 HRSN 6169 C1
Harry Van Arsdale Jr Av
106-00 QENS 6824 D2
Hart Av
10 STNL 7020 A1
10 YNKR 6394 B5
Hart Blvd
10 STNL 6920 B7
10 STNL 7020 B1
Hart Lp
10 STNL 7117 C3
Hart Pl
10 BKLN 7120 D1
10 STNL 7206 B3
Hart St
- BRNX 6614 D4
10 HmpT 6929 B3
10 JSYC 6819 D4
10 LNBK 6929 B3
10 MLVN 6929 B3
17-00 BKLN 6823 A5
18-00 QENS 6823 A4
500 BKLN 6822 E6
Hartford Av
10 GrwT 6170 D5
10 MTVN 6395 A4
10 STNL 7020 A2
Hartford Ct
500 SOrT 6712 B6
Hartford Ln
10 GrbT 6049 D4
Hartford Rd
200 SOrT 6712 B5
Hartford St
- CLST 6278 C2
10 NWRK 6713 C6
10 STNL 7117 B6
500 PTHA 7205 E3
Hartland Av
218-00 QENS 6722 C7
219-00 QENS 6826 D1
Hartley Av
10 MTVN 6394 D3
Hartley Pl
10 BAYN 6919 D5
Hartley Rd
10 GTNK 6617 B5
Hartley Ter
100 HlsT 6917 D1
Hartman Av
- STNL 7117 D1
10 GRFD 6500 A1
Hartman Ln
6-00 QENS 7027 B5
Hartman Pl
10 YNKR 6281 A5
Hartsdale Av
10 WHPL 6168 B5
200 SCDL 6168 A5
E Hartsdale Av
10 GrbT 6167 D4
W Hartsdale Av
10 GrbT 6167 B1
W Hartsdale Av SR-100A
10 GrbT 6167 B1
Hartsdale Rd
10 EMFD 6049 B6
W Hartsdale Rd
500 GrbT 6167 B1
700 GrbT 6049 B7
900 EMFD 6049 B7
Hartwell Pl
10 HmpT 6928 C7
10 HmpT 7028 D3
Hartwell St
600 TnkT 6502 B1
Hartwick St
10 LFRY 6501 D7
Harty St
10 YNKR 6279 E7
Hartz Dr
10 OrgT 6164 B3
Hartz Ter
- PRMT 6165 A1
Hartz Wy
10 SECS 6715 E1
Harvard Av
10 HmpT 6928 E6
10 LNBK 6929 A3
10 RKVC 6929 E3

Harvard Av
10 STNL 6920 C6
10 WbgT 7114 D1
10 YNKR 6280 E4
500 HlsT 6816 B6
Harvard Ct
10 WHPL 6168 B3
800 HmpT 6928 B7
Harvard Dr
10 GrbT 6167 D3
Harvard Ln
10 HAOH 6279 E1
Harvard Pl
700 CLFP 6611 D1
700 FTLE 6611 D1
1000 FTLE 6502 D7
Harvard Rd
10 HmpT 6928 B7
10 NHLS 6724 B1
10 NRCH 6281 E2
Harvard Rd S
10 HmpT 6828 C3
300 GDNC 6828 C3
Harvard St
10 CLST 6278 C2
10 CRSK 6278 A6
10 EORG 6712 D4
10 FLPK 6827 C3
10 GDNC 6828 A2
10 NHmT 6724 D1
10 VLYS 6928 A2
10 WLPK 6724 E4
500 NHmT 6723 E7
Harvard Ter
10 WOrT 6712 A3
Harve Rd
10 PTCH 6170 B4
Harvest Av
10 STNL 7020 A1
200 STNL 7019 E2
Harvest Dr
10 SCDL 6282 B2
Harvey Av
10 STNL 7019 C3
Harvey St
10 CLST 6278 A2
10 NWRK 6713 E4
10 STNL 7020 D7
Harway Av
10 BKLN 7022 D6
Harwich Ln
10 HRSN 6168 E1
Harwich Rd
10 HmpT 6929 B7
10 HmpT 7029 B1
Harwood Av
10 WHPL 6050 B6
E Harwood Av
10 PALP 6502 C7
W Harwood Av
10 PALP 6502 B6
Harwood Ct
10 SCDL 6167 C5
Harwood Dr E
10 GLCV 6509 E3
Harwood Dr W
10 GLCV 6509 E3
Hasbrouck Av
10 HSBH 6500 E4
100 HSBH 6501 A4
Hasbrouck Pl
10 ERTH 6500 A7
10 RTFD 6500 A7
Hasbrouck Rd
10 STNL 7020 A4
Hasbrouk Av
400 HSBH 6501 A4
Haseco Av
10 PTCH 6170 B5
Haskin St
2900 BRNX 6614 D3
2900 BRNX 6615 B1
Haspel St
51-00 QENS 6823 E1
Hassock St
15-00 QENS 7027 D4
Hastings Ct
10 STNL 7207 A2
Hastings Dr
10 TFLY 6392 C4
Hastings Lndg
10 HAOH 6279 E1
Hastings Pl
10 CART 7017 C6
Hastings Rd
10 ISPK 7029 C5
Hastings St
- VLYS 6928 D5
10 BKLN 7121 C1
10 STNL 7020 E5
10 STNL 7021 B5
Hastings Tr
- HAOH 6166 A7
Hastings Close
10 GrbT 6280 B2
Hastings Trailway
- HAOH 6166 A6
Hatch Ter
10 DBSF 6165 D3
Hatfield Pl
10 STNL 7019 C1
100 STNL 6919 C7
Hathaway Av
10 HmpT 6827 A5
10 QENS 6827 A5
Hathaway Dr
10 GDNC 6828 A1
Hathaway Ln
10 WHPL 6168 D4
Hathaway Rd
10 EchT 6395 B1
10 SCDL 6281 C1
Hathaway St
10 WLTN 6500 A4
Hatheway St
200 WLTN 6500 A5
Hattie Jones Ct
10 BKLN 6923 D2
Hatting Pl
3000 BRNX 6615 C4
Haughwout Av
10 STNL 7019 C1
Hauser Ter
10 OrgT 6164 C3

Hausman St
10 BKLN 6822 D2
Hausmann Ct
10 MplT 6816 A3
Hausner Pl
300 MNLA 6724 D5
Hauxhurst Av
10 WhkT 6716 E3
Havemeyer Av
500 BRNX 6614 D2
Havemeyer St
10 BKLN 6822 B4
Haven Av
10 HmpT 6928 C1
10 MHTN 6503 C6
10 MTVN 6395 A4
10 NHmT 6617 E3
10 RYE 6283 E3
10 STNL 7118 B1
10 VLYS 6928 C2
300 MHTN 104 B4
Haven Pl
400 HmpT 6928 C6
Haven St
10 EMFD 6049 A5
Haven Esplanade
10 STNL 7020 C1
Havens Pl
10 BKLN 6924 C1
Havenwood Rd
10 STNL 7020 B1
Haverford Av
10 NRCH 6282 A3
10 SCDL 6282 A3
Havermeyer Rd
10 IRVN 6166 B2
Haviland Av
1900 BRNX 6614 B1
Haviland Dr
10 YNKR 6280 C4
800 HlsT 6816 D7
800 HlsT 6917 D1
Haviland Ln
10 RYE 6283 E2
10 RYE 6284 A1
Haviland Rd
10 HRSN 6169 A7
Haviland St
10 HRSN 6283 C3
Havilands Ln
10 WHPL 6168 E4
10 WHPL 6169 A3
Hawke Ln
10 RKVC 6929 E1
Hawkes Close
10 IRVN 6166 C2
Hawkins St
10 BRNX 6506 E6
10 NWRK 6818 C1
Hawkstone St
100 BRNX 105 C6
100 BRNX 6504 A7
Hawley Av
10 PTCH 6170 A4
10 STNL 7116 B7
10 STNL 7207 B1
Hawley St
10 WHPL 6167 E2
Hawley Ter
10 YNKR 6279 D3
Hawthorn Av
147-00 QENS 6721 B5
Hawthorne Av
10 EORG 6713 A5
10 FLPK 6827 D1
10 JSYC 6819 E1
10 NHmT 6618 A3
10 NWRK 6817 A3
10 RKVC 6929 E5
10 RYEB 6170 A5
10 YNKR 6393 B4
100 FLPK 6723 C7
100 QENS 6723 C7
100 STNL 7019 B3
300 NWRK 6816 E2
500 IrvT 6816 E2
600 TnkT 6502 B2
E Hawthorne Av
10 VLYS 6928 E4
200 LNBK 6928 E4
W Hawthorne Av
10 VLYS 6928 D4
Hawthorne Dr
10 NRCH 6396 B4
1500 BRNX 6505 B7
Hawthorne Ln
10 HmpT 6928 B4
10 LWRN 7028 B3
10 NHmT 6616 D7
10 PLDM 6617 E4
10 SDRK 6616 D7
E Hawthorne Ln
- LWRN 7028 B3
Hawthorne Pl
10 EORG 6712 E6
10 EORG 6713 A5
10 MLVN 6929 B2
10 MNPK 6617 E5
10 NWRK 6817 A3
10 RYE 6283 D6
10 YNKR 6393 B3
Hawthorne Rd
10 BRXV 6281 A7
10 GDNC 6828 B1
10 MrnT 6396 C1
10 SCLF 6509 E7
Hawthorne St
10 BKLN 6923 B4
10 ERTH 6500 A7
10 LNBK 6929 A3
10 MLVN 6929 A3
10 RTFD 6500 A7
10 WHPL 6050 B6
10 WLPK 6724 D4
100 ROSL 6917 B4
300 COrT 6712 D2
500 HmpT 6828 C7
1500 BRNX 6505 D4
Hawthorne St N
10 GrwT 6170 C1
Hawthorne St S
10 GrwT 6170 D3
Hawthorne Ter
10 LEON 6502 D4
10 NHmT 6616 D7

Hawthorne Ter
10 SDRK 6616 D7
300 MTVN 6395 A3
Hawthorne Wy
10 GrbT 6167 A3
Hawthorne Close
10 NRCH 6281 E1
Hawtree St
133-00 QENS 6925 D2
Hawtree Creek Rd
- QENS 6926 B2
128-00 QENS 6825 B7
Haxtun Av
600 COrT 6712 B5
Hay Rd
- MHTN 6821 A7
200 MHTN 120 A5
Hay St
10 STNL 7020 C5
Hayden Av
10 GTNK 6616 D4
10 GTNK 6617 A4
Hayes Av
10 ELIZ 6917 D4
Hayes Dr
10 EchT 6281 B5
Hayes Rd
10 UnnT 6816 A5
Hayes St
10 EMFD 6049 B5
10 NWRK 6713 C7
10 NWRK 6817 A2
100 GDNC 6828 B2
100 GrbT 6049 B5
200 LNDN 7017 C3
Hayhurst Av
10 MtPT 6050 A3
Hayhurst Dr
10 NRCH 6282 A4
Haynes Av
10 DBSF 6166 B4
10 NWRK 6817 B5
Haynes St
10 STNL 7207 B1
Hayward Av
10 CART 7017 D7
300 MTVN 6394 E2
Hayward Pl
10 RYE 6283 D5
100 WLTN 6500 A6
Hayward St
10 COrT 6712 D1
10 EORG 6712 D1
10 YNKR 6394 A2
Haywood Rd
190-00 QENS 6826 A3
Haywood St
10 STNL 7206 C3
Hazard Pl
10 ELIZ 6917 E1
Hazel Av
10 WOrT 6712 A3
500 PTHA 7205 B2
Hazel Ct
10 BKLN 7023 E6
100 NRWD 6164 B7
Hazel Dr
500 HmpT 6928 B7
Hazel Ln
10 LRMT 6396 C3
Hazel Pl
10 BRNX 6615 B4
10 FLPK 6827 B3
10 HmpT 6928 C7
10 IrvT 6816 C4
10 LNBK 6929 A5
10 NWRK 6817 A3
Hazel Rd
10 NHmT 6617 D2
Hazelton Dr
10 SCDL 6168 B6
10 WHPL 6168 B6
Hazelton Rd
10 YNKR 6280 C4
Hazelton St
10 RDFP 6501 E4
10 RDFP 6502 A4
Hazelwood Av
10 NWRK 6712 C6
Hazen St
10 PLMM 6395 C6
10-00 BRNX 6613 E7
19-00 QENS 6719 C3
Hazlitt Av
400 FTLE 6502 D5
400 LEON 6502 D5
Headley Ter
100 IrvT 6816 B1
100 MplT 6816 B1
Heald St
10 CART 7017 D7
10 CART 7115 D1
Healey Ter
10 KRNY 6714 B3
Healy Av
10 HmpT 7027 D2
23-50 QENS 7027 B5
N Healy Av
10 GrbT 6167 C4
S Healy Av
10 GrbT 6167 B5
Healy Pl
10 CART 7017 C7
10 YNKR 6281 A5
Healy St
1300 HmpT 6827 E4
Heaney Av
10 STNL 7019 A2
Hearst St
10 YNKR 6280 A2
Hearst Wy
- HRSN 6169 A2
Hearthstone Cir
10 GrbT 6167 A5
Hearthstone Rd
10 YNKR 6280 E1
Heath Av
2500 BRNX 102 E3
2500 BRNX 6504 B3
Heath Pl
10 BKLN 6924 D1
10 GrbT 6280 B2
10 HAOH 6280 B1
10 QENS 6924 D1

Heathcote Av
100 MRNK 6282 E6
3500 BRNX 6506 A1
Heathcote Byp
- NRCH 6282 A2
- SCDL 6168 A7
- SCDL 6282 A1
Heathcote Dr
10 NHmT 6724 E3
Heathcote Rd
10 HmpT 6827 A5
10 SCDL 6167 D7
10 SCDL 6168 A7
10 SCDL 6282 A1
10 YNKR 6280 C5
Heather Ct
10 STNL 7019 A2
Heather Dr
10 EHLS 6618 E6
Heather Ln
10 GrbT 6049 C4
10 LWRN 7028 A3
10 MrnT 6282 C5
10 NHmT 6724 A5
10 OrgT 6164 B1
10 WHPL 6168 D3
200 HWTH 6929 A7
Heather Wy
10 DBSF 6166 C3
Heatherbloom Rd
10 WHPL 6168 D3
Heatherdell Rd
10 ARDY 6166 E4
100 ARDY 6167 A4
500 GrbT 6167 A3
Heatherfield Rd
10 HmpT 6928 A4
Heather Hill Ct
10 CRSK 6278 A4
Heather Hill Rd
10 CRSK 6278 A6
100 DMRT 6278 A5
Heatherhill Rd
10 CRSK 6278 A5
10 DMRT 6278 A5
Heaton Ct
10 CLST 6278 C2
Heberton Av
10 STNL 6919 D7
200 STNL 7019 C1
Heckel St
- NWRK 6713 C2
10 BlvT 6713 C2
Hecker St
10 NWRK 6713 C6
10 STNL 7206 B3
Hedden Pl
10 EORG 6713 B5
10 NWRK 6713 B5
Hedden Ter
10 NARL 6714 C1
10 NWRK 6817 A3
Hedge Ln
200 HWTH 6929 A7
Hedgerow Dr
10 EGLD 6502 E2
Heenan Av
10 STNL 7116 C6
Heffernan St
100 STNL 7116 D3
Hegeman Av
300 BKLN 6924 D4
900 BKLN 6925 A3
Hegner Ct
10 SHkT 6501 C5
Hegney Pl
700 BRNX 6613 B3
Heidelberg Av
500 WbgT 7114 D4
Heights Dr
10 YNKR 6280 D4
Heights Ln
100 TFLY 6392 C4
Heights Rd
10 PLDM 6617 D5
10 PLNH 6617 D5
Heindel Av
9000 FRVW 6611 C4
9000 NBgT 6611 C4
Heineman Pl
10 HRSN 6283 D3
Heinrich Pl
- YNKR 6280 A6
Heinz Av
10 STNL 7117 B7
Heirloom Ct
100 GrbT 6049 E4
Heirloom Ln
10 RYEB 6051 E6
Heiser St
39-00 QENS 6719 A6
Helaine Ct
10 OrgT 6164 A1
Helen Av
10 RYE 6283 D5
10 WbgT 7114 D2
Helen Ct
10 FLPK 6827 E2
10 VLYS 6928 D5
Helen Dr
10 MNCH 6500 E7
Helen Ln
10 GTNK 6616 E5
Helen Pl
10 NWRK 6712 C7
Helen Rd
400 MNLA 6724 D6
400 NHmT 6724 D6
Helen St
10 LFRY 6501 C6
10 SECS 6715 E3
10 SECS 6716 A3
300 LNDN 7017 A1
Helena Av
- NoCT 6050 B3
10 LRMT 6396 C3
10 WHPL 6168 B6
200 YNKR 6280 E3
Helena Rd
10 STNL 7020 A6
Helene Ct
10 STNL 7115 E7
Helios Pl
10 STNL 7115 E6

Heller Pkwy
100 NWRK 6713 E2
200 BlvT 6713 D1
Heller Pkwy CO-670
200 BlvT 6713 D1
200 NWRK 6713 D1
Heller Pl
10 MplT 6816 A1
Helm Av
100 WRDG 6500 C5
Helmich Ln
- STNL 7019 E7
- STNL 7117 E1
Hemingway Av
10 NRCH 6395 D3
Hemlock Cir
10 WHPL 6168 D6
Hemlock Ct
- NRWD 6164 C7
10 STNL 7115 D5
800 NRWD 6278 B1
Hemlock Dr
10 ALPN 6392 D1
10 CRSK 6392 D1
10 GrwT 6170 E2
10 KNGP 6616 E2
10 WbgT 7115 B2
400 HmpT 6928 A7
Hemlock Ln
10 STNL 7115 D7
Hemlock Pl
10 NRCH 6395 E6
10 NRCH 6396 A6
10 NWRK 6713 E1
Hemlock Rd
10 ARDY 6166 E3
10 BRXV 6280 C4
10 BRXV 6281 A7
10 FLHL 6617 E4
10 FLHL 6618 A3
10 GrbT 6166 E3
10 JSYC 6819 A4
10 YNKR 6393 D2
Hemlock St
10 BKLN 6824 A7
10 FLPK 6827 C3
100 STNL 7115 E6
400 BKLN 6925 A2
700 HmpT 6828 B7
Hemlock Ter N
200 TnkT 6502 B2
Hemlock Ter S
200 TnkT 6502 B2
Hempstead Av
10 HMPD 6828 E5
10 HmpT 6828 C7
10 HmpT 6929 B3
10 LNBK 6929 B3
10 MLVN 6929 C1
10 RKVC 6929 E4
10 STNL 7118 C2
212-00 QENS 6826 E3
220-00 QENS 6827 A4
Hempstead Av SR-24
212-00 QENS 6826 D3
220-00 QENS 6827 A4
Hempstead Dr
300 HmpT 6828 D5
Hempstead Tpk
- QENS 6827 A4
10 HMPD 6828 E5
10 HmpT 6828 A4
100 HmpT 6827 D4
Hempstead Tpk SR-24
- QENS 6827 A4
10 HMPD 6828 E5
10 HmpT 6828 A4
100 HmpT 6827 D4
Hempstead Gardens Dr
10 HmpT 6828 D7
Hempstead Lake State Pk
10 HmpT 6929 E1
Hemsley Ln
10 GTNK 6617 A5
Henches Pl
10 LFRY 6501 C7
Henderson Av
10 HmpT 6928 B1
10 NHmT 6508 E6
10 SNPT 6508 E6
10 STNL 6920 A7
10 VLYS 6928 B1
10 YNKR 6394 B2
183-00 QENS 6826 A4
600 STNL 6919 E7
Henderson Dr
400 SOrT 6712 A5
Henderson Pl
10 MHTN 114 A4
10 MHTN 6718 C2
Henderson St
10 HBKN 6716 C7
10 JSYC 6716 C7
Henderson St CO-637
10 HBKN 6716 C7
10 JSYC 6716 C7
Hendrick N
10 IRVN 6166 A2
Hendrick S
10 IRVN 6166 A2
Hendrick Ln
10 TYTN 6048 B4
Hendricks Av
10 STNL 6920 C7
Hendricks Cswy
400 RDGF 6611 A1
1100 RDGF 6502 A7
Hendricks Cswy CO-50
400 RDGF 6611 A1
1100 RDGF 6502 A7
Hendrickson Av
10 HmpT 6827 C4
10 LNBK 6929 B3
10 RKVC 6929 D5
10 VLYS 6928 C1
100 HmpT 6929 D5
300 LNBK 6928 B3
400 HmpT 6928 C1
Hendrickson Pl
166-00 QENS 6825 E6
4200 BKLN 7024 A4
Hendrickson St
10 BKLN 7023 E3

Hendrickson St
2100 BKLN 7024 A4
Hendrix St
10 BKLN 6924 D1
Henhawk Rd
10 KNGP 6617 A4
Henley Rd
170-00 QENS 6825 D3
182-00 QENS 6826 A3
200 HmpT 7028 D3
Henley St
10 WbgT 7114 D4
Henmar Dr
10 CLST 6278 C4
Henmarken Dr
200 NVLE 6164 C4
Hennessey St
10 NWRK 6818 A3
Hennessy Pl
10 IrvT 6816 B3
1900 BRNX 105 B3
1900 BRNX 6504 A5
Henning St
10 STNL 7019 E3
Henrietta Av
10 HmpT 7029 E1
W Henrietta Av
10 HmpT 7029 E1
Henrietta Pl
1100 HmpT 6928 C7
Henrietta St
10 GRFD 6500 B1
10 VLYS 6928 B2
10 YNKR 6393 D1
Henry Av
10 HRSN 6283 A5
10 MRNK 6283 A5
10 PALP 6502 B6
Henry Ct
10 DBSF 6166 B4
Henry Dr
10 GLCV 6509 D4
Henry Pl
10 HKSK 6501 C4
10 MplT 6816 A2
10 STNL 7020 C7
10 WHPL 6050 B7
Henry Rd
7-00 QENS 7027 E5
Henry St
- HKSK 6501 A2
10 BKLN 121 A4
10 BKLN 6821 C5
10 CART 7115 C2
10 EGLC 6503 B3
10 FTLE 6503 B3
10 GrbT 6167 B7
10 GrwT 6170 C5
10 GTNK 6616 E6
10 HmpT 6827 B7
10 HSBH 6500 D4
10 JSYC 6820 A1
10 LFRY 6501 C6
10 LODI 6500 C4
10 MHTN 118 E7
10 MHTN 119 C6
10 MHTN 6821 C4
10 MNCH 6501 C7
10 RDFP 6501 E6
10 RYE 6283 C4
10 SECS 6716 A3
10 TCKA 6281 A6
10 TETB 6501 A3
10 WbgT 7115 C2
10 WLPK 6724 D4
10 YNKR 6280 A6
100 BGTA 6501 E3
100 SAMB 7205 C7
100 TnkT 6501 E3
100 VLYS 6928 B2
200 BKLN 120 E7
200 COrT 6712 C3
200 FRVW 6611 B4
200 HmpT 7027 E2
400 ELIZ 6917 A3
400 ELIZ 6918 B2
400 HmpT 6828 C5
400 HmpT 6929 D6
400 ROSP 6917 A3
500 BKLN 6922 B1
500 MLVN 6929 C3
3100 UNCT 6716 D2
E Henry St
200 LNDN 6917 A6
N Henry St
10 BKLN 6822 D2
W Henry St
100 PALP 6502 B6
Henry C Luthin Pl
10 BGTA 6501 D3
Henry Herz St
- YNKR 6393 A1
Henry Hudson Br
- BRNX 102 A3
- BRNX 6504 A2
- MHTN 102 A3
- MHTN 6504 A2
Henry Hudson Br SR-9A
- BRNX 102 A3
- BRNX 6504 A2
- MHTN 102 A3
- MHTN 6504 A2
Henry Hudson Dr
- ALPN 6279 A7
- ALPN 6392 E2
- ALPN 6393 A1
- EDGW 103 C3
- EDGW 6503 A6
- EGLC 101 A4
- EGLC 103 C1
- EGLC 6392 D7
- EGLC 6503 B5
- FTLE 103 C1
- FTLE 6503 A6
- TFLY 6392 E2
Henry Hudson Pkwy
- BRNX 102 A3
- BRNX 6393 D6
- BRNX 6504 A1
- MHTN 101 C7
- MHTN 103 E7
- MHTN 104 A7
- MHTN 106 D3
- MHTN 108 C7
- MHTN 109 A2

Henry Hudson Pkwy
- MHTN 112 A4
- MHTN 6503 C7
- MHTN 6611 D7
- MHTN 6612 B2
- MHTN 6717 C2
- YNKR 6393 D5
Henry Hudson Pkwy SR-9A
- BRNX 102 A3
- BRNX 6393 B7
- BRNX 6504 A1
- MHTN 101 E4
- MHTN 103 E7
- MHTN 104 A7
- MHTN 106 D3
- MHTN 108 E4
- MHTN 109 A2
- MHTN 112 A4
- MHTN 6503 C7
- MHTN 6611 D7
- MHTN 6612 B2
- MHTN 6717 C2
Henry Hudson Pkwy E
2600 BRNX 102 B2
2600 BRNX 6504 A1
3800 BRNX 6393 B7
Henry Hudson Pkwy W
2600 BRNX 102 B2
2600 BRNX 6504 A1
3900 BRNX 6393 B7
Henshaw St
10 MHTN 101 D6
10 MHTN 6503 E3
Hensler St
10 NWRK 6818 A2
Henwood Pl
100 BRNX 105 C5
100 BRNX 6504 B6
Hepworth Pl
10 GRFD 6500 A3
Herald Av
1200 HmpT 6827 E5
Herald St
10 YNKR 6394 A2
Herbert Av
10 CART 7017 D7
10 CLST 6278 B2
10 HmpT 6827 D4
10 NHmT 6617 E1
10 SFPK 6827 D4
10 WHPL 6168 A3
200 HlsT 6816 C6
Herbert Dr
10 NHmT 6724 C6
Herbert Pl
10 NHmT 6617 E1
10 NWRK 6713 E3
10 NWRK 6714 C4
10 YNKR 6394 C3
1200 HmpT 6928 D7
Herbert St
- STNL 7207 A2
10 BKLN 6822 D3
10 NWRK 6818 B2
10 RDFP 6501 D5
10 WbgT 7205 B1
200 PTHA 7205 B3
400 HmpT 6828 C5
Herbhill Rd
10 GLCV 6509 E4
Hereford Rd
- RSLG 6723 A2
10 NHmT 6723 A2
10 YNKR 6280 D7
10 YNKR 6394 D1
1500 HmpT 6929 A6
Hereford St
10 STNL 7117 A4
Hering Av
2400 BRNX 6505 C4
Heritage Ct
10 DMRT 6278 B6
10 HmpT 6928 C5
10 RYEB 6051 D5
10 TYTN 6048 B3
10 VLYS 6928 C5
Heritage Ln
10 KNGP 6617 B4
10 RYE 6284 A3
Heritage Rd
10 OLDT 6164 A3
Heritage Wy
1700 PLNM 6617 C4
Heritage Hill Rd
10 IRVN 6048 C7
10 TYTN 6048 B4
Herkimer Av
10 HmpT 6928 E6
Herkimer Ct
10 BKLN 6923 C2
Herkimer Pl
10 BKLN 6923 C1
4200 BRNX 6393 E7
Herkimer Rd
10 SCDL 6282 B3
Herkimer St
10 BKLN 6923 B1
10 STNL 7020 B2
800 BKLN 6924 A1
Herkomer St
10 NHPK 6828 A1
Herman Av
600 HmpT 6828 B7
Herman Blvd
10 HmpT 6828 A4
Herman St
10 ERTH 6500 B7
10 LFRY 6501 C6
100 ERTH 6609 C2
Hermann Av
10 CART 7115 C1
Hermann St
10 CART 7017 B6
Hermany Av
2000 BRNX 6614 C2
Hermits Rd
10 GrbT 6048 D7
10 IRVN 6048 D7
10 IRVN 6166 D1
Hermon St
10 NWRK 6817 D2
Heron Dr
10 HBPK 7028 E1

Heron St
10 LBCH 7029 E6
Heronvue Rd
10 GrwT 6051 D1
Herpers St
10 IrvT 6816 D2
Herrick Av
10 STNL 7206 D1
10 TnkT 6502 A2
200 TnkT 6501 E1
Herrick Ct
10 BAYN 6919 E5
Herrick Dr
10 ERKY 6929 C6
10 LWRN 7027 B3
10 LWRN 7028 A3
Herrick St
10 ERTH 6500 A7
10 WLTN 6500 A6
Herricks Ct
10 NHmT 6724 B6
Herricks Rd
10 GDNC 6724 D7
10 MNLA 6724 C6
10 NHmT 6724 C6
Herriot Pl
10 YNKR 6393 D2
Herriot St
10 YNKR 6393 C2
Herrmann Pl
10 YNKR 6280 B5
Herschell St
1300 BRNX 6505 C7
1300 BRNX 6614 D1
Hertford St
10 NRCH 6396 A3
Hertz Drwy
- NWRK 6817 C7
Hervey St
10 GrwT 6170 C6
10 STNL 7115 E5
Herzl St
10 BKLN 6924 A3
Hesper Pl
10 MTVN 6394 E6
Hess Av
- HRSN 6283 C3
Hess Plz
10 WbgT 7114 B6
Hessler Av
69-00 QENS 7026 C6
Hester St
10 LFRY 6501 C6
100 MHTN 118 E5
100 MHTN 119 A6
100 MHTN 6821 C3
Heston Av
10 SRVL 7205 A7
Heterodox View Av
- NWRK 6713 C4
Hetfield Av
400 ELIZ 6917 E5
Hett Av
- STNL 7117 E5
10 STNL 7118 B3
Heuer St
10 LFRY 6501 C6
Heusden St
10 STNL 7019 A1
Hevelyne Rd
10 GrbT 6049 C5
Hewes St
10 BKLN 6822 B5
Hewitt Av
10 BRXV 6395 B1
10 EchT 6395 B1
10 STNL 7020 B4
10 WHPL 6168 C6
Hewitt Pl
800 BRNX 6613 C3
Hewitt Rd
10 RKVC 6929 E2
Hewlett Av
10 RYE 6283 E5
1400 HmpT 6928 E6
Hewlett Dr
800 HmpT 6928 B5
Hewlett Ln
10 FLHL 6618 B4
10 KNGP 6616 C3
1300 HmpT 6929 A7
1300 HWTH 6929 A7
Hewlett Pkwy
300 HmpT 6928 C6
Hewlett Pl
10 GTNK 6616 C4
10 KNGP 6616 C4
10 PTCH 6170 C4
Hewlett Plz
1200 HmpT 6928 D7
Hewlett St
76-00 QENS 6723 C5
77-00 NHmT 6723 C5
400 HmpT 6828 B7
Hewlett Heath Rd
1300 HBPK 6928 E6
1300 HmpT 6928 E6
Hewlett Neck Rd
100 HWTN 7028 D2
Hewlett Point Av
10 HmpT 6929 B7
10 HmpT 7029 B1
Hey Hoe Woods Rd
10 OrgT 6165 A4
Heyson Rd
11-00 QENS 7027 D6
Heyward St
10 BKLN 6822 B5
Heywood Av
100 COrT 6712 B5
Heywood Rd
10 PLMM 6395 C6
Heywood St
10 NHmT 6724 C5
Hiawatha Av
196-00 QENS 6826 B4
1400 HlsT 6816 C5
Hickcox Av
200 HmpT 6928 C7
Hickey Rd
- OrgT 6164 E1
Hickey St
10 OrgT 6164 E1
10 PRMT 6164 E1

New York City/5 Borough Street Index

STREET	Block	City	Map#	Grid
Hickory Av				
	10	STNL	7020	E6
	100	TFLY	6392	A1
Hickory Cir				
	10	STNL	7116	B5
Hickory Ct				
	10	NHLS	6724	B1
	10	STNL	7115	E5
	10	TFLY	6392	A1
Hickory Dr				
	10	GrwT	6170	C3
	10	GTNE	6616	D7
	10	PTCH	6170	C3
	10	RYE	6283	D4
Hickory Hl				
	10	ROSE	6618	C6
Hickory Ln				
	-	YNKR	6280	C5
	10	CLST	6278	C3
	10	GLCV	6509	E2
	10	NHmT	6724	D1
	10	SCDL	6167	D6
	100	ALPN	6278	C3
Hickory Rd				
	10	HWTN	7028	D2
	10	MHVN	6508	B6
	10	NHmT	6724	B5
	10	WDBG	7028	D2
Hickory St				
	10	CART	7115	C1
	10	COrT	6712	C4
	10	EGLC	6503	A3
	10	FLPK	6827	D3
	10	GrbT	6167	D3
	10	KRNY	6714	B4
	10	NRCH	6396	A5
	10	SFPK	6827	D3
	200	BGTA	6501	E3
	200	TnkT	6501	E2
	300	TnkT	6502	A2
	800	PTHA	7205	D1
Hickory Grove Dr E				
	100	MRNK	6282	C7
	100	MrnT	6282	C7
Hickory Grove Dr W				
	10	MrnT	6282	C7
Hickory Hill Dr				
	10	DBSF	6166	B4
Hickory Hill Ln				
	10	OrgT	6164	B2
Hickory Hill Rd				
	10	EchT	6281	B6
	10	OrgT	6164	B3
Hickory Pine Ct				
	10	HRSN	6051	B5
Hicks Dr				
	63-00	QENS	6719	C6
Hicks Ln				
	10	GTNK	6616	E5
	10	GTNK	6617	A5
	10	KNGP	6617	A5
	10	SNPT	6508	A6
Hicks St				
	10	BKLN	121	A4
	10	BKLN	6821	C6
	10	RSLN	6618	D5
	10	VLYS	6928	D3
	100	BKLN	120	E5
	500	BKLN	6922	B1
	1300	BRNX	6505	C2
Hicksville Rd				
	300	QENS	7027	E5
Hidden Glen Rd				
	10	GrbT	6166	D7
Hidden Green Ln				
	10	MrnT	6282	C6
Hidden Ledge Rd				
	10	EGLD	6503	A3
Hidden Pond Dr				
	10	RYEB	6169	E5
	10	RYEB	6170	A5
Hidden Ridge Ct				
	-	YNKR	6280	E1
Hidden Spring Ln				
	10	RYE	6284	A1
Hidden Village Dr				
	100	PTHA	7205	D3
Higa Ter				
	10	UnnT	6816	B7
Higbie St				
	10	HmpT	6928	E1
Higgins St				
	31-00	QENS	6720	E3
High Ct				
	10	NHmT	6723	C1
E High Rd				
	10	FLHL	6618	B4
High St				
	10	ARDY	6166	D5
	10	BKLN	121	B3
	10	BKLN	6821	D6
	10	BXTE	6617	D1
	10	CARL	6609	C1
	10	CART	7115	D2
	10	COrT	6712	C2
	10	DBSF	6165	D3
	10	DMRT	6278	B5
	10	ELIZ	6918	A4
	10	ERTH	6609	B1
	10	GRFD	6500	C1
	10	GrwT	6170	D5
	10	HAOH	6279	E1
	10	HAOH	6280	A1
	10	HRSN	6168	D1
	10	JSYC	6820	A1
	10	LEON	6502	C4
	10	LNBK	6928	E4
	10	LODI	6500	C1
	10	MtPT	6050	A3
	10	NHmT	6617	D1
	10	NHmT	6723	C1
	10	NRCH	6396	A3
	10	NRWD	6164	B6
	10	PTCH	6170	A7
	10	RYE	6170	A7
	10	RYE	6283	D1
	10	RYEB	6170	A7
	10	STNL	7021	A4
	10	TYTN	6048	C5
	10	VLYS	6928	E4
	10	WbgT	7114	C4
	10	YNKR	6279	D7
	100	CLST	6278	A3
	100	EWLS	6724	E3
	100	NVLE	6164	C5
	100	WOrT	6712	D1
	200	PTHA	7205	E3
High St CO-104				
	400	CLST	6278	B3
High St CO-502				
	100	CLST	6278	A3
High St CO-638				
	10	COrT	6712	C2
N High St				
	10	GrbT	6049	C4
	10	MTVN	6394	D4
	10	TCKA	6281	A6
S High St				
	10	GrbT	6049	C4
	10	MTVN	6394	C4
	10	TCKA	6281	A6
Highbrook Av				
	10	PLHM	6395	B6
	300	PLMM	6395	B5
N Highbrook Av				
	200	PLHM	6395	C4
Highclere Ln				
	10	MtPT	6049	E1
	10	MtPT	6050	A1
High Cliffe Ln				
	400	TYTN	6048	C4
Highfield Av				
	10	NHmT	6508	D5
	10	PTWN	6508	E6
Highfield Ln				
	10	RTFD	6609	A3
Highfield Rd				
	10	HRSN	6283	C2
	10	WbgT	7114	A1
Highland Av				
	-	OrgT	6164	E2
	10	BKLN	7120	B1
	10	CLFP	6611	D4
	10	DBSF	6166	B4
	10	DMRT	6278	B7
	10	EchT	6281	B6
	10	ELIZ	6917	B3
	10	ERKY	6929	B6
	10	GRFD	6500	B1
	10	GTPZ	6617	B7
	10	HRPK	6278	A1
	10	JSYC	6819	E1
	10	KRNY	6714	A5
	10	LODI	6500	C1
	10	MplT	6816	A1
	10	NHmT	6618	A2
	10	NRCH	6395	D5
	10	NWRK	6713	E2
	10	OybT	6618	E2
	10	PRMT	6164	E1
	10	RSLN	6618	D6
	10	SCLF	6509	D7
	10	STNL	7020	B3
	10	THSN	6617	B7
	10	TYTN	6048	C3
	10	WbgT	7205	A3
	10	WHPL	6168	A2
	10	YNKR	6393	C2
	100	ALPN	6165	A5
	100	OrgT	6165	A2
	159-00	QENS	6825	C4
	200	COrT	6712	B3
	200	PALP	6502	B6
	200	WRDG	6500	C5
	300	MTVN	6395	B5
	400	PRMT	6165	A1
	900	PLMM	6395	B7
	1200	UnnT	6816	A6
	1400	HlsT	6816	D5
	1500	NHmT	6724	A7
	1500	NHPK	6724	A7
Highland Av US-9W				
	10	PRMT	6164	E1
	100	ALPN	6165	A5
	100	OrgT	6165	A2
	400	PRMT	6165	A1
E Highland Av				
	10	COrT	6712	C4
	10	EORG	6712	C4
Highland Blvd				
	10	HmpT	6929	B3
	10	LNBK	6929	B3
Highland Cir				
	10	YNKR	6394	D1
Highland Cross				
	100	RTFD	6609	B3
Highland Ct				
	10	GrbT	6166	D6
	10	QENS	7027	C6
Highland Dr				
	10	ARDY	6166	D4
	300	MRNK	6282	E6
Highland Ln				
	10	IRVN	6166	B1
	10	STNL	7117	B7
E Highland Pkwy				
	100	ROSL	6917	A6
	200	LNDN	6917	A6
Highland Pl				
	10	BKLN	6823	E7
	10	BKLN	6924	E1
	10	GrwT	6170	D3
	10	NHmT	6723	A3
	10	RDFP	6501	E4
	10	RDFP	6502	A4
	10	SCLF	6509	E7
	10	WOrT	6712	A1
	10	YNKR	6393	C3
	600	QENS	7122	B4
	1000	HmpT	6928	C7
	6000	WNYK	111	C1
	6000	WNYK	6611	B7
	6000	WNYK	6717	B1
Highland Rd				
	-	HRSN	6169	B6
	10	GrbT	6166	E6
	10	GrbT	6167	A6
	10	GrwT	6170	D4
	10	MrnT	6282	B6
	10	RYE	6283	E1
	10	STNL	7117	B5
	10	VLYS	6928	D2
	10	WbgT	7114	A1
	100	RYE	6169	E7
Highland St				
	10	NWRK	6817	A1
	10	PTCH	6170	C5
	200	LEON	6502	D4
Highland Ter				
	10	IrvT	6816	E1
	10	NHmT	6617	D6
	300	COrT	6712	B3
Highland Wy				
	10	SCDL	6167	D5
Highland Park Pl				
	10	HRSN	6169	E7
	10	RYE	6169	E7
Highland Ridge Ln				
	10	HRSN	6169	E7
Highland View Av				
	2200	BKLN	7120	D2
Highlawn Av				
	10	BKLN	7022	D5
Highmeadow Rd				
	10	NHmT	6617	D7
Highmount Rd				
	10	STNL	7117	A6
High Pine Rd				
	10	GLCV	6509	E2
Highpoint Av				
	10	WhkT	6716	D3
	100	UNCT	6716	D3
High Point Cir				
	10	RYEB	6051	D6
High Point Dr				
	100	GrbT	6167	D1
High Point Ln				
	10	GrbT	6166	E7
High Point Rd				
	10	GrbT	6166	E7
	10	STNL	7020	A5
Highpoint Rd				
	10	NRCH	6396	A1
High Point Ter				
	10	GrbT	6166	E7
Highridge Av				
	500	CLFP	6611	C2
	500	FRVW	6611	C2
High Ridge Rd				
	10	HRSN	6050	E6
Highridge Rd				
	10	GrbT	6167	C5
	10	MrnT	6282	C6
	10	NRCH	6282	A7
High School Rd				
	-	GrbT	6167	C1
Highview Av				
	10	EchT	6281	B4
	10	NRCH	6396	B3
	10	RYEB	6170	A6
	10	STNL	6920	C6
	10	TCKA	6281	B4
Highview Cir				
	10	DBSF	6165	D3
Highview Ct				
	10	CLST	6278	D3
Highview Dr				
	10	GrbT	6280	D1
Highview Pl				
	10	BGTA	6501	E2
	10	WHPL	6050	C6
Highview Rd				
	-	GrwT	6170	B1
	10	JSYC	6819	C5
	300	EGLD	6392	B6
	400	TFLY	6392	B5
Highview St				
	100	MRNK	6282	D5
Highview Ter				
	10	YNKR	6393	E4
Highway Dr				
	-	NHmT	6724	D3
	-	WLPK	6724	D3
Highwood Av				
	10	EGLD	6392	A5
	10	MrnT	6282	B7
	10	NRCH	6282	B7
	10	TFLY	6392	B2
	100	WhkT	111	A4
	100	WhkT	6716	E2
	100	WhkT	6717	A2
	300	LEON	6502	D5
Highwood Pl				
	10	ALPN	6278	E7
Highwood Rd				
	10	WOrT	6712	A2
Highwood St				
	200	BGTA	6501	E2
	200	TnkT	6501	E2
Highwood Ter				
	10	UNCT	6716	E2
	10	WhkT	6716	E3
Highwood Ter CO-505				
	10	UNCT	6716	E2
	10	WhkT	6716	E3
Highwood Wy				
	10	LRMT	6396	C1
	10	MrnT	6396	C1
Hilary Cir				
	10	NRCH	6282	A4
Hilary Ct				
	1600	HmpT	6929	A7
	1600	HWTH	6929	A7
Hilary Wy				
	10	EchT	6281	B4
Hilburn Av				
	184-00	QENS	6826	B5
Hildreth Pl				
	10	YNKR	6394	B4
Hildreth Pl N				
	100	YNKR	6394	B3
Hill Av				
	10	HmpT	6827	D5
	3900	BRNX	6394	D7
	4600	MTVN	6394	D5
Hill Ct				
	10	OybT	6618	E2
	10	ROSH	6618	E2
E Hill Ct				
	10	CRSK	6392	C1
	10	TFLY	6392	A3
Hill Rd				
	10	SNPT	6509	A7
N Hill Rd				
	10	WbgT	7114	A1
S Hill Rd				
	10	WbgT	7114	A1
W Hill Rd				
	10	WbgT	7114	A1
Hill St				
	10	BGTA	6501	E2
	10	BKLN	6925	A1
	10	CARL	6500	C7
	10	COrT	6712	D3
	10	FLPK	6827	E2
	10	JSYC	6716	B7
	10	JSYC	6820	B1
	10	MTVN	6394	D2
	10	NRCH	6395	D6
	10	NWRK	6817	D1
	10	RYE	6283	E4
	10	STNL	7020	D2
	10	WRDG	6500	C7
	100	PLMM	6395	C6
	500	MRNK	6282	D6
Hill Ter				
	10	YNKR	6280	A5
	300	NVLE	6164	C4
Hillair Cir				
	-	WHPL	6168	C6
Hillair Ct				
	10	WHPL	6168	C6
Hillandale Av				
	10	NoCT	6050	B4
	10	WHPL	6050	B4
Hillandale Ct				
	10	NRCH	6282	A4
	10	SCDL	6282	A4
Hillandale Rd				
	10	RYEB	6170	A2
Hillanddale Ct				
	10	NRCH	6282	A4
	10	SCDL	6282	A4
Hillanddale Dr				
	10	NRCH	6282	A4
Hillbright Ter				
	10	YNKR	6279	E5
Hillbrook Ct				
	10	STNL	7020	D7
Hillbrook Dr				
	10	STNL	7020	E5
Hillburn Rd				
	10	EchT	6281	D3
	10	GrbT	6167	B5
Hillcrest Av				
	10	FTLE	6503	A3
	10	GrbT	6049	B7
	10	GrbT	6166	D6
	10	LEON	6502	D3
	10	LODI	6500	C3
	10	MNPK	6617	E6
	10	MrnT	6282	C7
	10	NHmT	6617	D6
	10	NRCH	6395	E2
	10	QENS	6722	D2
	10	RSLN	6618	E6
	10	RYEB	6170	A5
	10	STNL	7117	A6
	10	YNKR	6393	D3
	100	WRDG	6500	D6
	400	EGLD	6503	A3
	500	RDGF	6611	C1
Hillcrest Ct				
	10	OLDT	6164	A2
	10	STNL	7020	D5
Hillcrest Dr				
	10	GTNE	6616	D7
	10	NRCH	6395	D7
	10	PLMM	6395	D7
Hillcrest Ln				
	10	RYE	6284	B3
Hillcrest Pl				
	100	NBgT	6611	C5
	400	FTLE	6502	D7
	400	PALP	6502	D7
	600	HmpT	6928	A6
Hillcrest Rd				
	10	EchT	6395	B2
	10	GrbT	6167	C3
	10	KRNY	6714	B2
	10	MplT	6816	A1
	10	MTVN	6395	B2
	10	NHmT	6509	A7
	10	NHmT	6618	B1
	10	STNL	7020	C2
	10	WbgT	7114	A1
	300	EGLD	6392	B6
Hillcrest St				
	10	STNL	7117	A7
	400	TnkT	6501	D1
Hillcrest Ter				
	10	EORG	6712	D6
	10	NWRK	6712	D6
	10	STNL	7020	D5
Hillcrest Vw				
	10	GrbT	6167	C4
Hillcroft				
	-	ARDY	6166	D4
Hill Ct Pl				
	10	YNKR	6393	D3
Hilldale Av				
	10	WHPL	6050	C7
Hilldale Ct				
	10	STNL	7020	D7
Hilldale Dr				
	10	NHmT	6724	C2
Hilldale Ln				
	10	SNPT	6508	C5
Hilldale Pl				
	10	EchT	6281	B3
	10	HlsT	6816	D6
	10	WHPL	6050	C7
Hilldale Rd				
	10	DBSF	6166	B4
	10	NHmT	6724	E3
Hille Pl				
	10	RDFP	6501	E6
Hillel Pl				
	10	BKLN	7023	C1
Hilliard Av				
	10	EDGW	6611	E2
Hillis St				
	10	STNL	7116	D7
Hillman Av				
	10	STNL	7018	E4
	300	STNL	7019	A3
	3900	BRNX	6504	D1
Hillman St				
	900	HmpT	6929	D2
Hillmeyer Av				
	69-00	QENS	7026	C5
Hill Park Av				
	10	GTPZ	6617	B7
	10	GTPZ	6723	B1
	10	THSN	6617	B7
	10	THSN	6723	B1
Hillridge Ct				
	10	STNL	7020	D7
Hillsboro Av				
	10	HmpT	6827	C5
Hillside Av				
	10	BXTE	6617	D1
	10	CRSK	6278	C7
	10	EGLD	6392	A7
	10	EWLS	6724	E4
	10	GrbT	6049	D6
	10	GrwT	6170	C4
	10	GTNE	6617	A7
	10	GTPZ	6617	A7
	10	HAOH	6165	C7
	10	HAOH	6166	A7
	10	HlsT	6816	B5
	10	HSBH	6500	E4
	10	HSBH	6501	A4
	10	IrvT	6816	A4
	10	KRNY	6714	A4
	10	LNBK	6929	A3
	10	MHTN	104	D1
	10	MHTN	6503	E5
	10	MtPT	6050	B2
	10	MTVN	6395	A4
	10	NHmT	6617	C6
	10	NHmT	6618	D7
	10	NRCH	6395	D2
	10	NRWD	6164	A6
	10	NWRK	6817	B2
	10	OybT	6618	E2
	10	PLHM	6395	D7
	10	PTCH	6170	C4
	10	QENS	7122	D3
	10	RKVC	6929	E4
	10	ROSE	6618	D7
	10	RSLN	6618	D7
	10	STNL	7020	C3
	10	TFLY	6392	B3
	10	TnkT	6502	A2
	10	UnnT	6816	A4
	10	WbgT	7114	C2
	10	WHPL	6168	C2
	10	WLPK	6724	D5
	10	WOrT	6712	A3
	10	YNKR	6279	E5
	100	DMRT	6278	C7
	100	LEON	6502	D3
	100	MRNK	6282	E5
	100	NHmT	6723	E6
	100	TnkT	6501	D3
	117-00	QENS	6824	E5
	122-00	QENS	6825	A5
	181-00	QENS	6826	D1
	200	ALPN	6278	C7
	200	NHmT	6724	A6
	200	PALP	6502	C5
	200	VLYS	6928	B2
	235-30	QENS	6827	A1
	247-00	QENS	6723	B7
	300	COrT	6712	B4
	300	MNLA	6724	D5
	600	CLFP	6611	D2
	700	MtPT	6049	E4
Hillside Av CO-74				
	10	CRSK	6278	C7
	100	DMRT	6278	C7
	200	ALPN	6278	C7
Hillside Av CO-509				
	300	HlsT	6816	C5
Hillside Av CO-628				
	10	HlsT	6816	D6
Hillside Av SR-25				
	138-36	QENS	6825	C5
	181-00	QENS	6826	A3
Hillside Av SR-25B				
	10	EWLS	6724	E4
	10	NHmT	6723	E6
	10	WLPK	6724	D5
	200	NHmT	6724	A5
	220-00	QENS	6826	E1
	235-30	QENS	6827	A1
	247-00	QENS	6723	B7
	300	MNLA	6724	D5
Hillside Av SR-100				
	10	GrbT	6049	D6
	700	MtPT	6049	E4
Hillside Av US-1				
	10	GrwT	6170	C4
	10	PTCH	6170	C4
Hillside Av S				
	10	GrbT	6049	D7
Hillside Av S SR-100				
	10	GrbT	6049	D7
N Hillside Av				
	10	EMFD	6049	B5
	200	VLYS	6928	C2
S Hillside Av				
	10	EMFD	6049	A6
Hillside Blvd				
	10	NHPK	6827	E1
	500	NHmT	6723	E7
	500	NHPK	6723	D7
Hillside Cres				
	10	NRCH	6282	A7
Hillside Ct				
	10	RDGF	6611	B1
	1600	NHmT	6724	A5
Hillside Dr				
	-	HSBH	6500	E5
	10	YNKR	6393	D3
Hillside Dr S				
	300	NHmT	6724	B5
Hillside Ln				
	10	NHmT	6723	E6
	10	NRCH	6395	E1
	10	NRCH	6396	A1
Hillside Pl				
	10	ARDY	6166	D5
	10	EMFD	6049	A6
	10	LODI	6500	C1
	10	RYE	6283	E4
	10	SCLF	6509	E7
	10	TYTN	6048	B2
	100	EchT	6281	B5
	300	SOrT	6712	B4
	700	WbgT	7114	D3
	1100	NBgT	6716	E1
	1100	UNCT	6716	E1
Hillside Rd				
	10	DBSF	6165	E5
	10	EchT	6395	A1
	10	ELIZ	6917	B3
	10	MrnT	6396	B1
	10	RYE	6169	E7
	10	RYE	6170	A7
	600	PLMM	6395	B6
Hillside St				
	-	TYTN	6048	C5
	400	RDGF	6611	B1
Hillside Ter				
	10	ERTH	6500	A7
	10	GRFD	6500	B1
	10	IRVN	6166	B1
	10	IrvT	6816	C1
	10	NWRK	6712	C7
	10	NWRK	6816	C1
	10	STNL	7117	B5
	10	WHPL	6168	A1
	10	WLTN	6500	A6
	400	SOrT	6712	A4
	400	WOrT	6712	A4
Hillside Close				
	10	GrbT	6049	D6
Hillside Park Dr				
	10	NHmT	6724	A5
Hillspoint Ln				
	10	RYEB	6169	E4
Hill Top Av				
	300	LEON	6502	D4
Hilltop Av				
	10	NRCH	6395	E3
Hilltop Ct				
	5000	FTLE	6503	A4
Hilltop Dr				
	10	GTNE	6616	E6
	10	NHmT	6618	A6
	10	PTCH	6170	C7
Hilltop Dr E				
	10	GTNE	6616	E6
Hilltop Dr W				
	10	GTNE	6616	E7
Hilltop Ln				
	-	ALPN	6278	E7
	10	GrbT	6167	B1
	10	NHmT	6724	E1
Hilltop Pk				
	100	DBSF	6166	C3
Hilltop Pl				
	10	HRSN	6169	D7
	10	NHmT	6724	E2
	10	STNL	7117	B6
Hilltop Rd				
	10	ARDY	6166	E4
	10	BRXV	6395	B1
	10	BXTE	6617	E1
	10	EchT	6395	B1
	10	GrwT	6170	D5
	10	MrnT	6282	C5
	10	NHmT	6724	C2
	10	STNL	7117	A7
Hilltop Ter				
	10	STNL	7020	A6
	500	CLFP	6611	D3
Hilltop Acres				
	10	YNKR	6394	A3
Hillturn Ln				
	10	NHmT	6724	D1
Hillvale Rd				
	10	NHmT	6724	D2
Hillview Av				
	10	NHmT	6508	E7
	10	NHmT	6617	E1
	10	YNKR	6394	A4
Hillview Dr				
	10	SCDL	6282	A2
Hillview Ln				
	10	STNL	7020	A6
Hillview Pl				
	10	GrbT	6049	B4
	10	STNL	7020	B5
Hillwood Ct				
	10	STNL	7020	E4
Hillwood Pl				
	10	YNKR	6280	C5
Hillyer St				
	10	COrT	6712	D3
	10	EORG	6712	D3
	50-00	QENS	6719	D7
Hilton Av				
	10	GDNC	6828	E1
	10	NHmT	6724	C7
	10	WHPL	6050	B6
Hilton St				
	10	EORG	6712	E1
	10	LNBK	6929	C4
Hiltop Dr				
	10	PTCH	6170	B7
Himrod St				
	10	BKLN	6822	E6
	17-00	BKLN	6823	B4
	17-00	QENS	6823	B5
Hinckley Pl				
	10	BKLN	6922	E6
	10	BKLN	6923	A6
Hinman Pl				
	400	MRNK	6282	C4
	400	MRNK	6283	A5
Hinrichs Pl				
	10	BlmT	6713	B1
Hinsdale Av				
	10	FLPK	6827	D1
	10	QENS	6827	D1
Hinsdale Pl				
	10	NWRK	6713	E3
	10	NWRK	6714	C4
Hinsdale St				
	10	BKLN	6924	C2
Hinton St				
	10	STNL	7116	C3
Hiram Av				
	10	WHPL	6168	B2
Hiram Pl				
	10	HRSN	6714	B6
Hirsch Ln				
	10	STNL	7018	E3
Hiscock Pl				
	10	YNKR	6394	B1
Hitchcock Av				
	100	STNL	7117	D2
E Hitchcock Av				
	10	FLPK	6827	D1
W Hitchcock Av				
	10	FLPK	6827	D1
Hix Av				
	10	RYE	6283	E5
Hobart Av				
	10	BAYN	6919	E5
	10	PTCH	6170	B4
	100	GrwT	6170	B4
	1100	BRNX	6615	A1
	1200	BRNX	6506	A7
	1600	BRNX	6505	E6
Hobart Dr				
	10	GrwT	6170	E1
Hobart Pl				
	10	GRFD	6500	B4
Hobart St				
	10	BRXV	6281	A7
	10	HKSK	6501	B2
	10	RDFP	6501	E5
	10	TCKA	6281	A7
	28-00	QENS	6719	B4
	100	RDFP	6502	A5
	100	SHkT	6501	B3
	200	PTHA	7205	D4
Hoboken Av				
	10	JSYC	6716	C7
	100	JSYC	6820	B1
Hoboken Av SR-139				
	-	JSYC	6820	B1
Hoboken Rd				
	10	CARL	6609	C1
	10	ERTH	6609	C1
	200	CARL	6500	B7
	200	ERTH	6500	B7
Hoboken Rd CO-S55				
	10	CARL	6609	C1
	10	ERTH	6609	C1
	200	CARL	6500	B7
	200	ERTH	6500	B7
Hobson St				
	10	JSYC	6716	C6
	10	NWRK	6816	E3
Hoda Pl				
	10	STNL	7116	C7
Hodges Pl				
	10	STNL	7019	E3
Hodson Av				
	10	HmpT	6929	B3
	10	LNBK	6929	B3
Hoe Av				
	900	BRNX	6613	D2
	1600	BRNX	6504	D7
Hoeffner Av				
	10	HmpT	6827	C4
Hoefleys Ln				
	10	FTLE	6502	E4
	10	LEON	6502	E4
Hoehn St				
	10	HSBH	6500	E3
	10	LODI	6500	E3
Hoffman Av				
	1900	HmpT	6827	B5
Hoffman Blvd				
	10	BlmT	6713	B2
	10	EORG	6713	B2
Hoffman Dr				
	57-00	QENS	6824	A3
Hoffman Pl				
	10	HlsT	6816	C4
	10	IrvT	6816	C4
Hoffman Rd				
	10	NHPK	6828	A1
Hoffman St				
	10	HKSK	6501	B3
	10	HmpT	6828	B5
	10	SHkT	6501	B3
	10	VLYS	6928	C2
	2300	BRNX	6504	D5
Hoffstot Ln				
	10	SNPT	6508	B4
Hogan Pl				
	10	HAOH	6165	C7
	10	MHTN	118	D6
	10	MHTN	6821	A2
Hoke Av				
	200	HmpT	6929	D7
Holbernt Ct				
	10	STNL	7019	D1
Holbrook Av				
	10	YNKR	6280	D4
Holbrooke Rd				
	10	WHPL	6168	C6
Holcomb Av				
	10	STNL	7116	B5
Holden Blvd				
	10	STNL	7019	D5
Holder Pl				
	72-00	QENS	6824	D3
Holdridge Av				
	10	STNL	7116	E7
	200	STNL	7207	E1
Holdrum St				
	10	NRWD	6164	A6
Holgate St				
	10	STNL	7019	B3
Holiday Ct				
	10	HmpT	6928	C6
	10	VLYS	6928	C6
	400	NWRK	6713	D6
Holiday Dr				
	10	STNL	7019	B2
Holiday Wy				
	10	STNL	7019	A2
Holiday Gate				
	10	LKSU	6723	E4
	10	NHmT	6723	E4
Holiday Park Dr				
	10	NHmT	6724	D4
Holland Av				
	10	CRSK	6278	C7
	10	DMRT	6278	B7
	10	FLPK	6827	D1
	10	HmpT	6827	C4
	10	STNL	6918	E7
	10	SYHW	6048	A2
	10	WHPL	6050	B6
	90-00	QENS	7026	B7
	100	QENS	6827	D1
	2200	BRNX	6505	B4
Holland Ct				
	10	VLYS	6928	A2
Holland Pl				
	10	GrbT	6167	D3
Holland Rd				
	10	SOrT	6712	C6
Holland St				
	-	JSYC	6716	C6
	10	HRSN	6283	B3
	10	NWRK	6713	A7
	10	NWRK	6817	A1
Holland Ter				
	10	TnkT	6502	B1
Holland Tun				
	-	JSYC	6820	D1
	-	MHTN	118	B3
	-	MHTN	6820	D1
	-	MHTN	6821	A2
Hollers Av				
	2200	BRNX	6505	E1
	2500	BRNX	6395	A7
	2500	BRNX	6506	A1
Holley Ter				
	10	CLFP	6611	D3
Hollis Av				
	207-00	QENS	6826	D4
Hollis Ct Blvd				
	-	QENS	6826	C2
	46-00	QENS	6721	E5
	53-48	QENS	6722	A6
Hollis Ct Blvd SR-24				
	-	QENS	6826	C2
Hollis Hills Ter				
	-	QENS	6722	B7
	79-00	QENS	6826	B1
Hollister Av				
	100	RTFD	6609	A1
Hollister Rd				
	10	TETB	6501	A4
Hollow Ct				
	10	NHmT	6724	D2
	10	SNPT	6508	C5
Hollow Ln				
	10	LKSU	6723	E3
	10	NHLS	6723	E3
Hollow Wood Ln				
	10	GrwT	6170	C3
Holls Ter N				
	10	YNKR	6279	D5
Holls Ter S				
	10	YNKR	6279	D5
Holls Ter W				
	10	YNKR	6279	C5
Holly Av				
	10	STNL	7117	A6
	140-00	QENS	6721	B5
Holly Ct				
	700	NRWD	6278	C1
	900	HmpT	6828	A7
Holly Dr				
	10	NRCH	6395	D3
Holly Ln				
	10	CRSK	6278	A6
	10	DMRT	6278	A6
	10	GTNK	6616	E5
	10	LWRN	7027	E4
	10	MtPT	6049	E1
	10	RYE	6284	A1
	10	RYEB	6170	A1
Holly Pl				
	10	BRNX	6615	C4
	10	FLPK	6827	D1
	10	GrbT	6280	A2
	10	HAOH	6280	A2
	10	MrnT	6282	C6
	10	STNL	7117	E2
	300	HmpT	6929	D1
	400	NVLE	6164	B3
Holly Rd				
	10	HmpT	6928	D6
Holly St				
	10	CART	7115	C2
	10	JSYC	6819	B4
	10	STNL	7020	B5
	10	WbgT	7115	C2
	10	YNKR	6394	A3
	200	BKLN	6925	A3
Holly Hill Ln				
	10	GrwT	6170	D4
Holly Ridge Rd				
	10	MtPT	6049	E1
Hollywood Av				
	10	EGLC	6392	C7
	10	EORG	6713	A6
	10	HlsT	6816	D7
	10	HmpT	6928	E5
	10	LNBK	6928	E5
	10	LNBK	6929	A5
	10	VLYS	6928	C4
	10	YNKR	6281	A4
	100	IrvT	6816	A4
	100	NWRK	6713	A6
	100	UnnT	6816	A4
	149-00	QENS	6721	B5
	235-00	QENS	6722	C2
	400	BRNX	6615	A1
	1200	BRNX	6506	A7
	1500	BRNX	6505	E6
Hollywood Av E				
	10	TCKA	6281	A5
Hollywood Cross				
	100	LWRN	7028	B3
Hollywood Ct				
	10	QENS	7027	A5
	10	RKVC	6929	E1
Hollywood Dr				
	10	DBSF	6166	A6
	10	HAOH	6166	A6
	10	WbgT	7114	B5
Holmes Av				
	10	GrbT	6167	B2
	10	JSYC	6819	D1
Holmes Ln				
	10	BKLN	6924	C7
Holmes Pl				
	10	LNBK	6929	A3
	10	MLVN	6929	A3
Holmes St				
	10	CART	7017	C7
	10	YNKR	6394	C3
Holsman Rd				
	10	STNL	7020	C4
Holt Pl				
	200	BRNX	6504	E2
Holt St				
	10	HKSK	6501	C3
	500	HmpT	6828	D6
Holten Av				
	10	STNL	7207	B2
Holton St				
	10	WbgT	7114	E5
	10	WbgT	7115	A5
Holzheimer St				
	900	HmpT	6828	A4
Homans Av				
	10	CLST	6278	B3
	500	ALPN	6278	D4
Home Av				
	10	RTFD	6609	A2
	10	STNL	7021	A4
Home Pl				
	10	LODI	6500	C2
	10	STNL	7019	B3
E Home Pl				
	10	IRVN	6166	C1
W Home Pl				
	10	IRVN	6166	C1
Home St				
	10	MLVN	6929	A2
	10	TnkT	6502	B2
	10	VLYS	6928	E2
	10	WHPL	6168	D2
	200	VLYS	6929	A2
	700	BRNX	6613	C2
	700	HmpT	6827	E7
Home Ter				
	10	LNDN	6917	B5
	10	ROSL	6917	B5
Homecrest Av				
	10	BKLN	7023	B5
	10	YNKR	6280	A4
	2700	BKLN	7121	C2
Homecrest Ct				
	10	BKLN	7023	A5
	10	HmpT	6929	D3
Homecrest Ovl				
	10	YNKR	6280	A4
Home Depot Dr				
	-	NRCH	6395	D6
Homelawn St				
	82-23	QENS	6825	D3
Homer Av				
	10	MrnT	6282	B7
	10	WbgT	7114	D1
	2000	BRNX	6614	C3
Homer Pl				
	10	MNPK	6618	A5
Homer St				
	10	STNL	6920	D7
	10	STNL	7020	D1
Homesdale Rd				
	10	BRXV	6395	A1
Homeside Ln				
	10	WHPL	6168	E5
Homesite Pkwy				
	10	YNKR	6279	E7
Homestead Av				
	10	EchT	6281	C2
	10	GDNC	6828	B1
	10	STNL	7019	C1
	10	WbgT	7114	D1
	200	WbgT	7115	A1
	400	MTVN	6395	A5
E Homestead Av				
	200	PALP	6502	C7
W Homestead Av				
	10	PALP	6502	B6
Homestead Ln				
	10	GrwT	6170	D4
Homestead Pk				
	10	NWRK	6816	E3
Homestead Pl				
	10	BGTA	6501	D1
	10	HRSN	6283	C1
	10	JSYC	6820	A1
	10	NRCH	6396	C4
	10	RDFP	6501	E5
Homestead Rd				
	10	GrwT	6170	C1
	10	TFLY	6392	C3
Homewood Av				
	10	YNKR	6280	A7
Homewood Ct				
	10	GrbT	6167	C2
Homewood Dr				
	10	NHmT	6617	C6
Homewood Pl				
	-	NHmT	6618	A3
	10	FLHL	6618	A3
Homewood Rd				
	10	GrbT	6167	C2
	10	MTVN	6395	D6
Hommann Av				
	600	PTHA	7205	C2
S Hommel St				
	1100	HmpT	6928	B1
Hommell St				
	10	HmpT	6928	B1
Hommocks Rd				
	10	MRNK	6396	E2
	10	MrnT	6396	E2
Hone Av				
	2500	BRNX	6505	B3
Honeck St				
	10	EGLD	6502	D1
Honey Ln				
	10	STNL	7206	B4
Honeysuckle Av				
	10	WOrT	6712	B1
Honeywell Av				
	1900	BRNX	6504	E7
Honeywell Pl				
	100	HmpT	7027	C2
Honeywell St				
	39-00	QENS	6718	E5
Honiss Pl				
	10	NWRK	6713	E1
Honiss St				
	10	BlvT	6713	C1
Hood Ct				
	10	GrbT	6167	B2
Hook Rd				
	10	BAYN	6920	B4
	10	RYE	6284	A3
Hook St				
	500	HmpT	6928	A6
Hook Creek Blvd				
	10	HmpT	6928	A4
	121-00	QENS	6928	A1
	133-00	VLYS	6928	A2
Hooker Pl				
	100	STNL	7019	B1
Hooks Ln				
	10	EDGW	103	A5
	10	EDGW	6503	A6
Hooper Av				
	10	STNL	7117	D4
Hooper St				
	100	BKLN	6822	B5
Hoover Av				
	124-00	QENS	6825	A4
Hoover Dr				
	10	CRSK	6392	C2
Hoover Rd				
	10	YNKR	6280	A3
Hoover St				
	10	HmpT	7027	D2

New York City/5 Borough Street Index

STREET Block City Map# Grid

Hoover Wy
500 WbgT 7114 A7
Hopatcong Av
400 HmpT 6929 C2
Hope Av
10 STNL 7020 E4
10 STNL 7021 A4
400 ROSL 6917 A4
Hope Ln
- ELIZ 6918 C5
10 STNL 7020 E4
100 STNL 7021 B4
Hope St
10 BKLN 6822 B3
10 ERTH 6500 B6
10 JSYC 6716 C7
10 LODI 6500 D2
10 WLTN 6500 B6
Hopke Av
10 HAOH 6165 E7
Hopkins Av
10 JSYC 6716 B7
10 JSYC 6820 B1
10 MNLA 6724 E5
10 STNL 7117 D4
Hopkins Pl
10 IrvT 6816 D2
10 NWRK 6816 D2
Hopkins St
10 BKLN 6822 C5
Hopper St
100 HKSK 6501 A2
Hopping Av
10 STNL 7206 A4
Hops Ln
10 SECS 6610 B6
Hops Commons Ct
10 SECS 6610 C6
Horace Ct
10 BKLN 6922 E4
Horace Pl
10 SCLF 6509 E7
Horace Harding Blvd
10 LKSU 6723 B3
10 NHmT 6723 B3
100 QENS 6723 A3
Horace Harding Dr
- LKSU 6723 B3
Horace Harding Expwy
- QENS 6824 A1
Horace Harding Expwy N
94-01 QENS 6824 B1
130-01 QENS 6720 E6
137-01 QENS 6721 C7
195-01 QENS 6722 B6
248-01 QENS 6723 A4
260-55 LKSU 6723 B3
260-55 NHmT 6723 B3
Horace Harding Expwy S
92-00 QENS 6824 A1
130-00 QENS 6720 E6
172-78 QENS 6721 D7
242-00 QENS 6722 E5
248-00 QENS 6723 A4
263-00 LKSU 6723 B3
Horan Pl
10 OrgT 6164 D2
Horatio Av
700 HmpT 6828 B6
Horatio Pkwy
49-00 QENS 6722 C4
Horatio St
10 MHTN 115 D7
10 MHTN 6717 B7
10 NWRK 6818 C1
10 YNKR 6280 A5
Horizon Blvd
10 MNCH 6610 C1
10 SHkT 6610 C2
Horizon Rd
10 FTLE 6502 E7
10 LKSU 6723 B3
Horizon Wy
10 KNGP 6616 D2
Horn St
10 OrgT 6164 A1
Hornaday Pl
800 BRNX 6504 E6
Hornbill Dr
200 NHLS 6724 B1
Hornell Lp
10 BKLN 6924 E6
Horner Av
10 HAOH 6166 A7
Horne Tooke Rd
10 OrgT 6164 E4
10 OrgT 6165 C5
Hornridge Rd
300 MRNK 6283 B5
300 RYE 6283 B5
Hornsby Av
600 PTHA 7114 C7
Horseguard Ln
10 SCDL 6167 D6
Horse Shoe Ln
10 LKSU 6723 B3
Horseshoe Ln
10 RYEB 6169 E4
Horton Av
10 LNBK 6928 E4
10 NRCH 6395 D3
10 PTCH 6170 C5
10 VLYS 6928 E4
16-00 QENS 7027 C4
Horton Ct
10 HRSN 6050 D3
Horton Hwy
100 MNLA 6724 E6
300 WLPK 6724 E5
Horton Rd
10 HmpT 6928 E5
10 VLYS 6928 E5
Horton St
10 BRNX 6506 E7
10 MLVN 6929 A2
10 RYE 6284 A3
10 VLYS 6929 A2
Hosey Ln
200 HmpT 7029 E5
Hosmer Av
100 BRNX 6615 A4
Hospital Pl
10 HKSK 6501 B1
Hospital Rd
- MtPT 6049 C1
Hospital Service Rd
- MtPT 6049 C1
Hotel Dr
10 WHPL 6168 D4
Hotel Rd
- NWRK 6817 C7
Hothorn Av
10 YNKR 6281 A3
Housman Av
10 STNL 6919 B7
Housman Wy
- STNL 7117 D1
Houston Av
200 WLPK 6724 D5
300 MNLA 6724 D5
Houston Ln
10 STNL 7019 B2
Houston St
10 NWRK 6818 A2
10 STNL 7019 B2
E Houston St
10 MHTN 118 E3
10 MHTN 119 D5
10 MHTN 6821 E3
W Houston St
10 MHTN 118 C2
10 MHTN 6821 A1
Hovenden Rd
182-00 QENS 6825 E3
182-00 QENS 6826 A3
Hovey Ln
10 PRMT 6164 E1
Howard Al
10 BKLN 121 A3
10 BKLN 6821 C5
Howard Av
10 BKLN 6823 A7
10 EchT 6281 B5
10 MtPT 6050 A3
10 NHmT 6724 B5
10 OrgT 6164 A1
10 STNL 7020 B3
10 WHPL 6168 A3
300 BKLN 6924 A3
300 HmpT 6828 B6
300 HmpT 6928 A7
300 HmpT 7028 B1
800 MRNK 6282 E5
Howard Cir
10 STNL 7020 C2
Howard Ct
10 NWRK 6713 C7
10 STNL 6920 A7
Howard Pkwy
10 NRCH 6395 E2
Howard Pl
- GrbT 6166 E3
10 BAYN 6919 B5
10 BKLN 6922 E4
10 BlvT 6714 A1
10 JSYC 6819 E2
10 JSYC 6820 A2
10 LNBK 6929 C5
10 RYE 6284 A1
10 YNKR 6280 C5
800 RDGF 6611 A2
Howard St
10 DBSF 6166 B4
10 IrvT 6816 D2
10 LODI 6500 D1
10 LRMT 6396 C2
10 MHTN 118 D5
10 MHTN 6821 B3
10 MTVN 6394 D3
10 NWRK 6713 C7
10 PTHA 7205 B1
10 SYHW 6048 B1
10 WbgT 7205 A1
100 NWRK 6817 C1
600 TnkT 6502 B2
1200 HlsT 6816 E7
1200 HmpT 6929 C3
1200 MLVN 6929 C3
Howard Ter
10 LEON 6502 D4
Howard Park Dr
10 TFLY 6392 B4
Howe Av
400 BRNX 6614 C3
Howe Ct
10 HmpT 7028 D1
Howe Pl
10 YNKR 6280 D6
Howe St
10 STNL 7020 A2
Howell Av
10 MrnT 6396 C1
10 WbgT 7114 A6
Howell Pl
10 EchT 6281 C6
10 KRNY 6714 C2
10 NWRK 6712 D6
Howell Rd
1400 HmpT 6928 D1
Howell St
100 JSYC 6715 D7
Howland Rd
10 ERKY 6929 B6
Howton Av
10 STNL 7117 B4
Hoxie Av
230-00 QENS 6722 C4
Hoxie Dr
227-00 QENS 6722 C4
Hoxie St
4500 BRNX 6394 D6
Hoym St
200 FTLE 103 A4
200 FTLE 6502 E5
200 FTLE 6503 B5
Hoyt Av
10 STNL 6920 A7
10 STNL 7020 A1
100 MRNK 6282 E6
1000 RDGF 6611 A1
2000 FTLE 103 A3
2000 FTLE 6503 A5
Hoyt Av N
19-00 QENS 6719 A2
Hoyt Av N I-278 TRK
29-00 QENS 6719 A3
Hoyt Av S
21-00 QENS 114 E4
21-00 QENS 6719 A2
Hoyt Av S I-278 TRK
29-00 QENS 6719 A2
N Hoyt Av
2100 FTLE 103 B2
2100 FTLE 6503 A5
Hoyt St
10 BKLN 121 B6
10 BKLN 6821 D7
10 KRNY 6714 A5
10 NWRK 6713 D6
100 BKLN 6922 C1
Hubbard Cir
10 EchT 6395 B1
Hubbard Dr
10 WHPL 6168 D6
Hubbard Pl
10 BKLN 7023 D2
Hubbard St
10 BKLN 7023 A7
Hubbell St
1600 BRNX 6505 C7
Huber Pl
10 YNKR 6394 B3
Huber St
10 SECS 6610 B6
Hubert Pl
10 NRCH 6395 E2
Hubert St
10 MHTN 118 B4
10 MHTN 6821 A2
Huckleberry Ln
1300 HmpT 6929 A7
1300 HWTH 6929 A7
Hudson Av
10 BKLN 121 C3
10 EDGW 6611 E1
10 EORG 6712 D6
10 IRVN 6048 C7
10 MplT 6712 A7
10 MplT 6816 A1
10 MTVN 6395 A4
10 NRWD 6164 C6
10 NWRK 6712 D6
10 RDFP 6501 E5
10 TFLY 6392 C2
10 VLYS 6928 C3
400 BKLN 6821 E7
400 WhkT 6716 E3
600 SECS 6609 E7
600 SECS 6610 A6
1000 RDGF 6611 A2
1800 UNCT 6716 E3
4600 UNCT 111 A2
4600 UNCT 6717 A1
4900 WNYK 111 A1
4900 WNYK 6717 A1
5800 WNYK 6611 A7
6700 GTBG 6611 B6
7100 NBgT 6611 B6
E Hudson Av
10 EGLD 6392 A5
100 TFLY 6392 B5
E Hudson Av CO-68
10 EGLD 6392 A4
W Hudson Av
10 EGLD 6392 A4
Hudson Blvd
300 WbgT 7114 B2
Hudson Ct
10 HmpT 6929 B2
10 JSYC 6819 B4
Hudson Dr
- ALPN 6392 E4
- EGLC 6392 E4
- TFLY 6392 E4
10 DBSF 6165 E3
10 DBSF 6166 A3
10 IRVN 6166 A3
Hudson Pl
- TYTN 6048 A4
10 HBKN 6716 D7
10 MrnT 6282 B6
10 STNL 7019 B2
10 WhkT 111 A4
10 WhkT 6717 A2
200 CLFP 6611 C4
200 FRVW 6611 C4
500 CDHT 7028 A2
Hudson Rd
- STNL 7021 B6
10 BLRS 6827 B2
10 FLPK 6827 C2
10 GDNC 6828 B1
10 HmpT 6827 B2
Hudson Rd E
10 IRVN 6166 A3
Hudson Rd W
- IRVN 6165 E2
10 IRVN 6166 A3
Hudson St
10 CART 7115 D3
10 GRFD 6500 A3
10 HAOH 6279 E1
10 HAOH 6280 A1
10 HBKN 6716 E6
10 HKSK 6501 C2
10 JSYC 6820 D4
10 MHTN 6821 B2
10 NWRK 6713 C6
10 PASC 6500 A3
10 STNL 7020 D2
10 SYHW 6048 A2
10 TYTN 6048 A2
10 YNKR 6393 C1
100 PLMM 6395 B7
200 MHTN 118 C4
400 LFRY 6501 D4
500 MHTN 115 C7
500 MHTN 6717 B7
Hudson St CO-124
10 HKSK 6501 C2
400 LFRY 6501 D4
Hudson St E
10 HmpT 7029 B1
Hudson St W
10 HmpT 7029 C2
E Hudson St
10 LBCH 7029 D6
N Hudson St
2000 FTLE 103 B2
2000 FTLE 6503 A5
W Hudson St
100 LBCH 7029 B6
Hudson Ter
10 DBSF 6165 E4
10 EDGW 6611 E1
10 EGLC 6503 B4
10 FTLE 6503 A6
10 SYHW 6048 B1
10 YNKR 6279 D6
600 CLFP 6611 D3
2000 FTLE 103 B2
Hudson Ter CO-505
10 EGLC 6503 B4
10 FTLE 6503 B3
2000 FTLE 103 B2
Hudson Manor Ter
3600 BRNX 102 B1
3600 BRNX 6393 A7
Hudson Park Rd
10 NRCH 6396 A5
Hudson River Rd
10 BRNX 6393 B5
Hudson View Dr
10 YNKR 6279 D5
Hudson View Pk
10 IRVN 6048 C6
10 TYTN 6048 B6
Hudson View Ter
10 YNKR 6279 D6
Hueston St
800 UnnT 6917 C2
Hughes Av
10 RYE 6283 C4
2300 BRNX 6504 D5
Hughes Pl
10 TCKA 6280 C3
100 NHmT 6724 D3
Hughes St
10 LODI 6500 C1
10 MplT 6816 A3
500 NVLE 6164 A4
Hughes Ter
10 YNKR 6279 D5
Hugh J Grant Cir
10 BRNX 6614 B1
Huguenot Av
10 EGLD 6502 E1
10 STNL 7116 B7
200 UnnT 6917 C1
300 UnnT 6816 A7
900 STNL 7207 C2
3400 BRNX 6506 B1
3500 BRNX 6395 A7
Huguenot Ct
10 TFLY 6392 A3
Huguenot Dr
10 MrnT 6396 B1
10 NRCH 6396 B1
Huguenot St
10 NRCH 6396 A4
100 NRCH 6395 E5
Huguenot St US-1
10 NRCH 6396 A4
100 NRCH 6395 E5
Hull Av
10 NARL 6714 D2
10 NHmT 6723 E6
10 STNL 7020 A7
69-00 QENS 6823 D2
100 STNL 7118 B1
3000 BRNX 6504 E2
3100 BRNX 6505 A2
Hull St
10 BKLN 6924 A1
Humbert St
10 STNL 7020 D7
Humboldt St
10 BKLN 6822 D4
10 CARL 6500 C7
10 ERTH 6609 B1
10 NWRK 6713 A6
10 WRDG 6500 C7
700 SECS 6610 A7
Humphrey Av
10 BAYN 6919 C6
Humphrey St
200 EGLD 6502 D1
Humphreys St
24-00 QENS 6720 A3
Hungry Harbor Rd
10 HmpT 6928 A6
10 VLYS 6928 C5
262-00 QENS 6928 A5
700 HmpT 6927 E6
Hunnewell Av
10 HmpT 6827 E5
Hunt Av
10 YNKR 6280 A5
1900 BRNX 6505 A6
Hunt Ct
10 NHmT 6724 C4
Hunt Dr
10 HmpT 6929 A6
10 HWTH 6929 A7
Hunt Ln
10 STNL 7020 A5
400 MNPK 6617 E6
400 MNPK 6618 B6
Hunt Pl
10 RYE 6283 C4
10 WHPL 6168 C2
Hunt Pth
10 NRCH 6282 A7
Hunt Ter
10 GrwT 6170 B1
Hunter Av
- BKLN 7022 C7
10 HmpT 6928 B1
10 NRCH 6396 A2
10 STNL 7020 A7
10 STNL 7118 B1
10 VLYS 6928 B1
10 YNKR 6394 B3
600 PTHA 7114 C7
1000 PLMM 6395 C7
2200 BRNX 6506 A4
3300 BRNX 6505 E1
Hunter Dr
10 EchT 6281 C4
10 RYEB 6169 E3
Hunter Ln
10 GrbT 6049 B3
10 RYE 6283 D1
10 WbgT 7114 B4
Hunter Pl
10 STNL 6920 B7
10 STNL 7020 B1
Hunter Rd
10 GrbT 6049 D4
Hunter St
10 LODI 6500 D3
10 MRNK 6283 A4
10 NWRK 6817 C3
10 STNL 7020 C5
42-00 QENS 6718 D6
100 HSBH 6500 D3
500 HRSN 6283 A4
Hunter St CO-61
10 LODI 6500 C2
Hunterdon St
100 NWRK 6713 B7
800 NWRK 6817 A4
Hunterfly Pl
10 BKLN 6923 E1
Hunters Ln
10 FLHL 6618 B6
Hunters Run
100 DBSF 6166 B5
Hunters Point Av
4-00 QENS 117 D5
11-00 QENS 6718 C7
Hunting Hill Rd
10 NHmT 6724 C6
Hunting Ridge Rd
10 WHPL 6168 D6
Huntington Av
10 LNBK 6929 C4
10 SCDL 6167 E4
100 BRNX 6615 A3
900 BRNX 6614 E2
Huntington Dr
10 YNKR 6393 E4
10 YNKR 6394 A5
Huntington Pl
10 NRCH 6396 A4
Huntington Rd
100 NHmT 6617 D2
Huntington St
100 BKLN 6922 B2
200 PTHA 7205 D2
Huntington Ter
10 NWRK 6816 E4
10 NWRK 6817 A3
Huntley Dr
100 ARDY 6166 D4
100 GrbT 6166 E3
Huntley Pl
1700 HmpT 6929 A6
Huntley Rd
10 EchT 6281 B5
10 HmpT 6827 A4
200 HmpT 7028 B1
Hunton St
10 STNL 7020 C5
Hunts Ln
10 BKLN 121 A5
10 BKLN 6821 C6
Huntsbridge Rd
10 YNKR 6394 B4
Hunts Point Av
400 BRNX 6613 D3
Huntswood Pl
10 MTVN 6395 A2
Hurden St
10 ELIZ 6816 E7
10 HlsT 6816 E7
Hurlbert St
10 STNL 7020 D6
Hurley Ct
8-00 QENS 7027 D5
Hurley Pl
700 FRVW 6611 B3
Huron Av
10 JSYC 6716 A7
Huron Pl
10 STNL 7020 A1
Huron Rd
10 BLRS 6827 B2
10 HmpT 6827 B2
10 YNKR 6280 D5
Huron St
10 BKLN 6822 B1
149-00 QENS 6925 E3
Hurst St
10 STNL 7019 D1
Hussa St
10 LNDN 7017 A1
1100 LNDN 6917 B6
Hussey Rd
200 MTVN 6395 A3
Husson Av
100 BRNX 6614 C4
Husson St
10 STNL 7020 B7
200 STNL 7118 B1
Husted St
200 PTCH 6170 C4
Hutcheson Pl
10 LNBK 6929 C4
Hutchinson Av
10 NRCH 6282 A3
10 SCDL 6282 A3
300 MTVN 6395 B5
3200 BRNX 6506 A1
Hutchinson Blvd
10 EchT 6281 D3
10 MTVN 6395 B3
10 NRCH 6281 D3
300 EchT 6395 C2
Hutchinson Ct
10 BKLN 7023 A5
10 GTNK 6617 B6
10 NHmT 6617 B6
Hutchinson Rd
200 EGLD 6502 E1
200 EGLD 6503 A1
Hutchinson River Pkwy
- BRNX 6395 B6
- BRNX 6505 E6
- BRNX 6506 A4
- BRNX 6614 D1
- EchT 6281 C7
- EchT 6395 C1
- GrwT 6170 A1
- HRSN 6168 E7
- HRSN 6169 A6
- HRSN 6282 E1
- MTVN 6395 B5
- NRCH 6281 D5
- NRCH 6282 C2
- NRCH 6395 C2
- PLHM 6395 B5
- PLMM 6395 B6
- RYEB 6169 D3
- RYEB 6170 A2
- SCDL 6282 C2
- WHPL 6168 E7
- WHPL 6169 A6
- WHPL 6282 E1
Hutchinson River Pkwy I-678
- BRNX 6614 E4
Hutchinson River Pkwy E
1600 BRNX 6505 E6
4100 BRNX 6506 A4
Hutton Av
10 WOrT 6712 A1
Hutton St
10 JSYC 6716 C6
Huxley Av
6000 BRNX 6393 C5
Huxley St
146-00 QENS 6927 E4
Huyler Av
10 TFLY 6392 A3
Huyler Av CO-501
10 TFLY 6392 A3
Huyler St
- LFRY 6501 B5
10 HKSK 6501 B2
10 SHkT 6501 B3
10 TETB 6501 B3
Huyler Landing Rd
- ALPN 6392 E2
10 CRSK 6392 C1
Hyannis Ct
10 HmpT 7029 C2
Hyannis Ln
- HRSN 6168 E1
Hyatt Av
10 HRSN 6283 B3
10 NWRK 6818 C3
10 YNKR 6394 B5
Hyatt Pl
10 YNKR 6394 B5
Hyatt St
10 STNL 6920 D6
300 WbgT 7114 B1
Hycliff Rd
10 GrwT 6051 E3
Hyde Ct
10 NHLS 6724 B2
Hygeia Pl
10 STNL 7020 D1
Hylan Blvd
10 STNL 7021 A3
100 STNL 7020 E4
1900 STNL 7118 B1
2700 STNL 7117 C5
4400 STNL 7208 A1
4600 STNL 7207 A3
6100 STNL 7206 B4
Hylan Blvd N
- STNL 7020 D4
Hylan Blvd S
- STNL 7020 D5
Hylan Pl
10 STNL 7118 B1
Hyman Ct
10 BKLN 7024 A7
100 BKLN 7023 E7

I

I St
1300 HmpT 6827 E6
I-80 Express Ln
- BGTA 6501 E3
- HKSK 6501 D3
- LODI 6500 E1
- LODI 6501 A1
- RDFP 6501 D3
- SHkT 6501 D3
- TETB 6501 A3
- TnkT 6501 E3
- TnkT 6502 A4
Ibis Ct
200 NHLS 6724 C1
Ibsen Av
10 STNL 7116 D4
Ibsen St
600 HmpT 6928 A7
600 HmpT 7028 D3
Icard Ln
10 NRCH 6396 A6
Icarus Rd
600 MHTN 6820 E7
Ichabod Ln
10 TYTN 6048 C3
Ida Ct
10 STNL 7116 C7
Ida Wy
- PTHA 7114 B7
- WbgT 7114 B7
Idaho Av
10 STNL 7206 E1
Ide Ct
10 QENS 7027 C5
Idell Rd
10 HmpT 6928 D1
10 VLYS 6928 D1
Iden Av
10 LRMT 6396 C2
10 PLMM 6395 B6
Idlease Pl
10 STNL 7118 B1
Idlewood Rd
10 WHPL 6168 B5
Igro Ct
10 STNL 7206 E1
Ike Pl
10 HmpT 7028 D1
10 HWTN 7028 D1
Ikea Dr
10 ELIZ 6918 E2
Ilinka Ln
10 IRVN 6166 B2
Ilion Av
185-00 QENS 6826 B5
Ilion Pl
10 STNL 7117 D2
Illingworth Av
10 EGLD 6392 B5
10 TFLY 6392 B5
Illinois Av
10 LBCH 7028 D7
10 YNKR 6394 D1
Ilsley Pl
10 MLVN 6929 B1
Ilyse Ct
10 STNL 7117 C3
Ilyssa Wy
10 STNL 7116 C4
Imlay St
10 BKLN 6922 A1
Impala Ct
10 STNL 7020 D7
Imperia Dr
10 PLMM 6395 B6
Imperial Av
1500 NHPK 6724 A7
1800 NHmT 6724 B7
Imperial Ct
10 NHmT 6617 A6
10 STNL 7020 D3
In Pl
- NHmT 6724 E3
Ina St
10 STNL 7118 A3
Indale Av
10 STNL 7207 A3
Independence Av
10 OrgT 6164 B1
10 STNL 7116 E2
1500 BKLN 7022 A5
2600 BRNX 102 A2
2600 BRNX 6504 A1
5700 BRNX 6393 B5
Independence Ct
10 HBKN 6716 E5
Independence Dr
10 NHmT 6723 E4
Independence St
10 TYTN 6048 B3
10 WHPL 6167 E2
Independence Wy
10 EDGW 108 B1
10 EDGW 6611 D4
10 JSYC 6819 E7
Independence Wy N
10 EDGW 108 B1
10 EDGW 6611 D4
Independence Wy S
10 EDGW 108 B1
10 EDGW 6611 D4
India St
10 BKLN 6822 C1
Indian Rd
10 BRNX 6393 C6
10 MHTN 102 A5
10 MHTN 6504 A3
10 PTCH 6170 B4
Indian Tr
10 GrbT 6049 E6
10 HRSN 6283 B1
10 NRCH 6281 D6
Indiana Av
10 LBCH 7028 D7
72-00 QENS 6823 E5
72-00 QENS 6824 A5
Indiana Pl
10 BKLN 7024 B4
Indian Cove Rd
10 MRNK 6283 A7
Indian Hill Ln
10 OrgT 6164 E5
Indian Hill Rd
10 HRSN 6050 D3
10 NRCH 6282 B5
10 RYE 6283 E3
Indian Lake Rd
10 LFRY 6501 D5
Indian Spring Rd
10 GrwT 6170 D1
Industrial Av
- MNCH 6500 D6
- WRDG 6500 D6
10 FRVW 6611 B3
10 HSBH 6500 E6
10 LFRY 6501 D7
10 RDFP 6501 D4
10 TETB 6501 A5
100 TETB 6500 E5
1000 RDGF 6502 B7
Industrial Dr
10 JSYC 6920 C1
10 RTFD 6609 B4
100 BAYN 6920 C1
Industrial Hwy
10 CART 7017 D6
10 CART 7115 E1
Industrial Ln
10 LNDN 7017 B1
10 NRCH 6395 D6
Industrial Lp
10 STNL 7115 C5
Industrial Lp E
10 STNL 7115 C5
Industrial Lp W
10 STNL 7115 C5
Industrial Pkwy
10 NVLE 6164 C5
Industrial Pl
4100 HmpT 7029 D4
Industrial Plz
10 HmpT 6928 A4
10 QENS 6928 A4
Industrial Rd
10 CARL 6500 B6
10 LODI 6500 E1
10 WRDG 6500 B6
Industrial St
10 BRNX 6505 D6
Industrial Park Dr
10 NHmT 6618 C4
Industry Rd
10 STNL 7018 B5
Inez St
10 STNL 7207 A2
Ingalls Av
1800 LNDN 6917 C5
2100 ELIZ 6917 C5
Ingelside Ln
10 WHPL 6168 E6
Ingham Av
10 BAYN 6919 E6
Ingraham Ln
10 NHPK 6828 A1
100 NHPK 6724 A7
600 NHmT 6724 A7
Ingraham Pl
10 NWRK 6817 A3
Ingraham St
10 BKLN 6822 E4
200 BKLN 6823 A3
Ingram Av
10 STNL 7019 C4
Ingram St
67-00 QENS 6824 C3
Inip Dr
10 HmpT 7027 D1
S Inman Av
10 WbgT 7114 C1
Inman Pl
10 NARL 6714 C1
Innes Rd
10 SCDL 6282 A1
400 WRDG 6500 D5
Inness Pl
10 MNPK 6617 E6
10 MNPK 6618 A6
Inness Rd
10 TFLY 6392 A4
Innis St
10 STNL 7019 B1
100 STNL 6919 B7
Innisfree Pl
10 EchT 6281 C4
Innkeeper Rd
10 OLDT 6164 A3
Inslee Pl
100 ELIZ 6918 C5
Inslee St
300 PTHA 7114 D7
300 PTHA 7205 E1
Insley St
10 DMRT 6278 A5
Interlaken Av
10 NRCH 6395 C2
Interlaken Dr
10 EchT 6281 C6
International Dr
10 GrwT 6051 E6
10 RYEB 6051 E6
International Wy
10 NWRK 6817 C5
International Airport Ctr Blvd
- QENS 6927 C5
Interstate Pl
500 CARL 6500 B6
Intervale
10 FLHL 6618 C6
10 NHmT 6618 D7
10 ROSE 6618 C6
Intervale Av
10 NoCT 6050 B4
1100 BRNX 6613 C2
Intervale Pl
10 RYE 6283 E3
10 RYE 6284 B3
10 YNKR 6393 D4
Intervale St
10 WHPL 6168 A2
Inverness Ct
10 WHPL 6169 A5
Inverness Rd
10 GrbT 6281 A1
10 NRCH 6395 D1
10 YNKR 6281 B1
Inwood Av
10 PTCH 6170 A6
1200 BRNX 105 A7
1200 BRNX 6504 A7
Inwood Pl
10 NRCH 6395 C3
10 PLHM 6395 C3
Inwood Rd
10 GrbT 6167 A6
10 MHVN 6508 B6
10 STNL 7020 C3
Inwood St
10 YNKR 6394 A3
104-00 QENS 6825 C6
114-00 QENS 6926 D3
Inwood Ter
700 CLFP 6611 D1
700 FTLE 6611 D1
1000 FTLE 6502 D7
Iona St
10 STNL 7118 D1
10 VLYS 6928 C3
Ionia Av
600 STNL 7116 A7
Iorio Ct
10 JSYC 6819 C4
Iowa Cir
- STNL 7021 A6
Iowa Pl
10 HmpT 7029 D5
10 STNL 7019 C3
Iowa Rd
255-00 NHmT 6723 A3
255-00 QENS 6723 A3
Ipswich Av
10 GTNE 6722 E1
10 GTPZ 6722 E1
Ira Ct
10 BKLN 7023 E6
Ireland St
50-00 QENS 6719 D7
Irene Ct
10 CLST 6278 C4
10 DMRT 6278 C4
900 HmpT 6929 A1
Irene Dr
10 NHmT 6724 C2
Irene Ln
10 STNL 7206 C4
Irene St
100 LNDN 7017 C4
Irenhyl Av
10 PTCH 6170 A5
100 RYEB 6170 A5
Iris Av
- BKLN 7022 D2
10 FLPK 6827 C2
Iris Ct
10 STNL 7115 E5
600 TnkT 6502 C2
Iris Ln
10 HmpT 6928 B4
10 NHmT 6724 A5
10 WLTN 6500 A6
4500 NHmT 6723 A2
Iris Pl
10 WbgT 7114 B4
700 HmpT 6929 D1
Iris St
10 HmpT 7028 B2
700 HmpT 6828 B4
Irma Av
10 NHmT 6508 E7
10 NHmT 6617 E1
Irma Dr
10 HmpT 7029 E2
Irma Pl
10 STNL 7020 A2
Iron Mine Dr
10 STNL 7020 A7
Irons Pl
10 NHmT 6723 E6
Ironwood Ln
10 HRSN 6169 B5
Ironwood St
10 STNL 7117 B4
Iroquois Av
10 OrgT 6164 E4
Iroquois Rd
10 YNKR 6280 D6
Iroquois St
10 RYE 6283 E1
10 STNL 7118 C2
Iroquois Tr
10 HRSN 6283 B2
Irvine St
800 BRNX 6613 D3
Irvine Turner Blvd
10 NWRK 6817 B2
Irving Av
10 BKLN 6822 E5
10 CLST 6278 B3
10 EGLC 6503 A3
10 EGLD 6503 A3
10 FLPK 6723 D7
10 NWRK 6816 E4
10 QENS 6723 D7
10 SOrT 6712 A5
10 TYTN 6048 C2
10-00 BKLN 6823 B6
10-00 QENS 6823 B6
100 FLPK 6827 D1
100 PTCH 6170 A5
Irving Ln
10 NHmT 6723 D6
Irving Pl
10 BKLN 6822 B7
10 BKLN 6923 B1
10 BRNX 6394 C7
10 DBSF 6166 B4
10 ERKY 6929 B6
10 GLCV 6509 E5
10 GRFD 6500 B2
10 HmpT 7028 C1
10 HRSN 6283 B4
10 IRVN 6048 B7
10 MHTN 116 B7
10 MHTN 119 B1
10 MHTN 6717 D7
10 MHTN 6821 D1
10 MTVN 6394 C7
10 NRCH 6395 D2
10 PLHM 6395 C5
10 RKVC 6929 E3
10 SCLF 6509 E5
10 STNL 7020 D3
10 SYHW 6048 B1
10 VLYS 6928 E3
10 WHPL 6168 A2
10 YNKR 6279 C7
100 HmpT 6928 C7
100 RTFD 6609 A1
700 SECS 6610 A7
Irving St
10 CART 7115 D1
10 EORG 6712 D4
10 HmpT 6928 B1
10 JSYC 6716 B5
10 NWRK 6714 A1
100 LEON 6502 D5
S Irving St
1000 HmpT 6928 B1
Irving Ter
500 COrT 6712 B5
500 SOrT 6712 B5
Irving Heir Cir
- JSYC 6819 B3
Irvington Av
10 SOrT 6712 A6
300 ELIZ 6917 D2
400 MplT 6712 A7
400 NWRK 6712 A7
500 HlsT 6917 D2
500 MplT 6816 A1
500 NWRK 6816 A1
700 IrvT 6816 A1
Irvington Av CO-665
10 SOrT 6712 A6
400 MplT 6712 A7
400 NWRK 6712 A7
500 MplT 6816 A1
500 NWRK 6816 A1
700 IrvT 6816 A1
Irvington Pl
10 BKLN 6923 B7
Irvington St
10 DBSF 6166 C4
10 HmpT 6928 C5
10 STNL 7207 C2
10 VLYS 6928 D5
Irvington Manor Dr
- IRVN 6166 C2
Irwin Av
3100 BRNX 102 D2
3100 BRNX 6504 B1
4000 BRNX 6393 C7
Irwin Ct
10 LNBK 6929 B4
Irwin Pl
121-00 QENS 6826 B7
122-00 QENS 6927 B1
Irwin St
10 BKLN 7121 C1
10 NHmT 6724 C5
Isabel Rd
10 OrgT 6164 B1

New York City/5 Borough Street Index

STREET
Block City Map# Grid

Isabella Av
10 BAYN 6919 E5
10 NWRK 6712 D7
10 STNL 7117 E3
100 IrvT 6712 D7
200 IrvT 6816 D1
400 STNL 7118 A4
Isabella Wy
10 DMRT 6278 B6
Ise St
10 HKSK 6501 C3
10 SHkT 6501 C3
Iselin Av
5000 BRNX 6393 B6
Iselin Dr
10 NRCH 6281 E3
Iselin Ter
10 LRMT 6396 B2
600 MrnT 6396 B2
Isernia Av
10 STNL 7118 A3
Isham St
500 MHTN 102 A6
500 MHTN 6504 A3
Island Av
300 HmpT 6928 A7
300 HmpT 7028 B1
Island Blvd
- SECS 6610 B7
Island Ct
10 PTWN 6508 C6
Island Dr
10 RYE 6284 C1
N Island Dr
10 RYE 6284 C1
W Island Dr
10 RYE 6284 C2
Island Ln
10 GrwT 6170 E5
Island Pkwy
10 ISPK 7029 C4
100 HmpT 7029 C4
Island Pkwy N
10 HmpT 7029 C4
10 ISPK 7029 C4
Island Pkwy S
10 HmpT 7029 C5
Island Pkwy W
10 HmpT 7029 B5
Island Park Pl
10 HmpT 7029 C5
Islandview Ct
10 BAYN 6919 C6
Island View Pl
10 NRCH 6395 C6
Islington St
10 STNL 7117 A4
Ismay St
10 STNL 7019 C5
Isora Pl
10 STNL 7117 E3
Itaska St
300 HlsT 6816 D5
Ithaca Av
10 ATLB 7028 A7
Ithaca St
10 STNL 7117 E4
39-00 QENS 6719 E6
43-00 QENS 6720 C6
Ittner Pl
300 BRNX 105 E5
300 BRNX 6504 C6
IU Willets Rd
- NHLS 6723 E3
10 NHLS 6724 A3
10 NHmT 6724 C3
Ivan Ct
10 BKLN 7024 A7
100 BKLN 7023 E7
Ivanhoe Pl
10 VLYS 6928 A2
10 YNKR 6280 D5
Ivanitsky Ter
10 CART 7017 B6
Ives Rd
10 HmpT 6928 D7
Ives St
- BRNX 6505 D6
Ivy Cir
10 NRCH 6281 D2
Ivy Ct
10 STNL 7115 E5
200 COrT 6712 C3
Ivy Ln
10 LWRN 7028 B3
10 WLTN 6500 A6
E Ivy Ln
10 EGLD 6392 A4
E Ivy Ln CO-68
10 EGLD 6392 A4
W Ivy Ln
10 EGLD 6392 A4
Ivy Pl
10 BRNX 6615 C4
10 EchT 6281 B5
10 GrbT 6166 E2
10 HmpT 6928 C5
10 JSYC 6819 E3
10 JSYC 6820 B3
10 NHmT 6724 C5
10 RTFD 6609 B1
10 VLYS 6928 C5
10 WHPL 6168 C4
10 YNKR 6279 E7
Ivy St
10 GrwT 6170 D5
10 HmpT 7028 B2
10 KRNY 6714 C4
10 NWRK 6712 B7
10 RYE 6283 E3
100 HmpT 6828 E5
Ivy Wy
10 NHmT 6617 D2
Ivy Close
10 QENS 6824 E2
Ivy Hill Cres
100 RYEB 6170 A2
Ivy Hill Ln
100 RYEB 6170 A2
Ivy Hill Rd
700 WDBG 7028 D2
800 HWTN 7028 D2
W Ivy Hill Rd
10 HmpT 7028 C2
10 WDBG 7028 C2
Ixworth Rd
1200 HmpT 6827 E7
Izmir St
2300 ELIZ 6919 B2

J

Jabez St
10 NWRK 6818 A3
Jacey Dr
600 FTLE 6502 D5
Jackie Robinson Pkwy
- BKLN 6823 D7
- BKLN 6924 C1
- QENS 6823 D7
- QENS 6824 A6
- QENS 6825 A3
- QENS 6924 C1
Jack Jacobs Cir
- EORG 6712 D5
Jacklyn Ct
10 HmpT 7027 C2
Jackson Av
- YNKR 6280 E1
10 BXTE 6617 D1
10 CART 7017 C7
10 CART 7115 B1
10 EchT 6281 A6
10 ERTH 6500 A7
10 GrbT 6280 D1
10 HAOH 6280 B1
10 HKSK 6501 C3
10 HmpT 6827 C6
10 MNLA 6724 E6
10 NHmT 6617 D1
10 RTFD 6500 A7
10 SHkT 6501 C4
10 STNL 7020 E5
10 TCKA 6281 A6
10 WHPL 6167 E2
10-00 QENS 117 E5
10-00 QENS 6718 C6
100 GrbT 6166 D7
100 PLMM 6395 B7
100 STNL 7021 A6
200 BRNX 6613 B5
400 ELIZ 6918 B1
500 JSYC 6819 E3
500 LNDN 6917 A6
500 NHmT 6724 C7
900 HmpT 6828 A6
Jackson Av SR-25A
10-00 QENS 117 D5
10-00 QENS 6718 C6
Jackson Ct
10 BKLN 7021 D4
Jackson Dr
10 ALPN 6278 D7
10 CRSK 6278 D7
10 CRSK 6392 D1
Jackson Ln
10 GLCV 6509 E1
Jackson Pl
10 BKLN 6922 D4
10 GrbT 6049 E6
10 HmpT 6929 A6
10 ISPK 7029 C4
10 LODI 6500 D3
10 MNCH 6501 B7
Jackson Rd
10 VLYS 6928 D5
Jackson St
- HRSN 6818 A1
10 BKLN 6822 B3
10 GDNC 6828 A2
10 GLCV 6509 D3
10 HBKN 6716 C7
10 LFRY 6501 C6
10 MHTN 119 D7
10 MHTN 6821 E3
10 MTVN 6394 E5
10 MTVN 6395 A5
10 NRCH 6396 A4
10 NWRK 6818 A1
10 STNL 7020 D1
10 YNKR 6393 C2
100 EGLD 6502 D1
300 COrT 6712 C3
5400 WNYK 6610 E7
6500 WNYK 6611 A6
6700 GTBG 6611 A6
7100 NBgT 6611 A6
Jackson Mill Rd
24-00 QENS 6720 A4
Jacob St
- STNL 7206 B4
10 GRFD 6500 B1
10 HmpT 6827 D5
10 NWRK 6713 A7
10 NWRK 6817 A1
10 WLTN 6500 B5
Jacobus Av
10 KRNY 6715 A7
10 KRNY 6819 A1
Jacobus Dr
800 RDGF 6611 B1
Jacobus Pl
10 MHTN 102 C4
10 MHTN 6504 B2
Jacobus St
50-00 QENS 6719 D7
Jacoby St
10 MplT 6816 A3
Jacowski Ct
10 PTHA 7205 E3
Jacqueline Ln
10 RYEB 6170 A3
Jacques Av
10 STNL 7117 B1
10 STNL 7118 A2
Jacques St
500 PTHA 7205 D2
Jadwin St
10 HmpT 6928 C6
10 VLYS 6928 C6
Jaegers Ln
10 QENS 6925 E2
Jaffe St
10 STNL 7019 B2
Jaffray Pk
10 IRVN 6166 A1
Jaffrey St
10 BKLN 7121 D1
Jake Ct
10 STNL 7020 C2
Jamaica Av
10 BKLN 6924 D1
10 HmpT 7029 E3
74-00 BKLN 6824 A7
74-00 QENS 6824 A7
121-00 QENS 6825 D5
179-09 QENS 6826 D3
220-00 QENS 6827 A3
224-00 HmpT 6827 A3
500 BKLN 6823 E7
Jamaica Av SR-24
211-30 QENS 6826 D3
E Jamaica Av
10 VLYS 6928 D4
W Jamaica Av
10 VLYS 6928 D3
James Av
10 JSYC 6715 E7
10 NHmT 6508 E7
1500 HmpT 6827 D7
James Ct
10 LODI 6500 E2
10 PTCH 6170 C5
114-00 QENS 6825 D7
300 HmpT 6828 C6
James Dr
10 NRCH 6281 E4
James Pl
10 LODI 6500 D2
10 SECS 6610 B6
10 STNL 7020 E4
James Rd
10 HRSN 6168 E7
10 HRSN 6169 A7
James St
- PTHA 7205 E2
- YNKR 6393 A1
10 BGTA 6501 E3
10 GrwT 6170 D6
10 HAOH 6280 A1
10 HmpT 6828 B5
10 HmpT 7027 E3
10 LODI 6500 D2
10 MHTN 118 E7
10 MHTN 6821 D5
10 NHmT 6724 C5
10 NoCT 6050 C3
10 NWRK 6713 D6
10 SHkT 6501 B3
10 SRVL 7205 A7
10 WbgT 7205 A1
100 HlsT 6816 D7
200 TnkT 6501 E3
600 PLMM 6395 B6
1100 MRNK 6282 E4
1300 HmpT 6827 E5
James St N
10 ERKY 6929 C6
James St S
10 HmpT 6929 C7
N James St
10 WbgT 7114 C4
1500 MRNK 6282 D3
James Wy
10 RYEB 6170 A3
James E Hanson Wy
10 SHkT 6501 B4
10 TETB 6501 B4
Jamie Ct
10 STNL 7019 A2
Jamie Ln
200 STNL 7116 C4
Jamison Ct
10 HRSN 6050 D4
Jane Ct
10 SECS 6610 B6
Jane Dr
10 EGLC 6392 C5
Jane Pl
10 VLYS 6928 C2
Jane St
10 CARL 6609 C1
10 CLST 6278 B4
10 EHLS 6618 E7
10 ERTH 6609 C1
10 GrbT 6167 D3
10 MHTN 115 C7
10 MHTN 6717 B7
10 NHmT 6618 E7
10 OrgT 6164 C3
100 UNCT 6716 D3
100 WhkT 6716 D3
400 FTLE 6502 E5
2600 NBgT 6716 C2
Janet Ln
10 GLCV 6509 E4
Janet Pl
10 HmpT 6928 B5
10 VLYS 6928 B5
39-00 QENS 6720 E4
Janet Ter
10 IRVN 6048 C7
Janice Dr
10 NRWD 6164 B6
Janos Ln
10 HmpT 6929 D1
Jansen Av
200 WbgT 7114 B1
Jansen Av US-1
- WbgT 7114 A4
Jansen Ct
10 STNL 7207 D1
Jansen St
10 STNL 7116 E7
400 STNL 7207 C1
Janssen Dr
10 PLNM 6617 E4
Jaques St
10 ELIZ 6918 A4
Jara Ct
10 NHmT 6723 E7
Jardine Av
10 STNL 7018 E4
10 STNL 7019 A4
Jardine Pl
10 BKLN 6924 C1
Jared Dr
10 WHPL 6168 C5
Jarico Dr
10 WLTN 6500 B6
Jarret Pl
1500 BRNX 6505 D6
Jarvis Av
5-00 QENS 7027 E5
10 STNL 7207 D2
1500 BRNX 6506 B7
1600 BRNX 6505 E6
Jarvis Pl
10 ERKY 6929 C5
10 LNBK 6929 C5
Jasamine Pl
- BRNX 6615 C4
Jasen Av
1700 HmpT 6928 B1
1700 VLYS 6928 B1
Jasko Ct
10 SAMB 7205 B7
Jasmine Av
146-00 QENS 6721 B5
1500 NHPK 6724 A7
1600 NHmT 6724 A7
Jasmine Dr
10 WLTN 6500 A6
Jasmine Ln
10 HmpT 6928 B4
Jason Ln
10 MrnT 6282 D6
10 NRCH 6282 A6
Jason Woods Rd
10 CLST 6278 C4
Jasper Av
10 TnkT 6501 E3
10 TnkT 6502 A3
Jasper St
10 HmpT 6928 B1
10 STNL 7019 C6
Jasper St S
1100 HmpT 6928 B1
1100 VLYS 6928 B1
Jassamine Wy
1000 FTLE 6502 D7
1000 FTLE 6611 A2
Java Pl
3-01 QENS 7026 B6
Java St
10 BKLN 6822 B1
Jay Av
64-00 QENS 6823 C2
Jay Ct
10 GrbT 6166 E1
10 HmpT 6928 B5
Jay St
10 BKLN 121 B3
10 HKSK 6501 C4
10 MHTN 118 B5
10 MHTN 6821 E4
10 NRWD 6164 B6
10 NWRK 6713 C6
10 STNL 7118 C2
10 TFLY 6392 A2
10 WbgT 7114 D2
100 BKLN 6821 D6
100 WRDG 6500 C5
Jay St CO-70
10 TFLY 6392 A2
Jayne Ln
10 STNL 7206 C4
Jayson Av
10 GTPZ 6723 A1
10 NHmT 6723 A1
Jean Ct
10 HmpT 6929 B2
10 MLVN 6929 B2
10 WbgT 7114 D5
Jean Dr
10 EGLC 6392 C5
Jean Ln
10 GrbT 6167 A2
10 RYEB 6169 E4
Jean St
10 RYE 6283 E5
Jeanette Av
10 HmpT 7027 D3
10 STNL 7116 D6
Jeanette St
10 CART 7017 D7
Jeannes Pl
10 OrgT 6164 D2
Jeannette Dr
10 NHmT 6617 E1
Jeannette St
2800 UNCT 6716 D3
Jedwood Pl
10 HmpT 6928 C4
10 VLYS 6928 C4
Jefferson Av
10 BKLN 6923 B1
10 BlmT 6713 B2
10 CRSK 6278 A7
10 CRSK 6392 A1
10 HAOH 6166 A7
10 HmpT 7029 C5
10 HSBH 6500 D4
10 JSYC 6716 B7
10 KRNY 6714 B1
10 LNBK 6929 C4
10 LNDN 7017 A1
10 LODI 6500 D3
10 MNLA 6724 E6
10 MRNK 6282 E5
10 MtPT 6050 A2
10 NARL 6714 B1
10 NHmT 6618 D7
10 QENS 6928 A2
10 RSLN 6618 D7
10 STNL 7020 A7
10 VLYS 6928 A2
10 WHPL 6167 E1
100 ELIZ 6917 E3
100 TFLY 6392 A1
200 HmpT 6828 A3
300 GDNC 6828 A3
300 HmpT 6929 C2
400 BKLN 6822 E7
400 ELIZ 6918 A2
500 MRNK 6283 A5
500 SECS 6715 E2
500 SECS 6716 A2
500 STNL 7118 C2
600 CLFP 6611 D1
700 BKLN 6823 B7
1000 ELIZ 6817 A7
1100 NWRK 6817 A7
1600 QENS 6823 B6
Jefferson Blvd
10 ATLB 7028 A7
200 STNL 7116 B5
Jefferson Ct
10 NHmT 6618 D7
100 EDGW 108 C1
100 EDGW 6611 E5
Jefferson Pl
10 GrbT 6049 E6
10 MNCH 6501 B7
10 MTVN 6394 A7
10 TCKA 6281 A6
400 MNLA 6724 D6
400 NHmT 6724 D6
600 BRNX 6613 C1
Jefferson Rd
10 SCDL 6281 D1
Jefferson St
- MRNK 6282 C4
10 BKLN 6822 D6
10 CARL 6500 D7
10 GLCV 6509 E3
10 HmpT 6828 A3
10 HmpT 7027 D3
10 HRSN 6050 D7
10 LFRY 6501 C7
10 MHTN 119 B7
10 MHTN 6821 D4
10 NHmT 6617 C1
10 NHmT 6723 E6
10 NRCH 6396 A3
10 NWRK 6818 A1
10 STNL 7020 B7
10 UNCT 6716 E3
10 WhkT 6716 B3
10 WRDG 6500 D7
10 YNKR 6393 C2
100 GDNC 6828 A2
100 NWRK 6817 E3
100 PTHA 7205 D4
100 STMN 6828 A2
300 BKLN 6823 A4
300 ERTH 6500 B7
400 QENS 6823 A4
800 HmpT 6928 B7
1300 HBKN 6716 D5
1300 HmpT 6827 E3
5500 WNYK 6610 E7
6000 WNYK 6611 A7
N Jefferson St
10 COrT 6712 C2
S Jefferson St
10 COrT 6712 B2
Jeffrey Ln
10 LKSU 6723 C3
Jeffrey Pl
10 NHmT 6724 A4
10 STNL 7206 C3
Jeffrey Wy
10 GrbT 6166 E1
Jeffries St
200 PTHA 7205 D2
Jeffry Pl
- SCDL 6282 A2
10 NRCH 6282 A2
Jelliff Av
10 NWRK 6817 B3
Jelliff Pl
100 NWRK 6817 A3
Jena Ct
800 HmpT 6929 D1
Jenesee Ct
10 WbgT 7114 C3
Jenkins Dr
100 EGLC 6503 B2
Jenna Ln
10 STNL 7020 B6
Jennetty Ct
800 PTHA 7114 B7
Jenni Ln
10 NRWD 6164 B7
Jennifer Ct
10 STNL 7018 E6
Jennifer Ln
10 GrbT 6167 A2
10 RYEB 6169 E4
10 STNL 7118 A4
10 YNKR 6280 D3
Jennifer Pl
10 STNL 7019 A4
10 YNKR 6280 D2
Jennings Av
500 HmpT 6828 E7
Jennings Rd
10 WHPL 6168 E4
10 WHPL 6169 A4
Jennings St
700 BRNX 6613 C1
Jenny Close
10 MrnT 6282 D2
Jensen Av
10 WbgT 7114 A7
100 MRNK 6283 A5
Jensen Ln
10 UnnT 6917 A2
Jeraldo St
10 BlvT 6713 C2
10 NWRK 6713 C2
Jericho Tpk
- HmpT 6827 B2
- QENS 6827 A2
10 FLPK 6827 C1
10 MNLA 6724 E6
10 NHmT 6827 E1
10 NHPK 6827 B2
246-32 BLRS 6827 B2
500 NHmT 6724 B7
1000 NHPK 6828 A1
1600 NHPK 6724 B7
Jericho Tpk SR-25
10 FLPK 6827 C1
10 MNLA 6724 E6
10 NHmT 6827 E1
10 NHPK 6827 B2
10 QENS 6827 C1
244-00 HmpT 6827 B2
246-32 BLRS 6827 B2
500 NHmT 6724 B7
1000 NHPK 6828 A1
1600 NHPK 6724 B7
Jerome Av
10 BKLN 7023 C7
10 NRCH 6281 E7
10 STNL 7020 E6
800 HlsT 6917 D1
900 BRNX 107 D2
900 BRNX 6612 E1
1100 BRNX 6613 A1
1200 BRNX 6504 A7
1300 BRNX 105 E1
2300 BRNX 102 E7
3500 BRNX 6393 E7
Jerome Ct
500 HmpT 6828 A7
Jerome Dr
10 GLCV 6509 D4
Jerome Rd
10 STNL 7020 D6
1000 HmpT 6828 A7
1000 HmpT 6929 A1
Jerome St
800 BKLN 6924 E4
Jersey Av
10 CLFP 6611 D3
10 JSYC 6820 B3
10 TFLY 6392 A1
10 WbgT 7205 A2
200 FRVW 6611 C3
300 ELIZ 6917 C4
800 HBKN 6716 C7
800 JSYC 6716 C7
900 ROSL 6917 C4
Jersey Pl
10 HKSK 6501 B2
Jersey St
10 CART 7115 C1
10 HRSN 6713 C4
10 MHTN 118 E3
10 MHTN 6821 C2
10 NWRK 6818 A1
10 STNL 6920 C6
600 HRSN 6714 B6
E Jersey St
10 ELIZ 6918 C5
1000 ELIZ 6917 B5
W Jersey St
10 ELIZ 6917 D3
Jersey City Blvd
200 JSYC 6820 A4
Jersey Gardens Blvd
- ELIZ 6918 C4
Jervis Rd
10 YNKR 6393 E4
Jessamine Av
10 YNKR 6280 A7
Jessica Ct
10 STNL 7116 D6
Jessica Ln
10 STNL 7115 D7
Jessica Pl
10 NHLS 6618 D7
10 NHLS 6724 D1
10 NHmT 6618 D7
10 NHmT 6724 D1
Jessie Ct
44-00 QENS 6722 E3
Jessie Ln
10 WbgT 7114 D2
Jessie St
10 CART 7115 D3
Jesup Av
1300 BRNX 105 A6
1300 BRNX 6504 A7
Jewel Av
107-00 QENS 6824 D2
136-00 QENS 6825 B1
Jewel Dr
900 HmpT 6928 B5
Jewel St
10 BKLN 6822 C1
Jewell Pl
10 EchT 6281 C3
Jewel McCoy Ln
10 BKLN 6923 D1
Jewett Av
10 JSYC 6819 E2
10 STNL 6919 D7
100 STNL 7019 D1
JFK Expwy
- QENS 6926 D4
- QENS 6927 A3
JFK Commuter Plz
- QENS 6718 D6
JF Kennedy Blvd E
300 WhkT 6716 E4
700 WhkT 111 A5
700 WhkT 6717 A2
1000 WNYK 111 B1
1000 WNYK 6717 A1
6000 WNYK 6611 B7
6700 GTBG 6611 B7
7100 NBgT 6611 C6
JF Kennedy Blvd E CO-505
- WhkT 6716 E3
700 WhkT 111 A5
700 WhkT 6717 A2
1000 WNYK 111 B1
1000 WNYK 6717 A1
JF Kennedy Blvd E CO-677
300 WhkT 6716 E4
JF Kennedy Blvd E CO-693
6000 WNYK 111 C1
6000 WNYK 6611 B7
6000 WNYK 6717 B1
6700 GTBG 6611 B7
7100 NBgT 6611 C6
Jillian Ct
10 STNL 7019 D2
Joan Av
10 GrbT 6049 C7
Joan Ct
10 HmpT 6827 C5
400 HmpT 6828 E6
Joan Dr
10 EchT 6281 C6
10 YNKR 6394 C3
Joan Pl
10 STNL 7019 D3
Joann Ct
10 HmpT 6929 E7
Joanna Wy
1400 UnnT 6816 B6
Joanne Ter
10 GRFD 6500 C1
10 SdBT 6500 B1
Joan Ree Ter
10 BAYN 6920 A2
Jocelyn Av
100 WRDG 6500 B5
Jochum Av
10 LRMT 6396 C2
Jodi Ct
10 GLCV 6509 E2
Jodie Ct
10 BKLN 6923 E6
Jody Ln
10 YNKR 6279 D5
Joe Dimaggio Hwy
- MHTN 118 B2
10 MHTN 115 C5
300 MHTN 6821 A2
400 MHTN 111 D7
400 MHTN 6717 B4
700 MHTN 112 A5
Joe Dimaggio Hwy SR-9A
- MHTN 118 B2
10 MHTN 115 C5
300 MHTN 6821 A2
400 MHTN 111 D7
400 MHTN 6717 A4
700 MHTN 112 A5
W Joe Dimaggio Hwy
- MHTN 111 E6
- MHTN 112 A5
- MHTN 115 C2
- MHTN 118 B5
- MHTN 120 A1
- MHTN 6717 A7
- MHTN 6821 A2
W Joe Dimaggio Hwy SR-9A
- MHTN 111 E6
- MHTN 112 A5
- MHTN 115 C2
- MHTN 118 B5
- MHTN 6717 B4
- MHTN 6821 A2
Joel Pl
10 NHmT 6617 D2
10 STNL 7117 D2
Joe Sipos Ln
- GRFD 6500 B1
Joey Ln
10 WbgT 7114 E2
Johanna Ln
10 STNL 7207 A2
John Av
10 HmpT 6827 D4
John Cir
10 NRWD 6164 A7
John St
10 BKLN 121 C2
10 BKLN 6821 D5
10 CART 7017 E7
10 CLST 6278 A2
10 DMRT 6278 B5
10 EGLC 6503 B1
10 EGLD 6503 B1
10 ELIZ 6918 A5
10 ERKY 6929 C7
10 ERTH 6500 A6
10 GLCV 6509 D3
10 HKSK 6501 B2
10 HmpT 6929 C7
10 HmpT 7027 D3
10 KRNY 6714 A5
10 LFRY 6501 C6
10 LNBK 6929 A4
10 LODI 6500 D1
10 MHTN 118 B7
10 MHTN 120 C1
10 MHTN 6821 B4
10 NRCH 6395 D6
10 NRWD 6164 A7
10 SHkT 6501 C4
10 STNL 6919 C7
10 TYTN 6048 B3
10 WbgT 7205 A1
10 YNKR 6393 C1
100 HRSN 6714 A6
100 NVLE 6164 C6
100 SAMB 7205 C7
200 CLFP 6611 C4
200 FRVW 6611 C4
300 ENWK 6714 A6
400 HlsT 6816 B6
600 TnkT 6502 B2
700 SECS 6610 B7
1000 LNDN 6917 A6
1100 ROSL 6917 A6
1400 FTLE 6502 E5
S John St
- TnkT 6502 B3
John Alden Rd
10 NRCH 6395 C3
10 PLHM 6395 C3
John Bean Ct
10 FLHL 6618 D5
Johned Rd
400 NVLE 6164 B4
John F Cali Wy
- KRNY 6819 A2
John F Kennedy Blvd
10 JSYC 6820 A1
1500 BAYN 6819 B6
1500 JSYC 6819 B6
2900 JSYC 6716 B6
3700 NBgT 6716 C4
3700 UNCT 6716 C4
John F Kennedy Blvd CO-501
10 JSYC 6820 A1
1500 BAYN 6819 B6
1500 JSYC 6819 B6
2900 JSYC 6716 B6
3700 NBgT 6716 C4
3700 UNCT 6716 C4
John F Kennedy Cir
68-01 QENS 6722 C6
John F Kennedy Dr N
10 BlmT 6713 A1
10 EORG 6713 A1
John F Kennedy Dr S
10 BlmT 6713 A1
10 EORG 6713 A1
John F Kennedy Memorial Drwy
10 YNKR 6279 C5
John Glenn Dr
1000 HlsT 6816 D7
John Hay Av
10 KRNY 6714 C4
John Jay Pl
10 RYE 6283 C5
John Meagher Rd
- EORG 6712 C5
- NWRK 6712 C5
John P Devaney Blvd
1900 BKLN 6922 D5
John R Albanese Pl
10 EchT 6281 E6
Johns Ct
10 HmpT 6828 E7
Johnson Av
10 EGLC 6392 B6
10 EGLD 6392 B6
10 ERTH 6500 A7
10 MLVN 6929 B2
10 STNL 7206 A3
10 TnkT 6502 A1
10 WLTN 6500 A6
100 BKLN 6822 D4
200 TnkT 6501 E1
300 ELIZ 6917 E4
300 NWRK 6817 B4
500 BKLN 6823 A4
600 QENS 6823 A4
1500 HmpT 6827 D5
2200 BRNX 102 C2
2200 BRNX 6504 B1
3600 BRNX 6393 A7
Johnson Ct
10 ALPN 6278 D4
10 CLST 6278 D4
10 CRSK 6278 C7
10 DBSF 6166 B5
600 TnkT 6502 A1
Johnson Ln
300 HmpT 6828 C6
Johnson Pl
10 ARDY 6166 D5
10 HmpT 7028 D1
10 HRSN 6050 C3
10 NoCT 6050 C3
10 RYE 6283 C4
10 STNL 7020 B6
600 NVLE 6164 A4
6100 WNYK 6611 B7
Johnson Rd
10 EchT 6281 D3
10 HmpT 7027 D1
10 SCDL 6281 D2
Johnson St
10 BRNX 6394 E7
10 CART 7115 C1
10 MTVN 6394 E7
10 NWRK 6817 D2
10 OybT 6618 E2
10 ROSH 6618 E2
10 STNL 7115 C5
10 WbgT 7205 A1
100 MRNK 6282 D4
Johnston Av
10 KRNY 6713 E5
10 KRNY 6714 A5
100 HRSN 6714 A5
200 JSYC 6820 A3
Johnston Ter
10 STNL 7207 B3
Johnstone Rd
10 NHmT 6617 B6
Johnstone St
400 PTHA 7205 D3
John T O'Leary Blvd
10 SAMB 7205 C7
Jojo Ct
10 STNL 7206 C5
Joline Av
10 STNL 7206 C4
Joline Ln
10 STNL 7206 C5
Jomike Ct
400 CARL 6610 A2
Jones Pl
10 JSYC 6820 A2
10 OrgT 6164 A1
10 STNL 7020 A1
10 WHPL 6167 E2
10 YNKR 6279 D7
Jones Rd
10 EGLD 6392 A7
10 EGLD 6503 A1
300 EGLD 6502 E3
2000 FTLE 6502 E4
Jones St
10 JSYC 6820 A1
10 MHTN 118 D1
10 MHTN 6821 B1
10 NHmT 6723 D6
10 NRCH 6395 D5
10 NWRK 6713 C7
10 NWRK 6817 A2
10 STNL 7018 E4
10 YNKR 6280 A3
Jony Dr
100 CARL 6609 E2
Joralemon St
10 BKLN 120 E5
10 BKLN 121 A5
10 BKLN 6821 C6
Jordan Av
10 ERTH 6500 B7
10 JSYC 6820 A2
10 WLTN 6500 B7
185-00 QENS 6826 B6
300 HmpT 7028 B1
Jordan Ct
15-00 QENS 6615 E7
15-00 QENS 6721 E1
Jordan Dr
10 GTNE 6722 E1
207-00 QENS 6721 E1
207-40 QENS 6615 E7
Jordan Ln
10 ARDY 6166 E4
Jordan Rd
10 HAOH 6279 E1
10 HAOH 6280 A1
Jordan St
28-00 QENS 6721 D2
Jorgen St
500 LWRN 7028 B3
Joseph Av
10 STNL 7019 C5
500 WbgT 7114 B4
Joseph Ct
- TnkT 6502 A2
10 STNL 7206 B3
Joseph Ln
10 STNL 7020 E5
Joseph Rd
10 NHmT 6724 C6
Joseph St
10 LFRY 6501 C6
10 MNCH 6501 B7
10 NHmT 6723 D5
10 NWRK 6714 C7
E Joseph St
10 MNCH 6501 C7
S Joseph St
10 MNCH 6501 B7
Joseph Hock Memorial Dr
- QENS 6926 C5
Josephine St
10 STNL 7019 D4
Josephine Evaristo Av
10 GrwT 6170 E3
Joseph P Ward St
10 MHTN 120 A1
10 MHTN 6821 B5
Joseph Pycior Jr Wy
300 CARL 6609 D3
300 ERTH 6609 D3
Jost Pl
10 YNKR 6394 A4
Jouet St
300 ROSL 6917 A5
Journal Av
1300 HmpT 6827 E4
Journal Sq
10 JSYC 6820 D2
Journal Square Plz
10 JSYC 6820 A1
Journal Square Plz CO-501
10 JSYC 6820 A1
Journeay St
10 STNL 7019 A1
Joval Ct
10 BKLN 7023 E6
Joy Dr
10 NHmT 6724 A4
Joyce Ln
10 STNL 7206 B4
Joyce Rd
10 EchT 6281 B6
10 GrbT 6166 D3
10 GrbT 6167 A3
10 NRCH 6396 A3
10 TFLY 6392 A3
Joyce St
10 COrT 6712 B3
10 STNL 7020 B7
10 STNL 7118 B1
10 WOrT 6712 B3
Juana St
10 YNKR 6281 A3
Juanita Pl
1000 FTLE 6502 D7
Jubilee Pl
10 MNCH 6501 B7
Judge St
10 BKLN 6822 D3
41-00 QENS 6719 E6
Judith Ct
10 ERKY 6929 A6
10 STNL 7021 B4
Judith Dr
10 EGLC 6392 C6
Judith Ln
10 VLYS 6928 C2
Judson Av
10 ARDY 6166 C5
10 DBSF 6166 A5
100 HAOH 6166 A5
Judson Pl
10 RKVC 6929 E3
Judson St
10 MrnT 6282 C7
Judy Dr
10 WbgT 7205 B3
200 PTHA 7205 B3
Jules Dr
10 STNL 7019 A3
100 STNL 7018 E2
Julia Ct
10 OrgT 6164 D2
Julia St
10 CLST 6278 A3
800 ELIZ 6918 A2
Julian Pl
10 ELIZ 6917 B4
10 ISPK 7029 C5
Julian St
10 PTCH 6170 A7
10 RYE 6170 A7
Julian Ter
1400 UnnT 6816 A5
Juliana Pl
10 BKLN 6822 A5
Julianne Ter
200 SECS 6610 A5
Julie Ct
10 STNL 7019 D4
Julieann Ct
10 STNL 7020 A7
Juliette Rd
10 HmpT 6929 D1
Juliette St
10 BAYN 6919 C5
10 WbgT 7205 B2
Julius Rd
300 QENS 6614 D7
Julius St
100 WbgT 7114 A3
E Julius St
10 WbgT 7114 A3
Jumel Pl
10 MHTN 104 C7
10 MHTN 6503 D7
Jumel St
10 STNL 7117 A4
Jumel Ter
10 MHTN 107 B1
10 MHTN 6612 D1
Junard Blvd
500 HmpT 6828 C7
Junard Dr
10 RSLN 6618 D6
Junction Blvd
32-00 QENS 6720 A5
60-00 QENS 6824 B1

New York City/5 Borough Street Index

STREET
Block City Map# Grid

June Ct
10 WHPL 6168 D6
500 HmpT 6828 C6
600 HmpT 6928 A6
June Pl
300 HmpT 6828 C6
500 HmpT 6927 E6
500 HmpT 6928 A6
June St
10 YNKR 6280 D5
June Wk
- LBCH 7029 A7
Juni Ct
10 STNL 7019 A7
Juniper Av
137-00 QENS 6721 A6
Juniper Blvd N
74-00 QENS 6823 E2
81-00 QENS 6824 A2
Juniper Blvd S
- QENS 6824 A3
69-00 QENS 6823 E3
Juniper Cir E
200 LWRN 7028 A4
Juniper Cir N
200 LWRN 7028 A4
Juniper Cir S
200 LWRN 7028 A4
Juniper Dr
10 GTNE 6722 D1
Juniper Pl
10 STNL 7020 A7
10 STNL 7118 A1
Juniper Rd
10 GrbT 6167 A6
10 MHVN 6508 B6
100 GrbT 6166 E6
Juniper St
10 JSYC 6819 B4
Juniper Hill Rd
10 GrbT 6167 D1
Juniper Valley Rd
69-00 QENS 6823 D3
77-00 QENS 6824 A3
Junius St
10 BKLN 6924 C4
Juno St
67-00 QENS 6824 C3
Jupiter Ln
10 STNL 7019 A2
Just Ct
10 BKLN 7024 A7
100 BKLN 7023 E7
Justice Av
86-00 QENS 6719 E2
87-00 QENS 6720 A7
Justin Av
10 STNL 7117 C4
Justin Ct
10 OrgT 6165 A5
Justin Rd
10 HRSN 6282 E1
10 HRSN 6283 A1

K

K St
1200 HmpT 6827 E7
Kaateskill Pl
10 GrbT 6166 E6
10 GrbT 6167 A6
Kahn Ter
10 EGLC 6503 C1
Kalb Av
200 HmpT 6828 A3
Kalda Av
10 NHmT 6723 D6
Kaldenberg Pl
10 TYTN 6048 B2
Kallas Ct
800 HmpT 6827 E7
Kalmia Av
137-00 QENS 6721 A6
Kalmia Ln
10 HmpT 6928 B4
Kaltenmeier Ln
10 STNL 7020 E3
Kalver Pl
10 STNL 7019 B1
Kamda Blvd
10 NHmT 6723 E7
Kamena St
200 CLFP 6611 C4
200 FRVW 6611 C3
Kamm St
600 PTHA 7205 C1
Kamp Pl
100 NBgT 6611 C5
Kandahar Rd
10 GrwT 6170 C1
Kane Av
10 LRMT 6396 C3
Kane Ct
200 HmpT 6828 C5
Kane Pl
10 BKLN 6924 A2
Kane St
10 BKLN 120 D7
10 BKLN 6821 C7
200 BKLN 121 A7
Kansas Av
10 STNL 7020 D4
Kansas Pl
10 BKLN 7024 C4
Kansas St
10 HKSK 6501 B2
E Kansas St
10 HKSK 6501 C2
Kapkowski Rd
600 ELIZ 6918 D3
Kaplan Av
- LODI 6501 A1
200 HKSK 6501 A1
Kappock St
500 BRNX 102 A2
500 BRNX 6504 A1
Karen Ct
10 STNL 7019 D2
Karen Ln
10 NRCH 6396 A6
Karens Ln
10 EGLC 6503 B1
Karkus Av
100 WbgT 7114 A5
Karl Pl
10 GRFD 6500 B2
Karlston Pl
10 VLYS 6928 B4
Karweg Pl
10 BKLN 6824 A7
10 QENS 6824 A7
Karyn Ct
10 OLDT 6164 A4
Kass Rd
10 WHPL 6168 E4
10 WHPL 6169 A4
Kassel Ct
10 MRNK 6283 B5
Katan Av
10 STNL 7116 D5
10 STNL 7117 A5
Katan Lp
10 STNL 7117 A5
Kate Dr
100 NHmT 6724 C6
Katherine St
10 LFRY 6501 C6
Kathleen Ct
10 RDGF 6611 C2
10 STNL 7206 C4
Kathleen Pl
10 BKLN 7023 A7
10 SRVL 7205 A7
Kathryn St
10 ERKY 6929 B6
10 LNBK 6929 B6
Kathwood Rd
10 GrbT 6049 B7
10 YNKR 6280 E1
Kathy Ct
10 STNL 7116 E3
Kathy Ln
10 SCDL 6167 D7
10 YNKR 6393 E2
Kathy Pl
10 STNL 7116 E1
Katie Ln
10 MrnT 6282 D3
Katonah Av
4200 BRNX 6394 A6
Katrina Av
10 SYHW 6048 B1
Katsura Dr
10 HRSN 6051 B5
Kaufers Ln
1600 FTLE 103 B4
1600 FTLE 6503 A6
Kaufman Av
10 LFRY 6501 D5
Kaufman Pl
10 BKLN 6924 D7
Kavrik St
10 LFRY 6501 C6
Kay Ct
10 BKLN 7023 E7
Kay Ln
10 HlsT 6816 C6
Kay Pl
10 STNL 7020 D7
Kaywood Rd
10 MHVN 6508 B7
Kean Dr
- UnnT 6917 C1
Keane Ct
10 RYE 6283 C5
Keap St
100 BKLN 6822 C4
Kearney Av
10 BRNX 6615 B3
10 JSYC 6819 D4
10 SRVL 7205 A6
500 CLFP 6611 D3
1200 BRNX 6506 A7
Kearney Rd
10 SRVL 7205 A6
Kearney St
10 EORG 6712 D1
27-00 QENS 6720 A4
Kearny Av
10 ENWK 6714 A5
10 HRSN 6714 A5
10 KRNY 6714 C2
10 PTHA 7205 D5
800 NARL 6714 C1
Kearny Av CO-697
10 ENWK 6714 A5
10 HRSN 6714 A5
10 KRNY 6714 A4
800 NARL 6714 C1
Kearny Pl
700 HmpT 6928 B6
Kearny St
10 NWRK 6713 D4
Keasby Rd
10 COrT 6712 B5
10 SOrT 6712 B5
Keasby St
10 HRSN 6714 A5
10 KRNY 6714 A5
Keasler Av
10 LODI 6500 C1
Keating Pl
10 GrbT 6167 B4
10 STNL 7019 A6
Keating St
10 STNL 7207 B3
Keats Av
10 GrbT 6167 B2
100 ELIZ 6917 B3
100 UnnT 6917 B2
Keats Ln
10 SDRK 6616 D7
Keats St
10 STNL 7117 C5
Keegan St
500 HmpT 6827 C6
Keegans Ln
10 STNL 7117 C5
Keel Ct
121-00 QENS 6614 D6
Keel Pl
10 HmpT 6928 B6
Keeler Av
900 MRNK 6283 B5
Keeler Av SR-127
900 MRNK 6283 B5
Keeley St
10 STNL 7021 A3
Keen Ct
10 BKLN 7023 E7
Keene Av
10 FLPK 6827 A3
10 QENS 6827 A3
Keene Ln
800 HmpT 7028 C2
800 WDBG 7028 C2
Keene St
200 PTHA 7205 D1
Keer Av
10 NWRK 6816 E5
300 IrvT 6816 D4
Keeseville Av
187-00 QENS 6826 B6
Keewaydin Rd
10 LWRN 7028 A4
Keiber Ct
10 STNL 7019 D3
Keil St
10 HmpT 6827 B7
Keisel Pl
7300 NBgT 6611 A5
Kelby St
300 FTLE 6502 E5
Kell Av
200 STNL 7019 C5
Keller Av
200 HmpT 6827 E6
Keller Ln
10 DBSF 6166 B4
Keller St
10 VLYS 6928 E2
Kellogg St
10 JSYC 6819 B4
10 NWRK 6818 B5
Kellum Pl
1500 GDNC 6724 E7
1500 MNLA 6724 E7
Kelly Av
600 PTHA 7114 C7
Kelly Blvd
10 STNL 7019 A7
Kelly Ct
1100 HmpT 6827 E7
Kelly Ln
1100 GTBG 6611 A6
1100 NBgT 6611 A6
Kelly Pkwy
10 BAYN 6919 D6
Kelly St
- HmpT 7027 B3
10 WbgT 7114 B3
800 BRNX 6613 C3
Kelsey Av
500 PTHA 7114 C6
500 WbgT 7114 C6
Kelsey Pl
10 HmpT 6929 B3
10 LNBK 6929 B3
Kelvin Av
10 STNL 7117 C4
Kelwynne Rd
10 SCDL 6168 A7
Kemball Av
10 STNL 7019 D3
Kemp Ln
10 MNLA 6724 C5
10 NHmT 6724 C5
Kempner Ln
10 HRSN 6051 B4
Kempshall Pl
10 ELIZ 6917 D2
Kempster Rd
10 GrbT 6167 A7
Kendall Av
10 SYHW 6048 B1
Kendall Av Ext
10 SYHW 6048 B1
Kendolin Ln
- RYEB 6169 D4
Kendon Pl
10 YNKR 6281 A3
Kendrick Pl
84-00 QENS 6825 D3
Kenilworth Av
10 STNL 7116 C3
Kenilworth Ct
- GDNC 6828 B1
Kenilworth Dr
10 CRSK 6392 B1
10 TFLY 6392 B1
222-00 QENS 6722 C5
Kenilworth Ln
10 HRSN 6169 B5
Kenilworth Pl
- COrT 6712 D4
10 BKLN 6923 C7
10 BKLN 7023 C1
Kenilworth Rd
10 HRSN 6169 B4
10 YNKR 6280 A7
Kenilworth St
- MLVN 6929 B2
Kenilworth Ter
10 KNGP 6616 E2
Kenmare Rd
10 LRMT 6396 C1
10 MrnT 6396 D1
Kenmare St
10 MHTN 118 E4
10 MHTN 119 A5
10 MHTN 6821 C2
Kenmore Av
10 NWRK 6712 C6
10 SOrT 6712 C6
Kenmore Ct
10 BKLN 7023 C7
Kenmore Rd
10 GDNC 6828 B1
10 VLYS 6928 D5
235-00 QENS 6722 C1
Kenmore St
10 STNL 7116 D4
10 YNKR 6280 A5
Kenmore Ter
10 EORG 6712 E1
10 EORG 6713 A1
2100 BKLN 6923 B5
Kennedy Blvd
- JSYC 6819 B6
100 BAYN 6919 D4
900 BAYN 6920 A1
1100 BAYN 6819 A7
Kennedy Blvd CO-501
- JSYC 6819 B6
100 BAYN 6919 E3
900 BAYN 6920 A1
1100 BAYN 6819 A7
Kennedy Blvd W
500 JSYC 6716 C4
500 NBgT 6716 C4
3200 UNCT 6716 E2
4800 WNYK 6716 E1
5300 NBgT 6610 E7
5300 WNYK 6610 E7
6300 WNYK 6611 A6
6700 GTBG 6611 A6
9100 NBgT 6611 B5
Kennedy Blvd W CO-501
500 JSYC 6716 C4
500 NBgT 6716 C4
500 UNCT 6716 C4
4800 WNYK 6716 E1
5300 NBgT 6610 E7
5300 WNYK 6610 E7
6300 NBgT 6611 A6
6300 WNYK 6611 A6
6700 GTBG 6611 A6
Kennedy Blvd W CO-693
9100 NBgT 6611 B5
Kennedy Cir
10 CLST 6278 C2
Kennedy Dr
10 LODI 6500 D1
300 FRVW 6611 C4
300 LNDN 7017 A2
Kennedy Ln
10 MNLA 6724 C5
10 NHmT 6724 C5
Kennedy Pl
10 YNKR 6281 A3
Kennedy Rd
10 CRSK 6278 C7
10 CRSK 6392 C1
Kennedy St
10 HKSK 6501 C3
500 PTHA 7205 C2
E Kennedy St
10 HKSK 6501 D3
Kennellworth Pl
1400 BRNX 6506 A6
Kenneth Av
900 ELIZ 6917 D5
Kenneth Ct
10 FLPK 6827 E2
10 KNGP 6617 A4
Kenneth Pl
10 NHmT 6723 E6
10 STNL 7206 E2
10 STNL 7207 A2
2800 HmpT 6929 E7
Kenneth Rd
10 GrbT 6166 E3
10 GrbT 6167 A3
10 WHPL 6168 C6
Kenneth St
100 HKSK 6501 A2
Kennington St
10 STNL 7117 B4
Keno Av
193-00 QENS 6826 B2
Kenridge Rd
10 LWRN 7028 A4
Kensett Rd
10 MNPK 6618 A5
N Kensico Av
10 MtPT 6050 A3
10 WHPL 6050 B7
10 WHPL 6168 E2
S Kensico Av
10 MtPT 6050 A3
10 WHPL 6168 C1
Kensico Pl
10 WHPL 6050 B7
10 WHPL 6168 E2
Kensico St
10 STNL 7117 C2
Kensico Knoll Pl
10 NoCT 6050 B4
Kensington Av
10 JSYC 6819 D2
10 NRWD 6164 A7
10 NRWD 6278 A1
10 STNL 7020 D6
S Kensington Av
100 RKVC 6929 E4
Kensington Cir
10 NHLS 6723 E3
10 NHLS 6724 A2
Kensington Cross
- GRFD 6500 D1
- SdBT 6500 D1
Kensington Ct
10 GDNC 6828 C3
10 KENS 6617 A6
10 TFLY 6392 A4
Kensington Dr
10 FTLE 6611 E1
Kensington Ovl
10 NRCH 6396 B6
Kensington Pl
10 EORG 6713 A1
500 CDHT 7028 A1
25500 LKSU 6723 A2
25500 NHmT 6723 A2
Kensington Rd
10 ARDY 6166 E5
10 BRXV 6280 E7
10 GDNC 6828 C1
10 HmpT 6828 C4
10 SCDL 6167 E6
10 TCKA 6280 E6
100 HmpT 6929 B3
200 GDNC 6724 C6
200 NHmT 6724 B6
Kensington Rd S
100 HmpT 6828 C4
Kensington St
10 BKLN 7121 D1
Kensington Ter
10 TCKA 6280 C3
Kensington Gate E
- NHLS 6724 A4
Kensington Gate W
10 NHLS 6724 A4
Kent Av
10 BKLN 6822 A4
10 HAOH 6166 B6
10 HAOH 6280 A1
Kent Blvd
10 HmpT 7029 C5
Kent Dr
10 HmpT 6929 A7
200 ERKY 6929 A7
Kent Pl
10 NHmT 6723 B1
400 HmpT 6828 E7
Kent Rd
10 GrbT 6050 A7
10 ISPK 7029 C5
10 NHmT 6724 A5
10 SCDL 6167 C6
10 TFLY 6392 C5
10 VLYS 6928 D2
10 YNKR 6280 C7
10 YNKR 6394 C1
Kent St
10 BKLN 6822 B1
10 NHmT 6724 C5
10 NWRK 6817 A1
10 STNL 7117 D1
80-00 QENS 6825 E2
85-00 QENS 6826 A2
100 HKSK 6501 A2
Kentucky St
10 LBCH 7028 D7
Kenwood Av
100 STNL 7207 D2
Kenwood Dr
10 NRCH 6282 A4
Kenwood Pl
10 EORG 6712 C5
500 TnkT 6501 E1
Kenwood Rd
10 TFLY 6392 B3
Kenwood St
300 EGLD 6502 E3
Kenworth Rd
10 NHmT 6617 E2
Kenyon Ct
10 NRWD 6164 B6
Kenyon Pl
10 MTVN 6394 E3
Keogh Ln
10 NRCH 6395 E7
Kepler Av
4200 BRNX 6394 A6
Keppel Av
10 STNL 7206 B4
Kerlyn Ct
10 ELIZ 6917 D5
Kermit Av
10 STNL 7020 D6
Kermit Pl
10 BKLN 6922 E6
10 BKLN 6923 A5
Kero Rd
10 CARL 6610 A2
Kerrigan Av
1400 NBgT 6716 C4
1400 UNCT 6716 C4
Kerrigan Blvd
100 IrvT 6816 B1
100 NWRK 6816 B1
200 NWRK 6712 B7
Kerrigan St
10 LBCH 7029 E6
Kerry Ln
10 STNL 7206 C4
Kervan Rd
10 HRSN 6169 B6
Kerwin Pl
10 TYTN 6048 C3
Kessel St
67-00 QENS 6824 C3
Keswick Pl
1000 FTLE 6502 D7
Keswick Rd
600 HmpT 6827 A6
Ketch Ct
120-00 QENS 6614 C6
Ketcham St
44-00 QENS 6719 E6
Kettell Av
10 YNKR 6394 B3
Keuka Rd
1000 HmpT 6929 D2
Keune Ct
10 STNL 7020 B5
Kevin Ct
10 MLVN 6929 B2
Kevin Mahon Av
65-00 QENS 6719 C6
Kew Av
1300 HmpT 6928 D6
Kewanee Rd
10 NRCH 6282 A3
Kew Forest Ln
77-00 QENS 6824 E3
Kew Gardens Rd
80-00 QENS 6824 E4
82-35 QENS 6825 A4
Key Ct
10 WbgT 7115 C2
Key Pl
10 OrgT 6164 A1
Keystone Ct
10 WbgT 7114 A3
Keystone Pl
10 HmpT 6928 E7
Keystone Rd
10 YNKR 6280 E1
Kiefer Av
1300 HmpT 6827 D5
Kiely Pl
10 BKLN 6824 A7
Kiesel Ter
7500 NBgT 6611 A5
Kiesewetter Ln
10 SECS 6610 C5
Kilburn Pl
100 SOrT 6712 A7
Kilburn Rd
10 GDNC 6828 C3
10 HmpT 6828 C4
100 GDNC 6724 C6
200 NHmT 6724 C7
Kilburn Rd S
100 HmpT 6828 C4
Kilburn Rd S
300 GDNC 6828 C4
Kildare Rd
10 ISPK 7029 D4
100 GDNC 6828 B2
100 NHmT 6828 B1
176-00 QENS 6825 E2
Killarney St
155-00 QENS 6925 D3
Kilmer Ln
800 HmpT 6928 A5
Kilmer Rd
10 LRMT 6396 C2
Kilmurray Dr
- TnkT 6502 B3
Kilroe St
100 BRNX 6506 E5
Kilsyth Rd
800 ELIZ 6917 E1
800 ELIZ 6918 A1
900 ELIZ 6817 A7
Kim Ct
10 OrgT 6164 B1
Kimball Av
10 BRNX 6394 A5
10 YNKR 6394 C1
900 YNKR 6280 D7
Kimball Pl
10 MTVN 6395 A6
Kimball St
10 BKLN 7023 D3
10 WbgT 7114 A3
2200 BKLN 7024 A4
Kimball Ter
10 YNKR 6394 A2
Kimberly Ln
10 STNL 7020 D3
Kimberly Pl
200 BRNX 102 D3
200 BRNX 6504 B2
Kimhunter Rd
10 EGLC 6503 B1
Kimmel Rd
10 MHTN 120 B6
10 MHTN 6821 A6
Kimmig Av
10 LODI 6500 C1
Kimson Ct
10 PLDM 6617 D5
Kincaid Dr
10 YNKR 6281 A3
King Av
10 WhkT 111 A5
10 WhkT 6716 B3
10 WhkT 6717 A3
10 YNKR 6394 A5
300 MHTN 120 A7
300 MHTN 6821 A7
600 BRNX 6506 E5
King Ct
10 HmpT 6827 C6
King Pl
10 CLST 6278 C3
King Rd
10 RCKL 6164 E5
35-00 QENS 6720 E4
King St
- JSYC 6716 C7
10 ARDY 6166 D4
10 BKLN 6922 A1
10 DBSF 6166 C4
10 EGLD 6392 A6
10 ELIZ 6816 E7
10 FLPK 6827 D2
10 HKSK 6501 B2
10 HlsT 6816 E7
10 HRSN 6283 B3
10 IRVN 6166 A2
10 KRNY 6714 B4
10 MHTN 118 D3
10 MHTN 6821 B1
10 MLVN 6929 B1
10 NoCT 6051 B1
10 OybT 6618 E2
10 PTCH 6170 B2
10 WLTN 6500 A5
10 YNKR 6280 A3
100 HmpT 6827 C6
100 STNL 7117 A7
200 PTHA 7205 D4
400 STNL 7208 A1
700 RYEB 6170 A1
800 GrwT 6170 A1
800 HmpT 6928 B7
1000 GrwT 6051 D3
1000 RYEB 6051 E6
King St SR-120
10 NoCT 6051 B1
King St SR-120A
- NoCT 6051 B1
10 PTCH 6170 B2
700 RYEB 6170 A1
800 GrwT 6170 A1
1000 GrwT 6051 D3
1000 RYEB 6051 E6
N King St
10 HmpT 6827 C6
10 MLVN 6929 B1
S King St
200 HmpT 6827 C6
W King St
10 HlsT 6816 D7
Kingdom Av
10 STNL 7116 B7
10 STNL 7207 C1
King Georges Post Rd
400 WbgT 7114 A7
King Georges Post Rd CO-501
500 WbgT 7114 A7
Kinghorn Ct
10 GrbT 6166 C6
Kinghorn St
10 STNL 7117 A7
10 STNL 7208 A1
100 STNL 7207 E1
King James Ct
10 STNL 7117 C5
Kingman Rd
10 SOrT 6712 B6
S Kingman Rd
10 SOrT 6712 B6
Kingman Ter
10 YNKR 6279 D5
Kings Av
10 ATLB 7028 A7
Kings Cross
10 YNKR 6281 A1
Kings Ct
10 CLFP 6611 E2
10 FTLE 6611 E2
10 GTNK 6616 C4
10 KNGP 6616 C4
100 WbgT 7114 D2
900 HmpT 6828 B3
Kings Hwy
- BKLN 6924 A5
10 BKLN 7022 D4
10 NRCH 6395 C5
10 OrgT 6164 D2
100 PLHM 6395 C5
100 PLMM 6395 C5
3500 BKLN 7023 D2
4900 BKLN 6923 E7
Kings Ln
10 NHmT 6724 B4
Kings Pl
10 BKLN 7022 E5
10 GTNK 6616 C4
Kings Plz
5300 BKLN 7024 A4
Kingsborough 3rd Wk
10 BKLN 6923 E2
Kingsbridge Av
- MHTN 102 D3
- MHTN 6504 B2
10 STNL 7018 E3
3000 BRNX 102 D3
3000 BRNX 6504 B1
Kingsbridge Plz
10 MTVN 6394 C7
Kingsbridge Rd E
10 MTVN 6394 C7
10 MTVN 6395 A7
Kingsbridge Rd W
10 MTVN 6394 E6
100 BRNX 6394 D6
E Kingsbridge Rd
10 BRNX 6504 C3
W Kingsbridge Rd
10 BRNX 102 E5
10 BRNX 6504 C3
Kingsbridge Ter
2600 BRNX 102 E4
2600 BRNX 6504 C3
Kingsbury Av
216-00 QENS 6722 D7
Kingsbury Rd
10 NRCH 6282 A7
10 NRCH 6396 A1
Kings College Pl
3500 BRNX 6505 A1
Kingsland Av
10 BKLN 6822 C1
10 HRSN 6714 B5
10 KRNY 6714 B5
600 CLFP 6611 C1
600 RDGF 6611 C1
700 FTLE 6611 D1
3200 BRNX 6505 D2
Kingsland Ln
800 RDGF 6611 D1
1000 FTLE 6502 D7
1000 FTLE 6611 A2
Kingsland Pl
10 BRNX 105 C3
10 BRNX 6504 E6
Kingsland St
10 STNL 7207 B2
Kingsley Av
100 STNL 7019 D2
Kingsley Dr
10 YNKR 6280 D3
Kingsley Pl
10 STNL 6920 C7
Kingsley St
10 WOrT 6712 B2
100 LEON 6502 D3
Kingsley Close
10 IRVN 6166 C2
Kings Park Dr
10 RYEB 6170 B3
Kings Point Rd
10 GTNK 6616 D3
10 KNGP 6616 C4
Kings Terrace Rd
10 KNGP 6616 E3
Kingston Av
10 BKLN 6923 D4
10 HRSN 6168 D1
10 SFPK 6827 D3
10 YNKR 6280 B7
100 FLPK 6827 D3
100 YNKR 6394 B1
Kingston Blvd
10 HmpT 7029 D4
Kingston Ct
10 NHmT 6724 A7
300 WNYK 111 D1
300 WNYK 6717 B1
Kingston Pl
85-00 QENS 6825 D3
Kingston Rd
10 SCDL 6167 E4
Kingston St
10 HmpT 6827 C7
10 NHmT 6724 B6
Kingsway Pl
10 BKLN 6924 A7
Kingswood Rd
10 WhkT 6716 B3
1000 UnnT 6816 A6
Kingwood Rd
10 GrbT 6280 D1
10 YNKR 6280 D1
Kinkaid Av
10 CLST 6278 C3
E Kinney Pl
10 NWRK 6817 D1
E Kinney St
10 NWRK 6817 E2
300 NWRK 6818 A2
W Kinney St
10 NWRK 6817 C1
Kinross Pl
10 YNKR 6279 D5
Kinsella St
800 BRNX 6505 B6
Kinsey Pl
10 STNL 7018 E1
Kinzley St
10 LFRY 6501 C5
10 SHkT 6501 C5
Kip Av
10 RTFD 6609 B2
Kipling Rd
10 YNKR 6280 E2
900 ELIZ 6917 A2
1100 UnnT 6917 A2
Kipling St
10 GrbT 6167 B1
Kipp Av
10 HSBH 6500 E4
10 LODI 6500 C3
Kipp St
10 NWRK 6817 B1
200 HKSK 6501 A2
300 TnkT 6501 D1
Kira Ln
10 EGLC 6503 B1
10 EGLD 6503 B1
Kirby Av
300 HmpT 7028 B1
Kirby Ct
10 STNL 6920 C6
Kirby Ln
10 RYE 6284 B2
Kirby Ln N
10 RYE 6284 B1
Kirby Pl
10 HRSN 6168 D1
Kirby St
10 GrwT 6170 C6
200 BRNX 6506 E6
Kirby Ter
10 WHPL 6168 C2
Kirchner Dr
10 OrgT 6164 D2
Kirk St
10 WbgT 7114 C1
Kirkby Rd
400 HmpT 6827 B6
Kirke St
- COrT 6712 B3
Kirkland Ct
10 STNL 6919 C7
Kirkland Pl
300 PTHA 7205 C3
Kirkman Av
200 HmpT 6827 E6
Kirkwood Rd
10 MHVN 6508 B6
Kirkwood St
10 LBCH 7029 E6
Kirlaldy Ct
10 GrbT 6166 C7
N Kirlaldy Ct
10 GrbT 6166 C7
Kirshon Av
10 STNL 7018 E3
10 STNL 7019 A3
Kissam Av
10 STNL 7118 A4
Kissam Ct
10 JSYC 6819 A4
Kissam Ln
10 OybT 6618 E1
Kissel Av
200 STNL 6920 A7
300 STNL 7020 B1
Kissena Blvd
41-00 QENS 6720 E4
41-00 QENS 6721 B7
65-34 QENS 6825 B1
Kiswick St
10 STNL 7118 B2
Kitchell Pl
10 NWRK 6713 E7
Kitchell St
10 NWRK 6713 E7
Kitching Pl
10 DBSF 6166 A6
Kleber Pl
10 LFRY 6501 B6
Klem Av
1700 LNDN 6917 D6
2500 ELIZ 6917 D6
Kling St
10 WOrT 6712 C1
Klondike Av
10 STNL 7019 A7
700 STNL 7018 D7
Kluepfel Ct
10 QENS 6823 C5
Knapp Pl
10 EGLD 6502 D2
Knapp St
10 BKLN 7023 E6
10 STNL 7018 E6
1400 BRNX 6505 D3
Knapp Ter
100 LEON 6502 D5
Knauth Pl
10 STNL 7020 E5
Kneeland Av
10 YNKR 6393 E4
76-00 QENS 6719 D7
78-00 QENS 6823 D1
100 YNKR 6394 A3
Kneeland St
50-00 QENS 6719 D7
Knesel St
10 STNL 7115 E5
Knickerbocker Av
10 BKLN 6822 E4
200 BKLN 6823 A6
1200 MRNK 6282 D4
Knickerbocker Rd
10 MNCH 6500 E7
10 MNCH 6609 E1
10 NHmT 6618 A6
100 HmpT 7029 D5
Knight Ct
10 BKLN 7023 E6
10 OrgT 6164 E1
Knightsbridge Rd
10 GTPZ 6723 A1
10 THSN 6723 A1
Knightsbridge Manor Rd
10 HRSN 6169 D4
Knoll Pl
10 NRCH 6395 C4
Knoll Rd
10 CRSK 6392 B1
10 SNPT 6508 E5
10 TFLY 6392 B2
Knoll St
10 HmpT 7027 C3
Knoll Wy
10 NRWD 6278 D1
Knolls Cres
10 BRNX 102 B3
10 BRNX 6504 A2
Knolls Dr
10 NHmT 6724 A4
Knolls Dr N
10 NHmT 6724 A4
Knolls Ln
10 FLHL 6617 E4
10 FLHL 6618 A4
Knolltop Rd
10 EMFD 6049 C5
Knollwood Av
10 EMFD 6049 B6
10 MTVN 6394 E6
100 MRNK 6282 E4
235-00 QENS 6722 C1
Knollwood Ct
10 STNL 7018 D1
Knollwood Dr
10 MrnT 6282 B7
10 NRCH 6282 A7
10 RYEB 6170 A3
500 HmpT 6828 C6
Knollwood Dr N
10 MrnT 6282 B6
Knollwood Rd
10 EchT 6281 B4
10 FLHL 6618 C5
10 GrbT 6167 C1
10 YNKR 6393 D2
100 GrbT 6049 C7
300 EMFD 6049 C7
1100 MtPT 6049 C3
Knollwood Rd SR-100A
10 GrbT 6167 B1
100 GrbT 6049 C7
300 EMFD 6049 C7
1100 MtPT 6049 C3
Knollwood Rd Ext
10 EMFD 6049 C6
10 GrbT 6049 C5
Knopf St
10 LNDN 7017 A1
Knota Rd
800 HmpT 6928 B7
Knowles St
10 YNKR 6393 C2
Knox Av
10 CLFP 6611 D2
10 EDGW 6611 D2
Knox Dr
10 EGLC 6392 C7
Knox Pl
10 STNL 7019 E3
3400 BRNX 6504 E1
Knox Rd
10 EchT 6281 B5
Knox St
10 STNL 7207 B2
Knutsen Knls
10 OrgT 6164 B2
Koch Blvd
10 STNL 7116 E7
10 STNL 7117 A7
Koch St
10 NRCH 6395 E3
Koelle Blvd
1000 SECS 6610 B6
Koewing Pl
10 WOrT 6712 A2
N Koewing Pl
10 WOrT 6712 A2
Kohring Cir N
10 HRPK 6278 A1
Kohring Cir S
10 HRPK 6278 A1
Kolbert Dr
10 MrnT 6282 C4
Komorn St
10 NWRK 6818 B2
Korean War Veterans Pkwy
- STNL 7116 E3
- STNL 7206 D1
- STNL 7207 A1
Korean War Vet Pkwy SR-440
- STNL 7206 C1
Kosciusko St
600 PTHA 7205 C1
Kosciuszko Br
- BKLN 6822 E2
- QENS 6822 E2
Kosciuszko Br I-278
- BKLN 6822 E2
- QENS 6822 E2
Kosciuszko St
10 BKLN 6822 D6
Kosene St
10 WbgT 7114 B5
Kossuth Av
3300 BRNX 6504 E2
Kossuth Pl
10 BKLN 6822 E6
Kossuth St
10 NWRK 6818 B2
10 WLTN 6500 A5
Koster St
10 WLTN 6500 A5
Kouwenhoven Ln
3100 BKLN 7023 D6
Kovar St
10 BGTA 6501 E2
Kowall Pl
10 LNBK 6929 A3
Koyen St
10 WbgT 7114 A7
Kozosko Av
600 PTHA 7114 C7
Kraft Av
10 BRXV 6280 B3
10 BRXV 6394 E1

New York City/5 Borough Street Index

STREET
Block City Map# Grid

Krakow St
10 GRFD 6500 B1
100 ELIZ 6918 A7
Kramer Av
10 STNL 7115 E6
Kramer Ct
300 BGTA 6501 D1
Kramer Pl
10 STNL 7019 D1
Kramer St
10 STNL 7020 D6
Kraus Ct
1400 HmpT 6827 D7
Kreil St
800 PTHA 7205 D1
Kreischer St
10 STNL 7115 B7
Kress Av
10 NRCH 6395 D3
Kresse St
400 HmpT 7029 D1
Krier Pl
10 BKLN 6924 B6
Krissa Ct
10 STNL 7116 B4
Kristen Ct
10 STNL 7020 E3
Krochmally Av
400 PTHA 7205 C1
Kroll Ter
10 SECS 6610 B6
Krotik Pl
10 IrvT 6816 B3
Krueger Ct
10 NWRK 6713 C7
Krug Ct
10 WLTN 6500 B4
Krug Pl
10 MNLA 6724 D7
Kruger Rd
181-00 QENS 6825 E3
Kruser St
10 STNL 7118 A2
100 STNL 7117 E1
Kruze St
100 HmpT 6828 C5
Kubala Av
10 CART 7115 B1
Kubasek Trinity Manor Dr
10 YNKR 6393 B2
Kuchima Wy
100 OrgT 6164 D2
Kulenkampf Pl
10 VLYS 6928 E5
Kuna Ter
10 IrvT 6816 B3
Kunath Av
10 STNL 7115 E5
Kurdyla Av
10 CART 7115 B1
Kuykendal Ter
10 GrbT 6048 E4
Kyle Ct
10 STNL 7116 B4

L

L St
10 HmpT 6827 E6
Labau Av
10 STNL 7020 A3
Labelle Rd
10 EchT 6395 B2
10 MTVN 6395 B2
Laburnum Av
140-00 QENS 6721 B5
Lackawanna Av
10 WLTN 6500 B6
100 NWRK 6713 C6
Lacombe Av
1700 BRNX 6614 C3
Lacon Ct
10 BKLN 7023 E6
Laconia Av
10 STNL 7020 D6
700 STNL 7118 B1
2200 BRNX 6505 C3
4000 BRNX 6394 D7
Ladd Av
10 STNL 7116 D4
Ladd Rd
700 BRNX 6393 B5
Ladik St
10 PRMT 6165 B1
Ladomus Rd
10 HmpT 7029 D3
La Farge Ln
10 MNPK 6618 B5
Lafayette Av
10 BKLN 121 D7
10 BKLN 6821 E7
10 CLFP 6611 D2
10 EDGW 6611 E2
10 EORG 6713 B2
10 LNBK 6929 C3
10 NoCT 6050 A4
10 NRCH 6395 D5
10 SCLF 6509 E6
10 STNL 6920 B6
100 LynT 6609 A5
400 HmpT 6929 C2
400 RDGF 6611 C1
600 MTVN 6395 B3
1000 BRNX 6613 D3
1100 BKLN 6822 E6
1600 BRNX 6614 C2
2800 BRNX 6615 A1
Lafayette Blvd
10 LBCH 7029 B7
Lafayette Dr
10 HmpT 6928 C6
10 OrgT 6164 C2
10 PTCH 6170 B4
Lafayette Pl
10 HmpT 7028 C1
10 IrvT 6816 C1
10 KRNY 6714 B2
10 LODI 6500 C3
10 SCLF 6509 D6
10 YNKR 6393 C1
Lafayette Rd
10 MrnT 6396 B1
Lafayette St
10 CART 7017 E7
10 CART 7115 E1
10 COrT 6712 B3
10 HKSK 6501 C3
10 JSYC 6820 A3
10 LFRY 6501 D7
10 MHTN 118 D6
10 MHTN 6821 C2
10 NRCH 6396 B5
10 NWRK 6817 E1
10 STNL 7206 A3
10 WHPL 6168 A2
10 WLPK 6724 D4
10 WOrT 6712 B3
100 NHmT 6724 D4
137-00 QENS 6925 D2
200 NWRK 6818 A2
300 MHTN 119 A2
600 ELIZ 6918 A3
1000 ELIZ 6917 B4
E Lafayette St
10 HKSK 6501 C3
S Lafayette St
100 NHmT 6724 C5
100 WLPK 6724 C5
La Fontaine Av
1900 BRNX 6504 D6
Laforge Av
10 STNL 7019 C1
Laforge Pl
10 STNL 7019 C1
La France Av
10 BlmT 6713 B2
100 EORG 6713 B2
La Grange Pl
10 STNL 7019 C1
La Guardia Av
10 STNL 7019 E5
La Guardia Ext
- QENS 6720 A2
Laguardia Pl
400 MHTN 118 E3
400 MHTN 6821 C2
La Guardia Rd
- QENS 6719 E2
- QENS 6720 A2
La Guardia Airport
- QENS 6719 D3
Laguna Ln
10 STNL 6919 A7
Lahey St
10 NHmT 6723 D5
Lahn St
153-00 QENS 6925 D3
Laidlaw Av
10 JSYC 6716 B7
1100 HmpT 6828 A5
Laight St
10 MHTN 118 C4
10 MHTN 6821 A2
Laird Av
200 CLFP 6611 C4
Laird Dr
10 WOrT 6712 B1
Laird Pl
10 CLFP 108 A1
10 CLFP 6611 C4
10 EDGW 108 A1
10 EDGW 6611 C4
Lake Av
10 BRXV 6280 E7
10 NRCH 6395 C3
10 STNL 6919 B7
10 TCKA 6280 E6
10 TYTN 6048 C3
10 YNKR 6279 D6
100 TCKA 6281 A6
300 STNL 7019 B2
600 LynT 6609 A4
N Lake Cir
10 WHPL 6168 E5
Lake Ct
10 EGLD 6502 D2
Lake Dr
10 HWTH 7029 A1
10 NHmT 6724 A4
10 OrgT 6164 E2
10 OrgT 6165 A2
10 PLMM 6395 C6
Lake Dr E
10 VLYS 6928 D2
Lake Dr N
10 VLYS 6928 D2
Lake Dr S
10 VLYS 6928 D2
Lake Pl
10 BKLN 7022 E6
Lake Rd
- MTVN 6395 A7
10 DMRT 6278 B5
10 LKSU 6723 C4
10 MRNK 6283 B6
10 PLNM 6617 C4
10 RYE 6283 B6
100 CLST 6278 C5
200 MtPT 6048 D1
200 TYTN 6048 D1
Lake Rd N
10 LKSU 6723 C4
Lake Rd S
10 LKSU 6723 C4
Lake Rd W
10 LKSU 6723 B4
Lake St
10 BKLN 7022 E5
10 BlvT 6713 C2
10 EGLD 6502 D2
10 EORG 6712 E1
10 IrvT 6816 C2
10 JSYC 6716 A6
10 WHPL 6050 C7
10 WHPL 6168 C1
100 CLST 6278 C5
100 DMRT 6278 C5
100 HRSN 6050 E6
100 NWRK 6713 D3
600 HRSN 6051 A4
Lake Ter
10 TYTN 6048 C1
Lakeland Rd
10 STNL 7019 E3
Laken Ter
10 NRCH 6395 C2
Lake Shore Dr
10 EchT 6281 C4
10 NRCH 6281 D4
Lakeshore Dr N
10 EchT 6281 D4
Lakeside Av
10 COrT 6712 C1
10 WOrT 6712 C1
Lakeside Dr
10 HRSN 6169 E6
10 MrnT 6282 C5
10 MtPT 6050 A2
10 NRCH 6395 C3
10 PLHM 6395 C3
10 RKVC 6929 D3
10 YNKR 6393 D3
800 HmpT 6928 A7
Lakeside Dr E
10 LWRN 7027 E4
Lakeside Dr S
100 LWRN 7027 E4
Lakeside Dr W
10 LWRN 7027 E4
Lake Side Pl
10 STNL 7020 D6
Lakeside Pl
900 UnnT 6917 B2
Lake Success Quadrangle
- LKSU 6723 E4
- NHmT 6723 E4
Lakeview Av
10 ARDY 6166 C5
10 EchT 6281 C2
10 GrbT 6167 D3
10 HmpT 6929 B3
10 HRSN 6050 D7
10 HRSN 6168 C3
10 LEON 6502 D2
10 LFRY 6501 C5
10 LNBK 6929 C3
10 MtPT 6049 D2
10 MtPT 6050 A1
10 RKVC 6929 E3
10 YNKR 6280 C5
100 MLVN 6929 C3
Lakeview Blvd
118-00 QENS 6926 E1
Lakeview Dr
10 LKSU 6723 C4
10 TYTN 6048 B5
10 WHPL 6050 C6
100 HmpT 6929 A6
500 HlsT 6917 D2
Lakeview Dr N
10 NoCT 6050 B5
10 WHPL 6050 B5
Lakeview Ln
122-00 QENS 6926 E1
Lakeview Pl
200 BRNX 6393 C6
Lakeview Rd
10 NRCH 6281 C7
Lakeview Ter
10 STNL 7020 D5
200 TnkT 6502 C1
Lakeville Dr
10 NHmT 6723 E7
Lakeville Rd
10 NHPK 6723 E7
10 NHPK 6827 E1
200 LKSU 6723 B1
200 NHmT 6723 D5
200 THSN 6723 B1
400 QENS 6723 D5
Lakewood Av
138-00 QENS 6825 C7
Lakewood Blvd
10 LNBK 6929 C5
Lakewood Ln
10 MrnT 6282 A6
Lakewood Pl
1100 BRNX 6505 C5
Lakewood Rd
10 STNL 7020 B1
Lakin Rd
10 SCDL 6167 E7
Lama Ct
10 BKLN 7022 E6
Lamar Pl
10 NRWD 6278 D1
10 YNKR 6280 B5
Lamartine Av
10 YNKR 6279 C7
Lamartine Ter
10 YNKR 6279 C7
Lamberson St
10 VLYS 6928 E2
Lambert Av
- STNL 7018 B1
100 NVLE 6164 B5
Lambert Ln
10 NRCH 6281 D3
Lambert Rd
10 WHPL 6168 D6
Lambert St
10 NHmT 6618 D7
10 STNL 7019 A3
10 WbgT 7114 B5
Lamberts Ln
- STNL 7018 C2
- STNL 7019 A3
Lambeth Ln
10 HmpT 6928 E2
Lambs Ln
10 CRSK 6392 C1
Lamesa Av
10 EchT 6281 B4
Lamker Ct
10 LFRY 6501 C7
Lamoka Av
100 STNL 7117 A5
400 STNL 7116 D5
Lamont Av
91-00 QENS 6720 A6
600 STNL 7116 A7
Lamont Ct
10 BKLN 6923 C4
Lamont St
10 GrbT 6049 A4
Lamped Lp
10 STNL 7018 E7
100 STNL 7019 B7
Lamport Blvd
10 STNL 7020 D6
Lamport Pl
2800 BRNX 6615 A2
Lana Cir E
10 WHPL 6168 E5
Lana Cir W
10 WHPL 6168 E5
Lanark Av
10 EORG 6712 C5
10 NWRK 6712 C5
Lanark Rd
10 YNKR 6393 D2
700 QENS 7026 B4
Lancaster Av
10 BKLN 7023 A6
Lancaster Ct
10 CRSK 6278 C7
10 NHLS 6724 A3
Lancaster Pl
10 ISPK 7029 C5
Lancaster Rd
10 ISPK 7029 C5
10 NRWD 6164 D7
10 TFLY 6392 C4
10 UnnT 6917 A1
700 RDGF 6611 B1
Lancaster St
10 LNBK 6929 C3
Lancia Ln
10 MrnT 6282 C6
Land Pl
- HmpT 7029 E1
Landau Av
10 FLPK 6827 E4
10 HmpT 6827 E4
Lander Av
10 STNL 7018 E3
10 STNL 7019 A3
Lander St
84-00 QENS 6825 B3
Landers Manor Rd
10 GrbT 6166 E1
Landford Dr
100 HmpT 6827 C7
Landing Dr
10 DBSF 6165 E3
10 DBSF 6166 A3
Landing Rd
10 GLCV 6509 E3
10 RSLN 6618 D5
200 BRNX 102 C7
200 BRNX 6504 A5
Landings Ln
- WNYK 111 D1
- WNYK 6717 B1
Landis Av
10 STNL 7020 E5
Landis Ct
10 BKLN 7023 E6
Landis Pl
10 YNKR 6394 C4
Landmark Ct
10 GrbT 6050 A5
Landolfe Pl
10 HRSN 6283 B3
Landscape Av
- STNL 7117 E1
10 YNKR 6393 D4
Lane Dr
10 EGLC 6503 B1
10 EGLD 6503 B1
Lane St
10 YNKR 6280 A5
Lane Wy
10 RYE 6283 C6
Lane Crest Av
10 NRCH 6395 E6
Lanett Av
9-00 QENS 7027 D5
Lang St
10 NWRK 6818 A2
Langdale St
77-00 QENS 6723 D7
Langdon Av
10 DBSF 6166 A3
10 IRVN 6166 A3
10 MTVN 6395 A5
Langdon Blvd
1100 HmpT 6929 D3
1400 RKVC 6929 D3
Langdon Ln
1300 MRNK 6282 E4
Langdon Pl
10 LNBK 6929 A4
Langdon St
500 COrT 6712 A4
1000 HmpT 6828 A5
1200 HmpT 6827 E5
Langdon Ter
10 YNKR 6394 D1
Langere Pl
10 STNL 7020 E3
Langford St
10 WbgT 7114 E3
Langham St
10 BKLN 7121 D1
Langley Av
300 HmpT 6828 D6
Langston Av
260-00 QENS 6723 B5
Lani Ct
10 WbgT 7115 B2
Lanni Pl
- JSYC 6820 B3
Lannon Pl
10 NHmT 6508 E7
Lanograf Ln
- ISPK 7029 D4
Lanram Rd
10 OrgT 6164 D1
Lansdowne Dr
10 MrnT 6282 C7
Lansing Av
230-00 QENS 6927 D3
Lansing St
10 STNL 7020 E6
Lantern Ln
10 GrwT 6170 B2
Lanza Ln
10 SECS 6610 B6
La Placa Ct
10 NHmT 6617 B5
Laporte Av
10 MTVN 6394 E1
Lapwing Ct
200 NHLS 6724 C1
Larch Av
10 BGTA 6501 D2
10 FLPK 6827 B2
10 JSYC 6715 E7
100 TnkT 6501 D2
Larch Ct
10 STNL 7115 D5
Larch Dr
10 GTNE 6722 E1
10 NHmT 6724 B4
Larch Ln
10 MrnT 6282 C5
10 SCDL 6167 D5
Larch St
10 CART 7115 B2
10 WbgT 7115 B2
Larch Hill Rd
10 LWRN 7028 A4
Larchmont Av
10 LRMT 6396 D2
Larchmont St
10 ARDY 6166 D5
10 GrbT 6166 D5
Larchmont Acres
10 MRNK 6282 D7
10 MrnT 6282 D7
Larchwood Rd
10 NRCH 6282 A7
Laredo Av
10 STNL 7116 D5
Lark Av
10 GrbT 6166 E1
Lark Ct
700 HmpT 7028 B1
Lark Pl
10 WHPL 6168 E4
Larkin Av
62-00 QENS 7026 D7
Larkin St
10 STNL 6919 C7
Larkspur Ln
10 RYE 6284 A1
10 YNKR 6394 B4
Laron Dr
10 NRCH 6281 E3
La Rosa Dr
10 LFRY 6501 B6
Larrimore Rd
10 YNKR 6280 B3
Larrison Lp
10 STNL 7019 C5
Larry Pl
10 YNKR 6280 B6
Larsen Av
10 OybT 6618 E1
10 ROSH 6618 E2
Larsen Rd
10 WbgT 7114 A3
Larue Av
102-00 QENS 6720 B7
Lasalle Av
10 HSBH 6500 D3
10 RYE 6283 C4
2800 BRNX 6505 E7
3000 BRNX 6506 B7
Lasalle Dr
10 NRCH 6396 A3
10 YNKR 6280 E5
Lasalle St
10 MHTN 106 C7
10 MHTN 6612 B4
10 STNL 6919 B7
Lasher Ln
10 EDGW 103 A7
10 EDGW 6503 A7
Latham Ln
140-00 QENS 6927 A2
Latham Pl
10 STNL 7115 E6
10 STNL 7116 A6
Latham Rd
100 MNLA 6724 D6
Lathers Pk
10 NRCH 6395 D4
Lathrop Av
300 STNL 7019 B2
Latimer Av
10 STNL 7018 C5
Latimer Pl
136-00 QENS 6720 E3
Latonia Rd
10 RYEB 6169 E3
Latourette Ln
10 STNL 7019 B7
La Tourette Pl
10 BAYN 6919 D5
Latourette St
10 STNL 7206 E2
Lattin Dr
10 YNKR 6393 D4
Latting St
2700 BRNX 6505 E7
Laub Pond Rd
10 GrwT 6051 E2
Laura Ln
10 GrbT 6166 E6
Laura Pl
10 PTHA 7205 D1
Laura St
1000 ELIZ 6918 A2
Laura Joy Cir
100 MRNK 6283 B5
Laurel Av
10 BKLN 7120 B1
10 BlmT 6712 E1
10 EORG 6712 E1
10 GLCV 6509 E3
10 IrvT 6816 B1
10 KRNY 6714 B2
10 MrnT 6282 C7
10 MTVN 6394 E1
10 SCLF 6509 D7
10 STNL 7020 D3
10 TFLY 6392 B2
100 MplT 6816 B1
100 MrnT 6396 C1
Laurel Ct
10 HmpT 6828 D7
10 JSYC 6820 C2
Laurel Dr
- BRNX 6505 B7
10 GTNE 6722 E1
Laurel Dr
10 NHmT 6724 A5
10 PTCH 6170 C7
10 WRDG 6500 B5
100 NHmT 6723 E5
600 HmpT 6828 C7
600 HmpT 6929 C1
Laurel Ln
10 SNPT 6508 C6
100 LWRN 7027 E3
Laurel Pl
10 EchT 6281 B5
10 ERTH 6500 B7
10 NRCH 6395 E5
10 NWRK 6712 D7
10 VLYS 6928 A2
10 YNKR 6394 B5
100 EGLD 6392 A5
900 HmpT 6928 D1
Laurel Rd
10 DMRT 6278 A4
10 WHPL 6168 E4
300 HmpT 6828 D6
Laurel St
- WbgT 7115 C2
10 CART 7115 C2
10 FLPK 6827 D2
10 GrbT 6166 D5
10 GrbT 6167 D3
10 RDFP 6501 E6
10 RYE 6283 E2
10 SRVL 7205 A6
10 WbgT 7114 B7
10 WbgT 7205 A1
100 NHmT 6618 E7
400 COrT 6712 B4
E Laurel St
10 CART 7115 C2
10 WbgT 7115 B2
Laurel Wy
10 HRSN 6051 B6
10 SCLF 6509 D7
Laurel Hill Av
39-00 QENS 6719 A6
Laurel Hill Blvd
34-00 QENS 6822 E1
46-00 QENS 6823 A1
58-00 QENS 6719 B7
Laurel Hill Dr
10 HmpT 6928 B5
Laurel Hill Rd
10 DBSF 6166 B3
Laurel Hill Ter
10 KRNY 6714 B2
10 MHTN 104 D4
10 MHTN 6503 E6
Laurelton Blvd
10 LBCH 7029 B7
Laurelton Pkwy
121-00 QENS 6928 A1
137-00 QENS 6927 E3
Laurel Wood Ct
10 HRSN 6169 B6
Lauren Rd
10 OrgT 6164 E4
Laurence Ct
10 CLST 6278 C4
Lauren Pond Ct
10 DMRT 6278 B6
Laurie Av
2800 BRNX 6505 E6
Laurie Ct
10 STNL 7020 B6
Laurie Dr
10 EGLC 6392 C6
Laurie Ln
200 HmpT 6828 E5
Lausecker Ln
10 SECS 6610 A6
Lava St
10 STNL 7020 E7
Lavender Ln
10 RYE 6284 A1
Lavenders Ct
10 NHLS 6618 A7
10 NHLS 6724 A2
Laventhal Av
10 IrvT 6816 B4
Law Pl
10 STNL 7020 A2
Law St
10 HmpT 6827 B7
10 HmpT 6928 B1
Lawn Av
10 NRCH 6395 E4
10 STNL 7117 D1
400 LEON 6502 C5
400 PALP 6502 C5
N Lawn Av
10 EMFD 6049 B4
10 GrbT 6049 B5
S Lawn Av
10 EMFD 6049 A6
Lawn Ct
10 BKLN 7023 B7
Lawn Pl
800 WDBG 7028 C1
Lawn St
10 HmpT 6928 E1
Lawn Ter
100 MRNK 6283 A6
Lawnridge Rd
300 COrT 6712 A4
Lawrence Av
10 BKLN 7022 E1
10 EchT 6281 B4
10 GrbT 6049 E5
10 HmpT 7027 E2
10 HSBH 6500 E3
10 LNBK 6929 C3
10 LODI 6500 D3
10 LWRN 7027 E2
10 LWRN 7028 A4
10 MLVN 6929 B1
10 STNL 7020 A2
10 SYHW 6048 B1
10 TCKA 6281 B4
10 WHPL 6050 B7
10 WOrT 6712 A4
1400 HmpT 6929 D3
3200 HmpT 7029 E1
N Lawrence Av
10 GrbT 6049 C4
S Lawrence Av
10 GrbT 6049 C4
Lawrence Ct
10 GrbT 6049 E4
10 GrbT 6050 A4
10 TFLY 6392 B3
10 TnkT 6502 C2
800 HmpT 6828 C7
900 HmpT 6928 B5
Lawrence Dr
10 GrbT 6049 E4
10 GrbT 6050 A4
10 MtPT 6050 A4
Lawrence Ln
10 HmpT 7027 E1
10 HRSN 6169 B7
10 HRSN 6283 B1
10 OrgT 6165 B5
Lawrence Pkwy
- LWRN 7027 B3
10 HmpT 7027 C2
10 TFLY 6392 A3
Lawrence Pl
10 NRCH 6395 C2
10 PLMM 6395 A6
10 YNKR 6393 D2
Lawrence Rd
10 SCDL 6282 B1
400 HmpT 6828 C6
Lawrence St
10 BlmT 6713 B1
10 BlvT 6713 C2
10 DBSF 6166 C6
10 EORG 6713 B1
10 ERKY 6929 B7
10 GrbT 6166 C6
10 HKSK 6501 B1
10 HmpT 6929 B7
10 MTVN 6395 A2
10 NHmT 6723 E5
10 NWRK 6713 C2
10 OrgT 6164 D3
10 WbgT 7205 A1
10 YNKR 6393 C4
57-00 QENS 6720 E6
100 BKLN 121 B6
100 BKLN 6821 D7
100 NHmT 6724 A5
200 MRNK 6282 E4
300 MRNK 6283 A3
300 PTHA 7205 D1
600 HmpT 6827 D7
1000 HmpT 6828 A4
Lawrence Park Cres
10 YNKR 6394 C1
Lawrence Park Ter
10 YNKR 6394 C1
Lawridge Dr
10 RYEB 6170 A1
Lawrie St
200 PTHA 7205 D3
Lawson Av
10 ERKY 6929 B7
10 RKVC 6929 D5
100 HmpT 6929 B7
Lawson Blvd
2900 HmpT 6929 D7
3100 HmpT 7029 D1
Lawson Ln
10 GTNK 6616 D6
10 KNGP 6616 D6
Lawton Av
10 CLFP 6611 C1
10 GrbT 6167 D3
400 RDGF 6611 D2
2700 BRNX 6615 A3
Lawton Ln
10 YNKR 6394 C1
Lawton Pl
400 PTHA 7205 C3
Lawton St
10 BKLN 6822 E6
10 BlmT 6713 C3
10 EORG 6713 C3
10 NWRK 6817 B2
10 YNKR 6393 E4
Lax Av
122-00 QENS 6614 D7
Layton Av
10 STNL 6920 D6
3100 BRNX 6615 A1
Layton St
10 RSLN 6618 D5
42-00 QENS 6719 E6
Lea Pl
10 NHmT 6724 E2
10 RYE 6284 A3
Leach St
10 LNBK 6929 A4
Leaf Pl
10 GrbT 6049 B4
Leafwood Ter
10 IRVN 6166 B2
Leafy Ln
10 MrnT 6396 B1
Leaman Pl
10 LNBK 6929 A4
Leamar Dr
10 NHmT 6724 A4
Leary Ln
10 EDGW 103 A5
10 EDGW 6503 A6
Leary St
10 EchT 6281 B6
Leason Pl
10 STNL 7019 B7
Leather Stocking Ln
10 GrbT 6049 E6
Leatherstocking Ln
10 MrnT 6282 D5
10 SCDL 6168 A7
Leavitt St
32-00 QENS 6721 A3
Lebanon Rd
10 SCDL 6282 A2
Lebanon St
1100 BRNX 6504 E6
1100 BRNX 6505 A7
Leber Av
10 CART 7115 C2
10 WbgT 7115 C2
Le Count Pl
10 NRCH 6395 E4
10 NRCH 6396 B5
Ledge Crest Rd
10 GrbT 6166 D7
Ledgewood Rd
10 YNKR 6394 D1
Ledyard Pl
10 STNL 7020 D6
Lee Av
10 BKLN 6822 B5
10 EchT 6281 B1
10 EWLS 6724 A6
10 NHmT 6724 D3
10 PTHA 7205 A1
10 RKVC 6929 E4
10 SCDL 6281 B1
10 STNL 7206 B3
10 THSN 6617 C7
10 VLYS 6928 E5
10 WbgT 7205 A1
10 WHPL 6167 E2
10 YNKR 6393 E4
100 NHmT 6723 C1
100 THSN 6723 C1
Lee Ct
10 GTNK 6616 E4
10 HmpT 6827 C4
10 HmpT 6828 A3
10 JSYC 6819 A4
10 KNGP 6616 E4
10 MplT 6816 A2
10 NRCH 6395 E6
10 STMN 6828 A3
400 FTLE 6502 D5
Lee Ct W
10 GTNK 6616 E4
Lee Ln
10 RYEB 6169 E4
Lee Pl
10 BRXV 6395 A1
100 HKSK 6501 B1
Lee Rd
100 GDNC 6828 B1
100 SCDL 6281 C1
Lee St
10 BRNX 6505 E6
10 WbgT 7115 A3
22-00 QENS 6721 A1
500 PTHA 7205 C2
1600 HmpT 6827 D7
1600 HmpT 6928 B3
Leeds Dr
10 NHmT 6617 D3
Leeds Rd
252-00 QENS 6723 A3
Leeds St
10 STNL 7117 D3
Lee Goldman Ln
230-00 QENS 6722 D6
Lees Av
10 TnkT 6502 A3
Leeward Ln
10 BRNX 6506 C5
Leewood Cir
10 EchT 6281 B5
Leewood Dr
10 EchT 6281 B3
Leewood Lp
10 STNL 7020 D4
Lefante Wy
10 BAYN 6920 A3
Lefark Memorial Sq
- QENS 6824 B1
Le Fevres Ln
10 NRCH 6396 B4
Leffert St
10 CART 7017 E7
Lefferts Av
10 BKLN 6923 B4
Lefferts Blvd
80-40 QENS 6824 E4
91-00 QENS 6825 A7
106-00 QENS 6926 A4
Lefferts Pl
10 BKLN 6923 A1
Lefferts Rd
10 YNKR 6393 D3
100 HmpT 7028 D1
1100 HBPK 7028 D1
Leffingwell Pl
10 NRCH 6395 D3
Lefurgy Av
10 DBSF 6166 B3
10 HAOH 6166 A7
Lefurgy Ter
10 HAOH 6166 A7
Legacy Cir
10 GrbT 6050 B4
Legacy Ct
10 RYEB 6051 D6
Legal St
10 NWRK 6817 B5
Legate Av
10 STNL 7116 C5
Legend Cir
10 GrbT 6049 E5
Legend Ct
10 HRSN 6051 A6
Legendary Cir
10 RYEB 6051 D5
Legends Hills Dr
10 EDGW 108 A1
10 EDGW 6611 C5
Leggett Av
900 BRNX 6613 C4
Leggett Pl
7-00 QENS 6615 B6
10 STNL 7019 A4
Leggett Rd
- STNL 7021 A5
10 BRXV 6394 E1
10 BRXV 6395 C1
Legion Dr
10 CRSK 6278 B7
10 CRSK 6392 B1
10 MtPT 6050 A3
100 GrbT 6049 E3
100 MtPT 6049 E4
Legion Pl
10 CLST 6278 A3
10 ERKY 6929 C7
10 HRPK 6278 A1
10 MLVN 6929 A2
10 STNL 7020 E5
10 VLYS 6928 D4
10 WbgT 7114 D5
Legion St
10 BKLN 6924 A3
Legrand Av
- NVLE 6164 C6
100 RCKL 6164 C6
Legrande Av
10 TYTN 6048 C2
Lehigh Av
10 NWRK 6817 A4
10 WbgT 7114 D1
100 NWRK 6816 E4
300 PTHA 7205 C3
400 UnnT 6917 A2
900 UnnT 6816 B7
Lehigh Ln
500 HmpT 6928 C6
Lehigh Pl
10 IrvT 6816 C3
400 HlsT 6816 B6
Lehigh St
10 HKSK 6501 B1
10 WLPK 6724 E4
500 HlsT 6816 B6
Lehman Rd
1000 HmpT 6929 C2
Lehman Ter
10 YNKR 6393 C4
Lehrer Av
10 HmpT 6827 D5
Leicester St
200 PTCH 6170 B5
Leick Av
10 CART 7017 D7
10 CART 7115 D1
Leif Ericson Sq
- BKLN 6921 E7
Leigh Av
10 STNL 7018 E3
Leighton Av
10 BRNX 6393 C4
10 YNKR 6393 C4
Leighton Rd
2100 HmpT 6827 A6
Leighton St
10 EGLC 6503 A3
10 FTLE 6503 A3
Leir Ct
10 WHPL 6168 D3
Leith Pl
10 WHPL 6168 B5
52-00 QENS 6723 A3
Leith Rd
252-00 QENS 6723 A3
Leland Av
10 NRCH 6395 E5
10 NRCH 6396 A6
500 BRNX 6614 B3
1400 BRNX 6505 B7
Leland Pl
300 HlsT 6816 D7
Lembeck Av
10 JSYC 6819 B5
Lemke Pl
100 NRCH 6396 A2
Lemoine Av
- FTLE 6503 A5
1500 FTLE 103 A4
2400 EGLC 6503 B4
Lemoine Av SR-67
1500 FTLE 103 A4
1500 FTLE 6503 A6
Lemoine Av US-9W
- FTLE 103 A2
2300 FTLE 6503 A5
2400 EGLC 6503 B4
Lempke Pl
10 NRCH 6396 A2
Len Rd
- HmpT 6827 B5
Lenevar Av
10 STNL 7115 E6
10 STNL 7116 A7
300 STNL 7207 A1
Lenhart St
10 STNL 7206 B3
Lennon Av
10 YNKR 6279 E7
Lennon Ct
10 STNL 7116 E3
10 STNL 7117 A4
Lenore Ct
10 STNL 7019 A3
Lenore Ln
600 HmpT 6827 D7
Lenox Av
10 DMRT 6278 A5
10 EORG 6712 E4
10 HmpT 6929 A5
10 IrvT 6712 C7
10 IrvT 6816 C1
10 LNBK 6929 A5
10 MHTN 109 E4
10 MHTN 6612 D4
10 MTVN 6395 A3
10 NWRK 6712 D7
10 WbgT 7114 C2
10 WHPL 6050 B7
10 YNKR 6280 E6
200 MHTN 110 A1
400 MHTN 107 C5
Lenox Ct
10 FTLE 6611 E2
Lenox Dr
200 HmpT 6828 C7
Lenox Pl
10 SCDL 6282 B1
200 HmpT 6828 B3
Lenox Rd
10 BKLN 6923 B5
10 RKVC 6929 E5
900 BKLN 6924 A4
Lenox St
10 NWRK 6712 C7
1600 HmpT 6827 D7
Lenox Ter
10 BlmT 6713 C2
Lenox Terrace Pl
10 MHTN 107 B7
10 MHTN 6612 D4
Lenroc Dr
10 GrbT 6048 D7
10 GrbT 6166 E1
Lentz Av
10 NWRK 6818 C1
Lentz Pl
10 IrvT 6816 A3

New York City/5 Borough Street Index

STREET / Block City Map# Grid

Lenzie St
10 STNL 7117 A7
10 STNL 7207 E1
Leo Pl
10 LODI 6500 D2
10 NWRK 6816 E3
10 NWRK 6817 A2
Leo St
10 STNL 7019 A3
500 HlsT 6816 B5
Leon Av
300 PTHA 7205 D1
500 WbgT 7114 B4
Leon Ct
10 RKVC 6929 E2
Leon Pl
500 ROSL 6917 B4
Leona Dr
10 YNKR 6280 B3
Leona St
10 STNL 7019 A4
Leonard Av
10 CLST 6278 C3
10 TFLY 6392 A4
200 STNL 7019 B3
500 WbgT 7114 B4
Leonard Blvd
10 NHmT 6724 A6
Leonard Dr
10 ERKY 6929 A6
Leonard Pl
10 SCLF 6509 E7
10 YNKR 6394 C4
Leonard Rd
10 BRXV 6280 E6
10 TCKA 6280 E6
Leonard St
10 BKLN 6822 C2
10 GRFD 6500 B2
10 LODI 6500 C2
10 MHTN 118 C5
10 MHTN 6821 B3
10 PTCH 6170 B7
100 JSYC 6716 B4
Leonard Wy
1300 HmpT 6827 D6
Leonard Cir Ct
100 NHmT 6724 C6
Leonard Morange Sq
- BRXV 6280 B3
Leone St
600 WbgT 7114 D3
Leone Close
10 GrbT 6166 E7
Leonello Ln
10 STNL 7206 C5
Leonia Av
100 BGTA 6501 E2
200 LEON 6502 D3
400 TnkT 6501 E2
Leo Sylvious Dr
100 BAYN 6819 A7
Lerer Ln
10 STNL 7206 C4
Leroy Av
10 MtPT 6049 E1
10 TYTN 6048 B3
10 YNKR 6393 D4
200 CDHT 7028 A2
Leroy Pl
10 LNBK 6929 A4
10 NRCH 6395 E5
10 YNKR 6393 D4
Leroy St
10 MHTN 118 C2
10 MHTN 6821 A1
10 STNL 7018 C6
10 TFLY 6392 B4
Leslie Av
10 STNL 7020 C5
Leslie Ln
10 NHmT 6723 D6
Leslie Pl
10 IrvT 6816 A3
10 NRCH 6281 E3
10 TFLY 6392 B3
Leslie Rd
10 EchT 6281 B6
177-00 QENS 6927 B1
178-30 QENS 6826 B7
Leslie St
10 BlmT 6713 B3
10 EORG 6713 B3
10 NWRK 6816 E3
400 HlsT 6816 C5
Lesoir Av
10 HmpT 6827 E4
Lester Av
10 LNBK 6929 A3
700 MRNK 6282 E5
Lester Ct
10 BKLN 7023 E6
10 BKLN 7024 A7
300 HmpT 6828 C6
Lester Dr
10 ERKY 6929 C5
10 OrgT 6164 B2
Lester Pl
10 MrnT 6396 B1
10 NRCH 6395 E1
10 NRCH 6396 B1
10 WHPL 6167 E2
Lester St
10 STNL 7019 D3
10 WLTN 6500 A5
400 FTLE 6502 D5
400 LEON 6502 D5
600 BRNX 6505 A3
Leticia Rd
10 EchT 6281 B6
Letter Av
600 TnkT 6502 B2
Letty Ct
10 STNL 6919 A7
Leuning St
10 SHkT 6501 B3
E Leuning St
10 SHkT 6501 B3
Leverett Av
10 STNL 7117 B4
400 STNL 7116 E4
Leverett Ct
10 STNL 7117 B4
Leverich St
35-00 QENS 6719 D5
Levi Pl
10 NHmT 6617 E2
10 NHmT 6618 A2
Le Vinnes Pl
10 NRCH 6395 E3
Levit Av
10 STNL 7019 B3
Lewellyn Cir
300 EGLD 6392 B6
Lewis Av
10 ATLB 7028 A7
10 BKLN 6822 D7
10 DBSF 6166 C3
10 GrbT 6167 D4
10 JSYC 6715 E7
10 NHmT 6827 E1
10 NHPK 6827 E1
10 YNKR 6279 D6
99-00 QENS 6720 B7
300 BKLN 6923 D1
300 HmpT 7028 B1
Lewis Ct
700 TnkT 6502 C1
Lewis Ln
10 NHmT 6508 E7
Lewis Pkwy
10 YNKR 6393 D4
Lewis Pl
10 BKLN 6923 A6
10 ERKY 6929 B6
10 LNBK 6929 B6
10 NRCH 6281 D5
10 YNKR 6279 E4
400 MNLA 6724 D5
400 WLPK 6724 D5
800 HmpT 6828 A7
N Lewis Pl
10 RKVC 6929 E4
S Lewis Pl
10 RKVC 6929 E5
Lewis Rd
10 IRVN 6166 C1
Lewis St
10 CLST 6278 B3
10 EGLD 6502 D1
10 MHTN 119 D6
10 MHTN 6821 E3
10 PTHA 7205 D5
10 YNKR 6279 E4
10 YNKR 6280 A4
100 VLYS 6928 B2
300 HmpT 6828 D6
400 FTLE 6502 E5
600 WbgT 7114 D3
Lewiston Av
188-00 QENS 6826 B6
Lewiston St
10 STNL 7019 B7
900 HmpT 6828 A4
Lewmay Rd
29-00 QENS 7027 B6
Lewyt St
10 NHmT 6617 C2
10 NHmT 6618 A2
Lexa Pl
10 STNL 7116 C7
Lexington Av
10 BAYN 6919 D6
10 BKLN 6822 C7
10 BlmT 6713 C1
10 CART 7017 D7
10 CRSK 6278 A6
10 HmpT 6828 A4
10 MHTN 116 C5
10 MHTN 6717 E5
10 MLVN 6929 B3
10 MTVN 6395 A3
10 STNL 7019 C1
10 WbgT 7114 B2
10 WLTN 6500 B5
100 HKSK 6501 B2
100 JSYC 6819 C2
500 MHTN 117 A1
500 MHTN 6718 A4
700 MHTN 113 C4
1400 MHTN 109 E7
1400 MHTN 6612 C6
1600 MHTN 110 C2
E Lexington Av
10 HmpT 7029 E1
N Lexington Av
10 WHPL 6168 C2
S Lexington Av
10 WHPL 6168 B4
Lexington Ct
10 EGLD 6392 A7
Lexington Ln
10 STNL 7117 A4
Lexington Pl
1400 ELIZ 6816 E7
1400 HlsT 6816 E7
Lexington Rd
600 UnnT 6917 A1
Lexington St
10 FLPK 6827 D2
10 NWRK 6818 B1
10 OrgT 6164 D3
10 RKVC 6929 E2
Leyden Av
10 STNL 7019 A1
Leyland Dr
10 LEON 6502 C3
Libby Pl
1700 BRNX 6505 E6
Liberty Av
- UnnT 6816 C7
10 BKLN 6924 E2
10 JSYC 6716 A7
10 LNDN 7017 B1
10 STNL 7020 B7
10 WbgT 7114 B4
74-01 BKLN 6925 A1
74-01 QENS 6925 D1
100 NRCH 6395 E6
100 NRCH 6396 A6
110-01 QENS 6824 E7
113-00 QENS 6826 A6
180-00 QENS 6826 A5
400 THSN 7118 C1
500 NBgT 6716 B5
500 WLPK 6724 D5
900 HlsT 6816 D5
7100 NBgT 6610 E5
7800 NBgT 6611 A5
Liberty Av CO-509
- UnnT 6816 C7
900 HlsT 6816 C7
Liberty Blvd
10 VLYS 6928 B3
Liberty Ct
10 SECS 6610 A6
Liberty Ln
10 LODI 6500 D2
Liberty Pl
10 MHTN 120 B1
10 MHTN 6821 B6
10 PALP 6502 C5
10 UNCT 6716 B3
10 WhkT 111 A4
10 WhkT 6716 B3
10 WhkT 6717 A2
500 RDGF 6611 B1
800 HmpT 6828 B4
Liberty Rd
10 DMRT 6278 B5
10 OrgT 6164 A2
Liberty St
10 CART 7017 D7
10 GRFD 6500 A1
10 IrvT 6816 C1
10 KRNY 6714 B4
10 LFRY 6501 C6
10 LODI 6500 D2
10 MHTN 120 B1
10 NWRK 6817 E1
10 PRMT 6165 A1
10 WbgT 7205 A1
10 WHPL 6167 E2
10 WOrT 6712 C1
100 ELIZ 6917 E4
100 HKSK 6501 B2
100 MHTN 118 A7
100 MHTN 6821 A4
100 SHkT 6501 B2
500 COrT 6712 A4
Liberty St CO-503
10 LFRY 6501 C6
400 SHkT 6501 C4
Library Av
1500 BRNX 6506 B6
Library Ct
10 BAYN 6919 E4
Library Dr
10 BXTE 6617 D1
10 NHmT 6617 D1
Library Ln
10 BRXV 6394 E1
10 RKVC 6929 D3
10 TCKA 6280 C2
100 MRNK 6282 D4
Library Plz
10 NRCH 6395 E4
Lidgerwood Av
400 ELIZ 6917 D5
700 LNDN 6917 D5
Lidgerwood Av CO-656
400 ELIZ 6917 D5
700 LNDN 6917 D5
Lido Ln
500 HmpT 6928 B6
Lieb Pl
10 EchT 6281 B6
Liebic Ln
10 CART 7115 E2
Liebig Av
5900 BRNX 6393 C5
6300 YNKR 6393 C5
Lienau Pl
10 JSYC 6716 B7
Ligett Rd
10 STNL 7021 A5
Liggett Rd
10 VLYS 6928 D5
Liggons Ln
10 JSYC 6819 D7
Light St
2100 BRNX 6394 E7
Lighthipe Pl
300 COrT 6712 B3
Lighthouse Av
200 STNL 7117 C1
Lighthouse Dr
10 SAMB 7205 D7
73-01 QENS 7026 C7
Lighthouse Plz
10 STNL 6920 E6
Lighthouse Rd
10 KNGP 6616 C3
10 SNPT 6508 A4
Light House Ter
10 EDGW 108 C1
10 EDGW 6611 D4
Lighting Wy
100 SECS 6610 B7
Lightner Av
10 STNL 7020 A4
300 STNL 7019 E6
Lilac Ct
10 STNL 7018 E2
Lilac Ln
10 NHmT 6618 A6
10 WLTN 6500 A6
300 CARL 6609 C1
300 ERTH 6609 C1
Lillian Ct
10 SNPT 6509 A5
Lillian Pl
10 STNL 7117 B6
Lillian Ter
10 WbgT 7114 C5
Lillie Ln
10 STNL 7019 B7
Lily St
10 FLPK 6827 C2
Lily Pond Av
10 STNL 7021 A5
Limekiln Spur
10 TCKA 6281 A5
Limerick Ct
10 GrbT 6049 E5
Linbergh Av
10 CLST 6278 C3
Lincoln Av
- GrwT 6051 D5
- MTVN 6395 B3
- RYEB 6051 D5
- STNL 7020 E5
- STNL 7021 A5
10 ARDY 6166 D5
10 BKLN 6824 A7
10 BRNX 110 D1
10 BRNX 6612 E5
10 CART 7017 D7
10 COrT 6712 C3
10 EDGW 6611 D2
10 EHLS 6618 E7
10 HAOH 6166 A7
10 HmpT 7029 C5
10 HRSN 6169 E4
10 HSBH 6500 C5
10 KRNY 6714 A5
10 MNLA 6724 E6
10 NHmT 6618 E7
10 NHmT 6723 E6
10 NRCH 6395 C4
10 NWRK 6713 E3
10 OLDT 6164 A5
10 PLHM 6395 B4
10 RDFP 6501 E5
10 RKVC 6929 D4
10 RTFD 6609 A2
10 RYEB 6169 E4
10 STNL 7118 B2
10 TCKA 6281 B4
10 TYTN 6048 C5
10 WbgT 7114 A2
10 WHPL 6167 E1
10 WRDG 6500 C5
10 YNKR 6394 C3
100 EchT 6281 B5
100 ELIZ 6917 C2
100 HRSN 6051 D6
100 NRWD 6164 A5
200 SECS 6716 A2
300 CLFP 6611 C2
300 FTLE 103 A1
300 FTLE 6503 A4
300 NWRK 6714 A2
500 BKLN 6925 B2
500 HmpT 6828 D7
500 RDGF 6611 C2
1300 NHPK 6724 A7
1600 NHmT 6724 A7
2800 HmpT 6929 E7
Lincoln Av E
10 HRSN 6050 D7
E Lincoln Av
10 MTVN 6394 E3
10 VLYS 6928 D3
200 MTVN 6395 A3
300 ROSP 6917 A3
500 ELIZ 6917 A2
500 UnnT 6917 A2
600 PLHM 6395 B3
600 RHWY 7017 A4
S Lincoln Av
500 WbgT 7114 B3
W Lincoln Av
10 MTVN 6394 D4
10 VLYS 6928 D3
Lincoln Blvd
10 LBCH 7029 D6
Lincoln Cir
10 YNKR 6280 C2
10 YNKR 6281 A5
Lincoln Ct
10 GDNC 6828 A1
10 RKVC 6929 D5
Lincoln Dr
10 CRSK 6278 A7
700 PTHA 7205 B1
Lincoln Hwy
- JSYC 6819 C2
- KRNY 6818 E1
- NWRK 6818 E1
100 KRNY 6819 A1
Lincoln Hwy US-1
- JSYC 6819 C2
- KRNY 6818 E1
- NWRK 6818 E1
100 NWRK 6819 A1
Lincoln Hwy US-9
- JSYC 6819 C2
- KRNY 6818 E1
- NWRK 6818 E1
100 KRNY 6819 A1
Lincoln Hwy US-9 TRK
- JSYC 6819 C2
- KRNY 6818 E1
- NWRK 6818 E1
100 KRNY 6819 A1
Lincoln Ln
10 HRSN 6169 D2
Lincoln Pk
- JSYC 6819 D1
10 NWRK 6817 C2
Lincoln Pkwy
10 BAYN 6919 E2
Lincoln Pl
10 BKLN 6922 E2
10 CARL 6500 C7
10 ERTH 6500 C7
10 ERTH 6609 B1
10 GLCV 6509 E3
10 GrbT 6050 A6
10 GRFD 6500 B3
10 HmpT 7027 E2
10 IrvT 6816 B3
10 LNBK 6929 B5
10 LODI 6500 C3
10 MNCH 6501 B7
10 NHmT 6617 E2
10 STNL 7020 E4
10 WbgT 7114 A2
10 WhkT 6716 E4
10 WLTN 6500 A5
10 EchT 6281 C5
400 BKLN 6923 B2
400 COrT 6712 B4
400 MNLA 6724 D7
400 NHmT 6724 D7
600 HmpT 6828 E7
1500 BKLN 6924 A3
6600 WNYK 6611 B7
Lincoln Rd
10 BKLN 6923 B4
10 HmpT 6828 B4
10 SCDL 6282 A1
10 THSN 6617 C7
900 HmpT 6929 D2
Lincoln Sq
- MHTN 112 C4
- MHTN 6717 D2
Lincoln St
10 DMRT 6278 B5
10 EGLD 6392 B7
10 EORG 6712 E3
10 FRVW 6611 B4
10 GDNC 6828 A2
10 HmpT 6827 D5
10 HSBH 6500 D5
10 JSYC 6716 B6
10 LFRY 6501 D7
10 LNDN 6917 B7
10 LRMT 6396 C2
10 NBgT 6611 B4
10 NRCH 6396 A4
10 NWRK 6817 C1
10 SHkT 6501 C4
10 STNL 7019 E5
111-00 QENS 6926 C1
200 EORG 6713 A2
200 HmpT 6828 A6
300 CARL 6500 B7
300 ERTH 6500 B7
400 CDHT 7028 A1
400 PALP 6502 C6
500 LEON 6502 C6
500 NBgT 6716 E1
500 UNCT 6716 E1
1400 ROSL 6917 B7
Lincoln Ter
10 YNKR 6279 C6
3600 NBgT 6716 B2
Lincoln Tun
- MHTN 111 A6
- MHTN 115 D1
- MHTN 6717 A3
- WhkT 111 A6
- WhkT 6716 E3
- WhkT 6717 A4
Lincoln Tun SR-495
- MHTN 111 A6
- MHTN 115 D1
- MHTN 6717 A3
- WhkT 111 A6
- WhkT 6716 E3
- WhkT 6717 A3
Lincoln Center Plz
10 MHTN 112 C4
10 MHTN 6717 C2
Lincoln Tunnel Ct
- WhkT 111 A6
- WhkT 6717 A3
Lincoln Tunnel Expwy
- MHTN 115 E3
- MHTN 116 A2
- MHTN 6717 C5
Lincoln Tunnel Expwy SR-495
- MHTN 115 E3
- MHTN 116 A2
- MHTN 6717 C5
Lincoln Woods
10 HRSN 6169 D1
Linda Av
10 STNL 7021 A6
10 WHPL 6168 B3
Linda Ct
10 HmpT 6929 A6
10 LNBK 6929 A6
10 STNL 7019 C1
Linda Ln
10 FRVW 6611 B3
10 GrbT 6280 E1
10 STNL 7116 C4
10 YNKR 6280 E1
500 HmpT 6928 B6
Linda Rd
10 NHmT 6508 E7
10 NHmT 6617 E1
Lindberg Av
100 NHmT 6617 D6
100 PLNH 6617 D5
500 CLFP 6611 D3
Lindberg St
200 HmpT 6828 D5
Lindbergh Av
10 PTHA 7114 C7
10 RYE 6283 E4
10 STNL 7117 E2
10 STNL 7118 A3
Lindbergh Blvd
10 TnkT 6502 B1
Lindbergh Dr
100 MNCH 6500 E7
100 MNCH 6501 A7
Lindbergh Pl
10 WLPK 6724 E4
10 YNKR 6281 A4
Lindbergh Rd
- NWRK 6817 C7
Lindell Blvd
10 LBCH 7029 A7
Linden Av
- IrvT 6712 E7
- NWRK 6712 E7
10 BRNX 6615 B4
10 EORG 6712 E5
10 FLPK 6827 D1
10 IrvT 6816 D1
10 JSYC 6819 B5
10 KRNY 6714 B2
10 LRMT 6396 D3
10 MTVN 6394 D3
10 PLHM 6395 C3
10 STNL 7019 A1
10 WOrT 6712 A2
100 HmpT 6928 E5
100 LNBK 6928 E5
300 BGTA 6501 D2
300 ELIZ 6917 C4
400 RDGF 6502 B7
400 TnkT 6501 E1
500 LNDN 7017 A2
500 WbgT 7114 C4
600 RDGF 6611 C1
800 ROSL 6917 C4
Linden Av E
10 JSYC 6819 D7
E Linden Av
10 EGLD 6502 E1
10 LNDN 7017 A1
10 EGLD 6503 A1
600 LNDN 6917 C6
2500 ELIZ 6917 D5
E Linden Av CO-656
2000 LNDN 6917 C5
2500 ELIZ 6917 C5
W Linden Av
10 LNDN 7017 A1
Linden Blvd
10 BKLN 6923 C5
10 GTNE 6616 E7
10 GTNE 6617 C4
10 KENS 6617 C4
23-900 HmpT 6827 A6
78-01 BKLN 6925 B3
93-00 QENS 6925 D2
112-00 QENS 6926 B1
142-00 QENS 6825 E7
168-00 QENS 6826 B6
227-00 QENS 6827 A6
800 BKLN 6924 A5
Linden Blvd SR-27
- BKLN 6925 A3
- QENS 6925 C2
10 BKLN 6923 E5
800 BKLN 6924 D4
Linden Ct
10 JSYC 6819 C6
10 NHmT 6618 E7
10 WOrT 6712 A2
400 RDGF 6611 B1
Linden Dr
10 HRSN 6169 D2
1500 BRNX 6505 C7
N Linden Ln
- NWRK 6713 D1
S Linden Ln
10 NWRK 6713 D3
Linden Pl
10 GrwT 6170 C1
10 GTPZ 6617 A7
10 HmpT 6928 C6
10 HmpT 6929 A6
10 LNBK 6928 C6
10 MtPT 6050 A2
10 NRCH 6395 E5
25-00 QENS 6720 E3
300 HmpT 6828 E6
400 COrT 6712 C2
400 HmpT 7029 D2
Linden Rd
10 MNLA 6724 E5
10 ROSL 6917 A4
10 ROSP 6917 A3
10 VLYS 6928 D2
Linden St
10 BAYN 6919 D5
10 BKLN 6823 B5
10 CART 7115 C1
10 HmpT 7028 B1
10 LODI 6500 D1
10 MLVN 6929 A1
10 NHmT 6617 D6
10 NHmT 6618 E7
10 NHmT 6724 B5
10 NWRK 6713 D7
10 PTCH 6170 C4
10 PTHA 7205 D5
10 RKVC 6929 E3
10 STNL 6920 A7
10 TFLY 6392 A3
10 THSN 6617 D7
10 THSN 6723 C1
10 YNKR 6393 D2
59-00 QENS 6823 C4
100 HmpT 6929 A1
300 ELIZ 6917 E2
400 HmpT 6828 E6
500 MRNK 6283 A5
Linden Ter
10 LEON 6502 D4
Lindenwood Pl
10 STNL 7117 A5
Lindenwood Rd
10 STNL 7117 B6
Linderman Av
10 CLST 6278 A3
Lindley Av
10 TFLY 6392 A3
Lindner Pl
10 MLVN 6929 B2
500 HmpT 6828 C6
Lindsay Ln
10 KRNY 6714 A4
Lindsey St
10 YNKR 6394 A2
Lindsley Av
10 IrvT 6816 A3
10 MplT 6712 A7
10 NWRK 6712 C7
10 SOrT 6712 A7
10 WOrT 6712 B2
Lindsley Dr
10 LRMT 6396 D2
Lindsley Pl
10 COrT 6712 C5
10 EORG 6712 C5
Lindy Ter
10 UnnT 6816 A4
Linford Rd
10 RSLG 6723 A2
Link Ct
10 HmpT 6928 C6
Link Dr
10 RCKL 6164 D5
Link Rd
10 STNL 7020 A6
Links Ct
100 NHmT 6618 B2
Links Dr
- NHmT 6724 B3
10 LKSU 6723 B3
10 NHLS 6724 B4
Links Dr S
400 NHLS 6724 A3
Links Rd
1000 HBPK 7028 D1
1000 HmpT 7028 D1
Linmouth Rd
10 MLVN 6929 C2
Linn Av
10 YNKR 6393 D4
Linn Pl
10 YNKR 6393 E3
Linneaus Pl
34-20 QENS 6720 E3
Linnet Ct
200 NHLS 6724 C1
Linnet St
10 BAYN 6919 E5
Linton Pl
10 STNL 7117 A4
Linwick Pl
10 YNKR 6394 B5
Linwood Av
10 BGTA 6501 E3
10 CRSK 6278 B7
10 CRSK 6392 B1
10 STNL 7020 E6
200 CDHT 7028 A2
2000 FTLE 6502 E5
2100 FTLE 103 A1
2100 FTLE 6503 A4
Linwood Dr
- FTLE 6502 E4
500 FTLE 103 A1
500 FTLE 6503 A4
Linwood Pl
10 EORG 6712 E2
10 WHPL 6167 E3
200 HlsT 6816 D7
Linwood Plz
10 FTLE 103 A1
10 FTLE 6503 A4
Linwood Rd
10 MrnT 6396 D2
10 NRCH 6282 B7
10 NRCH 6396 D2
Linwood Rd N
10 MHVN 6508 B6
Linwood Rd S
10 MHVN 6508 B7
Linwood St
10 BKLN 6924 E1
900 BKLN 6925 A4
Lion Ct
10 HmpT 6929 A6
Lion St
10 STNL 7206 B3
Lipsett Av
10 STNL 7116 D7
300 STNL 7207 E1
Lipton Ln
10 NHmT 6724 D4
Lisa Ct
10 DBSF 6166 B4
Lisa Ln
10 MtPT 6049 C2
10 STNL 7116 B5
400 HmpT 6828 D6
Lisa Pl
10 STNL 7018 E4
Lisbon Pl
10 STNL 7118 A1
100 BRNX 6504 E1
Lisk Av
10 STNL 7018 E2
Lismore Rd
10 LWRN 7027 E4
Lispenard Av
10 EchT 6395 B1
10 NRCH 6396 A3
Lispenard St
10 MHTN 118 D5
10 MHTN 6821 E4
Liss St
10 STNL 7116 E7
Lister Av
10 NWRK 6714 C7
Litchfield Av
10 HmpT 6827 E5
Litchfield Rd
10 NHmT 6617 E2
Litchfield Wy
10 ALPN 6278 D5
Lithonia Av
164-00 QENS 6721 C6
Little Ln
10 WHPL 6168 E4
Little St
10 BKLN 121 D2
10 BKLN 6821 E5
10 EORG 6713 B3
10 NWRK 6713 B3
Little Clove Rd
10 STNL 7020 A3
Little Farms Rd
10 MrnT 6282 C6
Littlefield Av
10 STNL 7117 B7
Little John Pl
10 WHPL 6168 D4
10 YNKR 6280 B7
Little Kings Ln
10 RYEB 6170 B2
Little League Pl
10 BRNX 6505 D7
Little Nassau St
10 BKLN 6822 B6
Little Neck Blvd
24-00 QENS 6722 A1
Little Neck Pkwy
33-00 QENS 6722 E2
47-00 QENS 6723 A3
85-01 QENS 6827 C1
88-56 FLPK 6827 C2
Littleton Av
10 NWRK 6713 B7
300 NWRK 6817 B1
Little West 12th St
10 MHTN 115 C6
10 MHTN 6717 A7
Littleworth Ln
10 SCLF 6509 D7
Livermore Av
10 STNL 7019 C3
Liverpool St
104-00 QENS 6825 C6
Livingston Av
10 DBSF 6165 E5
10 KRNY 6714 B1
10 MtPT 6050 A3
10 NARL 6714 C1
10 STNL 7019 D5
10 WbgT 7114 C2
10 YNKR 6168 B3
10 YNKR 6393 C3
100 NRCH 6282 E6
4500 BRNX 6393 C7
Livingston Ct
10 STNL 6920 A6
300 EDGW 108 C1
300 EDGW 6611 E5
Livingston Mnr
10 DBSF 6166 A4
Livingston Pl
10 GrwT 6170 D2
10 LWRN 7028 B6
300 CDHT 7027 E2
300 CDHT 7028 A2
300 HmpT 7027 E2
Livingston Rd
10 NRCH 6282 A2
500 HlsT 6816 C7
600 ELIZ 6917 B2
Livingston St
10 BKLN 121 A5
10 BKLN 6821 D7
10 HRPK 6278 A1
10 HRSN 6050 D7
10 NRWD 6278 A1
10 NVLE 6164 C4
10 OrgT 6164 C4
100 NRWD 6164 B6
100 NWRK 6817 B2
300 ELIZ 6918 B4
300 MTVN 6394 E3
Livingston St CO-505
10 HRPK 6278 A1
10 NRWD 6278 A1
100 NRWD 6164 B6
100 NVLE 6164 C5
200 OrgT 6164 C4
E Livingston St
10 MtPT 6050 A2
W Livingston St
10 MtPT 6050 B2
Livingstone Av
10 DBSF 6166 B6
Livonia Av
10 BKLN 6924 B4
Lladro Dr
10 MNCH 6501 B6
Llewellyn Pl
10 STNL 7019 D1
10 WOrT 6712 B1
Lloyd Av
10 HmpT 6929 A5
10 LNBK 6929 A5
Lloyd Ct
10 BKLN 7022 E5
10 STNL 7020 A1
Lloyd Rd
137-00 QENS 6825 B6
Lloyd St
10 BKLN 6923 C5
10 NHmT 6724 C5
10 RDGF 6611 B1
1000 HmpT 6828 A4
Loch Ln
10 RYEB 6170 B3
Lock St
10 NWRK 6713 D6
Locke Av
154-00 QENS 6721 B1
Lockman Av
10 STNL 6919 A7
100 STNL 7019 A1
300 STNL 7018 E1
Lockman Lp
10 STNL 7019 A1
Lockman Pl
10 STNL 6919 A7
Lockwood Av
10 EchT 6395 C2
10 NRCH 6395 D4
10 WbgT 7114 C2
10 YNKR 6279 C5
10 YNKR 6280 A6
Lockwood Pl
10 HRSN 6283 A3
10 PTCH 6170 C5
10 STNL 7019 C2
Lockwood Rd
10 SCDL 6281 C1
Lockwood St
10 NWRK 6714 D7
10 NWRK 6818 C1
Locust Av
10 BKLN 7023 A3
10 BlmT 6713 A1
10 BRNX 6613 B6
10 BXTE 6617 D1
10 CDHT 7028 B2
10 EchT 6281 C2
10 ERTH 6500 A6
10 HmpT 7028 B2
10 KRNY 6714 B2
10 LRMT 6396 D2
10 NRCH 6396 A5
10 RKVC 6929 E3
10 RYE 6283 E1
10 SCLF 6509 E5
10 STNL 7117 E1
10 WHPL 6168 B4
10 WLTN 6500 A5
100 PASC 6500 A5
100 STNL 7118 A2
200 HRSN 6283 D1
200 PTCH 6170 C5
500 HlsT 6816 B6
Locust Av E
10 HRSN 6168 D1
Locust Ct
10 STNL 7115 E5
300 HmpT 6929 D2
Locust Dr
10 GTNE 6616 D7
2700 HmpT 6929 E7
3200 HmpT 7029 E1
Locust Ln
10 BRXV 6395 A1
10 ERTH 6500 A6
10 MTVN 6395 A2
10 NHmT 6724 B4
10 RYE 6283 E4
10 SCDL 6167 D7
10 WLTN 6500 A6
100 IRVN 6166 B2
Locust Pl
10 NHmT 6617 D6
10 SCLF 6509 D6
10 STNL 7117 B5
Locust Rd
10 GrwT 6051 B1
Locust St
10 BKLN 6822 D5
10 CART 7115 D2
10 CLST 6278 A2
10 EHLS 6618 E6
10 EMFD 6049 B6
10 FLPK 6827 D3
10 GLCV 6509 E3
10 GrbT 6049 B6
10 JSYC 6819 B4
10 MLVN 6929 A2
10 MtPT 6050 A1
10 NHmT 6617 D6
10 NHmT 6618 E6
10 VLYS 6928 D5
39-00 QENS 6719 A6
100 HmpT 6827 C3
100 SFPK 6827 C3
200 HmpT 6828 D6
200 HmpT 6928 D6
200 TnkT 6502 A3
300 MTVN 6394 D3
Locust Ter
10 MrnT 6396 B3
400 HmpT 6828 D6
Locust Cove Ln
10 KNGP 6616 D3
Locust Hill Av
10 YNKR 6279 C7
10 YNKR 6393 C1
Locust Point Dr
4300 BRNX 6615 C3
Locust Ridge Rd
10 MrnT 6282 B6
Locustwood Blvd
10 HmpT 6827 A5
Loden Ln
10 HRSN 6169 D2
Loder St
10 RYE 6284 B2
Lodge Rd
10 THSN 6617 C7
Lodi St
10 HKSK 6501 B2
10 PASC 6500 A5
Lodovick Av
2200 BRNX 6505 E4
Loehr Pl
10 YNKR 6279 D7
Loel Ct
10 RKVC 6929 E3
Loewen Ct
10 RYE 6283 E2
Loft Rd
1000 HmpT 7028 D1
Logan Av
10 JSYC 6819 D1
10 STNL 7020 A3
200 BRNX 6615 B3
Logan Pl
10 LODI 6500 C4
Logan St
10 BKLN 6823 E7
100 BKLN 6924 E1
800 BKLN 6925 A3
Loh Av
10 TYTN 6048 B3
Lohengrin Pl
1200 BRNX 6506 A7
Lohs Pl
10 HRPK 6164 A5
Lois Av
10 BKLN 7024 A7
10 DMRT 6278 B5
Lois Ln
10 STNL 7018 D3
Lois Pl
10 LNBK 6928 E4
10 STNL 6920 B7
10 VLYS 6928 E4
Loman Ct
10 CRSK 6392 C1
Lombard Ct
10 STNL 7116 A5
Lombardy Pl
10 NWRK 6713 C4
Lombardy St
10 BKLN 6822 D2
10 NWRK 6713 E6
Lomond Pl
10 NRCH 6395 D1
London Ct
10 STNL 7117 C1
10 TnkT 6502 B2
London Rd
10 STNL 7117 D1
London Ter
10 NRCH 6282 A7
Long Av
10 HlsT 6816 C6
S Long Av
1100 HlsT 6816 D7
Long St
10 COrT 6712 E1
10 EORG 6712 E1
10 JSYC 6819 C5
117-00 QENS 6926 E1
122-00 QENS 6927 A1
Longacre Av
300 HmpT 6928 A7
300 HmpT 7028 D3
Long Beach Blvd
10 LBCH 7029 C7
700 HmpT 7029 C6
Long Beach Plz
10 LBCH 7029 C7
Long Beach Rd
10 ISPK 7029 D5
2700 HmpT 6929 E7
3200 HmpT 7029 E1
Longdale Av
10 GrbT 6049 D7
Longdale St
10 STNL 7018 E3
Longfellow Av
10 NWRK 6712 C6
10 STNL 7020 B4
200 BRNX 6613 D3
1800 BRNX 6504 E6
Longfellow Rd
10 SDRK 6616 D6
Longfellow St
10 CART 7115 D2
10 GrbT 6167 B1
S Longfellow St
10 GrbT 6167 B2
Long Ferry Rd
100 PTHA 7205 E2
Long Island Expwy
- EHLS 6724 E1
- LKSU 6723 C3
- NHLS 6723 D3
- NHLS 6724 B2
- NHmT 6724 E1
- QENS 117 E6

New York City/5 Borough Street Index

Column format: **Street** — Block · City · Map# · Grid

Long Island Expwy
- QENS 6718 C7
- QENS 6719 A7
- QENS 6720 B7
- QENS 6721 C7
- QENS 6722 C5
- QENS 6723 C3
- QENS 6823 D1
- QENS 6824 B1

Long Island Expwy I-495
- EHLS 6724 E1
- LKSU 6723 C3
- NHLS 6723 D3
- NHLS 6724 B2
- NHmT 6724 C1
- QENS 117 E6
- QENS 6718 E7
- QENS 6719 A7
- QENS 6720 B7
- QENS 6721 C7
- QENS 6722 C5
- QENS 6723 C3
- QENS 6823 A1
- QENS 6824 B1

Longledge Dr
10 RYEB 6169 E5
10 RYEB 6170 A7

Longmeadow Rd
10 YNKR 6393 D5

Long Pond Ln
10 STNL 7020 D3

Longridge Rd
10 PLDM 6617 D5

Longspur Rd
10 YNKR 6280 B6

Longstreet Av
100 BRNX 6615 C3

Longue Vue Av
10 EchT 6281 E7
900 NRCH 6828 A6

Longvale Rd
10 YNKR 6280 D7

Longview Av
10 CART 7017 C7
10 DBSF 6166 C4
10 HKSK 6501 C4
10 HmpT 6928 B5
10 WHPL 6168 B3
100 LEON 6502 D2
200 HSBH 6501 A2
500 CLFP 6611 C2
500 FRVW 6611 C2

Longview Cir
10 WbgT 7205 A1

Longview Ct
400 NVLE 6164 B3

Longview Dr
10 EchT 6281 C6
10 GrbT 6167 A4
100 GrbT 6166 E6

Longview Pl
10 BKLN 7023 D2
10 GTPZ 6617 B7
10 THSN 6617 B7
500 CLBT 6617 A5
500 HSBH 6501 D3

Longview Rd
- NHmT 6617 C1
10 HSON 6509 A7
10 NHmT 6618 A1
10 STNL 7020 B3

Longview St
10 WOrT 6712 B2

Longvue Ter
200 YNKR 6280 E3

Longwood Av
800 BRNX 6615 C3

Longwood Cross
10 LWRN 7028 B4

Longwood Rd
10 SNPT 6508 C4

Longworth Av
100 HmpT 7028 D1
100 HSBH 6500 E3
200 HSBH 6501 A4

Longworth St
10 NWRK 6817 C2

Looker St
10 HlsT 6816 E7

Lookout Av
10 BRXV 6280 C4

Lookout Cir
10 BKLN 6924 A2
10 MrnT 6396 B1

Lookout Pl
10 ARDY 6166 E3

Loomis Av
100 YNKR 6394 B1

Loomis St
10 ELIZ 6918 A5
1300 BRNX 6505 D6

Loop Rd
- QENS 6926 E5
- STNL 7021 A5
10 NoCT 6051 C2

Lopez Dr
200 BRNX 6828 D7

Lord Av
10 BAYN 6919 D4
10 HmpT 7027 D3
10 LWRN 7027 E4

Lord St
10 HmpT 7114 B4

Lord Kitchener Rd
10 NRCH 6281 D5

Lords Wy
10 STNL 7207 E1

Lorelei Ter
10 LODI 6500 B4

Loren Ct
300 NVLE 6164 C4

Lorena St
10 LFRY 6501 C6
800 MRNK 6283 C4

Lorentz St
600 HmpT 6827 B7

Lorenz Av
10 NRCH 6395 B4

Lorenzen St
10 LRMT 6396 C2

Loretta Ct
10 EGLC 6503 C1

Loretta Rd
22-00 QENS 7027 C5

Loretta St
10 HmpT 7027 E2
10 WbgT 7205 A1

Loretto St
10 IrvT 6816 D3
10 NWRK 6816 D3
400 STNL 7206 B5

Lori Dr
206-00 QENS 6615 E2

Lori Ln
900 UnnT 6917 B1

Lorillard Pl
2300 BRNX 6504 D5

Lorimer St
10 BKLN 6822 C4

Loring Av
10 BKLN 6925 A3
10 STNL 7116 D4
10 YNKR 6394 A2
100 PLHM 6395 C5
1400 QENS 6925 B3

Loring Pl N
10 NHmT 6827 C1
2200 BRNX 102 D7
2200 BRNX 105 C1
100 NHPK 6504 B4
600 NHPK 6723 E7
1300 NHPK 6724 A7
1600 NHmT 6724 A7

Loring Pl S
1800 BRNX 105 B3
1800 NHmT 6504 A5

Lorrain Av
10 STNL 7116 D6

Lorraine Av
10 MTVN 6395 B4
800 STNL 6816 B7

Lorraine Ct
10 MLVN 6929 A1
500 EGLD 6502 E3

Lorraine Dr
10 EchT 6281 B5
900 NRCH 6828 A6

Lorraine Lp
10 STNL 7115 D6

Lorraine Pl
10 HRSN 6283 A3
10 SCDL 6167 E6

Lorraine Rd
10 ISPK 7029 D4

Lorraine St
10 BKLN 6922 B2
600 MRNK 6283 C4

Lorraine Ter
10 NRCH 6395 B4

Lortel Av
10 STNL 7019 E4
10 STNL 7020 E4

Lowerre Pl
4000 BRNX 6394 B7

Lt Glenn Zamorski Dr
10 STNL 6918 B5

Lott Av
10 BKLN 6924 C4

Lott Ln
10 STNL 7116 E2

Lott Pl
10 BKLN 7023 D2

Lott St
10 BKLN 6923 B6
10 JSYC 6820 A1

Lotts Ln
10 BKLN 7023 D2

Lotus Ovl N
10 HmpT 6928 A3

Lotus Ovl S
10 HmpT 6928 B4

Lotus Rd
10 NRCH 6282 A7

Lotus St
10 CDHT 7028 B2
- WbgT 7205 B2

Loubet St
67-00 QENS 6824 C3

Louden St
10 GrwT 6170 D5

Loudoun St
10 YNKR 6393 D4

Louis Av
10 HmpT 6827 C4
10 SFPK 6827 C4
300 FLPK 6827 D3
400 NHmT 6828 B6
700 LNDN 6917 D6

Louis Ct
10 ShkT 6501 C5

Louis Pl
10 BKLN 6924 A2
10 UnnT 6816 B6

Louis St
10 CART 7115 D1
10 HSBH 6500 E3
10 LFRY 6501 D6
10 LODI 6500 E3
10 ShkT 6501 C5
10 STNL 7020 C1
10 WbgT 7205 A1
10 WhkT 111 A3
1000 ELIZ 6918 A1

Louisana Ter
10 YNKR 6394 D1

Louise Ln
10 STNL 7020 A1

Louise Pl
10 VLYS 6928 B3

Louise St
10 STNL 7207 C1
10 LFRY 6501 D6
10 LFRY 7019 E1

Louise Ter
7000 BRNX 6921 D7

Louisiana Av
10 BKLN 6924 D1
10 HmpT 7029 D4

Louisiana St
10 LBCH 7028 D7

Louis Nine Blvd
- BRNX 6613 D4

Love Ln
10 BKLN 121 A4
10 BKLN 6821 D6
10 STNL 6282 E4

Lovelace Av
10 STNL 7116 D5

Lovell Av
10 STNL 7019 B6

Lovell Ln
10 NRCH 6281 D6

Lovell Rd
10 NRCH 6281 D5

Lovely Dr
10 SAMB 7205 B7

Lovingham Pl
116-00 QENS 6826 B7

Lowden Av
900 UnnT 6917 B1

Lowden St
10 ELIZ 6917 D3

Lowe Av
500 RDGF 6611 A1

Lowe Ct
148-00 QENS 6825 C5

Lowe Ln
10 OrgT 6164 B1

Lowe St
- LEON 6502 D3

Lowell Av
10 BKLN 6922 B1

Lowell Ct
10 TnkT 6502 C2

Lowell Pl
10 NWRK 6817 B5

Lowell Rd
10 HRSN 6168 D1

Lowell St
10 CART 7115 D1
10 HmpT 6929 A3
10 LNBK 6929 A3
10 STNL 7117 C1
10 YNKR 6279 E7
800 HmpT 6928 B7
1000 BRNX 6613 D2

Lower Rd
10 LNDN 7017 A4
1300 ELIZ 6918 A4
1400 HlsT 6816 E7
1800 RHWY 7017 A4

Lower Rd CO-613
100 LNDN 7017 C3
1800 RHWY 7017 A4

Lower Rdwy
- SECS 6715 D1

Lucas St
120-00 QENS 6826 C7
122-00 QENS 6927 C1

Lucerne St
3200 BRNX 6506 A4

Lucht Pl
10 STNL 6610 B6

Lucia Pl
10 STNL 7117 C3

Lucille Av
10 HmpT 6828 A5
10 STNL 7115 E6
500 HmpT 6827 E6

Lucille Ct
1700 HmpT 6827 C6

Lucille Dr
- WbgT 7205 B2

Lucille Pl
10 STNL 6395 B2

Luckenbach Ln
10 STNL 6508 D5
10 SNPT 6508 D5

Lucky Ln
7600 QENS 6611 B5

Lucy Av
500 TnkT 6502 B2

Lucy Lp
10 STNL 7116 D6

Lucy St
10 GrwT 6170 D5

Luddington Rd
10 WOrT 6712 A4

Ludlam Av
10 HmpT 6827 A5

Ludlam St
10 BKLN 6923 B3

Ludlow Av
100 NVLE 6164 C6

Ludlow Ln
10 OrgT 6165 B1

Ludlow St
10 ELIZ 6917 A4
10 JSYC 6819 C6
10 MHTN 119 B5
10 MHTN 6821 D3
10 NWRK 6817 A4
10 STNL 7116 D5
10 YNKR 6393 C2

Ludlum St
187-00 QENS 6826 B9

Ludwig Ln
10 EWLS 6724 E3

Ludwig St
10 LFRY 6501 D6
10 LFRY 7019 E1

Lu Esther T Mertz Plz
10 NHmT 6618 B1

Lufberry St
10 EHLS 6618 D4

Luhmann Ter
10 SECS 6610 B4

Luhrs Ct
10 SECS 6610 B4

Luigi Pl
10 STNL 7117 D1

Luke Ct
10 STNL 7117 D1

Luke Pl
216-01 QENS 6722 B5

Lulu Ct
10 STNL 7206 C4

Lum Av
300 UnnT 6816 A7

Lum Ln
10 NWRK 6817 D2

Lumber Rd
10 RSLN 6618 D5

Lumber St
10 LNDN 7017 A1

Luna Cir
10 STNL 7207 E1

Lundi Ct
10 STNL 7019 A7

Lundsten Av
10 STNL 7115 C7

Lundy Ln
10 MrnT 6396 B2

Luquer Rd
10 NHmT 6617 D3
10 PLNM 6617 D3

Luquer St
10 BKLN 6922 B1

Lurene St
- NBgT 6611 C5

Lurting Av
2200 BRNX 6614 C1
2300 BRNX 6505 C7

Lustre St
2100 BRNX 6394 B7

Luten Av
10 STNL 7207 B1

Luther Av
10 PTHA 7205 A1
10 WbgT 7205 A1

Luther Rd
69-00 QENS 6823 E5

Lutheran Av
6100 QENS 6823 E3

Luttgen Pl
10 LNDN 7017 A2
10 LNBK 6929 A3
900 HmpT 6917 A7

Lutz Dr
10 VLYS 6928 C2

Lutz St
900 HmpT 6928 A4

Lux Rd
143-00 QENS 6825 C7

Luxor Pl
10 NWRK 6817 A5

Luzern Rd
10 FRVW 6611 B3

Luzern Rd
10 BRNX 6166 B4

Lyceum Ct
10 EGLD 6392 A6

Lydecker St
10 EGLD 6392 A6

Lydia Av
1400 HmpT 6827 D7

Lydia Dr
100 WNYK 6611 C7

Lydia Ln
10 GDNC 6828 D3
10 STNL 6828 D3

Lydia St
10 VLYS 6929 A2

Lydig Av
600 BRNX 6505 A5

Lyle Ct
10 STNL 7117 C3

Lyle King St
- ELIZ 6918 E1
- ELIZ 6919 A1

Lyman Av
10 STNL 7021 A4
400 WbgT 7114 B4

Lyman Pl
10 DBSF 6166 B3
10 STNL 7020 B4
10 EGLD 6392 A7
1300 BRNX 6613 C1

Lyman St
88-00 QENS 6827 A1

Lyme Av
10 BKLN 7120 B1

Lynbrook Av
10 LNBK 6929 C4
10 STNL 7115 E7

Lynbrook Ct
10 STNL 7115 E6

Lynch St
10 BKLN 6822 B5
10 STNL 7207 D1
1500 HmpT 6827 D4

Lyncrest Rd
100 EGLC 6392 B7
200 EGLD 6392 B7

Lyncrest St
10 VLYS 6928 C6

Lyncroft Rd
10 NRCH 6281 D4
10 NRCH 6395 E1

Lynd St
10 PTHA 7205 D4

Lyndale Av
10 STNL 7116 E6
10 STNL 7117 A4

Lyndale Ln
10 STNL 7116 E6

Lynden Av
10 BKLN 6284 A9

Lynette Dr
100 FTLE 6502 D5

Lynhurst Av
10 STNL 7020 B4

Lynmar Wy
700 UnnT 6917 C2

Lynn Dr
10 EGLC 6392 A5
800 HmpT 6827 D7

Lynn Pl
10 VLYS 6928 D1
800 STNL 6928 E1

Lynn Rd
10 HmpT 6618 A3

Lynn St
10 STNL 7117 E4

Lynnette St
10 NRCH 6396 A3

Lynnhaven Pl
10 STNL 7019 E3

Lynns Wy
10 NRCH 6396 A6

Lynton Pl
10 WHPL 6168 A3

Lynton Rd
10 NHmT 6724 C1

E Macon Av
10 STNL 7116 D4

E Macon St
10 STNL 7116 E4

Lynwood Av
10 HmpT 6928 D2
10 VLYS 6928 D2

Lynwood Pl
- YNKR 6281 A1

Lynwood Rd
10 GrbT 6281 B1

Lyon Av
10 GrwT 6170 E4
10 WbgT 7114 C2
2200 BRNX 6614 C1
2300 BRNX 6505 C7

Lyon Ct
10 JSYC 6819 A4

Lyon Pl
10 NRCH 6396 A3
10 STNL 7019 B3
10 WHPL 6168 B2

Lyon St
10 PTCH 6170 A6
10 VLYS 6928 B2
200 HmpT 6928 B1

Lyon Farm Ct
10 PTCH 6170 A6

E Lyon Farm Dr
10 GrwT 6170 D2

W Lyon Farm Dr
10 GrwT 6170 C2

Lyons Av
10 NWRK 6816 D4
10 NWRK 6817 A5
400 IrvT 6816 D3

Lyons Av CO-602
10 NWRK 6816 D4
10 NWRK 6817 A5
400 IrvT 6816 D3

Lyons Pl
10 ELIZ 6917 D4
10 LRMT 6396 D6
10 MTVN 6395 A4

Lyons Rd
10 EchT 6281 C3
10 SCDL 6281 C3

Lytton Av
10 NHmT 6167 B1

Lytton Av
10 HlsT 6816 E7

Lyvere St
2400 BRNX 6505 C7

M

M St
1300 HmpT 6827 E7

Mabel Wayne Pl
10 HmpT 7027 D3

MacArthur Av
10 BlmT 6713 B1
10 CLST 6278 C4
10 GRFD 6500 B3
10 HSBH 6500 B3
10 HSBH 6501 A2
10 STNL 7021 A4
400 WbgT 7114 B4

MacArthur Av
10 TYTN 6048 B4

Macatee Pl
400 MNLA 6724 D5

MacDonald Rd
10 HmpT 7029 D2

MacDonald St
10 STNL 7019 A3
400 EGLD 6502 D4
500 SdBT 6500 C4

Macdonough Pl
1300 BRNX 6506 A6

Macdonough St
10 BKLN 6923 D1

MacDougal Al
10 MHTN 118 E1

MacDougal St
10 BKLN 6924 A3
10 MHTN 118 E1
10 MHTN 6821 E5

MacDougal St
10 MHTN 118 C7
10 MHTN 109 E6
10 MHTN 6821 E7
1300 BRNX 6612 C6
2100 BRNX 107 C4
2100 BRNX 6506 E7

Mace Av
10 STNL 7117 D2
600 BRNX 6505 C4

Mace St
10 STNL 7117 D2

Macedulski Ter
10 SAMB 7205 B7

E Madison Av
10 CRSK 6278 D7

MacFarland Av
10 STNL 7020 B4

N Madison Av
10 NHmT 6618 D7

MacGregor Av
10 NHmT 6618 D7

MacGregor St
10 STNL 7207 A1

Mack Pl
600 LNDN 6917 D7

Mackay Av
2100 FTLE 103 A2
2100 FTLE 6503 A5

Mackay Pl
10 BKLN 6921 D1

Mackay St
10 RSLN 6618 B5

Mackenzie St
10 BKLN 7121 D1

Mackey Av
10 BXTE 6617 E1

Mackintosh St
10 STNL 7206 B2

Maclay Av
2400 BRNX 6505 C7

Macnish St
44-00 QENS 6719 D7

Macombs Pl
10 MHTN 107 C7
59-00 QENS 6823 C7

Macombs Rd
1400 BRNX 105 B6

Macombs Dam Br
- BRNX 107 D3
- BRNX 6612 D2
- MHTN 107 C3
- MHTN 6612 D2

Macon Av
10 STNL 7116 D4

E Macon Av
10 STNL 7116 E4

Macon St
10 BKLN 6923 E1
600 BKLN 6924 A1

Macmorac Pl
10 STNL 6918 E7

Macquesten Pkwy N
10 MTVN 6394 C4
10 NRCH 6395 D4

Macquesten Pkwy S
10 MTVN 6394 C4
10 NRCH 6394 C4

Macri Av
10 HRSN 6168 D1

Madison Cir Dr
10 HBPK 7028 E1

Madison Park Gdns
10 NHmT 6617 C1

Madoc Av
800 BRNX 6613 C3

Madonia Ct
10 PLDM 6617 E5

Madonna Pl
200 HmpT 6928 B1

Mador Ct
7-00 QENS 7027 D5

Madsen Av
10 STNL 7206 C2

Magazine St
10 MHTN 117 C2

Magee Av
2600 BRNX 6505 D4

Magee Plz
10 NHmT 6618 A1

Magenta St
600 BRNX 6505 C2

Magie Av
10 ELIZ 6917 C5
100 RSLN 6618 D6
900 UnnT 6917 A2

Magnett Ct
10 MrnT 6282 D3

Magnolia Av
10 CRSK 6278 A7
10 ELIZ 6918 C5
10 FLPK 6827 B3
10 JSYC 6819 C5
10 KRNY 6714 B2
10 LRMT 6396 A4
10 MTVN 6395 A4
10 STNL 7020 C7
10 TFLY 6392 B2
10 WOrT 6712 D3
10 YNKR 6393 C1
36-00 QENS 6720 E4
41-59 QENS 6721 A6
65-00 QENS 6825 A1
100 EchT 6281 A6
100 GRFD 6500 B4
100 NRCH 6396 A4
200 CLFP 6611 C4
200 FTLE 6502 E5
400 SHkT 6501 C5
- YNKR 6393 E5

Magnolia Blvd
10 LBCH 7029 B7

Magnolia Ct
94-00 QENS 6925 D3

Magnolia Dr
10 DBSF 6165 E5
10 GTNE 6616 E7
10 HAOH 6165 E5
10 HRSN 6051 B5
10 NHmT 6724 A6
10 RYEB 6170 B2

Magnolia Ln
700 MHTN 113 E7

N Magnolia Ln
10 BlvT 6713 D1
10 NWRK 6713 D1

Magnolia Pl
10 BRNX 6615 B4
10 RYE 6283 A6
42-00 QENS 6721 A4
300 LEON 6502 D4
1000 HmpT 6928 C6
1200 HmpT 6816 B7

Magnolia Rd
10 SCDL 6168 C7

Magnolia St
10 EDGW 6503 B4
10 EDGW 6503 A6
10 FTLE 6503 A6
10 PTCH 6170 A6
10 STNL 7206 E1

Maguire Ct
10 STNL 7206 E2

Mahan Av
1600 BRNX 7205 B7
1600 BRNX 6506 B7

Mahan St
10 TFLY 6392 A1

W Mahan St
10 TFLY 6392 A1

Mahatma Ghandi Plz
10 JSYC 6716 A7

Mahland Pl
10 NRCH 6820 D2

Mahogany Ct
10 STNL 6929 E7

Mahoney Pl
10 STNL 6929 D1

Mahopac Rd
10 HmpT 6929 D1

Maiden Ln
- GrbT 6049 A1
10 ALPN 6278 E6
10 BGTA 6501 B4
10 JSYC 6820 A2
10 LFRY 6501 D7
10 MHTN 120 C1
10 NWRK 6821 A6
10 STNL 7206 D3

Maiden Wy
10 WbgT 7114 A1

Madison Av
10 BKLN 6822 C7
100 MRNK 6282 E5
100 NWRK 6817 E2
200 CLST 6278 B3
200 FRVW 6611 B2
200 LNDN 7017 C3
200 MHTN 107 C3
200 LynT 6609 A7
300 CARL 6500 C7
300 ERTH 6500 B7
10 HmpT 6828 A6
400 COrT 6712 B2
900 HWTN 7028 D1
900 NWRK 7028 D1
1300 BKLN 6823 B6
1300 HmpT 6827 E4
5400 WNYK 6610 E7
5400 WNYK 6716 C1
6200 WNYK 6611 A7
6600 GTBG 6611 A6
7100 NBgT 6611 A6

Madison Av Br
- BRNX 107 D7
- BRNX 6612 E4
- MHTN 107 C7
- MHTN 6612 E4

Madison Av Br CO-74
10 CRSK 6278 A7

E Madison St
10 SAMB 7205 B7

N Madison St
10 CRSK 6278 D7

Madison Pl
10 BKLN 7023 D4
10 GrbT 6049 E5
10 HRSN 6283 A1
10 NHmT 6618 D7

Madison Rd
10 EchT 6281 D3
10 SCDL 6281 D2

Madison St
10 BKLN 6923 B3
10 ALPN 6278 E6
10 BGTA 6501 A5
10 BXTE 6617 E1
10 HBKN 6716 C1
10 HRSN 6283 A3
10 JSYC 6820 A2
10 LFRY 6501 D7
10 LODI 6500 D3
10 MHTN 120 C1
10 NWRK 6821 D1
10 STNL 7206 D3
59-00 QENS 6823 D7

E Main St CO-56
10 BGTA 6501 C2

E Main St SR-119
10 EMFD 6049 A5

E Main St US-1
10 MrnT 6396 B3

N Main St
9-00 QENS 6718 E2
10 GDNC 6828 B1

Main Av
10 NHmT 6828 B1
10 SCLF 6509 E6
10 WLTN 6500 A5
100 NWRK 6817 E2
300 WRDG 6500 B4
500 SHkT 6500 B4

Main Av CO-61
300 COrT 6712 D3
300 LODI 6500 C3
500 WRDG 6500 B4

Main Av CO-507
10 WLTN 6500 A5

Main Pl
10 HRSN 6168 D2

Main St
10 BGTA 6501 C2
10 BRNX 6615 C2
10 EHLS 6618 D6
10 ALPN 6278 E6
10 BKLN 6821 C5
10 BXTE 6617 E1
10 BlvT 6713 C1
10 CORt 6712 D3
10 COrT 6712 D3
10 DBSF 6165 E4
10 EDGW 103 B4
10 EDGW 6503 B4
10 EORG 6712 D3
10 EORG 6713 A4
10 ERKY 6929 B6
10 FTLE 103 A4
10 FTLE 6503 A6
10 HAOH 6165 E7
10 HKSK 6501 C1
10 HSBH 6500 D5
10 IRVN 6048 A6
10 IRVN 6166 A1
10 LFRY 6501 C5
10 LNDN 7017 C4
10 MHTN 117 C2
10 MNLA 6724 E6
10 NHmT 6617 E1
10 NHmT 6618 A1
10 NVLE 6164 C3
10 NWRK 6713 B5
10 NWRK 6818 B1
10 OrgT 6164 C3
10 RSLN 6618 D6
10 SAMB 7205 B7
10 SRVL 7205 B6
10 STNL 7021 A5
10 TCKA 6280 E6
10 TCKA 6281 A6
10 TYTN 6048 B2
10 WbgT 7114 A6
10 WHPL 6168 A2
10 YNKR 6393 C1

Main St CO-8
10 HmpT 6827 A5

Main St CO-56
42-00 QENS 6721 A4
300 LEON 6502 D4
1000 HmpT 6928 C6
1200 HmpT 6816 B7

Main St CO-505
10 EDGW 103 B4
10 EDGW 6503 B4
10 FTLE 103 A4
10 FTLE 6503 A6

Main St CO-514
10 WbgT 7114 A6

Main St CO-659
10 STNL 7115 E7

Main St CO-684
1600 BRNX 7205 B7
1600 BRNX 6506 B7

Main St E
400 HRSN 6168 C1

Main St Ext
10 LNBK 6929 C4

Main St N
800 MHTN 6718 C3

Main St SR-35
10 TFLY 6392 A1

Main St SR-119
10 WHPL 6168 A2

Main St US-1
100 NRCH 6396 A4
400 NRCH 6396 A4
900 PLMM 6395 D6

Main St E
400 HRSN 6168 C1

E Main St
10 MrnT 6396 A3

E Main St CO-56
10 BGTA 6501 C2

E Main St SR-119
10 EMFD 6049 A5

E Main St US-1
10 MrnT 6396 B3

N Main St
10 PTCH 6170 C5

N Main St
10 LODI 6500 D1

N Main St CO-61
100 LODI 6500 D1

N Main St US-1
100 PTCH 6170 C5

S Main St
10 CORt 6712 D3
10 LODI 6500 C3
10 PTCH 6170 C6
10 ShkT 6500 C4
10 WLTN 6500 B4
100 HKSK 6501 C3
100 ShkT 6501 C3

S Main St CO-61
10 ShkT 6500 C4
10 WLTN 6500 B4
100 WRDG 6500 B4

S Main St US-1
10 PTCH 6170 C6

W Main St
10 ALPN 6278 E6
10 BGTA 6501 D2
10 EMFD 6049 A5
10 HAOH 6165 E7

W Main St CO-56
10 EORG 6712 D3

W Main St SR-119
10 EMFD 6049 A5

Maine Av
10 CART 7017 B6
10 RKVC 6929 D3
10 STNL 7019 D2
400 HmpT 6929 D3

Mainsail Ln
10 IRVN 6166 A1
700 SECS 6715 D1

Main St Ext
2600 BRNX 7205 A6

Maioran Pl
- BlvT 6713 C1

Maitland Av
2800 BRNX 6505 E7

Maitland Pl
10 GRFD 6500 B2

Majestic Av
10 NHmT 6724 A4

Majestic Pl
10 WbgT 7115 B2

Major Av
10 STNL 7021 A5

Major Ct
10 RKVC 6929 D3

Major Ln
10 NHmT 6724 A5

Major Applebys Rd
10 ARDY 6166 C3

Major Deegan Expwy
- BRNX 102 D7
- BRNX 104 D7
- BRNX 105 B1
- BRNX 110 E1
- BRNX 6393 D7
- BRNX 6503 E7
- BRNX 6504 E2
- BRNX 6612 E2
- BRNX 6613 E5
- YNKR 6393 E5

Major Deegan Expwy I-87
- BRNX 104 D7
- BRNX 105 B1
- BRNX 107 D2
- BRNX 6393 D7
- BRNX 6503 E7
- BRNX 6504 E2
- BRNX 6612 E2

Major William F Deegan Blvd
10 BRNX 110 D1
- BRNX 6612 E4

Makofske Av
10 HmpT 6827 C4

Malba Dr
10-66 QENS 6615 A7
143-00 QENS 6614 E6

Malbone Ln
10 BKLN 6923 C3

Malcolm St
10 HSBH 6500 E5
10 GRFD 6500 B2
10 TETB 6500 B2
10 TETB 6501 A5

Malcolm Ct
2900 HmpT 6929 E3

Malcolm Pl
100 LODI 6500 B4

Malcolm Wilson Ln
10 YNKR 6394 E1
900 PLMM 6395 D6

Malcolm X Blvd
10 BKLN 6822 E7
10 BKLN 6923 E1
200 BKLN 6923 E1

Malden Av
10 LNBK 6929 C4

Malden Ln
10 STNL 7117 E3

Malden Pl
10 MLVN 6929 A2

Malden Ter
10 ELIZ 6917 D1

Malecon Pl
10 BKLN 6929 A2

Mall Dr E
10 JSYC 6820 D2

Mall Dr W
10 JSYC 6820 C2

Mallard Ln
10 STNL 7115 D7

Mallard Pl
10 SECS 6610 A5

Mallard Rd
10 FLHL 6617 E4

New York City/5 Borough Street Index

STREET
Block City Map# Grid

Mallard Rise
10 IRVN 6048 C6
10 TYTN 6048 C6
Mallis St
1000 HmpT 6929 A1
Mallon Pl
10 NHmT 6617 E1
Mallory Av
10 JSYC 6819 C3
100 STNL 7020 D6
Mallory Ln
10 OrgT 6164 B1
Mallow Rd
10 ERKY 6929 B7
Mallow St
10 STNL 7116 A6
100 STNL 7115 E5
Mallow Wy
- LWRN 7028 B5
Malone Av
10 HmpT 7028 D7
10 STNL 7117 D3
Malone Pl
600 HRSN 6714 A6
Maloon Av
800 HmpT 6828 B3
Malta St
10 BKLN 6924 D4
1300 HmpT 6827 E5
Malthusian Wy
- NWRK 6817 A1
Malvern Ln
10 NRCH 6282 A1
Malvern Rd
10 YNKR 6281 B1
100 GrbT 6281 B1
Malvern St
10 NWRK 6817 E2
100 NWRK 6818 A3
Malverne Av
10 MLVN 6929 B1
500 HmpT 6828 A7
Malvine Av
100 STNL 7115 D6
Malysana Ln
10 NRCH 6396 A6
Mamaroneck Av
10 WHPL 6168 C3
100 MRNK 6282 E5
300 HRSN 6282 E3
1200 SCDL 6282 D3
1200 WHPL 6282 D3
1700 MrnT 6282 E3
Mamaroneck Av SR-125
10 WHPL 6168 B2
Mamaroneck Av S
100 MRNK 6282 D4
100 MRNK 6283 A6
Mamaroneck Rd
10 SCDL 6167 E5
10 SCDL 6168 A6
200 SCDL 6282 B1
400 MrnT 6282 B1
Mamie Ct
10 SAMB 7205 A7
Manatauck Av
- FTLE 6611 E1
10 EDGW 6611 E1
Manatauk Av
10 EDGW 6611 E1
10 FTLE 6611 E1
Mance Ln
10 GrbT 6167 A7
Manchester Dr
10 STNL 7116 B5
Manchester Pl
10 NWRK 6713 E1
Manchester Rd
10 EchT 6281 C5
10 YNKR 6280 B4
Mandy Ct
10 STNL 7115 D7
Manee Av
10 STNL 7207 A2
Manger Cir
10 PLMM 6395 B7
Mangin Av
186-00 QENS 6826 B5
Mangin St
100 MHTN 119 E5
100 MHTN 6821 E3
Mangrove Rd
10 YNKR 6280 B6
Manhasset Av
10 MHVN 6508 C7
10 NHmT 6617 C6
10 PTWN 6508 C7
Manhasset Woods Rd
10 NHmT 6618 A6
300 FLHL 6617 E4
300 FLHL 6618 A5
300 MNPK 6617 E5
300 MNPK 6618 A5
Manhattan Av
10 BKLN 6822 B1
10 GrbT 6049 D7
10 HRSN 6169 D7
10 JSYC 6716 B6
10 MHTN 109 B5
10 MHTN 6612 A6
10 NRCH 6395 C5
10 NRCH 6396 A3
10 WbgT 7114 D2
10 YNKR 6280 E4
100 UNCT 6716 C5
100 YNKR 6281 A3
1000 BKLN 117 D7
1000 BKLN 6718 B7
4000 BKLN 7120 B1
Manhattan Av CO-683
1300 UNCT 6716 D4
Manhattan Br
- BKLN 121 A1
- BKLN 6821 C4
- MHTN 118 E6
- MHTN 119 A7
- MHTN 121 A1
- MHTN 6821 C3
Manhattan Ct
10 BKLN 7023 A7
Manhattan Pl
10 CLFP 108 A2
10 CLFP 6611 C5
10 NBgT 108 A2
Manhattan Pl
10 NBgT 6611 C5
Manhattan St
10 STNL 7206 B4
Manhattan College Pkwy
4400 BRNX 6393 B7
Manhattanville Rd
10 HRSN 6169 B3
Manida St
200 BRNX 6613 D4
Manila Av
10 STNL 7118 A4
300 JSYC 6820 C2
Manila Pl
10 STNL 7118 A4
Manilla St
51-00 QENS 6719 E7
51-00 QENS 6823 E1
Manitou Tr
10 GrbT 6049 E6
10 GrbT 6050 C6
Manley St
10 STNL 7115 C7
Manly Pl
10 NHmT 6723 E7
Mann Av
10 STNL 7019 D4
Mann Pl
- LWRN 7027 E4
10 HmpT 7029 E1
Manner Av
10 GRFD 6500 B1
Manning Av
10 JSYC 6820 A4
10 YNKR 6280 A6
Manning Cir
10 PLHM 6395 B5
Manning St
2200 BRNX 6505 C7
Manor Av
10 HRSN 6714 B6
10 NHmT 6724 D2
10 WHPL 6168 D7
200 WbgT 7114 C5
1000 BRNX 6614 A2
1100 BRNX 6613 E1
Manor Cir
1100 PLMM 6395 D7
Manor Ct
10 BKLN 7023 B7
10 NHmT 6724 A5
10 OLDT 6164 A3
10 STNL 7117 C2
Manor Ct S
10 NHmT 6724 A5
Manor Dr
10 LKSU 6723 B1
10 MplT 6816 A1
10 NHmT 6723 B1
10 NWRK 6712 B7
10 NWRK 6816 A1
10 YNKR 6280 E5
100 GrbT 6049 D5
1700 IrvT 6816 A4
1700 UnnT 6816 A4
N Manor Dr
10 GrbT 6049 D5
S Manor Dr
10 GrbT 6049 D6
Manor Ln
10 LRMT 6396 C2
10 LWRN 7028 A3
10 WDBG 7028 C2
100 PLMM 6395 B6
Manor Pl
10 DBSF 6166 B4
10 LRMT 6396 C2
10 NRCH 6395 E3
10 WbgT 7114 B2
10 WHPL 6168 D7
100 NHmT 6723 C1
3400 HmpT 7029 E1
Manor Rd
10 BRXV 6395 B1
10 ERTH 6609 C2
10 HmpT 6929 C2
10 LNBK 6929 C5
10 STNL 7019 D1
10 VLYS 6928 E4
100 GDNC 6828 A2
100 STMN 6828 A2
221-00 QENS 6826 D1
235-00 QENS 6722 C2
1200 STNL 7117 C1
Manor Ter
10 COrT 6712 C2
Manorhaven Blvd
10 MHVN 6508 B7
10 NHmT 6508 C7
Manor House Dr
10 DBSF 6166 B4
Manor House Ln
10 DBSF 6166 B5
Manor House Sq
10 YNKR 6393 C1
Manor House Sq SR-9A
10 YNKR 6393 C1
Manor House Sq US-9
10 YNKR 6393 C1
Manor Pond Ln
10 IRVN 6166 C2
Manor Ridge Rd
400 PLHM 6395 C6
400 PLMM 6395 C5
Manse St
67-00 QENS 6824 C4
Mansfield Av
200 SECS 6609 E7
200 SECS 6610 A7
Mansfield Pl
10 HmpT 6929 A6
10 LNBK 6929 A6
Mansfield Rd
10 WHPL 6168 E3
Mansion Av
10 STNL 7117 C6
10 YNKR 6394 B2
Mansion Ln
10 NHLS 6724 B1
Mansion St
1700 BRNX 6505 A7
Manton Pl
10 STNL 7020 D4
Manton St
83-00 QENS 6825 A4
Manufacturers Pl
10 NWRK 6818 C1
Manursing Av
10 RYE 6284 A2
Manursing Wy
- RYE 6284 C3
Mapes Av
10 NWRK 6816 E4
10 NWRK 6817 A4
1900 BRNX 6504 D6
Mapes Pl
10 NWRK 6817 A4
Mapes Ter
10 NWRK 6816 E4
Maple Av
- BKLN 7022 E3
10 BKLN 7120 B1
10 BRNX 6615 B3
10 CDHT 7028 B2
10 CLST 6278 B4
10 CRSK 6278 B6
10 DMRT 6278 B6
10 EchT 6281 B5
10 ELIZ 6917 E5
10 FLPK 6827 C3
10 GrbT 6048 D4
10 GrbT 6167 C3
10 HAOH 6165 E7
10 HmpT 7028 B2
10 HRSN 6283 B3
10 IrvT 6816 D3
10 LNBK 6929 A4
10 LNDN 7017 A2
10 LRMT 6396 C3
10 LWRN 7028 B2
10 NRCH 6395 E5
10 NWRK 6816 E4
10 PLHM 6395 C2
10 RKVC 6929 E4
10 RYE 6283 D2
10 SCLF 6509 E6
10 SHkT 6501 B4
10 STNL 6919 C7
10 TCKA 6281 B5
10 WHPL 6168 B2
100 HlsT 6816 D5
100 LNDN 6917 A7
100 MRNK 6282 E6
100 WLTN 6500 A6
131-00 QENS 6720 E5
134-01 QENS 6721 A5
200 FTLE 6503 A4
600 RDGF 6502 B7
E Maple Av
500 WbgT 7114 C4
N Maple Av
10 IrvT 6816 D1
200 EORG 6713 B2
S Maple Av
10 EORG 6713 A5
Maple Cir
100 NHmT 6723 E6
Maple Ct
10 NHmT 6723 E6
10 RYEB 6169 E4
10 STNL 7116 B5
100 EGLD 6503 A1
3500 HmpT 7029 D2
Maple Dr
- BRNX 6505 C7
10 FLHL 6618 C5
10 GTNE 6616 E7
10 GTNE 6617 A7
10 GTNE 6722 E1
10 GTPZ 6617 A7
10 NHmT 6724 A6
10 RYE 6284 A2
100 LODI 6500 D2
100 HmpT 6828 A3
W Maple Dr
10 NHmT 6723 E7
10 NHmT 6724 B6
Maple Ln
10 HAOH 6165 D6
10 NHmT 6723 E6
1000 NHmT 6724 B4
Maple Pkwy
10 STNL 7019 A1
Maple Pl
10 IrvT 6816 B3
10 MTVN 6394 E3
10 NHmT 6617 C7
10 NHmT 6723 A1
10 NHmT 6724 D2
10 NWRK 6816 E4
10 PTCH 6170 B5
10 YNKR 6394 B3
200 MNLA 6724 E5
700 HmpT 6828 C7
Maple Rd
10 HmpT 7027 C3
Maple St
10 BKLN 6923 C4
10 CART 7115 D1
10 DBSF 6166 A4
10 EchT 6281 C2
10 EDGW 103 A5
10 EDGW 6503 A6
10 EGLC 6392 B7
10 EMFD 6049 B6
10 ERTH 6500 A7
10 ERTH 6609 B1
10 GrbT 6049 D6
10 GrbT 6166 D2
10 GrbT 6167 D3
10 GRFD 6500 A3
10 GTNK 6616 E5
10 IRVN 6166 A1
10 JSYC 6820 A3
10 KRNY 6714 A5
10 LEON 6502 C4
10 LFRY 6501 C6
10 MLVN 6929 A1
10 MrnT 6396 D3
10 MtPT 6050 A2
10 NHLS 6618 D7
10 NHmT 6617 C2
10 NHmT 6618 D7
10 NRWD 6164 C7
10 OLDT 6164 A4
10 OybT 6618 E2
10 RDFP 6501 E6
10 ROSH 6618 E2
10 RTFD 6500 A7
10 RTFD 6609 A2
10 SYHW 6048 B1
Maple St
10 TFLY 6392 B4
10 TnkT 6501 E3
10 TnkT 6502 A3
10 YNKR 6393 D1
100 BGTA 6501 E3
100 EGLD 6502 E1
100 EGLD 6503 A1
100 FRVW 6611 B3
100 UNCT 6716 E3
100 WhkT 6716 E3
200 HmpT 6828 D6
200 MNCH 6501 B7
200 PTHA 7205 D4
200 SECS 6610 A6
1600 FTLE 6502 D5
E Maple St
10 MtPT 6050 A1
10 TnkT 6502 A3
10 VLYS 6928 E3
N Maple St
10 WbgT 7114 D1
S Maple St
10 WbgT 7114 A6
W Maple St
10 VLYS 6928 D3
Maple Ter
10 EORG 6713 A5
10 STNL 7118 B3
Maple Grove St
10 GTNK 6617 A5
Maple Hill Dr
10 MrnT 6282 C7
100 WbgT 7114 A5
Maple Hill Rd
10 MtPT 6049 E2
10 MtPT 6050 A2
Mapleleaf Ln
10 NHmT 6724 A5
Maplemoor Ln
10 WHPL 6168 E5
10 WHPL 6169 A5
Maple Ridge Ct
10 GrbT 6167 A7
Mapleton Av
10 STNL 7118 C2
Maplewood Av
10 BGTA 6501 E3
10 DBSF 6166 A6
10 STNL 7117 D2
10 WbgT 7114 A1
S Maplewood Av
10 WbgT 7205 A2
Maplewood Ln
10 PTCH 6170 B2
10 RYEB 6170 B2
Maplewood Pl
10 STNL 7118 B2
Maplewood Rd
10 ALPN 6278 C5
10 CLST 6278 C5
10 GrbT 6167 C2
Maplewood St
10 HmpT 6828 D5
10 MrnT 6282 B5
10 OybT 6618 E1
Mara Ct
1200 HmpT 7028 C7
Maracaibo St
10 NWRK 6818 B7
Maran Pl
600 BRNX 6505 A5
Marathon Pkwy
42-00 QENS 6722 E3
52-00 QENS 6723 A4
Marathon Pl
10 PTCH 6170 B5
Marble Pl
10 TCKA 6281 A6
Marble St
100 STNL 7019 C3
Marble Ter
10 HAOH 6165 E7
Marbledale Rd
10 TCKA 6281 A6
300 EchT 6281 A6
Marble Hill Av
10 MHTN 102 C4
10 MHTN 6504 B2
100 BRNX 102 D3
100 BRNX 6504 B2
Marbourne Dr
10 MrnT 6282 D3
Marbridge Rd
10 LWRN 7028 A3
Marc Dr
1000 HmpT 6928 B5
Marc St
10 STNL 7019 A2
Marcella Dr
1200 UnnT 6816 B6
Marcellus Rd
100 MNLA 6724 E6
400 WLPK 6724 D5
March Dr
1000 HmpT 6928 C1
March Ln
10 SNPT 6508 B4
Marco Av
10 YNKR 6394 B1
Marconi Pl
10 BKLN 6924 B2
Marcus Av
10 LKSU 6723 E4
10 NHmT 6724 C6
10 QENS 6723 C4
1600 NHmT 6723 D4
Marcus St
- JSYC 6819 D5
Marcus Garvey Blvd
300 BKLN 6923 D1
Marcy Av
10 EORG 6713 A1
10 JSYC 6819 C2
10 STNL 7116 A7
100 BKLN 6822 B5
300 BKLN 6923 C1
Marcy Pl
10 BRNX 105 B7
10 BRNX 6504 A7
Marden Av
10 SCLF 6509 E7
Mardon Rd
10 MrnT 6282 C7
Maren St
400 HmpT 6828 D6
Marengo St
86-88 QENS 6826 B2
Maretzek Ct
10 STNL 7206 E1
Margaret Av
10 LWRN 7028 A3
10 YNKR 6281 A4
Margaret Ct
10 BKLN 7023 B7
10 DMRT 6278 B4
10 GTNK 6616 E5
Margaret Dr
10 HmpT 6928 B1
Margaret Ln
10 LRMT 6396 D3
Margaret Pl
80-00 QENS 6824 C5
Margaret St
10 BAYN 6919 C5
10 GLCV 6509 E3
10 STNL 7117 A5
600 HmpT 6828 C4
Margaret Corbin Dr
- MHTN 104 C1
10 MHTN 101 D7
10 MHTN 6503 D4
Margaretta Ct
10 STNL 7019 D3
Margaretta St
10 NWRK 6818 B2
Margene Ct
300 NVLE 6164 C4
Margie Av
10 CRSK 6278 B7
Margie St
3400 HmpT 7029 C2
N Marginal Hwy
10 UNCT 6716 E3
10 WhkT 6716 E3
S Marginal Hwy
- WhkT 6716 E3
10 UNCT 6716 E3
Marginal Rd
10 HKSK 6501 C3
100 RTFD 6609 A3
1200 HmpT 7028 C7
N Marginal Rd
- JSYC 6820 D1
Marginal St
- MHTN 106 C5
- MHTN 116 E7
- MHTN 117 C1
- MHTN 119 E1
- MHTN 120 B3
- MHTN 6612 B3
- MHTN 6717 E7
- MHTN 6718 C4
- MHTN 6821 B5
Marginal St E
10 BKLN 6924 D1
Marginal St W
10 BKLN 6924 C1
Margo Lp
10 STNL 6920 E7
Margo Wy
10 ALPN 6278 E4
Margood Ct
10 ERTH 6500 A7
Margot Pl
10 GTNK 6616 E5
Marguerite Av
200 HmpT 6827 D4
200 SFPK 6827 D4
300 FLPK 6827 D3
Marguerite St
2000 FTLE 6502 E5
Maria Ln
10 GDNC 6724 E7
10 MNLA 6724 E7
10 STNL 7116 E5
10 YNKR 6281 A3
Mariane Ct
10 ALPN 6278 E5
Mariani Dr
10 LFRY 6501 B6
Marianna Dr
10 HAOH 6280 A2
10 YNKR 6280 A2
Marianne St
10 STNL 7019 C2
Marianne Ter
10 SECS 6610 B5
Marick Ct
700 HmpT 6827 E7
Marie Ct
10 HmpT 6827 B5
200 HmpT 6828 E6
Marie St
10 STNL 7020 D5
Marie Major Rd
10 ALPN 6278 E5
Marietta St
200 EGLC 6503 B3
Marilyn Dr
10 EGLC 6392 C5
Marin Blvd
10 JSYC 6820 C4
600 HBKN 6716 C7
600 JSYC 6716 C7
Marin Blvd CO-637
200 JSYC 6820 C1
600 HBKN 6716 C7
600 JSYC 6716 C7
Marina Dr
10 BAYN 6919 C4
10 BRNX 6615 B4
Marina Pl
10 ISPK 7029 D4
Marina Rd
10 ISPK 7029 D4
Marina Key Rd
10 SECS 6609 E7
Marina View Dr
10 WbgT 7115 A4
Marine Av
10 BKLN 7021 D3
Marine Ct
200 TnkT 6502 B2
Marine Dr
- STNL 7207 A3
Marine Pkwy
10 BKLN 7023 D3
Marine Rd
7700 NBgT 108 A5
7700 NBgT 6611 C6
Marine St
100 BRNX 6506 E7
Marine Ter
200 HlsT 6917 D2
Marine Wy
10 STNL 7118 B3
Marine Pkwy Gil Hodges Mem Br
- BKLN 7122 E2
- QENS 7122 E2
Mariners Ln
10 STNL 6919 B7
Mariners Wy
10 GLCV 6509 E4
Mariners Cove
10 EDGW 6611 E2
Marine Terminal Rd
- QENS 6719 E3
Marinette St
25-00 QENS 6722 D1
Marino Av
10 NHmT 6617 E3
10 NHmT 6618 A3
Marion Av
10 CLFP 6611 D1
10 GrbT 6167 C4
10 HAOH 6280 A2
10 HRSN 6283 B3
10 MTVN 6395 B3
10 NWRK 6712 C6
10 SOrT 6712 C6
10 STNL 7020 D1
10 YNKR 6280 A2
2300 BRNX 6504 D3
Marion Ct
10 BAYN 6919 D6
Marion Dr
10 NRCH 6281 E4
Marion Pl
10 ISPK 7029 D3
10 JSYC 6715 E7
10 JSYC 6819 E1
10 MTVN 6395 B3
10 WHPL 6168 B3
10 YNKR 6393 D4
10 RDGF 6611 A1
N Marion Pl
10 RKVC 6929 E4
S Marion Pl
10 RKVC 6929 E5
Marion St
10 BKLN 6923 E1
10 CART 7115 C2
10 ERKY 6929 B6
10 HKSK 6501 C2
10 HmpT 6929 A5
10 LNBK 6929 B6
10 LODI 6500 C1
10 STNL 7019 D1
10 WbgT 7115 C2
100 BKLN 6924 B1
400 TnkT 6502 B2
700 HmpT 6828 B6
Marion Pepe Dr
10 LODI 6500 C4
10 WRDG 6500 C4
Marisa Cir
10 STNL 7115 E7
Marisa Ct
10 STNL 7117 A1
Marisa Dr
10 YNKR 6281 A1
Marissa St
140-00 QENS 6927 C2
Maritime St
10 NWRK 6818 B6
Maritime Wy
10 BAYN 6919 B5
Marjorie Ct
10 HmpT 6928 C5
10 NHmT 6617 C7
10 TnkT 6502 C1
Marjorie Ln
- HmpT 7029 C1
10 HmpT 6929 C7
Marjorie St
10 STNL 7115 C7
Marjorie Ter
10 EGLC 6503 B1
Marjory Ln
10 SCDL 6168 B7
Mark Dr
10 RYEB 6169 E3
Mark Ln
10 HmpT 7028 C7
Mark Pl
1600 HmpT 6928 D1
Mark St
10 STNL 7020 C6
Market Ln
10 LKSU 6723 A3
10 NHmT 6723 A3
Market Pl
10 YNKR 6393 C1
500 NBgT 6716 E1
500 WNYK 6716 E1
Market Rd
- HmpT 6928 B3
- VLYS 6928 B3
Market St
10 MHTN 119 A7
10 MHTN 6821 C4
10 NWRK 6713 D7
10 PTHA 7205 C3
10 QENS 7122 B3
10 STNL 6919 E7
100 GRFD 6500 A1
200 NWRK 6817 E1
300 NWRK 6818 A1
Market St CO-510
10 NWRK 6713 D7
200 NWRK 6817 E1
E Market St
10 LBCH 7029 D6
N Market St
10 BKLN 6924 A6
S Market St
10 BKLN 6924 A6
W Market St
10 NWRK 6713 B6
10 QENS 7122 A4
100 LBCH 7029 A6
Marketfield St
10 MHTN 120 B2
10 MHTN 6821 B6
Market Slip
10 MHTN 119 A7
10 MHTN 6821 C4
100 MHTN 121 A1
Markham Cir
10 EGLD 6502 E3
Markham Dr
10 STNL 6919 E7
Markham Pl
10 STNL 7019 C3
Markham Rd
10 STNL 6919 E7
Markley St
10 WbgT 7114 E2
Markowitz St
10 CART 7115 B1
Marks Pl
100 NBgT 6611 C5
Markthaler Pl
400 ELIZ 6917 A3
400 ROSP 6917 A3
Markwood Pl
10 ARDY 6166 E5
77-00 QENS 6824 E4
Markwood Rd
10 ARDY 6166 E5
10 GrbT 6166 E5
Marlboro Ln
10 YNKR 6280 A4
Marlboro Rd
10 NHmT 6617 D7
10 NHmT 6618 C7
10 VLYS 6928 D6
100 HmpT 6928 D6
200 WRDG 6500 C5
Marlborough Ct
600 BKLN 6923 A7
600 BKLN 7023 A1
Marlborough Rd
10 BKLN 6923 A7
10 HmpT 6828 E4
300 CDHT 7027 C1
300 CDHT 7028 A1
10 YNKR 6280 A6
Marlene Ct
10 RYE 6283 D2
Marlette Pl
10 WHPL 6168 B4
Marlin Ln
10 PTWN 6508 D6
Marlin St
10 NWRK 6818 B6
Marlow Rd
10 VLYS 6928 B2
Marlowe Rd
10 HmpT 6928 C1
Marmion Av
1700 BRNX 6504 D7
Marne Av
10 STNL 7116 D4
Marne Pl
112-00 QENS 6826 A6
Marne St
10 NWRK 6818 B2
Marolla Pl
3600 BRNX 6505 D1
Marquand Av
10 YNKR 6394 D1
Marquand Pl
10 PLHM 6395 D7
Marrow St
10 NWRK 6713 C7
Mars Pl
125-00 QENS 6927 B1
Marsac Pl
10 IrvT 6816 B1
10 NWRK 6816 B1
Marsan Dr
300 CARL 6500 D7
Marscher Pl
10 STNL 7207 B3
Marsden Ct
400 HmpT 7029 D2
Marsden St
115-00 QENS 6825 E7
116-00 QENS 6826 A7
117-00 QENS 6927 A1
Marsellus Pl
10 GRFD 6500 B3
Marsh Av
10 STNL 7019 A7
100 STNL 7116 E1
Marsh St
10 NWRK 6818 B6
10 WbgT 7114 E4
Marshall Av
10 FLPK 6827 E2
10 LFRY 6501 C6
10 LNBK 6929 A4
10 STMN 6827 E2
10 STNL 7019 E5
200 HmpT 6828 D4
204-00 QENS 7122 A3
Marshall Ct
10 SOrT 6712 A6
10 THSN 6723 A1
Marshall Dr
10 BKLN 7021 D4
300 HBKN 6716 C7
Marshall Rd
- STNL 7021 A5
10 YNKR 6393 D3
Marshall St
- WbgT 7114 A2
10 ELIZ 6918 B4
10 HBKN 6716 C7
10 IrvT 6816 D1
10 KRNY 6714 A5
100 BKLN 121 C2
100 BKLN 6821 D5
1300 HmpT 6827 D4
Marshes Dock Rd
2600 LNDN 7017 C4
Marston Pl
10 YNKR 6394 B4
Martens Av
10 EORG 6712 E6
10 NWRK 6712 E6
10 VLYS 6928 B2
Martens Pl
10 MTVN 6394 C6
10 MTVN 6395 A4
Martense Av
100-00 QENS 6720 B7
Martense Ct
10 BKLN 6923 C5
Martense St
10 BKLN 6923 B5
Martha Av
4200 BRNX 6394 B6
4300 YNKR 6394 B6
Martha Ct
10 NWRK 6817 C1
Martha Pl
1100 HmpT 6827 E6
1100 HmpT 6828 A6
Martha St
10 STNL 7020 B3
600 HmpT 6827 C6
Martha Ter
10 FLPK 6827 D1
Martha Washington Wy
1900 FTLE 103 A4
1900 FTLE 6503 B5
Martin Av
100 STNL 7019 C5
Martin Ct
10 EGLC 6503 B1
10 EGLD 6503 B1
10 HmpT 6929 D7
10 KNGP 6616 C5
10 YNKR 6280 A7
2900 QENS 7027 B5
Martin Ln
10 LWRN 7028 A4
Martin Pl
10 IrvT 6816 C3
10 MNPK 6618 B6
10 PTCH 6170 C6
1000 HmpT 6928 D1
Martin Rd
- NWRK 6817 C6
10 RYE 6284 A3
10 YNKR 6280 B6
500 HmpT 6828 A7
Martin St
- BGTA 6501 E3
- TnkT 6501 E3
800 ELIZ 6918 A4
Martin St E
10 HmpT 6929 B7
Martin St W
10 HmpT 6929 B6
Martin Ter
10 WbgT 7114 C4
Martin Butler Ct
10 RYE 6283 E5
Martine Av
10 WHPL 6168 A2
Martineau St
10 STNL 6918 E7
Martin L King Pl
10 BKLN 6822 C6
Martin Luther King Jr Dr
10 JSYC 6819 D4
Martin Luther King Jr Plz
10 ELIZ 6917 B5
Martling Av
10 STNL 7019 E2
100 TYTN 6048 B4
Martling Pl
400 RDGF 6611 C2
Martool Dr
200 WbgT 7114 B4
Marvin Av
- LODI 6500 E1
10 RKVC 6929 E1
200 HKSK 6501 A1
Marvin Pl
- KNGP 6616 C4
10 BRNX 6505 C7
10 NRCH 6395 E5
Marvin Rd
10 STNL 7115 E7
Marwill Pl
10 NHmT 6618 D7
Marwood Ln
10 YNKR 6280 B7
Marwood Rd N
10 MHVN 6508 B6
Marwood Rd S
10 MHVN 6508 B7
Marx St
10 STNL 7020 A3
Mary St
10 CART 7017 C7
10 LODI 6500 C4
10 NWRK 6818 B2
10 OrgT 6164 D2
10 STNL 7020 C3
10 VLYS 6928 C2
100 HKSK 6501 A2
200 EGLD 6502 E1
600 PTHA 7205 C2
1000 ELIZ 6918 A2
1100 ELIZ 6917 E2
Mary Wy
10 WbgT 7114 D2
Mary Alice Ct
100 UnnT 6917 C1
Mary Ann Ln
400 HmpT 6929 D1
Maryann Wy
300 NVLE 6164 C4
Mary Fee Ln
10 WbgT 7205 B1
N Mary Frances St
10 OrgT 6164 B2
S Mary Francis St
10 OrgT 6164 B1
Maryland Av
10 LBCH 7028 E7
10 STNL 7021 A3
10 STNL 7020 E4
N Maryland Av
10 NHmT 6617 E1
S Maryland Av
10 NHmT 6617 C2
Maryland Ln
10 STNL 7020 D7
Maryland Pl
10 COrT 6712 C2
Maryland Rd
240-00 QENS 6722 D4
Maryland St
400 COrT 6712 B2
Marylin Ct
10 WLTN 6500 B5
Mary Lou Av
200 YNKR 6279 E5
Marymount Av
10 TYTN 6048 C3
Maryton Rd
10 GrbT 6049 E5
10 GrbT 6050 A5
Masefield Ln
10 GrbT 6167 B2
Masefield Wy
10 SDRK 6616 D5
Mason Av
200 STNL 7020 C7
500 STNL 7118 C1
Mason Blvd
10 STNL 7115 E6
10 STNL 7116 A6
Mason Ct
1000 HmpT 6929 C2
Mason Dr
10 FLHL 6617 E5
200 NHmT 6617 E6
Mason St
10 GrbT 6167 E1
10 NHmT 6723 E5
10 STNL 7020 B5
100 SAMB 7205 C7
Maspeth Av
10 BKLN 6822 E3
48-00 QENS 6823 A2
Massa Ln
10 EDGW 103 A5
10 EDGW 6503 A6
Massachusetts Av
10 HmpT 7029 E4
Massachusetts Blvd
10 BLRS 6827 B2
10 FLPK 6827 B2
10 QENS 6827 B2
Massachusetts St
10 STNL 7206 A4
Massachusetts St S
10 STNL 7206 A5
Massey St
10 LODI 6500 D2
Massitoa Rd
10 YNKR 6280 D5
Masters Sq
10 HlsT 6917 D1
Masterton Rd
10 BRXV 6394 A4
10 BRXV 6395 A1
Mathews Av
10 STNL 7020 A2
Mathews St
10 HRSN 6283 B2
Mathewson Ct
131-00 QENS 6927 C1
Mathias Av
161-00 QENS 6825 E7
Matilda Av
4300 BRNX 6394 C6
Matinecock Av
10 MHVN 6508 C7
10 MHVN 6617 C1
Matt St
10 WbgT 7114 D2
Mattausch Pl
10 GRFD 6500 A1
Matthew Av
10 CART 7115 D1
Matthew Pl
10 STNL 7019 A2
Matthew St
100 COrT 6712 C3
300 HmpT 7029 C1
Matthews Av
1600 BRNX 6505 B5
Matthews Ct
10 BKLN 6923 A6
Matthews Pl
10 BKLN 6924 E7
10 BKLN 7024 C1
Matthews St
200 NWRK 6713 C7
Matthewson Rd
10 BRNX 105 A3
10 BRNX 6504 E5
Matthiessen Pk
10 IRVN 6048 A7
Mattison Av
300 WbgT 7114 B5
Mattocks Pl
10 CLST 6278 A2
Maujer St
10 BKLN 6822 C4
E Maujer St
10 VLYS 6928 E3
Maul Pl
10 NRCH 6395 C4
Maul St
10 NRCH 6395 C4
Maurer Rd
10 PTHA 7114 D7
Maurer Rd CO-654
10 PTHA 7114 D7
Maurice Av
58-00 QENS 6823 B1
Mauro Ct
300 NVLE 6164 C4
Mauro Rd
300 EGLC 6503 B2
Mavis Pl
10 MNCH 6501 B7
Mawbey St
100 WbgT 7114 B4
Maxie Blvd
- BKLN 7024 C2
Maxie Ct
10 STNL 7020 C2
Maxine Ct
10 HmpT 6828 E6
Maxwell Av
10 MrnT 6396 D3
Maxwell Pl
1000 HBKN 6716 E6

New York City/5 Borough Street Index

STREET / Block City Map# Grid

Maxwell St
10 ERKY 6929 B6
10 JSYC 6820 B2
900 HmpT 6828 A4
May Av
10 STNL 7018 E3
10 STNL 7019 A3
700 PTHA 7114 B7
May Ct
10 HmpT 6828 E4
May Pl
10 PTCH 6170 B3
10 STNL 7116 D6
May St
10 IrvT 6816 C2
10 NRCH 6395 E4
10 NWRK 6713 E3
10 PTHA 7205 B1
10 WbgT 7205 B1
10 WLTN 6500 A5
10 YNKR 6280 D5
Maybaum Av
- EORG 6712 E5
10 NWRK 6712 E6
Mayberry Promenade
10 STNL 7208 A1
Maybrook Cir
10 EchT 6395 B2
Maybury Av
200 STNL 7117 C5
Maybury Ct
10 STNL 7117 C5
Mayda Rd
240-00 QENS 6927 E4
Mayer Ct
300 RDGF 6611 A2
Mayfair Av
10 FLPK 6827 B3
10 HmpT 6828 E4
200 GDNC 6828 E4
Mayfair Cir
10 HRSN 6169 D1
Mayfair Dr N
10 BKLN 7024 B4
Mayfair Dr S
10 BKLN 7024 B4
Mayfair Ln
10 FTLE 6611 E3
10 NHmT 6618 B6
Mayfair Rd
10 GrbT 6049 C5
10 NHmT 6723 E5
10 NHmT 6724 A5
10 YNKR 6280 A4
115-00 QENS 6824 D5
Mayfair Wy
10 GrbT 6049 D3
Mayfield Ln
10 HmpT 6928 B4
Mayfield Rd
171-00 QENS 6825 E3
900 HmpT 6928 B7
Mayfield St
10 RYE 6283 E4
Mayflower Av
10 MNLA 6724 D5
10 NHmT 6724 D4
10 NRCH 6395 D3
300 PLHM 6395 C3
1200 BRNX 6505 E7
1200 BRNX 6614 E1
Mayflower Dr
10 TFLY 6392 B5
10 YNKR 6280 E5
Mayflower Pl
10 FLPK 6827 D2
Mayflower Rd
10 SCDL 6282 C2
Mayforth Ter
10 DMRT 6278 A5
Mayhew Av
10 LRMT 6396 C2
Maynard St
10 TCKA 6281 A6
Mayo Av
10 GrwT 6170 E4
Mayville St
110-00 QENS 6826 B5
Maywood Av
10 RYEB 6170 A5
Maywood Rd
10 NRCH 6396 A1
300 NRCH 6282 A7
Mazeau St
57-00 QENS 6823 D2
Mazza Ct
10 STNL 7116 A4
Mazzoni Pl
9100 NBgT 6611 A4
McAdoo Av
10 JSYC 6819 C5
McAllister Pl
10 IrvT 6816 C4
McAlpin Av
10 NHmT 6724 D3
McArthur Av
10 STNL 7116 D5
10 YNKR 6281 B3
McArthur Rd
10 BKLN 7021 E4
McBaine Av
10 STNL 7115 E6
10 STNL 7116 A6
McBride Av
10 WHPL 6050 B6
McBride St
14-00 QENS 7027 C4
McCabe Ct
10 LFRY 6501 D7
McCain Ct
10 CLST 6278 D3
McCandless Pl
800 LNDN 6917 D6
McCandless St
10 LNDN 6917 A6
1500 ROSL 6917 A6
McCarter Hwy
200 NWRK 6817 D2
800 NWRK 6713 E7
1900 NWRK 6714 A2
2000 BlvT 6714 B1
McCarter Hwy SR-21
200 NWRK 6817 D2
800 NWRK 6713 E7
1500 NWRK 6714 A3
McCayan Memorial Br
- BGTA 6501 D1
- HKSK 6501 D1
McCayan Memorial Br CO-56
- BGTA 6501 D1
- HKSK 6501 D1
McChesney St
500 COrT 6712 A4
McClancy Pl
10 BKLN 6924 E3
McClean Av
10 STNL 7021 A5
100 STNL 7020 D6
McClellan Av
10 MNLA 6724 E5
10 WLPK 6724 E5
McClellan St
10 BRNX 6613 A1
10 NRWD 6164 A5
10 NWRK 6817 A7
200 PTHA 7205 D4
500 NVLE 6164 B4
McClellan Ter
10 WOrT 6712 A2
McClelland Av
10 DBSF 6166 A3
McClellen Av
200 MTVN 6395 B5
McClellen St
- NRWD 6164 B4
- NVLE 6164 B4
McCloud Dr
200 FTLE 6502 E6
McClure Av
1300 HmpT 6827 E5
McClure St
10 HRSN 6050 C4
10 NoCT 6050 C4
McCollum Pl
10 YNKR 6394 A5
McCormick Pl
10 STNL 7020 D6
McCullough Pl
10 RYE 6284 B2
McCully Av
10 STNL 7117 D1
McCurry Ln
10 EDGW 6611 E2
McDermott Av
10 STNL 7020 D6
McDivitt Av
10 STNL 7019 B6
McDonald Av
10 BKLN 6922 D5
800 BKLN 7022 E1
McDonald Ct
10 STNL 7206 A5
McDonald Pl
10 SCDL 6282 A2
McDonald St
10 STNL 7019 C5
1500 BRNX 6505 D5
McDougal Dr
10 NoCT 6050 B5
McDougall Ln
10 BGTA 6501 D2
McDougall St
10 JSYC 6819 E3
McElroy Av
200 FTLE 6502 E7
McGann Dr
10 RKVC 6929 E5
McGann Ln
- ISPK 7029 D4
McGeory Av
10 YNKR 6394 C1
McGillvray Pl
500 LNDN 6917 D6
McGlynn Pl
100 CDHT 7028 B2
McGotty Pl
10 IrvT 6816 C3
McGowan St
- BRNX 6615 D5
McGrath Dr
10 CRSK 6392 C2
McGraw Av
1800 BRNX 6614 A1
McGuigan Pl
400 HRSN 6714 B6
McGuiness Ln
10 WHPL 6169 A5
McGuinness Blvd
10 BKLN 6822 C1
300 BKLN 117 D7
300 BKLN 6718 B7
McGuinness Blvd S
10 BKLN 6822 C2
McGuire Pl
10 LODI 6500 D1
200 PTHA 7205 C3
McIntosh Ct
10 MLVN 6929 A1
McIntosh St
25-00 QENS 6720 A4
McIntyre St
10 YNKR 6280 E6
McKay Av
10 EORG 6712 C5
McKee Av
10 STNL 7117 C6
McKee St
10 FLPK 6827 E1
10 NHmT 6827 D1
100 FLPK 6723 D7
100 NHmT 6723 D7
McKeel Av
10 TYTN 6048 B2
McKeever Pl
10 BKLN 6923 B3
McKenna Dr
100 NRWD 6164 B7
McKenna Pl
10 MmT 6282 D6
McKenny St
10 BKLN 121 A2
10 BKLN 6821 D5
McKeon Av
- SAMB 7205 B6
10 VLYS 6928 C2
McKeon St
400 PTHA 7205 B2
McKibbin Ct
10 BKLN 6822 D5
McKibbin St
200 BKLN 6822 D5
McKinley Av
10 BKLN 6925 A1
10 CART 7115 C2
10 ERKY 6929 B5
10 HmpT 6828 B4
10 LNBK 6929 B5
10 LODI 6500 C3
10 MtPT 6050 A4
10 NHmT 6724 D3
10 STNL 7117 C3
10 WHPL 6167 E1
10 YNKR 6394 B1
100 HmpT 7029 C5
300 QENS 6925 B1
S McKinley Av
10 WbgT 7114 A2
McKinley Pl
10 ARDY 6166 D5
10 GLCV 6509 E3
6600 WNYK 6611 B7
McKinley St
10 BRXV 6281 A7
10 CLST 6278 B3
10 HKSK 6501 B2
10 TCKA 6281 A7
300 FRVW 6611 B4
300 HmpT 6828 C6
400 LNDN 6917 B5
600 ELIZ 6917 E6
McKnight Dr
10 GTNE 6616 E7
McLain St
900 ELIZ 6917 D4
McLaughlin Av
188-00 QENS 6826 A2
McLaughlin Pl
700 COrT 6712 A4
McLaughlin St
10 STNL 7020 E6
McLean Av
10 GrbT 6049 D7
10 YNKR 6393 D3
600 YNKR 6394 A5
1000 BRNX 6394 A5
McLean Pl
- HlsT 6816 B6
McLester St
800 ELIZ 6918 E3
2400 ELIZ 6919 A1
McLoughlin St
10 GLCV 6509 E4
McMahon Av
10 YNKR 6394 B2
McMartin Ct
10 JSYC 6819 A4
McMichael Pl
500 HlsT 6816 B6
McMurray St
2700 HmpT 6929 E6
McNeil Pl
300 MNLA 6724 E6
McNulty Pl
400 NHPK 6723 E7
McOwen Av
3400 BRNX 6395 A7
3400 BRNX 6506 B1
McPherson Pl
10 JSYC 6820 B1
McVeigh Av
10 STNL 7019 A7
McWhirter Rd
10 KRNY 6714 C3
McWhorter St
10 NWRK 6817 E2
McWilliams Pl
10 JSYC 6820 C2
Meacham Av
10 HmpT 6827 E6
600 LNDN 6917 D6
Mead Av
10 GrwT 6170 C6
Mead Pl
10 RYE 6283 E2
Mead St
10 JSYC 6715 D7
10 NWRK 6712 C7
10 SOrT 6712 A6
600 BRNX 6505 A7
Mead Wy
10 YNKR 6394 D1
Meadbrook Rd
10 GDNC 6828 C2
100 NHmT 6828 C1
Meade Dr
10 CLST 6278 C2
Meade St
10 COrT 6712 D1
10 STNL 7206 C2
10 WbgT 7114 E5
10 WOrT 6712 D1
100 PTHA 7205 C4
Meade Ter
300 UnnT 6917 A1
Meadon Ln
3600 NBgT 6716 D2
Meadow Av
- STNL 7019 E7
- STNL 7117 E1
10 BRXV 6280 E7
10 BRXV 6394 E1
10 STNL 7020 C5
Meadow Av W
10 YNKR 6280 D7
Meadow Cir
100 HmpT 6827 E7
Meadow Cswy
- LWRN 7027 E4
Meadow Ct
10 NRWD 6164 B5
10 STNL 7115 E5
Meadow Dr
10 GrwT 6170 E1
10 HmpT 7028 C2
10 LWRN 7028 C3
10 NHmT 6617 D3
10 NHmT 6724 E2
10 WDBG 7028 C2
Meadow Ln
10 HRSN 6169 C3
10 LWRN 7028 A3
10 NHLS 6724 B1
10 NHmT 6724 D1
10 NRCH 6395 E6
10 NRWD 6164 B5
10 STNL 7117 D5
100 NRCH 6396 A6
100 SECS 6610 A5
400 CARL 6610 B2
Meadow Pl
10 MmT 6396 C1
10 RYE 6169 E7
10 STNL 7118 B1
Meadow Rd
10 ERTH 6609 B3
10 HmpT 7027 D1
10 HRSN 6283 C2
10 LynT 6609 A4
10 RTFD 6609 B3
10 SCDL 6282 A4
177-00 QENS 6927 B3
Meadow Rd CO-55
10 ERTH 6609 B3
10 RTFD 6609 B3
Meadow St
10 BAYN 6919 E4
10 BKLN 6822 E4
10 CRSK 6278 B6
10 DMRT 6278 B6
10 EORG 6713 A2
10 HKSK 6501 C2
10 HRSN 6283 C4
10 TYTN 6048 C4
500 ELIZ 6918 A2
600 MRNK 6282 E4
600 ROSL 6917 A4
E Meadow St
10 TYTN 6048 C4
Meadow Wy
10 IRVN 6166 C1
10 LWRN 7028 B4
10 WHPL 6168 D6
Meadoway
10 DBSF 6166 B4
Meadowbrook Ln
10 VLYS 6928 D2
300 SOrT 6712 A5
Meadowbrook Pl
10 MplT 6816 A2
10 SOrT 6712 A6
10 YNKR 6279 C4
Meadowbrook Rd
10 IRVN 6048 B7
10 MplT 6816 A2
10 WHPL 6168 D2
100 EGLD 6502 E1
Meadowfarm Rd
10 NHmT 6724 A4
Meadowlands Pkwy
10 SECS 6609 E7
10 SECS 6610 B5
100 SECS 6715 C2
Meadowlands Plz
10 ERTH 6609 D5
Meadowlark Rd
10 RYEB 6169 E2
10 RYEB 6170 A2
Meadow Ln Ct
100 SECS 6610 C6
Meadowood Pth
10 NRCH 6282 A6
Meadows Ln
10 CLST 6278 C4
Meadow Sweet St
100 WLPK 6724 E5
Meadowview Av
- NBgT 6716 C3
100 HBPK 6928 D7
100 HmpT 6928 D7
100 HmpT 7028 D1
6700 NBgT 6610 D6
6700 NBgT 6611 B5
Meadowview Ct
10 LEON 6502 C4
Meadow View Dr
10 GrbT 6167 B4
Meadow Wood Dr
10 GrwT 6170 E4
Meadow Wood Ln
10 HRSN 6169 E6
Meadow Woods Rd
10 LKSU 6723 B2
Mead Pond Rd
10 RYE 6283 D2
Meagan Lp
10 STNL 7206 A3
Meagher Av
- BRNX 6615 C2
Meagher Pl
10 WLPK 6724 A6
Mechanic St
10 BAYN 6919 D3
10 BAYN 6920 A4
10 GLCV 6509 D3
200 COrT 6712 C3
300 PTHA 7205 E3
Mechanics Al
- MHTN 119 A7
- MHTN 6821 C4
Mechanics Av
10 TYTN 6048 B2
Meda Pl
10 WHPL 6168 C6
Medbourne Av
10 IrvT 6816 C3
Medford Ln
10 GrbT 6167 A7
Medford Rd
10 STNL 7020 B5
Medina St
10 STNL 7117 E4
Meehan Av
9-00 QENS 7027 D5
Meehan Ln
10 RKVC 6929 D4
Meeker Av
10 BKLN 6822 D2
10 NWRK 6817 A4
Meeker St
10 COrT 6712 A4
10 STNL 7117 C1
10 WOrT 6712 A4
200 SOrT 6712 A5
Meeting House Ln
10 RYEB 6051 D6
Mehrhof Ln
10 LFRY 6501 D6
Mehrhof Rd
10 LFRY 6501 D7
Mehrman Av
10 VLYS 6928 C2
Meinert Ln
- STNL 7019 E7
Meinzer St
10 WbgT 7114 D2
200 PTHA 7205 D1
Meisner Av
10 STNL 7117 D1
Meisser Av
700 HmpT 6828 B7
Melba Ct
10 BKLN 7023 E7
10 BKLN 7024 A7
Melba St
500 STNL 7019 D5
Melbourne Av
144-00 QENS 6825 A1
200 MRNK 6283 A5
400 MRNK 6282 C4
Melbourne Ct
10 WbgT 7114 D4
Melbourne Rd
10 RSLG 6723 A1
10 THSN 6723 B1
Meldon Av
10 NHmT 6724 D3
Melhorn Rd
10 STNL 7019 E6
100 STNL 7020 A4
Melissa Ct
207-00 QENS 6615 D6
Melissa Dr
10 GrbT 6166 D3
Melissa St
10 STNL 7019 A2
Mellon Pl
200 ELIZ 6917 D3
Melmore Gdns
10 EORG 6712 E3
Melrose Av
10 EORG 6712 C4
10 ERKY 6929 C5
10 GrwT 6170 E3
10 IrvT 6712 D7
10 LNBK 6929 C5
10 MTVN 6394 D3
10 NARL 6714 C1
10 NWRK 6712 D7
10 SRVL 7205 A6
10 STNL 7020 B3
10 YNKR 6280 D4
100 IrvT 6816 D1
500 BRNX 6613 A3
Melrose Dr
10 NRCH 6396 A1
Melrose Ln
234-00 QENS 6722 C2
Melrose Pl
10 STNL 7117 B6
Melrose St
10 BKLN 6822 D6
10 HmpT 6827 E4
E Melrose St
10 VLYS 6928 E3
W Melrose St
10 VLYS 6928 D3
Melrose Ter
10 ELIZ 6917 C2
10 UnnT 6917 C2
Melville Ln
10 SDRK 6616 D6
Melville Pl
10 IrvT 6816 C3
Melville St
10 STNL 7207 B3
1600 BRNX 6505 A7
Melville Ter
600 ROSL 6917 A5
Melvin Av
10 STNL 7018 B6
10 WbgT 7114 A3
200 HmpT 6929 D1
Melvina Pl
56-00 QENS 6823 B2
Melyn Pl
10 STNL 7019 B2
Memo St
10 STNL 7207 B3
Memorial Dr
- QENS 6824 D5
10 LODI 6500 C2
200 HlsT 6816 C5
Memorial Dr CO-61
10 LODI 6500 C2
Memorial Hwy
- NRCH 6395 E3
Memorial Ln
10 HRSN 6050 C3
10 NoCT 6050 C3
Memorial Pl
10 NHmT 6617 D6
Memory Ct
10 STNL 7020 E2
Memphis Av
10 SFPK 6827 D3
10 STNL 7116 D5
100 FLPK 6827 D3
240-00 QENS 6927 E3
250-00 QENS 6928 A4
Menahan St
10 BKLN 6823 A6
16-00 QENS 6823 B5
Mendelsohn St
10 STNL 7020 D7
Mendham Av
10 GrbT 6280 B1
Mendota Av
10 RYE 6169 E7
10 RYE 6283 D1
Mentone Av
225-00 QENS 6927 D3
Menzel Av
10 MplT 6816 A3
Merancou Av
1000 OrgT 6164 C2
Mercer Av
10 EGLC 6503 A3
10 GrbT 6167 D4
300 ROSL 6917 A4
Mercer Ct
10 NWRK 6817 C1
10 SCDL 6281 D1
Mercer Lp
300 JSYC 6820 A2
Mercer Pl
10 LODI 6500 D3
10 SOrT 6712 B7
10 STNL 7117 B6
Mercer St
10 CART 7115 D3
10 JSYC 6820 B3
10 MHTN 118 D5
10 MHTN 6821 B2
10 NWRK 6817 C1
10 WLTN 6500 A5
200 MHTN 119 A2
500 JSYC 6819 E2
Mercer St N
10 LODI 6500 C2
E Mercer St
10 HKSK 6501 C1
W Mercer St
10 HKSK 6501 C1
Merchant Pl
10 NWRK 6818 A2
Merchant St
10 NWRK 6818 A1
Mercia Ln
10 GrwT 6170 E4
Mercury Ln
10 STNL 7117 A1
Mercy College Dr
- DBSF 6166 A3
- IRVN 6166 A3
Mercy College Pl
10 BRNX 6505 B5
Meredith Av
10 STNL 7018 B5
900 ELIZ 6917 D5
Meredith Ln
200 HmpT 6828 D4
Meredith Pl
10 EchT 6395 B1
Meredith St
200 PTHA 7205 D2
Mereland Rd
10 NRCH 6281 D7
Mereline Av
10 WbgT 7114 D2
Merical St
- FRVW 6611 A3
Meridian Blvd
- QENS 7026 D7
Meridian Rd
- QENS 6720 D5
Meridian St
1100 ELIZ 6918 E2
Meridith Rd
10 DMRT 6278 B5
Meril Pl
- HmpT 7027 D4
Merill Pl
10 HmpT 7027 D3
Merillon Av
- NHmT 6724 C7
10 GDNC 6724 C7
10 GDNC 6828 C1
Merion Dr
10 HRSN 6050 E7
Merit Ct
10 BKLN 7023 E7
Merivale Ln
10 STNL 7020 E2
Merkel Pl
10 STNL 7117 E5
Merkle St
100 FTLE 103 B2
100 FTLE 6503 A5
Merle Av
10 HmpT 6929 D3
Merle Pl
10 STNL 7020 E4
Mermaid Av
10 BKLN 7120 C2
Merrall Dr
10 LWRN 7028 A3
Merriam Av
10 YNKR 6280 D7
1200 BRNX 104 E6
1200 BRNX 6503 E7
Merriam Pl
10 YNKR 6280 D7
Merrick Av
10 STNL 7020 A5
Merrick Blvd
103-01 QENS 6825 E5
111-01 QENS 6826 A7
122-01 QENS 6927 E1
240-00 QENS 6928 A2
245-00 VLYS 6928 A2
Merrick Ct
10 VLYS 6928 B2
Merrick Rd
10 LNBK 6929 A4
10 RKVC 6929 E4
600 LNBK 6928 E4
600 VLYS 6928 E4
E Merrick Rd
10 VLYS 6928 D3
200 LNBK 6928 E4
W Merrick Rd
10 VLYS 6928 B2
800 QENS 6928 A2
Merrick Close
10 YNKR 6280 C2
Merrifield Av
200 HmpT 6929 D7
Merrifield Wy
10 CRSK 6278 A6
Merrill Av
10 STNL 7018 E4
10 STNL 7019 A4
Merrill Ct
400 COrT 6712 C1
Merrill St
10 HAOH 6166 A7
119-00 QENS 6826 A7
119-61 QENS 6927 B1
1500 BRNX 6505 A7
1500 BRNX 6614 A1
Merriman Av
10 STNL 7019 D2
Merrison St
10 TnkT 6502 A1
Merritt Av
10 EchT 6281 B5
10 SCDL 6167 E4
10 WHPL 6167 E4
10 WHPL 6168 C4
100 ELIZ 6918 B5
3300 BRNX 6506 A1
3700 BRNX 6394 E7
3700 BRNX 6505 E1
Merritt Av W
10 GrbT 6049 A6
Merritt Ct
10 TFLY 6392 A1
Merritt Pkwy
- GrwT 6170 A1
- RYEB 6170 A1
Merritt Pkwy SR-15
- GrwT 6170 A1
- RYEB 6170 A1
Merritt Pl
10 YNKR 6281 A5
Merritt St
10 JSYC 6819 B7
10 PTCH 6170 A5
Merrivale Rd
10 LKSU 6723 B2
10 NHmT 6723 B2
10 RSLG 6723 A1
Merrivale Ter
10 LKSU 6723 B2
Merry Av
1300 BRNX 6506 A7
1400 BRNX 6505 E7
Merrymount St
10 STNL 7019 A7
300 STNL 7018 D7
Merrywood Dr
10 WOrT 6712 B1
Merseles St
200 JSYC 6820 B2
Mersereau Av
10 MTVN 6395 A4
10 STNL 6918 E7
400 STNL 7018 D1
Merton Av
10 LNBK 6929 D4
10 RKVC 6929 D4
Merton St
10 NRCH 6396 B3
Mertz Av
10 HlsT 6816 D5
W Mertz Av
100 HlsT 6816 D5
Mervin St
10 HmpT 7027 D3
Meryl Ln
10 GTNK 6616 D5
Meserole Av
10 BKLN 6822 C1
Meserole St
10 BKLN 6822 D4
500 BKLN 6823 A4
Messenger Ln
10 SNPT 6508 A6
Messick Av
3000 HmpT 6929 D7
3200 HmpT 7029 D1
Meta Ln
10 LODI 6500 E1
Metcalf Av
164-00 QENS 6721 C6
1000 BRNX 6614 A1
Metcalfe St
10 STNL 7020 C3
Metro Av
10 MNCH 6500 E7
Metro Rd
10 CARL 6610 A4
10 ERTH 6610 A4
Metro Wy
10 SECS 6715 E2
Metro Plaza Dr
- JSYC 6820 C2
Metroplex Rd
100 ELIZ 6918 C2
Metropolitan Av
- BKLN 6823 A3
10 STNL 7020 B1
46-00 QENS 6823 A3
75-01 QENS 6824 A4
123-07 QENS 6825 A5
1100 BKLN 6822 D3
1300 BRNX 6614 B1
1300 QENS 6822 E3
1500 BRNX 6505 B7
Metropolitan Ovl
10 BRNX 6505 C6
Metuchen Av
10 WbgT 7114 B5
Meuter Pl
600 RDGF 6611 B2
Mexico St
114-00 QENS 6826 B6
Meyer Av
10 HmpT 6927 E7
10 QENS 6927 E7
10 VLYS 6928 C2
10 YNKR 6394 D3
157-00 QENS 6825 E7
Meyer Ln
10 STNL 7020 D7
Meyers St
2900 BRNX 6614 D3
2900 BRNX 6615 B1
Mezzine Dr
10 CRSK 6278 A6
Michael Ct
10 RSLN 6618 D6
10 STNL 7117 A4
13-00 QENS 6615 D6
Michael Dr
10 NRCH 6281 E2
Michael Ln
10 NHmT 6723 D6
Michael Lp
10 STNL 7020 B4
Michael Pl
13-00 QENS 6615 D7
Michael St
10 HKSK 6501 B3
10 ShkT 6501 B3
Michael Frey Dr
10 EchT 6281 B5
Michaels Ct
100 WbgT 7114 A3
Michaels Ln
10 CLST 6278 A1
Michel Ct
10 MLVN 6929 A2
Michele Ct
10 CRSK 6278 B7
Michele Pl
300 CARL 6610 A3
300 ERTH 6610 A3
Michelle Ct
10 STNL 7019 A1
Michelle Ln
10 STNL 7118 A4
Michelle Pl
500 HmpT 6927 E6
500 HmpT 6928 A6
Michigan Av
10 HSBH 6500 E4
Michigan Rd
10 BLRS 6827 B2
10 HmpT 6827 B2
Michigan St
10 LBCH 7028 E7
10 PRMT 6165 A1
Micieli Pl
10 BKLN 6922 D6
Mickardan Ct
10 STNL 7020 E1
Mickey Spillane Wy
700 ELIZ 6917 E6
Mickle Av
3200 BRNX 6505 D2
Midchester Av
10 WHPL 6168 B4
Middagh St
10 BKLN 121 A3
10 BKLN 6821 C5
Middale Rd
10 WHPL 6168 D3
Middle Dr
10 PLDM 6617 D4
Middle Rd
10 BRXV 6281 A7
10 EchT 6281 B7
10 SNPT 6509 A7
10 WHPL 6168 C6
Middleboro Dr
10 YNKR 6280 B4
Middleburg Av
45-00 QENS 6719 A6
Middle Cross Ln
10 GLCV 6509 D2
Middle Hill Rd
10 WbgT 7114 A1
Middle Loop Rd
10 STNL 7116 E4
100 STNL 7117 A3
Middlemay Cir
10 QENS 6824 D3
Middlemay Pl
103-00 QENS 6824 E2
Middle Neck Rd
10 FLHL 6618 C5
10 GTNE 6617 A7
10 GTPZ 6617 A7
10 KENS 6617 A7
10 NHmT 6508 A4
10 ROSE 6618 C6
10 SNPT 6508 A4
100 GTNE 6616 E6
100 KENS 6616 E6
100 NHmT 6616 E6
200 GTNK 6616 E4
800 KNGP 6616 E4
1400 PTWN 6508 E6
Middle Neck Rd S
10 GTPZ 6617 A7
10 THSN 6617 A7
100 GTPZ 6723 B1
100 LKSU 6723 B1
100 NHmT 6723 B1
100 RSLG 6723 A1
100 THSN 6723 A1
Middlesex Av
10 CART 7115 D3
100 EGLC 6503 B3
200 EGLD 6503 A2
E Middlesex Av
400 WbgT 7114 C4
Middlesex Ln
10 YNKR 6280 B4
Middlesex St
200 HRSN 6714 A7
500 LNDN 6917 A6
Middleton Pl
10 EchT 6281 B7
Middleton Rd
10 GDNC 6828 B3
Middleton St
10 BKLN 6822 B5
Middletown Rd
2800 BRNX 6505 E7
3100 BRNX 6506 A6
Middleway
10 GrbT 6166 E3
Midfield Rd
700 HmpT 7028 D3
Midgely Dr
100 HmpT 6928 D7
Midland Av
10 BRXV 6280 E7
10 BRXV 6281 A7
10 BRXV 6394 E1
10 EORG 6712 E1
10 GRdT 6712 E1
10 GRFD 6500 A4
10 KRNY 6714 C3
10 MTVN 6394 E1
10 PTCH 6170 B6
10 RYE 6284 A1
10 STNL 7118 A1
10 WHPL 6168 A3
10 WLTN 6500 A4
10 YNKR 6393 E4
100 TCKA 6281 A6
100 TYTN 6048 C3
200 EchT 6281 A7
200 SdBT 6500 B3
300 RYE 6170 B7
1000 YNKR 6394 C1
Midland Av CO-67
10 GRFD 6500 A4
200 SdBT 6500 B3
Midland Av CO-507
10 GRFD 6500 A4
10 WLTN 6500 A4
Midland Av E
10 KRNY 6714 C3
N Midland Av
10 KRNY 6714 B2
S Midland Av
10 KRNY 6714 B3
Midland Blvd
10 MplT 6816 A1
10 UnnT 6816 A7
Midland Ct
200 WNYK 6611 C7
Midland Dr
10 NHmT 6724 A5
Midland Gdns
10 BRXV 6394 E1
Midland Pkwy
83-00 QENS 6825 E3
184-00 QENS 6826 A2
Midland Pl
10 NWRK 6712 B7
10 TCKA 6281 A6
100 MplT 6816 B1
100 NWRK 6816 B1
Midland Rd
10 STNL 7117 B5
Midland Ter
10 YNKR 6394 A3
Midland Av Byp
- YNKR 6394 B1
Midtown Bridge Pl
- HKSK 6501 C2
Midtown Bridge Appr St
10 HKSK 6501 C1
Midtown Bridge Appr St CO-56
10 HKSK 6501 C1
Midvale Ct
10 GrbT 6167 C5
Midvale Ln
1100 HmpT 6928 E1
Midvale Rd
10 GrbT 6167 C5
Midway
900 HmpT 6928 B6
Midway Ct
1100 HmpT 6828 A7
Midway Pl
10 STNL 7020 B6
Midway Rd
10 GrbT 6167 D1
Midwood Av
10 YNKR 6280 A5
Midwood Dr
10 GrwT 6170 D1
Midwood Rd
10 NVLE 6164 B4
10 RKVC 6929 E1
100 TnkT 6502 B1
300 HmpT 6928 C7
Midwood St
10 BKLN 6923 D4
10 VLYS 6928 B3
Mijack Ct
500 CARL 6610 A2
Mikasa Dr
10 SECS 6715 E2
Milano Ct
10 ShkT 6501 D4
Milbank Rd
10 STNL 7118 B3
Milbar Hth
10 HmpT 6928 E6
10 HWTH 6928 E6
Milburn Ct
10 HmpT 6929 E2
10 VLYS 6929 E2
Milburn Rd
10 HmpT 6928 E1
10 VLYS 6928 E1
10 VLYS 6929 A1
1000 HmpT 6929 E2
Milburn St
10 BRXV 6280 D7
10 STNL 7117 D1
121-00 QENS 6826 C7
123-00 QENS 6927 C1
Milburn St Ext
100 BRXV 6280 B3
Milden Av
10 STNL 7020 B4
Mildred Av
10 RYE 6283 D4
10 STNL 7018 C6
1500 LNDN 6917 C6
Mildred Ct
10 FLPK 6827 E2
Mildred Pkwy
10 NRCH 6281 D5
Mildred Pl
10 ERKY 6929 A6
Mildred St
10 YNKR 6394 B2
500 TnkT 6502 A2
Mileed Wy
10 WbgT 7017 A6
Miles Av
10 NHmT 6724 D3
10 STNL 7117 B4
10 WHPL 6168 B5
2500 BRNX 6615 A3
Miles St
10 ALPN 6278 D6
Mile Square Pl
10 YNKR 6394 C3
Mile Square Rd
10 YNKR 6280 B7
700 YNKR 6394 B2
Miles Standish Cir
10 PTCH 6170 C3
Milestone Rd
- GrbT 6049 E5
10 RYEB 6051 E5
Mileview Av
10 WHPL 6168 B5

New York City/5 Borough Street Index

STREET
Block City Map# Grid

Milford Av
10 NWRK 6817 C3
10 STNL 7020 B4
Milford Dr
10 SCDL 6168 A5
10 STNL 7020 A4
10 WHPL 6168 A5
Milford Ln
1100 HmpT 6928 C1
Milford Pl
10 RKVC 6929 E3
Milford St
10 BKLN 6924 E1
200 BKLN 6925 A3
Milford Close
10 WHPL 6168 B5
Milik St
200 CART 7017 A7
200 WbgT 7017 A7
Mill Av
10 BKLN 7024 A3
Mill Ct
10 ARDY 6166 D4
E Mill Dr
10 NHmT 6722 E2
10 NHmT 6723 C2
W Mill Dr
10 NHmT 6722 E2
Mill Ln
5600 BKLN 7024 A3
Mill Rd
- HlsT 6816 B4
10 EchT 6281 C5
10 IrvT 6816 A3
10 JSYC 6820 A2
10 NRCH 6281 B5
10 STNL 7118 A3
100 HmpT 6928 D6
100 UnnT 6816 A3
100 VLYS 6928 C4
400 STNL 7117 E5
2600 BKLN 7022 D7
Mill St
10 BKLN 6922 B2
10 BlvT 6714 A1
10 GrwT 6170 C5
10 LODI 6500 E1
10 PTCH 6170 C5
10 YNKR 6393 C1
200 HmpT 7027 E3
300 BlvT 6713 E1
Mill St CO-672
10 BlvT 6714 A1
Millard Av
10 YNKR 6280 C6
200 HlsT 6816 C6
Millay Ct
10 TnkT 6502 C2
Millbrook Av
10 TYTN 6048 C4
Mill Brook Cir
- ALPN 6278 D2
10 NRWD 6278 D2
Millbrook Ct
10 GTNK 6616 E6
Mill Creek Dr
10 SECS 6610 B7
Millenium Pl
10 RYEB 6051 D5
Millennium Lp
10 STNL 7115 E5
Miller Av
10 BKLN 6924 D3
10 FLPK 6827 C3
10 SFPK 6827 C3
10 TYTN 6048 B3
2600 HmpT 6929 E6
Miller Pl
10 BKLN 6924 D1
10 NHmT 6618 E7
10 VLYS 6928 C2
10 YNKR 6280 C2
100 MTVN 6395 A6
Miller St
10 GLCV 6509 E3
10 JSYC 6819 C3
10 NWRK 6817 C3
10 STNL 7019 D2
10 WLTN 6500 B6
32-00 QENS 6720 E3
100 ELIZ 6918 B4
300 PTHA 7205 E3
Miller Ter
10 GrbT 6049 E7
Millers Cross
10 TFLY 6392 C2
Millers Ln
10 NHPK 6828 A1
Milligan Pl
10 SOrT 6712 A6
Millington Av
10 NWRK 6816 D2
10 NWRK 6817 A3
Millington Pl
10 MNLA 6724 D7
Millington St
10 MTVN 6395 A5
Millison Close
10 YNKR 6280 D7
Millo Ct
10 LFRY 6501 C5
10 SHkT 6501 C5
Millo Pl
10 LFRY 6501 C4
Mill Pond Ln
10 NRCH 6396 A6
Mill Pond Rd
10 CLST 6278 D2
10 NHmT 6508 D7
10 PTWN 6508 D7
10 PTWN 6617 D1
Millridge Rd
10 SECS 6610 C5
Mill River Av
10 ERKY 6929 C5
10 RKVC 6929 D5
Mills Av
10 NRWD 6164 A6
10 STNL 7020 E6
10 STNL 7021 A6
Mill Spring Rd
10 NHmT 6618 A6
Millstone Ct
10 STNL 7116 E2
Milos Wy
10 WbgT 7115 A3
Milton Av
10 JSYC 6716 B6
10 STNL 7118 B3
10 WbgT 7114 C5
E Milton Av
800 RHWY 7017 A4
Milton Ct
10 PTCH 6170 C5
10 RTFD 6609 A1
Milton Pl
10 SOrT 6712 B7
800 HmpT 7028 B1
2900 BRNX 6615 B3
Milton Rd
- RYE 6284 A2
10 RYE 6283 E3
Milton St
10 BKLN 6822 B1
10 CRSK 6278 B7
10 GrbT 6167 A2
10 LNBK 6929 A3
Mimosa Dr
10 EHLS 6618 E6
Mimosa Ln
10 SNPT 6509 A5
10 STNL 7116 A5
Mina Dr
10 JSYC 6819 B5
Minden Rd
10 GLCV 6509 E1
Minell Pl
10 TnkT 6502 B1
Mineola Av
- NHmT 6618 D7
10 FLHL 6618 C6
10 ROSE 6618 D6
10 RSLN 6618 D6
E Mineola Av
10 VLYS 6928 D4
200 LNBK 6928 E4
W Mineola Av
10 VLYS 6928 D3
Mineola Blvd
10 GDNC 6724 E7
10 MNLA 6724 E6
300 WLPK 6724 D5
Miner Ter
300 LNDN 7017 A1
Minerva Dr
10 YNKR 6280 D4
Minerva Pl
10 BRNX 6504 D3
10 STNL 6920 C6
10 WHPL 6168 C1
Minerva St
10 JSYC 6819 E4
Minetta Ln
10 MHTN 118 D2
10 MHTN 6821 E5
Minetta Pl
10 YNKR 6280 B2
Minetta St
10 MHTN 118 D2
10 MHTN 6821 E5
Minford Pl
1400 BRNX 6613 D1
Minna Av
10 WbgT 7114 B1
Minna St
10 BKLN 6922 D6
10 STNL 7020 C6
Minnesota Av
10 LBCH 7028 E7
Minnewaska Dr
10 YNKR 6280 E5
Minnie Pl
600 SECS 6610 A7
Minnieford Av
200 BRNX 6506 E6
Minthorne St
10 STNL 6920 E7
Minton Pl
300 COrT 6712 B3
Minton St
13-00 QENS 7027 D4
Minturn Av
- STNL 7115 E7
10 STNL 7207 A1
Minturn Rd
10 TCKA 6280 C3
Minturn St
10 HAOH 6165 E6
Minue St
10 CART 7017 B7
Minute Arms Rd
200 UnnT 6917 A1
300 UnnT 6816 C7
Minuteman Cir
10 OrgT 6164 A1
Miriam Ct
1500 HmpT 6827 D6
Miriam Pkwy
10 HmpT 6827 D7
Miriam Pl
1200 HlsT 6816 D6
Miriam St
10 VLYS 6928 E5
200 BRNX 6504 D3
Mirrielees Cir
10 GTNE 6722 E1
Mirrielees Rd
- GTPZ 6722 E1
10 GTNE 6722 E1
Mission Wy
10 TFLY 6392 B4
Missouri Ln
10 STNL 7021 A6
Mistletoe Ln
10 RYE 6284 B2
Mistletoe Wy
400 LWRN 7028 B4
Mitchell Av
10 YNKR 6280 B7
100 LBCH 7029 E7
300 LNDN 7017 A1
Mitchell Dr
10 KNGP 6616 E2
Mitchell Pl
10 GrwT 6170 B3
10 MHTN 117 B3
10 MHTN 6718 A5
10 NHmT 6617 D7
10 NWRK 6817 A6
10 PLMM 6395 C6
10 PTCH 6170 B3
10 WbgT 7114 C1
10 WHPL 6168 C3
400 PTHA 7205 B2
3000 BRNX 6615 C4
Mitchell Rd
10 NHmT 6617 E2
Mitchell St
10 COrT 6712 A2
10 LODI 6500 D1
10 WOrT 6712 A3
Mitchie Dr
10 WHPL 6168 A3
Mittman Rd
10 HRSN 6169 C4
Mobile Av
10 STNL 7117 D2
10 WbgT 7114 B4
Mobile Rd
7-00 QENS 7027 D5
Moffat St
10 BKLN 6823 B7
10 BKLN 6924 B1
200 QENS 6823 C6
Moffett St
10 STNL 7116 D6
10 WbgT 7205 A1
Moffitt Av
1400 HmpT 6928 E6
Mohawk Av
10 HmpT 7028 D7
10 NRWD 6278 D1
100 NRWD 6164 D7
Mohawk Rd
10 YNKR 6280 D6
Mohawk Rd E
500 HmpT 6929 C1
Mohawk Rd W
500 HmpT 6929 D2
Mohawk St
10 HlsT 6816 C5
10 NWRK 6818 B7
10 RYE 6169 E7
Mohawk Tr
10 GrbT 6049 E6
Mohegan Av
10 MHVN 6508 C7
1800 BRNX 6504 D7
Mohegan Ln
10 RYEB 6169 E3
Mohegan Pl
10 NRCH 6281 E3
10 NRCH 6282 A3
Mohegan Rd
10 MrnT 6282 C6
Mohegan Wy
200 FTLE 6502 E6
Mohican Ln
10 GrbT 6048 C6
Mohican Tr
10 SCDL 6167 A7
Mohican Park Av
10 DBSF 6166 B4
Mohn Pl
10 STNL 7020 B4
Molinari St
10 MNCH 6501 C7
Moline Ct
10 KNGP 6617 A4
Moline St
88-00 QENS 6827 A1
89-00 QENS 6826 E1
Moller St
10 SECS 6716 A3
10 TFLY 6392 A3
Molter Pl
10 BlmT 6713 B1
Molyneaux Rd
10 HmpT 6928 C1
10 VLYS 6928 C1
Momm Ct
10 IrvT 6816 B2
Monaco Av
10 HmpT 6827 C6
Monaco Pl
10 BKLN 6924 B2
Monahan Av
10 STNL 7019 A6
Monastery Pl
300 UNCT 6716 D3
300 WhkT 6716 D4
Money St
10 LODI 6500 D2
Monfort Rd
10 NHmT 6618 A1
Monica Ct
10 BKLN 7023 A7
Monica Rd
10 GrwT 6170 C3
Monitor Pl
100 WNYK 111 C1
6000 WNYK 6611 B7
Monitor St
10 BKLN 6822 D2
10 JSYC 6820 A4
Monmouth Av
1100 LNDN 6917 B6
Monmouth Ct
10 OrgT 6164 A1
Monmouth Rd
10 ELIZ 6917 B3
300 UnnT 6917 C2
Monmouth Rd CO-618
10 ELIZ 6917 B3
Monmouth St
- EGLD 6502 E2
- EGLD 6503 A2
10 NWRK 6817 C2
100 JSYC 6820 B3
Monnett St
10 LFRY 6501 B5
Monona Av
10 RTFD 6500 A7
Monroe Av
10 CART 7017 C7
10 CRSK 6278 A7
10 EORG 6713 A2
10 LRMT 6396 D2
10 STNL 6920 D6
400 ELIZ 6918 A1
1000 ELIZ 6817 B7
1600 BRNX 105 D6
1600 BRNX 6504 B7
Monroe Blvd
10 LBCH 7029 D7
Monroe Dr
10 WHPL 6168 E4
Monroe Ln
900 HWTN 7028 D2
Monroe Pl
10 BKLN 121 A4
10 BKLN 6821 C6
10 GrbT 6049 E6
10 PTCH 6170 A5
10 RYEB 6170 A5
10 STNL 7019 D5
10 YNKR 6393 D4
500 RDGF 6611 C2
6000 WNYK 6611 A7
Monroe St
- MHTN 119 C7
10 BKLN 6822 E7
10 BKLN 6923 B1
10 BRNX 6506 C1
10 BXTE 6617 E1
10 GDNC 6828 B2
10 GRFD 6500 A3
10 HBKN 6716 D6
10 HmpT 6828 B4
10 HmpT 7027 D3
10 HSBH 6500 D3
10 LFRY 6501 C7
10 LNBK 6929 C4
10 LODI 6500 D3
10 LWRN 7028 A4
10 MHTN 118 E7
10 MHTN 6821 D5
10 MTVN 6394 E5
10 NHmT 6617 E2
10 NRCH 6396 A4
10 NWRK 6818 A2
10 PASC 6500 A3
10 PLMM 6395 C7
10 PLMM 6506 C1
10 QENS 7027 D3
10 RKVC 6929 C4
10 TCKA 6281 A5
10 TYTN 6048 B4
10 YNKR 6280 B5
100 MTVN 6395 A5
100 RSLN 6917 A4
200 LNDN 7017 C3
300 CARL 6500 C7
300 ERTH 6500 B7
400 CDHT 7028 A1
400 COrT 6712 B2
600 WRDG 6500 C7
700 BRNX 6823 A7
1300 HmpT 6827 E3
Monroe St CO-57
300 CARL 6500 B7
300 ERTH 6500 B7
600 WRDG 6500 C7
Monrovia Blvd
10 YNKR 6281 A2
Monsey Pl
10 STNL 7019 B2
Monsignor Halpin Pl
2900 BRNX 6615 B3
Monsignor Kemezis Pl
200 ELIZ 6918 D5
Montague Av
10 WbgT 7114 A3
Montague Pl
- JSYC 6820 D1
10 YNKR 6279 E5
100 SOrT 6712 A7
200 MplT 6712 A7
Montague St
10 BKLN 120 E5
10 BKLN 121 A5
10 BKLN 6821 B6
10 YNKR 6279 C5
N Montague St
10 VLYS 6928 C2
S Montague St
10 VLYS 6928 B3
Montague Ter
10 BKLN 120 E5
10 BKLN 6821 B6
Montammy Rd
- ALPN 6392 D2
- CRSK 6392 D2
- TFLY 6392 D2
Montana Pl
10 BKLN 7024 C4
Montauk Av
10 BKLN 6924 E2
500 BKLN 6925 A3
Montauk Ct
10 BKLN 7023 A7
Montauk Pl
10 STNL 7019 B4
Montauk St
100 VLYS 6929 A2
118-00 QENS 6826 B7
122-00 QENS 6927 C1
Montclair Av
10 NWRK 6714 A2
100 NWRK 6713 E1
Montclair Pl
10 YNKR 6280 D4
Montclair Rd
10 YNKR 6280 D4
Monte Pl
10 MNCH 6501 B7
Monteith Av
10 BlvT 6713 D2
10 NWRK 6713 D2
Montell St
10 STNL 7019 C1
Monterey Av
10 STNL 7116 D4
10 TnkT 6502 B1
100 FTLE 6395 C5
300 PLMM 6395 C5
1900 BRNX 6504 D6
Monterey Dr
10 MTVN 6395 B2
10 NHmT 6723 E4
10 NHmT 6724 A4
Monterey Pl
10 YNKR 6280 E1
Monterey St
107-00 QENS 6826 E4
Montgomery Av
10 EchT 6281 C2
10 EMFD 6049 C5
10 GrbT 6049 C4
10 HmpT 7029 D1
10 IrvT 6816 E2
10 NWRK 6816 E2
10 STNL 6920 D7
10 YNKR 6280 B6
1400 BRNX 105 A4
1400 BRNX 6504 A6
Montgomery Blvd
10 ATLB 7028 A7
Montgomery Cir
10 NRCH 6395 E1
Montgomery Pl
10 BKLN 6922 E2
10 NRCH 6395 E2
300 ELIZ 6917 C6
1700 BRNX 6505 C6
Montgomery Rd
10 SCDL 6281 D1
Montgomery St
10 BKLN 6923 B3
10 HlsT 6816 C5
10 JSYC 6820 B3
10 MHTN 119 C6
10 MHTN 6821 D4
10 NWRK 6817 C1
600 ELIZ 6917 E4
700 JSYC 6819 E2
N Montgomery St
10 VLYS 6928 C3
S Montgomery St
10 VLYS 6928 C3
Monticello Av
10 JSYC 6819 E3
10 NWRK 6712 C6
200 JSYC 6820 A2
4400 BRNX 6394 D5
4600 MTVN 6394 D5
Monticello Ter
10 STNL 7117 B6
Montieth St
10 BKLN 6822 D5
Montreal Av
100 STNL 7117 D4
Montrose Av
10 BKLN 6822 C4
10 JSYC 6716 B7
10 SOrT 6712 B5
W Montrose Av
10 SOrT 6712 A4
Montrose Ct
10 ROSH 6618 E3
Montrose Dr
10 ROSH 6618 E3
Montrose Rd
10 SCDL 6167 E4
10 YNKR 6280 D4
Montrose St
10 NWRK 6712 B7
10 SOrT 6712 C6
Montrose Ter
10 IrvT 6712 E7
Montross Av
10 ERTH 6500 A7
10 RTFD 6500 A7
10 RTFD 6609 A1
Montross St
10 WHPL 6050 B6
Mont Sec Av
10 STNL 7021 A4
Montvale Pl
10 STNL 7117 A5
Monument Wk
10 BKLN 121 D4
10 BKLN 6821 E6
Moody Pl
10 STNL 6920 A7
Moonachie Av
10 CARL 6610 A1
10 MNCH 6500 D7
10 MNCH 6610 A1
10 WRDG 6500 D7
10 WRDG 6501 A7
Moonachie Av CO-36
10 CARL 6610 A1
10 MNCH 6500 D7
10 MNCH 6610 A1
100 MNCH 6501 A7
500 WRDG 6500 D6
Moonachie Rd
10 HKSK 6501 C4
10 LFRY 6501 C7
10 MNCH 6501 B7
100 MNCH 6610 B1
200 CARL 6610 B1
400 SHkT 6501 C4
Moonachie Rd CO-503
10 HKSK 6501 C4
10 LFRY 6501 C7
10 MNCH 6501 B7
100 MNCH 6610 B1
200 CARL 6610 B1
400 SHkT 6501 C4
E Moonachie Rd
10 HKSK 6501 D4
E Moonachie Rd CO-503
10 HKSK 6501 D4
Mooney Pl
10 YNKR 6393 E1
Moonlight Ct
10 STNL 7019 E3
Moore Av
10 HmpT 7029 E1
10 LEON 6502 C5
10 WbgT 7114 D5
Moore Pl
10 NARL 6714 D1
500 LNDN 6917 A7
1600 BKLN 7023 B4
Moore Plz
4300 BRNX 6394 C7
Moore Rd
10 YNKR 6280 D7
Moore St
10 BKLN 6822 C5
10 GrbT 6167 B2
10 HKSK 6501 C1
10 MHTN 120 B2
10 MHTN 6821 B6
10 NHmT 6724 C4
10 STNL 7117 C2
100 FTLE 6503 A3
800 HmpT 6928 A7
N Moore St
10 MHTN 118 C5
10 MHTN 6821 E4
Moorland Dr
10 GrbT 6167 A6
Mopsick Av
900 LNDN 7017 B2
Moquette Row N
10 YNKR 6279 D7
Moquette Row S
10 YNKR 6279 D7
Mora Ct
10 NHmT 6617 C6
Mora Pl
1000 HmpT 6928 C7
Moran Pl
10 MrnT 6396 B3
10 NRCH 6396 B3
Morani St
10 STNL 7019 A4
Moravian Av
- STNL 7019 E7
- STNL 7117 E1
Morea St
400 HmpT 7029 D1
Morehead Dr
10 RYE 6283 D3
Moreland Ct
10 GTNK 6616 D4
Moreland St
10 STNL 7118 B2
10 YNKR 6394 D1
Morenci Ln
50-00 QENS 6722 E3
50-50 QENS 6723 A3
Morewood Oaks
- MHVN 6508 C6
10 NHmT 6508 C6
Morgan Av
10 BKLN 6822 D2
10 GrwT 6170 C2
2200 BRNX 6505 D4
Morgan Ct
10 PLNM 6617 D3
Morgan Ln
10 STNL 7018 E3
Morgan Pl
10 KRNY 6714 C2
10 NARL 6714 C1
10 PTWN 6508 D7
10 WHPL 6168 D6
Morgan St
10 EchT 6281 A5
10 JSYC 6820 D3
10 NRCH 6395 D6
10 TCKA 6281 A5
10 YNKR 6393 C1
40-00 QENS 6722 E2
1600 HmpT 6827 C7
Morgan Days Dr
10 RKVC 6929 D4
Morley Av
10 STNL 7117 D2
Morley Ct
10 NHLS 6724 C1
10 NHmT 6724 C1
Morningside Av
- NRWD 6278 C1
10 CRSK 6278 B6
10 HmpT 7029 E4
10 MHTN 109 C3
10 MHTN 6612 B4
10 WHPL 6050 B7
10 YNKR 6279 D7
100 MHTN 106 D7
100 OrgT 6164 E5
200 CLFP 6611 C3
200 FRVW 6611 C3
W Morningside Av
200 CRSK 6278 A6
Morningside Cir
10 BRXV 6281 B7
Morningside Dr
10 MHTN 109 C2
10 MHTN 6612 B5
Morningside Ln
- PALP 6611 C1
10 RDFP 6502 A5
100 FTLE 6502 D7
100 PALP 6502 D7
700 RDGF 6611 C1
900 FTLE 6611 C1
Morningside Pl
10 NoCT 6050 B4
100 YNKR 6279 D6
Morningside Rd
10 ARDY 6166 D3
Morningside Ter
200 TnkT 6502 A3
Morningstar Rd
10 STNL 6919 B7
100 STNL 7019 B2
Morrell Pl
10 GRFD 6500 B2
Morrell St
10 ELIZ 6917 B5
Morris Av
10 GLCV 6509 E4
10 MLVN 6929 B1
10 RKVC 6929 E4
200 BRNX 107 E7
200 BRNX 6612 E4
200 ELIZ 6917 D2
200 HmpT 7027 D3
200 NWRK 6713 B7
300 NWRK 6817 B1
500 UnnT 6917 D2
800 BRNX 6613 A1
1100 UnnT 6816 B7
1200 BRNX 105 C5
2400 BRNX 102 E7
2500 BRNX 6504 D3
Morris Av CO-629
300 ELIZ 6917 D2
500 UnnT 6917 D2
Morris Av SR-82
600 UnnT 6917 C1
1100 UnnT 6816 B7
Morris Av W
10 MLVN 6929 B1
E Morris Av
10 LNDN 7017 A1
W Morris Av
300 LNDN 7017 A3
Morris Cres
10 YNKR 6393 B3
Morris Ct
10 RYE 6283 C5
Morris Dr
10 NHmT 6724 C6
400 HmpT 6827 E6
Morris Ln
10 GTNK 6616 D4
10 NRCH 6281 E1
10 SCDL 6167 E6
10 SCDL 6281 E1
S Morris Ln
10 NRCH 6281 E1
100 SCDL 6281 E1
Morris Pkwy
10 HmpT 6928 E1
10 VLYS 6928 E1
Morris Pl
10 STNL 7117 B6
10 YNKR 6393 C3
400 ROSL 6917 A5
1400 HlsT 6816 E5
Morris Rd
10 OrgT 6164 A2
Morris St
10 EORG 6713 A3
10 JSYC 6820 D3
10 MHTN 120 A1
10 MHTN 6821 B6
10 NRCH 6395 E3
10 STNL 7115 E5
10 WbgT 7114 E3
10 WbgT 7115 A3
10 YNKR 6393 C3
200 FRVW 6611 A3
400 COrT 6712 A4
500 PTHA 7205 B3
900 ROSL 6917 A5
1200 LNDN 6917 A6
1200 UNCT 6716 C4
Morrison Av
10 STNL 7020 A1
200 STNL 7019 E1
1000 BRNX 6614 A1
Morrison Dr
10 NRCH 6281 D5
Morrison Pl
10 MTVN 6394 E5
Morrison St
10 CLST 6278 A2
Morris Park Av
300 BRNX 6505 C6
Morris Pesin Dr
- JSYC 6819 E5
200 JSYC 6820 A6
Morrisse Av
10 ERTH 6500 A7
10 WLTN 6500 B6
Morristown Dr
100 OrgT 6164 A1
Morristown Rd
10 ELIZ 6917 B3
Morrow Av
- YNKR 6281 A1
10 YNKR 6280 E1
Morrow Rd
200 EGLD 6392 B6
3000 HmpT 6929 D7
Morrow St
10 STNL 7018 D2
500 COrT 6712 A4
Morry Ln
10 NHmT 6724 E2
Morse Av
10 BlmT 6713 A1
10 EORG 6712 E1
10 EORG 6713 A1
10 RTFD 6500 A7
10 RTFD 6609 A1
10 STNL 7019 E5
300 RDGF 6611 B2
Morse Ct
10 QENS 7027 D5
Morse Ln
10 MNPK 6618 B6
Morsemere Av
10 YNKR 6279 E5
Morsemere Pl
10 YNKR 6279 D4
Morsemere Ter
100 YNKR 6279 E5
Morses Mill Rd
- LNDN 6917 C7
- LNDN 7017 D1
700 ELIZ 6917 E7
Mortimer Av
10 RTFD 6609 A2
N Mortimer Av
10 EMFD 6049 A3
S Mortimer Av
10 EMFD 6049 A6
Mortimer Pl
10 EchT 6395 C1
Mortimer St
200 PTCH 6170 C4
Morton Av
10 ERKY 6929 C7
10 HmpT 6828 E5
Morton Pl
10 EORG 6712 E3
10 GrbT 6049 D4
10 JSYC 6819 D4
10 NARL 6714 D2
100 BRNX 105 B4
100 BRNX 6504 A6
Morton Sq
10 MHTN 118 B2
10 MHTN 6821 A4
Morton St
10 BKLN 6822 A5
10 ERTH 6500 B6
10 JSYC 6819 C3
10 MHTN 118 C2
10 MHTN 6821 B5
10 NWRK 6817 B2
10 STNL 7117 C2
Mortorano Wy
10 JSYC 6819 B3
Mosco St
10 MHTN 118 E6
10 MHTN 6821 E4
Mosefan St
900 HmpT 6828 A5
Mosel Av
10 STNL 7020 D4
Mosel Lp
10 STNL 7020 D4
Mosher Av
200 HmpT 6928 C7
200 HmpT 7028 C1
Moshier St
10 GrwT 6170 D3
Mosholu Av
5400 BRNX 6393 C5
Mosholu Pkwy
- BRNX 6504 D1
Mosholu Pkwy N
- BRNX 6393 D7
- BRNX 6504 D1
Mosholu Pkwy S
- BRNX 6393 D7
- BRNX 6504 E2
E Mosholu Pkwy N
10 BRNX 6504 E2
E Mosholu Pkwy S
10 BRNX 6504 E2
W Mosholu Pkwy N
10 BRNX 6504 E1
W Mosholu Pkwy S
10 BRNX 6504 D1
Mosley Av
200 STNL 7116 E6
Moss Pl
10-00 LWRN 7027 D4
10-00 QENS 7027 D4
Moss Run
10 WHPL 6168 E6
Mosswood Av
600 COrT 6712 B5
700 SOrT 6712 B5
Mosswood Ter
10 MplT 6816 A2
Mostyn St
10 YNKR 6279 E6
Mother Gaston Blvd
200 BKLN 6924 B2
Motley Av
10 STNL 7019 E6
10 STNL 7020 A4
Motley St
10 MLVN 6929 A2
10 VLYS 6929 A2
200 VLYS 6928 E2
Motor Pkwy
300 EWLS 6724 E3
300 NHmT 6724 E3
300 WLPK 6724 E3
Mott Av
10 HmpT 7027 E3
10 RSLN 6618 D5
13-00 QENS 7027 C4
200 CDHT 7028 A2
200 HmpT 7028 A2
Mott Pl
10 HmpT 7027 D3
10 OybT 6618 E2
Mott St
10 HmpT 7029 E1
10 MHTN 118 E6
10 MHTN 6821 C2
10 NWRK 6818 B1
10 STNL 7116 D5
200 MHTN 119 A4
Motts Ln
10 NHmT 6618 E2
10 OybT 6618 E2
Motts Cove Ct N
100 OybT 6618 E2
100 ROSH 6618 E2
Motts Cove Rd N
700 OybT 6618 E2
700 ROSH 6618 E2
Moulton Av
10 DBSF 6166 C4
Moultrie Av
10 YNKR 6280 A4
Moultrie St
10 BKLN 6822 C1
Mountain Av
- MrnT 6282 B7
- WOrT 6712 B1
10 MrnT 6396 B1
10 NRCH 6396 B1
N Mountain Dr
10 DBSF 6166 B3
Mountain Rd
10 GrbT 6048 C6
10 IRVN 6048 C6
10 JSYC 6716 C7
10 TFLY 6392 B3
200 EGLD 6503 A1
200 UNCT 6716 D4
300 WhkT 6716 D4
Mountain Wy
10 RTFD 6609 A3
200 LynT 6609 A4
Mountain Cut
10 NHmT 6618 A7
Mountaindale Rd
10 YNKR 6280 D4
Mountain House Rd
10 SOrT 6712 A5
Mountainside Rd
10 STNL 7020 B5
Mountain View Av
400 COrT 6712 B3
Mountainview Av
10 EORG 6712 D6
10 NWRK 6712 D6
100 STNL 7019 D4
Mountainview Pl
10 IrvT 6816 C1
10 NWRK 6712 B7
10 NWRK 6816 C1
Mountain View Rd
10 DMRT 6278 A4
Mountain View St
10 WOrT 6712 B2
Mt Carmel Pl
10 MHTN 116 D6
10 MHTN 6717 E7
10 YNKR 6393 D2
Mt Cedar Av
10 WLTN 6500 A6
E Mt Eden Av
10 BRNX 6504 B7
100 BRNX 105 D6
W Mt Eden Av
10 BRNX 105 B5
10 BRNX 6504 E5
Mt Eden Pkwy
100 BRNX 105 C6
100 BRNX 6504 B7
Mt Etna Pl
10 NRCH 6396 A5
Mt Holly Dr
10 HRSN 6169 E6
Mt Hope Blvd
- HAOH 6165 E7
10 HAOH 6166 A7
Mt Hope Pl
10 BRNX 105 C4
10 BRNX 6504 B6
Mt Joy Av
10 GrbT 6167 A6
Mt Joy Pl
10 NRCH 6395 D2
Mt Kisco Rd
- NoCT 6050 B4
Mt Kisco Rd SR-22
- NoCT 6050 B4
Mt Morris Av
10 WHPL 6050 B7
Mt Morris Pk W
10 MHTN 110 A2
10 MHTN 6612 C5
Mt Olivet Cres
60-00 QENS 6823 C3
Mt Pleasant Av
10 COrT 6712 C2
10 ERTH 6500 A6
10 NWRK 6713 E5
10 WLTN 6500 B6
10 WOrT 6712 C2
100 MRNK 6282 E6
Mt Pleasant Av CO-577
100 WOrT 6712 A1
Mt Pleasant Av CO-660
10 WOrT 6712 B1
Mt Pleasant Ln
10 GrbT 6048 C6
Mt Pleasant Rd
10 YNKR 6279 D5
Mt Prospect Av
10 NWRK 6713 D5
800 NWRK 6714 D2
900 BlvT 6714 A1
Mt Prospect Pl
10 NWRK 6713 E4
Mt Tom Rd
10 NRCH 6395 D7
10 PLMM 6395 D7
Mt Vernon Av
10 IrvT 6816 C3
10 MTVN 6394 D4
100 COrT 6712 C1
100 YNKR 6394 C4
Mt Vernon Pl
10 NWRK 6712 B7
100 SOrT 6712 A7
Mt Vernon Pl E
10 IrvT 6816 C1
10 NWRK 6712 C7
10 NWRK 6816 C1
Mt Vernon St
10 RDFP 6501 E5
100 RDFP 6502 A5
Mt Vernon St CO-41
10 RDFP 6501 E5
100 RDFP 6502 A5
Mt View Av
10 ARDY 6166 E5
Mowbray Dr
10 QENS 6824 E4
10 QENS 6825 A4
Mozart St
10 CARL 6500 B7
10 ERTH 6500 B7
10 ERTH 6609 B1
W Mravlag Pl
10 ELIZ 6918 A4
Msgr Francis J Dillon Pl
- QENS 6615 B7
Msgr John C McCarthy Pl
200 BRNX 6504 E4
Msgr Wojtycha Dr
10 JSYC 6819 B4
Msnbc Plz
10 SECS 6715 E1
Muchmore Rd
10 HRSN 6169 B7
Muhammad Ali Av
10 NWRK 6817 B1
Muir Pl
10 NRCH 6395 D4
Mulbach Ct
10 QENS 7027 A5
Mulberry Av
10 STNL 7018 E6
137-00 QENS 6721 B6
Mulberry Cir
10 STNL 7018 E5
Mulberry Ln
- NRCH 6396 A1
10 NRCH 6282 B5
10 WHPL 6169 A4
100 HmpT 6828 E6
100 MrnT 6282 C6
Mulberry Pl
300 ELIZ 6917 D3
700 HmpT 6928 A6
Mulberry St
10 CART 7115 C1
10 JSYC 6819 A4
10 MHTN 118 E5
10 MHTN 6821 C3
10 NWRK 6713 E7
10 YNKR 6393 E1
200 MHTN 119 A4
200 NWRK 6817 D2
Muldoon Av
- STNL 7116 B2
Mulford Av
1600 BRNX 6505 E6
Mulford Pl
10 NWRK 6816 E5

New York City/5 Borough Street Index

STREET
Block City Map# Grid

Mulford St
10 YNKR 6279 B7
Muliner Av
1800 BRNX 6505 B6
Mullan Pl
3000 BRNX 6615 C3
Muller Av
10 STNL 7019 C3
Muller Pl
- VLYS 6928 D5
500 HmpT 6828 E7
Muller St
100 WLTN 6500 B6
Mulligan Ln
10 GrbT 6048 D7
Mullon Av
10 NHmT 6617 E1
Mulock Pl
10 ENWK 6713 E5
10 HRSN 6713 E5
10 HRSN 6714 A6
Mulry Ln
300 CDHT 7028 A3
300 LWRN 7028 A3
Mulvey Av
2300 BRNX 6394 E7
Mundet Pl
400 HlsT 6816 C5
Mundy Av
10 STNL 7019 D2
Mundy Ln
300 BRNX 6394 D6
300 MTVN 6394 D6
Municipal Plz
10 WOrT 6712 A1
Munn Av
10 BGTA 6501 D2
10 TnkT 6502 A3
100 TnkT 6501 E3
1400 HlsT 6816 E5
N Munn Av
10 EORG 6712 E6
10 EORG 6713 A4
10 NWRK 6712 E6
S Munn Av
- EORG 6713 A4
10 EORG 6712 E5
10 NWRK 6712 D7
100 IrvT 6712 D7
Munn Pl
10 YNKR 6394 C3
Munro Av
400 MRNK 6282 E7
Munro Blvd
10 VLYS 6928 D5
200 LNBK 6928 E5
E Munsell Av
10 LNDN 7017 B1
W Munsell Av
10 LNDN 7017 A1
Munsey Pl
10 MNPK 6617 E6
10 NHmT 6617 E6
Munson Av
10 HmpT 6828 C5
Munson Pl
10 ERKY 6929 C5
Munson St
10 NHmT 6617 C2
10 NHmT 6618 B1
10 PTCH 6170 B3
Murchison Pl
10 WHPL 6168 D5
Murdock Av
173-01 QENS 6826 A6
223-01 QENS 6827 A5
3200 HmpT 7029 D1
3900 BRNX 6394 D6
Murdock Ct
10 BKLN 7023 A7
Murdock Pl
10 STNL 7019 B1
Murdock Rd
10 ERKY 6929 B6
10 MrnT 6282 B4
10 SCDL 6282 B4
Murel Ct
10 ROSH 6618 E3
Muriel Av
10 LWRN 7028 A3
Muriel Ct
107-00 QENS 6925 E1
Muriel Pkwy
500 ELIZ 6917 C3
Muriel Pl
10 GrwT 6170 B2
Muriel Rd
10 NHmT 6617 D3
Muriel St
- STNL 7115 C7
Muroney Av
10 OrgT 6164 E4
Murphy Pl
4900 UNCT 6716 E1
4900 WNYK 6716 E1
Murray Av
10 MrnT 6282 B7
10 MrnT 6396 B1
10 NHmT 6617 D2
10 QENS 6616 A7
10 YNKR 6394 B2
Murray Ct
- GLCV 6509 E2
10 BRNX 6614 B4
10 RKVC 6929 E5
Murray Dr
10 HmpT 7029 E1
Murray Ln
25-00 QENS 6721 B3
Murray Pl
10 STNL 7020 D2
Murray St
10 ELIZ 6917 D4
10 MHTN 118 C6
10 MHTN 6821 A3
10 NWRK 6817 D2
10 STNL 7206 C3
15-00 QENS 6615 C6
17-00 QENS 6721 B2
400 PLMM 6395 B6
800 ROSL 6917 C4
Murray Hill Pkwy
- CARL 6609 D2
10 ERTH 6609 C3
Murray Hill Rd
10 SCDL 6167 E6
10 SCDL 6168 A6
Murray Hill St
10 HmpT 6827 B5
Murray Hulbert Av
10 STNL 6920 E7
Murylu Dr
10 JSYC 6819 C6
Musgnug Av
100 MNLA 6724 E5
Musket Rd
10 OrgT 6164 A2
Musket St
86-00 QENS 6826 E1
Muskrat Pond Dr
10 GrwT 6170 D4
Mutillod Ln
10 SECS 6610 B7
Mutton Hollow Rd
- WbgT 7114 A6
Myer St
10 HKSK 6501 B1
Myers Av
200 HSBH 6500 E3
300 HSBH 6501 A4
Myrna Dr
800 HmpT 6828 C7
Myrna Ln
10 STNL 7116 B5
Myron Ct
10 TnkT 6502 C1
Myrtle Av
10 DBSF 6166 B4
10 DMRT 6278 B5
10 EDGW 103 A7
10 EDGW 6502 E7
10 EDGW 6503 A7
10 EDGW 6611 E1
10 IrvT 6816 D1
10 JSYC 6819 D5
10 NWRK 6713 A6
10 SECS 6610 C6
10 STNL 7019 E1
10 STNL 7020 A1
54-00 BKLN 6823 A6
54-00 QENS 6823 C5
73-00 QENS 6824 A5
100 BKLN 121 E5
100 BKLN 6821 D6
100 FTLE 103 C1
100 FTLE 6503 A4
200 IrvT 6712 D7
300 BKLN 6822 E6
300 EGLD 6502 E3
400 EGLD 6503 A3
400 NWRK 6712 E7
500 WbgT 7114 C4
Myrtle Blvd
10 MrnT 6282 C7
10 MrnT 6396 B1
Myrtle Dr
10 GTNE 6616 E7
Myrtle Pl
10 EchT 6281 B5
Myrtle St
10 BlmT 6713 A1
10 ELIZ 6918 A7
10 ERTH 6500 A7
10 LODI 6500 C2
10 NHmT 6617 D6
10 RTFD 6500 A7
10 WHPL 6167 C2
10 WHPL 6168 A3
10 YNKR 6279 D7
100 ROSL 6917 A4
300 PTHA 7205 D1
500 ELIZ 6917 D6
1200 HlsT 6816 C6
S Myrtle St
1200 HlsT 6816 C6
Myrtledale Rd
10 SCDL 6282 B1

N

N St
1300 HmpT 6827 E7
Nadal Pl
10 STNL 7018 E3
164-00 QENS 6825 E6
Naden Av
10 IrvT 6816 B4
Nadine St
10 STNL 7117 D1
Nagel St
200 CLFP 6611 C4
200 FRVW 6611 C4
Nagle Av
10 MHTN 104 D1
10 MHTN 6503 E4
100 MHTN 102 A7
100 MHTN 6504 A4
Nahant St
10 STNL 7117 B4
Nairn Pl
10 NWRK 6817 A3
Nameoke Av
19-00 QENS 7027 C4
Nameoke St
10-00 QENS 7027 D4
Names Ct
10 HRPK 6164 A6
Nancy Ct
10 FLHL 6617 E3
10 STNL 7117 C4
Nancy Ln
10 MrnT 6282 C7
10 STNL 7206 B4
Nancy Pl
10 EchT 6395 B1
600 HmpT 6928 A6
Nancy Rd
400 MNLA 6724 C6
400 NHmT 6724 C6
Nansen St
68-00 QENS 6824 C4
Nantucket Pl
10 YNKR 6281 A2
Napier Av
400 BRNX 6394 A6
Naple Av
600 HmpT 6828 B5
Naples Av
10 BlvT 6713 C1
Naples Pl
10 GRFD 6500 B3
Naples Ter
200 BRNX 102 D3
200 BRNX 6504 B1
Napoleon St
10 NWRK 6818 A2
800 HmpT 6928 A7
Narcissus Dr
10 WLTN 6500 A6
Nardozzi Pl
100 NRCH 6395 D6
Narragansett Av
200 LWRN 7028 B5
1800 BRNX 6505 C5
Narrow Ln
100 HmpT 7027 D2
200 HmpT 7028 B1
Narrows Av
6800 BKLN 6921 D7
7500 BKLN 7021 D1
Narrows Rd N
10 STNL 7020 B4
Narrows Rd S
10 STNL 7020 E4
10 STNL 7021 A5
Nasby Pl
6-00 QENS 7027 C5
Nash Ct
10 STNL 7117 B6
Nashville Blvd
117-00 QENS 6826 D6
185-00 QENS 6927 C1
Nashville St
10 STNL 7206 B3
Naso Ct
10 STNL 7019 B7
Nassau Av
10 ATLB 7028 A7
10 BKLN 6822 C2
10 HmpT 7027 C3
10 MLVN 6929 B1
10 NHmT 6617 D6
100 MNPK 6617 D6
200 FLHL 6617 D6
Nassau Blvd
- NHLS 6724 B2
10 GDNC 6828 C1
10 HmpT 6828 C6
10 HmpT 6929 B3
10 MLVN 6929 B3
100 GDNC 6724 C7
100 NHmT 6724 C7
200 MNLA 6724 C5
254-00 QENS 6723 A3
260-00 NHmT 6723 A3
300 WLPK 6724 E5
Nassau Blvd S
10 HmpT 6828 C4
300 GDNC 6828 C3
Nassau Ct
10 VLYS 6928 B3
Nassau Dr
10 GTPZ 6617 A7
10 KENS 6617 B7
10 NHmT 6724 D2
Nassau Expwy
- ATLB 7027 E5
- HmpT 7027 E2
- LWRN 7027 E4
- QENS 6925 D3
- QENS 6926 B3
- QENS 6927 A4
Nassau Expwy SR-27
- QENS 6925 D3
Nassau Expwy SR-878
- HmpT 7027 E2
- LWRN 7027 E4
Nassau Ln
10 ISPK 7029 D5
N Nassau Ln
200 ISPK 7029 D3
Nassau Pl
- COrT 6712 B3
10 EORG 6712 E5
10 STNL 7206 B2
400 HmpT 6828 C3
Nassau Rd
- QENS 6722 E2
10 HmpT 6929 E7
10 LRMT 6396 C1
10 NHmT 6722 E2
100 YNKR 6280 E2
100 YNKR 6281 A2
3200 HmpT 7029 E1
Nassau St
10 BKLN 121 B4
10 COrT 6712 A3
10 FLPK 6827 C3
10 HmpT 6827 C7
10 MHTN 118 C7
10 MHTN 120 C1
10 MHTN 6821 B4
10 RKVC 6929 D4
10 STNL 6920 D7
10 WOrT 6712 A3
100 BKLN 6821 D6
200 HmpT 6928 C7
Nassau Terminal Rd
10 NHmT 6724 B7
10 NHmT 6828 B1
Natalie Ct
10 STNL 7020 D1
Natalie Crossman Pl
130-00 QENS 6927 D1
Nathan Ct
10 STNL 7207 A1
Nathan D Perlman Pl
10 MHTN 119 C1
10 MHTN 6821 E1
Natick St
10 STNL 7117 C2
National Blvd
100 LBCH 7029 C7
National Ct
10 HRSN 6724 A3
National Dr
10 BKLN 7024 A4
National St
40-00 QENS 6720 B6
Natoma St
10 RYE 6169 E7
Naughton Av
10 STNL 7020 B7
200 STNL 7118 C1
Naugle St
10 CLST 6278 A2
Nautilus Av
10 BKLN 7120 B2
Nautilus Ln
1000 MRNK 6397 A1
Nautilus Pl
10 NRCH 6395 E7
Nautilus St
10 STNL 7021 A4
Navesink Pl
10 STNL 7118 A4
Navigator Ct
- STNL 7207 B3
Navy St
10 BKLN 121 D4
10 BKLN 6821 E5
10 NWRK 6818 C6
Neal Dr
10 EGLC 6392 C6
Neal Dow Av
100 STNL 7019 C3
Nebel Wy
200 WbgT 7114 A1
Nebraska St
10 LBCH 7028 E7
Neck Ln
200 ELIZ 6817 B7
200 NWRK 6817 B7
1000 ELIZ 6918 B1
Neckar Av
10 STNL 7020 D4
Ned Ct
10 WbgT 7115 A3
Nedley Ln
10 GrwT 6170 B2
10 RYEB 6170 B2
Nedra Ln
10 STNL 7116 B5
Needes Ln
- LODI 6500 D2
Needham Av
1300 BRNX 6505 C2
Negundo Av
137-00 QENS 6721 B6
Nehring Av
10 STNL 7019 A6
Neil Pl
10 RYE 6283 C6
Neill Av
700 BRNX 6505 C5
Neilson St
10-00 QENS 7027 D4
Nelkin Dr
10 WLTN 6500 B4
Nellis St
122-00 QENS 6927 C1
Nelson Av
10 HRSN 6283 B2
10 JSYC 6716 B5
10 STNL 7117 B6
100 NBgT 6716 B4
300 CLFP 6611 C2
300 ELIZ 6917 E5
400 RDGF 6611 C2
1000 BRNX 107 E1
1000 BRNX 6612 E1
1100 BRNX 104 E7
1100 BRNX 6503 E7
1200 BRNX 105 A6
1200 BRNX 6504 A7
Nelson Av CO-659
10 JSYC 6716 B5
100 NBgT 6716 B4
Nelson Ct
100 EDGW 108 C1
100 EDGW 6611 D4
1600 HmpT 6928 E6
Nelson Pl
10 IrvT 6816 E1
10 MplT 6816 A3
10 NWRK 6816 E1
10 TFLY 6392 C4
Nelson Rd
10 EchT 6281 C3
10 HmpT 6928 E5
10 VLYS 6928 E5
100 SCDL 6281 C2
Nelson St
10 HmpT 6827 E6
10 YNKR 6394 B3
100 BKLN 6922 B2
1400 MRNK 6283 A3
Nemeth St
10 MLVN 6929 A2
10 VLYS 6929 A2
Nepera Pl
10 HAOH 6280 A1
10 YNKR 6280 A3
Neperan Rd
- GrbT 6048 C2
- MtPT 6048 D1
10 TYTN 6048 D1
Neponsit Av
142-00 QENS 7123 B2
Nepperhan Av
100 EMFD 6049 B5
100 GrbT 6049 B5
100 YNKR 6393 D1
300 YNKR 6279 D7
900 YNKR 6280 A3
1500 HAOH 6280 A3
Nepperhan St
10 YNKR 6393 B1
Nepton St
125-00 QENS 6927 C1
Neptune Av
10 BKLN 7121 B1
10 HmpT 7028 D1
10 JSYC 6819 C7
10 NRCH 6395 E6
10 WDBG 7028 D2
400 BKLN 7120 B1
Neptune Blvd
10 LBCH 7029 E6
Neptune Ct
100 BRNX 6614 C4
Neptune Ln
100 BRNX 6614 C5
Neptune Pl
10 STNL 7019 B5
Neptune St
10 NWRK 6818 C6
10 STNL 7118 B3
Nereid Av
- YNKR 6394 B6
500 BRNX 6394 D6
2100 MTVN 6394 D6
Nero Av
190-00 QENS 6826 A2
Nesaquake Av
10 MHVN 6508 C7
Nesbit St
100 WhkT 6716 E2
Nesbit Ter
10 IrvT 6816 B2
Nesbitt St
10 JSYC 6716 B7
10 NWRK 6713 D6
Nesmythe Ter
10 STNL 7020 C3
Nestor St
900 HmpT 7028 D1
Netherland Av
200 STNL 7019 A1
300 STNL 7018 E1
2600 BRNX 102 B3
2600 BRNX 6504 B1
5900 BRNX 6393 B5
Nethermont Av
10 NoCT 6050 B4
100 WHPL 6050 B4
Netherwood Dr
10 NHmT 6724 D2
Netherwood Pl
10 NWRK 6712 B7
Netherwood Ter
10 BlmT 6712 E1
10 EORG 6712 E1
10 EORG 6713 A1
Netz Pl
10 NHmT 6724 D2
Neulist Av
10 NHmT 6617 E3
10 NHmT 6618 A3
Neuton Av
100 PTCH 6170 A4
100 RYEB 6170 A4
Neutral Av
10 STNL 7118 B4
Nevada Av
10 HmpT 7028 D7
10 LBCH 7028 D7
10 STNL 7117 D1
100 STNL 7019 D7
3900 HmpT 7029 E3
Nevada Dr
10 LKSU 6723 E4
10 NHmT 6723 E4
Nevada Pl
10 YNKR 6394 D2
Nevada St
10 NWRK 6817 D1
Neville St
200 PTHA 7205 D2
Nevin St
10 JSYC 6819 E2
Nevins St
10 BKLN 121 C7
10 BKLN 6821 D7
10 RTFD 6609 B3
100 BKLN 6922 D1
New Av
10 YNKR 6394 B5
New Ct
10 HMPD 6828 E4
New Ln
10 STNL 7021 A4
New Pl
10 YNKR 6394 B5
New St
10 BAYN 6920 A3
10 CLST 6278 A2
10 CRSK 6278 B7
10 EchT 6281 A6
10 EGLC 6503 B2
10 EORG 6713 A4
10 ERTH 6500 A6
10 GrbT 6049 D7
10 GrwT 6170 C5
10 HKSK 6501 C2
10 HmpT 6928 D7
10 HmpT 6929 C7
10 HRSN 6169 C1
10 IrvT 6816 C2
10 JSYC 6819 C6
10 LNBK 6929 A5
10 MHTN 120 B2
10 MHTN 6821 A5
10 NHmT 6617 D2
10 NRCH 6395 E4
10 NWRK 6713 E7
10 OrgT 6164 E2
10 RYE 6170 A7
10 RYE 6284 A1
10 STNL 6919 C7
10 TFLY 6392 A3
10 WbgT 7114 C5
10 WHPL 6168 A1
100 COrT 6712 D2
100 MRNK 6282 E5
300 PTHA 7205 D3
E New St
10 WbgT 7114 E6
S New St
10 GrwT 6170 C5
Newark Av
- NWRK 6713 D1
10 BlvT 6713 D1
10 JSYC 6820 B2
10 STNL 6919 B7
200 LynT 6609 A5
300 HBKN 6716 C7
500 ELIZ 6917 E1
700 ELIZ 6918 A1
700 JSYC 6716 A7
800 JSYC 6715 E7
900 ELIZ 6817 A7
1000 NWRK 6817 A7
Newark Av CO-639
100 JSYC 6820 B2
Newark Av CO-677
- JSYC 6716 C7
300 HBKN 6716 C7
Newark Av SR-7
1000 JSYC 6715 D7
Newark Av SR-27
500 ELIZ 6917 E2
700 ELIZ 6918 A1
900 ELIZ 6817 A7
Newark Av SR-27
1000 NWRK 6817 A7
Newark St
10 HBKN 6716 D7
10 NWRK 6713 C6
100 OLDT 6164 A5
Newark Wy
10 MplT 6816 A3
Newark Bay Ct
10 BAYN 6919 E2
Newark-Jersey City Tpk
- JSYC 6715 D7
500 KRNY 6715 C6
1800 KRNY 6714 D5
Newark-Jersey City Tpk CO-508
- KRNY 6714 D5
500 KRNY 6715 A6
Newark-Jersey City Tpk SR-7
- JSYC 6715 D7
900 KRNY 6715 C6
Newberry Av
10 STNL 7020 B6
Newberry Pl
10 RYE 6283 D6
Newbold Av
10 VLYS 6928 E4
2000 BRNX 6614 C1
New Broad St
10 PTCH 6170 B6
New Broadway
10 HAOH 6279 E1
10 SYHW 6048 B1
New Broadway US-9
10 HAOH 6279 E1
New Brunswick Av
10 PTHA 7205 C2
10 WbgT 7205 B2
New Brunswick Av CO-616
10 PTHA 7205 C2
10 WbgT 7205 A2
Newburg Av
800 HmpT 6928 A5
Newburg St
114-00 QENS 6826 B6
Newburgh Ct
400 WNYK 111 D1
400 WNYK 6717 B1
Newburgh St
600 HmpT 6827 C7
Newbury Rd
10 NHmT 6618 B3
New Castle Rd
500 NBgT 6716 A5
Newcomb Pl
10 ELIZ 6917 C4
10 GrbT 6167 E3
10 WHPL 6167 E3
Newcomb Rd
10 TFLY 6392 A1
Newcomb St
10 BlvT 6713 D1
New County Rd
400 SECS 6715 D4
New Cutter Mill Rd
10 GTNE 6722 E1
10 GTPZ 6722 E1
10 GTPZ 6723 A1
10 NHmT 6722 E1
10 NHmT 6723 A1
New Dock St
10 BKLN 121 A2
10 BKLN 6821 C5
10 MHTN 121 A2
10 MHTN 6821 C5
New Dorp Ln
10 STNL 7117 E2
10 STNL 7118 A2
New Dorp Plz
10 STNL 7117 B1
New Dorp Plz N
10 STNL 7117 E2
New Dorp Plz S
10 STNL 7117 E2
New Dover Rd
100 WbgT 7114 A1
New Dover Rd CO-650
100 WbgT 7114 A1
E Newell Av
10 RTFD 6609 A2
W Newell Av
10 RTFD 6609 A2
Newell Pl
10 KRNY 6714 D1
10 NARL 6714 D1
Newell St
10 BKLN 6822 C2
New England Ter
400 COrT 6712 B3
New England Thwy
- BRNX 6505 E2
- BRNX 6506 A4
- GrwT 6170 C7
- HRSN 6283 A4
- LRMT 6396 C1
- MRNK 6282 D7
- MRNK 6283 A4
- MrnT 6282 D6
- MrnT 6396 B2
- NRCH 6395 C7
- NRCH 6396 B2
- PLMM 6395 D7
- PLMM 6506 C1
- PTCH 6170 C7
- PTCH 6284 B1
- RYE 6283 D2
- RYE 6284 B1
New England Thwy I-95
- BRNX 6505 E2
- BRNX 6506 A1
- GrwT 6170 C7
- HRSN 6283 C2
- LRMT 6396 C1
- MRNK 6282 D7
- MRNK 6283 A4
- MrnT 6282 D7
- MrnT 6396 B1
- NRCH 6395 C7
- NRCH 6396 A2
- PLMM 6395 C7
- PLMM 6506 C1
New England Thwy I-95
- PTCH 6170 C7
- PTCH 6284 B1
- RYE 6283 D2
- RYE 6284 B1
Newfield St
10 BlmT 6713 B3
10 EORG 6713 B3
New Folden Pl
10 STNL 7206 C3
Newhall Av
240-00 QENS 6927 E4
New Hampshire St
10 LBCH 7028 E7
New Haven Av
1300 QENS 7027 D5
New Haven St
10 HRSN 6283 B3
New Haven RR St
10 MTVN 6394 C5
New Heckman Dr
10 JSYC 6819 D7
New Hook Rd
10 BAYN 6920 A3
New Hope Ln
10 JSYC 6819 D7
New Hyde Park Rd
10 GDNC 6828 A2
10 HmpT 6828 A2
10 NHPK 6828 A1
100 NHPK 6724 A7
600 NHmT 6724 A6
1800 NHmT 6723 E4
2300 LKSU 6723 E4
3000 NHLS 6723 E3
New Jefferson St
- MrnT 6396 B1
New Jersey Av
10 BKLN 6924 C2
10 CART 7017 B6
700 LynT 6609 A5
New Jersey Tpk
- CARL 6610 E1
- CART 7017 B7
- CART 7115 B1
- EGLD 6502 D2
- ELIZ 6817 E7
- ELIZ 6918 B5
- ERTH 6609 D6
- ERTH 6610 A4
- FTLE 103 A3
- FTLE 6502 E5
- FTLE 6503 B5
- KRNY 6714 D7
- KRNY 6715 A5
- LEON 6502 C2
- LNDN 6917 E7
- LNDN 6918 A7
- LNDN 7017 E1
- LynT 6609 C7
- LynT 6715 A3
- NBgT 6610 D5
- NWRK 6714 E7
- NWRK 6817 E7
- NWRK 6818 D2
- RDFP 6502 A7
- RDGF 6501 E7
- RDGF 6502 A7
- RDGF 6610 D4
- RTFD 6609 D6
- SECS 6610 C7
- SECS 6715 D4
- SECS 6716 B1
- TnkT 6502 C2
- WbgT 7114 A6
- WbgT 7115 A2
New Jersey Tpk I-95
- CARL 6610 E1
- CART 7017 B7
- CART 7115 B1
- EGLD 6502 D2
- ELIZ 6817 E7
- ELIZ 6918 E1
- ERTH 6609 D6
- ERTH 6610 A4
- FTLE 103 A2
- FTLE 6502 E5
- FTLE 6503 A5
- KRNY 6714 D7
- KRNY 6715 C5
- LEON 6502 D2
- LNDN 6917 E7
- LNDN 6918 A7
- LNDN 7017 E1
- LynT 6609 C7
- LynT 6715 A3
- NBgT 6610 D5
- NWRK 6714 E6
- NWRK 6817 E7
- NWRK 6818 D2
- RDFP 6502 A7
- RDGF 6501 E7
- RDGF 6502 A7
- RDGF 6610 E1
- RTFD 6609 D6
- SECS 6610 C7
- SECS 6715 E3
- SECS 6716 B1
- TnkT 6502 A5
- WbgT 7114 A6
- WbgT 7115 A2
New Jersey Tpk SR-4
- FTLE 6502 E5
New Jersey Tpk US-1
- FTLE 103 A2
- FTLE 6502 E5
- FTLE 6503 A5
New Jersey Tpk US-9
- FTLE 103 B3
- FTLE 6502 E5
- FTLE 6503 A5
New Jersey Tpk US-46
- FTLE 103 A2
- FTLE 6502 E5
- FTLE 6503 A5
New Jersey RR Av
200 HRSN 6714 A7
New Jersey Turnpike Ext
- BAYN 6818 E6
- BAYN 6819 A6
- JSYC 6819 D6
- JSYC 6820 A5
- NWRK 6818 C5
New Jersey Turnpike Ext I-78
- BAYN 6818 E6
- BAYN 6819 A6
- JSYC 6819 D6
- JSYC 6820 B2
- NWRK 6818 C5
New Jersey Tpk Bus Only Ln
- NBgT 6716 B2
- SECS 6716 B2
New King St
10 HRSN 6051 B3
10 NoCT 6051 B1
Newkirk Av
- BKLN 7022 E1
10 BKLN 7023 A1
10 ERKY 6929 B6
1000 BKLN 6923 B7
4300 NBgT 6716 D1
5400 NBgT 6610 E7
6700 NBgT 6611 A6
9100 FRVW 6611 B4
Newkirk Plz
10 BKLN 6923 A7
Newkirk Rd
10 YNKR 6280 C5
Newkirk St
10 JSYC 6820 A1
New Lawn Av
10 KRNY 6714 B3
New Lebanon Av
10 GrwT 6170 D6
New Lots Av
10 BKLN 6924 C4
1000 BKLN 6925 A3
New Main St
10 YNKR 6393 C1
Newman Av
10 BAYN 6919 D5
100 BRNX 6614 C4
Newman Pl
500 ROSL 6917 A5
Newman St
10 HKSK 6501 B1
S Newman St
10 HKSK 6501 B2
Newmarket Rd
10 GDNC 6828 B1
New McNeil Av
1000 LWRN 7027 E4
1000 QENS 7027 E4
New Mexico Ct
- STNL 7021 B5
New Northern Blvd
10 FLHL 6618 D5
New Point Rd
400 ELIZ 6918 A4
Newport Av
10 OrgT 6164 A2
116-00 QENS 7123 B2
1700 BRNX 6505 C5
Newport Ct
100 WbgT 7114 A5
Newport Dr
10 HmpT 6928 C6
Newport Pkwy
- JSYC 6820 D1
Newport Rd
10 ISPK 7029 D4
10 YNKR 6280 E3
Newport St
10 BKLN 6924 B4
New Rochelle Rd
- NRCH 6395 B1
300 BRXV 6395 B1
300 EchT 6395 B1
500 MTVN 6395 B1
500 PLHM 6395 B1
News Av
1300 HmpT 6827 E6
New Schley St
10 GRFD 6500 B1
New School St
10 YNKR 6393 C1
Newton Av
10 LNBK 6929 C5
Newton Pl
10 IrvT 6816 C1
10 MTVN 6395 A6
Newton St
- STNL 7117 A1
10 BKLN 6822 C3
10 NWRK 6713 C7
10 STNL 7207 D1
10 WbgT 7205 A3
Newtown Av
21-00 QENS 114 E4
21-00 QENS 6718 E2
24-00 QENS 6719 A3
Newtown Rd
40-00 QENS 6719 B4
New Utrecht Av
3800 BKLN 6922 C7
5300 BKLN 7022 C2
New Wilmot Rd
10 EchT 6281 C3
100 NRCH 6281 D4
New Woods Rd
10 GLCV 6509 E2
New York Av
- HBKN 6716 C7
10 BKLN 6923 C1
10 CART 7017 B6
10 HmpT 6828 D4
10 JSYC 6716 C6
10 LBCH 7028 E7
10 NWRK 6817 E2
10 WHPL 6168 A4
100 STNL 7021 A4
100 UNCT 6716 E2
200 FTLE 103 A1
200 FTLE 6503 A4
200 NVLE 6164 C5
200 NWRK 6818 A2
300 ELIZ 6917 D5
600 LynT 6609 A4
1100 HmpT 6827 E6
1700 BKLN 7023 C2
4200 HmpT 7029 E4
9000 CLFP 6611 C5
9000 NBgT 6611 C5
New York Av S
10 WHPL 6168 A4
E New York Av
100 LNBK 6928 E4
100 VLYS 6928 E4
400 BKLN 6923 C4
1100 BKLN 6924 A3
New York Pl
10 STNL 7019 D2
400 HlsT 6816 C6
New York State Thwy
- ARDY 6166 C7
- BRNX 6393 E5
- GrbT 6048 C5
- GrbT 6166 C7
- GrbT 6280 C1
- IRVN 6048 E7
- TYTN 6048 C5
- YNKR 6280 C2
- YNKR 6393 E4
- YNKR 6394 A4
New York State Thwy I-87
- ARDY 6166 C7
- BRNX 6393 E5
- GrbT 6048 C5
- GrbT 6166 C7
- GrbT 6280 C1
- IRVN 6048 E7
- TYTN 6048 C5
- YNKR 6280 C2
- YNKR 6393 E4
- YNKR 6394 A4
New York State Thwy I-287
- GrbT 6048 C5
- TYTN 6048 C5
New York Times Plz
10 QENS 6720 E2
Next Day Hill Ct
200 EGLD 6392 B5
Next Day Hill Dr
400 EGLD 6392 B5
Niagara St
10 NWRK 6818 B2
10 STNL 7020 B3
800 HmpT 6827 C7
800 HmpT 6928 C1
Nicholas Av
10 ERKY 6929 C7
10 GrwT 6170 C3
10 STNL 6919 C7
200 STNL 7019 C1
Nicholas St
10 LFRY 6501 C6
10 STNL 6920 D6
Nicholas Oresko St
- EORG 6712 C5
Nichols Av
10 BKLN 6824 A7
200 BKLN 6925 B3
Nichols Av N
100 YNKR 6280 A6
Nichols Av S
10 YNKR 6280 A6
Nichols Dr
10 HAOH 6280 C1
Nichols St
10 NWRK 6817 E2
100 NWRK 6818 A2
Nickel St
10 GrwT 6170 D5
Nick Laporte Pl
10 STNL 6920 D6
Nicola Pl
10 PTCH 6170 C7
Nicole Lp
10 STNL 7020 B4
Nicolls Av
101-00 QENS 6720 B6
Nicolosi Dr
10 STNL 7207 D2
Nicolosi Lp
10 STNL 7207 D2
Nicols Ct
10 HRSN 6050 E4
Niehaus Av
10 LFRY 6501 C6
Nielson St
10 WbgT 7114 C4
Nieman Av
10 LNBK 6929 A4
Nightingale Ct
10 NHLS 6618 B7
Nightingale Rd
600 HmpT 6828 E7
600 HmpT 6929 D1
Nightingale St
10 STNL 7117 E1
Nile St
10 YNKR 6394 A3
Niles Pl
10 STNL 7019 C5
Niles St
10 ELIZ 6918 A5
Nimitz Pl
10 YNKR 6281 A2
Nimitz Rd
10 YNKR 6281 A2
Nina Av
10 STNL 7019 B4
Nina Ln
10 WHPL 6168 E4
Nine Acres Ln
1000 MRNK 6397 A1
Nippon Av
10 STNL 7116 B6
Nirvana Av
10 GTNK 6616 E6
Nixon Av
10 STNL 7020 D1
Nixon Ct
10 BKLN 7023 A7
Nixon Rd
700 UnnT 6917 B1
Njrr Av
10 NWRK 6817 E1
Noah Ct
10 STNL 6919 A7
Nob Ct
10 NRCH 6282 A3
10 SCDL 6282 A3
Nob Hill Dr
10 EMFD 6049 A6
Noble Av
10 YNKR 6394 C1

New York City/5 Borough Street Index

STREET
Block City Map# Grid

Noble Av
700 BRNX 6614 A3
1500 BRNX 6505 A7
Noble Pl
10 STNL 7019 E1
Noble St
10 BKLN 6822 B1
10 LNBK 6929 B4
10 NWRK 6817 B5
Nocella Ct
400 HmpT 6828 D6
Nodine St
- HAOH 6279 E1
300 HAOH 6165 E7
Noe Av
500 WbgT 7114 C4
Noe St
10 CART 7115 D1
Noel Av
10 BKLN 7023 E7
10 BKLN 7024 A7
1300 HmpT 6928 D6
Noel Cir
10 HRSN 6283 A4
Noel Rd
10 QENS 7026 B4
Noel St
10 STNL 7116 E7
10 STNL 7117 A7
10 STNL 7207 E1
Noell Av
3400 BRNX 6506 A1
Nolan Av
- STNL 7117 B5
- YNKR 6394 B3
4700 NBgT 6716 D1
6900 NBgT 6610 E6
Nolan Ct
5000 WLTN 6500 B4
Nolans Ln
10 BKLN 6924 B6
Noll Pl
10 NWRK 6712 C6
Noll St
10 BKLN 6822 D5
Nome Av
10 STNL 7019 A7
10 STNL 7117 A1
300 STNL 7018 E7
Nora Dr
1000 LNDN 6917 B5
1000 ROSL 6917 B5
Norbay St
1100 HmpT 6828 A5
Norcroft Rd
10 JSYC 6819 B5
Norcross St
10 RKVC 6929 E3
Norden Rd
10 QENS 6824 E3
Norden St
10 STNL 7020 B6
Nordhoff Dr
400 FTLE 6502 E4
400 LEON 6502 E4
Nordhoff Pl
10 EGLD 6502 D1
E Nordhoff Pl
500 EGLD 6502 D2
W Nordhoff Pl
400 EGLD 6502 D2
Norfeld Blvd
10 HmpT 6827 C6
Norfolk Dr E
10 HmpT 6827 B7
Norfolk Dr W
10 HmpT 6827 B7
Norfolk Rd
10 ISPK 7029 D4
10 NHmT 6723 A2
Norfolk St
10 BKLN 7121 D1
10 MHTN 119 B6
10 MHTN 6821 D3
10 NWRK 6713 C7
Norfolk Wy
- YNKR 6280 B4
Norgate Rd
10 NHmT 6617 D6
Norias Rd
10 GrwT 6170 D6
Norma Ct
700 TnkT 6502 A1
Norma Pl
10 SCDL 6168 B6
10 STNL 7020 B1
Norma Rd
100 TnkT 6502 A1
Norma St
10 HmpT 6827 C6
Normal Rd
159-00 QENS 6825 C4
Normalee Rd
10 STNL 7020 D5
Norman Av
10 BKLN 6822 C2
Norman Dr
- CLFP 6611 D2
10 RYE 6283 C6
Norman Pl
10 EORG 6713 A2
10 NHmT 6618 D7
10 RYE 6283 C6
10 STNL 7207 B3
10 TFLY 6392 A3
600 WbgT 7114 D3
Norman Rd
- FTLE 6611 C1
- PALP 6611 C1
10 NRCH 6395 C1
10 NWRK 6712 B7
100 MplT 6816 B1
100 NWRK 6816 B1
700 RDGF 6611 C1
Norman St
10 EORG 6713 A1
10 LNBK 6929 A4
10 NHmT 6724 C4
16-00 QENS 6823 C6
1200 HlsT 6816 C5
Norman Wy
500 HmpT 6928 B6
Normandy Av
10 HRPK 6278 A1
Normandy Ln
10 NHmT 6617 D6
10 NRCH 6396 B1
10 SCDL 6282 A3
Normandy Pl
10 IrvT 6816 C3
10 ROSL 6917 A5
Normandy Rd
10 BRXV 6394 A4
10 GrbT 6049 C3
10 MrnT 6396 B1
10 YNKR 6280 A5
Normandy Ter
10 UnnT 6917 A1
Norman Rockwell Blvd
10 NRCH 6395 C5
Nortema Ct
10 NHmT 6723 E5
North Av
- FLPK 6827 E2
- NHPK 6827 E2
- STMN 6827 E2
- STMN 6828 A2
10 BGTA 6501 D3
10 ELIZ 6917 E1
10 HlsT 6917 C2
10 LRMT 6396 B1
10 NRCH 6396 A5
10 RDFP 6501 D3
10 STNL 7019 C2
10 UnnT 6917 D2
100 GDNC 6828 C2
100 NRCH 6395 D2
200 WRDG 6500 C6
300 FTLE 6502 D5
500 LEON 6502 D5
1000 ELIZ 6918 A1
1000 NRCH 6281 D6
North Av CO-624
1000 ELIZ 6918 A1
North Av SR-439
10 ELIZ 6917 E1
10 HlsT 6917 C2
10 UnnT 6917 D2
1300 ELIZ 6918 A1
North Av E
10 ELIZ 6918 D3
North Av E CO-624
10 ELIZ 6918 D3
North Blvd
- JSYC 6820 D1
10 HmpT 6929 B7
North Brch
10 NHmT 6618 B6
10 ROSE 6618 B6
North Cir
10 WbgT 7114 B4
North Ct
10 BAYN 6919 C5
10 NHmT 6617 D2
10 NHmT 6724 D1
North Dr
10 DBSF 6166 A5
10 HmpT 6928 C1
10 KENS 6617 A6
10 LBCH 7029 C6
10 NHmT 6617 B6
10 NHmT 6724 A4
10 PLDM 6617 C4
10 PLNM 6617 D4
10 QENS 6614 E7
10 QENS 6615 A7
10 STNL 7020 E4
10 VLYS 6928 C1
10 YNKR 6394 C2
North Ln
10 BAYN 6919 C5
North Pl
- GrbT 6049 D7
North Rd
- SECS 6715 E4
- STNL 7021 A4
10 BRXV 6281 A7
10 EchT 6281 B7
10 GrbT 6049 E5
10 GrbT 6050 A5
10 GTNK 6616 E5
10 GTNK 6617 A5
10 KNGP 6617 A5
North St
10 BRNX 105 D1
10 BRNX 6504 B4
10 EDGW 103 A7
10 EDGW 6502 E7
10 EDGW 6503 A7
10 FLPK 6827 D2
10 GLCV 6509 E3
10 HAOH 6165 E6
10 HmpT 6927 D7
10 HRSN 6283 C1
10 JSYC 6716 B5
10 MTVN 6394 D4
10 STNL 6919 C7
10 SYHW 6048 C1
10 WHPL 6168 D3
10 YNKR 6281 A2
100 BAYN 6919 C5
100 LWRN 7028 A4
100 SHkT 6501 B4
100 TETB 6501 B4
100 WbgT 7114 C3
200 HRSN 6169 B7
200 NHmT 6724 B4
200 RYE 6283 D1
300 TnkT 6501 E1
800 WHPL 6169 A5
North St SR-127
10 WHPL 6168 D3
200 HRSN 6169 B7
200 HRSN 6283 C1
800 WHPL 6169 A5
North Wy
10 BAYN 6919 C5
Northbrook Ln
10 IRVN 6166 C2
Northdale Rd
10 WHPL 6168 D3
Northend Dr
10 SECS 6610 A5
Northentry Rd
10 STNL 7020 A7
Northern Av
10 BRXV 6280 C3
Northern Blvd
- NasC 6618 D5
10 NHmT 6722 E2
10 NHmT 6723 A2
10 STNL 7020 A4
29-39 QENS 6718 E5
39-00 QENS 6719 A5
126-00 QENS 6720 E4
141-00 QENS 6721 D4
200 RSLG 6723 A2
202-00 QENS 6722 D4
400 LKSU 6723 B1
500 THSN 6723 A2
900 NHmT 6617 D7
1000 FLHL 6618 A6
1000 MNPK 6618 B6
1000 NHmT 6618 B6
1000 ROSE 6618 A6
1000 RSLN 6618 E5
1600 MNPK 6617 E6
1600 ROSH 6618 E5
Northern Blvd SR-25A
- NasC 6618 D5
10 NHmT 6722 E2
10 NHmT 6723 A2
29-39 QENS 6718 E5
39-00 QENS 6719 E5
92-00 QENS 6720 E4
137-84 QENS 6721 C4
200 RSLG 6723 A2
202-00 QENS 6722 A4
400 LKSU 6723 B1
500 THSN 6723 A2
900 NHmT 6617 C7
1000 FLHL 6618 A6
1000 MNPK 6618 B6
1000 NHmT 6618 B6
1000 ROSE 6618 A6
1000 RSLN 6618 E5
1600 MNPK 6617 E6
1600 ROSH 6618 E5
Northern Blvd E
29-00 QENS 6718 D6
Northern Blvd E SR-25A
29-00 QENS 6718 D6
Northern Pkwy
- EHLS 6724 E1
- LKSU 6723 C4
- NHLS 6723 C4
- NHLS 6724 A3
- NHmT 6723 E3
- NHmT 6724 E1
- QENS 6723 C4
Northern Rd
10 GrbT 6166 E2
Northfield Av
10 DBSF 6166 C4
10 STNL 6918 E7
10 WOrT 6712 A2
100 STNL 7018 E1
Northfield Av CO-508
10 WOrT 6712 A2
Northfield Ct
10 STNL 6918 E7
Northfield Rd
10 GLCV 6509 D3
10 NRCH 6281 D6
300 HmpT 6928 B7
Northminster Dr
10 WHPL 6050 C6
Northport Ln
10 STNL 7019 B7
Northrop Av
10 YNKR 6280 D4
300 MRNK 6282 D6
Northumberland Gate
10 LNBK 6928 C5
10 VLYS 6928 C5
100 LNBK 6929 A5
Northview Ct
10 STNL 6920 C6
Northview Pl
10 WHPL 6050 A7
10 YNKR 6279 D5
Northview Ter
10 GRFD 6500 C1
10 LODI 6500 C1
10 SdBT 6500 C1
10 YNKR 6279 D5
Northway
10 BRXV 6395 B1
10 EchT 6395 B1
10 GrbT 6166 E2
Northwest Wy
10 BRXV 6395 B1
Northwood Av
10 DMRT 6278 B5
Northwood Cir
10 NRCH 6281 D4
Northwood Ct
10 NRCH 6281 D4
Northwood Wy
300 PALP 6502 C7
Northwoods Rd
10 FLHL 6618 A5
Norton Av
- QENS 7027 B5
10 NHmT 6724 C7
2100 BRNX 6614 C4
Norton Dr
11-00 QENS 7027 B4
Norton Rd
1000 UnnT 6816 A7
Norton St
10 HmpT 7027 E2
Norwalk Av
10 STNL 7019 E4
Norway Av
100 STNL 7020 D6
Norwich Av
10 HmpT 6929 A6
10 LNBK 6929 A5
Norwich St
10 STNL 7019 C6
Norwood Av
10 BKLN 6823 E7
10 BKLN 6924 E1
10 IrvT 6816 C3
10 LODI 6500 C3
10 MLVN 6929 B1
10 STNL 7020 D3
10 WbgT 7114 C2
Norwood Ct
10 STNL 7020 C1
Norwood Pl
10 EORG 6712 D6
10 NRWD 6164 B6
10 NWRK 6712 C6
Norwood Rd
10 GrbT 6167 B5
10 MHVN 6508 B7
10 YNKR 6280 E2
Norwood St
10 NWRK 6712 C7
400 EORG 6712 D6
Norwood Ter
600 ELIZ 6917 E4
Nosband Av
10 WHPL 6168 C3
Nostrand Av
10 BKLN 6822 B6
10 MRNK 6282 E5
10 STNL 7018 E4
400 BKLN 6923 C6
2100 BKLN 7023 C3
2700 HmpT 6929 E6
Nostrand Pl
10 YNKR 6280 B6
Notre Dame Av
10 STNL 7117 A5
Nottingham Av
10 HmpT 6928 B1
10 VLYS 6928 B1
Nottingham Ct
10 NHmT 6724 A4
600 NRWD 6278 D1
Nottingham Pl
10 NHmT 6616 D7
10 SDRK 6616 D7
Nottingham Rd
10 MLVN 6929 B2
10 NHmT 6724 A4
Nottingham Wy
100 HlsT 6816 D7
Notus Av
100 STNL 7116 C5
Nova Ct
10 BKLN 7023 E7
10 BKLN 7024 A7
Noye Ln
10 WDBG 7028 D2
Nuber Av
10 MTVN 6395 A5
Nugent Av
10 STNL 7020 D6
400 STNL 7118 C1
Nugent Ct
10 STNL 7118 C1
Nugent St
10 NHmT 6723 E6
100 STNL 7117 C2
Nunda Av
10 JSYC 6819 D2
Nunley Ct
10 STNL 7020 D3
Nunzie Ct
10 STNL 7019 A1
Nurge Av
54-27 QENS 6823 B3
Nursery Ln
10 RYE 6283 D2
Nursery St
10 NWRK 6713 E3
Nutgrove St
10 WHPL 6168 A3
Nutley Pl
500 HmpT 6927 E6
500 HmpT 6928 A6
Nutly Pl
10 STNL 7020 A2
Nutman Pl
10 WOrT 6712 B3
Nuttman St
10 NWRK 6713 C6
Nutwood Ct
10 STNL 7117 B3
Nuvern Av
10 BRNX 6394 E7
10 MTVN 6394 E7
Nyac Av
100 PLHM 6395 B5
Nye Av
10 NWRK 6816 E3
10 NWRK 6817 A3
200 IrvT 6816 E3
NYS Thruway Access Dr
- RYE 6283 D2

O

O St
1200 HmpT 6827 E7
Oak Av
10 BRNX 6615 B3
10 HmpT 7027 D3
10 IrvT 6712 E7
10 LRMT 6396 C3
10 PLHM 6395 C2
10 STNL 7117 E3
10 TCKA 6280 E6
10 TYTN 6048 C1
10 WHPL 6050 B7
137-00 QENS 6721 B6
200 WbgT 7114 B5
300 CDHT 7028 A2
400 STNL 7118 A4
Oak Bnd
10 YNKR 6394 C1
Oak Ct
10 STNL 7117 B5
300 CDHT 7028 A2
1000 HmpT 6828 A7
Oak Dr
5-00 QENS 7027 E5
10 GTNE 6616 E7
10 MTVN 6395 B4
10 NHmT 6724 A6
300 HmpT 6928 D6
N Oak Dr
700 BRNX 6505 B2
S Oak Dr
700 BRNX 6505 B3
Oak Ln
- OrgT 6165 B5
10 BRNX 6506 C1
10 MRNK 6396 E1
10 NHmT 6724 C4
10 PLMM 6395 C7
10 PLMM 6506 C1
10 SCDL 6167 D5
10 SECS 6610 A5
10 STNL 7116 C4
240-00 QENS 6722 D2
800 HmpT 6928 B5
Oak Ln E
10 EchT 6281 C2
Oak Pl
10 DMRT 6278 C7
10 HmpT 6928 D7
10 HmpT 7027 D2
10 IrvT 6816 C3
10 MNLA 6724 D6
10 NHmT 6724 D2
1200 UnnT 6816 B7
Oak St
10 BAYN 6919 E5
10 BKLN 6822 B2
10 CART 7017 C7
10 CRSK 6392 B1
10 DBSF 6166 A4
10 EMFD 6049 B6
10 EORG 6712 E5
10 ERTH 6500 B7
10 FLPK 6827 D2
10 GrbT 6049 D7
10 GrbT 6166 E2
10 GrbT 6167 D3
10 GrwT 6170 E3
10 HmpT 6827 B5
10 HmpT 7028 B1
10 HRSN 6168 C1
10 HRSN 6283 B4
10 IRVN 6166 A1
10 JSYC 6819 D3
10 LNBK 6929 B4
10 LODI 6500 C1
10 MLVN 6929 A2
10 MNCH 6500 D7
10 MTVN 6394 C4
10 NoCT 6050 B5
10 NRCH 6396 A3
10 NRWD 6164 B6
10 NVLE 6164 B6
10 NWRK 6712 E5
10 PTCH 6170 B6
10 RDFP 6501 E7
10 STNL 7020 D3
10 TFLY 6392 A4
10 TnkT 6501 E3
10 TnkT 6502 A3
10 VLYS 6928 D5
10 WbgT 7114 D1
10 WDBG 7028 B1
10 WhkT 6716 D3
10 WLTN 6500 B7
10 WRDG 6500 D7
10 YNKR 6393 D2
100 BGTA 6501 E3
100 HmpT 6828 E5
100 PTHA 7205 C4
100 UNCT 6716 D3
100 YNKR 6394 C4
200 ELIZ 6918 A3
300 RDGF 6611 B2
300 SRVL 7205 A6
900 ROSL 6917 A5
Oak St W
10 GrwT 6170 C6
Oak Ter
10 TCKA 6280 C3
500 BRNX 6613 A4
Oak Wy
10 SCDL 6167 D5
Oak Bend Rd S
10 WOrT 6712 B1
Oak Bluff Av
10 LRMT 6396 C4
Oakcrest Ln
10 GrbT 6280 B1
Oakdale Av
10 NRCH 6395 C4
10 RYE 6283 D5
10 STNL 7020 B6
Oakdale Dr
10 DBSF 6166 A6
10 HAOH 6166 A6
Oakdale Rd
10 JSYC 6819 A5
10 MrnT 6282 B6
10 NHLS 6724 C1
10 NHmT 6724 C1
Oakdale St
10 STNL 7117 A6
100 STNL 7116 E7
Oakdene Av
- FTLE 6502 D6
- PALP 6502 D6
10 EDGW 6611 D3
10 TnkT 6502 A2
100 TnkT 6501 D3
300 CLFP 6611 C2
500 RDGF 6611 C1
E Oakdene Av
- FTLE 6502 D6
10 LEON 6502 C5
10 PALP 6502 C5
100 TnkT 6502 A2
W Oakdene Av
10 LEON 6502 C5
10 PALP 6502 C5
Oakdene Pl
200 CLFP 6611 D2
Oakdene Ter
10 EDGW 6611 E3
Oakford St
200 HmpT 6828 D7
Oak Grove Av
10 HSBH 6500 D4
10 LODI 6500 D3
Oak Hill Dr
1700 UnnT 6816 A5
Oakhill Rd
10 ARDY 6166 E3
Oakhurst Rd
500 MRNK 6283 A6
Oakland Av
10 EchT 6281 A4
10 HmpT 6828 D5
10 HRSN 6283 C4
10 JSYC 6716 B7
10 JSYC 6820 B1
10 LNBK 6929 B5
10 MTVN 6395 A3
10 NHmT 6508 D5
10 TCKA 6281 A4
10 WbgT 7205 A3
10 YNKR 6280 E4
100 CLST 6278 B3
200 STNL 6920 A7
300 CDHT 7028 A1
500 HmpT 7028 A1
500 STNL 7020 A2
600 HmpT 6928 A7
Oakland Dr
10 NHmT 6617 D3
Oakland Pl
10 BKLN 6923 B6
10 GTNE 6616 E7
600 BRNX 6504 D6
Oakland St
10 IrvT 6816 C1
Oakland Ter
10 NWRK 6712 C6
10 STNL 7020 C2
200 HlsT 6816 D5
Oakland Beach Av
10 RYE 6283 D4
300 RYE 6284 A4
Oakledge Rd
10 BRXV 6395 A1
10 MTVN 6395 A1
Oakleigh Rd
700 HmpT 6928 B5
700 VLYS 6928 B5
Oakley Av
10 MTVN 6394 E4
10 WHPL 6168 C1
200 HmpT 6827 E6
Oakley Ln
10 EWLS 6724 A5
Oakley Pl
10 MTVN 6394 D3
10 NHmT 6723 A3
10 QENS 6723 A3
10 STNL 7117 D2
Oakley Rd
10 WHPL 6168 A4
Oakley St
1300 BRNX 6505 C2
Oakmont Dr
10 HRSN 6050 E7
Oak Park Dr
239-00 QENS 6722 E6
240-00 QENS 6723 A6
Oak Point Av
500 BRNX 6613 E4
Oak Ridge Ct
10 HRSN 6050 E4
Oakridge Dr
10 PTCH 6170 C7
Oak Ridge Ln
10 NHmT 6724 E2
Oakridge Ln
10 NHLS 6724 B3
200 NHmT 6724 B3
Oakridge Pl
10 EchT 6281 B5
Oakridge Rd
10 GrbT 6167 B1
10 WOrT 6712 A3
Oak Ridge St
10 GrwT 6170 E3
Oak Rise
10 TYTN 6048 C6
Oaks Ct
400 HmpT 6828 A6
Oaks Dr
800 HmpT 6828 A6
Oaks Pl
400 HmpT 6828 A6
Oaks Hunt Rd
10 LKSU 6723 A2
Oakstwain Rd
10 SCDL 6167 E5
Oak Trail Rd
10 EGLD 6503 A3
Oak Tree Ct
10 NHmT 6724 E2
10 SNPT 6508 B6
Oak Tree Ln
10 FLHL 6618 B5
10 SNPT 6508 B5
Oak Tree Pl
500 BRNX 6504 D5
Oaktree Pl
100 LEON 6502 D4
Oak Tree Rd
10 OrgT 6164 C3
600 OrgT 6165 A4
Oak Valley Ln
10 HRSN 6051 A5
Oakville St
10 STNL 7019 C5
Oakwood Av
10 BGTA 6501 E3
10 CART 7017 B6
10 COrT 6712 C4
10 KRNY 6714 B3
10 MTVN 6395 A4
10 RYE 6283 E4
10 RYE 6284 A4
10 STNL 7020 B1
10 WbgT 7114 A4
10 WHPL 6168 B3
10 CLFP 6611 C4
200 CDHT 7028 B1
1200 HlsT 6816 E6
Oakwood Cir
10 FLHL 6618 C5
Oakwood Dr
600 NVLE 6164 A4
Oakwood Ln
10 EGLC 6503 B2
10 FLHL 6617 E5
10 PALP 6611 C1
10 PLDM 6617 E5
700 RDGF 6611 C1
Oakwood Pl
10 CART 7017 B6
10 ELIZ 6917 D2
10 SCDL 6167 C5
100 COrT 6712 C4
2100 HmpT 6827 B6
Oakwood Rd
200 EGLD 6392 B6
800 MRNK 6283 A7
Oban St
10 STNL 7116 E7
10 STNL 7117 A7
Oberlin St
10 STNL 7020 D6
O'Brien Av
1800 BRNX 6614 B4
O'Brien Ct
10 BAYN 6919 D4
O'Brien Pl
10 BKLN 6824 A7
O'Brien St
10 KRNY 6714 C3
Obry Dr
10 SCDL 6281 D1
Observer Hwy
10 HBKN 6716 D7
10 JSYC 6716 A7
Observer Hwy CO-681
100 HBKN 6716 C7
Observer Hwy SR-139
10 JSYC 6716 A7
Occident Av
10 STNL 7020 D1
Ocean Av
10 BKLN 6923 B6
10 ERKY 6929 C4
10 HmpT 6929 C3
10 JSYC 6819 C6
10 LNBK 6929 C3
10 LRMT 6396 D3
10 MLVN 6929 C2
10 QENS 6928 A2
10 STNL 7021 A5
10 VLYS 6928 A2
100 HBPK 7028 D1
100 HmpT 6928 A2
100 HmpT 7028 D1
100 HWTN 7028 D1
100 LWRN 7028 B3
100 RKVC 6929 C3
1100 BKLN 7023 C7
4000 BKLN 7121 C1
Ocean Blvd
1500 ATLB 7028 B7
1900 ATLB 7027 E7
Ocean Ct
10 BKLN 7023 A7
10 STNL 7020 A5
Ocean Drwy
10 STNL 7207 E1
10 STNL 7208 A2
Ocean Pkwy
- BKLN 7022 E1
- BKLN 7023 A7
10 BKLN 6922 E7
2700 BKLN 7121 A1
Ocean Rd
10 STNL 7117 B5
Ocean Ter
10 STNL 7019 E5
100 STNL 7020 A5
Oceana Dr E
10 BKLN 7121 B2
Oceana Dr W
10 BKLN 7121 B2
Oceana St
- QENS 6826 B1
Oceana Ter
- BKLN 7121 B1
Oceancrest Blvd
23-62 QENS 7027 B5
Oceanfront St
1000 LBCH 7028 D7
Ocean Harbor Dr
3100 HmpT 6929 D7
3100 HmpT 7029 C1
Oceania St
48-00 QENS 6722 B5
Oceanic Av
10 BKLN 7120 B2
10 STNL 7117 A7
Oceanlea Dr
3500 HmpT 7029 E2
Oceanpoint Av
300 CDHT 7028 A1
500 HmpT 7028 A1
Oceanside Av
- QENS 7121 E4
10 STNL 7020 D7
10 STNL 7021 B6
100 QENS 7122 A4
200 STNL 7118 D1
Ocean View Av
10 GrwT 6170 D5
10 LBCH 7028 D7
Oceanview Av
- LWRN 7028 B3
10 BKLN 7121 A1
10 LNBK 6928 E4
10 STNL 7207 E1
10 VLYS 6928 E5
600 QENS 7122 D2
3800 BKLN 7120 A1
Oceanview Ct
10 LBCH 7028 D7
Oceanview Ln
10 STNL 7020 B5
Oceanview Pl
10 STNL 7117 A6
Oceanview Rd
10 ERKY 6929 C5
10 RKVC 6929 D5
O'Connell Ct
48-00 QENS 6720 A7
O'Connor Av
10 STNL 7019 C3
O'Dell Av
10 WHPL 6168 A3
100 YNKR 6279 E4
400 YNKR 6280 A4
O'Dell Pl
10 NRCH 6395 E4
10 STNL 7207 A1
O'Dell Plz
10 YNKR 6279 E3
O'Dell St
1300 BRNX 6614 C1
1400 BRNX 6505 C7
O'Dell Ter
10 YNKR 6279 E3
Oder Av
400 STNL 7020 C5
Odin St
10 STNL 7117 E1
O'Donnell Rd
164-00 QENS 6825 E7
Oehler Pl
400 CARL 6610 A2
Ogden Av
- BRNX 105 A5
10 DBSF 6166 B4
10 EWLS 6724 A6
10 HRSN 6714 B6
10 JSYC 6716 B7
10 KRNY 6714 B6
10 WHPL 6168 B4
400 MRNK 6282 D6
900 BRNX 107 E1
900 BRNX 6612 E1
1100 BRNX 104 E7
1100 BRNX 6503 E7
Ogden Pk
10 DBSF 6165 E4
Ogden Pl
10 DBSF 6166 B4
300 PTHA 7205 C3
Ogden Rd
10 SCDL 6167 C6
Ogden St
10 NWRK 6713 E4
10 STNL 7116 E6
200 COrT 6712 C4
700 ELIZ 6917 E6
700 LNDN 6917 E6
Ogden Wy
200 HlsT 6816 D7
Ogorman Av
10 STNL 7117 C4
Ogston Ter
10 MLVN 6929 B2
Ohio Av
10 LBCH 7028 D7
10 NHmT 6617 E1
10 NHmT 6618 B1
Ohio Dr
10 LKSU 6723 E4
10 NHmT 6723 E4
Ohio Pl
10 STNL 7019 D2
4000 HmpT 7029 E4
Ohio St
10 RKVC 6929 E4
Ohm Av
1400 BRNX 6506 A6
Okinawa St
- ELIZ 6919 A1
Olcott St
68-00 QENS 6824 C4
200 COrT 6712 C4
Old Fld
10 NHLS 6724 A3
Old Ln
10 GrbT 6167 A6
Old Rd
10 EMFD 6049 C6
10 GrbT 6049 D7
10 GTNK 6617 B5
10 NHmT 6617 B5
10 WbgT 7114 E4
700 ELIZ 6917 D6
700 LNDN 6917 D6
Old Rd W
10 EMFD 6049 B6
Old Albany Post Rd
5000 BRNX 6393 C6
Old Amboy Rd
4200 STNL 7117 A6
Old Army Rd
10 YNKR 6281 B1
100 GrbT 6167 B7
100 GrbT 6281 B1
Old Barn Ln
10 SNPT 6508 B5
Old Beach 88th St
300 QENS 7026 B6
Old Bergen Rd
10 JSYC 6819 B7
Old Boston Post Rd
10 NRCH 6396 B3
Old Broadway
10 MHTN 106 D6
10 MHTN 6612 B3
10 NHmT 6724 B7
10 NHmT 6828 C1
100 HAOH 6279 E1
400 SYHW 6048 A1
Old Broadway US-9
100 HAOH 6279 E1
Old Cedar Rd
300 GrbT 6167 C2
Old Central Av
10 HmpT 6928 C4
10 VLYS 6928 C4
Old Chapel Ct
10 ALPN 6392 D1
Old Colony Dr
10 LRMT 6396 D1
Old Colony Ln
10 GTNK 6617 B6
10 NHmT 6617 B6
Old Colony Rd
10 GrbT 6167 C5
Old Country Rd
10 GDNC 6724 E7
10 GrbT 6049 B4
10 MNLA 6724 E7
10 NRCH 6282 A6
10 NHmT 6724 D7
Old County Ct
10 DMRT 6278 A4
Old Courthouse Rd
10 NHmT 6724 B4
Old Cutter Mill Ln
10 NHmT 6722 C2
Old Cutter Mill Rd
10 GTNE 6722 C2
10 NHmT 6722 C2
Old Dock Rd
10 ALPN 6278 E6
10 ALPN 6279 A6
Old Estate Rd
10 GLCV 6509 D2
10 NHmT 6618 A7
Old Farm Cir
10 WHPL 6168 E6
Old Farm Ln
10 GrbT 6167 A3
Old Farm Rd
- ALPN 6165 A6
10 LKSU 6723 A3
10 MtPT 6049 B1
10 NRCH 6281 D3
N Old Farm Rd
100 NHmT 6724 A5
S Old Farm Rd
100 NHmT 6724 A5
Old Farmers Ln
10 STNL 7020 B5
Oldfield Av
10 HSBH 6500 E5
Old Field Ln
10 LKSU 6723 B2
Oldfield St
10 STNL 7118 B2
Old Field Point Rd
10 GrwT 6170 E3
Old Forge Ln
10 TYTN 6048 B6
Old Fulton St
10 BKLN 121 A3
10 BKLN 6821 C5
Old Garden Ln
10 RYE 6283 B6
Old Hills Ln
10 NHmT 6618 A1
Old Hoboken Rd
10 HKSK 6501 D4
Old Homestead Rd
10 NHmT 6724 C3
Old Homestead Wy
10 NHmT 6724 C4
Old Hook Rd
10 BAYN 6920 A4
100 BAYN 6919 E4
Old House Ln
10 SNPT 6508 E5
10 SNPT 6509 A5
Old Jackson Av
10 GrbT 6166 C7
10 GrbT 6280 C1
Old Jerome Av
10 YNKR 6394 A5
Old Kensico Rd
- GrbT 6167 D1
200 GrbT 6049 E7
200 GrbT 6050 A7
Old Kingsbridge Rd
700 BRNX 6504 E6
Old Knollwood Av
10 EMFD 6049 C5
Old Knollwood Rd
10 EMFD 6049 C5
10 GrbT 6049 B7
Old Lake St
10 HRSN 6050 E6
200 HRSN 6051 A4
Old Lakeville Rd
300 LKSU 6723 C3
Old Lyme Rd
10 HRSN 6168 E1
10 NRCH 6282 A4
10 SCDL 6282 A4
Old Mamaroneck Rd
10 WHPL 6168 B3
300 SCDL 6168 B6
Old Mamaroneck Rd SR-125
10 WHPL 6168 B3
300 SCDL 6168 B6
Old Mill Ct
10 RKVC 6929 D3
Old Mill Ln
10 ARDY 6166 D4
10 OrgT 6164 C2
Old Mill Rd
10 BKLN 6925 A4
10 GTNK 6616 E6
10 HRSN 6050 E3
10 HRSN 6051 A4
10 NHmT 6616 E6
10 NHmT 6617 E6
10 NHmT 6618 A6
10 STNL 7117 B2
100 SDRK 6616 D6
Old Milton Rd
700 RYE 6283 E5
Old Nepperhan Av
400 YNKR 6280 A5
Old New Utrecht Rd
10 BKLN 6922 D7
4800 BKLN 7022 D1
Old Northern Blvd
1000 FLHL 6618 C6
1000 ROSE 6618 C6
1000 RSLN 6618 C6
Old Northfield Av
10 WOrT 6712 A1
Old Oak Rd
10 RYEB 6169 E3
10 RYEB 6170 A4
Old Orchard Ln
10 SCDL 6167 C7
Old Orchard Rd
10 NRCH 6281 C7
10 RYEB 6169 E2
Old Orchard St
1400 HRSN 6050 D4
1400 NoCT 6050 C3
1400 WHPL 6050 C3
Old Ox Rd
10 NHmT 6617 E6
Old Palisade Rd
100 FTLE 103 A4
100 FTLE 6503 A6
Old Pine Dr
10 FLHL 6617 E5
Old Pond Rd
10 GTNK 6616 D6
Old Post Ln
10 MRNK 6282 E7
Old Post Rd
10 RYE 6283 D3
700 MRNK 6282 D7
Old Post Rd 5
10 GrwT 6170 D4
Old Post Rd No 2
10 GrwT 6170 E3
Old Post Rd No 3
300 GrwT 6170 E3
Old Powerhouse Rd
10 EHLS 6724 E1
10 NHmT 6618 D7
100 NHLS 6724 D1
100 NHmT 6724 C1

New York City/5 Borough Street Index

STREET
Block City Map# Grid

Old Quarry Rd
10 ALPN 6278 D4
10 EGLD 6502 E3
10 EGLD 6503 A3
Old Rd to Bloomfield
10 NWRK 6713 D2
Old Rd to Kensico
- WHPL 6050 C6
Old Ridge Lp
10 STNL 7020 B5
Old River Rd
- EDGW 6611 C5
- NBgT 6611 C5
10 EDGW 108 A2
100 NBgT 108 A2
300 CLFP 6611 D4
Old River St
10 HKSK 6501 C1
Old Rockaway Blvd
- QENS 6927 A4
Old Saw Mill Rd
10 ALPN 6278 D5
10 CLST 6278 C5
Old Saw Mill River Rd
- GrbT 6048 E3
- GrbT 6049 A3
10 MtPT 6049 A2
Old Schoolhouse Ln Ct
10 RSLN 6618 D4
Old Searingtown Rd
10 NHmT 6724 C4
Old Shelter Rock Rd
10 NHLS 6617 E7
10 NHLS 6724 B3
10 NHmT 6617 E7
Old Shore Rd
10 PTWN 6508 D7
Old Sleigh Hill Rd
400 NVLE 6164 B3
Old Slip
10 MHTN 120 C2
10 MHTN 6821 B5
Old Smith Rd
10 TFLY 6392 B3
Old South Rd
76-00 QENS 6925 B2
124-00 QENS 6926 B3
Old Sprain Rd
10 GrbT 6166 E5
100 ARDY 6166 E5
Old Stable Rd
10 DMRT 6278 B6
Old Stewart Av
10 NHmT 6724 B7
Old Tappan Ln
10 NVLE 6164 B3
10 OLDT 6164 B3
10 OrgT 6164 B3
Old Tappan Rd
10 NVLE 6164 B3
10 OLDT 6164 B3
10 OrgT 6164 B3
Old Tappan Rd CO-110
10 NVLE 6164 B3
10 OLDT 6164 B3
10 OrgT 6164 B3
Old Tappan Rd E
10 OLDT 6164 A3
Old Tappan Rd E CO-110
10 OLDT 6164 A3
Old Tarrytown Rd
10 GrbT 6049 D7
10 GrbT 6050 A6
500 EMFD 6049 C6
Old Town Rd
10 STNL 7020 C6
Old Track Rd
10 GrwT 6170 E3
Old Tree Ln
10 GTNK 6616 E4
Old Well Rd
10 HRSN 6168 D1
Old Westbury Rd
- EHLS 6724 E1
- NHmT 6724 E1
Old White Plains Rd
- BRNX 6394 C7
200 GrbT 6048 E4
600 MRNK 6282 E5
900 MrnT 6282 C3
1100 SCDL 6282 C3
E Old White Plains Rd
- MRNK 6282 D5
Old Wilmot Rd
100 EchT 6281 D3
100 NRCH 6281 D3
Old Wood Rd
10 EDGW 6611 E2
Oldwood Rd S
10 MHVN 6508 B7
Old Woods Dr
10 HRSN 6282 E3
Olean Av
100 JSYC 6819 D1
Olean St
10 BKLN 7023 C3
Oleri Ter
1300 FTLE 6502 E7
Olga Pl
- STNL 7020 D5
Olinda Av
10 HAOH 6165 C7
Olinville Av
2200 BRNX 6505 A4
Oliphant Av
10 DBSF 6165 E4
10 DBSF 6166 A5
Olive Ct
10 RKVC 6929 D5
Olive Dr
10 LNBK 6929 A4
Olive Ln
100 NHmT 6724 B4
Olive Pl
10 LNBK 6929 A5
10 QENS 6824 D3
500 WbgT 7114 C4
Olive St
10 BKLN 6822 D4
10 BlmT 6713 A1
10 EORG 6713 A1
10 LKSU 6723 D4
10 PTHA 7205 C4
Olive St
10 WbgT 7205 A1
800 ELIZ 6918 A2
E Olive St
10 LBCH 7029 D7
W Olive St
10 LBCH 7029 A7
700 LBCH 7028 E6
Oliver Av
10 GrbT 6050 A5
10 HmpT 6827 C5
10 HmpT 6928 B1
10 YNKR 6393 D1
Oliver Pl
10 STNL 7018 E4
300 BRNX 6504 D3
Oliver St
10 BKLN 7021 C3
10 MHTN 118 E7
10 MHTN 6821 C4
10 NWRK 6817 E2
300 NWRK 6818 A2
800 HmpT 6928 A7
Olivia Ct
10 STNL 6920 A7
10 STNL 7020 A1
Olivia St
10 PTCH 6170 B6
Olmstead Av
1200 BRNX 6614 C1
1500 BRNX 6505 C7
Olmsted Rd
10 SCDL 6167 D6
Olsen Ct
600 PTHA 7205 E2
Olsen St
10 HmpT 6827 B7
Olson Pl
10 IrvT 6816 D3
Olympia Av
500 CLFP 6611 C2
500 FRVW 6611 C2
Olympia Blvd
10 STNL 7020 D7
700 STNL 7118 B2
Olympia St
- CLST 6278 C2
Olympic Ter
10 IrvT 6816 A3
Omaha St
- STNL 6918 D7
Omar Av
300 CART 7017 A7
300 WbgT 7017 A7
Omega St
1400 HmpT 6827 E4
Oncrest Pl
300 CLFP 6611 D4
Oncrest Ter
400 CLFP 6611 D3
Onderdonk Av
10 BKLN 6823 A4
10 QENS 6823 B5
One Depot Plz
10 MRNK 6282 D4
Oneida Av
10 ATLB 7028 A7
10 MTVN 6395 A5
10 STNL 7020 B3
4200 BRNX 6394 A6
Oneida Cir
10 HRSN 6283 A1
Oneida Rd
10 SCDL 6168 B6
Oneida St
10 RYE 6169 E7
10 YNKR 6279 E6
O'Neill Pl
2900 BRNX 6505 D3
One Lighting Pl
10 BRNX 6613 E5
Onondaga St
10 RYE 6169 E7
10 YNKR 6394 B2
Onslow Pl
100 QENS 6824 E4
Ontario Av
10 STNL 7020 A3
Ontario Rd
- HmpT 6827 A2
10 BLRS 6827 B2
10 FLPK 6827 C2
900 HmpT 6929 C2
Opal Ct
10 BKLN 7023 E7
Opal Ln
10 STNL 7206 E2
Opal St
10 HmpT 6827 D7
Ophir Dr
10 HRSN 6169 B2
Opp Ct
10 STNL 7116 E4
Opus Ct
10 STNL 7020 E3
Orama Dr
10 SNPT 6508 C4
Orange Av
- BKLN 7022 E2
10 IrvT 6816 C1
10 STNL 7019 C1
200 IrvT 6712 C7
300 NWRK 6712 D7
S Orange Av
10 NWRK 6713 A7
100 SOrT 6712 B6
500 NWRK 6712 E6
800 EORG 6712 D6
S Orange Av CO-510
10 NWRK 6713 A7
100 SOrT 6712 B6
500 NWRK 6712 E6
800 EORG 6712 D6
Orange Pl
10 IrvT 6816 C1
Orange St
10 BKLN 120 E3
10 BKLN 121 A3
10 BKLN 6821 C6
10 BlmT 6713 B1
10 NWRK 6713 D6
10 WbgT 7114 C3
600 EORG 6713 B5
Orangeburg Rd
10 HRPK 6164 A5
10 NRWD 6164 A5
10 OLDT 6164 A5
100 OrgT 6164 D1
300 PRMT 6164 D1
Orangeburg Rd SR-340
100 OrgT 6164 D1
300 PRMT 6164 D1
Orange Heights Av
10 WOrT 6712 A3
Oratam Ter
200 LEON 6502 E4
Oratio Pl
10 LODI 6500 D2
Oraton Pkwy
- IrvT 6712 E7
- NWRK 6712 E6
N Oraton Pkwy
10 EORG 6713 A4
S Oraton Pkwy
10 EORG 6712 E5
10 EORG 6713 A4
Oraton St
10 NWRK 6713 E3
10 NWRK 6714 A3
Oratory Pl
100 BKLN 121 C6
100 BKLN 6821 D7
Orawaupum St
10 WHPL 6168 A2
Orbach Av
10 HmpT 6929 A1
10 MLVN 6929 A1
Orbach Wy
- ALPN 6279 A1
Orbit Ln
10 STNL 7019 A6
Orchard Av
10 RYE 6283 E1
10 STNL 7206 B3
500 LEON 6502 C5
500 PALP 6502 C5
Orchard Ct
10 LODI 6500 E2
10 NHmT 6618 E7
Orchard Dr
10 HRSN 6169 C1
10 RYE 6283 E4
10 WHPL 6050 B6
Orchard Ln
10 GrbT 6049 B4
10 KNGP 6617 A3
10 OLDT 6164 A3
10 RYE 6284 A3
10 SCLF 6509 D7
10 STNL 7117 A7
Orchard Ln S
10 STNL 7117 A7
10 STNL 7208 A1
Orchard Pkwy
10 WHPL 6168 A3
Orchard Pl
10 BRXV 6281 A7
10 HRSN 6283 B4
10 IrvT 6816 B4
10 NRCH 6395 E3
10 TFLY 6392 B2
10 VLYS 6928 B2
10 WHPL 6050 B7
10 YNKR 6279 E7
100 LEON 6502 C4
Orchard Rd
10 DMRT 6278 B5
10 MplT 6816 A1
10 MrnT 6282 C7
10 NHmT 6616 E6
Orchard St
10 CART 7017 B6
10 DBSF 6166 B4
10 EchT 6281 B5
10 EDGW 103 A6
10 EDGW 6503 A7
10 ELIZ 6917 D3
10 ERTH 6609 B2
10 GrbT 6166 E1
10 GRFD 6500 A2
10 GTNK 6616 E5
10 HRSN 6283 B3
10 JSYC 6819 E2
10 JSYC 6820 A2
10 LODI 6500 D3
10 MHTN 119 B5
10 MHTN 6821 D3
10 MTVN 6394 E2
10 NHmT 6508 D6
10 NHmT 6617 D6
10 NHmT 6618 A2
10 NWRK 6817 D2
10 PTCH 6170 C5
10 PTWN 6508 D6
10 RDFP 6501 E6
10 WHPL 6050 B6
10 WLTN 6500 A5
10 YNKR 6279 D7
42-00 QENS 6718 D6
300 EGLD 6392 A5
400 CARL 6500 B7
500 MRNK 6283 A5
Orchard Ter
200 BGTA 6501 D2
1400 HlsT 6816 D5
Orchard Wy
10 GLCV 6509 D3
Orchard Beach Blvd
10 MHVN 6508 B7
Orchard Beach Rd
10 BRNX 6506 C4
Orchard Farm Rd
10 NHmT 6618 A1
Orchard Meadows Dr N
500 UnnT 6816 B4
Orchard Meadows Dr S
100 UnnT 6816 B4
Orchid Ct
10 FLPK 6827 E2
Orchid Dr
10 WLTN 6500 A6
Orchid Ln
10 NHmT 6723 E6
Orchid St
10 FLPK 6827 E3
Ordell Av
10 STNL 7019 D2
Ordinance Rd
10 QENS 6616 A6
Oregon Av
10 EchT 6395 B2
10 WbgT 7205 A1
500 CLFP 6611 C2
500 FRVW 6611 C2
Oregon Rd
10 STNL 7020 C6
Oregon St
10 LBCH 7028 E7
Orient Av
10 BKLN 6822 D3
10 JSYC 6819 D4
Orient Pl
10 LWRN 7028 A6
Orient St
10 OrgT 6165 A2
10 YNKR 6394 A3
100 BAYN 6919 D5
Orient Wy
10 LynT 6609 A4
10 RTFD 6609 A3
Orient Wy CO-130
10 LynT 6609 A4
10 RTFD 6609 A4
Orienta Av
300 MRNK 6282 E7
600 MRNK 6396 E1
700 MRNK 6397 A2
Oriental Blvd
100 BKLN 7121 D1
Oriental Pl
10 NWRK 6713 E4
Oriental St
10 NWRK 6713 E4
Orinoco Pl
10 STNL 6919 A7
Oriole Av
10 BRXV 6281 A7
10 BRXV 6395 C1
600 HmpT 6828 D7
600 HmpT 6929 D1
Oriole Ct
200 NHLS 6724 C1
Oriole Pl
10 RYEB 6170 A2
Oriole Rd
10 YNKR 6280 B6
Oritan Av
500 RDGF 6611 A1
Oritani Pl
500 TnkT 6501 D1
Orlando Av
10 ARDY 6166 D5
800 HmpT 6929 C1
Orlando St
10 STNL 7020 E6
Orleans Rd
10 VLYS 6928 D5
Orloff Av
3800 BRNX 6504 C1
Ormond Pl
10 MrnT 6282 C5
10 RYE 6283 D5
10 RYE 6284 A4
10 STNL 7020 E3
Ormond St
10 RKVC 6929 E5
Ormonde Blvd
10 VLYS 6928 B2
100 HmpT 6928 B1
Ormonde Pl
10 NRCH 6395 C3
Ormsby Av
10 STNL 7207 B2
Orsini Dr
10 MrnT 6282 B7
Osage Ln
10 STNL 7117 A7
Osborn Av
100 MRNK 6283 B5
Osborn Ln
10 DBSF 6166 A4
Osborn Rd
10 HRSN 6169 A7
10 RYE 6283 D3
100 HRSN 6283 C3
Osborn St
400 BKLN 6924 B4
Osborne Av
10 STNL 7117 B6
Osborne Pl
10 IrvT 6816 C3
10 PTCH 6170 A5
10 RKVC 6929 E4
10 RYEB 6170 A5
10 WOrT 6712 B2
1900 BRNX 105 B2
1900 BRNX 6504 A5
Osborne Rd
10 HmpT 6828 D4
Osborne St
10 STNL 7116 E7
10 WHPL 6168 A3
Osborne Ter
10 NWRK 6817 A3
10 NWRK 6816 E4
Osceola Av
10 DBSF 6166 B3
10 IRVN 6166 B3
Osgood Av
10 STNL 7020 D3
Osgood St
4800 BRNX 6394 C5
Oshaughnessy Ln
10 CLST 6278 C4
Osman Pl
4700 BRNX 6394 D5
Osmun Pl
10 YNKR 6280 A7
Osprey Ct
10 NHmT 6618 C3
10 SECS 6610 A5
Osprey Dr
10 SAMB 7205 D7
Ossipee Rd
1100 HmpT 6929 C1
1100 MLVN 6929 C1
Ostend Pl
300 QENS 7027 D5
Ostend Rd
10 ISPK 7029 D4
Ostermeier Wy
- EGLC 6503 B2
Ostrich Ct
10 STNL 7206 C1
Ostwood Ter
1900 UnnT 6816 A4
2000 MplT 6816 A4
Oswald Pl
10 STNL 7207 A2
Oswego Av
10 HmpT 7028 D7
Oswego Ct
300 WNYK 111 D1
300 WNYK 6611 C7
300 WNYK 6717 B1
Oswego St
10 STNL 7020 B4
Othello Av
700 HmpT 6828 B6
Otis Av
10 STNL 7117 E1
10 WHPL 6050 B6
100 STNL 7118 A2
102-00 QENS 6720 C7
2900 BRNX 6615 A1
Otsego Av
- STNL 7020 A3
10 NRCH 6395 D2
Otsego Rd
900 HmpT 6929 C1
Otsego St
10 BKLN 6922 A2
10 YNKR 6394 B2
Otsigo Rd
10 YNKR 6280 D5
Ottavio Promenade
10 STNL 7206 C5
Ottawa Av
10 HSBH 6500 D3
10 LODI 6500 D3
400 HSBH 6501 A4
Otter Rock Dr
10 GrwT 6170 E4
Otto Rd
64-00 QENS 6823 D5
Outerbridge Av
10 STNL 7206 E1
Outerbridge Cross
- PTHA 7205 E2
- PTHA 7206 A2
- STNL 7206 A2
Outerbridge Cross SR-440
- PTHA 7205 E2
- PTHA 7206 A2
- STNL 7206 A2
Outlook Av
10 WbgT 7114 A1
10 YNKR 6280 E5
1400 BRNX 6506 B6
Outwater Ln
10 CARL 6610 A4
10 ERTH 6610 A4
10 GRFD 6500 A1
100 LODI 6500 C1
100 SdBT 6500 A1
Outwater Ln CO-42
10 GRFD 6500 A1
100 LODI 6500 C1
100 SdBT 6500 A1
Oval Ct
10 BRXV 6280 E6
10 YNKR 6280 D3
Ovation Ct
10 GrbT 6049 E5
Overbaugh Pl
10 BKLN 7023 D2
Overbrook Rd
400 NVLE 6164 B4
Overbrook St
46-00 QENS 6722 E3
Overcliff St
10 YNKR 6393 D3
Overdale Rd
10 RYE 6283 B5
Overhill Av
10 RYE 6283 E5
Overhill Ln
10 FLHL 6618 C5
Overhill Pl
10 YNKR 6394 C4
Overhill Rd
10 EchT 6395 B2
10 GrbT 6049 A7
10 MTVN 6395 B2
10 NRCH 6281 E7
10 NRCH 6282 A7
10 SCDL 6281 C1
108-00 QENS 6824 D3
Overing St
1400 BRNX 6505 D7
E Overlook
200 NHmT 6618 B1
N Overlook
- NHmT 6618 B2
S Overlook
10 NHmT 6618 C2
W Overlook
10 NHmT 6618 B2
Overlook Av
- STNL 7019 E7
- STNL 7117 E1
10 CLFP 6611 D3
10 EchT 6281 B6
10 GTPZ 6723 B1
10 LEON 6502 D3
10 RDFP 6502 A5
10 STNL 7020 B6
10 TCKA 6281 B6
10 THSN 6723 B1
100 HKSK 6501 B1
Overlook Cir
10 NHLS 6724 B1
200 NRCH 6395 E1
Overlook Ct
10 NoCT 6050 B4
10 STNL 7020 D5
100 WbgT 7114 B3
Overlook Dr
10 BXTE 6617 E1
10 MtPT 6050 A3
10 STNL 7020 C4
1100 FTLE 6502 E3
1100 FTLE 6503 C3
Overlook Pl
10 RYE 6283 D6
10 RYE 6284 A4
500 EGLD 6502 E3
Overlook Rd
10 ALPN 6278 E6
10 ARDY 6166 E3
10 DBSF 6166 B4
10 HAOH 6166 A7
10 NHmT 6723 A3
10 NRCH 6281 E7
10 NRCH 6395 E1
10 QENS 6723 A3
10 SCDL 6167 D6
10 WHPL 6168 C4
Overlook Rd N
10 NoCT 6050 B4
Overlook St
10 MTVN 6394 E3
Overlook Ter
10 EHLS 6618 E7
10 LEON 6502 D4
10 MHTN 104 C3
10 MHTN 6503 D5
10 MrnT 6396 B1
10 STNL 7020 D5
10 YNKR 6393 C1
Overman Pl
10 NRCH 6395 C2
Overpeck Av
10 RDFP 6502 A5
Overpeck Pl
10 EGLD 6502 D1
Overpeck Ter
200 TnkT 6502 C1
Overton Rd
10 GrbT 6167 B7
10 GrbT 6281 B1
Overview Ter
- EDGW 6611 E2
- FTLE 6611 E3
Ovid Pl
114-00 QENS 6826 B6
Ovington Av
200 BKLN 6921 E7
300 BKLN 7021 E1
1000 BKLN 7022 B1
Ovington Ct
10 BKLN 7022 C2
Ovis Pl
10 STNL 7117 D4
Owasco Rd
300 MHTN 120 A7
300 MHTN 6821 A7
900 HmpT 6929 C2
Owen Rd
10 NRCH 6281 D6
Owens Rd
10 HKSK 6501 B2
Owls Head Ct
6800 BKLN 6921 D7
Oxer Pl
10 GrwT 6170 D5
Oxford Av
10 JSYC 6819 D3
10 YNKR 6280 E4
3100 BRNX 102 C1
3100 BRNX 6504 B1
3600 BRNX 6393 B7
Oxford Blvd
10 GDNC 6828 D2
10 GTNK 6617 A6
10 NHmT 6617 A6
Oxford Blvd S
300 GDNC 6828 D3
300 HmpT 6828 D3
Oxford Ct
300 CDHT 7028 C3
800 HmpT 6827 E7
Oxford Dr
10 MNCH 6501 B6
10 TFLY 6392 C4
Oxford Ln
10 GrbT 6167 B5
Oxford Pl
- NRCH 6281 E7
10 CRSK 6278 B7
10 DMRT 6278 B7
10 LWRN 7028 B6
10 STNL 6920 B6
10 STNL 7020 C1
Oxford Rd
10 HAOH 6280 A1
10 HmpT 6929 B7
10 MrnT 6282 C6
10 NHmT 6617 E6
10 NRCH 6281 E7
10 NRCH 6395 D1
10 SCDL 6167 E5
10 SCDL 6168 A5
10 WHPL 6168 D4
10 YNKR 6394 C2
400 CDHT 7028 C3
500 CDHT 7027 D1
500 HmpT 7027 E1
800 HmpT 6928 B7
Oxford St
10 BKLN 7121 D1
10 MLVN 6929 C3
10 MtPT 6050 A2
10 NHmT 6724 C5
10 NWRK 6818 B1
100 COrT 6712 C4
E Oxford St
10 MtPT 6050 A2
10 VLYS 6928 E3
N Oxford St
10 BKLN 121 E4
10 BKLN 6821 E6
S Oxford St
10 BKLN 121 E6
10 BKLN 6821 E7
100 BKLN 6922 E1
W Oxford St
10 VLYS 6928 D3
Oxford Ter
10 WOrT 6712 A3
Oxford Wy
10 ALPN 6278 D4
Oxholm Av
10 STNL 7020 A2
Ox Ridge Rd
10 GrbT 6049 C4
Ozzie Nelson Dr
10 RDFP 6502 A4

P

P St
1300 HmpT 6827 E7
Pacific Av
10 HmpT 6828 A4
10 JSYC 6819 E5
10 STNL 7117 A7
100 JSYC 6820 A4
200 CDHT 7028 A2
200 HmpT 7027 E2
200 HmpT 7028 A2
500 PTHA 7205 C2
Pacific Blvd
10 LBCH 7029 E7
2000 ATLB 7027 E7
Pacific St
10 BKLN 120 E6
10 NWRK 6817 E2
100 BKLN 121 A6
100 BKLN 6821 C7
400 BKLN 6922 E1
600 BKLN 6923 B1
1800 BKLN 6924 A2
Packard Ct
10 RYE 6283 D3
Packard St
10 BAYN 6920 A3
39-00 QENS 6719 A6
Packer Av
400 PTHA 7205 B2
Packman Av
300 MTVN 6394 E2
Paddington Cir
10 BRXV 6281 B7
10 BRXV 6395 A1
Paddington Rd
10 BRXV 6281 B7
10 BRXV 6395 A1
10 SCDL 6167 C6
Paddock Ln
10 LKSU 6723 A3
Paddock Rd
10 RYEB 6169 E3
10 WHPL 6168 C6
Paderewski Av
200 PTHA 7205 D2
Paerdegat Av N
10 BKLN 7024 B1
Paerdegat Av S
10 BKLN 7024 A1
Paerdegat 1st St
10 BKLN 7024 B1
7700 BKLN 6924 B7
Paerdegat 2nd St
10 BKLN 7024 B1
Paerdegat 3rd St
10 BKLN 7024 B1
Paerdegat 4th St
10 BKLN 7024 B1
Paerdegat 5th St
10 BKLN 7024 B1
Paerdegat 6th St
10 BKLN 7024 B1
Paerdegat 7th St
10 BKLN 7024 B1
Paerdegat 8th St
10 BKLN 7024 B1
Paerdegat 9th St
10 BKLN 7024 B1
Paerdegat 10th St
10 BKLN 7024 B1
Paerdegat 11th St
10 BKLN 7024 B1
Paerdegat 12th St
10 BKLN 7024 C2
Paerdegat 13th St
10 BKLN 7024 C2
Paerdegat 14th St
10 BKLN 7024 C2
Paerdegat 15th St
10 BKLN 7024 C2
Page Av
10 STNL 7206 C3
10 YNKR 6394 B2
Page Pl
57-00 QENS 6823 A3
Page Rd
10 VLYS 6928 D5
Page Ter
400 SOrT 6712 A4
Paidge Av
10 BKLN 117 E7
10 BKLN 6718 C7
Paine Av
- HlsT 6816 C4
10 IrvT 6816 B4
10 NRCH 6395 E1
100 NRCH 6281 E7
Paine Rd
1300 HBPK 6928 E7
1300 HmpT 6928 E7
Paine St
2900 BRNX 6505 E7
Palace Ct
10 STNL 7020 A5
Palace Pl
10 PTCH 6170 B5
Paladino Av
10 MHTN 110 D4
10 MHTN 6612 E6
Palermo Ct
1100 HmpT 6828 A7
Palermo St
85-00 QENS 6826 A2
Palisade Av
10 BGTA 6501 D3
10 CLFP 108 A1
10 CLFP 6611 C5
10 CRSK 6278 B7
10 GrbT 6166 E2
10 GRFD 6500 A3
10 JSYC 6820 B1
10 LEON 6502 C4
10 LNBK 6929 A4
10 RDFP 6501 D3
10 YNKR 6393 C1
100 CRSK 6392 B1
100 DBSF 6165 E6
100 HAOH 6165 E6
100 JSYC 6716 C7
100 UNCT 6716 D5
100 YNKR 6279 E4
200 DBSF 6166 A5
Palisade Av
400 TnkT 6501 E2
700 FTLE 6611 E2
700 TnkT 6502 A1
1100 FTLE 6502 E7
1400 FTLE 103 A4
1400 FTLE 6503 A6
1900 WhkT 6716 D4
2300 BRNX 102 A1
2300 BRNX 6504 A1
3900 BRNX 6393 A7
4900 WNYK 6716 E1
4900 WNYK 6717 A1
5000 WNYK 111 A2
5700 WNYK 6611 A7
6700 GTBG 6611 B6
7000 NBgT 6611 B6
Palisade Av CO-27
10 CLFP 108 A1
10 CLFP 6611 E1
10 NBgT 6611 C5
700 FTLE 6611 E2
Palisade Av SR-5
1000 FTLE 6611 E1
Palisade Av SR-67
1100 FTLE 6502 E7
1400 FTLE 103 A5
1400 FTLE 6503 A6
E Palisade Av
10 EGLD 6392 A7
300 EGLC 6503 B1
300 EGLD 6503 B1
E Palisade Av CO-505
10 EGLD 6392 A7
300 EGLC 6503 B1
300 EGLD 6503 B1
Palisade Blvd
10 DMRT 6278 A5
Palisade Ct
10 CRSK 6392 B1
Palisade Pl
1800 BRNX 105 B3
1800 BRNX 6504 A5
Palisade Plz
10 EDGW 103 A6
10 EDGW 6503 A7
1400 CLFP 6611 C5
9000 NBgT 6611 C5
Palisade Rd
10 ELIZ 6917 B3
10 RYE 6284 A2
300 UnnT 6917 B3
Palisade St
10 DBSF 6165 E4
10 STNL 7021 B5
100 DBSF 6166 A4
Palisade Ter
10 EDGW 103 A6
10 EDGW 6503 A7
10 FTLE 6503 A7
1400 FTLE 103 A5
1400 FTLE 6502 D6
Palisades Blvd
- ALPN 6165 B6
- ALPN 6278 E7
- ALPN 6279 A5
- ALPN 6392 E2
- OrgT 6165 B6
- TFLY 6392 D3
400 FTLE 6502 D7
Palisades Blvd US-9W
- ALPN 6165 B6
- ALPN 6278 E7
- ALPN 6279 A5
- ALPN 6392 E2
- OrgT 6165 B6
- TFLY 6392 D3
E Palisades Blvd
- FTLE 6502 C6
10 PALP 6502 C6
W Palisades Blvd
10 PALP 6502 B5
Palisades Gdns
10 OrgT 6164 E4
10 OrgT 6165 A4
Palisades Pl
10 RYE 6284 A2
Palisades Interstate Pkwy
- ALPN 6165 A6
- ALPN 6278 E7
- ALPN 6279 B2
- ALPN 6392 E2
- EGLC 101 A2
- EGLC 6392 C7
- EGLC 6503 B4
- FTLE 103 B1
- FTLE 6503 A6
- OrgT 6164 E3
- OrgT 6165 A5
- TFLY 6392 E2
Palisades InterSt Pkwy US-9W
- FTLE 103 B1
- FTLE 6503 A4
Palisadium Dr
700 CLFP 6611 E2
700 FTLE 6611 E2
Palliser Rd
10 IRVN 6166 B2
Palm Ln
500 HmpT 6828 D6
Palm St
10 EORG 6712 C6
10 NWRK 6712 C6
Palm Ter
700 HmpT 6828 B7
Palma Dr
10 HRSN 6283 A3
10 STNL 7020 D4
Palmer Av
10 BRXV 6280 D7
10 MTVN 6395 A2
10 NoCT 6050 B5
10 SCDL 6168 B7
10 SCDL 6282 A1
10 STNL 7019 C1
10 YNKR 6280 D7
100 MRNK 6282 E6
400 TnkT 6501 E2
600 TnkT 6502 A1
900 MrnT 6282 D7
1100 MrnT 6396 C1
1400 LRMT 6396 C1
2100 BRNX 6506 A4
2100 NRCH 6396 B2
Palmer Av
3200 BRNX 6505 E2
Palmer Av SR-125
10 SCDL 6168 B7
10 SCDL 6282 A1
Palmer Ct
700 MRNK 6282 D6
Palmer Dr
10 QENS 7121 E4
10 QENS 7122 A3
Palmer Pl
10 LEON 6502 D5
10 PALP 6502 D5
10 VLYS 6928 C2
Palmer Rd
10 YNKR 6279 E6
400 YNKR 6280 B7
Palmer St
10 ELIZ 6918 A5
Palmer Ter
10 CARL 6609 E2
100 WRDG 6500 B5
300 MRNK 6282 D6
Palmetto Dr
600 HmpT 6828 B7
700 HmpT 6929 B1
Palmetto St
10 BKLN 6823 A7
16-00 QENS 6823 A7
Palmieri Ln
10 STNL 7207 A3
Palmyra Av
100 HmpT 7028 D1
Palo Alto Av
188-00 QENS 6826 A3
Palo Alto Pl
10 MTVN 6395 B2
Palo Alto St
85-00 QENS 6826 A3
Palumbo Pl
10 BRXV 6394 E1
10 MTVN 6394 E1
Pamela Ln
10 MtPT 6049 E1
10 NRCH 6281 E5
10 STNL 7020 C5
Pamrapo Av
10 JSYC 6819 B6
Pan Am Rd
- QENS 6926 A4
Panama St
10 NWRK 6818 B7
Panasonic Wy
10 SECS 6609 E7
Pandolfi Av
100 SECS 6610 A7
Pandosa Memorial Av
10 FLPK 6827 C3
Panorama Dr
100 EDGW 6611 E3
Pansy Av
10 FLPK 6827 C2
Paper Mill Rd
10 RSLN 6618 D6
Papermill Rd
10 PLNM 6617 D3
Papetti Plz
10 ELIZ 6918 B4
Par Ct
10 NHLS 6724 B2
Parade Ln
10 RYEB 6051 D6
Parade Pl
10 BKLN 6923 A5
Paradise Av
10 PRMT 6165 A1
Paradise Dr
10 GrbT 6167 B6
Paradise Pl
10 STNL 7206 B4
Paradise Rd
10 BRXV 6280 E7
Parcot Av
10 NRCH 6395 D2
Parente Ln N
10 ISPK 7029 D3
S Parente Ln
10 ISPK 7029 D4
Paret Ln
10 GrbT 6167 A4
Paris Av
10 NVLE 6164 B5
10 RCKL 6164 D5
Paris St
10 NWRK 6818 B2
Parish Av
10 STNL 7018 B6
Park E
10 NHmT 6724 C5
Park W
10 NHmT 6724 C5
Park Av
- UNCT 6717 A2
- WhkT 6717 A2
10 ARDY 6166 D4
10 BKLN 121 E4
10 BKLN 6821 E6
10 BRXV 6280 E7
10 BRXV 6281 A7
10 CART 7017 A6
10 COrT 6712 C1
10 CRSK 6278 B7
10 EchT 6281 B5
10 EORG 6713 A3
10 GRFD 6500 B1
10 HBKN 6716 D7
10 HmpT 7027 E2
10 HRSN 6050 D7
10 HRSN 6168 C3
10 HRSN 6283 C4
10 IRVN 6048 B6
10 KRNY 6714 A3
10 LODI 6500 C2
10 LRMT 6396 D3
10 MHTN 6717 E6
10 MLVN 6929 A2
10 MNPK 6617 E6
10 MRNK 6283 A5
10 MtPT 6049 E1
10 MTVN 6394 E4
10 NARL 6714 D1
10 NHmT 6617 E6
10 NHmT 6618 A2
10 NRCH 6396 A5
10 NWRK 6713 D5

New York City/5 Borough Street Index

STREET Block City Map# Grid

Park Av
10 OrgT 6164 E4
10 PTCH 6170 A4
10 RDFP 6501 E4
10 RTFD 6609 A2
10 STNL 6919 C7
10 TCKA 6281 A6
10 TnkT 6501 E4
10 TYTN 6048 B3
10 WHPL 6168 A1
10 WLPK 6724 D4
10 WOrT 6712 C1
71-00 QENS 6825 C1
100 BKLN 6822 C6
100 CLFP 6611 D3
100 EORG 6712 E2
100 ERTH 6609 B1
100 LEON 6502 D5
100 SCLF 6509 E7
100 TnkT 6502 A3
200 FRVW 6611 C3
200 MHTN 116 D3
200 MNLA 6724 D7
300 PTHA 7205 D3
300 RYE 6283 C4
400 MHTN 113 D2
400 MHTN 6718 B2
400 MNPK 6618 A5
500 CDHT 7028 A2
500 HmpT 6828 E7
500 YNKR 6279 E4
600 ELIZ 6917 B3
800 NHPK 6827 E1
900 NHPK 6828 A1
900 ROSP 6917 A3
1200 MHTN 109 E6
1200 MHTN 6612 D4
1400 MHTN 110 B3
1400 NHPK 6724 A7
1600 NHmT 6724 A7
1600 WhkT 6716 E5
2100 MHTN 107 C7
2300 BRNX 107 D7
2500 BRNX 6612 E3
3300 BRNX 6613 B1
3300 UNCT 6716 E2
3700 BRNX 105 E6
4000 BRNX 6504 D5
4400 WhkT 111 A3
4500 UNCT 111 A3
4900 WNYK 111 B1
4900 WNYK 6717 A1
6000 WNYK 6611 B7
6700 GTBG 6611 B7
7100 NBgT 6611 B6
Park Av CO-30
10 RTFD 6609 A2
Park Av CO-32
- ERTH 6609 B2
- RTFD 6609 B2
Park Av CO-658
10 COrT 6712 C1
10 EORG 6713 A3
10 NWRK 6713 D5
10 WOrT 6712 C1
100 EORG 6712 E2
Park Av CO-677
1400 HBKN 6716 E5
1600 WhkT 6716 E5
Park Av N
800 MNPK 6618 B6
900 FLHL 6618 B6
Park Av S
200 MHTN 116 C5
200 MHTN 6717 D7
Park Av W
10 GrbT 6166 D1
E Park Av
10 LBCH 7029 D7
10 WbgT 7114 C4
N Park Av
10 LNDN 6917 C5
10 RKVC 6929 E4
600 ROSL 6917 C5
N Park Av CO-616
10 LNDN 6917 C5
S Park Av
10 ERKY 6929 D5
10 LNDN 6917 D6
10 RKVC 6929 E4
S Park Av CO-616
10 LNDN 6917 C6
W Park Av
10 LBCH 7029 B7
10 WbgT 7114 C2
700 LBCH 7028 D7
1200 HmpT 7028 D7
Park Blvd
10 MLVN 6929 B2
Park Cir
- NHmT 6724 C5
10 GTNK 6616 E5
10 HmpT 7028 A1
10 NHmT 6723 E7
10 QENS 6825 C4
10 WHPL 6050 A7
10 WHPL 6168 A1
200 BKLN 6922 E5
Park Cir E
10 NHmT 6724 C5
Park Cir W
10 NHmT 6724 B6
Park Ct
10 NRWD 6164 B5
10 STNL 7020 B1
900 HmpT 6928 B5
E Park Ct
600 HmpT 6927 E5
700 HmpT 6928 A6
N Park Ct
- WNYK 111 D1
- WNYK 6717 B1
Park Dr
- BlvT 6713 E1
- BRNX 6506 C4
- COrT 6712 C4
- MHTN 101 C7
- MHTN 6503 E4
- NBgT 6611 B6
- NWRK 6713 E1
- QENS 6824 C5
10 BRNX 6395 B7
10 EchT 6281 B4
10 HmpT 6929 A1
10 MLVN 6929 A1
10 PLDM 6617 D4
1000 SECS 6610 B6
Park Dr E
- NoCT 6050 B3
7-901 QENS 6825 A2
66-00 QENS 6824 E1
Park Dr N
- MHTN 109 C7
- MHTN 112 E5
- MHTN 113 A5
- MHTN 6612 B6
- MHTN 6717 E3
- MHTN 6718 B1
10 HRSN 6169 D6
10 STNL 7018 E6
Park Dr S
- MHTN 109 C4
- MHTN 112 E3
- MHTN 113 A1
- MHTN 6612 A7
- MHTN 6717 E3
- MHTN 6718 A1
10 HRSN 6169 D6
Park Dr W
- MtPT 6050 B3
- NoCT 6050 B3
N Park Dr
10 WbgT 7114 B4
400 PTHA 7114 C7
400 PTHA 7205 C1
S Park Dr
10 TFLY 6392 B4
100 WbgT 7114 B4
400 PTHA 7205 C1
Park Ln
- GDNC 6828 B1
- MHVN 6508 B7
10 HRSN 6050 E4
10 HRSN 6051 A5
10 KENS 6617 A6
10 MTVN 6395 A3
10 NHmT 6617 A6
10 RYE 6283 D6
10 STNL 7020 C2
10 YNKR 6281 A3
80-00 QENS 6824 E4
235-00 QENS 6722 D2
400 HmpT 7028 A1
500 HmpT 6928 A7
1300 BRNX 6506 D1
1300 PLMM 6395 D7
1300 PLMM 6506 D1
Park Ln E
900 HmpT 6828 A7
Park Ln N
900 HmpT 6828 A7
Park Ln S
74-00 QENS 6824 E4
600 HmpT 6828 A7
Park Pl
10 BGTA 6501 D1
10 BKLN 6922 E1
10 BRXV 6280 E7
10 CART 7115 C1
10 COrT 6712 D2
10 EORG 6712 D2
10 FLPK 6827 D1
10 GTNK 6616 C4
10 GTPZ 6617 A7
10 HRSN 6168 C1
10 HRSN 6283 B3
10 IrvT 6816 B3
10 KENS 6617 A7
10 KNGP 6616 C4
10 KRNY 6714 A3
10 LNBK 6929 C4
10 LODI 6500 C1
10 MHTN 118 B6
10 MHTN 6821 B4
10 MTVN 6394 E3
10 NHmT 6724 E2
10 NRCH 6395 E4
10 NWRK 6713 E7
10 OrgT 6164 E2
10 PLHM 6395 C4
10 PTCH 6170 A5
10 RKVC 6929 D5
10 SCLF 6509 D6
10 SECS 6610 C7
10 SOrT 6712 A6
10 STNL 6920 C6
10 VLYS 6928 B1
10 WbgT 7114 D2
10 WLPK 6724 D3
10 WOrT 6712 B1
100 BKLN 6923 A2
100 ELIZ 6918 C5
100 FTLE 103 A1
400 FTLE 6503 A4
400 LBCH 7029 C6
500 CDHT 7028 A2
1500 BKLN 6924 A2
Park Pl CO-508
10 NWRK 6713 E7
Park Pl E
10 WRDG 6500 D7
100 MNCH 6500 D6
Park Pl W
10 WRDG 6500 D7
E Park Pl
10 GTNK 6617 A5
10 RTFD 6609 A2
S Park Pl
1400 NHPK 6828 A1
W Park Pl
10 GTNK 6616 C5
10 RTFD 6609 A2
100 BGTA 6501 D1
Park Rd
- KENS 6617 B6
- PRMT 6165 A1
- WbgT 7114 A7
10 BAYN 6919 D2
10 IRVN 6166 B1
10 SCDL 6167 E5
10 SCDL 6168 A5
10 STNL 7117 A7
10 WHPL 6168 A4
Park Row
10 LWRN 7028 B3
10 MHTN 118 D7
10 MHTN 6821 B4
10 WLTN 6500 A5
Park St
- NRWD 6164 A5
10 BKLN 6822 D5
10 COrT 6712 D3
10 DMRT 6278 A5
10 EDGW 103 A6
10 EDGW 6503 A7
10 HlsT 6816 D6
10 JSYC 6819 E3
10 LFRY 6501 D6
10 RDFP 6501 E5
10 RYE 6283 D5
10 SHkT 6501 C4
10 STNL 7117 D2
10 TFLY 6392 B2
100 ELIZ 6917 B4
100 EORG 6712 D2
100 HKSK 6501 C1
100 HmpT 7028 C1
100 RDFP 6502 A5
100 ROSL 6917 B4
1500 ATLB 7028 B7
1900 ATLB 7027 E7
E Park St
10 EORG 6712 D2
10 NWRK 6713 E7
10 NHmT 6724 C2
200 MNCH 6501 C7
N Park St
10 EORG 6712 D1
S Park St
10 ELIZ 6918 C5
10 HKSK 6501 B1
W Park St
10 MNCH 6501 B7
10 NWRK 6713 D7
Park Ter
10 STNL 7117 B5
10 WHPL 6168 A1
Park Ter E
10 MHTN 102 B5
10 MHTN 6504 A3
Park Ter W
10 MHTN 102 A5
10 MHTN 6504 A3
Park Wy
10 SCLF 6509 D5
10 WOrT 6712 B1
Park Av Ter
10 BRXV 6281 A7
10 YNKR 6279 E4
Park Av Tun
- MHTN 116 C4
- MHTN 6717 E5
Parkchester Rd
1400 BRNX 6505 B7
1400 BRNX 6614 B1
Park End Pl
10 COrT 6712 C5
10 EORG 6712 C5
10 QENS 6824 E2
Park End Ter
10 QENS 7122 D3
Parker Al
10 MHTN 116 D7
10 MHTN 6717 E7
Parker Av
100 MplT 6816 A1
200 HKSK 6501 A1
200 HmpT 6828 D4
1500 FTLE 103 A4
1500 FTLE 6503 A6
Parker Dr
10 EGLD 6502 D2
Parker Ln
10 TnkT 6502 A2
Parker Rd
- UnnT 6917 D2
10 ELIZ 6917 E2
Parker St
10 NWRK 6713 E1
10 PTCH 6170 B5
10 STNL 7206 B3
600 PTHA 7205 E2
1300 BRNX 6614 D1
1400 BRNX 6505 C7
Parkfield Rd
10 SCDL 6167 C5
Park Hill Av
10 STNL 7020 D3
10 YNKR 6393 D3
Park Hill Cir
10 STNL 7020 D3
Park Hill Ct
10 STNL 7020 D3
Park Hill Ln
10 MrnT 6282 A6
10 STNL 7020 D3
Park Hill Pl
10 YNKR 6393 D3
Park Hill Ter
10 DBSF 6166 C3
10 YNKR 6393 C3
Parkhurst Rd
2100 HmpT 6827 A5
Parkhurst St
10 NWRK 6817 D2
Parkinson Av
10 STNL 7020 D5
Parkinson Ter
400 COrT 6712 C1
Parkland Av
10 MrnT 6396 B3
Park Ln Dr
10 NHmT 6724 D3
Park Plaza Dr
300 SECS 6610 C7
300 SECS 6716 A1
Park Ridge Av
10 NRCH 6395 D6
Parkridge Ct
10 RYEB 6170 A4
Park Ridge Ln
10 GrbT 6050 A6
Parkside Av
10 BKLN 6923 C4
Parkside Ct
10 BKLN 6923 B4
10 HRSN 6051 A6
Parkside Dr
10 NHmT 6616 D6
10 NHmT 6724 E1
10 SDRK 6616 D6
100 UnnT 6816 A5
200 EHLS 6724 E1
Parkside Ln
10 BAYN 6919 D4
10 CLST 6278 C3
Parkside Pl
300 NWRK 6817 A7
3100 BRNX 6505 A2
Parkside Rd
10 HmpT 6929 C2
Parkside Wy
10 IRVN 6166 B1
Park View Av
200 YNKR 6280 E5
Parkview Av
10 NRCH 6395 E6
10 YNKR 6280 E6
100 WhkT 6716 B3
1600 BRNX 6506 A6
1700 BRNX 6505 E6
Parkview Av E
10 HRSN 6168 C1
Parkview Ct
10 WHPL 6050 A7
10 WHPL 6168 B1
Parkview Dr
10 EchT 6395 C2
10 MTVN 6395 C2
10 NHmT 6724 C2
10 TnkT 6502 A4
10 WLTN 6500 A6
Parkview Lp
10 STNL 7019 A4
Parkview Pl
10 GrbT 6049 A7
10 HmpT 6827 B7
10 MLVN 6929 B1
10 STNL 7020 A2
10 TCKA 6281 A5
Parkview Rd
10 GrbT 6049 A7
Parkview Ter
10 BAYN 6919 E2
10 NWRK 6816 E5
100 COrT 6712 C4
800 ELIZ 6917 C4
800 ROSL 6917 C4
1400 HlsT 6816 D5
2700 BRNX 6504 D3
Parkville Av
10 BKLN 7022 E1
100 BKLN 7023 A1
Parkway
10 HKSK 6501 B1
Parkway E
10 BlmT 6713 D2
10 MTVN 6395 A2
10 YNKR 6280 B6
Parkway N
10 YNKR 6393 E5
10 YNKR 6394 A5
Parkway S
10 MTVN 6394 E2
10 MTVN 6395 A2
Parkway W
10 BlmT 6713 C1
10 MHTN 6394 E2
E Parkway
10 SCDL 6167 C7
Parkway Av
2500 LNDN 7017 C3
Parkway Cir
10 EchT 6281 C2
10 MTVN 6395 A2
Parkway Ct
10 BKLN 7023 A7
Parkway Dr
10 DBSF 6165 E5
10 HAOH 6165 E5
10 PLHM 6395 D7
10 PTCH 6170 B4
10 RYE 6283 D3
11500 HmpT 6827 A6
Parkway Dr E
10 EORG 6713 A3
Parkway Dr W
10 EORG 6713 A3
Parkway Ln
10 HRSN 6283 B2
Parkway Plz
10 EchT 6395 C2
10 EMFD 6049 A4
Parkway Rd
- BRXV 6280 E7
- YNKR 6394 E1
10 BRXV 6394 E1
Parkway St
10 LRMT 6396 B4
Parkway Homes Rd
10 GrbT 6050 A5
10 NoCT 6050 A5
Parkway Viaduct
- YNKR 6280 C2
Parkwold Dr E
10 HmpT 6929 E1
Parkwold Dr S
10 HmpT 6929 E1
Parkwold Dr W
10 HmpT 6929 E1
Parkwood Av
10 STNL 7207 A1
200 STNL 7116 A7
Parkwood Ct
10 RKVC 6929 D3
Parkwood Dr
10 NHmT 6616 D7
Parkwood Pl
10 RYEB 6170 A1
Parkwoods Rd
10 FLHL 6617 D5
10 PLDM 6617 D5
Parma Rd
10 ISPK 7029 D5
Parmelee Pl
200 ELIZ 6917 C3
Parnell Pl
10 JSYC 6819 C5
Paroubek St
10 LFRY 6501 C5
10 SHkT 6501 C5
Parrott Pl
10 BKLN 7021 E3
Parrow St
10 COrT 6712 D3
Parsells Ct
10 CLST 6278 D4
Parsells Ln
10 CLST 6278 C4
200 ALPN 6278 D4
Parsifal Pl
3100 BRNX 6506 A7
Parsler Pl
10 WbgT 7114 A5
Parson Pl
10 EchT 6281 C5
Parsonage Point Rd
10 RYE 6283 E6
Parsons Blvd
13-00 QENS 6615 A7
15-00 QENS 6721 A3
67-00 QENS 6825 C4
Parsons Pl
10 STNL 7020 A1
Parsons St
10 HRSN 6283 C3
10 RYE 6283 E2
10 YNKR 6279 C5
10 YNKR 6280 A6
Partridge Av
600 HmpT 6828 D7
Partridge Rd
10 WHPL 6168 E4
Pasadena Av
10 HSBH 6500 E2
10 LODI 6500 E2
200 HSBH 6501 A3
Pasadena Pl
10 MTVN 6395 B3
Pasadena Rd
10 EchT 6395 B2
Paschal Av
200 HmpT 6828 A3
Passaic Av
10 HRSN 6713 E5
10 JSYC 6716 B6
10 KRNY 6713 E5
10 KRNY 6714 A4
10 LODI 6500 D4
10 WRDG 6500 D4
100 RTFD 6609 D3
200 ENWK 6713 E5
200 HSBH 6500 D5
300 CARL 6500 C7
300 GRFD 6500 B3
300 NWRK 6714 A4
900 NARL 6714 B1
1100 LNDN 6917 B6
Passaic Av CO-38
10 HSBH 6500 D4
10 LODI 6500 D4
10 WRDG 6500 D4
Passaic Av CO-40
300 GRFD 6500 B3
300 LODI 6500 C3
Passaic Av CO-699
10 HRSN 6713 E5
10 KRNY 6713 E5
10 KRNY 6714 A4
200 ENWK 6713 E5
300 NWRK 6714 A4
900 NARL 6714 B1
E Passaic Av
10 RTFD 6609 B2
W Passaic Av
10 RTFD 6609 A2
Passaic St
10 CART 7115 D2
10 GRFD 6500 A4
10 NWRK 6713 E5
10 PASC 6500 A4
200 LODI 6500 B3
Passaic St CO-40
10 GRFD 6500 A4
200 LODI 6500 B3
Pat Capone Rd
10 GrbT 6167 C1
Patchen Av
10 BKLN 6822 E7
100 BKLN 6923 E1
Patchin Pl
10 MHTN 118 E1
10 MHTN 6821 A1
Paterson Av
10 CARL 6609 C1
10 ERTH 6609 B1
10 HBKN 6716 C7
10 HSBH 6500 E3
10 LODI 6500 D3
100 ERTH 6500 A6
100 JSYC 6716 C7
100 WLTN 6500 A6
400 CARL 6500 B7
Paterson Av CO-120
10 CARL 6609 C1
10 ERTH 6609 B1
100 ERTH 6500 A6
100 WLTN 6500 A6
400 CARL 6500 B7
Paterson Av CO-681
10 HBKN 6716 C7
100 JSYC 6716 C7
Paterson St
10 JSYC 6716 B5
Paterson Plank Rd
- CARL 6610 A4
10 CARL 6609 D2
10 JSYC 6716 C4
100 SECS 6716 C1
200 UNCT 6716 C4
500 ERTH 6610 A3
800 NBgT 6716 C3
900 ERTH 6609 C1
1000 SECS 6610 A7
Paterson Plank Rd CO-681
10 JSYC 6716 C4
100 SECS 6716 C1
200 UNCT 6716 C4
800 NBgT 6716 C3
1000 SECS 6610 B7
Paterson Plank Rd SR-120
10 CARL 6609 D2
10 ERTH 6609 D2
300 CARL 6610 A3
300 ERTH 6610 A3
Paterson Plank Rd W
- SECS 6716 C1
3300 NBgT 6716 C1
Paterson Plank Rd W CO-681
- SECS 6716 C1
3300 NBgT 6716 C1
N Path Rd
10 STNL 7021 A5
Pathmark Plz
10 MTVN 6394 E4
Patmor Av
10 YNKR 6280 B5
Patricia Ct
10 CARL 6500 B6
300 UnnT 6917 A2
500 SOrT 6712 B5
Patricia Ln
10 BRNX 6615 C3
10 HmpT 7028 D1
10 WHPL 6168 C6
Patricia Pl
10 YNKR 6394 A3
Patrick St
10 CART 7017 C7
Patriot Wy
500 PTHA 7205 C2
Patsy Pl
10 GTNK 6616 E6
10 GTNK 6617 A6
Patt Pl
700 HmpT 6828 B7
Patten Av
500 HmpT 6929 D6
500 RKVC 6929 D6
600 PTHA 7114 C7
Patten Pl
10 NWRK 6816 E3
Patten St
10 STNL 7206 A4
Patterson Av
600 HmpT 6828 B7
700 STNL 7118 C3
1700 BRNX 6614 B4
Patterson St
- BRNX 6615 D5
10 HRSN 6714 A5
10 KRNY 6714 A4
10 NWRK 6818 A2
100 PTHA 7205 D4
Patti Ln
10 YNKR 6279 D5
Patton Blvd
10 NHmT 6723 D5
Patton Cres
10 CLST 6278 C3
Patton Dr
10 YNKR 6281 A2
Patton Ln
10 CLST 6278 C3
Patton Pl
200 HmpT 6828 C7
200 HmpT 6929 D1
Patton Rd
1900 UnnT 6816 A6
Patton St
10 LODI 6500 C3
Patty Ct
10 STNL 7116 E5
Paul Av
10 NHmT 6723 E6
3200 BRNX 6504 D2
Paul Ct
10 OrgT 6164 D3
300 HmpT 6828 C6
Paul Pl
200 HmpT 6828 C6
Paul St
500 HlsT 6816 B5
1000 LNDN 6917 A6
1100 ROSL 6917 A6
Paula Av
10 YNKR 6394 C2
Paula Rd
10 GLCV 6509 D4
Paulanne Ter
200 SECS 6610 A5
Paulding Av
10 STNL 7018 E4
10 TYTN 6048 A4
400 NVLE 6164 B4
2100 BRNX 6505 B5
4000 BRNX 6394 C7
Paulding Pl
10 OrgT 6164 E2
Paulding St
10 EMFD 6049 A5
10 WHPL 6168 C2
Pauley Dr
500 HmpT 6828 C5
Paulin Blvd
10 LEON 6502 D5
Pauline St
10 CART 7017 A6
Pauline Ter
10 LODI 6500 E2
Paulis Pl
200 BRNX 6506 E6
Paulison Av
10 RDFP 6501 E4
Paulusen Ct
10 JSYC 6819 B4
Pauw St
10 STNL 6920 C7
Pavillion Hill Ter
- STNL 6920 D7
Pavonia Av
10 KRNY 6714 B3
200 JSYC 6820 B1
800 JSYC 6819 E1
Pavonia Ct
10 BAYN 6919 D4
Pawnee Pl
1200 BRNX 6505 C5
Paxford Ln
10 GrbT 6167 A7
Paxton Av
10 BRXV 6280 D7
Paxton St
10 STNL 7020 D1
Payan Av
10 VLYS 6928 D3
Payne Cir
10 ERKY 6929 A7
Payne Rd
10 GrbT 6049 C4
Payne St
10 GrbT 6049 B4
N Payne St
10 GrbT 6049 B4
Payne Whitney Ln
10 NHmT 6618 A7
100 NHLS 6617 E7
100 NHmT 6617 D7
Payson Av
10 MHTN 101 E6
10 MHTN 102 A6
10 MHTN 6503 E3
10 MHTN 6504 A3
Peabody Ct
10 TnkT 6502 B2
Peabody Pl
10 NWRK 6714 C4
Peace Dr
10 JSYC 6819 B7
Peace St
10 BRNX 6395 B7
10 PLMM 6395 B7
Peach Dr
10 EHLS 6618 E6
Peachgrove Dr
10 HmpT 6828 D5
Peachtree Ln
10 FLHL 6618 C5
10 NHmT 6724 E1
Peachtree Rd
10 MplT 6816 B1
Peacock Lp
10 STNL 7206 C1
Peale Rd
10 MNPK 6618 A6
Pearce Pl
10 GTPZ 6617 A7
Peare Pl
10 STNL 7207 E1
Pearl Av
10 HRSN 6050 D7
500 WbgT 7114 D4
Pearl Ct
10 LODI 6500 E1
Pearl Pl
10 LNBK 6929 B4
10 PTHA 7205 E3
Pearl Rd
127-51 QENS 6614 D7
Pearl St
- EGLD 6392 A6
- JSYC 6820 D3
10 BKLN 121 B3
10 BKLN 6821 D6
10 DBSF 6166 C4
10 HAOH 6279 E1
10 HmpT 6928 B5
10 HmpT 7027 E2
10 MHTN 120 C2
10 MHTN 6821 B4
10 MTVN 6394 C5
10 NHmT 6723 D7
10 NHmT 6724 A6
10 NWRK 6817 D1
10 STNL 7020 D2
10 VLYS 6928 B5
10 YNKR 6279 E6
14-00 QENS 7027 C4
100 BRNX 6394 C5
200 CDHT 7027 E2
300 MHTN 118 D7
300 WbgT 7114 C4
400 HmpT 6929 C6
600 ELIZ 6917 D4
600 ERKY 6929 C6
Pearl St CO-614
300 ELIZ 6917 D4
N Pearl St
10 PTCH 6170 C5
N Pearl St SR-120A
10 PTCH 6170 C5
S Pearl St
10 PTCH 6170 B6
100 ELIZ 6917 E4
S Pearl St CO-614
100 ELIZ 6917 E4
Pearl Harbor Memorial Expwy
- STNL 7018 B6
- STNL 7115 D6
- STNL 7116 B1
- STNL 7206 D2
Pearl Harbor Mem Expwy SR-440
- STNL 7018 B6
- STNL 7115 D6
- STNL 7116 A4
- STNL 7206 D2
Pearsall Av
10 HmpT 6929 B3
10 JSYC 6819 B6
10 LNBK 6929 B3
300 CDHT 7028 A2
300 HmpT 7028 A3
2200 BRNX 6505 C4
Pearsall Dr
10 MTVN 6395 B4
Pearsall Pl
10 NHmT 6618 E7
200 HmpT 7027 E3
200 HmpT 7028 B1
200 LWRN 7028 A3
Pearsall St
10 STNL 7020 E6
Pearson Pl
47-00 QENS 6718 C6
Pearson St
10 BKLN 7024 A3
10 STNL 7018 C7
45-00 QENS 6718 C6
Pear Tree Av
3200 BRNX 6506 A1
Peartree Av
3200 BRNX 6506 B1
Pease St
10 MTVN 6395 A5
Peat St
10 NWRK 6713 A7
Pebble Ln
10 STNL 7021 B5
100 HmpT 6928 E6
1400 HWTH 6928 E6
1500 HBPK 6928 E6
Pebble Wy
10 NRCH 6282 A7
Pebble Beach Dr
10 HRSN 6168 E1
Pebble Beach Ln
10 WHPL 6169 A5
Peck Av
10 GrwT 6170 C6
10 NWRK 6713 C3
10 RYE 6284 A1
175-00 QENS 6721 D6
214-00 QENS 6722 C7
217-00 QENS 6826 C1
Peck Ct
10 STNL 7117 C3
Peck Dr
- RYE 6284 A1
Peck Slip
10 MHTN 120 D1
10 MHTN 6821 B4
Peconic St
133-00 QENS 6925 E2
E Peddie St
10 NWRK 6817 B4
W Peddie St
10 NWRK 6817 B3
Peden Ter
10 KRNY 6714 A3
Pedestrian Wy
- QENS 6824 C2
Peekskill St
700 HmpT 6827 C7
Peel Pl
10 STNL 7117 D3
Peerless Pl
10 NWRK 6817 C4
Pegasus Av
200 NVLE 6164 C4
Peggy Ln
10 STNL 7118 C2
Pekola Ter
10 CART 7017 B6
Pel Pl
10 PLHM 6395 C4
Pelham Av
10 SNPT 6508 A7
Pelham Pkwy
10 PLMM 6395 A7
Pelham Pkwy N
600 BRNX 6505 B5
Pelham Pkwy S
600 BRNX 6505 D5
Pelham Rd
10 NRCH 6396 A6
400 NRCH 6395 E7
700 PLMM 6395 E7
Pelham St
100 HmpT 6827 C4
100 MRNK 6282 D5
Pelham Bay Pk W
- PLMM 6395 B7
2500 BRNX 6395 B7
2500 BRNX 6506 B1
Pelhamdale Av
10 MTVN 6395 B4
100 PLHM 6395 B5
300 PLMM 6395 C6
700 NRCH 6395 C2
1400 PLMM 6506 D1
Pelham Manor Rd
400 PLHM 6395 C5
400 PLMM 6395 C5
Pelhamside Dr
10 NRCH 6395 C6
Pelhamwood Av
10 PLHM 6395 B4
Pelican Cir
- STNL 7118 A4
Pelick Pl
10 CART 7017 B6
Pell Pl
10 BRNX 6506 E7
10 NRCH 6396 A1
Pell St
10 MHTN 118 E6
10 MHTN 6821 C3
Pelton Av
10 STNL 6920 A6
700 STNL 7020 A2
Pelton Pl
10 STNL 6920 A6
Pelton St
10 YNKR 6393 D4
Pemberton Av
10 STNL 7117 A3
Pemberwick Rd
10 GrwT 6170 D3
Pembroke Av
253-00 QENS 6722 C2
25400 NHmT 6723 A2
25400 QENS 6723 A2
Pembroke Dr
10 GLCV 6509 D2
Pembroke St
10 BKLN 7121 D1
10 NRCH 6396 C4
10 WLPK 6724 D4
Pembroke Wy
10 PALP 6502 C7
700 PALP 6611 C1
700 RDGF 6611 C1
Pembrook Dr
10 YNKR 6280 C4
Pembrook Lp
10 STNL 7115 D7
Penbroke Av
10 STNL 6920 B7
Pence St
10 BKLN 7021 D4
Pendale St
10 STNL 7117 E4
Pendleton Pl
10 STNL 6920 C7
Pendro Av
10 CART 7017 B6
Penelope Av
69-00 QENS 6823 E3
78-00 QENS 6824 A3
Penfield Pl
10 PLMM 6395 C7
Penfield St
10 NRWD 6164 A6
700 BRNX 6394 C5
Pengilly Dr
10 MrnT 6282 A5
10 NRCH 6282 A5
10 SCDL 6282 A5
Penhorn Av
- NBgT 6716 C1
10 SECS 6716 A3
Penhorn Av SR-3
- NBgT 6716 B1
- SECS 6716 B1
Peninsula Blvd
- HmpT 6929 C4
- RKVC 6929 E2
10 HmpT 6928 B7
10 LNBK 6929 A5
10 VLYS 6928 D6
300 CDHT 7027 E1
300 CDHT 7028 A1
300 HmpT 7027 E1
400 HmpT 7028 A1
1700 LNBK 6928 E5
Penn Av
300 STNL 7117 E3
300 STNL 7118 A4
Penn Blvd
10 NRCH 6282 A3
10 SCDL 6282 A3
Penn Ct
100 EDGW 108 C1
100 EDGW 6611 E5
100 OrgT 6164 A1
Penn Pl
10 LNDN 7017 A1
10 PLMM 6395 A7
Penn Rd
10 SCDL 6282 B3
800 HmpT 6828 B6
Penn St
10 BKLN 6822 B5
10 STNL 7019 E4
400 PTHA 7205 D2
E Penn St
10 LBCH 7029 D7
W Penn St
10 LBCH 7029 A7
700 LBCH 7028 E6
Pennington St
10 NWRK 6817 D2
300 ELIZ 6917 C4
900 ROSL 6917 B4
Pennsy Pl
10 NWRK 6817 C7
Pennsylvania Av
- BKLN 6925 A6
10 BKLN 6924 D3
10 CART 7017 B6
10 HlsT 6816 D6
10 KRNY 6714 E7
10 KRNY 6715 A7
10 LBCH 7028 E7
10 NWRK 6817 C3
10 WbgT 7205 A1
10 YNKR 6280 C2
10 YNKR 6281 A4
100 HmpT 7029 D5
100 MTVN 6395 B3
200 MNLA 6724 E5
200 WLPK 6724 E5
300 LNDN 7017 A1
500 ELIZ 6917 E2
500 LNDN 6917 C6
600 ELIZ 6918 A1
700 LynT 6609 A5
E Pennsylvania Av
10 WbgT 7114 C2
Pennsylvania Blvd
10 BLRS 6827 B2
10 FLPK 6827 B2
10 QENS 6827 B2
Pennsylvania RR Av
10 LNDN 7017 A1
Pennval Rd
- WbgT 7114 D5
Penny Ln
10 GrbT 6166 E7
10 GrbT 6167 A7
10 GrbT 6280 E1
10 GrbT 6281 A1
Pennyfield Av
10 BRNX 6615 C3
Penrod St
57-00 QENS 6720 C7
Penton St
10 STNL 7206 E2
Peppard Pl
600 FTLE 6502 E4
600 LEON 6502 E4
Peppe Dr
10 HmpT 7027 C2
Pepperday Av
10 NHmT 6508 D6
10 PTWN 6508 D6
Pepperidge Ln
10 WHPL 6169 A4
Pepperidge Rd
10 ERKY 6929 B7
200 HWTH 6929 A7
300 HWTH 7029 A1
Peppermill Rd
10 NHmT 6724 B4
Pequot Av
10 MHVN 6508 C7
Percival Pl
10 STNL 7207 A2
Perez Dr
10 NWRK 6713 C6
Peri Ln
- BKLN 7024 B2
10 VLYS 6928 D5
Perimeter Rd
- QENS 6926 E5
- QENS 6927 A5
Perine Av
10 STNL 7020 C7
Peripheral Rd
10 MtPT 6049 B1
E Peripheral Rd
- ERTH 6609 E4
W Peripheral Rd
- ERTH 6609 E4
Perkins Av
200 HmpT 6929 D7
N Perkins Av
10 EMFD 6049 B6
S Perkins Av
10 EMFD 6049 C5
Perkiomen Av
10 STNL 7116 D4
E Perkiomen Av
10 STNL 7117 A4
Perona Ln
10 STNL 7117 B6
Perot St
10 BRNX 102 E3
10 BRNX 6504 C2

New York City/5 Borough Street Index

STREET — Block City Map# Grid

Perrine Av
10 JSYC 6820 A1
10 SRVL 7205 A7
Perry Av
- BKLN 7121 D1
10 GrbT 6050 A5
10 PTCH 6170 A5
64-00 QENS 6823 C2
100 STNL 7019 D4
2900 BRNX 6504 E3
3200 BRNX 6505 A2
Perry Ln
700 TnkT 6502 C1
Perry Pl
10 BKLN 6923 C1
10 YNKR 6280 D6
Perry St
- NRWD 6164 A5
10 CLST 6278 B3
10 JSYC 6716 B7
10 MHTN 115 D7
10 MHTN 118 C1
10 MHTN 6717 B7
10 MHTN 6821 B1
10 OLDT 6164 A4
Perry Ter
7000 BKLN 6921 D7
Pershing Av
10 CART 7115 D2
10 EGLC 6392 B7
10 EGLD 6392 B7
10 ELIZ 6917 C4
10 NRCH 6395 C3
10 NWRK 6817 A7
10 VLYS 6928 C5
10 YNKR 6393 C4
100 ROSP 6917 A3
300 CART 7017 D7
800 PTHA 7205 C1
Pershing Blvd
300 HmpT 6929 C2
300 RKVC 6929 C2
Pershing Cir
- WhkT 111 B4
- WhkT 6717 A3
139-00 QENS 6825 B4
Pershing Ct
10 RDFP 6502 A5
Pershing Lp N
10 BKLN 7021 E4
Pershing Pl
10 ISPK 7029 C4
Pershing Plz
- JSYC 6716 B7
10 JSYC 6820 C3
Pershing Rd
10 EGLC 6503 C1
10 WhkT 111 A4
10 WhkT 6717 A2
100 EGLC 6392 B7
100 EGLD 6392 B7
Pershing St
10 GRFD 6500 A1
10 STNL 7020 E6
1600 HmpT 6827 C7
1600 HmpT 6928 D1
Persimmon Ct
10 JSYC 6819 A4
Persimmon Ln
10 WHPL 6169 A4
Perth Av
10 NRCH 6395 D1
Perth Rd
187-00 QENS 6825 E2
187-00 QENS 6826 B2
Perth Amboy Pl
- STNL 7206 A4
Peru St
10 STNL 7019 E5
Peshine Av
10 NWRK 6817 B3
Peter Av
10 STNL 7117 D3
300 STNL 7118 A4
Peter Ct
10 STNL 7020 B6
Peter Ln
10 NHmT 6723 D6
Peter St
- WhkT 6716 E3
10 HmpT 6827 B5
10 STNL 7019 A2
100 UNCT 6716 E3
600 LNDN 6917 B6
Peter Cooper Rd
10 MHTN 116 D7
10 MHTN 119 D1
10 MHTN 6717 E7
10 MHTN 6821 E1
Peterhoff St
10 HmpT 6929 A1
10 MLVN 6929 A1
1000 VLYS 6929 A1
Peter Jay Ln
10 RYE 6283 C5
Peter J Barbaro Cir
- STNL 6920 B5
Peter Lynas Ct
10 TFLY 6392 C2
Peters Ln
10 PLDM 6617 D4
Peters Pl
4200 BRNX 6394 B6
Peters Rd
200 HKSK 6501 C1
Petersilge Dr
10 LFRY 6501 D6
Peterson Ct
10 PTHA 7205 D3
Peterson Pl
10 LNBK 6929 A5
Petersons Ln
10 STNL 7206 E1
Petersville Rd
10 NRCH 6396 A3
Petracca Pl
15-00 QENS 6721 A1
Petrus Av
10 STNL 7116 E6
Pettit Av
81-00 QENS 6719 E6
Pettit Pl
10 HmpT 7029 D5
Petunia Ct
10 STNL 7206 B4

Petzinger St
10 IrvT 6816 C1
Peyser St
10 WbgT 7114 B5
Pfeiffer Blvd
400 PTHA 7205 C1
700 WbgT 7205 B1
Pfeiffer Blvd SR-184
600 PTHA 7205 B1
700 WbgT 7205 B1
Pflug Pl
10 VLYS 6928 C3
Pheasant Dr
10 HRSN 6169 E6
10 OrgT 6164 D2
Pheasant Ln
10 STNL 7115 D7
10 STNL 7206 C1
Pheasant Run
10 EGLD 6502 C3
10 GrbT 6166 E7
10 GrbT 6280 E1
10 KNGP 6617 B3
10 MrnT 6396 C3
10 NHLS 6724 A2
10 OLDT 6164 A3
Pheasants Run
10 HRSN 6283 A1
Phelan Pl
1800 BRNX 105 B3
1800 BRNX 6504 A5
Phelps Av
10 CRSK 6392 A1
10 EGLD 6392 A4
10 TFLY 6392 A4
100 EGLD 6502 E2
Phelps Pl
10 STNL 6920 D6
Phelps Rd
800 TnkT 6502 B1
Philadelphia Av
100 NVLE 6164 C5
Philip Av
10 STNL 7116 C7
200 STNL 7207 D1
2700 BRNX 6615 A2
Philip Pl
10 IrvT 6816 C4
Philips Ln
10 RYE 6283 E5
10 RYE 6284 A5
100 HWTN 7028 D1
Philipse Pl
10 YNKR 6279 D6
Philipse Rd
10 YNKR 6279 C6
Phillip Ct
1000 VLYS 6928 B1
Phillip St
10 JSYC 6820 B4
Phillips Av
- HKSK 6501 C3
10 SHkT 6501 C5
300 LFRY 6501 C5
Phillips St
- HAOH 6165 C7
Phillips Park Rd
10 MRNK 6282 C4
Phipps Av
10 ERKY 6929 C6
Phlox Pl
42-00 QENS 6721 A5
Phoebe St
900 HmpT 6828 A4
Phoebus Ct
700 HmpT 6828 A7
Phroane Av
163-00 QENS 6825 E7
Phyllis Ct
10 HmpT 6827 C5
10 STNL 7115 B6
Phyllis Pl
10 RYEB 6169 E4
Piave Av
10 STNL 7020 E6
Picadilly Pl
1100 STNL 7117 B2
Piccadilly Rd
10 GTNK 6616 C5
10 GTNK 6617 A6
10 NHmT 6617 A6
Piccadilly Downs
10 LNBK 6928 E5
10 VLYS 6928 E5
Pickens St
10 LFRY 6501 D6
Pickersgill Av
10 STNL 7020 E5
Pickett Ct
10 MLVN 6929 A1
Pickwick Rd
10 MNPK 6618 A6
10 NHmT 6618 A6
Pickwood Ln
10 GTNK 6616 C4
Pidgeon Meadow Rd
162-00 QENS 6721 C5
Piedmont Av
10 STNL 7020 E5
Pier St
- BAYN 6919 E5
10 YNKR 6393 C3
Pierce Av
10 CRSK 6278 A6
10 DMRT 6278 A5
10 JSYC 6716 B5
600 LNDN 6917 A6
900 BRNX 6505 C6
Pierce Pl
10 KRNY 6714 C3
Pierce St
10 CART 7115 C1
10 NRCH 6396 A2
10 NWRK 6817 A1
10 STNL 7020 D4
400 HmpT 7029 C1
Pier Dt
10 WhkT 6716 E4
Piermont Av
10 HBPK 6928 D7
10 HmpT 6928 D7
10 OrgT 6164 E2
10 PRMT 6164 E2
10 PRMT 6165 A1

Piermont Av SR-340
10 OrgT 6164 E2
10 PRMT 6164 E2
Piermont Pl
10 PRMT 6165 A1
Piermont Rd
10 CLST 6278 B4
10 CRSK 6278 A7
10 CRSK 6392 A2
10 NRWD 6164 D7
10 NRWD 6278 D1
10 OrgT 6164 E5
10 RCKL 6164 E5
10 TFLY 6392 A1
300 DMRT 6278 A7
Piermont Rd CO-501
10 CLST 6278 B4
10 NRWD 6164 D7
10 NRWD 6278 D1
10 OrgT 6164 E5
10 RCKL 6164 E5
500 DMRT 6278 B5
Piermont St
10 OrgT 6164 E2
Pier Point St
10 YNKR 6393 B1
Pierpont Pl
10 STNL 7117 A1
Pierre Av
10 GRFD 6500 A3
E Pierrepont Av
10 RTFD 6609 A2
W Pierrepont Av
10 RTFD 6609 B3
Pierrepont Pl
10 BKLN 120 E4
10 BKLN 6821 C6
Pierrepont St
10 BKLN 120 E4
10 BKLN 121 A4
10 BKLN 6821 C6
Pierron St
200 NVLE 6164 C5
Pierson Av
10 NRWD 6278 D1
10 SYHW 6048 B1
Pierson St
100 COrT 6712 C3
Pietro Dr
10 YNKR 6280 E3
10 YNKR 6281 A3
Pietro Pl
10 DBSF 6166 B3
Pike St
10 ALPN 6278 E7
10 MHTN 119 A7
10 MHTN 6821 C4
10 STNL 6920 D7
Pike Slip
- MHTN 119 A7
- MHTN 6821 C4
Pikeview Ln
10 WbgT 7114 B6
Pikeview Ter
10 SECS 6610 A6
Pilcher St
10 STNL 7019 C6
Pilgrim Av
10 YNKR 6280 E5
1600 BRNX 6505 E6
Pilgrim Ct
10 TFLY 6392 B5
Pilgrim Dr
10 GrwT 6170 C3
10 PTCH 6170 C3
Pilgrim Pl
10 VLYS 6928 C3
Pilgrim Rd
10 HRSN 6169 C5
10 NRCH 6281 E2
10 WHPL 6168 C5
Pilgrim St
10 NHmT 6723 E6
Pilling St
10 BKLN 6823 B7
10 BKLN 6924 B1
Pillot Pl
10 WOrT 6712 B2
Pilot Rd
- QENS 6926 D4
Pilot St
10 BRNX 6506 E7
Pilvinis Dr
10 GTNK 6616 C4
10 KNGP 6616 C4
Pinchot Pl
1200 BRNX 6505 C5
Pindle Av
200 EGLD 6392 A5
Pine Av
10 FLPK 6827 B2
10 NRCH 6395 C2
10 PLHM 6395 C2
Pine Cir
10 EchT 6281 B7
Pine Ct
10 NRCH 6395 E5
Pine Dr
10 GTNE 6722 E1
10 NHmT 6617 D2
1500 BRNX 6505 B7
Pine Dr N
10 RSLN 6618 D5
Pine Dr S
10 ROSE 6618 C6
10 RSLN 6618 C6
Pine Ln
10 GrbT 6048 C6
10 RYE 6283 E3
10 VLYS 6928 D4
Pine Pl
10 IrvT 6816 B3
10 PTCH 6170 B4
10 STNL 7020 D2
300 MNLA 6724 D5
Pine Rd
10 HmpT 7027 C3
Pine St
- LNDN 7017 A4
10 BGTA 6501 E1
10 BKLN 6824 A7
10 CART 7115 C1
10 ELIZ 6918 C5
10 GrbT 6166 D2
10 HAOH 6280 B2

Pine St
10 HmpT 6827 B5
10 HmpT 6929 E6
10 HmpT 7028 B1
10 HRSN 6050 C7
10 HRSN 6168 C1
10 KRNY 6714 C3
10 LODI 6500 E3
10 MHTN 120 C1
10 MHTN 6821 B5
10 MLVN 6929 A2
10 MRNK 6283 A5
10 NHmT 6617 E3
10 NRCH 6395 E5
10 RDFP 6501 E5
10 RKVC 6929 E3
10 STNL 6920 C7
10 SYHW 6048 B1
10 TFLY 6392 B4
10 TnkT 6501 E1
10 WLTN 6500 B5
10 WOrT 6712 A3
10 YNKR 6279 C6
100 BKLN 6925 A1
100 CLFP 108 A1
100 CLFP 6611 C5
100 GrwT 6170 D5
100 JSYC 6820 A4
100 NHmT 6724 B5
200 TnkT 6502 A2
700 HmpT 6828 C4
900 PTHA 7205 D1
E Pine St
10 LBCH 7029 E6
W Pine St
100 LBCH 7029 B6
Pine Ter
10 BRXV 6395 A1
10 DMRT 6278 B4
10 STNL 7116 D7
N Pine Ter
10 STNL 7116 D7
Pineapple St
10 BKLN 120 E3
10 BKLN 121 A4
10 BKLN 6821 C6
Pinebrook Av
10 HmpT 6929 C2
600 MLVN 6929 C2
Pinebrook Blvd
100 NRCH 6396 A1
800 NRCH 6281 E4
900 NRCH 6282 A4
Pinebrook Ct
400 HmpT 6929 C2
Pine Brook Dr
10 WHPL 6168 E5
Pinebrook Dr
10 LRMT 6396 B2
Pinebrook Rd
10 NRCH 6396 A1
Pinebrook Hollow Dr
10 NRCH 6281 E4
10 NRCH 6282 A4
Pine Close
10 SYHW 6048 B1
Pinecrest Dr
10 HAOH 6279 E1
Pinecrest Pkwy
100 HAOH 6279 E1
Pinecrest Rd
10 JSYC 6819 B5
10 SCDL 6281 D1
Pine Grove Ln
10 GrbT 6167 C2
Pinegrove St
104-00 QENS 6825 C6
Pinegrove Ter
10 EORG 6712 D7
10 NWRK 6712 D7
Pine Hill Rd
10 ALPN 6278 C5
10 CLST 6278 C5
10 DMRT 6278 C5
10 LKSU 6723 B2
400 LEON 6502 E4
Pinehurst Av
100 MHTN 104 B3
100 MHTN 6503 D5
S Pinehurst Av
10 MHTN 104 B5
10 MHTN 6503 C7
Pinehurst Ct
400 NHLS 6724 A3
Pinehurst Dr
10 HRSN 6050 E7
Pine Island Rd
10 RYE 6283 E6
10 RYE 6284 A6
Pine Knoll Ln
1400 MRNK 6283 B5
Pinelake Dr
10 HmpT 6929 C1
Pine Low
10 GLCV 6509 E2
Pine Park Dr
10 NRCH 6282 A7
Pine Ridge Rd
10 LRMT 6396 C2
10 RYEB 6169 E3
Pineridge Rd
10 GrbT 6049 C4
Pine Tree Dr
10 KNGP 6616 D2
10 RYEB 6051 E7
Pine Tree Ln
10 OrgT 6164 C2
Pinetree Ln
10 FLHL 6618 A5
10 NHmT 6724 E1
Pineview Cir
10 HRSN 6051 B7
Pineville Ln
186-00 QENS 6927 C1
191-00 QENS 6826 D7
Pinewood Av
100 STNL 7117 C2
Pinewood Cir
10 NoCT 6050 B6
Pinewood Dr
- WHPL 6050 B5
10 NoCT 6050 B6
Pinewood Ln
10 NHmT 6724 A6

Pinewood Rd
10 FLHL 6617 E5
10 PLDM 6617 E5
10 WHPL 6168 D7
100 GrbT 6167 D2
Pingry Pl
10 ELIZ 6917 E2
Pinho Av
10 CART 7017 A6
Pink St
10 HKSK 6501 C3
10 SHkT 6501 B2
Pinkney Av
3500 BRNX 6506 A1
3600 BRNX 6395 A7
Pin Oak Dr
10 NHmT 6724 C4
Pin Oak Ln
10 WHPL 6168 A4
Pinson St
13-00 QENS 7027 C4
Pintail Rd
10 TYTN 6048 C6
Pintard Av
10 NRCH 6395 E5
Pinto St
86-00 QENS 6826 B2
Pioneer St
10 BKLN 6922 A1
Pipeline Rd
- GrbT 6167 C6
Piper Ct
10 GrbT 6166 E1
10 RSLN 6618 D6
Piper Dr
10 NHmT 6724 C3
Pirates Cove
800 MRNK 6397 A1
Pitcairn Rd
- NWRK 6817 C6
Pitcher Ct
300 NVLE 6164 C4
Pitkin Av
10 BKLN 6924 C2
75-00 BKLN 6925 D2
75-00 QENS 6925 B2
Pitman Av
1700 BRNX 6394 C6
2100 MTVN 6394 D6
Pitney Av
10 STNL 7206 D1
Pitt Av
10 STNL 7019 E5
Pitt St
10 MHTN 119 C5
10 MHTN 6821 D3
10 PTCH 6170 B7
Pittsville Av
10 STNL 7206 B4
Piza St
10 HmpT 7027 D2
Plain Av
10 NRCH 6396 B2
Plain Ct
200 GDNC 6828 B3
200 HmpT 6828 B3
Plainfield Av
10 ERKY 6929 C6
10 FLPK 6827 D2
10 HmpT 6827 C4
100 JSYC 6819 D1
Plainfield Ln
700 HmpT 6928 A6
Plainfield Rd
10 NHmT 6724 D2
Plainview Av
10 ARDY 6166 D5
17-00 QENS 7027 C6
Plandome Ct
10 PLNH 6617 C5
Plandome Ct N
100 PLNH 6617 C5
Plandome Ct S
10 PLNH 6617 D5
Plandome Dr
10 PLDM 6617 D4
Plandome Rd
10 NHmT 6617 D6
500 PLNH 6617 D5
900 PLDM 6617 C5
1000 PLNM 6617 C4
N Plandome Rd
10 NHmT 6617 D3
10 PLNM 6617 D3
Plane Av
800 HmpT 6828 A5
Plank Rd
10 BAYN 6920 A1
10 STNL 7018 E4
Plankford Track Av
- BRNX 6615 D4
Plant Rd
10 HSBH 6500 E5
Plant Rd Ext
10 HSBH 6500 E6
Platchmen Viola Av
10 STNL 7206 D3
Plateau Av
10 FTLE 6502 D7
Plateau Cir E
10 BRXV 6280 E7
Plateau Cir W
10 BRXV 6280 E7
Platinum Av
- STNL 7117 A2
10 STNL 7116 E1
Plato St
500 HmpT 6828 B6
Platt Ln
10 RYE 6284 A3
Platt Pl
10 WHPL 6168 D2
Platt St
10 MHTN 120 C1
10 MHTN 6821 B6
10 STNL 7117 D4
Plattsburg St
10 STNL 7020 B6
Plattsdale Rd
10 GDNC 6828 A3
Plattwood Av
103-00 QENS 6925 E1
Plauderville Av
10 GRFD 6500 A1

Plauderville Av
100 SdBT 6500 B1
Playland Pkwy
- RYE 6283 E3
- RYE 6284 A4
Playland Access Dr
- RYE 6283 D2
Plaza Av
10 MRNK 6282 D5
1500 NHPK 6828 A1
E Plaza Av
10 MRNK 6282 E5
Plaza Ctr
10 SECS 6610 B7
Plaza Dr
100 WbgT 7114 A3
600 SECS 6610 C7
800 SECS 6716 C1
Plaza Pl
10 BRNX 6615 B4
Plaza Rd
10 GDNC 6828 A2
10 HmpT 7027 E1
Plaza St
- FTLE 103 B3
- FTLE 6503 A5
Plaza St E
10 BKLN 6923 A2
Plaza St W
10 BKLN 6923 A3
Plaza A
- ERTH 6609 D2
S Plaza East Rd
- MtPT 6049 C1
Plaza F
- ERTH 6609 E4
Plaza G
- ERTH 6609 D4
Plaza H
- ERTH 6609 D4
Plaza J
- ERTH 6609 C4
Plaza K
- ERTH 6610 A4
Plaza L
- ERTH 6610 A4
Plaza Lafayette
800 MHTN 104 B3
800 MHTN 6503 D5
Plaza M
- CARL 6610 A4
- ERTH 6610 A4
S Plaza West Rd
- MtPT 6049 C2
Pleasant Av
10 GRFD 6500 A3
10 HAOH 6165 E6
10 MHVN 6508 D7
10 NHmT 6508 D7
10 PTWN 6508 D7
10 TCKA 6281 A5
10 WbgT 7114 A2
10 WHPL 6168 C4
200 MHTN 110 D5
200 MHTN 6612 D6
300 CLFP 6611 D1
3200 UNCT 6716 B2
3200 WhkT 6716 B2
E Pleasant Av
10 WbgT 7114 E4
Pleasant Ct
10 STNL 7020 D2
Pleasant Pl
10 BKLN 6924 B2
10 KRNY 6714 B1
10 STNL 7020 D2
10 TCKA 6281 A6
100 NARL 6714 C1
200 BGTA 6501 E2
200 TnkT 6501 E2
1300 HmpT 6929 A7
1300 HWTH 6929 A7
Pleasant St
10 NRCH 6396 B2
10 RYE 6284 A2
10 STNL 7117 A5
10 SYHW 6048 B1
100 LNDN 7017 A3
Pleasant Plains Av
10 STNL 7206 D2
Pleasant Ridge Rd
10 HRSN 6169 A7
10 HRSN 6282 E1
10 HRSN 6283 A1
10 MtPT 6049 C3
Pleasant Valley Av
10 STNL 7020 C3
E Pleasant View Av
200 HKSK 6501 A5
W Pleasant View Av
200 HKSK 6501 A5
300 HKSK 6500 E2
300 LODI 6500 E2
Pleasantview St
63-00 QENS 6823 E4
Pleasant View Ter
10 WLTN 6500 B6
Pleasantview Ter
700 RDGF 6611 A2
Plimpton Av
1200 BRNX 104 E6
1300 BRNX 6503 E7
1500 BRNX 105 A5
1500 BRNX 6504 E5
Ploughmans Bush
10 BRNX 6393 A7
Plumb 1 St
10 BKLN 7023 E5
Plumb 2 St
10 BKLN 7023 E5
Plumb 3rd St
10 BKLN 7023 E7
Plum Beach Point Rd
10 SNPT 6508 A7
10 SNPT 6617 A1
Plum Tree Ln
100 HmpT 6828 E4
100 UnnT 6816 A5
Plunkett Av
32-00 QENS 7027 B3
Plymouth Av
10 YNKR 6280 D5
1500 BRNX 6505 E7
Plymouth Dr
10 NRCH 6281 E2

Plymouth Dr
10 NRCH 6282 C1
Plymouth Pl
10 WHPL 6168 B5
Plymouth Rd
10 ERKY 6929 B6
10 GrbT 6049 D4
10 GTNK 6617 A5
10 HRSN 6169 D5
10 MrnT 6396 D1
10 NHmT 6617 A5
10 NHmT 6618 A2
10 PLDM 6617 E4
10 STNL 7018 E6
200 UnnT 6917 A1
500 HlsT 6816 C7
Plymouth St
10 BKLN 121 B2
10 BKLN 6821 D5
10 NHmT 6723 E6
10 NHmT 6724 A6
10 NWRK 6712 D7
200 HmpT 6828 D6
900 PLMM 6395 B7
Plympton Av
10 NHmT 6618 D7
Pocahont Pl
10 WbgT 7114 C1
Pocantico St
10 SYHW 6048 B1
Pocasset Ct
10 HmpT 7029 C1
Poccia Cir
10 MrnT 6282 C5
Pocono Av
10 YNKR 6280 A6
Poe Av
10 NWRK 6712 C6
Poe Ct
10 STNL 7206 C3
Poe Pl
2500 BRNX 6504 D4
Poe St
10 GrbT 6167 B1
10 STNL 7206 C3
700 HmpT 6928 A7
S Poe St
10 GrbT 6167 B2
Poets Cir
10 STNL 7116 B4
Poi Ct
10 STNL 7018 D7
10 STNL 7019 A7
Poillon Av
10 STNL 7116 D7
200 STNL 7207 D1
Poillon St
10 WbgT 7114 C4
Poinier St
10 NWRK 6817 C3
Poinier St SR-27
10 NWRK 6817 C3
Point Cres
10 QENS 6614 E7
Point Rd
- LRMT 6396 C4
- NRCH 6396 C4
Point St
10 STNL 7117 B7
10 YNKR 6279 C6
Point Breeze Av
10 LKSU 6723 C1
10 QENS 7122 A3
Point Breeze Pl
14-60 QENS 7027 B3
Point View Ter
10 BAYN 6919 C6
Poland Pl
10 STNL 7019 E4
Polar St
10 BKLN 7120 B1
Polar Wy
100 JSYC 6920 C1
Polaris St
1100 ELIZ 6918 E3
Polhemas Av
174-00 QENS 6825 E5
Polhemus Pl
10 BKLN 6922 E2
Polhemus St
10 OrgT 6164 D2
Polifly Rd
10 HKSK 6501 A2
200 HSBH 6501 A3
Polifly Rd CO-55
10 HKSK 6501 A2
200 HSBH 6501 A3
Polito Av
10 LynT 6609 A5
10 RTFD 6609 A5
Polk Av
800 HmpT 6828 A6
Polk Pl
10 GrbT 6049 E5
Polk St
10 CART 7017 C7
10 CART 7115 C1
10 NWRK 6818 A1
5200 WNYK 6716 E1
5400 WNYK 6610 D6
6200 WNYK 6611 A7
6700 GTBG 6611 A6
7100 NBgT 6611 A6
Polk Wk
- STNL 7021 A4
Pollock Av
10 JSYC 6819 C3
Polly Rd
10 HRSN 6169 E7
Polly Park Rd
10 HRSN 6169 B5
Polo Ln
10 LWRN 7028 C3
Polo Pl
90-00 QENS 6824 B4
3200 BRNX 6506 B7
Polo Rd
10 GTNK 6616 E6
Polo Field Ln
- LKSU 6723 B2
Polonia Av
700 ELIZ 6917 E6
Poly Pl
600 BKLN 7021 E4
800 BKLN 7022 A4

PO Machate Cir
- BKLN 6922 E5
Pomander Dr
10 GrbT 6049 B7
100 GrbT 6167 B1
Pomander Rd
100 MNLA 6724 E5
Pommer Av
10 STNL 7020 D1
Pomona Av
10 NWRK 6816 E5
10 NWRK 6817 A5
10 YNKR 6280 A4
Pompeii Av
196-00 QENS 6826 B3
Pompeii Rd
200-00 QENS 6826 B2
Pompey Av
10 STNL 7116 D6
Pond Cross
- LWRN 7028 A5
Pond Ln
10 DBSF 6166 B5
10 GrbT 6280 B1
10 NHmT 6724 A5
10 SNPT 6508 C4
200 LWRN 7028 B4
700 WDBG 7028 C2
800 HmpT 7028 C2
1300 HBPK 6928 E7
1300 HmpT 6928 E7
Pond Pl
2700 BRNX 6504 D3
Pond Rd
- GLCV 6398 E7
10 KNGP 6616 C1
10 RCKL 6164 D5
10 YNKR 6393 D1
N Pond Rd
10 CRSK 6392 C1
S Pond Rd
10 CRSK 6392 C1
W Pond Rd
10 PTHA 7205 B1
10 WbgT 7114 B7
10 WbgT 7205 B1
W Pond Rd SR-184
10 PTHA 7205 B1
10 WbgT 7114 B7
10 WbgT 7205 B1
Pond St
10 STNL 7115 E5
Pond Wy
10 STNL 6918 E7
Pond Crest Ln
1300 GrbT 6049 C7
Pondfield Pkwy
10 MTVN 6394 E2
10 MTVN 6395 A1
Pondfield Rd
10 BRXV 6280 E7
100 BRXV 6394 E1
200 BRXV 6395 A1
300 EchT 6395 A1
Pondfield Rd W
10 BRXV 6280 E7
10 YNKR 6280 D7
W Pondfield Rd
- YNKR 6280 D7
Pond Hill Rd
10 NHmT 6723 C1
Pond Park Rd
10 NHmT 6616 D7
Ponds Ln
10 HRSN 6051 C7
10 HRSN 6169 C1
Pondside Dr
300 GrbT 6049 C7
Pondview E
10 HRSN 6169 B1
Pondview W
10 HRSN 6169 B1
Pond View Dr
10 GLCV 6398 E7
Pondview Ln
10 NRCH 6281 E6
10 YNKR 6280 C3
Pond View Rd
10 GTNK 6616 D6
Pondview Rd
10 RYE 6283 D2
Poningo St
10 PTCH 6170 B5
Ponsi St
1000 FTLE 6502 E5
Pont St
10 GTPZ 6617 C4
10 THSN 6617 C4
10 THSN 6723 A1
Pontiac Pl
600 BRNX 6613 B4
Pontiac St
10 STNL 7019 C2
88-00 QENS 6826 E1
Ponton Av
2600 BRNX 6505 D7
Pony Cir
10 NHLS 6618 C7
10 NHLS 6724 C1
Pool Dr
10 MNCH 6500 E7
10 RSLN 6618 D6
Poole St
10 HmpT 6929 E6
Poor St
200 HKSK 6501 A2
Popham Av
1400 BRNX 105 A4
1400 BRNX 6504 A6
Popham Ln
10 SCDL 6167 D7
Popham Rd
10 GrbT 6167 B7
10 SCDL 6167 B7
10 SCDL 6281 C1
Poplar Av
10 BKLN 7120 B1
10 BRNX 6615 C4
10 LFRY 6501 D5
10 PLHM 6395 C2
10 STNL 7115 E5
140-00 QENS 6721 B6
Poplar Ct
10 GTNK 6616 E4

Poplar Dr
10 EHLS 6618 E6
Poplar Ln
10 STNL 7115 D7
Poplar Pl
10 NHmT 6508 D6
10 NRCH 6395 E5
Poplar Rd
10 DMRT 6278 C5
10 MrnT 6282 B7
10 NRCH 6282 B7
Poplar St
10 BKLN 121 A3
10 BKLN 6821 C5
10 CARL 6500 B7
10 CART 7115 B1
10 CRSK 6392 A1
10 EMFD 6049 B6
10 ERTH 6500 B7
10 GrbT 6049 B6
10 GrbT 6166 E2
10 HmpT 6828 D5
10 JSYC 6716 B5
10 LODI 6500 C2
10 PTCH 6170 C4
10 RDFP 6501 E5
10 VLYS 6928 D5
10 YNKR 6393 D1
100 RDFP 6502 A5
100 ROSL 6917 A5
1000 SECS 6610 A6
2400 BRNX 6505 C7
E Poplar St
10 FLPK 6827 D2
W Poplar St
10 FLPK 6827 D3
100 SFPK 6827 D3
Pople Av
132-00 QENS 6720 E5
Poppenhusen Av
115-00 QENS 6614 C7
Poppy Av
10 HmpT 6828 B4
Poppy Ln
10 GLCV 6509 E2
Poppy Pl
10 FLPK 6827 B3
Porach St
10 YNKR 6393 E1
Porcaro Dr
10 LFRY 6501 C7
10 MNCH 6501 C7
Porete Av
10 KRNY 6714 D2
10 NARL 6714 D2
Port Av
10 ELIZ 6918 C5
Port Dr
10 NHmT 6508 C6
10 PTWN 6508 C6
800 MRNK 6283 A7
Port Ln
10 STNL 6919 C7
E Port St
10 NWRK 6818 C5
Portage Av
10 STNL 7019 D5
Portal St
10 BKLN 6923 E3
Port Carteret Dr
10 CART 7115 D3
Porter Av
- HKSK 6501 A1
- LODI 6501 A1
10 BKLN 6822 E4
10 NWRK 6817 A4
Porter Pl
10 DBSF 6165 E5
10 NWRK 6817 A4
10 SCLF 6509 D7
800 HmpT 7028 C2
800 WDBG 7028 C2
Porter Rd
10 NHmT 6724 B6
167-00 QENS 6927 A4
Porter St
10 HKSK 6501 B2
10 SHkT 6501 B2
500 HmpT 6827 E7
Portico Ct
- KENS 6617 C4
10 GTPZ 6617 C4
Portico Pl
10 GTPZ 6617 C4
Port Imperial Blvd
- WhkT 111 A5
- WhkT 6716 E4
- WhkT 6717 A2
- WNYK 6611 B7
10 WNYK 111 B3
10 WNYK 6717 A1
Port Jersey Blvd
10 JSYC 6920 D2
100 BAYN 6920 C1
N Portland Av
10 BKLN 121 E4
10 BKLN 6821 E6
S Portland Av
10 BKLN 121 E7
10 BKLN 6821 E7
100 BKLN 6922 D1
Portland Pl
10 STNL 6920 B7
10 STNL 7020 C1
10 YNKR 6279 E6
Portland Rd
10 UnnT 6816 A5
Portman Rd
10 NRCH 6396 A2
Portnellan Av
10 NRCH 6395 C1
Port of Lake Dr
10 OrgT 6165 A2
Port Reading Av
10 WbgT 7114 D3
400 WbgT 7115 A3
900 CART 7115 C2
Port Reading Av CO-604
10 WbgT 7114 D3
300 WbgT 7115 B2
900 CART 7115 C2
Port Richmond Av
10 STNL 6919 C7
300 STNL 7019 C2

New York City/5 Borough Street Index

Portside Dr · Range St

STREET / Block City / Map# Grid

Portside Dr
100 EDGW 6611 E2
Portsmouth Av
10 STNL 7020 A5
Port Terminal Blvd
10 BAYN 6920 D3
Portugal Pl
10 MTVN 6394 E4
Port Washington Blvd
10 FLHL 6618 A4
10 MNPK 6618 B6
10 ROSE 6618 B6
300 NHmT 6618 A1
1200 NHmT 6617 E1
1300 NHmT 6508 E7
1300 SNPT 6508 E7
Port Washington Blvd SR-101
10 FLHL 6618 A4
10 MNPK 6618 B6
10 ROSE 6618 B6
300 NHmT 6617 E1
1200 NHmT 6617 E1
1300 NHmT 6508 E7
1300 SNPT 6508 E7
Posen St
10 STNL 7116 D6
Post Al
10 LRMT 6396 C2
Post Av
10 MHTN 101 E7
10 MHTN 102 A7
10 MHTN 6503 E4
10 MHTN 6504 A4
10 STNL 7019 C1
1000 STNL 6919 E7
1300 HmpT 6827 E5
Post Blvd
10 CART 7017 C5
Post Ct
10 BKLN 7023 E7
Post Dr
10 ROSH 6618 E3
Post Ln
10 EWLS 6724 E4
10 OrgT 6165 A1
10 STNL 6918 E7
Post Pl
10 HRSN 6283 B3
700 SECS 6610 B7
Post Rd
1000 SCDL 6167 E6
1200 SCDL 6168 A4
1200 WHPL 6168 A4
5000 BRNX 6393 C6
Post Rd SR-22
1000 SCDL 6167 E6
1200 SCDL 6168 A4
1200 WHPL 6168 A4
E Post Rd
200 WHPL 6168 B2
E Post Rd SR-22
200 WHPL 6168 B2
W Post Rd
10 WHPL 6168 A4
300 SCDL 6168 A4
W Post Rd SR-22
10 WHPL 6168 A4
10 SFPK 6827 D4
300 SCDL 6168 A4
Post St
10 YNKR 6393 C3
Potiphar Ct
200 ELIZ 6917 C6
Potomac St
10 YNKR 6280 A5
Potter Av
10 NRCH 6396 A4
10 STNL 7019 E3
900 UnnT 6816 B7
900 UnnT 6917 B1
Potter Pl
10 EchT 6281 C2
10 SCDL 6281 A4
10 WhkT 111 A4
10 WhkT 6717 A2
Potter Rd
100 SCDL 6281 C1
Potter St
10 SAMB 7205 B7
Potters Ct
10 GTNK 6616 D4
Potters Ln
10 GTNK 6616 D5
10 KNGP 6616 D5
10 QENS 6396 B5
Pouch Ter
10 STNL 7020 D5
Poultney St
200 STNL 7018 C6
Powderhorn Ct
10 WbgT 7114 A3
Powderhorn Rd
10 ARDY 6166 D4
Powder Horn Wy
10 STNL 6048 B6
Powell Av
2100 BRNX 6614 C1
Powell Ln
10 STNL 7116 A6
Powell Pl
10 NHmT 6723 D5
Powell St
10 BKLN 6924 C3
10 GrwT 6170 D2
10 STNL 7116 A3
Powells Cove Blvd
126-00 QENS 6614 B6
153-00 QENS 6615 C6
Power Rd
10 QENS 7026 D4
Powerhouse Rd
10 EHLS 6724 D1
10 NHLS 6724 C1
Poyer St
48-00 QENS 6719 E7
Prague Ct
10 STNL 7207 B3
Prague St
100 VLYS 6929 A2

Praise the Lord Plz
700 ELIZ 6918 A3
Prall Av
10 STNL 7207 B1
Prall St
400 WbgT 7114 D3
Pratt Av
100 QENS 6616 A4
3600 BRNX 6505 E1
3700 BRNX 6394 E7
4000 MTVN 6394 E7
Pratt Ct
10 STNL 7116 A4
Pratt Pl
500 LNDN 6917 A7
Pratt St
10 BRNX 6394 E7
10 YNKR 6394 E7
10 NRCH 6396 A3
Praver Pl
1500 HmpT 6827 D5
Premier Blvd
400 NHPK 6827 D2
1100 NHPK 6827 E2
Premium Point Rd
10 NRCH 6396 B3
Premium River Rd
10 MrnT 6396 C3
Prentiss Av
200 BRNX 6615 B3
Prescott Av
10 BRXV 6280 E7
10 BRXV 6281 A7
10 WHPL 6168 B4
100 STNL 7118 A1
Prescott Ct
900 HmpT 6927 E6
Prescott Pl
10 BKLN 6924 A2
10 HAOH 6166 A6
500 HmpT 6927 E6
600 HmpT 6928 A7
Prescott Rd
300 UnnT 6917 A1
Prescott Sq
10 BRXV 6280 E7
Prescott St
10 JSYC 6819 E3
200 YNKR 6393 E2
800 HmpT 6827 D7
President Pl
100 HmpT 7029 B5
President St
10 ENWK 6713 C3
10 ENWK 6714 A5
10 LNBK 6929 B3
10 NRCH 6395 D2
10 QENS 7027 C5
200 BKLN 6922 C1
400 SdBT 6500 B1
400 GRFD 6500 B1
900 BKLN 6923 D3
Presley St
10 STNL 7117 A7
Press St
10 HmpT 6827 D4
10 SFPK 6827 D4
Preston Av
10 HRSN 6168 D1
10 SCLF 6509 D7
10 STNL 7116 E7
10 STNL 7117 A7
Preston Rd
10 GTNK 6616 E5
Preston St
10 BGTA 6501 E7
10 MrnT 6282 B5
10 NHmT 6617 D2
10 RDFP 6501 E7
10 RYE 6283 E4
Price Ct
100 GTBG 6714 C7
100 WNYK 6611 C7
Price St
10 DBSF 6166 B4
100 ELIZ 6917 E3
E Price St
10 LNDN 6917 A7
10 LNDN 7017 A1
W Price St
10 LNDN 7017 A1
Prices Ln
10 STNL 7018 C6
Primrose Av
10 FLPK 6827 C2
10 MTVN 6394 E4
10 YNKR 6280 D5
200 MTVN 6395 A3
Primrose Av W
10 GrbT 6167 B1
Primrose Ct
10 GrbT 6049 D7
10 TFLY 6392 A4
Primrose Dr
10 NHmT 6724 A5
10 WLTN 6500 A6
Primrose Ln
10 CLST 6048 B4
10 HmpT 6929 A1
Primrose Pl
10 NHmT 6724 A5
10 HmpT 6928 E5
Primrose Rd
10 NRCH 6281 D2
100 WLPK 6724 E5
Prince Ct
10 BKLN 121 C5
10 BKLN 6821 D6
Prince Ln
10 STNL 7115 B6

Prince St
10 NRCH 6395 D4
10 NWRK 6713 C7
10 STNL 7020 E3
33-00 QENS 6720 E3
100 NWRK 6817 C1
800 TnkT 6502 B1
Princes Gate
10 OrgT 6164 E1
Princess Ct
1900 WbgT 7114 D2
Princess Ln
10 STNL 7019 B1
Princess St
10 STNL 7019 B1
Princeton Av
10 HmpT 6928 D6
10 YNKR 6280 E4
100 JSYC 6819 C7
300 HlsT 6816 C6
Princeton Av S
600 HlsT 6828 C3
Princeton Dr
10 OrgT 6164 A2
10 GrbT 6167 E3
Princeton Ln
10 STNL 7116 B5
Princeton Pl
10 PALP 6502 D7
10 KRNY 6714 C2
10 RTFD 6500 A7
10 RTFD 6609 A1
100 STNL 7117 E2
300 BRNX 105 D5
300 BRNX 6504 C6
1500 BKLN 6924 A2
Princeton Rd
10 ELIZ 6917 B3
10 UnnT 6917 A1
300 UnnT 6917 A1
400 HmpT 6929 D3
700 HmpT 6828 B6
800 HmpT 6828 A6
Princeton St
10 CLST 6278 C2
10 EORG 6712 D4
10 GDNC 6828 A3
10 NHmT 6724 D1
10 VLYS 6928 A2
10 WLPK 6724 E3
Prince Willow Ln
10 STNL 7207 B1
Princewood Av
10 OrgT 6165 A5
Prior Ct
10 YNKR 6280 B2
Prior Pl
10 JSYC 6820 A7
Priory Ln
10 PLMM 6395 D7
10 PLMM 6506 D1
Priscilla Av
10 YNKR 6280 D5
Priscilla Ln
10 EGLC 6392 C5
10 PTCH 6170 D4
400 EGLD 6392 B5
Priscilla Rd
100 HWTN 7028 D2
Private Pkwy
10 HRSN 6169 D6
Private Rd
154-51 QENS 6615 C6
Private Right of Wy
10 ISPK 7029 C5
Probst Av
600 FRVW 6611 B3
Progress St
500 ELIZ 6918 B3
Prol Pl
10 STNL 7117 A7
Prominard Av
10 STNL 7117 E4
10 STNL 7118 A4
Property St
10 STNL 7117 A7
Proposed St
10 WRDG 6500 C5
Propp Av
600 HmpT 6828 C5
Prospect Av
- STNL 7117 E1
- STNL 7118 A2
10 CARL 6609 C1
10 ARDY 6166 D5
10 BAYN 6919 E4
10 BAYN 6920 A3
10 BKLN 6922 D4
10 CDHT 7028 B2
10 CLFP 108 A1
10 CLFP 6611 C4
10 CRSK 6278 B6
10 EchT 6281 B6
10 ERKY 6929 C6
10 GLCV 6509 E5
10 HKSK 6501 B1
10 HmpT 6928 E5
10 HmpT 7028 B1
10 IrvT 6816 B1
10 KRNY 6714 C1
10 LFRY 6501 C7
10 LRMT 6396 D2
10 MtpT 6050 A4
10 NARL 6714 C1
10 QENS 6722 D2
10 SCLF 6509 D5
10 TYTN 6048 B4
10 WbgT 7114 B2
100 HmpT 6928 E5
100 LNBK 6928 E5
100 MRNK 6282 E7
300 STNL 6920 B7
400 OybT 6618 B1
400 RDGF 6611 B1
400 SCLF 6509 E5
500 BRNX 6613 C5
600 FRVW 6611 B3
600 RDGF 6502 B7
800 PALP 6502 B7
900 PLMM 6395 C7
E Prospect Av
10 BRNX 6394 E4
10 MTVN 6394 E4
10 HAOH 6280 A1
10 MHTN 118 D3
10 MHTN 6821 C6
N Prospect Av
10 LNBK 6928 E3

S Prospect Av
10 HKSK 6501 A2
W Prospect Av
10 GrbT 6167 E1
10 MTVN 6394 A4
10 WbgT 7114 C3
200 WbgT 7114 C3
600 FRVW 6611 A3
Prospect Ct
10 MtPT 6050 A7
222-00 QENS 6927 D3
Prospect Dr
10 YNKR 6393 D3
Prospect Expwy
10 BKLN 6922 E5
Prospect Expwy SR-27
10 BKLN 6922 E5
Prospect Ln
10 SNPT 6508 A7
100 STNL 7117 E3
300 HlsT 6816 C6
Prospect Pk SW
10 BKLN 6922 E4
Prospect Pk W
10 BKLN 6922 E2
10 BKLN 6923 A2
Prospect Pl
- EORG 6712 C4
10 BKLN 6922 E1
10 GTNE 6616 E7
10 GTNE 6722 C1
10 KRNY 6714 C2
10 STNL 7117 E2
100 STNL 7117 E3
300 BRNX 105 D5
300 BRNX 6504 C6
1500 BKLN 6924 A2
Prospect Row
10 IRVN 6166 C1
Prospect Row
10 NWRK 6817 E1
Prospect St
10 BKLN 121 C3
10 BKLN 6821 D6
10 BlmT 6713 A2
10 DMRT 6278 A4
10 ELIZ 6918 A4
10 EMFD 6049 B6
10 EORG 6712 E3
10 EWLS 6724 E4
10 GRFD 6500 A1
10 GTPZ 6617 B7
10 HSBH 6500 E4
10 JSYC 6716 B7
10 LODI 6500 C3
10 NHmT 6617 D1
10 NRCH 6395 E6
10 NWRK 6817 E1
10 NWRK 6818 A1
10 PALP 6502 B6
10 PTCH 6170 D4
10 SOrT 6712 A1
10 STNL 7020 D1
10 THSN 6617 B7
10 THSN 6723 B1
10 WHPL 6168 A4
10 WLPK 6724 D5
10 YNKR 6393 C1
100 FTLE 103 B1
100 FTLE 6503 A4
100 HSBH 6500 E4
100 LEON 6502 C4
100 NHmT 6724 D5
100 ROSL 6917 B4
100 RYE 6170 A1
200 PTHA 7205 C3
300 HmpT 7027 D3
1000 HlsT 6816 C6
Prospect St SR-9A
10 STNL 7117 A4
Prospect St US-9
10 RYE 6393 C1
Prospect St W
10 GrwT 6170 D7
E Prospect St
900 HBPK 7028 D1
900 STNL 7028 D1
900 NWRK 7028 D1
Prospect Ter
10 CARL 6609 C1
10 EORG 6712 E3
10 ERTH 6609 B1
10 SCLF 6509 D6
10 TFLY 6392 B2
10 YNKR 6393 D2
Prospect Park Dr
- BKLN 6922 E4
Protano Ln
900 MRNK 6282 E7
Provenzano St
10 HmpT 7027 D2
Providence Av
10 YNKR 6280 E4
Providence St
10 NWRK 6818 B1
10 STNL 7020 C5
Provost Av
- BRNX 6506 A1
2300 BRNX 6505 E1
3600 BRNX 6394 E7
3900 BRNX 6395 A7
3900 MTVN 6395 A7
Provost Av SR-22
- BRNX 6506 A1
2300 BRNX 6505 E1
3600 BRNX 6394 E7
3900 MTVN 6395 A7
Provost St
10 BKLN 6822 C1
10 BKLN 117 D7
10 BKLN 6718 C2
Purroy Pl
10 STNL 7020 D2
Purser Pl
10 QENS 6393 C2
Pryer Ln
10 LRMT 6396 C2
Pryer Pl
10 NRCH 6395 D2
10 NRCH 6396 A1
Pryer Ter
10 NRCH 6395 D2
Pryer Manor Rd
10 LRMT 6396 C2
10 MmT 6396 C2
10 NRCH 6396 C2

Pubins Ln
10 NHmT 6724 B6
Puffin Wy
10 TnkT 6502 A2
Pugsley Av
500 BRNX 6614 C2
Pulaski Av
10 CART 7115 D2
10 ERTH 6500 A6
10 STNL 7019 B1
10 WLTN 6500 A6
100 PTHA 7205 D2
Pulaski Br
- BKLN 117 D7
- BKLN 6718 B7
- BKLN 6822 C1
- QENS 117 E6
- QENS 6718 C7
Pulaski Ct
10 OrgT 6164 A1
Pulaski Ln W
10 OrgT 6164 A1
Pulaski Pl
- BAYN 6920 C1
- JSYC 6920 C1
Pulaski Pl
10 HKSK 6501 C4
10 NHmT 6508 D6
10 PTWN 6508 D6
Pulaski Skwy
10 JSYC 6715 D7
10 JSYC 6716 A7
10 JSYC 6819 C1
10 KRNY 6714 C2
10 KRNY 6819 A1
10 KRNY 6818 A7
10 NWRK 6818 A7
10 STNL 7116 C7
Pulaski Skwy US-1
10 JSYC 6715 D7
10 JSYC 6716 A7
10 JSYC 6819 C1
10 KRNY 6819 A1
10 KRNY 6818 E1
10 KRNY 6818 A7
10 NWRK 6818 A7
10 STNL 7116 C7
Pulaski Skwy US-9
10 BAYN 6920 C2
10 JSYC 6715 D7
10 JSYC 6716 A7
10 KRNY 6818 A7
10 KRNY 6819 A1
10 KRNY 6818 E1
600 ELIZ 6918 A1
600 ELIZ 6918 A1
Pulaski St
10 BKLN 6922 D6
10 BKLN 6923 A6
10 NWRK 6818 A1
Puleo Pl
10 STNL 6918 D5
Pulsifer Av
10 YNKR 6280 A7
Pupek St
10 SAMB 7205 B7
Purce St
500 HlsT 6816 B6
Purcell Ct
10 MNCH 6500 E7
Purcell St
10 STNL 7019 E1
Purchase Ln
10 HRSN 6169 E6
Purchase St
10 NoCT 6051 B3
10 RYE 6284 A1
10 RYE 6170 A7
200 HRSN 6169 E6
200 HRSN 6169 E7
3000 HRSN 6051 B7
Purchase St SR-120
10 NoCT 6051 B3
10 RYE 6283 E1
10 RYE 6284 A1
10 RYE 6170 A7
200 HRSN 6169 E6
200 HRSN 6169 E7
3000 HRSN 6051 B7
Purchase Hills Dr
10 HRSN 6169 B1
Purdue St
10 STNL 7019 A7
Purdue St
10 STNL 7019 A7
Purdy Av
- SCDL 6282 C7
10 PTCH 6170 C6
10 RYE 6283 E2
10 RYE 6284 A1
Purdy Pl
10 RYE 6283 E2
W Purdy Av
10 RYE 6283 E2
Purdy Pl
10 STNL 7207 B3
Purdy St
10 HRSN 6283 C3
1300 BRNX 6614 C1
1500 BRNX 6505 C7
Puritan Av
10 YNKR 6280 E5
103-00 QENS 6824 D4
1200 BRNX 6505 E2
1200 BRNX 6614 C1
Puritan Dr
10 NRCH 6281 E2
10 NRCH 6282 A2
10 PTCH 6170 D4
Puritan Rd
10 STNL 7019 D5
Puritan Woods Rd
10 NRCH 6169 D1
Purroy Pl
10 STNL 7020 D2
Purser Pl
10 QENS 6393 C2
Purves St
44-00 QENS 6718 D6
Pusan St
10 QENS 6919 A1
Putnam Av
- BKLN 6923 B1

Putnam Av
10 WHPL 6167 E2
10 YNKR 6393 B6
16-00 QENS 6823 B6
59-00 QENS 6823 D5
300 BKLN 6822 D7
Putnam Av US-1
10 PTCH 6170 C4
Putnam Av W
21-00 QENS 6718 E5
Putnam Av W US-1
700 PTCH 6170 D4
Putnam Blvd
- BKLN 117 D7
- BKLN 6718 B7
- BKLN 6822 C1
- QENS 117 E6
- QENS 6718 C7
Putnam Ct
10 OrgT 6164 A1
Putnam Dr
10 PTCH 6170 C4
Putnam Grn
10 GrwT 6170 D4
Putnam Pl
10 STNL 6918 D5
3400 BRNX 6504 E2
3400 BRNX 6505 A2
Putnam Rd
10 NRCH 6167 E5
300 UnnT 6816 E7
300 UnnT 6917 A1
Putnam St
10 LODI 6500 C1
10 MpIT 6816 B1
10 MTVN 6394 D3
10 NWRK 6818 B1
10 STNL 7116 C7
Putnam Ter
10 PTCH 6170 B4
Putney Rd
200 HmpT 6928 C1
Putters Ct
10 STNL 7020 A2

Q

Q St
1300 HmpT 6827 E7
Quabeck Av
10 HlsT 6816 B4
10 IrvT 6816 B4
Quail Dr
10 EGLD 6502 E2
Quail Ln
10 STNL 7115 D7
10 STNL 7206 C1
Quail Pl
10 ERKY 6929 B6
Quail Run
10 OLDT 6164 A4
10 IRVN 6166 C1
Quail Close
10 IRVN 6166 C1
Quaker Ctr
10 SCDL 6168 A7
Quaker Ln
10 GrwT 6051 D1
10 HRSN 6050 D4
Quaker Sq
10 SCDL 6282 B5
Quaker St
10 HmpT 6724 C5
Quaker Ridge Rd
10 NoCT 6051 B3
10 NHLS 6617 E7
10 NHmT 6617 E7
10 NHmT 6618 A7
10 NRCH 6281 D6
800 SCDL 6282 A5
Quality Wy
10 WbgT 7114 A4
Quarropas St
10 WHPL 6168 A2
Quarry Ln
10 IRVN 6048 C6
10 STNL 7118 D1
Quarry Rd
10 LRMT 6396 D2
2000 BRNX 6504 D5
Quarry Hgts
1500 HRSN 6050 D2
1500 HRSN 6050 D2
Quarter Deck
10 MHVN 6508 B6
Quay Av
10 HmpT 6928 D6
Quay Ct
10 HmpT 6929 B7
Quay St
10 BKLN 6822 B2
Quealy Pl
10 RKVC 6929 B6
Quebec Rd
10 YNKR 7029 C5
Queen Av
10 ELIZ 6816 E7
10 HlsT 6816 E7
Queen Rd
10 WbgT 7114 A3
Queen St
10 NWRK 6817 B4
10 STNL 7019 D5
Queen Anne Rd
10 NRCH 6281 E2
10 NRCH 6282 A2
10 PTCH 6170 B4
Queens Av
1300 HmpT 6827 E7
Queens Blvd
29-00 QENS 6718 C6
49-01 QENS 6719 D7
86-01 QENS 6824 C1
120-01 QENS 6824 A7
120-15 QENS 6825 A1
Queens Blvd SR-25
29-00 QENS 6718 C6
49-01 QENS 6719 D7
86-01 QENS 6824 C1
101-00 QENS 6720 B7
120-01 QENS 6824 A7
Queens Ct
200 TnkT 6501 E2

N Queens Ct
10 OrgT 6164 E1
S Queens Ct
10 OrgT 6164 E1
Queens Dr
10 YNKR 6393 E1
Queens Ln
10 NHmT 6724 B4
Queens Plz N
21-00 QENS 6718 C5
Queens Plz S
8-00 QENS 6718 D5
10-00 QENS 117 E2
Queens St
43-00 QENS 6718 D6
Queensboro Br
- MHTN 117 D2
- MHTN 6718 B4
- QENS 117 E2
- QENS 6718 C5
Queensdale St
10 GrwT 6170 D4
Queens Midtown Expwy
- QENS 117 D6
Queens Midtown Expwy I-495
- QENS 117 D6
- QENS 6718 D7
Queens Midtown Tun
- MHTN 116 A4
- MHTN 117 A4
- MHTN 6718 A6
- MHTN 6717 E6
- QENS 117 C6
- QENS 6718 B7
Queens Midtown Tun I-495
- MHTN 116 A4
- MHTN 117 A4
- MHTN 6717 E6
- MHTN 6718 A6
- QENS 117 C6
- QENS 6718 B7
Queens Midtown Tunnel
- QENS 117 E6
Queens Midtown Tunnel I-495
- QENS 117 E6
- QENS 6718 B7
Quencer Rd
187-00 QENS 6826 B6
Quentin Av
2000 BRNX 6614 C2
Quentin Rd
1000 HmpT 6928 C1
Quentin St
10 BKLN 7021 D1
1600 BKLN 7023 C4
Quentin Charlton Ter
10 YNKR 6393 E3
Quimby Av
2000 BRNX 6614 C2
Quimby Pl
10 WOrT 6712 B2
Quinby Av
10 WHPL 6167 E3
10 WHPL 6168 A3
Quince Av
140-00 QENS 6721 E6
Quincy Av
10 STNL 7020 E6
200 BRNX 6615 A3
200 WHPL 7118 D1
900 BKLN 6614 E1
Quincy Ct
10 TYTN 6048 C6
Quincy Ln
10 WHPL 6168 E6
10 WHPL 6169 A6
10 YNKR 6280 A4
Quincy Pl
10 KRNY 6714 C4
10 KRNY 6279 C7
Quincy St
10 JSYC 6716 B7
10 BKLN 6822 E7
800 BKLN 6823 B7
Quincy Wy
10 HRSN 6168 E1
Quinlan Av
10 STNL 7019 D6
Quinn St
10 STNL 7020 D2
Quintard Dr
10 GrwT 6170 D4
Quintard Pl
10 PTCH 6170 B4
Quintard St
10 STNL 7020 D6
Quinton St
10 WbgT 7114 B2
Quisenbury Pl
10 BKLN 6922 E1
Quitman St
10 NWRK 6817 B1

R

R St
1300 HmpT 6827 E7
Racal Ct
10 STNL 7018 C2
Race St
10 HlsT 6816 E7
10 ELIZ 6917 D7
Rachel Ct
10 STNL 6920 A6
Radcliff Av
10 NHmT 6508 D6
10 PTWN 6508 D6
10 SNPT 6508 E6

Radcliff Dr
10 GTNK 6616 C4
Radcliff Pl
10 STNL 7114 E4
Radcliff Rd
10 ISPK 7029 C5
10 STNL 7020 D5
Radcliffe Av
10 RYE 6283 E3
Radcliffe Av
10 STNL 7116 A5
Radde Pl
10 BKLN 6924 A2
Radel Ter
200 MpIT 6712 A7
200 SOrT 6712 A7
Rademann Pl
10 JSYC 6820 D1
Radford St
10 STNL 7019 D7
10 STNL 7019 E2
Radigan Av
10 STNL 7115 E6
Radio Av
10 SECS 6610 B6
Radio Dr
3200 BRNX 6506 A7
Radisson Plz
700 HmpT 7028 A7
Radley St
10 HRSN 6714 B6
10 KRNY 6714 B6
10 STNL 7116 C6
Radnor Rd
10 GTNK 6617 A5
10 NHmT 6617 A6
700 BKLN 6924 A7
Radnor St
84-00 QENS 6825 E2
Radstock Av
10 NRCH 6281 E6
10 NRCH 6282 A6
100 HmpT 6827 D4
Rae Av
10 STNL 7116 D7
Rae St
500 BRNX 6613 A3
Raff Av
10 FLPK 6827 C2
100 HmpT 6827 D4
Ragazzi Wy
10 STNL 7021 B6
Ragland Dr
400 ELIZ 6917 A3
600 ELIZ 6917 A3
Ragonese St
10 LODI 6500 D2
Rahway Av
10 ELIZ 6917 D5
10 LNDN 6917 C5
400 WbgT 7114 D3
700 LNDN 6917 C5
Rahway Av CO-514
400 WbgT 7114 D3
Rahway Av SR-27
10 ELIZ 6917 D5
700 LNDN 6917 C5
Raia Dr
10 GRFD 6500 B1
Railey Ct
- STNL 7116 A5
Railroad Av
10 FTLE 6611 D2
10 MtpT 6049 E1
10 NBgT 6610 E3
10 QENS 6718 D7
10 RDGF 6610 E3
10 CLFP 6611 B3
10 CLST 6278 B2
10 HAOH 6279 D1
10 LNBK 6928 E3
10 NHmT 6724 E3
10 NRCH 6395 E4
10 NRWD 6164 E3
10 PALP 6502 B6
10 RDFP 6501 E7
10 RSLN 6616 E6
10 STNL 7116 B5
10 TCKA 6281 E6
10 TYTN 6048 B4
10 VLYS 6928 E4
10 YNKR 6393 D1
37-00 QENS 6822 D1
100 BGTA 6501 D3
100 ERTH 6609 B1
100 NHmT 6724 E3
100 RDGF 6610 E3
100 NRWD 6164 E3
100 NVLE 6164 C6
900 SAMB 7205 B7
900 HmpT 6928 E7
9300 NBgT 6611 A3
9500 FRVW 6611 A3
Railroad Av CO-41
100 RDFP 6501 D3
100 BGTA 6501 D3
E Railroad Av
10 HKSK 6501 B1
N Railroad Av
10 TFLY 6392 A2
Railroad Pl
- GRFD 6500 B1
10 HmpT 7029 C6
10 SdBT 6500 B1
Railroad St
10 HSBH 6500 E4
10 MNCH 6500 E6
N Railroad Av
10 TFLY 6392 A2
Railroad Wy
10 LNBK 6928 E3

S Railroad St
10 STNL 7116 C7
Railroad Wy
10 LRMT 6396 D1
10 MRNK 6282 D6
Railside Av
10 WHPL 6168 B5
Raily Ct
10 STNL 7116 A5
Rainbow Av
10 STNL 7019 C1
Raisig Ct
10 VLYS 6928 C2
E Raleigh Av
10 STNL 7019 E2
10 STNL 7020 A1
W Raleigh Av
10 STNL 7019 E2
Raleigh Ln
800 HmpT 6928 A7
Raleigh Pl
10 NRCH 6923 C5
Raleigh Rd
1200 MRNK 6282 E4
Ralph Av
10 BKLN 6822 E7
10 BKLN 6823 A7
10 STNL 7116 D6
100 WHPL 6168 B5
Ralph Pl
10 STNL 7020 C4
Ralph Rd
10 NRCH 6281 D4
Ralph Hoist Triangle
- BRNX 6505 C2
Ralston Av
10 SOrT 6712 A7
Ralston St
10 RYE 6284 A1
Ramapo Av
10 STNL 7116 A6
10 STNL 7115 E7
Ramapo Cir
10 HRSN 6283 B1
Ramapo Tr
10 HRSN 6283 B2
Ramble Rd
10 STNL 7117 B5
Ramblewood Av
10 STNL 7117 A6
Ramella Av
10 QENS 6501 C2
Ramland Rd S
10 OrgT 6164 A2
Ramona Av
10 STNL 7116 C6
10 STNL 7115 E7
Ramona Ct
10 NRCH 6282 A4
Rams Hl
10 NHmT 6618 A4
Ramsey Av
10 YNKR 6280 A4
600 HmpT 6816 C4
Ramsey Cir
400 ELIZ 6917 B2
Ramsey Ln
10 STNL 7019 D4
Ramsey Pl
10 STNL 7020 C2
Ramsey Rd
10 STNL 7116 C6
10 SCDL 6168 B5
Ranch Ln
10 CLST 6278 C4
Rand Pl
100 LWRN 7027 C4
Randall Av
10 HmpT 7027 C4
10 LNBK 6929 D4
10 RKVC 6929 D4
10 STNL 7020 B1
200 CDHT 7027 E2
200 HmpT 6827 E6
1100 BRNX 6613 E4
1700 BRNX 6614 D3
Randall Pl
10 STNL 7020 C4
N Randall Av
10 MHTN 6613 A7
N Randall Wy
10 STNL 7020 C7
W Randall Av
900 HmpT 7027 E2
W Randall Wy
10 STNL 6920 B6
Randalls I
- MHTN 6613 A7
Randolph Av
10 YNKR 6280 A4
10 JSYC 6819 C6
10 STNL 7116 A6
200 ERTH 6500 B7
2500 CART 7017 D4
Randolph Av CO-602
10 JSYC 6819 C6
2500 CART 7017 A6
Randolph Pl
10 COrt 6712 A5
10 NWRK 6816 E2
10 SOrt 6712 B1
10 WOrT 6712 B1
Randolph Rd
3100 BRNX 6506 A7
Randolph St
10 BKLN 6923 A6
10 CART 7115 D5
10 CART 7017 C7
Range Rd
10 LNDN 7017 A4
Range St
86-00 QENS 6826 C1
86-01 QENS 6827 A1

New York City/5 Borough Street Index

STREET
Block City Map# Grid

Ranger Pl
10 NRCH 6281 E7
Rankin St
10 ELIZ 6918 A5
10 STNL 7116 E7
Ransom Av
10 SCLF 6509 E7
Ransom St
88-00 QENS 6826 E1
Ranson Rd N
10 HmpT 7027 D1
Rapelye St
10 BKLN 6922 B1
Raritan Av
10 STNL 7020 B6
10 WbgT 7114 E3
500 PTHA 7205 B2
Raritan St
200 SAMB 7205 B7
200 SRVL 7205 B7
Raritan Reach Rd
10 SAMB 7205 D7
Raskulinecz Rd
10 CART 7017 A7
10 CART 7115 A1
Rason Rd
10 HmpT 7027 E1
Rasweiler Blvd
600 HmpT 6828 B7
Rathbun Av
10 WHPL 6168 A3
200 STNL 7116 B6
900 STNL 7115 E7
Rathburn Pl
400 PTHA 7205 B2
Rau Ct
99-00 QENS 6925 E5
102-00 QENS 6926 A5
Ravenhill Pl
10 PALP 6502 D6
10 RDGF 6502 D6
700 RDGF 6611 C1
Ravenhurst Av
10 STNL 7019 D2
Ravenna St
10 STNL 7207 E1
Ravensdale Rd
10 GrbT 6280 B1
10 HAOH 6280 A1
Ravenswood Rd
10 YNKR 6280 C5
Ravine Av
10 JSYC 6716 B7
10 YNKR 6279 C6
400 HSBH 6500 E4
Ravine Dr
10 DBSF 6166 A6
10 HAOH 6165 E6
10 HAOH 6166 A6
Ravine Rd
10 GTNK 6617 B6
10 TFLY 6392 B3
N Ravine Rd
10 GTNK 6617 B5
Rawlins Av
3100 BRNX 6506 A7
Rawson Pl
10 STNL 7018 C7
Ray Av
10 LEON 6502 D2
500 RDGF 6611 C1
700 RDGF 6502 B7
Ray Ln
10 MLVN 6929 C2
Ray Pl
10 EchT 6281 C2
Ray St
- WbgT 7114 B4
10 STNL 7116 D6
Raybrook Pl
10 YNKR 6394 B4
Raybrook Rd
10 YNKR 6394 C4
Raydol Av
10 SECS 6610 A7
Rayfield Ct
10 STNL 7019 E1
Raymond Av
10 ERTH 6500 A7
10 LNBK 6929 B5
10 RTFD 6500 A7
10 SOrT 6712 A5
10 STNL 7019 D3
Raymond Blvd
- KRNY 6818 E1
200 NWRK 6818 B1
900 NWRK 6817 E1
1000 NWRK 6713 D7
Raymond Blvd US-1
- KRNY 6818 E1
10 NWRK 6818 D1
Raymond Blvd US-9
- KRNY 6818 E1
10 NWRK 6818 D1
Raymond Blvd US-9 TRK
- KRNY 6818 E1
- NWRK 6818 E1
Raymond Ct
10 SCLF 6509 E7
200 SOrT 6712 A6
Raymond Pl
10 HmpT 6928 E7
10 HmpT 7028 D1
10 YNKR 6394 C4
100 STNL 7019 E1
E Raymond Plz
10 NWRK 6817 D3
W Raymond Plz
10 NWRK 6713 E7
10 NWRK 6817 D3
Raymond St
10 EGLC 6503 B1
10 GLCV 6509 E3
10 HSBH 6500 D4
10 RKVC 6929 E3
Raymond Ter
10 ELIZ 6917 C2
10 UnnT 6917 C2
Raynor Av
10 MTVN 6395 A2
Raynor St
200 WbgT 7114 A2
Rayson Ln
10 DBSF 6165 D4
10 DBSF 6166 A5
Read Av
10 YNKR 6280 E5
10 YNKR 6281 A5
Read St
10 NWRK 6818 B1
10 PTCH 6170 C5
Reade St
10 MHTN 118 C6
10 MHTN 6821 A3
10 YNKR 6280 A3
300 PTHA 7205 C3
Reading Av
10 STNL 7116 E4
E Reading Av
10 STNL 7117 A4
Reads Ln
4-00 QENS 7027 E5
Rear Row
10 LODI 6500 E1
Rebeau Dr
10 MrnT 6282 B6
Rebecca Pl
800 ELIZ 6918 A4
Rebecca St
1200 LNDN 7017 A3
Rector Av
10 WbgT 7114 D5
Rector Pl
200 MHTN 120 A1
200 MHTN 6821 A4
Rector St
10 MHTN 120 A1
10 MHTN 6821 A4
10 NWRK 6713 E7
10 PTHA 7205 D5
10 STNL 6919 D7
10 STNL 7019 D1
Rectory Ln
10 SCDL 6167 C7
Rectory Ln S
10 SCDL 6167 D7
Rectory St
10 RYE 6283 E2
10 RYE 6284 A2
100 PTCH 6170 C5
Red Rd
700 TnkT 6502 A1
Red Brook Rd
10 GTNK 6616 D3
10 KNGP 6616 D3
Red Brook Ter
10 GTNK 6616 E4
10 KNGP 6616 E4
Redcedar Ln
10 STNL 7115 D7
Redcliffe St
300 ELIZ 6918 A5
Red Coat Ln
10 OrgT 6164 A2
Red Cross Ln
10 QENS 6616 A7
Red Cross Pl
10 BKLN 121 B3
10 BKLN 6821 D5
Redding St
136-00 QENS 6925 D2
Redfern Av
10 HmpT 7027 D3
10 QENS 7027 D4
Redfield Rd
10 ISPK 7029 D3
Redfield St
10 RYE 6284 A4
51-00 QENS 6722 E4
Redgrave Av
10 STNL 7117 C4
Red Hook Ln
10 BKLN 121 B6
10 BKLN 6821 D7
Redmond St
700 TnkT 6502 B1
Redmont Rd
200 HmpT 6828 D6
Redneck Av
10 LFRY 6501 B6
10 MNCH 6501 B7
Red Oak Dr
10 RYE 6283 E4
400 OrgT 6164 D4
W Red Oak Ln
- WHPL 6169 A4
10 HRSN 6169 B4
Red Oak Rd
10 BRXV 6280 E7
Red Pole Cir
100 NHLS 6618 C6
Red Roof Dr
10 RYEB 6169 E3
10 RYEB 6170 A3
Red Spring Ln
10 GLCV 6509 D3
Redwood Av
10 STNL 7117 B4
100 HmpT 7027 E3
Redwood Ct
10 SNPT 6508 C5
Redwood Dr
10 EHLS 6618 E6
500 HmpT 7028 A1
Redwood Lp
10 STNL 7115 E5
Redwood Rd
10 NHmT 6724 A6
10 WHPL 6168 E7
Redwood St
10 JSYC 6819 A4
Redwood Oak Dr
- BRNX 6505 B7
Reed Av
10 HmpT 6827 E3
10 PLMM 6395 B6
Reed Ct
10 GTNK 6616 D5
Reed Dr
10 NHmT 6724 C3
Reed Pl
1400 BRNX 6506 A7
Reed St
10 BKLN 6922 A2
10 JSYC 6819 E2
Reeder St
- BRNX 6615 D5
51-00 QENS 6719 E7
Reeds Mill Ln
2100 BRNX 6505 E1
Reeve Pl
10 BKLN 6922 E5
Reeves Av
146-00 QENS 6721 A7
Reeves Pl
10 NWRK 6817 A3
Reeves Ter
1000 UnnT 6816 A6
Regal Dr
10 NRCH 6281 D4
Regal Wk
100 STNL 7018 E2
Regan Av
10 STNL 6920 A7
10 STNL 7020 A1
Regatta Pl
37-00 QENS 6722 C3
Regency Cir
10 EGLD 6502 E3
Regency Pl
10 WhkT 111 A5
10 WhkT 6717 A3
Regent Cir
10 STNL 7116 B5
Regent Dr
10 LWRN 7027 E3
10 LWRN 7028 A3
Regent Ln
10 NHmT 6724 B4
Regent Pl
10 HmpT 6828 E5
10 ROSE 6618 D6
10 RSLN 6618 D6
10 YNKR 6280 D2
2000 BKLN 6923 B6
Regent St
10 VLYS 6928 C3
N Regent St
10 PTCH 6170 B4
S Regent St
10 PTCH 6170 A6
Regina Av
22-00 QENS 7027 C5
Regina Ln
10 STNL 7116 C4
Regina Pl
10 YNKR 6279 E4
Regina St
100 WbgT 7114 A2
Regis Dr
10 STNL 7019 A2
100 STNL 7018 E2
Reid Av
10 NHmT 6617 D2
10 RKVC 6929 E5
10 STNL 7020 C6
Reid St
10 ELIZ 6918 A4
S Reid St
10 ELIZ 6918 A4
Reidel Ct
10 SECS 6610 A5
Reilly Ct
10 HKSK 6501 C3
Reily Rd
10 CDHT 7027 E1
10 CDHT 7028 A1
10 HmpT 7027 E1
Reimar Ct
100 UnnT 6917 A1
Reimer Rd
- SCDL 6167 E6
Reina Rd
400 HmpT 7029 C2
Reiner Pl
10 EGLC 6392 C7
10 EGLC 6503 C1
Reinhart Rd
44-00 QENS 7027 A6
Reiss Ln
10 STNL 7020 B5
Reiss Pl
600 BRNX 6505 A5
Reldyes Av
100 LEON 6502 D5
Relyea Pl
10 NRCH 6395 E5
Remington Pl
10 NRCH 6395 D4
Remington Rd
10 MNPK 6618 A6
Remington St
95-00 QENS 6825 C7
Remington Ter
10 NRCH 6395 C5
Remmey St
10 WbgT 7114 A6
Remsen Av
10 BKLN 6923 E3
10 RSLN 6618 E5
10 VLYS 6928 C2
10 WbgT 7114 B1
300 BKLN 6924 C7
1500 BKLN 7024 C1
Remsen Cir
10 YNKR 6280 D1
Remsen Ln
10 BLRS 6827 C2
10 FLPK 6827 C2
10 QENS 6827 C2
Remsen Pl
- RDGF 6611 A1
56-00 QENS 6823 C2
Remsen Pl CO-50
- RDGF 6611 A1
Remsen Rd
10 GTNK 6617 A4
10 KNGP 6617 A4
10 YNKR 6280 E3
Remsen St
10 BKLN 120 E5
10 BKLN 121 A5
10 BKLN 6821 C6
10 HmpT 6827 E4
10 HmpT 6928 E1
10 LNBK 6929 C4
10 STNL 7020 C6
10 VLYS 6928 E1
10 WLPK 6724 D4
Renaissance Ct
10 BKLN 6822 D5
Renaissance Sq
10 WHPL 6168 C2
Rene Ct
21-00 QENS 6823 B4
Rene Dr
10 STNL 7117 C3
Renee Pl
10 IrvT 6816 C4
10 STNL 7018 E4
10 STNL 7019 A3
Renewal Wy
500 WbgT 7115 A3
Renfrew Av
2000 HmpT 6827 B5
Renfrew Pl
10 STNL 7019 B2
Reni Rd
10 FLHL 6618 A3
Renken Blvd
10 HmpT 6828 A4
Renner Av
10 NWRK 6817 A4
100 NWRK 6816 E3
Renner Pl
10 NARL 6714 D1
Rennie Pl
10 LODI 6500 D2
Reno Av
10 STNL 7117 E3
Renshaw Av
10 EORG 6713 B2
Renshaw Pl
10 PTCH 6170 C4
Rensselaer Av
200 STNL 7116 B6
1000 STNL 7115 E7
Rensselear Av
10 ATLB 7028 B7
Rental Car N
- QENS 6926 C4
Rentar Plz
- QENS 6823 D4
Renwick Av
10 STNL 7020 A3
Renwick St
10 MHTN 118 C3
10 MHTN 6821 A1
Reock St
200 COrT 6712 C3
Reon Av
10 STNL 7019 E4
Rescigno Pl
10 EchT 6281 C3
Research Av
1500 BRNX 6506 A6
Reserve Av
10 JSYC 6716 A6
Reservoir Av
- BRNX 102 E4
10 JSYC 6716 B7
10 WLTN 6500 B5
2600 BRNX 6504 C2
Reservoir Ct
10 WLTN 6500 B5
Reservoir Pl
200 BRNX 6505 A1
Reservoir Rd
10 NoCT 6050 B5
10 WHPL 6050 B5
Reservoir St
- SCLF 6509 E6
Rest Av
10 ARDY 6166 D4
Retford Av
10 STNL 7116 E6
100 STNL 7117 A7
400 STNL 7208 A1
Retiro Ln
10 NRCH 6281 D3
Retner St
10 STNL 7021 B6
Return Bnd
10 YNKR 6394 D1
Reunion Rd
10 GrbT 6050 A5
10 RYEB 6051 E5
100 GrbT 6049 E4
Reuten Dr
10 CLST 6278 B2
Reuter Av
300 ELIZ 6917 E5
Revere Av
100 BRNX 6615 B3
1000 BRNX 6614 E1
Revere Ct
10 FLPK 6827 E2
10 OLDT 6164 A3
Revere Dr
800 HlsT 6816 D7
800 HlsT 6917 D1
Revere Dr E
10 FLPK 6827 E2
Revere Dr W
10 FLPK 6827 E2
Revere Ln
10 HRSN 6168 E1
10 STNL 7117 B2
Revere Pl
10 BKLN 6923 D2
10 OrgT 6164 A1
Revere Rd
10 ARDY 6166 D3
10 MNPK 6618 A6
10 MRNK 6282 D6
10 MrnT 6282 D6
10 NHmT 6618 A2
10 NRCH 6281 E2
10 NRCH 6282 A2
Revere St
10 RKVC 6929 E2
10 STNL 7020 B1
Reverend James A Polite Av
800 BRNX 6613 C3
Reverend James H Screven Plz
10 NWRK 6817 A3
Reverie Ct
100 GrbT 6049 E4
Review Av
28-00 QENS 6718 D7
34-00 QENS 6822 D1
Review Pl
3800 BRNX 102 E1
3800 BRNX 6504 C2
Reville St
100 BRNX 6506 E6
Revolutionary Rd
10 ARDY 6166 D4
Rewe St
10 BKLN 6822 E3
Rex Pl
10 YNKR 6394 A4
Rex Rd
- QENS 6825 E5
10 PTCH 6170 B4
175-00 QENS 6826 A5
Rex St
10 GrwT 6170 C3
Reyam Rd
10 LNBK 6929 A5
Reyem Dr
10 HmpT 7027 E1
Reyer Av
10 YNKR 6394 C2
Reymont Av
10 RYE 6283 D4
Reyna Ln
10 NRCH 6282 A2
Reynal Cross
10 SCDL 6168 B6
Reynal Rd
10 WHPL 6168 C6
Reynold St
10 BRNX 6506 E7
Reynolds Av
10 ENWK 6713 E6
10 HRSN 6713 E6
100 BRNX 6615 B3
Reynolds Ct
10 STNL 7020 E4
Reynolds Ln
200 CLFP 6611 D2
Reynolds Pl
10 EchT 6281 C3
10 GrwT 6170 D3
10 NWRK 6712 B7
100 SOrT 6712 B7
Reynolds Rd
10 GLCV 6509 E2
Reynolds St
10 STNL 7020 D4
100 COrT 6712 C4
Reynolds Ter
200 COrT 6712 C3
Rhame Av
10 ERKY 6929 C7
100 HmpT 6929 C7
Rhett Av
10 STNL 7117 A5
N Rhett Av
10 STNL 7117 A5
Rhine Av
200 STNL 7020 C4
Rhinehart Pl
10 HmpT 7027 D2
Rhinelander Av
600 BRNX 6505 B6
Rhoda St
10 HmpT 6828 C6
Rhoda Ter
10 ELIZ 6917 A3
10 ROSP 6917 A3
Rhode Island Av
10 EORG 6712 D5
Rhodes Dr
10 NHmT 6724 C6
W Rhodes Dr
10 NHmT 6724 B6
Rhodes Ln
300 HmpT 6929 C1
Rhodes St
10 NHmT 6723 D6
10 NRCH 6396 A3
Rhynas Dr
10 MTVN 6395 A2
Ria Dr
10 WHPL 6168 C5
Ribbon St
10 HmpT 6828 B5
Rica Ln
500 HmpT 6928 B6
Rica Pl
1500 HmpT 6928 D1
Ricard St
4-00 QENS 6823 B4
Ricardo Pl
100 HKSK 6501 B1
Rice Av
10 STNL 7019 E3
10 SYHW 6048 B1
Rich Av
10 MTVN 6394 E4
Rich St
10 IrvT 6816 C1
W Rich St
10 IrvT 6816 C1
Richard Av
10 STNL 7206 D3
10 WbgT 7114 A7
E Richard Av
600 WbgT 7114 B3
Richard Ct
10 CLST 6278 C5
10 DMRT 6278 C5
Richard Ln
10 STNL 7019 A4
Richard Pl
10 RYE 6284 A2
Richard St
10 GrwT 6170 C6
10 JSYC 6819 D5
100 HmpT 7028 B7
200 HmpT 6828 C6
Richard Ter
10 GrbT 6167 B3
Richard Ter N
100 UnnT 6816 A4
Richard Ter S
100 UnnT 6816 A4
Richard Newcome Sq
- QENS 6824 E3
Richards Ln
100 HWTH 7029 A1
200 HWTH 6928 E7
200 HWTH 7028 E1
Richards Rd
10 NHmT 6617 D2
Richards St
10 NWRK 6818 C1
10 WHPL 6050 A7
200 BKLN 6922 A2
Richardson Av
10 SCLF 6509 E7
4300 BRNX 6394 C6
Richardson Ln
10 HRSN 6283 C2
Richardson Pl
10 EchT 6281 B5
Richardson St
10 BKLN 6822 C3
Richbell Rd
10 MRNK 6282 D7
10 MrnT 6282 D7
10 SCDL 6167 E7
10 WHPL 6168 D5
Richbell Close
10 SCDL 6167 E6
Riche Av
10 STNL 7018 C6
Richelieu Pl
10 NWRK 6712 C7
Richelieu Rd
10 SCDL 6281 D1
Richelieu Ter
10 NWRK 6712 C6
Richfield Av
10 YNKR 6394 B3
Richford Ter
200 ELIZ 6917 C5
200 LNDN 6917 C5
Richland Av
206-00 QENS 6826 B1
209-00 QENS 6722 C7
Richland Rd
10 GrwT 6170 D5
Richlee Ct
10 MNLA 6724 D7
Richman Plz
10 BRNX 105 A3
10 BRNX 6504 E5
Richmond Av
200 SOrT 6712 A7
900 STNL 7019 A3
2100 STNL 7018 E5
2600 STNL 7116 E5
3900 STNL 7117 A7
Richmond Ct
10 STNL 6918 E7
Richmond Hl
10 IRVN 6166 A1
Richmond Ln
10 NRCH 6282 A5
Richmond Pl
10 YNKR 6280 C5
100 LWRN 7027 B3
400 LEON 6502 D5
1100 UnnT 6917 A1
Richmond Rd
10 STNL 7020 C5
235-00 QENS 6722 C1
2000 STNL 7118 A1
2400 STNL 7117 B2
Richmond St
- CLST 6278 C2
- WbgT 7114 B2
10 BKLN 6823 E7
10 LODI 6500 C3
10 NWRK 6713 C7
100 BKLN 6924 E1
200 BKLN 6925 A1
400 ELIZ 6917 E6
Richmond Ter
10 STNL 6920 C6
1300 STNL 6919 D7
3000 STNL 6918 C6
Richmond Hill Rd
10 GrwT 6051 D1
10 STNL 7018 E7
100 STNL 7019 A7
300 STNL 7117 A1
Richmond Valley Rd
10 STNL 7206 C2
Rickbern St
10 RYE 6284 A4
Rico Pl
132-00 QENS 6925 D2
Ricord St
10 NWRK 6712 D6
Rider Av
10 HmpT 6929 B2
10 MLVN 6929 B2
10 YNKR 6280 A2
100 BRNX 110 D1
100 BRNX 6612 E4
200 BRNX 107 E7
Rider Ct
10 NWRK 6713 B7
Ridge Av
10 STNL 7020 B5
100 HmpT 6928 C4
100 VLYS 6928 C4
100 YNKR 6279 D7
Ridge Blvd
10 PTCH 6170 A4
10 RYEB 6170 A4
6600 BKLN 6921 D7
7300 BKLN 7021 D1
Ridge Cir
10 MNPK 6617 E6
Ridge Cres
10 MNPK 6617 E6
Ridge Ct
10 STNL 7020 B3
100 COrT 6712 C2
600 RDGF 6611 C1
7000 BKLN 6921 E7
7000 BKLN 7021 E1
Ridge Dr
10 NHmT 6617 D7
10 NHmT 6618 A1
10 YNKR 6393 D4
Ridge Dr E
10 FLHL 6618 C6
10 GTNE 6616 D7
10 GTNE 6722 E1
Ridge Dr W
10 FLHL 6618 C5
10 GTNE 6616 D7
10 GTNE 6722 D1
W Ridge Dr
10 RYEB 6169 E3
Ridge Ln
500 FTLE 6502 D5
Ridge Lp
10 STNL 7020 B5
W Ridge Mw
100 WRDG 6500 D6
Ridge Pl
- BRNX 6506 B1
10 BRNX 6395 C7
10 GrwT 6170 D3
10 PLMM 6395 C7
Ridge Rd
10 ARDY 6166 C5
10 BRXV 6280 E6
10 BRXV 6281 A6
10 CRSK 6278 A6
10 DBSF 6166 B5
10 EGLC 6503 B2
10 GLCV 6509 D1
10 GrbT 6167 C3
10 KRNY 6714 C1
10 LynT 6609 A3
10 NARL 6714 C1
10 NHmT 6724 C2
10 NRCH 6282 B5
10 NRCH 6396 A1
10 NRWD 6278 D2
10 RTFD 6609 A4
10 TCKA 6280 E6
10 TCKA 6281 A6
10 TFLY 6392 C4
10 WOrT 6712 A1
10 YNKR 6393 D3
234-00 QENS 6722 D2
500 EGLD 6503 A3
500 HmpT 6827 B6
Ridge Rd SR-17
- RTFD 6609 A3
10 KRNY 6714 C1
10 LynT 6609 A3
10 NARL 6714 C1
S Ridge Rd
10 MrnT 6282 D6
Ridge St
10 ALPN 6278 E6
10 COrT 6712 C2
10 EchT 6281 B7
10 HAOH 6165 E7
10 MHTN 119 C5
10 MHTN 6821 D3
10 NWRK 6713 D4
10 RYE 6169 E7
10 RYE 6170 A7
10 RYEB 6170 A7
10 YNKR 6281 B3
N Ridge St
10 RYEB 6170 A3
200 RYEB 6169 E3
S Ridge St
10 RYEB 6170 A5
Ridge Wy
2000 FTLE 6502 E4
Ridgecrest E
10 SCDL 6167 E5
Ridgecrest N
10 SCDL 6167 E5
Ridgecrest W
10 SCDL 6167 E5
Ridgecrest Av
10 STNL 7117 A6
300 STNL 7116 E6
Ridge Crest Ter
7000 BKLN 6921 D7
Ridgecroft Rd
10 BRXV 6281 B7
Ridgedale Av
500 WbgT 7114 C3
Ridgedale Pl
10 WbgT 7114 C2
Ridgedale Rd
10 SCDL 6282 B1
Ridgedale St
186-00 QENS 6927 C1
Ridgedell Av
10 HAOH 6165 D6
Ridgefield Av
10 RDFP 6501 E6
10 STNL 7020 C3
100 BGTA 6501 D2
Ridgefield Ter
400 FRVW 6611 C2
400 RDGF 6611 C2
Ridge Hill Rd
10 YNKR 6280 B4
Ridgeland Mnr
10 RYE 6284 A4
Ridgeland Rd
10 YNKR 6280 E4
Ridgeland Ter
10 RYE 6284 A4
400 LEON 6502 E4
500 EGLD 6502 E3
600 FTLE 6502 E3
Ridgeley St
200 PTHA 7205 D2
Ridgeview Av
10 WHPL 6167 E3
10 WHPL 6168 A3
10 WOrT 6712 A4
10 YNKR 6280 B5
Ridgeview Pl
10 PTCH 6170 C5
Ridgeview Ter
10 EMFD 6049 A5
Ridgeway
10 WHPL 6168 C5
500 WHPL 6169 A4
Ridgeway Av
10 HlsT 6816 E6
10 STNL 7018 C6
500 SAMB 7205 B7
500 SRVL 7205 A7
Ridgeway Av CO-686
500 SAMB 7205 B7
500 SRVL 7205 A6
Ridgeway Cir
10 WHPL 6168 D5
Ridgeway Dr
10 IRVN 6166 B1
1600 HmpT 6929 A6
Ridgeway Rd
10 BXTE 6617 D1
10 MrnT 6282 C6
Ridgeway St
10 KNGP 6616 D4
10 MTVN 6394 E2
Ridgewood Av
10 BKLN 6924 E1
10 IrvT 6816 B1
10 NWRK 6816 B1
10 NWRK 6817 B3
10 STNL 7116 E5
10 YNKR 6394 B4
300 BKLN 6824 A7
300 BKLN 6925 A1
600 QENS 6824 A7
600 WbgT 7114 D3
Ridgewood Dr
10 GrbT 6049 A3
10 RYE 6283 E1
Ridgewood Pl
10 BKLN 6823 B6
10 STNL 6920 B7
10 STNL 7020 B1
N Ridgewood Rd
400 SOrT 6712 B4
400 WOrT 6712 B4
Ridgewood St
10 HmpT 6928 B2
10 VLYS 6928 B2
Ridgewood Ter
10 TYTN 6048 C3
Ridgley Pl
10 UNCT 6716 B2
10 WhkT 6716 B2
Riedel Av
10 STNL 7117 D2
Riegelmann St
10 STNL 7019 C2
Rifton St
600 HmpT 6827 C7
Riga St
10 STNL 7117 E4
10 STNL 7118 A4
Rigby Av
10 STNL 7117 B2
Rigby St
10 YNKR 6394 C3
Rigene Rd
10 HRSN 6282 E1
10 HRSN 6283 A1
Rigene Close
10 HRSN 6283 A1
Riggs Pl
10 SOrT 6712 A6
10 WOrT 6712 B2
Right of Wy Rd
- IRVN 6048 B7
Rigimar Ct
- STNL 7206 E2
Riis Av
- QENS 7123 B2
Rikers Island Br
- BRNX 6613 E7
- QENS 6613 E7
- QENS 6719 D1
Riley Pl
10 STNL 7019 C1
Ring Pl
118-00 QENS 6826 A7
118-27 QENS 6927 A1
Ring Rd
- STNL 7018 E7
- STNL 7019 B7
- STNL 7116 E1
Rintin St
10 HmpT 6828 B5
Rio Dr
188-00 QENS 6826 A3
Rionda Ct
10 ALPN 6278 E7
Rio Vista Dr
10 ALPN 6392 D1
100 NRWD 6278 D1
Ripley Pl
100 ELIZ 6918 C4
Riser Rd
10 LFRY 6501 B5
10 SHkT 6501 B5
Risley Pl
10 NRCH 6395 D4
Risse St
3300 BRNX 6504 D2
Ristaino Dr
100 JSYC 6820 A2
Rita Ln
10 GrbT 6049 A6
10 NRCH 6281 D4
Ritch Av
- GrwT 6170 D5
Ritch Av W
10 GrwT 6170 D5
Ritchey Pl
10 WHPL 6168 B5
Ritchie Dr
10 YNKR 6393 D3
Rittenhouse Rd
10 EchT 6281 B7
10 EchT 6395 B1
Ritter Pl
800 BRNX 6613 C1
Ritters Ln
10 YNKR 6279 D7
Riva Ct
10 HmpT 6928 B5
River W
100 GrwT 6170 B1
River Av
10 GrwT 6170 C6
10 HmpT 6929 D5
10 RKVC 6929 D5
400 BRNX 107 D5
400 BRNX 6612 E2
400 PLHM 6395 B3
1000 BRNX 6613 A1
1200 BRNX 105 A7
1200 BRNX 6504 D7
River Blvd
- FTLE 103 B4
- FTLE 6503 A6
River Ct
10 JSYC 6820 D2
River Dr
10 GRFD 6500 A4
River Dr CO-507
10 GRFD 6500 A4
River Dr S
10 JSYC 6820 D2
River Ln
- SECS 6610 B5
River Pl
- NWRK 6713 E7
10 YNKR 6279 E5
River Rd
- BRNX 102 A1
- STNL 7018 B3
10 BGTA 6501 D1
10 EDGW 108 B1
10 EDGW 6611 C5
10 HmpT 6929 D6
10 MHTN 114 A6
10 MHTN 6718 C3
10 NBgT 108 A3
10 NBgT 6611 C5
10 RKVC 6929 D5
10 SCDL 6167 E4
10 SECS 6610 A5
500 TnkT 6501 D1
700 BRNX 6504 A1
1100 EDGW 103 A7
1100 EDGW 106 A1
1100 EDGW 6503 A7
1100 EDGW 6612 A1
1500 FTLE 103 B4
1500 FTLE 6503 A6
6500 GTBG 6611 C7
6500 WNYK 6611 C7
River Rd CO-41
10 BGTA 6501 D3
500 TnkT 6501 D1
River Rd CO-505
10 EDGW 108 A4
10 EDGW 6611 E2
10 NBgT 108 A3
10 NBgT 6611 C5
1100 EDGW 103 A5
1100 EDGW 106 A1
1100 EDGW 6503 A7
1100 EDGW 6612 A1
1500 FTLE 103 B4
1500 FTLE 6503 A6
6500 GTBG 6611 C7
6500 WNYK 6611 C7
River Run
10 CART 7115 D2
River St
- NRCH 6395 E4
10 BKLN 6822 A3
10 EMFD 6049 A5
10 GrwT 6170 C3
10 HAOH 6165 E7
10 HBKN 6716 E7
10 HKSK 6501 C1
10 IRVN 6048 A7
10 LFRY 6501 D5
10 LODI 6500 C2
10 NRCH 6396 A4
10 NWRK 6713 E7
10 SYHW 6048 A2
10 TCKA 6280 E5
10 TCKA 6281 E6
10 TYTN 6048 A2
10 YNKR 6393 A1
400 HmpT 6929 D7
700 MRNK 6282 E4
700 MRNK 6283 A4
1000 RDGF 6611 A1
River St CO-49
10 HKSK 6501 D4
10 LFRY 6501 D5
River St CO-503
10 HKSK 6501 C1
S River St
10 HKSK 6501 D4
S River St CO-49
500 HKSK 6501 D4
S River St CO-503
10 HKSK 6501 D4
River Ter
10 MHTN 118 A6
10 MHTN 6821 A3
10 TYTN 6048 C1
Riverbend Dr
- WNYK 111 C2
- WNYK 6717 A1
Rivercrest Ln
10 DBSF 6165 D4
Rivercrest Rd
10 BRNX 6393 B5
Riverdale Av
10 BKLN 6924 B4
10 GrbT 6049 D7
10 GrwT 6170 C4
10 PTCH 6170 C4
100 YNKR 6393 C3
500 BRNX 6393 B6
3000 BRNX 102 D2
3000 BRNX 6504 B1
Riverdale Av SR-9A
10 YNKR 6393 C1
Riverdale Av US-9
10 YNKR 6393 C1
Riverdale Dr
200 FTLE 6502 E6
Riverdale Ext
10 GrwT 6170 C4
Riverdale Rd
10 HmpT 6928 B5
Riveredge Rd
10 TFLY 6392 A2
Riveredge Rd CO-70
10 TFLY 6392 A2
Riveria Ct
10 MLVN 6929 B1
Riverpointe Rd
10 HAOH 6279 D2
Rivers Dr
10 LKSU 6723 B1
Riverside Av
10 NWRK 6714 C4
300 HmpT 6929 D7
Riverside Blvd
10 LBCH 7029 C7
10 MHTN 112 B3
10 MHTN 6717 D2
Riverside Ct
- SECS 6610 A5
Riverside Dr
10 MHTN 108 C7
10 MHTN 112 C2
10 MHTN 6717 D1
10 RKVC 6929 D5

New York City/5 Borough Street Index

STREET
Block City Map# Grid

Riverside Dr
158-00 QENS 6615 C6
200 MHTN 6611 E6
200 MHTN 106 B7
400 MHTN 109 A3
500 ELIZ 6917 D2
500 HlsT 6917 D2
700 MHTN 107 A1
800 MHTN 6503 C7
800 MHTN 6612 C1
1000 MHTN 104 A6
1700 MHTN 101 D6
3300 HmpT 7029 D2
Riverside Dr E
- MHTN 106 B7
- MHTN 6612 A4
Riverside Dr W
- MHTN 106 B7
156-00 MHTN 6612 C1
158-00 MHTN 103 E7
158-00 MHTN 6503 C7
159-00 MHTN 104 A7
Riverside Pl
10 DBSF 6165 E4
10 GRFD 6500 A3
8900 EDGW 108 A2
8900 EDGW 6611 C5
8900 NBgT 108 A2
8900 NBgT 6611 C5
Riverside Rd
10 ERKY 6929 D5
10 RKVC 6929 D5
Riverside Vw
10 RYE 6283 E4
Riversville Rd
10 GrwT 6170 B1
400 GrwT 6051 E1
Riverton St
118-00 QENS 6826 B7
Rivervale Av
300 NRWD 6164 A5
Riverview Av
10 ARDY 6166 D5
10 CART 7017 B6
10 CLFP 6611 D3
10 EDGW 6611 D3
10 RTFD 6609 B3
10 TYTN 6048 B3
Riverview Cir
10 NBgT 108 A5
10 NBgT 6611 C6
Riverview Ct
10 GrwT 6170 B1
10 KRNY 6714 A3
10 NWRK 6714 C7
10 NWRK 6818 C1
10 SECS 6610 A5
Riverview Dr
- WhkT 6716 E5
300 PTHA 7205 B4
Riverview Dr N
- NBgT 6611 C6
Riverview Ln
- FTLE 103 B2
- FTLE 6503 A5
Riverview Pl
10 HAOH 6165 E6
10 YNKR 6393 D1
200 CLFP 6611 C4
200 FRVW 6611 C4
Riverview Rd
10 IRVN 6048 C7
10 JSYC 6819 B5
400 GrbT 6048 C7
Riverview Ter
10 IRVN 6166 B1
Rivervue Pl
10 YNKR 6280 C2
Riverwalk Pl
10 WNYK 111 C1
10 WNYK 6717 B1
Riviera Ct
120-00 QENS 6614 D6
Rivington Av
10 STNL 7018 E6
Rivington St
10 MHTN 119 A4
10 MHTN 6821 D3
10 WbgT 7114 A2
900 ROSL 6917 A5
1200 LNDN 6917 A6
Rizkin Pl
10 HmpT 7029 D4
10 ISPK 7029 D3
Rizzolo Rd
10 KRNY 6714 C3
Road 3 de
- MHTN 117 C3
- MHTN 6718 B5
Road A
- ERTH 6609 D4
Road C
- ERTH 6609 D4
Road D
- ERTH 6609 E4
Road on the Hl
10 NHmT 6616 E6
Roadway
- LFRY 6501 C6
10 BGTA 6501 D2
Roanoke Av
- HlsT 6917 E1
10 RYEB 6170 B6
200 NWRK 6818 D2
800 ELIZ 6917 E1
900 HlsT 6816 E7
Roanoke St
10 STNL 7019 C6
10 WbgT 7114 B2
10 YNKR 6280 B5
Robard Ln
107-00 QENS 6826 E4
Robbins Av
10 EMFD 6049 B6
Robbins Ln
10 LKSU 6723 A2
Robbins Pl
10 YNKR 6393 C2
Robbins St
700 PTHA 7205 B1
Robby Ln
10 NHmT 6724 A4
Robby Rd
10 LFRY 6501 B6
10 MNCH 6501 B6

Robert Av
10 HmpT 6827 D4
10 PTCH 6170 B3
400 HmpT 6828 B6
Robert Cir
10 SRVL 7205 A7
Robert Ct
10 LODI 6500 E3
Robert Dr
10 NRCH 6281 E5
Robert Ln
10 GrbT 6049 B7
10 STNL 6920 C7
Robert Pl
10 IrvT 6816 C4
Robert Rd
10 HmpT 7027 D2
208-00 QENS 6615 D6
Robert St
300 HmpT 6929 D2
1200 HlsT 6816 E6
1200 UnnT 6816 A6
N Robert St
10 WbgT 7114 E4
S Robert St
10 WbgT 7114 E5
Roberta Pl
10 NoCT 6050 B5
Roberta St
100 VLYS 6928 E2
Robert Crisfield Pl
10 RYE 6283 D6
Robert F Wagner Sr Pl
10 MHTN 118 D7
10 MHTN 120 D1
10 MHTN 6821 B4
Roberto Clemente State Park Br
200 BRNX 105 A3
200 BRNX 6504 A5
Roberts Av
100 YNKR 6279 D4
300 YNKR 6280 A5
2800 BRNX 6505 E6
3100 BRNX 6506 A5
Roberts Ct
10 TFLY 6392 A3
Roberts Dr
10 STNL 7118 A4
Roberts Ln
10 CDHT 7027 C2
10 CDHT 7028 A2
10 YNKR 6279 D4
Roberts Pl
4000 NBgT 6716 B2
Roberts Rd
10 EGLC 6392 C6
200 COrT 6712 B4
Robertson Av
10 WHPL 6167 E1
10 WHPL 6168 C2
Robertson Pl
10 YNKR 6281 A3
1500 BRNX 6506 A6
Robertson Rd
10 ERKY 6929 C5
10 LNBK 6929 C5
Robertson St
4800 BRNX 6394 C5
Robin Ct
10 STNL 7115 D7
500 HmpT 6828 E7
Robin Ln
10 ALPN 6278 E7
10 ALPN 6392 E1
12-00 QENS 6615 E7
1000 UnnT 6816 B7
Robin Rd
10 DMRT 6278 B6
10 NHmT 6617 D7
10 STNL 7021 A6
100 STNL 7020 E6
200 EGLD 6502 E2
900 HmpT 6828 A7
Robin Wy
10 NHmT 6616 D6
Robin Hill Rd
10 GrbT 6167 B7
10 GTNK 6616 E4
Robinhood Rd
10 WHPL 6168 D4
Robins Cres
10 NRCH 6395 C2
Robins Rd
- PLHM 6395 C2
10 NRCH 6395 C2
Robins Nest Ln
10 MrnT 6396 B2
Robinson Av
10 QENS 6928 A2
10 STNL 7117 B7
10 VLYS 6928 A2
100 BRNX 6615 A3
Robinson Bch
10 STNL 7206 C5
Robinson Dr
- JSYC 6819 A4
Robinson Rd
10 LODI 6500 E1
10 LODI 6501 B2
Robinson St
43-00 QENS 6721 A5
Robins Roost
10 RYEB 6170 A2
Robley St
10 YNKR 6394 B3
Rocco St
10 BlvT 6713 D1
Rochambeau Av
10 DBSF 6166 A4
3100 BRNX 6504 E2
Rochambeau Dr
10 GrbT 6167 A4
Rochambeau Rd
10 SCDL 6167 C5
10 SCDL 6281 C1
Roc Harbour Dr
- NBgT 108 A4
- NBgT 6611 C6
Rochelle Pl
10 NRCH 6395 C5
10 STNL 7116 D6
Rochelle Rd
10 MrnT 6396 B1

Rochelle St
10 BRNX 6506 E7
10 STNL 7020 B6
Rochelle Ter
10 MTVN 6394 D3
Rochester Av
10 BKLN 6923 E3
10 HmpT 7028 D7
Rock Ln
10 HRSN 6283 A1
10 YNKR 6279 D4
Rock Pl
10 YNKR 6393 D3
Rock Rd
10 EGLC 6503 B2
Rock Rdg
10 MRNK 6282 D5
Rock St
10 BKLN 6822 E5
10 JSYC 6820 A1
Rockaway Av
- NHmT 6724 D7
10 BKLN 6924 B2
10 GDNC 6828 E3
10 HmpT 6828 E4
10 RKVC 6929 E5
10 VLYS 6928 D5
100 GDNC 6724 D7
100 HmpT 6929 D6
100 MNLA 6724 D7
1100 LNBK 6928 E5
1700 HmpT 6928 E6
N Rockaway Av
10 HmpT 6929 B3
10 LNBK 6929 B3
S Rockaway Av
1600 HmpT 6928 C6
1600 LNBK 6928 C6
Rockaway Blvd
74-00 QENS 6824 B7
74-01 BKLN 6824 A7
81-00 QENS 6925 E1
110-00 QENS 6926 E2
156-00 QENS 6927 D6
Rockaway Ct
10 HmpT 6929 D6
Rockaway Frwy
- QENS 7123 E1
- QENS 7124 A1
24-00 QENS 7027 A6
92-00 QENS 7026 A7
Rockaway Pkwy
- BKLN 7024 D1
10 BKLN 6923 E3
10 VLYS 6928 D3
400 HmpT 6928 E1
700 BKLN 6924 C6
E Rockaway Rd
10 HBPK 6928 D6
10 HmpT 6928 D6
100 HmpT 6929 A7
100 HWTH 6928 E6
100 HWTH 6929 A7
200 ERKY 6929 A7
Rockaway St
10 STNL 7206 B5
Rockaway Tpk
- QENS 6927 E7
10 LWRN 7028 A3
100 CDHT 7028 A2
100 HmpT 6927 E7
100 HmpT 7028 A2
200 CDHT 7027 E1
200 HmpT 7027 E1
Rockaway Beach Blvd
37-00 QENS 7027 A6
67-00 QENS 7026 C7
105-00 QENS 7124 A1
126-00 QENS 7123 C2
Rockaway Beach Dr
108-00 QENS 7123 E2
Rockaway Community Pk Entrance
- QENS 7027 A5
Rockaway Point Blvd
- QENS 7122 D3
217-00 QENS 7121 E4
Rock Cliff Pl
10 NoCT 6050 B4
Rock Creek Ln
100 SCDL 6168 B7
Rock Creek Ter
10 EGLD 6502 E2
Rockcrest Rd
10 NHmT 6618 A6
Rockdale Av
10 NRCH 6395 D5
Rockefeller St
700 ELIZ 6918 A7
Rock Hall Rd
10 LWRN 7027 E5
10 LWRN 7028 A4
Rock Hill Ln
10 GrbT 6167 B5
Rockhill Ter
10 LRMT 6396 B4
Rockhollow Rd
10 PLNM 6617 D4
Rockingchair Rd
10 GrbT 6049 B7
Rockinghorse Tr
10 RYEB 6169 E1
10 RYEB 6170 D2
Rockingstone Av
100 MrnT 6282 B7
100 MrnT 6396 D2
Rockland Av
- STNL 7117 D1
10 MrnT 6282 C6
10 PTCH 6170 B4
10 YNKR 6393 D3
100 MRNK 6282 D7
100 NRWD 6164 B6
100 NVLE 6164 C6
300 STNL 7019 C7
Rockland Pl
10 GrwT 6170 D3
10 NRCH 6396 A2
10 YNKR 6393 D2
Rockland Rd
- PRMT 6165 A1
10 HRSN 6050 D3
10 NoCT 6050 C3
10 OrgT 6165 A2

Rockland Ter
10 NWRK 6712 C6
Rockland Park Av
10 OrgT 6164 D4
Rockledge Av
10 MTVN 6394 E6
10 WHPL 6168 B1
Rockledge Cir
- GrbT 6167 D4
Rockledge Dr
10 NRCH 6395 D7
10 PLMM 6395 D7
Rockledge Pl
10 NRCH 6396 A1
10 YNKR 6393 C4
300 TnkT 6502 A2
Rockledge Rd
10 GrbT 6167 D4
10 HRSN 6169 C5
10 NoCT 6050 B5
10 YNKR 6280 C7
10 YNKR 6394 C1
Rockleigh Rd
10 OrgT 6164 E5
10 RCKL 6164 E6
Rocklyn Av
10 LNBK 6929 C4
200 ERKY 6929 C5
Rockmart Av
10 HmpT 6827 C5
Rock Meadow Ln
10 SCDL 6168 C7
Rockne Rd
10 YNKR 6280 B6
Rockne St
10 STNL 7019 A7
Rock Ridge Av
10 GrwT 6170 E1
Rock Ridge Cir
10 NRCH 6281 E5
Rock Ridge Dr
10 RYEB 6170 A3
Rockridge Rd
10 ARDY 6166 E4
10 MrnT 6396 D1
10 MTVN 6395 A2
10 RYE 6284 A2
Rockrose Pl
105-00 QENS 6824 D4
Rockville Av
10 RKVC 6929 E5
10 STNL 7018 E6
Rockville Ct
500 HmpT 6929 D6
Rockwell Av
10 STNL 7020 D4
Rockwell Pl
10 BKLN 121 D6
10 BKLN 6821 E7
Rockwell St
10 HRSN 6283 B3
Rockwood Av
10 NHmT 6508 E6
10 SNPT 6508 E6
Rockwood Dr
10 LRMT 6396 B2
10 MrnT 6396 B2
Rockwood Pl
10 EDGW 6611 E3
10 EGLD 6502 E2
10 NRCH 6281 E3
Rockwood Rd
10 FLHL 6617 E5
10 PLDM 6617 E5
10 PLNM 6617 D4
Rockwood Rd E
10 PLDM 6617 E4
Rockwood Rd W
10 PLDM 6617 E4
Rockwood St
100 BRNX 105 C6
100 BRNX 6504 A7
Rocky Rd
10 MrnT 6282 C7
Rocky Hill Rd
201-00 QENS 6722 A5
Rocky Hollow Dr
10 MrnT 6282 B5
Rocky Ridge Rd
10 HRSN 6050 E6
Rocky Wood Rd
10 NHmT 6617 E6
Rodeo Ln
10 STNL 7020 C3
Roder Av
700 BKLN 7023 A3
Roderick Av
10 STNL 7020 D7
Roderick Ln
10 GDNC 6724 E7
Rodman Ovl
10 NRCH 6396 A6
Rodman Pl
1200 BRNX 6504 E6
Rodman St
10 STNL 7019 B2
Rodmans Neck
10 BRNX 6506 C5
Rodney Ln
10 KNGP 6616 C1
Rodney Pl
10 DMRT 6278 B5
10 RKVC 6929 D5
Rodney Rd
10 SCDL 6281 D1
Rodney St
200 BKLN 6822 B4
Rodwell Av
10 GrwT 6170 E4
10 IrvT 6712 E7
10 NWRK 6712 E7
Roe Ct
10 STNL 7019 E1
Roe Rd
176-00 QENS 6826 B7
Roe St
10 STNL 6919 E7
10 STNL 7019 E1
Roebling Av
2800 BRNX 6505 E7
Roebling St
10 BKLN 6822 B4
Roeckel Av
10 VLYS 6928 B2

Roehrs Dr
10 WLTN 6500 A6
Roff Av
10 PALP 6502 C6
10 RDGF 6502 B7
500 LEON 6502 D5
Roff St
100 STNL 7020 D3
Roger Av
10 HmpT 7027 C3
1200 UnnT 6816 B6
Roger Dr
10 NHmT 6508 E7
Roger Pl
10 WHPL 6168 E4
Rogers Av
- LNBK 6928 C5
10 BKLN 6923 C5
10 GrbT 6167 B1
Rogers Dr
10 NRCH 6281 E3
Rogers Pl
10 BLRS 6827 C2
10 FLPK 6827 C2
10 STNL 7116 D7
800 BRNX 6613 C3
Rogers Rd
10 GTNK 6617 A4
10 KNGP 6617 A4
Rogers St
10 TCKA 6281 A6
Roger Sherman Pl
10 RYE 6283 E3
Rohr Pl
2400 BRNX 6614 D3
Rokeby Pl
10 STNL 6920 A7
Roland Av
10 GrbT 6050 A5
Roland Dr
10 WHPL 6168 E6
10 WHPL 6169 A6
Roland Pl
10 VLYS 6928 E5
Roland Rd
10 IRVN 6166 A3
Roliver St
10 RTFD 6609 B3
Roll Av
10 SRVL 7205 A7
Rollhaus Pl
10 PTCH 6170 C5
Rolling St
10 LNBK 6929 C3
100 MLVN 6929 C3
Rolling Wy
10 NRCH 6281 E5
Rolling Field Rd
10 WHPL 6168 D7
Rolling Hill Grn
10 STNL 7116 B5
Rolling Hill Ln
10 LWRN 7028 A4
Rolling Hill Rd
10 NHmT 6617 E6
Rolling Hills Ln
10 HRSN 6283 A2
Rolling Ridge Rd
10 WHPL 6168 C6
Rollins St
10 YNKR 6393 D4
Rollinson St
10 WOrT 6712 A3
Roma Av
10 STNL 7118 A4
Romaine Av
10 JSYC 6819 E1
10 YNKR 6393 C3
Romaine Pl
10 NWRK 6713 E3
10 NWRK 6714 A3
100 LEON 6502 C4
Roman Av
10 STNL 7018 E3
10 STNL 7019 A5
100-00 QENS 6824 D4
Roman Ct
10 STNL 7206 C4
Romanelli Av
10 HKSK 6501 B2
10 SHKT 6501 B3
Romanko Av
10 LFRY 6501 B6
Romano Ln
10 YNKR 6393 D2
Romanowski St
10 CART 7115 D1
Romar Av
10 JSYC 6819 B6
10 SCDL 6168 C7
10 WHPL 6168 C7
Rombouts Av
3200 BRNX 6506 A1
3400 BRNX 6505 E1
3700 BRNX 6394 E7
3900 MTVN 6394 E7
Rome Av
10 STNL 7020 B5
Rome Dr
187-00 QENS 6826 B6
Rome St
10 NWRK 6818 B2
800 HmpT 6827 C7
Romeo Ct
198-00 QENS 6826 B2
Romeo St
10 MNCH 6500 E7
Romer Rd
10 STNL 7020 A6
Romig Rd
- STNL 7019 E7
Romney Pl
10 YNKR 6281 B2
Romola Dr
10 KNGP 6616 D6
Ronald Av
10 STNL 7019 B1
Ronalds Av
10 NRCH 6395 C5
Ronalds Ln
10 NRCH 6395 D5
Ronbru Dr
200 NRCH 6281 E4

Ronkonkoma Av
400 HmpT 6929 C2
Ronny Cir
10 HAOH 6280 A2
Ronson Ln
10 VLYS 6929 A2
Rooney Pl
10 MNCH 6501 B7
Roosevelt Av
- HmpT 6827 D6
- SECS 6610 B7
10 BKLN 7021 D4
10 CART 7115 D2
10 EORG 6713 B3
10 HmpT 7027 D3
10 HSBH 6500 C5
10 JSYC 6819 C2
10 LNBK 6929 B5
10 LODI 6500 C3
10 LRMT 6396 C1
10 MLVN 6929 B2
10 MtPT 6050 A3
10 RDFP 6501 E4
10 RDFP 6502 A4
10 RYE 6284 A4
10 VLYS 6928 C4
10 WbgT 7115 C2
65-00 QENS 6719 D6
91-00 QENS 6720 B6
100 HmpT 6928 C4
100 STNL 7019 D4
136-22 QENS 6721 A4
200 HmpT 6828 A3
200 WRDG 6500 C4
300 GDNC 6828 A3
500 CART 7017 D7
1300 PLMM 6395 D7
1300 PLMM 6506 D1
1400 BRNX 6506 D1
1400 WbgT 7017 A6
2800 BRNX 6615 A2
Roosevelt Av CO-602
200 CART 7115 D2
500 CART 7017 D7
1400 WbgT 7017 A6
Roosevelt Av CO-604
10 CART 7115 D2
10 WbgT 7115 C2
Roosevelt Blvd
10 LBCH 7029 E7
300 HmpT 6828 C5
Roosevelt Ct
7-00 QENS 7027 D5
10 STNL 7019 D5
Roosevelt Dr
10 HlsT 6816 D5
Roosevelt Pl
10 BKLN 6924 A2
10 ISPK 7029 C4
10 LODI 6500 D2
10 MNCH 6501 B7
10 RKVC 6929 E3
10 SCDL 6281 D1
1400 PLMM 6506 D1
Roosevelt Sq E
10 MTVN 6394 A4
Roosevelt Sq N
10 MTVN 6394 A4
Roosevelt Sq S
10 MTVN 6394 A5
Roosevelt Sq W
10 MTVN 6394 A4
Roosevelt St
10 CLST 6278 C3
10 CRSK 6278 A7
10 ERKY 6929 B6
10 GLCV 6509 E3
10 HmpT 6828 A3
10 HmpT 6929 E7
10 KRNY 6714 D1
10 LFRY 6501 C6
10 NARL 6714 D1
10 OrgT 6164 B2
10 PALP 6502 B5
10 RSLN 6618 D5
10 STNL 7020 C4
10 WHPL 6168 C4
10 YNKR 6279 E6
10 YNKR 6280 A6
100 GDNC 6828 A2
100 NHPK 6828 A2
200 TnkT 6502 B2
200 UNCT 6716 B1
300 FRVW 6611 C3
500 NVLE 6164 A4
900 ELIZ 6917 D4
Roosevelt Ter
10 BAYN 6919 E1
10 IrvT 6712 E7
Roosevelt Av Br
- QENS 6720 D5
Roosevelt Island Br
- MHTN 114 A7
- MHTN 6718 C4
- QENS 114 A7
- QENS 6718 C4
Roosevelt St Ext
- TnkT 6502 C2
Ropes Av
3400 BRNX 6395 A7
Ropes Pl
10 NWRK 6713 D1
Ropes Rd
300 EGLC 6503 B2
Roquette Av
10 HmpT 6827 C4
100 SFPK 6827 C4
300 FLPK 6827 D3
Rosa Dr
10 GrbT 6166 D1
Rosalind Av
1500 HmpT 6827 D4
Rosalind Pl
10 LWRN 7028 A3
Roscoe Pl
10 FLPK 6827 D2
Rose Av
- BRXV 6281 A7
10 EGLC 6503 B2
10 FLPK 6827 C2
10 GLCV 6509 E1
10 GTNK 6617 B6
10 HRSN 6283 B4
10 JSYC 6819 C6
10 MRNK 6282 E6
10 NHmT 6617 B6

Rose Av
10 NWRK 6713 D2
10 STNL 7117 E2
10 TCKA 6281 A7
10 VLYS 6928 C2
100 EchT 6281 B6
140-00 QENS 6721 B6
200 STNL 7118 A2
300 HmpT 6929 D1
Rose Ct
10 CLST 6278 B2
10 STNL 7020 B2
Rose Ln
10 ERKY 6929 B7
10 NRCH 6395 C1
10 STNL 7116 C7
10 YNKR 6393 D2
100 NHmT 6723 D5
1400 MRNK 6283 B5
Rose Pl
10 NHmT 6724 D7
Rose Rdg
10 TYTN 6048 B3
Rose St
- ERKY 6929 C5
- LNBK 6929 C5
- MHTN 118 E7
- MHTN 6821 C4
10 BKLN 6924 B6
10 CARL 6500 C7
10 CRSK 6278 B7
10 DMRT 6278 B6
10 ERTH 6500 A6
10 HAOH 6280 A1
10 HmpT 6929 D7
10 HmpT 7028 B2
10 KRNY 6714 A5
10 LFRY 6501 C7
10 NWRK 6817 B2
10 RYE 6283 E4
10 WHPL 6168 D6
10 WLTN 6500 A6
10 WRDG 6500 C7
10-00 QENS 7027 D5
700 HmpT 6828 B4
Rose Ter
10 NWRK 6817 A2
10 WOrT 6712 B2
Rose Wy
10 WHPL 6168 D6
Rose Bank Pl
10 STNL 7020 E3
Rosecliff Rd
10 STNL 7018 E2
Rosedale Av
10 HAOH 6166 A7
10 HAOH 6280 C1
10 NRCH 6395 C2
10 SCDL 6168 D7
10 STNL 7116 A6
10 WHPL 6168 E7
400 BRNX 6614 A1
400 WHPL 6169 A6
1400 BRNX 6505 A7
Rosedale Rd
- QENS 6928 B5
10 HmpT 6928 B5
10 VLYS 6928 C5
10 YNKR 6280 E4
Rosedale St
10 NRCH 6395 C2
Rosegold St
900 HmpT 6828 A5
Rose Haven Ln
10 RCKL 6164 E6
Rosehill Av
10 TYTN 6048 C3
100 NRCH 6395 C1
Rose Hill Dr
10 NHLS 6724 B1
Rosehill Pl
10 IrvT 6816 C3
300 ELIZ 6917 D5
Rosehill Ter
10 YNKR 6279 E5
10 YNKR 6280 A5
Roseland Pl
300 ELIZ 6917 B2
300 UnnT 6917 A2
Roselle Av
200 CDHT 7028 A2
Roselle Pl
1000 HmpT 6928 C7
Roselle St
10 LNDN 6917 A7
10 MNLA 6724 E5
1500 BRNX 6505 C6
Roselle St CO-619
100 LNDN 6917 A7
Rosemere St
10 RYE 6284 A3
Rosemont Blvd
10 GrbT 6049 D7
Rosemont Pl
10 NHmT 6616 D7
10 SDRK 6616 D7
Roseth Pl
10 NHmT 6723 B1
Roseville Av
10 NWRK 6713 C3
Rosewell St
10 SAMB 7205 C7
Rosewood Av
500 ROSL 6917 A4
Rosewood Ln
100 WbgT 7115 B2
300 CART 7115 B2
Rosewood Pl
10 ELIZ 6917 D2
10 STNL 6920 D7
10 STNL 7020 D1
Rosewood Rd
10 WHPL 6168 E7
Rosewood St
600 BRNX 6505 A2
Rosewood Ter
10 ERTH 6500 A6
Rosita Rd
104-00 QENS 6925 E1
Roslyn Av
10 EGLC 6503 B1
10 SCLF 6509 E6
Roslyn Ct
10 EGLC 6503 B1
200 WNYK 6611 C7

Roslyn Pk E
10 SCLF 6509 E6
Roslyn Pk W
10 SCLF 6509 E6
Roslyn Pl
10 MTVN 6394 E6
10 MTVN 6395 A6
Roslyn Rd
10 EHLS 6618 E7
10 NHmT 6618 E7
10 RSLN 6618 E6
200 EHLS 6724 E1
200 NHmT 6724 E1
Roslyn U-Turn
- NHmT 6618 C1
Roslyn West Shore Dr
- NHmT 6618 C1
10 NHmT 6509 B7
Ross Av
10 CRSK 6278 C7
10 DMRT 6278 C7
10 STNL 7117 E2
200 STNL 7118 A2
Ross Ct
10 MLVN 6929 A1
Ross Ln
10 HWTN 7028 D2
10 KRNY 6714 B1
10 NARL 6714 B1
Ross Pl
10 OrgT 6164 A2
Ross Plz
10 LNBK 6929 B4
Ross Rd
10 SCDL 6167 E6
10 WLTN 6500 A5
Ross St
10 BKLN 6822 A5
10 EORG 6712 C5
10 NWRK 6817 A6
10 WHPL 6168 B1
100 WbgT 7114 C4
Rosser Av
1300 HmpT 6827 D5
Rossett St
10 EGLC 6503 A3
10 FTLE 6503 A3
Rossi Ct
10 SHKT 6501 C4
Rossiter Av
10 YNKR 6280 A6
Rossmore Av
10 YNKR 6394 D1
Rossville Av
10 STNL 7116 A6
700 STNL 7115 E4
Rost Pl
10 BKLN 6924 D7
Roswell Av
10 STNL 7018 B7
2700 HmpT 6929 E6
Rothwell Av
100 CLFP 108 A1
100 CLFP 6611 C4
Rottkamp St
10 HmpT 6827 C5
10 HmpT 6928 B1
1000 VLYS 6928 B1
Rotunno Pl
10 NRCH 6395 D2
Round A Bend Rd
10 TYTN 6048 C6
Round Hill Dr
10 YNKR 6280 D3
Round Hill Ln
10 SNPT 6508 B5
Round Hill Rd
10 DBSF 6166 B5
10 GrbT 6167 B6
10 LKSU 6723 A2
400 EHLS 6618 E7
500 NHmT 6618 E7
Roundtop Rd
10 YNKR 6280 D3
Row Pl
10 STNL 7116 C5
Rowan Av
10 STNL 7118 C1
Rowe Av
10 ERKY 6929 A6
10 HmpT 6929 A6
10 LNBK 6929 A6
Rowe Pl
10 NHmT 6723 D6
Rowe St
10 EORG 6713 B3
2400 BRNX 6505 D7
Rowland Av
10 HKSK 6501 A1
Rowland Pl
100 WbgT 7114 B4
Rowland St
10 NWRK 6713 C5
1400 BRNX 6505 C7
Rowley St
10 NWRK 6713 A7
Rowson Av
800 PTHA 7114 C7
Roxboro Rd
10 MrnT 6282 B6
Roxbury Av
10 QENS 7122 D3
Roxbury Blvd
10 QENS 7122 D3
Roxbury Dr E
10 YNKR 6280 E3
Roxbury Dr W
10 YNKR 6280 E2
Roxbury Rd
- GDNC 6724 C7
- NHmT 6724 C7
- NHmT 6828 C2
10 ERKY 6929 C5
10 GDNC 6828 C3
10 GrbT 6167 B7
10 HmpT 6828 C4
10 HmpT 6929 C5
10 NHmT 6618 A2
10 RKVC 6929 E5
Roxbury Rd S
100 HmpT 6828 C4
300 GDNC 6828 C3
Roxbury St
10 STNL 7018 E1
10 STNL 7019 A1

Roxy Pl
10 LNBK 6929 A4
Roy Pl
10 EchT 6281 B5
Roy St
10 HmpT 6827 D6
500 HmpT 6828 C5
Royal Av
3000 HmpT 6929 D7
3200 HmpT 7029 D1
Royal Ct
10 RKVC 6929 E3
Royal Pl
200 MRNK 6282 E7
Royal Rd
10 RKVC 6929 E3
Royal St
10 YNKR 6394 C2
Royal Wy
10 NHmT 6724 B4
Royal Oak Rd
10 STNL 7019 E3
100 STNL 7020 A3
Royalton Pl
10 BlmT 6713 C2
Royce Pl
10 BKLN 7024 B2
Royce St
10 BKLN 7024 B2
Royden Rd
10 TFLY 6392 B1
Rt 440-Connector
- WbgT 7205 B3
600 PTHA 7205 B3
RT-3 E
100 SECS 6610 B7
800 NBgT 6716 B1
800 SECS 6716 B1
RT-3 W
- NBgT 6716 C1
- SECS 6716 C1
100 SECS 6610 B7
RT-440 S
- JSYC 6819 B4
RT-495 Bus Ln
- WhkT 6716 E4
Rubenstein St
10 STNL 7020 E4
E Ruby Av
200 PALP 6502 C7
W Ruby Av
10 PALP 6502 B6
Ruby Ct
10 JSYC 6819 A4
Ruby Pl
10 NWRK 6713 E1
Ruby St
10 HmpT 6827 C6
300 BKLN 6925 B2
300 QENS 6925 B2
Ruby Brown Ter
10 JSYC 6819 B7
Ruckman Rd
10 ALPN 6279 A2
10 CLST 6278 E3
500 ALPN 6278 D2
Ruddy Pl
10 WbgT 7114 C5
Rudolph Ter
10 YNKR 6279 D4
Rudolph Ter W
10 YNKR 6279 D4
Rudyard Dr
1000 PTHA 7114 C7
Rudyard St
10 STNL 7118 B2
Rufus King Av
147-00 QENS 6825 C5
Rugby Av
10 STNL 7020 B3
Rugby Ln
10 SCDL 6167 E5
Rugby Rd
10 BKLN 6923 A6
10 HRSN 6283 B3
10 NHmT 6617 D6
10 NRCH 6282 A7
10 YNKR 6280 E2
300 CDHT 7027 E1
300 CDHT 7028 A1
300 HmpT 7027 E1
500 BKLN 7023 A1
Ruggerio Plz
10 NWRK 6713 D5
Ruggles St
10 STNL 7116 C7
Rule St
100 HmpT 6828 C5
Rumba Pl
10 STNL 7116 A5
Rumbrook Rd
10 GrbT 6049 A7
Rumsey Av
10 YNKR 6394 A1
Rumsey Rd
10 YNKR 6393 E2
Rumson Rd
10 STNL 7117 A1
Runiak Av
10 NWRK 6817 B7
Runway Dr
- QENS 6719 E3
Runyon Av
10 YNKR 6280 A5
Runyon Pl
10 NRCH 6281 E2
10 NRCH 6282 A2
E Runyon St
10 NWRK 6817 B3
W Runyon St
10 NWRK 6817 B3
200 NWRK 6816 E3
Rupert Av
10 STNL 7019 C5
Ruppert Pl
10 BRNX 107 D3
10 BRNX 6612 E2
Rural Dr
10 SCDL 6282 B2
Rusciano Blvd
10 PLMM 6395 A7
Ruscoe St
106-00 QENS 6825 E5
106-00 QENS 6826 A5

Each entry is listed as: **Street** — Block · City · Map# · Grid

Rushby Wy
- 10 YNKR 6280 B6

Rushfield Ln
- 10 HmpT 6928 B4

Rushmore Av
- 10 NHmT 6724 E1
- 100 MRNK 6282 E7
- 240-00 QENS 6722 D4
- 500 MRNK 6283 A7
- 900 MRNK 6397 A1

Rushmore Ter
- 249-00 QENS 6722 E3
- 250-00 QENS 6723 A3

Russek Dr
- 10 STNL 7116 A5

Russell Av
- 10 EDGW 6611 E3
- 10 HmpT 6827 D7
- 10 NRCH 6395 D5
- 500 RDGF 6611 A1

Russell Ln
- 200 HWTH 6928 E7

Russell Pl
- 10 DBSF 6166 C3
- 10 QENS 6824 D3
- 100 HKSK 6501 B1
- 400 ELIZ 6917 D4

S Russell Pl
- 10 DBSF 6166 C4

Russell St
- 10 BKLN 6822 C1
- 10 EHLS 6618 E7
- 10 GrbT 6167 E1
- 10 HmpT 6929 B3
- 10 LNBK 6929 A3
- 10 NHmT 6618 E7
- 10 STNL 7117 B7
- 10 WHPL 6167 E1
- 99-00 QENS 6925 E5
- 100 WbgT 7114 C5
- 102-00 QENS 6926 A4
- 900 HmpT 6828 A4
- 1200 HmpT 6827 E4

Russel Woods Rd
- 10 NHmT 6723 B1
- 10 THSN 6723 B1

Rust St
- 56-01 QENS 6823 B3

Rustic Ct
- 10 STNL 7117 B5

Ruta Ct
- 10 SHkT 6501 B4
- 10 TETB 6501 B4

Rutgers Av
- 10 JSYC 6819 C5
- 400 HlsT 6816 B6

Rutgers Dr
- 10 NWRK 6713 C7

Rutgers Pl
- 10 EchT 6281 B2
- 10 GrbT 6167 E3

Rutgers Rd
- 700 HmpT 6828 B5

Rutgers Rd E
- 100 OrgT 6164 A1

Rutgers St
- 10 CLST 6278 C4
- 10 IrvT 6816 B3
- 10 MHTN 119 B7
- 10 MHTN 6821 D4

Rutgers Slip
- 10 MHTN 119 B7
- 10 MHTN 6821 D4

Ruth Av
- 1100 HmpT 6828 A6

Ruth Ct
- 10 GTNK 6617 B6

Ruth Ln
- 10 DMRT 6278 A4

Ruth Pl
- 10 HmpT 6929 C3
- 10 LNBK 6929 C3
- 10 STNL 7020 C6

Ruth St
- 10 IrvT 6816 D1
- 10 STNL 7019 C4

Rutherford Av
- 10 WHPL 6168 B2
- 100 WbgT 7114 C2
- 400 LynT 6609 A4
- 400 RTFD 6609 A2

Rutherford Av SR-17
- 600 LynT 6609 A4
- 600 RTFD 6609 A2

Rutherford Ct
- 10 STNL 7115 E5

Rutherford Ln
- - HmpT 7028 C2
- - LWRN 7028 C2
- - WDBG 7028 C2

Rutherford Pl
- 10 BKLN 7022 B4
- 10 KRNY 6714 C1
- 10 MHTN 119 C1
- 10 MHTN 6821 D1
- 10 NARL 6714 C1

Rutherford St
- 10 NWRK 6818 B1

Rutland Av
- 10 KRNY 6714 B3
- 10 RKVC 6929 E5

Rutland Pl
- 10 GrbT 6281 A1
- 10 NHmT 6723 B2
- 10 YNKR 6280 C7
- 10 YNKR 6281 A1
- 900 BKLN 6923 E4
- 1000 BKLN 6924 A3

Rutledge Av
- 10 EORG 6713 D3
- 10 NWRK 6713 C3
- 88-00 QENS 6824 D7

Rutledge Ct
- 100 EDGW 108 B1
- 100 EDGW 6611 E5

Rutledge Pl
- 10 NRCH 6281 E3
- 10 NRCH 6282 A3

Rutledge St
- 10 BKLN 6822 B5

Rutter du Bois Ln
- 100 IRVN 6166 C1

Ruxton Av
- 10 STNL 7116 B5

Ruxton Rd
- 10 GTNK 6617 A5
- 10 NHmT 6617 A5

Ruxton St
- 10 NHmT 6724 C4

Ryan Av
- 10 PTCH 6170 C7

Ryan Ct
- 22-00 QENS 6721 A2

Ryan Pl
- 10 STNL 7207 E1

Ryan Rd
- 219-24 QENS 6927 C2

Ryan St
- 10 HlsT 6816 C6

Ryawa Av
- 10 BRNX 6613 E5

Ryder Av
- 10 BKLN 7022 E3
- 10 ERKY 6929 C6
- 300 BKLN 7023 A3

Ryder Pl
- 10 ERKY 6929 C6
- 10 YNKR 6394 B4

Ryder Rd
- 10 NHmT 6617 E6
- 100 MNPK 6617 E6
- 200 MNPK 6618 A6

Ryder St
- 1500 BKLN 7023 D3
- 2200 BKLN 7024 E4

Ryders Al
- 10 MHTN 120 C1
- 10 MHTN 6821 B6

Rye Av
- 10 HlsT 6816 B4
- 10 IrvT 6816 B4

Rye Ct
- 10 STNL 7116 C6

Rye Pl
- 109-00 QENS 6826 B1

Rye Rd
- 10 PTCH 6284 C1
- 10 RYE 6283 C6

Rye St
- 400 HmpT 6827 E6

Rye Beach Av
- 300 RYE 6284 A4

Rye Lake Av
- 10 GrwT 6051 C3
- 10 RYEB 6051 C3

Rye Lake Rd
- 10 HRSN 6051 B4

Ryer Av
- 2000 BRNX 105 E3
- 2000 BRNX 6504 C5

Rye Ridge Av
- 10 HRSN 6169 A7

Rye Ridge Plz
- 10 RYEB 6169 E5
- 10 RYEB 6170 A5

Rye Ridge Rd
- 10 HRSN 6169 A7

Ryerson Av
- 500 WRDG 6500 D6

Ryerson Pl
- 10 BRNX 6613 A5
- 10 OrgT 6164 C7

Ryerson St
- 10 BKLN 6822 A6

Ryerson Walk Gate
- 10 BKLN 6822 A6

Ryewood Farm Dr
- 10 MRNK 6283 B5

S

S St
- 1200 HmpT 6827 E7

Sabina St
- 10 LFRY 6501 C6

Sable Av
- 10 STNL 7020 D4

Sable Lp
- 10 STNL 7117 B3

Sabo St
- 10 CART 7017 A6

Sabre St
- 88-00 QENS 6826 E1

Sabrina Ln
- 10 STNL 7020 D2

Saccheri Ct
- 10 STNL 7117 D5

Sachem St
- 10 ERKY 6929 B6

Sacket St
- 10 YNKR 6281 A3

Sackett Cir
- 900 BRNX 6505 C7

Sackett Ct
- 10 MrnT 6282 B6

Sackett Lndg
- 10 MrnT 6282 B6

Sackett St
- 10 BKLN 121 D6
- 10 BKLN 6821 B7
- 10 RYE 6284 B1

Sackett St
- 10 BKLN 120 D7
- 10 BKLN 6821 D7
- 10 JSYC 6819 D3
- 10 BKLN 6922 C1

Sackman St
- 10 BKLN 6924 C4

Sackville Rd
- 100 GDNC 6828 B2
- 100 NHmT 6828 B1

Saddle Ridge Rd
- 10 HmpT 6928 B3

Saddle River Av
- 10 GRFD 6500 B3
- 10 SHkT 6500 B4
- 10 WRDG 6500 B4

Saddle Rock Rd
- 10 HmpT 6928 C5

Saddle Rock Ter
- 10 HmpT 6928 C5

Saddletree Ln
- 10 HRSN 6283 A3

Saddlewood Ct
- 10 JSYC 6820 C2

Sadore Ln
- 10 YNKR 6280 D5

Sadowski Pkwy
- 10 PTHA 7205 C5

Safety City Dr
- - STNL 7020 A4

Sagamore Av
- 195-00 QENS 6826 B4
- 300 EWLS 6724 E5
- 300 MNLA 6724 E5

Sagamore Rd
- 10 HmpT 7029 D4
- 10 BRXV 6280 E7
- 10 ISPK 7029 C5
- 10 TCKA 6280 E6

Sagamore St
- 600 BRNX 6505 A6

Sagamore Hill Dr
- 10 MHVN 6508 C7
- 10 NHmT 6617 B1

Sage Av
- 100 LWRN 7028 A5

Sage Cir
- 10 NRCH 6281 E1

Sage Ct
- 10 STNL 7019 B1
- 10 WHPL 6169 A5

Sage Pl
- 10 EchT 6281 B6

Sage Rd
- 10 EGLC 6392 D6

Sage St
- 11-00 QENS 7027 D4

Sage Ter
- - SCDL 6167 E5

Sageman St
- 10 MTVN 6395 A3

Sager Pl
- 10 HlsT 6816 B4
- 10 IrvT 6816 B4

Sagona Ct
- 10 STNL 7116 C6

Sailer Ct
- 10 ELIZ 6918 A2

St. Adalbert Pl
- 10 STNL 7019 B1

St. Agnes Ln
- 10 EORG 6712 C5

St. Agnes Pl
- 400 HmpT 6828 A4

St. Albans Pl
- 10 STNL 7116 E6
- 10 STNL 7117 A6

St. Andrews Pl
- 10 STNL 7206 B3
- 10 BKLN 6923 C1
- 10 YNKR 6393 C3

St. Andrews Rd
- 10 STNL 7117 D2

St. Andrews Wy
- - GrbT 6280 C1
- - GrbT 6166 C7

St. Ann St
- 10 STNL 6920 D7

St. Anns Av
- 400 BRNX 6613 A3
- 1400 BRNX 6505 A7

St. Anns Br
- 200 YNKR 6394 B1

St. Anns Pl
- 10 BRNX 6613 A4

St. Anthony Pl
- 10 STNL 7019 C2

St. Austins Pl
- 10 BKLN 6920 A7

N St. Austins Pl
- 10 BKLN 6920 A7

S St. Austins Pl
- 10 BKLN 6920 A7

St. Barnabas Pl
- 400 BRNX 6394 B5

St. Casimir Av
- 10 STNL 6393 D1

St. Charles Pl
- 10 BKLN 6923 B2

St. Charles St
- 10 NWRK 6818 B1

St. Clair Av
- 10 STNL 7020 C6

St. Clair Pl
- 10 MHTN 106 C6
- 10 MHTN 6612 A3

St. Clair St
- 10 LNBK 6929 B3

St. Edward Ln
- 10 STNL 7207 A3

St. Edwards St
- 10 BKLN 121 D5
- 10 BKLN 6821 E6

St. Eleanoras Ln
- 10 ERKY 6929 B6

St. Felix Av
- 57-00 QENS 6823 C6

St. Felix St
- 10 BKLN 121 D6
- 10 BKLN 6821 E7

St. Francis Pl
- 10 BKLN 6923 B2

St. Francis St
- 100 NWRK 6818 B1

St. George Dr
- 10 STNL 7020 D2

St. George Pkwy
- 10 HmpT 7027 D3

St. George Pl
- 10 BKLN 6280 E4

St. George Rd
- 10 STNL 7117 C2
- 10 THSN 6617 B7

Saddle Ridge Rd / **St. Georges Av**
- 600 WbgT 7114 B3

St. Georges Av SR-35
- 700 WbgT 7114 B3

E St. Georges Av
- 700 LNDN 6917 A6
- 700 ROSL 6917 A6

E St. Georges Av SR-27
- 700 LNDN 6917 A6
- 700 ROSL 6917 A6

St. Georges Cres
- 2100 ELIZ 6917 A2

St. James Av
- 82-00 QENS 6719 E7
- 88-00 QENS 6720 E7
- 200 WbgT 7114 B5

St. James Pl
- 10 BKLN 6822 A7
- 10 GDNC 6828 A5
- 10 HMPD 6828 E3
- 10 LNBK 6929 B4
- 10 MHTN 118 D7
- 10 MHTN 6821 B4
- 10 NWRK 6816 E3
- 10 STNL 7020 A6
- 100 BKLN 6923 A1
- 800 HmpT 6828 B5

St. James Ter
- 10 YNKR 6394 C4

St. John Av
- 10 STNL 7019 C3

St. John Pl
- 10 NHmT 6618 A1
- 300 HmpT 6828 A6

St. John Rd
- - STNL 7019 E7

St. John St
- 10 LFRY 6501 B5

St. Johns Av
- 10 QENS 6928 A1
- 10 STNL 7020 E4
- 10 STNL 7021 A4
- 10 VLYS 6928 A1
- 10 YNKR 6394 A3

St. Johns Ln
- 10 MHTN 118 C5
- 10 MHTN 6821 E4

St. Johns Pl
- 10 BKLN 6922 E1
- 10 NRCH 6395 D3
- 200 BKLN 6923 D2
- 1500 BKLN 6924 A2

St. Johns Rd
- 10 CART 6823 B4

St. Joseph Blvd
- 10 LODI 6500 E2

St. Joseph Pl
- 300 HmpT 6828 A6

St. Joseph St
- 10 NRCH 6395 E6
- 10 WbgT 7114 C6

St. Joseph Ter
- 10 WbgT 7114 C5

St. Josephs Av
- 10 CART 6919 C7
- 500 STNL 7116 E6
- 800 STNL 7117 A6
- 900 YNKR 6279 D7

St. Josephs Pl
- 10 YNKR 6279 D7

St. Josephs Wy
- - BRNX 6614 E2

St. Jude Pl
- 10 BKLN 7024 D1
- 10 YNKR 6280 A4

St. Julian Pl
- 10 STNL 6920 D7

St. Lawrence Av
- 400 BRNX 6613 B3
- 1400 BRNX 6505 A7

St. Lawrence Av
- 10 WhkT 6716 D4

St. Louis Av
- 1100 HlsT 6816 C6

St. Luke Pl
- 300 HmpT 6828 A6

St. Luke Rd
- - STNL 7019 E7

St. Lukes Av
- 10 STNL 7115 E4

St. Marks Av
- 10 BKLN 6922 E1
- 10 RKVC 6929 E4
- 900 BKLN 6923 E2
- 1300 BKLN 6924 A2

St. Marks Pl
- 10 BKLN 6922 E1
- 10 BRNX 6394 A5
- 10 MHTN 119 D2
- 10 MHTN 6821 D1
- 10 NHmT 6618 A1
- 10 RSLN 6618 A1
- 10 STNL 6920 C6
- 10 YNKR 6394 A5

E St. Marks Pl
- 10 STNL 6920 E3

W St. Marks Pl
- 10 VLYS 6928 D3

St. Marys Av
- 10 STNL 7020 E2

St. Mary's Pl
- 10 GrbT 6049 C4

St. Marys St
- 10 YNKR 6393 D2
- 500 BRNX 6613 B4

St. Michael's Wk
- 300 UNCT 6716 D4

St. Nicholas Av
- 2-61 QENS 6823 A4
- 10 BKLN 6823 A3
- 10 MHTN 109 D4
- 10 YNKR 6279 D7
- 100 MHTN 6612 B5
- 500 MHTN 107 A5
- 1200 MHTN 104 C6
- 1200 MHTN 6503 E6

St. Nicholas Pl
- 10 MHTN 107 B3
- 10 MHTN 6612 D2

St. Nicholas St
- 10 LNBK 6929 B3
- 10 THSN 6617 B7

St. Nicholas Ter
- 10 MHTN 106 C7
- 10 MHTN 6612 C4

St. Ouen St
- 700 BRNX 6394 C4

St. Patricks Av
- 10 STNL 7117 D3

St. Paul Av
- 10 STNL 7117 D3

St. Paul St
- 2100 ELIZ 6923 D4

St. Pauls Av
- 10 STNL 7020 D7

St. Pauls Av
- 10 BKLN 6923 A7

St. Pauls Cres
- 500 CLFP 6611 C2
- 500 FRVW 6611 C2

St. Pauls Cres
- 10 GDNC 6828 C3

St. Pauls Dr
- 10 IrvT 6816 C2

St. Pauls Pl
- - MTVN 6395 A7
- 10 GDNC 6828 D1
- 10 GTPZ 6617 B7
- 10 HMPD 6828 E4
- 10 MTVN 6394 E7
- 400 BRNX 6613 C1
- 800 HmpT 6828 B5

St. Pauls Rd N
- 100 HMPD 6828 C4

St. Peters Av
- 1400 BRNX 6505 C7

St. Peters Pl
- 10 QENS 6920 D6

St. Raymond Av
- 2000 BRNX 6505 C2

St. Roch Av
- 10 GrwT 6170 E3

St. Stephens Pl
- 97-00 QENS 6825 B4

St. Theresa Av
- 2800 BRNX 6505 E6

St. Thomas Pl
- 1500 BRNX 6924 D2

St. Volodymyr Av
- 10 CART 7017 D1

Sakirk St
- 10 GrbT 6166 C1

Salamander Ct
- 10 STNL 7115 D7

Saldo Cir
- 10 NRCH 6281 E5

Sale St
- 10 BKLN 6822 B6

Salem Av
- 10 CART 7115 D2
- 500 ELIZ 6917 E1
- 800 HlsT 6917 E1
- 900 HlsT 6816 E7

Salem Dr
- 10 MrnT 6282 C4

Salem Ln
- 10 NHmT 6618 A3

Salem Pl
- 10 WHPL 6168 D5

Salem Rd
- 10 ERKY 6929 B6
- 10 GrbT 6049 C4
- 10 HmpT 6827 C1
- 400 UnnT 6917 A1
- 400 VLYS 6928 A1
- 800 UnnT 6816 B7

Salem Rd CO-509
- 400 UnnT 6917 A1
- 800 UnnT 6816 B7

Salem St
- 10 HKSK 6501 C5
- 3100 BRNX 6505 A5
- 3100 BRNX 6506 A5

E Salem St
- 10 HKSK 6501 C1

Salem Wy
- 10 BKLN 6280 B2

Salem Gate
- 10 HmpT 6928 E1

E Salem St Ext
- 10 HKSK 6501 C1

E Salem St Ext CO-56
- 10 HKSK 6501 C1

Salerno Av
- 193-00 QENS 6826 B3

Salidge St
- - NRWD 6164 A5

Salisbury Av
- 10 FLPK 6827 E2
- 10 STMN 6827 E2
- 100 GDNC 6828 C2

Salisbury Rd
- 10 YNKR 6280 D5

Salk Dr
- 10 EMFD 6049 C5

Sally Ct
- 10 STNL 7116 E4

Sally Rd
- 400 MNLA 6724 D4

Salter Pl
- 10 BlmT 6713 C1
- 10 BlvT 6713 C1
- 200 EORG 6712 C4
- 300 NWRK 6816 D7

Salt Meadow Rd
- 10 CART 7017 D6

Saluatation Rd
- 10 GLCV 6398 D2

Salvatore R Naclerio Plz
- 10 BRNX 6505 D1

Salzburg Ct
- 10 STNL 7020 A6

Samantha Dr
- 13-00 QENS 7027 C4

Samantha Ln
- 10 STNL 7115 E2

Samford Dr
- 10 EGLC 6392 C4

Sammis Ln
- 10 WHPL 6168 D6

Sampson Av
- 10 HmpT 6724 D3
- 300 BRNX 6505 E6

Sampson Pl
- 300 JSYC 6920 D7

Sampson Sct
- 10 STNL 7117 D3

Sampson St
- 200 JSYC 6715 E7

Sampson St E
- 300 JSYC 7029 B1

Sampson St W
- 10 HmpT 7029 C2

Samuel Pl
- 10 ERKY 6929 B5
- 10 LNBK 6929 B5

Samuel Dickstein Plz
- 10 MHTN 119 C1
- 10 MHTN 6821 D3

Samuel Lupo Pl
- 10 WbgT 7114 B3

Sancho St
- 86-00 QENS 6826 B2

Sand Ln
- 10 STNL 7021 A7

Sand St
- 10 BKLN 6821 E3

Sandalwood Av
- 2800 BRNX 6505 E6

Sandalwood Dr
- 10 STNL 7117 B3

Sandborn St
- 10 STNL 7116 E7

Sandburg Ct
- 10 NRCH 6282 A6

Sand Castle Key Rd
- 10 SECS 6609 D7

Sanderling Ct
- 500 SECS 6715 D1

Sanders Pl
- 92-00 QENS 6825 B4

Sanders St
- 10 STNL 7019 B2

Sandford Av
- 10 KRNY 6714 B6

Sandford Blvd E
- - PLMM 6395 B5
- 10 MTVN 6395 A6

Sandford Blvd W
- 10 MTVN 6394 D6
- 10 BRNX 6394 D6

Sandford St
- 10 BKLN 6822 B6

Sandgap St
- 10 MNPK 6618 A4
- 10 MTVN 6395 A6

Sand Hill Ct
- 10 LFRY 6501 C5

Sand Hill Rd
- 247-00 QENS 6722 D2

Sand Piper Dr
- 10 SAMB 7205 D7

Sandpiper Key Rd
- 10 SECS 6609 D7

Sandra Ln
- 10 STNL 7020 D3

Sandra Pl
- 500 TnkT 6502 A2

Sandrock Av
- 10 DBSF 6166 C4

Sands Ct
- 43-00 QENS 6720 A5

Sands Ln
- 75-00 QENS 6825 E1
- 80-00 QENS 6826 A3

Sands Pl
- 10 HAOH 6508 D6

Sands St
- 10 BKLN 121 B3
- 10 BKLN 6821 D5
- 10 PTCH 6170 D7
- 10 STNL 7020 D1

Sands Light Rd
- 10 SNPT 6508 A3

Sands Point Rd
- 10 MHVN 6508 C6
- 10 SNPT 6508 B5

Sandy Ct
- 10 GDNC 6724 D7
- 10 MNLA 6724 D7
- 10 PTWN 6508 C6

Sandy Ln
- 10 STNL 7206 D3

Sandy Hollow Ln
- 10 BXTE 6508 E7

Sandy Hollow Rd
- 10 BXTE 6508 E7
- 100 PTWN 6508 D7
- 100 NHmT 6508 E7

Sandywood Ln
- 10 STNL 7115 E5

Sanford Av
- 131-00 QENS 6720 C5
- 136-00 QENS 6721 A4
- 200 EORG 6712 C6
- 300 NWRK 6816 D7
- 800 NWRK 6816 B1

Sanford Av CO-605
- 200 EORG 6712 C6
- 800 NWRK 6816 B1

Sanford Ct
- 10 HmpT 6928 C4

Sanford Pl
- 10 IrvT 6816 C2
- 10 JSYC 6716 B3
- 100 MtPT 6049 A2
- 300 HAOH 6166 C1
- 400 ARDY 6166 C1

Sanford St
- 10 EORG 6712 D5

Sanford St CO-605
- 10 EORG 6712 D5

Sanford Ter
- 10 IrvT 6816 B1

Sanial Av
- 10 NVLE 6164 C6

Sanilac St
- 10 STNL 7118 B2

San Juan St
- 10 NHmT 6724 D3

Santa Monica Dr
- 10 EchT 6281 C6

Santa Monica Ln
- 10 STNL 7115 E7

Santiago Av
- 10 RTFD 6609 A1

Santiago St
- 85-00 QENS 6826 A3

Santo Ct
- 10 STNL 7117 C2

Santo Donato Pl
- 10 STNL 7019 D3

Sapir St
- 216-00 QENS 6826 D1

Sapphire Ct
- 10 STNL 7206 B4

Sara Ln
- 10 NRCH 6282 A6

Sara Hill Ln
- 10 EGLC 6503 B2

Saranac Pl
- 900 HmpT 6929 C1

Saranac St
- 10 DBSF 6166 A3

Saranac St
- 10 IRVN 6166 A3

Saratoga Av
- 10 BKLN 6823 A7
- 10 YNKR 6393 A4
- 10 BKLN 6924 A1

Saratoga Blvd
- 10 WHPL 6168 D7

Saratoga Rd
- 10 GrbT 6167 D1

Saratoga St
- 10 GrbT 6164 D3

Sarcona Ct
- 10 STNL 7206 E3

Sargent Pl
- 10 MNPK 6618 A4
- 10 MTVN 6395 A6

Sargent Rd
- 10 YNKR 6281 B2

Sarosca Farm Ln
- 10 HRSN 6051 B7

Sarven Ct
- 10 TYTN 6048 B3

Satterie Ct
- 10 VLYS 6928 E4

Satterlee St
- 10 STNL 7206 A4

Saturn Ln
- 10 STNL 7019 B7
- 10 STNL 7117 A1

Sault St
- 43-00 QENS 6720 E5

Saultell Av
- 109-00 QENS 6720 C7

Saul Weprin St
- 75-00 QENS 6825 E1
- 80-00 QENS 6826 A3

Saunders St
- - STNL 7020 D4
- 10 HAOH 6508 D6
- 61-00 QENS 6824 D1

Savanna St
- 10 YNKR 6280 B2

Saville St
- 200 MNLA 6724 D6

Savin Ct
- 10 STNL 7020 C6

Savo Ln
- 10 STNL 7021 A4

Savo Lp
- 10 STNL 7206 D2

N Savoie St
- 10 LODI 6500 E2

S Savoie St
- 10 LODI 6500 E2

Savoy Av
- 10 HmpT 6827 B5

Savoy St
- 10 STNL 7117 D3

Saw Mill Rd
- 10 GrbT 6048 E2
- 10 MtPT 6048 A2
- 200 MtPT 6049 A2

Saw Mill River Pkwy
- - BRNX 6393 D5
- - DBSF 6166 B3
- - EMFD 6049 C5
- - GRFD 6049 A6
- - HAOH 6166 A1
- - IRVN 6048 D7
- - MtPT 6049 A2
- - MtPT 6048 A2
- - NRWD 6164 B6
- - NVLE 6164 C5
- - NRWD 6278 B1

Saw Mill River Rd
- 10 EMFD 6049 A3
- 10 GrbT 6280 B1
- 10 HAOH 6166 B7
- 10 HAOH 6280 B1
- 10 YNKR 6280 B1
- 100 YNKR 6393 E3

Saw Mill River Rd SR-9A
- 10 EMFD 6049 A3
- 10 GrbT 6280 B1
- 10 HAOH 6280 B1
- 10 HWTH 6929 A7

Saw Mill River Rd SR-9A
- 1800 GrbT 6048 E7

Saw Mill River Rd S
- 10 YNKR 6049 A1

Saw Mill River Rd SR-9A
- 1800 BRNX 6393 D5

N Saw Mill River Rd
- 10 EMFD 6049 B5

N Saw Mill River Rd SR-9A
- 10 EMFD 6049 A5

Sawyer Av
- 10 BlmT 6713 B2
- 10 EORG 6713 B2
- 2600 BRNX 6614 E3
- 2600 BRNX 6615 A3

Saxon Av
- 10 STNL 7019 A6
- 3900 BRNX 6504 D1

Saxon Dr
- 100 MRNK 6282 E4
- 100 MRNK 6282 E4

Saxon Wy
- 10 NRCH 6282 A5

Saxon Wood Park Dr
- 10 NRCH 6168 D7

Saxon Woods Rd
- - WHPL 6282 D1
- - SCDL 6168 C3
- 10 WHPL 6168 D7

Saxony Ct
- 10 NHLS 6724 A1

Saybrook St
- 10 STNL 7019 A4

Sayles St
- 10 JSYC 6819 B6

Sayre Av
- 400 PTHA 7205 B2
- 600 WbgT 7205 B2

Sayre Pl
- 100 VLYS 6928 B3

Sayre Rd N
- - UnnT 6816 A6

Sayre Rd S
- 1000 UnnT 6816 A6

Sayre St
- 10 ELIZ 6917 D3
- 10 NWRK 6817 B1

Sayres Av
- 163-00 QENS 6825 E7
- 169-00 QENS 6826 A6

Scaneateles Av
- 400 HmpT 6929 D2

Scarboro Av
- 10 STNL 7021 A3

Scarcliffe Dr
- 10 MLVN 6929 A1
- 100 HmpT 6929 A1

Scarsdale Av
- 10 EchT 6281 B2
- 800 SCDL 6281 B1

Scarsdale Rd
- 10 YNKR 6280 E5
- 300 YNKR 6281 A2
- 1100 GrbT 6167 B7
- 1100 GrbT 6281 B1

Scarsdale Farm Rd
- 10 GrbT 6167 A6

Scenic Av
- 10 DBSF 6166 A4
- 10 HAOH 6166 A4

Scenic Ln
- 10 STNL 7020 C6
- 10 YNKR 6280 D3

Scenic Pl
- 3000 BRNX 102 A1
- 3000 BRNX 6504 A1

Schaefer St
- 10 BKLN 6823 D7
- 10 BKLN 6924 D1

Schaffer Rd
- 10 ALPN 6278 A5
- 10 ALPN 6279 A5

Schalk St
- 10 NWRK 6818 C1

Scharer Av
- 100 NRWD 6164 B6
- 100 NVLE 6164 C5

Scharf St
- - NRWD 6164 C7
- - NRWD 6278 B1

Scheerer Av
- 10 STNL 7020 E4

Scheffelin Av
- 1800 BRNX 6505 D1

Schefflin Av
- 1800 BRNX 6505 D1

Schenck Av
- 10 NHmT 6617 B2
- 10 BKLN 6924 D1
- 10 GTPZ 6617 B7
- 10 THSN 6617 B7

Schenck Cir
- 10 HAOH 6280 B1

Schenck Ct
- 10 HAOH 6279 E7
- 10 HAOH 6280 A7

Schenck Pl
- 400 ARDY 6166 C1
- 500 ARDY 6166 C1

Schenck St
- 10 BKLN 6924 C1
- 10 BKLN 7024 C1

Schencks Ln
- 10 BKLN 6928 E2
- 100 HmpT 6827 E7
- 1300 HWTH 6928 A7

Schenectady Av
- 10 BKLN 6923 E5
- 1600 BKLN 7023 E3

Schermerhorn St
- 10 BKLN 121 A6
- 10 BKLN 6821 D7

Schieffelin Av
- 1700 BRNX 6505 C1

Schieffelin Pl
- 1800 BRNX 6505 D1

Schiller St
- 300 ELIZ 6918 C4

Schindler Ct
- 10 STNL 7115 D5

Schleifer Rd
- 1000 HlsT 6816 D7

Schley Av
- 10 NHmT 6724 D4
- 10 NRCH 6395 B3
- 2600 BRNX 6614 E3
- 2600 BRNX 6615 A3

Schley Pl
- 10 NWRK 6816 D3
- 500 WNYK 6610 D6
- 500 WNYK 6611 A7

Schley St
- 10 GRFD 6500 A1
- 200 NWRK 6816 E4
- 1600 HlsT 6816 C5

Schlosser St
- 10 STNL 7117 D3

Schlosser St SR-67
- 1600 FTLE 103 A4
- 1600 FTLE 6503 A4

Schmidt St
- 1200 UnnT 6816 C5

Schmidts Ln
- 10 STNL 7019 E4
- 10 STNL 7020 A4

Schmidts Pl
- 500 BKLN 6610 A5

Schoder Av
- 10 WbgT 7114 C3

Schoen Ln
- 10 NRCH 6282 A3

Schofield Av
- 10 BRNX 6506 D6

Schofield St
- 10 NWRK 6712 C7

Schoharie St
- 10 STNL 7020 B3

Scholes St
- 10 BKLN 6822 C4
- 500 BKLN 6823 A4
- 500 QENS 6823 A3

School Dr
- 10 HAOH 6166 A7
- 10 NHmT 7027 E3

School Ln
- 10 SCDL 6281 C1

School Pl
- 1300 HmpT 6827 E4

School Rd
- 10 HmpT 6827 C4
- 10 STNL 7021 A4

School St
- 10 HAOH 6166 A7
- 10 HmpT 7027 E3
- 10 MLVN 6929 C2
- 10 NHmT 6508 D7
- 10 NWRK 6713 C7
- 10 RYE 6284 B2
- 10 STNL 7117 A5
- 100 YNKR 6393 D1
- 100 HmpT 6828 D6
- 100 NRWD 6164 B5
- 10 NVLE 6164 B5
- 300 HmpT 7114 C4

School House Ln
- 10 ALPN 6278 E6
- 10 LKSU 6723 B2

School House Hill Rd
- 10 OybT 6618 E1

Schooner Dr
- 10 PTWN 6508 D6

Schooner Pl
- - QENS 7026 D7

Schopmann Dr
- 900 SECS 6610 A6

Schor Av
- 10 LEON 6502 C7

Schorr Dr
- 15-00 QENS 6823 C6

Schorr Pl
- 1500 BRNX 6505 D3

Schreiber St
- 10 OrgT 6164 B2

Schreiffer St
- 10 SHkT 6501 B3

Schroeders Av
- 10 BKLN 6924 E6

Schroeter Av
- 800 HmpT 6828 B3

Schudy Pl
- 10 STNL 7020 E4

Schultz Pl
- 10 NRCH 6395 D3

Schulz Av
- 10 LFRY 6501 C6

Schum Av
- 10 BKLN 7021 D4

Schumacher Dr
- 10 NHmT 6724 C5

Schurz Av
- 2500 BRNX 6615 A4

Schuster Av
- 200 MNLA 6724 C7

Schuyler Av
- 10 HRSN 6714 B5
- 10 KRNY 6714 B5
- 10 NARL 6714 D1
- 10 NWRK 6816 E4
- 10 NWRK 6817 A1

Schuyler Av CO-130
- 10 KRNY 6714 B5
- 10 NARL 6714 D1

Schuyler Av CO-507
- 800 HmpT 6714 D2

Schuyler Pl
- 10 BAYN 6919 C4
- 3100 BRNX 6505 E6

New York City/5 Borough Street Index

Format of each entry: *Block — City — Map# — Grid*

Schuyler Pl W
10 BAYN 6919 B5
Schuyler St
10 BVrT 6714 B1
10 NRCH 6396 A2
10 NRCH 6920 D5
Schuyler Ter
10 EORG 6712 D2
Schuyler Wy
500 UnnT 6917 A1
Schyler Pl
10 WHPL 6168 B3
Scimitar Av
1200 BRNX 6827 E5
Sciortino Pl
10 GrbT 6049 C7
10 GrbT 6167 C1
Scoralick Ln
10 GrbT 6049 D3
10 HmpT 6049 D3
Scotland Rd
10 COrT 6712 B3
10 ELIZ 6917 E1
10 SOrT 6712 A6
500 UnnT 6917 A2
Scotland Rd CO-638
10 COrT 6712 B3
10 SOrT 6712 A6
Scott Av
10 BKLN 6823 A4
10 SRVL 7205 A6
10 STNL 7020 D6
10 YNKR 6394 B5
100 BKLN 6822 E4
Scott Av CO-686
10 SRVL 7205 A6
Scott Cir
10 HRSN 6168 E1
Scott Ct
10 RDFP 6502 A6
400 UnnT 6816 A7
Scott Dr
10 HmpT 7028 C7
1000 HmpT 6929 A4
Scott Ln
10 HRSN 6168 E1
Scott Pl
10 GrbT 6167 B1
10 RKVC 6929 E5
10 WbgT 7114 E4
10 WbgT 7115 A3
2900 BRNX 6615 A2
Scott St
10 DBSF 6166 C4
10 JSYC 6819 C4
10 NHmT 6724 C4
10 NWRK 6817 D2
Scott A Gadell Pl
14-00 QENS 7027 C4
Scotti Av
10 OrgT 6164 E4
Scott Mobus Pl
400 HRSN 6714 A5
400 KRNY 6714 A5
Scout Av
10 STNL 6819 B1
Scranton Av
10 LNBK 6928 E4
10 LNBK 6929 B6
10 STNL 7116 D5
10 VLYS 6928 E4
600 ERKY 6929 B6
E Scranton Av
10 STNL 7117 A4
Scranton St
10 STNL 7020 C5
Screvin Av
400 BRNX 6614 C3
Scribner Av
10 STNL 6920 C7
Scudder Av
10 STNL 7207 A1
Scudder St
10 GRFD 6500 A1
Scudders Ln
10 NHmT 6618 E2
10 OybT 6618 E2
10 ROSH 6618 E2
Scully Pl
10 ISPK 7029 C4
Sczkurka Pl
10 CART 7017 B6
Sea Breeze Av
10 BKLN 7121 A2
200 BKLN 7120 E1
Seabreeze Av
200 QENS 7122 D3
Sea Breeze Ln
10 STNL 7206 B5
Seabreeze Wk
400 QENS 7122 A4
Seabring St
10 BKLN 6922 B1
Seabury Av
600 HmpT 6828 B7
1200 BRNX 6614 D1
1300 BRNX 6505 D7
Seabury Pl
1400 BRNX 6613 D1
Seabury St
10 NWRK 6714 A3
52-00 QENS 6719 E2
55-00 QENS 6823 E1
55-27 QENS 6824 A1
Sea Cliff Av
10 SCLF 6509 E6
Seacoast Ln
10 SNPT 6508 E3
Seacoast Ter
10 BKLN 7121 A3
Seacord Rd
10 NRCH 6281 D7
10 NRCH 6395 C1
Seacrest Av
10 STNL 7117 A3
Seacrest St
10 STNL 7206 B4
Seafoam Ct
62-00 QENS 7026 D6
Seafoam St
10 STNL 7118 B3
Sea Gate Av
10 BKLN 7120 B1

Seagate Ct
10 STNL 7021 B6
Sea Gate Rd
10 STNL 7021 A4
Seagirt Av
2-00 LWRN 7027 C6
24-00 QENS 7027 C6
Seagirt Blvd
5-00 LWRN 7027 E6
5-00 QENS 7027 E6
Seagull Ct
10 PTWN 6508 D6
Seahaven Dr
1000 MRNK 6397 A1
Sea Isle Key Rd
300 SECS 6715 D1
Sealy Ct
10 LWRN 7028 B3
Sealy Dr
10 CDHT 7028 B3
10 LWRN 7028 B3
Seaman Av
10 JSYC 6715 D6
10 MHTN 101 D7
100 MHTN 102 B5
100 MHTN 6503 E3
100 MHTN 6504 A3
Seaman St
400 PTHA 7205 C3
Searing Av
10 ENWK 6713 E6
10 HRSN 6713 E6
10 HRSN 6714 A6
10 MNLA 6724 E6
Searingtown Av
10 NHLS 6724 C3
Searingtown Rd
- FLHL 6618 B6
- MNPK 6618 B6
- NHLS 6724 C1
10 NHmT 6724 C4
200 NHmT 6618 B7
200 ROSE 6618 A6
Searingtown Rd N
10 NHLS 6724 C2
100 NHLS 6724 C2
Searingtown Rd S
10 NHLS 6724 C3
Sears Av
10 LFRY 6501 B6
10 EMFD 6049 B4
400 BKLN 6049 B5
Seaside Av
3-00 QENS 7026 A6
Seaside Ln
10 STNL 7021 B6
Seasongood Rd
73-00 QENS 6823 D3
Seaton Pl
10 HmpT 6827 C5
10 HmpT 6928 C5
Seaton Gate
10 HmpT 6928 B2
Seaver Av
10 STNL 7020 B7
400 STNL 7118 C1
Seaview Av
- BKLN 6925 B5
10 QENS 7029 E5
10 JSYC 6819 B6
10 NRCH 6396 B3
10 SECS 6715 E4
10 STNL 7020 B7
100-01 BKLN 6924 D7
10 IrvT 6816 D3
10 NWRK 6816 D3
Seaview Blvd
10 NHmT 6618 C4
Seaview Ct
10 BAYN 6919 D6
10 BKLN 7024 D1
Seaview Dr
- JSYC 6715 E4
- SECS 6715 E4
Seaview Ln
10 PTWN 6508 C6
Seawall Av
10 BKLN 7121 E1
Seawane Av
200 HWTH 6928 E7
Seawane Rd
10 HWTH 6929 B2
Seaward Av
100 GLCV 6509 D2
Seba Av
10 BKLN 7023 E7
10 BKLN 7024 A7
Secatoag Av
10 MHVN 6508 C7
Secaucus Av
10 JSYC 6716 B3
10 NBgT 6716 A3
300 SECS 6716 A2
700 SECS 6716 C5
Secaucus Rd CO-678
700 JSYC 6716 C3
700 NBgT 6716 B4
700 UNCT 6716 C3
Secor Av
3600 BRNX 6505 E1
3700 BRNX 6394 E7
3900 MTVN 6394 E7
Secor Dr
10 DBSF 6166 C4
10 RYE 6283 C3
Secor Ln
10 HRSN 6169 B7
Secor Pl
10 YNKR 6394 C4
Secor Rd
10 GrbT 6166 D2
10 SCDL 6168 B7
200 SCDL 6167 A2
Secor Rd SR-125
100 SCDL 6168 B7

Secor Rd SR-125
200 WHPL 6168 B6
Secor Glen Rd
10 GrbT 6167 A2
Seddon St
1600 BRNX 6505 C7
Sedgwick Av
10 YNKR 6393 E4
900 BRNX 104 E6
900 BRNX 107 D1
900 BRNX 6503 E7
900 BRNX 6612 E1
1500 BRNX 105 A3
1500 BRNX 6504 A5
2200 BRNX 102 D7
Sedgwick Pl
6600 BKLN 6921 D7
Sedita Pl
10 MNCH 6501 B7
Sedore Av
10 FRVW 6611 B2
Seele Ct
10 MLVN 6929 C1
Seeley Av
10 YNKR 6394 C2
Seeley St
10 BKLN 6922 E5
Seely Ln
10 STNL 7117 A5
Seely Pl
10 GrbT 6167 B7
Seguine Av
10 STNL 7207 D2
Seguine Lp
10 STNL 7207 D2
Seguine Pl
10 STNL 7116 D6
Seib Av
10 ELIZ 6917 C5
Seidman Av
10 STNL 7116 E7
Seidman Pl
200 HmpT 6828 A3
Seigel Ct
10 BKLN 6822 D5
Seigel St
100 BKLN 6822 D5
Seiler Ct
10 STNL 7021 B4
Selden Ln
10 GrwT 6051 E2
Selden Pl
1300 FTLE 6502 E7
Seldin Av
10 STNL 7019 A5
Self Blvd
73-00 CART 7017 B7
Self Pl
200 SOrT 6712 B6
Selfridge St
66-00 QENS 6824 B3
Selkirk St
10 STNL 7115 E5
10 STNL 7116 A5
Sellers St
10 KRNY 6714 D3
Selma Pl
1700 HmpT 6827 C4
Selover Rd
178-00 QENS 6927 B1
57-40 QENS 6826 B7
Selvage St
10 IrvT 6816 D3
10 NWRK 6816 D3
Selvin Lp
10 STNL 7018 D7
Selwyn Av
1500 BRNX 105 C6
1500 BRNX 6504 D1
Semel Av
10 GrwT 6500 A1
Seminary Av
10 GRFD 6394 B2
Seminole Av
1700 BRNX 6505 C5
Seminole Rd
10 NHmT 6618 B1
500 HmpT 6828 A7
Seminole St
1500 BRNX 6505 D5
Semton Blvd
10 HmpT 6828 C5
Senate Pl
10 JSYC 6715 E7
10 MrnT 6282 B7
Senator St
10 BKLN 6921 E7
500 BKLN 6922 A7
500 BKLN 7022 A1
Seneca Av
3-00 QENS 6823 C6
10 BKLN 6924 A4
10 NoCT 6050 B5
10 STNL 7020 B3
10 WHPL 6168 B6
700 SECS 6716 A3
Seneca Lp
10 STNL 7019 B5
Seneca Pl
10 GrwT 6170 D3
Seneca Rd
10 SCDL 6168 A6
Seneca St
10 DBSF 6166 A3
10 RYE 6283 C3
Seneca Tr
10 HRSN 6169 A1
Seney Av
600 MRNK 6283 D7
700 MRNK 6397 A3
Senger St
2400 BRNX 6614 D2
Sentry Dr
10 GrbT 6167 B6
Serena Ln
100 SCDL 6168 B7

Serena Rd
300 HmpT 6928 C7
Sergeant Bollinger Ct
10 OrgT 6164 D2
Serpentine Ct
10 NHmT 6724 C2
Serpentine Rd
10 DMRT 6278 A5
10 EGLC 6392 A4
10 TFLY 6392 A4
Serpentine Tr
10 LRMT 6396 B2
Serrell Av
10 STNL 7116 D5
N Service Ct
- QENS 6926 D5
S Service Ct
- QENS 6926 D5
Service Dr
- UnnT 6816 A5
Service Rd
- JSYC 6819 B4
- LynT 6609 B4
- QENS 6926 D5
- RTFD 6609 A4
E Service Rd
10 STNL 7018 B7
N Service Rd
- ERTH 6609 C4
- QENS 6926 C4
S Service Rd
- ERTH 6609 D5
- LKSU 6723 D3
- NHLS 6724 A2
- QENS 6926 C6
- NHLS 6723 E3
W Service Rd
10 STNL 7116 A4
10 STNL 7018 B7
Seth Ct
10 STNL 7020 B7
Seth Lp
10 STNL 7020 D7
Seth St
10 STNL 7021 B4
Seth Boyden Ter
100 NWRK 6817 A6
Seton Av
700 PTHA 7114 B7
800 WbgT 7114 B7
Seton Dr
10 SOrT 6712 B6
10 NRCH 6281 E4
Seton Ln
10 GrwT 6170 B2
Seton Pl
100 MpIT 6712 A7
100 SOrT 6712 A7
800 BKLN 7022 E1
Seton Wy
10 WHPL 6168 E6
Seton Hall Dr
- NWRK 6713 B7
Seven Gables Rd
10 STNL 7020 C4
Seven Oaks Ct
400 COrT 6712 C4
Seven Oaks Ln
1000 BRNX 6397 A2
Seven Oaks Rd
400 COrT 6712 B4
Seven Oaks Wy
300 COrT 6712 C4
Severn St
10 NRCH 6281 E1
Seville Av
10 HRSN 6169 B7
Seville St
10 HmpT 6827 B5
Sewanee Av
10 HmpT 6827 C5
Seward Av
10 MNLA 6724 E1
229-00 QENS 6826 E1
231-00 QENS 6722 E7
Seward Pl
10 BRNX 6614 A3
Sewaren Av
10 WbgT 7114 A5
Sexton Pl
2700 BRNX 6505 C2
Seymour Av
10 STNL 7019 C1
500 WbgT 7114 B3
300 BRNX 6505 C2
Seymour Pl
10 WHPL 6168 D5
Seymour Rd
100 PTCH 6170 B3
Seymour St
10 YNKR 6393 E1
400 MTVN 6395 A4
1200 BRNX 6613 D3
Sgt Beers Av
10 BRNX 6616 A7
Sgt Beers Ln
10 BRNX 6616 A7
Sgt Hartz Dr
10 OrgT 6164 D2
Shad Creek Rd
10 NRCH 7026 A2
Shadetree Ln
10 NHmT 6724 C2
Shadow Ln
10 GTPZ 6823 A5
10 LRMT 6396 B2
10 NRCH 6396 B2
10 STNL 7117 D2
Shady Gln
10 WOrT 6712 A1
Shady Ln
10 DBSF 6166 B4

Shady Ln
10 EchT 6281 B3
10 GrwT 6170 B1
10 IRVN 6506 B5
10 RYEB 6170 A1
Shady Rd
10 ARDY 6166 C5
Shady Brook Rd
10 KNGP 6617 A4
Shady Glen Ct
10 NRCH 6396 A7
Shadyside Av
10 NHmT 6508 E6
10 PTWN 6508 E6
10 STNL 7206 D3
10 STNL 7207 A2
Shaefer Av
10 YNKR 6394 C2
Shafer Pl
10 HKSC 6501 C4
Shafter Av
10 NHmT 6724 D3
10 STNL 7117 B4
Shafto St
- GrbT 6500 B2
Shaina Ct
1000 STNL 7115 E7
Shakespeare Av
10 DBSF 6165 E6
1100 BRNX 107 E1
1100 BRNX 6612 B1
1100 BRNX 6613 B1
1200 BRNX 105 A7
1200 BRNX 6504 A7
Shale St
10 STNL 7019 B7
Shaler Av
10 FRVW 6611 C4
64-00 QENS 6823 D5
200 CLFP 6611 C4
Shaler Blvd
200 RDGF 6611 B1
700 RDGF 6502 C7
800 PALP 6502 C7
Shaler Blvd CO-31
500 RDGF 6611 B1
700 RDGF 6502 C7
800 PALP 6502 C7
Shanley Av
10 NWRK 6817 A2
Shannon Av
700 PTHA 7114 B7
800 WbgT 7114 B7
Shannon Pl
4400 BRNX 6394 D5
Shannon Dr
400 CLFP 6611 C1
400 RDGF 6611 C1
Shapham Pl
10 WHPL 6168 C3
Sharon Av
10 IrvT 6816 D2
10 STNL 7020 B1
Sharon Ln
100 RYE 6283 D2
10 SCDL 6167 D7
10 STNL 7115 E7
Sharon St
10 BKLN 6822 D3
Sharon Wy
10 STNL 7020 B3
Sharon Gardens Ct
10 WbgT 7114 A5
Sharot St
10 CART 7115 D1
Sharpe Av
10 STNL 6919 C7
10 STNL 7019 C1
Sharrett Pl
10 STNL 7020 C2
Sharrott Av
10 RKVC 6929 D5
Sharrotts Ln
10 STNL 7115 D7
Sharrotts Rd
10 STNL 7115 C7
Shatterhand Close
10 STNL 6049 E6
Shaughnessy Ln
10 STNL 7020 E3
Shaun Rdg
10 OybT 6618 E2
10 ROSH 6618 E2
Shaw Av
10 VLYS 6928 B2
100 IrvT 6816 D3
10 NWRK 6816 D3
Shaw Ln
10 GrbT 6048 D6
10 WLTN 6500 A7
Shaw Pl
10 NWRK 6817 A2
10 NWRK 6816 E2
Shaw Rd
10 SCDL 6167 E7
Shaw St
10 GRFD 6500 A1
Shawnee Av
10 YNKR 6280 D6
Shawnee Rd
10 SCDL 6167 D5
Shawnee St
10 STNL 7020 C2
Shawnee Ter
10 HRSN 6283 B7
Shea Pl
10 NRCH 6395 E5
Shea Rd
34-00 QENS 6720 D4
Shearer Av
400 ELIZ 6917 B7
10 STNL 7019 C2
Shearwater Ct E
10 STNL 6819 C2
Shearwater Ct W
10 STNL 6819 C2
Sheehy Pl
10 ARDY 6166 C4
Sheepshead Bay Rd
10 BKLN 7123 B7
10 BKLN 7023 B7
Sheridan Av
10 BKLN 6925 A1
700 KRNY 6714 A5
Sheffield Av
700 BRNX 6924 D4

E Sheffield Av
10 EGLD 6502 D2
W Sheffield Av
10 EGLD 6502 D2
Sheffield Ct
10 ARDY 6166 D4
Sheffield Rd
10 THSN 6617 B7
800 TnkT 6502 C1
Sheffield St
10 JSYC 6819 C6
10 STNL 7020 A1
Sheila Ct
800 HmpT 6828 B7
Shelbourne Ln
10 NHmT 6724 A4
Shelbourne Rd
10 YNKR 6280 B4
Shelburne Av
1300 MRNK 6283 B6
Shelburne Dr
900 HmpT 6828 A7
Sheldon Av
10 NRCH 6395 D2
10 STNL 7116 C6
10 TYTN 6048 C5
1000 STNL 7115 E7
Sheldon Pl
10 DBSF 6165 E6
10 HAOH 6165 E6
10 MLVN 6929 D1
10 NRCH 6395 D2
Sheldon St
10 HmpT 6166 D6
Sheldon Ter
10 NWRK 6816 B1
Sheldrake Av
10 BRNX 6282 B6
10 LODI 6500 D3
10 MrnT 6282 B6
100 PTHA 7205 C4
Sheldrake Dr
10 NRCH 6282 A5
Sheldrake Ln
10 NRCH 6282 A5
100 MRNK 6282 C4
Sheldrake Rd
10 SCDL 6168 A6
Shell Pl
10 HmpT 7029 E3
Shell Rd
10 BKLN 7022 E7
10 BXTE 6508 D7
10 NHmT 6508 D7
Shellbank Pl
2800 BKLN 7120 E1
Shelley Av
10 RKVC 6929 D5
Shelley Ln
10 HRSN 6050 D4
10 MTVN 6395 A3
10 NWRK 6920 D7
Shelly Av
10 GrbT 6167 B1
10 STNL 7018 C6
Shelter Ln
10 NHmT 6724 E2
Shelter Bay Dr
100 WbgT 7114 A5
Shelter Rock Rd
10 NHLS 6617 E7
10 NHLS 6618 A7
10 NHmT 6724 A1
100 MHTN 6504 A4
100 ROSP 6617 E1
200 TnkT 6501 E1
Shelterview Dr
1300 MRNK 6283 B5
Shelton Ct
10 RKVC 6929 D5
Shelton Ln
10 HRSN 6283 A3
Shelton Ter
10 HISt 6816 C5
W Shelton Ter
10 HISt 6816 C5
Shenandoah Av
10 STNL 7018 C5
Shepard Av
10 BRNX 6615 D4
10 LNBK 6928 E4
10 LNDN 6917 B6
10 NRCH 6396 C4
10 PTCH 6170 A6
100 WbgT 7114 E4
100 PTHA 7205 C4
Shepard Pl
10 KRNY 6714 C2
Shepard Ter
10 ERTH 6500 A7
Shephard Av
10 NWRK 6817 A2
10 NWRK 6816 E2
Shephards Ln
10 NHmT 6508 E5
10 SNPT 6508 E5
10 SNPT 6509 A4
Shepherd Av
10 BKLN 6823 E7
200 BKLN 6924 E2
800 BKLN 6925 A3
Shepherd Ln
10 NHmT 6724 E1
Shepherds Dr
10 NRCH 6282 A2
Sheppard Pl
10 LRMT 6396 D7
Sheraden Av
10 STNL 7019 C5
Sherborn Pl
10 ISPK 7029 C4
Sherbourne Rd
300 NHmT 6928 C7
Sherbrooke Pk
10 HRSN 6169 D7
Sherbrooke Rd
10 ARDY 6166 C4
10 SCDL 6167 D7

Sheridan Av
10 MTVN 6395 B3
10 ROSP 6917 A3
10 STNL 7020 D5
10 WLPK 6724 E5
10 ROSL 6917 A4
800 BRNX 6613 A1
800 ELIZ 6917 A4
900 ELIZ 6817 A7
1100 LNDN 6917 B5
1100 NWRK 6817 A1
1200 BRNX 6504 C7
1200 BRNX 6504 D7
Sheridan Blvd
10 QENS 7027 D3
Sheridan Ct
10 QENS 7027 C4
Sheridan Ct
10 STNL 7117 C4
Sheridan Expwy
- BRNX 6613 E1
Sheridan Expwy I-895
- BRNX 6613 E1
Sheridan Ln
10 SCLF 6509 D6
Sheridan Lp
10 BKLN 7021 D4
Sheridan Pl
10 HmpT 7029 C6
10 STNL 7116 D7
400 FRVW 6611 B4
Sheridan Rd
10 GrbT 6167 A3
Sheridan Sq
10 MHTN 6821 A1
Sheridan St
10 HSBH 6500 D3
10 IrvT 6816 D3
10 LODI 6500 D3
10 VLYS 6928 E4
100 PTHA 7205 C4
Sheriff St
- MHTN 119 C6
- MHTN 6821 A1
Sheriff S Byrd Pl
- BRNX 105 A7
Sherill Ct
10 WHPL 6168 B5
Sherlock Pl
10 BKLN 6924 E2
Sherman Av
10 HWTN 7028 E2
- MHTN 104 D1
10 BRXV 6395 A2
10 CLST 6278 D3
10 ENWK 6713 A2
10 EORG 6713 A2
10 GrbT 6166 E1
10 GrbT 6167 A1
100 MHTN 6504 A4
100 MHTN 6503 A4
Sherman Dr
900 HmpT 6828 A7
10 GTNE 6616 D7
Sherman Pl
10 GRFD 6500 B2
10 IrvT 6816 C2
10 JSYC 6716 B6
400 FRVW 6611 B4
Sherman Rd
4000 STNL 7029 E3
Sherman St
10 BKLN 6922 E4
10 LNBK 6928 E4
10 LNDN 6917 B6
10 NRCH 6396 C4
10 PTCH 6170 A6
100 WbgT 7114 E4
100 PTHA 7205 C4
Sherry St
10 PTCH 7114 C5
Sherry Hill Ln
10 NWRK 6817 A6
Sherwood Av
10 EGLC 6503 B2
10 EGLC 6051 E5
10 STNL 6051 E5
10 MHVN 6508 C7
10 RYEB 6051 E5
10 STNL 7206 E3
10 TnkT 6502 A3
10 YNKR 6394 B3
Sherwood Ct
10 ALPN 6278 D4
700 HmpT 6928 D7
Sherwood Ln
10 CDHT 7028 B2
10 MrnT 6282 A3
10 QENS 6395 A6
10 RYE 6283 E6
Sherwood Ovl
10 LRMT 6396 D2
Sherwood Pl
10 GrbT 6167 B7
10 STNL 7117 A5
100 EGLD 6503 A1

Sherwood Rd
10 NRWD 6278 B5
10 TFLY 6392 A4
200 UnnT 6816 A7
200 UnnT 6917 C1
Sherwood Av
10 MtPT 6050 A7
600 HmpT 6928 A6
Sherwood Ter
10 STNL 7021 A4
Sherwood Farm Ln
10 GrbT 6170 C1
Shetland Ln
- PALP 6611 A1
- PALP 6502 C7
700 RDGF 6611 C1
Shiel Av
10 STNL 7115 E6
Shields Av
10 WLPK 6724 E5
Shields Pl
10 STNL 7020 D1
Shift Pl
10 STNL 7116 B6
Shiloh Av
10 STNL 7116 C6
249-00 QENS 6723 B6
Shiloh St
10 STNL 7018 E6
10 STNL 7019 A7
Shine Pl
10 HmpT 6928 C3
Shipherd Av
10 LNBK 6929 B5
Shipherd Pl
10 LNBK 6929 B5
Shipley Av
1700 HmpT 6928 B1
Shipman St
10 NWRK 6817 D1
Shippen St
10 WhkT 6716 E3
Shipyard Ln
10 HBKN 6716 E5
Shirley Av
10 STNL 7117 A7
10 STNL 7116 E7
200 STNL 7207 E1
Shirley Ln
10 NRCH 6281 D4
Shirra Av
10 STNL 7019 B6
Shonnard Pl
10 YNKR 6279 D6
Shonnard Row
10 YNKR 6279 C5
Shonnard Ter
10 YNKR 6279 C5
Shore Av
143-00 QENS 6825 C7
W Shore Av
10 BGTA 6501 D3
10 RDFP 6501 D3
W Shore Av CO-41
107-00 QENS 6824 E2
Shore Blvd
10 BKLN 7121 B1
20-00 QENS 6613 A7
20-00 QENS 6719 A1
23-00 QENS 113 D3
23-00 QENS 6718 E2
Shore Ct
8900 BKLN 7021 C2
Shore Dr
10 BRNX 6615 B1
10 GTNE 6616 B7
10 GTNE 6722 D1
10 KNGP 6616 E2
10 LRMT 6396 D2
10 PLDM 6617 C4
10 PTCH 6170 A6
10 PTCH 6284 C1
E Shore Dr
10 BRNX 6617 A2
W Shore Dr
10 BAYN 6919 D3
10 NHmT 6617 C6
Shore Pkwy
80-01 QENS 6925 C4
10 BKLN 7022 B5
2300 BKLN 7120 E1
2400 BKLN 7121 A1
3200 BKLN 7023 D7
5000 BKLN 7024 E1
Shore Rd
- BRNX 6506 B4
- SCLF 6509 B6
- BRNX 6921 D7
10 BXTE 6617 D1
10 EDGW 103 B5
10 EDGW 6503 A7
10 GLCV 6509 D2
10 MHVN 6508 C7
10 MRNK 6283 D6
10 NHmT 6618 D1
10 PLMM 6506 D1
10 PLNH 6617 C4
10 PTWN 6508 C7
10 RYE 6283 D6
10 STNL 7206 A4
10 TnkT 6502 C1
500 KNGP 6616 E3

W Shore Rd
10 FLHL 6618 C6
10 NHmT 6618 C1
200 RSLN 6618 D5
200 UnnT 6816 C1
100 KNGP 6616 D5
100 UnnT 6917 C1
Shore Acres Dr
500 MRNK 6283 A6
Shore Acres Rd
10 STNL 7021 A4
Shorecliff Pl
10 NRCH 6616 C7
Shore Cliff Ter
10 NRCH 6616 D7
Shore Club Dr
10 NRCH 6396 B5
Shoredale Dr
10 NRCH 6616 C6
Shore Front Pkwy
- QENS 7123 E2
74-00 QENS 7026 B7
99-10 QENS 7124 A1
Shorehaven Ln
10 NHmT 6617 C6
Shore Park Rd
10 NHmT 6616 D7
Shore Rd Ln
10 NHmT 7021 C2
Shoreview Av
10 NHmT 6616 C6
Shoreview Cir
10 PLMM 6506 D1
Shore View Dr
10 YNKR 6280 B3
10 YNKR 6281 A3
Shoreview Rd
10 BXTE 6617 C1
Shoreward Dr
10 GTPZ 6823 A7
10 THSN 6617 A7
Shorewood Dr
10 NHmT 6508 E5
10 SNPT 6508 E5
10 SNPT 6509 A5
Short Dr
10 RSLN 6618 D5
10 UnnT 6816 B6
Short Ln
10 NRCH 6281 D4
Short Pl
10 CRSK 6278 A7
10 STNL 7027 C2
Short St
10 FTLE 6503 A4
10 LODI 6500 E2
10 MTVN 6283 B5
10 MTVN 6394 A7
10 TYTN 6048 B5
Short Wy
10 NHLS 6724 D1
Short Hill Rd
106-00 QENS 6824 D5
Shorthill Rd
10 ARDY 6166 D5
107-00 QENS 6824 E2
Shotwell Av
10 STNL 7116 C4
Shrady Pl
10 BRNX 102 E3
10 BRNX 6504 C2
Shrub Hollow Rd
10 NHmT 6617 B4
Shultz Pl
10 NHmT 6617 B5
Sicard Av
10 NRCH 6395 D1
Sickles Av
10 NRCH 6395 D4
Sickles Pl
10 NRCH 6395 D4
Sickles St
10 MHTN 101 D7
10 MHTN 104 E1
10 MHTN 6503 E4
W Side Av
10 JSYC 6819 C4
700 PTHA 7205 D1
10 WbgT 6715 E7
W Side Hwy
10 MHTN 111 E6
10 MHTN 115 C1
10 MHTN 120 A1
10 MHTN 6717 B4
10 BKLN 6821 A4
W Side Hwy SR-9A
10 MHTN 111 E6
10 MHTN 115 C1
10 MHTN 6717 B4
E Side Ln
10 WbgT 7114 C1
Sidehill Dr
10 YNKR 6280 D3
Sideview Av
10 STNL 7018 E4
Sidney Av
10 ERTH 6609 A1
10 RTFD 6609 A1
E Sidney Av
10 MTVN 6394 A4
10 MTVN 6395 A4
W Sidney Av
10 MTVN 6394 A4
Sidney Pl
10 HmpT 6928 B3
10 STNL 121 A6
10 VLYS 6928 B3
Sidney Lanier Ln
10 LODI 6500 D1
Sidway Pl
126-00 QENS 6927 B1
Siebrecht Pl
10 NRCH 6395 D1
Siedler St
10 JSYC 6819 E3

New York City/5 Borough Street Index

STREET Block City Map# Grid

Siegfried Pl
1300 BRNX 6506 B7
Sierra Ct
10 STNL 7018 E5
100 WbgT 7114 B3
Sievers Ln
10 LFRY 6501 C4
10 SHKT 6501 C4
Sigma Pl
10 BRNX 6393 B5
Signal Hill Rd
10 STNL 7020 C3
Signs Rd
10 STNL 7018 E5
Sigourney St
10 BKLN 6922 A2
Sigsbee Av
100 NHmT 6724 D4
Silkman Pl
10 IrvT 6816 D1
Silver Av
100 HIsT 6816 C6
Silver Ct
10 STNL 7020 B2
300 HmpT 7028 B1
Silver Ln
300 HmpT 6929 D6
Silver Rd
90-00 QENS 6925 D2
Silver St
10 BAYN 6919 D5
10 GrwT 6170 D5
10 HmpT 6827 D6
10 MLVN 6929 B1
10 NWRK 6712 C6
1500 BRNX 6505 C7
Silver Beach Rd
10 STNL 7020 A4
Silver Birch Dr
10 NRCH 6281 E7
Silver Lake Rd
10 STNL 7020 C1
Silver Lake Park Rd
- STNL 7020 B2
Silver Spring Rd
10 WOrT 6712 B4
Silver Stream Dr
10 HRSN 6050 E5
Silvia Pl
10 NARL 6714 D1
Silzer St
200 PTHA 7205 C3
Simmons Ln
10 STNL 7018 C6
Simmons Lp
10 STNL 7018 C6
Simon Ct
10 STNL 7206 C3
Simon Wy
400 NVLE 6164 B4
Simons Av
200 HKSK 6501 A1
Simonson Av
10 STNL 6919 B7
10 STNL 7019 A1
Simonson Pl
10 STNL 6919 D7
10 STNL 7019 D1
Simonson Rd
100 MNLA 6724 D6
Simonson St
51-00 QENS 6719 E2
Simpson Pl
10 YNKR 6280 E2
10 YNKR 6281 A2
Simpson St
10 STNL 7020 C7
900 BRNX 6613 D3
Sinatra Dr
100 HBKN 6716 E7
Sinatra Dr N
1300 HBKN 6716 E5
Sinclair Av
500 STNL 7116 B6
1000 STNL 7115 E7
Sinclair Ct
10 TnkT 6502 C2
Sinclair Dr
10 KNGP 6616 B4
Sinclair Pl
10 GrbT 6166 E3
Sinclair Ter
500 SOrT 6712 B6
600 NWRK 6712 B6
Sinclair Martin Dr
10 RSLN 6618 E5
Singleton Av
900 HmpT 7028 D1
Singleton St
10 STNL 7207 B2
Singley Ct
10 THSN 6617 B7
Sintsink Dr E
10 MHVN 6508 C7
Sintsink Dr W
10 MHVN 6508 C7
Sinvalco Rd
100 SECS 6716 A1
Sioux Ct
10 OrgT 6164 E4
Sioux Pl
10 GrwT 6170 B1
Sioux St
10 STNL 7118 C2
Sip Av
10 JSYC 6820 A1
100 JSYC 6819 E1
Sip St
700 UNCT 6716 D2
Sisson Ct
10 BAYN 6919 E4
Sisson Ter
10 TFLY 6392 B2
Site Dr
- BKLN 6925 A5
Sitka St
133-00 QENS 6925 D2
Siwanoy Blvd
10 EchT 6281 B7
Siwanoy Pl
400 PLMM 6395 B6
Siwanoy Clubway
10 BRXV 6281 B7
10 BRXV 6395 B1
10 EchT 6281 B7
10 EchT 6395 B1
Sixty-Six
10 LODI 6500 C4
10 WRDG 6500 C4
Skeggs Rd
- GrbT 6048 D4
Skelly Pl
10 MNLA 6724 D7
Sketch Pl
500 RDGF 6611 C2
Sketch Pl N
500 RDGF 6611 B2
Sketch Pl S
500 RDGF 6611 B2
Skibo Ln
10 MRNK 6397 A1
Skidmore Av
10 BKLN 7024 D1
Skidmore Ln
10 BKLN 6924 C7
Skidmore Pl
10 HmpT 6928 C5
10 VLYS 6928 C5
Skillman Av
10 BKLN 6822 D3
10 JSYC 6716 A5
24-00 QENS 6718 E6
40-00 QENS 6719 A6
Skillman St
10 BKLN 6822 B6
10 RSLN 6618 D5
Skippy's Wy
10 ERKY 6929 C7
Skitka Av
10 CART 7017 B6
Sky Ln
10 STNL 7020 D3
Skyline Dr
10 EGLC 6503 B2
10 JSYC 6819 D5
10 MtPT 6049 B1
10 STNL 7020 D4
7000 FTLE 6502 E4
7000 FTLE 6503 C3
Skyline Ln
100 STNL 7020 C3
Skymeadow Pl
10 EMFD 6049 B6
10 GrbT 6049 B6
Skymeadow Farm
10 HRSN 6169 D3
10 RYEB 6169 D3
Sky Top Rd
10 GrbT 6280 E1
Skyview Ln
10 NRCH 6281 E5
Skyview Ovl
10 OrgT 6164 B1
Skyview Rd
10 UnnT 6816 B7
Skywood Ct
10 GrbT 6280 D1
10 YNKR 6280 D1
Slabey Av
10 MLVN 6929 A2
1100 HmpT 6929 A1
1100 VLYS 6929 A1
Slaight St
10 STNL 6919 C7
Slater Av
10 YNKR 6280 D4
Slater Blvd
10 STNL 7020 B7
10 STNL 7118 C1
Slater Dr
10 ELIZ 6918 D5
Slater St
10 PTCH 6170 B6
Slayton Av
10 STNL 7019 A6
Sleepy Hollow Av
- SYHW 6048 A1
Sleepy Hollow Rd
10 RYEB 6170 A1
10 STNL 7018 E6
10 SYHW 6048 D1
Sleight Av
10 STNL 7206 B4
Sloan Dr E
10 VLYS 6928 D2
Sloan Dr N
10 VLYS 6928 D2
Sloan Dr S
10 VLYS 6928 D2
Sloan Pl
10 BKLN 7022 E5
Sloan St
137-00 QENS 6927 C2
Sloane Av
10 STNL 7019 D7
10 STNL 7117 D1
Sloanes Ct
10 SNPT 6508 B4
Sloanes Beach Rd
10 SNPT 6508 B4
Slocum Av
10 NHmT 6508 D5
10 OrgT 6164 D3
10 YNKR 6394 C1
600 RDGF 6611 B1
800 RDGF 6502 B7
Slocum Cres
10 QENS 6824 D3
Slocum Pl
10 BKLN 6923 A6
Slocum St
10 NRCH 6395 B3
10 NRCH 6396 A2
1700 HmpT 6928 E6
1700 HmpT 6929 A6
Slocum Wy
200 FTLE 103 A5
200 FTLE 6502 E6
200 FTLE 6503 A6
Slosson Av
10 STNL 7019 E3
Slosson Ter
10 STNL 6920 D7
Small St
400 CARL 6500 C7
400 CARL 6609 D2
Smalley Ter
10 IrvT 6712 E7
Smallwood Pl
10 NoCT 6050 B5
Smart Av
10 YNKR 6394 B1
Smart St
43-00 QENS 6721 B5
Smeathers St
10 WbgT 7114 B3
Smedley St
83-00 QENS 6825 B3
Smit Ct
10 JSYC 6819 A4
Smith Av
10 STNL 7019 E3
10 WHPL 6168 B3
5000 NBgT 6716 E1
6000 NBgT 6610 D6
8100 NBgT 6611 B4
9100 FRVW 6611 B4
Smith Ct
10 OrgT 6164 E5
10 STNL 7019 C3
100 EDGW 108 B1
100 EDGW 6611 D5
Smith Ln
800 HWTN 7028 D2
900 HmpT 7028 D2
Smith Pl
10 STNL 7019 C2
10 WLPK 6724 D3
10 YNKR 6280 D6
16-00 QENS 7027 D5
Smith St
10 BKLN 121 A7
10 BKLN 6821 D7
10 BlvT 6714 A1
10 EGLD 6502 D1
10 ELIZ 6918 A4
10 EORG 6712 D5
10 ERKY 6929 B7
10 GrwT 6170 D4
10 HmpT 6929 C1
10 HmpT 7027 E3
10 IrvT 6816 C2
10 JSYC 6820 A1
10 LNBK 6929 B3
10 OybT 6618 E1
10 PTCH 6170 B6
10 PTHA 7205 B3
10 RKVC 6929 E5
10 RYE 6283 E2
10 RYE 6284 A1
10 STNL 7020 E3
10 VLYS 6928 C3
100 NWRK 6712 C7
117-00 QENS 6826 A7
119-00 QENS 6927 A1
200 BKLN 6922 C1
200 HmpT 7028 B1
500 WbgT 7205 A3
600 HmpT 6828 B7
800 LNDN 7017 A3
Smith St CO-656
100 PTHA 7205 B3
500 WbgT 7205 A3
Smith St N
10 GrwT 6170 D4
Smith St S
10 GrwT 6170 D5
E Smith St
200 WbgT 7114 C5
N Smith St
10 WbgT 7114 D2
W Smith St
300 WbgT 7114 B1
Smith Ter
10 CRSK 6278 A7
10 STNL 7020 D1
Smiths Ln
10 BKLN 6924 C6
Smith St Connector
- PTHA 7205 B2
- WbgT 7205 B2
Smull Pl
10 PTWN 6508 D7
Smyrna Av
10 STNL 7116 C5
Snapdragon Ln
10 NHmT 6724 E2
Snedeker Pl
200 NVLE 6164 C5
Sneden Av
10 STNL 7116 D6
Snediker Av
10 BKLN 6924 C4
Snow Crest Ct
10 OLDT 6164 A3
Snug Harbor Rd
10 STNL 6920 A5
Snyder Av
10 BKLN 6923 E5
5600 BKLN 6924 A5
Snyder Rd
10 EGLC 6503 B2
Snyder St
100 COrT 6712 D2
Sobel Ct
10 STNL 7020 D3
Sobo Av
800 HmpT 6828 B4
Sobro Av
10 HmpT 6928 B1
10 QENS 6928 B1
10 VLYS 6928 B1
Society Hill Dr
- JSYC 6819 B4
Society Hill Dr N
10 JSYC 6819 B4
Sofield Av
800 PTHA 7114 C7
Soho Dr
188-00 QENS 6826 A3
Sokkon Yun Plz
- JSYC 6716 B6
Solar Ln
10 NHmT 6724 C2
Soloff Blvd
10 HmpT 7027 D2
Solomon Av
10 HmpT 7027 D3
Soltes Av
10 CART 7115 B1
Soma St
10 NHmT 6723 E5
Somers St
10 BKLN 6924 B1
Somerset Av
10 GDNC 6828 C1
Somerset Ct
- CART 7115 D2
Somerset Dr
10 NHmT 6723 A2
10 YNKR 6280 E3
200 ERKY 6929 A6
200 HmpT 6929 A6
200 LNBK 6929 A6
Somerset Dr N
10 NHmT 6723 A2
Somerset Dr S
10 NHmT 6723 B2
Somerset Rd
10 NRCH 6282 A4
10 NRWD 6278 A1
10 TFLY 6392 A2
100 NRWD 6164 A7
Somerset St
10 CART 7115 D2
10 GRFD 6500 A3
10 NWRK 6817 C2
85-00 QENS 6826 A3
300 HRSN 6714 A7
Somerville Pl
100 YNKR 6279 E6
Somme St
10 NWRK 6818 B1
Sommer Av
10 STNL 7018 E4
Sommer Pl
2900 BRNX 6615 A1
Sommers Ln
10 STNL 7019 E4
Sonia Ct
10 STNL 7115 D7
Sonn Dr
10 RYE 6283 D4
Soper St
10 HmpT 6929 E7
Sophia Ln
10 STNL 7020 B6
Sophia St
10 MRNK 6283 A5
Soren St
10 STNL 7019 C5
Soulard St
10 HRSN 6283 C3
Soulice Pl
10 NRCH 6281 E3
10 NRCH 6282 A3
Sound Rd
10 RYE 6283 C5
Sound St
23-00 QENS 6719 B3
Soundside Ln
10 GLCV 6509 D2
Sound View Av
10 BRNX 6614 C4
Soundview Av
10 RYE 6283 D4
10 WHPL 6168 A4
10 YNKR 6394 B2
100 MRNK 6282 D4
400 MRNK 6283 A4
Soundview Cir
10 WHPL 6168 B5
Sound View Dr
10 BRNX 6615 C2
Soundview Dr
10 EchT 6281 C6
10 LKSU 6723 A3
10 LRMT 6396 B2
10 MHVN 6508 C7
10 NHmT 6508 C7
10 NHmT 6723 B3
10 PTWN 6508 C6
700 MRNK 6283 B6
Soundview Gdns
10 PTWN 6508 C6
Soundview Ln
10 KNGP 6616 C3
10 SNPT 6508 A5
Sound View Rd
5-02 QENS 6614 C7
Soundview Rd
10 GLCV 6509 D3
10 NHmT 6723 B3
Soundview St
10 NRCH 6396 A5
10 PTCH 6170 B6
Soundview Ter
10 BRNX 6615 C4
Soundview Crest
10 NHmT 6618 A7
Sousa Dr
10 SNPT 6508 B4
South Av
10 ELIZ 6918 A4
10 GDNC 6828 D2
10 NRWD 6164 B7
10 STNL 6918 E7
200 STNL 7018 D5
South Brch
10 NHLS 6618 C7
10 ROSE 6618 C7
South Cir
10 WbgT 7114 B5
10 YNKR 6279 E4
South Ct
10 NHmT 6617 D2
10 NHmT 6724 D1
South Dr
10 GTNE 6616 E7
10 GTNE 6722 E1
10 HAOH 6166 A6
10 HmpT 6928 C5
10 MrnT 6282 B6
10 NHmT 6617 D7
10 NHmT 6724 B5
10 PLDM 6617 C5
10 RSLN 6618 D6
10 VLYS 6928 C5
10 YNKR 6394 C2
141-00 QENS 6614 E7
141-00 QENS 6615 A7
South Ln
10 DBSF 6166 A4
South Pl
10 LODI 6500 D2
South Rd
- SECS 6715 E4
- STNL 7021 A4
10 BRXV 6281 A7
10 GrbT 6049 E6
10 GrbT 6050 A6
10 HRSN 6283 C3
10 SNPT 6508 E7
10 SNPT 6509 A7
143-00 QENS 6825 C6
South St
- STNL 6920 E6
10 BGTA 6501 D1
10 CRSK 6278 B6
10 DMRT 6278 A6
10 GTNK 6616 E5
10 GTNK 6617 A5
10 HmpT 6927 D7
10 JSYC 6716 C6
10 MHTN 120 E1
10 MTVN 6394 C5
10 NHmT 6617 E2
10 NHmT 6724 B5
10 NWRK 6817 D2
10 PASC 6500 A4
10 RDFP 6501 E6
10 STNL 7019 E1
10 STNL 7020 A1
100 HKSK 6501 B2
100 SHKT 6501 B2
200 COrT 6712 C3
200 ELIZ 6918 A4
200 MHTN 121 A1
300 MHTN 119 C7
300 MHTN 6821 D4
300 NWRK 6818 A3
400 ELIZ 6917 E4
2100 FTLE 103 A1
2100 FTLE 6502 E3
2100 FTLE 6503 A4
Southampton Ter
10 EDGW 108 B1
10 EDGW 6611 D4
Southard Dr
10 ISPK 7029 C4
Southdale Rd
10 WHPL 6168 D3
Southeast Rd
10 SNPT 6509 B7
Southeast Wy
10 EchT 6395 B1
Southern Blvd
- BRNX 6505 A3
300 BRNX 6613 D1
2600 BRNX 6504 E4
Southern Dr
800 HmpT 6828 A7
900 HmpT 6929 A1
1500 HmpT 6928 B4
Southern Rd
10 GrbT 6166 E3
Southern State Pkwy
- HmpT 6827 B7
- HmpT 6828 E7
- HmpT 6928 D1
- HmpT 6929 A1
- QENS 6827 A7
Southfield Av
10 DBSF 6166 C4
Southfield Rd
10 GLCV 6509 D3
10 MTVN 6395 A2
Southgate Av
10 HAOH 6166 A7
10 HAOH 6280 C1
Southgate Dr
700 HmpT 6927 E5
Southgate Plz
139-00 QENS 6927 C2
Southgate Rd
10 HmpT 6928 B5
Southgate St
137-00 QENS 6927 C2
Southlawn Av
10 DBSF 6165 E6
10 HAOH 6165 E6
Southminster Dr
10 WHPL 6050 C7
Southside Av
10 HAOH 6165 E7
10 HAOH 6279 E1
Southview
10 HRSN 6169 B1
Southway
10 EchT 6395 B1
10 GrbT 6166 E3
Southwood Pl
10 GrbT 6167 D1
Southwoods Ln
10 SCDL 6281 D1
Sova Pl
10 MNCH 6501 B7
Soverel Ter
10 EORG 6712 E2
Spa Pl
107-00 QENS 6825 C6
Spanish Ln
10 STNL 7207 E2
Spanish Colony
10 STNL 7207 D2
Spanish Cove Rd
10 LRMT 6396 D2
Spark Pl
- STNL 7018 D5
Sparkill Av
10 OrgT 6164 D2
10 STNL 7020 B5
Sparks Av
100 PLHM 6395 B4
Sparman Pl
10 SECS 6609 E7
10 SECS 6610 A7
Sparrow Cir
10 WHPL 6168 D6
Sparrow Dr
200 NHLS 6724 C1
Spartan Av
10 STNL 7018 E2
Spartan Row
10 LODI 6500 E1
Spaulding Ln
10 BRNX 6393 B6
10 HmpT 7027 D2
Spectrum Sq
10 CLST 6278 B2
Speedling Pl
10 YNKR 6279 E4
Speedway Av
10 IrvT 6712 E6
10 NWRK 6712 E6
Speedwell Av
10 STNL 7018 E4
Speer Av
100 EGLD 6392 B5
Spencer Av
10 LNBK 6929 B5
100 ERKY 6929 B5
214-00 QENS 6826 D1
6000 BRNX 6393 C5
Spencer Ct
10 BKLN 6822 B7
10 GrbT 6167 B1
Spencer Dr
3100 BRNX 6506 A7
Spencer Dr E
10 NRCH 6396 B2
Spencer Dr W
10 NRCH 6396 B2
Spencer Pl
10 BKLN 6923 B1
10 GRFD 6500 B3
10 SCDL 6167 C5
100 MRNK 6282 E6
200 BRNX 6393 C4
Spencer St
10 BKLN 6822 B6
10 ELIZ 6918 A5
10 NWRK 6712 D7
10 STNL 7018 B5
Spencer Ter
6100 BRNX 6393 C4
Sperry Blvd
10 NHmT 6723 E7
10 NHmT 6724 B6
Sperry Ct
10 NHmT 6723 E6
10 NHmT 6724 A7
Sperry Pl
10 STNL 7116 B6
Sperry St E
10 HmpT 7029 B1
Sperry St W
10 HmpT 7029 C2
Spier Rd
10 SCDL 6168 C7
Spinnaker Ct
700 SECS 6715 D1
Spinnaker Dr
10 SAMB 7205 D7
73-01 QENS 7026 C7
Spinney Hill Dr
10 LKSU 6723 C1
10 NHmT 6723 C1
10 THSN 6723 C1
Spirit Ln
10 STNL 7019 A1
Spitler Pl
10 NHmT 6617 E1
Split Rail Dr
10 STNL 7020 D6
Split Rock Dr
10 KNGP 6616 D2
Split Rock Ln
10 NRCH 6282 A6
Split Rock Rd
10 BRNX 6395 B7
10 PLMM 6395 B7
Split Tree Rd
10 MrnT 6282 B4
Spofford Av
900 ELIZ 6917 D5
1100 BRNX 6613 D4
Spoganetz Av
10 CART 7017 A6
Spooner St
10 FLPK 6827 C1
Sprague Av
10 EchT 6281 C2
10 SCDL 6281 C2
10 STNL 7206 C5
100 NRCH 6281 D2
600 HmpT 6828 B7
Sprague Ct
10 STNL 7206 C5
Sprague Dr
10 VLYS 6928 C2
Sprague Rd
300 HmpT 7027 D2
Sprain Pl
10 YNKR 6280 B5
Sprain Rd
- GrbT 6280 C1
10 GrbT 6166 E5
10 GrbT 6167 A4
100 ARDY 6166 E6
400 YNKR 6280 B2
S Sprain Rd
- GrbT 6280 C1
- YNKR 6280 C1
Sprain Brook Pkwy
- ARDY 6167 A4
- EMFD 6049 B5
- GrbT 6049 B7
- GrbT 6166 E6
- GrbT 6167 A4
- GrbT 6280 D2
- MtPT 6049 B7
- YNKR 6280 C6
- YNKR 6394 E1
Sprain Brook Parkway Dr
10 EMFD 6049 A6
10 GrbT 6049 A6
Sprain Valley Rd
10 GrbT 6166 E7
10 GrbT 6280 D1
Spratt Av
10 STNL 7117 C4
Spray View Av
36-00 QENS 7027 B6
Spring Ct
10 WLTN 6500 B5
Spring Hllw
10 NHLS 6724 B3
Spring Ln
- DMRT 6278 A5
10 EGLD 6392 A7
10 GTNK 6617 A4
10 KNGP 6617 A4
Spring Rd
10 YNKR 6393 D3
900 BRNX 6395 B7
900 PLMM 6395 B7
Spring St
- ELIZ 6917 E5
10 COrT 6712 C1
10 CRSK 6278 B7
10 ERTH 6500 A6
10 GrbT 6048 D4
10 GRFD 6500 A2
10 GrwT 6170 E4
10 HAOH 6165 D6
10 JSYC 6819 B5
10 LEON 6502 C4
10 LODI 6500 D2
10 MHTN 118 D3
10 MHTN 119 A4
10 MHTN 6821 B2
10 NRCH 6396 A4
10 NWRK 6713 E6
10 PTCH 6170 B6
10 STNL 7020 B5
10 WbgT 7114 C5
10 WLTN 6500 B5
10 WOrT 6712 C1
100 ELIZ 6918 A2
200 HmpT 7027 E2
400 HIsT 6816 B6
500 TnkT 6502 B2
700 PTHA 7205 D1
1000 ELIZ 6817 B7
1000 NWRK 6817 B7
Spring St US-1
- ELIZ 6917 E5
100 ELIZ 6918 A2
1000 ELIZ 6817 B7
1000 NWRK 6817 B7
Spring St US-9
- ELIZ 6917 E5
100 ELIZ 6918 A4
S Spring St
10 ELIZ 6918 A4
Springdale Av
10 EORG 6713 A3
10 NWRK 6713 B3
10 WHPL 6050 C7
400 EORG 6712 E2
700 COrT 6712 D1
Springdale Rd
10 MrnT 6282 B7
10 NRCH 6282 B7
10 SCDL 6168 B7
10 SCDL 6282 B1
Spring Dell Av
10 RTFD 6609 D3
Springer Av
10 YNKR 6394 C2
Springfield Av
10 HSBH 6500 C4
10 NWRK 6713 D7
10 STNL 7019 C3
100 NWRK 6817 A1
100 RTFD 6609 C2
600 NWRK 6816 E1
700 IrvT 6816 C2
1400 MplT 6816 A2
Springfield Av CO-510
10 NWRK 6713 D7
Springfield Av CO-603
10 NWRK 6713 D7
100 NWRK 6817 A1
600 NWRK 6816 E1
700 IrvT 6816 C2
Springfield Av SR-124
1400 IrvT 6816 A2
1400 MplT 6816 A2
Springfield Blvd
45-00 QENS 6722 C6
80-40 QENS 6826 D7
122-86 QENS 6927 C2
Springfield Ln
146-00 QENS 6927 C4
Springfield Rd
10 ELIZ 6917 C3
300 UnnT 6917 C3
Spring Garden St
10 VLYS 6928 B2
Springhill Av
10 STNL 6920 B7
Spring Hollow Rd
10 OLDT 6164 A4
Springhurst Park Ln
10 DBSF 6166 B5
Spring Lake Dr
10 HRSN 6168 D1
Springline St
10 NWRK 6818 B6
Springside Av
10 TnkT 6502 B2
Springwood Av
10 ARDY 6166 D5
10 GrbT 6166 D5
Spritz Rd
88-00 QENS 6925 D2
Spruce Av
- BKLN 7022 E2
10 FLPK 6827 B2
10 RDFP 6501 E5
100-00 QENS 6720 B6
Spruce Ct
10 STNL 7206 C4
Spruce Dr
10 FLHL 6618 C5
10 WHPL 6168 E5
Spruce Ln
10 HmpT 6928 C5
10 NHmT 6723 E6
10 STNL 7115 D7
10 VLYS 6928 C5
100 SCDL 6168 B7
Spruce Pl
10 CRSK 6278 C7
10 DMRT 6278 C7
10 GTNE 6617 A7
Spruce Rd
10 MrnT 6282 B7
Spruce St
10 CART 7115 B2
10 CDHT 7028 B2
10 FRVW 6611 B2
10 HmpT 6828 D5
10 JSYC 6716 A7
10 KRNY 6714 C3
10 LODI 6500 C2
10 LWRN 7028 B3
10 MHTN 118 C7
10 MHTN 6821 B4
10 MLVN 6929 A1
10 MNCH 6500 E7
10 NRCH 6395 E6
10 NWRK 6817 C2
10 STNL 7117 C2
10 SYHW 6048 B1
10 THSN 6617 B7
10 THSN 6723 B1
10 WbgT 7115 B2
10 YNKR 6393 D2
100 GrwT 6170 D5
100 MRNK 6283 A6
500 ROSL 6917 A5
800 PTHA 7205 D1
Squire Av
10 YNKR 6280 A3
Squire Ct
10 EGLD 6502 C3
Squirrel Dr
10 ERKY 6929 B6
Squirrel Hl
10 NHLS 6724 B3
Staal Ln
10 HSBH 6500 D4
10 LODI 6500 D4
Stable Ln
10 LWRN 7028 A5
Stacey Ln
10 STNL 7118 B1
Stack Dr
10 STNL 7116 B5
Stadium Av
1100 BRNX 6506 A7
1100 BRNX 6615 B1
Stadium Ct
10 JSYC 6819 A4
Stadium Rd
- ERTH 6609 D4
10 GrbT 6049 C7
Stadium Club Rd
- ERTH 6609 D4
Staff St
10 MHTN 101 D6
10 MHTN 6503 E3
Stafford Av
700 STNL 7116 A6
900 STNL 7115 E7
Stafford Pl
10 LRMT 6396 C2
10 WHPL 6050 B6
Stafford Rd
1000 HmpT 6928 C1
Stage Ln
10 STNL 7020 D3
Stagg St
10 BKLN 6822 C4
10 JSYC 6716 A6
Stagg Wk
10 BKLN 6822 C4
Stairway St
10 STNL 7206 A4
Standard Av
1300 HmpT 6827 E5
Standard Ln
39-00 QENS 6718 E5
Standard Pl
10 BAYN 6919 E4
10 IrvT 6816 E1
Standish Av
10 WOrT 6712 C1
10 YNKR 6280 D5
200 HKSK 6501 A2
Standish Dr
10 NRCH 6281 E2
Standish Pl
10 ARDY 6166 E3
10 GrbT 6166 E3
72-00 QENS 6824 E2
100 HRSN 6283 B4
100 MRNK 6283 B4
Standish Rd
10 HmpT 6928 E1
Standish St
100 ELIZ 6917 B4
Stanford St
300 PTHA 7205 D3
Stanhope St
10 BKLN 6822 E6
17-00 BKLN 6823 A5
17-00 QENS 6823 A5
Stanley Av
10 DBSF 6166 B6
10 HAOH 6166 B7
10 HAOH 6280 A1
100 STNL 6920 C7
100 YNKR 6393 C2
200 BKLN 6924 C5
200 HSBH 6500 B3
200 MRNK 6282 D6
300 HSBH 6501 A4
800 BKLN 6925 A3
Stanley Cir
10 STNL 7116 E5
10 STNL 7117 A5
Stanley Dr
- HBKN 6716 E6
Stanley Ln
10 NHmT 6724 B6
Stanley Pl
- WbgT 7114 E4
10 YNKR 6393 C3
Stanley Rd
10 SOrT 6712 B6
10 WHPL 6168 E4
S Stanley Rd
10 SOrT 6712 B6
Stanley St
10 ERTH 6609 B2
10 HmpT 7027 E2
10 IrvT 6816 C1
Stanley Ter
1300 ELIZ 6917 E1
1400 HIsT 6816 D5
Stanley Keyes Ct
10 RYE 6284 A4
Stanton Av
800 ELIZ 6917 E1
900 ELIZ 6816 E7
1000 HmpT 7028 D1
Stanton Cir
10 NRCH 6281 E3
Stanton Ct
10 BRNX 6614 C4
Stanton Rd
10 TFLY 6392 C2
Stanton St
10 MHTN 119 B4
10 MHTN 6821 D3
10 NWRK 6817 C3
Stanwich St
10 STNL 7020 C5
Stanwick Pl
400 HmpT 6827 B6
Stanwix St
10 BKLN 6822 D5
Stanwood Rd
10 NHmT 6724 C5
Staple St
10 MHTN 118 C5
10 MHTN 6821 E5
Star Av
1300 HmpT 6827 E6
Star Ct
10 STNL 7116 E5
N Star Rd
10 CLST 6278 D2
Star St
10 HmpT 6827 D3
10 SFPK 6827 D3
Starboard Ct
10 BRNX 6614 C4
Starboard St
10 NWRK 6919 B1
Starbuck St
10 STNL 7020 C4
Star Farm Rd
10 HRSN 6169 C3
Starfire Ct
10 HmpT 6928 C5
10 VLYS 6928 C5
Starfire Ln
10 NHmT 6724 D4
Starke Rd
300 CARL 6609 E1
Starkey Rd
10 NoCT 6050 C3
10 WHPL 6050 C3
Starks Pl
10 HmpT 6929 A5
10 LNBK 6929 A5
Starlight Rd
10 STNL 7020 C4
Starling Av
2000 BRNX 6614 C1
Starling Ct
200 NHLS 6724 B1
Starling Rd
200 EGLD 6502 E1
Starr Av
10 STNL 7020 A2
30-00 QENS 6718 D7
36-00 QENS 6822 D1
Starr St
10 BKLN 6822 E5
17-00 BKLN 6823 A5
17-00 QENS 6823 A4
Starr Ter
10 NRCH 6281 E7
State Hwy
- JSYC 6716 A7
- JSYC 6820 B1
State Hwy SR-139
- JSYC 6716 A7
- JSYC 6820 B1
State St
- SHKT 6610 C1
10 BKLN 120 E5
10 BKLN 121 D7
10 BKLN 6821 C6
10 CART 7115 C1
10 COrT 6712 D2
10 EORG 6712 D2
10 HKSK 6501 C1
10 JSYC 6820 A3
10 MHTN 120 B3
10 MHTN 6821 A5
10 MNCH 6501 C7
10 MNCH 6610 C1
10 NRCH 6396 A2
10 NWRK 6713 D6
10 PTHA 7114 E7
10 PTHA 7205 D5
10 STNL 6919 E7
10 VLYS 6928 C2
10 WbgT 7114 E7
1200 HIsT 6816 D6
State St CO-56
10 HKSK 6501 C1
State St CO-611
10 PTHA 7114 E7
10 WbgT 7114 E7
300 PTHA 7205 E2
E State St
200 LBCH 7029 D6
S State St
10 HKSK 6501 B2
100 SHKT 6501 B2
1100 HIsT 6816 C6
State Line Lookout
- ALPN 6279 B1
State Line Lookout Access
- ALPN 6279 B2
Staten Island Blvd
10 STNL 7020 B4
Staten Island Expwy
- STNL 6918 B7
- STNL 7018 D1
- STNL 7019 A4
- STNL 7020 A4
- STNL 7021 A5
Staten Island Expwy I-278
- STNL 6918 B7
- STNL 7018 D1
- STNL 7019 D4
- STNL 7020 A4
- STNL 7021 A5
Staten Island Expwy SR-440
- STNL 7018 E2
- STNL 7019 A3
Staten Island Fy
- MHTN 120 B3
- MHTN 6821 A5
- STNL 6920 E5

New York City/5 Borough Street Index

STREET
Block City Map# Grid

Staten Island Ferry Viaduct
- STNL 6920 E6
Staten Island Mall Dr
10 STNL 7116 E1
Statewide Ct
10 SECS 6610 C6
Station Av
10 STNL 7206 D2
Station Ct
10 CLST 6278 A3
Station Dr
10 GrbT 6167 D4
Station Pkwy
10 LEON 6502 C4
Station Pl
200 MTVN 6395 B3
800 HmpT 7028 B1
Station Plz
- MRNK 6282 E5
10 DBSF 6165 D3
10 HmpT 7028 D3
10 ISPK 7029 D5
10 LNBK 6929 B4
10 LWRN 7027 B3
10 NRCH 6395 C5
10 RDFP 6501 D5
10 RYE 6284 B1
1200 HmpT 6928 E7
Station Plz N
200 MNLA 6724 E7
N Station Plz
10 GTPZ 6617 A7
S Station Plz
10 GTPZ 6617 C4
Station Rd
- NWRK 6817 C5
10 GTNK 6617 B6
10 IRVN 6166 A1
10 KENS 6617 B6
10 KNGP 6617 B5
10 NHmT 6617 B5
100 MNLA 6724 D7
172-00 QENS 6721 D4
Station Sq
10 QENS 6824 D3
10 RTFD 6609 B2
Staub Ct
10 MRNK 6282 C4
Stauderman Av
10 LNBK 6929 B4
Staunton St
10 YNKR 6394 B2
Steadman Pl
400 PTHA 7205 C3
Steamboat Dr
10 PTWN 6508 C6
Steamboat Rd
10 GTNK 6616 E4
100 KNGP 6616 C4
Stearns Rdg
10 IRVN 6048 B7
Stearns St
2300 BRNX 6505 C7
Stebbins Av
10 EchT 6281 B6
10 STNL 6920 A7
10 TCKA 6281 B6
1300 BRNX 6613 D1
Stecher St
- IrvT 6816 D4
10 NWRK 6816 D3
10 STNL 7116 B7
10 STNL 7207 C1
Stedman Pl
2500 BRNX 6505 C4
Steele Av
10 STNL 7117 E1
Steele St
1500 HmpT 6827 D5
Steenwick Av
3400 BRNX 6505 E1
Steers St
10 STNL 7019 C6
Stegman Ct
10 JSYC 6819 C4
Stegman Pkwy
200 JSYC 6819 C4
Stegman Pl
10 JSYC 6819 C4
Stegman St
10 JSYC 6819 D5
Stegman Ter
10 JSYC 6819 C4
Stein Av
10 WLTN 6500 A5
Stein St
10 VLYS 6928 C3
Steinberg Av
10 GRFD 6500 A1
Steiner St
10 CART 7017 C7
10 CART 7115 A1
Steinway Av
10 STNL 7019 A6
100 STNL 7018 E6
Steinway Pl
10 QENS 6719 C1
Steinway St
17-00 QENS 6719 B2
36-96 QENS 6718 E5
Stelfox St
10 DMRT 6278 A5
Stell Pl
1000 BRNX 6505 B4
Stella Ct
100 LNBK 6929 B5
Stellar Av
400 PLHM 6395 B5
400 PLMM 6395 B5
Stellar Pl
10 PLMM 6395 B6
Stelton St
600 TnkT 6502 B2
Stengel Av
10 NWRK 6817 A4
Stenson Av
10 SCLF 6509 D7
Stephanie Dr
10 GrbT 6167 B5
244-00 QENS 6928 A4
244-00 VLYS 6928 A4
Stephanie Ln
10 WbgT 7114 E2

Stephen Av
10 NHmT 6723 E6
700 PTHA 7114 B7
700 PTHA 7205 B1
700 WbgT 7114 B7
Stephen Dr
10 EGLC 6392 C6
10 TYTN 6048 C5
Stephen Ln
10 NHmT 6724 D1
Stephen Lp
10 STNL 7018 E6
Stephen Pl
10 VLYS 6928 C1
1300 HmpT 6928 D1
Stephen St
16-00 QENS 6823 C6
Stephen Crane Plz
- NWRK 6713 D3
Stephen Gregg Dr
- COrT 6712 C5
- EORG 6712 C5
- SOrT 6712 B5
Stephen Marc Ln
10 NHmT 6723 D6
Stephens Av
100 BRNX 6614 C4
Stephens Ct
10 BKLN 6923 B7
Stephens Ln
10 GrbT 6049 E3
10 MtPT 6049 E4
Stephens Rd
10 NVLE 6164 B3
10 OrgT 6164 B3
Stephens St
10 BlvT 6714 B1
Stephenson Blvd
10 NRCH 6396 A3
Stepney St
10 STNL 7019 A7
Stepping Stone Ln
10 KNGP 6616 C4
Stepping Stones
10 HAOH 6280 A1
Sterling Av
10 HRSN 6283 A4
10 JSYC 6819 C5
10 OrgT 6164 B2
10 STNL 7117 E2
10 STNL 7118 A2
10 WhkT 6716 B3
10 WHPL 6168 A3
10 YNKR 6394 B5
300 MRNK 6283 B5
Sterling Ct
10 PTHA 7114 C7
Sterling Dr
10 BKLN 7021 D4
Sterling Ln
10 SNPT 6508 C5
Sterling Pl
10 BKLN 6922 E1
10 EDGW 103 A7
10 EDGW 6502 E7
10 EDGW 6503 A7
10 ELIZ 6917 E3
10 LWRN 7028 B3
10 MLVN 6929 C2
10 TnkT 6502 A1
100 BKLN 6923 B2
1600 BKLN 6924 A2
Sterling Plz
10 NHLS 6724 B2
Sterling Rd
10 HmpT 6827 B5
10 KNGP 6617 A4
200 HRSN 6283 B1
300 HRSN 6169 A7
1000 UnnT 6816 B7
Sterling St
10 BKLN 6923 B4
Stern Av
10 KRNY 6715 B7
Stern Ct
10 STNL 7117 B5
Sterner Rd
900 HlsT 6816 E7
900 HlsT 6917 E1
Stetson St
500 COrT 6712 B3
Steuben Av
10 OrgT 6164 B2
3200 BRNX 6504 E2
Steuben St
10 BKLN 6822 A6
10 EORG 6713 A5
10 JSYC 6820 C3
400 STNL 7020 D5
Steuerwald Pl
10 PTHA 7205 B2
Steve Flanders Sq
10 MHTN 118 C7
10 MHTN 6821 A3
Steven Av
400 HmpT 6828 C6
Steven Dr
10 HmpT 6928 C6
10 VLYS 6928 C6
Steven Ln
10 KNGP 6617 A3
Stevens Av
10 GDNC 6828 E4
10 HMPD 6828 E4
10 HmpT 6828 E4
10 YNKR 6394 B4
100 JSYC 6819 C5
100 MTVN 6394 D4
100 SAMB 7205 C7
N Stevens Av
200 SAMB 7205 B7
N Stevens Av CO-686
200 SAMB 7205 B7
Stevens Ct
10 HmpT 6828 A3
10 STMN 6828 A4
2900 HmpT 6929 E7
Stevens Pl
- BRNX 6615 C2
10 GrbT 6167 D3
10 LWRN 7027 E4
10 NARL 6714 B1
200 HmpT 7028 B1
Stevens Rd
10 WLTN 6500 A4

Stevens St
10 WHPL 6167 C2
10 WHPL 6168 C4
2700 HmpT 6929 E6
Stevenson Av
10 GrbT 6167 A2
Stevenson Cir
1400 HmpT 6928 E6
Stevenson Dr
10 SDRK 6616 D6
Stevenson Pl
10 BRNX 6504 C1
10 KRNY 6714 A3
10 STNL 7206 E3
400 PTHA 7205 C2
Stevenson Rd
10 HmpT 6928 E6
1300 HBPK 6928 E6
Stevenson St
10 LNBK 6929 A3
100 MLVN 6929 A3
700 HmpT 6928 A7
Stewart Av
10 EchT 6281 B4
10 GDNC 6828 B2
10 IrvT 6816 B4
10 NHPK 6828 A2
10 STMN 6827 E2
10 STMN 6828 A2
10 STNL 7019 B3
10 TCKA 6281 B4
100 BKLN 6822 E4
100 KRNY 6714 C2
400 FLPK 6827 E2
400 NHPK 6827 E2
1600 NHmT 6723 D6
2700 HmpT 6929 E6
7100 BKLN 7022 A1
7300 BKLN 7021 E1
Stewart Ct
- FLPK 6827 C4
- STMN 6827 C4
Stewart Dr
10 GTNE 6616 D7
Stewart Pl
10 EchT 6281 B4
10 ELIZ 6917 D5
10 SOrT 6712 A5
10 VLYS 6928 E4
10 WHPL 6168 E2
10 YNKR 6279 B7
800 HmpT 6828 A3
Stewart Rd
217-00 QENS 6722 C7
218-00 QENS 6826 C1
Stewart St
10 BKLN 6924 C1
10 FLPK 6827 D2
10 HmpT 6827 D5
10 HmpT 6928 E5
10 NHPK 6827 E2
500 RDGF 6611 C1
Stew Leonard Dr
10 YNKR 6280 B2
Stickball Blvd
600 BRNX 6614 C3
Stickney Pl
1400 BRNX 6505 C1
Stieg Av
10 STNL 7117 A4
Stier Pl
66-00 QENS 6823 C4
Stiles Av
600 MRNK 6282 E7
Stiles St
10 ELIZ 6917 C5
10 WbgT 7115 A4
N Stiles St
10 LNDN 7017 A2
N Stiles St CO-615
10 LNDN 7017 A2
S Stiles St
10 LNDN 7017 B2
S Stiles St CO-615
10 LNDN 7017 A2
Stille Ln
- NWRK 6817 B1
Stillman Ln
10 GrwT 6170 D1
Stillview Dr
10 GrwT 6170 C1
Stillwell Av
10 BKLN 7022 D5
10 YNKR 6394 C3
300 FTLE 6502 D6
1700 BRNX 6505 E5
2000 BRNX 6506 B5
2600 BKLN 7120 D1
Stillwell Pl
10 BKLN 6924 C7
Stima Av
10 CART 7017 B6
E Stimpson Av
10 LNDN 7017 B1
W Stimpson Av
10 LNDN 7017 A2
Stirling Av
100 COrT 6712 B5
100 SOrT 6712 B5
Stirling Dr E
700 COrT 6712 B5
700 SOrT 6712 B5
Stirling Dr N
100 COrT 6712 B5
100 SOrT 6712 B5
Stirling Dr W
700 COrT 6712 B5
Stirrup Ln
10 NHmT 6724 E2
Stobe Av
10 STNL 7020 B7
10 STNL 7118 B1
Stockbridge Rd
10 YNKR 6280 B4
Stockholm St
10 BKLN 6822 E6
17-00 QENS 6823 A5
100 BKLN 6823 A6
Stockman Pl
10 IrvT 6712 D7
10 NWRK 6712 D7
Stockman St
10 COrT 6712 B3
10 WOrT 6712 B3

Stockton Av
10 HlsT 6816 B5
100 JSYC 6819 C1
300 ROSL 6917 A4
Stockton Ct
100 EDGW 108 B1
100 EDGW 6611 D5
Stockton Pl
10 EORG 6713 A4
Stockton Rd
300 UnnT 6917 A1
Stockton St
10 BKLN 6822 C6
10 NWRK 6818 A3
100 SAMB 7205 C7
300 PTHA 7205 C3
Stoddard Pl
10 BKLN 6923 B3
Stokes Rd
10 YNKR 6280 C6
Stokes St
10 LODI 6500 D2
Stone Av
10 GrbT 6050 A5
10 GrwT 6170 E3
10 YNKR 6280 A6
500 HmpT 6828 A6
N Stone Av
10 EMFD 6049 A5
S Stone Av
10 EMFD 6049 A6
10 GrbT 6049 A6
Stone Ln
10 STNL 7117 A1
Stone Pl
10 BRXV 6280 E7
500 LNDN 6917 A7
Stone St
10 HmpT 6827 D5
10 MHTN 120 B2
10 MHTN 6821 A5
10 NWRK 6713 D5
10 STNL 7020 D1
1100 HlsT 6816 D7
Stone Cabin Rd
10 NRCH 6396 A1
Stone Cottage
10 HAOH 6165 E6
Stonecrest Ct
10 STNL 7117 B5
Stone Falls Ct
10 RYEB 6170 A4
Stonegate
10 OLDT 6164 A3
Stonegate Dr
10 STNL 7020 C5
Stonegate Ln
10 HRSN 6169 E7
Stoneham Pl
10 GrbT 6049 D7
Stoneham St
10 STNL 7118 A4
400 STNL 7117 E4
Stonehenge Rd
10 GTNK 6616 D6
10 NHmT 6617 D6
Stone Hill Dr E
10 NHLS 6724 B1
Stone Hill Dr N
10 NHLS 6618 A7
10 NHLS 6724 A1
Stone Hill Dr S
10 NHLS 6724 A1
Stone Hill Gate
- NHLS 6724 A1
Stonehouse Rd
10 SCDL 6167 C7
Stonehurst Ct
100 NVLE 6164 C6
Stonehurst Dr
10 TFLY 6392 B3
Stonelea Pl
10 NRCH 6396 A3
Stoneleigh Plz
10 BRXV 6280 B3
Stoneleigh Rd
10 YNKR 6281 A2
Stoneleigh Close
10 GrbT 6167 A6
Stoneleigh Manor Ln
10 HRSN 6169 D2
Stone Oaks Dr
10 GrbT 6167 C2
Stoner Av
10 GTPZ 6617 A7
10 KENS 6617 A7
10 THSN 6617 B7
Stone Tower Dr
10 ALPN 6392 D1
Stonewall Cir
10 GrbT 6049 B7
10 GrbT 6167 B1
10 HRSN 6050 D4
Stonewall Ln
10 MrnT 6282 C3
1000 SECS 6610 B6
Stoneybrook Av
1200 MRNK 6283 B5
Stoneybrook Ln
10 GrbT 6167 B6
Stoneycrest Rd
10 RYE 6284 B2
Stoneyside Dr
10 MrnT 6282 C6
Stony Run
10 NRCH 6282 A6
Stony Brook Rd
10 TFLY 6392 C2
Stonycrest Rd
10 HRSN 6050 D6
Stonygate Ovl
10 NRCH 6281 D5
Stony Hill Rd
10 HRSN 6050 E6
Stony Run Rd
10 GTNK 6616 E6
Stonytown Rd
10 PLDM 6617 D4
10 PLNM 6617 E4
200 FLHL 6617 E4
300 FLHL 6618 A4
Stoothoff Dr
10 NHmT 6724 C5

Storer Av
10 NRCH 6395 C4
10 PLHM 6395 C4
10 STNL 7115 C7
Storey Ln
10 YNKR 6280 A4
Storig Av
10 CLST 6278 A2
Storm St
10 DBSF 6166 A4
10 TYTN 6048 B2
400 HmpT 7029 C1
Storms Av
10 JSYC 6819 E2
Stormy Cir Dr
10 GrwT 6170 D6
Story Av
300 QENS 6616 A7
1400 BRNX 6613 E3
1500 BRNX 6614 A3
Story Ct
10 BAYN 6919 D5
10 BKLN 6922 D6
Story St
10 BKLN 6922 D6
Stover Av
10 KRNY 6714 C4
Strang Av
1900 BRNX 6394 D7
Stratford Av
10 GDNC 6828 C2
10 NHPK 6828 A2
10 STNL 7020 C2
10 WHPL 6168 C3
10 WLPK 6724 E4
1000 BRNX 6614 A2
1200 BRNX 6613 E1
Stratford Ct
10 DMRT 6278 A4
10 STNL 7018 E7
Stratford Dr
10 NHmT 6724 D1
Stratford Ln
10 HAOH 6165 C7
10 HAOH 6279 D1
Stratford Pl
10 IrvT 6816 C2
10 NARL 6714 D1
10 NWRK 6817 B2
W Stratford Pl
10 IrvT 6816 D3
Stratford Rd
10 BKLN 6923 A6
10 EchT 6281 B2
10 EGLC 6503 B1
10 EGLD 6503 B1
10 GrbT 6049 E7
10 HMPD 6828 E4
10 HmpT 6828 E4
10 HRSN 6169 B7
10 LNBK 6928 E5
10 MrnT 6282 B6
10 NHmT 6509 A7
10 NHmT 6618 A1
10 NRCH 6281 C7
10 VLYS 6928 E5
100 HRSN 6283 A1
Stratford St N
10 NHmT 6724 D1
Stratford St S
10 NHmT 6724 D1
Strathmore Rd
- EchT 6281 B2
10 GTNK 6616 D6
10 NHmT 6616 E6
10 NHmT 6617 E6
10 YNKR 6281 B2
Strathmore St
10 HmpT 6928 B5
N Strathmore St
10 HmpT 6928 B5
Strattford Rd
100 NHmT 6724 B5
Stratton Rd
10 HRSN 6169 D1
10 NRCH 6281 D4
10 NRCH 6282 A3
10 SCDL 6282 A3
Stratton St
10 YNKR 6280 A7
30-01 QENS 6720 E3
Stratton St S
10 YNKR 6279 E7
10 YNKR 6280 A7
Strauss St
10 BKLN 6924 A3
10 STNL 7020 E4
Strawberry Ln
10 IRVN 6048 B7
10 NHmT 6724 E2
10 STNL 7208 A1
Strawberry Hill Av
10 WbgT 7114 D5
Strawbridge Ln
10 GrwT 6170 C2
Stream Ct
10 KNGP 6616 D5
Strickland Av
10 BKLN 7024 B4
Strickland Pl
10 MNPK 6618 A5
Stringham Av
10 VLYS 6928 C3
Strong Av
101-00 QENS 6720 B7
Strong Pl
10 BKLN 120 E7
10 BKLN 6821 C7
10 BKLN 6922 C1
Strong St
10 BRNX 6504 D2
10 WLTN 6500 A5
Stronghurst Av
220-00 QENS 6826 D1
229-00 QENS 6722 E7
Stroud Av
10 STNL 7116 D5
E Stroud Av
10 STNL 7117 A4
Stryker Ct
10 BKLN 7022 E6
10 BKLN 7023 A6
Stryker St
10 BKLN 7022 E7

Stuart Av
10 HmpT 6827 B7
10 MLVN 6929 B3
600 MRNK 6283 A6
Stuart Dr
100 NRCH 6281 E3
500 HmpT 6928 B7
Stuart Ln
10 QENS 6722 D2
Stuart Pl
10 MNPK 6617 E6
10 MNPK 6618 A6
Stuart Rd
100 HmpT 6928 E5
100 VLYS 6928 E5
Stuart St
10 BKLN 7023 D4
10 GTNK 6616 E6
10 HmpT 6929 B3
10 LNBK 6929 B3
100 MLVN 6929 B2
Stuart Wy
10 GrbT 6167 B1
Studio Ct
10 RDGF 6611 C1
Studio Ln
10 BRXV 6281 A7
10 STNL 7020 D3
Studio Rd
500 RDGF 6611 C2
Studio Arc
10 BRXV 6280 E7
Sturbridge Pl
10 NRCH 6281 E1
Sturges St
10 STNL 7019 E3
Sturgis Rd
10 BRXV 6395 A1
10 MTVN 6395 A1
Sturl Av
1300 HmpT 6928 D6
Sturlane Pl
1200 HmpT 6928 D7
Stuyvesant Av
10 BKLN 6822 D7
10 EORG 6712 D6
10 JSYC 6819 E1
10 KRNY 6714 B1
10 LRMT 6396 C2
10 NWRK 6712 C7
10 RYE 6283 E6
10 STNL 7116 E6
200 BKLN 6923 E1
300 IrvT 6712 C7
300 IrvT 6816 C2
1100 UnnT 6816 A4
Stuyvesant Av CO-619
1000 IrvT 6816 A3
1100 UnnT 6816 A4
Stuyvesant Pl
10 LWRN 7028 B3
10 STNL 6920 D5
Stuyvesant Plz
10 MTVN 6395 B2
Stuyvesant St
10 MHTN 119 B2
10 MHTN 6821 D1
1600 HmpT 6827 D7
Suburban Av
10 PLMM 6395 B6
Suburban Pl
10 GrbT 6049 A7
800 BRNX 6613 D1
Suburban Rd
700 UnnT 6816 A7
Suburban Gate
10 LKSU 6723 E4
10 NHmT 6723 E4
Suburbia Ct
10 JSYC 6819 B5
Suburbia Dr
10 JSYC 6819 B5
Suburbia Ter
10 JSYC 6819 B5
Sudbury Dr
10 YNKR 6280 B4
Sudbury Pl
10 YNKR 6280 B4
Suffolk Av
10 STNL 7019 D4
Suffolk Blvd
10 ATLB 7028 B7
Suffolk Ct
10 HmpT 6929 E7
Suffolk Dr
188-00 QENS 6826 B6
Suffolk Ln
10 GDNC 6724 E7
10 TFLY 6392 B4
Suffolk Rd
10 ISPK 7029 C5
Suffolk St
10 MHTN 119 B5
10 MHTN 6821 D3
Suffolk Tr
10 YNKR 6280 B3
Sugar Maple Dr
10 NHmT 6724 C3
Sulgrave Rd
10 YNKR 6281 A1
Sullivan Dr
10 JSYC 6819 B5
Sullivan Pl
10 BKLN 6923 B3
2900 BRNX 6615 A2
Sullivan Rd
187-00 QENS 6826 B6
600 ELIZ 6918 C3
Sullivan St
10 BKLN 6922 A1
10 MHTN 118 D3
10 MHTN 6821 B2
Sully Dr
10 MNPK 6618 B6
Summer Av
10 LKSU 6723 B1
10 NHmT 6723 C1
10 NWRK 6713 D5
10 THSN 6723 B1
100 HlsT 6816 D5
700 NWRK 6714 A2
800 BlvT 6714 A1
Summer Pl
10 NWRK 6713 E3

Summer St
10 LKSU 6723 B1
10 LODI 6500 C3
10 NHmT 6723 B1
10 PTCH 6170 B5
10 STNL 7021 A4
10 THSN 6723 B1
100 COrT 6712 C2
105-00 QENS 6824 D4
200 ERTH 6609 D3
500 ELIZ 6917 E5
Summerfield Pl
10 PTCH 6170 B5
10 STNL 7019 A2
Summerfield St
10 EchT 6281 C2
10 YNKR 6394 A1
16-00 QENS 6823 C6
Summit Av
- NHmT 6722 E2
- QENS 6722 E2
10 ARDY 6166 A5
10 BRXV 6281 A7
10 GRFD 6500 A2
10 HKSK 6501 A1
10 HlsT 6816 D4
10 JSYC 6819 E3
10 LNBK 6929 B4
10 LRMT 6396 C2
10 LynT 6609 A4
10 MTVN 6395 A4
10 NRCH 6395 D2
10 NWRK 6816 D4
10 OrgT 6164 B2
10 PTCH 6170 B5
10 ROSH 6618 E5
10 RTFD 6609 A4
10 RYE 6283 D1
10 SCLF 6509 E6
10 STNL 7117 D1
10 TCKA 6281 A7
10 WHPL 6168 A3
100 BGTA 6501 E2
100 CLFP 108 A1
100 CLFP 6611 C4
100 JSYC 6820 A3
100 MTVN 6394 E3
300 CDHT 7028 A2
300 LEON 6502 D5
300 PTHA 7205 D1
400 CARL 6500 C7
400 FTLE 6502 E5
500 JSYC 6716 C5
500 UNCT 6716 C4
900 BRNX 107 D1
900 BRNX 6612 E1
Summit Av CO-57
10 HKSK 6501 A1
E Summit Av
10 WbgT 7114 E4
S Summit Av
10 HKSK 6501 A1
200 HSBH 6501 A2
S Summit Av CO-57
10 HKSK 6501 A1
200 HSBH 6501 A2
Summit Cir
10 LFRY 6501 C5
Summit Cross
10 RTFD 6609 A2
Summit Ct
10 HKSK 6501 B2
10 QENS 6720 E5
Summit Dr
10 HAOH 6166 A6
10 PLNH 6617 C5
Summit Ln
10 NHmT 6724 E2
Summit Pl
10 LFRY 6501 C5
10 PLNH 6617 D5
10 STNL 7116 D7
100 BRNX 102 E3
100 BRNX 6504 C2
100 JSYC 6819 E2
100 JSYC 6920 C1
144-00 QENS 6615 A6
1300 UnnT 6816 B7
Summit Rd
10 ALPN 6278 E6
10 ELIZ 6917 B3
10 KNGP 6616 C4
10 NHmT 6509 B7
10 NHmT 6618 A1
10 STNL 7206 A4
100 UnnT 6917 B2
Summit St
10 BKLN 6922 B1
10 EchT 6281 B6
10 EGLC 6503 A3
10 EGLD 6503 B2
10 EMFD 6049 B6
10 EORG 6712 E3
10 EORG 6713 A3
10 FTLE 6503 A3
10 GrbT 6049 B6
10 HAOH 6279 D1
10 HSBH 6500 D5
10 NRWD 6164 A7
10 NWRK 6713 D6
10 RDFP 6501 E4
10 STNL 7206 B4
10 TYTN 6048 B4
10 WRDG 6500 D5
10 YNKR 6279 B7
10 YNKR 6393 D1
400 NVLE 6164 B5
500 EGLC 6392 C7
N Summit St
10 TFLY 6392 B1
S Summit St
10 TFLY 6392 A2
Summit Ter
10 CLFP 6611 D3
10 DBSF 6166 C4
Summitt Pl
10 MtPT 6050 A3
Sumner Av
10 BKLN 6822 D6
10 STNL 7019 A3
10 YNKR 6394 B2
300 BKLN 6923 D1
Sumner Pl
10 BKLN 6822 E4
200 STNL 6920 C7
Sumo Village Ct
10 NWRK 6817 D2

Sumpter Pl
10 QENS 6928 A3
10 VLYS 6928 A3
Sumpter St
10 BKLN 6923 E1
10 BKLN 6924 A1
Sumter Av
10 EWLS 6724 A6
Sumutka Av
10 CART 7115 C1
Sumutka Ct
10 CART 7115 B1
10 WbgT 7115 B1
Sun Av
1300 HmpT 6827 E5
Sunapee Rd
1000 HmpT 6929 C1
Sunbury Rd
- QENS 6927 B1
176-00 QENS 6826 B7
Suncliff Dr
10 TYTN 6048 C2
Sundale Pl
10 GrbT 6167 A5
Sunderland Av
10 RTFD 6500 A7
Sunderland Rd
10 TFLY 6392 C4
Sunfield Av
10 STNL 7116 D4
Sunhaven Ct
10 TYTN 6048 C2
Sunhaven Dr
10 NRCH 6396 A3
Sunlight Hl
10 YNKR 6394 A3
Sunny Ln
300 HmpT 6828 B3
Sunnybrae Pl
10 BRXV 6395 A1
Sunnybrook Rd
10 YNKR 6280 C7
10 YNKR 6394 C1
Sunnyfield Ln
10 HmpT 6928 A4
Sunny Hill Dr
10 HRSN 6283 B4
10 MRNK 6283 B4
Sunnymeade Vil
10 STNL 7020 D7
10 STNL 7021 B6
Sunny Ridge Plz
10 HRSN 6283 C2
Sunny Ridge Rd
10 NRCH 6281 E3
100 HRSN 6283 C2
Sunnyside Av
10 BKLN 6924 D1
10 HRSN 6283 D3
10 TYTN 6048 C3
1200 MRNK 6283 B6
Sunnyside Ct
10 BKLN 6924 D1
Sunnyside Dr
10 CART 7017 C7
10 HRSN 6283 C3
10 YNKR 6393 B3
E Sunnyside Ln
10 IRVN 6048 B6
10 TYTN 6048 B6
400 GrbT 6048 C6
W Sunnyside Ln
10 IRVN 6048 A6
10 TYTN 6048 A6
Sunnyside Pl
10 GrbT 6048 C7
10 IRVN 6048 C7
10 WbgT 7114 D3
Sunnyside St
13-00 QENS 7027 B4
Sunnyside Ter
10 EchT 6281 C5
10 EORG 6712 D6
10 NWRK 6712 D6
10 STNL 7020 B3
Sunnyside Wy
10 NRCH 6281 D5
Sunny Slope Ter
10 YNKR 6280 B4
Sunnyvale Rd
10 FLHL 6618 B5
Sunny View Ln
10 NRCH 6281 E2
Sunrise Dr
10 LNBK 6929 A5
Sunrise Hwy
10 LNBK 6929 A4
10 RKVC 6929 E4
240-00 QENS 6927 E3
245-00 QENS 6928 A3
248-00 HmpT 6928 A3
248-00 VLYS 6928 A3
800 LNBK 6928 E4
Sunrise Hwy SR-27
10 LNBK 6929 C4
10 RKVC 6929 E4
240-00 QENS 6927 E3
245-00 QENS 6928 A3
248-00 HmpT 6928 A3
248-00 VLYS 6928 A3
800 LNBK 6928 E4
E Sunrise Hwy
10 VLYS 6928 D4
200 LNBK 6928 E4
E Sunrise Hwy SR-27
10 VLYS 6928 D4
200 LNBK 6928 E4
W Sunrise Hwy
10 VLYS 6928 B3
600 HmpT 6928 A3
700 QENS 6928 A3
W Sunrise Hwy SR-27
10 VLYS 6928 B3
600 HmpT 6928 A3
700 QENS 6928 A3
Sunrise Ln
10 GrbT 6280 E1
Sunrise Plz
10 VLYS 6928 C4
Sunrise Ter
10 STNL 7020 C1
10 YNKR 6279 E5
Sunset Av
10 BAYN 6819 A7
10 BRXV 6280 E7

Sunset Av
10 EORG 6712 D6
10 HmpT 6929 A5
10 HmpT 7029 D5
10 LNBK 6929 A5
10 NWRK 6712 D7
10 OybT 6618 E1
10 STNL 7019 C5
200 EGLD 6502 E2
200 EGLD 6503 A2
Sunset Blvd
100 BRNX 6614 C5
Sunset Cir
- IRVN 6166 B1
Sunset Ct
- BKLN 7120 A1
10 CART 7017 C7
400 FTLE 6502 E4
Sunset Dr
10 FLHL 6617 E5
10 NHmT 6724 C4
10 SCDL 6281 D1
10 WbgT 7115 B2
10 WHPL 6050 C7
10 YNKR 6394 A2
500 HmpT 6928 B6
Sunset Ln
10 GDNC 6828 D4
10 GrbT 6167 B4
10 HRSN 6168 E7
10 HRSN 6282 E1
10 HRSN 6283 D1
10 NHmT 6618 A1
10 RYE 6283 D1
10 STNL 7206 B4
10 TFLY 6392 A2
Sunset Pl
100 PALP 6502 C7
N Sunset Pl
1600 UnnT 6816 B6
Sunset Rd
10 CRSK 6278 B6
10 DMRT 6278 A6
10 KNGP 6616 B3
10 LWRN 7027 B3
10 RYE 6283 C6
10 RYEB 6169 E5
10 VLYS 6928 D2
100 MRNK 6282 E4
Sunset Rd N
10 NHmT 6724 D2
Sunset Rd S
10 NHmT 6724 D3
Sunset Rd W
10 NHmT 6724 C2
S Sunset Rd
10 LWRN 7027 E3
Sunset St
10 HAOH 6166 A7
Sunset Ter
- BKLN 6922 A6
10 IrvT 6816 A3
300 MNLA 6724 D6
400 FRVW 6611 C2
400 RDGF 6611 C2
Sunset Tr
10 BRNX 6615 B4
Sunset Wy
10 TYTN 6048 C2
Sunset Hill Dr
10 STNL 7020 B2
Sunset Key
100 SECS 6609 D7
Sunshine Av
700 HmpT 6929 D1
Sunshine Cottage Rd
- MtPT 6049 B1
Sunview Dr
10 GLCV 6509 D3
Superior Rd
10 BLRS 6827 A3
10 FLPK 6827 A3
23800 HmpT 6827 A3
Superior St
200 HlsT 6816 D7
Supor Blvd
10 HRSN 6714 B6
Surf Av
10 BKLN 7121 A2
300 BKLN 7120 B2
500 STNL 7206 A5
Surf Dr
100 BRNX 6614 C5
Surf Rd
31-00 QENS 7027 B6
Surf Side Plz
10 STNL 7206 B5
Surprise St
1300 HmpT 6827 D5
Surrey Coms
10 LNBK 6928 E5
10 VLYS 6928 E5
100 LNBK 6929 A5
Surrey Dr
10 NRCH 6281 E4
Surrey Ln
10 GTNK 6617 A5
10 NHmT 6724 B5
10 VLYS 6929 A2
10 YNKR 6280 B3
Surrey Pl
80-00 QENS 6825 E2
Surrey Rd
10 NHmT 6723 A2
10 NHmT 6724 A5
100 HlsT 6917 D1
Surrey Wy
10 GrbT 6049 A7
10 GrbT 6167 B1
Surrey Close
10 GrbT 6167 B1
Surry Ct
10 JSYC 6819 A4
Susan Av
400 NVLE 6164 C4
Susan Ct
10 OLDT 6164 A3
10 STNL 7020 D2
10 VLYS 6928 D4
10 WHPL 6168 C6
400 HmpT 6928 D6
Susan Dr
10 CLST 6278 D2
Susan Pl
1000 UnnT 6816 A6

Susanna Ln

New York City/5 Borough Street Index

Tier St

STREET
Block City Map# Grid

Susanna Ln
10 STNL 7116 C5
Susquehanna Av
10 RSLG 6723 B1
10 THSN 6723 B1
100 NHmT 6723 C1
Sussex Av
10 BRXV 6395 A1
10 EORG 6713 A5
10 NWRK 6713 B5
10 STNL 7019 E5
Sussex Dr
10 NHmT 6618 B6
Sussex Grn
- STNL 7116 A5
Sussex Pl
10 YNKR 6394 C1
Sussex Rd
10 HmpT 6827 B5
10 NHmT 6723 B2
10 NRCH 6281 E5
10 NRCH 6282 A6
10 TFLY 6392 A3
400 WRDG 6500 D5
Sussex St
10 HKSK 6501 B1
10 JSYC 6820 D3
10 WbgT 7114 A1
100 HRSN 6713 E6
100 HRSN 6714 A6
Sussex Av Connector
- NWRK 6713 C6
Sutherland St
100 BRNX 6506 D5
Sutphin Blvd
90-46 QENS 6825 D7
115-00 QENS 6926 D1
Sutro Pl
10 GrwT 6170 B1
Sutro St
86-00 QENS 6826 B2
Sutter Av
10 BKLN 6924 D2
84-00 QENS 6925 D2
137-00 QENS 6926 D2
1100 BKLN 6925 A2
Sutton Av
- LODI 6500 E1
200 HKSK 6501 A1
Sutton Ct
10 KENS 6617 A6
Sutton Ln
10 HmpT 6928 C6
10 VLYS 6928 C6
Sutton Ovl
10 YNKR 6279 C6
Sutton Pl
- WbgT 7114 A4
10 EGLD 6392 A7
10 LWRN 7027 E3
10 MHTN 117 C1
10 MHTN 6718 C4
10 NHLS 6724 B1
10 STNL 7116 B5
71-00 QENS 6825 C1
200 HRPK 6164 A6
200 NRWD 6164 A6
300 HmpT 6928 B7
300 HmpT 7028 D3
Sutton Pl S
10 LWRN 7027 E4
10 MHTN 117 B2
10 MHTN 6718 A5
Sutton Sq
10 MHTN 117 C1
10 MHTN 6718 C4
Sutton St
10 BKLN 6822 D2
100 PTHA 7205 D2
Sutton Crest
10 NHmT 6618 A7
Sutton Hill Ln
10 NHmT 6724 A4
Sutton Manor Ln
10 NRCH 6396 A5
Sutton Manor Rd
10 NRCH 6396 A4
Suydam Av
200 JSYC 6820 A4
Suydam Pl
10 BKLN 6923 E2
Suydam St
10 BKLN 6822 E6
17-00 BKLN 6823 A5
18-00 QENS 6823 A4
Suzette Ln
10 MtPT 6049 E1
Swaim Av
10 STNL 7207 C2
Swaine Pl
10 WOrT 6712 B2
Swale Rd
10 HmpT 6828 A7
Swan Ct
10 ERTH 6500 A7
10 JSYC 6819 A4
200 NHLS 6724 C1
Swan St
10 OrgT 6165 A5
10 STNL 6920 D7
Swanston Ln
10 ARDY 6166 C5
Swarthmore Dr
10 CART 7017 C7
Swarthmore Rd
10 SCDL 6282 A3
Sweet Briar Rd
10 ARDY 6166 C6
Sweetbrook Rd
10 STNL 7116 E5
Sweetfield Cir
10 YNKR 6394 A2
Sweetland Av
500 HlsT 6816 B5
Sweetman Av
1300 HmpT 6827 D5
Sweetwater Av
10 STNL 7117 B7
Swift Av
10 EchT 6281 C3
Swinnerton St
10 STNL 7206 B5
Swinton Av
700 BRNX 6615 A2
800 BRNX 6614 E1
Sybil St
10 WHPL 6167 E2
Sybilla St
69-00 QENS 6824 C4
Sycamore Av
- BKLN 7022 E2
- STNL 7019 E7
- STNL 7117 D1
10 FLPK 6827 E1
10 MTVN 6395 A4
10 NHmT 6827 E1
10 NRCH 6395 D6
10 OybT 6618 E1
5000 BRNX 6393 B6
Sycamore Ct
10 HRSN 6051 B5
10 LBCH 7029 C6
Sycamore Dr
10 FLHL 6618 C5
10 GTNE 6616 E7
10 SNPT 6508 B5
100 NHmT 6724 C5
Sycamore Ln
10 IRVN 6166 B1
10 NHmT 6724 E2
10 PTCH 6170 B4
10 WHPL 6168 E6
10 WHPL 6169 A6
Sycamore Rd
10 BAYN 6819 B6
10 GLCV 6509 D3
10 HmpT 6928 B5
10 JSYC 6819 B6
10 SCDL 6168 B7
Sycamore St
10 BRXV 6281 A7
10 CART 7115 C1
10 CRSK 6392 A1
10 HmpT 6828 D5
10 STNL 7117 A6
200 STNL 7116 E7
Sydney Av
10 MLVN 6929 B1
Sydney Pl
10 STNL 7117 E1
Sylva Ln
10 STNL 7021 A3
Sylvan Av
10 EchT 6281 B5
10 EGLC 6503 B3
10 FTLE 6503 B4
10 LFRY 6501 C5
10 NWRK 6714 A1
10 TCKA 6281 B5
100 LEON 6502 C5
500 EGLC 101 A1
500 EGLC 6392 D7
600 MRNK 6282 E7
900 TFLY 6392 D6
5400 BRNX 6393 C5
Sylvan Av US-9W
10 EGLC 6503 B3
10 FTLE 6503 B4
500 EGLC 101 A1
500 EGLC 6392 C7
900 TFLY 6392 D6
Sylvan Av US-46
10 LFRY 6501 C5
E Sylvan Av
10 NWRK 6714 A1
Sylvan Blvd
- ALPN 6392 D3
- EGLC 6392 D6
- TFLY 6392 D4
Sylvan Blvd US-9W
- ALPN 6392 D3
- EGLC 6392 D6
- TFLY 6392 D4
Sylvan Ct
10 STNL 7206 C4
1600 HmpT 6827 D7
Sylvan Dr
200 HmpT 6828 C7
Sylvan Ln
10 SCDL 6168 C7
900 MRNK 6282 E7
Sylvan Pl
10 NRCH 6396 A2
10 RYE 6284 A2
10 STNL 6919 A7
10 VLYS 6928 D5
Sylvan Rd
10 PTCH 6170 A3
10 RYEB 6170 A3
10 WHPL 6168 D7
Sylvan St
10 RTFD 6609 A3
100 FTLE 103 B2
100 FTLE 6503 A5
1100 LNDN 7017 A3
Sylvan Ter
10 MHTN 107 B1
10 MHTN 6612 B1
Sylvan Wy
500 COrT 6712 B4
Sylvanleigh Rd
10 HRSN 6169 D4
Sylvaton Ter
10 STNL 7020 E2
10 STNL 7021 A3
Sylvestar Av
- QENS 6616 A6
Sylvester Pl
10 LNBK 6929 A4
Sylvia Ln
10 ARDY 6166 D3
10 NHmT 6723 E6
Sylvia Pl
800 WbgT 7114 C2
Sylvia St
10 OybT 6618 E1
10 STNL 7116 E6
Syms Wy
10 SECS 6610 A7
10 SECS 6716 A1
Synott Pl
10 NWRK 6712 B7
Syracuse St
10 WLPK 6724 E3
Syringa Pl
42-00 QENS 6721 A4
Szold Pl
10 MHTN 119 E3
10 MHTN 6821 E2

T

Taaffe Pl
10 BKLN 6822 B6
Tabb Pl
10 STNL 7019 C1
Tabor Ct
1200 BKLN 7022 B1
Tacoma St
10 STNL 7020 C5
Taconic Tr
10 HRSN 6283 B1
Taconic State Pkwy
- MtPT 6049 E1
- MtPT 6050 A2
- NoCT 6050 B3
Taft Av
10 HmpT 7027 D2
10 LNBK 6929 A4
10 STNL 6920 C7
10 YNKR 6394 B1
100 LBCH 7029 E7
Taft Ct
10 STNL 7019 C5
Taft Ln
10 ARDY 6166 D5
Taft Pl
10 IrvT 6816 D2
10 NHmT 6724 D3
300 HRSN 6714 A7
Taft St
10 HAOH 6166 B7
800 HmpT 6828 D7
Tahoe St
150-00 QENS 6925 E3
Tain Dr
10 NHmT 6723 A2
10 RSLG 6723 A1
Taipei Ct
114-00 QENS 6614 C7
Talarico Ct
10 STNL 7019 D5
Talbot Av
800 HmpT 6928 A6
Talbot Dr
10 LKSU 6723 C1
Talbot Ln
10 GrwT 6170 D5
Talbot Pl
- ISPK 7029 C4
10 STNL 7020 E2
Talbot St
10 NHmT 6724 C4
83-00 QENS 6824 D5
83-00 QENS 6825 A4
Talcott Rd
10 RYEB 6169 E4
Talfor Rd
10 ERKY 6929 B6
Tallman St
10 STNL 7116 D7
Tall Trees Rd
10 NRCH 6282 A3
10 SCDL 6282 A3
Tall Tulip Ln
10 YNKR 6280 D3
Tallwood Dr
10 GrbT 6167 D2
Tamarac Cir
10 HRSN 6283 B1
Tamarac Tr
10 HRSN 6283 B2
Tamarack Pl
10 GrwT 6170 C1
Tamarack Rd
10 ALPN 6278 D7
10 ALPN 6392 D1
10 CRSK 6278 D7
10 RYEB 6170 A4
Tamarack Tr
10 GrbT 6167 C6
Tamcrest Ct
10 ALPN 6392 D1
10 CRSK 6392 D2
Tameling Rd
10 ERKY 6929 B7
Tamerton St
10 MTVN 6395 A2
Tammie Hill Rd
10 OrgT 6164 D1
Tam O'Shanter Dr
10 HRSN 6050 E7
Tampa Rd
200 MHTN 120 A5
200 MHTN 6821 A6
Tanglewood Cross
100 LWRN 7028 B4
Tanglewood Dr
10 STNL 7117 B3
Tanglewood Ln
10 SCLF 6509 D7
Tanglewood Rd
10 GrbT 6280 E1
10 GrbT 6281 A1
10 HmpT 6929 C3
1400 LNBK 6929 C3
Tanglewylde Av
10 BRXV 6280 E7
10 BRXV 6281 A7
Tanners Rd
10 LKSU 6723 D4
Tanners Pond Rd
10 GDNC 6828 B2
100 NHmT 6828 B2
Tanwood Dr
600 HmpT 6828 D7
Tappan Plz
10 OrgT 6164 C4
Tappan Rd
10 HRPK 6164 A7
10 NRWD 6164 A7
400 NVLE 6164 B4
500 OrgT 6164 C3
Tappan Rd CO-39
10 HRPK 6164 A7
10 NRWD 6164 A7
400 NVLE 6164 B5
500 OrgT 6164 C3
Tappan St
10 KRNY 6714 B5
Tappan Ter
10 ARDY 6166 D3
Tappan Landing Rd
10 TYTN 6048 B3
N Tappan Landing Rd
10 TYTN 6048 C4
Tappan Zee Br
- TYTN 6048 A3
Tappan Zee Br I-87
- TYTN 6048 A3
Tappan Zee Br I-287
- TYTN 6048 A3
Tappen Ct
10 STNL 7020 D2
Tappen St
10 WbgT 7114 B2
E Tappen St
10 WbgT 7115 B2
Tapscott St
10 BKLN 6924 A4
Tara Wy
10 TCKA 6281 A6
Taras Shevchenko Pl
10 MHTN 119 B3
10 MHTN 6821 C2
Tarboro St
10 HmpT 6827 C4
Targee St
10 STNL 7020 C5
Tarlee Pl
10 STNL 7117 B6
Tarlton St
10 STNL 7117 E5
10 STNL 7118 A5
Tarring St
10 STNL 7117 D3
Tarry Pl
10 TYTN 6048 B4
Tarry Hill Rd
10 TYTN 6048 B6
Tarryhill Wy
100 GrbT 6049 D6
Tarrytown Av
10 STNL 7117 E4
Tarrytown Rd
- WHPL 6167 E1
10 GrbT 6167 E1
10 WHPL 6168 A1
200 GrbT 6049 C7
Tarrytown Rd SR-100
- WHPL 6167 E1
- WHPL 6168 A1
10 GrbT 6049 E7
10 GrbT 6167 E1
Tarrytown Rd SR-100B
200 GrbT 6049 D7
Tarrytown Rd SR-119
- WHPL 6167 E1
10 GrbT 6167 E1
10 WHPL 6168 A1
200 GrbT 6049 C7
Tarrytown-White Plains Rd
- EMFD 6048 E5
- GrbT 6048 E5
Tarrytwn-White Plns Rd SR-119
- EMFD 6048 E5
- GrbT 6048 E5
Tate Av
10 PRMT 6165 B1
Tate St
10 STNL 7019 B1
Tatro St
10 STNL 7117 D4
Tatterson St
10 RSLN 6618 C5
Taunton Rd
10 SCDL 6281 C1
Taunton Rd E
10 SCDL 6281 C1
Taunton St
10 STNL 7117 C4
Taxi Ln
10 NoCT 6051 C2
Taxter Pl
10 STNL 7020 D1
Taxter Rd
10 GrbT 6048 D6
500 EMFD 6048 E5
Taylor Av
10 CART 7017 C7
10 CART 7115 C1
10 HRSN 6168 D1
300 BRNX 6614 B2
300 HKSK 6501 C4
400 SHkT 6501 C4
1300 BRNX 6505 A7
N Taylor Av
400 SHkT 6501 C4
Taylor Ct
10 STNL 6919 E7
Taylor Dr
10 CLST 6278 D3
Taylor Ln
10 HRSN 6283 A1
Taylor Pl
10 GrbT 6049 D3
10 MrnT 6396 C1
10 MtPT 6049 D3
Taylor Rd
10 GrbT 6049 C3
10 MtPT 6049 C3
100 HmpT 6929 C1
Taylor Sq
10 HRSN 6050 D6
Taylor St
10 BKLN 6822 A5
10 LFRY 6501 B5
10 NWRK 6713 D4
10 STNL 6919 E7
100 COrT 6712 C3
200 STNL 7019 E1
Taylors Ln
400 MRNK 6283 B5
Taymil Rd
10 NRCH 6281 D6
Tea Pl
10 OrgT 6164 A2
Teakwood Ct
10 STNL 7117 B3
Teakwood Wy
10 WbgT 7114 A2
Teal Plz
400 SECS 6715 D1
Teaneck Rd
10 RDFP 6501 E5
10 TnkT 6502 A4
300 RDFP 6502 A5
Teaneck Rd CO-39
10 TnkT 6502 A4
100 RDFP 6501 E5
300 RDFP 6502 A5
Teaneck Rd CO-50
10 RDFP 6501 E7
Teaticket Ct
10 HmpT 6929 B6
Tech Pl
10 BKLN 121 B5
10 BKLN 6821 D6
Tecumseh Av
100 MTVN 6395 A5
Ted Pl
10 STNL 7020 B4
Tee Ct
900 HmpT 6928 B7
Teena Pl
10 OrgT 6164 D2
Tehama St
10 BKLN 6922 D6
Teillaud St
10 GrbT 6167 E1
Tekening Dr
10 TFLY 6392 C3
Telegram Av
1200 HmpT 6827 E5
Teleport Dr
10 STNL 7018 C5
Telford St
10 EORG 6712 D5
10 NWRK 6712 C6
Teller Av
800 BRNX 6613 B2
1300 BRNX 105 D7
1400 BRNX 6504 D7
Tellicherry Ct
10 JSYC 6819 A4
Temple Ct
10 BKLN 6922 E4
10 STNL 7018 C6
Temple Dr
10 NHmT 6617 E3
Temple Pl
10 IrvT 6816 C4
Temple Rd
10 DBSF 6166 B3
Temple St
10 HRSN 6283 B3
10 WLPK 6724 E4
Temple Ter
100 PALP 6502 C7
E Tenafly Av
10 STNL 7116 D7
Tenafly Ct
10 TFLY 6392 A3
Tenafly Dr
10 NHmT 6724 C5
Tenafly Pl
10 STNL 7116 C7
Tenafly Rd
10 TFLY 6392 A3
Tenakill Dr
400 NVLE 6164 B3
Tenakill Pk E
10 CRSK 6278 A7
Tenakill Pk W
1100 CRSK 6278 A7
Tenakill Rd
10 CRSK 6278 A7
Tenakill St
10 CLST 6278 A3
Tenbroeck Av
2200 BRNX 6505 C5
Tenby Dr
10 GrbT 6166 C7
Teneyck Av
10 VLYS 6928 D2
Ten Eyck St
400 BKLN 6822 E4
Ten Eyck Wk
10 BKLN 6822 D4
Tennessee Av
10 LBCH 7028 E7
Tennessee Rd
10 STNL 7021 A5
Tennessee St
10 FLPK 6827 D3
10 HmpT 6827 D3
10 SFPK 6827 D3
Tenney Pl
10 BRNX 105 A4
10 BRNX 6504 A6
Tennis Ct
- GrbT 6166 C6
10 BKLN 6923 A6
200 HmpT 6828 B3
Tennis Pl
10 QENS 6824 D3
Tennyson Dr
10 STNL 7117 B7
500 STNL 7208 A1
Tennyson St
10 CART 7017 C7
10 GrbT 6167 B2
Teramar Wy
10 GrbT 6167 D1
10 SCDL 6168 D7
10 WHPL 6168 D7
Teresa Av
10 YNKR 6394 A3
Teresa Ct
10 LFRY 6501 B6
10 MNCH 6501 B6
Teresa Dr
1400 FTLE 6502 D6
Teresa Ln
100 MRNK 6282 D4
Teresa St
10 SYHW 6048 B1
Terhune Av
10 JSYC 6819 B5
10 LODI 6500 C4
10 SHkT 6500 C4
10 WRDG 6500 C4
100 HSBH 6500 C4
Terhune Av CO-38
10 LODI 6500 C4
10 SHkT 6500 C4
10 WRDG 6500 C4
Terhune Av CO-38
100 HSBH 6500 C4
Terhune St
300 TnkT 6501 E1
Teri Ct
10 STNL 7019 A7
Terminal Av
10 CART 7115 D2
Terminal Rd
- MNCH 6610 B1
10 HmpT 6828 C4
10 LynT 6609 A4
10 RTFD 6609 A4
400 CARL 6610 B1
400 SHkT 6610 B1
Terrace Av
10 FLPK 6827 D2
10 HSBH 6500 B4
10 LODI 6500 C3
10 STNL 7207 A1
10 TYTN 6048 C2
10 WHPL 6168 B1
10 WRDG 6500 D6
100 JSYC 6716 B5
100 PTCH 6170 C4
200 GDNC 6828 C3
200 HmpT 6828 C3
400 HSBH 6501 A3
500 HKSK 6501 A3
800 WbgT 7114 C2
Terrace Av CO-55
10 HSBH 6500 E4
10 WRDG 6500 D6
400 HSBH 6501 A3
500 HKSK 6501 A3
E Terrace Av
10 HmpT 6827 C5
N Terrace Av
10 MTVN 6394 D3
S Terrace Av
10 MTVN 6394 C4
Terrace Blvd
10 NHPK 6724 A7
10 NHPK 6828 C1
1000 NHmT 6724 A7
Terrace Cir
10 NHmT 6722 E2
Terrace Ct
10 NHmT 6617 D3
10 NHmT 6724 E2
10 RYEB 6169 E4
10 STNL 7117 C1
Terrace Dr
- MHTN 112 E4
- MHTN 113 A4
- MHTN 6717 E2
- MHTN 6718 A2
- THSN 6617 C7
10 HAOH 6166 A6
10 NHmT 6617 D3
S Terrace Dr
10 MTVN 6394 C5
Terrace Pk
10 GDNC 6828 B1
Terrace Pl
10 BlvT 6714 B1
10 BRNX 6395 B7
10 GLCV 6509 E4
10 GRFD 6500 B3
10 KRNY 6714 B2
10 NHmT 6617 D2
10 PLMM 6395 B7
10 TCKA 6281 A6
10 YNKR 6393 C2
100 BKLN 6922 E5
N Terrace Pl
10 VLYS 6928 C2
S Terrace Pl
- HmpT 6928 B3
10 VLYS 6928 B3
Terrace Rd
10 BKLN 7021 D4
W Terrace Rd
10 GTNK 6617 B6
10 NHmT 6617 B6
Terrace St
10 GrbT 6049 D7
100 BRNX 6506 E5
Terrace Park Ln
10 NRCH 6395 D7
Terrace View Av
10 MHTN 102 C3
10 MHTN 6504 A2
Terrell Av
10 HmpT 6929 D6
10 RKVC 6929 D5
Terry Ln
- UnnT 6917 A1
10 NHmT 6724 C2
Terry Pl
500 HmpT 6827 E6
500 HmpT 6828 A6
Teunissen Pl
10 MHTN 102 C4
10 MHTN 6504 A2
Tewkesbury Rd
10 NRCH 6281 E1
Texas Av
10 HmpT 7029 E3
100 YNKR 6394 D1
Thacher Ln
100 SOrT 6712 A5
Thames Av
10 STNL 7020 A2
Thames St
10 BKLN 6822 E5
10 MHTN 120 B1
10 MHTN 6821 A4
W Thames St
100 MHTN 120 A1
100 MHTN 6821 A4
Thatcher Av
10 HRSN 6283 B4
Thatcher Rd
10 TFLY 6392 B4
Thatford Av
300 BKLN 6924 B4
Thayer Av
100 WbgT 7114 D2
Thayer Ln
- NHmT 6508 E6
10 SNPT 6508 E6
10 SNPT 6509 A6
Thayer Pl
10 STNL 7117 D4
Thayer Rd
10 MNPK 6617 E6
10 NHmT 6617 E6
Thayer St
10 MHTN 101 E7
10 MHTN 104 E1
10 MHTN 6503 E4
The Dr
10 SCLF 6509 E5
The Gln
10 TFLY 6392 A3
The Spur
10 FLHL 6618 B4
10 NHLS 6618 C7
10 ROSE 6618 C7
Theall Rd
10 RYE 6283 D3
Theatre Al
10 MHTN 118 C7
10 MHTN 6821 C4
Theatre Ln
10 STNL 7020 D3
The Balsams
10 ROSE 6618 B6
The Beach Wy
10 PLNH 6617 C5
Thebes Av
248-00 QENS 6722 E3
250-17 QENS 6723 A3
The Birches
10 NHmT 6618 D7
10 ROSE 6618 C6
The Boulevard
10 GLCV 6509 D5
10 NRCH 6395 E3
10 NRCH 6396 A3
10 SCLF 6509 D5
The Boulevard E
100 NRCH 6396 A2
The Boulevard
10 STNL 7019 D3
The Bridge
10 MHVN 6508 B7
The Byway
10 BRXV 6395 A1
The Circle
10 LKSU 6723 B2
10 NRCH 6395 E3
The Court
10 NRCH 6396 A3
The Crescent
- NHLS 6724 C1
- NHmT 6724 C1
10 YNKR 6393 D4
100 NHLS 6618 C7
700 MRNK 6283 A7
The Crossing at Blind Brk
10 HRSN 6169 C2
The Crossroad
10 PLDM 6617 D5
The Dell
10 NHmT 6724 C2
The Dogwoods
10 ROSE 6618 C6
The East Al
- BRXV 6280 C4
The Esplanade
10 ALPN 6392 D1
10 NRCH 6395 E2
The Fenway
10 HAOH 6280 C2
10 ROSE 6618 C6
10 RSLN 6618 C6
The Gate
10 MNPK 6618 A6
10 NHmT 6618 A6
The Glenada
10 ROSE 6618 C6
The Greenway
10 FLHL 6618 B5
The Hamlet
10 PLMM 6395 C6
The Hemlocks
10 ROSE 6618 B6
The High Rd
10 BRXV 6395 A1
The Lane
- RYE 6283 E5
The Lindens
10 ROSE 6618 C6
Thelma Ct
10 STNL 7020 D2
Thelma Dr
1400 UnnT 6816 B6
Thelma Pl
10 WHPL 6168 B6
Thelma St
10 EHLS 6618 E7
10 NHmT 6618 E7
The Loch
10 ROSE 6618 C6
10 RSLN 6618 C6
The Locusts
10 FLHL 6618 C6
10 ROSE 6618 C6
The Maples
10 ROSE 6618 C6
10 RSLN 6618 C6
The Moorings
10 EDGW 103 A7
10 EDGW 6503 A7
The Neck
10 PLNH 6617 C5
The Oaks
10 ROSE 6618 C6
Theodora St
1000 HmpT 6828 A5
1200 HmpT 6827 E5
Theodore Ct
10 VLYS 6928 D3
Theodore Conrad Dr
10 JSYC 6820 A5
Theodore Fremd Av
10 RYE 6283 C3
500 HRSN 6283 C3
The Oval
10 STNL 7020 A7
The Parkway
500 MRNK 6283 B6
The Pines
10 ROSE 6618 C7
The Place
10 GLCV 6509 E4
The Plaza
10 ATLB 7027 E7
10 STNL 7020 A7
The Poplars
10 ROSE 6618 C7
The Promenade
10 EDGW 108 B2
10 EDGW 6611 D5
Theresa Av
500 HmpT 6828 C6
Theresa Ln
10 GrbT 6280 E1
10 HRSN 6283 C2
Theresa Pl
10 STNL 7020 C2
The Ridge
10 PLDM 6617 D4
The Ridgeway
10 GrwT 6170 E1
The River Clb
- EDGW 108 B1
- EDGW 6611 E4
The Serpentine
10 NRCH 6395 E3
10 NRCH 6396 C3
10 ROSE 6618 C7
The Terrace
10 PLDM 6617 C5
10 RTFD 6609 B2
The Tideway
100 PLNH 6617 C5
The Tulips
- NHLS 6618 C7
- NHmT 6618 C7
10 ROSE 6618 C7
The Water Wy
10 PLNH 6617 C5
The Yard
10 CDHT 7028 B2
Thieriot Av
300 BRNX 6614 B4
1400 BRNX 6505 B7
Thies Ct
10 SCDL 6282 B1
Thistle Ct
10 STNL 7020 E3
Thistle Ln
10 GrwT 6170 C2
10 RYE 6284 A1
Thixton Av
10 HmpT 6929 B7
Thixton Dr
10 HWTH 7029 A1
Thollen St
10 STNL 7117 D4
Thomas Av
10 SRVL 7205 A7
Thomas Blvd
300 COrT 6712 D1
300 EORG 6712 D1
Thomas Cir
10 OrgT 6164 B1
Thomas Ct
10 GrbT 6167 B5
10 HmpT 7027 E3
Thomas Ln
10 GrbT 6167 B6
Thomas Pl
10 EchT 6395 C2
10 MtPT 6049 D3
10 NRCH 6395 D3
10 STNL 7117 E3
10 WHPL 6168 B4
10 YNKR 6280 A6
Thomas Pl S
10 YNKR 6280 A7
Thomas St
10 GrbT 6167 B5
10 MHTN 118 C6
10 MHTN 6821 A3
10 NWRK 6817 D2
100 STNL 7117 C2
200 WbgT 7114 B4
300 PTHA 7205 D1
300 TnkT 6501 E1
700 ELIZ 6917 E6
700 LNDN 6917 E6
1100 HlsT 6816 C6
1100 HmpT 6928 E7
Thomas Wy
10 GrbT 6166 E1
Thomas A Edison Br
- SRVL 7205 A4
- WbgT 7205 A5
Thomas A Edison Br US-9
- SRVL 7205 A5
- WbgT 7205 A5
Thomas Gangemi Dr
10 JSYC 6820 C2
Thomas McGovern Dr
10 JSYC 6820 A5
Thomas S Boyland St
10 BKLN 6823 A7
10 BKLN 6924 B3
N Thomas Sharp Blvd
10 MTVN 6394 D4
Thompson Av
10 EDGW 108 A1
10 EDGW 6611 D5
10 HmpT 7029 D1
10 WbgT 7114 A6
10 WHPL 6050 B6
100 ROSL 6917 B5
1100 LNDN 6917 B5
Thompson Dr
10 ERKY 6929 B7
Thompson Ln
- EDGW 6611 D5
10 EDGW 108 B1
Thompson Pl
10 HmpT 6929 A5
10 LNBK 6929 A5
10 LRMT 6396 D2
10 STNL 7020 E4
61-00 QENS 6720 D6
Thompson St
- TCKA 6281 A5
10 HmpT 6928 E1
10 MHTN 118 D4
10 MHTN 6821 B2
10 MrnT 6396 D3
10 STNL 7020 E1
10 YNKR 6281 A4
200 SAMB 7205 B7
Thompson St
300 HKSK 6501 A1
Thompson Shore Rd
10 NHmT 6617 C6
Thomson Av
27-00 QENS 6718 D6
Thorens Av
10 NHmT 6724 C7
Thornall St
10 CART 7115 D1
Thornbury Rd
10 YNKR 6281 A2
Thornbury Rd E
10 NRCH 6281 E1
Thorncliffe Ln
10 GrbT 6049 D3
Thorne Pl
10 RYE 6283 D4
Thorne St
10 JSYC 6716 B5
10 NWRK 6817 A6
Thornhill Av
242-00 QENS 6722 E4
249-00 QENS 6723 A4
Thornton Ct
300 EDGW 108 B1
300 EDGW 6611 D4
Thornton Pl
10 EORG 6712 E1
66-00 QENS 6824 B2
Thornton Rd
200 EGLD 6392 B6
Thornton St
10 BKLN 6822 E4
10 BlmT 6713 A1
10 NWRK 6818 C2
Thornwood Pl
10 SCDL 6168 C7
Thornycroft Av
100 STNL 7117 A6
Thorpe Av
10 WbgT 7114 B1
Thorpe Dr
10 OrgT 6164 E1
Throggs Neck Expwy
400 BRNX 6615 B2
Throgmorton Av
900 BRNX 6615 A1
1100 BRNX 6506 A7
Throgs Neck Blvd
800 BRNX 6615 B1
Throgs Neck Br
- BRNX 6615 D6
- QENS 6615 D7
Throgs Neck Br I-295
- BRNX 6615 D6
- QENS 6615 D7
Throgs Neck Expwy
- BRNX 6506 A7
- BRNX 6615 A1
Throgs Neck Expwy I-295
- BRNX 6615 B3
Throgs Neck Expwy I-695
- BRNX 6506 A7
- BRNX 6615 A1
Throgs Neck Bridge Approach
- BRNX 6615 C3
Throgs Neck Br Approach I-295
- BRNX 6615 C3
Throgs Neck Expressway Ext
3200 BRNX 6615 B3
Throop Av
10 BKLN 6822 C5
500 BKLN 6923 D1
2200 BRNX 6505 C4
Thrush Av
600 HmpT 6828 D7
Thurman St
10 YNKR 6393 D2
Thurman Munson Wy
200 BRNX 6613 A2
Thursby Av
62-00 QENS 7026 D6
Thurston St
10 STNL 7019 B3
134-00 QENS 6927 C2
Thurton Pl
10 YNKR 6394 B3
Thwaites Pl
600 BRNX 6505 A4
Tianderah Rd
10 BXTE 6617 E1
Tibbett Av
3000 BRNX 102 D1
3000 BRNX 6504 B1
4400 BRNX 6393 C7
Tibbetts Rd
10 YNKR 6393 E5
Tibbits Av
10 WHPL 6167 C2
10 WHPL 6168 A2
Tibbits Ln
10 SNPT 6508 B5
Tiber Pl
100 STNL 7020 A5
Tichenor Av
100 SOrT 6712 A7
Tichenor Ln
10 NWRK 6817 D2
Tichenor St
10 NWRK 6817 D2
Tichenor Ter
10 IrvT 6712 E7
Tides Ln
10 STNL 7206 B1
Tideway
10 KNGP 6616 D3
10 SNPT 6508 C4
Tiebout Av
2000 BRNX 6504 C5
Tiemann Av
2200 BRNX 6505 D4
Tiemann Pl
10 MHTN 106 C6
10 MHTN 6612 B3
Tier St
10 BRNX 6506 D6

STREET
Block City Map# Grid

Tiernans Ln
10 DBSF 6165 D3
Tierney Pl
3000 BRNX 6615 C4
Tietjen Av
100 EGLD 6502 C1
Tiffany Blvd
10 NWRK 6713 E1
10 NWRK 6714 A1
Tiffany Cir
10 NHLS 6724 B2
Tiffany Ct
10 STNL 7206 D3
Tiffany Pl
10 BKLN 120 D7
10 BKLN 6821 B7
10 IrvT 6816 B2
10 MplT 6816 B2
Tiffany St
300 BRNX 6613 D3
Tiger Ct
10 STNL 7019 B2
Tilden Av
4700 BKLN 6923 E6
5600 BKLN 6924 A6
Tilden Pl
10 NRWD 6278 D2
Tilden St
10 STNL 6920 C7
700 BRNX 6505 B2
Tillary St
10 BKLN 121 B4
10 BKLN 6821 D6
Tiller Ct
10 STNL 7115 B7
10 STNL 7206 B1
Tilley Pl
100 SCLF 6509 D6
Tillinghast St
10 NWRK 6816 E3
10 NWRK 6817 A3
Tillman St
10 STNL 7019 E5
100 STNL 7020 A4
500 HlsT 6816 B5
Tillotson Av
2000 BRNX 6505 E2
2200 BRNX 6506 A1
Tilrose Av
10 MLVN 6929 B2
2800 HmpT 6929 E6
Tilson Pl
10 STNL 7020 E3
Timber Ln
10 NHmT 6618 A7
Timber Tr
10 HRSN 6169 C5
Timberline Dr
10 ALPN 6278 E5
10 ALPN 6279 A5
Timber Ridge Dr
200 STNL 7117 C4
Times Av
1200 HmpT 6827 E5
Tim Hendrix Pl
100 BRNX 102 E2
100 BRNX 6504 C2
Timmons Rd
10 EchT 6281 D3
Timothy Ct
10 STNL 7018 E4
Timothy Ln
10 EGLD 6392 A7
Timpson Pl
400 BRNX 6613 B4
Timpson St
600 PLMM 6395 B6
Tingue St
10 GrwT 6170 D5
Tintern Ln
10 NRCH 6281 E1
Tinton Av
400 BRNX 6613 C2
Tioga Av
10 ATLB 7028 B7
10 YNKR 6394 B2
Tioga Dr
188-00 QENS 6826 B6
Tioga St
10 STNL 7020 B4
Tisdale Pl
500 WbgT 7114 C4
Tisdale Rd
10 SCDL 6281 C1
Tito Puente Wy
- MHTN 109 E4
- MHTN 6612 C6
Titus Av
10 STNL 7118 A3
Tobin Av
10 NHmT 6723 A1
Tocco Pl
10 YNKR 6394 B1
Todd Dr
10 SNPT 6509 B6
Todd Pl
100 LNDN 6917 A7
100 LNDN 7017 A2
Todd Rd
10 VLYS 6928 C2
Toddy Av
10 STNL 7018 E5
Todt Hill Ct
10 STNL 7020 A7
Todt Hill Rd
200 STNL 7019 E4
300 STNL 7020 A7
900 STNL 7118 A1
Toftree Ct
400 NHLS 6724 A3
Token St
10 STNL 7116 D3
Toler Pl
10 NWRK 6817 B4
Tollgate Ct
10 LNBK 6929 A4
Tolson Wy
10 SECS 6609 E7
Tom Ct
10 STNL 6920 A7
Tomahawk Dr
10 GrbT 6049 E6
Tom Hunter Rd
200 FTLE 103 A5
200 FTLE 6502 E6
200 FTLE 6503 B5
Tomlinson Av
1500 BRNX 6505 C6
Tompkins Av
10 BKLN 6822 C6
10 HAOH 6279 E2
10 HAOH 6280 A2
10 STNL 7020 D2
10 WHPL 6050 B6
10 YNKR 6280 A2
300 BKLN 6923 C1
300 MRNK 6283 A6
800 STNL 7021 A4
Tompkins Cir
10 STNL 6920 D7
Tompkins Pl
10 BKLN 120 E7
10 BKLN 6821 C7
10 BKLN 6922 C1
10 STNL 7020 D1
400 COrT 6712 B3
Tompkins Rd
- STNL 7021 A5
10 SCDL 6167 E6
Tompkins St
10 COrT 6712 B3
10 STNL 7020 D2
10 WOrT 6712 B3
Tompkins Point Rd
10 NWRK 6817 E3
Toms Point Ln
10 MHVN 6617 C1
Tone Ln
10 STNL 7020 D4
Toni Dr
10 EGLC 6503 B2
Toni Ln
10 YNKR 6280 C5
400 MRNK 6282 E7
Tonking Rd
10 STNL 7117 D1
Tonlyn Pl
10 WbgT 7114 E4
Tonnele Av
10 JSYC 6819 E1
100 JSYC 6715 E7
200 JSYC 6716 A6
800 NBgT 6716 B4
Tonnele Av US-1
200 JSYC 6716 A6
800 NBgT 6716 B4
Tonnele Av US-9
200 JSYC 6716 A6
800 NBgT 6716 B4
Tonnelle Av
- JSYC 6716 B4
2400 NBgT 6716 D1
4800 NBgT 6610 D7
7500 NBgT 6611 A5
9100 FRVW 6611 A4
Tonnelle Av US-1
- JSYC 6716 B4
2400 NBgT 6716 C1
4800 NBgT 6610 D7
7500 NBgT 6611 A5
9100 FRVW 6611 A4
Tonnelle Av US-9
- JSYC 6716 B4
500 NBgT 6716 B4
4800 NBgT 6610 D7
7500 NBgT 6611 A5
9100 FRVW 6611 A4
Tonsor St
4-00 QENS 6823 B4
Tony Ct
10 STNL 7020 D6
Tony Galento Plz
10 COrT 6712 C2
Toomer Pl
10 HmpT 6929 A2
10 MLVN 6929 A2
Top Row
10 LODI 6500 E2
Topland Rd
10 GrbT 6167 A4
10 WHPL 6168 E4
10 WHPL 6169 A4
Top of the Ridge Dr
10 NRCH 6281 E2
Top of the Ridge Rd
10 MRNK 6283 B5
Topol Cir
- GrbT 6166 E1
Topping Av
1600 BRNX 6504 B7
1700 BRNX 105 D5
Topping St
10 STNL 7118 B3
Topsail Ln
10 RYE 6283 E6
800 SECS 6715 D1
Topside Ln
10 STNL 7206 B1
Torquay Pl
100 HmpT 6929 A6
Torre Pl
10 YNKR 6279 E6
Torrence Pl
10 SCDL 6167 E6
Torricelli St
10 STNL 7021 B4
Torry Av
400 BRNX 6614 C3
Tory Cir
10 OrgT 6164 A2
Tory Ln
10 SCDL 6167 D6
Totem Pole Pl
10 GrbT 6049 E6
Toten St
- STNL 7115 E5
Totten Av
100 QENS 6616 A7
Totten St
7-00 QENS 6615 D7
Tottenham Ct
10 JSYC 6819 A4
Tottenham Pl
10 NHmT 6724 B5
Tottenham Rd
10 LNBK 6928 E4
10 LNBK 6929 A5
10 VLYS 6928 E4
Tottenville Pl
10 STNL 7206 A4
Touissant Av
10 YNKR 6280 A5
Touraine Av
10 PTCH 6170 A6
Tournade Ln
400 UNCT 6716 D4
Tournament Dr
10 WHPL 6169 A5
Tower Dr
10 CLFP 6611 E2
10 EDGW 6611 E2
10 FTLE 6611 E2
Tower Ln
10 HRSN 6051 B5
Tower Pl
10 MTVN 6394 E2
10 YNKR 6279 E6
Tower Rd
- NWRK 6817 D6
10 GLCV 6509 E2
Tower St
10 RSLN 6618 D6
Tower Hill Dr
10 PTCH 6170 B3
Tower Hill Rd
- MtPT 6048 D1
- TYTN 6048 D1
Towers Ln
10 STNL 7018 C6
Towers St
10 JSYC 6819 C4
Towle Pl
10 GLCV 6509 E5
Town Dock Rd
10 NRCH 6396 A6
Town Green Dr
10 GrbT 6048 E5
Town House Cir
10 GTNE 6617 C4
10 GTPZ 6617 C4
Town House Pl
10 GTNE 6617 C4
10 GTPZ 6617 C4
Townley Av
10 STNL 7019 E6
10 STNL 7020 A4
700 UnnT 6816 B7
700 UnnT 6917 C1
Townsend Av
10 GrbT 6167 C4
10 STNL 7020 E2
100 PLMM 6395 B7
1400 BRNX 105 B7
1600 BRNX 6504 B6
Townsend St
10 PTCH 6170 C6
Town Square Pl
10 JSYC 6820 D2
Tracy Av
10 STNL 7206 B3
700 FRVW 6611 B3
Tracy Av CO-16
700 FRVW 6611 B3
Tracy Pl
10 HmpT 6928 E6
10 HmpT 6929 A6
Tradition Rd
100 GrbT 6049 E5
100 GrbT 6050 A5
Trafalgar Blvd
10 HmpT 7029 E4
Trafalgar Pl
1800 BRNX 6504 D7
Trafalgar Rd
- PALP 6502 C7
10 TFLY 6392 C4
Trafalgar Sq
10 LNBK 6928 E5
10 VLYS 6928 E5
Traffic Av
63-00 QENS 6823 C4
Trailhead Ln
10 GrbT 6048 D4
Trails End
10 HRSN 6283 C2
10 RYE 6283 C6
100 IRVN 6166 C1
Transvaal St
10 DBSF 6166 A4
Trantor Pl
10 STNL 7019 B1
Trask Av
10 BAYN 6919 C6
Tratman Av
2400 BRNX 6505 D7
Trausneck Pl
10 YNKR 6279 E5
Trautwein Cres
10 CLST 6278 C3
Travers Av
10 YNKR 6393 E3
100 MRNK 6282 E4
400 MRNK 6283 A3
1000 ELIZ 6817 A7
Travers St
10 NHmT 6617 C6
800 UnnT 6917 C2
Traverse Av
10 PTCH 6170 C6
Travis Av
10 STNL 7019 B7
100 HmpT 6827 D5
800 STNL 7018 D5
Travis Dr
- GDNC 6828 E2
Travis Pl
10 HAOH 6165 E6
Traymore Blvd
100 HmpT 7029 D5
Treacy Av
10 NWRK 6817 A2
Treadwell Av
10 STNL 6919 C7
100 STNL 7019 C1
Treadwell Pl
10 YNKR 6280 C2
Treadwell St
10 NWRK 6713 D4
Treat Pl
10 NWRK 6817 D1
Tredwell Av
10 ERKY 6929 B5
10 LNBK 6929 B5
Tree Top Cres
200 RYEB 6170 D2
Tree Top Ln
10 DBSF 6166 B5
200 RYEB 6170 D2
Tree Top Ter
10 GrwT 6170 C1
Treetz Pl
10 STNL 7019 D3
Trefoil Pass
10 WOrT 6712 B1
Tremley Ct
10 BAYN 6919 E5
Tremley Point Rd
2600 LNDN 7017 D4
4700 LNDN 7018 A5
Tremley Point Rd CO-617
3300 LNDN 7017 D3
Tremont Av
10 COrT 6712 A4
10 EORG 6712 D6
10 NWRK 6712 E6
10 STNL 7019 B3
10 WOrT 6712 A4
200 FTLE 6502 E6
E Tremont Av
10 BRNX 105 E4
10 BRNX 6505 E7
400 BRNX 6504 E7
3200 BRNX 6614 E1
3400 BRNX 6615 B3
W Tremont Av
10 BRNX 105 C4
10 BRNX 6504 B5
Tremont Ct
600 COrT 6712 B5
Tremont Pl
300 COrT 6712 B4
Tremont St
10 IrvT 6816 C2
Tremont Ter
10 IrvT 6816 D1
W Tremont Ter
10 IrvT 6816 A2
Trenchard St
10 YNKR 6394 B3
Treno St
10 NRCH 6395 E3
Trenor Dr
10 NRCH 6281 E7
Trent Pl
1000 UnnT 6816 A6
Trent St
10 STNL 7117 C5
Trenton Av
10 HmpT 7028 D7
10 WHPL 6167 E2
400 ELIZ 6918 A6
Trenton Blvd
- CLST 6278 C2
Trenton Ct
200 STNL 7207 B3
Trenton St
10 JSYC 6820 A2
Treptow St
10 LFRY 6501 D6
Trevon Pl
10 NRCH 6281 D7
Triangle Blvd
10 CARL 6609 E2
10 CARL 6610 A2
Triangle Pl
10 TCKA 6280 C3
Triborough Br
- MHTN 110 D3
- MHTN 114 E2
- MHTN 6612 E5
- MHTN 6613 A6
- MHTN 6718 E1
- QENS 114 E3
- QENS 6718 E2
- QENS 6719 A2
Triborough Br I-278
- MHTN 110 E7
- MHTN 114 E2
- MHTN 6612 E7
- MHTN 6613 A6
- MHTN 6718 E1
- QENS 114 E3
- QENS 6718 E2
- QENS 6719 A2
Triborough Bridge Approach
- BRNX 6613 A5
- MHTN 6613 A6
Triborough Br Approach I-278
- BRNX 6613 A5
- MHTN 6613 A6
Tribune Av
1200 HmpT 6827 E5
Tricia Wy
10 STNL 7206 C5
Trimble Pl
10 MHTN 118 C6
10 MHTN 6821 A3
Trimble Rd
63-00 QENS 6719 C6
Trina Ln
10 STNL 7115 D6
Trinity Av
800 BRNX 6613 B2
Trinity Ct
10 HmpT 6828 D6
Trinity Ln
10 WbgT 7114 D3
Trinity Pl
10 HKSK 6501 C1
10 HMPD 6828 E4
10 HmpT 6928 D7
10 KRNY 6714 B3
10 MHTN 120 B1
10 MHTN 6821 A4
10 NRCH 6396 A5
10 STNL 6919 E7
10 UnnT 6917 A1
10 WbgT 7114 D1
100 HmpT 6828 E4
300 ELIZ 6917 E3
300 HlsT 6816 D7
300 MLVN 6929 B1
Trinity St
10 YNKR 6393 E1
Tripoli St
2300 ELIZ 6919 A2
Trist Pl
13-00 QENS 7027 B4
Triton Pl
10 NWRK 6714 A3
Triton Ter
10 NWRK 6714 C4
Triumph Ct
10 ERTH 6500 A7
Troon Rd
186-00 QENS 6825 E2
186-00 QENS 6826 B2
Troost St
10 HKSK 6501 B2
Trossach Rd
10 STNL 7020 C1
Trotters Ln
10 ELIZ 6917 D2
10 HlsT 6917 D2
10 UnnT 6917 D2
Trotting Rd
300 UnnT 6917 A2
Trotting Course Ln
69-00 QENS 6824 B4
Troutman St
10 BKLN 6822 E5
17-00 BKLN 6823 A4
17-00 QENS 6823 A4
Troutville Rd
177-00 QENS 6826 B7
177-00 QENS 6927 B1
Troy Av
10 HmpT 7028 D7
1000 BKLN 6923 D7
1500 BKLN 7023 D1
Troy Ct
10 MplT 6816 A3
Troy Ln
10 NRCH 6395 C3
10 YNKR 6279 C6
Troy St
10 HmpT 6827 C7
10 JSYC 6716 A7
10 STNL 7117 A3
Trucklemans Ln
10 BKLN 6924 C6
Trudy Dr
10 LODI 6500 E1
Truesdale Pl
10 YNKR 6393 E2
Truman Av
10 YNKR 6280 A3
Truman Ct
10 CLST 6278 C3
Truman Dr
10 CRSK 6392 D1
200 CRSK 6278 C7
300 DMRT 6278 C7
Truman Pl
10 MNCH 6501 B7
Truman Rd
10 NARL 6714 D1
Truman St
10 STNL 7206 C4
Trumbull Pl
10 STNL 6920 C7
Trumbull Rd
10 MNPK 6618 A5
Trumbull St
10 ELIZ 6918 B3
Truxton Dr
1000 PTHA 7114 C7
1000 WbgT 7114 C7
Truxton Rd
10 ISPK 7029 C5
Truxton St
10 BKLN 6924 B1
500 BRNX 6613 D4
Tryon Av
10 STNL 7116 C5
3400 BRNX 6504 E2
Tryon Ct
10 NHmT 6724 A5
Tryon Pl
80-00 QENS 6825 E2
Trysting Pl
500 CDHT 7028 A1
T Sharp Blvd
10 MTVN 6394 E6
700 BRNX 6394 E7
Tuckahoe Av
10 EchT 6281 B6
10 STNL 7207 C1
Tuckahoe Rd
- TCKA 6280 E6
- YNKR 6280 C6
Tucker Ln
10 MLVN 6929 C1
Tuckerton St
95-00 QENS 6825 C5
Tuddington Rd
10 GTNK 6617 A5
Tudor Cres
- HmpT 6827 C5
Tudor Dr
10 NHmT 6724 A5
Tudor Ln
10 EchT 6281 B2
10 SNPT 6508 C5
10 YNKR 6280 B7
Tudor Pl
10 GrbT 6167 A2
100 BRNX 6613 A1
300 HmpT 6828 D6
Tudor Rd
179-00 QENS 6825 E2
Tudor St
10 STNL 7117 B4
Tudor Ter
10 BKLN 7120 B2
Tudor City Pl
10 MHTN 117 A4
10 MHTN 6718 A6
Tudor Gate
10 HmpT 6827 C5
Tuers Av
10 JSYC 6819 D1
10 JSYC 6820 A2
Tulfan Ter
500 BRNX 102 D1
500 BRNX 6504 B1
Tulip Av
- BKLN 7022 D2
10 FLPK 6827 C2
10 MLVN 6929 C2
10 QENS 6827 C2
10 WOrT 6712 B1
400 HmpT 6827 E3
500 STMN 6827 E3
600 HmpT 6828 A3
600 STMN 6828 A3
800 HmpT 6929 D1
Tulip Cir
10 HmpT 6928 D2
10 STNL 7116 B5
10 TnkT 6502 D2
10 VLYS 6928 D2
Tulip Ct
10 NHmT 6724 B4
Tulip Dr
10 GTNE 6616 E7
Tulip Ln
10 LRMT 6396 B2
10 NHmT 6618 A3
10 NHmT 6723 E6
10 NHmT 6724 C4
10 NRCH 6282 A4
Tulip Pl
10 NHmT 6724 D7
10 WLTN 6500 A6
Tulip St
10 HmpT 7028 B2
Tulip Tree Ln
10 ALPN 6392 E1
10 MRNK 6283 B5
Tullamore Rd
100 GDNC 6828 B2
Tunbridge Pl
10 BlmT 6713 C2
Tunis Av
10 YNKR 6394 C1
Tunnel St
10 FLPK 6827 D2
Tunnel Approach St
- MHTN 116 E4
- MHTN 6717 E6
Tunnel Exit St
- MHTN 116 E4
- MHTN 6717 E6
Tunstall Rd
10 SCDL 6281 D1
Turf Av
10 RYE 6283 E5
Turf Ct
10 STNL 7019 A7
Turf Rd
10 STNL 7019 A7
600 HmpT 6928 A6
Turin Dr
188-00 QENS 6826 B6
Turnberry Dr
10 GrbT 6166 C7
Turnbull Av
1900 BRNX 6614 C2
Turner Dr
10 GrwT 6170 D1
10 NRCH 6281 D3
Turner Pl
10 BKLN 6922 E6
10 BKLN 6923 A6
Turner St
10 STNL 7115 D6
10 WbgT 7115 B2
10 YNKR 6394 C2
Turnesa Dr
10 EMFD 6049 C6
Turneur Av
300 BRNX 6614 D3
Turrell Av
10 SOrT 6712 A6
Turs Ct
10 WLTN 6500 B6
Turtle Cove Ln
10 KNGP 6617 B3
Tuscan Rd
200 MplT 6816 A2
Tut Basin
400 HmpT 7029 D1
Tuttle Pl
10 HmpT 7029 D5
Tuttle St
10 STNL 7019 B3
10 WLTN 6500 A5
Tuve Ln
10 SHkT 6501 D4
Tuxedo Av
10 NHmT 6724 B5
Tuxedo Dr
600 HmpT 6827 C7
Tuxedo Pkwy
10 NWRK 6712 B7
100 MplT 6816 A1
100 NWRK 6816 A1
Tuxedo Pl
600 LNDN 6917 C6
Twin Pl
10 ISPK 7029 D4
Twin Oak Dr
10 STNL 7020 B4
Twin Oaks Rd
400 UnnT 6816 A7
Twin Pines Dr
10 BKLN 6924 E6
Twin Pond Ln
10 GrbT 6166 E1
Twin Ponds St
10 KNGP 6617 A3
Two Brothers Ct
2600 HmpT 6929 D6
Twombly Av
10 STNL 7117 C4
Tybee Pl
10 YNKR 6280 E6
Tyler Av
10 CART 7017 C7
10 CART 7115 C1
10 STNL 7020 A2
10 WbgT 7114 A3
59-00 QENS 6719 B7
60-00 QENS 6823 C1
Tyler Cir
10 RYE 6284 A3
Tyler Pl
10 GrbT 6049 E5
300 HmpT 6828 D5
Tyler Pl
6000 WNYK 6611 A7
Tyler Rd
10 SCDL 6282 B1
1000 HmpT 6929 D2
Tyler St
10 NWRK 6818 B7
800 HmpT 6828 B6
Tynan St
10 STNL 7116 D3
Tyndale Pl
10 YNKR 6280 B6
Tyndale St
10 STNL 7207 E1
Tyndall Av
10 YNKR 6280 B4
5700 BRNX 6393 C5
Tyrellan Av
10 STNL 7206 C2
Tyrells Ln
10 PTHA 7114 D7
Tyrrell St
10 STNL 7206 A3
Tysen St
10 STNL 6920 B6
Tysens Ln
10 STNL 7117 E3
600 STNL 7118 A3
Tyson Av
10 FLPK 6827 C2
N Tyson Av
10 FLPK 6827 C1
10 QENS 6827 C1
S Tyson Av
10 FLPK 6827 D2
Tyson Ln
10 JSYC 6819 D3

U

Udall Dr
10 NHmT 6723 C1
10 THSN 6723 C1
Uhland St
10 ERTH 6500 B7
10 ERTH 6609 B1
Ulmer St
25-00 QENS 6720 E2
Ulster Av
10 ATLB 7028 B7
Umberto Pl
10 YNKR 6280 B7
Uncas Av
100 STNL 7207 A1
Undercliff Av
10 EDGW 6611 E2
10 EMFD 6049 A6
600 EDGW 6502 E7
700 EDGW 6503 A7
900 EDGW 103 A5
1300 BRNX 104 E5
1300 BRNX 6503 E7
1500 BRNX 105 A4
1500 BRNX 6504 A6
Undercliff St
10 YNKR 6393 C2
Underhill Av
10 BKLN 6923 A2
10 BRNX 6614 B3
10 HRSN 6168 C1
171-00 QENS 6721 D6
196-00 QENS 6722 B7
200 HRSN 6050 D7
800 MRNK 6282 D5
Underhill Pl
10 HRSN 6168 C1
Underhill Rd
10 GrbT 6167 A5
300 GrbT 6166 E5
Underhill St
10 TCKA 6281 A6
10 YNKR 6280 D5
Underwood Rd
108-00 QENS 6824 D4
Underwood St
10 NWRK 6712 C7
Union Av
- MrnT 6282 E2
10 BKLN 6822 C4
10 BlvT 6714 A1
10 CRSK 6278 A7
10 ERTH 6609 C2
10 GRFD 6500 A1
10 HRSN 6283 A2
10 IrvT 6816 C2
10 LFRY 6501 B6
10 LNBK 6929 A6
10 LNDN 7017 B1
10 MNCH 6501 B6
10 MplT 6712 A7
10 MplT 6816 A1
10 MTVN 6394 E4
10 NRCH 6395 C5
10 NWRK 6712 A7
10 RTFD 6609 A1
10 STNL 6919 A7
10 STNL 7019 A1
10 TYTN 6048 C3
100 HmpT 6929 A6
100 UnnT 6816 A5
100 WRDG 6500 C6
200 ELIZ 6917 E2
200 HRSN 6282 E2
200 MRNK 6282 E5
200 MRNK 6283 A5
500 BRNX 6613 C2
500 HlsT 6816 B4
600 HlsT 6917 D1
1300 HmpT 6827 E4
1500 HWTH 6929 A7
Union Av CO-32
10 ERTH 6609 B2
10 RTFD 6609 A1
Union Av CO-74
10 CRSK 6278 A7
Union Av CO-647
10 BlvT 6714 A1
E Union Av
10 ERTH 6609 C2
N Union Av
500 HlsT 6816 B4
600 UnnT 6816 B4
Union Blvd
10 WLTN 6500 A5
Union Ct
10 STNL 7019 A1
Union Ln
10 MTVN 6394 E5
Union Pl
10 IrvT 6816 B4
10 KRNY 6714 C1
10 LNBK 6929 B5
10 NARL 6714 C1
10 RDFP 6501 E4
10 RDFP 6502 A4
10 STNL 7020 D1
10 TCKA 6281 A6
10 YNKR 6279 C7
400 HmpT 6929 D7
Union Sq E
10 MHTN 116 B7
10 MHTN 119 B1
10 MHTN 6717 D7
10 MHTN 6821 D1
Union Sq W
10 MHTN 116 A7
10 MHTN 119 A1
10 MHTN 6717 C7
10 MHTN 6821 C1
Union St
10 BKLN 120 C7
10 BKLN 6821 B7
10 BKLN 6922 B1
10 CART 7115 D2
10 COrT 6712 A3
10 ERKY 6929 C6
10 HKSK 6501 B1
10 JSYC 6819 D3
10 LODI 6500 D2
10 MNCH 6500 D7
10 NHmT 6724 C4
10 NRCH 6396 A5
10 NWRK 6817 E1
10 OrgT 6164 E2
10 PALP 6502 B5
10 PRMT 6164 E2
10 RDFP 6501 E6
10 VLYS 6928 B3
10 WOrT 6712 A3
10 WRDG 6500 D7
25-00 QENS 6721 A2
100 ELIZ 6917 B4
100 NVLE 6164 D5
200 HmpT 7027 E2
200 HSBH 6500 E3
300 CARL 6500 B7
300 ERTH 6500 B7
900 BKLN 6923 D3
1100 LNDN 6917 B6
1800 BKLN 6924 A3
Union St CO-8
10 OrgT 6164 E2
10 PRMT 6164 E2
Union St CO-40
10 LODI 6500 D2
200 HSBH 6500 E3
Union Ter
10 BlvT 6714 D2
2100 UNCT 6716 D3
Union Tpk
102-00 QENS 6824 D4
141-01 QENS 6825 E2
188-00 QENS 6826 A1
220-01 QENS 6722 D7
238-00 QENS 6723 D5
272-16 NHmT 6723 D5
1400 NBgT 6716 D1
Union Tpk CO-676
1400 NBgT 6716 D1
Union County Pkwy
1400 UnnT 6816 A7
Union Hall St
106-00 QENS 6825 D6
Unionport Rd
1300 BRNX 6614 B1
1500 BRNX 6505 B7
United Dr
- LODI 6500 B2
United Ln
10 TETB 6500 E5
United Nations Plz
700 MHTN 117 A3
700 MHTN 6718 A5
Unity Av
10 NWRK 6712 C7
Universal Av
10 WbgT 7114 A3
Universal Pl
10 CARL 6610 A1
University Av
10 NWRK 6713 D7
200 NWRK 6394 B1
300 NWRK 6817 D1
900 BRNX 107 D1
900 BRNX 6612 E1
1000 BRNX 104 E7
1000 BRNX 6503 E7
1500 BRNX 105 A5
1500 BRNX 6504 A6
2200 BRNX 102 E6
University Ct
10 SOrT 6712 A6
University Pl
10 EORG 6712 D4
10 IrvT 6712 D7
10 LKSU 6723 B1
10 MHTN 118 E3
10 MHTN 119 A1
10 MHTN 6821 C1
10 NWRK 6712 D7
10 PTCH 6170 B4
10 STNL 7020 B1
700 HmpT 6928 A6
University Rd
10 LKSU 6723 B1
University Heights Br
- MHTN 102 B7
- MHTN 6504 A4
Upland Av
10 WHPL 6050 C7
200 YNKR 6279 E5
300 YNKR 6280 B4
Upland Dr
10 GrwT 6170 E2
Upland Pl
10 YNKR 6279 C4
10 YNKR 6280 A5
Upland Rd
10 GrwT 6170 E2
10 NHmT 6723 A3
Upland Rd
10 NRCH 6281 D7
10 QENS 6723 A3
Upland St
10 GrwT 6170 C3
10 PTCH 6170 B3
Upland St E
10 GrwT 6170 C3
Upland St W
10 GrwT 6170 C3
10 PTCH 6170 C3
Upland Ter
10 WHPL 6050 C7
Upper Dogwood Ln
10 RYE 6169 E7
Ups Dr
10 SECS 6716 A1
Upshaw Rd
108-00 QENS 6824 E2
Upton St
10 STNL 7020 B5
Urban Pl
10 YNKR 6280 B5
Urban St
10 MTVN 6394 E3
1500 MRNK 6282 E3
1600 HRSN 6282 E3
Urbana St
10 STNL 7020 C5
Urbanowitz Av
2200 LNDN 6917 D5
2500 ELIZ 6917 D6
Ursina Rd
177-00 QENS 6927 B1
Ursino Pl
10 ELIZ 6917 D2
10 UnnT 6917 D2
Ursula Dr
10 NHmT 6724 C2
USS Connecticut Ct
- STNL 7021 A6
USS North Carolina Rd
400 STNL 7021 A6
Utah Rd
900 HmpT 6929 D1
Utah St
10 STNL 7206 A3
Ute Pl
10 GrwT 6170 D2
Utica Av
10 BKLN 6923 E6
1500 BKLN 7023 E3
Utica St
10 JSYC 6716 A7
10 STNL 7207 A2
1700 HmpT 6827 C7
Utica Wk
10 QENS 7121 E4
Utilities Rd
100 UnnT 6917 A2
Utopia Ct
10 STNL 7020 A6
Utopia Pkwy
10-00 QENS 6615 D7
15-00 QENS 6721 D1
69-00 QENS 6825 D2
Utter Av
10 STNL 7019 E3
Utterby Rd
10 MLVN 6929 B2
Uxbridge Rd
10 GrbT 6167 B5
Uxbridge St
10 STNL 7019 C5

V

Vaccaro Dr
100 CRSK 6392 D2
Vail Av
10 STNL 7206 E3
100 STNL 7207 A3
Vail St
10 NWRK 6712 C5
Vailsburg Ter
10 IrvT 6712 D7
10 NWRK 6712 D7
Val Ct
800 HmpT 6827 D6
Valdale Av
10 YNKR 6393 C4
Valdemar Av
10 STNL 7207 A1
Vale Ct
100 NHmT 6724 B6
Vale Pl
10 RYE 6283 E4
10 WbgT 7114 E5
Valencia Av
10 STNL 6920 B7
Valentine Av
400 OrgT 6164 E2
400 PRMT 6164 E2
1800 BRNX 105 E4
1800 BRNX 6504 C5
Valentine Av SR-340
400 OrgT 6164 E2
400 PRMT 6164 E2
Valentine Dr
10 NHmT 6723 E4
10 NHmT 6724 E3
Valentine Ln
10 RSLN 6618 E6
10 YNKR 6393 B3
Valentine Pl
10 QENS 6824 A4
100 WbgT 7114 C4
Valentine St
10 GLCV 6509 D3
10 MTVN 6394 D4
10 YNKR 6394 B2
Valerie Ct
800 HmpT 6929 D2
Valerie Dr
10 YNKR 6279 E4
Valet Rd
- ERTH 6609 E3
Valhalla Av
10 NoCT 6050 B4
Valhalla Dr
3100 BRNX 6506 A7
Valhalla Pl
10 MtPT 6050 A3
10 NoCT 6050 B4

New York City/5 Borough Street Index

STREET
Block City Map# Grid

Valimar Blvd
10 GrbT 6049 E5
10 GrbT 6050 B4
Valimar Ct
10 GrbT 6050 A5
Valles Av
5400 BRNX 6393 C5
Valley Av
10 EMFD 6049 A5
500 YNKR 6279 E5
Valley Blvd
100 WRDG 6500 D6
300 HSBH 6500 D5
Valley Blvd CO-57
100 WRDG 6500 D6
300 HSBH 6500 D5
Valley Ct
10 SECS 6610 B6
Valley Dr
10 GrwT 6170 D3
Valley Ln E
10 HmpT 6928 B6
10 VLYS 6928 B6
Valley Ln N
10 VLYS 6928 B6
Valley Ln W
10 HmpT 6928 B6
10 VLYS 6928 B6
Valley Pl
10 EDGW 6611 E1
10 HAOH 6166 A6
10 HRSN 6169 A7
10 NRCH 6396 B1
10 NRWD 6164 A6
10 TFLY 6392 A3
200 MRNK 6282 E5
400 EGLD 6392 A5
800 PTHA 7205 E2
Valley Rd
- LKSU 6723 C1
- NHmT 6723 C1
10 BRXV 6280 E7
10 GLCV 6509 D2
10 LFRY 6501 D5
10 MrnT 6282 B7
10 NHmT 6508 D6
10 NRCH 6281 D7
10 NRCH 6395 D1
10 PLDM 6617 D5
10 PTWN 6508 D6
10 SCDL 6167 E4
10 STNL 7020 A7
10 WbgT 7114 A1
10 WHPL 6050 C7
10 YNKR 6393 D3
300 COrT 6712 B2
300 WOrT 6712 B2
8900 NBgT 108 A2
8900 NBgT 6611 C5
S Valley Rd
10 COrT 6712 A3
10 WOrT 6712 A4
200 SOrT 6712 A4
Valley St
10 BlvT 6714 B1
10 IrvT 6712 C7
10 NWRK 6712 C7
10 SYHW 6048 B2
10 TYTN 6048 B2
300 COrT 6712 A4
300 WOrT 6712 A3
700 SOrT 6712 A4
1600 FTLE 6502 D5
Valley Ter
10 RYEB 6170 A4
Valley Brook Av
600 LynT 6609 B7
Valley Close
10 YNKR 6393 E4
Valley Forge Pl
10 OrgT 6164 A1
Valley Greens Dr
10 HmpT 6928 B6
10 VLYS 6928 B6
Valley Ridge Rd
10 HRSN 6169 A7
E Valley Stream Blvd
10 VLYS 6928 D4
W Valley Stream Blvd
10 VLYS 6928 B3
Valley Stream Rd E
10 MrnT 6282 C6
Valley Stream Rd W
10 MrnT 6282 C6
Valley Stream State Park Rd
- HmpT 6928 D1
Valleyview Av
10 RYE 6283 E5
Valley View Dr
10 YNKR 6280 B3
Valleyview Pl
10 STNL 7019 E6
10 STNL 7020 A4
Valley View Rd
10 HlsT 6816 C7
10 THSN 6617 C7
Valleyview Rd
10 GrbT 6049 A7
100 IRVN 6166 B1
Valmont Pl
500 HmpT 6827 D6
Valois Pl
10 MTVN 6395 C1
Val Park Av
800 HmpT 6827 D7
900 HmpT 6928 B4
Van Ter
10 OrgT 6164 E3
10 OrgT 6165 A2
Van Allen Av
10 STNL 7116 D4
Van Arsdale Pl
10 NHmT 6617 B5
Van Brunt Rd
10 QENS 7026 A5
Van Brunt St
10 BKLN 120 C7
10 BKLN 6821 B7
10 STNL 7116 D6
100 BKLN 6922 A2
S Van Brunt St
200 EGLD 6502 D1
Van Buren Av
10 CART 7017 C7
Van Buren Av
10 CART 7115 A1
10 FLPK 6827 C1
10 TnkT 6502 A2
200 TnkT 6501 E1
500 LNDN 6917 A6
600 ELIZ 6918 B2
800 HmpT 6828 A5
Van Buren Ct
10 CRSK 6392 D1
Van Buren Pl
10 GrbT 6049 E5
6000 WNYK 6611 A7
Van Buren St
10 LFRY 6501 B5
10 NHmT 6617 E1
10 NWRK 6818 A3
10 RYE 6283 D6
10 STNL 6920 B6
10 WbgT 7114 B3
10 YNKR 6393 E1
200 LynT 6609 A5
300 NWRK 6817 E3
400 BKLN 6822 E7
1600 BRNX 6505 A7
Vance St
2300 BRNX 6505 E4
Van Cleef St
10 JSYC 6819 D5
55-00 QENS 6720 C7
Van Corlear Pl
10 MHTN 102 C4
10 MHTN 6504 A2
Van Cortland Pl
10 KRNY 6714 C1
Van Cortlandt Av
10 STNL 7020 B3
Van Cortlandt Av E
10 BRNX 6504 D2
Van Cortlandt Pk E
4200 BRNX 6393 E6
4200 BRNX 6394 A6
4400 YNKR 6394 A6
Van Cortlandt Pk S
10 BRNX 6504 D1
Van Cortlandt Pk W
10 BRNX 6504 D1
Van Cortlandt Park Av
10 YNKR 6393 D4
Van Courtland Pl
10 RDGF 6611 B2
Vandalay Ct
10 GrbT 6167 A5
Vandalia Av
- BKLN 6925 A4
10 BKLN 6924 D5
Van Dam St
10 BKLN 6822 D2
43-00 QENS 6718 D6
53-61 QENS 6822 D1
Vandam St
10 MHTN 118 C3
10 MHTN 6821 A1
600 HmpT 6927 E5
600 HmpT 6928 A6
Vandelinda Av
10 TnkT 6502 A1
200 TnkT 6501 E1
Vanderbilt Av
- STNL 7019 E7
10 BKLN 6822 A6
10 FLPK 6827 D1
10 HmpT 7029 D5
10 ISPK 7029 D5
10 MHTN 116 D2
10 MHTN 6717 E5
10 NHmT 6617 D6
10 QENS 6827 D1
10 STNL 7020 D3
300 BKLN 6923 A1
Vanderbilt Ct
10 IrvT 6816 A3
Vanderbilt Dr
10 LKSU 6723 B3
10 SNPT 6508 A4
Vanderbilt Pl
10 EORG 6712 C5
10 NARL 6714 D1
10 WbgT 7114 C3
4400 HmpT 7029 D5
Vanderbilt Rd
10 NHmT 6618 A6
10 SCDL 6282 A1
Vanderbilt St
500 BKLN 6922 E5
Vanderbilt Wy
10 HmpT 6928 A5
Vanderburgh Av
10 ERTH 6500 A7
10 LRMT 6396 C2
10 RTFD 6500 A7
Van Der Donck St
10 YNKR 6393 A1
Vanderlyn Dr
10 MNPK 6618 B5
Vanderpool St
10 NWRK 6817 C3
Vanderveer Pl
2200 BKLN 6923 B6
Vanderveer St
10 BKLN 6924 C1
88-00 QENS 6826 D2
Vanderventer Av
10 NHmT 6617 C2
10 NHmT 6618 B1
Vandervoort Av
10 BKLN 6822 D3
Vandervoort Pl
10 BKLN 6822 E5
Vanderwater Av
10 FLPK 6827 C3
10 HmpT 6827 C3
10 SFPK 6827 C3
Van Doren St
55-00 QENS 6720 C7
Van Duyne St
10 NWRK 6817 B6
Van Duzen Pl
10 TCKA 6281 A6
Van Duzer St
10 STNL 6920 D7
100 STNL 7020 D1
Van Duzer St Ext
- STNL 6920 E7
Van Dyke St
10 BKLN 6922 A2
10 WLTN 6500 B6
Vaneck Dr
10 NRCH 6281 D4
Vanessa Ln
10 STNL 7116 E6
Van Etten Blvd
10 NRCH 6281 E5
Van Guilder Av
10 NRCH 6395 D4
Van Hoesen Av
2000 BRNX 6505 C5
Van Horn St
51-00 QENS 6719 E2
53-00 QENS 6823 E1
57-00 QENS 6824 B3
Van Horne St
10 JSYC 6819 E4
10 JSYC 6820 A4
Van Houten Av
10 JSYC 6819 C4
Van Keuren Av
10 JSYC 6715 E6
Van Kleeck St
51-00 QENS 6719 E7
Van Kruiningen Ct
10 WLTN 6500 B4
Van Loon St
51-00 QENS 6719 E2
Van Meter Fens
10 NRCH 6281 D6
Van Meter Fenway
10 NRCH 6281 D6
Van Name Av
10 STNL 6919 A7
10 STNL 7019 A1
E Van Ness Av
10 RTFD 6609 A3
Van Ness Ct
10 MplT 6816 A3
Van Ness Pl
10 NWRK 6817 A3
Van Ness Ter
10 MplT 6816 A3
Van Nest Av
400 BRNX 6505 C6
Van Nostrand Av
10 EGLC 6503 A3
10 EGLD 6502 D1
10 GTNK 6616 D4
10 JSYC 6819 C5
10 NHmT 6618 D7
300 EGLD 6503 A2
Van Nostrand Ct
10 QENS 6722 C2
10 QENS 6723 C2
Van Olst St
100 HKSK 6501 C2
Van Orden Av
10 LEON 6502 D3
Van Orden Rd
10 HRPK 6164 A7
Van Pelt Av
10 STNL 6919 A7
10 STNL 7019 A1
Van Ranst Pl
500 MRNK 6282 C4
Van Reipen Av
10 JSYC 6820 A1
100 JSYC 6819 D1
Van Renssalaer Ct
400 RDGF 6611 B1
Van Rensselaer Rd
10 RYE 6284 C3
Van Rensselaer St
10 BlvT 6714 A1
Van Reypen St
10 JSYC 6819 E1
10 JSYC 6820 D2
Van Riper Av
10 RTFD 6609 A3
Van Riper St
10 STNL 7019 B2
Van Ripper Av
10 SYHW 6048 B1
Van Sciver St
10 CLST 6278 B2
Van Sicklen St
10 BKLN 7022 E6
Van Siclen Av
10 FLPK 6827 C1
600 BKLN 6924 E5
1500 BKLN 6925 A6
Van Siclen Ct
10 BKLN 6924 D1
Van Siclen St
105-00 QENS 6825 B7
Van Sinderen Av
100 BKLN 6924 C3
Van Tassel Av
10 SYHW 6048 A2
Van Tuyl St
10 STNL 6920 C7
Van Vechten St
10 NWRK 6817 A7
Van Velsor Pl
10 NWRK 6816 E5
Van Vorst St
100 JSYC 6820 C3
Van Wagenen Av
10 JSYC 6819 E1
10 RYE 6283 E6
100 JSYC 6715 D6
200 JSYC 6716 A5
Van Wagenen St
10 NWRK 6713 E4
Van Wagner Pl
300 WLPK 6724 D5
Van Wagoner Dr
10 EGLC 6392 C6
Van Wardt Pl
10 OrgT 6164 C3
Van Wart Av
10 TYTN 6048 A4
10 WHPL 6168 A3
Van Wart St
10 EMFD 6049 C6
Van Wettering Pl
10 HKSK 6501 C2
Van Wicklen Rd
- QENS 6925 E2
Van Winkle Av
10 GRFD 6500 A3
Van Winkle Av
10 JSYC 6716 A7
200 JSYC 6715 E7
Van Winkle Pl
200 RTFD 6609 A3
Van Winkle St
100 ERTH 6609 B2
Van Wyck Av
10 STNL 7207 B3
Van Wyck Expwy
- QENS 6720 D4
- QENS 6824 E1
- QENS 6825 A2
- QENS 6926 C5
- QENS 6927 A6
Van Wyck Expwy I-678
- QENS 6720 D4
- QENS 6824 E1
- QENS 6825 A2
- QENS 6926 C5
Van Zandt Av
242-00 QENS 6722 E4
249-00 QENS 6723 A3
Varet St
10 BKLN 6822 D5
Varga Dr
10 CART 7017 B7
Varian Av
3600 BRNX 6505 E1
Varian Ln
10 SCDL 6168 A5
Varick Av
10 BKLN 6822 E4
Varick Ct
10 RKVC 6929 E3
Varick St
10 BKLN 6822 D2
10 MHTN 118 C5
10 MHTN 6821 B3
200 JSYC 6820 B3
Vark St
10 YNKR 6393 C2
Varkens Hook Rd
10 BKLN 6924 B6
Varsity Ct
10 NWRK 6712 C7
Varsity Rd
10 NWRK 6712 B7
100 SOrT 6712 B7
Vassar Av
10 NWRK 6816 E4
10 NWRK 6817 A5
Vassar Pl
10 EchT 6281 B2
10 LNBK 6929 A3
10 RKVC 6929 E3
100 HmpT 6828 E4
100 WbgT 7114 D1
Vassar St
10 GDNC 6828 A3
10 STNL 7019 A7
10 STNL 7018 D7
Vaughan Dr
10 NWRK 6713 C7
Vaughan St
10 STNL 7020 E3
400 HmpT 7029 C2
Vaughn Av
10 NRCH 6395 C3
10 PLHM 6395 C4
Vauxhall Rd
1000 UnnT 6816 A6
Vauxhall Rd CO-630
1000 UnnT 6816 A6
Vedder Av
10 STNL 7019 B2
Veeder Dr
1200 HBPK 6928 D7
Veith Pl
10 STNL 7207 C2
Vella Wy
- EDGW 103 A6
- EDGW 6503 A7
Velock Dr
10 LFRY 6501 C6
Veltman Av
10 STNL 7019 C2
Veltri Ln
10 YNKR 6394 C2
Venice Av
10 STNL 7020 C5
Ventana Ct
10 LWRN 7028 B3
Venture Wy
100 SECS 6715 D2
Venus Dr
10 CLST 6278 D3
Venus Ln
10 STNL 7117 A1
Venus Pl
10 STNL 7116 A6
Veprek Ln
10 SHkT 6501 C4
N Veprek Ln
10 SHkT 6501 C4
Vera Rd
10 YNKR 6280 D6
Vera St
10 STNL 7020 B7
Verandah Pl
10 BKLN 120 E6
10 BKLN 6821 C7
Verbena Av
10 FLPK 6827 C3
Verdi Av
10 TCKA 6281 A5
Verdun Av
10 NRCH 6281 D5
Verity Ln
10 RSLN 6618 D5
Vermilyea Av
10 MHTN 101 E7
10 MHTN 102 A6
10 MHTN 6503 E4
10 MHTN 6504 A4
Vermont Av
10 CART 7017 B6
10 HmpT 7029 D1
10 NWRK 6712 D6
10 WHPL 6168 A4
100 IrvT 6712 D7
100 STNL 7020 E3
200 IrvT 6816 A2
Vermont Ct
10 BKLN 6924 D1
10 QENS 6924 D1
10 STNL 7019 D5
Vermont Pl
- BKLN 6823 D7
- QENS 6823 D7
Vermont St
10 BKLN 6924 D3
10 LBCH 7028 E7
Vermont Ter
10 YNKR 6281 A5
Verne Pl
10 GrbT 6167 B1
Vernon Av
10 ATLB 7028 B7
10 BKLN 6822 C6
10 MTVN 6395 A4
10 NWRK 6816 E2
10 NWRK 6817 A2
10 YNKR 6394 C4
100 RKVC 6929 E5
100 STNL 7116 A7
100 STNL 7207 B1
Vernon Blvd
30-00 QENS 114 A7
30-00 QENS 6718 D4
41-00 QENS 117 E3
Vernon Dr
10 EchT 6281 C3
Vernon Ln
10 EMFD 6049 B5
Vernon Pkwy
10 MTVN 6395 A2
Vernon Pl
10 EORG 6713 A4
10 MTVN 6394 E2
10 MTVN 6395 A2
10 YNKR 6394 C4
400 COrT 6712 C1
Vernon Rd
10 SCDL 6168 B7
Vernon St
10 FLPK 6827 C2
10 RSLN 6618 E5
10 WbgT 7114 E4
Vernon Ter
10 EORG 6713 A4
Vernon Wy
10 WbgT 7115 B2
Verona Av
10 NWRK 6714 A1
10 YNKR 6280 E4
100 NWRK 6713 E1
300 ELIZ 6917 B2
Verona Pl
10 BKLN 6923 C1
10 VLYS 6928 C3
Verona St
10 BKLN 6922 B1
Veronica Pl
10 BKLN 6923 B6
Verrazano-Narrows Br
- BKLN 7021 D4
- STNL 7021 B5
Verrazano-Narrows Br I-278
- BKLN 7021 D4
- STNL 7021 B5
Vervalen St
10 CLST 6278 B3
10 NRWD 6164 A6
Verveelen Pl
100 BRNX 102 D3
100 BRNX 6504 A2
Vesey St
10 MHTN 118 B7
10 MHTN 6821 A4
10 NWRK 6817 E2
Vespa Av
10 STNL 7116 B5
Vesper Av
500 WbgT 7114 D4
Vesper Pl
10 BlmT 6713 C1
Vesta Pl
10 YNKR 6280 A3
Vestry St
10 MHTN 118 B4
10 MHTN 6821 A2
Veteran Pl
700 CLFP 6611 D1
Veterans Av
10 BKLN 7024 A3
Veterans Blvd
10 CARL 6609 E2
10 CARL 6610 A2
10 RTFD 6609 B4
Veterans Ct
- PASC 6500 A4
10 WLTN 6500 A6
Veterans Dr
100 NRWD 6164 C6
100 NVLE 6164 C6
Veterans Pl
400 HSBH 6500 E5
Veterans Plz
10 PALP 6502 D6
Veterans Rd E
10 STNL 7115 D5
300 STNL 7206 D1
Veterans Rd W
10 STNL 7115 D5
10 STNL 7116 A4
2600 STNL 7206 C1
Veterans Wy
- BGTA 6501 D1
10 EDGW 103 A5
10 EDGW 6503 A6
Veterans Memorial Dr
- ELIZ 6918 D4
- HRSN 6050 C7
Veterans Memorial Plz
10 HmpT 6928 D7
Via Bagheria
- LODI 6500 B2
Vian Av
1300 HmpT 6928 D7
Via Trenta Ct
10 YNKR 6280 E1
Victor Dr
10 IRVN 6166 B1
Victor Pl
10 IrvT 6816 C4
Victor Rd
10 BKLN 6923 C7
Victor St
- GRFD 6500 B1
10 LODI 6500 D2
10 VLYS 6929 A2
10 YNKR 6393 D1
1700 BRNX 6505 A6
Victoria Av
10 NWRK 6713 D5
Victoria Dr
172-00 QENS 6826 A7
172-00 QENS 6927 A2
Victoria Ln
10 TFLY 6392 B4
10 YNKR 6280 B6
Victoria Pl
200 LWRN 7028 B6
Victoria Pl E
10 CLFP 6611 E2
10 FTLE 6611 E2
Victoria Pl W
100 FTLE 6611 E1
Victoria Rd
10 ARDY 6166 D3
10 STNL 7116 B5
173-00 QENS 6826 A7
Victoria St
10 NWRK 6817 B4
Victoria Ter
10 RDGF 6610 E1
10 RDGF 6611 A1
Victoria Wy
10 WbgT 7115 A4
Victorian Ct
- MplT 6816 A4
- UnnT 6816 A4
Victory Av
500 RDGF 6611 C1
Victory Blvd
10 NRCH 6281 D6
10 STNL 6920 D7
300 STNL 7020 A3
1500 STNL 7019 B4
2900 STNL 7018 B7
Victory Br
- PTHA 7205 B4
- SRVL 7205 B4
Victory Br SR-35
- PTHA 7205 B4
- SRVL 7205 B4
Victory Ct
10 GrbT 6049 E5
Victory Ln
10 RDFP 6501 E4
Victory Plz
10 NWRK 6817 D1
Viele Av
1200 BRNX 6613 D5
Vienna Ct
10 STNL 7020 E3
Vietor Av
83-00 QENS 6719 E6
E View Ct
10 FLHL 6618 B4
10 JSYC 6819 E5
W View Ct
10 JSYC 6819 C4
View St
10 GrbT 6049 D7
10 GrwT 6170 D5
View St W
10 GrwT 6170 E3
Villa Av
10 STNL 7019 B2
10 YNKR 6394 C3
100 MRNK 6282 E3
2900 BRNX 6504 D2
Villa Ct
10 NRWD 6164 A7
Villa Ln
10 MrnT 6282 B7
Villa Pl
10 NHmT 6618 D7
10 NHmT 6724 B7
200 CDHT 7028 A2
Villa Rd
10 MrnT 6282 B7
Villa St
10 MTVN 6394 E3
10 NHLS 6618 D7
10 NHmT 6618 D7
Village Av
10 HmpT 6827 B6
N Village Av
10 RKVC 6929 D4
200 LNBK 6929 D5
S Village Av
10 RKVC 6929 D5
Village Ct
10 BKLN 7022 E6
10 CRSK 6278 B6
10 DMRT 6278 B6
300 FTLE 6502 D5
Village Grn
10 ARDY 6166 C4
10 PTCH 6170 B4
10 NHmT 6618 B2
Village Grn N
- NHmT 6618 B2
Village Grn S
600 NHmT 6618 C2
Village Ln
10 BRXV 6394 E1
10 BRXV 6395 A1
10 STNL 7116 E6
Village Pl
10 SECS 6610 A5
Village Rd
- ROSE 6618 B6
10 NHmT 6618 B6
100 SOrT 6712 A7
144-00 QENS 6825 B3
1400 UnnT 6816 A4
Village Rd E
10 BKLN 7022 E6
10 BKLN 7023 A6
Village Rd N
10 BKLN 7022 E6
10 BKLN 7023 A6
Village Rd S
10 BKLN 7022 E6
Village Wy
10 LWRN 7028 B3
Village Cir Dr
200 FTLE 6502 D5
Villa Nova St
10 STNL 7019 A7
Villard Av
10 HAOH 6165 E6
10 HAOH 6166 A6
100 DBSF 6166 A6
Villus Av
10 NRCH 6395 D6
Vincent Av
10 LNBK 6929 B4
10 STNL 7117 D2
300 HKSK 6501 A2
500 BRNX 6615 B1
1100 BRNX 6506 A7
Vincent Pl
- TETB 6500 E5
10 ERKY 6929 C5
10 LNBK 6929 C5
600 PTHA 7205 B2
600 WbgT 7205 B2
Vincent Rd
10 YNKR 6394 D1
Vincent St
10 EMFD 6049 A6
10 NWRK 6818 C1
E Vincent St
10 EMFD 6049 B6
Vinci Dr
10 GrwT 6170 D4
Vine Av
10 IrvT 6712 E7
Vine Pl
10 MrnT 6282 B6
Vine Rd
10 MrnT 6282 B7
10 NRCH 6282 B7
Vine St
10 BKLN 121 A3
10 BKLN 6821 C5
10 BRXV 6280 E7
10 BRXV 6281 A7
10 EGLC 6392 C7
10 HlsT 6816 D6
10 JSYC 6820 A2
10 LNBK 6929 A4
10 MrnT 6396 C1
10 NWRK 6817 D1
10 OybT 6618 E2
10 ROSH 6618 E2
10 STNL 6920 D6
200 ELIZ 6917 D4
800 ROSL 6917 D4
Vineland Av
10 STNL 7116 C5
Vineyard Av
10 YNKR 6279 D7
Vintage Ct
10 RYEB 6051 D5
100 GrbT 6050 B4
Vinton St
10 LBCH 7029 E6
Viola St
10 VLYS 6928 B2
Violet Av
10 FLPK 6827 C3
Vireo Av
4200 BRNX 6394 B6
4300 YNKR 6394 B6
Virgil Av
600 RDGF 6611 C1
900 RDGF 6502 B7
Virgil Pl
2000 BRNX 6614 C2
Virgil Rd
10 NRWD 6164 B5
Virginia Av
10 CART 7017 B5
10 DBSF 6166 B4
10 FTLE 6502 E7
10 HmpT 7029 D1
10 JSYC 6819 D4
10 LBCH 7028 E7
10 NHmT 6617 E1
10 STNL 7020 E3
1000 BRNX 6614 B1
1700 HmpT 6827 C7
N Virginia Ct
10 EGLC 6392 C6
S Virginia Ct
10 EGLC 6392 B6
10 EGLD 6392 B6
Virginia Dr
10 HmpT 6827 D4
10 NHmT 6617 C6
Virginia Pl
10 BKLN 6923 D2
10 HmpT 6928 C4
10 LRMT 6396 C1
10 STNL 7019 D2
10 YNKR 6280 A4
Virginia Rd
10 BLRS 6827 C2
10 FLPK 6827 C2
10 GrbT 6050 A4
10 MtPT 6050 A4
10 NoCT 6050 B5
10 WHPL 6050 A5
Virginia St
10 ELIZ 6817 A7
10 NWRK 6817 A7
10 OrgT 6164 D2
10 VLYS 6928 E2
10 YNKR 6394 C3
11-28 QENS 7027 D4
100 HlsT 6816 D7
Virginia Ter
10 JSYC 6819 D3
10 STNL 7019 E5
Visitation Pl
10 BKLN 6922 A1
Vista Av
10 ELIZ 6917 A3
10 STNL 7020 B5
Vista Ct
10 NHmT 6724 C1
Vista Dr
10 GTNE 6616 D7
10 GTNE 6722 D1
Vista Ln
10 EDGW 103 A6
10 EDGW 6503 A7
10 NRCH 6281 D3
Vista Pl
10 GrbT 6166 E3
10 GrbT 6167 A3
10 MTVN 6394 C5
10 STNL 7020 E5
500 HmpT 6827 B6
6800 BKLN 7021 E1
Vista Rd
10 NHLS 6724 C1
10 NHmT 6724 C1
1500 HmpT 6827 D7
Vista St
10 YNKR 6281 A4
Vista Wy
10 NHmT 6617 E2
Vista Hill Rd
10 GTNK 6617 B6
10 NHmT 6617 B6
Vito P Battista Blvd
10 BKLN 6924 D1
300 QENS 6924 D1
400 BKLN 6823 D7
400 QENS 6823 D7
Vivian Dr
10 NRCH 6281 D3
Vivian Ln
10 CLST 6278 B4
Vivian Ter
10 UnnT 6917 C2
700 ELIZ 6917 C2
Viviparous Wy
200 NWRK 6713 E1
Vleigh Pl
73-00 QENS 6825 A3
Vogel Av
10 STNL 7207 A1
Vogel Ln
10 STNL 7019 D3
Vogel Lp
10 STNL 7019 D3
Vogel Pl
10 STNL 7206 E1
Vogler Rd
- STNL 7019 E7
Vogt Ct
- RDGF 6611 B2
Vogt Ln
10 LFRY 6501 C5
Volvo Dr
10 OrgT 6164 D4
10 RCKL 6164 D4
Volz Pl
10 YNKR 6280 B7
Von Braun Av
10 STNL 7116 D4
Von Spiegel Pl
1700 LNDN 6917 D6
Von Vetchen Av
10 WbgT 7114 D3
Voorhees Pl
10 MLVN 6929 A2
10 RDFP 6501 E6
Voorhees St
10 NWRK 6816 E2
1000 HlsT 6816 C7
Voorhies Av
10 BKLN 7023 C7
Vose Av
100 SOrT 6712 A5
400 COrT 6712 A5
Voss Av
10 YNKR 6279 D6
E Voss Av
10 ERKY 6929 B6
Vosseler Ct
10 WOrT 6712 A1
Vosseler Ter
10 WOrT 6712 A1
Vredenburgh Av
10 YNKR 6394 B3
Vreeland Av
10 CARL 6609 C1
10 EMFD 6049 A5
10 ERTH 6609 C1
10 HKSK 6501 C4
10 RTFD 6609 A2
10 SHkT 6501 C4
100 LEON 6502 D3
1300 BRNX 6505 D7
1300 BRNX 6614 D2
Vreeland Pl
10 JSYC 6819 D5
Vreeland St
10 LODI 6500 D1
10 STNL 6919 D7
Vreeland Ter
10 EDGW 6611 E3
10 JSYC 6819 D5
Vroom St
10 JSYC 6820 A2
100 JSYC 6819 E1
Vulcan St
100 STNL 7020 E7
Vyse Av
1100 BRNX 6613 D2
1800 BRNX 6504 E7

W

Wachusetts St
10 RKVC 6929 E2
Wade Sq
10 BRNX 6504 D6
Wade St
10 JSYC 6819 C5
10 STNL 7019 C3
Wadhams St
- BRNX 6615 D5
Wadleigh Av
500 HmpT 6828 D7
Wadsworth Av
10 MHTN 104 D2
10 MHTN 6503 D5
10 STNL 7021 A5
Wadsworth Ct
10 TnkT 6502 C2
Wadsworth Rd
10 STNL 7021 A4
Wadsworth St
10 WLTN 6500 A7
Wadsworth Ter
10 MHTN 104 D2
10 MHTN 6503 E5
10 STNL 7020 E7
Wagg Av
10 MLVN 6929 B2
Wagner Av
10 WLTN 6500 B5
100 MRNK 6283 A5
300 PTHA 7205 D1
N Wagner Av
500 MRNK 6283 A4
Wagner Pl
10 HAOH 6165 E6
10 IrvT 6816 B2
Wagner St
10 HmpT 6827 B7
10 STNL 7020 D7
Wagon Wheel Cir
10 TYTN 6048 B6
Wagon Wheel Rd
10 MrnT 6282 D3
Wahl Av
10 HmpT 7027 D2
Wahler Pl
10 STNL 7118 C2
Waimer Pl
10 STNL 7116 E6
Wainwright Av
10 CLST 6278 C4
10 STNL 7116 E5
10 YNKR 6280 C6
Wainwright Ct
- QENS 7123 E1
10 CLST 6278 C3
Wainwright Dr
10 BKLN 7021 E4
Wainwright St
10 NWRK 6816 E3
10 RYE 6284 A3
300 HlsT 6816 D4
Wainwright Vil
- STNL 7116 D4
Wakefield Av
10 FLHL 6618 A3
10 NHmT 6618 A3
10 YNKR 6394 B5
100 BRNX 6394 C5
10 STNL 7018 C6
Wakefield Rd
10 SCDL 6282 A2
10 STNL 7208 A1
Wakelee Dr
10 DMRT 6278 A5
Wakeman Av
10 NWRK 6713 E4
Wakeman Pl
10 BKLN 6921 E7
10 LRMT 6396 C2
Walbrook Cir
10 GrbT 6167 B7
Walbrook Rd
10 GrbT 6167 B7
Walbrooke Av
10 STNL 6920 A6
10 STNL 7020 B1
Walch Pl
10 STNL 7207 B3
Walcott Av
10 HmpT 7027 D3
10 QENS 7027 D3
10 STNL 7019 C6
Walden Av
10 STNL 7117 E1
254-00 NHmT 6723 C2
254-00 QENS 6723 C2
Walden Ln
- RYE 6283 B6
Walden Pl
1000 HmpT 6929 D2
25500 NHmT 6723 A3
Walden Rd
10 TYTN 6048 C2
N Waldinger St
10 VLYS 6928 C3
S Waldinger St
10 VLYS 6928 C3
Waldo Av
10 BlmT 6713 B2
10 ERKY 6929 C6
10 JSYC 6820 A2
10 WHPL 6167 E2
100 EORG 6713 B2
3600 BRNX 102 D1
3600 BRNX 6393 C7
3600 BRNX 6504 B1
Waldo Ln
10 MNPK 6618 B5
Waldo Pl
10 STNL 7019 E4
Waldorf Av
10 HmpT 6827 B5
Waldorf Ct
10 BKLN 7023 A1
Waldron Av
10 STNL 7020 B3
Waldron St
56-00 QENS 6720 C7
Wales Av
10 JSYC 6715 E7
10 JSYC 6819 E1
300 BRNX 6613 B4
Wales Pl
10 MTVN 6395 A3
10 STNL 6920 A6
10 HmpT 7028 D1
Walgrove Av
10 DBSF 6166 A4
Walker Av
10 CLST 6278 C3
10 RYE 6283 D4
1400 UnnT 6816 A4
1700 IrvT 6816 A4
Walker Ct
10 BKLN 7021 E4
10 GrwT 6170 B1
10 STNL 7116 D5
10 WOrT 6712 A4
Walker Dr
10 STNL 7019 B1
Walker Pl
10 DBSF 6166 A3
10 NHmT 6724 D3
10 STNL 7116 B6
200 HmpT 6828 D6
Walker Rd
10 GrbT 6049 B2
10 MtPT 6049 B2
10 WOrT 6712 A4

New York City/5 Borough Street Index

STREET
Block City Map# Grid

Walker Rd
100 MNLA 6724 E6
Walker St
10 MHTN 118 C5
10 MHTN 6821 B3
10 MLVN 6929 A2
10 STNL 7019 A1
10 VLYS 6929 A2
100 CLFP 6611 C3
200 FRVW 6611 C3
Walkers Ln
100 EGLD 6392 A6
Wall Av
10 MtPT 6049 E1
10 MtPT 6050 A1
Wall St
10 ERTH 6500 A6
10 FTLE 103 B1
10 FTLE 6503 A4
10 GRFD 6500 A4
10 MHTN 120 C2
10 MHTN 6821 B5
10 MtPT 6049 E1
10 NWRK 6818 A2
10 PASC 6500 A4
10 STNL 6920 D6
10 WLTN 6500 A6
600 HmpT 6828 C7
9000 NBgT 108 A2
9000 NBgT 6611 C5
Wall St W
1000 LynT 6609 B5
1200 RTFD 6609 B4
Wallabout St
10 BKLN 6822 B5
Wallace Av
10 MTVN 6394 E3
10 STNL 7020 E5
3300 BRNX 6505 B2
Wallace Ct
10 VLYS 6928 D3
Wallace Pkwy
10 YNKR 6393 D2
Wallace Pl
10 WHPL 6167 E3
10 WHPL 6168 C4
Wallace St
10 RKVC 6929 E2
10 TCKA 6281 A6
10 WbgT 7114 C5
100 COrT 6712 D2
Wallaston Ct
10 BKLN 7022 C2
Wall Bridge Ln
- ROSE 6618 D5
- RSLN 6618 D5
Waller Av
10 WHPL 6168 B2
Waller St
100 JSYC 6716 A6
Wallick Close
10 GrbT 6167 B7
Wallington Av
100 WLTN 6500 A5
Wallis Av
10 JSYC 6715 E7
10 JSYC 6819 D1
Wallis Av US-1
100 JSYC 6715 E7
Wallis Av US-9
100 JSYC 6715 E7
Wallis Av US-9 TRK
100 JSYC 6715 E7
Walloon St
10 STNL 7019 A1
Walnut Av
- BKLN 7022 E2
10 BGTA 6501 D3
10 BRNX 6613 B5
10 FLPK 6827 B2
10 LRMT 6396 D3
10 PLHM 6395 C3
10 RKVC 6929 E3
10 STNL 7117 B7
Walnut Ct
10 EGLD 6392 A7
10 SOrT 6712 A4
10 WHPL 6169 A5
Walnut Dr
10 TFLY 6392 A4
Walnut Ln
10 FLHL 6618 A5
10 HRSN 6283 B4
Walnut Pl
10 GTPZ 6617 A7
10 LODI 6500 C3
10 STNL 7117 E1
Walnut Rd
10 ERKY 6929 B6
10 HmpT 7027 C3
Walnut St
10 CLST 6278 B3
10 DBSF 6165 E4
10 ERTH 6500 A7
10 FRVW 6611 B2
10 GrbT 6167 E1
10 GRFD 6500 B1
10 HmpT 6828 D5
10 JSYC 6819 B4
10 LNBK 6929 B4
10 NRCH 6395 D4
10 NRWD 6164 B7
10 NWRK 6817 D1
10 OybT 6618 E2
10 PTHA 7205 C4
10 RDGF 6611 B2
10 ROSH 6618 E2
10 RTFD 6500 A7
10 RYE 6283 E2
10 STNL 6920 A7
10 TnkT 6502 A3
10 TYTN 6048 C5
70-00 QENS 6824 C4
100 BGTA 6501 E3
100 EGLD 6392 A7
100 NVLE 6164 C5
100 TnkT 6501 E3
200 ELIZ 6917 E2
200 NWRK 6818 A2
200 SAMB 7205 B7
200 YNKR 6393 D1
400 YNKR 6279 E7
500 FTLE 6502 E5
500 MRNK 6283 A5
700 LNDN 6917 A7
900 ELIZ 6817 A7
Walnut St
900 ELIZ 6918 A1
E Walnut St
10 LBCH 7029 D7
10 TnkT 6502 A3
N Walnut St
10 EORG 6712 E4
10 WbgT 7114 D1
300 EORG 6713 A2
500 BlmT 6713 A1
S Walnut St
10 EORG 6712 E4
W Walnut St
10 LBCH 7029 A7
700 LBCH 7028 E6
Walsh Av
1000 HmpT 7028 C1
Walsh Ct
10 BKLN 7022 E1
Walsh Ln
10 GrwT 6170 D4
Walsh Rd
10 YNKR 6279 D7
10 YNKR 6393 D1
Walter Av
10 HSBH 6500 D4
200 MNLA 6724 D6
Walter Ct
10 RTFD 6609 A4
Walter Dr
10 WbgT 7114 B2
Walter Ln
10 FLHL 6617 E5
Walter Pl
10 IrvT 6712 D7
10 SECS 6609 E7
Walter St
10 TYTN 6048 B5
100 LNDN 7017 D4
Walter Cherry Sr St
- WbgT 7114 A4
Walters Av
10 STNL 7020 A3
Walters Ln
10 NHmT 6616 D7
10 SDRK 6616 D6
Waltham St
95-00 QENS 6825 C6
Walton Av
10 WHPL 6167 E4
10 WHPL 6168 A4
200 BRNX 107 D7
200 BRNX 6612 E3
500 MRNK 6282 E7
600 MRNK 6283 A7
800 BRNX 6613 A1
800 MRNK 6397 A1
1200 BRNX 105 B7
1200 BRNX 6504 B6
2400 BRNX 102 D6
Walton Ct
400 HmpT 6828 D6
Walton Rd
600 QENS 7026 B4
Walton St
10 BKLN 6822 C5
100 EGLD 6502 E2
200 HmpT 6828 D6
Waltrous Av
400 PTHA 7205 C1
Walworth Av
10 SCDL 6167 D4
100 WHPL 6167 C2
Walworth Cross
10 WHPL 6167 E3
Walworth St
10 BKLN 6822 B6
Walworth Ter
10 WHPL 6167 E3
Wanamaker St
400 HmpT 7029 C1
Wandel Av
10 STNL 7020 C3
Wanser Av
10 HmpT 7027 D3
Wappanocca Av
10 RYE 6169 E7
10 RYE 6283 E1
Warburton Av
10 HAOH 6279 D2
10 YNKR 6279 D2
10 YNKR 6393 C1
300 HAOH 6165 E7
Warburton Av SR-9A
10 YNKR 6393 C1
Warburton Av US-9
10 YNKR 6393 C1
Ward Av
10 STNL 6920 D7
10 STNL 7020 D1
300 MRNK 6282 E5
1000 BRNX 6613 E1
Ward Dr
10 NRCH 6282 A4
100 NRCH 6281 E4
Ward Pl
10 SOrT 6712 A7
1100 HmpT 6928 C7
N Ward Pl
10 EORG 6713 B4
S Ward Pl
- EORG 6713 B5
Ward St
10 COrT 6712 D2
10 FLPK 6827 D2
10 HAOH 6165 C7
Wardman St
10 WHPL 6050 A7
Wards Pk E
10 RYE 6284 A3
Wards Pk W
10 RYE 6284 A3
Wards I
- MHTN 6612 E7
10 MHTN 110 E7
10 MHTN 114 E1
10 MHTN 6718 E1
Wards Point Av
10 STNL 7206 A4
Wardwell Av
10 STNL 7019 D3
Wardwell Rd
100 MNLA 6724 D7
Wareham Pl
84-00 QENS 6825 E3
Warehouse Ln
10 GrbT 6049 A4
Waring Av
10 STNL 7116 C4
600 BRNX 6505 B4
Waring Ct
1500 ERKY 6929 A7
1500 HmpT 6929 A7
1500 HWTH 6929 A7
Waring Dr
10 FLHL 6618 A4
Waring Pl
10 YNKR 6279 D7
Waring Row
10 YNKR 6393 D1
Warner Av
10 JSYC 6819 C5
10 NHmT 6618 D7
10 ROSE 6618 D7
100 RSLN 6618 D7
Warner Ln
10 TYTN 6048 C1
Warner Rd
800 HmpT 6827 E7
Warner St
10 WbgT 7205 A1
10 WbgT 7114 A7
Warnke Ln
10 GrbT 6166 E7
Warren Av
10 GrbT 6049 D7
10 TCKA 6281 B4
10 TYTN 6048 C2
100 FTLE 6611 D1
100 MRNK 6282 E4
500 MRNK 6283 A3
Warren Blvd
10 HmpT 6828 C3
Warren Ct
10 SOrT 6712 B6
Warren Dr
300 HmpT 7028 D3
Warren Ln
10 ALPN 6278 D5
Warren Pkwy
800 TnkT 6502 B1
Warren Pl
10 HRSN 6168 D1
10 MTVN 6394 C7
10 MTVN 6395 A6
10 NWRK 6713 D7
Warren Rd
10 MplT 6816 A1
Warren St
10 CART 7115 D2
10 HAOH 6279 E1
10 HAOH 6280 A1
10 HKSK 6501 B4
10 HRSN 6713 E6
10 JSYC 6820 C3
10 LFRY 6501 C6
10 LODI 6500 C1
10 MHTN 118 A5
10 MHTN 6821 A3
10 NWRK 6713 C6
10 STNL 7020 D2
10 WHPL 6168 B1
37-00 QENS 6720 A5
100 BKLN 120 E7
100 BKLN 121 A7
100 BKLN 6821 C7
100 NRCH 6395 D4
500 BKLN 6922 D1
600 HRSN 6714 B6
900 ROSL 6917 A5
1200 LNDN 6917 A6
Warrington Pl
10 EORG 6713 B3
Warriston Ln
10 RYE 6283 E6
Warsoff Pl
10 BKLN 6822 B6
Warwick Av
10 EchT 6281 B2
10 MTVN 6395 D7
100 STNL 7019 C5
200 FTLE 6502 E7
200 SOrT 6712 B5
235-00 QENS 6722 C1
Warwick Blvd
- ISPK 7029 C5
10 HmpT 7029 B5
Warwick Cir
173-00 QENS 6825 E4
Warwick Ln
200 LEON 6502 D4
Warwick Pl
10 NHmT 6508 D6
Warwick Rd
10 GTNK 6617 A5
10 HlsT 6816 C7
10 HmpT 6827 B5
10 HmpT 7029 C5
10 ISPK 7029 C5
10 NHmT 6617 A5
10 YNKR 6280 C7
10 YNKR 6394 C1
1600 ERKY 6929 A6
Warwick St
10 BKLN 6924 D2
10 BlmT 6713 B2
10 EORG 6713 B3
10 NWRK 6817 E2
10 NWRK 6818 B2
Washburn St
10 JSYC 6820 B1
Washington Av
10 BKLN 6822 A6
10 BlvT 6714 A1
10 CARL 6610 A3
10 CART 7115 D1
10 CDHT 7028 A2
10 CLFP 6611 D2
10 DBSF 6166 B3
10 ERTH 6609 B1
10 GrbT 6049 C6
10 HAOH 6165 E7
10 HmpT 7029 C5
10 IRVN 6166 B3
10 IrvT 6816 D2
10 KRNY 6714 B2
10 LFRY 6501 D6
10 LNBK 6929 C4
10 LWRN 7028 A2
Washington Av
10 MNLA 6724 E6
10 NHmT 6724 C7
10 NRCH 6395 C4
10 NWRK 6714 A1
10 OrgT 6164 A2
10 QENS 6928 A1
10 RTFD 6609 A1
10 STNL 7019 C6
10 VLYS 6928 B2
10 WHPL 6168 C2
100 ELIZ 6917 D5
100 FTLE 103 D1
100 FTLE 6503 A4
100 HKSK 6501 C3
100 SECS 6716 A2
100 UNCT 6716 D4
100 WhkT 6716 D4
200 CART 7017 D7
200 RTFD 6500 A7
300 PLHM 6395 C4
400 BKLN 6923 A2
400 LNDN 6917 A7
400 RDGF 6611 C2
500 HmpT 6828 D7
800 BRNX 6613 B3
800 MNCH 6610 B1
900 PLMM 6395 B7
1300 NHPK 6828 A1
1400 BRNX 105 E6
1400 BRNX 6504 C7
1500 NHPK 6724 A7
Washington Av CO-503
10 CARL 6610 B1
800 MNCH 6610 B1
Washington Av CO-604
10 CART 7115 D1
200 CART 7017 D7
Washington Av CO-667
10 BlvT 6714 A1
10 NWRK 6714 A1
Washington Av SR-7
10 BlvT 6714 A1
Washington Av N
10 NoCT 6050 A4
Washington Av S
10 CDHT 7028 A3
10 LWRN 7028 A3
E Washington Av
100 WbgT 7114 B4
N Washington Av
10 GrbT 6167 D3
10 LFRY 6501 D6
10 STNL 7018 C1
10 WbgT 7114 A1
S Washington Av
10 DBSF 6166 B4
10 GrbT 6167 C4
Washington Blvd
10 LBCH 7029 A7
10 MTVN 6394 E7
400 JSYC 6820 D3
Washington Br
- BRNX 104 E5
- BRNX 105 A5
- BRNX 6503 E6
- BRNX 6504 A6
- MHTN 104 D5
- MHTN 6503 E6
Washington Ln
10 EDGW 103 A6
10 EDGW 6503 A7
10 OrgT 6164 C3
Washington Mw
10 MHTN 118 E2
10 MHTN 119 A2
10 MHTN 6821 E5
Washington Pk
10 BKLN 121 E5
10 BKLN 6821 E6
Washington Pkwy
10 BAYN 6919 D4
Washington Pl
- BRNX 6615 C2
- EORG 6712 C4
10 CARL 6500 C7
10 ERTH 6500 C7
10 ERTH 6609 D2
10 GrbT 6049 E6
10 GRFD 6500 B3
10 HKSK 6501 B4
10 HSBH 6500 D3
10 ISPK 7029 C4
10 KRNY 6714 B2
10 LODI 6500 D3
10 MHTN 118 D1
10 MHTN 119 A2
10 MHTN 6821 C1
10 MNCH 6610 B1
10 MTVN 6394 A7
10 NHmT 6617 E2
10 NWRK 6713 C4
10 STNL 7019 C1
10 TYTN 6048 A4
10 WLTN 6500 A5
200 CLFP 6611 C4
200 FRVW 6611 C4
200 HmpT 7027 E2
400 MNLA 6724 D6
400 NHmT 6724 D6
Washington Pl E
10 NoCT 6050 B5
E Washington Pl
10 PALP 6502 C6
W Washington Pl
10 PALP 6502 C5
Washington Rd
10 BKLN 7021 D4
Washington Sq
10 MrnT 6396 B1
Washington Sq E
10 MHTN 118 E2
10 MHTN 6821 E5
Washington Sq S
10 MHTN 118 E2
10 MHTN 6821 E5
Washington St
- PRMT 6164 D3
10 BKLN 121 B3
10 BKLN 6821 D5
10 BlvT 6714 A1
10 COrT 6712 D1
10 CRSK 6278 B7
10 EORG 6712 E3
10 HBKN 6716 E5
10 HRSN 6050 D7
10 HRSN 6714 A6
Washington St
10 LODI 6500 D2
10 MHTN 120 A2
10 MTVN 6394 E4
10 NWRK 6713 D7
10 PTCH 6170 B6
10 PTHA 7205 E3
10 RKVC 6929 D4
10 TCKA 6281 A6
10 TFLY 6392 A2
10 TnkT 6502 B2
10 WOrT 6712 D2
100 JSYC 6820 D4
100 MRNK 6282 D5
100 NVLE 6164 C5
100 OrgT 6164 D3
100 SYHW 6048 B1
100 TYTN 6048 B2
200 FRVW 6611 B2
200 MTVN 6395 A4
200 NWRK 6817 D1
300 CARL 6500 B7
300 ERTH 6500 B7
300 GrbT 6050 A5
400 MHTN 118 C1
400 MHTN 6821 A2
600 HmpT 6828 B4
700 MHTN 115 C7
700 MHTN 6717 B7
700 WRDG 6500 B7
5700 WNYK 6610 E7
6100 NBgT 6610 E6
Washington St CO-8
- PRMT 6164 D3
100 OrgT 6164 D3
Washington St CO-671
10 COrT 6712 D1
10 WOrT 6712 D2
Washington St CO-679
10 HBKN 6716 D7
N Washington St
10 BXTE 6617 C1
10 TYTN 6048 B2
100 SYHW 6048 B2
S Washington St
10 BXTE 6617 D1
10 NHmT 6617 D1
10 TYTN 6048 B3
Washington Ter
10 EORG 6712 E3
10 MHTN 104 D4
10 MHTN 6503 C5
400 FTLE 6502 E5
400 LEON 6502 D5
Washington Springs Rd
10 OrgT 6165 B4
Washington Square Vil
10 MHTN 118 E3
10 MHTN 6821 C2
Wasylenko Ln
10 YNKR 6393 B1
10 YNKR 6394 A1
Watch Hill Dr
10 GrbT 6048 E4
10 GrwT 6170 B1
2000 GrbT 6049 A4
Watchogue Rd
10 STNL 7019 C3
Watchung Av
10 BlvT 6713 D1
10 NWRK 6713 D1
100 COrT 6712 C1
200 WOrT 6712 C1
Water Ln
10 PLNM 6617 C3
Water St
- STNL 7018 A1
10 BKLN 121 C2
10 BKLN 6821 C5
10 EchT 6281 C4
10 HKSK 6501 C3
10 JSYC 6819 C3
10 LBCH 7029 C6
10 MHTN 120 B2
10 MHTN 6821 A5
10 NRCH 6396 A6
10 PTHA 7205 E5
10 STNL 7020 D1
10 WHPL 6168 A1
300 MHTN 119 A7
300 MHTN 121 A1
N Water St
10 GrwT 6170 C5
S Water St
10 GrwT 6170 C6
Waterbury Av
10 STNL 7207 A2
2200 BRNX 6614 C1
2700 BRNX 6505 E7
3100 BRNX 6506 A7
Waterbury St
10 BKLN 6822 D4
Wateredge Pl
900 HWTH 7028 E1
900 HWTH 7029 A2
Waterford Ct
10 STNL 7021 B5
Waterford Rd
10 ISPK 7029 D4
Waterford Towers
1000 EDGW 108 A2
1000 EDGW 6611 D5
Water Front Blvd
10 HmpT 7027 C3
Waterfront Blvd
10 HmpT 7029 D6
Waterfront Ter
- WhkT 6716 E4
Water Grant St
10 YNKR 6393 C1
Waterloo Pl
14-00 QENS 7027 B4
1800 BRNX 6504 D7
Waters Av
- BRNX 6505 D6
10 STNL 7019 C3
Waters Pl
10 HmpT 6928 C5
10 VLYS 6928 C5
1000 BRNX 6505 D6
Water's Edge
10 GLCV 6509 D3
Waters Edge Dr
14-00 QENS 6616 A7
23-00 QENS 6722 A1
Waters Edge Ln
- ELIZ 6918 C5
Waterside Ct
150-00 QENS 6615 B6
Waterside Dr
10 PLNH 6617 C5
100 LFRY 6501 D5
300 GrbT 6049 A3
Waterside Pkwy
10 STNL 7117 C6
Waterside St
10 STNL 7118 B3
Waterside Close
10 EchT 6281 C5
Waterview Ct
10 STNL 7021 A3
Waterview Dr
10 PTWN 6508 C7
1200 HmpT 6929 D2
1200 RKVC 6929 D2
Waterview Pl
10 HmpT 6929 C3
10 LNBK 6929 C3
Waterview Rd
10 HmpT 7029 D6
10 KNGP 6617 B4
500 HmpT 6929 D6
Waterview St
10 HmpT 6929 C7
12-00 QENS 7027 B4
Watjean Ct
2-00 QENS 7027 C6
Watkins Av
10 STNL 7116 D4
Watkins Dr
500 MNLA 6724 D5
Watkins Pl
10 NRCH 6395 D3
Watkins St
10 BKLN 6924 B2
10 LNBK 6929 C4
Watsessing Av
10 BlmT 6713 C1
Watsessing Av CO-509
200 BlmT 6713 C1
Watson Av
10 ELIZ 6917 C4
10 EORG 6712 E5
10 LNDN 6917 C5
10 NWRK 6817 A4
10 STNL 7018 C7
100 NWRK 6712 E5
200 PTHA 7205 C4
300 WbgT 7114 D4
1400 BRNX 6613 E2
1500 BRNX 6614 A2
Watson Ct
10 RYE 6283 E5
Watson Pl
107-00 QENS 6825 E5
107-00 QENS 6826 A5
Watson St
10 YNKR 6281 A5
Watt Av
3200 BRNX 6506 A6
Watts Pl
10 ERKY 6929 B5
10 HmpT 6928 C5
10 LNBK 6929 B5
10 VLYS 6928 C5
Watts St
10 KRNY 6714 A5
10 MHTN 118 C4
10 MHTN 6821 B2
Waukena Av
10 HmpT 7029 E1
W Waukena Av
10 HmpT 7029 D1
Wave St
10 STNL 7020 E1
Wavecrest Pl N
10 HmpT 7029 D4
Wavecrest Pl S
10 HmpT 7029 D4
Wavecrest St
10 STNL 7118 B3
10 VLYS 6928 E4
Waverly Av
10 BKLN 6822 A7
10 EchT 6281 B6
10 ERKY 6929 A7
10 TCKA 6281 B6
100 MRNK 6282 E6
300 BKLN 6923 A1
300 HWTH 6929 B7
2900 HmpT 6929 D7
Waverly Pl
10 CDHT 7028 B3
10 CRSK 6278 A7
10 LWRN 7028 B3
10 MHTN 118 D1
10 MHTN 119 A2
10 MHTN 6821 C1
10 MtPT 6050 A2
10 RKVC 6929 E4
10 STNL 7020 D3
10 VLYS 6928 B2
10 YNKR 6393 C2
200 MHTN 115 D7
200 MHTN 6717 B7
200 MplT 6712 A7
200 SOrT 6712 A7
400 COrT 6712 B3
1200 ELIZ 6917 E1
Waverly Rd
10 NRCH 6281 E2
10 NRCH 6282 A3
Waverly St
10 JSYC 6716 B7
10 OybT 6618 E1
10 YNKR 6393 D2
1200 HmpT 6928 C6
S Waverly St
10 YNKR 6393 D2
Way St
10 WRDG 6500 D6
Waydell St
10 NWRK 6818 C1
Wayne Av
10 ATLB 7028 B7
10 EORG 6712 C4
10 WHPL 6167 E2
Wayne Av
200 CLFP 6611 D1
600 NHPK 6827 E2
3300 BRNX 6504 E1
Wayne Ct
10 ARDY 6166 D3
Wayne Ln
10 OrgT 6164 B1
Wayne St
10 JSYC 6820 C3
10 STNL 6919 E7
100 PTHA 7205 D2
Wayne Ter
200 UnnT 6917 A1
300 UnnT 6816 C7
Wayne Wy
10 GrbT 6049 B7
Wayside Dr
10 GrbT 6166 E2
Wayside Ln
10 SCDL 6167 C7
WCC East Gate
- GrbT 6049 E4
- MtPT 6049 E4
WCC Knollwood Rd Gate
- GrbT 6049 D5
Weaver Av
300 QENS 6616 A6
Weaver Pl
- GrwT 6170 D4
Weaver St
10 GrwT 6170 D4
10 MrnT 6282 D7
10 MrnT 6396 D1
10 NRCH 6282 A5
10 SCDL 6282 A5
10 STNL 7116 E7
10 STNL 7207 E1
Weaver St SR-125
10 MrnT 6282 D7
10 MrnT 6396 D1
10 NRCH 6282 A5
10 SCDL 6282 A5
E Weaver St
10 GrwT 6170 D3
Webb Av
- HRSN 6169 D5
2300 BRNX 102 E5
2300 BRNX 6504 B4
Webb Pl
10 HSBH 6500 D5
10 YNKR 6280 E3
Webber Av
100 SYHW 6048 C1
Webb Hill Rd
10 NHmT 6723 B3
Weber Av
10 MLVN 6929 B2
Weber Dr
10 PTCH 6170 B7
Weber Pl
10 IrvT 6816 C2
Weber Ter
10 SAMB 7205 B7
Webster Av
10 BKLN 7022 E1
10 HRSN 6283 B3
10 JSYC 6716 C6
10 KRNY 6714 B1
10 NARL 6714 B1
10 NHmT 6617 D5
10 NRCH 6395 D4
10 PLNH 6617 D5
10 STNL 6920 C7
100 FLHL 6617 E5
100 YNKR 6393 D1
200 BKLN 7023 A1
300 BKLN 6923 A7
300 UNCT 6716 C5
1000 BRNX 6613 B1
1000 NRCH 6281 D7
1400 BRNX 105 D6
1500 BRNX 6504 C5
3100 BRNX 6505 A1
3700 BRNX 6394 A7
4300 YNKR 6394 A7
Webster Av US-1
1700 BRNX 105 E5
1700 BRNX 6504 C5
E Webster Av
300 ROSP 6917 A3
Webster Pl
- RDFP 6501 D5
10 BKLN 6922 D3
10 COrT 6712 D3
10 EORG 6712 D3
10 PTCH 6170 B5
Webster Rd
10 EchT 6281 C3
10 OrgT 6164 A1
100 SCDL 6281 C2
Webster St
10 FLPK 6827 E3
10 IrvT 6816 B4
10 LNBK 6929 A3
10 MLVN 6929 A3
10 NWRK 6713 D5
10 RDFP 6501 E4
10 VLYS 6928 E2
10 VLYS 6929 A2
1200 HmpT 6928 D6
1300 HmpT 6827 E3
Wedgewood Av
10 CART 7017 C6
10 WbgT 7114 C3
Wedgewood Ct
10 GTNK 6617 B5
10 NHmT 6617 B5
Wedgewood Ln
10 LWRN 7027 B3
Weed Av
10 STNL 7118 A3
Weed Rd
- STNL 7021 B4
Weehawken St
10 MHTN 118 B1
10 MHTN 6821 A1
Weeks Av
1600 BRNX 105 D6
1600 BRNX 6504 B6
2800 HmpT 6929 E6
Weeks Ln
47-00 QENS 6722 C5
47-32 QENS 6721 E6
Weeks Pl
10 NRCH 6396 A2
Weeks Rd
10 EWLS 6724 E3
Weequahic Av
10 NWRK 6816 E4
10 NWRK 6817 A5
Weequahic Park Dr
- NWRK 6816 D4
- NWRK 6817 B5
Wegman Ct
10 JSYC 6819 D5
Wegman Pkwy
10 JSYC 6819 D5
Weidner Av
10 HmpT 6929 D7
3100 HmpT 7029 D1
Weigands Ln
100 SECS 6716 A2
Weight Ct
10 THSN 6617 B7
Weiher Ct
400 BRNX 6613 B2
Weil Pl
10 CRSK 6278 B7
10 DMRT 6278 B7
Weiner St
10 STNL 7206 C2
Weir Ln
- STNL 7206 D2
Weir Wy
300 CARL 6609 D3
Weirfield St
10 BKLN 6823 B6
16-00 QENS 6823 B6
Weirup St
500 PTHA 7205 B2
Weldon St
10 BKLN 6925 A1
10 JSYC 6819 E1
Welland Av
10 IrvT 6816 C3
Wellbrook Av
10 STNL 7019 D5
Weller Av
240-00 QENS 6927 E4
Weller Ln
147-00 QENS 6927 E5
Welles Ct
10 STNL 7020 A1
Wellesley Av
10 YNKR 6393 D4
Wellfleet Rd
10 HmpT 7029 B1
Wellford Rd
10 GrbT 6049 B7
Wellhouse Ln
10 MrnT 6282 C3
Wellhouse Close
10 MrnT 6282 C3
Welling Ct
11-00 QENS 114 D5
11-00 QENS 6718 D2
Wellington Av
10 CLST 6278 A2
10 COrT 6712 A3
10 NRCH 6281 E7
10 NRCH 6395 E1
10 WOrT 6712 A3
Wellington Cir
10 BRXV 6280 C4
Wellington Ct
10 BKLN 7023 A1
10 GrwT 6170 D6
10 STNL 7117 A1
Wellington Dr
10 WbgT 7115 B2
Wellington Rd
- NHmT 6724 C7
10 GDNC 6828 C3
10 HmpT 6827 A5
10 HmpT 6828 C3
100 GDNC 6724 C7
200 MNLA 6724 D5
400 WLPK 6724 D5
Wellington Rd S
10 HmpT 6828 C4
300 GDNC 6828 C3
Wellington St
- RKVC 6929 D3
10 GrwT 6170 C6
Wellington Ter
10 GrbT 6049 B7
Wellman Av
2800 BRNX 6505 E7
Wells Av
10 YNKR 6393 C1
Wells Av SR-9A
10 YNKR 6393 C1
Wells Av US-9
10 YNKR 6393 C1
Wells Ct
10 DMRT 6278 A5
Wells Pl
10 HmpT 7027 E2
10 RTFD 6500 A7
Wells Rd
1600 HmpT 6928 C1
Wells St
10 BKLN 6925 A1
Wellsboro Rd
10 HmpT 6928 C1
Wells Park Dr
- YNKR 6393 D5
Wellwood Rd
10 DMRT 6278 B5
Wellyn Rd
10 YNKR 6394 D1
Wellyn Close
10 YNKR 6394 A3
Welsh Ln
10 JSYC 6819 E3
Welwyn Rd
10 GTPZ 6617 B7
Wemple St
10 STNL 7018 E2
10 STNL 7019 A2
Wendel Pl
10 YNKR 6279 C5
10 YNKR 6280 A7
Wendell Pl
10 FRVW 6611 B4
Wendover Rd
10 EchT 6281 B5
Wendover Rd
10 HRSN 6169 B7
10 YNKR 6393 D3
106-00 QENS 6824 D4
200 YNKR 6394 A4
Wendt Av
10 LRMT 6396 C1
Wendy Dr
10 STNL 7207 D1
Wendy Ln
10 CLST 6278 D2
Wendy Ter
10 GRFD 6500 B1
Wenlock St
10 STNL 7019 A1
Wenner Pl
2400 BRNX 6614 D2
Wensley Dr
10 NHmT 6723 A1
10 RSLG 6723 A1
Wentworth Av
10 NHmT 6724 D3
10 STNL 7020 E6
100 WLPK 6724 D3
Wentworth Pl
10 LWRN 7027 C4
Wenz Pl
600 ROSL 6917 A4
Werneking Pl
10 LFRY 6501 D6
Werns Av
300 HmpT 6827 D6
Wescott St
- NWRK 6818 B1
10 OLDT 6164 A3
500 NVLE 6164 A3
Weser Av
10 STNL 7020 D4
Wesley Av
10 PTCH 6170 A5
Wesley Ct
10 BAYN 6919 E1
Wesley Dr
10 ERKY 6929 B7
Wesley Pl
10 NARL 6714 C1
10 WbgT 7114 E3
Wesley St
10 SHkT 6501 B3
E Wesley St
10 HKSK 6501 B3
10 SHkT 6501 B3
Wesley White Dr
100 CART 7017 A7
100 WbgT 7017 A7
Wessels Pl
10 GrwT 6170 C6
Wessington Av
10 GRFD 6500 A2
West Av
10 BKLN 7121 A1
10 HmpT 6927 D7
10 LRMT 6396 C1
10 MLVN 6929 A2
300 BKLN 7120 E1
300 WbgT 7114 E5
400 NVLE 6164 B4
600 WbgT 7115 A3
1400 BRNX 6505 B7
West Av CO-611
300 WbgT 7114 E5
600 WbgT 7115 A3
West Blvd
10 HmpT 6929 B7
10 HmpT 7029 B1
West Ct
10 NHmT 6724 D1
West Dr
- MHTN 112 D6
- MHTN 6717 E3
10 BAYN 6919 E2
10 GTPZ 6617 A6
10 KENS 6617 A6
10 MHVN 6508 B7
10 MrnT 6282 B6
10 NHmT 6617 D7
10 PLDM 6617 C4
10 YNKR 6394 C2
25-00 QENS 6722 C2
West Rd
- HRSN 6051 C6
- MHTN 113 E7
- MHTN 114 A6
- MHTN 117 D1
- MHTN 6718 C3
600 QENS 7026 B4
West St
10 BKLN 6822 B1
10 CLST 6278 A1
10 GDNC 6724 E7
10 HRSN 6283 A3
10 JSYC 6820 A1
10 MHTN 120 A2
10 MHTN 6821 A5
10 MNLA 6724 E7
10 MRNK 6283 B4
10 NHmT 6618 E2
10 NHmT 6724 B5
10 NWRK 6713 B7
10 NWRK 6817 C1
10 OybT 6618 E2
10 PTCH 6170 A6
10 RYEB 6170 A6
10 STNL 6919 E7
10 STNL 7019 E1
100 SHkT 6501 B2
100 WHPL 6168 D7
200 HKSK 6501 B3
200 WHPL 6282 E1
300 MHTN 118 B3
400 BKLN 7022 E5
400 FTLE 103 A4
400 FTLE 6503 A5
400 HRSN 6282 E2
500 MHTN 115 C7
500 MHTN 6717 A7
900 BRNX 6395 B7
900 PLMM 6395 B7
1300 UNCT 6716 D3
1500 FTLE 6502 E5
2000 BKLN 7023 A6
4200 QENS 6718 D6
West St SR-9A
300 MHTN 118 B3
300 MHTN 6821 A2

New York City/5 Borough Street Index

N West St   Wilt Av

Each entry: **Street** — Block, City, Map#, Grid

N West St — 10 MTVN 6394 A7
S West St — 10 MTVN 6394 C4
West Ter — 10 STNL 7116 B7
West Wy — 10 NRCH 6395 D5 / - WHPL 6168 D5
Westaway Rd — 300 QENS 6616 A7
Westbank Rd — 10 RYE 6283 D6
Westbourne Av — 25-00 QENS 7027 A4
Westbrook Av — 10 STNL 7019 A1
Westbrook Rd — 10 KNGP 6616 E3
Westbrooks Av — 10 NWRK 6817 B1
Westbury Av — 10 STNL 6920 B7
Westbury Ct — 2000 BKLN 6923 A4
Westbury Rd — 10 WbgT 7114 A4
Westchester Av — 10 PTCH 6170 C6 / 100 WHPL 6168 B1 / 100 BRNX 6505 E6 / 100 YNKR 6280 C2 / 100 HRSN 6168 E2 / 200 MTVN 6394 E4 / 400 BRNX 6613 A2 / 500 RYEB 6169 E5 / 500 RYEB 6170 A4 / 700 WHPL 6169 A3 / 800 HRSN 6169 A3 / 1500 BRNX 6614 A1 / 3200 BRNX 6506 A5
Westchester Av SR-22 — 10 CLST 6278 A2 / 10 WHPL 6168 B1
Westchester Av SR-119 — 10 WHPL 6168 B1
Westchester Av SR-120 — - HRSN 6169 A4
Westchester Av SR-120A — 10 PTCH 6170 A5 / 500 RYEB 6169 E5 / 500 RYEB 6170 A5 / 3000 HRSN 6169 D5
Westchester Av SR-127 — 100 WHPL 6168 C1
Westchester Pl — 10 NRCH 6395 C5
Westchester Plz — 10 GrbT 6049 B3
Westchester Sq — 10 BRNX 6505 B7
Westchester View Ln — 10 GDNC 6828 D2 / 10 GrbT 6166 E1 / 10 GrbT 6167 A2
Westcliff Av — 10 LKSU 6723 C4
Westcott Blvd — 10 STNL 7019 D3
Westcott St — 10 BlmT 6713 A1 / 10 EORG 6713 A1 / 10 HmpT 7027 D3
Westend Av — 10 VLYS 6928 A2 / 700 CLFP 6611 D1 / 700 FTLE 6611 D1
W Westend Av — 600 CLFP 6611 C1
Westend Pl — 10 HRSN 6283 B4 / 10 HRSN 6283 B4
Westentry Rd — 10 STNL 7020 A7
Westerleigh Ct — 10 RYEB 6613 E2
Westerleigh Rd — 10 HRSN 6169 D4 / 10 RYEB 6169 E4
Westerly St — 10 YNKR 6394 B2
Western Av — - STNL 7117 E1 / 10 JSYC 6716 A4 / 10 NRCH 6918 C7 / 10 STNL 7018 C1 / 10 YNKR 6393 D3
Western Blvd — - LEON 6502 D3
Western Dr — 10 ARDY 6166 D5
Western Hwy — 10 OrgT 6164 B1
Western Pkwy — 10 IrvT 6712 D7 / 10 IrvT 6816 D1
Western Junior Hwy — 10 GrwT 6170 D4
Western Park Dr — 500 HmpT 6828 C6
Westervelt Av — 10 CLST 6278 A4 / 10 STNL 6920 C6 / 10 TFLY 6392 A3 / 2200 BRNX 6505 D4
Westervelt Av CO-501 — 10 TFLY 6392 A3
Westervelt Pl — 10 CRSK 6278 B7 / 10 GRFD 6500 B3 / 10 IrvT 6816 C1 / 10 JSYC 6820 B4 / 10 LODI 6500 C2 / 10 NWRK 6816 C1 / 10 EGLC 6503 A4 / 1200 HmpT 6928 D7
Westfield Av — 10 ELIZ 6917 B3 / 900 ROSP 6917 B3
Westfield Av SR-27 — 10 ELIZ 6917 E3
Westfield Av SR-28 — 100 ELIZ 6917 B3 / 900 ROSP 6917 B3

E Westfield Av — 200 ROSP 6917 B3 / 400 ELIZ 6917 B3
E Westfield Av CO-616 — 400 ELIZ 6917 A3 / 400 ROSP 6917 A3
E Westfield Av SR-28 — 200 ROSP 6917 A3
Westfield Cir — 10 WHPL 6168 E7
Westfield Ln — 10 WHPL 6168 E7
Westfield Pl — 10 GLCV 6509 E3
Westfield Rd — 10 WHPL 6168 E7 / 10 WHPL 6169 A7
West Gate — 10 LFRY 6501 C3
Westgate — 10 HmpT 6827 D4
Westgate Blvd — 10 PLDM 6617 C5
Westgate Dr — 1400 FTLE 6502 D6
Westgate Dr S — 900 FTLE 6502 D5
Westgate St — 136-00 QENS 6927 B2
Westhaven Ln — 10 WHPL 6168 E1
Westhelp Dr — 10 GrbT 6049 E4
Westinghouse Plz — 175-00 QENS 6825 E4 / 182-00 QENS 6826 A3
Westlake Dr — 10 NoCT 6050 A2 / 10 MtPT 6050 A1
Westland Pl — 10 WbgT 7114 C4
Westminister Av — 10 CLST 6278 A2
Westminster Av — 300 HlsT 6917 E1 / 700 HlsT 6917 E1 / 800 HlsT 6816 D7
Westminster Ct — 10 NRCH 6395 C3 / 10 STNL 7020 A4
Westminster Dr — 10 GrbT 6049 D3 / 10 MtPT 6049 D3 / 1400 UnnT 6816 A4
Westminster Ln — 10 JSYC 6819 C3
Westminster Pl — 10 GRFD 6500 B3 / 10 LODI 6500 C1 / 500 SdBT 6500 C1
Westminster Rd — 10 BKLN 6923 A4 / 10 GDNC 6828 D2 / 10 GrbT 6167 A4 / 10 HmpT 6828 E4 / 10 LKSU 6723 A2 / 10 LNBK 6928 E5 / 10 NHmT 6723 A2 / 10 RKVC 6929 E2 / 10 VLYS 6928 E5
Westminster Rd S — 10 HmpT 6828 E5
Westmoreland Av — 10 WHPL 6168 A2
Westmoreland Dr — 10 YNKR 6394 A4
Westmoreland Pl — 235-00 QENS 6722 C4
Westmoreland St — 39-00 QENS 6722 E4
Weston Pl — 10 LWRN 7028 A3
Westover Pl — 10 LWRN 7027 E4 / 10 WNYK 111 C1 / 100 WNYK 6611 A7
Westport Ln — 10 STNL 7019 B7
Westport St — 10 STNL 7019 A7 / 10 STNL 7117 A1
Westside Av — 10 WbgT 7114 C2 / 108-00 QENS 6720 C7 / 3800 NBgT 6716 C1 / 4300 NBgT 6610 D6 / 4300 SECS 6716 D1 / 4300 SECS 6716 D1 / 8500 RDGF 6610 E3
Westview — 10 HRSN 6169 B1
Westview Av — 10 TCKA 6280 E6 / 10 WHPL 6168 A7 / 200 FTLE 6502 E6 / 300 LEON 6502 E3 / 400 EGLD 6503 C3 / 400 EGLD 6502 E3 / 500 CLFP 6611 C2 / 500 FRVW 6611 C2 / 500 RDGF 6611 C2
Westview Cir — 10 SYHW 6048 C1
Westview Ln — 10 SCDL 6282 A2
Westview Pl — 10 EGLD 6503 C3 / 400 FRVW 6611 B3
Westville Rd — 10 WbgT 7027 D2
Westward Ln — 10 GrbT 6395 B6
Westward Pl — 10 GrbT 6049 B4

Westway — 10 BRXV 6395 B1 / 10 EchT 6395 B1 / 10 SCDL 6281 D2 / 400 MNLA 6724 D5 / 400 NHmT 6724 D5
Westwind Ct — 200 NRWD 6278 C1
Westwind Rd — 10 YNKR 6280 D3
Westwood Av — 10 NRCH 6283 A3 / 600 STNL 7019 C4
Westwood Cir — 10 IRVN 6166 B1
Westwood Dr — 10 HRSN 6283 A3
Westwood Dr N — 10 HRSN 6283 A3
Westwood Ln — 10 IRVN 6166 C1
Westwood Pl — 10 YNKR 6280 E2 / 10 HmpT 6827 C7
Westwood Close — 60-00 QENS 6824 A1
Wetherole St — 60-00 QENS 6824 A1
Wetmore Av — 10 MplT 6712 A7 / 10 SOrT 6712 A7
Wetmore Pl — 10 RYE 6284 A3
Wetmore Rd — 10 STNL 7020 C4
Wexford Ter — 175-00 QENS 6825 E4 / 182-00 QENS 6826 A3
Weyant Dr — 10 CDHT 7028 B2 / 10 LWRN 7028 B2
Weybridge Rd — 10 GTNK 6617 A5
Weyburn Rd — 10 YNKR 6281 B1
Weyford Ter — 10 GDNC 6828 C2 / 10 GDNC 6828 C1
Weyman Av — 10 NRCH 6506 E1 / 10 NRCH 6395 E7
Whale Sq — 200 BRNX 6393 C5
Whalen St — 10 BKLN 6921 E5
Whalley Av — 10 STNL 7116 D6
Wharton Pl — 10 BKLN 6824 A7
Wharton St — 10 NWRK 6817 A7
Wheatland Av — 10 WOrT 6712 A3
Wheatley Av — 10 NHmT 6724 C3
Wheatley St — 13-00 QENS 7027 D4 / 1200 HmpT 6928 D6
Wheaton Pl — 10 RTFD 6609 A3
Wheeler Av — 10 CART 7017 D7 / 10 CART 7115 D1 / 100 MNLA 6724 E5 / 10 NHmT 6724 E5 / 400 CART 7028 A1 / 500 BKLN 7023 A1 / 800 HmpT 6928 B7 / 3300 HmpT 7029 D2
Wheeler Av W — 10 VLYS 6928 D2
Wheeler St — 10 WOrT 6712 B2 / 10 CLFP 6611 C4
Wheeler Point Rd — 10 NWRK 6818 A3
Wheeling Av — 10 GTNK 6617 B5 / 10 KNGP 6617 B5
Wheelock Av — 10 EchT 6395 B5 / 10 TYTN 6048 B4 / 100 BRNX 6614 B3 / 100 TCKA 6281 A7
Wheelock Rd — 10 SCDL 6168 B1
Whelan Pl — 10 YNKR 6279 D7
Whelan Rd — 10 SCDL 6167 D6
Whig Rd — 10 SCDL 6167 D6
Whimbrel Ln — 10 SECS 6609 E7 / 300 SECS 6715 D1
Whinhill Ct — 10 GrbT 6166 C6
Whippoorwill Rd — 10 RYEB 6170 A1
Whipple St — 10 BKLN 6822 C5
Whistler Av — - QENS 6616 A6
Whistler Rd — 10 MNPK 6618 A6
Whitaker Pl — 10 STNL 7020 B2
White Av — 10 BKLN 7021 E4 / 10 NHmT 6723 D7 / 100 NRWD 6164 E4 / 100 NVLE 6164 E5 / 100 OLDT 6164 E5
White Ct — 10 NRWD 6164 B5 / 10 STNL 7116 A5
White Dr — 10 CDHT 7028 B2
White Pl — 10 STNL 7019 D1

White Rd — 10 EchT 6281 D2 / 10 NWRK 7029 E3 / 10 SCDL 6281 D2 / 400 MNLA 6724 D5 / 400 NHmT 6724 D5
White St — 10 BKLN 6822 D5 / 10 COrT 6712 C2 / 10 HRSN 6283 B2 / 10 MHTN 118 D6 / 10 MHTN 6821 B3 / 10 STNL 7021 A3 / 10 TYTN 6048 B3 / 10 VLYS 6929 A2 / 10 WbgT 7114 C3 / 10 WOrT 6712 C2 / 300 ROSL 6917 A5 / 1200 HlsT 6816 C6
White Ter — 10 ERTH 6500 A7
White Birch Dr — 10 GrbT 6167 B6 / 10 RYE 6283 D5
White Birch Ln — 10 NRCH 6282 A4
White Deer Ln — 10 NRCH 6282 A4
Whitehall Blvd — 10 GDNC 6828 D3 / 100 GDNC 6724 C7 / 200 NHmT 6724 D7
Whitehall Blvd S — 10 GDNC 6828 D3 / 200 HmpT 6828 D3
Whitehall Dr — 900 HmpT 6928 B5
Whitehall Ln — 10 NHmT 6724 B6
Whitehall Pl — 700 BRNX 6394 C6
Whitehall Rd — 10 EchT 6281 B4
Whitehall Rd S — 10 EchT 6281 B4
Whitehall St — 10 LNBK 6928 E3 / 10 MHTN 6821 B6 / 10 STNL 7117 D3 / 10 VLYS 6928 E3 / 100 LNBK 6929 A3 / 100 MLVN 6929 A3 / 100 VLYS 6929 A3
Whitehall Ter — 10 STNL 7116 D6
Whitehead Pl — 1200 HlsT 6917 E7
White House Rd — 10 GrbT 6048 A7
Whitelaw Pl — 300 TnkT 6502 A3
Whitelaw St — 136-00 QENS 6925 D2
Whiteman St — 200 FTLE 6502 E6 / 200 FTLE 6503 B5
White Oak Cir — 10 HRSN 6051 B4
White Oak Dr — 10 NRCH 6051 D4
White Oak Ln — 10 GrbT 6167 B6 / 10 STNL 7115 D7
White Oak Rd — 400 OrgT 6164 D4
White Oak St — 10 NRCH 6395 D2
White Pine Ln — 10 GTNK 6617 B5 / 10 KNGP 6617 B5
White Plains Av — 10 EMFD 6049 B5 / 10 HRSN 6168 A3 / 10 STNL 7020 E3 / 10 WHPL 6168 B1
White Plains Rd — 10 BRXV 6281 B4 / 10 BRXV 6395 B1 / 10 EchT 6395 B1 / 10 TYTN 6048 B4 / 100 BRNX 6614 B3 / 100 TCKA 6281 A7 / 200 EchT 6281 A6 / 400 SCDL 6281 D1 / 800 SCDL 6281 D1 / 1000 SCDL 6281 B7 / 2200 BRNX 6505 B3 / 3900 BRNX 6394 C7 / 4800 MTVN 6394 C6
White Plains Rd SR-22 — 10 BRXV 6281 B4 / 100 BRXV 6281 A7 / 100 TCKA 6281 A7 / 600 SCDL 6281 D1 / 1000 SCDL 6281 D1
White Plains Rd SR-119 — 10 TYTN 6048 B4 / 400 EMFD 6048 C4
Whiteside Av — 1100 HmpT 6828 A4
White Star Av — - QENS 6615 A7
Whitestone Expwy — - QENS 6615 A7 / - QENS 6720 E3 / - QENS 6721 A1
Whitestone Expwy I-678 — - QENS 6615 A7 / - QENS 6720 E3 / - QENS 6721 D1
White Stone Pl — 10 STNL 6395 C3
Whitetail Rd — 10 TYTN 6048 C6
Whitewood Av — 10 NRCH 6395 E7

Whitewood Av — 10 STNL 7020 A2
Whitewood Dr — 10 NHLS 6724 B3
Whitewood Rd — 10 TFLY 6392 A5 / 400 EGLD 6392 A5
Whitfield Ter — 10 NRCH 6395 C2
Whitlock Av — 10 STNL 7020 A6 / 1000 BRNX 6613 D2
Whitman Av — 10 EORG 6713 B3 / 10 JSYC 6819 E1 / 10 STNL 7117 B6
Whitman Dr — 10 BKLN 7024 B4
Whitman Ln — 10 GLCV 6509 E5
Whitman Rd — 10 CART 7017 C7 / 10 HAOH 6165 B7 / 10 TnkT 6502 C2
Whitney Av — 10 BKLN 7023 E5 / 10 FLPK 6827 C1 / 10 QENS 6827 C1 / 10 STNL 7020 D5 / 84-00 QENS 6719 E6 / 89-27 QENS 6720 A6
Whitney Cir — 900 HmpT 6928 B5
Whitney Dr — 10 GLCV 6509 D2
Whitney Pl — 10 BKLN 7022 E5 / 10 BKLN 7023 E5 / 10 EORG 6713 B3 / 10 NHmT 6617 D7
Whitney St — 10 EMFD 6049 B5 / 10 WHPL 6167 D2
Whiton St — 10 JSYC 6820 A4
Whitson St — 73-00 QENS 6824 D4
Whittemore St — 10 RYEB 6170 A5
Whittier Av — 10 YNKR 6394 D3 / 200 FLPK 6827 D1 / 200 QENS 6827 D1 / 300 NHmT 6723 D7 / 300 NHPK 6723 D7 / 800 NHPK 6724 A7
Whittier Dr — 10 NHmT 6724 C2
Whittier Pl — 136-00 QENS 6925 D2
Whittier St — 10 EORG 6713 D4 / 10 GrbT 6167 B6 / 10 MLVN 6929 A3 / 500 BKLN 6613 E3
Whittingham Pl — 10 WOrT 6712 B2
Whittington Rd — 10 GrbT 6049 B7
Whittlesey Av — 10 EORG 6713 B3 / 100 NWRK 6712 E6
Whitty Ln — 10 BKLN 6923 E7
Whitwell Pl — 10 BKLN 6821 B2 / 10 STNL 7020 A5
Wick Dr — 10 WbgT 7114 A5
Wicker Ct — 10 BKLN 6924 C1
Wicker St — 700 BKLN 6713 D5 / 10 YNKR 6279 C6
Wickes Av — 10 YNKR 6280 A6
Wickford Rd — 10 NRCH 6395 C3 / 10 PLHM 6395 C3
Wickham Av — 2200 BRNX 6505 B3 / 3900 BRNX 6394 C7
Wickham Rd — 10 GDNC 6828 B2 / 100 GDNC 6828 B1
Wicklow Pl — 85-00 QENS 6826 A7
Wicks Dr — 10 HRPK 6164 A7
Wicks Ln — 10 MLVN 6929 C2
Wicks Rd — 10 MNLA 6724 C6 / 10 NHmT 6724 C6
Wiederer Av — 10 STNL 7020 E1
Wieland Av — 10 STNL 7115 E6 / 10 STNL 7116 A6
Wilbert Ter — 200 BRNX 6504 E4
Wilbur Pl — 10 NRCH 6281 D2 / 143-00 QENS 6721 C1 / 166-30 QENS 6615 D7
Wilbur St — 10 LNBK 6928 E4 / 10 MHTN 6821 D3
Wilbur Ter — 10 YNKR 6393 C7
Wilben Ct — 10 QENS 6616 E7 / 20-01 QENS 6721 C1

Wilburton Pl — 10 NWRK 6713 E4
Wilcox Av — 10 EORG 6393 E3 / 10 YNKR 6393 E3 / 500 BRNX 6615 B1 / 1100 BRNX 6506 E7
Wilcox St — 10 STNL 7019 A2
Wild Av — 10 STNL 7018 B7 / 1000 BRNX 6613 D2
Wildacre Av — 10 NWRK 7027 E4
Wildcat Wy — - LNDN 7017 A3 / - ERTH 6609 C2
Wildcliff Rd — 10 NRCH 6396 A5
Wilden St — 10 BKLN 7024 B4
Wilden Pl — 300 NWRK 6712 A7 / 300 SOrT 6712 A7
Wilder Av — 10 STNL 7117 C2 / 3900 BRNX 6394 D7
Wilder St — 10 ELIZ 6816 E7 / 10 HlsT 6816 E7 / 10 HlsT 6917 D1
Wildey St — 10 SYHW 6048 B2 / 10 TYTN 6048 B2
Wildflowers — - GrbT 6167 A3 / 10 ARDY 6167 A3
Wildway — 10 EchT 6281 C3 / 10 YNKR 6394 D1
Wildwood Av — 10 WOrT 6712 B1 / 100 PTCH 6170 B6 / 100 VLYS 6928 B2 / 200 HmpT 6828 D4 / 600 NHmT 6724 A7 / 600 NHmT 6724 A7 / 900 ELIZ 6917 B4 / 1000 HmpT 6928 C5 / 1100 HmpT 6928 C5 / 1600 FTLE 6502 E5 / 1900 UnnT 6816 A4
Wildwood Dr — 10 GTNE 6616 D6 / 100 KNGP 6616 E6
Wildwood Ln — 10 ARDY 6166 D3 / 10 STNL 7206 B4
Wildwood Pl — 73-00 QENS 6824 D4
Wildwood Rd — 10 EchT 6281 C4 / 10 GrbT 6167 C2 / 10 KNGP 6616 D3 / 10 MrnT 6396 B1 / 10 NRCH 6396 B1 / 10 NRCH 6396 C3
Wildwood Rd W — 500 NVLE 6164 A4 / 1200 UnnT 6816 B7
Wildwood Ter — 1200 UnnT 6816 B7
Wilentz Dr — - PTHA 7114 C7
Wiley Pl — 500 BRNX 6613 E3
Wiley Post Rd — 10 STNL 7117 D3
Wilfred Ter — 10 CART 7115 C3
Wilgarth Rd — 10 NRCH 6394 C1
Wilhelm St — 10 BKLN 6714 B6
Wilkins Av — 10 PTCH 6170 C5 / 1500 BRNX 6613 C1
Wilkinson Av — 10 JSYC 6819 D5 / 2800 BRNX 6505 E6 / 3100 BRNX 6506 A5
Wilkinson Ter — 10 KRNY 6714 A3
Wilkliff St — 10 NWRK 6713 C7
Will Pl — 10 BKLN 6924 C5
Willa Wy — 10 EchT 6281 C4
Willada Ln — 10 GLCV 6509 D3
Willams Av — - NRWD 6164 A5 / 10 PLHM 6395 C3
Willard Av — 10 BlmT 6713 C1 / 10 MTVN 6395 A4 / 10 STNL 7019 C3 / 2800 HmpT 6929 E6
Willard St — 10 ERKY 6929 A4 / 10 GRFD 6500 A3 / 10 LODI 6500 C2
Willers Wy — 10 GrwT 6170 C4
Willets Av — 10 NHmT 6828 E5
Willets Pl — 10 PLDM 6617 C5
Willets Pond Pth — - QENS 6615 A7
Willett St — 10 MHTN 119 C6 / 10 MHTN 6821 D3
Willetts Point Blvd — 126-00 QENS 6721 D4
Williamson Wy — 10 LWRN 6928 B5

William Av — 10 STNL 7117 C6 / 200 BRNX 6506 E6
William Ct — 10 QENS 7027 D5 / 1200 BKLN 7023 B7
William Pl — 1400 BRNX 6505 E7
William St — 10 NWRK 6713 B7 / 10 OrgT 6164 B3 / 10 BlvT 6714 A1 / 10 CART 7017 B6 / 10 CDHT 7028 A2 / 10 CLST 6278 A2 / 10 DMRT 6278 B6 / 10 EORG 6712 C3 / 10 EORG 6713 A4 / 10 ERTH 6500 A6 / 10 GTNK 6616 E6 / 10 HAOH 6165 E7 / 10 HmpT 6827 B7 / 10 HRSN 6050 C3 / 10 KRNY 6714 A3 / 10 LWRN 7028 A2 / 10 MHTN 120 B2 / 10 MHTN 6821 B4 / 10 MplT 6816 A1 / 10 MTVN 6394 D3 / 10 NARL 6714 D1 / 10 NoCT 6050 C4 / 10 NWRK 6817 D1 / 10 PRMT 6164 E2 / 10 RTFD 6609 A3 / 10 STNL 7020 D1 / 10 WHPL 6168 B1 / 10 WLPK 6724 D4 / 10 WLTN 6500 A6 / 10 COrT 6712 C2 / 10 MHTN 118 C7 / 100 PTCH 6170 B6 / 100 PTHA 7205 D3 / 100 VLYS 6928 B2 / 200 HmpT 6828 D4 / 300 WbgT 7114 C5 / 500 NHmT 6724 A7 / 700 NHmT 6929 D2
E William St — 10 PTCH 6170 B6 / 10 WbgT 7205 A2
N William St — 300 WbgT 7114 C5
S William St — 10 MHTN 120 B2 / 10 MHTN 6821 B6
W William St — 400 PTCH 6170 A6 / 400 RYEB 6170 A6
William A Clarke Pl — 108-00 QENS 6925 E1
William L Butcher Br — - HRSN 6168 E2
William Penn Rd — 10 GTNK 6616 E6
Williams Av — 10 BKLN 6924 A4 / 10 JSYC 6819 C3 / 10 SHkT 6168 A5 / 10 STNL 7117 C4 / 10 TFLY 6392 A3 / 100 HSBH 6500 E1 / 100 OLDT 6164 A5 / 200 HKSK 6500 A4 / 300 HSBH 6501 A4
Williams Av CO-40 — 10 BKLN 6821 C6
Williams Ct — 10 BKLN 7023 B7 / 10 EDGW 6611 D4 / 10 EDGW 108 B1
Williams Dr — 10 ELIZ 6917 D5
Williams Ln — 10 ISPK 7029 D3
Williams Pl — 10 BKLN 6924 C2 / 700 CLFP 6611 D1
Williams Ter — 10 CLFP 6611 D3
Williamsbridge Ovl — 3200 BRNX 6504 E4 / 3300 BRNX 6505 A1
Williamsbridge Rd — 10 BRNX 6505 B3
Williamsbridge Br — - BKLN 6821 C6
Williamsburg Pl — 10 BKLN 6822 A6
Williamsburg St E — 10 BKLN 6822 A6
Williamsburg St W — 10 BKLN 6822 D6 / 10 STNL 7019 B3
Williamson Pl — 10 NRCH 6281 D1
Williamson St — 10 ERKY 6929 C7 / 185-00 QENS 6927 C1 / 192-00 QENS 6823 B7 / 200 HlsT 6816 D7

Willis Av — - BRNX 6612 E5 / - MHTN 110 E3 / - MHTN 6612 E4 / 10 NHmT 6618 D7 / 10 FLPK 6723 D7 / 10 NHmT 6723 D7 / 10 STNL 6920 D7 / 100 BRNX 110 E2 / 100 BRNX 6613 A4 / 100 MNLA 6724 E4 / 200 QENS 6723 D7 / 300 WLPK 6724 E5
Willis Ct — 100 HmpT 7028 D1
Willis Av Br — - BRNX 110 D3 / - MHTN 110 D3 / - MHTN 6612 E5
E Williston Av — 10 EWLS 6724 E4 / 10 WLPK 6724 E4
E Williston Av SR-25B — 10 EWLS 6724 E4 / 10 WLPK 6724 E4
Willmohr St — 10 BKLN 6924 A4
Willoughby Av — 10 BKLN 121 E6 / 10 BKLN 6822 A6 / 17-00 QENS 6823 A4 / 400 BKLN 6822 D6
Willoughby St — 10 BKLN 121 C5 / 10 BKLN 6821 E5
Willow Av — 10 BRNX 6613 B5 / 10 HBKN 6716 D6 / 10 LRMT 6396 C3 / 10 NRCH 6395 C3 / 10 PLHM 6395 C3 / 10 QENS 6723 E5 / 10 RCKL 6164 E5 / 10 STNL 7020 B5 / 10 WLTN 6500 B5 / 1900 NVLE 6164 B4
Willow Av CO-675 — 10 HBKN 6716 D6
Willow Cir — 10 BRXV 6280 C4
Willow Ct — 300 WbgT 7114 C5
Willow Ct N — 10 PLNH 6617 C5
Willow Ct S — 10 PLNH 6617 C5
Willow Dr — 10 EGLC 6392 C6 / 10 NHmT 6617 E3 / 10 NRCH 6395 C6 / 10 NRCH 6396 A6
Willow Ln — 10 HWTH 7028 E1 / - TnkT 6502 A2
Willow Pl — 10 BKLN 6821 C6 / 10 GTNE 6616 E7 / 10 GTNE 6617 A7 / 10 MLVN 6929 A3 / 10 MTVN 6394 E4
Willow Rd E — 10 STNL 7019 B3
Willow Rd W — 10 STNL 7019 B3
Willow St — 10 LEON 6502 C3 / 10 BKLN 6821 C6 / 10 BAYN 6819 B3 / 10 BlmT 6713 B1 / 10 CART 7115 C3 / 10 CRSK 6278 B7 / 10 ERTH 6500 A4 / 10 JSYC 6820 A4 / 10 LFRY 6501 C6 / 10 NHmT 6821 B7 / 10 PTCH 6170 B7 / 10 STNL 7019 B3
Willow Ter — 10 HmpT 6828 E6
Willow Wy — 10 TYTN 6048 A5
Willowbrook Av — 10 HmpT 7028 E1

Willowbrook Ct — - STNL 7019 B7
Willowbrook Expwy — - STNL 6919 B7 / - STNL 7019 B7
Willowbrook Expwy SR-440 — - STNL 6919 B7 / - STNL 7019 A1
Willowbrook Rd — 10 WHPL 6168 E6 / 300 STNL 7019 B3
Willowdale Av — 10 NHmT 6617 E2 / 10 NHmT 6618 B1
Willow Gate — 10 EHLS 6618 E4
Willow Glade Rd — 10 LNDN 6917 D2
Willow Pond Ln — 10 HBPK 6928 E2 / 10 HWTH 6928 E7
Willow Pond Rd — 10 STNL 7020 A5
Willow Run Rd — 10 GrwT 6051 E6
Willows Ln — 10 STNL 7020 C3
Willow Shore Av — 10 SCLF 6509 D7
Willow Tree Rd — 300 LEON 6502 C3
Willowtree Rd — 10 LEON 6502 C4
Willow Wood Ln — 10 STNL 7117 B4
Willow Wood Sq — 10 ERTH 6500 A7
Willry St — 10 IrvT 6712 D7 / 10 STNL 7020 E6
Wills Pl — 10 IrvT 6712 D7
Wilmont Av — 10 WHPL 6168 B6
Wilmont St — 300 SAMB 7205 A7
Wilmot Cir — 10 NRCH 6281 E2
Wilmot Dr — 200 HmpT 6929 A6
Wilmot Rd — 10 NRCH 6281 D4 / 900 NRCH 6282 A1 / 1200 SCDL 6282 A1
Wilmoth Av — 10 ARDY 6166 E5
Wilputte Rd — 10 NRCH 6281 D4
Wilsey St — 10 NWRK 6713 C6
Wilshire Dr — - LKSU 6723 B2 / 10 WHPL 6169 A6
Wilson Av — 10 BKLN 6822 E5 / 10 KRNY 6714 A4 / 10 LNBK 6929 A4 / 10 MtPT 6049 A4 / 10 NWRK 6818 C7 / 10 RTFD 6609 A3 / 10 SECS 6610 B7 / 10 STNL 7117 A5 / 10 BKLN 6823 A4 / 10 LBCH 7029 E7 / 100 CLFP 6611 C4 / 200 FRVW 6611 C4 / 10 STNL 7117 A5 / 200 FTLE 103 A1 / 200 FTLE 6503 A7 / 300 STNL 7116 E6 / 3200 BRNX 6505 C2
Wilson Blvd — 10 MNLA 6724 C6 / 10 NHmT 6724 C6
Wilson Dr — 10 RYE 6283 C4 / 100 ALPN 6278 E7
Wilson Ln — 10 RKVC 6929 D3
Wilson Pl — 10 RKVC 6929 E5 / 10 BlvT 6714 D2 / 10 CLST 6278 A4 / 10 COrT 6712 D3 / 10 HAOH 6166 A6 / 10 IrvT 6816 B2 / 10 MTVN 6394 A6 / 10 YNKR 6279 E6
Wilson Rd — - TFLY 6392 A3 / 10 VLYS 6928 D6
Wilson St — 10 BKLN 6822 A5 / 10 ERKY 6929 C6 / 10 GDNC 6828 E2 / 10 GRFD 6500 A1 / 10 JSYC 6820 A4 / 10 LFRY 6501 C5 / 10 SHkT 6167 D7 / 10 STNL 7020 C6 / 200 PTHA 7205 C3 / 600 HmpT 6928 B3 / 700 HmpT 6828 B3 / 4500 HmpT 7029 D4
Wilson Ter — 10 STNL 6917 D2
Wilson Block — 10 NWRK 6394 E2
Wilson Park Dr — 300 SYHW 6048 C7
Wilson View Pl — 10 STNL 7020 C4
Wilson Woods Park Rd — - MTVN 6395 A4
Wilt Av — 1000 RDGF 6502 E3

New York City/5 Borough Street Index

STREET
Block City Map# Grid

Wilt Av
1000 RDGF 6611 A1
Wilton Cir
10 RYEB 6169 E4
Wilton Ct
10 NRWD 6164 A7
10 NRWD 6278 A1
10 STNL 7020 D7
10 STNL 7021 B4
Wilton Rd
10 EchT 6281 C5
10 HmpT 6928 E1
10 RYEB 6169 E4
Wilton St
10 NHmT 6723 E7
10 NHmT 6724 A7
200 NHPK 6724 A7
Wiltshire Pl
10 YNKR 6280 D6
Wiltshire Rd
- SCDL 6282 A1
10 NRCH 6281 E1
10 NRCH 6282 A1
Wiltshire St
10 YNKR 6280 D6
Wilwade Rd
10 NHmT 6723 B3
Wiman Av
10 STNL 7117 B7
Wiman Pl
10 STNL 7021 A3
Wimbledon Ct
10 GrbT 6167 E1
Wimbledon Dr
10 NHLS 6724 B3
Wimbleton Ln
10 GTNK 6617 A5
10 KNGP 6617 A5
Winans Av
- IrvT 6816 C4
10 NWRK 6817 B1
200 HlsT 6816 D5
900 LNDN 7017 B2
Winans Dr
10 YNKR 6280 B7
Winans St
10 EORG 6712 E4
10 LRMT 6396 B2
10 MrnT 6396 B2
Winant Av
10 LFRY 6501 D5
10 RDFP 6501 D5
10 STNL 7115 E6
Winant Av US-46
10 LFRY 6501 D5
10 RDFP 6501 D5
E Winant Av
10 RDFP 6501 E6
Winant Ln
10 STNL 7115 B7
Winant Pl
10 STNL 7115 B7
Winant St
10 STNL 6919 B7
Winchcombe Wy
10 NRCH 6281 E1
Winchester Av
10 YNKR 6280 C6
100 STNL 7117 A6
400 STNL 7116 C7
400 UnnT 6917 A1
800 HlsT 6917 D1
Winchester Blvd
79-00 QENS 6722 E7
83-01 QENS 6826 E2
Winchester Dr
10 NHmT 6618 B7
100 YNKR 6280 C3
Winchester Ovl
10 NRCH 6396 B6
Winchester Pl
100 LWRN 7027 B3
Winchester Rd
100 WbgT 7114 C7
100 WbgT 7205 A1
Winchester St
200 WHPL 6168 B2
Windcrest Rd
10 RYE 6283 D1
Windemere Av
10 STNL 7117 D3
Windermere Dr
10 YNKR 6280 D3
Windermere Pl
10 RKVC 6929 E5
Windermere Rd
10 STNL 7020 D5
900 HmpT 6828 A7
Windham Lp
10 STNL 7116 E1
10 STNL 7117 A1
Winding Ln
10 EchT 6281 C2
Winding Rd N
400 ARDY 6166 C5
400 GrbT 6166 C6
Winding Rd S
10 GrbT 6166 C6
Winding Wy
10 SCLF 6509 E5
10 WOrT 6712 A3
Winding Brook Dr
10 MrnT 6282 B5
Winding Brook Rd
10 NRCH 6282 A5
100 NRCH 6281 E5
Winding Rd Farm
10 GrbT 6166 C6
Winding Rd Farm E
10 GrbT 6166 C6
Winding Rd Farm W
300 GrbT 6166 C6
Winding Ridge Rd
10 GrbT 6049 E7
Windingwood Rd N
10 RYEB 6169 E2
Windingwood Rd S
10 RYEB 6169 E3
Winding Woods Lp
10 STNL 7206 B5
Windle Pk
10 TYTN 6048 B3
Windmill Cir
10 SCDL 6168 C5
Windmill Ct
10 STNL 7118 A3
Windmill Ln
10 SCDL 6168 A4
Windom Av
10 STNL 7021 A6
Windom St
10 GrbT 6166 E1
Windsong Rd
10 ARDY 6166 E4
Windsor Av
10 CARL 6500 B7
10 ERTH 6500 B7
10 MNLA 6724 E5
10 RKVC 6929 D6
200 HmpT 6929 D4
Windsor Ct
10 HRSN 6051 B5
10 NRWD 6164 A6
10 STNL 7019 E3
Windsor Dr
500 PALP 6502 D6
500 SECS 6716 B1
Windsor Ln
10 SCDL 6281 C1
200 HmpT 6828 D6
Windsor Ovl
10 NRCH 6396 A6
Windsor Pk
1100 EGLD 6502 C1
Windsor Pkwy
10 HmpT 6929 E7
W Windsor Pkwy
10 HmpT 6929 D7
Windsor Pl
10 BKLN 6922 D4
10 COrT 6712 D3
10 LNBK 6929 C5
10 PLMM 6395 C7
300 HmpT 6929 D6
Windsor Rd
10 HAOH 6279 E1
10 PTCH 6170 A4
10 RYEB 6170 A4
10 STNL 7019 E4
10 STNL 7020 A3
10 THSN 6617 C7
10 YNKR 6281 B2
400 WRDG 6500 D6
Windsor St
10 KRNY 6714 A4
10 MrnT 6282 C7
Windsor Ter
10 WHPL 6168 B1
100 YNKR 6279 D4
Windsor Wy
100 HlsT 6816 D7
Windsor Brook Ln
10 OrgT 6164 D2
Windsor Gate
10 LKSU 6723 C2
Windsor Gate Dr
10 NHLS 6723 E3
10 NHmT 6723 E3
Windward Av
10 WHPL 6168 E7
Windward Ct
- STNL 7206 B1
Windward Ln
10 BRNX 6506 E6
10 SCDL 6282 B2
Windward Rd
10 GLCV 6509 D3
Windy Knls
10 GrwT 6170 D4
Windy Hollow Wy
10 STNL 7020 A7
Winegar Ln
10 STNL 6919 E7
Winfield Av
10 HRSN 6282 E2
10 MTVN 6395 A3
10 STNL 7020 C6
100 JSYC 6819 B6
1600 MRNK 6282 E3
Winfield Pl
10 MLVN 6929 A2
10 NRCH 6396 B2
Winfield St
10 STNL 7020 D7
Winfield Ter
10 NHmT 6616 D7
10 SDRK 6616 D7
W Winfield Scott Plz
10 ELIZ 6917 B4
Winfred Av
10 YNKR 6394 C3
Wingate Pl
10 YNKR 6393 E2
Wingate Rd
10 VLYS 6928 C5
10 YNKR 6393 E2
Winged Foot Dr
10 MrnT 6282 C6
Wingham St
10 STNL 7020 E3
N Wing Viaduct
- UNCT 6716 D5
N Wing Viaduct CO-683
- UNCT 6716 D5
S Wing Viaduct
- JSYC 6716 D5
- UNCT 6716 D5
S Wing Viaduct CO-683
- JSYC 6716 D5
- UNCT 6716 D5
Winham Av
10 STNL 7118 A3
Winnebago Rd
10 YNKR 6280 E6
Winnetou Rd
10 GrbT 6049 E6
Winslow Cir
10 TCKA 6281 A6
Winslow Pl
10 LRMT 6396 C2
10 RTFD 6609 A3
10 SCDL 6281 C1
10 STNL 7116 D7
Winslow Rd
10 SCDL 6168 A4
10 WHPL 6168 A4
Winsor Pl
10 HRSN 6168 D1
Winston Dr
- CLFP 6611 E2
10 WbgT 7114 C3
Winston Pl
10 YNKR 6394 A1
Winston St
10 STNL 7116 C3
Winter Av
10 STNL 6920 C7
Winter Pl
10 ERTH 6609 B2
Winter St
10 LNBK 6929 A4
10 QENS 6824 D3
10 WbgT 7114 A2
Winterburn Grv
500 CLFP 6611 D3
Winterburn Pl
10 EDGW 6611 E2
Winter Hill Rd
10 TCKA 6281 A6
Winters St
10 BRNX 6506 E7
Winthrop Av
10 EMFD 6049 B5
10 MrnT 6396 D1
10 NRCH 6395 D3
10 WHPL 6168 A3
10 WLPK 6724 E4
10 YNKR 6280 D5
100 GrbT 6049 B5
Winthrop Dr
10 RYEB 6169 E3
Winthrop Ln
10 GrbT 6167 A6
Winthrop Pl
10 LEON 6502 D5
10 STNL 7019 E3
100 EGLD 6392 A6
400 ELIZ 6917 C2
Winthrop Rd
10 NHmT 6618 A3
Winthrop St
10 LNBK 6929 A3
10 MLVN 6929 A3
10 NHmT 6723 E6
10 NRWD 6164 B6
10 NVLE 6164 B6
10 NWRK 6714 A1
10 RYE 6283 D5
900 BKLN 6923 E4
1000 BKLN 6924 A4
Winthrop Ter
10 EORG 6713 A5
Winthrope Rd
10 NHmT 6617 D5
10 PLNH 6617 D5
Winton Pl
10 YNKR 6280 E5
Winyah Ter
10 NRCH 6395 D4
Wirt Av
10 STNL 7115 E5
Wirt Ln
10 STNL 7115 B6
Wirth Av
100 SYHW 6048 B1
Wisconsin St
10 LBCH 7028 E7
Wisse Ct
10 LODI 6500 E2
Wisse St
10 LODI 6500 E2
Wissman Av
3000 BRNX 6615 C3
Wisteria Pth
10 SNPT 6509 A5
Wisteria St
10 PTHA 7205 D5
Witherbee Av
10 PLMM 6395 C6
Witherell Dr
10 GrwT 6170 E1
Witherell St
10 YNKR 6280 D6
Withers St
10 BKLN 6822 C3
Withington Rd
10 GrbT 6167 A7
Witte Ln
- RSLN 6618 D5
Witteman Pl
10 STNL 7020 B4
Witthoff St
111-00 QENS 6826 D4
Woehrle Av
10 STNL 7116 C4
Wogan Ter
9400 BKLN 7021 D3
Wolcott Av
10 STNL 7116 D5
Wolcott St
10 BKLN 6922 A1
Wolcott Ter
10 NWRK 6816 E3
Wolf Av
10 HmpT 6929 A1
10 MLVN 6929 A1
Wolf Pl
10 BKLN 7022 E6
10 HlsT 6816 B4
10 IrvT 6816 B4
Wolfe Ln
10 HRSN 6051 B5
Wolfe Pl
10 WbgT 7114 C2
Wolff St
800 PTHA 7205 D2
Wolffe St
10 YNKR 6393 D4
Wolfs Ln
10 PLHM 6395 B5
300 PLMM 6395 B6
Wolkoff Ln
10 STNL 7018 E2
Wolski Dr
10 ELIZ 6917 D6
Wolverine St
10 STNL 7117 C3
Wood Av
10 GrbT 6166 D2
10 NHmT 6724 D3
10 SECS 6610 A6
10 STNL 7206 B3
1800 BRNX 6614 B1
N Wood Av
10 LNDN 7017 A1
N Wood Av CO-617
10 LNDN 7017 A1
S Wood Av
10 LNDN 7017 A1
S Wood Av CO-617
10 LNDN 7017 A1
Wood Ct
10 STNL 7115 E5
10 TYTN 6048 B2
Wood Ln
- STNL 7206 B3
10 HmpT 6928 C5
10 HmpT 7028 C1
10 NRCH 6281 D7
10 VLYS 6928 C5
10 WDBG 7028 C2
N Wood Ln
10 HmpT 7028 C1
10 WDBG 7028 C1
Wood Pl
10 GrbT 6167 C2
10 JSYC 6716 C7
10 NHmT 6617 D7
10 NRCH 6395 D4
10 YNKR 6279 B6
500 LNDN 7017 B1
Wood Rd
10 GTNK 6616 D4
10 SNPT 6508 E7
10 SNPT 6509 A7
10 TFLY 6392 C2
100 EGLC 6503 B2
1400 BRNX 6505 B7
1400 BRNX 6614 B1
Wood St
10 ERTH 6609 A1
10 GRFD 6500 A1
10 HSBH 6500 D5
10 LNBK 6929 A4
10 MrnT 6396 C1
10 NWRK 6713 D5
10 RTFD 6609 A1
10 WRDG 6500 C5
110-00 QENS 6826 B6
400 HmpT 6929 C7
600 MRNK 6283 A4
900 HmpT 7028 C1
Wood Ter
10 LEON 6502 D4
Woodale Pl
10 WHPL 6050 C6
Woodbine Av
10 LRMT 6396 C3
10 NRCH 6395 D3
10 NWRK 6712 B7
100 SOrT 6712 B7
100 STNL 7019 B4
800 MRNK 6282 D7
Woodbine Ct
10 FLPK 6827 C3
Woodbine Rd
10 IRVN 6166 A1
Woodbine St
10 BKLN 6823 A6
10 YNKR 6394 B5
16-51 QENS 6823 B5
200 TnkT 6502 A3
Woodbine Ter
10 DBSF 6166 C4
Woodbourne Rd
10 GTNK 6617 B5
Woodbridge Av
10 WbgT 7114 E5
10 WbgT 7115 A5
Woodbridge Av CO-652
10 WbgT 7114 E5
E Woodbridge Av
400 WbgT 7114 C1
W Woodbridge Av
10 WbgT 7114 A3
Woodbridge Pl
10 STNL 7019 C2
Woodbridge Ter
10 WbgT 7114 A5
Woodbridge Center Dr
10 WbgT 7114 A5
Woodbridge Center Dr CO-646
10 WbgT 7114 A5
Woodbrook Rd
10 WHPL 6169 A4
Woodbury Ln
- GrbT 6166 C6
Woodbury St
10 NRCH 6395 D6
Woodcleft Av
10 BXTE 6617 E1
Woodcliff Av
- STNL 7018 E1
10 NBgT 6611 C4
400 FRVW 6611 B4
Woodcliff Ct
10 NHLS 6724 A1
Woodcliff Dr
900 HmpT 6828 A7
Woodcrest Av
10 WHPL 6050 C7
Woodcrest Dr
10 NHLS 6724 B3
Woodcrest Ln
10 OLDT 6164 A4
Woodcrest Rd
10 KNGP 6617 A4
10 STNL 7018 D1
Woodcrest St
10 VLYS 6928 E4
Wood Cut Ln
10 NHmT 6508 E7
10 SNPT 6508 E7
Woodcut Ln
10 NHmT 6617 E6
10 NHmT 6724 D2
10 NRCH 6282 A7
Woodcutters Ln
10 STNL 7117 C4
Wooddale Av
10 STNL 7020 B5
Woodedge Rd
10 PLDM 6617 E5
Wood End Ln
10 BRXV 6395 A1
10 MTVN 6395 A1
Woodfield Rd
10 HmpT 6828 D6
700 HmpT 6929 D2
Woodfield Ter
10 GrbT 6048 D4
Woodford Rd
10 YNKR 6281 A1
100 GrbT 6281 A1
Woodhampton Dr
200 GrbT 6049 D5
Woodhaven Av
100 STNL 7020 A5
Woodhaven Blvd
- QENS 6925 D1
60-01 QENS 6824 B4
Woodhaven Ct
95-00 QENS 6824 D7
Woodhill Ln
10 FLHL 6618 A4
Woodhill Rd
10 TFLY 6392 B3
Wood Hollow Ln
10 NRCH 6282 A7
Woodhollow Rd
10 NHmT 6724 D2
10 WHPL 6169 A4
Woodhull Av
188-00 QENS 6826 B4
900 STNL 7116 B7
1000 STNL 7207 B1
2200 BRNX 6505 D4
Woodhull St
10 BKLN 6922 B1
Woodland Av
10 BRXV 6281 A7
10 EMFD 6049 A4
10 EORG 6712 E2
10 HRSN 6714 A5
10 JSYC 6819 B5
10 KRNY 6714 A5
10 LFRY 6501 C5
10 LRMT 6396 C1
10 MrnT 6396 C1
10 NRCH 6395 E5
10 NWRK 6817 A1
10 OybT 6618 E1
10 PTCH 6170 A5
10 RKVC 6929 E5
10 RTFD 6609 A3
10 RYEB 6170 A5
10 STNL 7117 A5
10 TYTN 6048 C2
100 YNKR 6279 E6
400 ROSP 6917 A3
600 NVLE 6164 B4
900 UnnT 6917 B1
Woodland Cres
10 SOrT 6712 B5
Woodland Ct
10 FLHL 6618 C5
Woodland Dr
10 HSBH 6500 C5
10 PLDM 6617 D4
10 PTCH 6170 A3
10 RYEB 6170 A3
10 SNPT 6508 B5
100 NHmT 6724 A6
Woodland Pl
10 NHmT 6616 D7
10 NHmT 6617 D2
10 SCDL 6167 C7
10 WHPL 6167 E2
10 WHPL 6168 A3
300 LEON 6502 D4
300 SOrT 6712 A5
Woodland Rd
10 CRSK 6278 A6
10 FLHL 6618 C5
10 GLCV 6509 D3
10 HmpT 6928 C4
10 HRSN 6050 D3
10 NoCT 6050 C3
10 RYE 6283 C5
10 SCDL 6168 A5
10 VLYS 6928 C4
Woodland St
10 EGLD 6392 C6
10 TFLY 6392 C5
N Woodland St
10 EGLD 6392 B6
10 EGLD 6503 B1
400 TFLY 6392 C6
S Woodland St
10 EGLD 6503 A1
Woodland Ter
10 BRXV 6395 A1
10 MTVN 6395 A1
10 YNKR 6279 D5
Woodland Wy
10 NHmT 6618 A7
Woodland Hills Rd
- GrbT 6050 A6
Woodland Park Dr
10 TFLY 6392 A4
Woodlands Av
10 GrbT 6166 D2
N Woodlands Av
10 GrbT 6166 E1
Woodlands Ln
10 GrbT 6166 D2
Woodlands Rd
10 HRSN 6283 B1
400 HRSN 6282 E1
Woodlawn Av
10 JSYC 6819 C4
10 NHmT 6617 B6
10 NRCH 6282 A7
10 NRCH 6396 A1
10 STNL 7020 D5
10 VLYS 6928 E5
10 YNKR 6394 B5
100 LNDN 7017 B1
Woodlawn Pl
10 IrvT 6816 D1
10 LNBK 6929 A3
Woodlawn Rd
10 NHmT 6618 B2
200 HmpT 6828 E5
Woodlawn St
10 TYTN 6048 C5
Woodlot Rd
10 EchT 6281 C5
Woodmansten Pl
900 BRNX 6505 B5
Woodmere Av
10 OybT 6618 E1
Woodmere Blvd
10 HmpT 7028 C1
10 WDBG 7028 C1
200 HmpT 6928 B7
Woodmere Blvd S
10 HmpT 7028 C1
10 WDBG 7028 D2
100 HWTN 7028 D2
Woodmere Ct
800 HmpT 7028 D3
Woodmere Dr
800 HmpT 6928 B5
Woodmere Pl
800 HmpT 7028 D3
Woodnut Pl
10 MNLA 6724 E7
Woodoak Pl
10 GDNC 6828 D3
10 HmpT 6828 D3
Woodpoint Rd
10 BKLN 6822 D3
Wood Ridge Av
100 WRDG 6500 C6
Woodridge Ln
10 SCLF 6509 D7
Woodridge Pl
10 LEON 6502 D4
Woodridge St
10 CARL 6500 D7
10 WRDG 6500 D7
Woodrose Ln
10 STNL 7115 E7
Woodrow Av
10 YNKR 6280 A4
Woodrow Dr
10 YNKR 6280 E3
Woodrow Rd
10 STNL 7116 A6
1300 STNL 7115 E6
Woodruff Av
10 BKLN 6923 A5
10 EchT 6281 C2
10 YNKR 6394 C2
100 WbgT 7114 B1
1100 HlsT 6816 D6
Woodruff Ln
10 STNL 6919 E7
800 ELIZ 6918 B2
Woodruff Pl
10 PTHA 7205 D5
100 HlsT 6816 D7
1300 ROSP 6917 A2
1300 UnnT 6917 A2
Woodruff St
- WbgT 7114 A2
Woods Av
10 ERKY 6929 C6
10 GrwT 6170 B1
10 MLVN 6929 A1
10 RKVC 6929 E5
100 HmpT 6929 E5
Woods Ct
- LynT 6609 B7
Woods Ln
10 NHmT 6724 B3
10 RYE 6283 C3
10 SCDL 6281 D1
Woods Pl
10 BKLN 6923 B6
10 RKVC 6929 E5
Woods Rd
- GrbT 6049 C3
- MtPT 6049 C3
10 OrgT 6165 B4
W Woods Rd
10 LKSU 6723 B3
Woods Wy
10 LRMT 6396 B2
10 MrnT 6396 B2
10 WHPL 6168 E7
Woods Edge Rd
10 OLDT 6164 A3
Woods End
10 HRSN 6169 C4
Woods End Ln
10 GrbT 6167 C2
Woods End Rd
10 GrbT 6167 C2
Woodshole Dr
10 YNKR 6281 A2
Woodside Av
- LODI 6500 D4
10 BKLN 7022 E4
10 BKLN 7023 A4
10 EMFD 6049 C6
10 GrbT 6049 C6
10 HRSN 6050 D7
10 HRSN 6168 D1
10 HSBH 6500 D3
10 MLVN 6929 B2
10 NWRK 6713 E3
10 STNL 7020 C3
33-00 QENS 6719 B6
300 NWRK 6714 A1
N Woodside Av
10 LODI 6500 D3
Woodside Dr
100 HBPK 7028 D1
100 HmpT 7028 D1
Woodside Ln
10 HRSN 6169 E6
Woodside Pl
10 NWRK 6713 E4
Woodside Rd
10 IrvT 6816 B1
10 MplT 6816 B1
Woods of Arden Rd
10 STNL 7116 E7
200 STNL 7117 A7
300 STNL 7208 A1
Woodstock Av
10 STNL 7020 C1
Woodstock St
10 YNKR 6279 D5
1500 HmpT 6827 D7
Wood Turtle Run
200 NRWD 6278 E1
Woodvale Av
10 STNL 7206 E2
200 STNL 7207 A2
Woodvale Lp
10 STNL 7207 A3
Wood Valley Ln
10 FLHL 6618 B5
Woodview Rd
10 HMPD 6828 E5
10 HmpT 6828 E5
Woodville Ln
10 NHmT 6724 D2
Woodward Av
1-00 QENS 6823 B4
10 RTFD 6609 A2
100 STNL 7019 B5
Woodward St
10 JSYC 6819 E4
10 NHLS 6618 D7
10 NHmT 6618 D7
200 JSYC 6820 A3
Woodworth Av
10 YNKR 6279 C7
10 YNKR 6393 A1
Woody Ln
10 MrnT 6282 C6
Woodycrest Av
10 YNKR 6279 E7
900 BRNX 107 D2
900 BRNX 6612 E1
1100 BRNX 104 E7
1100 BRNX 6503 E7
Woody Shaw Jr Plz
10 NWRK 6817 B2
Wool Av
- HmpT 6828 B5
Wooleys Ln
10 GTNK 6616 E6
10 GTNK 6617 A6
10 NHmT 6617 A6
Wooleys Ln E
10 GTNK 6617 B6
10 NHmT 6617 B6
Woolley Av
10 STNL 7019 C3
Woolsey Av
10 GLCV 6509 E3
Woolsey St
10 IrvT 6816 D3
Woolworth St
1400 HmpT 6827 D5
Wooster St
10 MHTN 118 D4
10 MHTN 6821 B2
Worden Av
10 PTHA 7205 A1
10 WbgT 7205 A1
World Av
1200 HmpT 6827 D4
Worlds Fair Marina
10 QENS 6720 C4
Worth Av
600 LNDN 6917 D6
Worth St
10 HKSK 6501 C4
10 MHTN 118 C5
10 MHTN 6821 A2
10 SHkT 6501 B3
10 WbgT 7114 A2
10 YNKR 6279 E6
Worthen St
500 BRNX 6613 D4
Worthington Rd
10 GrbT 6048 E7
100 GrbT 6166 E1
Worthington Ter
10 GrbT 6049 A6
Worthington Ter W
10 GrbT 6049 A7
Wortman Av
10 BKLN 6924 E4
400 BKLN 6925 A4
Wortylko St
10 CART 7115 B1
Wren Ct
- GrbT 6166 E1
600 HmpT 6828 D7
Wren Pl
- QENS 6826 A5
107-00 QENS 6825 E5
Wrenn St
10 STNL 7207 B1
Wrexham Rd
10 YNKR 6394 C1
Wright Av
10 JSYC 6715 E7
10 JSYC 6819 E1
10 LNBK 6929 A4
10 MLVN 6929 C2
10 STNL 6919 B7
3400 BRNX 6505 E1
Wright Pl
10 EchT 6281 B1
10 GRFD 6500 B2
10 YNKR 6394 B3
Wright St
10 STNL 7020 D1
100 NWRK 6817 D3
1000 HmpT 6929 A1
Wyanoke St
10 WHPL 6168 A2
Wyatt St
1100 BRNX 6504 E7
1100 BRNX 6505 A7
Wycham Pl
10 GTPZ 6617 B7
10 THSN 6617 B7
Wyckoff Av
7-01 QENS 6823 B6
10 BKLN 6823 A4
Wyckoff Pl
- DMRT 6278 B6
10 HmpT 7028 C1
10 WDBG 7028 C1
Wyckoff St
10 BKLN 121 A7
10 BKLN 6821 C7
100 BKLN 6922 D1
Wycliff Ln
10 STNL 7116 A6
Wydler Ct
10 GDNC 6828 C3
Wygant Pl
10 STNL 6919 D7
Wykagyl Ter
10 NRCH 6281 C7
Wyldwood Ln
10 GrbT 6048 D4
Wylie St
10 WbgT 7114 B1
Wyman St
10 HRSN 6169 E6
10 RYEB 6169 E6
10 RYEB 6170 A6
Wyman St N
10 RYEB 6170 B6
Wyndcliff Rd
10 YNKR 6281 A1
Wyndham Rd
10 GrbT 6281 B1
10 NRWD 6278 A1
10 YNKR 6281 B1
Wyndham Wy
10 NHmT 6618 B3
Wyndham Close
10 WHPL 6168 D3
Wyndmere Rd
10 MTVN 6395 A2
Wyndmoor Av
10 HlsT 6816 D4
10 NWRK 6816 D4
Wyndover Rd
10 GrbT 6049 E6
Wyngate Dr
700 HmpT 6827 E7
Wyngate Dr E
600 HmpT 6827 E7
Wyngate Dr W
600 HmpT 6827 E7
Wyngate Pl
10 GTPZ 6617 B7
10 THSN 6617 B7
Wynmor Rd
10 SCDL 6282 A1
Wynnewood Rd
400 PLHM 6395 C5
400 PLMM 6395 C6
Wyoming Av
10 GrbT 6049 C7
10 LBCH 7028 E7
10 LNBK 6929 C4
600 ELIZ 6917 B2
Wyona Av
10 STNL 7019 B4
Wyona St
100 BKLN 6924 D4
Wysocki Pl
10 HKSK 6501 C3
Wythe Av
10 BKLN 6822 A5
Wythe Pl
10 BKLN 6822 A5
1400 BRNX 105 B7
1400 BRNX 6504 D7

X

X St
300 BRNX 6614 C5
Xavier Ct
10 JSYC 6819 A4
Xavier Dr
10 YNKR 6394 C2
Xenia St
10 STNL 7020 D6
57-00 QENS 6720 B7

Y

Yacht Basin Rd
- LWRN 7028 A5
Yacht Club Dr
10 NHmT 6617 C2
Yacht Club Cove
3700 STNL 7117 C5
Yadanza Ct
10 OrgT 6164 E4
Yafa Ct
10 STNL 7019 B3
Yale Av
10 IrvT 6816 B2
10 JSYC 6819 C3
10 WbgT 7114 D1
300 HlsT 6816 C6
300 HmpT 6928 B7
400 HmpT 6929 D3
400 RKVC 6929 D3
Yale Blvd
10 NHmT 6723 E7
Yale Dr
- NHLS 6724 B1
Yale Pl
10 CLST 6278 C2
10 LNBK 6929 A3
10 RKVC 6929 E3
800 HmpT 6828 B3
Yale Rd
10 GrbT 6167 D3
10 HAOH 6279 E1
10 HmpT 6828 C3
300 GDNC 6828 C3
Yale St
10 GDNC 6828 B2
10 HmpT 7027 D2
10 NHmT 6724 D2
10 STNL 7018 E2
10 WLPK 6724 E3
500 HmpT 7029 D2
Yale Ter
10 WOrT 6712 A3
Yancy Dr
10 NWRK 6713 C7
Yardley Av
300 WbgT 7114 E1
Yarmouth Rd
10 HmpT 7029 B1
10 HRSN 6168 D2
Yates Av
10 ATLB 7028 B7
10 NWRK 6817 A3
2300 BRNX 6505 C4
Yates Rd
150-00 QENS 6825 D6
Yeaton Rd
600 MHTN 6820 E7
Yellowstone Av
10 GrbT 6049 C7
Yellowstone Blvd
61-00 QENS 6720 E7
62-27 QENS 6824 B3
Yennicock Av
10 MHVN 6508 C7
Yeomalt Av
10 STNL 7207 C2
Yeshiva Ct
10 STNL 7206 E3
Yeshiva Ln
10 STNL 7206 E3
Yetman Av
300 STNL 7206 B4
Yolanda Pl
10 LODI 6500 E1
Yona Av
- STNL 7019 A4
Yonkers Av
10 TCKA 6280 E6
10 YNKR 6393 E1
200 YNKR 6394 A2
Yonkers Ter
10 YNKR 6394 C4
York Av
10 RYE 6283 C4
10 STNL 6920 C6
1100 MHTN 113 D6
1100 MHTN 117 C1
1100 MHTN 6718 B4
1600 MHTN 114 A3
York Dr
10 THSN 6617 C7
York Pl
10 EchT 6281 B7
10 TFLY 6392 B4
10 WLPK 6724 D5
York Rd
10 MrnT 6282 C5
York St
10 BKLN 121 C3
10 BKLN 6821 D5
10 ELIZ 6918 B3
10 GrbT 6049 B7
10 JSYC 6820 B3
10 LNBK 6929 C3
10 MHTN 118 C4
10 MHTN 6821 B3
10 MLVN 6929 C3
York Ter
10 STNL 6920 C6
Yorkshire Pl
10 YNKR 6279 C6
Yorkshire Rd
10 NHmT 6724 C5
Yorktown Ct
10 OrgT 6164 C3
Yorktown Rd
500 UnnT 6917 A1
Yorkview Dr
10 EDGW 103 A5
10 EDGW 6503 A6
Yosemite Av
10 GrbT 6049 C7
Yost Blvd
3000 HmpT 6929 D7
3200 HmpT 7029 D1
Young Av
10 HlsT 6816 B4
10 PLHM 6395 C4
10 YNKR 6280 E1
2200 BRNX 6505 C4
Young Pl
10 TCKA 6281 B5
Young St
10 DBSF 6166 A5
10 STNL 7020 C2
Yucca Dr
10 STNL 7116 B5
Yukon Av
10 STNL 7116 E2
Yung Pl
1000 HmpT 7028 C1
Yvonne Pl
900 UnnT 6917 B2
Yznaga Pl
500 BRNX 6614 D3

Z

Zabriskie Av
10 BAYN 6919 D6
Zabriskie St
10 JSYC 6716 B6
Zaccheus Mead Ln
10 GrwT 6170 E1
Zachary Ct
10 STNL 7019 D2
Zadig St
400 HmpT 7029 C1
Zambory St
300 PTHA 7205 C1
Zavatt St
10 HmpT 7027 E2
Zebra Pl
10 STNL 7115 D5
Zeck Ct
10 STNL 7019 A3
Zemek St
10 VLYS 6929 A2
Zephyr Av
10 STNL 7207 D2
Zerega Av
300 BRNX 6614 D2
1300 BRNX 6505 C7
Zerman Pl
10 WhkT 6716 E4
Ziegler Av
400 LNDN 6917 A7
400 LNDN 7017 A2
Zimmerman Ct
10 DBSF 6166 A5
Zinnia Av
10 FLPK 6827 C3
Zinsser Wy
10 HAOH 6165 E6
Zinzedorf Cir
- STNL 7117 E1
- STNL 7118 A2
Zion Ln
10 WHPL 6169 A6
Zion St
45-00 QENS 6722 E3
Zoe St
10 STNL 7020 B7
Zola St
600 HmpT 6928 B7
600 HmpT 7028 A1
Zoller Rd
178-00 QENS 6927 B1

New York City/5 Borough Street Index

Column header (repeated across all columns): **STREET — Block | City | Map# | Grid**

Zotti Av

Block	City	Map#	Grid
-	NRWD	6164	B5
100	OLDT	6164	A5
400	NVLE	6164	B5

Zulette Av

| 2800 | BRNX | 6505 | E7 |
| 3000 | BRNX | 6506 | A7 |

Zwicky Av

| 10 | STNL | 7118 | B1 |

#

1st Av

Block	City	Map#	Grid
-	MHTN	110	D3
10	BlmT	6713	C3
10	BRNX	6615	A2
10	EORG	6713	B3
10	ERKY	6929	C7
10	HmpT	6929	C7
10	KRNY	6714	C4
10	MHmT	6724	B7
10	NHmT	6828	B1
10	NWRK	6713	C3
10	PLHM	6395	B4
10	SECS	6610	B7
10	WbgT	7114	E3
100	NHPK	6827	E1
200	ELIZ	6918	B5
200	MHTN	119	C1
200	MHTN	116	E5
300	MHTN	116	E5
800	HmpT	6828	A6
800	MHTN	117	B1
900	NHPK	6828	A1
1000	MHTN	113	C7
1700	MHTN	114	A1
1900	MHTN	6612	D6
4000	BKLN	6922	A6
5100	BKLN	6921	E6
8200	NBgT	6611	B5

1st Av W

| 100 | NWRK | 6713 | C3 |
| 10 | BlmT | 6713 | C3 |

E 1st Av

| 200 | ROSL | 6917 | A4 |
| 700 | ELIZ | 6917 | B3 |

E 1st Av CO-610

| 200 | ROSL | 6917 | A4 |
| 700 | ELIZ | 6917 | B3 |

S 1st Av

| 10 | MTVN | 6394 | E5 |
| 300 | ELIZ | 6918 | A5 |

1st Ct

| 10 | BKLN | 7023 | A5 |

1st Pl

10	BKLN	6922	C1
10	NHmT	6724	B7
100	MHTN	120	A2
100	MHTN	6821	A4
200	BGTA	6501	E2

1st Pl S

| 600 | HmpT | 6828 | C3 |

1st Rd

| - | QENS | 7026 | A3 |

1st St

Block	City	Map#	Grid
-	GrbT	6167	D1
10	LODI	6500	D2
10	BRNX	6394	B6
10	CLST	6278	B4
10	EGLC	6503	A4
10	ELIZ	6918	D5
10	EMFD	6049	A3
10	ERKY	6927	C5
10	FTLE	6503	B5
10	GDNC	6828	D3
10	HBKN	6716	C7
10	HKSE	6501	B1
10	HlsT	6816	D6
10	HmpT	6827	B6
10	HRPK	6164	A5
10	HRSN	6283	B4
10	HTLE	6501	E6
10	JSYC	6820	C7
10	LFRY	6501	C5
10	LNBK	6929	B5
10	NHmT	6617	D7
10	NHmT	6724	B7
10	NRCH	6395	D4
10	NRWD	6164	A5
10	OybT	6618	E2
10	PLHM	7205	D4
10	PTHA	7205	D4
10	QENS	6927	E7
10	RDFP	6501	D3
10	RYE	6284	B2
10	SAMB	7205	C7
10	SHkT	6501	C5
10	STNL	7117	E2
10	VLYS	6928	D4
10	WbgT	7115	A2
10	WLTN	6500	A6
26-00	QENS	6718	D2
26-00	QENS	6925	E5
99-00	QENS	6925	E7
100	BKLN	6922	C4
100	MNLA	6724	E6
100	NWRK	6713	C4
100	WRDG	6500	C6
102-00	QENS	6926	A4
200	GRFD	6500	E7
200	PALP	6502	C6
200	SdBT	6500	C7
200	YNKR	6394	B4
300	CARL	6500	C7
300	CLFP	6611	C2
300	ERTH	6500	B7
300	HRSN	6714	A6
400	CDHT	7028	A1
400	HmpT	6828	A6
500	HmpT	7028	A1
500	LEON	6502	C5
500	MRNK	6282	E4
500	SECS	6610	A7

1st St CO-55

| 10 | HKSE | 6501 | B1 |

E 1st St

10	BAYN	6919	D6
10	MHTN	119	A4
10	MHTN	6821	C2
10	MTVN	6394	D4
2200	BKLN	7023	A6

N 1st St

10	HRSN	6283	A3
10	MHTN	6822	A3
100	NHPK	6827	E1

N 1st St (continued)

| 500 | NHmT | 6723 | D7 |
| 500 | NHPK | 6723 | D7 |

S 1st St

10	ELIZ	6918	B6
10	NHPK	6827	E1
300	BKLN	6822	B4

W 1st St

10	BAYN	6919	C6
10	BKLN	7022	E4
10	MNCH	6501	A7
10	MTVN	6394	D4
300	BRNX	6394	D5
1800	BKLN	7023	A7
2700	BKLN	7121	A1

1st Av Lp

| - | MHTN | 119 | D1 |
| 10 | MHTN | 6821 | E1 |

2nd Av

Block	City	Map#	Grid
-	STNL	7018	B1
10	BRNX	6615	B2
10	ERKY	6929	C7
10	HmpT	6929	C7
10	KRNY	6714	C4
10	MHTN	119	B2
10	MHTN	6821	D2
10	NHmT	6617	D1
10	NHmT	6724	B7
10	NHmT	6828	B1
10	PLHM	6395	B4
10	SECS	6610	B7
10	WbgT	7114	E3
100	ELIZ	6918	A5
300	MHTN	116	C7
300	MHTN	6717	E6
400	NHPK	6827	E1
600	LynT	6609	A4
800	MHTN	6828	A6
800	MHTN	117	A3
800	NHPK	6828	A1
1100	MHTN	113	E2
1800	MHTN	110	C3
1800	MHTN	114	A1
1800	MHTN	6612	C7
5300	BKLN	6921	E6
8000	NBgT	6611	B5

2nd Av E

| 10 | NWRK | 6713 | D4 |

2nd Av W

| 200 | NWRK | 6713 | C3 |
| 400 | ELIZ | 6917 | B4 |

E 2nd Av

| 300 | ELIZ | 6917 | B4 |
| 700 | ELIZ | 6917 | B4 |

N 2nd Av

| 100 | MTVN | 6394 | E4 |

S 2nd Av

| 10 | MTVN | 6394 | E4 |

2nd Ct

| 10 | STNL | 7207 | E1 |

2nd Pl

10	BKLN	6922	B1
10	MHTN	120	A1
10	MHTN	6821	A4
200	BGTA	6501	E2

2nd Pl S

W 2nd Pl

| 10 | BKLN | 7121 | A1 |

2nd Rd

| 10 | GTNK | 6617 | B6 |

2nd St

Block	City	Map#	Grid
-	CRSK	6278	A7
10	BGTA	6501	D2
10	BKLN	6922	C1
10	CLST	6278	B4
10	EGLC	6503	A4
10	ERKY	6929	C5
10	FTLE	6503	B5
10	GDNC	6828	E3
10	HBKN	6716	C7
10	HKSE	6501	B1
10	HlsT	6816	D6
10	HmpT	6827	B7
10	HRPK	6164	A5
10	HRSN	6283	B4
10	JSYC	6820	C7
10	KRNY	6715	A7
10	KRNY	6819	A1
10	LNBK	6929	B5
10	LODI	6500	D2
10	NHmT	6617	D7
10	NHmT	6724	B7
10	NRCH	6395	D4
10	NRWD	6164	A5
10	NWRK	6713	C6
10	OybT	6618	E2
10	PLHM	6395	B4
10	QENS	6927	E7
10	RDFP	6501	D4
10	RYE	6284	B1
10	SAMB	7205	D7
10	SOrT	6712	A6
10	STNL	7117	E2
10	WbgT	7114	C6
10	WRDG	6500	C6
26-00	QENS	114	C6
26-50	QENS	117	C6
50-00	QENS	6718	D7
100	MNLA	6724	E7
100	SdBT	6500	C7
200	SdBT	6500	B7
300	CARL	6500	C7
300	CLFP	6611	C2
400	GRFD	6500	E6
400	HmpT	6828	A6
400	SECS	6610	A7

E 2nd St

10	BKLN	6919	D6
10	BKLN	6922	E1
10	MHTN	119	B4
10	MHTN	6821	D2
1300	BKLN	7022	D2
1600	BKLN	7023	A6

N 2nd St

10	HRSN	6714	A6
100	NHPK	6827	E1
500	NHmT	6723	D7
500	NHPK	6723	D7

S 2nd St

10	ELIZ	6918	B6
10	HRSN	6714	A7
10	NHPK	6827	E1
300	BKLN	6822	B4

W 2nd St

10	BRNX	6394	C5
10	BAYN	6919	C6
10	MNCH	6501	A7
10	MTVN	6394	D5
10	PLHM	6395	B5
1500	BKLN	7022	E4
1800	BKLN	7023	A7
3000	BKLN	7121	A3

3rd Av

Block	City	Map#	Grid
-	STNL	7018	B1
10	BKLN	121	D7
10	BKLN	6821	E7
10	BKLN	6922	D2
10	ERKY	6929	C7
10	GDNC	6724	E7
10	HmpT	6929	C7
10	KRNY	6714	C4
10	MHTN	119	B1
10	MHTN	6821	D1
10	MNLA	6724	E6
10	NHmT	6617	D2
10	NHmT	6724	B7
10	NHmT	6828	B1
10	PLHM	6395	B4
10	SECS	6610	B7
10	WbgT	7114	E3
100	ELIZ	6918	A4
100	MHTN	6717	D7
145-00	QENS	6615	E2
400	NHPK	6827	E1
700	BRNX	6615	C2
700	HmpT	6828	A6
700	MHTN	117	A1
700	MHTN	6718	A5
800	NHPK	6828	A1
900	BRNX	113	B7
1700	MHTN	109	E7
1700	MHTN	110	A6
2400	BRNX	110	D1
2500	BRNX	107	E7
2600	BRNX	6613	E4
3700	BRNX	105	E7
145-00	QENS	6615	E1
6300	BKLN	6921	E6
7200	BKLN	7021	D2
3000	NBgT	6611	B4

3rd Av E

| 10 | NWRK | 6713 | D4 |

3rd Av W

| 10 | NWRK | 6713 | C3 |
| 10 | MHTN | 120 | A1 |

E 3rd Av

| 200 | ROSL | 6917 | A4 |
| 700 | ELIZ | 6917 | B4 |

4th Av E

| 10 | MTVN | 6394 | E4 |

4th Av W

| 300 | MTVN | 6394 | E4 |

E 4th Av

| 200 | ROSL | 6917 | A4 |

S 4th Av

| 10 | MTVN | 6394 | E6 |

4th Ct

| 10 | STNL | 7207 | E1 |

4th Pl

| 10 | BGTA | 6501 | E2 |
| 100 | TnkT | 6501 | E2 |

4th Pl S

| 600 | HmpT | 6828 | C3 |

3rd Rd

| 10 | GTNK | 6617 | B6 |

3rd St

Block	City	Map#	Grid
-	CLST	6278	B4
-	CRSK	6278	A7
10	ELIZ	6918	B5
10	GDNC	6828	E3
10	HBKN	6716	C7
10	HmpT	6827	B7
10	HRPK	6164	A5
10	LODI	6500	D2
10	NHmT	6724	D7
10	NRCH	6395	D4
10	NWRK	6713	C6
10	PLHM	6395	B4
10	QENS	6927	E7
10	RDFP	6501	D4
10	STNL	7117	E2
10	WRDG	6500	C6
26-00	QENS	6718	D7
26-00	QENS	6925	E7
100	BKLN	6922	C1
100	MNLA	6724	E7
200	SdBT	6500	B1
200	CARL	6500	C7
200	ERTH	6609	C1
300	SdBT	6500	B1
400	HmpT	6828	A6
400	SECS	6610	A7

3rd Pl

10	BGTA	6501	E2
10	BKLN	6922	C1
10	GDNC	6828	E3
10	HBKN	6716	D6
10	HKSE	6501	B1
10	HlsT	6816	D6
10	HmpT	6827	B7
10	HRPK	6164	A5

3rd Pl S

| 600 | HmpT | 6828 | C3 |

3rd Rd (E)

| - | QENS | 7026 | B3 |

E 3rd Rd

| 10 | GTNK | 6617 | B6 |

E 3rd St

-	PLHM	6395	B5
10	BAYN	6919	C4
10	BKLN	6922	E5
10	MHTN	119	C4
10	MHTN	6821	C2
10	MNCH	6501	A7
10	MTVN	6394	D4
200	MTVN	6395	B5
1300	BKLN	7022	E3
1500	BKLN	7023	A6

N 3rd St

10	BKLN	6822	A3
10	HRSN	6714	A6
10	MHTN	6822	A3
1500	BKLN	7022	E4
1800	BKLN	7023	A7
3000	BKLN	7121	A3

S 3rd St

10	BKLN	6822	A4
10	BKLN	6821	E7
10	BKLN	6922	D2
600	HRSN	6714	A7

S 3rd St SR-22

| 10 | BKLN | 6822 | A4 |

W 3rd St

10	BAYN	6919	C5
10	MHTN	118	D2
10	MHTN	119	A3
10	MHTN	6821	C1
10	MNCH	6501	A7
10	MTVN	6394	D5
100	BRNX	6394	D5
10	MHTN	6717	B7

3rd Av Br

-	BRNX	110	D1
-	BRNX	6612	E4
-	MHTN	110	C2
-	MHTN	6612	C7

4th Av

Block	City	Map#	Grid
10	BKLN	121	D7
10	BKLN	6821	E7
10	BKLN	6922	D1
10	BRNX	6615	C2
10	EORG	6713	B3
10	ERKY	6929	C7
10	GDNC	6724	E7
10	HmpT	6929	C7
10	MHTN	119	B7
10	MHTN	6821	D1
10	MNLA	6724	E6
10	NHmT	6617	D2
10	NHmT	6828	B1
10	NWRK	6713	C4
10	PLHM	6395	C4
100	MHTN	112	E6
100	MHTN	113	C1
6400	BKLN	6921	E1
6900	BKLN	7021	E1
7600	NBgT	6611	B5

4th Av E

| 200 | ROSL | 6917 | A4 |
| 700 | ELIZ | 6917 | B4 |

4th Av W

| 300 | MTVN | 6394 | E4 |
| 400 | EORG | 6713 | C3 |

E 4th Av

| 200 | ROSL | 6917 | A4 |

S 4th Av

| 10 | MTVN | 6394 | E6 |

E 5th Av

| 10 | MTVN | 6394 | E6 |

4th Ct

| 10 | STNL | 7207 | E1 |

W 5th Rd

| 10 | QENS | 7026 | A4 |

5th St

Block	City	Map#	Grid
-	NRWD	6164	C7
-	NRWD	6278	B1
10	CLST	6278	B4
10	EGLC	6503	A4
10	ELIZ	6918	B4
10	FTLE	6503	B4
10	GDNC	6828	E3
10	HBKN	6716	C7
10	HmpT	6827	A5
10	LODI	6500	D2
10	MHTN	119	B3
10	NHmT	6724	D7
10	NRCH	6395	D4
10	PASC	6500	A4
10	RDFP	6501	D4
10	VLYS	6928	D4
10	WHPL	6167	E1
44-00	QENS	117	D4
45-00	QENS	6718	D4
100	BKLN	6922	D2
100	FRVW	6611	C3
100	JSYC	6820	C7
100	RDFP	6501	E4
200	MRNK	6283	A4
200	SAMB	7205	B7
300	GRFD	6500	C7
300	SdBT	6500	B1
400	CARL	6500	C7
400	ERTH	6609	C1

4th St CO-57

E 4th St

10	BKLN	6919	D5
100	BKLN	6922	E1
500	MRNK	6282	D5
600	SECS	6610	A7

E 4th St

-	PLHM	6395	A3
10	BAYN	6919	C4
10	BKLN	6922	E5
10	MNCH	6501	C1
10	MTVN	6394	E5
200	MTVN	6395	B5
300	NWRK	6713	C4
900	NHPK	6723	E7
1300	BKLN	7022	E3
1500	BKLN	7023	A6

N 4th St

| 10 | BKLN | 6822 | B3 |
| 10 | MHTN | 6822 | B4 |

W 4th St

10	NHPK	6827	E1
200	MTVN	6394	E6
400	MplT	6712	A7
400	SOrT	6712	A7

5th Av

Block	City	Map#	Grid
-	NRWD	6164	C7
10	BKLN	6922	B5
10	BRNX	6615	C2
10	FLPK	6827	E7
10	LynT	6609	A3
10	NHPK	6827	E1
500	LynT	6609	A4
800	NHmT	6828	A2
1300	GDNC	6828	D2
4400	BKLN	6922	A7
6700	BKLN	7022	A1
7000	BKLN	7021	E1

6th Av W

| 200 | EORG | 6713 | B4 |
| 300 | EORG | 6713 | B4 |

E 6th Av

200	ROSL	6917	A5
300	CARL	6609	C1
400	CLFP	6611	C2

N 6th Av

| 10 | MTVN | 6394 | D4 |

S 6th Av

| 10 | MTVN | 6394 | E6 |

6th Pl S

| 500 | HmpT | 6828 | C4 |

6th Rd

| 151-00 | QENS | 6615 | B6 |

E 6th Rd

| - | QENS | 7026 | B4 |

6th St

Block	City	Map#	Grid
10	BGTA	6501	D2
10	BKLN	6922	D2
10	CARL	6500	C7
10	CRSK	6392	A1
10	EGLC	6503	B4
10	ELIZ	6918	B4
10	FRVW	6611	C3
10	FTLE	6503	B4
10	GDNC	6828	E3
10	HBKN	6716	D6
10	HKSE	6501	B1
10	HmpT	6827	B5
10	HRPK	6164	A5
10	KRNY	6819	B1
10	LODI	6500	D2
10	NHmT	6724	D7
10	NRCH	6395	D4
10	NHmT	6617	D7
10	CRSK	6392	B3
10	HRPK	6164	A5
10	HmpT	6827	B7
26-00	QENS	114	C6
26-00	QENS	6718	D2
50-00	QENS	117	C6
100	MNLA	6724	E7
100	SdBT	6500	B1
200	CARL	6500	C7
300	CLFP	6611	C2
300	ERTH	6609	C1
300	GRFD	6500	C1
400	HmpT	6828	A6
400	QENS	6925	E7

E 5th Av SR-27

E 5th St

10	BAYN	6919	D5
10	MHTN	6821	C2
300	NWRK	6713	D3

N 5th St

10	BKLN	6822	B3
10	HRSN	6714	A6
100	NHPK	6827	E1

N 5th St

| 500 | NHmT | 6723 | E7 |
| 500 | NHPK | 6723 | E7 |

S 5th St

10	ELIZ	6918	A5
10	HRSN	6714	B7
10	NHPK	6827	E1

N 4th St

10	BKLN	6822	B4
300	NWRK	6713	C4
900	NHPK	6723	E7

W 5th St

10	BAYN	6919	B4
10	BKLN	7022	E4
10	MNCH	6610	A2
10	MTVN	6394	E6
200	MTVN	6394	E6
2700	BKLN	7121	A1
2800	BKLN	7120	E1

5th St Connection

| 10 | BKLN | 6919 | E5 |

6th Av

Block	City	Map#	Grid
10	CDHT	7028	A2
10	EGLC	6503	A4
10	ERKY	6929	C7
10	GDNC	6724	E7
10	GDNC	6828	E2
10	HBKN	6716	D6
10	HRSN	6714	B6
10	NHmT	6724	B7
10	PLHM	6395	C3
10	WbgT	7114	C7
100	CRSK	6278	A7
100	FRVW	6611	C3
100	JSYC	6820	B2
100	WbgT	7115	B2
100	WRDG	6500	B1
200	EORG	6713	B4
200	PALP	6502	D6
300	GRFD	6500	B1
300	SCLF	6509	D6

E 6th Av

200	ROSL	6917	A5
300	CLFP	6611	C1
400	CARL	6609	C1
500	FTLE	6503	D4

N 6th Av

| 10 | MTVN | 6394 | D4 |

S 6th Av

| 10 | MTVN | 6394 | E6 |

6th Pl S

| 600 | HmpT | 6828 | C4 |

6th Rd

E 6th Rd

| - | QENS | 7026 | B4 |

6th St

10	BKLN	6922	D2
10	CARL	6609	C1
10	CRSK	6392	A1
10	EGLC	6503	B4
10	ELIZ	6918	B4
10	HBKN	6716	D6
10	MHTN	119	B3
10	MNCH	6610	A2
200	MHTN	119	B3
200	VLYS	6928	D4
600	MHTN	6821	C1
700	MHTN	6717	D7

N 6th St

10	BKLN	6822	B3
119-00	QENS	6614	C7
145-00	QENS	6615	A6
204-00	QENS	7122	A4
300	PLHM	6395	C3
400	NHPK	6827	E1
400	NHPK	6723	E7

E 8th Av

| 200 | ROSL | 6917 | A4 |

S 6th St

10	BKLN	6822	A4
100	FRVW	6611	C3
100	JSYC	6820	B7
100	NWRK	6713	B7
100	RDFP	6501	E4

W 6th St

10	BAYN	6919	D5
10	BKLN	7022	E4
10	MTVN	6394	D5
200	MRNK	6283	A4
200	SAMB	7205	B7
300	GRFD	6500	B7
300	SdBT	6500	C7

7th Av

Block	City	Map#	Grid
10	BKLN	6922	D4
10	GDNC	6724	E7
10	HmpT	6929	C7
10	MHTN	115	C5
10	MHTN	116	A5
10	MHTN	6717	C5
700	UNCT	6716	C4
700	WRDG	6500	C7
3200	FTLE	103	B1
3200	HmpT	7029	E1

5th St CO-686

| 300 | SAMB | 7205 | B7 |

E 5th St

10	BAYN	6919	D5
10	MHTN	119	B3
10	MNCH	6610	A2
10	MTVN	6394	E5
119-00	QENS	6614	C7
145-30	QENS	6615	A5
204-00	QENS	7122	A4
200	MHTN	6821	C1
600	MHTN	6717	D7
700	NWRK	6713	D3
600	MHTN	6821	C1
2100	MHTN	107	A7

7th Av E

| 10 | NWRK | 6713 | D5 |

7th Av S

10	MHTN	118	B1
100	MHTN	115	B7
100	MHTN	6717	B7

7th Av W

200	MHTN	6713	C5
1500	FTLE	6502	D5
2400	FTLE	103	C1

7th Av S

| 200 | ROSL | 6917 | A5 |

N 7th Av

| 10 | MTVN | 6394 | D4 |

S 7th Av

| 10 | MTVN | 6394 | D5 |

E 7th Rd

| - | QENS | 7026 | B4 |

7th St

Block	City	Map#	Grid
-	NBgT	6716	B4
-	NRWD	6164	C1
-	NRWD	6278	C1
10	BGTA	6501	E3
10	BKLN	6922	E3
10	CRSK	6392	A1
10	EGLC	6503	A4
10	ELIZ	6918	A4
10	FTLE	6503	A4
10	GDNC	6828	E2
10	HBKN	6716	D6
10	HRSN	6714	B6
10	NHmT	6724	B7
10	NRCH	6395	C3
10	NWRK	6713	B6
10	PASC	6500	A4
10	RDFP	6501	E4
10	STNL	7117	E2
10	TRLY	6820	D4
10	VLYS	6928	D4
100	CRSK	6278	A7
100	FRVW	6611	C3
100	GRFD	6500	B1
100	SdBT	6500	B1
200	GRFD	6500	B1
200	SdBT	6500	B1
300	CARL	6609	C1
300	ERTH	6609	C1
400	NHPK	6827	C1
400	NWRK	6717	C4
500	CARL	6500	C7
500	HmpT	6828	A6
500	NBgT	6716	C4
500	MNLA	6724	E7
100	SCLF	6509	E6

E 8th Av

| 200 | ROSL | 6917 | A4 |

N 8th Av

| 10 | MTVN | 6394 | D4 |

S 8th Av

| 10 | MTVN | 6394 | D6 |

W 6th St

10	BAYN	6919	D5
10	BKLN	7022	E6
10	MTVN	6394	E6

E 8th Rd

| - | QENS | 7026 | B4 |

W 8th Rd

| - | QENS | 7026 | A4 |

7th Av

10	ERKY	6929	C7
10	HmpT	6929	C7
-	NRWD	6164	C1
-	NRWD	6278	C1
-	STNL	7018	B3
10	BGTA	6501	E3
10	BKLN	6922	D3
10	GDNC	6724	E7
10	MNLA	6724	E7
10	FTLE	6503	B3
10	HBKN	6716	D6
10	NHmT	6724	B7
10	NHPK	6395	C3
10	PASC	6500	D6
10	RDFP	6501	E4
10th Av			

8th St

500	HmpT	6828	C4
100	SECS	6609	E7
100	MHTN	115	D7
100	MHTN	6717	B7
800	NBgT	6716	B3
800	BKLN	6822	A4
800	GDNC	6828	E1
800	HBKN	6716	D6

S 8th St

10	BKLN	6822	A4
10	NHPK	6827	E1
10	NWRK	6713	B6
600	STMN	6827	E2

W 8th St

10	BAYN	6919	D4
10	MHTN	118	C1
10	MTVN	6394	E6
10	MTVN	6395	A6
300	PLHM	6395	C3
600	MHTN	112	A5
3700	BKLN	105	A1
3800	NHPK	102	A4
6200	BKLN	7023	A3

9th Av W

| 10 | NWRK | 6713 | B5 |
| 10 | EORG | 6713 | B5 |

E 9th Av

| 200 | ROSL | 6917 | A5 |

N 9th Av

| 10 | MTVN | 6394 | D4 |

S 9th Av

| 10 | MTVN | 6394 | D5 |

S 10th Av

| 10 | BKLN | 6822 | A4 |

N 8th St

10	BKLN	6822	B3
10	BlvT	6713	D2
10	NWRK	6713	B5
10	NHmT	6723	E7
500	NHmT	6723	E7

S 7th St

10	ELIZ	6918	A4
10	NWRK	6713	B7
300	NWRK	6817	E1

W 7th St

10	BAYN	6919	D5
10	BKLN	7022	E6
10	MTVN	6394	E6

8th Av

Block	City	Map#	Grid
10	ROSL	6917	A5
10	GDNC	6724	E7
10	HmpT	6929	C7
10	MHTN	115	E4
10	MHTN	116	B1
10	MHTN	6717	C6
100	MHTN	6713	E6
119-00	QENS	6614	C7
145-00	QENS	6615	A6
204-00	QENS	7122	A4
300	NHPK	6827	C1
400	NHPK	6827	C1
500	UNCT	6716	C4
700	MHTN	112	C6
3800	BKLN	6922	B6

E 8th Av

N 8th Av

S 9th St

10	BKLN	6922	D4
10	GDNC	6828	E2
10	HBKN	6716	D6
10	NWRK	6713	A7
10	STNL	7117	E2
10	WRDG	6500	B1
25-00	QENS	114	B6
33-00	QENS	114	B6
42-00	QENS	6718	C6
100	FRVW	6611	C3
100	JSYC	6820	B1
200	PASC	6500	D6
300	CARL	6609	C1
300	CLFP	6611	C2
300	GRFD	6500	C1
300	SdBT	6500	C1
400	UNCT	6716	C4
500	FTLE	6502	D5

W 9th St

10	BAYN	6919	D4
10	MHTN	6821	C1
10	MTVN	6395	A6

E 11th St

10th Av

Block	City	Map#	Grid
3700	MHTN	102	B6
3700	MHTN	105	A1
3800	MHTN	6504	A4
3800	BKLN	6716	D6
5900	BKLN	7022	B1
8300	BKLN	7021	E3

E 10th Av

| 400 | ROSL | 6917 | A5 |

N 10th Av

| 10 | MTVN | 6394 | D4 |

S 10th Av

| 10 | MTVN | 6394 | D5 |

E 10th Rd

| - | QENS | 7026 | B4 |

W 10th Rd

| - | QENS | 7026 | A4 |

10th St

Block	City	Map#	Grid
-	GRFD	6500	C1
-	NRWD	6164	C7
-	NRWD	6278	C1
10	BKLN	6922	C2
10	CARL	6500	C6
10	GDNC	6828	E1
10	HBKN	6716	D6
10	STNL	7117	E2
10	STNL	7118	A2
10	WRDG	6500	C6
33-00	QENS	114	B6
33-00	QENS	6718	D4
42-00	QENS	117	E3
100	PASC	6500	A4
200	PASC	6500	A4
200	HSBH	6500	A4
300	CARL	6609	C1
300	ERTH	6609	C1
300	FRVW	6611	C3
300	SdBT	6500	C1
400	UNCT	6716	C4
400	HmpT	6928	A7
500	NBgT	6716	B4

10th St E

115-00	QENS	6614	D7
154-00	QENS	6615	A6
204-00	QENS	7122	A4

10th St W

| - | QENS | 6509 | E7 |

E 10th St

10	BAYN	6919	D4
10	MHTN	118	E1
10	MHTN	6821	E2
100	BKLN	6922	E6

N 10th St

10	BKLN	6822	B3
10	EORG	6713	C5
10	NWRK	6713	C3
100	NHPK	6723	E7
300	BlvT	6713	C2

S 10th St

10	BKLN	6822	A4
100	NWRK	6713	A7
300	NWRK	6828	A1
600	STMN	6828	A2

W 10th St

10	BAYN	6919	D4
10	LNDN	7017	B1
10	MHTN	118	C1
10	MHTN	6821	B2

11th Av

Block	City	Map#	Grid
10	BRNX	6615	B2
10	EORG	6713	A4
10	GDNC	6724	E7
10	MNLA	6724	D7
10	STNL	7117	C2
10	WRDG	6500	C6
25-00	QENS	114	B6
33-00	QENS	114	B6
42-00	QENS	6718	C6
121-00	QENS	6614	E7
145-00	QENS	6615	A7
200	PASC	6500	D6
300	CARL	6609	C1
500	NHPK	6827	E2
600	STMN	6827	E2

11th Av W

| 10 | EORG | 6713 | B6 |

E 11th Av

S 11th Av

| 10 | MTVN | 6394 | D6 |

11th Pl

| 49-00 | QENS | 117 | E6 |
| 49-00 | QENS | 6718 | C7 |

W 11th Rd

| - | QENS | 7026 | A4 |

11th St

Block	City	Map#	Grid
-	CLST	6278	C1
-	JSYC	6820	C1
-	NRWD	6164	C1
10	BKLN	6922	D3
10	GDNC	6828	E1
10	HBKN	6716	D6
32-00	QENS	114	C6
42-00	QENS	6718	C6
117	E5		
400	UNCT	6716	C4
1100	NBgT	6716	B4
1400	PALP	6502	D6
500	FTLE	6502	E6

E 11th St

10	MHTN	118	A7
10	LNDN	7017	B1
10	MHTN	118	C1
10	MHTN	6821	B1
10	GDNC	6828	E2
10	HBKN	6716	D6
200	BKLN	6923	A6
2400	BKLN	7023	A3
2700	BKLN	7121	C2

S 11th St

| 10 | BKLN | 6822 | A4 |

New York City/5 Borough Street Index

STREET
Block City Map# Grid

S 11th St
10 NWRK 6713 B5
200 NHPK 6828 A2
500 NWRK 6817 A2
500 STMN 6828 A2
W 11th St
10 BAYN 6919 D4
10 BKLN 7022 D4
10 LNDN 7017 B2
10 MHTN 115 C7
10 MHTN 119 A1
10 MHTN 6717 C7
10 MHTN 6821 A1
300 MHTN 118 C1
12th Av
- MHTN 111 D7
- STNL 7018 C2
10 BRNX 6615 C2
10 GDNC 6724 D7
10 MNLA 6724 D7
10 NWRK 6713 B7
10 SCLF 6509 E6
117-00 QENS 6614 C7
147-00 QENS 6615 C7
214-00 QENS 7122 A4
216-00 QENS 7121 E4
300 MHTN 115 D2
700 MHTN 112 A5
700 MHTN 6717 C3
2200 MHTN 106 C5
2200 MHTN 6612 B3
3600 BKLN 6922 D7
6100 BKLN 7022 B2
12th Av SR-9A
300 MHTN 115 D2
300 MHTN 6717 B5
E 12th Av
200 ROSL 6917 A6
S 12th Av
10 MTVN 6394 D5
200 BRNX 6394 D5
12th Rd
149-00 QENS 6615 C7
E 12th Rd
- QENS 7026 B5
W 12th Rd
10 QENS 7026 A5
12th St
- GDNC 6828 E1
- NRWD 6164 C7
- NRWD 6278 C1
10 BKLN 6922 C2
10 HBKN 6716 D5
25-00 QENS 114 D4
25-00 QENS 6718 E3
43-00 QENS 117 E3
100 JSYC 6820 C1
100 WRDG 6500 C6
400 UNCT 6716 C4
1100 NBgT 6716 C4
1400 FTLE 6502 D6
1400 PALP 6502 D6
E 12th St
10 BAYN 6919 E4
10 LNDN 7017 B1
10 MHTN 6821 D1
700 MHTN 119 E3
800 BKLN 7023 B7
2700 BKLN 7121 C2
N 12th St
10 BKLN 6822 B2
10 NHPK 6828 A1
100 NHPK 6724 A7
100 NWRK 6713 B4
200 NHPK 6723 E7
S 12th St
- GDNC 6828 A1
10 NHPK 6828 A1
10 NWRK 6713 A6
500 NWRK 6817 A1
600 STMN 6828 A1
W 12th St
10 BAYN 6919 D4
10 BKLN 7022 D5
10 LNDN 7017 B2
10 MHTN 115 C7
10 MHTN 118 E1
10 MHTN 119 A1
10 MHTN 6717 B7
10 MHTN 6821 C1
2800 BKLN 7120 E2
13th Av
10 BRNX 6615 C2
10 GDNC 6724 D7
10 MNLA 6724 D7
123-00 QENS 6614 D7
141-36 QENS 6615 A7
300 NWRK 6713 B6
3600 BKLN 6922 D7
5000 BKLN 7022 A3
S 13th Av
10 MTVN 6394 D5
200 BRNX 6394 D5
13th Rd
145-00 QENS 6615 A6
W 13th Rd
10 QENS 7026 A5
13th St
- ERTH 6609 C1
- NRWD 6164 C7
- NRWD 6278 C1
10 BKLN 6922 D3
10 GDNC 6828 E1
10 HBKN 6716 D5
10 JSYC 6820 C1
33-00 QENS 114 C6
42-00 QENS 6718 C5
100 WRDG 6500 C5
200 PALP 6502 D7
300 CARL 6609 D1
300 UNCT 6716 C4
800 NBgT 6716 C4
1500 FTLE 6502 E6
E 13th St
10 LNDN 7017 C2
10 MHTN 119 D2
10 MHTN 6821 E1
800 BKLN 7023 B5
N 13th St
10 BKLN 6822 B2
10 BlmT 6713 C3
10 NWRK 6713 C3
500 BlvT 6713 C2
S 13th St
10 NWRK 6713 B5
400 NHPK 6828 A2
500 NWRK 6817 A1
600 GDNC 6828 A2
800 NWRK 6816 E2
W 13th St
10 BAYN 6919 D4
10 BKLN 7022 D5
10 MHTN 116 A7
300 MHTN 115 C6
300 MHTN 6717 B7
14th Av
10 NWRK 6713 B7
10 SCLF 6509 E6
122-00 QENS 6720 D1
130-00 QENS 6614 E7
140-00 QENS 6615 A7
300 IrvT 6712 E7
300 NWRK 6712 E7
3400 BKLN 6922 D7
4800 BKLN 7022 C1
N 14th Av
10 MTVN 6394 A7
S 14th Av
10 MTVN 6394 D5
100 BRNX 6394 D5
14th Pl
25-00 QENS 114 E4
25-00 QENS 6718 E2
14th Rd
110-00 QENS 6720 D1
150-00 QENS 6615 B7
E 14th Rd
100 QENS 7026 B5
W 14th Rd
10 QENS 7026 A5
14th St
- CLST 6278 C1
10 BKLN 6922 D3
10 GDNC 6724 E7
10 JSYC 6820 C1
10 NRWD 6164 D7
10 NRWD 6278 D1
25-00 QENS 114 E3
36-00 QENS 6718 D4
100 WRDG 6500 C5
200 FTLE 6502 D6
200 PALP 6502 D6
300 CARL 6609 D1
300 HBKN 6716 D5
800 NBgT 6716 C4
1100 UNCT 6716 C4
14th St CO-670
- UNCT 6716 D5
100 HBKN 6716 D5
E 14th St
10 BAYN 6919 E4
10 LNDN 7017 B2
10 MHTN 116 A7
10 MHTN 119 A1
10 MHTN 6717 C7
10 MHTN 6821 E1
800 BKLN 7023 B6
N 14th St
10 BKLN 6822 B2
10 EORG 6713 B4
10 NWRK 6713 B4
S 14th St
400 GDNC 6828 A2
400 NHPK 6828 A1
400 NWRK 6713 A7
600 NWRK 6817 A1
700 NWRK 6816 E2
W 14th St
10 BAYN 6919 D4
10 MHTN 115 E7
10 MHTN 116 A7
10 MHTN 6717 B7
14th St Lp
- MHTN 119 D2
- MHTN 6821 E1
14th St Lp S
- MHTN 119 D2
- MHTN 6821 E1
15th Av
10 SCLF 6509 E6
109-00 QENS 6720 C1
140-00 QENS 6721 A1
145-00 QENS 6615 A7
200 NWRK 6817 B1
212-00 QENS 6722 A1
214-00 QENS 6616 A7
300 NWRK 6713 B7
600 IrvT 6712 E7
600 NWRK 6712 E7
3500 BKLN 6922 D7
4700 BKLN 7022 D1
S 15th Av
10 MTVN 6394 D5
W 15th Av
100 SCLF 6509 D6
15th Dr
147-00 QENS 6721 B1
150-00 QENS 6615 B7
W 15th Pl
10 BKLN 7022 D7
15th Rd
147-00 QENS 6615 B7
200-00 QENS 6721 D1
215-00 QENS 6616 A7
W 15th Rd
10 QENS 7026 A5
15th St
- CARL 6609 D1
10 BKLN 6922 C3
100 GDNC 6724 E7
100 JSYC 6820 C1
200 HBKN 6716 D5
300 NRWD 6164 D7
300 NRWD 6278 D1
300 UNCT 6716 C4
900 NBgT 6716 C4
1100 FTLE 6502 D7
E 15th St
10 BAYN 6919 E4
10 LNDN 7017 B2
10 MHTN 116 A7
10 MHTN 6717 C7
100 MHTN 6821 D1
700 MHTN 119 E2
1200 BKLN 7023 B3
N 15th St
10 BKLN 6822 B2
10 BlmT 6713 C2
10 EORG 6713 B4
S 15th St
10 EORG 6713 B5
300 NWRK 6713 A7
600 NWRK 6816 E2
600 NWRK 6817 A1
W 15th St
10 BAYN 6919 D4
10 BKLN 7022 D7
10 LNDN 7017 B2
10 MHTN 115 E7
10 MHTN 116 A7
10 MHTN 6717 B7
2600 BKLN 7120 D1
16th Av
10 NWRK 6817 B1
100 NWRK 6713 A7
100 SCLF 6509 D6
157-00 QENS 6721 D1
200 NWRK 6712 E7
212-01 QENS 6722 A1
214-00 QENS 6616 A7
300 IrvT 6712 E7
3800 BKLN 6922 D7
4300 BKLN 7022 D1
S 16th Av
10 MTVN 6394 A7
16th Dr
155-00 QENS 6721 C1
16th Rd
147-00 QENS 6721 B1
E 16th Rd
10 QENS 7026 B5
W 16th Rd
10 QENS 7026 A5
16th St
10 BKLN 6922 C3
100 JSYC 6820 C1
200 HBKN 6716 D5
300 CARL 6609 D1
300 ERTH 6609 D1
900 NBgT 6716 D4
1100 FTLE 6502 D7
1100 UNCT 6716 C3
2600 JSYC 6716 B3
E 16th St
10 BAYN 6919 E4
10 LNDN 7017 B2
100 MHTN 116 B7
100 MHTN 6717 D7
100 MHTN 6821 D1
200 BKLN 6923 A7
300 MHTN 119 C1
1300 BKLN 7023 B3
N 16th St
10 BlmT 6713 C2
10 EORG 6713 C2
S 16th St
10 EORG 6713 A5
10 NHPK 6828 A1
10 NWRK 6713 A5
500 NWRK 6816 E1
500 NWRK 6817 A1
W 16th St
10 BAYN 6919 D4
10 BKLN 7022 D7
10 LNDN 7017 B2
10 MHTN 115 E6
10 MHTN 116 A7
10 MHTN 6717 B7
2700 BKLN 7120 D1
17th Av
10 NWRK 6817 B1
10 SCLF 6509 D6
199-00 QENS 6721 D1
200 IrvT 6712 E7
200 NWRK 6712 E7
200 NWRK 6816 E1
215-00 QENS 6722 A1
216-00 QENS 6616 A7
4100 BKLN 7022 D2
17th Ct
1200 BKLN 7022 A5
17th Rd
145-00 QENS 6721 A1
W 17th Rd
10 QENS 7026 A5
17th St
- CARL 6609 D1
- ERTH 6609 D1
10 BKLN 6922 C3
10 NRWD 6164 D7
10 NRWD 6278 D1
200 JSYC 6820 C1
300 UNCT 6716 C3
900 NBgT 6716 C3
E 17th St
10 BAYN 6919 E4
10 BKLN 6923 B7
10 LNDN 7017 C2
10 MHTN 116 B7
10 MHTN 6717 C7
100 MHTN 119 C1
100 MHTN 6821 D1
800 BKLN 7023 B6
N 17th St
10 EORG 6713 B4
100 BlmT 6713 C2
S 17th St
10 EORG 6713 A5
10 NHPK 6828 A1
400 NWRK 6713 A7
500 NWRK 6817 A1
600 NWRK 6816 E2
W 17th St
10 BKLN 7022 D7
10 LNDN 7017 B2
10 MHTN 116 A7
10 MHTN 6717 C7
100 BAYN 6919 D3
100 MHTN 115 E6
2800 BKLN 7120 D1
18th Av
10 SCLF 6509 D6
17-85 QENS 6722 A1
126-00 QENS 6720 D1
145-00 QENS 6721 B1
200 NWRK 6817 A1
500 NWRK 6816 E1
600 IrvT 6712 D7
600 IrvT 6816 E1
800 NWRK 6712 C7
3700 BKLN 6923 A7
3800 BKLN 7023 A1
3900 BKLN 7022 E1
E 18th Rd
10 QENS 7026 A5
W 18th Rd
10 QENS 7026 A5
18th St
- CARL 6609 D1
10 BKLN 6922 C3
10 JSYC 6820 C1
20-00 QENS 6719 A1
25-00 QENS 114 E4
25-00 QENS 6718 E2
200 WhkT 6716 D4
600 UNCT 6716 C3
900 NBgT 6716 C3
E 18th St
10 BAYN 6919 E4
10 BKLN 6923 A6
10 LNDN 7017 C2
10 MHTN 116 B7
10 MHTN 6717 D7
200 MHTN 119 C1
200 MHTN 6821 D1
800 BKLN 7023 B3
N 18th St
200 EORG 6713 B3
S 18th St
10 EORG 6713 A5
10 NHPK 6828 A1
10 NWRK 6713 A6
500 NWRK 6712 E7
500 NWRK 6816 E1
W 18th St
10 LNDN 7017 B2
10 MHTN 116 A6
10 MHTN 6717 C7
10 WhkT 6716 D4
100 BAYN 6919 D3
100 MHTN 115 C5
19th Av
10 NWRK 6816 E1
10 NWRK 6817 A1
10 SCLF 6509 D6
35-00 QENS 6719 C2
100 IrvT 6816 E1
145-00 QENS 6721 B1
4900 BKLN 7022 D2
W 19th Av
200 IrvT 6712 D7
200 IrvT 6816 A2
19th Dr
77-00 QENS 6719 D2
19th Ln
1900 BKLN 7022 B5
19th Rd
77-00 QENS 6719 D2
W 19th Rd
10 QENS 7026 A5
19th St
- CARL 6609 D1
- ERTH 6609 D1
10 BKLN 6922 C3
21-00 QENS 6719 A1
200 WhkT 6716 E4
300 UNCT 6716 D4
900 NBgT 6716 C3
E 19th St
10 BAYN 6919 E4
10 BKLN 6923 B7
10 LNDN 7017 C2
10 MHTN 116 B7
10 MHTN 6717 D7
300 MHTN 119 D1
300 MHTN 6821 E1
800 BKLN 7023 B4
N 19th St
10 EORG 6713 B4
S 19th St
200 EORG 6713 A6
200 NWRK 6713 A7
400 NWRK 6712 E7
600 NWRK 6816 E2
W 19th St
10 BAYN 6919 D3
10 LNDN 7017 C2
10 MHTN 116 A6
10 MHTN 6717 C7
10 UNCT 6716 D4
10 WhkT 6716 D4
100 MHTN 115 C5
2800 BKLN 7120 D1
20th Av
10 IrvT 6816 E1
10 SCLF 6509 D6
14-00 QENS 6613 A7
18-00 QENS 6719 C2
118-00 QENS 6720 C1
139-14 QENS 6721 B1
4800 BKLN 7022 E2
20th Dr
1900 BKLN 7022 B5
20th Ln
2000 BKLN 7022 B5
20th Rd
31-00 QENS 6719 B1
146-00 QENS 6721 B1
E 20th Rd
10 QENS 7026 B5
W 20th Rd
10 QENS 7026 A5
20th St
- ERTH 6609 D1
10 BKLN 6922 C3
20-00 QENS 6719 A1
300 CARL 6609 D1
900 NBgT 6716 C3
900 UNCT 6716 C3
E 20th St
10 LNDN 7017 C2
10 MHTN 116 B6
10 MHTN 6717 D7
400 MHTN 119 D1
400 MHTN 6821 E1
E 20th St S
100 MHTN 116 C7
100 MHTN 6717 D7
N 20th St
10 EORG 6713 B3
S 20th St
10 EORG 6713 A5
10 IrvT 6816 E2
10 NWRK 6713 A6
10 NWRK 6816 D3
400 IrvT 6712 E7
400 NWRK 6712 E7
W 20th St
10 BAYN 6919 D3
10 LNDN 7017 C2
10 MHTN 116 A6
10 MHTN 6717 C6
100 MHTN 115 C5
2800 BKLN 7120 D1
20th St Lp
- MHTN 119 D1
- MHTN 6821 E1
21st Av
10 BKLN 7022 C5
18-00 QENS 6719 B1
122-00 QENS 6720 D1
160-31 QENS 6721 D2
21st Dr
18-00 QENS 6719 A1
2000 BKLN 7022 B5
21st Rd
18-00 QENS 6719 A1
160-00 QENS 6721 D2
E 21st Rd
10 QENS 7026 A5
21st St
10 BKLN 6922 C3
10 IrvT 6712 E7
20-00 QENS 6719 A1
25-00 QENS 114 C7
25-00 QENS 6718 E3
45-27 QENS 117 E5
200 NWRK 6816 E1
300 IrvT 6816 E1
300 UNCT 6716 D3
300 WhkT 6716 D3
900 NBgT 6716 C3
E 21st St
10 BAYN 6919 E4
10 BKLN 6923 B7
10 LNDN 7017 C2
10 MHTN 116 C7
10 MHTN 6717 E7
900 BKLN 7023 C7
N 21st St
10 EORG 6713 B3
S 21st St
500 IrvT 6816 D3
W 21st St
10 BAYN 6919 D3
10 LNDN 7017 C2
10 MHTN 116 A6
10 MHTN 6717 B6
100 MHTN 115 D4
2800 BKLN 7120 D2
22nd Av
118-00 QENS 6720 D1
145-00 QENS 6721 B1
22nd Dr
19-00 QENS 6719 A1
98-00 QENS 6720 A3
22nd Rd
19-00 QENS 6719 A1
143-00 QENS 6721 A1
22nd St
10 BKLN 6922 C4
25-00 QENS 114 E4
36-00 QENS 6718 D5
100 IrvT 6712 E7
100 IrvT 6816 E1
300 UNCT 6716 D3
300 WhkT 6716 D3
900 NBgT 6716 D3
E 22nd St
10 BAYN 6919 E4
10 BAYN 6920 A4
10 MHTN 116 B6
10 MHTN 6717 E7
400 BKLN 6923 B7
900 BKLN 7023 C7
N 22nd St
10 EORG 6713 B3
W 22nd St
- QENS 7026 A6
10 BAYN 6919 E3
10 MHTN 116 A6
10 MHTN 6717 C6
200 MHTN 115 C4
2700 BKLN 7120 D2
23rd Av
80-00 QENS 6719 E3
94-00 QENS 6720 A3
145-00 QENS 6721 C2
210-00 QENS 6722 A1
7500 BKLN 7022 C6
23rd Dr
19-00 QENS 6719 A2
23rd Rd
40-00 QENS 6719 B3
102-00 QENS 6720 A3
215-00 QENS 6722 A1
23rd St
10 BKLN 6922 C4
20-00 QENS 6719 A1
25-08 QENS 114 E4
36-00 QENS 6718 D5
300 UNCT 6716 C3
300 WhkT 6716 D3
900 NBgT 6716 C3
E 23rd St
10 BAYN 6919 E3
10 BAYN 6920 A4
10 BKLN 6923 B6
10 MHTN 116 D7
10 MHTN 6717 E7
500 MHTN 119 E1
800 BKLN 7023 C5
N 23rd St
10 EORG 6713 B3
W 23rd St
10 BAYN 6919 D3
10 BKLN 7120 D2
10 MHTN 116 A6
10 MHTN 6717 C6
100 MHTN 115 C4
23rd Ter
19-00 QENS 6719 A2
24th Av
10 BKLN 7022 E4
19-00 QENS 6719 A2
93-00 QENS 6720 A3
145-00 QENS 6721 A2
214-00 QENS 6722 A1
24th Dr
19-00 QENS 6719 A2
24th Rd
19-00 QENS 6719 A2
149-00 QENS 6721 C2
24th St
10 BKLN 6922 C4
20-00 QENS 6719 B1
34-00 QENS 114 D7
34-00 QENS 6718 D4
300 UNCT 6716 D3
300 WhkT 6716 D3
900 NBgT 6716 D3
E 24th St
10 BAYN 6919 E3
10 BAYN 6920 A4
10 BKLN 6923 B7
10 MHTN 116 C6
10 MHTN 6717 D7
700 BKLN 7023 B1
W 24th St
10 BAYN 6919 E3
10 BKLN 7120 C2
10 MHTN 116 A5
10 MHTN 6717 B6
200 MHTN 115 E5
25th Av
10 BKLN 7022 D6
71-00 QENS 6719 E4
94-00 QENS 6720 A3
141-00 QENS 6721 A2
25th Dr
149-00 QENS 6721 C2
25th Rd
18-00 QENS 114 E4
18-00 QENS 6718 E2
25-00 QENS 6719 A2
119-00 QENS 6720 D2
144-00 QENS 6721 A2
25th St
10 BKLN 6922 C4
49-00 QENS 6718 C7
300 UNCT 6716 D3
300 WhkT 6716 D3
E 25th St
10 BAYN 6919 E3
10 BAYN 6920 A4
10 MHTN 116 D7
10 MHTN 6717 E7
200 BKLN 6923 B6
W 25th St
10 BAYN 6919 E3
10 BKLN 7120 C2
10 MHTN 116 A5
10 MHTN 6717 C6
200 MHTN 115 E4
26th Av
10 BKLN 7022 D6
10 QENS 114 C3
18-00 QENS 6718 E2
119-00 QENS 6720 D2
149-00 QENS 6721 E2
209-00 QENS 6722 A1
26th Rd
18-00 QENS 114 E4
18-00 QENS 6718 E2
26th St
10 BKLN 6922 B4
21-00 QENS 6719 A2
300 UNCT 6716 D3
300 WhkT 6716 D3
1100 NBgT 6716 C2
E 26th St
10 BAYN 6919 E3
10 BAYN 6920 A3
10 MHTN 116 E7
10 MHTN 6717 E7
200 BKLN 6923 C6
1700 BKLN 7023 C5
W 26th St
10 BAYN 6919 E3
10 MHTN 116 A5
10 MHTN 6717 B5
200 MHTN 115 E4
27th Av
1-00 QENS 114 C4
1-00 QENS 6718 E2
10 BKLN 7022 D7
60-00 QENS 6719 C4
99-00 QENS 6720 A3
149-00 QENS 6721 C2
209-00 QENS 6722 A2
27th Rd
21-00 QENS 114 E5
21-00 QENS 6718 E3
27th St
10 BKLN 6922 B4
20-00 QENS 6719 B1
27-00 QENS 114 E5
37-00 QENS 6718 D5
300 WhkT 6716 D3
1100 NBgT 6716 D2
1100 UNCT 6716 D2
E 27th St
10 BAYN 6919 D3
10 BAYN 6920 A3
10 MHTN 116 C6
10 MHTN 6717 D7
800 BKLN 7023 C4
W 27th St
10 MHTN 116 A4
10 MHTN 6717 C6
100 BAYN 6919 E2
200 MHTN 115 E4
2900 BKLN 7120 C2
28th Av
10 BKLN 7022 D7
14-00 QENS 114 D4
14-00 QENS 6718 E2
31-00 QENS 6719 A3
119-00 QENS 6720 D2
149-00 QENS 6721 B2
210-00 QENS 6722 A2
28th Rd
31-00 QENS 6719 A3
138-00 QENS 6720 E2
209-00 QENS 6721 E2
216-00 QENS 6722 B2
28th St
10 BKLN 6922 B4
26-00 QENS 6719 A3
33-00 QENS 114 D7
33-00 QENS 6718 D5
300 WhkT 6716 E3
1100 NBgT 6716 D2
1100 UNCT 6716 C2
E 28th St
10 BAYN 6919 D3
10 BAYN 6920 A3
10 BKLN 6923 C6
10 MHTN 116 C5
10 MHTN 6717 E7
800 BKLN 7023 C4
W 28th St
10 BAYN 6919 E3
10 BKLN 7120 C2
10 MHTN 116 B5
10 MHTN 6717 C6
300 MHTN 115 E4
29th Av
12-00 QENS 114 D4
12-00 QENS 6718 E3
102-00 QENS 6720 B4
142-00 QENS 6721 A2
210-00 QENS 6722 A2
29th Rd
137-00 QENS 6720 E2
142-00 QENS 6721 A2
29th St
10 BKLN 6922 B4
20-00 QENS 6719 A2
30-28 QENS 114 E7
30-28 QENS 6718 E4
300 WhkT 6716 E3
400 UNCT 6716 D2
1900 NBgT 6716 C2
E 29th St
10 BAYN 6920 A3
10 BKLN 6923 C6
10 MHTN 116 D6
10 MHTN 6717 D6
800 BKLN 7023 C1
W 29th St
10 BAYN 6919 E2
10 BKLN 7120 C2
10 MHTN 116 B4
10 MHTN 6717 C6
300 MHTN 115 E3
30th Av
11-00 QENS 114 D4
11-00 QENS 6718 E3
27-12 QENS 6719 A3
119-00 QENS 6720 D3
198-00 QENS 6721 D3
209-00 QENS 6722 A2
30th Dr
11-00 QENS 114 D5
11-00 QENS 6718 E3
29-00 QENS 6719 A3
30th Pl
46-00 QENS 6718 D7
30th Rd
11-00 QENS 6718 E3
25-00 QENS 114 E6
44-00 QENS 6719 B4
30th St
- WhkT 6716 E3
26-00 QENS 6719 A3
30-71 QENS 114 E6
46-00 QENS 6718 D7
100 BKLN 6922 C4
100 UNCT 6716 D2
1100 NBgT 6716 D2
E 30th St
10 BAYN 6920 A3
10 MHTN 116 E6
10 MHTN 6717 E6
W 30th St
10 BAYN 6919 E2
10 BAYN 6920 A3
10 BKLN 7120 C1
10 MHTN 116 A4
10 MHTN 6717 B5
300 MHTN 115 D2
31st Av
11-00 QENS 114 C5
11-00 QENS 6718 D3
30-00 QENS 6719 C4
92-00 QENS 6720 A4
31st Dr
11-00 QENS 114 C5
11-00 QENS 6718 D3
138-00 QENS 6720 E3
140-00 QENS 6721 A3
31st Pl
45-00 QENS 6718 D7
31st Rd
14-00 QENS 114 D6
14-00 QENS 6718 E3
133-00 QENS 6720 E3
140-00 QENS 6721 A3
216-00 QENS 6722 B2
31st St
- NBgT 6716 D2
20-00 QENS 6719 B2
31-00 QENS 114 E7
31-00 QENS 6718 E4
100 BKLN 6922 B4
500 UNCT 6716 D2
E 31st St
10 BAYN 6920 A3
10 BKLN 6923 C6
10 MHTN 116 D5
10 MHTN 6717 D6
800 BKLN 7023 C2
W 31st St
10 BAYN 6920 A2
10 BKLN 7120 C2
10 MHTN 116 B4
10 MHTN 6717 C5
100 BAYN 6919 E2
300 MHTN 115 E3
32nd Av
51-00 QENS 6719 D5
132-00 QENS 6720 E3
140-00 QENS 6721 E3
208-00 QENS 6722 A2
32nd Dr
208-00 QENS 6721 E3
32nd Pl
43-00 QENS 6718 D7
32nd Rd
198-00 QENS 6721 D3
214-30 QENS 6722 A2
32nd St
- WhkT 6716 E3
10 BKLN 6922 B4
23-00 QENS 6719 A3
31-00 QENS 114 E7
31-00 QENS 6718 E5
300 UNCT 6716 D2
500 NBgT 6716 D2
32nd St CO-674
300 UNCT 6716 D2
500 NBgT 6716 D2
E 32nd St
10 BAYN 6920 A2
10 MHTN 116 D5
10 MHTN 6717 D6
400 BKLN 6923 C7
800 BKLN 7023 C2
W 32nd St
10 BAYN 6919 E2
10 BAYN 6920 A2
10 BKLN 7120 C1
10 MHTN 116 B4
10 MHTN 6717 D6
33rd Av
13-01 QENS 114 C6
13-01 QENS 6718 E4
134-00 QENS 6720 E3
141-00 QENS 6721 B3
208-00 QENS 6722 A3
33rd Rd
9-00 QENS 6718 D3
14-01 QENS 114 C6
151-00 QENS 6721 B3
210-00 QENS 6722 A2
33rd St
10 BKLN 6922 B4
20-00 QENS 6719 B2
31-00 QENS 114 E7
32-00 QENS 6718 E5
100 WhkT 6716 E3
200 UNCT 6716 E2
E 33rd St
10 BAYN 6920 A2
10 BKLN 7023 E4
10 MHTN 116 C4
10 MHTN 6717 D6
W 33rd St
10 BAYN 6919 E2
10 BAYN 6920 A2
10 BKLN 7120 C2
10 MHTN 116 B4
100 MHTN 6717 B5
300 MHTN 115 E3
34th Av
8-00 QENS 114 D7
8-00 QENS 6718 D3
35-00 QENS 6719 A4
91-00 QENS 6720 B5
140-00 QENS 6721 A3
249-00 QENS 6722 D2
34th Rd
94-00 QENS 6720 A5
139-00 QENS 6721 A3
209-00 QENS 6722 A3
34th St
10 BKLN 6922 B4
25-00 QENS 6719 A3
50-00 QENS 6718 E7
100 UNCT 6716 E2
100 WhkT 6716 E3
1500 NBgT 6716 D2
E 34th St
10 BAYN 6920 A2
10 BKLN 6923 C6
10 MHTN 116 C4
10 MHTN 6717 E6
1500 BKLN 7023 D4
W 34th St
10 BAYN 6919 E2
10 BAYN 6920 A2
10 MHTN 116 A3
10 MHTN 6717 B5
300 MHTN 115 E3
35th Av
7-00 QENS 114 C7
7-00 QENS 6718 E4
62-00 QENS 6719 D5
91-00 QENS 6720 A5
138-00 QENS 6721 D3
207-00 QENS 6722 A3
35th Rd
70-00 QENS 6719 D6
35th St
10 BKLN 6922 B4
20-00 QENS 6719 A3
51-00 QENS 6718 D7
53-00 QENS 6822 D1
100 UNCT 6716 E2
100 WhkT 6716 E3
500 NBgT 6716 D2
E 35th St
10 BAYN 6920 A2
10 BKLN 6923 C6
10 MHTN 116 D5
10 MHTN 6717 E6
1400 BKLN 7023 D4
W 35th St
10 BAYN 6919 E2
10 BAYN 6920 A2
10 BKLN 7120 B2
10 MHTN 116 B3
10 MHTN 6717 C5
400 MHTN 115 E2
36th Av
7-00 QENS 114 A7
8-00 QENS 6718 D4
38-00 QENS 6719 A5
133-00 QENS 6720 E4
200-00 QENS 6721 E3
207-00 QENS 6722 B3
36th Rd
133-00 QENS 6720 E4
36th St
19-00 QENS 6719 B3
34-00 QENS 6718 E5
100 WhkT 6716 E3
500 NBgT 6716 D2
500 UNCT 6716 D2
900 BKLN 6922 D6
E 36th St
10 BAYN 6920 A2
10 MHTN 116 E4
10 MHTN 6717 E6
400 MHTN 117 A5
400 MHTN 6718 A6
1500 BKLN 7023 D3
W 36th St
10 BAYN 6920 A2
10 MHTN 116 C3
10 MHTN 6717 C5
400 MHTN 115 E2
2800 BKLN 7120 B2
37th Av
- GTNE 6722 E2
8-00 QENS 6718 E5
53-00 QENS 6719 E5
90-00 QENS 6720 B5
189-00 QENS 6721 D4
221-00 QENS 6722 B3
37th Dr
104-00 QENS 6720 B5
37th Rd
73-00 QENS 6719 D6
104-00 QENS 6720 B5
37th St
19-00 QENS 6719 B2
41-00 QENS 6718 E7
52-00 QENS 6822 D1
100 WhkT 6716 E2
500 BKLN 6922 D6
500 NBgT 6716 D2
500 UNCT 6716 D2
37th St CO-505
100 UNCT 6716 D2
100 WhkT 6716 E2
500 NBgT 6716 D2
E 37th St
10 BAYN 6920 A2
10 MHTN 116 E4
10 MHTN 6717 E6
400 BKLN 6923 D7
400 MHTN 117 A5
400 MHTN 6718 A6
900 BKLN 7023 D1
W 37th St
10 BAYN 6920 A2
10 BKLN 7120 B1
10 MHTN 116 C3
10 MHTN 6717 C5
100 BAYN 6919 E1
400 MHTN 115 E2
38th Av
8-00 QENS 6718 D4
53-00 QENS 6719 B6
96-00 QENS 6720 A5
142-00 QENS 6721 A4
207-00 QENS 6722 A3
38th Dr
240-00 QENS 6722 D2
38th Rd
236-01 QENS 6722 D2
38th St
10 IrvT 6816 B2
24-00 QENS 6719 A5
41-00 QENS 6718 E6
100 UNCT 6716 E2
100 WhkT 6716 E2
500 NBgT 6716 D2
900 BKLN 6922 E7
E 38th St
10 BAYN 6920 A2
10 BKLN 6923 D5
10 MHTN 116 D3
10 MHTN 6717 E6
400 MHTN 117 A5
400 MHTN 6718 A6
1200 BKLN 7023 D2
W 38th St
10 BAYN 6920 A1
10 MHTN 116 C3
10 MHTN 6717 D5
400 MHTN 115 E1
39th Av
21-00 QENS 6718 D5
53-00 QENS 6719 B6
104-00 QENS 6720 B5
170-00 QENS 6721 E4
204-00 QENS 6722 B3
39th Dr
52-00 QENS 6719 B6
39th Pl
41-00 QENS 6718 E6
39th Rd
52-00 QENS 6719 B6
250-00 QENS 6722 E2
256-00 NHmT 6722 E2
39th St
10 BKLN 6922 D7
10 IrvT 6816 B2
36-00 QENS 6718 E7
100 UNCT 6716 E2
100 WhkT 6716 E2
1500 NBgT 6716 D1
E 39th St
10 BAYN 6920 A2
10 MHTN 116 E4
10 MHTN 6717 E6
300 MHTN 117 A4
300 MHTN 6718 A6
400 BKLN 6923 D6
1000 BKLN 7023 D1
W 39th St
10 BAYN 6920 A1
10 MHTN 116 B2
10 MHTN 6717 D5
400 MHTN 115 E1
40th Av
8-00 QENS 6718 C5
247-00 QENS 6722 E2
40th Dr
94-00 QENS 6720 A6
40th Rd
29-00 QENS 6718 D5
131-00 QENS 6720 E5
40th St
10 IrvT 6816 A3
41-00 QENS 6719 A6
43-00 QENS 6718 E7
100 UNCT 6716 E2
100 WhkT 6716 E2
200 BKLN 6922 D6
1500 NBgT 6716 D1
E 40th St
10 BAYN 6920 A2
10 MHTN 116 E4
10 MHTN 6717 E5
300 MHTN 117 A4
300 MHTN 6718 A6
400 BKLN 6923 D6
900 BKLN 7023 D1
W 40th St
10 BAYN 6920 A1
10 MHTN 116 B2
10 MHTN 6717 D5
400 MHTN 115 E1
40th St Br
- BAYN 6920 A2
41st Av
8-00 QENS 6718 C5
41-00 QENS 6720 E5
77-00 QENS 6719 D6
136-18 QENS 6721 A4
208-00 QENS 6722 A4
256-00 NHmT 6722 E2
41st Dr
58-00 QENS 6719 B6
250-00 QENS 6722 E2
256-00 NHmT 6722 E2
41st Rd
- QENS 6718 C5
132-00 QENS 6720 E5

New York City/5 Borough Street Index

STREET / Block City Map# Grid

41st Rd
221-00 QENS 6722 C3
41st St
10 BKLN 6922 C6
10 IrvT 6816 B2
41-00 QENS 6719 A7
47-00 QENS 6718 E7
100 UNCT 6716 E2
100 WhkT 6716 E2
1500 NBgT 6716 D1
E 41st St
10 BAYN 6920 A2
10 BKLN 7023 D2
10 MHTN 116 E4
10 MHTN 6717 D5
300 MHTN 117 A4
300 MHTN 6718 A6
W 41st St
10 BAYN 6920 A1
100 MHTN 116 A1
100 MHTN 6717 D5
400 MHTN 115 E1
600 MHTN 111 D7
42nd Av
104-00 QENS 6720 B6
200-00 QENS 6721 E4
203-01 QENS 6722 A4
42nd Pl
36-00 QENS 6719 A5
42nd Rd
23-00 QENS 6718 D6
196-00 QENS 6721 E4
42nd St
- BKLN 7022 E1
10 BKLN 6922 B5
10 IrvT 6816 A2
24-00 QENS 6719 A5
50-00 QENS 6718 E7
100 UNCT 6716 E2
100 WhkT 6716 E2
1900 NBgT 6716 D1
E 42nd St
10 BAYN 6920 A1
10 MHTN 116 E3
10 MHTN 6717 E5
300 MHTN 117 A4
300 MHTN 6718 A6
400 BKLN 6923 D7
900 BKLN 7023 D1
W 42nd St
10 BAYN 6920 A1
10 MHTN 116 B2
10 MHTN 6717 C4
400 MHTN 115 E1
500 MHTN 111 E7
43rd Av
8-00 QENS 117 E3
32-00 QENS 6718 E6
40-00 QENS 6719 A6
89-00 QENS 6720 C5
156-00 QENS 6721 C4
202-00 QENS 6722 A4
43rd Rd
8-00 QENS 117 E3
8-00 QENS 6718 C5
189-00 QENS 6721 D4
43rd St
10 IrvT 6816 A2
41-00 QENS 6719 A6
53-00 QENS 6822 E1
100 UNCT 6716 E2
100 WhkT 6716 E2
600 BKLN 6922 C6
1100 NBgT 6716 D1
1600 BKLN 7022 E1
E 43rd St
10 BAYN 6920 A1
10 MHTN 6717 E5
100 MHTN 116 E3
300 MHTN 117 A3
300 MHTN 6718 A5
400 BKLN 6923 D7
900 BKLN 7023 D1
W 43rd St
10 BAYN 6920 A1
10 MHTN 116 A1
10 MHTN 6717 C4
500 MHTN 111 E7
500 MHTN 115 E1
44th Av
8-00 QENS 117 E3
8-00 QENS 6718 C5
58-00 QENS 6719 B7
94-00 QENS 6720 C6
189-00 QENS 6721 D5
241-00 QENS 6722 D3
44th Dr
4-00 QENS 117 D4
4-00 QENS 6718 B6
44th Rd
9-00 QENS 117 E4
9-00 QENS 6718 C6
44th St
10 BKLN 6922 A5
10 MplT 6816 A2
24-00 QENS 6719 A5
53-00 QENS 6823 A1
54-40 QENS 6822 E1
100 UNCT 6716 E2
100 WhkT 6716 E2
1500 BKLN 7022 D1
1500 NBgT 6716 D1
E 44th St
10 BAYN 6920 B1
10 MHTN 116 D2
10 MHTN 117 A3
10 MHTN 6718 A5
100 MHTN 6717 E5
W 44th St
10 BAYN 6920 A1
10 MHTN 116 A1
10 MHTN 6717 D4
400 MHTN 112 A7
500 MHTN 111 E7
45th Av
5-00 QENS 6718 B6
10-00 QENS 117 E4
70-00 QENS 6719 D7
88-00 QENS 6720 C6
147-00 QENS 6721 E5
202-00 QENS 6722 A4
45th Dr
189-00 QENS 6721 D5
200-00 QENS 6722 A5
45th Rd
10-00 QENS 117 E4
10-00 QENS 6718 C6
45th Rd
189-00 QENS 6721 D5
206-00 QENS 6722 B4
45th St
10 BKLN 6922 D7
10 MplT 6816 A2
18-00 QENS 6719 C2
100 UNCT 111 A3
100 UNCT 6716 E2
100 UNCT 6717 A2
100 WhkT 111 A3
100 WhkT 6717 A2
500 NBgT 6716 E2
1500 BKLN 7022 E1
E 45th St
10 BAYN 6920 B1
10 MHTN 116 E3
10 MHTN 6717 E5
200 MHTN 117 A3
200 MHTN 6718 A5
600 BKLN 6923 D7
1100 BKLN 7023 E1
W 45th St
10 BAYN 6920 A1
10 MHTN 116 C2
10 MHTN 6717 C4
400 MHTN 112 A7
500 MHTN 111 E7
46th Av
5-00 QENS 117 E5
5-00 QENS 6718 C6
74-00 QENS 6719 D7
94-00 QENS 6720 A6
147-00 QENS 6721 B5
206-00 QENS 6722 B4
46th Rd
5-00 QENS 117 D4
5-00 QENS 6718 B6
197-01 QENS 6721 E5
209-00 QENS 6722 B4
46th St
10 BKLN 6922 C7
10 UNCT 111 A3
10 UNCT 6717 A2
10 WhkT 111 A3
10 WhkT 6717 A2
24-00 QENS 6719 B4
53-00 QENS 6823 A1
200 UNCT 6716 E1
1500 BKLN 7022 D1
1500 NBgT 6716 D1
E 46th St
10 BAYN 6920 B1
10 MHTN 116 D2
10 MHTN 6717 E5
200 MHTN 117 A3
200 MHTN 6718 A6
600 BKLN 6923 E6
1200 BKLN 7023 E2
W 46th St
10 BAYN 6920 A1
10 MHTN 116 D2
10 MHTN 6717 C4
300 MHTN 112 A7
500 MHTN 111 E7
47th Av
4-00 QENS 117 D5
24-00 QENS 6718 D6
67-00 QENS 6719 C7
102-00 QENS 6720 B6
192-01 QENS 6721 E5
204-33 QENS 6722 B4
47th Rd
4-00 QENS 117 D5
4-00 QENS 6718 B6
217-00 QENS 6722 B4
47th St
10 BKLN 6922 A5
10 UNCT 111 A3
10 UNCT 6717 A2
10 WhkT 111 A3
10 WhkT 6717 A2
24-00 QENS 6719 B3
55-00 QENS 6823 A3
200 UNCT 6716 E1
1500 BKLN 7022 D1
1500 NBgT 6716 D1
E 47th St
10 BAYN 6920 B1
10 MHTN 116 D2
10 MHTN 6717 E5
200 MHTN 117 A3
200 MHTN 6718 A5
W 47th St
10 BAYN 6920 A1
10 MHTN 116 D1
10 MHTN 6717 C4
300 MHTN 112 A7
500 MHTN 111 E7
48th Av
4-00 QENS 117 E5
4-00 QENS 6718 B6
64-00 QENS 6719 C7
89-00 QENS 6720 A7
186-00 QENS 6721 E5
204-00 QENS 6722 B5
48th St
10 BKLN 6922 C7
10 UNCT 111 A3
10 UNCT 6717 A1
10 WhkT 111 A3
10 WhkT 6717 A2
23-60 QENS 6719 A6
54-30 QENS 6823 A2
500 UNCT 6716 E1
1400 BKLN 7022 D1
1400 NBgT 6716 D1
2000 NBgT 6610 D7
E 48th St
10 BAYN 6920 B1
10 MHTN 116 E2
10 MHTN 6717 E5
200 BKLN 6923 E7
200 MHTN 117 A3
200 MHTN 6718 A5
1100 BKLN 7023 E3
W 48th St
10 BAYN 6920 A1
10 MHTN 116 D1
10 MHTN 6717 D4
100 BAYN 6819 A7
200 MHTN 112 A7
600 MHTN 111 E6
49th Av
66-00 QENS 6719 C7
104-00 QENS 6720 B6
196-00 QENS 6721 E5
49th Av
217-00 QENS 6722 B5
49th Pl
58-00 QENS 6823 A3
49th Rd
228-00 QENS 6722 C4
49th St
10 UNCT 111 A2
10 UNCT 6717 A1
10 WhkT 111 A2
10 WhkT 6717 A1
18-00 QENS 6719 D2
56-00 QENS 6823 A2
300 BKLN 6922 C7
500 UNCT 6716 E1
500 WNYK 6716 E1
1300 BKLN 7022 D1
1500 NBgT 6716 D1
2000 NBgT 6610 D7
E 49th St
10 BAYN 6920 B1
10 MHTN 116 E2
10 MHTN 6717 E5
100 MHTN 117 A2
100 MHTN 6718 A5
200 BKLN 6923 E6
1400 BKLN 7023 E2
W 49th St
10 BAYN 6920 B1
10 MHTN 116 C1
10 MHTN 6717 E4
100 BAYN 6819 A7
200 MHTN 112 A7
600 MHTN 111 E6
50th Av
2-00 QENS 117 D5
2-00 QENS 6718 B6
59-00 QENS 6719 C7
106-00 QENS 6720 C6
195-00 QENS 6721 E6
198-00 QENS 6722 A5
50th St
10 BKLN 6922 C7
10 WhkT 111 B2
10 WhkT 6717 A1
38-00 QENS 6719 A6
53-00 QENS 6823 A2
200 WNYK 111 A2
200 WNYK 6717 A1
1100 NBgT 6716 E1
1100 WNYK 6716 E1
1300 BKLN 7022 D1
2000 NBgT 6610 D7
E 50th St
10 BAYN 6920 B1
10 MHTN 116 E1
10 MHTN 6717 E4
100 MHTN 117 B2
100 MHTN 6718 A5
W 50th St
10 BAYN 6819 A7
10 BAYN 6920 B1
10 MHTN 116 D1
10 MHTN 6717 C3
100 MHTN 112 A6
600 MHTN 111 E6
51st Av
2-00 QENS 117 D5
2-00 QENS 6718 B6
69-00 QENS 6719 E7
87-00 QENS 6720 A7
196-00 QENS 6721 E6
214-00 QENS 6722 B5
249-00 QENS 6723 A4
51st Dr
72-00 QENS 6823 D1
51st Rd
46-00 QENS 6823 A1
72-00 QENS 6719 D7
51st St
10 BKLN 6921 E5
10 WhkT 111 B2
10 WhkT 6717 A1
10 WNYK 6717 A1
31-00 QENS 6719 B5
100 BKLN 6922 C7
200 WNYK 111 A2
400 WNYK 6716 E1
500 NBgT 6716 E1
1400 NBgT 6610 D7
1800 BKLN 7022 D1
E 51st St
10 BAYN 6920 B2
10 BKLN 6923 E5
10 MHTN 116 E1
10 MHTN 6717 A4
100 MHTN 117 A2
100 MHTN 6718 A5
1000 BKLN 7023 E1
W 51st St
10 BAYN 6819 A7
10 BAYN 6920 B1
10 MHTN 116 D1
10 MHTN 6717 C3
100 MHTN 112 A6
600 MHTN 111 E6
52nd Av
58-00 QENS 6719 B7
65-00 QENS 6823 C1
103-00 QENS 6720 C6
240-00 QENS 6722 D4
249-00 QENS 6723 A3
52nd Ct
73-00 QENS 6823 D1
52nd Dr
73-00 QENS 6823 D1
52nd Rd
58-00 QENS 6823 B1
254-00 QENS 6723 A3
52nd St
10 BKLN 6921 E5
39-00 QENS 6719 B6
100 BKLN 6922 B7
100 WNYK 111 A1
100 WNYK 6717 A1
500 NBgT 6716 E1
500 WNYK 6716 E1
1200 BKLN 7022 D1
1400 NBgT 6610 D7
E 52nd St
10 BAYN 6920 B1
10 BKLN 6923 E6
10 MHTN 116 E1
10 MHTN 6717 A4
100 MHTN 117 B2
100 MHTN 6718 A4
1000 BKLN 7023 E1
E 52nd St
2000 BKLN 7024 A4
W 52nd St
- MHTN 111 E6
10 BAYN 6819 A7
10 BAYN 6920 B1
10 MHTN 112 A6
10 MHTN 116 D1
10 MHTN 6717 E4
53rd Av
5-00 QENS 117 D6
5-00 QENS 6718 B7
65-00 QENS 6823 C1
86-00 QENS 6719 E2
103-05 QENS 6720 C7
189-00 QENS 6721 E6
240-00 QENS 6722 E5
53rd Dr
60-00 QENS 6823 C1
53rd Pl
32-00 QENS 6719 B5
E 53rd Pl
10 BKLN 7024 A4
53rd Rd
66-00 QENS 6823 C1
53rd St
10 BKLN 6921 E6
10 BKLN 6922 A6
41-00 QENS 6719 B6
60-00 QENS 6823 B3
100 WNYK 111 A1
100 WNYK 6717 A1
1100 NBgT 6716 E1
1100 WNYK 6716 E1
1200 BKLN 7022 D2
1500 NBgT 6610 D7
E 53rd St
10 BAYN 6920 B1
10 JSYC 6920 B1
10 MHTN 116 E1
10 MHTN 6717 A4
100 MHTN 117 B2
100 MHTN 6718 A4
900 BKLN 6923 E7
900 BKLN 7023 E2
1500 BKLN 7024 A3
W 53rd St
10 BAYN 6819 A7
10 MHTN 112 B6
10 MHTN 116 D1
10 MHTN 6717 D3
54th Av
1-00 QENS 117 C6
1-00 QENS 6718 B7
42-00 QENS 6822 E1
43-00 QENS 6823 A1
87-00 QENS 6719 E7
88-00 QENS 6720 A7
242-00 QENS 6722 E4
54th Dr
44-00 QENS 6823 A1
54th Pl
60-00 QENS 6823 B3
54th Rd
42-00 QENS 6822 E1
43-00 QENS 6823 A1
54th St
10 BKLN 6921 E6
10 WNYK 111 A1
10 WNYK 6717 A1
41-00 QENS 6719 B6
58-00 QENS 6823 A3
300 BKLN 6922 B7
400 WNYK 6716 C1
500 NBgT 6610 E7
500 WNYK 6610 E7
1100 BKLN 7022 C1
E 54th St
10 BKLN 6923 E6
10 MHTN 112 E7
10 MHTN 116 E1
10 MHTN 6717 A4
100 MHTN 117 B2
100 MHTN 6718 A4
900 BKLN 7023 E1
1200 BKLN 7024 A2
W 54th St
10 BAYN 6819 B7
10 MHTN 112 D7
10 MHTN 6717 D3
55th Av
43-00 QENS 6822 E1
48-00 QENS 6823 A1
87-00 QENS 6719 E7
87-00 QENS 6720 B7
55th Dr
56-00 QENS 6823 B2
55th Rd
86-00 QENS 6823 E1
87-00 QENS 6824 A3
55th St
10 BKLN 6921 E6
38-00 QENS 6719 B6
60-00 QENS 6823 B3
200 BKLN 6922 A6
200 WNYK 111 A1
200 WNYK 6717 A1
500 WNYK 6610 E7
500 WNYK 6716 C1
600 NBgT 6610 E7
1100 BKLN 7022 C1
E 55th St
10 BKLN 6923 E4
10 MHTN 112 E7
10 MHTN 116 E1
10 MHTN 6717 E4
100 MHTN 117 A1
100 MHTN 6718 A4
700 BKLN 6924 A7
800 BKLN 7024 A2
W 55th St
10 BAYN 6819 B7
10 JSYC 6819 B7
10 MHTN 112 C6
10 MHTN 6717 E4
600 MHTN 111 E5
56th Av
58-00 QENS 6823 B2
86-00 QENS 6824 A1
89-00 QENS 6720 A7
137-00 QENS 6721 A6
196-22 QENS 6722 A6
56th Dr
10 BKLN 7024 B4
56-00 QENS 6823 B2
56th Pl
28-00 QENS 6719 B4
56th Rd
41-00 QENS 6822 E1
44-00 QENS 6823 A2
142-00 QENS 6721 A6
223-00 QENS 6722 C5
56th St
10 BKLN 6921 E6
38-00 QENS 6719 B6
59-56 QENS 6823 B3
200 BKLN 6922 A6
200 WNYK 111 A1
200 WNYK 6717 A1
400 WNYK 6611 A7
500 WNYK 6610 E7
600 NBgT 6610 E7
1000 BKLN 7022 C1
E 56th St
10 BKLN 6923 E4
10 MHTN 112 E7
10 MHTN 113 A7
10 MHTN 6717 E3
10 MHTN 6718 A4
100 MHTN 117 A1
600 BKLN 6924 A7
800 BKLN 7024 A1
W 56th St
10 BAYN 6819 B7
10 MHTN 112 D7
10 MHTN 6717 D3
56th Ter
56-00 QENS 6823 B2
E 56th St Ext
- BKLN 6924 A7
57th Av
72-00 QENS 6823 E1
86-00 QENS 6824 A1
90-00 QENS 6720 A7
227-00 QENS 6722 D5
249-00 QENS 6723 A4
57th Dr
69-01 QENS 6823 D2
244-00 QENS 6722 E4
57th Pl
57-01 QENS 6823 B2
E 57th Pl
10 BKLN 7024 B4
57th Rd
58-00 QENS 6823 B2
85-00 QENS 6824 A1
130-00 QENS 6720 E6
136-00 QENS 6721 A6
226-00 QENS 6722 D5
57th St
- BKLN 6925 C4
- QENS 6925 B4
10 BKLN 6921 E6
41-00 QENS 6719 B7
58-00 QENS 6823 B3
100 WNYK 111 A1
100 WNYK 6717 A1
200 BKLN 6922 A6
500 WNYK 6610 E7
500 WNYK 6611 A7
600 NBgT 6610 E7
1000 BKLN 7022 B1
E 57th St
10 BKLN 6923 E4
10 MHTN 112 E7
10 MHTN 113 A7
10 MHTN 6717 E4
10 MHTN 6718 A4
100 MHTN 117 B1
200 BKLN 6924 A6
2000 BKLN 7024 A3
W 57th St
10 BAYN 6819 B7
10 MHTN 112 D6
10 MHTN 6717 D3
58th Av
57-00 QENS 6823 B2
85-00 QENS 6824 A1
130-00 QENS 6720 E6
182-00 QENS 6721 D7
205-00 QENS 6722 C5
251-00 QENS 6723 B4
58th Dr
59-00 QENS 6823 B3
58th Ln
47-00 QENS 6719 B7
51-00 QENS 6823 B1
58th Pl
48-00 QENS 6719 B7
56-00 QENS 6823 B2
58th Rd
68-00 QENS 6823 D2
130-00 QENS 6720 E6
136-00 QENS 6721 A6
230-00 QENS 6722 D5
58th St
10 BKLN 6921 E6
31-00 QENS 6719 B7
57-00 QENS 6823 B3
100 WNYK 111 B1
100 WNYK 6717 A1
300 BKLN 6922 B7
300 WNYK 6611 A7
1100 NBgT 6610 E7
1100 WNYK 6610 E7
2000 BKLN 7022 E2
E 58th St
10 BKLN 6924 A5
10 MHTN 112 E7
10 MHTN 113 A7
10 MHTN 6717 E4
10 MHTN 6718 A4
200 MHTN 117 B1
800 BKLN 7024 A2
W 58th St
10 BAYN 6819 A7
10 MHTN 112 C5
10 MHTN 6717 C2
59th Av
58-00 QENS 6823 B3
91-08 QENS 6824 A1
130-00 QENS 6720 E6
136-00 QENS 6721 A6
221-00 QENS 6722 C5
259-00 QENS 6723 B4
59th Dr
58-00 QENS 6823 B3
59th Pl
47-00 QENS 6719 B7
56-40 QENS 6823 B2
E 59th Pl
10 BKLN 7024 B4
59th Rd
59-00 QENS 6823 B3
59th St
10 BKLN 6921 E6
46-00 QENS 6719 B7
55-00 QENS 6823 B3
100 WNYK 111 B1
100 WNYK 6717 A1
200 WNYK 6611 A7
300 BKLN 6922 B7
500 WNYK 6610 E7
600 NBgT 6610 E7
900 BKLN 7022 E3
E 59th St
10 BKLN 6924 A5
10 MHTN 112 E7
10 MHTN 113 A7
10 MHTN 6717 E4
10 MHTN 6718 A4
300 MHTN 117 B1
800 BKLN 7024 A3
W 59th St
400 MHTN 112 B5
400 MHTN 6717 D2
60th Av
59-00 QENS 6823 B3
84-00 QENS 6824 A1
130-00 QENS 6720 E6
136-00 QENS 6721 A6
245-00 QENS 6723 A4
60th Ct
- QENS 6823 B3
60th Dr
60-00 QENS 6823 C3
83-00 QENS 6824 A2
60th Ln
58-00 QENS 6823 C3
60th Pl
33-00 QENS 6719 C5
62-10 QENS 6823 C4
E 60th Pl
10 BKLN 7024 B4
60th Rd
64-00 QENS 6823 C3
84-00 QENS 6824 A1
262-00 QENS 6723 B4
60th St
10 BKLN 6921 E6
10 WNYK 111 B1
10 WNYK 6717 B1
40-00 QENS 6719 C7
58-00 QENS 6823 B3
100 WNYK 6611 A7
300 BKLN 6922 A7
500 WNYK 6610 E7
600 NBgT 6610 E7
900 BKLN 7022 D2
E 60th St
10 BKLN 7024 A3
10 MHTN 112 E6
10 MHTN 113 A7
10 MHTN 6717 E3
10 MHTN 6718 A4
300 MHTN 117 C1
W 60th St
10 MHTN 112 C5
10 MHTN 6717 D3
61st Av
241-00 QENS 6722 E5
245-00 QENS 6723 A4
61st Dr
69-00 QENS 6823 D3
82-00 QENS 6824 A2
W 61st Dr
200 MHTN 112 B4
200 MHTN 6717 C2
61st Rd
67-00 QENS 6823 D3
84-00 QENS 6824 A2
134-00 QENS 6720 E7
142-00 QENS 6721 B7
61st St
10 BKLN 6921 E6
31-00 QENS 6719 C4
78-00 QENS 6823 D6
300 BKLN 6922 A7
500 WNYK 6611 A7
600 NBgT 6610 E7
600 WNYK 6610 E7
1500 BKLN 7022 E3
E 61st St
10 BKLN 7024 A3
10 MHTN 112 E6
10 MHTN 113 B7
10 MHTN 6717 E3
10 MHTN 6718 A4
400 MHTN 117 C1
W 61st St
10 MHTN 6717 D3
100 MHTN 112 B4
62nd Av
69-00 QENS 6823 D3
99-00 QENS 6720 C7
99-00 QENS 6824 B1
136-00 QENS 6721 A7
245-00 QENS 6723 A5
62nd Av S
110-00 QENS 6720 C7
62nd Dr
70-00 QENS 6823 E3
94-00 QENS 6824 B1
105-00 QENS 6720 C7
62nd Rd
61-00 QENS 6823 C4
99-00 QENS 6824 B1
135-00 QENS 6720 E7
136-00 QENS 6721 A7
62nd St
10 BKLN 6921 E6
10 WNYK 6611 A7
34-38 QENS 6719 C6
52-00 QENS 6823 C1
400 BKLN 6922 A7
800 BKLN 7022 C1
1400 NBgT 6610 E6
E 62nd St
10 MHTN 112 E6
10 MHTN 113 A6
10 MHTN 6718 B4
400 MHTN 117 C1
W 62nd St
10 MHTN 112 C5
10 MHTN 6717 E3
63rd Av
82-00 QENS 6824 A2
108-00 QENS 6720 C7
137-00 QENS 6721 A7
245-00 QENS 6723 A5
63rd Dr
96-00 QENS 6824 C1
63rd Pl
54-00 QENS 6823 C2
63rd Rd
84-00 QENS 6824 A2
135-00 QENS 6720 E7
63rd St
10 BKLN 6921 E6
35-00 QENS 6719 C6
57-00 QENS 6823 C2
400 BKLN 6922 A7
400 WNYK 6611 A7
1100 NBgT 6610 E6
1100 WNYK 6610 E6
1500 BKLN 7022 E3
E 63rd St
10 BKLN 7024 B3
10 MHTN 113 B7
10 MHTN 6718 B4
W 63rd St
10 BAYN 6819 B6
10 JSYC 6819 B6
10 MHTN 6717 D3
100 MHTN 112 B4
64th Av
97-00 QENS 6824 C1
136-00 QENS 6720 E7
154-00 QENS 6721 B7
224-00 QENS 6722 D6
249-00 QENS 6723 A5
64th Cir
192-00 QENS 6721 E7
194-00 QENS 6722 A7
64th Ln
74-00 QENS 6823 D5
64th Pl
71-00 QENS 6823 D5
64th Rd
93-00 QENS 6824 B2
136-00 QENS 6720 E7
137-00 QENS 6721 A7
64th St
10 BKLN 6921 E7
10 WNYK 6611 B7
33-00 QENS 6719 C5
55-19 QENS 6823 C2
400 BKLN 6922 A7
700 BKLN 7022 E3
1100 NBgT 6611 A6
1200 NBgT 6610 E6
E 64th St
10 BKLN 7024 B3
10 MHTN 113 B7
10 MHTN 6718 A4
W 64th St
100 MHTN 112 B4
100 MHTN 6717 D2
65th Av
98-00 QENS 6824 C1
154-00 QENS 6721 B7
239-00 QENS 6722 E5
65th Cres
194-35 QENS 6722 A7
65th Dr
75-00 QENS 6823 E3
85-00 QENS 6824 B3
65th Ln
64-00 QENS 6823 D4
65th Pl
39-00 QENS 6719 C7
72-00 QENS 6823 D5
65th Rd
98-00 QENS 6824 C1
65th St
- BKLN 6922 A7
- MHTN 112 D5
- MHTN 113 A5
- MHTN 6717 E3
- MHTN 6718 A3
10 BKLN 6921 E7
44-00 QENS 6719 C7
67-00 QENS 6823 D5
500 WNYK 6611 A6
600 NBgT 6611 A6
700 BKLN 7022 C2
E 65th St
10 BKLN 7024 B4
10 MHTN 113 C7
10 MHTN 6718 A3
W 65th St
100 MHTN 112 B4
100 MHTN 6717 E2
66th Av
102-00 QENS 6824 C1
239-00 QENS 6722 E5
66th Dr
71-00 QENS 6823 E3
77-00 QENS 6824 A4
66th Pl
72-00 QENS 6823 D5
66th Rd
69-00 QENS 6823 D3
99-00 QENS 6824 C1
66th St
10 WNYK 6611 A7
43-00 QENS 6719 C7
52-00 QENS 6823 C2
400 BKLN 6921 E7
500 BKLN 6922 A7
500 NBgT 6611 A6
600 BKLN 7022 A1
E 66th St
10 MHTN 113 C7
10 MHTN 6718 B3
1400 BKLN 7024 A2
W 66th St
10 MHTN 112 B3
10 MHTN 6717 D2
67th Av
59-00 QENS 6823 C5
98-00 QENS 6824 C1
164-00 QENS 6825 C1
178-00 QENS 6721 E7
216-00 QENS 6722 C6
67th Dr
73-00 QENS 6823 E4
102-00 QENS 6824 C2
67th Pl
69-00 QENS 6823 D5
67th Rd
73-00 QENS 6823 E4
85-00 QENS 6824 B3
67th St
10 WNYK 6611 B7
44-01 QENS 6719 C7
67th St
61-00 QENS 6823 D3
400 BKLN 6921 E7
400 GTBG 6611 A6
500 BKLN 6922 A7
500 NBgT 6611 A6
1400 NBgT 6610 E6
1500 BKLN 7022 C2
E 67th St
10 BKLN 7024 B3
10 MHTN 113 A5
10 MHTN 6718 B4
W 67th St
10 MHTN 112 D4
10 MHTN 6717 D2
68th Av
59-00 QENS 6823 C5
103-00 QENS 6824 C2
171-00 QENS 6825 D1
216-00 QENS 6722 C6
68th Dr
104-00 QENS 6824 D2
137-00 QENS 6825 A1
68th Pl
69-00 QENS 6823 E5
68th Rd
73-00 QENS 6823 E4
103-00 QENS 6824 D2
144-00 QENS 6825 A1
68th St
10 GTBG 6611 A6
10 WNYK 6611 A6
31-00 QENS 6719 C4
54-00 QENS 6823 C2
300 BKLN 6921 E7
500 BKLN 7021 E1
500 NBgT 6611 A6
1500 BKLN 7022 C3
E 68th St
10 MHTN 113 A5
10 MHTN 6718 A3
1400 BKLN 7024 B3
W 68th St
10 MHTN 112 C4
10 MHTN 6717 E2
69th Av
73-00 QENS 6823 E4
88-00 QENS 6824 C4
140-00 QENS 6825 A1
188-00 QENS 6721 E7
240-00 QENS 6722 E5
260-00 QENS 6723 B5
69th Dr
79-00 QENS 6824 A4
69th Ln
54-00 QENS 6823 D2
69th Pl
50-00 QENS 6719 D7
58-00 QENS 6823 D2
69th Rd
73-00 QENS 6823 E4
105-00 QENS 6824 C2
144-00 QENS 6825 A1
69th St
10 GTBG 6611 B6
36-01 QENS 6719 C7
50-21 QENS 6823 C1
1400 NBgT 6610 E5
E 69th St
10 MHTN 113 B5
10 MHTN 6718 B3
1400 BKLN 7024 B3
W 69th St
10 MHTN 6717 D2
400 MHTN 112 B2
70th Av
65-00 QENS 6823 D5
90-00 QENS 6824 C3
137-00 QENS 6825 A1
240-00 QENS 6722 E6
70th Dr
89-00 QENS 6824 C4
70th Rd
107-00 QENS 6824 D2
147-01 QENS 6825 B1
70th St
10 BKLN 6921 D7
10 GTBG 6611 B7
46-00 QENS 6719 D7
51-24 QENS 6823 D1
700 BKLN 7022 D3
1100 NBgT 6611 A6
2000 NBgT 6610 E5
E 70th St
10 MHTN 113 C5
10 MHTN 6718 A3
1400 BKLN 7024 B3
W 70th St
10 MHTN 112 B2
10 MHTN 6717 D2
71st Av
74-00 QENS 6823 E4
89-01 QENS 6824 C4
154-00 QENS 6825 B1
251-00 QENS 6723 B5
71st Cres
188-01 QENS 6825 E1
188-29 QENS 6721 E7
190-00 QENS 6826 A1
192-33 QENS 6722 A7
71st Dr
93-00 QENS 6824 C4
71st Pl
70-00 QENS 6823 E5
71st Rd
107-00 QENS 6824 D2
136-00 QENS 6825 A2
251-00 QENS 6723 A5
71st St
10 BKLN 6921 D7
10 GTBG 6611 A6
40-00 QENS 6719 D6
59-00 QENS 6823 D2
700 BKLN 7022 B2
900 NBgT 6611 A6
1500 NBgT 6610 E5
E 71st St
10 BKLN 7024 C3
10 MHTN 113 C5
10 MHTN 6718 B3
W 71st St
10 MHTN 112 C2
10 MHTN 6717 D2
72nd Av
95-00 QENS 6824 C4
157-00 QENS 6825 C1
72nd Av
252-00 QENS 6723 B5
72nd Cres
141-00 QENS 6825 A2
72nd Ct
7200 BKLN 6921 D7
72nd Dr
110-00 QENS 6824 D3
144-00 QENS 6825 A2
72nd Pl
50-00 QENS 6719 D7
70-00 QENS 6823 E5
72nd Rd
103-00 QENS 6824 D3
144-00 QENS 6825 B2
261-00 QENS 6723 B5
72nd St
10 BKLN 6921 D7
10 NBgT 6611 B6
25-00 QENS 6719 C4
51-42 QENS 6823 D1
200 BKLN 7021 E1
700 BKLN 7022 A1
1500 NBgT 6610 D5
E 72nd St
10 BKLN 7024 B2
10 MHTN 113 D5
10 MHTN 6718 B3
W 72nd St
10 MHTN 112 D3
10 MHTN 6717 E2
73rd Av
111-00 QENS 6824 D3
141-00 QENS 6825 B2
190-00 QENS 6826 A1
195-00 QENS 6722 D6
255-00 QENS 6723 B5
73rd Pl
50-00 QENS 6719 D7
70-00 QENS 6823 E4
72-01 QENS 6824 A5
73rd Rd
110-00 QENS 6824 D3
214-00 QENS 6722 C7
254-00 QENS 6723 B5
73rd St
10 BKLN 6921 D7
10 NBgT 6611 B6
20-00 QENS 6719 C3
52-00 QENS 6823 D1
100 BKLN 7021 D1
700 BKLN 7022 B2
1700 NBgT 6610 D5
E 73rd St
10 BKLN 7024 A1
10 MHTN 113 C5
10 MHTN 6718 C3
W 73rd St
10 MHTN 112 D3
10 MHTN 6717 D1
73rd Ter
137-00 QENS 6825 A2
74th Av
62-00 QENS 6823 D5
88-00 QENS 6824 B4
175-00 QENS 6825 D1
219-00 QENS 6722 C7
254-00 QENS 6723 B6
74th Pl
88-00 QENS 6824 B7
93-00 QENS 6925 B3
74th St
- NBgT 6610 E5
10 BKLN 6921 D7
10 NBgT 6611 B6
30-00 QENS 6719 D4
63-00 QENS 6823 E3
77-00 QENS 6824 A5
100 BKLN 7021 D1
700 BKLN 7022 A2
E 74th St
10 BKLN 7024 C3
10 MHTN 113 B4
10 MHTN 6718 B3
W 74th St
10 MHTN 112 D3
10 MHTN 6717 E2
75th Av
60-00 QENS 6823 D6
88-00 QENS 6824 B4
154-00 QENS 6825 E1
189-00 QENS 6826 A1
211-00 QENS 6722 C7
255-00 QENS 6723 B6
75th Pl
63-00 QENS 6823 E3
75th Rd
108-00 QENS 6824 D3
137-00 QENS 6825 A2
75th St
- QENS 6925 B4
37-00 QENS 6719 D6
63-00 QENS 6823 E3
86-00 QENS 6824 B7
105-00 BKLN 6925 B1
1400 NBgT 6611 A5
E 75th St
10 MHTN 113 C5
10 MHTN 6718 B3
W 75th St
10 MHTN 112 C2
10 MHTN 6717 E1
76th Av
111-00 QENS 6824 E3
141-00 QENS 6825 B2
224-00 QENS 6722 D7
245-00 QENS 6723 A6
76th Dr
111-00 QENS 6824 E3
76th Rd
111-00 QENS 6824 E3
144-00 QENS 6825 C2
224-00 QENS 6722 D7
76th St
10 NBgT 6611 B6
31-00 QENS 6719 D5
57-00 QENS 6823 E2
85-00 QENS 6824 B7
100 BKLN 7021 E1
101-00 QENS 6925 B1
133-00 BKLN 6925 B2
700 BKLN 7022 B3
E 76th St
10 BKLN 6924 A7
10 MHTN 113 C4
10 MHTN 6718 B3

New York City/5 Borough Street Index

STREET Block	City	Map#	Grid
E 76th St			
800	BKLN	7024	A1
W 76th St			
10	MHTN	112	D2
10	MHTN	6717	E1
77th Av			
111-00	QENS	6824	E3
144-00	QENS	6825	C2
216-00	QENS	6722	C7
261-01	QENS	6723	C5
271-12	LKSU	6723	D5
271-12	NHmT	6723	D5
77th Cres			
245-00	QENS	6723	A6
77th Pl			
58-00	QENS	6823	E2
65-00	QENS	6824	A3
77th Rd			
79-00	QENS	6824	A5
166-00	QENS	6825	C2
271-00	NHmT	6723	D5
271-00	QENS	6723	D5
77th St			
10	BKLN	7021	D1
10	NBgT	6611	B6
23-00	QENS	6719	D4
60-00	QENS	6823	E2
86-00	QENS	6824	B7
94-00	QENS	6925	B1
700	BKLN	7022	C4
E 77th St			
10	BKLN	6924	A7
10	MHTN	113	E5
10	MHTN	6718	B2
800	BKLN	7024	A1
W 77th St			
10	MHTN	112	C1
10	MHTN	6717	E1
78th Av			
10	NHmT	6723	C5
10	QENS	6723	C5
62-00	QENS	6823	D6
73-00	QENS	6824	A5
144-00	QENS	6825	C2
78th Cres			
112-00	QENS	6824	E3
78th Dr			
135-00	QENS	6825	A3
78th Rd			
79-00	QENS	6824	A5
141-00	QENS	6825	A3
78th St			
10	BKLN	7021	C1
19-00	QENS	6719	D3
57-00	QENS	6823	E2
86-60	QENS	6824	B7
137-01	BKLN	6925	C3
151-00	QENS	6925	C3
700	BKLN	7022	A2
800	NBgT	6611	A5
E 78th St			
10	BKLN	6924	A7
10	MHTN	113	D4
10	MHTN	6718	B2
900	BKLN	7024	B1
W 78th St			
100	MHTN	112	C1
100	MHTN	6717	E1
79th Av			
10	NHmT	6723	D6
58-00	QENS	6823	C6
87-00	QENS	6824	B5
144-00	QENS	6825	B3
258-00	QENS	6723	C6
79th Ln			
78-00	QENS	6824	A5
79th Pl			
70-00	QENS	6824	A4
79th St			
-	MHTN	113	A2
-	MHTN	6718	A1
10	BKLN	7021	E1
23-00	QENS	6719	D4
52-00	QENS	6823	D1
67-00	QENS	6824	A4
105-01	QENS	6925	B1
500	NBgT	6611	A5
700	BKLN	7022	C4
E 79th St			
10	BKLN	6924	A7
10	MHTN	113	E4
10	MHTN	6718	B2
900	BKLN	7024	A1
W 79th St			
100	MHTN	112	C1
100	MHTN	6717	E1
80th Av			
59-00	QENS	6823	D6
251-00	QENS	6723	C6
2700	NHmT	6723	D6
80th Dr			
176-00	QENS	6825	E2
186-00	QENS	6826	B1
80th Rd			
62-00	QENS	6823	D6
118-00	QENS	6824	E4
176-00	QENS	6825	E2
185-00	QENS	6826	A1
245-00	QENS	6723	A7
80th St			
10	BKLN	7021	D1
23-00	QENS	6719	D4
53-00	QENS	6823	E2
62-58	QENS	6824	A4
157-00	QENS	6925	C4
500	NBgT	6611	B5
700	BKLN	7022	C4
E 80th St			
10	BKLN	6924	B7
10	MHTN	113	C3
10	MHTN	6718	B2
500	MHTN	114	A5
1000	BKLN	7024	C1
W 80th St			
100	MHTN	112	D1
100	MHTN	6717	E1
81st Av			
10	QENS	6824	E4
164-00	QENS	6825	C2
188-00	QENS	6826	A2
244-00	QENS	6723	C6
271-00	NHmT	6723	D6
81st Rd			
87-00	QENS	6824	B5
81st St			
10	BKLN	7021	D1
23-66	QENS	6719	D4
57-00	QENS	6823	E2
76-00	QENS	6824	A4
157-00	QENS	6925	C4
700	NBgT	6611	A5
900	BKLN	7022	A2
E 81st St			
10	BKLN	6924	A7
10	MHTN	113	D4
10	MHTN	6718	B2
500	MHTN	114	A4
1000	BKLN	7024	B1
W 81st St			
-	MHTN	113	A2
10	MHTN	112	D1
10	MHTN	6717	E1
300	MHTN	108	C7
300	MHTN	6611	D7
82nd Av			
100	QENS	6824	E4
134-00	QENS	6825	A3
208-00	QENS	6826	C1
245-00	QENS	6723	B7
268-00	NHmT	6723	D6
82nd Dr			
158-00	QENS	6825	C3
252-00	QENS	6723	B7
82nd Pl			
61-00	QENS	6824	A2
82nd Rd			
90-00	QENS	6824	C5
164-00	QENS	6825	C3
252-00	QENS	6723	B7
82nd St			
10	BKLN	7021	D1
24-00	QENS	6719	D4
52-00	QENS	6823	E1
91-00	QENS	6824	B7
137-00	QENS	6925	C3
500	NBgT	6611	A5
1800	BKLN	7022	D5
E 82nd St			
10	BKLN	6924	B7
10	MHTN	113	C3
10	MHTN	114	A4
10	MHTN	6718	C2
1000	BKLN	7024	B1
W 82nd St			
10	MHTN	112	D1
10	MHTN	113	A1
10	MHTN	6717	E1
10	MHTN	6718	A1
200	MHTN	108	D7
200	MHTN	6611	E7
83rd Av			
118-00	QENS	6824	E4
135-00	QENS	6825	A4
245-00	QENS	6723	B7
270-00	NHmT	6723	D7
83rd Dr			
-	QENS	6824	B5
125-00	QENS	6825	A4
83rd Pl			
58-00	QENS	6823	E1
62-00	QENS	6824	A2
83rd Rd			
254-00	QENS	6723	C7
83rd St			
10	BKLN	7021	D2
24-00	QENS	6719	D4
58-00	QENS	6823	E2
70-00	QENS	6824	A4
97-00	QENS	6925	C1
900	BKLN	7022	A3
1100	NBgT	6611	A5
2400	NBgT	6610	E4
E 83rd St			
10	BKLN	6924	B7
10	MHTN	113	D3
10	MHTN	6718	C2
500	MHTN	114	A4
1000	BKLN	7024	C1
W 83rd St			
10	MHTN	112	E1
10	MHTN	113	A1
10	MHTN	6717	E1
10	MHTN	6718	A2
200	MHTN	108	D7
200	MHTN	6611	E7
84th Av			
110-00	QENS	6824	E5
125-00	QENS	6825	A4
84th Dr			
138-00	QENS	6825	B4
253-00	QENS	6827	B1
254-00	QENS	6723	C7
84th Pl			
58-00	QENS	6823	E1
62-00	QENS	6824	A2
84th Rd			
170-00	QENS	6825	D3
244-00	QENS	6827	B1
254-00	QENS	6723	C7
84th St			
10	BKLN	7021	D2
24-00	QENS	6719	E4
52-00	QENS	6823	E1
70-00	QENS	6824	B4
105-00	QENS	6925	C2
1400	NBgT	6611	A4
1800	BKLN	7022	C5
E 84th St			
-	BKLN	6924	A6
10	MHTN	113	E4
10	MHTN	114	A4
10	MHTN	6718	C2
1100	BKLN	7024	C1
W 84th St			
10	MHTN	112	E1
10	MHTN	113	A1
10	MHTN	6717	E1
10	MHTN	6718	A2
100	MHTN	108	D7
100	MHTN	6611	E7
85th Av			
10	FLPK	6723	D7
10	NHmT	6723	D7
102-00	QENS	6824	D6
164-00	QENS	6825	C4
209-00	QENS	6826	C1
244-00	QENS	6827	B1
264-00	QENS	6723	D7
85th Dr			
84-00	QENS	6824	B6
148-00	QENS	6825	C4
85th Rd			
74-00	BKLN	6824	A6
84-00	QENS	6824	C6
141-00	QENS	6825	B4
188-00	QENS	6826	A2
244-00	QENS	6827	B1
85th St			
-	MHTN	113	B2
-	MHTN	6718	A1
10	BKLN	7021	D2
23-00	QENS	6719	E4
55-00	QENS	6823	E1
84-00	QENS	6824	B7
97-00	QENS	6925	C1
500	NBgT	6611	B5
1000	BKLN	7022	A3
E 85th St			
10	BKLN	6924	B7
10	MHTN	113	D3
10	MHTN	6718	B2
500	MHTN	114	A4
1100	BKLN	7024	C1
W 85th St			
10	MHTN	112	E1
10	MHTN	113	A1
10	MHTN	6717	E1
10	MHTN	6718	A2
100	MHTN	108	D7
100	MHTN	6611	E7
86th Av			
104-00	QENS	6824	D6
148-00	QENS	6825	B4
211-01	QENS	6826	C1
244-00	QENS	6827	C1
263-00	FLPK	6827	D1
86th Cir			
161-00	QENS	6825	C4
86th Dr			
91-00	QENS	6824	C6
209-00	QENS	6826	C2
86th Rd			
102-00	QENS	6824	D6
131-00	QENS	6825	A5
212-00	QENS	6826	C1
241-00	QENS	6827	A1
86th St			
10	BKLN	7021	E2
24-30	QENS	6719	E4
94-00	QENS	6824	C7
97-00	QENS	6925	C1
1000	BKLN	7022	D5
1100	NBgT	6611	A4
E 86th St			
-	BKLN	6924	A6
10	MHTN	113	E3
10	MHTN	6718	B2
400	MHTN	114	A3
1200	BKLN	7024	C1
W 86th St			
10	MHTN	109	A7
10	MHTN	113	A1
10	MHTN	6612	A7
10	MHTN	6718	A1
100	MHTN	108	D7
100	MHTN	6611	E7
87th Av			
-	FLPK	6827	C1
74-00	BKLN	6824	A7
78-00	QENS	6824	B7
138-00	QENS	6825	B5
229-00	QENS	6826	E1
256-00	QENS	6827	C1
87th Dr			
139-00	QENS	6825	B5
188-00	QENS	6826	A3
247-00	QENS	6827	B1
87th Rd			
74-00	BKLN	6824	A7
74-00	QENS	6824	A7
144-00	QENS	6825	B4
187-00	QENS	6826	A3
255-00	QENS	6827	C1
258-00	FLPK	6827	C1
87th St			
10	BKLN	7021	D2
23-00	QENS	6719	E3
84-00	QENS	6824	B6
105-00	QENS	6925	C1
500	NBgT	6611	B5
E 87th St			
10	MHTN	113	D2
10	MHTN	6718	C1
400	MHTN	114	A3
500	BKLN	6924	B7
1200	BKLN	7024	C1
W 87th St			
10	MHTN	108	D6
10	MHTN	109	A7
10	MHTN	113	A1
10	MHTN	6612	A7
10	MHTN	6718	A1
100	MHTN	6611	E7
87th Ter			
255-00	QENS	6827	C1
88th Av			
74-00	BKLN	6824	A7
78-01	QENS	6824	B7
168-00	QENS	6825	D4
225-00	QENS	6826	E1
244-00	QENS	6827	B1
88th Dr			
242-00	QENS	6827	A1
88th Ln			
82-00	QENS	6824	C5
88th Pl			
82-00	QENS	6824	B5
88th Rd			
74-00	BKLN	6824	B7
78-00	QENS	6824	B7
139-00	QENS	6825	B5
210-00	QENS	6826	C2
242-00	QENS	6827	A1
88th St			
10	BKLN	7021	D2
23-00	QENS	6719	E5
48-00	QENS	6720	A7
87-00	QENS	6824	C7
156-00	QENS	6925	D3
900	NBgT	6611	B4
E 88th St			
10	MHTN	113	E3
10	MHTN	6718	C1
400	MHTN	114	A3
500	BKLN	6924	B6
1200	BKLN	7024	C1
W 88th St			
10	MHTN	109	A7
10	MHTN	6612	A7
100	MHTN	108	E7
100	MHTN	6611	E7
89th Av			
85-00	QENS	6824	C7
139-00	QENS	6825	D4
199-00	QENS	6826	C3
234-00	QENS	6827	A1
89th Rd			
130-00	QENS	6825	A5
211-00	QENS	6826	C2
89th St			
10	BKLN	7021	D2
25-00	QENS	6719	E4
72-00	QENS	6824	B4
97-00	QENS	6925	C1
1500	NBgT	6611	A4
E 89th St			
10	MHTN	113	C1
10	MHTN	6718	C1
400	MHTN	114	A3
1100	BKLN	6924	C7
1200	BKLN	7024	C1
W 89th St			
10	MHTN	109	A7
10	MHTN	6612	A7
100	MHTN	108	E7
100	MHTN	6611	E7
90th Av			
74-00	BKLN	6824	B7
100-00	QENS	6824	D6
166-00	QENS	6825	D4
196-00	QENS	6826	D2
244-00	QENS	6827	B2
90th Ct			
211-00	QENS	6826	D3
90th Pl			
24-00	QENS	6719	E4
90th Rd			
78-00	QENS	6824	B7
153-00	QENS	6825	C5
90th St			
25-00	QENS	6719	E4
46-00	QENS	6720	A7
84-00	QENS	6824	C6
155-00	QENS	6925	D3
300	BKLN	7021	D2
500	NBgT	6611	B4
E 90th St			
10	MHTN	113	E2
10	MHTN	6718	C1
300	MHTN	114	A3
W 90th St			
10	MHTN	109	A7
10	MHTN	6612	A7
100	MHTN	108	E6
100	MHTN	6611	E7
91st Av			
74-00	BKLN	6824	B7
97-00	QENS	6824	D7
119-00	QENS	6825	A6
208-00	QENS	6826	D2
242-00	QENS	6827	A2
247-00	BLRS	6827	B2
91st Dr			
96-00	QENS	6824	D7
91st Pl			
43-00	QENS	6720	A6
91st Rd			
-	QENS	6827	A1
96-00	QENS	6824	D7
219-00	QENS	6826	E2
91st St			
23-00	QENS	6719	E3
48-00	QENS	6720	A7
84-00	QENS	6824	C6
156-00	QENS	6925	D5
300	BKLN	7021	D2
1100	NBgT	6611	A3
E 91st St			
10	BKLN	6923	E4
10	MHTN	113	E2
10	MHTN	6718	C1
200	BKLN	6924	A4
300	MHTN	114	A2
1500	BKLN	7024	D1
W 91st St			
10	MHTN	109	A7
10	MHTN	6612	A7
100	MHTN	108	E6
100	MHTN	6611	E7
92nd Av			
100-00	QENS	6824	D7
129-00	QENS	6825	A6
212-00	QENS	6826	E2
223-00	QENS	6827	A2
92nd Rd			
168-00	QENS	6825	D5
214-00	QENS	6826	D2
222-00	QENS	6827	A2
92nd St			
22-00	QENS	6719	E3
47-00	QENS	6720	A7
89-00	QENS	6824	C7
103-00	QENS	6925	D1
300	BKLN	7021	E3
1100	NBgT	6611	B4
E 92nd St			
10	BKLN	6923	E4
10	MHTN	113	E2
10	MHTN	6718	B1
300	MHTN	114	A2
500	BKLN	6924	C7
1500	BKLN	7024	D1
W 92nd St			
10	MHTN	109	A6
10	MHTN	6612	A7
200	MHTN	108	E6
200	MHTN	6611	E7
93rd Av			
74-00	BKLN	6925	A1
74-00	QENS	6925	A1
100-00	QENS	6824	D7
212-00	QENS	6826	D3
222-00	QENS	6827	A2
93rd Rd			
211-00	QENS	6826	D3
221-00	QENS	6827	A2
93rd St			
22-00	QENS	6719	E3
26-00	QENS	6720	A5
94-00	QENS	6824	C7
97-00	QENS	6925	D1
300	BKLN	7021	D3
E 93rd St			
10	BKLN	6923	E4
10	MHTN	113	D1
100	BKLN	6924	A4
300	MHTN	114	A2
400	MHTN	6718	C1
1600	BKLN	7024	D1
W 93rd St			
10	MHTN	109	A6
10	MHTN	6612	A7
200	MHTN	108	E6
200	MHTN	6611	E7
94th Av			
100-00	QENS	6824	D7
137-00	QENS	6825	B6
217-00	QENS	6826	E2
221-00	QENS	6827	A2
94th Dr			
218-00	QENS	6826	E3
94th Pl			
134-00	QENS	6925	D2
94th Rd			
214-00	QENS	6826	E3
94th St			
22-00	QENS	6719	E3
23-10	QENS	6720	A3
94-00	QENS	6824	C7
97-00	QENS	6925	D1
100	BKLN	7021	D3
2400	NBgT	6611	A3
E 94th St			
10	BKLN	6923	E3
10	MHTN	109	D7
10	MHTN	113	E1
10	MHTN	6612	B7
10	MHTN	6718	C1
100	BKLN	6924	A4
300	MHTN	114	A1
1500	BKLN	7024	D1
W 94th St			
10	MHTN	109	A6
10	MHTN	6612	A7
200	MHTN	108	E5
200	MHTN	6611	E6
95th Av			
10	BKLN	6925	B1
10	QENS	6925	B1
100-00	QENS	6824	D7
117-00	QENS	6825	A6
222-00	QENS	6827	A3
224-00	HmpT	6827	A3
95th Pl			
134-00	QENS	6925	D2
95th St			
40-00	QENS	6720	A6
94-00	QENS	6824	D7
157-54	QENS	6925	D4
400	BKLN	7021	D3
2400	NBgT	6611	A3
E 95th St			
10	BKLN	6923	E3
10	MHTN	109	D7
10	MHTN	6612	B7
100	MHTN	113	E1
100	MHTN	6718	C1
300	MHTN	114	A1
800	BKLN	6924	B6
1500	BKLN	7024	D1
W 95th St			
10	MHTN	109	A6
10	MHTN	6612	A7
200	MHTN	108	E5
200	MHTN	6611	E6
96th Av			
222-00	QENS	6827	A3
96th Pl			
135-00	QENS	6925	D2
96th St			
22-00	QENS	6720	A3
91-00	QENS	6824	D7
103-00	QENS	6925	D1
300	BKLN	7021	D3
E 96th St			
10	BKLN	6923	E3
10	MHTN	109	D7
10	MHTN	6612	B7
100	MHTN	113	E1
100	MHTN	6718	C1
200	MHTN	114	A1
500	BKLN	6924	B5
2000	BKLN	7024	D1
W 96th St			
10	MHTN	109	A6
10	MHTN	6612	A7
200	MHTN	108	E5
200	MHTN	6611	E6
97th Av			
74-00	BKLN	6925	B1
74-00	QENS	6925	B1
88-00	QENS	6824	C7
137-00	QENS	6825	C6
218-00	QENS	6826	E3
219-00	QENS	6827	A3
97th Pl			
50-00	QENS	6720	B7
61-00	QENS	6824	B1
97th St			
-	MHTN	109	C6
-	MHTN	6612	B7
45-00	QENS	6720	A6
87-00	QENS	6824	C6
157-00	QENS	6925	E4
300	BKLN	7021	D3
E 97th St			
10	MHTN	109	E7
10	MHTN	6612	C7
100	MHTN	113	E1
100	MHTN	6718	C1
200	MHTN	114	A1
W 97th St			
10	MHTN	109	A5
10	MHTN	6612	A6
200	MHTN	108	E5
200	MHTN	6611	E6
98th Av			
217-00	QENS	6826	E3
98th Pl			
55-00	QENS	6720	B7
63-00	QENS	6824	B1
98th St			
10	BKLN	7021	D3
22-00	QENS	6720	A5
63-00	QENS	6824	B1
157-00	QENS	6925	E5
E 98th St			
10	BKLN	6923	E3
10	BKLN	6924	A4
10	MHTN	109	D7
10	MHTN	6612	B7
W 98th St			
200	MHTN	108	E5
200	MHTN	109	A5
200	MHTN	6611	E6
200	MHTN	6612	A6
99th Av			
95-00	QENS	6824	D7
189-00	QENS	6826	C4
220-00	QENS	6827	A3
99th Pl			
150-00	QENS	6925	E3
99th Rd			
197-01	QENS	6826	B4
99th St			
22-00	QENS	6720	A3
61-00	QENS	6824	C1
155-00	QENS	6925	E5
300	BKLN	7021	D3
E 99th St			
10	BKLN	6924	C5
10	MHTN	109	E7
100	MHTN	6612	C7
200	MHTN	110	A7
300	MHTN	114	A1
300	MHTN	6718	C1
W 99th St			
200	MHTN	108	E4
200	MHTN	109	A5
200	MHTN	6611	E6
200	MHTN	6612	A6
100th Av			
192-00	QENS	6826	B4
220-00	QENS	6827	A3
100th Dr			
219-00	QENS	6826	E3
219-01	QENS	6827	A3
100th Rd			
222-00	QENS	6827	A3
100th St			
10	BKLN	7021	D3
28-00	QENS	6720	A4
93-00	QENS	6824	D7
155-00	QENS	6925	E3
E 100th St			
10	MHTN	109	E7
10	MHTN	6612	C7
100	MHTN	110	A7
300	MHTN	114	A1
300	MHTN	6718	D1
700	BKLN	6924	C6
W 100th St			
10	MHTN	109	B5
10	MHTN	6612	A6
300	MHTN	108	E4
300	MHTN	6611	E6
101st Av			
10	BKLN	6925	B1
10	QENS	6925	C1
95-00	QENS	6824	D7
115-00	QENS	6825	B6
218-00	QENS	6826	E3
220-00	QENS	6827	A3
101st Rd			
105-00	QENS	6824	E7
101st St			
10	BKLN	7021	D3
23-00	QENS	6720	A3
84-01	QENS	6824	D6
101-00	QENS	6925	D1
E 101st St			
10	MHTN	6612	B7
100	MHTN	109	E7
300	MHTN	110	A7
700	BKLN	6924	C6
W 101st St			
200	MHTN	109	A4
200	MHTN	6612	A6
300	MHTN	108	E4
300	MHTN	6611	E6
102nd Av			
81-00	QENS	6925	C1
127-00	QENS	6825	B7
190-00	QENS	6826	B4
220-00	QENS	6827	A3
102nd Rd			
81-00	QENS	6925	C1
127-00	QENS	6825	B7
102nd St			
61-00	QENS	6720	E7
63-20	QENS	6824	C1
155-00	QENS	6925	E3
E 102nd St			
10	BKLN	6924	D7
10	MHTN	109	E6
10	MHTN	6612	C7
100	MHTN	110	A7
1500	BKLN	7024	E1
W 102nd St			
10	MHTN	109	B5
100	MHTN	6612	A6
300	MHTN	108	E4
300	MHTN	6611	E6
103rd Av			
84-00	QENS	6925	C1
104-00	QENS	6824	E7
114-00	QENS	6825	A7
220-00	QENS	6826	E4
220-00	QENS	6827	A4
103rd Dr			
105-00	QENS	6925	E1
103rd Rd			
105-00	QENS	6925	E1
127-00	QENS	6825	B7
103rd St			
31-00	QENS	6720	B5
95-00	QENS	6824	D7
101-00	QENS	6925	E1
E 103rd St			
10	BKLN	6924	C6
100	MHTN	109	E6
100	MHTN	6612	C7
200	MHTN	110	A7
W 103rd St			
200	MHTN	109	A4
200	MHTN	6612	A6
300	MHTN	108	E4
104th Av			
168-00	QENS	6825	E5
193-01	QENS	6826	D4
221-00	QENS	6827	A4
104th Rd			
164-00	QENS	6825	D5
212-00	QENS	6826	D4
104th St			
35-00	QENS	6720	B6
86-88	QENS	6824	D7
101-00	QENS	6925	E1
161-00	QENS	6926	A5
E 104th St			
10	BKLN	6924	C5
10	MHTN	109	E6
10	MHTN	6612	C7
100	MHTN	110	A7
W 104th St			
10	MHTN	109	B4
10	MHTN	6612	A6
105th Av			
133-00	QENS	6825	B7
190-00	QENS	6826	B5
221-00	QENS	6827	A4
105th Pl			
103-00	QENS	6925	E1
105th St			
31-00	QENS	6720	B4
95-00	QENS	6824	D7
103-00	QENS	6925	E1
E 105th St			
10	MHTN	109	E5
10	MHTN	6612	C6
100	MHTN	110	B7
500	BKLN	6924	D5
W 105th St			
10	MHTN	109	A3
10	MHTN	6612	A6
106th Av			
10	HmpT	6827	A4
84-00	QENS	6925	C1
144-00	QENS	6825	C6
215-00	QENS	6826	D4
221-00	QENS	6827	A4
106th Rd			
177-00	QENS	6826	A5
106th St			
31-00	QENS	6720	B4
93-00	QENS	6824	E7
110-00	QENS	6925	E2
E 106th St			
10	BKLN	6924	D6
10	MHTN	109	E5
10	MHTN	6612	C7
100	MHTN	110	A6
W 106th St			
10	MHTN	109	B4
10	MHTN	6612	A6
107th Av			
84-00	QENS	6925	C1
112-00	QENS	6926	A1
168-00	QENS	6825	E5
220-00	QENS	6826	E4
221-00	QENS	6827	A4
107th Rd			
139-00	QENS	6825	C7
107th St			
31-00	QENS	6720	B4
94-00	QENS	6824	E7
104-00	QENS	6925	E2
E 107th St			
10	BKLN	6924	D6
10	MHTN	109	E5
100	MHTN	110	A6
100	MHTN	6612	C7
W 107th St			
10	MHTN	109	C4
10	MHTN	6612	A5
108th Av			
94-00	QENS	6925	D1
159-00	QENS	6825	E6
220-00	QENS	6826	E4
222-00	QENS	6827	A4
108th Dr			
164-00	QENS	6825	E6
108th Rd			
167-00	QENS	6825	E6
108th St			
31-00	QENS	6720	B5
84-00	QENS	6824	D5
104-00	QENS	6925	E1
E 108th St			
10	BKLN	6924	D6
10	MHTN	109	E5
10	MHTN	110	A5
10	MHTN	6612	C6
W 108th St			
10	MHTN	109	A3
10	MHTN	6612	A5
109th Av			
10	HmpT	6827	B5
105-00	QENS	6925	E1
111-00	QENS	6926	A1
128-00	QENS	6825	C7
190-00	QENS	6826	B5
222-00	QENS	6827	A4
109th Dr			
150-00	QENS	6825	D7
109th Rd			
164-00	QENS	6825	E6
190-00	QENS	6826	B5
109th St			
33-00	QENS	6720	B5
84-00	QENS	6824	D5
104-00	QENS	6925	E1
E 109th St			
10	MHTN	109	E5
10	MHTN	110	A5
10	MHTN	6612	C6
W 109th St			
10	MHTN	109	C3
10	MHTN	6612	A5
110th Av			
195-00	QENS	6826	C5
223-00	QENS	6827	A4
110th Rd			
147-00	QENS	6825	D7
216-00	QENS	6826	E4
110th St			
33-00	QENS	6720	B5
63-00	QENS	6824	C1
104-00	QENS	6925	E1
E 110th St			
10	MHTN	109	E5
10	MHTN	110	B6
10	MHTN	6612	D7
111th Av			
110-00	QENS	6925	E1
110-00	QENS	6926	A1
138-00	QENS	6825	C7
171-00	QENS	6826	A6
223-00	QENS	6827	A5
111th Rd			
150-00	QENS	6825	D7
190-00	QENS	6826	B5
111th St			
37-01	QENS	6720	C5
66-00	QENS	6824	D1
105-00	QENS	6925	E1
109-00	QENS	6926	A1
E 111th St			
10	MHTN	109	E4
10	MHTN	110	A5
10	MHTN	6612	D6
W 111th St			
10	MHTN	109	C3
10	MHTN	6612	C6
112th Av			
148-00	QENS	6825	D7
190-00	QENS	6826	B5
223-00	QENS	6827	A5
112th Pl			
32-00	QENS	6720	B4
112th Rd			
162-00	QENS	6825	E7
209-00	QENS	6826	D5
223-00	QENS	6827	A5
112th St			
14-00	QENS	6720	C1
67-00	QENS	6824	D2
104-00	QENS	6925	E1
107-00	QENS	6926	A1
E 112th St			
10	MHTN	109	E4
10	MHTN	110	B5
10	MHTN	6612	D6
W 112th St			
10	MHTN	6612	B6
500	MHTN	109	B2
113th Av			
150-00	QENS	6825	D7
191-00	QENS	6826	C5
223-00	QENS	6827	A5
113th Dr			
216-00	QENS	6826	E5
223-00	QENS	6827	A5
113th Rd			
191-00	QENS	6826	C5
113th St			
14-00	QENS	6720	C1
72-00	QENS	6824	E3
104-00	QENS	6925	E1
104-00	QENS	6926	A1
E 113th St			
200	MHTN	110	B5
200	MHTN	6612	D6
W 113th St			
100	MHTN	109	D3
400	MHTN	6612	A5
114th Av			
216-00	QENS	6826	E5
223-00	QENS	6827	A5
114th Dr			
188-00	QENS	6826	B6
227-00	QENS	6827	A5
114th Pl			
115-00	QENS	6926	A2
114th Rd			
150-00	QENS	6825	D7
177-00	QENS	6826	B6
223-00	QENS	6827	A5
114th St			
33-00	QENS	6720	C5
84-00	QENS	6824	E6
103-00	QENS	6825	A7
104-00	QENS	6926	A1
E 114th St			
400	MHTN	110	C5
400	MHTN	6612	D6
W 114th St			
100	MHTN	6612	B5
400	MHTN	109	C2
114th Ter			
228-00	QENS	6827	A5
115th Av			
-	HmpT	6827	A6
117-00	QENS	6926	B1
150-00	QENS	6825	D7
216-00	QENS	6826	E5
224-00	QENS	6827	A5
115th Ct			
216-00	QENS	6826	E5
115th Dr			
150-00	QENS	6825	E7
150-00	QENS	6926	D1
205-00	QENS	6826	D6
115th Rd			
150-00	QENS	6926	D1
157-00	QENS	6825	E7
215-00	QENS	6826	E5
225-00	QENS	6827	A6
2300	HmpT	6827	A6
115th St			
5-00	QENS	6614	C7
12-00	QENS	6720	C1
83-00	QENS	6824	E5
101-00	QENS	6825	A7
115-00	QENS	6926	A2
E 115th St			
10	MHTN	110	C5
10	MHTN	6612	D6
W 115th St			
10	MHTN	110	A4
10	MHTN	6612	B5
600	MHTN	109	B1
115th Ter			
216-00	QENS	6826	E5
23600	HmpT	6827	A6
116th Av			
150-00	QENS	6926	D1
155-00	QENS	6825	E7
208-36	QENS	6826	E6
226-00	QENS	6827	A6
23600	HmpT	6827	A6
116th Dr			
150-00	QENS	6926	E1
116th Rd			
142-00	QENS	6926	D1
205-00	QENS	6826	D6
23800	HmpT	6827	B6
116th St			
10-00	QENS	6614	C7
14-00	QENS	6720	C1
87-00	QENS	6824	E6
97-00	QENS	6825	A7
115-00	QENS	6926	A2
E 116th St			
10	MHTN	110	C5
10	MHTN	6612	D6
W 116th St			
10	MHTN	110	A3
10	MHTN	6612	C5
400	MHTN	109	C2
117th Av			
23800	HmpT	6827	B7
117th Rd			
132-00	QENS	6926	C2
193-00	QENS	6826	C6
23800	HmpT	6827	A7
117th St			
5-00	QENS	6614	C7
12-00	QENS	6720	C1
94-00	QENS	6824	E6
95-00	QENS	6825	A7
115-00	QENS	6926	A2
E 117th St			
10	MHTN	110	D5
10	MHTN	6612	D6
W 117th St			
10	MHTN	109	D2
10	MHTN	110	A3
10	MHTN	6612	C6
118th Av			
150-00	QENS	6926	D1
167-00	QENS	6927	A1
197-00	QENS	6826	E6
228-00	QENS	6827	A7
2100	HmpT	6827	A7
118th Rd			
160-00	QENS	6926	E1
168-00	QENS	6927	A1
186-00	QENS	6826	B7
118th St			
9-00	QENS	6614	C7
12-00	QENS	6720	C1
83-00	QENS	6824	E4
94-00	QENS	6825	A6
104-00	QENS	6926	A1
E 118th St			
10	MHTN	110	C4
10	MHTN	6612	D6
W 118th St			
10	MHTN	109	D2
10	MHTN	110	A3
10	MHTN	6612	C5
119th Av			
143-00	QENS	6926	D1
168-00	QENS	6927	A1
188-00	QENS	6826	D7
229-00	QENS	6827	A7
119th Dr			
160-00	QENS	6926	E1
187-00	QENS	6826	B7
119th Rd			
160-00	QENS	6926	E1
171-00	QENS	6927	A1
187-00	QENS	6826	B7
119th St			
5-00	QENS	6614	C7
12-00	QENS	6720	C1
E 119th St			
10	MHTN	110	C4
10	MHTN	6612	D6
W 119th St			
10	MHTN	110	A3
10	MHTN	6612	C5
100	MHTN	109	E2
120th Av			
139-00	QENS	6926	C2
169-00	QENS	6927	A1
176-00	QENS	6826	E7
230-00	QENS	6827	A7
120th Rd			
186-00	QENS	6826	C7
120th St			
9-00	QENS	6614	C7
14-00	QENS	6720	C2
84-00	QENS	6824	E5
88-00	QENS	6825	A7
135-00	QENS	6926	A3
E 120th St			
10	MHTN	110	C4
10	MHTN	6612	E6
W 120th St			
10	MHTN	110	A3
10	MHTN	6612	C5
400	MHTN	109	C1
121st Av			
160-00	QENS	6926	E1
161-00	QENS	6927	A1
186-00	QENS	6826	C7
231-10	QENS	6827	A7
236-00	QENS	6928	A1
121st St			
3-00	QENS	6614	D6
14-00	QENS	6720	D1
84-00	QENS	6824	E5
89-00	QENS	6825	A6
116-00	QENS	6926	A3
E 121st St			
10	MHTN	110	C3
10	MHTN	6612	D5
W 121st St			
10	MHTN	110	A2
100	MHTN	109	D1
400	MHTN	6612	B4
122nd Av			
160-00	QENS	6926	E1
161-00	QENS	6927	A1
188-00	QENS	6826	C7
122nd Pl			
117-00	QENS	6926	B3
122nd St			
28-00	QENS	6720	D3
84-00	QENS	6824	E5
86-00	QENS	6825	A5
100	MHTN	109	C1
100	MHTN	6612	B4
107-00	QENS	6926	A1
500	MHTN	106	C7
E 122nd St			
10	MHTN	110	B3
10	MHTN	6612	D5
W 122nd St			
10	MHTN	110	A2
100	MHTN	109	D1
600	MHTN	106	B7
600	MHTN	6612	B4
123rd Av			
140-00	QENS	6926	D2
123rd St			
5-00	QENS	6614	D7

New York City/5 Borough Street Index

STREET Block City Map# Grid

123rd St
14-00 QENS 6720 D1
84-00 QENS 6824 E5
84-01 QENS 6825 A5
117-00 QENS 6926 B2
E 123rd St
10 MHTN 110 B3
10 MHTN 6612 D5
W 123rd St
10 MHTN 110 A2
10 MHTN 6612 B4
100 MHTN 109 D1
500 MHTN 106 C7
124th Av
- QENS 6927 A1
153-00 QENS 6926 E2
124th Pl
83-00 QENS 6825 A5
124th St
5-00 QENS 6614 D7
26-00 QENS 6720 D2
84-00 QENS 6825 A5
107-00 QENS 6926 B1
E 124th St
300 MHTN 110 D3
300 MHTN 6612 E5
W 124th St
10 MHTN 110 A2
10 MHTN 6612 C4
100 MHTN 109 E1
125th Av
150-00 QENS 6926 E2
172-00 QENS 6927 A1
231-00 QENS 6826 E7
231-00 QENS 6827 A7
125th St
4-00 QENS 6614 D7
14-00 QENS 6720 D2
93-00 QENS 6825 A6
150-00 QENS 6926 B3
E 125th St
100 MHTN 110 D3
600 MHTN 6612 E7
126th Av
231-00 QENS 6927 E1
231-00 QENS 6928 A1
126th Pl
33-00 QENS 6720 D4
126th St
3-00 QENS 6614 D7
14-00 QENS 6720 D1
95-00 QENS 6825 A6
149-17 QENS 6926 B3
E 126th St
10 MHTN 110 D3
10 MHTN 6612 D5
W 126th St
10 MHTN 110 A1
10 MHTN 6612 C4
200 MHTN 109 E1
300 MHTN 106 D7
127th Av
172-00 QENS 6927 B1
127th Pl
33-00 QENS 6720 D4
127th St
3-00 QENS 6614 D7
13-07 QENS 6720 D1
94-00 QENS 6825 A6
109-00 QENS 6926 B3
E 127th St
10 MHTN 110 B2
100 MHTN 6612 D5
W 127th St
10 MHTN 110 A1
10 MHTN 6612 C4
200 MHTN 106 D7
200 MHTN 109 E1
128th Av
157-00 QENS 6926 E2
231-00 QENS 6927 E1
231-00 QENS 6928 A1
240-00 HmpT 6928 A1
128th Dr
231-00 QENS 6927 E1
240-00 QENS 6928 A1
243-00 HmpT 6928 A1
128th Rd
231-00 QENS 6927 E1
240-00 HmpT 6928 A4
240-00 QENS 6928 A4
128th St
6-00 QENS 6614 D7
15-00 QENS 6720 D1
104-00 QENS 6825 B7
109-00 QENS 6926 B1
E 128th St
10 MHTN 110 B2
10 MHTN 6612 D5
W 128th St
10 MHTN 110 A1
10 MHTN 6612 C4
400 MHTN 106 D7
129th Av
157-00 QENS 6926 E2
176-00 QENS 6927 B1
233-00 QENS 6928 A1
129th Rd
240-00 QENS 6928 A1
129th St
6-00 QENS 6614 D7
13-00 QENS 6720 D2
84-00 QENS 6825 A4
149-00 QENS 6926 B3
E 129th St
10 MHTN 110 B1
10 MHTN 6612 D5
W 129th St
10 MHTN 110 A1
100 MHTN 107 A7
300 MHTN 106 E7
300 MHTN 6612 C4
130th Av
137-00 QENS 6926 D2
216-00 QENS 6826 D7
220-00 QENS 6927 E1
233-00 QENS 6928 A1
245-00 VLYS 6928 A1
130th Dr
219-00 QENS 6927 D1
130th Pl
133-00 QENS 6926 C3
130th Rd
219-00 QENS 6927 D1
241-00 QENS 6928 A1

130th St
7-00 QENS 6614 D7
14-00 QENS 6720 D1
87-00 QENS 6825 A6
109-00 QENS 6926 C3
E 130th St
10 MHTN 110 C1
10 MHTN 6612 D4
W 130th St
10 MHTN 110 A1
10 MHTN 6612 C4
100 MHTN 107 A7
500 MHTN 106 C6
131st Av
142-00 QENS 6926 D2
216-00 QENS 6927 E1
241-00 QENS 6928 A1
244-00 VLYS 6928 A2
131st Rd
242-00 QENS 6928 A2
131st St
11-00 QENS 6614 E7
14-00 QENS 6720 E1
85-00 QENS 6825 A5
109-00 QENS 6926 B1
E 131st St
10 MHTN 110 C1
10 MHTN 6612 D4
W 131st St
10 MHTN 110 B1
100 MHTN 107 A7
500 MHTN 106 C6
500 MHTN 6612 B3
132nd Av
150-00 QENS 6926 E2
216-00 QENS 6927 D1
241-00 QENS 6928 A2
243-00 VLYS 6928 A2
132nd Rd
216-00 QENS 6927 D1
241-00 QENS 6928 A2
243-00 VLYS 6928 A2
132nd St
- QENS 6614 E7
14-31 QENS 6720 E1
104-00 QENS 6825 B7
120-00 QENS 6926 C3
E 132nd St
10 MHTN 110 B1
10 MHTN 6612 D4
200 BRNX 6613 A5
W 132nd St
10 MHTN 107 B7
10 MHTN 110 B1
10 MHTN 6612 C4
200 MHTN 106 E7
133rd Av
81-00 QENS 6925 C2
142-00 QENS 6926 D3
216-00 QENS 6927 D1
241-00 QENS 6928 A2
133rd Dr
245-00 QENS 6928 A2
133rd Pl
13-00 QENS 6614 E7
14-00 QENS 6720 E1
133rd Rd
234-00 QENS 6927 E2
245-00 QENS 6928 A2
133rd St
55-00 QENS 6720 E6
104-00 QENS 6825 B7
111-00 QENS 6926 C1
E 133rd St
600 BRNX 6613 A5
W 133rd St
100 MHTN 107 A7
400 MHTN 106 C5
400 MHTN 6612 B3
134th Av
94-00 QENS 6925 D2
137-00 QENS 6926 D3
155-00 QENS 6927 A2
242-00 QENS 6928 A2
247-00 VLYS 6928 A2
134th Pl
135-00 QENS 6926 C3
134th Rd
94-00 QENS 6925 D2
217-00 QENS 6927 D1
134th St
56-00 QENS 6720 E6
87-00 QENS 6825 B5
148-00 QENS 6926 C4
E 134th St
200 BRNX 6612 E5
400 BRNX 110 E2
600 BRNX 6613 B5
W 134th St
10 MHTN 107 B7
100 MHTN 6612 C4
300 MHTN 106 E6
135th Av
137-00 QENS 6926 D3
216-00 QENS 6927 D2
241-00 QENS 6928 A2
247-00 VLYS 6928 A2
135th Dr
97-00 QENS 6925 E2
135th Pl
124-00 QENS 6926 C2
135th Rd
97-00 QENS 6925 E2
130-00 QENS 6926 C3
246-00 QENS 6928 A2
247-00 VLYS 6928 A3
135th St
13-00 QENS 6614 E7
14-00 QENS 6720 E1
80-00 QENS 6825 A3
123-00 QENS 6926 C2
E 135th St
10 MHTN 107 C7
10 MHTN 6612 D4
100 BRNX 107 D7
100 BRNX 110 E1
100 BRNX 6612 E4
300 BRNX 6613 B5
W 135th St
10 MHTN 107 B7
10 MHTN 6612 D4
300 MHTN 106 E6
136th Av
151-00 QENS 6926 E3
240-00 QENS 6927 E2
242-00 QENS 6928 A2

136th Av
247-00 VLYS 6928 A3
136th Rd
216-00 QENS 6927 C1
244-00 QENS 6928 A3
247-00 VLYS 6928 A3
136th St
11-00 QENS 6614 E7
56-00 QENS 6720 E6
66-00 QENS 6824 E1
69-42 QENS 6825 A2
E 136th St
200 BRNX 110 D1
200 BRNX 6612 E4
700 BRNX 6613 B5
W 136th St
10 MHTN 107 B7
10 MHTN 6612 D3
500 MHTN 106 D5
137th Av
153-00 QENS 6926 E3
224-01 QENS 6927 D2
242-00 QENS 6928 A3
247-00 VLYS 6928 A3
137th Pl
46-00 QENS 6721 A6
137th Rd
- QENS 6927 D2
244-00 QENS 6928 A3
247-00 VLYS 6928 A3
137th St
11-00 QENS 6614 E7
29-00 QENS 6720 E3
55-00 QENS 6721 A6
72-00 QENS 6825 A2
E 137th St
200 BRNX 6612 E4
300 BRNX 110 E1
400 BRNX 6613 A4
W 137th St
10 MHTN 107 B7
10 MHTN 6612 D4
600 MHTN 106 D5
138th Av
217-00 QENS 6927 C2
243-00 QENS 6928 A3
138th Pl
9-00 QENS 6614 E7
89-00 QENS 6825 B5
138th Rd
217-00 QENS 6927 C2
138th St
7-00 QENS 6614 E7
37-00 QENS 6720 E4
55-00 QENS 6721 A6
88-70 QENS 6825 B5
E 138th St
10 MHTN 107 C7
10 MHTN 6612 D4
100 BRNX 107 D7
100 BRNX 6612 E4
200 BRNX 110 E1
300 BRNX 6613 A5
W 138th St
10 MHTN 107 B6
10 MHTN 6612 D3
400 MHTN 106 E5
139th Av
220-00 QENS 6927 D2
245-00 QENS 6928 A3
139th Rd
175-00 QENS 6927 B2
139th St
13-00 QENS 6614 E7
29-00 QENS 6720 E3
72-00 QENS 6825 A2
111-00 QENS 6926 C1
E 139th St
10 MHTN 107 C6
10 MHTN 6612 D3
200 BRNX 107 E7
200 BRNX 110 E1
200 BRNX 6612 E4
300 BRNX 6613 A4
W 139th St
10 MHTN 107 C6
10 MHTN 6612 C3
500 MHTN 106 D4
140th Av
154-00 QENS 6927 A2
140th St
13-00 QENS 6614 E7
31-00 QENS 6720 E3
68-13 QENS 6825 A1
116-00 QENS 6926 C1
E 140th St
100 BRNX 6612 E4
200 BRNX 107 E7
200 BRNX 110 E1
400 BRNX 6613 A4
W 140th St
100 MHTN 107 B6
400 MHTN 106 D4
400 MHTN 6612 B2
141st Av
218-00 QENS 6927 C2
141st Pl
73-00 QENS 6825 A2
141st Rd
218-00 QENS 6927 C2
141st St
7-00 QENS 6614 E7
13-00 QENS 6615 A7
57-00 QENS 6721 A6
69-00 QENS 6825 A1
111-00 QENS 6926 C1
E 141st St
300 BRNX 107 E7
300 BRNX 6612 E5
300 BRNX 6613 B5
W 141st St
10 MHTN 107 C6
10 MHTN 6612 D3
400 MHTN 106 E4
142nd Av
240-00 QENS 6927 E3
142nd Pl
117-00 QENS 6926 D1
142nd Rd
219-00 QENS 6927 C3
142nd St
13-00 QENS 6615 A7
56-00 QENS 6721 A6
109-00 QENS 6825 C7
126-00 QENS 6926 D2

E 142nd St
200 BRNX 107 E7
200 BRNX 6612 E4
400 BRNX 6613 A4
W 142nd St
10 MHTN 107 A5
400 MHTN 106 E4
400 MHTN 6612 C2
143rd Av
240-00 QENS 6927 E3
143rd Pl
11-00 QENS 6615 A7
143rd Rd
170-00 QENS 6927 B3
143rd St
14-00 QENS 6615 A6
29-00 QENS 6721 A3
89-00 QENS 6825 B5
121-00 QENS 6926 D2
E 143rd St
200 BRNX 107 E6
200 BRNX 6612 E3
200 BRNX 6613 A4
W 143rd St
10 MHTN 107 C5
400 MHTN 106 E4
400 MHTN 6612 C2
144th Av
162-00 QENS 6927 A3
256-00 QENS 6928 A4
144th Dr
165-34 QENS 6927 A3
144th Pl
13-00 QENS 6615 A6
25-00 QENS 6721 A2
90-00 QENS 6825 B5
144th Rd
168-00 QENS 6927 B3
144th St
21-00 QENS 6721 A1
111-00 QENS 6825 C7
114-00 QENS 6926 D1
E 144th St
100 BRNX 107 E6
100 BRNX 6612 E3
300 BRNX 6613 A4
W 144th St
100 MHTN 6612 D3
400 MHTN 106 E3
400 MHTN 107 A4
144th Ter
165-00 QENS 6927 A3
145th Av
155-00 QENS 6926 E3
178-00 QENS 6927 B3
257-00 QENS 6928 A4
260-00 HmpT 6928 A4
145th Dr
178-00 QENS 6927 B3
145th Pl
13-00 QENS 6615 A7
33-00 QENS 6721 A3
145th Rd
219-00 QENS 6927 C4
145th St
33-00 QENS 6721 A3
111-00 QENS 6825 D7
114-00 QENS 6926 D1
E 145th St
300 BRNX 6613 A3
W 145th St
100 MHTN 107 B4
100 MHTN 6612 B2
500 MHTN 106 E4
145th St Br
- BRNX 107 C5
- BRNX 6612 E3
- MHTN 107 D5
- MHTN 6612 E3
146th Av
153-00 QENS 6926 E3
228-00 QENS 6927 D4
146th Dr
178-00 QENS 6927 B4
146th Pl
13-00 QENS 6615 A7
61-00 QENS 6721 A7
146th Rd
167-00 QENS 6927 A4
146th St
13-00 QENS 6615 A7
61-00 QENS 6721 A7
90-00 QENS 6825 C5
114-00 QENS 6926 D1
E 146th St
100 BRNX 107 D6
100 BRNX 6612 E3
500 BRNX 6613 A4
W 146th St
100 MHTN 107 B5
400 MHTN 6612 C2
500 MHTN 106 E3
146th Ter
178-00 QENS 6927 B4
147th Av
- QENS 6926 D3
165-00 QENS 6927 A4
255-00 QENS 6928 A4
147th Dr
239-00 QENS 6927 D4
255-00 QENS 6928 A4
147th Pl
2-00 QENS 6615 A6
32-00 QENS 6721 A3
95-00 QENS 6825 C6
147th Rd
239-00 QENS 6927 D4
255-00 QENS 6928 A4
147th St
3-00 QENS 6615 A6
23-00 QENS 6721 A2
110-00 QENS 6825 D7
126-00 QENS 6926 D3
E 147th St
300 BRNX 6613 A4
W 147th St
100 MHTN 107 C4
100 MHTN 6612 D2
500 MHTN 106 E3
148th Av
225-00 QENS 6927 C4
255-00 QENS 6928 A4
148th Dr
235-00 QENS 6927 D5
255-00 QENS 6928 A5

148th Pl
61-00 QENS 6721 A7
148th Rd
239-00 QENS 6927 D5
255-00 QENS 6928 A5
148th St
- QENS 6926 D4
9-00 QENS 6615 B7
56-00 QENS 6721 A7
94-00 QENS 6825 C6
E 148th St
200 BRNX 6613 A3
W 148th St
400 MHTN 107 A3
400 MHTN 6612 C2
500 MHTN 106 E3
149th Av
78-00 BKLN 6925 C3
78-00 QENS 6925 C3
114-00 QENS 6926 A3
233-00 QENS 6927 D5
255-00 QENS 6928 A5
149th Dr
245-00 QENS 6927 E5
149th Pl
2-00 QENS 6615 A6
37-00 QENS 6721 B4
149th Rd
177-00 QENS 6927 B4
255-06 QENS 6928 A5
149th St
- QENS 6926 D4
1-00 QENS 6615 A6
15-18 QENS 6721 B2
90-00 QENS 6825 C5
E 149th St
10 BRNX 107 E5
10 BRNX 6612 E3
400 BRNX 6613 A4
W 149th St
200 MHTN 6612 D2
400 MHTN 107 A3
500 MHTN 106 E3
150th Av
- QENS 6926 E4
177-00 QENS 6927 B4
150th Dr
181-00 QENS 6927 B4
150th Pl
14-00 QENS 6615 B7
30-00 QENS 6721 B3
150th Rd
95-00 QENS 6925 D3
179-00 QENS 6927 B4
150th St
2-00 QENS 6615 B7
15-50 QENS 6721 B2
83-00 QENS 6825 B3
126-00 QENS 6926 E3
E 150th St
10 BRNX 107 D5
10 BRNX 6612 E3
200 BRNX 6613 A3
W 150th St
400 MHTN 106 E2
400 MHTN 107 A3
400 MHTN 6612 C2
151st Av
78-00 BKLN 6925 C3
89-51 QENS 6925 C3
151st Pl
6-00 QENS 6615 B6
134-00 QENS 6926 E3
151st St
6-00 QENS 6615 B6
54-00 QENS 6721 B6
84-00 QENS 6825 C4
E 151st St
100 BRNX 6612 E2
200 BRNX 107 E5
200 BRNX 6613 A3
W 151st St
400 MHTN 107 A3
400 MHTN 6612 C2
600 MHTN 106 E2
152nd Av
124-01 QENS 6926 B3
152nd St
6-00 QENS 6615 B7
30-00 QENS 6721 B3
84-00 QENS 6825 C4
118-00 QENS 6926 E1
E 152nd St
600 BRNX 6613 B3
W 152nd St
200 MHTN 107 B3
400 MHTN 6612 C1
600 MHTN 106 E2
153rd Av
78-00 BKLN 6925 C3
78-00 QENS 6925 C3
153rd Ct
144-00 QENS 6926 E3
153rd Ln
144-00 QENS 6926 E3
153rd Pl
15-00 QENS 6615 C6
144-00 QENS 6926 E4
153rd St
61-00 QENS 6721 B7
108-00 QENS 6825 D6
118-00 QENS 6926 E1
E 153rd St
10 BRNX 107 E4
10 BRNX 6612 E2
300 BRNX 6613 B3
W 153rd St
400 MHTN 107 A2
400 MHTN 6612 C2
600 MHTN 106 E2
154th Pl
6-00 QENS 6615 C6
59-00 QENS 6721 B7
154th St
7-00 QENS 6615 C7
17-00 QENS 6721 B3
106-00 QENS 6825 D6
129-00 QENS 6926 E2
134-00 QENS 6927 A3
E 154th St
300 BRNX 6613 A3
W 154th St
200 MHTN 107 C3
400 MHTN 6612 D1

155th Av
- QENS 6926 B4
78-00 BKLN 6925 C3
89-50 QENS 6925 C3
155th St
14-00 QENS 6615 C7
29-00 QENS 6721 B3
106-00 QENS 6825 D6
127-00 QENS 6926 E2
134-00 QENS 6927 A2
E 155th St
- MHTN 107 C3
- MHTN 6612 D2
300 BRNX 6613 A3
W 155th St
200 MHTN 107 A2
400 MHTN 6612 C1
600 MHTN 106 E1
156th Av
75-00 BKLN 6925 B4
75-00 QENS 6925 C4
156th Pl
104-00 QENS 6825 D6
156th St
14-00 QENS 6615 C7
41-00 QENS 6721 B5
106-00 QENS 6825 D6
132-00 QENS 6926 E2
132-00 QENS 6927 A2
E 156th St
100 BRNX 107 E4
100 BRNX 6612 E2
200 BRNX 6613 A3
W 156th St
500 MHTN 107 A2
600 MHTN 6612 C1
600 MHTN 106 E1
157th Av
82-00 QENS 6925 D4
157th St
7-00 QENS 6615 C7
41-00 QENS 6721 B5
106-00 QENS 6825 D6
127-00 QENS 6926 E2
129-00 QENS 6927 A2
E 157th St
10 BRNX 107 D3
10 BRNX 6612 E2
200 BRNX 6613 B3
W 157th St
400 MHTN 107 A1
400 MHTN 6612 D1
158th Av
74-00 QENS 6925 C4
158th St
6-00 QENS 6615 C6
32-00 QENS 6721 C5
94-00 QENS 6825 C5
129-00 QENS 6926 E2
144-00 QENS 6927 A3
E 158th St
10 BRNX 107 E3
10 BRNX 6612 E2
200 BRNX 6613 A2
W 158th St
400 MHTN 107 B1
400 MHTN 6612 C1
600 MHTN 106 E1
159th Av
78-00 QENS 6925 C4
159th Dr
102-00 QENS 6925 E4
159th Rd
102-00 QENS 6925 E4
159th St
14-00 QENS 6615 C7
41-00 QENS 6721 C5
94-00 QENS 6825 D5
132-01 QENS 6927 A2
E 159th St
300 BRNX 6613 A2
W 159th St
400 MHTN 107 B1
400 MHTN 6612 C1
160th Av
94-00 QENS 6925 E4
160th St
6-00 QENS 6615 C7
41-00 QENS 6721 C5
72-00 QENS 6825 C2
127-00 QENS 6926 E2
128-00 QENS 6927 A2
E 160th St
200 BRNX 6613 A2
W 160th St
400 MHTN 107 A1
400 MHTN 6612 D1
600 MHTN 104 A7
600 MHTN 6503 C7
161st Av
78-00 QENS 6925 C5
161st Pl
122-00 QENS 6927 A1
161st St
14-00 QENS 6615 C7
28-00 QENS 6721 C3
80-00 QENS 6825 C3
133-00 QENS 6927 A2
E 161st St
10 BRNX 107 E3
10 BRNX 6612 E2
500 BRNX 6613 B3
W 161st St
100 BRNX 107 D2
100 BRNX 6612 E1
500 MHTN 107 A1
500 MHTN 6612 D1
600 MHTN 104 A7
600 MHTN 6503 C7
162nd Av
94-00 QENS 6925 E5
162nd St
4-500 QENS 6721 C3
7-00 QENS 6615 C7
71-00 QENS 6825 C1
E 162nd St
10 BRNX 107 E3
100 BRNX 6612 E2
200 BRNX 6613 A2
W 162nd St
10 BRNX 107 D2
10 BRNX 6612 E1
400 MHTN 6612 D1
400 MHTN 107 B1
500 MHTN 6503 C7
600 MHTN 104 A7

163rd Av
94-00 QENS 6925 E5
163rd Dr
99-00 QENS 6925 E5
102-00 QENS 6926 A5
163rd Pl
47-00 QENS 6721 C6
163rd Rd
99-00 QENS 6925 E5
102-00 QENS 6926 A5
163rd St
14-00 QENS 6615 D7
22-00 QENS 6721 C3
88-00 QENS 6825 D4
E 163rd St
300 BRNX 6613 B2
W 163rd St
10 BRNX 107 D2
10 BRNX 6612 E1
400 MHTN 107 B1
400 MHTN 6612 D1
500 MHTN 104 A7
500 MHTN 6503 C7
164th Av
83-00 QENS 6925 D5
102-00 QENS 6926 A5
164th Dr
99-00 QENS 6925 E5
102-00 QENS 6926 A5
164th Pl
104-00 QENS 6825 D5
164th Rd
99-00 QENS 6925 E5
102-00 QENS 6926 A5
164th St
14-00 QENS 6615 D7
47-00 QENS 6721 C7
67-01 QENS 6825 C3
117-00 QENS 6926 E1
117-00 QENS 6927 A1
E 164th St
10 BRNX 107 E2
10 BRNX 6612 E1
200 BRNX 6613 A2
W 164th St
10 BRNX 107 D2
10 BRNX 6612 E1
400 MHTN 104 B7
400 MHTN 107 C1
400 MHTN 6503 D7
400 MHTN 6612 B1
165th Av
95-00 QENS 6925 E5
99-61 QENS 6926 A5
165th St
14-00 QENS 6615 D7
27-00 QENS 6721 C3
80-00 QENS 6825 C3
117-00 QENS 6826 A7
117-00 QENS 6927 A1
E 165th St
10 BRNX 107 E2
10 BRNX 6612 E1
500 BRNX 6613 C2
W 165th St
10 BRNX 107 D1
10 BRNX 6612 E1
400 MHTN 104 B7
400 MHTN 6503 C7
166th Pl
134-00 QENS 6927 A2
166th St
7-00 QENS 6615 D7
25-00 QENS 6721 D3
110-20 QENS 6825 E6
116-00 QENS 6826 A7
143-00 QENS 6927 A3
E 166th St
500 BRNX 6613 B2
W 166th St
10 BRNX 107 E1
10 BRNX 6612 E1
400 MHTN 6503 D7
500 MHTN 104 B7
167th St
27-00 QENS 6721 D3
80-00 QENS 6825 D3
115-00 QENS 6826 A7
143-00 QENS 6927 A3
E 167th St
10 BRNX 6613 B2
W 167th St
10 BRNX 107 E1
10 BRNX 6612 E1
100 BRNX 104 E7
100 BRNX 6503 E7
500 MHTN 104 B7
500 MHTN 6503 D7
168th Pl
83-00 QENS 6825 D3
168th St
25-00 QENS 6721 D3
67-00 QENS 6825 D2
114-00 QENS 6826 A7
144-00 QENS 6927 A3
E 168th St
10 BRNX 105 A7
10 BRNX 6504 D7
300 BRNX 6613 B1
W 168th St
10 BRNX 104 E7
10 BRNX 105 A7
10 BRNX 6503 E7
10 BRNX 6504 D7
400 MHTN 104 B6
400 MHTN 6503 D7
169th Pl
108-00 QENS 6825 E6
169th St
18-00 QENS 6721 D3
83-00 QENS 6825 D3
113-00 QENS 6826 A7
137-00 QENS 6927 B2
E 169th St
10 BRNX 105 B7
10 BRNX 6504 A7
200 BRNX 6613 A1
W 169th St
10 BRNX 104 E7
10 BRNX 105 A7
10 BRNX 6503 E7
10 BRNX 6504 A7
100 MHTN 104 C6
500 MHTN 6503 D7
170th Pl
48-00 QENS 6721 D6

170th St
27-00 QENS 6721 D3
67-00 QENS 6825 D1
114-00 QENS 6826 A7
137-00 QENS 6927 B2
E 170th St
10 BRNX 105 D7
10 BRNX 6504 A7
700 BRNX 6613 C1
W 170th St
10 BRNX 105 A6
10 BRNX 6504 A7
100 BRNX 104 E6
100 BRNX 6503 E7
600 MHTN 104 B6
600 MHTN 6503 D7
171st Pl
45-00 QENS 6721 D5
105-00 QENS 6825 E5
171st St
39-00 QENS 6721 D5
84-00 QENS 6825 D3
116-00 QENS 6826 A7
137-00 QENS 6927 B2
E 171st St
10 BRNX 105 C7
10 BRNX 6504 A7
500 BRNX 6613 C1
W 171st St
100 BRNX 104 E6
100 BRNX 6503 E7
500 MHTN 104 C6
500 MHTN 6503 D7
172nd St
40-00 QENS 6721 D4
103-00 QENS 6825 E5
114-00 QENS 6826 A7
126-00 QENS 6927 A1
E 172nd St
10 BRNX 6504 A7
400 BRNX 105 E7
800 BRNX 6613 D1
1600 BRNX 6614 A1
W 172nd St
10 BRNX 105 A6
10 BRNX 6504 A7
500 MHTN 104 B5
500 MHTN 6503 D7
173rd St
61-00 QENS 6721 D7
91-00 QENS 6825 E4
114-00 QENS 6826 A7
137-00 QENS 6927 B2
E 173rd St
100 BRNX 6504 B7
400 BRNX 105 E6
1500 BRNX 6613 E1
W 173rd St
500 MHTN 104 B5
500 MHTN 6503 D6
174th Pl
125-00 QENS 6927 B1
174th St
64-00 QENS 6721 D7
68-00 QENS 6825 D1
108-00 QENS 6826 A6
140-00 QENS 6927 B2
E 174th St
10 BRNX 105 D5
900 BRNX 6504 D7
900 BRNX 6613 E1
1600 BRNX 6614 A1
W 174th St
100 BRNX 105 A5
100 BRNX 6504 A6
500 MHTN 104 B5
500 MHTN 6503 D6
175th Pl
49-00 QENS 6721 D7
112-00 QENS 6826 A6
175th St
50-00 QENS 6721 D6
69-00 QENS 6825 D2
108-00 QENS 6826 A6
144-51 QENS 6927 A3
E 175th St
10 BRNX 6504 B6
300 BRNX 105 E5
W 175th St
100 BRNX 105 A4
100 BRNX 6504 A6
500 MHTN 104 C5
500 MHTN 6503 D6
176th Pl
130-00 QENS 6927 B1
176th St
92-00 QENS 6825 E4
108-00 QENS 6826 A5
144-00 QENS 6927 A3
E 176th St
300 BRNX 105 E5
600 BRNX 6504 D7
W 176th St
10 BRNX 105 B4
100 BRNX 6504 A6
500 MHTN 104 B5
500 MHTN 6503 D6
177th Pl
114-50 QENS 6826 B6
144-00 QENS 6927 B3
177th St
73-00 QENS 6825 D1
109-00 QENS 6826 A6
146-00 QENS 6927 B4
E 177th St
10 BRNX 105 D4
10 BRNX 6504 B6
1100 BRNX 6505 A7
W 177th St
10 BRNX 105 C4
10 BRNX 6504 B6
500 MHTN 6503 D6
700 MHTN 104 B4
178th Pl
92-00 QENS 6825 E4
119-00 QENS 6826 B7
144-00 QENS 6927 B3
178th St
87-00 QENS 6825 E4
111-00 QENS 6826 A6
120-18 QENS 6927 B1
E 178th St
- BRNX 105 E4
700 BRNX 6504 D7
1100 BRNX 6505 A7

W 178th St
500 MHTN 104 C5
500 MHTN 6503 D6
W 178th St US-9
700 MHTN 104 B4
700 MHTN 6503 D6
179th Pl
88-00 QENS 6825 E4
110-00 QENS 6826 A5
179th St
67-00 QENS 6721 D7
67-00 QENS 6825 D1
111-00 QENS 6826 A6
144-00 QENS 6927 B3
E 179th St
10 BRNX 105 D3
400 BRNX 6504 D6
1100 BRNX 6505 A7
W 179th St
10 BRNX 105 C2
10 BRNX 6504 A5
500 MHTN 104 C4
500 MHTN 6503 D6
W 179th St US-9
700 MHTN 104 C4
700 MHTN 6503 D6
180th St
65-00 QENS 6721 D7
67-00 QENS 6825 E1
103-00 QENS 6826 A5
140-00 QENS 6927 B3
E 180th St
200 BRNX 105 E3
400 BRNX 6504 E7
1100 BRNX 6505 A7
W 180th St
10 BRNX 105 C2
10 BRNX 6504 B5
500 MHTN 104 B4
500 MHTN 6503 D6
181st Pl
143-00 QENS 6927 B3
181st St
64-00 QENS 6721 D7
67-00 QENS 6825 E1
89-00 QENS 6826 A4
140-00 QENS 6927 B3
E 181st St
10 BRNX 105 E3
400 BRNX 6504 D6
W 181st St
10 BRNX 105 D2
10 BRNX 6504 B5
500 MHTN 104 B4
500 MHTN 6503 D5
182nd Pl
88-00 QENS 6826 A3
143-00 QENS 6927 C3
182nd St
58-00 QENS 6721 D7
67-00 QENS 6825 E1
88-00 QENS 6826 A4
147-00 QENS 6927 B4
E 182nd St
10 BRNX 105 E2
200 BRNX 6504 C5
W 182nd St
10 BRNX 105 D2
10 BRNX 6504 B5
500 MHTN 104 D4
500 MHTN 6503 E6
183rd Pl
102-00 QENS 6826 A4
183rd St
61-00 QENS 6721 D7
67-00 QENS 6825 E1
88-00 QENS 6826 A3
144-00 QENS 6927 B4
E 183rd St
10 BRNX 105 E2
300 BRNX 6504 D5
W 183rd St
10 BRNX 105 D1
10 BRNX 6504 B4
500 MHTN 104 D4
700 MHTN 6503 D5
184th Pl
88-00 QENS 6826 A3
184th St
61-00 QENS 6721 E7
69-00 QENS 6825 E1
88-00 QENS 6826 A4
147-00 QENS 6927 B4
E 184th St
10 BRNX 105 E1
400 BRNX 6504 D5
W 184th St
10 BRNX 105 E1
10 BRNX 6504 C4
500 MHTN 104 C3
500 MHTN 6503 D5
185th St
50-00 QENS 6721 D6
69-00 QENS 6825 E1
88-00 QENS 6826 A4
141-00 QENS 6927 C3
E 185th St
400 BRNX 6504 D5
W 185th St
500 MHTN 104 D3
500 MHTN 6503 E5
186th Ln
64-00 QENS 6721 E7
69-00 QENS 6825 E1
186th St
50-00 QENS 6721 D6
73-00 QENS 6825 E1
88-00 QENS 6826 A4
E 186th St
400 BRNX 6504 B3
W 186th St
400 MHTN 104 D3
400 MHTN 6503 E5
187th Pl
88-00 QENS 6826 A3
187th St
50-00 QENS 6721 E6
73-00 QENS 6825 E1
88-00 QENS 6826 A3
E 187th St
400 BRNX 6504 D5
W 187th St
400 MHTN 104 D3
800 MHTN 6503 D5

New York City/5 Borough Street Index

STREET
Block City Map# Grid

188th St
46-00 QENS 6721 E6
68-01 QENS 6825 E1
102-00 QENS 6826 B4
E 188th St
100 BRNX 6504 C4
W 188th St
10 BRNX 102 E7
10 BRNX 6504 C4
500 MHTN 104 D3
500 MHTN 6503 E5
189th St
43-00 QENS 6721 D5
73-00 QENS 6825 E1
88-00 QENS 6826 A3
E 189th St
400 BRNX 6504 E5
W 189th St
500 MHTN 104 D3
500 MHTN 6503 E5
190th Ln
67-00 QENS 6721 E7
190th Pl
109-00 QENS 6826 B5
190th St
40-00 QENS 6721 D4
73-00 QENS 6825 E1
92-00 QENS 6826 B4
E 190th St
10 BRNX 102 E7
10 BRNX 6504 C4
W 190th St
10 BRNX 102 E7
10 BRNX 6504 C4
500 MHTN 104 D2
700 MHTN 6503 D5
191st St
36-00 QENS 6721 D4
104-00 QENS 6826 B5
122-00 QENS 6927 C1
E 191st St
500 BRNX 6504 D4
W 191st St
500 MHTN 104 D2
500 MHTN 6503 E5
192nd St
34-00 QENS 6721 E4
67-40 QENS 6722 A7
88-00 QENS 6826 B3
E 192nd St
100 BRNX 6504 C4
W 192nd St
10 BRNX 102 E6
10 BRNX 6504 C3
500 MHTN 104 D2
500 MHTN 6503 E5
193rd Ln
67-00 QENS 6722 A7
193rd St
- QENS 6927 D1
40-00 QENS 6721 E6
73-00 QENS 6826 A1
E 193rd St
10 BRNX 6504 C3
W 193rd St
200 BRNX 102 D5
200 BRNX 6504 B3
500 MHTN 6503 E5
600 MHTN 104 D2
194th Ln
64-00 QENS 6721 E7
64-00 QENS 6722 A7
194th St
47-00 QENS 6721 E6
60-01 QENS 6722 A7
109-00 QENS 6826 B5
E 194th St
200 BRNX 6504 D4
2800 BRNX 6505 E5
195th Ln
67-00 QENS 6722 A7
195th Pl
88-00 QENS 6826 B3
195th St
47-00 QENS 6721 E5
88-00 QENS 6826 B3
E 195th St
300 BRNX 6504 D4
2800 BRNX 6505 E5
W 195th St
10 BRNX 102 E5
10 BRNX 6504 D2
196th Pl
45-00 QENS 6721 E5
56-00 QENS 6722 A6
73-00 QENS 6826 A1
196th St
47-00 QENS 6721 E5
73-00 QENS 6722 A7
109-00 QENS 6826 C6
E 196th St
10 BRNX 6504 D3
2800 BRNX 6505 E5
2900 BRNX 6506 A5
W 196th St
600 MHTN 104 D1
600 MHTN 6503 D4
197th St
46-00 QENS 6721 E5
67-00 QENS 6722 A7
109-00 QENS 6826 C5
E 197th St
200 BRNX 6504 D3
2800 BRNX 6505 E5
W 197th St
10 BRNX 6504 C3
100 BRNX 102 E5
198th St
47-00 QENS 6721 E5
67-00 QENS 6722 A7
109-22 QENS 6826 C6
E 198th St
10 BRNX 6504 D3
199th St
47-00 QENS 6721 E5
50-00 QENS 6722 A6
120-00 QENS 6826 D7
E 199th St
300 BRNX 6504 E3
200th St
15-00 QENS 6615 D7
15-00 QENS 6721 D1
117-00 QENS 6826 D6
201st Pl
117-00 QENS 6826 D6

201st St
15-00 QENS 6615 D6
28-00 QENS 6721 E3
47-06 QENS 6722 A5
109-50 QENS 6826 D6
E 201st St
200 BRNX 6504 E3
W 201st St
300 MHTN 105 A1
300 MHTN 6504 A4
202nd St
15-00 QENS 6615 D6
15-00 QENS 6721 D1
47-20 QENS 6722 A6
117-00 QENS 6826 D6
E 202nd St
200 BRNX 6504 D3
W 202nd St
300 MHTN 105 A1
300 MHTN 6504 A4
203rd Pl
- QENS 6721 E2
203rd St
26-00 QENS 6721 E3
47-00 QENS 6722 A5
109-50 QENS 6826 D5
E 203rd St
400 BRNX 6504 E4
W 203rd St
300 MHTN 105 A1
300 MHTN 6504 A4
204th St
28-00 QENS 6721 E3
45-00 QENS 6722 A5
99-00 QENS 6826 C4
E 204th St
200 BRNX 6504 E3
W 204th St
300 MHTN 105 A1
300 MHTN 6504 A4
400 MHTN 102 A6
600 MHTN 101 E6
600 MHTN 6503 E3
205th Pl
99-00 QENS 6826 C4
205th St
32-00 QENS 6721 E3
39-11 QENS 6722 A4
88-00 QENS 6826 C3
E 205th St
200 BRNX 6504 E2
300 BRNX 6505 A3
W 205th St
10 BRNX 6504 D2
300 MHTN 102 A7
300 MHTN 105 B1
300 MHTN 6504 A4
206th St
26-00 QENS 6721 E2
48-00 QENS 6722 A6
E 206th St
200 BRNX 6504 E2
W 206th St
300 MHTN 102 B7
300 MHTN 6504 A4
207th St
23-01 QENS 6721 E2
47-00 QENS 6722 A5
88-00 QENS 6826 C3
E 207th St
300 BRNX 6504 E4
300 BRNX 6505 A2
W 207th St
- BRNX 102 B7
- BRNX 6504 A4
400 MHTN 102 A6
400 MHTN 6504 A3
208th Pl
13-00 QENS 6615 E7
14-00 QENS 6721 E1
208th St
28-00 QENS 6721 E2
47-00 QENS 6722 A5
88-00 QENS 6826 C3
E 208th St
10 BRNX 6504 E2
W 208th St
300 MHTN 102 B7
300 MHTN 6504 A4
209th Pl
28-00 QENS 6722 A2
109-00 QENS 6826 D4
209th St
13-00 QENS 6615 E7
15-00 QENS 6721 E1
32-00 QENS 6722 A3
86-00 QENS 6826 C2
E 209th St
300 BRNX 6505 A2
210th Pl
26-00 QENS 6722 A2
89-00 QENS 6826 C2
210th St
61-00 QENS 6722 B7
112-00 QENS 6826 D5
E 210th St
10 BRNX 6504 E2
211th Pl
104-01 QENS 6826 D4
211th St
18-00 QENS 6721 E1
61-00 QENS 6722 B6
88-00 QENS 6826 D4
E 211th St
100 BRNX 6504 E1
900 BRNX 6505 C2
W 211th St
500 MHTN 102 B6
500 MHTN 6504 A3
212th Pl
88-00 QENS 6826 D2
212th St
13-00 QENS 6615 E7
14-00 QENS 6721 E1
26-00 QENS 6722 A2
98-00 QENS 6826 D3
212th St SR-24
88-00 QENS 6826 D2
E 212th St
10 BRNX 6504 E1
900 BRNX 6505 C2
W 212th St
500 MHTN 102 B6
500 MHTN 6504 A3

213th Pl
- QENS 6722 A1
213th St
48-00 QENS 6722 B5
91-00 QENS 6826 D3
E 213th St
10 BRNX 6504 E1
600 BRNX 6505 A2
W 213th St
500 MHTN 102 B6
500 MHTN 6504 A3
214th Ln
34-00 QENS 6722 B3
214th Pl
32-00 QENS 6722 A2
92-00 QENS 6826 D3
214th St
50-00 QENS 6722 B5
91-00 QENS 6826 D2
E 214th St
800 BRNX 6505 B2
W 214th St
500 MHTN 102 A5
500 MHTN 6504 A3
215th Pl
28-00 QENS 6722 B2
87-00 QENS 6826 D2
215th St
15-00 QENS 6616 A7
61-00 QENS 6722 C6
80-00 QENS 6826 C1
E 215th St
900 BRNX 6505 C2
W 215th St
500 MHTN 102 B5
500 MHTN 6504 A3
216th St
15-00 QENS 6616 A7
35-00 QENS 6722 B3
87-00 QENS 6826 D1
E 216th St
600 BRNX 6505 B2
W 216th St
300 MHTN 102 C5
300 MHTN 6504 B3
217th Ln
102-00 QENS 6826 E4
217th Pl
101-00 QENS 6826 E3
217th St
73-00 QENS 6722 C7
98-00 QENS 6826 E3
132-00 QENS 6927 D1
E 217th St
700 BRNX 6505 B1
W 217th St
500 MHTN 102 B5
500 MHTN 6504 A3
218th Pl
102-00 QENS 6826 E4
218th St
39-00 QENS 6722 B3
88-00 QENS 6826 D2
135-00 QENS 6927 C2
E 218th St
700 BRNX 6505 B1
W 218th St
400 MHTN 102 B5
400 MHTN 6504 A3
219th St
61-00 QENS 6722 C6
112-00 QENS 6826 E6
134-00 QENS 6927 C2
E 219th St
600 BRNX 6505 B1
W 219th St
400 MHTN 102 C5
400 MHTN 6504 B3
220th Pl
45-00 QENS 6722 C4
137-00 QENS 6927 D2
220th St
38-00 QENS 6722 B3
96-00 QENS 6827 A3
114-00 QENS 6826 E6
137-00 QENS 6927 D2
E 220th St
600 BRNX 6505 B1
W 220th St
400 MHTN 102 C5
400 MHTN 6504 B3
221st Pl
89-01 QENS 6826 E1
221st St
35-00 QENS 6722 B3
89-00 QENS 6826 E1
94-50 QENS 6827 B3
145-00 QENS 6927 C4
E 221st St
600 BRNX 6505 B1
222nd St
42-00 QENS 6722 C4
93-00 QENS 6827 A2
114-00 QENS 6826 E7
145-00 QENS 6927 C4
E 222nd St
500 BRNX 6505 E2
223rd Pl
61-00 QENS 6722 C6
223rd St
41-00 QENS 6722 C3
80-00 QENS 6826 D1
102-00 QENS 6827 A4
130-00 QENS 6927 D1
E 223rd St
600 BRNX 6505 B1
224th St
61-00 QENS 6722 D6
91-00 QENS 6827 A2
114-00 QENS 6826 E6
141-00 QENS 6927 D3
E 224th St
600 BRNX 6394 B7
1100 BRNX 6505 D1
225th St
57-00 QENS 6722 C5
94-00 HmpT 6827 A2
102-00 QENS 6827 A5
115-00 QENS 6826 E7
135-00 QENS 6927 D1
E 225th St
600 BRNX 6394 B7
700 BRNX 6505 C1
W 225th St
10 BRNX 102 D4

W 225th St
10 BRNX 6504 B2
100 MHTN 102 C4
100 MHTN 6504 B2
E 226th Dr
1100 BRNX 6505 D1
226th St
69-00 QENS 6722 D6
114-00 QENS 6827 A6
115-50 QENS 6826 E7
143-00 QENS 6927 C4
9400 HmpT 6827 A2
E 226th St
600 BRNX 6394 B7
800 BRNX 6505 C1
227th St
104-00 QENS 6827 A5
116-00 QENS 6826 E7
130-00 QENS 6927 E1
E 227th St
600 BRNX 6394 B7
900 BRNX 6505 C1
W 227th St
100 MHTN 102 C3
100 MHTN 6504 B2
500 BRNX 102 B2
500 BRNX 6504 A2
228th St
57-00 QENS 6722 D5
114-00 QENS 6827 A6
117-00 QENS 6826 E7
143-00 QENS 6927 C4
E 228th St
600 BRNX 6394 B7
900 BRNX 6505 C1
W 228th St
10 MHTN 102 D3
10 MHTN 6504 B2
229th Dr N
1100 BRNX 6505 D1
229th Dr S
1100 BRNX 6505 D1
229th St
50-00 QENS 6722 C5
81-10 QENS 6826 E1
114-00 QENS 6827 A6
129-00 QENS 6927 D3
E 229th St
600 BRNX 6394 B7
1000 BRNX 6505 D1
W 229th St
200 BRNX 102 E4
200 BRNX 6504 C2
230th Pl
142-00 QENS 6927 D4
230th St
56-00 QENS 6722 D5
114-00 QENS 6827 A6
119-00 QENS 6826 E7
130-00 QENS 6927 E2
E 230th St
600 BRNX 6394 B7
W 230th St
100 BRNX 102 D3
200 BRNX 6504 B2
231st St
56-00 QENS 6722 D5
86-00 QENS 6826 E1
114-00 QENS 6827 A7
144-00 QENS 6927 D4
E 231st St
600 BRNX 6394 B7
W 231st St
100 BRNX 102 D2
100 BRNX 6504 B1
232nd St
61-00 QENS 6722 D5
82-00 QENS 6826 E1
115-00 QENS 6827 A7
129-00 QENS 6927 E1
E 232nd St
600 BRNX 6394 C7
W 232nd St
500 BRNX 102 C1
500 BRNX 6504 A1
233rd Pl
37-00 QENS 6722 C2
233rd St
80-00 QENS 6722 E7
82-00 QENS 6826 E1
115-00 QENS 6827 A7
126-00 QENS 6928 A1
128-50 QENS 6927 E1
E 233rd St
10 BRNX 6393 E6
10 BRNX 6394 D7
1600 BRNX 6395 A7
W 233rd St
100 BRNX 102 E2
100 BRNX 6504 B1
234th Pl
135-00 QENS 6927 E2
234th St
80-00 QENS 6722 E7
82-00 QENS 6826 E1
116-00 QENS 6827 A7
121-00 QENS 6928 A1
130-00 QENS 6927 E3
E 234th St
500 BRNX 6394 B7
W 234th St
200 BRNX 102 E2
200 BRNX 6504 C1
234th St Ext
- QENS 6722 D3
235th Ct
86-00 QENS 6827 A1
235th St
40-01 QENS 6722 D3
82-00 QENS 6826 E1
117-00 QENS 6827 A7
121-00 QENS 6928 A1
147-00 QENS 6927 D4
E 235th St
10 BRNX 6393 E6
600 BRNX 6394 C7
W 235th St
500 BRNX 102 C1
500 BRNX 6504 B1
236th St
80-00 QENS 6722 E7
118-00 QENS 6827 A7
121-00 QENS 6928 A1
148-00 QENS 6927 D5

E 236th St
10 BRNX 6394 A6
W 236th St
- BRNX 6393 A7
200 BRNX 102 E1
200 BRNX 6504 C1
237th St
80-00 QENS 6722 E7
119-00 QENS 6827 A7
120-00 QENS 6928 A1
11700 HmpT 6827 A7
E 237th St
10 BRNX 6394 A6
W 237th St
100 BRNX 102 E1
100 BRNX 6504 C1
600 BRNX 6393 B7
238th St
119-00 QENS 6827 A7
120-00 QENS 6928 A1
11400 HmpT 6827 A6
E 238th St
10 BRNX 6394 A6
W 238th St
100 BRNX 6504 C1
400 BRNX 102 D1
600 BRNX 6393 B7
239th St
93-00 QENS 6827 A2
11700 HmpT 6827 A7
E 239th St
600 BRNX 6394 C6
W 239th St
- BRNX 102 E1
100 BRNX 6504 C1
500 BRNX 6393 A7
240th Pl
51-00 QENS 6722 D4
240th St
- QENS 6722 E5
83-00 QENS 6723 A7
92-00 QENS 6827 A2
147-00 QENS 6927 D4
800 HmpT 6827 B7
E 240th St
400 YNKR 6394 B6
500 BRNX 6394 C5
W 240th St
200 BRNX 102 E1
200 BRNX 6504 C1
600 BRNX 6393 A7
241st St
52-00 QENS 6722 E4
82-00 QENS 6723 A7
84-00 QENS 6827 A1
93-86 HmpT 6827 A2
134-00 QENS 6927 E3
134-00 QENS 6928 A2
E 241st St
- YNKR 6394 C5
500 BRNX 6394 D6
1000 MTVN 6394 D6
242nd St
- HmpT 6827 A2
43-00 QENS 6722 D3
80-00 QENS 6723 A7
83-00 QENS 6827 A1
131-00 QENS 6928 A2
135-00 QENS 6927 E3
E 242nd St
300 YNKR 6394 A5
500 BRNX 6394 C5
800 MTVN 6394 D5
W 242nd St
200 BRNX 6393 C7
243rd St
45-00 QENS 6722 E3
72-00 QENS 6723 A5
92-00 QENS 6827 A2
131-00 QENS 6928 A2
139-00 QENS 6927 E4
9400 HmpT 6827 A2
E 243rd St
600 BRNX 6394 C5
244th St
71-00 QENS 6722 E5
73-00 QENS 6723 A6
130-00 QENS 6928 A2
9200 HmpT 6827 A2
9200 QENS 6827 A2
W 244th St
- BRNX 6393 C7
245th Pl
61-12 QENS 6722 E5
61-12 QENS 6723 A5
245th St
45-00 QENS 6722 E3
91-00 QENS 6827 B2
133-00 QENS 6928 A2
146-00 QENS 6927 E4
9200 HmpT 6827 B2
W 245th St
300 BRNX 6393 C7
246th Cir
57-00 QENS 6722 E4
246th Pl
57-00 QENS 6723 A4
246th St
80-00 QENS 6723 B7
83-00 QENS 6827 B1
91-00 HmpT 6827 B2
137-00 QENS 6928 A3
139-00 QENS 6927 E3
W 246th St
400 BRNX 6393 A7
247th St
40-00 QENS 6722 D2
65-00 QENS 6723 A5
83-00 QENS 6827 B1
91-00 BLRS 6827 B2
91-00 HmpT 6827 B2
138-00 QENS 6928 A3
139-00 QENS 6927 E4
W 247th St
500 BRNX 6393 B6
248th St
40-00 QENS 6722 E3
80-00 QENS 6723 B7
84-00 QENS 6827 B1
138-00 QENS 6928 A3
140-00 QENS 6927 E3
W 248th St
600 BRNX 6393 B6
249th St
40-00 QENS 6722 E3
75-00 QENS 6723 B7

249th St
84-00 QENS 6827 B1
89-00 BLRS 6827 B2
138-00 QENS 6928 A3
141-00 QENS 6927 E4
W 249th St
500 BRNX 6393 B6
250th St
53-00 QENS 6723 A4
84-00 QENS 6827 B1
89-00 BLRS 6827 B1
138-00 QENS 6928 A3
141-00 QENS 6927 E4
W 250th St
300 BRNX 6393 B6
251st Pl
53-00 QENS 6723 A4
251st St
45-00 QENS 6722 E3
64-00 QENS 6723 A5
84-00 QENS 6827 B1
89-00 BLRS 6827 C1
W 251st St
200 BRNX 6393 C6
252nd St
76-00 QENS 6723 B6
84-00 QENS 6827 B1
W 252nd St
500 BRNX 6393 B6
253rd Pl
147-00 QENS 6927 E4
253rd St
54-00 QENS 6723 A3
84-00 QENS 6827 C1
137-00 HmpT 6928 A3
137-00 QENS 6928 A4
146-01 QENS 6927 E5
W 253rd St
200 BRNX 6393 C6
254th St
38-00 QENS 6722 E2
56-00 QENS 6723 A4
86-00 QENS 6827 C1
139-00 QENS 6928 A4
142-00 QENS 6927 E4
W 254th St
400 BRNX 6393 B5
255th St
33-00 QENS 6722 D2
79-00 QENS 6723 B7
137-00 HmpT 6928 A4
137-00 QENS 6928 A4
149-00 QENS 6927 E5
W 255th St
5400 BRNX 6393 B5
256th St
79-00 QENS 6723 C7
85-00 QENS 6827 C1
87-51 FLPK 6827 C1
137-00 HmpT 6928 A4
147-00 QENS 6928 A4
W 256th St
400 BRNX 6393 B5
257th St
79-00 QENS 6723 C7
84-00 QENS 6827 C1
87-61 FLPK 6827 C1
137-00 HmpT 6928 A4
137-00 QENS 6928 A4
258th St
79-00 QENS 6723 C7
84-00 QENS 6827 C1
87-61 FLPK 6827 C1
147-00 QENS 6928 A4
W 258th St
400 BRNX 6393 C5
259th St
79-00 QENS 6723 C7
85-00 QENS 6827 C1
87-00 FLPK 6827 C1
147-00 QENS 6928 A5
W 259th St
200 BRNX 6393 B5
260th Pl
69-00 QENS 6723 B5
260th St
73-42 QENS 6723 B6
85-00 QENS 6827 C1
87-00 FLPK 6827 C1
W 260th St
200 BRNX 6393 C5
261st St
- FLPK 6827 C1
77-00 QENS 6723 C7
85-00 QENS 6827 C1
W 261st St
200 BRNX 6393 B4
262nd Pl
148-00 QENS 6928 A5
262nd St
58-00 QENS 6723 B4
85-00 QENS 6827 C1
86-00 FLPK 6827 D1
149-00 QENS 6928 A5
W 262nd St
200 BRNX 6393 C4
263rd St
73-00 QENS 6723 C6
85-00 QENS 6827 D1
W 263rd St
200 BRNX 6393 C4
264th St
76-00 QENS 6723 C6
265th St
78-00 QENS 6723 C6
85-00 FLPK 6723 C6
266th St
69-00 QENS 6723 B5
84-15 FLPK 6723 D7
267th St
76-00 QENS 6723 C5
84-15 FLPK 6723 D7
268th St
- FLPK 6723 D7
- NHmT 6723 D7
77-45 QENS 6723 D6
269th St
76-00 QENS 6723 C5
270th St
76-00 QENS 6723 C5
271st St
76-00 QENS 6723 C5

New York City/5 Borough Points of Interest Index

Airports

FEATURE NAME Address City ZIP Code	MAP#	GRID
E 34th Street Heliport, MHTN	117	A5
John F Kennedy International, QENS	6926	E6
LaGuardia, QENS	6720	A2
Linden Municipal, LNDN	7017	A3
Newark Liberty International, ELIZ	6817	D6
Port Authority Downtown Heliport, MHTN	120	C3
Teterboro, TETB	6501	A5
W 30th Street Heliport, MHTN	115	C2
Westchester County, RYEB	6051	B4

Beaches, Harbors & Water Rec

FEATURE NAME Address City ZIP Code	MAP#	GRID
20th Street Pier, BKLN	6922	B3
21st Street Pier, BKLN	6922	B3
23rd Street Pier, BKLN	6922	B3
29th Street Pier, BKLN	6922	B3
30th Street Pier, BKLN	6922	A4
31st Street Pier, BKLN	6922	A4
33rd Street Pier, BKLN	6922	A4
35th Street Pier, BKLN	6922	A4
36th Street Pier, BKLN	6922	A4
39th Street Pier, BKLN	6922	A4
57th Street Pier, BKLN	6921	E5
79th Street Boat Basin, MHTN	108	C7
Ann's Harbor Inn Marina, BRNX	6506	D5
Apache Yacht Club, ISPK	7029	C6
Atlantic Beach, HmpT	7028	B7
Atlantis Marina & Yacht Club, STNL	7117	C6
Atlas Yacht Club, BAYN	6919	E5
Bailey's Marina, HmpT	7029	D2
Bay End Marine, BKLN	7024	B3
Bay Park Yacht Harbor, HmpT	7029	C2
Bayside Marina, QENS	6722	B1
Bergen Beach, BKLN	7024	D4
Bergen Beach Yacht Club, BKLN	7024	B4
Brewer Capri Marina, MHVN	6508	B7
Brewer Post Road Boat Yard Marina, MRNK	6283	A6
Brighton Beach, BKLN	7121	C2
Canarsie Beach, BKLN	7024	E1
Cape Liberty Cruise Port, BAYN	6920	E3
Captains Marina, STNL	7117	C6
Castaways Yacht Club, NRCH	6396	A6
City Marina, ELIZ	6918	C6
Cliffside Marina, WbgT	7115	A5
Colony Marina, NHmT	6618	C2
Coney Island Beach, BKLN	7120	D2
Crow's Nest Marina, HmpT	6929	D7
East Atlantic Town Beach, HmpT	7028	C7
Edgewater Marina, EDGW	6611	E2
Empire Point Marina, HmpT	7029	E3
Evers Seaplace Base & Marina, BRNX	6506	B6
Fane Court Marina, BKLN	7023	E6
Gateway Marina, BKLN	7024	C7
Greenwich Bay Marina, GrwT	6170	C6
Harry Tappen Boat Basin, SCLF	6618	D1
Haven Marina, MHVN	6617	C1
Hazard Beach, FTLE	103	C1
Hewlett Point Yacht Club, HmpT	7029	A1
Hicks Beach, LWRN	7028	E6
Imperial Yacht Club, NRCH	6396	A7
Jude Thaddeus Glen Cove Marina, GLCV	6509	E5
Katsacos Marina, GrwT	6170	C4
Knickerbocker Yacht Club, NHmT	6617	C2
Liberty Harbor Marina, JSYC	6820	C4
Liberty Landing Marina, JSYC	6820	C4
Lil Cricket Marina, QENS	6925	E5
Lincoln Harbor Yacht Club, WhkT	6716	E4
Manhasset Bay Marina, MHVN	6617	C1
Manhattan Beach, BKLN	7121	D1
Mansion Marina, STNL	7117	C6
Marina Ebb Tide, QENS	7026	B6
Marine Basin Marina, BKLN	7022	C7
McMichael Rushmore Yard Marina, MRNK	6283	A7
Metro Marine Sales & Service Marina, BRNX	6505	D7
Midway Boat Club, QENS	6720	C1
Mill River Marine, ERKY	6929	C7
Neptune Boat Club, NRCH	6396	A7
Newport Marina, JSYC	6820	D2
New York City Convention Pier, MHTN	111	E5
Nicholl's Great Kills Park Marina, STNL	7117	D6
Nichols Yacht Yard Marina, MRNK	6282	E7
North Shore Yacht Club, MHVN	6508	B7
Oakland Beach, RYE	6284	A5
Orchard Beach, BRNX	6506	D3
Oriental Beach, BKLN	7121	E1
Parkway Fishing Center Marina, BKLN	7023	E7
Pier 1, BKLN	6921	D6
Pier 1, MHTN	120	E3
Pier 1A, BKLN	6921	D6
Pier 2, BKLN	6921	D6
Pier 2, MHTN	120	E3
Pier 3, BKLN	6921	D6
Pier 3, MHTN	120	D4
Pier 4, BKLN	6921	E6
Pier 4, MHTN	120	D4
Pier 5, BKLN	6921	E4
Pier 5, MHTN	120	D5
Pier 6, BKLN	6922	A4
Pier 6, MHTN	120	C3
Pier 7, BKLN	6922	A4
Pier 7, MHTN	120	D5
Pier 8, MHTN	120	C6
Pier 9A, MHTN	120	C6
Pier 9B, MHTN	120	C7
Pier 10, BKLN	120	C7
Pier 11, MHTN	120	C3
Pier 12, BKLN	6922	A1
Pier 13, MHTN	120	D2
Pier 14, MHTN	120	D2
Pier 15, MHTN	120	D2
Pier 16, MHTN	120	D2
Pier 26, MHTN	118	A4
Pier 35, MHTN	121	B1
Pier 39, BKLN	6921	E1
Pier 40, BKLN	6921	E1
Pier 40, MHTN	118	A2
Pier 41, BKLN	6921	E2
Pier 43, MHTN	121	C1
Pier 45, MHTN	118	A1
Pier 46, MHTN	118	B1
Pier 51, MHTN	115	B7
Pier 52, MHTN	115	B6
Pier 54, MHTN	115	B6
Pier 57, MHTN	115	B5
Pier 59, MHTN	115	B5
Pier 60, MHTN	115	B4
Pier 61, MHTN	115	B4
Pier 62, MHTN	115	B4
Pier 64, MHTN	115	B3
Pier 66, MHTN	115	B3
Pier 70, MHTN	119	E1
Pier 76, MHTN	115	C1
Pier 78, MHTN	115	C1
Pier 79, MHTN	115	D1
Pier 81, MHTN	111	C7
Pier 83, MHTN	111	D7
Pier 84, MHTN	111	D6
Pier 86, MHTN	111	D6
Pier 88, MHTN	111	D6
Pier 90, MHTN	111	D5
Pier 92, MHTN	111	D5
Pier 94, MHTN	111	E5
Pier 95, MHTN	111	E5
Pier 96, MHTN	111	E5
Pier 97, MHTN	111	E4
Pier 98, MHTN	111	E4
Pier 99, MHTN	112	A4
Pier A, BKLN	6922	A2
Pier A, MHTN	120	A2
Pier B, BKLN	6922	A2
Pier B, JSYC	6920	E2
Pier B, MHTN	112	A3
Pier C, JSYC	6920	E2
Pier D, JSYC	6920	D2
Pier D, MHTN	112	A3
Pier E, MHTN	112	A3
Pier F, MHTN	112	A3
Pier G, MHTN	112	A3
Pier I, MHTN	112	A2
Pilgrim Yacht Club, BKLN	7023	E7
Plaza Marina, QENS	6925	D4
Plumb Beach, BKLN	7024	A7
Polychron Marina, NRCH	6396	B4
Port Atlantic Marina, STNL	7206	A3
Port Sheepshead Yacht Club, BKLN	7023	D7
Rockaway Beach, QENS	7026	B7
Ross Beach, EGLC	6503	B4
Rudy's Tackle Barn Marina, GrwT	6170	C6
Rye Beach, RYE	6284	A4
Saltaire Marina, HmpT	6929	C7
Sandy's Marina, STNL	7207	A3
Sea Travelers Marina, BKLN	7024	B5
Shongut Marine, RYE	6283	E5
Skips Marina, HmpT	6929	C7
Skyline Cove Marina, QENS	6720	C1
Staten Island Marina, STNL	6919	E7
Stella Maris Fishing Station Marina, BKLN	7023	C7
Stelter Boats & Motors Marina, BRNX	6506	D5
Sunset Marina, QENS	7026	A4
Tamaqua Marina, BKLN	7023	D6
Tide Mill Yacht Basin, RYE	6284	B2
Tom's Point Marina, MHVN	6617	C1
Tottenville Marina, STNL	7206	A3
Venice Marina, BKLN	7023	E7
Von Dohlin Marina, EDGW	103	A7
W & W Marina, MHVN	6508	B7
Waterview Marine, HmpT	6929	C7
West Harbor Yacht Service Marina, NRCH	6395	E7
World's Fair Marina, QENS	6720	C4
Wright Island Marina, NRCH	6395	E7

Buildings

FEATURE NAME Address City ZIP Code	MAP#	GRID
53rd Street at Third Avenue, 885 3rd Av, MHTN, 10022	117	A1
ABC Building, 77 W 66th St, MHTN, 10023	112	D4
American Geographical Society Building, 120 Wall St - MHTN, 10005	120	C2
American Radiator Building, 40 Avenue of the Americas - MHTN, 10018	116	C3
CBS Building, 51 W 52nd St, MHTN, 10019	112	D7
Century Building, 33 E 17th St, MHTN, 10003	116	B7
Chanin Building, 122 E 42nd St, MHTN, 10017	116	D3
Chrysler Building, 405 Lexington Av, MHTN, 10017	116	E3
City Spire Building, 156 W 56th St, MHTN, 10019	112	D7
College Point Industrial Park, QENS, 11354	6720	D2
Consolidated Edison Power Plant, QENS, 11105	6719	B1
Criminal Courts Building, 100 Centre St, MHTN, 10013	118	D6
Daily News Building, 220 E 42nd St, MHTN, 10017	116	E3
Empire State Building, 350 5th Av, MHTN, 10001	116	C4
Flatiron Building, 175 5th Av, MHTN, 10010	116	B6
GE Building, 30 W 50th St, MHTN, 10020	116	D1
General Foods Corporate Offices, Bowman Av, RYEB - 10573	6169	E5
Grace Building, 41 Avenue of the Americas, MHTN, 10036	116	C2
Grand Central Station, 109 E 42nd St, MHTN, 10017	116	D2
Haughwout Building, 488 Broadway, MHTN, 10012	118	E4
Industrial Park at Elizabeth, ELIZ, 07201	6918	E2
International Building, 5th Av, MHTN, 10020	116	D1
Liberty Industrial Park, JSYC, 07305	6820	A5
Linden Oil, LNDN, 07036	6917	D7
Little Singer Building, 561 Broadway, MHTN, 10012	118	E4
Metlife Building, 72 E 45th St, MHTN, 10017	116	D2
Metropolitan Life Insurance Tower, 1 Madison Av - MHTN, 10010	116	B6
Municipal Building, 1 Centre St, MHTN, 10007	118	D7
National Newark Building, The, 744 Broad St, NWRK - 07102	6713	D7
Navy Yard Industrial Park, BKLN, 11201	121	D3
New Era Building, 495 Broadway, MHTN, 10012	118	E4
New York Stock Exchange, 11 Wall St, MHTN, 10005	120	B1
Pennsylvania Station-New York, 3 W 31st St, MHTN - 10001	116	A3
Rockefeller Center, W 49th St, MHTN, 10020	116	C1
Roslyn Clock Tower, 1 Main St, RSLN, 11576	6618	D5
Seagram Building, 375 Park Av, MHTN, 10022	116	E1
Singer Building, 149 Liberty St, MHTN, 10006	120	B1
Socony-Mobil Building, 150 E 42nd St, MHTN, 10017	116	D3
Solow Building, 9 W 57th St, MHTN, 10019	112	E7
Theresa Towers, 2090 7th Av, MHTN, 10027	109	E1
Toy Center Building, 200 5th Av, MHTN, 10010	116	A6
Transportation Building, 255 Broadway, MHTN, 10007	118	C6
Universal Pictures Building, 445 Park Av, MHTN, 10022	113	A7
Wang Building, 780 3rd Av, MHTN, 10017	116	E2
Western Union Building, 60 Hudson St, MHTN, 10013	118	B5
Woodridge Industrial Park, WRDG, 07075	6500	C4
Woolworth Building, 233 Broadway, MHTN, 10007	118	C7

Buildings - Governmental

FEATURE NAME Address City ZIP Code	MAP#	GRID
Alpine Borough Hall, 100 Church St, ALPN, 07620	6278	E6
Ardsley Village Hall, 507 Ashford Av, ARDY, 10502	6166	D4
Arthur Kill Correctional Facility, 2911 Arthur Kill Rd - STNL, 10309	7115	C5
Atlantic Beach Village Court, 65 The Plz, ATLB, 11509	7027	E7
Atlantic Beach Village Hall, 65 The Plz, ATLB, 11509	7027	E7
Baxter Estates Village Hall, 2 Harbor Rd, BXTE, 11050	6617	D1
Bayonne City Hall, 630 Avenue C, BAYN, 07002	6919	E3
Bayonne Municipal Court, 630 Avenue C, BAYN, 07002	6919	E3
Bayview Correctional Facility, 550 W 20th St, MHTN - 10011	115	C4
Bellerose Village Court, 50 Superior Rd, FLPK, 11001	6827	B2
Bellerose Village Hall, 50 Superior Rd, FLPK, 11001	6827	B2
Bergen County Administration Building, Court St, HKSK - 07601	6501	C2
Bergen County Courthouse, 10 Main St, HKSK, 07601	6501	C2
Bergen County Jail, 160 River St, HKSK, 07601	6501	C1
Bergen County Municipal Court, 375 Larch Av, BGTA - 07603	6501	D2
Bergen County Municipal Court, 500 Madison St, CARL - 07072	6500	C7
Bergen County Municipal Court, 525 Palisade Av, CLFP - 07010	6611	D3
Bergen County Municipal Court, 295 Closter Dock Rd - CLST, 07624	6278	B3
Bergen County Municipal Court, 67 Union Av, CRSK - 07626	6278	B7
Bergen County Municipal Court, 118 Serpentine Rd - DMRT, 07627	6278	A5
Bergen County Municipal Court, 916 River Rd, EDGW - 07020	6611	E2
Bergen County Municipal Court, 10 Kahn Ter, EGLC - 07632	6503	C2
Bergen County Municipal Court, 1 Everett Pl, ERTH - 07073	6609	B1
Bergen County Municipal Court, 59 Anderson Av, FRVW - 07022	6611	B4
Bergen County Municipal Court, 309 Main St, FTLE - 07024	6502	E5
Bergen County Municipal Court, 111 Outwater Ln, GRFD - 07026	6500	A1
Bergen County Municipal Court, 65 Central Av, HKSK - 07601	6501	C1
Bergen County Municipal Court, 320 Boulevard, HSBH - 07604	6500	E4
Bergen County Municipal Court, 312 Broad Av, LEON - 07605	6502	D4
Bergen County Municipal Court, 215 Liberty St, LFRY - 07643	6501	C6
Bergen County Municipal Court, 1 Memorial Dr, LODI - 07644	6500	D2
Bergen County Municipal Court, 70 Moonachie Rd - MNCH, 07074	6501	C7
Bergen County Municipal Court, 455 Broadway, NRWD - 07648	6164	C7
Bergen County Municipal Court, 116 Paris Av, NVLE - 07647	6164	B5
Bergen County Municipal Court, 275 Broad Av, PALP - 07650	6502	C6
Bergen County Municipal Court, 26 Rockleigh Rd, RCKL - 07647	6164	E6
Bergen County Municipal Court, 234 Main St, RDFP - 07660	6501	E4
Bergen County Municipal Court, 604 Broad Av N, RDGF - 07657	6611	B1
Bergen County Municipal Court, 176 Park Av, RTFD - 07070	6609	A2
Bergen County Municipal Court, 227 Phillips Av, SHkT - 07606	6501	C4
Bergen County Municipal Court, 100 Riveredge Rd, TFLY - 07670	6392	A2
Bogota Borough Hall, 375 Larch Av, BGTA, 07603	6501	D2
Bronx Borough Hall, 851 Grand Concourse, BRNX, 10451	6613	A2
Bronx County Building, 851 Grand Concourse, BRNX - 10451	107	E3
Bronx County Civil Court, 851 Grand Concourse, BRNX - 10451	6613	A2
Bronx County Criminal Court, 215 E 161st St, BRNX - 10451	6613	A2
Bronx County Family Court, 900 Sheridan Av, BRNX - 10451	6613	A2
Bronx County Supreme Court, 851 Grand Concourse - BRNX, 10451	107	E3
Bronxville Village Hall, 200 Pondfield Rd, BRXV, 10708	6394	E1
Brooklyn Borough Hall, 209 Joralemon St, BKLN, 11201	121	B5
Brooklyn Civic Center, BKLN, 11201	121	B5
Brooklyn Social Security Administration - 2250 Nostrand Av, BKLN, 11210	7023	C1
Burgen County Superior Court, 10 Main St, HKSK - 07601	6501	C2
Carlstadt Borough Hall, 500 Madison St, CARL, 07072	6500	B7
Carteret Borough Hall, 61 Cooke Av, CART, 07008	7115	D1
Carteret Municipal Court, 230 Roosevelt Av, CART - 07008	7115	E2
Cedarhurst Village Court, 200 Cedarhurst Av, CDHT - 11516	7028	A2
Cedarhurst Village Hall, 200 Cedarhurst Av, CDHT, 11516	7028	A2
City of New York Department of Health, 125 Worth St - MHTN, 10013	118	D6
Cliffside Park Borough Hall, 525 Palisade Av, CLFP - 07010	6611	D3
Closter Borough Hall, 295 Closter Dock Rd, CLST, 07624	6278	B3
Cresskill Borough Hall, 67 Union Av, CRSK, 07626	6278	B7
Demarest Borough Hall, 118 Serpentine Rd, DMRT - 07627	6278	A5
Department of Health, 51 Stuyvesant Pl, STNL, 10301	6920	D6
Department of Transportation, 40 Worth St, MHTN - 10013	118	C6
Department of State, 123 William St, MHTN, 10038	120	C1
Dobbs Ferry Village Hall, 112 Main St, DBSF, 10522	6166	A4
Eastchester Town Hall, 40 Mill Rd, EchT, 10709	6281	B5
East Newark Borough Hall, 34 Sherman Av, ENWK - 07029	6714	A5
East Orange City Hall, 44 City Hall Plz, EORG, 07017	6712	E4
East Orange Social Security Administration - 15 Halsted St, EORG, 07018	6712	E3
East Rockaway Village Hall, 376 Atlantic Av, ERKY - 11518	6929	C6
East Rutherford Borough Hall, 1 Everett Pl, ERTH, 07073	6609	B1
East Williston Village Hall, 2 Prospect St, EWLS, 11596	6724	E4
Edgecombe Correctional Facility, 611 Edgecombe Av - MHTN, 10032	107	B1
Edgewater Borough Hall, 916 River Rd, EDGW, 07020	6611	E2
Elizabeth City Hall, 50 W Winfield Scott Plz, ELIZ, 07201	6917	E3
Elizabeth Social Security Administration, 547 Morris Av - ELIZ, 07208	6917	D2
Elmsford Village Hall, 15 S Stone Av, EMFD, 10523	6049	A6
Englewood Cliffs Borough Hall, 482 Kahn Ter, EGLC - 07632	6503	C2
Essex County Court Building - 465 Dr Martin Luther King Jr Bl, NWRK, 07103	6713	D7
Essex County Municipal Court, 593 Lincoln Av, COrT - 07050	6712	B4
Essex County Municipal Court, 221 Freeway Dr E, EORG - 07018	6712	E4
Essex County Municipal Court, 66 Main St, WOrT, 07052	6712	B1
Fairview Borough Hall, 59 Anderson Av, FRVW, 07022	6611	C4
Federal Office Building, 100 Church St, MHTN, 10007	118	B6
Flatbush Town Hall, 35 Snyder Av, BKLN, 11226	6923	B5
Floral Park Village Hall, 1 Floral Blvd, FLPK, 11001	6827	C2
Flower Hill Village Hall, 1 Bonnie Heights Rd, FLHL, 11030	6618	A4
Flushing Social Security Administration - 136-65 Congressman Rosenthal Pl, QENS, 11354	6721	A3
Flushing Town Hall, 137-35 Northern Blvd, QENS, 11354	6720	E4

Buildings - Governmental

New York City/5 Borough Points of Interest Index

Cemeteries

FEATURE NAME Address City ZIP Code	MAP#	GRID
Fort Lee Borough Hall, 309 Main St, FTLE, 07024	6502	E5
Fulton Correctional Facility, 1511 Fulton Av, BRNX - 10457	105	E7
Garfield City Hall, 111 Outwater Ln, GRFD, 07026	6500	A1
Great Neck Estates Village Court, 4 Gateway Dr, GTNE - 11021	6617	A7
Great Neck Estates Village Hall, 4 Gateway Dr, GTNE - 11021	6617	A7
Great Neck Plaza Village Hall, 2 Gussack Plz, GTPZ - 11021	6617	A7
Great Neck Village Court, 61 Baker Hill Rd, GTNK, 11023	6617	A5
Great Neck Village Hall, 61 Baker Hill Rd, GTNK, 11023	6617	A5
Greenburgh Town Hall, 177 Hillside Av, GrbT, 10603	6049	D6
Guttenberg Borough Hall, 6808 Park Av, GTBG, 07093	6611	B7
Hackensack City Hall, 65 Central Av, HKSK, 07601	6501	C1
Hackensack Social Security Administration, 22 Sussex St - HKSK, 07601	6501	C2
Harlem Community Justice Center, 170 E 21st St, MHTN - 10010	116	C7
Harrison Town Hall, 318 Harrison Av, HRSN, 07029	6714	A6
Harrison Town Hall, 1 Heineman Pl, HRSN, 10528	6283	C3
Hasbrouck Heights Borough Court, 248 Hamilton Av - HSBH, 07604	6500	D4
Hasbrouck Heights Borough Hall, 320 Boulevard, HSBH - 07604	6500	E4
Hastings-on-Hudson City Hall, 7 Maple Av, HAOH - 10706	6165	E7
Hewlett Bay Park Village Hall, 30 Piermont Av, HBPK - 11557	6928	D7
Hewlett Harbor Village Hall, 449 Pepperidge Rd, HWTH - 11557	7029	A1
Hewlett Neck Village Hall, 30 Piermont Av, HBPK, 11557	6928	D7
Hillside Twp Hall, 1409 Liberty Av, HlsT, 07205	6816	C5
Hoboken City Hall, 94 Washington St, HBKN, 07030	6716	D7
Hoboken Municipal Court, 94 Washington St, HBKN - 07030	6716	D7
Hudson County Courthouse, 583 Newark Av, JSYC - 07306	6820	A1
Hudson Regional Health Commission, 595 County Av - SECS, 07094	6610	B7
Irvington Social Security Administration, 686 Nye Av - IrvT, 07111	6816	B2
Irvington Town Hall, 85 Main St, IRVN, 10533	6166	A1
Irvington Twp Hall, 1 Civic Sq, IrvT, 07111	6816	C2
Island Park Village Hall, 127 Long Beach Rd, ISPK, 11558	7029	D5
Jersey City Hall, 280 Grove St, JSYC, 07302	6820	C3
Jersey City Municipal Court, 769 Montgomery St, JSYC - 07306	6819	E2
Jersey City Social Security Administration - 3000 John F Kennedy Blvd, JSYC, 07306	6716	A7
Kearny Municipal Court, 404 Kearny Av, KRNY, 07032	6714	B4
Kearny Town Hall, 402 Kearny Av, KRNY, 07032	6714	B3
Kensington Village Hall, 2 Nassau Dr, KENS, 11021	6617	A7
Kings County Appellate Division Court, 45 Monroe Pl - BKLN, 11201	121	A4
Kings County Civil Court, 141 Livingston St, BKLN, 11201	121	B6
Kings County Criminal Court, 120 Schermerhorn St, BKLN - 11201	121	B6
Kings County Family Court, 330 Brooklyn Bridge Blvd - BKLN, 11201	121	B5
Kings County Supreme Court, 360 Montague St, BKLN - 11201	121	B5
Kings County Surrogates Court, 2 Johnson Av, BKLN - 11211	6822	C5
Kings Point Village Court, 32 Sunset Rd, KNGP, 11024	6616	C4
Kings Point Village Hall, 32 Sunset Rd, KNGP, 11024	6616	C3
Lake Success Village Court, 15 Vanderbilt Dr, NHmT - 11020	6723	B3
Lake Success Village Hall, 318 Lakeville Rd, LKSU, 11020	6723	C3
Larchmont Village Hall, 120 Larchmont Av, LRMT, 10538	6396	D2
Lawrence Village Court, 196 Central Av, LWRN, 11559	7027	E3
Lawrence Village Hall, 196 Central Av, LWRN, 11559	7027	E3
Leonia Borough Hall, 312 Broad Av, LEON, 07605	6502	D4
Lincoln Correctional Facility, 31-33 Central Pk N, MHTN - 10026	109	E4
Linden City Hall, 301 N Wood Av, LNDN, 07036	7017	A1
Little Ferry Borough Hall, 215 Liberty St, LFRY, 07643	6501	C6
Lodi Borough Hall, 1 Memorial Dr, LODI, 07644	6500	D2
Long Beach City Court, 1 W Chester St, LBCH, 11561	7029	C6
Long Beach City Hall, 1 W Chester St, LBCH, 11561	7029	C7
Long Beach Social Security Administration, 25 E Park Av - LBCH, 11561	7029	C7
Lynbrook Village Court, 1 Columbus Dr, LNBK, 11563	6929	B4
Lynbrook Village Hall, 1 Columbus Dr, LNBK, 11563	6929	B4
Malverne Village Hall, 99 Church St, MLVN, 11565	6929	B2
Mamaroneck Town Hall, 740 W Boston Post Rd, MRNK - 10543	6282	E7
Mamaroneck Village Court, 169 Mt Pleasant Av, MRNK - 10543	6282	E6
Mamaroneck Village Hall, 123 Mamaroneck Av, MRNK - 10543	6282	E6
Manhattan Borough Hall, 281 Broadway, MHTN, 10007	118	C6
Manhattan Civic Center, MHTN, 10007	118	D6
Manorhaven Village Hall, 33 Manorhaven Blvd, MHVN - 11050	6508	C7
Mineola Social Security Administration, 211 Station Rd - MNLA, 11501	6724	E7
Mineola Village Court, 155 Washington Av, MNLA, 11501	6724	E6
Mineola Village Hall, 155 Washington Av, MNLA, 11501	6724	E6
Moonachie Borough Hall, 70 Moonachie Rd, MNCH - 07074	6501	C7
Mt Vernon City Court, 2 Roosevelt Sq E, MTVN, 10550	6394	D4
Mt Vernon City Hall, 1 Roosevelt Sq E, MTVN, 10550	6394	D4
Municipal Court of Hackensack, 215 State St, HKSK - 07601	6501	C1
Munsey Park Village Hall, 1777 Northern Blvd, MNPK - 11030	6618	A6
Nassau County Courthouse, 1 West St, GDNC, 11501	6724	E7
Newark City Hall, 970 Broad St, NWRK, 07102	6817	D1
Newark Social Security Administration, 970 Broad St - NWRK, 07102	6817	D1
New Hyde Park Village Hall, 1420 Jericho Tpk, NHPK - 11040	6828	A1
New Jersey Superior Court, 10 Main St, HKSK, 07601	6501	C2
New Rochelle City Court, 475 North Av, NRCH, 10801	6395	E3
New Rochelle City Hall, 515 North Av, NRCH, 10801	6395	E3
New Rochelle Social Security Administration - 85 Harrison St, NRCH, 10801	6396	A4
New York City Department of Correction, 60 Hudson St - MHTN, 10013	118	C5
New York City Hall, 36 Chambers St, MHTN, 10007	118	C7
New York County Appellate Division Court - 27 Madison Av, MHTN, 10010	116	B6
New York County Civil & Municipal Court, 111 Centre St - MHTN, 10013	118	D6
New York County Civil Supreme Court, 60 Centre St - MHTN, 10007	118	D6
New York County Criminal Supreme Court, 100 Centre St - MHTN, 10013	118	D6
New York County Family Court, 60 Lafayette St, MHTN - 10013	118	D6

FEATURE NAME Address City ZIP Code	MAP#	GRID
New York County Small Claims Court, 111 Centre St - MHTN, 10013	118	D6
New York County Surrogates Court, 31 Chambers St - MHTN, 10007	118	D6
New York State Supreme Court, 45 Monroe Pl, BKLN - 11201	121	A4
New York State Supreme Court, 851 Grand Concourse - BRNX, 10451	107	E3
New York State Supreme Court, 60 Centre St, MHTN - 10007	118	D6
North Bergen Municipal Court, 4233 Kennedy Blvd W - NBgT, 07047	6716	E1
North Bergen Twp Hall, 4233 Kennedy Blvd W, NBgT - 07047	6716	E1
North Hempstead Town Hall, 220 Plandome Rd, NHmT - 11030	6617	D6
North Hills Village Hall, 1 Shelter Rock Rd, NHLS, 11576	6724	B3
Northvale Borough Hall, 116 Paris Av, NVLE, 07647	6164	C5
Norwood Borough Hall, 455 Broadway, NRWD, 07648	6164	C7
Orange Twp Hall, 29 N Day St, COrT, 07050	6712	C2
Palisades Park Borough Hall, 275 Broad Av, PALP, 07650	6502	C6
Pelham Manor Village Hall, 4 Penfield Pl, PLMM, 10803	6395	C7
Pelham Town Hall, 34 5th Av, PLHM, 10803	6395	B4
Pelham Village Hall, 195 Sparks Av, PLHM, 10803	6395	B4
Perth Amboy City Hall, 260 Market St, PTHA, 08861	7205	E4
Perth Amboy Municipal Court, 56 Fayette St, PTHA - 08861	7205	E4
Plandome Manor Village Hall, 1526 N Plandome Rd - PLNM, 11030	6617	D4
Plandome Village Hall, 65 South Dr, PLDM, 11030	6617	D4
Port Chester Village Hall, 222 Grace Church St, PTCH - 10573	6170	B7
Port Washington North Village Hall, 71 Old Shore Rd - PTWN, 11050	6508	D7
Queensboro Correctional Facility, 47-04 Van Dam St - QENS, 11101	6718	D6
Queens Borough Hall, 120-55 Queens Blvd, QENS, 11415	6824	E3
Queens County Civil Court, 25-10 Court Sq, QENS, 11101	6718	C6
Queens County Civil Court, 120-55 Queens Blvd, QENS - 11415	6824	E3
Queens County Civil Court, 89-17 Sutphin Blvd, QENS - 11435	6825	C5
Queens County Civil Term, 88-11 Sutphin Blvd, QENS - 11435	6825	C5
Queens County Criminal Court, 125-01 Queens Blvd - QENS, 11415	6825	A4
Queens County Criminal Court, 88-11 Sutphin Blvd - QENS, 11435	6825	C5
Queens County Family Court, 151-20 Jamaica Av, QENS - 11433	6825	C5
Queens County Surrogates Court, 88-11 Sutphin Blvd - QENS, 11435	6825	C5
Richmond County Civil Court, 927 Castleton Av, STNL - 10310	6920	A7
Richmond County Courthouse, 18 Richmond Ter, STNL - 10301	6920	E6
Richmond County Criminal Court, 67 Targee St, STNL - 10304	7020	D2
Richmond County Family Court, 100 Richmond Ter, STNL - 10301	6920	D6
Richmond County Supreme Court, 18 Richmond Ter - STNL, 10301	6920	D6
Richmond County Surrogates Court, 18 Richmond Ter - STNL, 10301	6920	D6
Ridgefield Borough Hall, 604 Broad Av N, RDGF, 07657	6611	B1
Ridgefield Park Village Hall, 234 Main St, RDFP, 07660	6501	E6
Rockleigh Borough Hall, 26 Rockleigh Rd, RCKL, 07647	6164	E6
Rockville Centre Village Court, 1 College Pl, RKVC - 11570	6929	E4
Rockville Centre Village Hall, 1 College Pl, RKVC, 11570	6929	E4
Roslyn Estates Village Hall, 25 The Tulips, ROSE, 11576	6618	C7
Roslyn Village Hall, 1200 Old Northern Blvd, RSLN, 11576	6618	D5
Russell Gardens Village Hall, 6 Tain Dr, RSLG, 11021	6723	A2
Rutherford Borough Hall, 176 Park Av, RTFD, 07070	6609	A2
Rye Brook Village Hall, 938 King St, RYEB, 10573	6170	A1
Rye City Hall, 1051 Boston Post Rd, RYE, 10580	6283	E2
Rye Town Hall, 10 S Pearl St, PTCH, 10573	6170	B6
Saddle Rock Village Hall, 18 Masefield Wy, SDRK, 11023	6616	D6
Sands Point Village Hall, 26 Tibbits Ln, SNPT, 11050	6508	B5
Scarsdale Village Hall, 1001 White Plains Rd, SCDL - 10583	6281	D1
Sea Cliff Village Hall, 300 Sea Cliff Av, SCLF, 11579	6509	D6
Secaucus Municipal Court, 1203 Paterson Plank Rd, SECS - 07094	6610	B7
Secaucus Town Hall, 1203 Paterson Plank Rd, SECS, 07094	6610	B7
Sleepy Hollow City Hall, 28 Beekman Av, SYHW, 10591	6048	B1
South Amboy City Hall, 140 Broadway N, SAMB, 08879	7205	C7
South Amboy Municipal Court, 140 Broadway N, SAMB - 08879	7205	C7
South Floral Park Village Hall, 383 Roquette Av, SFPK - 11001	6827	D3
South Hackensack Twp Hall, 227 Phillips Av, SHkT - 07606	6501	C4
Staten Island Borough Hall, 10 Richmond Ter, STNL - 10301	6920	E6
Staten Island Civic Center, STNL, 10301	6920	D6
Stewart Manor Village Hall, 120 Covert Av, STMN - 11530	6827	E3
Superior Court, 595 Newark Av, JSYC, 07306	6820	A1
Superior Court, 877 Broad St, NWRK, 07102	6817	D1
Superior Courthouse, 10 Main St, HKSK, 07601	6501	C2
Superior Court of New Jersey, 50 W Market St, NWRK - 07103	6713	D7
Supreme Court New York State, 360 Brooklyn Bridge Blvd - BKLN, 11201	121	B5
Tarrytown Village Hall, 21 Wildey St, TYTN, 10591	6048	B2
Teaneck Municipal Court, 818 Teaneck Rd, TnkT, 07666	6502	B1
Teaneck Twp Hall, 818 Teaneck Rd, TnkT, 07666	6502	B1
Tenafly Borough Hall, 100 Riveredge Rd, TFLY, 07670	6392	A2
Teterboro Borough Hall, TETB, 07608	6501	B4
Thomaston Village Court, 100 E Shore Rd, THSN, 11021	6617	C7
Thomaston Village Hall, 100 E Shore Rd, THSN, 11021	6617	C7
Tuckahoe Village Hall, 65 Main St, TCKA, 10707	6281	A6
Tweed Courthouse, 52 Chambers St, MHTN, 10007	118	C7
Unified Court System New York State - 283 Brooklyn Bridge Blvd, BKLN, 11201	121	B5
Unified Court System New York State, 25 Beaver St - MHTN, 10004	120	B2
Union City Hall, 3715 Palisade Av, UNCT, 07087	6716	E2
Union City Municipal Court, 3715 Palisade Av, UNCT - 07087	6716	E2
Union County Administration Building - 10 Elizabethtown Plz, ELIZ, 07201	6917	E3
Union County Courthouse, 2 Broad St, ELIZ, 07201	6917	E4
United Nations Headquarters, 760 United Nations Plz - MHTN, 10017	117	A4
United State Courthouse Court of Appeals, 40 Centre St - MHTN, 10007	118	D7
United States Bankruptcy Court, 1 Bowling Grn, MHTN - 10004	120	B2
United States District Court, 225 Cadman Plz E, BKLN - 11201	121	B4

FEATURE NAME Address City ZIP Code	MAP#	GRID
United States District Court, 575 Middle Neck Rd, GTNK - 11023	6616	E5
United States Dist Ct Eastern New York Dist - 225 Cadman Plz E, BKLN, 11201	121	B4
United States District Courthouse, 500 Pearl St, MHTN - 10007	118	D6
United States Federal District Court, 225 Cadman Plz E - BKLN, 11201	121	B4
United States Federal District Court, 40 Centre St - MHTN, 10007	118	D6
United States Federal District Court, 50 Walnut St - NWRK, 07102	6817	D1
United States Federal District Court, 300 Quarropas St - WHPL, 10601	6168	A2
Valley Stream Village Hall, 123 S Central Av, VLYS - 11580	6928	C3
Wallington Municipal Court, 56 Union Blvd, WLTN - 07057	6500	A5
Weehawken Municipal Court, 400 Park Av, WhkT, 07086	6716	E3
Weehawken Twp Hall, 400 Park Av, WhkT, 07086	6716	E3
Westchester County City Court, 21 McCullough Pl, RYE - 10580	6284	A1
Westchester County City Court, 77 S Lexington Av, WHPL - 10601	6168	A2
Westchester County Civil Court, 100 S Broadway, YNKR - 10701	6393	C2
Westchester County Courthouse, 90 Beaufort Pl, NRCH - 10801	6395	E3
Westchester County Criminal Court, 200 Pondfield Rd - BRXV, 10708	6394	E1
Westchester County Criminal Court, 100 S Broadway - YNKR, 10701	6393	C1
Westchester County Department of Health - 145 Huguenot St, NRCH, 10801	6396	A4
Westchester County Family Court, 420 North Av, NRCH - 10801	6395	E3
Westchester County Family Court, 53 S Broadway, YNKR - 10701	6393	C1
Westchester County Justice Court, 505 Ashford Av - ARDY, 10502	6166	C4
Westchester County Justice Court, 40 Mill Rd, EchT - 10709	6281	B5
Westchester County Justice Court, 188 Tarrytown Rd - GrbT, 10607	6049	E7
Westchester County Justice Court, 85 Main St, IRVN - 10533	6048	A7
Westchester County Justice Court, 120 Larchmont Av - LRMT, 10538	6396	C2
Westchester County Justice Court, 10 S Pearl St, PTCH - 10573	6170	B6
Westchester County Justice Court, 1001 White Plains Rd - SCDL, 10583	6281	D1
Westchester County Justice Court, 21 Wildey St, TYTN - 10591	6048	B2
Westchester Co Michaelian Office Building - 148 Martine Av, WHPL, 10601	6168	B2
Westchester County Small Claims Court, 100 S Broadway - YNKR, 10701	6393	C2
Westchester County Supreme Court, 148 Martine Av - WHPL, 10601	6168	B2
Westchester County Surrogates Court, 111 Grove St - WHPL, 10601	6168	B2
West New York Municipal Court, 428 60th St, WNYK - 07093	6611	A7
West New York Town Hall, 428 60th St, WNYK, 07093	6611	A7
West Orange Twp Hall, 66 Main St, WOrT, 07052	6712	B2
White Plains City Hall, 255 Main St, WHPL, 10601	6168	B1
White Plains Social Security Administration - 297 Knollwood Rd, GrbT, 10607	6049	C7
Williston Park Village Court, 494 Willis Av, WLPK, 11596	6724	E4
Williston Park Village Hall, 494 Willis Av, WLPK, 11596	6724	E4
Woodbridge Twp Hall, 1 Main St, WbgT, 07095	7114	C4
Woodbridge Twp Municipal Court, 375 Berry St, WbgT - 07095	7114	D4
Wood-Ridge City Hall, 85 Humboldt St, WRDG, 07075	6500	C6
Woodsburgh Village Hall, 30 Piermont Av, HBPK, 11557	6928	D7
Yonkers City Hall, 20 S Broadway, YNKR, 10701	6393	C1
Yonkers Social Security Administration, 20 S Broadway - YNKR, 10701	6393	C1

Cemeteries

Ahawith Chesed Cem, QENS	6823	A4
All Saints Cem, KNGP	6616	E4
Alpine Cem, PTHA	7205	C2
Arlington Memorial Park, KRNY	6714	D2
Baron De Hirsch Cem, STNL	7019	A2
Bay Park Section Cem, JSYC	6819	C6
Bayside-Acacia Cem, QENS	6925	C1
Bayview Cem, JSYC	6819	C6
Beechwood Cem, NRCH	6395	C5
Beth David Cem, HmpT	6827	C6
Bethel Cem, STNL	7206	C3
B'nai Jeshurun Cem, ELIZ	6816	E7
Brookside Cem, EGLD	6392	A5
Calvary Cem, QENS	6822	E1
Calvary Cem, WbgT	7114	B7
Canarsie Cem, BKLN	6924	C7
Cemetery of the Resurrection, STNL	7206	E3
Clinton Cem, IrvT	6816	C2
Cloverleaf Cem, WbgT	7114	A2
Cypress Hills Cem, QENS	6823	E5
Cypress Hills National Cem, BKLN	6823	E7
Elmont Cem, HmpT	6827	C5
Evergreen Cem, HlsT	6816	E6
Evergreen Cem, QENS	6823	C7
Fairmount Cem, NWRK	6713	A6
Fairview Cem, FRVW	6611	B3
Fairview Cem, STNL	7019	D4
Ferncliff Cem, GrbT	6166	E2
Flower Hill Cem, NBgT	6610	E7
Flushing Cem, QENS	6721	D5
Frederick Douglass Memorial Park Cem, STNL	7117	C3
Gate of Heaven Cem, MtPT	6049	D1
Greenwood Cem, BKLN	6922	D5
Greenwood Union Cem, RYE	6283	D2
Grove Church Cem, NBgT	6716	E1
Hebrew Cem, NWRK	6713	A6
Hebrew Free Burial Association Cem, STNL	7117	C3
Hillside Cem, LynT	6609	A4
Hoboken Cem, NBgT	6610	E7
Hollywood Memorial Park, UnnT	6816	A4
Holy Cross Cem, BKLN	6923	D6
Holy Cross Cem, NARL	6714	D1
Holy Mt Cem, EchT	6281	C4
Holy Name Cem, JSYC	6819	D1
Holy Sepulchre Cem, NRCH	6395	D5
Holy Sepulchre Cem, NWRK	6712	E6
Hungarian Cem, QENS	6823	D6
Hungarian Cem, WbgT	7205	A1
Jersey City Cem, JSYC	6820	B2
Kensico Cem, MtPT	6049	D2

Cemeteries

New York City/5 Borough Points of Interest Index

Entertainment & Sports

FEATURE NAME Address City ZIP Code	MAP#	GRID
Knollwood Park Cem, QENS	6823	C7
Lake Cem, The, STNL	7019	B2
Linden Hill Cem, QENS	6823	B4
Linden Park Cem, LNDN	6917	B7
Lodi Cem, LODI	6500	C3
Loretto Cem, STNL	7206	E3
Lutheran Cem, QENS	6823	D3
Machpelah Cem, QENS	6823	D6
Macphelah Cem, NBgT	6610	E7
Madonna Cem, LEON	6502	D4
Maimonides Cem, BKLN	6824	A6
Maple Grove Cem, HKSK	6501	C4
Maple Grove Cem, QENS	6825	A4
Marine Cem, STNL	7020	B2
Montefiore Cem, QENS	6826	D7
Moravian Cem, STNL	7019	E7
Most Holy Trinity Cem, The, BKLN	6823	C7
Mt Calvary Cem, GrbT	6049	E5
Mt Calvary Cem, LNDN	7017	C1
Mt Carmel Cem, QENS	6823	E6
Mt Carmel Cem, TFLY	6392	A4
Mt Eden Cem, MtPT	6049	E1
Mt Hebron Cem, QENS	6720	E7
Mt Hope Cem, BKLN	6824	A6
Mt Hope Cem, GrbT	6166	C7
Mt Judah Cem, QENS	6823	D6
Mt Lebanon Cem, QENS	6824	A5
Mt Moriah Cem, FRVW	6611	B3
Mt Neboh Cem, QENS	6823	E6
Mt Olivet Cem, NWRK	6817	B7
Mt Olivet Cem, QENS	6823	C3
Mt Pleasant Cem, NWRK	6713	E4
Mt Siani Cemetary, ELIZ	6817	B7
Mt Zion Cem, QENS	6823	B1
Nassau Knolls Cem, NHmT	6618	A2
New Calvary Cem, QENS	6719	A7
New Union Field Cem, QENS	6823	D6
New York Bay Cem, JSYC	6819	C6
Oakland Cem, YNKR	6279	E7
Ocean View Cem, STNL	7117	C4
Oheb Sholom Cem, HlsT	6816	E6
Palisades Cem, NBgT	6716	D1
Pelham Cem, BRNX	6506	E6
Potters Field Cem, BRNX	6507	A5
Presbyterian Cem, WHPL	6168	B1
Riverside Cem, SdBT	6500	C1
Rockland Cem, OrgT	6164	E1
Rockville Cem, LNBK	6929	C4
Rosedale Cem, COrT	6712	D1
Rosedale Cem, LNDN	6917	B7
Rose Hill Cem, LNDN	7017	C2
Sailor's Snug Harbor Cem, STNL	6920	B7
St. James Cem, WbgT	7114	B7
St. Johns Cem, HmpT	6827	B7
St. Johns Cem, QENS	6824	A4
St. Joseph Cem, NRCH	6395	E6
St. Josephs Cem, YNKR	6280	A2
St. Marys Cem, EORG	6713	B3
St. Marys Cem, HmpT	7028	A3
St. Marys Cem, PTHA	7205	D1
St. Marys Cem, QENS	6721	C7
St. Marys Cem, SdBT	6500	C1
St. Marys Cem, STNL	7019	B1
St. Mary's Cem, RYEB	6170	A6
St. Mary's Cem, STNL	7020	D6
St. Michaels Cem, QENS	6719	C6
St. Michaels Cem, SHkT	6500	B4
St. Nicholas Cem, LODI	6500	C3
St. Paul's Cem, HmpT	6827	B6
St. Peters Cem, GRFD	6500	B3
St. Peters Cem, JSYC	6716	A7
St. Peters Cem, STNL	7020	A2
St. Raymond's Cem, BRNX	6614	E1
St. Stephen Cem, WbgT	7205	A2
Salem Fields Cem, BKLN	6823	E7
Seacord Cem, NRCH	6281	D7
Shearith Israel Cem, BKLN	6823	E7
Silver Lake Cem, STNL	7020	B2
Silver Mt Cem, STNL	7020	B2
Sleepy Hollow Cem, SYHW	6048	B1
South Center Fountain Cem, STNL	6919	E7
Tappan Cem, OrgT	6164	C3
Trinity Cem, HmpT	6928	C7
Trinity Cem, MHTN	107	A2
Ukrainian Cem, WbgT	7205	B1
Union Field Cem, QENS	6823	D6
United Hebrew Cem, STNL	7117	B3
Washington Cem, BKLN	7022	D2
Wavecrest Garden Cem, QENS	7027	C6
Weehawken Cem, NBgT	6716	D1
White Plains Rural Cem, WHPL	6050	A6
Woodland Cem, NWRK	6817	A2
Woodland Cem, STNL	7020	B2
Woodlawn Cem, BRNX	6394	A7

Colleges & Universities

FEATURE NAME Address City ZIP Code	MAP#	GRID
Adelphi University, 1 South Av, GDNC, 11530	6828	D2
Albert Einstein College of Medicine, 1300 Morris Park Av - BRNX, 10461	6505	D6
All Saints University America, 3333 Broadway, MHTN - 10031	106	D5
Bank Street College of Education, 610 W 112th St - MHTN, 10025	109	A2
Barnard College-Columbia University, 3009 Broadway - MHTN, 10027	109	A1
Berkeley College-Middlesex, 430 Rahway Av, WbgT - 07095	7114	D4
Berkeley College-Midtown Manhattan, 3 E 43rd St - MHTN, 10017	116	D2
Berkeley College-Newark, 536 Broad St, NWRK, 07102	6713	E6
Berkeley College-Westchester, 99 Church St, WHPL - 10601	6168	A1
Beth Hamedrash Shaarei Yosher Institute, 4102 16th Av - BKLN, 11218	6922	D7
Beth Hatalmud Rabbinical College, 2127 82nd St, BKLN - 11214	7022	C5
Boricua College-Manhattan, 3755 Broadway, MHTN - 10032	107	A2
Borough Manhattan Community College - 199 Chambers St, MHTN, 10013	118	B5
Bronx Community College, 2179 University Av, BRNX - 10453	105	C2
Brooklyn Law School, 250 Joralemon St, BKLN, 11201	121	A6
College of Mt St. Vincent, 6301 Riverdale Av, BRNX - 10471	6393	B4
College of New Rochelle, 29 Castle Pl, NRCH, 10805	6395	E6
College of Westchester, 325 Central Av, WHPL, 10606	6167	E1
Columbia University, 2960 Broadway, MHTN, 10027	109	B1
Concordia College, 171 White Plains Rd, BRXV, 10708	6281	A7
Cornell University, 525 E 68th St, MHTN, 10021	113	D6
CUNY-Baruch, 151 E 25th St, MHTN, 10010	116	C6
CUNY Bernard M Baruch College, 17 E 23rd St, MHTN - 10010	116	B6
CUNY-Brooklyn College, 2900 Bedford Av, BKLN, 11210	7023	B1
CUNY City College, 160 Convent Av, MHTN, 10031	106	E5
CUNY College of Staten Island, 2800 Victory Blvd, STNL - 10314	7019	A4
CUNY Graduate Center, 365 5th Av, MHTN, 10016	116	C4
CUNY Lehman College, Bedford Park Blvd W, BRNX - 10468	6504	D2
CUNY Medgar Evers College, 1650 Bedford Av, BKLN - 11225	6923	B3
CUNY School of Law, 65-21 Main St, QENS, 11367	6721	A7
Empire State College, 20 New York Av, BKLN, 11216	6923	C1
Essex County College-Newark, 303 University Av, NWRK - 07102	6713	D7
Eugene Lang College, 65 W 11th St, MHTN, 10011	118	E1
Fashion Institute of Technology, 227 W 27th St, MHTN - 10001	116	A4
Felician College-Lodi, 262 S Main St, LODI, 07644	6500	B3
Felician College-Rutherford, 223 Montross Av, RTFD - 07070	6609	A1
Fordham University-Lincoln Center, 113 W 60th St - MHTN, 10023	112	C5
Fordham University-Rose Hill, 441 E Fordham Rd, BRNX - 10458	6504	D4
Gamla College, 1213 Elm Av, BKLN, 11230	7023	B3
Globe Institute of Technology, 291 Broadway, MHTN - 10007	118	C6
Hebrew Union College, 1 W 4th St, MHTN, 10003	119	A2
Hostos Community College, 500 Grand Concourse, BRNX - 10451	107	E6
Hudson County Community College, 70 Sip Av, JSYC - 07306	6820	A1
Hunter College, 695 Park Av, MHTN, 10021	113	B5
Interboro Institute, 450 W 56th St, MHTN, 10019	112	B6
Iona College, 715 North Av, NRCH, 10801	6395	E2
John Jay College, 899 10th Av, MHTN, 10019	112	B5
Katharine Gibbs School-New York, 50 W 40th St, MHTN - 10018	116	C3
Kean University, 1000 Morris Av, UnnT, 07083	6917	C1
Kingsborough Community College, 2001 Oriental Blvd - BKLN, 11235	7121	D1
Laguardia Community College, 31-10 Thomson Av, QENS - 11101	6718	D6
Lehman College, 250 Bedford Park Blvd, BRNX, 10458	6504	D3
Long Island College-School of Nursing, 340 Court St - BKLN, 11231	6922	C1
Long Island University-Brooklyn, 1 Fleet St, BKLN - 11201	121	C6
Long Island University-School of Business, 1 Fleet St - BKLN, 11201	121	D6
Machzikei Hadath Rabbinical College, 5407 16th Av - BKLN, 11204	7022	D1
Manhattan College, 4513 Manhattan College Pkwy, BRNX - 10471	6393	C7
Manhattan School of Music, 120 Claremont Av, MHTN - 10027	106	B7
Manhattanville College, 2900 Purchase St, HRSN, 10577	6169	B2
Mannes College The New School for Music - 150 W 85th St, MHTN, 10024	108	D7
Marymount College of Fordham University - Marymount Av, TYTN, 10591	6048	C2
Marymount Manhattan College, 221 E 71st St, MHTN - 10021	113	C5
Mercy College, 555 Broadway, DBSF, 10522	6166	A3
Mercy College-Bronx Branch Campus, 1200 Waters Pl - BRNX, 10461	6505	D6
Mercy College-White Plains, 277 Martine Av, WHPL - 10601	6168	B2
Metropolitan College New York-Bronx - 529 Courtlandt Av, BRNX, 10451	6613	A3
Metropolitan College New York-Staten Island - 120 Stuyvesant Pl, STNL, 10301	6920	D6
Metropolitan College of New York-Manhattan - 431 Canal St, MHTN, 10013	118	C4
Monroe College, 2501 Jerome Av, BRNX, 10468	102	E7
Monroe College-New Rochelle, 434 Main St, NRCH - 10801	6396	A4
Mt Sinai School of Medicine, 1 5th Av, MHTN, 10029	109	D7
New Jersey City University, 2039 John F Kennedy Blvd - JSYC, 07305	6819	C4
New Jersey Institute of Technology - 323 Dr Martin Luther King Jr Bl, NWRK, 07103	6713	D6
New School University, 66 W 12th St, MHTN, 10011	118	E1
New York Academy of Art Graduate School - 111 Franklin St, MHTN, 10013	118	C5
New York City College of Technology, 300 Jay St, BKLN - 11201	121	B4
New York College of Podiatric Medicine, 53 E 124th St - MHTN, 10035	110	B2
New York Institute of Technology-Manhattan - 1855 Broadway, MHTN, 10023	112	C5
New York Law School, 57 Worth St, MHTN, 10013	118	C6
New York Medical College, Sunshine Cottage Rd, MtPT - 10532	6049	B1
New York Theological Seminary, 475 Claremont Av - MHTN, 10027	109	B1
New York University, 22 Waverly Pl, MHTN, 10003	118	E2
New York University School of Medicine, 550 1st Av - MHTN, 10016	116	E6
Nyack College-Manhattan, 93 Worth St, MHTN, 10013	118	D6
Pace University-New York, 1 Spruce St, MHTN, 10038	118	D7
Pace University-White Plains, 78 N Broadway, WHPL - 10603	6050	B7
Parson School of Design, E 13th St, MHTN, 10003	119	A1
Phillips Beth Israel School of Nursing - 776 Avenue of the Americas, MHTN, 10001	116	B5
Plaza College, 74-09 37th Av, QENS, 11372	6719	D6
Polytechnic University-Brooklyn Campus, 6 Jay St - BKLN, 11201	121	B5
Pratt Institute, 200 Willoughby Av, BKLN, 11205	6822	A6
Pratt Institute-Manhattan Division, 144 W 14th St - MHTN, 10011	115	E7
Queensborough Community College, 56th Av, QENS - 11364	6722	C5
Queens College, QENS, 11367	6721	B7
Rabbinical College-Bobover Bnei, 1577 48th St, BKLN - 11219	7022	D1
Rabbinical College of Long Island, 205 W Beech St - LBCH, 11561	7029	B7
Rockefeller University, 1230 York Av, MHTN, 10065	113	D7
Rutgers School of Law-Newark, 123 Washington St - NWRK, 07102	6713	D7
Rutgers University-Newark, 249 University Av, NWRK - 07102	6713	D7
St. Francis College, 180 Remsen St, BKLN, 11201	121	A5
St. John's University, Utopia Pkwy, QENS, 11432	6825	D2
St. John's University-Manhattan, 101 Murray St, MHTN - 10007	118	B6
St. John's University-Staten Island, 300 Howard Av - STNL, 10301	7020	C2
St. Joseph's College, 245 Clinton Av, BKLN, 11205	6822	A7
St. Peter's College, 2641 John F Kennedy Blvd, JSYC - 07306	6819	E2
St. Peter's College-Englewood Cliffs Campus, Allison Rd - EGLC, 07632	6503	C2
St. Thomas Aquinas College, OrgT, 10962	6164	D1
Sarah Lawrence College, 1 Mead Wy, YNKR, 10708	6394	D1
School of Visual Arts, 209 E 23rd St, MHTN, 10010	116	C6
Seton Hall University, 400 Seton Dr, SOrT, 07079	6712	A7
Seton Hall University School of Law, 1 McCarter Hwy - NWRK, 07102	6713	E7
Sh'or Yoshuv Rabbinical College, 1 Cedar Lawn Av - LWRN, 11559	7027	E4
Stevens Institute of Technology, 1 Castle Point Ter - HBKN, 07030	6716	E6
SUNY College of Optometry, 33 W 42nd St, MHTN - 10036	116	C2
SUNY Maritime College, Pennyfield Av, BRNX, 10465	6615	C4
SUNY Purchase, 735 Anderson Hill Rd, HRSN, 10577	6169	D1
SUNY Stony Brook College, E 28th St, MHTN, 10016	116	C5
Teachers College at Columbia University, 525 W 120th St - MHTN, 10027	109	C1
Tobe-Coburn School of Fashion Careers, 8 E 40th St - MHTN, 10016	116	C3
Touro College, 27 W 23rd St, MHTN, 10010	116	B6
Touro College, 133-35 Roosevelt Av, QENS, 11354	6720	E4
Touro College-Brighton, 532 Neptune Av, BKLN, 11224	7120	E1
Touro College-Harlem, 240 E 123rd St, MHTN, 10035	110	C3
Touro College-Lander College for Women, 227 W 60th St - MHTN, 10023	112	B4
Touro College-Machon l'Parnasa, 4421 13th Av, BKLN - 11219	6922	D7
Touro College of Osteopathic Medicine - 230 Dr Martin L King Jr Blvd, MHTN, 10027	109	E1
Touro Coll-Sch of Gen Studies Taino Towers - 240 E 123rd St, MHTN, 10035	110	C3
Touro College-Sunset Park, 475 53rd St, BKLN, 11220	6922	A6
Union County College-Elizabeth, 12 W Jersey St, ELIZ - 07201	6917	E3
US Merchant Marine Academy, 300 Steamboat Rd, KNGP - 11024	6616	B4
University of Med & Dentistry of New Jersey - 65 Bergen St, NWRK, 07107	6713	B6
Vaughn College of Aeronautics & Technology - 86-01 23rd Av, QENS, 11369	6719	E3
Wagner College, 1 Campus Rd, STNL, 10304	7020	C3
Weill Cornell Medical College, 1300 York Av, MHTN - 10021	113	D6
Westchester Community College, 75 Grasslands Rd - GrbT, 10603	6049	D3
William Alanson White Institute, 20 W 74th St, MHTN - 10023	112	D3
Yeshiva University, 245 Lexington Av, MHTN, 10016	116	D4
Yeshiva University-Wilf Campus, 500 W 185th St, MHTN - 10033	104	D4
York College, 94-20 Guy R Brewer Blvd, QENS, 11433	6825	D5

Entertainment & Sports

FEATURE NAME Address City ZIP Code	MAP#	GRID
3-Legged Dog, 80 Greenwich St, MHTN, 10006	120	A1
13th Street Repertory, 50 W 13th St, MHTN, 10011	115	E7
29th Street Repertory, 212 W 29th St, MHTN, 10001	116	A4
30th Street, 259 W 30th St, MHTN, 10001	116	A4
92nd Street Y, 1395 Lexington Av, MHTN, 10128	113	D1
Access Theater, 380 Broadway, MHTN, 10013	118	D5
Acorn, 410 W 42nd St, MHTN, 10036	116	A1
Actors Playhouse, 100 7th Av S, MHTN, 10014	118	D1
Adobe, 138 S Oxford St, BKLN, 11217	121	E7
Africa Arts, 660 Riverside Dr, MHTN, 10031	106	E4
Afrikan Poetry Theatre, The, 176-03 Jamaica Av, QENS - 11432	6825	E4
A Gathering of Artists, 322 Hillside Av, WLPK, 11596	6724	D5
Albert G Waters Stadium, 600 Francis St, PTHA, 08861	7205	D2
Alice Tully Hall, 1931 Broadway, MHTN, 10023	112	C4
All Seasons Theatre Company, 243 Wayne Av, CLFP - 07010	6611	D2
Amato Opera, 319 Bowery, MHTN, 10003	119	A3
Ambassador Theatre, 219 W 49th St, MHTN, 10019	112	B7
American Airlines Theater, 227 W 42nd St, MHTN, 10036	116	B2
American Ballet Theatre, 890 Broadway, MHTN, 10003	116	B7
American Jewish Theatre, 307 W 26th St, MHTN, 10001	115	E4
American Place Theater, 255 W 37th St, MHTN, 10018	116	A3
American Play, 19 W 44th St, MHTN, 10036	116	C2
American Theater Wing, 570 7th Av, MHTN, 10018	116	B2
American Theatre of Actors, 314 W 54th St, MHTN - 10019	112	B6
American Theatre of Harlem, 138 S Oxford St, BKLN - 11217	121	E7
Apollo Theatre, 253 Dr Martin L King Jr Blvd, MHTN - 10027	109	E1
Aqueduct Racecourse, 135th Dr, QENS, 11420	6925	E2
Arclight, 152 W 71st St, MHTN, 10023	112	C3
Ars Nova Theater, 511 W 54th St, MHTN, 10019	112	A5
Arthur Ashe Stadium, Meridian Rd, QENS, 11355	6720	C6
Asbury Summer Theatre, 167 Scarsdale Rd, YNKR, 10710	6280	E5
Astor Place Theatre, 434 Lafayette St, MHTN, 10003	119	A2
Atlantic Theater Company, 336 W 20th St, MHTN, 10011	115	D5
Audience Extras, 109 W 26th St, MHTN, 10001	116	A5
Baca Downtown Theatre, 195 Cadman Plz W, BKLN - 11201	121	A4
Beacon Theatre, 2124 Broadway, MHTN, 10023	112	D2
Bears and Eagles Riverfront Stadium, NWRK, 07102	6713	E6
Belasco Theater, 111 W 44th St, MHTN, 10036	116	C2
Belmont Park, Hempstead Tpk, HmpT, 11003	6827	A4
Belson Soccer Stadium, Union Tpk, QENS, 11432	6825	D2
Bendheim Performing Arts Center, 999 Wilmot Rd - NRCH, 10583	6282	A1
Bernard B Jacobs Theatre, 242 W 45th St, MHTN, 10036	116	B1
Bessie Schonberg Theater, 219 W 19th St, MHTN, 10011	115	E5
Billie Holiday Theatre, 1360 Fulton St, BKLN, 11216	6923	C1
Biltmore Theatre, 261 W 47th St, MHTN, 10036	116	B1
Black Experimental, 161 Hubert St, MHTN, 10013	118	C4
Blue Heron Arts Center, 123 E 24th St, MHTN, 10010	116	B6
Bombay Theatre, 68-25 Fresh Meadow Ln, QENS, 11365	6825	D1
Booth Theater, 222 W 45th St, MHTN, 10036	116	B1
Bouwerie Lane Theatre, 330 Bowery, MHTN, 10012	119	A3
Bowery Arts & Science, 330 Bowery, MHTN, 10012	119	A3
Bridge Stage, 101 W 78th St, MHTN, 10024	112	D2
Broadhollow Player, 700 Hempstead Tpk, HmpT, 11003	6827	C4
Broadhurst Theatre, 235 W 44th St, MHTN, 10036	116	B1
Broadway Theatre, 1681 Broadway, MHTN, 10019	112	B7
Bronx Dance Theatre, 585 E 187th St, BRNX, 10458	6504	D5
Bronx Zoo, Boston Rd, BRNX, 10460	6505	A5
Brooklyn Academy of Music, 30 Lafayette Av, BKLN - 11217	121	D7
Brooklyn Botanic Garden, 1000 Washington Av, BKLN - 11225	6923	A3
Brooklyn Center for Performing Arts, 2900 Bedford Av - BKLN, 11210	7023	C1
Brooks Atkinson Theatre, 256 W 47th St, MHTN, 10036	116	B1
Capital Theater, 149 Westchester Av, PTCH, 10573	6170	B6
Caribbean Cultural Theatre, 138 S Oxford St, BKLN - 11217	121	E7

Entertainment & Sports

New York City/5 Borough Points of Interest Index

Golf Courses

FEATURE NAME Address City ZIP Code	MAP#	GRID
Carnegie Hall, 887 7th Av, MHTN, 10019	112	C6
Castillo Theatre, 500 W 42nd St, MHTN, 10036	115	E1
Center for Contemporary Opera, 40 River Rd, MHTN - 10044	114	A6
Center for Traditional Music Dance, 32 Broadway - MHTN, 10004	120	B2
Center Stage Community Playhouse - 2474 Westchester Av, BRNX, 10461	6505	D7
Center Stage New York, 48 W 21st St, MHTN, 10010	116	A6
Central Park Zoo, 830 5th Av, MHTN, 10021	112	E6
Chashama, 135 W 42nd St, MHTN, 10036	116	B2
Chelsea Piers Sports & Entertainment Complex - W Joe Dimaggio Hwy, MHTN, 10011	115	B4
Chelsea Playhouse, 125 W 22nd St, MHTN, 10011	116	A5
Cherry Lane Theatre, 38 Commerce St, MHTN, 10014	118	C2
Childrens Theatre of Lynbrook, 317 Merrick Rd, LNBK - 11563	6929	B4
Circle in the Square, 159 Bleecker St, MHTN, 10012	118	E2
Circle Repertory Company, 632 Broadway, MHTN, 10012	118	E3
Citi Field, Shea Rd, QENS, 11368	6720	D4
City Center Theater, 130 W 56th St, MHTN, 10019	112	D7
City Island Theatre Group, 104 City Island Av, BRNX - 10464	6506	E7
Clark Botanic Garden, IU Willets Rd, NHmT, 11507	6724	E2
Classic Stage Company, 136 E 13th St, MHTN, 10003	119	B1
Colden Center-Queens College, Kissena Blvd, QENS - 11367	6721	A7
Colleagues, 321 W 76th St, MHTN, 10024	112	C1
Columbia University-Wien Stadium, W 218th St, MHTN - 10034	102	B4
Conservatory Garden, 5th Av, MHTN, 10029	109	D5
Cort Theater, 138 W 48th St, MHTN, 10036	116	C1
Criterion, 1514 Broadway, MHTN, 10036	116	C1
CSC Repertory, 136 E 13th St, MHTN, 10003	119	B1
Dance Theatre of Harlem, 466 W 152nd St, MHTN, 10031	107	A3
Dance Theatre Workshop, 219 W 19th St, MHTN, 10011	115	E6
Delacorte Theater, 425 Lafayette Av, BKLN, 11205	6822	B7
Delacourt Theatre, 81 Central Pk W, MHTN, 10023	112	D4
Deno's Wonder Wheel Amusement Park, 1025 W 12th St - BKLN, 11224	7120	E2
Destinta Theatre, 11 Kipp Av, LODI, 07644	6500	C3
Dionysus Group, 270 W 36th St, MHTN, 10018	116	A3
Dixon Place, 258 Bowery, MHTN, 10012	119	A4
Douglas Fairbanks Theatre, 432 W 42nd St, MHTN - 10036	116	A1
Duffy Theatre, 1553 Broadway, MHTN, 10036	116	B1
Duke on 42nd Street, The, 229 W 42nd St, MHTN, 10036	116	B2
Duo Theatre, 62 E 4th St, MHTN, 10003	119	A3
Eagle Theater, 73-07 37th Rd, QENS, 11372	6719	D6
Ed Sullivan Theater, 1697 Broadway, MHTN, 10019	112	C6
Emelin Theatre, 153 Library Ln, MRNK, 10543	6282	E6
Emerging Artists, 518 9th Av, MHTN, 10018	116	A2
Ensemble Studio Theater, 549 W 52nd St, MHTN, 10019	112	A6
Equitable Center Atruim, 787 7th Av, MHTN, 10019	112	C7
Ethel Barrymore Theater, 243 W 47th St, MHTN, 10036	116	C1
Eugene O'Neill Theatre, 230 W 49th St, MHTN, 10019	112	B7
Fair Theatre, 90-18 Astoria Blvd, QENS, 11369	6719	E4
Faison Firehouse Theater, 6 Hancock Pl, MHTN, 10027	109	D1
Fantasy Playhouse, 48 Atlantic Av, LNBK, 11563	6929	B4
Fleetwood Stage Playhouse, 44 Wildcliff Dr, NRCH - 10805	6396	B5
Florence Gould Hall, 55 E 59th St, MHTN, 10022	113	A7
Folksbiene Yiddish Theater, 45 E 33rd St, MHTN, 10016	116	C4
Forest Hills Stadium, Burns St, QENS, 11375	6824	C3
Freestyle Repertory Theatre, 120 W 86th St, MHTN - 10024	108	E7
French Institute Alliance Francaise, 22 E 60th St, MHTN - 10022	113	A6
Gaiety, 201 W 46th St, MHTN, 10036	116	B1
Gemini 1, 1210 2nd Av, MHTN, 10065	113	C7
Gene Frankel Theater, 24 Bond St, MHTN, 10012	119	A3
Gerald Schoenfeld Theatre, 236 W 45th St, MHTN - 10036	116	B1
Gershwin Theatre, 222 W 51st St, MHTN, 10019	112	B7
Get Set Go Theatre Company, 386 Brookfield Av, STNL - 10308	7117	A3
Giants Stadium, 50 Plaza F, ERTH, 07073	6609	D4
Gotham City Improv, 158 W 23rd St, MHTN, 10011	116	A5
Gramercy, 127 E 23rd St, MHTN, 10010	116	C6
Gramercy Arts, 138 E 27th St, MHTN, 10016	116	C6
Grand Prospect Hall, 263 Prospect Av, BKLN, 11215	6922	D3
Great Neck Arts Center, 113 Middle Neck Rd, GTPZ - 11021	6617	A7
Greenwich House Theatre, 27 Barrow St, MHTN, 10014	118	D1
Harman Street Playhouse, 59 Harman St, BKLN, 11221	6823	A6
Harold Clurman Theatre, 410 W 42nd St, MHTN, 10036	116	A1
Harry Warren Theatre, 2445 Bath Av, BKLN, 11214	7022	C6
Helen Hayes Theater, 240 W 44th St, MHTN, 10036	116	B1
Henry Miller Theatre, 124 W 43rd St, MHTN, 10036	116	C2
Henry Street Theatre, 70 Henry St, BKLN, 11201	121	A4
Here Art Center, 145 Avenue of the Americas, MHTN - 10013	118	C3
Hilton Theatre, 213 W 42nd St, MHTN, 10036	116	B1
Hirsch Feld Theatre, 302 W 45th St, MHTN, 10036	116	B1
Hostos Center for Arts & Culture, 450 Grand Concourse - BRNX, 10451	107	D6
Hudson Guild Theatre, 441 W 26th St, MHTN, 10001	115	D4
Hudson Theatre, 145 W 44th St, MHTN, 10036	116	C2
Icahn Stadium, 20 Randalls I, MHTN, 10035	110	E5
Il Piccolo Teatro Dell Opera, 138 Court St, BKLN, 11201	121	A6
Imperial Theatre, 249 W 45th St, MHTN, 10036	116	B1
Intar Theatre, 508 W 53rd St, MHTN, 10019	112	B6
Irish Arts Center, 553 W 51st St, MHTN, 10019	112	A6
Irish Repertory Theater, 132 W 22nd St, MHTN, 10011	116	A6
Ironbound Arena, 226 Rome St, NWRK, 07105	6818	B2
Irvington Town Hall Theatre, 85 Main St, IRVN, 10533	6166	A1
Izod Center, 50 E Peripheral Rd, ERTH, 07073	6609	E4
Jacob K Javits Convention Center, 11th Av, MHTN - 10018	115	D1
John Golden Theatre, 252 W 45th St, MHTN, 10036	116	B1
Joseph Pap Public Theater, 425 Lafayette St, MHTN - 10003	119	A2
Joyce Theater, 175 8th Av, MHTN, 10011	115	D5
Judson Poets, 55 Washington Sq S, MHTN, 10012	118	E2
Julia Miles Theatre, 424 W 55th St, MHTN, 10019	112	B6
KeySpan Park, 1902 Surf Av, BKLN, 11224	7120	D2
Kitchen Center, 512 W 19th St, MHTN, 10011	115	C5
Kraine Theatre, 85 E 4th St, MHTN, 10003	119	B3
La Mama Experimental Theater Club, 74 E 4th St, MHTN - 10003	119	B3
Lamb's Theater, 130 W 44th St, MHTN, 10036	116	C2
Landmark Loews Jersey Theatre, 54 John F Kennedy Blvd - JSYC, 07306	6820	A1
Larchmont Playhouse, 1975 Palmer Av, LRMT, 10538	6396	B2
La Tea Teatro, 107 Suffolk St, MHTN, 10002	119	B5
Laura Pels, 1530 Broadway, MHTN, 10036	116	C1
Lincoln Center, 60 Lincoln Center Plz, MHTN, 10023	112	C4
Little Shubert, 422 W 42nd St, MHTN, 10036	116	A1
Longacre Theatre, 220 W 48th St, MHTN, 10036	116	B1
Looking Glass, 422 W 57th St, MHTN, 10019	112	B5
Louis Armstrong Stadium, Meridian Rd, QENS, 11355	6720	D5
Lucille Lortel Theatre, 121 Christopher St, MHTN, 10014	118	C1

FEATURE NAME Address City ZIP Code	MAP#	GRID
Lunt-Fontanne Theater, 205 W 46th St, MHTN, 10036	116	C1
Lyceum Theatre, 149 W 45th St, MHTN, 10036	116	C1
Madison Square Garden, 4 W 31st St, MHTN, 10001	116	A3
Main Street, 548 Main St, MHTN, 10044	113	E7
Majestic Theater, 245 W 44th St, MHTN, 10036	116	B1
Mamaroneck Playhouse, 243 Mamaroneck Av, MRNK - 10543	6282	E6
Manhattan Center, 311 W 34th St, MHTN, 10018	116	A3
Manhattan Ensemble Theater, 55 Mercer St, MHTN - 10013	118	D4
Manhattan Playhouse, 460 W 49th St, MHTN, 10019	112	A7
Manhattan Theatre Club, 131 W 55th St, MHTN, 10019	112	D6
Marquis Theatre, Broadway, MHTN, 10036	116	C1
Maxwell's, 1039 Washington St, HBKN, 07030	6716	D6
McAlla Theatre, 957 McLean Av, YNKR, 10704	6394	B5
Meadowlands Exposition Center, 355 Plaza Dr, SECS - 07094	6610	C7
Meadowlands Racetrack, ERTH, 07073	6609	E4
Meadowlands Sports Complex, 50 W Peripheral Rd - ERTH, 07073	6609	D4
Mela Foundation, 275 Church St, MHTN, 10013	118	D5
Merkin Concert Hall, 129 W 67th St, MHTN, 10023	112	C3
Messenger Theater Corporation, 307 E 12th St, MHTN - 10003	119	C2
Metropolitan Opera House, 30 W 62nd St, MHTN, 10023	112	C4
Metropolitan Playhouse, 220 E 4th St, MHTN, 10009	119	B4
Minetta Lane Theatre, 18 Minetta Ln, MHTN, 10012	118	D2
Minskoff Theatre, 200 W 45th St, MHTN, 10036	116	B1
Mint Theatre, 311 W 43rd St, MHTN, 10036	116	A1
Miranda, 661 10th Av, MHTN, 10036	112	A7
Mt Vernon Fine Arts Cultural Center, 250 S 6th Av - MTVN, 10550	6394	E5
Mulberry Street Theatre, 70 Mulberry St, MHTN, 10013	118	E6
Music Box Theatre, 239 W 45th St, MHTN, 10036	116	B1
Music Hall Theatre, 13 Main St, TYTN, 10591	6048	B2
Music Palace, 93 Broadway, MHTN, 10006	120	B1
Music-Theatre Group, 30 W 26th St, MHTN, 10010	116	A5
Nada 45, 445 W 45th St, MHTN, 10036	112	A7
National Asian American Theater, 674 President St - BKLN, 11215	6922	E2
National Black Theatre, 2031 5th Av, MHTN, 10035	110	B2
Nederlander Theater, 208 W 41st St, MHTN, 10018	116	A2
Neighborhood Playhouse, 340 E 54th St, MHTN, 10022	117	B2
Neil Simon Theatre, 250 W 52nd St, MHTN, 10019	112	C7
New 42nd Street Theater, 330 W 42nd St, MHTN, 10036	116	A1
New Amsterdam Theater, 214 W 42nd St, MHTN, 10036	116	B2
Newark Symphony Hall, 1020 Broad St, NWRK, 07102	6817	D2
Newark Zoo, 49 Washington St, NWRK, 07102	6713	D6
New Balance Track & Field Center - 216 Fort Washington Av, MHTN, 10032	104	B6
New City, 155 1st Av, MHTN, 10003	119	C2
New Dance Group Art Center, 305 W 38th St, MHTN - 10018	116	A2
New Federal Theatre, 790 Riverside Dr, MHTN, 10032	107	A1
New Jersey Performing Arts Center, 1 Center St, NWRK - 07102	6713	E7
New Victory Theater, 209 W 42nd St, MHTN, 10036	116	B2
New York Aquarium, 602 Surf Av, BKLN, 11224	7120	E2
New York Art, 50 Park Av, MHTN, 10016	116	D4
New York Botanical Garden, Southern Blvd, BRNX - 10458	6504	E4
New York Deaf, 305 7th Av, MHTN, 10001	116	A4
New York Grand Opera, 154 W 57th St, MHTN, 10019	112	D6
New York State Theater-New York City Ballet - 20 Lincoln Center Plz, MHTN, 10023	112	B4
New York Theater Workshop, 79 E 4th St, MHTN, 10003	119	B3
Nokia Theatre, 1515 Broadway, MHTN, 10036	116	B1
NYC Millenieum Theatre, 1029 Brighton Beach Av, BKLN - 11235	7121	B1
Ohio Theatre, 66 Wooster St, MHTN, 10012	118	D4
Old Church Cultural Center, 561 Piermont Rd, DMRT - 07627	6278	A4
Olympia, 2770 Broadway, MHTN, 10025	109	A3
Ontological-Hysteric Theater, 131 E 10th St, MHTN - 10003	119	A2
Open Cage Theatre, 324 S 3rd Av, MTVN, 10550	6394	E5
Orpheum Theatre, 126 2nd Av, MHTN, 10003	119	B2
Pace Downtown Theatre, 1 Spruce St, MHTN, 10038	118	C7
Palace Theatre, 145 W 46th St, MHTN, 10036	116	C1
Pan Asian Repertory Theatre, 520 8th Av, MHTN, 10018	116	A2
Park Performing Arts Center, 560 32nd St, UNCT, 07087	6716	D2
Paul Robeson Theatre, 54 Greene Av, BKLN, 11238	6822	A7
Pearl Theater Company, 80 St. Marks Pl, MHTN, 10003	119	C3
People's Improve Theater, 154 W 29th St, MHTN, 10001	116	A4
Performing Arts Center, 735 Anderson Hill Rd, HRSN - 10577	6169	D1
Periwinkle National Theater, 1674 Broadway, MHTN - 10019	112	C7
Perry Street Theatre, 31 Perry St, MHTN, 10014	115	D7
Philipsburgh Performing Arts Center, 7 Hudson St - YNKR, 10701	6393	C1
Players Theatre, 115 MacDougal St, MHTN, 10012	118	D2
Playhouse 91, 316 E 91st St, MHTN, 10128	113	E2
Playland Amusement Park, Playland Pkwy, RYE, 10580	6284	A4
Playwrights Horizons Theatre, 416 W 42nd St, MHTN - 10036	116	A1
Plymouth Theatre, 236 W 45th St, MHTN, 10036	116	B1
Polk Theatre, 93-09 37th Av, QENS, 11372	6720	A5
Pratt Activity Resource Center, 200 Willoughby Av, BKLN - 11205	6822	A7
Pregones Theater, 571-575 Walton Av, BRNX, 10451	107	D5
Primary Stages, 354 W 45th St, MHTN, 10036	116	A1
Process Studio, 257 Church St, MHTN, 10013	118	C5
Producers Club Theaters, 616 9th Av, MHTN, 10036	116	A1
Project 400, 630 9th Av, MHTN, 10036	116	A1
Promenade Theatre, 2162 Broadway, MHTN, 10024	112	D2
Promethean, 237 W 109th St, MHTN, 10025	109	B3
Prospect Park Zoo, 450 Flatbush Av, BKLN, 11215	6923	A3
Protean, 484 W 43rd St, MHTN, 10036	116	A1
Provincetown Playhouse, 133 MacDougal St, MHTN - 10012	118	E2
Prudential Center, 165 Mulberry St, NWRK, 07102	6817	D1
Puerto Rican Traveling Theater, 304 W 47th St, MHTN - 10036	116	B1
Queens Botanical Garden, 43-50 Main St, QENS, 11355	6721	A5
Queens Wildlife Conservation Center, 53-51 111th St - QENS, 11368	6720	C6
Radio City Music Hall, 1260 Avenue of the Americas - MHTN, 10020	116	D1
Red Bull Park, Cape May St, HRSN, 07029	6714	B7
Richard Rodgers Theatre, 226 W 46th St, MHTN, 10036	116	B1
Richmond County Bank Ballpark, 75 Richmond Ter, STNL - 10301	6920	D6
Richmond Shepard Theatre, 309 E 26th St, MHTN, 10016	116	D6
Ridiculous Theatrical Company, 1 Sheridan Sq, MHTN - 10014	118	D1
Ritz Theatre, 1148 E Jersey St, ELIZ, 07201	6917	E3
River Rep, 100 E 4th St, MHTN, 10003	119	B3
Riverside Dance, 490 Delancey St S, MHTN, 10002	119	D6
Road Company, 220 5th Av, MHTN, 10001	116	B5
Roundabout Theatre Company, 231 W 39th St, MHTN - 10018	116	A2

FEATURE NAME Address City ZIP Code	MAP#	GRID
Royale Theatre, 242 W 45th St, MHTN, 10036	116	B1
Russian American Musical, 100 Church St, MHTN, 10007	118	B7
Sage Theatre Company, 205 W 15th St, MHTN, 10011	115	D6
St. George Theatre, 19 Hyatt St, STNL, 10301	6920	D6
St. James Theater, 246 W 44th St, MHTN, 10036	116	B1
Salt & Pepper Mime, 218 W 64th St, MHTN, 10023	112	B4
Seasoned Citizens Theatre Company, 200 E 5th St - MHTN, 10003	119	A3
Second Stage Theatre, 307 W 43rd St, MHTN, 10036	116	B1
Seventy-Eight Street Theatre Lab, 236 W 78th St, MHTN - 10024	112	D1
Shadow Box, 325 W End Av, MHTN, 10023	112	C2
Shea Stadium, Casey Stengel Plz, QENS, 11368	6720	C5
Shooting Star, 40 Peck Slip, MHTN, 10038	120	D1
Showtrans, 301 W 45th St, MHTN, 10036	116	B1
Shubert Theatre, 225 W 44th St, MHTN, 10036	116	B1
Sideshows By the Seashore, W 12th St, BKLN, 11223	7022	D6
Signature Theatre, 555 W 42nd St, MHTN, 10036	115	E1
Small Wonder Puppet Theatre, 1318 Carroll St, BKLN - 11213	6923	C3
Soho Playhouse, 15 Vandam St, MHTN, 10013	118	C3
Soho Repertory Theatre, 46 Walker St, MHTN, 10013	118	D5
South Oxford Space, 138 S Oxford St, BKLN, 11217	121	E7
Spanish Theatre Repertory Company, 138 E 27th St - MHTN, 10016	116	C6
Staten Island Botanical Garden, 175 Snug Harbor Rd - STNL, 10310	6920	A6
Staten Island Zoo, 614 Broadway, STNL, 10310	7019	E2
Street Theater, 228 Fisher Av, WHPL, 10606	6168	A2
Studio 54, 254 W 54th St, MHTN, 10019	112	C6
Sullivan Street Theater, 181 Sullivan St, MHTN, 10012	118	D2
Swedish Cottage Marionette Theatre, 24 W 81st St - MHTN, 10024	112	E2
Sylvia & Danny Kaye Playhouse, 149 E 68th St, MHTN - 10021	113	B5
Symphony Space, 2537 Broadway, MHTN, 10025	108	E5
Synapse Productions, 220 E 4th St, MHTN, 10009	119	C4
TADA & Dance Alliance, 120 W 28th St, MHTN, 10001	116	A5
Teatro Circulo, 250 W 26th St, MHTN, 10001	115	E4
Teatro Moderno Puertorriqueno, 181 E 111th St, MHTN - 10029	110	A5
Thalia Spanish Theater, 41-17 Greenpoint Av, QENS - 11104	6718	E7
Theatre By Blind, 306 W 18th St, MHTN, 10011	115	D6
Thelma Hill Performing Arts Center, 30 3rd Av, BKLN - 11217	121	C7
Third Eye Repertory, 22 W 34th St, MHTN, 10001	116	B4
Times Square Theater, 215 W 42nd St, MHTN, 10036	116	B2
Tower East, 1230 3rd Av, MHTN, 10021	113	B5
Town Hall Auditorium, 123 W 43rd St, MHTN, 10036	116	B2
Triad NYC, The, 158 W 72nd St, MHTN, 10023	112	C3
Tribeca Film Center, 375 Greenwich St, MHTN, 10013	118	B5
Tribeca Performing Arts Center, 199 Chambers St, MHTN - 10013	118	B6
Tribeca Playhouse, 111 Reade St, MHTN, 10007	118	C6
Trilogy, 341 W 44th St, MHTN, 10036	116	B1
Union Square Theatre, 100 E 17th St, MHTN, 10003	116	B7
USTA Billie Jean King National Tennis Center - Meridian Rd, QENS, 11355	6720	C5
Untitled Theater Company 61, 2373 Broadway, MHTN - 10024	108	D7
Upright Citizens Brigade, 161 W 22nd St, MHTN, 10011	116	A5
Variety Arts Theatre, 110 3rd Av, MHTN, 10003	119	B1
Village East Cinemas, 189 2nd Av, MHTN, 10003	119	B2
Vineyard Theatre, 108 E 15th St, MHTN, 10003	119	B1
Virginia Theatre, 245 W 52nd St, MHTN, 10019	112	C7
Vortex Theatre, 164 11th Av, MHTN, 10011	115	C4
Walter Kerr Theatre, 219 W 48th St, MHTN, 10019	116	C1
Watermark, 165 W End Av, MHTN, 10023	112	B3
Westchester Arts Council, 31 Mamaroneck Av, WHPL - 10601	6168	B1
Westchester County Center, 198 Central Av, WHPL - 10606	6168	A1
Westchester Philharmonic, 111 Central Park Av, GrbT - 10530	6167	C3
West End Kids, 173 W 78th St, MHTN, 10024	112	D2
Westside Theatre, 407 W 43rd St, MHTN, 10036	116	A1
Williams Center for the Arts, 1 Glen Rd, RTFD, 07070	6609	B2
Willow Cabin, 1633 Broadway, MHTN, 10019	112	C7
Wings Theatre Company, 154 Christopher St, MHTN - 10014	118	B1
Winter Garden Theater, 1634 Broadway, MHTN, 10019	112	C7
Womens Project, 55 W End Av, MHTN, 10023	112	A4
Workshop Theater, 312 W 36th St, MHTN, 10018	116	A3
WPA Theatre, 519 W 23rd St, MHTN, 10011	115	C4
Yankee Stadium, E 161st St, BRNX, 10452	107	E3
Yiddish Public Theatre, 440 E 79th St, MHTN, 10075	113	D5
Yonkers Raceway, YNKR, 10704	6394	B3
York Theater, 221 E 71st St, MHTN, 10021	113	C5
York Theatre Company, 619 Lexington Av, MHTN, 10022	117	A1

Golf Courses

Alpine CC, DMRT	6278	C6
Apawamis GC, RYE	6283	E1
Ardsley CC, DBSF	6166	B3
Bayonne GC, BAYN	6920	B4
Bay Park GC, HmpT	7029	C1
Blind Brook CC, RYEB	6051	E7
Bonnie Briar CC, MrnT	6282	A5
Brae Burn GC, HRSN	6050	E6
Century CC, HRSN	6169	A1
Cherry Valley CC, GDNC	6828	E3
Christopher Morley Park GC, NHLS	6724	C1
Clearview Park GC, QENS	6615	D7
Deepdale GC, NHLS	6723	D3
Doral GC, RYEB	6051	E7
Douglaston Park GC, QENS	6723	A5
Dunwoodie GC, YNKR	6394	A1
Dyker Beach GC, BKLN	7022	A3
Elmwood CC, GrbT	6166	E1
Engineers CC, ROSH	6618	E3
Fairview CC, GrwT	6051	D3
Fenway GC, WHPL	6168	B6
Flushing Meadows Golf Center, QENS	6720	D5
Forest Park GC, QENS	6824	A6
Fresh Meadow CC, LKSU	6723	C2
Garden City CC, GDNC	6828	C2
Garden City GC, GDNC	6828	E2
Golf Club of Purchase, HRSN	6051	B6
Griffith E Harris GC, GrwT	6051	C2
Hampshire CC, MRNK	6396	E1
Harbor Links GC, NHmT	6618	B2
Hempstead Golf & CC, HmpT	6828	E6
Inwood CC, HmpT	7027	C2
Kissena Park GC, QENS	6721	C6
Knollwood CC, EMFD	6049	C6
Lake Isle CC, EchT	6281	C3
Lake Success GC, LKSU	6723	C3
La Tourette GC, STNL	7117	B1
Lawrence Village CC, LWRN	7028	A4
Leewood GC, EchT	6281	B3

INDEX 65

New York City/5 Borough Points of Interest Index

FEATURE NAME Address City ZIP Code	MAP#	GRID
Liberty National GC, JSYC	6819	E6
Maple Moor GC, WHPL	6169	A6
Marine Park GC, BKLN	7024	B5
Metropolis CC, GrbT	6167	C1
Montammy GC, ALPN	6392	D2
Mosholu GC, BRNX	6393	E7
New York Hospital GC, WHPL	6168	C2
North Hempstead CC, FLHL	6618	A4
North Hills CC, NHLS	6724	A2
North Shore CC, OybT	6618	D1
North Woodmere Park GC, HmpT	6927	E6
Old Oaks CC, HRSN	6051	B7
Overpeck County GC, TnkT	6502	C1
Pelham CC, PLMM	6395	C6
Pelham-Split Rock GC, BRNX	6506	B2
Plandome CC, PLDM	6617	D4
Quaker Ridge GC, SCDL	6282	B4
Richmond County CC, STNL	7020	A7
Ridgeway CC, WHPL	6168	D5
Rockaway Hunting Club, LWRN	7028	C3
Rockland CC, OrgT	6165	A3
Rockleigh GC, RCKL	6164	D6
Rye GC, RYE	6283	D4
St. Andrews GC, GrbT	6166	C7
Sands Point GC, SNPT	6508	C5
Saxon Woods GC, SCDL	6282	C2
Scarsdale GC, GrbT	6167	D4
Seawane CC, HWTH	7028	E1
Silver Lake GC, STNL	7020	B2
Siwanoy CC, EchT	6281	B7
South Shore GC, STNL	7116	A5
Sprain Lake GC, YNKR	6280	D2
Suburban GC, UnnT	6816	A7
Sunningdale CC, GrbT	6167	A5
Towers CC, QENS	6723	C4
Van Cortlandt GC, BRNX	6393	D7
Village Club of Sands Point, SNPT	6509	A6
Weequahic Park GC, NWRK	6816	E6
Westchester CC, HRSN	6169	D6
Westchester Hills GC, WHPL	6168	D5
Willow Ridge CC, HRSN	6283	C1
Winged Foot GC, MrnT	6282	C5
Woodmere Club, HmpT	7028	C2
Wykagyl CC, NRCH	6281	D7

Historic Sites

FEATURE NAME Address City ZIP Code	MAP#	GRID
African Burial Ground, Duane St, MHTN, 10007	118	C6
Bartow-Pell Mansion, 895 Shore Rd, BRNX, 10464	6506	D1
Boxwood Hall State Historic Site, 1073 E Jersey St, ELIZ - 07201	6917	E3
Castle Clinton National Monument, State St, MHTN - 10004	120	A2
Castlegould, 95 Middle Neck Rd, SNPT, 11050	6508	D5
Center for Jewish History, 15 W 16th St, MHTN, 10011	116	A7
Colonnade Row, 428 Lafayette St, MHTN, 10003	119	A2
Confucius Statue, 2 Division St, MHTN, 10002	118	E6
Cushman Row, 406 W 20th St, MHTN, 10011	115	D5
Defenders Historic Upper Eastside, E 96th St, MHTN - 10128	109	C7
Edison National Historic Site, 98 Lakeside Av, WOrT - 07052	6712	C1
Ellis Island National Monument, Freedom Wy, JSYC - 07305	6820	C6
Falaise Mansion, 95 Middle Neck Rd, SNPT, 11050	6508	D5
Federal Hall National Memorial, 26 Wall St, MHTN - 10005	120	B1
First Shearith Israel Graveyard, 55 St. James Pl, MHTN - 10038	118	E7
Flight 587 Memorial, Beach 116th St, QENS, 11694	7123	E1
Fort Jay, Andes Rd, MHTN, 10004	120	A6
Fort Lee Historic Park, Hudson Ter, FTLE, 07024	103	B3
General Grant National Memorial, Riverside Dr, MHTN - 10027	106	B7
George Washington Masonic Historic Site - 20 Livingston St, OrgT, 10983	6164	C3
Governors Island National Monument, MHTN, 10004	120	A6
Gracie Mansion, 181 E End Av, MHTN, 10128	114	A3
Hamilton Grange National Memorial, 287 Convent Av - MHTN, 10031	107	A4
Hempstead House, 95 Middle Neck Rd, SNPT, 11050	6508	D4
Henry Street Settlement, 466 Grand St, MHTN, 10002	119	C6
Historic House Trust New York City, 830 5th Av, MHTN - 10065	113	A6
Historic Richmond Town, 441 Clarke Av, STNL, 10306	7117	B2
Holocaust Memorial & Education Center - 100 Crescent Beach Rd, GLCV, 11542	6509	E2
Irish Hunger Memorial, N End Av, MHTN, 10282	118	A6
Issacs Hendricks House, 77 Bedford St, MHTN, 10014	118	C2
Jacob Purdy House, 60 Park Av, WHPL, 10601	6168	A1
James N Wells House, 401 W 21st St, MHTN, 10011	115	D5
Jay Heritage Center, 210 Boston Post Rd, RYE, 10580	6283	C5
King of Greene Street, 72 Greene St, MHTN, 10012	118	D4
Kykuit-The Rockefeller Estate, 200 Lake Rd, MtPT - 10591	6048	D1
Langston Hughes House, 20 E 127th St, MHTN, 10035	110	B2
Litchfield Villa, 95 Prospect Pk W, BKLN, 11215	6922	E3
Louis Armstrong House, 34-56 107th St, QENS, 11368	6720	B5
New York Vietnam Veterans Memorial Plaza - 55 Water St, MHTN, 10004	120	B2
Northern Dispensary, 165 Waverly Pl, MHTN, 10014	118	D1
Old Quaker Meeting House, 137-16 Northern Blvd, QENS - 11354	6720	E3
Philipsburg Manor, 381 N Broadway, SYHW, 10591	6048	A1
Philipse Manor Hall, 29 Warburton Av, YNKR, 10701	6393	C1
Queen of Greene Street, 28 Greene St, MHTN, 10013	118	D4
Saddle Rock Grist Mill, Grist Mill Ln, SDRK, 11023	6616	C6
St. Paul's Church National Historic Site - 897 S Columbus Av, MTVN, 10550	6395	A7
Sinatra's Birthplace, 415 Monroe St, HBKN, 07030	6716	D6
Soldiers & Sailors Monument, Riverside Dr, MHTN - 10024	108	D6
South Street Seaport Historic District, 12 John St - MHTN, 10038	120	D2
Statue of Liberty National Monument, Craig Rd N, JSYC - 07305	6820	C7
Strivers' Row, 7th Av, MHTN, 10030	107	A6
Theodore Roosevelt Birthplace, 28 E 20th St, MHTN - 10003	116	B6
Tudor City Historic District, Tudor City Pl, MHTN, 10017	117	A4
Valentine Varian House, 3266 Bainbridge Av, BRNX - 10467	6504	E2
Washington Irving's Sunnyside, Sunnyside Av, TYTN - 10591	6048	A6
Washington Mews, Washington Mw, MHTN, 10003	118	E2
White Plains Historical Society, 60 Park Cir, WHPL - 10603	6168	A1
White Plains National Battlefield, 112 Battle Av, WHPL - 10606	6167	E2
Williamsburg Art & Historical Center, 135 Broadway - BKLN, 11211	6822	A4

Hospitals

FEATURE NAME Address City ZIP Code	MAP#	GRID
Allen Pavilion, The, 5141 Broadway, MHTN, 10034	102	B4
Bayonne Med Ctr, 29 E 30th St, BAYN, 07002	6920	A3
Bellevue Hosp Center, 462 1st Av, MHTN, 10016	116	E6
Beth Israel Med Ctr, 3201 Kings Hwy, BKLN, 11210	7023	C3
Beth Israel Med Ctr, 281 1st Av, MHTN, 10003	119	C1
Blythedale Children's Hosp, 95 Bradhurst Av, MtPT - 10595	6049	D3
Bronx Lebanon Hosp Center, 1650 Grand Concourse - BRNX, 10457	105	C6
Bronx State Hosp, 1500 Waters Pl, BRNX, 10461	6505	D6
Brookdale University Hosp, 1 Rockaway Pkwy, BKLN - 11212	6924	B5
Brooklyn Hosp Center, 121 DeKalb Av, BKLN, 11201	121	D6
Cabrini Med Ctr, 227 E 19th St, MHTN, 10003	116	C7
Calvary Hosp, 1740 Bassett Rd, BRNX, 10461	6505	D6
Christ Hosp, 176 Palisade Av, JSYC, 07306	6820	B1
Clara Maass Med Ctr, 1 Magnolia St, BlvT, 07109	6713	D1
Coler Memorial Hosp, 900 Main St N, MHTN, 10044	114	B5
Columbia Presbyterian Med Ctr, 622 W 168th St, MHTN - 10032	104	A6
Columbus Hosp, 495 N 13th St, NWRK, 07107	6713	C2
Community Hosp at Dobbs Ferry, 128 Ashford Av, DBSF - 10522	6166	B4
Coney Island Hosp, 2601 Ocean Pkwy, BKLN, 11235	7023	A7
East Orange General Hosp, 300 S Munn Av, EORG - 07018	6712	E5
Elmhurst Hosp Center, 79-01 Broadway, QENS, 11373	6719	D6
Englewood Hosp & Med Ctr, 350 Engle St, EGLD, 07631	6392	A5
Flushing Hosp Med Ctr, 4500 45th Av, QENS, 11355	6721	B5
Franklin Hosp Med Ctr, 900 Franklin Av, HmpT, 11580	6928	E1
Goldwater Memorial Hosp, 1 Main St, MHTN, 10044	117	C2
Gracie Square Hosp, 420 E 76th St, MHTN, 10021	113	D5
Greenville Hosp, 1825 John F Kennedy Blvd, JSYC, 07305	6819	C5
Hackensack University Med Ctr, 30 Prospect Av, HKSK - 07601	6501	A1
Harlem Hosp Center, 506 Lenox Av, MHTN, 10037	107	B7
Hebrew Hosp, 801 Co Op City Blvd, BRNX, 10475	6505	E2
Hoboken University Med Ctr, 308 Willow Av, HBKN - 07030	6716	C7
Holy Name Hosp, 718 Vandelinda Av, TnkT, 07666	6502	A1
Hosp for Joint Diseases Orthopaedic Inst, 301 E 17th St - MHTN, 10003	119	C1
Hospital for Special Surgery, 535 E 70th St, MHTN - 10021	113	D6
Interfaith Med Ctr, 1545 Atlantic Av, BKLN, 11213	6923	D1
Irvington Community Health Center, 832 Park Pl, IrvT - 07111	6816	B3
Jack D Weiler Hosp, 1825 Sacket Av, BRNX, 10461	6505	C6
Jacobi Med Ctr, 1400 Pelham Pkwy S, BRNX, 10461	6505	C5
Jamaica Hosp, 8900 Van Wyck Expwy, QENS, 11418	6825	B5
Jamaica Medical Hosp Center, 4-21 27th Av, QENS - 11102	114	D3
Jersey City Med Ctr, 355 Grand St, JSYC, 07302	6820	B3
Kingsbrook Jewish Med Ctr, 585 Winthrop St, BKLN - 11203	6923	D4
Kings County Hosp Center, 451 Clarkson Av, BKLN - 11203	6923	C4
Lawrence Hosp, 55 Pondfield Rd W, BRXV, 10708	6280	E7
Lenox Hill Hosp, 100 E 77th St, MHTN, 10021	113	C4
Libertyhealth-Meadowlands Hosp Med Ctr, 55 Cove Ct - SECS, 07094	6609	D7
Lincoln Medical & Mental Health Center, 234 E 149th St - BRNX, 10451	107	E6
Long Beach Med Ctr, 455 E Bay Dr, LBCH, 11561	7029	D6
Long Island College Hosp, 350 Hicks St, BKLN, 11201	120	E6
Long Island Jewish Med Ctr, 27005 76th Av, QENS - 11004	6723	C5
Lutheran Med Ctr, 150 55th St, BKLN, 11220	6921	E6
Maimonides Med Ctr, 967 49th St, BKLN, 11219	6922	B7
Mary Immaculate Hosp, 152-11 89th Av, QENS, 11432	6825	C5
Memorial Sloan-Kettering Cancer Center, 1275 York Av - MHTN, 10021	113	D6
Metropolitan Hosp Center, 1900 E 99th St, MHTN, 10029	114	A1
Montefiore Med Ctr-Moses Division Hosp - 111 E 210th St, BRNX, 10467	6504	E2
Morgan Stanley Children's Hosp of NY-Presb - 3959 Broadway, MHTN, 10032	104	A6
Mt Sinai Hosp of Queens, 25-10 30th Av, QENS, 11102	114	E5
Mt Sinai Med Ctr, 1425 Madison Av, MHTN, 10029	109	D6
Mt Vernon Hosp, 12 N 7th Av, MTVN, 10550	6394	D4
Newark Beth Israel Med Ctr, 201 Lyons Av, NWRK - 07112	6816	E4
New York Community Hosp, 2525 Kings Hwy, BKLN - 11210	7023	C3
New York Downtown Hosp, 170 William St, MHTN - 10038	118	C7
New York Eye and Ear Hosp, 310 E 14th St, MHTN - 10003	119	C1
New York Hosp Queens, 56-45 Main St, QENS, 11355	6721	A6
New York Methodist Hosp, 506 6th St, BKLN, 11215	6922	E3
New York Presbyterian Hosp, 5141 Broadway, MHTN - 10034	102	C4
New York University Med Ctr, 560 1st Av, MHTN, 10016	116	E5
New York Weill Cornell Med Ctr, 525 FDR Dr, MHTN - 10021	113	D7
North Central Bronx Hosp, 3424 Kossuth Av, BRNX - 10467	6504	E1
North General Hosp, 1879 Park Av, MHTN, 10035	110	B3
North Shore University Hosp, 300 Community Dr, NHmT - 11030	6723	D2
North Shore University Hosp, 102-01 66th Rd, QENS - 11375	6824	C1
NYU Elaine A & Kenneth G Langone Med Ctr - 301 E 17th St, MHTN, 10003	119	C1
Orange Community Health Center, 37 N Day St, COrT - 07050	6712	C2
Our Lady of Mercy Hosp, 1870 Pelham Pkwy S, BRNX - 10461	6505	D5
Our Lady of Mercy Med Ctr, 600 E 233rd St, BRNX - 10466	6394	B7
Palisades Med Ctr, 7600 River Rd, NBgT, 07047	6611	C6
Parkway Hosp, 70-35 113th St, QENS, 11375	6824	D2
Peninsula Hosp Center, 51-15 Beach 53rd St, QENS - 11691	7026	E6
Queens Hosp Center, 8268 161st St, QENS, 11432	6825	C3
Raritan Bay Med Ctr, 530 Groom St, PTHA, 08861	7205	C2
Richmond University Med Ctr, 355 Bard Av, STNL, 10310	6920	A7
St. Barnabas Hosp, 4422 3rd Av, BRNX, 10457	6504	D5
St. Francis Hosp, 100 Port Washington Blvd, FLHL, 11576	6618	B5
St. James Hosp, 155 Jefferson St, NWRK, 07105	6817	E1
St. John's Episcopal Hosp, 327 Beach 20th St, QENS - 11691	7027	D5
St. John's Queens Hosp, 90-02 Queens Blvd, QENS, 11373	6824	A1
St. John's Riverside Hosp, 967 N Broadway, YNKR, 10701	6279	D3
St. John's Riverside Hosp-ParkCare Pavilion, 2 Park Av - YNKR, 10703	6279	D7
St. Josephs Med Ctr, 127 S Broadway, YNKR, 10701	6393	C2
St. Luke's-Roosevelt Hosp Center, 1111 Amsterdam Av - MHTN, 10025	109	C2
St. Michael's Med Ctr, 268 Central Av, NWRK, 07102	6713	D6
St. Vincent's Hosp & Med Ctr, 153 W 12th St, MHTN - 10011	115	D7
St. Vincent's Midtown Hosp, 415 W 51st St, MHTN - 10019	112	B6
St. Vincent's Westchester, 275 North St, HRSN, 10580	6283	C1
Schneider Children's Hosp, 269-01 76th Av, QENS, 11004	6723	C5
Sound Shore Med Ctr, 16 Van Guilder Av, NRCH, 10801	6395	E4
Staten Island University Hosp-North, 475 Seaview Av - STNL, 10305	7020	C7
Staten Island University Hosp-South, 375 Seguine Av - STNL, 10309	7207	B3
Trinitas Hosp, 225 Williamson St, ELIZ, 07202	6917	E4
University Hosp, 150 Bergen St, NWRK, 07103	6713	B7
University Hosp of Brooklyn, 450 Lenox Rd, BKLN - 11203	6923	C5
Veterans Affairs Med Ctr, 134 W Kingsbridge Rd, BRNX - 10468	102	E6
Veteran's Hosp-East Orange, 385 Tremont Av, EORG - 07018	6712	C5
Victory Memorial Hosp, 699 92nd St, BKLN, 11228	7021	E3
Westchester County Med Ctr, 19 Hospital Service Rd - MtPT, 10595	6049	B1
Westchester Square Med Ctr, 2475 Seddon St, BRNX - 10461	6505	C7
White Plains Hosp Med Ctr, 41 Davis Av, WHPL, 10601	6168	B2
Winthrop University Hosp, 259 1st St, MNLA, 11501	6724	E6
Woodhull Medical-Mental Health Center, 760 Sumner Av - BKLN, 11206	6822	D6
Wyckoff Heights Med Ctr, 374 Stockholm St, BKLN - 11237	6823	A5
Zucker Hillside Hosp, The, 75-59 263rd St, QENS, 11004	6723	C5

Law Enforcement

FEATURE NAME Address City ZIP Code	MAP#	GRID
Alpine Police Dept, 100 Church St, ALPN, 07620	6278	E6
Ardsley Police Dept, 507 Ashford Av, ARDY, 10502	6166	D4
Bayonne Police Dept, 630 Avenue C, BAYN, 07002	6919	E3
Bergen County Sheriff Dept, 1 Court St, HKSK, 07601	6501	C2
Bogota Police Dept, 375 Larch Av, BGTA, 07603	6501	D2
Bronx Police 40th Precinct, 257 Alexander Av, BRNX - 10454	110	E1
Bronx Police 41st Precinct, 1035 Longwood Av, BRNX - 10459	6613	C3
Bronx Police 42nd Precinct, 830 Washington Av, BRNX - 10451	6613	B2
Bronx Police 43rd Precinct, 900 Fteley Av, BRNX, 10473	6614	A2
Bronx Police 44th Precinct, 2 E 169th St, BRNX, 10452	105	A7
Bronx Police 45th Precinct, 2877 Barkley Av, BRNX - 10465	6615	A1
Bronx Police 46th Precinct, 2120 Ryer Av, BRNX, 10457	105	E3
Bronx Police 47th Precinct, 4111 Laconia Av, BRNX - 10466	6394	C7
Bronx Police 49th Precinct, 2121 Eastchester Rd, BRNX - 10461	6505	D5
Bronx Police 50th Precinct, 3450 Kingsbridge Av, BRNX - 10463	102	E2
Bronx Police 52nd Precinct, 3016 Webster Av, BRNX - 10467	6504	E3
Bronxville Police Dept, 200 Pondfield Rd, BRXV, 10708	6394	E1
Brooklyn Police 60th Precinct, 2951 W 8th St, BKLN - 11224	7120	E1
Brooklyn Police 61st Precinct, 2575 Coney Island Av - BKLN, 11223	7023	B6
Brooklyn Police 62nd Precinct, 1925 Bath Av, BKLN - 11214	7022	B5
Brooklyn Police 63rd Precinct, 1844 Brooklyn Av, BKLN - 11210	7023	D1
Brooklyn Police 66th Precinct, 5822 16th Av, BKLN - 11219	7022	C2
Brooklyn Police 67th Precinct, 2820 Snyder Av, BKLN - 11226	6923	C5
Brooklyn Police 68th Precinct, 333 65th St, BKLN, 11220	6921	E7
Brooklyn Police 69th Precinct, 9720 Foster Av, BKLN - 11236	6924	C5
Brooklyn Police 70th Precinct, 154 Lawrence Av, BKLN - 11230	7022	E1
Brooklyn Police 71st Precinct, 421 Empire Blvd, BKLN - 11225	6923	C3
Brooklyn Police 72nd Precinct, 830 4th Av, BKLN, 11232	6922	B4
Brooklyn Police 73rd Precinct, 1470 E New York Av - BKLN, 11212	6924	B2
Brooklyn Police 75th Precinct, 1000 Sutter Av, BKLN - 11208	6924	E2
Brooklyn Police 76th Precinct, 191 Union St, BKLN - 11231	6922	B1
Brooklyn Police 77th Precinct, 127 Utica Av, BKLN - 11213	6923	E2
Brooklyn Police 78th Precinct, 65 6th Av, BKLN, 11217	6922	E1
Brooklyn Police 79th Precinct, 263 Tompkins Av, BKLN - 11221	6822	C7
Brooklyn Police 81st Precinct, 30 Ralph Av, BKLN, 11221	6822	E7
Brooklyn Police 83rd Precinct, 480 Knickerbocker Av - BKLN, 11237	6823	A6
Brooklyn Police 84th Precinct, 301 Gold St, BKLN, 11201	121	C5
Brooklyn Police 88th Precinct, 298 Classon Av, BKLN - 11205	6822	B7
Brooklyn Police 90th Precinct, 211 Union Av, BKLN - 11211	6822	C5
Brooklyn Police 94th Precinct, 100 Meserole Av, BKLN - 11222	6822	B2
Carlstadt Police Dept, 500 Madison St, CARL, 07072	6500	C7
Carteret Police Dept, 230 Roosevelt Av, CART, 07008	7115	E2
Cliffside Park Borough Police Dept, 525 Palisade Av - CLFP, 07010	6611	D3
Closter Police Dept, 295 Closter Dock Rd, CLST, 07624	6278	B3
Cresskill Police Dept, 67 Union Av, CRSK, 07626	6278	B7
Demarest Police Dept, 118 Serpentine Rd, DMRT, 07627	6278	A5
Dobbs Ferry Police Dept, 112 Main St, DBSF, 10522	6166	A4
Eastchester Town Police Dept, 40 Mill Rd, EchT, 10709	6281	B5
East Newark Police Dept, 34 Sherman Av, ENWK, 07029	6714	A5
East Orange Police Dept, 61 N Munn Av, EORG, 07017	6713	A4
East Rutherford Police Dept, 312 Grove St, ERTH, 07073	6609	B1
Edgewater Police Dept, 916 River Rd, EDGW, 07020	6611	E2
Elizabeth Police Dept, 1 E Grand St, ELIZ, 07201	6917	E3
Elmsford Police Dept, 15 S Stone Av, EMFD, 10523	6049	A5
Englewood Cliffs Police Dept, 10 Kahn Ter, EGLC, 07632	6503	C2
Fairview Police Dept, 59 Anderson Av, FRVW, 07022	6611	B4
Floral Park Police Dept, 1 Floral Blvd, FLPK, 11001	6827	C2
Fort Lee Police Dept, 1327 16th St, FTLE, 07024	6502	D6
Garfield Police Dept, 411 Midland Av, GRFD, 07026	6500	B2
Great Neck Estates Police Dept, 1 Cedar Dr, GTNE - 11021	6617	A7
Greenburgh Police Dept, 188 Tarrytown Rd, GrbT, 10607	6049	E7
Guttenberg Police Dept, 6810 Park Av, GTBG, 07093	6611	B7
Hackensack Police Dept, 225 State St, HKSK, 07601	6501	C1
Harrison Police Dept, 318 Harrison Av, HRSN, 07029	6714	A6
Harrison Police Dept, 650 North St, HRSN, 10528	6169	B6
Hasbrouck Heights Police Dept, 320 Boulevard, HSBH - 07604	6500	E4
Hastings-on-Hudson Police Dept, 7 Maple Av, HAOH - 10706	6165	E6

New York City/5 Borough Points of Interest Index

FEATURE NAME Address City ZIP Code	MAP#	GRID
Hillside Twp Police Dept, 1409 Liberty Av, HlsT, 07205	6816	D5
Hoboken Police Dept, 106 Hudson St, HBKN, 07030	6716	D7
Irvington Police Dept, 85 Main St, IRVN, 10533	6166	A1
Irvington Twp Police Dept, 1 Civic Sq, IrvT, 07111	6816	C2
Jersey City Police Dept, 8 Erie St, JSYC, 07302	6820	C2
Kearny Police Dept, 237 Laurel Av, KRNY, 07032	6714	C2
Kensington Police Dept, 1 Beverly Rd, KENS, 11021	6617	A7
Kings County Police Dept, 210 Joralemon St, BKLN - 11201	121	A5
Kings Point Police Dept, 32 Sunset Rd, KNGP, 11024	6616	C3
Lake Success Police Dept, 15 Vanderbilt Dr, NHmT - 11020	6723	B3
Larchmont Police Dept, 120 Larchmont Av, LRMT, 10538	6396	C2
Linden Police Dept, 301 N Wood Av, LNDN, 07036	7017	A1
LIRR Chief of Police, 93-59 183rd St, QENS, 11423	6826	A4
Little Ferry Police Dept, 215 Liberty St, LFRY, 07643	6501	C6
Lodi Police Dept, 1 Memorial Dr, LODI, 07644	6500	C2
Long Beach Police Dept, 1 W Chester St, LBCH, 11561	7029	C7
Lynbrook Police Dept, 1 Columbus Dr, LNBK, 11563	6929	B4
Malverne Police Dept, 1 Britton Cir, MLVN, 11565	6929	B2
Mamaroneck Town Police Dept, 740 W Boston Post Rd - MRNK, 10543	6282	E7
Mamaroneck Village Police Dept, 169 Mt Pleasant Av - MRNK, 10543	6282	E6
Manhattan Police 1st Precinct, 16 Beach St, MHTN - 10013	118	C5
Manhattan Police 5th Precinct, 19 Elizabeth St, MHTN - 10013	118	E6
Manhattan Police 6th Precinct, 233 W 10th St, MHTN - 10014	118	C1
Manhattan Police 7th Precinct, 19 Pitt St, MHTN, 10002	119	C6
Manhattan Police 9th Precinct, 130 Avenue C, MHTN - 10009	119	D3
Manhattan Police 10th Precinct, 230 W 20th St, MHTN - 10011	115	E5
Manhattan Police 13th Precinct, 230 E 21st St, MHTN - 10010	116	C7
Manhattan Police 17th Precinct, 167 E 51st St, MHTN - 10022	117	A2
Manhattan Police 19th Precinct, 153 E 67th St, MHTN - 10065	113	B6
Manhattan Police 20th Precinct, 120 W 82nd St, MHTN - 10024	112	E1
Manhattan Police 23rd Precinct, 164 E 102nd St, MHTN - 10029	109	E7
Manhattan Police 24th Precinct, 151 W 100th St, MHTN - 10025	109	B5
Manhattan Police 25th Precinct, 120 E 119th St, MHTN - 10035	110	B3
Manhattan Police 26th Precinct, 520 W 126th St, MHTN - 10027	106	D7
Manhattan Police 28th Precinct - 2271 Frederick Douglass Blvd, MHTN, 10027	109	D1
Manhattan Police 30th Precinct, 451 W 151st St, MHTN - 10031	107	A3
Manhattan Police 32nd Precinct, 250 W 135th St, MHTN - 10030	107	A6
Manhattan Police 34th Precinct, 4295 Broadway, MHTN - 10033	104	C3
Manhattan Police Mid Town North, 306 W 54th St - MHTN, 10019	112	C6
Manhattan Police Mid Town South, 357 W 35th St - MHTN, 10018	116	A2
Moonachie Police Dept, 70 Moonachie Rd, MNCH, 07074	6501	C7
Mt Vernon Police Dept, 2 Roosevelt Sq N, MTVN, 10550	6394	D4
Nassau County Police 3rd Precinct, 220 Hillside Av - WLPK, 11596	6724	D5
Nassau County Police 4th Precinct, 1699 Broadway - HmpT, 11557	6928	E6
Nassau County Police 5th Precinct, 1655 Dutch Broadway - HmpT, 11003	6827	D7
Nassau County Police 6th Precinct, 100 Community Dr - NHmT, 11030	6723	D1
Nassau County Police Academy, 6 Cross St, WLPK - 11596	6724	E4
Nassau County Police Dept Headquarters - 1490 Franklin Av, GDNC, 11530	6724	E7
Newark Police Dept, 22 Franklin St, NWRK, 07102	6817	D1
New Jersey State Police-Newark Station, 14 E Port St - NWRK, 07114	6818	A5
New Rochelle Police Dept, 475 North Av, NRCH, 10801	6395	E3
New York City Police Dept, 1 Madison St, MHTN, 10038	118	D7
New York City Police Headquarters, 240 Centre St - MHTN, 10013	118	E5
New York Police Dept-Downtown Center - 104 Washington St, MHTN, 10006	120	A1
New York State Police-Troop L, 1 Southern State Pkwy - HmpT, 11580	6928	D1
North Bergen Police Dept, 4233 Kennedy Blvd W, NBgT - 07047	6716	E2
North Manhattan Borough Patrol Command - 151 W 100th St, MHTN, 10025	109	A5
Northvale Police Dept, 116 Paris Av, NVLE, 07647	6164	B5
Norwood Police Dept, 455 Broadway, NRWD, 07648	6164	C7
Orange Police Dept, 29 Park St, COrT, 07050	6712	D3
Orange Twp Police Dept, 593 Lincoln Av, COrT, 07050	6712	B4
Palisades Park Police Dept, 275 Broad Av, PALP, 07650	6502	C6
Pelham Manor Police Dept, 4 Penfield Pl, PLMM, 10803	6395	C7
Pelham Police Dept, 34 5th Av, PLHM, 10803	6395	B4
Perth Amboy Police Dept, 351 Rector St, PTHA, 08861	7205	E4
Port Chester Police Dept, 350 N Main St, PTCH, 10573	6170	C5
Port Washington Police Dept, 500 Port Washington Blvd - NHmT, 11050	6618	A2
Queens Police 100th Precinct, 92-94 Rockaway Blvd - QENS, 11417	6925	D1
Queens Police 100th Precinct, 92-24 Rockaway Beach Blvd - QENS, 11693	7026	B7
Queens Police 101st Precinct, 16-12 Mott Av, QENS - 11691	7027	D5
Queens Police 102nd Precinct, 87-34 118th St, QENS - 11418	6824	E6
Queens Police 103rd Precinct, 168-02 91st Av, QENS - 11432	6825	D4
Queens Police 104th Precinct, 64-02 Catalpa Av, QENS - 11385	6823	D5
Queens Police 105th Precinct, 92-08 222nd St, QENS - 11428	6826	E2
Queens Police 106th Precinct, 103-51 101st St, QENS - 11417	6925	D1
Queens Police 107th Precinct, 71-01 Parsons Blvd, QENS - 11365	6825	B1
Queens Police 108th Precinct, 05-47 50th Av, QENS - 11101	117	D5
Queens Police 109th Precinct, 37-05 Union St, QENS - 11354	6721	A4
Queens Police 110th Precinct, 94-41 43rd Av, QENS - 11373	6720	A6
Queens Police 111th Precinct, 45-06 215th St, QENS - 11361	6722	B4
Queens Police 112th Precinct, 68-40 Austin St, QENS - 11375	6824	C2

FEATURE NAME Address City ZIP Code	MAP#	GRID
Queens Police 113th Precinct, 167-02 Baisley Blvd, QENS - 11434	6927	A1
Queens Police 114th Precinct, 34-16 Astoria Blvd S, QENS - 11103	6719	A3
Queens Police 115th Precinct, 92-15 Northern Blvd, QENS - 11369	6720	A5
Ridgefield Park Police Dept, 234 Main St, RDFP, 07660	6501	E5
Ridgefield Police Dept, 604 Broad Av N, RDGF, 07657	6611	B1
Rockleigh Police Dept, 26 Rockleigh Rd, RCKL, 07647	6164	E6
Rockville Centre Police Dept, 34 Maple Av, RKVC, 11570	6929	E4
Rutherford Police Dept, 176 Park Av, RTFD, 07070	6609	A2
Rye Brook Village Police Dept, 90 S Ridge St, RYEB - 10573	6170	A5
Rye City Police Dept, 21 McCullough Pl, RYE, 10580	6284	A1
Sands Point Police Dept, 26 Tibbits Ln, SNPT, 11050	6508	B5
Scarsdale Police Dept, 50 Tompkins Rd, SCDL, 10583	6167	E5
Secaucus Police Dept, 1203 Paterson Plank Rd, SECS - 07094	6610	B7
Sleepy Hollow Police Dept, 28 Beekman Av, SYHW - 10591	6048	B1
South Amboy Police Dept, 140 Broadway N, SAMB - 08879	7205	C7
South Hackensack Police Dept, 227 Phillips Av, SHkT - 07606	6501	C4
South Orange Police Dept, 201 S Orange Av, SOrT - 07079	6712	A6
Staten Island Police 120th Precinct, 78 Richmond Ter - STNL, 10301	6920	D6
Staten Island Police 122nd Precinct, 2320 Hylan Blvd - STNL, 10306	7118	A2
Staten Island Police 123rd Precinct, 116 Main St, STNL - 10307	7206	A3
Tarrytown Police Dept, 150 W Franklin St, TYTN, 10591	6048	B2
Teaneck Twp Police Dept, 818 Teaneck Rd, TnkT, 07666	6502	B1
Tenafly Police Dept, 100 Riveredge Rd, TFLY, 07670	6392	A2
Teterboro Police Dept, TETB, 07608	6501	B4
Tuckahoe Police Dept, 65 Main St, TCKA, 10707	6281	A6
Union City Police Dept, 3715 Palisade Av, UNCT, 07087	6716	E2
Wallington Police Dept, 56 Union Blvd, WLTN, 07057	6500	A5
Weehawken Police Dept, 400 Park Av, WhkT, 07086	6716	E3
West New York Police Dept, 428 60th St, WNYK, 07093	6611	A7
West Orange Police Dept, 60 Main St, WOrT, 07052	6712	B2
White Plains Police Dept, 77 S Lexington Av, WHPL - 10601	6168	A2
Woodbridge Police Dept, 1 Main St, WbgT, 07095	7114	C4
Wood-Ridge Police Dept, 85 Humboldt St, WRDG, 07075	6500	C7
Yonkers Police Dept, 104 S Broadway, YNKR, 10701	6393	C2
Yonkers Police Dept 1st Precinct, 730 E Grassy Sprain Rd - YNKR, 10710	6280	D2
Yonkers Police Dept 2nd Precinct, 441 Central Park Av - YNKR, 10704	6394	A3
Yonkers Police Dept 3rd Precinct, 435 Riverdale Av - YNKR, 10705	6393	C3
Yonkers Police Dept 4th Precinct, 53 Shonnard Pl, YNKR - 10703	6279	D6

Libraries

FEATURE NAME Address City ZIP Code	MAP#	GRID
125th St Branch, 224 E 125th St, MHTN, 10035	110	C3
Alden Manor, 799 Elmont Rd, HmpT, 11003	6827	B7
American Hugarian & Historical Society, 215 E 82nd St - MHTN, 10028	113	D3
Ardsley Public, 9 American Legion Dr, ARDY, 10502	6166	D4
Bayonne Public, 697 Avenue C, BAYN, 07002	6919	E2
Belmont Branch, 610 Frank Simeone Sq, BRNX, 10458	6504	D5
Bloomfield Public, 90 Broad St, NWRK, 07104	6713	E4
Bogota Public, 375 Larch Av, BGTA, 07603	6501	D2
Branch Brook, 235 Clifton Av, NWRK, 07104	6713	D4
Brandy, 25 N Moore St, MHTN, 10013	118	C5
Bronx Center, 310 E Kingsbridge Rd, BRNX, 10458	6504	D4
Bronxville Public, 201 Pondfield Rd, BRXV, 10708	6394	E1
Brooklyn Public, 7223 Ridge Blvd, BKLN, 11209	7021	D1
Brooklyn Public, 61 Glenmore Av, BKLN, 11212	6924	B2
Brooklyn Public, 396 Clinton St, BKLN, 11231	6922	C1
Brooklyn Public-Arlington, 203 Arlington Av, BKLN - 11207	6924	D1
Brooklyn Public-Bedford, 102 Putnam Av, BKLN, 11238	6923	B1
Brooklyn Public-Borough Park, 1265 43rd St, BKLN - 11219	6922	D7
Brooklyn Public-Brighton Beach, 16 Brighton 1st Rd - BKLN, 11235	7121	A1
Brooklyn Public-Brooklyn Heights, 280 Cadman Plz W - BKLN, 11201	121	A4
Brooklyn Public-Brower Park, 725 St. Marks Av, BKLN - 11216	6923	C2
Brooklyn Public-Bushwick, 340 Bushwick Av, BKLN - 11206	6822	D5
Brooklyn Public-Canarsie, 1580 Rockaway Pkwy, BKLN - 11236	6924	C6
Brooklyn Public-Carroll Garden, 396 Clinton Av, BKLN - 11238	6822	A7
Brooklyn Public-Central, 1 Grand Army Plz, BKLN, 11238	6923	A2
Brooklyn Public-Clarendon, 2035 Nostrand Av, BKLN - 11210	6923	C7
Brooklyn Public-Clinton Hill, 380 Washington Av, BKLN - 11238	6822	A7
Brooklyn Public-Coney Island, 1901 Mermaid Av, BKLN - 11224	7120	D1
Brooklyn Public-Cortelyou, 1305 Cortelyou Rd, BKLN - 11226	6923	A7
Brooklyn Public-Crown Heights, 560 New York Av, BKLN - 11225	6923	C4
Brooklyn Public-Cypress Hills, 1197 Sutter Av, BKLN - 11208	6925	A2
Brooklyn Public-DeKalb, 790 Bushwick Av, BKLN, 11221	6822	E6
Brooklyn Public-Dyker, 8202 13th Av, BKLN, 11228	7022	A3
Brooklyn Public-Eastern Pkwy, 1044 Eastern Pkwy, BKLN - 11213	6923	E3
Brooklyn Public-E Flatbush, 9612 Church Av, BKLN - 11212	6924	A4
Brooklyn Public-Flatbush, 22 Linden Blvd, BKLN, 11226	6923	B5
Brooklyn Public-Flatlands, 2065 Flatbush Av, BKLN - 11234	7023	E2
Brooklyn Public-Fort Hamilton, 9424 4th Av, BKLN - 11209	7021	D3
Brooklyn Public-Gerritsen Beach, 2808 Gerritsen Av - BKLN, 11229	7024	A6
Brooklyn Public-Gravesend, 303 Avenue X, BKLN, 11223	7022	E6
Brooklyn Public-Greenpoint, 107 Norman Av, BKLN - 11222	6822	C2
Brooklyn Public-Highlawn, 1664 W 13th St, BKLN, 11223	7022	D4
Brooklyn Public-Homecrest, 2525 Coney Island Av, BKLN - 11223	7023	B6
Brooklyn Public-Jamaica Bay, 9727 Seaview Av, BKLN - 11236	6924	D7
Brooklyn Public-Kensington, 410 Ditmas Av, BKLN - 11218	6922	E7
Brooklyn Public-Kings Bay, 3650 Nostrand Av, BKLN - 11229	7023	D6
Brooklyn Public-Kings Highway, 2115 Ocean Av, BKLN - 11229	7023	B4
Brooklyn Public-Leonard, 81 Devoe St, BKLN, 11211	6822	C3

FEATURE NAME Address City ZIP Code	MAP#	GRID
Brooklyn Public-Macon Branch, 361 Lewis Av, BKLN - 11233	6923	D1
Brooklyn Public-Mapleton, 1702 60th St, BKLN, 11204	7022	D2
Brooklyn Public-Marcy, 617 DeKalb Av, BKLN, 11206	6822	C7
Brooklyn Public-McKinley Park, 6802 Fort Hamilton Pkwy - BKLN, 11219	7022	A1
Brooklyn Public-Mill Basin, 2385 Ralph Av, BKLN, 11234	7024	A2
Brooklyn Public-New Lots, 665 New Lots Av, BKLN - 11207	6924	D3
Brooklyn Public-New Utrecht, 1743 86th St, BKLN - 11214	7022	B4
Brooklyn Public-Pacific, 25 4th Av, BKLN, 11217	6922	E1
Brooklyn Public-Paerdegat, 850 E 59th St, BKLN, 11234	7024	A1
Brooklyn Public-Park Slope, 431 6th Av, BKLN, 11215	6922	D3
Brooklyn Public-Red Hook, 7 Wolcott St, BKLN, 11231	6922	A2
Brooklyn Public-Rugby, 1000 Utica Av, BKLN, 11203	6923	E5
Brooklyn Public-Ryder, 5902 23rd Av, BKLN, 11204	7022	E3
Brooklyn Public-Saratoga, 8 Thomas S Boyland St, BKLN - 11233	6823	A7
Brooklyn Public-Sheepshead Bay, 2636 E 14th St, BKLN - 11235	7023	B7
Brooklyn Public-Spring Creek, 12143 Flatlands Av, BKLN - 11207	6924	D5
Brooklyn Public-Stone Av, 581 Mother Gaston Blvd, BKLN - 11212	6924	B3
Brooklyn Public-Sunset Park, 5108 4th Av, BKLN, 11220	6922	A6
Brooklyn Public-Ulmer Park, 2602 Bath Av, BKLN, 11214	7022	D6
Brooklyn Public-Wash Irving, 360 Irving Av, BKLN - 11237	6823	B6
Brooklyn Public-Williamsburg, 240 Division Av, BKLN - 11211	6822	B4
Brooklyn Public-Windsor Ter, 160 E 5th St, BKLN, 11218	6922	E5
Bryant, 2 Paper Mill Rd, RSLN, 11576	6618	D6
Byram Shubert, 21 Mead Av, GrwT, 06830	6170	C6
Carteret Public, 100 Cooke Av, CART, 07008	7115	D1
Central Torah of Boro Park, 4511 14th Av, BKLN, 11219	6922	D7
Chatham Square, 33 E Broadway, MHTN, 10002	118	E7
Cliffside Public, 505 Palisade Av, CLFP, 07010	6611	D3
Clinton Branch, 739 Bergen St, NWRK, 07108	6817	A3
Closter Public, 280 High St, CLST, 07624	6278	A3
Cooper Union, 7 E 7th St, MHTN, 10003	119	B2
Corona, 42-11 104th St, QENS, 11368	6720	B6
Cresskill Public, 53 Union Av, CRSK, 07626	6278	B7
Criminal Justice NCCD, 123 Washington St, NWRK, 07102	6713	D7
Demarest Public, 90 Hardenburgh Av, DMRT, 07627	6278	A5
Dobbs Ferry Public, 85 Main St, DBSF, 10522	6165	E4
Eastchester Public, 11 Oakridge Pl, EchT, 10709	6281	B5
East Orange-Franklin Branch, 192 Dodd St, EORG, 07017	6713	A1
East Orange Public, 21 S Arlington Av, EORG, 07018	6712	E4
East Rockaway Public, 477 Atlantic Av, ERKY, 11518	6929	C6
East Rutherford Memorial, 143 Boiling Springs Av, ERTH - 07073	6609	B1
East Williston Public, 2 Prospect St, EWLS, 11596	6724	E4
Edgewater Free Public, 49 Hudson Av, EDGW, 07020	6611	E1
Elizabeth Free Public, 11 S Broad St, ELIZ, 07202	6917	E4
Elizabeth Port Branch, 102 3rd St, ELIZ, 07206	6918	B5
Elmont Public, 1735 Hempstead Tpk, HmpT, 11003	6827	D4
Elmora Branch, 740 W Grand St, ELIZ, 07202	6917	C3
Elmwood Branch, 317 S Clinton St, EORG, 07018	6712	D5
Fairview Public, 213 Anderson Av, FRVW, 07022	6611	C3
Floral Park Public, 17 Caroline Pl, FLPK, 11001	6827	C2
Fort Lee Public, 320 Main St, FTLE, 07024	6502	E5
Franklin Square Public, 19 Lincoln Rd, HmpT, 11010	6828	B4
Frederick L Ehrman, 550 1st Av, MHTN, 10016	116	E6
Frick Art Reference, 10 E 71st St, MHTN, 10021	113	A5
Garden City Public, 60 7th St, GDNC, 11530	6828	E2
Garfield Free Public, 500 Midland Av, GRFD, 07026	6500	B1
Gimbel Adam Sophie Design, 2 W 13th St, MHTN, 10011	119	A1
Glen Cunningham Public, 291 Martin Luther King Jr Dr - JSYC, 07305	6819	D4
Great Neck, 159 Bayview Av, SDRK, 11023	6616	D6
Great Neck-Lakeville Branch, 475 Great Neck Rd, NHmT - 11021	6723	A2
Great Neck-Parkville, 10 Campbell St, NHmT, 11040	6723	D6
Great Neck-Station Branch, 40 Great Neck Rd, GTPZ - 11021	6617	A7
Greenburgh Public, 300 E Main St, EMFD, 10523	6049	B6
Greenville Public, 1841 John F Kennedy Blvd, JSYC, 07305	6819	C5
Hamilton Fish Park Branch, 415 E Houston St, MHTN - 10002	119	D5
Hampton-Booth Theatre, 16 E 20th St S, MHTN, 10003	116	B7
Harold L Drimmer, 75 Grasslands Rd, GrbT, 10603	6049	D3
Harrison Public, 415 Harrison Av, HRSN, 07029	6714	A6
Harrison Public, 2 Bruce Av, HRSN, 10528	6283	C3
Hasbrouck Heights Free Public, 301 Division Av, HSBH - 07604	6500	D4
Hastings Public, 7 Maple Av, HAOH, 10706	6165	E7
Hatch Billops Collection, 491 Broadway, MHTN, 10012	118	E4
Heichel Menachem, 1581 52nd St, BKLN, 11219	7022	D1
Henry Waldinger Memorial, 60 Verona Pl, VLYS, 11580	6928	C3
Hewlett-Woodmere Public, 1125 Broadway, HmpT - 11557	6928	D7
Hillside Public, 155 Lakeville Rd, NHPK, 11040	6827	E1
Hoboken Public, 500 Park Av, HBKN, 07030	6716	D6
Hollis Branch, 202-05 Hillside Av, QENS, 11423	6826	C3
Holocaust, 557 Bedford Av, BKLN, 11211	6822	B5
Horrmann, 1 Campus Rd, STNL, 10304	7020	C3
Hudson Park Branch, 66 Leroy St, MHTN, 10014	118	C2
Huguenot Children's, 794 North Av, NRCH, 10804	6395	D2
Huntington Free, 9 Westchester Sq, BRNX, 10461	6505	D7
Investment Division, 320 E 43rd St, MHTN, 10017	117	A4
Irvington Free Public, 1 Civic Sq, IrvT, 07111	6816	C2
Irvington Public, 12 S Astor St, IRVN, 10533	6166	A1
Island Park Public, 176 Long Beach Rd, ISPK, 11558	7029	D5
Ivan Branch, 669 E 242nd St, BRNX, 10470	6394	C5
Jefferson Market Branch, 425 Avenue of the Americas - MHTN, 10011	118	E1
Jersey City Free Public, 472 Jersey Av, JSYC, 07302	6820	C3
Jersey City Free Public-Five Corners, 678 Newark Av - JSYC, 07306	6820	A1
Jersey City Free Public-Pavonia, 326 8th St, JSYC, 07302	6820	B2
Jersey City Public-The Heights, 14 Zabriskie St, JSYC - 07032	6716	B6
Jewish Russian, 4429 18th Av, BKLN, 11230	7022	E1
Jewish Youth, 1461 46th St, BKLN, 11219	6922	D7
John F Kennedy Memorial, 92 Hathaway St, WLTN - 07057	6500	A5
Johnson Public, 274 Main St, HKSK, 07601	6501	C1
Kearny Branch, 759 Kearny Av, KRNY, 07032	6714	C2
Kearny Public, 318 Kearny Av, KRNY, 07032	6714	B4
Kensington Jewish, 601 E 3rd St, BKLN, 11218	6922	E7
Kim Barrett Memorial, 535 E 70th St, MHTN, 10021	113	D6
King Criminal Courts, 120 Schermerhorn St, BKLN, 11201	121	B6
Lafayette Branch, 307 Pacific Av, JSYC, 07304	6820	A4
Lakeview Public, 1120 Woodfield Rd, HmpT, 11570	6929	D2
Larchmont Public, 121 Larchmont Av, LRMT, 10538	6396	D2
Leonia Public, 227 Fort Lee Rd, LEON, 07605	6502	D4
Levi Yitzchak, 305 Kingston Av, BKLN, 11213	6923	D3
Library of Agudas Chabad, 770 Eastern Pkwy, BKLN - 11213	6923	C3
Lodi Memorial, 1 Memorial Dr, LODI, 07644	6500	D2
Long Beach Public, 111 W Park Av, LBCH, 11561	7029	B7

Libraries

New York City/5 Borough Points of Interest Index

Military Installations

FEATURE NAME Address City ZIP Code	MAP#	GRID
Long Beach Public-West End, 868 W Beech St, LBCH - 11561	7028	E7
Lynbrook Public, 56 Eldert St, LNBK, 11563	6929	B5
Malkin Dance, 27 W 72nd St, MHTN, 10023	112	D3
Malverne Public, 61 St. Thomas Pl, MLVN, 11565	6929	B2
Mamaroneck Public District, 136 Prospect Av, MRNK - 10543	6282	E6
Manhasset Public System, 30 Onderdonk Av, NHmT - 11030	6617	E6
Manhattan Center, 75 Varick St, MHTN, 10013	118	C4
Marion Branch, 1017 W Side Av, JSYC, 07306	6819	E1
Martin J Keena Memorial, 86 Trinity Pl, MHTN, 10006	120	B1
McEntegart Hall, 222 Clinton Av, BKLN, 11205	6822	A7
Mendik, 57 Worth St, MHTN, 10013	118	C5
Metropolitan New York Council, 57 E 11th St, MHTN - 10003	119	A1
Miller Branch, 489 Bergen Av, JSYC, 07304	6819	D3
Mineola Memorial, 195 Marcellus Rd, MNLA, 11501	6724	E6
Morgan & Museum, 29 E 36th St, MHTN, 10016	116	C4
Mt Pleasant Public-Valhalla, 6 Cleveland St, MtPT, 10595	6050	A3
Mt Vernon Branch, 142 Mt Vernon Pl, NWRK, 07106	6712	B7
Mt Vernon Public, 28 S 1st Av, MTVN, 10550	6394	E4
Newark Public, 5 Washington St, NWRK, 07102	6713	E6
Newark Public-First Av Branch, 282 1st Av W, NWRK - 07107	6713	C3
Newark Public-Madison Branch, 790 Clinton Av, NWRK - 07108	6816	E2
Newark Public-Roseville Branch, 99 N 5th St, NWRK - 07107	6713	C5
Newark Public-Weequahic Branch, 355 Osborne Ter - NWRK, 07112	6816	E4
New Hyde Park Public, 1420 Jericho Tpk, NHPK, 11040	6828	A1
New York City Municipal, 31 Chambers St, MHTN, 10007	118	C6
New York Public, 2905 Grand Concourse, BRNX, 10468	6504	D3
New York Public, 498 5th Av, MHTN, 10018	116	C3
New York Public-58th St, 127 E 58th St, MHTN, 10022	113	A7
New York Public-67th St, 328 E 67th St, MHTN, 10065	113	C6
New York Public-96th St, 112 E 96th St, MHTN, 10128	113	E1
New York Public-115th St, 203 W 115th St, MHTN, 10026	109	D3
New York Public-Aguilar, 174 E 110th St, MHTN, 10029	110	A5
New York Public-Allerton, 2740 Barnes Av, BRNX, 10467	6505	B3
New York Public-Andrew Heiskell, 40 W 20th St, MHTN - 10011	116	A6
New York Public-Bloomingdale, 150 W 100th St, MHTN - 10025	109	A5
New York Public-Castle Hill, 947 Castle Hill Av, BRNX - 10473	6614	C2
New York Public-Chatham Square, 33 E Broadway - MHTN, 10002	118	E7
New York Public-City Island, 320 City Island Av, BRNX - 10464	6506	E6
New York Public-Clason's Point, 1215 Morrison Av, BRNX - 10472	6614	A1
New York Public-Columbus, 742 10th Av, MHTN, 10019	112	A6
New York Public-Countee Cullen, 104 W 136th St, MHTN - 10030	107	B7
New York Public-Dongan Hills, 1617 Richmond Av, STNL - 10314	7019	A4
New York Public-Donnell Center, 20 W 53rd St, MHTN - 10019	116	D1
New York Public-Eastchester, 1385 E Gun Hill Rd, BRNX - 10469	6505	D3
New York Public-Edenwald, 1255 E 233rd St, BRNX - 10466	6394	D7
New York Public-Epiphany, 228 E 23rd St, MHTN, 10010	116	C7
New York Public-Fordham, 2556 Bainbridge Av, BRNX - 10458	6504	D4
New York Public-Fort Washington, 535 W 179th St - MHTN, 10033	104	C4
New York Public-Francis Martin, 2150 University Av - BRNX, 10453	105	D2
New York Public-George Bruce - 518 Dr Martin L King Jr Blvd, MHTN, 10027	106	C7
New York Public-Grand Concourse, 155 E 173rd St - BRNX, 10457	105	C5
New York Public-Great Kills, 56 Giffords Ln, STNL, 10308	7117	B5
New York Public-Hamilton Grange, 503 W 145th St - MHTN, 10031	106	E4
New York Public-Harlem, 9 W 124th St, MHTN, 10027	110	A2
New York Public-Huguenot Park, 830 Huguenot Av, STNL - 10312	7116	B7
New York Public-Hunt's Point, 877 Southern Blvd, BRNX - 10459	6613	D3
New York Public-Inwood, 4790 Broadway, MHTN, 10034	101	E6
New York Public-Jerome Park, 118 Eames Pl, BRNX - 10468	102	E6
New York Public-Kingsbridge Branch, 280 W 231st St - BRNX, 10463	102	D2
New York Public-Kips Bay, 446 3rd Av, MHTN, 10016	116	D5
New York Public-Macombs Bridge - 2650 Adam Clayton Powell Jr Blv, MHTN, 10039	107	C3
New York Public-Melrose, 910 Morris Av, BRNX, 10451	6613	A2
New York Public-Mid-Manhattan, 455 5th Av, MHTN - 10016	116	C3
New York Public-Morningside, 2900 Broadway, MHTN - 10025	109	B2
New York Public-Morrisania, 610 E 169th St, BRNX - 10456	6613	C1
New York Public-Mosholu Branch, 285 E 205th St, BRNX - 10467	6504	E2
New York Public-Mott Haven, 321 E 140th St, BRNX - 10454	107	E7
New York Public-Muhlenburg, 209 W 23rd St, MHTN - 10011	115	E5
New York Public-New Amsterdam, 9 Murray St, MHTN - 10007	118	C6
New York Public-New Dorp, 309 New Dorp Ln, STNL - 10306	7118	A2
New York Public-Ottendorfer, 135 2nd Av, MHTN - 10003	119	B2
New York Public-Parkchester Branch - 1985 Westchester Av, BRNX, 10462	6614	B1
New York Public-Pelham Bay, 3060 Middletown Rd - BRNX, 10461	6506	A6
New York Public-Performing Arts, 40 Lincoln Center Plz - MHTN, 10023	112	C4
New York Public-Port Richmond, 75 Bennett Av, STNL - 10312	7116	C7
New York Public-Richmondtown, 200 Clarke Av, STNL - 10306	7117	C3
New York Public-Riverdale, 5540 Mosholu Av, BRNX - 10471	6393	C5
New York Public-Riverside, 127 Amsterdam Av, MHTN - 10023	112	C4
New York Public-Roosevelt Island, 524 Main St, MHTN - 10044	113	E7
New York Public-St. Agnes, 444 Amsterdam Av, MHTN - 10024	112	D1
New York Public-St. George, 5 Central Av, STNL, 10301	6920	D6
New York Public-Science Industry Business - 188 Madison Av, MHTN, 10016	116	C4
New York Public-Sedgwick, 1701 University Av, BRNX - 10453	105	B4
New York Public-Soundview, 660 Sound View Av, BRNX - 10473	6614	B3
New York Public-South Beach Branch, 21 Robin Rd - STNL, 10305	7021	A6
New York Public-Spuyten Duyvil, 650 W 235th St, BRNX - 10463	102	B1
New York Public-Stapleton, 132 Canal St, STNL, 10304	7020	D2
New York Public-Steward Park, 192 E Broadway, MHTN - 10002	119	B6
New York Public-Throg's Neck - 3025 Cross Bronx Expressway Ext, BRNX, 10465	6615	A2
New York Public-Todt Hill-Westerly, 2550 Victory Blvd - STNL, 10314	7019	B4
New York Public-Tompkins Square, 331 E 10th St, MHTN - 10009	119	D3
New York Public-Tottenville, 7430 Amboy Rd, STNL - 10307	7206	B4
New York Public-Tremont, 1866 Washington Av, BRNX - 10457	6504	C6
New York Public-Van Cortlandt, 3874 Sedgwick Av - BRNX, 10463	6504	D1
New York Public-Van Nest, 2147 Barnes Av, BRNX - 10462	6505	B5
New York Public-Wakefield, 4100 Lowerre Pl, BRNX - 10466	6394	B7
New York Public-Washington Heights - 1000 St. Nicholas Av, MHTN, 10032	107	B1
New York Public-Webster, 1465 York Av, MHTN, 10075	113	E5
New York Public-West Farms, 2085 Honeywell Av, BRNX - 10460	6504	E6
New York Public-Woodlawn Heights, 4355 Katonah Av - BRNX, 10470	6394	A6
New York Public-Woodstock, 761 E 160th St, BRNX - 10456	6613	C3
New York Public-Yorkville, 222 E 79th St, MHTN, 10075	113	D4
New York Society, 53 E 79th St, MHTN, 10075	113	C3
NJIT, 200 Central Av, NWRK, 07103	6713	D6
North Bergen Free Public, 8411 Bergenline Av, NBgT - 07047	6611	B5
North End Branch, 722 Summer Av, NWRK, 07104	6713	E2
North White Plaines Public, 10 Clove Rd, NoCT, 10603	6050	B4
Norwood Public, 198 Summit St, NRWD, 07648	6164	B6
Oceanside, 30 Davison Av, HmpT, 11572	6929	E6
Palisades Free, 19 Closter Rd, OrgT, 10964	6165	A4
Palisades Park Public, 257 2nd St, PALP, 07650	6502	C6
Pearsall Branch, 104 Pearsall Av, JSYC, 07305	6819	C6
Peninsula Public, 280 Central Av, LWRN, 11559	7028	A3
Perfecto Oyola Biblioteca Criolla, 280 1st St, JSYC - 07302	6820	C2
Perth Amboy Free Publick, 196 Jefferson St, PTHA, 08861	7205	D3
Port Chester Public, 1 Haseco Av, PTCH, 10573	6170	B5
Port Washington, 1 Library Dr, BXTE, 11050	6617	D1
Prometheus Research, 11 Lispenard St, MHTN, 10013	118	D5
Purchase Free, 3093 Purchase St, HRSN, 10577	6169	B1
Queen Borough Public-Glen Oaks, 256-04 Union Tpk - QENS, 11004	6723	B6
Queens, 37-45 21st St, QENS, 11101	6718	D4
Queens Borough Public, 89-11 Merrick Blvd, QENS - 11432	6825	D4
Queens Borough Public-Astoria, 14-01 Astoria Blvd - QENS, 11102	114	D4
Queens Borough Public-Auburndale - 25-55 Francis Lewis Blvd, QENS, 11358	6721	D2
Queens Borough Public-Bayside, 214-20 Northern Blvd - QENS, 11361	6722	B4
Queens Borough Public-Bay Terrace, 18-36 Bell Blvd - QENS, 11360	6722	A1
Queens Borough Public-Bellerose, 250-06 Hillside Av - QENS, 11426	6723	B7
Queens Borough Public-Cambria Heights - 220-20 Linden Blvd, QENS, 11411	6826	E6
Queens Borough Public-Court Square, 25-01 Jackson Av - QENS, 11101	6718	C6
Queens Borough Public-East Flushing - 196-36 Northern Blvd, QENS, 11358	6721	E4
Queens Borough Public-Flushing, 41-17 Main St, QENS - 11355	6720	E4
Queens Borough Public-Forest Hills, 108-19 71st Av - QENS, 11375	6824	D2
Queens Borough Public-Fresh Meadows - 193-20 Horace Harding Expwy S, QENS, 11365	6721	E7
Queens Borough Public-Glendale, 78-60 73rd Pl, QENS - 11385	6824	A5
Queens Borough Public-Hillcrest, 187-05 Union Tpk - QENS, 11366	6825	E1
Queens Borough Public-Howard Beach, 92-06 156th Av - QENS, 11414	6925	D3
Queens Borough Public-Jackson Hights, 35-51 81st St - QENS, 11372	6719	E5
Queens Borough Public-Langston Highs - 100-01 Northern Blvd, QENS, 11369	6720	A4
Queens Borough Public-Laurelton, 134-26 225th St - QENS, 11413	6927	D1
Queens Borough Public-Lefferts, 103-34 Lefferts Blvd - QENS, 11419	6825	A7
Queens Borough Public-Maspeth, 69-70 Grand Av, QENS - 11378	6823	D2
Queens Borough Public-McGoldrick, 155-06 Roosevelt Av - QENS, 11354	6721	B4
Queens Borough Public-Middle Village - 72-31 Metropolitan Av, QENS, 11379	6823	E4
Queens Borough Public-N Forest Park - 98-27 Metropolitan Av, QENS, 11375	6824	C4
Queens Borough Public-Pomonok, 158-21 Jewel Av - QENS, 11365	6825	B1
Queens Borough Public-Queensboro Hills, 60-05 Main St - QENS, 11355	6721	A6
Queens Borough Public-Queensbridge, 10-43 41st Av - QENS, 11101	6718	C5
Queens Borough Public-Queens Village, 94-11 217th St - QENS, 11428	6826	E3
Queens Borough Public-Ravenswood, 35-32 21st Av - QENS, 11105	6719	B2
Queens Borough Public-Richmond Hill, 118-14 Hillside Av - QENS, 11418	6824	E5
Queens Borough Public-Ridgewood, 20-12 Madison St - QENS, 11385	6823	C5
Queens Borough Public-Rochdale Village - 169-09 137th Av, QENS, 11434	6927	B2
Queens Borough Public-Rosedale, 144-20 243rd St - QENS, 11422	6927	E4
Queens Borough Public-St. Albans, 191-05 Linden Blvd - QENS, 11412	6826	C6
Queens Borough Public-Seaside - 116-15 Rockaway Beach Blvd, QENS, 11694	7123	E1
Queens Borough Public-South Hollis, 204-01 Hollis Av - QENS, 11412	6826	C4
Queens Borough Public-South Jamaica - 108-41 Guy R Brewer Blvd, QENS, 11433	6825	E6
Queens Borough Public-South Ozone Park - 128-16 Rockaway Blvd, QENS, 11420	6926	C2
Queens Borough Public-Steinway, 21-45 31st St, QENS - 11105	6719	B2
Queens Borough Public-Windsor Park, 79-50 Bell Blvd - QENS, 11364	6826	C1
Queens Borough Public-Woodhaven, 85-41 Forest Pkwy - QENS, 11421	6824	B6
Queens Borough Public-Woodside, 54-22 Skillman Av - QENS, 11377	6719	B6
Queens Public-Arverne, 312 Beach 54th St, QENS, 11691	7026	E6
Queens Public-Baisley Park Branch, 117-11 Sutphin Blvd - QENS, 11434	6926	D1
Queens Public-Briarwood Branch, 85-12 Main St, QENS - 11435	6825	B4
Queens Public-Broad Channel, 16-26 Cross Bay Blvd - QENS, 11693	7026	A5
Queens Public-Broadway, 40-20 Broadway, QENS, 11103	6719	A4
Queens Public-East Elmhurst, 95-06 Astoria Blvd, QENS - 11369	6720	A4
Queens Public-Elmhurst, 86-01 Broadway, QENS, 11373	6719	E7
Queens Public-Far Rockaway, 16-37 Central Av, QENS - 11691	7027	D4
Queens Public-Kew Gardens Hills, 72-33 Vleigh Pl, QENS - 11367	6825	A2
Queens Public-Mitchell Linden, 29-42 Union St, QENS - 11354	6721	A3
Queens Public-North Hills, 57-04 Marathon Pkwy, QENS - 11362	6723	A4
Queens Public-Ozone Park, 92-24 Rockaway Blvd, QENS - 11417	6925	D1
Queens Public-Peninsula, 92-25 Rockaway Beach Blvd - QENS, 11693	7026	B7
Queens Public-Poppenhusen, 121-23 14th Av, QENS - 11356	6614	D7
Queens Public-Rego Park, 91-41 63rd Dr, QENS, 11374	6824	B2
Queens Public-Whitestone, 151-10 14th Rd, QENS - 11357	6615	B7
Research Center for Judaic Studies, 1353 51st St, BKLN - 11219	7022	C1
Ricardo Ogorman, 23 W 129th St, MHTN, 10027	110	B1
Richard Walker Bolling Medical, 1111 Amsterdam Av - MHTN, 10025	109	C2
Ridgefield Free Public, 527 Morse Av, RDGF, 07657	6611	B1
Ridgefield Park Public, 135 Euclid Av, RDFP, 07660	6501	E5
Robert E Lee Civil War, 94 Green St, WbgT, 07095	7114	C4
Robert R Livingston Masonic, 71 W 23rd St, MHTN - 10010	116	A5
Rockville Centre Public, 221 N Village Av, RKVC, 11570	6929	D3
Rutherford Free Public, 150 Park Av, RTFD, 07070	6609	A2
Ryan, 715 North Av, NRCH, 10801	6395	E2
Rye Free Reading Room, 1061 Boston Post Rd, RYE - 10580	6283	E2
Scarsdale Public, 54 Olmsted Rd, SCDL, 10583	6167	D6
Sea Cliff, Sea Cliff Av, SCLF, 11579	6509	E6
Secaucus Public, 1379 Paterson Plank Rd, SECS, 07094	6610	A6
Sewaren Free Public, 546 West Av, WbgT, 07077	7114	E5
Shelter Rock Public, 165 Searingtown Rd S, NHmT, 11507	6724	D4
South Orange Public, 65 Scotland Rd, SOrT, 07079	6712	A6
Springfield Branch, 50 Hayes St, NWRK, 07103	6713	C7
Steinberg, 245 Lexington Av, MHTN, 10016	116	D4
Stephen B Luce, 6 Pennyfield Av, BRNX, 10465	6615	C4
Stewart Manor, 100 Covert Av, STMN, 11530	6827	E3
Story Court Branch, 16 W 4th St, BAYN, 07002	6919	D5
Sunnyside Branch, 43-06 Greenpoint Av, QENS, 11377	6719	A7
Tappan, 93 Main St, OrgT, 10983	6164	C3
Teaneck, 840 Teaneck Rd, TnkT, 07666	6502	B1
Tenafly, 100 Riveredge Rd, TFLY, 07670	6392	A2
Terrence Cardinal Cooke Cathedral Branch - 560 Lexington Av, MHTN, 10022	116	E2
Town of Pelham Public, 530 Colonial Av, PLMM, 10803	6395	B5
Train J, 11 E 73rd St, MHTN, 10021	113	B4
Tuckahoe Public, 71 Columbus Av, TCKA, 10707	6281	A6
Union City Branch, 420 15th St, UNCT, 07087	6716	D4
Union City Public-Main, 324 43rd St, UNCT, 07087	6716	E2
Vailsburg Branch, 75 Alexander St, NWRK, 07106	6712	D6
Van Buren Branch, 140 Van Buren St, NWRK, 07105	6818	A2
Walt Whitman Branch, 93 St. Edwards St, BKLN, 11205	121	D5
Warner, 121 N Broadway, TYTN, 10591	6048	B2
Weehawken, 525 Gregory Av, WhkT, 07086	6716	E3
Weehawken Free Public, 49 Hauxhurst Av, WhkT, 07086	6716	E3
West Bergen Branch, 476 W Side Av, JSYC, 07304	6819	D3
Westchester Square Branch, 2521 Glebe Av, BRNX - 10461	6505	D7
West Harrison Branch, 2 Madison St, HRSN, 10604	6050	D7
West Hempstead Public, 252 Chestnut St, HmpT, 11552	6828	D6
West New Brighton Branch, 976 Castleton Av, STNL - 10310	6919	E7
West New York Public, 425 60th St, WNYK, 07093	6611	A7
West Orange-Branch, 242 Main St, WOrT, 07052	6712	C1
West Orange Public, 46 Mt Pleasant Av, WOrT, 07052	6712	B1
White Plains Public, 100 Martine Av, WHPL, 10601	6168	A2
William E Dermody Public, 420 Hackensack St, CARL - 07072	6500	C7
Williston Park Public, 494 Willis Av, WLPK, 11596	6724	E4
Wollman, 3009 Broadway, MHTN, 10027	109	B1
Woodbridge Free Public-Main, 1 George Frederick Plz - WbgT, 07095	7114	B3
Wood Ridge Memorial, 231 Hackensack St, WRDG, 07075	6500	D6
Yonkers Public-Crestwood, 16 Thompson St, YNKR - 10707	6281	A4
Yonkers Public-Grinton I Will, 1500 Central Park Av - YNKR, 10708	6280	D6
Yonkers Public-Riverfront, 1 Dock St, YNKR, 10701	6393	C1

Military Installations

FEATURE NAME Address City ZIP Code	MAP#	GRID
7th Regiment Armory, 643 Park Av, MHTN, 10065	113	B6
Bronx National Guard, 10 W 195th St, BRNX, 10468	6504	C3
Brooklyn National Guard, 355 Marcy Av, BKLN, 11206	6822	B5
Brooklyn National Guard, 1579 Bedford Av, BKLN, 11225	6923	B3
Fifth Avenue National Guard, 2366 5th Av, MHTN - 10037	107	C6
Fort Hamilton, BKLN, 11252	7021	E4
Fort Tilden, QENS, 11697	7122	D3
Fort Wadsworth Naval Station New York, STNL, 10305	7021	A4
Jamaica National Guard, 9305 168th St, QENS, 11433	6825	D5
Jersey City National Guard, 678 Montgomery St, JSYC - 07306	6820	A2
Lexington Avenue National Guard, 68 Lexington Av - MHTN, 10010	116	C6
Newark National Guard, 120 Roseville Av, NWRK, 07107	6713	B5
New York Armory, STNL, 10314	7019	E2
Park Avenue National Guard, 643 Park Av, MHTN - 10065	113	B6
Peninsula at Bayonne Harbor, The, BAYN, 07002	6920	C2
Staten Island National Guard, 321 Manor Rd, STNL - 10314	7019	E2
US Army Reserve Center, OrgT, 10962	6164	D1
US Coast Guard, Daytona St, ATLB, 11509	7027	E6
US Coast Guard Heliport, Flatbush Av, BKLN, 11234	7024	E6

68 INDEX

INDEX 68

Military Installations

New York City/5 Borough Points of Interest Index

Other

FEATURE NAME Address City ZIP Code	MAP#	GRID
US Coast Guard Station, Rockaway Point Blvd, QENS - 11697	7122	E2
US Coast Guard Station New York, Courtney Lp, STNL - 10305	7021	A4
Valhalla National Guard, 2 Dana Rd, MtPT, 10595	6049	B2
Whitestone National Guard, 150-74 6th Av, QENS - 11357	6615	B6
Yonkers National Guard, 2 Quincy Pl, YNKR, 10701	6279	B7

Museums

FEATURE NAME Address City ZIP Code	MAP#	GRID
Abigail Adams Smith Mus, 421 E 61st St, MHTN, 10065	113	C7
Adept Mus, 325 Hawthorne Ter, MTVN, 10552	6395	A3
African Art Mus of SMA Fathers, 23 Bliss Av, TFLY - 07670	6392	A4
Afro-American Historical Society - 1841 John F Kennedy Blvd, JSYC, 07305	6819	C5
Alice Austen House Mus, 2 Hylan Blvd, STNL, 10305	7021	A3
Alternative Mus, 594 Broadway, MHTN, 10012	118	E4
American Academy of Arts & Letters, 633 W 155th St - MHTN, 10032	107	A1
American Craft Mus, 40 W 53rd St, MHTN, 10019	112	D7
American Folk Art Mus, 45 W 53rd St, MHTN, 10019	112	D7
American Friends of Shanghai Mus, 530 E 86th St - MHTN, 10028	114	A4
American Hungarian Mus, 178 Oakdene Av, TnkT, 07666	6502	A2
American Institute of Graphic Arts, 164 5th Av, MHTN - 10010	116	A6
American Merchant Marine Mus, 300 Steamboat Rd - KNGP, 11024	6616	B4
American Mus of Natural History, 200 Central Pk W - MHTN, 10024	112	E2
American Mus of the Moving Image, 36-01 35th Av - QENS, 11106	6718	E5
Anthology Film Archives, 32 2nd Av, MHTN, 10003	119	B4
Asian American Arts Centre, 26 Bowery, MHTN, 10013	118	E6
Aunt Len's Doll & Toy Mus, 6 Hamilton Ter, MHTN, 10031	106	E5
Aviation Hall of Fame & Mus, 400 Fred Wehran Dr, LFRY - 07643	6501	B5
Bard Center for Decorative Arts, 18 W 86th St, MHTN - 10024	113	A1
Barron Arts Center, 582 Rahway Av, WbgT, 07095	7114	C4
Bartow-Pell Mansion Mus, 895 Shore Rd, BRNX, 10464	6506	D1
Bayonne Community Mus, 229 Broadway, BAYN, 07002	6919	D4
Bronx Mus of the Arts, 1040 Grand Concourse, BRNX - 10456	6613	A1
Brooklyn Children's Mus, 145 Brooklyn Av, BKLN, 11213	6923	C2
Brooklyn History Mus, 128 Pierrepont St, BKLN, 11201	121	A5
Brooklyn Mus of Art, 200 Eastern Pkwy, BKLN, 11238	6923	A2
Chaim Gross Studio Mus, 526 Laguardia Pl, MHTN, 10012	118	E2
Chancellor Robert Livingston Mus, 71 W 23rd St, MHTN - 10010	116	A5
Charles A Dana Discovery Center, Central Pk N, MHTN - 10029	109	D4
Chelsea Art Mus, 556 W 22nd St, MHTN, 10011	115	C4
Children's Mus of Manhattan, 212 W 83rd St, MHTN - 10024	112	D1
Children's Mus of the Arts, 182 Lafayette St, MHTN - 10013	118	D4
Children's Mus of the Native American, 550 W 155th St - MHTN, 10031	107	A2
China Institute, 125 E 65th St, MHTN, 10065	113	B6
City Island Historical Mus, 190 E Fordham Rd, BRNX - 10468	6504	C4
City Island Mus, 190 Fordham St, BRNX, 10464	6506	E6
City Reliquary Mus, 370 Metropolitan Av, BKLN, 11211	6822	B3
Cloisters, The, Henry Hudson Pkwy, MHTN, 10040	101	D7
Coney Island Mus, 1208 Surf Av, BKLN, 11224	7120	D1
Conference House, 7455 Hylan Blvd, STNL, 10307	7206	A5
Congregation Emanuel Mus, 1 E 65th St, MHTN, 10065	113	A5
Cooper-Hewitt National Design Mus, 2 E 91st St, MHTN - 10128	113	C1
Cooper Union-Foundation Center, Cooper Sq, MHTN - 10003	119	B2
CRRNJ Terminal Mus, Audrey Zapp Dr, JSYC, 07305	6820	D4
Czech Center New York, 1109 Madison Av, MHTN, 10028	113	B3
Dahesh Mus, 580 Madison Av, MHTN, 10022	112	E7
Dia Center for the Arts, 535 W 22nd St, MHTN, 10011	115	C4
Doll & Toy Mus of NYC, 157 Montague St, BKLN, 11201	121	A5
Drawing Center, 35 Wooster St, MHTN, 10013	118	D4
Dyckman Farmhouse Mus, 4881 Broadway, MHTN - 10034	102	A6
Eastchester Marble School House, 388 California Rd - EchT, 10708	6395	B2
El Museo del Barrio, 1230 5th Av, MHTN, 10029	109	E5
Enrico Caruso Mus of America, 1942 E 19th St, BKLN - 11229	7023	B5
Fashion Institute of Technology Mus, 227 W 27th St - MHTN, 10001	116	A4
F Goodwin & J Ternbach Mus, 65-30 Kissena Blvd, QENS - 11367	6721	B7
Fort Lee Mus, 1589 Parker Av, FTLE, 07024	103	A4
Fort Schuyler Maritime Industry Mus, 6 Pennyfield Av - BRNX, 10465	6615	C4
Fraunces Tavern Mus, 54 Pearl St, MHTN, 10004	120	B2
Frick Collection, 1 E 70th St, MHTN, 10021	113	A5
Friends of Old Croton Aqueduct, 15 Walnut St, DBSF - 10522	6165	E4
Garibaldi-Meucci Mus, 420 Tompkins Av, STNL, 10305	7020	E3
Garvies Point Mus & Preserve, 50 Barry Dr, GLCV, 11542	6509	D4
Genesis II Mus of Int'l Black Culture, 2376 7th Av - MHTN, 10030	107	A5
Glove Mus, 304 5th Av, MHTN, 10001	116	B4
Goethe Institut-German Cultural Center, 1014 5th Av - MHTN, 10021	113	B2
Greenpoint Moniter Mus, 1101 Lorimer St, BKLN, 11222	6822	B2
Guggenheim Mus Soho, 575 Broadway, MHTN, 10012	118	E3
Hackensack Meadowlands Dev Com Env Ct & Mus - 2 Valley Brook Av, LynT, 07071	6609	A7
Hall of Fame for Great Americans, 100 Hall of Fame Ter - BRNX, 10453	105	C2
Harbor Defense Mus-Fort Hamilton, Sterling Dr, BKLN - 11252	7021	D4
Henry Urbach Arcitechture, 526 W 26th St, MHTN - 10001	115	D4
Hispanic Society of America, 613 W 155th St, MHTN - 10032	107	A1
Historic Hudson Valley, 150 White Plains Rd, TYTN, 10591	6048	B6
Historic Park & Mus, 2400 Hudson Ter, FTLE, 07024	6503	B4
Hoboken Historical Mus, 1301 Hudson St, HBKN, 07030	6716	E5
Hudson River Mus, 511 Warburton Av, YNKR, 10701	6279	C5
International Center of Photography - 1133 Avenue of the Americas, MHTN, 10036	116	C2
International Print Center New York, 526 W 26th St - MHTN, 10001	115	C3
Intrepid Mus, 12 W 46th St, MHTN, 10036	116	D2
Intrepid Sea-Air-Space Mus, W Joe Dimaggio Hwy, MHTN - 10036	111	D6
Isamu Noguchi Garden Mus, 32-37 Vernon Blvd, QENS - 11106	114	B6
Isamu Noguchi Sculpture Mus, 32-37 Vernon Blvd, QENS - 11106	114	C6
Jacques Marchais Mus of Tibetan Art, 338 Lighthouse Av - STNL, 10306	7117	C2
Jamaica Arts Center, 161-04 Jamaica Av, QENS, 11433	6825	C5
Jersey City Mus, 350 Montgomery St, JSYC, 07302	6820	B3
Jersey Explorer Children's Mus, 192 Dodd St, EORG - 07017	6713	A1
Jewish Mus, 1109 5th Av, MHTN, 10128	113	C1
John Street Church, 44 John St, MHTN, 10038	120	C1
Judaica Mus at the Hebrew Home, 5961 Palisade Av - BRNX, 10471	6393	B4
Judaica Mus of Centra Synagogue, 123 E 55th St, MHTN - 10022	117	A1
Kearny Cottage, 63 Catalpa Av, PTHA, 08861	7205	D5
Kearny Mus, 318 Kearny Av, KRNY, 07032	6714	B4
King Manor Mus, 150-03 Jamaica Av, QENS, 11432	6825	C5
Kurdish Mus, The, 144 Underhill Av, BKLN, 11238	6923	A1
Laguardia & Wagner Archives, 31-10 Thomson Av, QENS - 11101	6718	D6
Leo Kaplan Modern, 41 E 57th St, MHTN, 10022	112	E7
Liberty Hall Mus, 1003 Morris Av, UnnT, 07083	6917	C1
Liberty Science Center, 251 Phillip St, JSYC, 07304	6820	B4
Lladro Art Gallery & Mus, 43 W 57th St, MHTN, 10019	112	E6
Longwood Arts Project, 571 Walton Av, BRNX, 10451	107	E5
Lower East Side Tenement Mus, 90 Orchard St, MHTN - 10002	119	A5
Lyndhurst Mus, 635 S Broadway, TYTN, 10591	6048	B6
Madame Tussauds New York, 234 W 42nd St, MHTN - 10036	116	B2
Math Mus, 999 Herricks Rd, NHmT, 11040	6724	C4
Meadowlands Mus, 91 Crane Av, RTFD, 07070	6609	A3
Merchant's House Mus, 29 E 4th St, MHTN, 10003	119	A3
Metropolitan Historic Structures Association - 303 5th Av, MHTN, 10016	116	C4
Metropolitan Mus of Art, 1000 5th Av, MHTN, 10021	113	B2
Mexican Cultural Institute, 27 E 39th St, MHTN, 10016	116	D3
Micro Mus, 123 Smith St, BKLN, 11201	121	B7
Morris-Jumel Mansion, 65 Jumel Ter, MHTN, 10032	107	B1
Municipal Art Society, 457 Madison Av, MHTN, 10022	116	E1
Mus of American Financial Historical, The, 28 Broadway - MHTN, 10004	120	B2
Museum African American History, 352 W 71st St - MHTN, 10023	112	B2
Museum for African Art, 36-01 43rd Av, QENS, 11101	6718	E6
Museum of American Folk Art, 2 Columbus Av, MHTN - 10023	112	D4
Museum of American Illustration, 128 E 63rd St, MHTN - 10065	113	A6
Museum of Arts & Design, 40 W 53rd St, MHTN, 10019	112	D7
Museum of Bronx History, 3266 Bainbridge Av, BRNX - 10467	6504	E2
Museum of Chinese In the Americas, 70 Mulberry St - MHTN, 10013	118	E6
Museum of Comedy, 80-60 Pitkin Av, QENS, 11417	6925	C2
Mus of Contemporary African Diasporan Arts - 80 Hanson Pl, BKLN, 11217	121	E7
Museum of Jewish Heritage, 36 Battery Pl, MHTN, 10280	120	A2
Museum of Migrating People, 750 Baychester Av, BRNX - 10475	6505	E2
Museum of Modern Art, 11 W 53rd St, MHTN, 10019	112	D6
Museum of the American Piano, 211 W 58th St, MHTN - 10019	112	D4
Museum of the City of New York, 1220 5th Av, MHTN - 10029	109	E6
National Academy Mus & School of Fine Arts - 1083 5th Av, MHTN, 10128	113	C1
National Audubon Society, 700 Broadway, MHTN, 10003	119	A2
National Lighthouse Mus, 30 Bay St, STNL, 10301	6920	E7
National Mus of Catholic Art & History, 443 E 115th St - MHTN, 10029	110	C5
National Mus of the American Indian, 1 Bowling Grn - MHTN, 10004	120	B2
Neuberger Mus of Art, 735 Anderson Hill Rd, HRSN - 10577	6169	C1
Neue Galerie New York, 1048 5th Av, MHTN, 10128	113	B2
Neustadt Mus of Tiffany Art, The, 2166 Broadway, MHTN - 10024	112	C2
NY Studio Sch of Drawing, Painting & Sculptu - 8 W 8th St, MHTN, 10011	118	E1
Newark Mus, 49 Washington St, NWRK, 07102	6713	E6
New Mus of Contemporary Art, 583 Broadway, MHTN - 10012	118	E3
Newseum-New York, 580 Madison Av, MHTN, 10022	112	E7
New World Art Center-TF Chen Cultural Center - 250 Mulberry St, MHTN, 10012	118	E4
New York City Fire Mus, 278 Spring St, MHTN, 10013	118	C3
New York City Police Mus, 100 Old Slip, MHTN, 10004	120	C2
New York Earth Room, 141 Wooster St, MHTN, 10012	118	D3
New York Hall of Science, 111th St, QENS, 11368	6720	C6
New York Historical Society, 2 W 77th St, MHTN, 10024	112	E2
New York Mercantile Exchange Mus, 1 N End Av, MHTN - 10280	118	A6
NY State Council on the Arts-Mus Program - 915 Broadway, MHTN, 10010	116	A6
New York Transit Mus, 99 Schermerhorn St, BKLN, 11201	121	A6
Nicholas Roerich Mus, 319 W 107th St, MHTN, 10025	109	A3
Noble Maritime Collection, 1000 Richmond Ter, STNL - 10301	6920	A6
North Wind Undersea Mus, 610 City Island Av, BRNX - 10464	6506	D5
Old Stone House Historic Interpretive Center, 336 3rd St - BKLN, 11215	6922	D2
Paley Center for Media, 25 W 52nd St, MHTN, 10019	112	D7
Polish American Mus, 16 Belleview Av, NHmT, 11050	6617	E1
Proprietary House, The Royal Gov's Mansion - 149 Kearny Av, PTHA, 08861	7205	D4
Queensborough Community College Art Gallery - 56th Av, QENS, 11364	6722	C5
Queens County Farm Mus, 73-50 Little Neck Pkwy, QENS - 11426	6723	B6
Queens Mus of Art, Meridian Rd, QENS, 11355	6720	D6
Rock Hall Mus, 199 Broadway, LWRN, 11559	7027	E4
Rose Mus at Carnegie Hall, 154 W 57th St, MHTN, 10019	112	D7
Rubin Mus of Art, 150 W 17th St, MHTN, 10011	115	E6
Rye Arts Center, 51 Milton Rd, RYE, 10580	6284	A2
Salmagundi Mus of American Art, 47 5th Av, MHTN - 10003	119	A1
Scandinavia House, 58 Park Av, MHTN, 10016	116	C3
Schomburg Center for Black Culture, 515 Lenox Av - MHTN, 10030	107	B6
Science Mus of Long Island, 1526 N Plandome Rd, PLNM - 11030	6617	D4
Sea Cliff Village Mus, 95 10th Av, SCLF, 11579	6509	D6
Seton Hall University Mus, 400 S Orange Av, SOrT - 07079	6712	A6
Simmons Collection African Art Mus, 1063 Fulton St - BKLN, 11238	6923	B1
Sir John Soane Mus, 636 Broadway, MHTN, 10012	118	E3
Skyscraper Mus, 39 Battery Pl, MHTN, 10280	120	A2
Solomon R Guggenheim Mus, 1071 5th Av, MHTN - 10128	113	C1
Sony Wonder Technology Lab, 550 Madison Av, MHTN - 10022	112	E7
Square House Mus, 1 Purchase St, RYE, 10580	6283	E1
Staten Island Children's Mus, 1000 Richmond Ter, STNL - 10301	6920	B6
Staten Island Ferry Collection, 1 Richmond Ter, STNL - 10301	6920	E6
Staten Island Mus, 75 Stuyvesant Pl, STNL, 10301	6920	E6
Studio Mus In Harlem, 144 Dr Martin L King Jr Blvd, MHTN - 10027	110	A1
Synagogue Architecture and Art Library, 633 3rd Av - MHTN, 10017	116	D4
Taipei Gallery-Chinese Info & Culture Ct - 1230 Avenue of the Americas, MHTN, 10020	116	D1
Tarrytown Historical Mus, 1 Grove St, DBSF, 10522	6166	A4
Tenafly Nature Center, 313 Hudson Av, TFLY, 07670	6392	C2
Theatre Mus, 723 7th Av, MHTN, 10020	116	C1
Thomas Paine Cottage & Mus, 983 North Av, NRCH - 10804	6395	D1
Thread Waxing Space, 476 Broadway, MHTN, 10013	118	D5
Tibet House New York, 22 W 15th St, MHTN, 10011	116	A7
Trinity Mus of the Parish of Trinity Church, Broadway - MHTN, 10006	120	B1
Ukrainian Mus, 203 2nd Av, MHTN, 10003	119	B1
US Naval Mus, 78 S River St, HKSK, 07601	6501	C2
USS Ling New Jersey Naval Mus, 150 River St, HKSK - 07601	6501	C1
Van Cortlandt House Mus, Broadway, BRNX, 10471	6393	C7
Visual Arts Mus, 209 E 23rd St, MHTN, 10010	116	C7
Washington's Headquarters Mus, 140 Virginia Rd, NoCT - 10603	6050	A5
Waterfront Mus, 290 Conover St, BKLN, 11231	6922	A2
Wavertree Ship Mus, FDR Dr, MHTN, 10038	120	D2
Whitney Mus at Philip Morris, 120 Park Av, MHTN - 10017	116	D3
Whitney Mus of America, 217 5th Av, BKLN, 11215	6922	D2
Whitney Mus of American Art, 945 Madison Av, MHTN - 10021	113	B4
Wyckoff Farmhouse Mus, 5816 Clarendon Rd, BKLN - 11203	6924	A6
Yeshiva University Mus, 15 W 16th St, MHTN, 10011	116	A7
Yeshiva University Mus, 2520 Amsterdam Av, MHTN - 10033	104	D4

Open Space

FEATURE NAME Address City ZIP Code	MAP#	GRID
Bronx & Pelham Parkway, BRNX	6505	C4
Bronx River Parkway, BRNX	6614	A2
Bronx River Parkway, YNKR	6281	A5
Churchill Nature Preserve, TFLY	6392	B5
Cross County Parkway, MTVN	6395	B3
Cross Island Parkway, QENS	6827	A6
Flat Rock Brook Nature Center, EGLD	6503	A2
Garvies Point Preserve, GLCV	6509	D4
Grand Central Parkway, QENS	6720	D3
Greenburgh Nature Center, GrbT	6167	B5
Hackensack Meadowlands Cons & Wildlife Area, CARL	6610	B3
High Rock Pk Conservation Center, STNL	7117	E1
Hutchinson River Parkway, PLHM	6395	B4
Lenoir Preserve, YNKR	6279	E2
Lost Brook Preserve, TFLY	6392	D4
National Audubon Society, GrwT	6051	D1
Nature Conservancy, GrwT	6051	E3
Otter Creek Preserve, MRNK	6283	B6
Prall's Island Bird Haven, STNL	7018	A4
Rye Nature Center, RYE	6283	E2
Sadowski Parkway, PTHA	7205	D5
Sands Point Preserve, SNPT	6508	D4
Saw Mill Creek Wildlife Mangement Area, LynT	6715	A2
Saw Mill River Parkway, YNKR	6280	A3
Shore Parkway, BKLN	7023	E7
Shore Parkway, QENS	6926	A3
Tanglewood Preserve, HmpT	6929	C3
Taxter Road Nature Preserve, GrbT	6048	D7
Welwyn Preserve, GLCV	6509	E1
Wildflower Sanctuary, GrwT	6051	E1
William Cullen Bryant Preserve, ROSH	6618	E4
WT Davis Wildlife Refuge, STNL	7018	D5

Other

FEATURE NAME Address City ZIP Code	MAP#	GRID
Affinia Hotel, 155 3rd Av, MHTN, 10022	117	A2
Algonquin Hotel, 59 W 44th St, MHTN, 10036	116	C2
Alley Pond Environmental Center, 228-06 Northern Blvd - QENS, 11362	6722	C4
Alphabet City, Avenue B, MHTN, 10009	119	C3
Andrus Planetarium, 511 Warburton Av, YNKR, 10701	6279	C5
Astrophysical Observatory, 2800 Victory Blvd, STNL - 10314	7019	A4
Atlantic Beach Boardwalk, Ocean Blvd, ATLB, 11509	7028	A7
Belvedere Castle, Park Dr N, MHTN, 10024	113	A2
Canaan Baptist Church of Christ, 132 W 116th St, MHTN - 10026	109	D3
Cathedral Basilica of the Sacred Heart, 89 Ridge St - NWRK, 07104	6713	D5
Cathedral of the Incarnation, 50 Cathedral Av, GDNC - 11530	6828	E2
Cathedral of St. John the Divine, 1047 Amsterdam Av - MHTN, 10025	109	B3
Chase Manhattan Plaza, 1 Pine St, MHTN, 10005	120	C1
Christ & St. Stephen's Episcopal Church, 120 W 69th St - MHTN, 10023	112	C3
Christ Church, 326 Clinton St, BKLN, 11231	120	E7
Christ Church Riverdale, 5030 Henry Hudson Pkwy, BRNX - 10471	6393	C5
Church of the Ascension, 36 5th Av, MHTN, 10011	118	E1
Church of the Epiphany, 1393 York Av, MHTN, 10021	113	D5
Church of the Holy Apostles, 296 9th Av, MHTN, 10001	115	E4
Church of the Holy Trinity, 316 E 88th St, MHTN, 10128	113	E3
Church of the Incarnation, 209 Madison Av, MHTN - 10016	116	C4
Church of the Resurrection, 119 E 74th St, MHTN, 10021	113	B4
Church of the Transfiguration, 29 Mott St, MHTN, 10013	118	E6
Church of the Transfiguration, 1 E 29th St, MHTN - 10016	116	B5
Church of St. Andrew, 40 Old Mill Rd, STNL, 10306	7117	B2
Church of St. Luke In the Fields, 487 Hudson St, MHTN - 10014	118	C1
Church of St. Mary the Virgin, 145 W 46th St, MHTN - 10036	116	C1
Church on the Green, 42 Court St, HKSK, 07601	6501	C2
Colgate Clock, 105 Hudson St, JSYC, 07302	6820	D3
Coney Island Lighthouse, Beach 47th St, BKLN, 11224	7120	A1
Divine Riviera Hotel, 169 Clinton Av, NWRK, 07108	6817	C2
Donald Kendall Sculpture Gardens, 700 Anderson Hill Rd - HRSN, 10577	6169	D1
Draper Park Observatory, Washington Av, HAOH, 10706	6165	E7
Duffy Square, W 46th St, MHTN, 10036	116	C1
Eldridge Street Synagogue, 12 Eldridge St, MHTN - 10002	119	A6
Episcopal Church of the Good Shepherd, 240 E 31st St - MHTN, 10016	116	D5
Episcopal Church of the Heavenly Rest, 2 E 90th St - MHTN, 10128	113	C1

New York City/5 Borough Points of Interest Index

Other

FEATURE NAME Address City ZIP Code	MAP#	GRID
Episcopal Church of Our Savior, 48 Henry St, MHTN - 10002	119	A7
Execution Rocks Lighthouse, Sands Light Rd, WesC - 10580	6507	D2
Federal Reserve Bank of New York, 33 Liberty St, MHTN - 10038	120	C1
Floyd Bennett Field Observatory, Flatbush Av, BKLN - 11234	7024	B5
Gansevoort Market, 9th Av, MHTN, 10014	115	C6
Grace Church, 802 Broadway, MHTN, 10003	119	A1
Grand Army Plaza, 413 Flatbush Av, BKLN, 11238	6923	A2
Greenwich Village, W 9th St, MHTN, 10011	118	E1
Hayden Planetarium, 175 Central Pk W, MHTN, 10024	112	E2
Henry Luce Nature Observatory, Park Dr N, MHTN - 10021	113	B2
Hilton-Newark Gateway, 1 Raymond Blvd, NWRK, 07102	6817	E1
Hilton-Times Square, 234 W 42nd St, MHTN, 10036	116	B2
Holyrood Episcopal Church, 715 W 179th St, MHTN - 10033	104	B4
Independence Plaza, Greenwich St, MHTN, 10013	118	B5
Judson Memorial Church, 55 Washington Sq S, MHTN - 10012	118	E2
Lamont-Doherty Earth Observatory, Woods Rd, OrgT - 10964	6165	B4
Lincoln Square, 200 Amsterdam Av, MHTN, 10023	112	C3
Little Red Lighthouse, George Washington Br, MHTN - 10033	104	A4
Lower Plaza, 5th Av, MHTN, 10020	116	D1
Madison Square, 10 Madison Av, MHTN, 10010	116	B6
Malcolm Shabazz Mosque, 102 W 116th St, MHTN - 10026	109	E3
Marble Collegiate Church, 1 W 29th St, MHTN, 10001	116	B5
Memorial Baptist Church, 141 W 115th St, MHTN, 10026	109	E3
Midway Hotel, 216 W 100th St, MHTN, 10025	109	A5
New York Plaza, 1 Broad St, MHTN, 10004	120	B3
Northeast Bronx Planetarium, 750 Baychester Av, BRNX - 10475	6505	E2
Obelisk, The, Park Dr N, MHTN, 10021	113	B2
Our Lady of Lebanon Maronite Church, 113 Remsen St - BKLN, 11201	121	A5
Our Lady of Mercy, 260 Westchester Av, PTCH, 10573	6170	B5
Park Avenue, 375 Park Av, MHTN, 10022	116	E1
Parkhurst Hotel, 11 Lincoln Pk, NWRK, 07102	6817	D2
Plymouth Church of the Pilgrims, 75 Hicks St, BKLN - 11201	121	A3
Riegelmann Boardwalk, W 28th St, BKLN, 11224	7120	C2
Riverdale Presbyterian Church - 4765 Henry Hudson Pkwy W, BRNX, 10471	6393	B6
Riverside Church, 490 Riverside Dr, MHTN, 10027	106	B7
Robert Treat Hotel, 50 Park Pl, NWRK, 07102	6713	E7
Roosevelt Island Tramway, 1141 2nd Av, MHTN, 10022	113	B7
St. Ann's & the Holy Trinity Episcopal Ch, 38 Water St - BKLN, 11201	121	A2
St. Ann's Episcopal Church, St. Anns Av, BRNX, 10454	6613	A4
St. Bartholomew's Church, 109 E 50th St, MHTN, 10022	116	E1
St. Demetrios Cathedral, 30-11 30th Dr, QENS, 11102	6719	A3
St. George's Ukrainian Catholic Church, 30 E 7th St - MHTN, 10003	119	B3
St. James Church, 865 Madison Av, MHTN, 10021	113	B5
St. James Church, 32 James St, MHTN, 10038	118	E7
St. John's Episcopal Church, 9818 Fort Hamilton Pkwy - BKLN, 11209	7021	D3
St. Joseph & Michael the Archangel Church - 1314 Central Av, UNCT, 07087	6716	C4
St. Mark's-In-The-Bowery Church, 131 E 10th St, MHTN - 10003	119	B2
St. Michael's Church, 225 W 99th St, MHTN, 10025	109	A5
St. Nicholas Russian Orthodox Cathedral, 15 E 97th St - MHTN, 10029	109	D7
St. Patrick's Cathedral, 5th Av, MHTN, 10022	116	D1
St. Paul's Chapel, 209 Broadway, MHTN, 10007	118	B7
St. Peter's Church, 619 Lexington Av, MHTN, 10022	117	A1
St. Peter's Episcopal Church, 346 W 20th St, MHTN - 10011	115	D5
St. Thomas Church, 1 W 53rd St, MHTN, 10019	112	D7
Sands Point Lighthouse, Sands Light Rd, SNPT, 11050	6508	A4
San Gennaro Church, 113 Baxter St, MHTN, 10013	118	E5
Shakespeare Gardens, Park Dr S, MHTN, 10024	113	A2
Shrine of St. Elizabeth Ann Seton, 7 State St, MHTN - 10004	120	A2
Snug Harbor Cultural Center, 175 Richmond Ter, STNL - 10301	6920	B6
Socrates Sculpture Park, Vernon Blvd, QENS, 11106	114	C5
Stepping Stones Lighthouse, City Island Av, NasC - 11024	6616	A2
Tarrytown Lighthouse, Devries Av, SYHW, 10591	6048	A1
Temple Emanu-El, 1 E 65th St, MHTN, 10065	113	A6
Throgs Neck Lighthouse, Hanus St, BRNX, 10465	6615	E5
Times Square, Broadway, MHTN, 10036	116	B2
Titanic Memorial Lighthouse, 268 Pearl St, MHTN - 10038	120	D1
Trinity Church, 74 Trinity Pl, MHTN, 10006	120	B1
Tuscan Square, 16 W 51st St, MHTN, 10020	116	D1
Union Square, 50 E 17th St, MHTN, 10003	116	B7
United Nations Headquarters, MHTN, 10017	117	A3
Wall Street, 22 Wall St, MHTN, 10005	120	B1
Washington Arch, Waverly Pl, MHTN, 10011	118	E1
Washington Square, 2 5th Av, MHTN, 10011	118	E1
Winter Garden, Vesey St, MHTN, 10281	118	A6
World Financial Center, 200 Vesey St, MHTN, 10281	118	A7
World Trade Center (Site), Church St, MHTN, 10007	118	B7

Park & Ride

FEATURE NAME Address City ZIP Code	MAP#	GRID
Eltingville Transit Center, STNL	7116	D4
Park & Ride-Branch Brook Park, NWRK	6713	D1
Park & Ride-Carteret, CART	7017	C7
Park & Ride-E 45th St, BAYN	6920	B1
Park & Ride-Fort Lee, FTLE	103	A3
Park & Ride-Franklin Av, NWRK	6713	D1
Park & Ride-Irvington Bus Terminal, IrvT	6816	D2
Park & Ride-Liberty State Park, JSYC	6820	A4
Park & Ride-Lincoln Tunnel, NBgT	6716	C2
Park & Ride-Meadowlands, ERTH	6609	D4
Park & Ride-NJ Transit-W Side Av, JSYC	6819	C3
Park & Ride-Palisades-Atlantic, STNL	7018	B7
Park & Ride-Prospect Av, BAYN	6920	A3
Park & Ride RT-440, STNL	7206	D2
Park & Ride-Rutherford, ERTH	6609	B2
Park & Ride-Union Station, UnnT	6917	C1
Park & Ride-Vince Lombardi, RDGF	6610	D2

Parks & Recreation

FEATURE NAME Address City ZIP Code	MAP#	GRID
17th Street Pk, LNDN	7017	C2
24th Street Pk, MHTN	116	E7
Abendroth Pk, PTCH	6170	A6
Abington Square, MHTN	115	C7
Albert Memorial Pk, QENS	6927	C2
Alex Lindower Pk, BKLN	7024	B3
Alfred E Smith Memorial Pk, MHTN	120	E1
Allenwood Pk, NHmT	6617	A6
Alley Pond Pk, QENS	6722	D6
Allison Pk, STNL	6920	B7
Alpine Pk, ALPN	6278	E3
Ambrosini Field, BRNX	6506	E6
Amersfort Pk, BKLN	7023	D1
Amman Pk, TnkT	6502	A3
Andrew Lehman Field, BKLN	7021	C3
Andrus Pk, YNKR	6280	C6
Arlington Pk, JSYC	6819	E3
Arlington Pk, VLYS	6928	B2
Arrandale Avenue Town Pk, GTNK	6616	D5
Arthur Von Briesen Pk, STNL	7021	A4
Asser Levy Pk, BKLN	7120	E2
Astoria Pk, QENS	114	E3
Athletic Field, BGTA	6501	D1
Athletic Field, GTNK	6616	E5
Athletic Field, QENS	114	C3
Audubon Pk, JSYC	6819	C4
Austin House Pk, STNL	7021	A3
Avenel Pk, WbgT	7114	B2
Averill Boulevard Pk, HmpT	6827	E4
Bacheller Avenue Pk, LNDN	6917	D6
Baisley Pond Pk, QENS	6926	E2
Baldwin Farm, WHPL	6050	C7
Barret Pk, VLYS	6928	D6
Battery Pk, MHTN	120	A2
Battle Hill Pk, WHPL	6167	E2
Battle Whitney Pk, WHPL	6167	E2
Baxter Pond Pk, BXTE	6617	D1
Bay County Pk, HmpT	7029	C1
Bayside Pk, JSYC	6819	D6
Bayside Playfield, QENS	6721	E2
Bayswater Point State Pk, QENS	7027	A3
Belleville Pk, BlvT	6714	A1
Bell Tower Pk, BRNX	6393	B7
Belmont Hill Pk, GRFD	6500	A2
Bensonhurst Pk, BKLN	7022	B6
Bergan Beach Pk, BKLN	7024	C4
Bicentennial Veterans Memorial Pk, BRNX	6615	B2
Blackwell Pk, MHTN	113	E7
Blake Hobbs Pk, MHTN	110	A7
Bloomingdale Pk, STNL	7115	E7
Blue Heron Pk, STNL	7207	D1
Bogota Pk, BGTA	6501	D2
Boston Road Garden, BRNX	6505	B4
Bowling Green, MHTN	120	B2
Bowne Pk, QENS	6721	C3
Boynton Pk, WbgT	7114	E3
Brady's Pk, STNL	7020	D4
Branch Brook Pk, NWRK	6713	D2
Breezy Point Pk, QENS	7121	D5
Bregano Pk, YNKR	6394	C2
Broad Channel Memorial Pk, QENS	7026	B4
Broadway Pk, NHmT	6724	C7
Bronx Pk, BRNX	6505	A3
Bronx River Pk, BRNX	6613	E1
Brooklyn Marine Pk, BKLN	7024	A6
Brookville Pk, QENS	6927	D4
Brophy Field, ELIZ	6918	C4
Brower Pk, BKLN	6923	C2
Brush Pk, MTVN	6394	E6
Brust Square, BRNX	6393	C7
Bryan Pk, WHPL	6168	D3
Bryant Pk, MHTN	116	C3
Buchanan Street Pk, LNDN	7017	C3
Butler Field, SCDL	6167	D7
Buttermilk Ridge County Pk, GrbT	6048	E4
Byram Pk, GrwT	6170	D5
Byrne Memorial Pk, BKLN	6922	D2
Caldwell Pk, ELIZ	6917	D4
Captain Carlson Pk, WbgT	7115	A6
Carl Schurz Pk, MHTN	114	A3
Carroll Pk, BKLN	6922	C1
Carteret Pk, CART	7115	C1
Carteret Pk, ELIZ	6917	C4
Carteret Street Pk, WbgT	7115	A2
Castle Hill Pk, BRNX	6614	C4
Cedar Pk, YNKR	6393	C2
Centennial Pk, RKVC	6929	D4
Central Avenue Playground, HlsT	6816	C7
Central Pk, MHTN	109	C6
Cerrato Pk, YNKR	6393	C2
Charles Street Pk, LNDN	6917	A6
Chelsea Pk, MHTN	115	D3
Chelsea Waterside Pk, MHTN	115	C4
Christopher Morley Pk, NHLS	6618	C7
Church Square Pk, HBKN	6716	D7
City Hall Pk, MHTN	118	C7
City Pk, QENS	6720	A3
City Stadium Pk, GLCV	6509	E4
Claremont Pk, BRNX	105	D6
Clarence T Barrett Pk, STNL	7019	E2
Clark Memorial Pk, NHmT	6724	E2
Clay Pit Ponds State Pk, STNL	7115	C6
Clearview Garden, QENS	6721	D1
Clement Clarke Moore Pk, MHTN	115	D4
Cleveland Avenue Pk, LNDN	6917	A6
Clinton Community Garden, MHTN	112	A7
Clinton G Martin Pk, NHmT	6723	E5
Clove Lakes Pk, STNL	7020	A3
Cochrane Pk, JSYC	6819	D7
Cochran Pk, YNKR	6393	D1
Coffey Pk, BKLN	6922	A2
Columbia Pk, JSYC	6819	B6
Columbus Pk, GRFD	6500	B1
Columbus Pk, HBKN	6716	D6
Columbus Pk, MHTN	118	D6
Columbus Pk, YNKR	6393	C2
Commodore John Barry Pk, BKLN	121	D4
Community Pk, GDNC	6828	D3
Conference House Pk, STNL	7206	A5
Constitution Pk, FTLE	6502	E5
Cooper Green, SCDL	6167	E5
Cooper Pk, BKLN	6822	D3
Cooper Pk, MHTN	119	A2
Corlears Hook Pk, MHTN	119	D7
Coyne Pk, YNKR	6394	A5
Cranberry Lake Pk, NoCT	6050	C2
Crane Square, ELIZ	6918	A1
Crawford Pk, RYEB	6169	E4
Creedmore Farm Pk, QENS	6723	B6
Crocheron Pk, QENS	6722	B2
Crossway Field, SCDL	6282	B2
Crotona Pk, BRNX	105	E7
Culver Pk, YNKR	6393	C3
Cunningham Pk, QENS	6826	A1
Cutter Mill Pk, NHmT	6723	A1
Dag Hammarskjold Plaza, MHTN	117	A3
Dahnerts Pk, GRFD	6500	B1
Damrosch Pk, MHTN	112	B4
Dana Garden, QENS	6825	B1
Dante Pk, MHTN	112	C4
Davenport Pk, NRCH	6396	A6
De Duivel Pk, BKLN	6923	C7
Deer Pk, STNL	7020	A4
Delfino Pk, WHPL	6168	C1
Devoe Pk, BRNX	102	D7
De Witt Clinton Pk, MHTN	112	A6
Didomenico Pk, BAYN	6919	D3
Disbrow Pk, RYE	6283	E4
Dobson Pk, LNDN	6917	A7
D'Onforio Memorial Pk, NRCH	6395	D6
Donnelly Pk, WNYK	111	C1
Doughboy Pk, QENS	6719	B6
Douglass Pk, NWRK	6817	C2
Drake Pk, BRNX	6613	E4
Drake Road Pk, SCDL	6281	D1
Dr Andrew Memorial Pk, QENS	6926	C1
Draper Pk, HAOH	6165	E7
Dreier Offerman Pk, BKLN	7120	C1
Dr Martin Luther King Jr Memorial Pk, LNDN	6917	A7
Drotar Field, ELIZ	6917	E6
Duane Pk, MHTN	118	B6
Duarte Square, MHTN	118	C4
Duck Pond Pk, SECS	6715	E2
Dunn Pk, YNKR	6279	D7
Dyker Beach Pk, BKLN	7021	E5
Eastchester Gardens, BRNX	6505	C3
East River Pk, MHTN	119	E5
Echo Pk & Pool, HmpT	6828	C6
Ecological Pk, MHTN	114	A6
Eddy Avenue Pk, LNDN	7017	B2
Edgewood Pk, PTCH	6170	B7
Edward Feir Statue Pk, STNL	6920	D6
EF Jones Pk, JSYC	6820	B1
Elizabeth Port LL Field, ELIZ	6918	C4
Elizabeth River Pk, ELIZ	6918	A5
Elmont Road Pk, HmpT	6827	B6
Elmore RC Pk, ELIZ	6917	B3
Elmwood Pk, EORG	6712	E5
Elysian Pk, HBKN	6716	E6
Empire-Fulton Ferry State Pk, BKLN	121	A2
English Neighborhood Pk, RDGF	6611	B2
Esplanade Pk, MHTN	118	A7
Evergreen Pk, QENS	6823	C6
Evergreen Pk, STNL	7117	B4
Everit Macy County Pk, IRVN	6166	D1
Ewen Pk, BRNX	102	C2
Faber Pk, STNL	6919	C7
Father Fagan Pk, MHTN	118	D3
Fay Pk, YNKR	6393	B4
Feeney Pk, NRCH	6395	C4
Felton Field, BlmT	6713	B2
Ferry Point Pk, BRNX	6614	E4
Fifth Ward Pk, LNDN	6917	C5
First Pk, MHTN	119	B4
Fishbridge Garden, MHTN	120	D1
Fisk Pk, JSYC	6716	C6
Fitzpatrick Tompkins Pk, YNKR	6279	E4
Five Islands Pk, NRCH	6396	B4
Fleming Pk, YNKR	6393	E2
Flint Pk, MrnT	6396	D1
Florence Street Pk, MRNK	6283	A5
Flower Hill Pk, FLHL	6618	A4
Floyd Bennett Field, BKLN	7122	D1
Flushing Meadows-Corona Pk, QENS	6824	D1
Flushing Meadows Pk, QENS	6720	C6
Fords Pk, WbgT	7114	A7
Forest Pk, QENS	6824	C5
Fort Greene Pk, BKLN	121	E6
Fort Independence Pk, BRNX	6504	D1
Fort Totten Pk, QENS	6616	A7
Fort Tryon Pk, MHTN	101	D7
Fort Washington Pk, MHTN	104	A3
Foschini Memorial Pk, HKSK	6501	D1
Fox Memorial Pk, BKLN	7024	A1
Francis Lewis Pk, QENS	6615	A6
Frank D O'Connor Pk, QENS	6719	D6
Frank Golden Memorial Pk, QENS	6720	E1
Franklin Square Pk, HmpT	6828	B5
Frank M Charles Memorial Pk, QENS	6925	E5
Frank Sinatra Pk, HBKN	6716	E7
Frank Turner Inlet Pk, QENS	6722	C3
Franz Sigel Pk, BRNX	107	E4
Fresh Kills Pk, STNL	7018	D6
Friends Field, BKLN	7022	E3
Frog Hollow, ELIZ	6918	B6
Fulton Pk, BKLN	6923	D1
Gantry Plaza State Pk, QENS	117	C5
Gardella Pk, WHPL	6050	A7
Garibaldi Pk, RYEB	6170	A6
Gateway National Rec Area, STNL	7118	C2
Gateway National Rec Area-Canarsie Pier, BKLN	7024	D2
Gateway National Recreation Area, BKLN	6925	B5
Gateway NRA-Jamaica Bay Wildlife Refuge, BKLN	7025	B5
Gateway NRA-Jamaica Bay Wildlife Refuge, QENS	6926	A7
Gateway Plaza, MHTN	117	B1
General Basimin Pulaski Memorial Pk, LNDN	7017	A2
General Douglas A MacArthur Pk, STNL	7020	B7
General Douglas MacArthur Pk, MHTN	117	B3
George Field Pk, SCDL	6167	E4
George T Farewell Memorial Pk, LNDN	6917	A7
George W Harvey Memorial Field, QENS	6721	A1
Georgia Pk, QENS	6824	E7
Gillie Pk, WHPL	6168	C4
Glen Island County Pk, NRCH	6506	E1
Gorden Pk, JSYC	6716	A6
Gould Pk, DBSF	6166	B4
Governor Nelson A Rockefeller Pk, MHTN	118	A5
Gramercy Pk, MHTN	116	B7
Grant County Pk, HmpT	6928	E6
Grant Pk, YNKR	6279	D7
Gravesend Pk, BKLN	7022	D2
Great Kills Pk, STNL	7117	D5
Greeley Square, MHTN	116	B4
Green Acres Pk, ELIZ	6917	C4
Greis Pk, LNBK	6928	E4
Grist Mill Pond County Pk, SDRK	6616	D6
Grove Pk, SOrT	6712	A6
Grover Cleveland Pk, QENS	6823	B4
Haffen Pk, BRNX	6505	D2
Hagel Avenue Pk, LNDN	6917	C5
Halls Pond Pk, HmpT	6828	C7
Halsey Pk, IRVN	6166	B2
Hamilton Fish Pk, MHTN	119	C5
Hamilton Pk, JSYC	6820	C2
Hanover Square, MHTN	120	C2
Harbor Island Pk, MRNK	6282	E6
Harbor View Pk, BAYN	6920	E3
Harkness Pk, RYEB	6170	A1
Harold Walls Field, RTFD	6609	B2
Harrison Pk, NWRK	6817	C2
Harris Pk, BRNX	6504	D2
Hartley Pk, MTVN	6394	E3

Parks & Recreation

Parks & Recreation

New York City/5 Borough Points of Interest Index

FEATURE NAME Address City ZIP Code	MAP#	GRID
Harwood Pk, SCDL	6167	D6
Hawthorne Pk, TnkT	6502	B2
Hayes Pk, NWRK	6818	C1
Hayes Pk West, NWRK	6817	B1
Hempstead Harbor County Pk, NHmT	6618	C1
Hempstead Lake State Pk, HmpT	6929	E1
Hendrickson Pk, VLYS	6928	D2
Hennesy Street Pk, NWRK	6818	A2
Henning Pk, YNKR	6280	B5
Henry Hudson Memorial Pk, BRNX	102	A2
Herald Square, MHTN	116	B3
Hermon A Macneil Pk, QENS	6614	C7
Hero Pk, STNL	7020	C1
Herricks Pk, NHmT	6724	C4
Hewlett Point Pk, HmpT	7029	B1
High Bridge Pk, MHTN	104	D6
Highland Memorial Pk, HRPK	6164	A7
Highland Pk, QENS	6823	D7
Hillside Pk, HAOH	6166	A6
Hitchcock Field, HSBH	6500	E3
Hogan Pk, YNKR	6280	B2
Holland Pk, ELIZ	6918	A3
Home Terrace Pk, ROSL	6917	A6
Hopelawn Pk, WbgT	7205	A1
Hudson Fulton Pk, YNKR	6279	D3
Hudson Pk & Beach, NRCH	6396	B5
Hudson River Pk, MHTN	111	E5
Hunt Woods Pk, MTVN	6395	A1
Hutchinson Field, MTVN	6395	A6
Hyatt Field, SCDL	6281	C1
Independence Pk, NWRK	6818	A2
Inlet Pk, BKLN	6822	B2
Inwood Hill Pk, MHTN	101	E5
Inwood Pk, HmpT	7027	B3
Irving Square, BKLN	6823	B6
Irvington Pk, IrvT	6816	C3
Isham Pk, MHTN	102	A5
Ivy Hill Pk, NWRK	6712	B7
Jackie Robinson Pk, MHTN	107	B4
Jackson Pk, ELIZ	6918	C5
Jackson Square, MHTN	115	D6
Jacob Purdy Pk, WHPL	6168	A1
Jacob Riis Pk, QENS	7123	A2
Jahring Pk, DBSF	6166	B3
James Gordon Bennet Pk, MHTN	104	B3
James Iozzi Memorial Pk, LNDN	6917	B6
James J Braddock North Hudson Pk, NBgT	6611	B5
James J Walker Pk, MHTN	118	C2
Jefferson Pk, ELIZ	6918	A2
Jesse Lee Allen Pk, NWRK	6817	C2
J Harvey Turnure Memorial Pk, WHPL	6168	B1
J Hood Wright Pk, MHTN	104	B5
Jim Franco Field, BKLN	7022	E7
John D Caemmerer Town Pk, NHmT	6724	D3
John Golden Pk, QENS	6722	B2
John Jay Pk, MHTN	113	E5
John J Carty Pk, BKLN	7021	D3
John Mullaly Pk, BRNX	107	E2
John O'Rourke Memorial Pk, OrgT	6164	E3
John Paul Jones Pk, BKLN	7021	D4
John Russell Wheeler Pk, LNDN	7017	A2
Jonathan Ielpi Firefighter's Memorial Pk, GTPZ	6617	A7
Joseph Medwick Memorial Pk, CART	7017	B5
Joseph Thomas McGuire Pk, BKLN	7024	C2
Joyce Kilmer Pk, BRNX	107	E3
Julius J Richman Memorial Pk, BRNX	105	E4
Julius Weissglass Memorial Pk, STNL	7019	B1
Juniper Valley Pk, QENS	6823	E3
Kellogg Pk, ELIZ	6918	A1
Kenah Field, ELIZ	6918	A1
Kensico Plaza Pk, NoCT	6050	B3
Kill Van Kull Pk, BAYN	6919	C6
Kingsland Point County Pk, SYHW	6048	A1
Kings Point Pk, KNGP	6616	D4
Kinnally Cove, HAOH	6165	D6
Kinsley Pk, YNKR	6279	E5
Kissena Corridor Pk, QENS	6721	A6
Kissena Pk, QENS	6721	B6
Kittrell Pk, WHPL	6168	A2
Lafayette Pk, JSYC	6820	A3
Lakeville Pk, LKSU	6723	A2
Lance Corporal Melnyk Memorial Pk, LNDN	7017	B2
La Tourette Pk, STNL	7117	C1
Laurel Hill County Pk, SECS	6715	D4
Lawn Pk, The, NRCH	6395	E3
Lawrence C Thompson Memorial Pk, STNL	6919	E7
Leeds Pond Pk, PLNM	6617	D3
Leggett Pk, ELIZ	6918	A3
Leif Ericson Pk & Square, BKLN	6921	E7
Lemon Creek Pk, STNL	7207	A3
Lennon Pk, YNKR	6279	D6
Liberty Pk, NRCH	6396	A5
Liberty Pk, QENS	6825	E5
Liberty Square, ELIZ	6918	B5
Liberty State Pk, JSYC	6820	B5
Lighthouse Pk, MHTN	114	B4
Lincoln Pk, JSYC	6819	C1
Lincoln Pk, NRCH	6395	D3
Lincoln Pk, NWRK	6817	D2
Lincoln Terrace Pk, BKLN	6923	E3
Lindbergh Field, CARL	6500	B6
Linden Pk, QENS	6720	B6
Lindsay Pk, BKLN	6822	C5
Linton Pk, BKLN	6924	D3
Little League Field, The, CARL	6500	C7
Little Bay Pk, QENS	6615	D7
Lodi Memorial Pk, LODI	6500	C2
Long Beach Pk, LBCH	7029	C7
Lorenzo Pk, LRMT	6396	C3
Losee Pk, TYTN	6048	A3
Louis Cuvillier Pk, MHTN	110	D4
L Ron Hubbard Pk, ELIZ	6917	E2
Lynch Memorial Pk, ELIZ	6918	A2
Lyon Pk, PTCH	6170	B4
MacEachron Pk, HAOH	6165	D6
Mack Place Pk, LNDN	6917	D6
Macombs Dam Pk, BRNX	107	D3
Madison Square Pk, MHTN	116	B6
Magnolia Pk, RYEB	6170	B2
Mahon Pk, ELIZ	6917	E4
Main Street Pk, NHmT	6617	D1
Maithiessen Pk, IRVN	6048	A7
Manhasset Valley Pk, NHmT	6617	C7
Manhattan Beach Pk, BKLN	7121	C1
Manorhaven Town Pk, MHVN	6508	C7
Manor Pk, LKSU	6723	C1
Manor Pk, LRMT	6396	D3
Maplecrest Pk, MplT	6816	A2
Marconi Memorial Field, QENS	6825	D6
Marcus Garvey Memorial Pk, MHTN	110	A2
Maria Hernandez Pk, BKLN	6823	A5
Marine Pk, QENS	7123	D1
Marshland County Pk, RYE	6283	C5
Mary Benson Pk, JSYC	6820	B2
Masera Pk, QENS	6823	D4
Masnicki Pk, ELIZ	6918	B5
Massaro Pk, GrbT	6049	B4
Mattano Circle, ELIZ	6917	B3
Mattano Pk, ELIZ	6918	A5
Maurice Pk, QENS	6823	B2
Maze Memorial Pk, BKLN	6923	D7
McCarren Pk, BKLN	6822	B3
McGillvray Place Pk, LNDN	6917	D6
McGoldrick Pk, BKLN	6822	C2
McKinley Pk, BKLN	7022	A1
McNair Pk, MHTN	110	B3
McPherson Pk, ELIZ	6917	B3
Meadowland Pk, SOrT	6712	A5
Memorial Field, QENS	6721	B2
Memorial Pk, CLST	6278	A2
Memorial Pk, DBSF	6165	E4
Memorial Pk, EORG	6712	E4
Memorial Pk, WNYK	111	A1
Mercer Pk, BAYN	6819	A6
Merillon Town Pk, LKSU	6723	E4
Merrill County Pk, WbgT	7114	A1
Michaelis Bayswater Pk, QENS	7027	B5
Mildred Helms Pk, NWRK	6817	A3
Milford Pk, NWRK	6817	B3
Military Pk, NWRK	6713	E7
Milkosky Pk, LNDN	6917	D6
Miller Field, STNL	7118	B3
Miller Pk, ELIZ	6918	B4
Miller Pk, WNYK	6610	E7
Mill Pond Pk, PTWN	6508	D7
Mill Rock Pk, MHTN	114	B2
Mitchell Garden, QENS	6721	A2
Morgan Days Pk, RKVC	6929	D4
Morgan Memorial Pk, GLCV	6509	D4
Morningside Pk, MHTN	109	C3
Nansen Pk, STNL	7018	D5
Nature Study Woods Pk, NRCH	6395	C2
Neptune Pk, NRCH	6395	E7
New York Athletic Club, PLMM	6506	D1
Nicholas Lia Memorial Pk, STNL	6920	D6
North Cove, MHTN	118	A6
North Hempstead Town Pk, NHmT	6724	A6
North Woodmere County Pk, HmpT	6927	E6
Oak Avenue Pk, WbgT	7114	B5
O'Boyle Pk, YNKR	6393	C2
O'Brien Field, ELIZ	6918	A4
O'Donohoe Pk, QENS	7027	D6
Olmsted-Beil House Pk, STNL	7208	A1
Olympia Square, ELIZ	6918	A4
Orange Pk, COrT	6712	C4
Overpeck County Pk, TnkT	6502	B4
Owls Head Pk, BKLN	6921	D7
Ozone Pk, QENS	6925	D2
Paerdegat Pk, BKLN	6923	D7
Palisades Interstate Park-New Jersey, FTLE	103	B2
Palisades Interstate Park-New York, OrgT	6165	B6
Parade Grounds, BKLN	6923	A5
Patriots Pk, TYTN	6048	B2
Pelham Bay Pk, BRNX	6506	D1
Pellegrino Pk, PTWN	6508	C7
Pelton Pk, YNKR	6393	D3
Pemberwick Pk, GrwT	6170	C3
Pershing Field, JSYC	6716	B7
Peter Detmold Pk, MHTN	117	B2
Phil Rizzuto Pk, UnnT	6917	D2
Pinebrook Pk, NRCH	6282	A6
Pine Ridge Pk, RYEB	6169	E3
Pitkin Pk, YNKR	6393	C1
Plandome Pk, PLNH	6617	D5
Poe Pk, BRNX	6504	D4
Pond Pk, GTNE	6722	D1
Port Reading Pk, WbgT	7115	B2
Powell's Cove Pk, QENS	6614	D7
Prospect Avenue Pk, WbgT	7114	B1
Prospect Pk, BKLN	6923	A3
Pugsley Creek Pk, BRNX	6614	C4
Pulaski Pk, HKSK	6501	C4
Pulaski Pk, PASC	6500	A3
Queens Bridge Pk, QENS	117	E2
Rahway Avenue Pk, WbgT	7114	D2
Rainey Pk, QENS	114	B6
Ralph Donin Playfield, NRCH	6281	E5
Ralph J Bunche Pk, MHTN	117	A4
Ramon Aponte Pk, MHTN	112	B7
Randalls Island Pk, MHTN	110	E5
Randolph Walker Pk, STNL	6920	A6
Ravine Pk, GTNK	6617	B5
Raymond M O'Connor Field, QENS	6722	A2
Red Hook Recreational Area, BKLN	6922	B2
Redmond Pk, YNKR	6280	A7
Reed's Basket Willow Swamp Pk, STNL	7020	B5
Regina Street Pk, WbgT	7114	B3
Residence Pk, NRCH	6395	E6
Reynolds Field, HAOH	6165	E7
Richard A Rutkowski Pk, BAYN	6819	A7
Richard De Korte Pk, LynT	6609	A7
Richard Tucker Pk, MHTN	112	C4
Rich Manor Pk, RYEB	6170	A3
Ridge Road County Pk, GrbT	6167	B3
Riggin Memorial Field, ERTH	6609	B2
River Bank Pk, KRNY	6714	B1
River Bank Pk, NWRK	6818	A1
Riverbank State Pk, MHTN	106	C4
Riverside Pk, BRNX	102	A1
Riverside Pk, MHTN	106	B7
Riverside Pk South, MHTN	112	B2
River View Pk, JSYC	6716	C6
Robert F Wagner Jr Pk, MHTN	120	A1
Roberto Clemente State Pk, BRNX	105	A2
Robert Venable Pk, BKLN	6925	B2
Rockaway Community Pk, QENS	7026	E5
Rockaway Pk, QENS	7123	D2
Roger Morris Pk, MHTN	107	B1
Roosevelt Commons, TFLY	6392	A2
Roslyn Pk, RSLN	6618	D6
Roy Wilkens Pk, QENS	6826	B7
Rudyk Pk, PTHA	7205	E1
Rufus King Pk, QENS	6825	C5
Rum Brook Pk, GrbT	6048	E7
Rum Brook Pk East, GrbT	6049	A7
Rye Hills Pk, RYEB	6169	E4
Rye Recreation Pk, RYE	6284	A2
Rye Town Pk, RYE	6284	A4
Saddle Rock Pk, SDRK	6616	D6
St. Albans Memorial Pk, QENS	6826	A6
St. Catherine's Pk, MHTN	113	C6
St. Gabriels Pk, MHTN	116	E5
St. James Pk, BRNX	6504	C4
St. John's Pk, BKLN	6923	D2
St. Mark's Pk, LNDN	6917	B6
St. Mary's Pk, BRNX	6613	B4
St. Michael's Pk, QENS	6719	C3
St. Nicholas Pk, MHTN	106	E6
St. Peter's Pk, NWRK	6816	D4
Sakura Pk, MHTN	106	B7
Samuel N Bennerson Pk, MHTN	112	B4
Samuel Nelkin County Pk, WLTN	6500	A6
Sanford Field, HlsT	6816	C5
Sarah D Roosevelt Pk, MHTN	119	A5
Saratoga Square Pk, BKLN	6823	A7
Saxon Woods County Pk, SCDL	6282	C1
Scarangella Pk, BKLN	7022	D6
Schaefer Town Pk, OrgT	6164	A2
Schmidt's Woods Pk, SECS	6610	B5
Schmul Pk, STNL	7018	C7
Schultze Pk, YNKR	6281	A3
Secor Woods Pk, GrbT	6167	A3
Seton Falls Pk, BRNX	6505	D1
Seton Pk, BRNX	102	B1
Seventh Ward Pk, LNDN	7017	B2
Seward Pk, MHTN	119	B6
Shell Creek Pk, HmpT	7029	E5
Sheltering Arms Pk, MHTN	106	D6
Sheridian Pk, ELIZ	6917	E4
Sherman Square, MHTN	112	C3
Shore Pk, PLMM	6506	D1
Shore Road Pk, BKLN	7021	C1
Silver Lake Pk, STNL	7020	B1
Silver Lake Pk, WHPL	6050	D6
Silver Point County Pk, ATLB	7027	D6
Smith Pk, YNKR	6279	E6
Snipes Beach Pk, SECS	6609	E6
Soho Square, MHTN	118	D3
Sound View Pk, BRNX	6614	A3
South Cove Pk, MHTN	120	A1
South Point Pk, MHTN	117	C3
Soverel Pk, EORG	6712	D1
S Parkes Cadman Plaza, BKLN	121	A4
Sprain Ridge Pk, YNKR	6280	B2
Spring Creek Pk, BKLN	6925	A5
Springfield Pk, QENS	6927	B4
Stannards Brook Pk, NHmT	6617	D2
Stephen R Gregg Bayonne Pk, BAYN	6920	A1
Steppingstone Pk, KNGP	6616	C3
Stevens Pk, HBKN	6716	E7
Strauss Pk, NoCT	6050	C3
Stuyvesant Square, MHTN	119	C1
Sullivan Oval Pk, YNKR	6393	D2
Sunnybrook Pk, YNKR	6394	C1
Sunrise Hill Pk, STNL	7019	B4
Sunset Pk, BKLN	6922	B5
Sutherland Pk, YNKR	6393	C3
Sutton Place Pk, MHTN	117	C2
Sylvester Land Field, ROSL	6917	A6
Tallman Mountain State Pk, OrgT	6165	A2
Tarrytown Lakes County Pk, GrbT	6048	D2
Tenafly Natural Pk, TFLY	6392	C3
Tenney Pk, QENS	6723	B5
Theodore Roosevelt Pk, MHTN	112	E1
Thomas Jefferson Pk, MHTN	110	C6
Thomas Paine Pk, MHTN	118	D6
Tibbets Brook Pk, YNKR	6393	E3
Tibbits Pk, WHPL	6168	B1
Tilly Pk, QENS	6825	D4
Todd's Pond, WHPL	6050	B7
Tompkins Pk, BKLN	6822	C7
Tompkins Square Pk, MHTN	119	C3
Toring Pk, QENS	6925	D2
Tot Pk, ROSL	6917	A5
Town Pk, OrgT	6164	C3
Travis Hill Pk, GrbT	6050	A6
Tremley Pk, LNDN	7017	C3
Trevor Pk, YNKR	6279	C6
Trumbul Pk, EGLD	6502	E2
Twin Lakes County Pk, NRCH	6281	C7
Union Square, ELIZ	6918	A4
Untermeyer Pk, YNKR	6279	D4
Vailsburg Pk, NWRK	6712	E6
Valley Stream Pk, VLYS	6928	C4
Valley Stream State Pk, HmpT	6928	D1
Valley Stream Volunteer Firemen's Field, VLYS	6928	E2
Van Arsdale Pk, ELIZ	6917	D4
Van Voorhees Pk, BKLN	120	E6
Van Vorst Pk, JSYC	6820	B3
Verdi Pk, MHTN	112	C2
Veteran's Field Pk, EDGW	106	A1
Veterans Memorial Pk, LNDN	7017	C3
Veterans Memorial Pk, RDGF	6611	B1
Veteran's Memorial Waterfront Pk, ELIZ	6918	B6
Veterans Pk, BAYN	6919	D2
Veterans Pk, RDFP	6502	A5
Veterans Pk, STNL	6919	C7
Veteran's Pk, FRVW	6611	B3
Victory Field, QENS	6824	C5
Village Green Pk, GTNK	6616	E5
Village Pk, ARDY	6166	E4
Village Pk, LKSU	6723	B3
Wakelee Field, DMRT	6278	A4
Waldmann Memorial Pk, MNPK	6618	A5
Wards Island Pk, MHTN	114	D1
Warinanco Pk, ROSL	6917	A4
War Memorial Pk, YNKR	6393	D1
Washington Market Pk, MHTN	118	B6
Washington Pk, NWRK	6713	D6
Washington Pk, PTHA	7205	B2
Washington Pk, UNCT	6716	C5
Washington Pk, YNKR	6393	C1
Washington Square Pk, MHTN	118	E2
Waterfront Pk, GTNE	6722	D1
Watsessing Pk, BlmT	6713	A1
Wave Hill, BRNX	6393	B6
Weequahic Pk, NWRK	6817	A5
Weinburg Nature Center, SCDL	6282	C2
Welty Pk, YNKR	6280	B6
Westchester County Playland Pk, RYE	6284	B3
West End Pk, ELIZ	6917	C4
Westerleigh Pk, STNL	7019	C2
West Hudson Pk, HRSN	6714	A5
West Side Pk, NWRK	6817	A1
Whitney Pond County Pk, NHmT	6617	D7
William Flower Pk, NRCH	6396	A1
William Kelly Memorial Pk, BKLN	7023	B5
Williams Field, ELIZ	6917	E5
William Warren County Pk, WbgT	7114	C6
Willowbrook Pk, STNL	7019	A5
Wilson Pk, ELIZ	6817	A7
Wilson Pk, YNKR	6394	B5
Wilson Woods County Pk, MTVN	6395	B4
W Munsell Avenue Pk, LNDN	7017	A2
Wolfe's Pond Pk, STNL	7207	B2
Woodbridge Pk, WbgT	7114	C4

Parks & Recreation

New York City/5 Borough Points of Interest Index

Post Offices

FEATURE NAME Address City ZIP Code	MAP#	GRID
Woodland Pk, HSBH	6500	C5
Wood Pk, LEON	6502	D4
Woodruff Circle, ELIZ	6918	A3
Woodruss Circle, ELIZ	6918	A2
Wyngate Pk, GTPZ	6617	B7
Yosemite Pk, GrbT	6049	C6
Young Pk, MHTN	107	C5

Post Offices

FEATURE NAME Address City ZIP Code	MAP#	GRID
Adelphi Station, 950 Fulton St, BKLN, 11238	6923	A1
Albertson Main Office, 860 Willis Av, NHmT, 11507	6724	E3
Alden Manor Branch, 778 Elmont Rd, HmpT, 11003	6827	B7
Alpine Main Office, 100 Church St, ALPN, 07620	6278	E6
Ampere Station, 75 4th Av, EORG, 07017	6713	B3
Ansonia Station, 178 Columbus Av, MHTN, 10023	112	C4
Archer Avenue Station, 147-21 Archer Av, QENS, 11435	6825	C5
Ardsley Main Office, 879 Saw Mill River Rd, ARDY, 10502	6166	D3
Ardsley-On-Hudson Main Office, 110 Ardsley Av W, IRVN - 10533	6166	A2
Arverne Station, 329 Beach 59th St, QENS, 11692	7026	E6
Astoria Station, 27-40 21st St, QENS, 11102	114	E4
Atlantic Beach Main Office, 2009 Park St, ATLB, 11509	7027	E7
Audubon Station, 511 W 165th St, MHTN, 10032	104	B7
Avenel Main Office, 1065 Rahway Av, WbgT, 07001	7114	D1
Bath Beach Station, 1865 Benson Av, BKLN, 11214	7022	B5
Baychester Station, 1525 E Gun Hill Rd, BRNX, 10469	6505	D3
Bayonne Main Office, 570 Broadway, BAYN, 07002	6919	E3
Bay Ridge, 5501 7th Av, BKLN, 11220	6922	B7
Bayside Annex, 41-29 216th St, QENS, 11361	6722	B4
Bayside Station, 212-35 42nd Av, QENS, 11361	6722	A4
Bay Station, 2628 E 18th St, BKLN, 11235	7023	C7
Bay Terrace Station, 212-71 26th Av, QENS, 11360	6722	A2
Bayway Station, 544 Bayway Cir, ELIZ, 07202	6917	D5
Bellerose Station, 237-15 Braddock Av, QENS, 11426	6827	A2
Bergenline Station, 2100 Bergenline Av, UNCT, 07087	6716	D3
Bergen Point, 195 Broadway, BAYN, 07002	6919	D5
Bergen Station, 528 Bergen Av, JSYC, 07304	6819	E3
Blythebourne Station, 1200 51st St, BKLN, 11219	6922	C7
Bogota Branch, 71 W Main St, BGTA, 07603	6501	D2
Borough Hall Station, 120-55 Queens Blvd, QENS, 11415	6825	A3
Botanical Station, 2963 Webster Av, BRNX, 10458	6504	E3
Boulevard Station, 1132 Southern Blvd, BRNX, 10459	6613	D2
Bowling Green Station, 25 Broadway, MHTN, 10006	120	B2
Brevoort Station, 1205 Atlantic Av, BKLN, 11216	6923	C1
Briarwood Finance, 138-69 Queens Blvd, QENS, 11435	6825	B4
Brick Church Station, 60 Evergreen Pl, EORG, 07018	6712	D4
Brighton Station, 3157 Coney Island Av, BKLN, 11235	7121	B1
Broadway Station, 21-17 Broadway, QENS, 11106	114	D6
Bronx, 558 Grand Concourse, BRNX, 10451	107	E5
Bronxville Branch, 119 Pondfield Rd, BRXV, 10708	6280	E7
Brownsville Station, 167 Bristol St, BKLN, 11212	6924	B3
Bryant Station, 23 W 43rd St, MHTN, 10036	116	C2
B Station, 102-12 159th Dr, QENS, 11414	6925	E4
Bush Terminal Station, 900 3rd Av, BKLN, 11232	6922	B4
Cambria Heights Station, 229-01 Linden Blvd, QENS - 11411	6827	A6
Canal Street Station, 350 Church St, MHTN, 10013	118	D5
Canarsie Station, 10201 Flatlands Av, BKLN, 11236	6924	C6
Carlstadt Branch, 331 1st St, CARL, 07072	6500	C7
Carteret Main Office, 212 Pershing Av, CART, 07008	7115	D1
Castle Hill Station, 1163 Castle Hill Av, BRNX, 10462	6614	C1
Cathedral Station, 215 W 104th St, MHTN, 10025	109	A4
Cedarhurst Main Office, 124 Grove Av, CDHT, 11516	7028	B2
Centuck Station, 1585 Central Park Av, YNKR, 10710	6280	D5
City Island Station, 199 City Island Av, BRNX, 10464	6506	E7
Cliff Park Station, 589 Anderson Av, CLFP, 07010	6611	D2
Cliffside Park Main Office, 289 Gorge Rd, CLFP, 07010	6611	C4
Closter Main Office, 185 Homans Av, CLST, 07624	6278	B3
College Point, 120-07 15th Av, QENS, 11356	6720	D1
Colonial Park Station, 99 Macombs Pl, MHTN, 10039	107	C3
Coney Island Station, 2727 Mermaid Av, BKLN, 11224	7120	C1
Co Op City Station, 3300 Conner St, BRNX, 10475	6506	A1
Cooper Station, 93 4th Av, MHTN, 10003	119	B2
Cornell Station, 1950 Lafayette Av, BRNX, 10473	6614	B3
Corona A Station, 103-28 Roosevelt Av, QENS, 11368	6720	B6
Cresskill Main Office, 20 Washington St, CRSK, 07626	6278	B7
Crotona Park Station, 1682 Boston Rd, BRNX, 10460	6613	D1
Cypress Hills Processing, 222 Crescent St, BKLN, 11208	6925	A1
Dag Hammarskjold, 884 2nd Av, MHTN, 10017	117	A3
Demarest Main Office, 126 Hardenburgh Av, DMRT - 07627	6278	A5
Dobbs Ferry Main Office, 120 Main St, DBSF, 10522	6166	A4
Doddtown Station, 333 Dodd St, EORG, 07017	6712	E1
Dundee Station, 122 8th St, PASC, 07055	6500	A4
Dyker Heights Station, 8320 13th Av, BKLN, 11228	7022	A3
Eastchester Branch, 155 Fisher Av, EchT, 10709	6281	B5
East Elmhurst Station, 91-07 25th Av, QENS, 11369	6719	E3
East New York Station, 2645 Atlantic Av, BKLN, 11207	6924	C2
East Orange Main Office, 26 City Hall Plz, EORG, 07017	6713	A4
East Rockaway Main Office, 10 Main St, ERKY, 11518	6929	C7
East Rutherford Branch, 193 Park Av, ERTH, 07073	6609	B1
Edgewater Main Office, 770 River Rd, EDGW, 07020	6611	E3
Elizabeth Main Office, 310 N Broad St, ELIZ, 07208	6917	E3
Elmhurst A Station, 80-27 Broadway, QENS, 11373	6719	E6
Elmhurst Station, 59-01 Junction Blvd, QENS, 11368	6720	B7
Elmont Branch, 260 Elmont Rd, HmpT, 11003	6827	B7
Elmora Station, 175 Elmora Av, ELIZ, 07202	6917	C3
Elmsford Annex, 150 Clearbrook Rd, GrbT, 10523	6049	B3
Elmsford Main Office, 2 E Main St, EMFD, 10523	6049	A5
Eltingville Station, 4455 Amboy Rd, STNL, 10312	7116	E6
Empire State Station, 19 W 34th St, MHTN, 10001	116	B4
Englewood Annex, 55 Smith St, EGLD, 07631	6502	D1
Englewood Cliffs Branch, 650 E Palisade Av, EGLC - 07632	6503	B1
Evergreen, 538 Prospect St, EORG, 07017	6712	E3
Fairview Main Office, 6 Anderson Av, FRVW, 07022	6611	B4
Far Rockaway, 18-36 Mott Av, QENS, 11691	7027	D5
Fieldston Station, 444 W 238th St, BRNX, 10463	102	D1
Five Corners Station, 645 Newark Av, JSYC, 07306	6820	A1
Flatbush Station, 2273 Church Av, BKLN, 11226	6923	B5
Floral Park Main Office, 35 Tulip Av, FLPK, 11001	6827	C2
Fordham Station, 465 E 188th St, BRNX, 10458	6504	D4
Forest Hills Station, 106-28 Queens Blvd, QENS, 11375	6824	D2
Fort George Station, 4558 Broadway, MHTN, 10040	104	D1
Fort Hamilton Station, 8801 5th Av, BKLN, 11209	7021	E2
Fort Lee Annex, 360 Sylvan Av, EGLC, 07632	6503	B2
Fort Lee Main Office, 229 Main St, FTLE, 07024	6502	E6
Forty Fifth Street Station, 4535 Bergenline Av, UNCT - 07087	6716	E1
Franklin D Roosevelt Station, 909 3rd Av, MHTN, 10022	117	A1
Franklin Square Main Office, 867 Hempstead Tpk, HmpT - 11010	6828	B4
Fresh Meadows Station, 192-20 Horace Harding Expwy S - QENS, 11365	6721	E7
Fresh Pond Station, 60-80 Woodbine St, QENS, 11385	6823	C4
Garfield Main Office, 254 Palisade Av, GRFD, 07026	6500	A2
Gedney Station, 620 Mamaroneck Av, WHPL, 10605	6168	C3
General Lafayette Station, 322 Pacific Av, JSYC, 07304	6820	A4
Glendale Station, 69-36 Myrtle Av, QENS, 11385	6823	E5
Glen Oaks Branch, 25629 Union Tpk, QENS, 11004	6723	C6
Glenville Station, 25 Glen Ridge Rd, GrwT, 06831	6170	B1
Glenwood Landing Main Office, 123 Glenwood Rd, OybT - 11547	6618	E1
Gracie Station, 229 E 85th St, MHTN, 10028	113	D3
Grand Central Station, 450 Lexington Av, MHTN, 10017	116	E3
Grand Station, 45-08 30th Rd, QENS, 11103	6719	B4
Grasselli Station, 938 S Wood Av, LNDN, 07036	7017	B2
Gravesend Station, 344 Avenue U, BKLN, 11223	7022	E6
Great Kills Station, 15 Nelson Av, STNL, 10308	7117	B5
Great Neck Main Office, 1 Welwyn Rd, GTPZ, 11021	6617	B7
Greeley Square Station, 39 W 31st St, MHTN, 10001	116	B4
Greenpoint Station, 66 Meserole Av, BKLN, 11222	6822	B2
Greenwich Main Office, 29 Valley Dr, GrwT, 06831	6170	E3
Guttenberg Branch, 6900 Park Av, GTBG, 07093	6611	B7
Hackensack Main Office, 226 State St, HKSK, 07601	6501	C1
Hamilton Grange Station, 521 W 146th St, MHTN, 10031	106	E3
Harrison Main Office, 427 Harrison Av, HRSN, 07029	6714	A6
Harrison Main Office, 258 Halstead Av, HRSN, 10528	6283	B3
Hartsdale Main Office, 441 Central Park Av, GrbT, 10583	6167	B5
Hasbrouck Heights Branch, 185 Boulevard, HSBH, 07604	6500	D4
Hastings on Hudson Branch, 591 Warburton Av, HAOH - 10706	6165	E6
Heathcoate Branch, 1112 Wilmot Rd, NRCH, 10583	6282	A1
Hell Gate Station, 153 E 110th St, MHTN, 10029	110	A5
Hewlett Main Office, 1245 Hewlett Plz, HmpT, 11557	6928	D7
Highbridge Station, 1315 Inwood Av, BRNX, 10452	105	A7
Hillside Branch, 1146 Liberty Av, HlsT, 07205	6816	C6
Hillside Manor Branch, 2038 Hillside Av, NHmT, 11040	6724	B5
Hoboken Main Office, 89 River St, HBKN, 07030	6716	E7
Hollis Station, 197-40 Jamaica Av, QENS, 11423	6826	B4
Homecrest-Carriers, 2370 E 19th St, BKLN, 11229	7023	C6
Homecrest Finance Station, 2302 Avenue U, BKLN - 11229	7023	C5
Horace Harding, 56-01 Marathon Pkwy, QENS, 11362	6723	A4
Howard Beach Station, 160-50 Cross Bay Blvd, QENS - 11414	6925	D4
Hub Station, 633 St. Anns Av, BRNX, 10455	6613	B3
Hudson City Station, 392 Central Av, JSYC, 07032	6716	C6
Industrial Hillside Branch, 397 Hillside Av, HlsT, 07205	6816	C5
Inwood Station, 143 Doughty Blvd, HmpT, 11096	7027	D3
Inwood Station, 90 Vermilyea Av, MHTN, 10034	102	A6
Irvington Branch, 1086 Springfield Av, IrvT, 07111	6816	C2
Irvington Main Office, 25 N Buckhout St, IRVN, 10533	6048	A7
Island Park Main Office, 367 Long Beach Rd, ISPK, 11558	7029	D4
Jackson Heights Station, 78-02 37th Av, QENS, 11372	6719	D6
Jamaica Main Office, 88-40 164th St, QENS, 11432	6825	D4
James A Farley Station, 441 8th Av, MHTN, 10001	116	A3
Jerome Avenue Station, 2549 Jerome Av, BRNX, 10468	102	E7
Journal Square Station, 899 Bergen Av, JSYC, 07306	6820	A1
Junction Boulevard Station, 33-23 Junction Blvd, QENS - 11372	6720	A5
Kearny Main Office, 64 Midland Av, KRNY, 07032	6714	B3
Kensington Station, 419 McDonald Av, BKLN, 11218	6922	E6
Kew Gardens Station, 83-30 Austin St, QENS, 11415	6824	E4
Kingsbridge Station, 5517 Broadway, BRNX, 10463	102	D3
Kings Point Branch, 661 Middle Neck Rd, GTNK, 11023	6616	E5
Knickerbocker Station, 128 E Broadway, MHTN, 10002	119	A6
LaGuardia Airport Station, QENS, 11371	6720	A2
Larchmont Main Office, 1 Chatsworth Av, LRMT, 10538	6396	D2
Lawrence Main Office, 12 Bayview Av, HmpT, 11559	6927	D7
Lefferts Station, 315 Empire Blvd, BKLN, 11225	6923	C3
Lenox Hill Station, 217 E 70th St, MHTN, 10021	113	C5
Leonia Branch, 398 Broad Av, LEON, 07605	6502	D4
Lincolnton Station, 2266 5th Av, MHTN, 10037	107	C7
Linden Hill Station, 29-50 Union St, QENS, 11354	6721	A2
Linden Main Office, 400 N Wood Av, LNDN, 07036	7017	A1
Little Ferry Main Office, 20 Main St, LFRY, 07643	6501	D6
Little Neck, 250-10 Northern Blvd, QENS, 11362	6722	E3
Lodi Main Office, 25 Washington St, LODI, 07644	6500	D2
Long Beach Main Office, 101 E Park Av, LBCH, 11561	7029	C7
Lynbrook Main Office, 100 Broadway, LNBK, 11563	6929	B5
Madison Square Station, 149 E 23rd St, MHTN, 10010	116	C6
Main Office Station, 271 Cadman Plz E, BKLN, 11201	121	B4
Main Office Station, 4602 21st St, QENS, 11101	6718	D4
Main Office Station, 41-65 Main St, QENS, 11355	6721	A5
Main Office Station, 550 Manor Rd, STNL, 10314	7019	E3
Malverne Main Office, 339 Hempstead Av, MLVN, 11565	6929	B1
Mamaroneck Main Office, 309 Mt Pleasant Av, MRNK - 10543	6282	E6
Manhasset Main Office, 28 Maple Pl, NHmT, 11030	6617	D6
Manhattanville Station, 365 Dr Martin L King Jr Blvd - MHTN, 10027	109	D1
Mariners Harbor Station, 2980 Richmond Ter, STNL - 10303	6919	A7
Martine Station, 170 Mamaroneck Av, WHPL, 10601	6168	B2
Maspeth Station, 55-02 69th St, QENS, 11378	6823	C2
Meacham Branch, 798 Meacham Av, HmpT, 11003	6827	E7
Meadows Station, 700 Plaza Dr, SECS, 07094	6610	C7
Meadowview Station, 6139 Kennedy Blvd W, NBgT - 07047	6610	E7
Melcourt Station, 860 Melrose Av, BRNX, 10451	6613	B2
Metropolitan Station, 47 Debevoise St, BKLN, 11206	6822	D5
Middle Village, 71-35 Metropolitan Av, QENS, 11379	6823	E4
Midtown Station, 223 W 38th St, MHTN, 10018	116	B2
Midtown Station, 40 Clinton St, NWRK, 07102	6713	E7
Midwood Station, 1288 Coney Island Av, BKLN, 11230	7023	A2
Mineola Main Office, 160 1st St, MNLA, 11501	6724	E6
Monitor Station, 6010 Park Av, WNYK, 07093	111	C1
Morningside Station, 232 W 116th St, MHTN, 10026	109	D3
Morrisania, 442 E 167th St, BRNX, 10456	6613	B1
Morris Heights Station, 2024 Jerome Av, BRNX, 10453	105	D3
Morris Park Station, 1807 Williamsbridge Rd, BRNX - 10461	6505	C6
Mosholu, 3464 Jerome Av, BRNX, 10467	6504	E1
Mott Haven Station, 517 E 139th St, BRNX, 10454	6613	A4
Mt Carmel Station, 652 E 187th St, BRNX, 10458	6504	D5
Mount Vernon Main Office, 15 S 1st Av, MTVN, 10550	6394	E4
Murray Hill Finance, 115 E 34th St, MHTN, 10016	116	D4
Murray Hill Station, 205 E 36th St, MHTN, 10016	116	D4
Newark Main Office, 2 Federal Sq, NWRK, 07102	6817	D1
New Dorp Station, 2562 Hylan Blvd, STNL, 10306	7118	A3
New Hyde Park Main Office, 1001 2nd Av, NHPK, 11040	6828	A1
New Lots, 1223 Sutter Av, BKLN, 11208	6925	A2
New Rochelle Main Office, 255 North Av, NRCH, 10801	6395	E4
New Springville Station, 2845 Richmond Av, STNL - 10314	7116	E1
North Bergen Main Office, 4608 Tonnelle Av, NBgT - 07047	6716	D1
North Elizabeth Station, 772 North Av, ELIZ, 07208	6918	A1
North New Hyde Park Station, 1568 Union Tpk, NHmT - 11040	6723	E5
North Station, 243 Broadway, NWRK, 07104	6713	E4
North Station, 7 O'Dell Ter, YNKR, 10701	6279	E3
North Tarrytown Branch, 45 Beekman Av, SYHW, 10591	6048	B1
Northvale, 126 Paris Av, NVLE, 07647	6164	C5
North White Plains Station, 585 N Broadway, WHPL - 10603	6050	B5
Norwood, 239 Railroad Av, NRWD, 07648	6164	B7
Nostrand Station, Avenue X, BKLN, 11229	7023	D6
Oakland Gardens Station, 61-43 Springfield Blvd, QENS - 11364	6722	C6
Oak Point Station, 839 E 149th St, BRNX, 10455	6613	B4
Oceanside Branch, 80 Atlantic Av, HmpT, 11572	6929	E7
Old Chelsea Station, 217 W 18th St, MHTN, 10011	115	E6
Orange, 384 Main St, COrT, 07050	6712	C2
Ozone Park Station, 91-11 Liberty Av, QENS, 11417	6925	D1
Palisades Main Office, 705 Oak Tree Rd, OrgT, 10964	6165	A4
Palisades Park Main Office, 201 Broad Av, PALP, 07650	6502	C6
Palisade Station, 1213 Anderson Av, FTLE, 07024	6502	D7
Pamrapo Station, 893 Broadway, BAYN, 07002	6920	A1
Parkchester Station, 1449 West Av, BRNX, 10462	6505	B7
Parkside Station, 101-19 Metropolitan Av, QENS, 11375	6824	C4
Park Slope Station, 148 7th St, BKLN, 11215	6922	C2
Parkville Station, 6618 20th Av, BKLN, 11204	7022	D3
Parkway Station, 2100 White Plains Rd, BRNX, 10462	6505	A5
Peck Slip Station, 1 Peck Slip, MHTN, 10038	120	D1
Pelham Branch, 1 Wolfs Ln, PLHM, 10803	6395	B4
Perth Amboy Main Office, 205 Smith St, PTHA, 08861	7205	D4
Peter Stuyvesant Station, 432 E 14th St, MHTN, 10009	119	C2
Piermont Main Office, 393 Piermont Av, PRMT, 10968	6165	A1
Pilgrim Station, 1545 Crosby Av, BRNX, 10461	6505	E7
Plandome Branch, 155 Stonytown Rd, PLNM, 11030	6617	D4
Planetarium Station, 127 W 83rd St, MHTN, 10024	112	E1
Plaza Station, 24-18 Queens Plz S, QENS, 11101	6718	D5
Plaza Station, 1257 Paterson Plank Rd, SECS, 07094	6610	B7
Pomonok Station, 158-05 71st Av, QENS, 11365	6825	B1
Port Chester Main Office, 245 Westchester Av, PTCH - 10573	6170	B5
Port Reading Main Office, 605 Port Reading Av, WbgT - 07064	7115	B2
Port Richmond Station, 364 Port Richmond Av, STNL - 10302	7019	C1
Port Washington, 1051 Port Washington Blvd, NHmT - 11050	6618	A1
Post Office, St. Johns Pl, BKLN, 11213	6923	D2
Post Office, Green Acres Rd S, HmpT, 11581	6928	B4
Pratt, 524 Myrtle Av, BKLN, 11205	6822	A6
Princes Bay Station, 655 Rossville Av, STNL, 10309	7116	A6
Prince Station, 124 Greene St, MHTN, 10012	118	E3
Prospect Park West Station, 211 Prospect Pk SW, BKLN - 11215	6922	E4
Purchase, 3003 Purchase St, HRSN, 10577	6169	B1
Queens Village Station, 209-20 Jamaica Av, QENS, 11428	6826	D3
Radio City Station, 322 W 52nd St, MHTN, 10019	112	B7
Red Hook Station, 615 Clinton St, BKLN, 11231	6922	B2
Rego Park Station, 92-24 Queens Blvd, QENS, 11374	6824	A1
Richmond Hill Station, 122-01 Jamaica Av, QENS, 11418	6825	A5
Ridgefield Main Office, 757 Broad Av N, RDGF, 07657	6502	B7
Ridgefield Park Main Office, 155 Main St, RDFP, 07660	6501	E5
Ridgewood Station, 6060 Myrtle Av, QENS, 11385	6824	C5
Riverdale Station, 5951 Riverdale Av, BRNX, 10471	6393	B5
Rochdale Village Station, 1651-00 Baisley Blvd, QENS - 11434	6927	A1
Rockaway Beach, 90-14 Rockaway Beach Blvd, QENS - 11693	7026	B7
Rockaway Park, 113-25 Beach Channel Dr, QENS, 11694	7123	E1
Rockefeller Center Station, 610 5th Av, MHTN, 10020	116	D1
Rockville Centre Main Office, 250 Merrick Rd, RKVC - 11570	6929	E4
Roosevelt Island Station, 694 Main St, MHTN, 10044	114	A6
Rosebank Station, 567 Tompkins Av, STNL, 10305	7020	E3
Rosedale Station, 145-06 243rd St, QENS, 11422	6927	E4
Roslyn Heights Main Office, 66 Mineola Av, ROSE, 11576	6618	D7
Roslyn Main Office, 1391 Old Northern Blvd, RSLN, 11576	6618	D5
Rugby Station, 726 Utica Av, BKLN, 11203	6923	E4
Rutherford Main Office, 156 Park Av, RTFD, 07070	6609	A2
Ryder Station, 1739 E 45th St, BKLN, 11234	7023	E3
Rye Main Office, 41 Purdy Av, RYE, 10580	6284	A1
St. Albans Station, 195-04 Linden Blvd, QENS, 11412	6826	C6
St. George Station, 45 Bay St, STNL, 10301	6920	E7
Sandford Station, 440 Sandford Blvd E, MTVN, 10550	6395	A6
Scarsdale Main Office, 29 Chase Rd, SCDL, 10583	6167	C7
Sea Cliff Main Office, 200 Sea Cliff Av, SCLF, 11579	6509	E6
Secaucus Main Office, 300 County Av, SECS, 07094	6716	A2
Sewaren Main Office, 85 Woodbridge Av, WbgT, 07077	7114	E5
Soundview Station, 1687 Gleason Av, BRNX, 10472	6614	A1
South Hackensack Branch, 560 Huyler St, TETB, 07608	6501	B4
South Ozone Park Station, 126-15 127th St, QENS - 11420	6926	B2
South Richmond Hill Station, 117-04 101st Av, QENS - 11419	6825	A7
South Shore Annex, 3031 Veterans Rd W, STNL, 10309	7206	D1
South Station, 514 Frelinghuysen Av, NWRK, 07114	6817	B5
Sparkill Main Office, 2 Washington St, OrgT, 10976	6164	E2
Springfield Avenue, 290 Springfield Av, NWRK, 07103	6817	B1
Springfield Gardens Station, 218-10 Merrick Blvd, QENS - 11413	6927	D1
Spuyten Duyvil Station, 562 Kappock St, BRNX, 10463	102	B3
Stadium Station, 901 Gerard Av, BRNX, 10452	107	E3
Stapleton Station, 160 Tompkins Av, STNL, 10304	7020	D2
Station A, 40-03 164th St, QENS, 11358	6721	C4
Station C, 7523 Main St, QENS, 11367	6825	A1
Station D Finance, 197-33 Hillside Av, QENS, 11423	6826	B3
Steinway Station, 43-04 Broadway, QENS, 11103	6719	A4
Strathmore Branch, 1900 Northern Blvd, NHmT, 11030	6618	A6
Stuyvesant Station, 1915 Fulton St, BKLN, 11233	6924	A1
Summit Avenue Station, 720 8th St, UNCT, 07087	6716	C4
Sunnyside, 45-15 44th St, QENS, 11104	6719	A6
Tappan Main Office, 57 Old Tappan Rd, OrgT, 10983	6164	C3
Tarrytown Main Office, 50 N Broadway, TYTN, 10591	6048	B2
Taurus Station, 6406 Bergenline Av, WNYK, 07093	6611	A7
Teaneck Main Office, 751 Palisade Av, TnkT, 07666	6501	E1
Tenafly Main Office, 400 Tenafly Rd, TFLY, 07670	6392	A2
Throggs Neck Station, 3630 E Tremont Av, BRNX, 10465	6615	A2
Times Plaza Station, 542 Atlantic Av, BKLN, 11217	121	D7
Times Square Station, 340 W 42nd St, MHTN, 10036	116	A1
Tottenville Station, 228 Main St, STNL, 10307	7206	A4
Town Center Station, 16 Main St, WOrT, 07052	6712	B2
Townley Station, 1020 Salem Rd, UnnT, 07083	6816	B7
Trainsmeadow, 75-77 31st Av, QENS, 11370	6719	D4
Tremont Station, 575 E Tremont Av, BRNX, 10457	6504	D6
Triborough Station, 167 E 124th St, MHTN, 10035	110	C3
Tuckahoe Branch, 7 Columbus Av, TCKA, 10707	6281	A6
Union City Main Office, 301 30th St, UNCT, 07087	6716	D3
Union Square, 946 Elizabeth Av, ELIZ, 07201	6918	A4
University Heights Station, 1541 Featherbed Ln, BRNX - 10452	105	A5
Uptown Station, 57 14th St, HBKN, 07030	6716	E5
Utopia Station, 182-04 Union Tpk, QENS, 11432	6825	E2
Vailsburg Station, 210 Stuyvesant Av, NWRK, 07106	6712	C7
Valhalla Main Office, 10 Cleveland St, MtPT, 10595	6050	A3
Valley Stream Main Office, 111 S Franklin Av, VLYS - 11580	6928	D4
Van Brunt Station, 275 9th St, BKLN, 11215	6922	D3
Van Cott Station, 3102 Decatur Av, BRNX, 10467	6504	E3
Vanderveer Station, 2319 Nostrand Av, BKLN, 11210	7023	C1
Van Nest Station, 715 Morris Park Av, BRNX, 10462	6505	B6
Village Station, 201 Varick St, MHTN, 10014	118	C2
Wakefield Station, 4165 White Plains Rd, BRNX, 10466	6394	B7
Wallington Branch, 218 Maple Av, WLTN, 07057	6500	A6
Wall Street Station, 73 Pine St, MHTN, 10005	120	C2
Washington Bridge Station, 555 W 180th St, MHTN - 10033	104	C4
Washington Park Station, 6 Atlantic St, NWRK, 07102	6713	E6

INDEX 72

Post Offices

New York City/5 Borough Points of Interest Index

Schools

FEATURE NAME Address City ZIP Code	MAP#	GRID
Washington Street Station, 734 Washington St, HBKN - 07030	6716	D6
Watsessing Station, 34 Dodd St, BlmT, 07003	6713	B1
Weehawken Branch, 4100 Park Av, WhkT, 07086	6716	E3
Westchester Station, 2619 Ponton Av, BRNX, 10461	6505	D7
West Farms Station, 362 Devoe Av, BRNX, 10460	6504	E7
West Harrison, 173 Underhill Av, HRSN, 10604	6168	D1
West Hempstead Branch, 245 Hempstead Tpk, HmpT - 11552	6828	E5
West Hudson Station, 255 Kearny Av, KRNY, 07032	6714	B4
West New Brighton Station, 1015 Castleton Av, STNL - 10310	6919	E7
West New York Main Office, 5415 Bergenline Av, WNYK - 07093	6716	E1
West Side Station, 502 Grand St, HBKN, 07030	6716	D6
White Plains Main Office, 100 Fisher Av, WHPL, 10606	6168	A2
Whitestone Station, 14-44 150th St, QENS, 11357	6615	B7
Williamsbridge Station, 711 E Gun Hill Rd, BRNX, 10467	6505	B2
Williamsburg Station, 263 S 4th St, BKLN, 11211	6822	B4
Williston Park Main Office, 446 Willis Av, WLPK, 11596	6724	E5
Woodbridge Main Office, 60 Main St, WbgT, 07095	7114	C4
Woodhaven Station, 86-42 Forest Pkwy, QENS, 11421	6824	B6
Woodlawn Station, 4364 Katonah Av, BRNX, 10470	6394	A6
Woodmere Main Office, 132 Franklin Pl, HmpT, 11598	6928	C7
Wood Ridge Branch, 290 Hackensack St, WRDG, 07075	6500	D6
Woodside Station, 39-25 61st St, QENS, 11377	6719	C6
Woolsey Station, 22-68 31st St, QENS, 11105	6719	B2
Wyckoff Heights Station, 86 Wyckoff Av, BKLN, 11237	6823	A5
Wykagyl Station, 3 Quaker Ridge Rd, NRCH, 10804	6281	D6
Yonkers Main Office, 80 Main St, YNKR, 10701	6393	C1
Yorkville Station, 1617 3rd Av, MHTN, 10128	113	E2

Schools

FEATURE NAME Address City ZIP Code	MAP#	GRID
24th International High School, 3110 Thomson Av, QENS - 11101	6718	D6
47th Amer Sign Language & English Secnd Sch - 225 E 23rd St, MHTN, 10010	116	C6
51st Avenue Academy, 7605 51st Av, QENS, 11373	6719	D7
AB Davis Middle School, 350 Gramatan Av, MTVN, 10552	6394	D3
Abington Avenue School, 209 Abington Av, NWRK - 07107	6713	C3
Abraham Joshua Heschel High School, 20 W End Av - MHTN, 10023	112	A4
Abraham Joshua Heschel School, 270 W 89th St, MHTN - 10024	108	E6
Abraham Lincoln High School, 2800 Ocean Pkwy, BKLN - 11224	7121	A1
Acad for Coll Prep & Career Exploration - 911 Flatbush Av, BKLN, 11226	6923	B5
Academy for New Americans, 3014 30th St, QENS - 11102	6719	A3
Academy for Scholarship & Entrepreneurship - 1619 Boston Rd, BRNX, 10460	6613	D1
Academy for Social Action, 509 W 129th St, MHTN - 10027	106	D6
Academy for Young Writers, 183 S 3rd St, BKLN, 11211	6822	A4
Academy I, 209 Bergen Av, JSYC, 07305	6819	D4
Academy II, 16 Bentley Av, JSYC, 07304	6819	E3
Academy of American Studies, 2804 41st Av, QENS - 11101	6718	D5
Academy of Applied Mathematics & Technology - 345 Brook Av, BRNX, 10454	6613	A4
Academy of Collaborative Education, 222 W 134th St - MHTN, 10030	107	A6
Academy of Environmental Science High School - 410 Gustave L Levy Pl, MHTN, 10029	114	B1
Academy of Finance & Enterprise, 3020 Thomson Av - QENS, 11101	6718	D6
Academy of Mt St. Ursula, 330 Bedford Park Blvd, BRNX - 10458	6504	D3
Academy of the Holy Angels, 315 Hillside Av, ALPN - 07620	6278	D7
Academy of Sacred Heart High School - 713 Washington St, HBKN, 07030	6716	E6
Academy of St. Benedict, 124 Niagara St, NWRK, 07105	6818	B2
Academy of St. Dorothy, 1305 Hylan Blvd, STNL, 10305	7020	C6
Academy of Urban Planning High School, 400 Irving Av - BKLN, 11237	6823	B6
Academy of Vocational Careers, 74 Montgomery St - NWRK, 07103	6817	C1
Academy Our Lady Good Counsel High School - 52 N Broadway, WHPL, 10603	6168	B1
Accion Academy, 1825 Prospect Av, BRNX, 10457	6504	D7
A Childs Place Day School, 3220 108th St, QENS, 11369	6720	B4
Acorn Community High School, 561 Grand Av, BKLN - 11238	6923	B1
Acorn High School for Social Justice, 1396 Broadway - BKLN, 11221	6823	A7
Adelphi Academy, 8515 Ridge Blvd, BKLN, 11209	7021	D2
Adlai E Stevenson High School, 1980 Lafayette Av, BRNX - 10473	6614	C3
A Fantis Parochial School, 195 State St, BKLN, 11201	121	A6
Ahi Ezer Yeshiva School, 2433 Ocean Pkwy, BKLN, 11235	7023	A7
AJ Herschel Middle School, 314 W 91st St, MHTN, 10024	108	D6
Albert Leonard Middle School, 25 Gerada Ln, NRCH - 10804	6281	E6
Albert Shanker School for VPA, 3151 21st St, QENS - 11106	114	D6
Alce School, 358 5th Av, MHTN, 10001	116	C4
Alden Terrace Elementary School, 1835 N Central Av - HmpT, 11580	6928	B1
Alexander Annex School, 15 Boylan St, NWRK, 07106	6712	D6
Alexander Hamilton High School, 98 S Goodwin Av - EMFD, 10523	6049	B6
Alexander Robertson School, 3 W 95th St, MHTN, 10025	109	B6
Alexander Street Elementary School, 43 Alexander St - NWRK, 07106	6712	D6
Alfred E Smith Career & Technical Edu HS, 333 E 151st St - BRNX, 10451	6613	A3
Alfred E Zampella School No 27, 201 North St, JSYC - 07032	6716	B5
Alfred M Franko Middle School, 624 S 3rd Av, MTVN - 10550	6394	E6
Al Ghazaly School, 17 Park St, JSYC, 07304	6819	E3
Alice E Grady Elementary School, 45 Cobb Ln, EMFD - 10523	6049	A6
Al Iman School, 8989 Van Wyck Expwy, QENS, 11435	6825	B5
All City Leadership Secondary School, 1474 Gates Av - BKLN, 11237	6823	A6
Allen Christian School, 17110 Linden Blvd, QENS, 11434	6826	A7
Allen-Stevenson School, 132 E 78th St, MHTN, 10075	113	C4
All Hallows High School, 111 E 164th St, BRNX, 10452	6613	A1
All Saints Day School, 707 Washington St, HBKN, 07030	6716	E6
All Saints School, 52 E 130th St, MHTN, 10035	110	B1
Al-Madinah School, 383 3rd Av, BKLN, 11215	6922	D2
Al Madrasa Alislamiya School, 5224 3rd Av, BKLN - 11220	6922	A6
Al Mamoor School, 8531 168th St, QENS, 11432	6825	D4
Al-Noor School, 675 4th Av, BKLN, 11232	6922	C3
Alpha School, 2400 Linden Blvd, BKLN, 11208	6925	A3

FEATURE NAME Address City ZIP Code	MAP#	GRID
Alpine Public Elementary School, 500 Hillside Av, ALPN - 07620	6278	E7
Amber Charter School, 220 E 106th St, MHTN, 10029	110	A6
Amistad Dual Language School, 4862 Broadway, MHTN - 10034	101	E6
Anderson School, 100 W 84th St, MHTN, 10024	112	E1
Andries Hudde School, 2500 Nostrand Av, BKLN, 11210	7023	C2
Anna C Scott Elementary School, 250 Highland St, LEON - 07605	6502	D4
Anne Hutchinson Elementary School, 60 Mill Rd, EchT - 10709	6281	B5
Anne Klein Elementary School, 301 69th St, GTBG - 07093	6611	B6
Ann Street Elementary School, 30 Ann St, NWRK, 07105	6818	A2
Annunciation School, 461 W 131st St, MHTN, 10027	106	D6
Annunciation School, 465 Westchester Av, YNKR, 10707	6281	A3
A Philip Randolph Campus High School, 433 W 135th St - MHTN, 10031	106	E6
A P Morris Elementary School, 143 Coe Av, HlsT, 07205	6816	D7
Aquinas High School, 685 E 182nd St, BRNX, 10457	6504	D6
Archbishop Molloy High School, 8353 Manton St, QENS - 11435	6825	A4
Archbishop Stepinac High School, 950 Mamaroneck Av - WHPL, 10605	6168	C5
Ardsley High School, 300 Farm Rd, ARDY, 10502	6166	E3
Ardsley Middle School, 700 Ashford Av, ARDY, 10502	6166	E5
Argus Community High School, 760 E 160th St, BRNX - 10456	6613	B3
Ark Christian Academy, 1710 Eastern Pkwy, BKLN, 11233	6924	B2
Art & Design High School, 1075 2nd Av, MHTN, 10022	117	B1
Arts High School, 550 Martin Luther King Junior B, NWRK - 07102	6817	D1
Ascension School, 220 W 108th St, MHTN, 10025	109	B3
Aspire Preparatory School, 2441 Wallace Av, BRNX - 10467	6505	B4
Assumption Catholic School, 380 Meredith St, PTHA - 08861	7205	D2
Assumption School, 151 1st St, WRDG, 07075	6500	C6
Astor Collegiate Academy, 925 Astor Av, BRNX, 10469	6505	B4
Augusta Street Elementary School, 100 Linden Av, IrvT - 07111	6816	D1
Automotive High School, 50 Bedford Av, BKLN, 11222	6822	B2
Auxiliary Services School, 198 Forsyth St, MHTN, 10002	119	A4
Avenel Street Elementary School, 230 Avenel St, WbgT - 07001	7114	C1
Avon Avenue School, 219 Avon Av, NWRK, 07108	6817	B2
Baccalaureate School Global Education, 3412 36th Av - QENS, 11106	6718	E5
Badr School, 539 Bergen Av, JSYC, 07304	6819	E3
Bailey Elementary School 12, 75 W 10th St, BAYN - 07002	6919	D4
Bais Brocho of Karlin Stolin, 4314 10th Av, BKLN, 11219	6922	C6
Bais Esther School, 1353 50th St, BKLN, 11219	7022	C1
Bais Sarah School, 1363 50th St, BKLN, 11219	7022	D1
Bais Tziporah School, 1449 39th St, BKLN, 11218	6922	D7
Bais Yaakov Academy for Girls, 12450 Metropolitan Av - QENS, 11415	6825	A5
Bais Yaakov D Gur, 1975 51st St, BKLN, 11204	7022	E2
Bais Yaakov Dkhal Adas Yereim, 1169 43rd St, BKLN - 11219	6922	C7
Bais Yaakov of 18th Avenue School, 4419 18th Av, BKLN - 11230	7022	E1
Bais Yaakov of Adas Yereim, 563 Bedford Av, BKLN - 11211	6822	B5
Bais Yaakov School of Midland, 3609 13th Av, BKLN - 11218	6922	D6
Ballet Tech NYC School for Dance, 890 Broadway, MHTN - 10003	116	B7
Banana Kelly Community Learning Center - 991 LongWood Av, BRNX, 10459	6613	C3
Banana Kelly High School, 965 Longwood Av, BRNX - 10459	6613	C3
Bank Street School for Children, 610 W 112th St, MHTN - 10025	109	B2
Bard High School Early College, 525 E Houston St, MHTN - 10002	119	D5
Barkai Yeshiva School, 5302 21st Av, BKLN, 11204	7022	E2
Barnard Early Childhood Center, 129 Barnard Rd, NRCH - 10801	6396	A1
Barringer Freshman Academy, 24 Crane St, NWRK - 07104	6713	D5
Barringer High School, 90 Parker St, NWRK, 07104	6713	C5
Baruch College Campus High School, 17 Lexington Av - MHTN, 10010	116	C7
Battalion Christian Academy, 661 Linden Blvd, BKLN - 11203	6923	D5
Battin Middle School 75, 300 S Broad St, ELIZ, 07202	6917	E4
Bayard Rustin Educational Complex, 351 W 18th St - MHTN, 10011	115	D5
Bayonne High School, 667 Avenue A, BAYN, 07002	6919	D2
Bay Ridge Christian Academy, 6324 7th Av, BKLN - 11220	6922	A7
Bay Ridge Preparatory High School, 7420 4th Av, BKLN - 11209	7021	E1
Bay Ridge Preparatory Lower School, 8101 Ridge Blvd - BKLN, 11209	7021	D1
Bayside Academy, 19411a Northern Blvd, QENS, 11358	6721	E4
Beacon Christian Academy, 30 Prospect Av, BAYN - 07002	6919	E4
Beacon School, 227 W 61st St, MHTN, 10023	112	B4
Becton Regional High School - 120 Paterson Av & Cornelia St, ERTH, 07073	6609	C1
Bedford Academy High School, 1119 Bedford Av, BKLN - 11216	6822	B7
Beer Hagolah Institute, 671 Louisiana Av, BKLN, 11239	6924	E6
Beginning With Children Charter School, 11 Bartlett St - BKLN, 11206	6822	C5
Beis Chaya Mushkah School, 1492 St. Johns Pl, BKLN - 11213	6923	E2
Beitcher Yeshirva School, 4414 12th Av, BKLN, 11219	6922	C7
Beit Rabban School, 8 W 70th St, MHTN, 10023	112	D4
Bell Academy, 1825 212th St, QENS, 11360	6722	A1
Bellaire School, 20711 89th Av, QENS, 11427	6826	C3
Belleville Elementary School 4, 30 Magnolia St, BlvT - 07109	6713	D1
Belmont Preparatory High School, 500 E Fordham Rd - BRNX, 10458	6504	C4
Benedictine Academy, 840 N Broad St, ELIZ, 07208	6917	E1
Ben Porat Yosef School, 150 Grand Av, LEON, 07605	6502	C5
Bergen Boulevard School, 635 Bergen Blvd, RDGF, 07657	6611	C2
Bergen County Tech High School-Teterboro, 504 US-46 - TETB, 07608	6501	B4
Berkeley-Carroll School, 181 Lincoln Pl, BKLN, 11217	6922	E2
Berkeley Terrace Elementary School, 811 Grove St, IrvT - 07111	6816	D1
Bernie L Edmonson Community Education Center - 74 Halsted St, EORG, 07018	6712	E4
Bethany Christian Grade School, 521 Thomas S Boyland St - BKLN, 11212	6924	B3
Beth Chana School for Girls, 620 Bedford Av, BKLN - 11211	6822	B5

FEATURE NAME Address City ZIP Code	MAP#	GRID
Bethel Christian Academy, 580 Mt Prospect Av, NWRK - 07104	6713	E2
Bethel Christian Learning Center, 219-09 Linden Blvd - QENS, 11411	6826	E6
Beth Jacob Academy, 1213 Elm Av, BKLN, 11230	7023	A3
Beth Jacob-Beth Miriam School, 2126 Barnes Av, BRNX - 10462	6505	B5
Beth Jacob Day School, 85 Parkville Av, BKLN, 11230	7022	E1
Beth Jacob High School, 4421 15th Av, BKLN, 11219	6922	D7
Beth Jacob of Boro Park School, 1371 46th St, BKLN - 11219	6922	D7
Beth Jacob Parochial School, 142 Broome St, MHTN - 10002	119	C6
Beth Rachel School for Girls, 227 Marcy Av, BKLN - 11211	6822	B4
Beth Rivka School, 310 Crown St, BKLN, 11225	6923	C3
Bet Yaakov Ateret Torah, 2166 Coney Island Av, BKLN - 11223	7023	B5
Bias Frima School, 1377 42nd St, BKLN, 11218	6922	D7
Big Apple Academy, 2937 86th St, BKLN, 11223	7022	E6
Bilingual Bicultural School PS 182, 219 E 109th St - MHTN, 10029	110	B5
Biondi Elementary Education Center - 1529 Williamsbridge Rd, BRNX, 10461	6505	C6
Birch Wathen Lenox School, 210 E 77th St, MHTN, 10021	113	C4
Bishop Ford Central High School, 500 19th St, BKLN - 11215	6922	D4
Bishop Kearney High School, 2202 60th St, BKLN, 11204	7022	E3
Bishop Loughlin Memorial High School, 357 Clermont Av - BKLN, 11238	6822	A7
Blessed Sacrament Elementary School, 24 Maple Av - NRCH, 10801	6395	E5
Blessed Sacrament School, 187 Euclid Av, BKLN, 11208	6925	A1
Blessed Sacrament School, 1160 Beach Av, BRNX, 10472	6614	B2
Blessed Sacrament School, 1086 North Av, ELIZ, 07201	6918	A1
Blessed Sacrament School, 147 W 70th St, MHTN, 10023	112	D3
Blessed Sacrament School, 600 Clinton Av, NWRK - 07108	6817	A2
Blessed Sacrament School, 3420 94th St, QENS, 11372	6720	A5
Blessed Sacrament School, 830 Delafield Av, STNL - 10310	7019	D1
Blessed Sacrament School, 50 Rose Av, VLYS, 11580	6928	C2
Blind Brook High School, 840 King St, RYEB, 10573	6170	B2
Blind Brook Middle School, 840 King St, RYEB, 10573	6170	B2
Block Institute, 376 Bay 44th St, BKLN, 11214	7022	C7
Bnos Bias Yaakov Elementary School, 613 Beach 9th St - QENS, 11691	7027	D5
Bnos Chayil School, 345 Hewes St, BKLN, 11211	6822	B4
Bnos Israel-East Flatbush School, 1629 E 15th St, BKLN - 11229	7023	B4
Bnos Malka Academy, 7102 113th St, QENS, 11375	6824	D2
Bnos Menachem, 739 E New York Av, BKLN, 11203	6923	D4
Bnos Yakov Pupa School, 1402 40th St, BKLN, 11218	6922	D7
Bnos Yakov School for Girls, 638 Bedford Av, BKLN - 11211	6822	B5
Bnos Yerushalayim School, 600 McDonald Av, BKLN - 11218	6922	E7
Bnos Zion of Bobov School, 5000 14th Av, BKLN, 11219	7022	C1
Bnot Shulamith of Long Island, 140 Irving Pl, HmpT - 11598	7028	C1
Bobover Yeshiva Bnei Zion School, 4206 15th Av, BKLN - 11219	6922	D7
Boys & Girls High School, 1700 Fulton St, BKLN, 11213	6923	E1
Bradford Public School No 16, 96 Sussex St, JSYC, 07302	6820	C3
Bragaw Avenue School, 103 Bragaw Av, NWRK, 07112	6816	E3
Branch Brook Elementary School, 228 Ridge St, NWRK - 07104	6713	D4
Brandeis School, 25 Frost Ln, LWRN, 11559	7028	A3
Bread & Roses Integrated High School, 6 Edgecombe Av - MHTN, 10030	107	A6
Brearley School, 610 E 83rd St, MHTN, 10028	114	A4
Brensinger School No 17, 600 Bergen Av, JSYC, 07304	6819	E2
Broadway Elementary School, 180 Oraton St, NWRK - 07104	6714	A2
Bronx Academy High School, 1619 Boston Rd, BRNX - 10460	6613	C1
Bronx Academy of Health Careers, 800 E Gun Hill Rd - BRNX, 10467	6505	B2
Bronx Academy of Letters, 339 Morris Av, BRNX, 10451	107	E7
Bronx Aerospace High School, 800 E Gun Hill Rd, BRNX - 10467	6505	B2
Bronx Alternative Special Education Program - 1725 Metropolitan Av, BRNX, 10462	6505	C7
Bronx Center for Science & Mathematics - 1363 Fulton Av, BRNX, 10456	6613	C1
Bronx Charter School for Better Learning - 3740 Baychester Av, BRNX, 10466	6505	D1
Bronx Charter School for Children, 388 Willis Av, BRNX - 10454	6613	A4
Bronx Charter School for Excellence, 1508 Webster Av - BRNX, 10457	105	D7
Bronx Coalition Community High School - 1300 Boynton Av, BRNX, 10472	6613	E1
Bronx Dance Academy School, 3617 Bainbridge Av - BRNX, 10467	6504	E1
Bronx Engineering & Technology Academy - 99 Terrace View Av, MHTN, 10463	102	C3
Bronx Expeditionary Learning High School - 240 E 172nd St, BRNX, 10456	105	C7
Bronx Green Middle School, 2441 Wallace Av, BRNX - 10467	6505	B4
Bronx Health Sciences High School, 750 Baychester Av - BRNX, 10475	6505	E2
Bronx HS for Law & Community Service - 500 E Fordham Rd, BRNX, 10458	6504	D5
Bronx HS for Writing & Communication Arts - 1180 Tinton Av, BRNX, 10456	6613	C2
Bronx High School of Business, 240 E 172nd St, BRNX - 10456	105	C7
Bronx High School of Medical Science, 240 E 172nd St - BRNX, 10456	105	C6
Bronx HS of Performance & Stagecraft, 1619 Boston Rd - BRNX, 10460	6613	D1
Bronx House Nursery-Kindergarten School - 2222 Wallace Av, BRNX, 10467	6505	B5
Bronx International High School, 1110 Boston Rd, BRNX - 10456	6613	B2
Bronx Lab High School, 800 E Gun Hill Rd, BRNX, 10467	6505	B2
Bronx Leadership Academy, 1710 Webster Av, BRNX - 10457	105	E5
Bronx Leadership Academy II High School - 1100 Boston Rd, BRNX, 10456	6613	B2
Bronx Little School, 1300 Boynton Av, BRNX, 10472	6613	E1
Bronx-Manhattan Seventh Day Adventist School - 1440 Plimpton Av, BRNX, 10452	105	A6
Bronx Mathematics Preparatory School - 456 White Plains Rd, BRNX, 10473	6614	C4
Bronx Preparatory Charter School, 3872 3rd Av, BRNX - 10457	105	E7
Bronx Regional High School - 1010 Reverend James A Polite Av, BRNX, 10459	6613	C2

INDEX 73

Schools

New York City/5 Borough Points of Interest Index

Schools

FEATURE NAME Address City ZIP Code	MAP#	GRID
Bronx School for Law & Finance, 99 Terrace View Av - MHTN, 10463	102	B4
Bronx School For Law Government & Justice - 350 Gerard Av, BRNX, 10451	107	D6
Bronx School For Law Government & Justice - 244 E 163rd St, BRNX, 10451	6613	A2
Bronx School of Science & Inquiry, 40 W Tremont Av - BRNX, 10453	105	C3
Bronx Theatre High School, 99 Terrace View Av, MHTN - 10463	102	C3
Bronxville Middle School, 177 Pondfield Rd, BRXV - 10708	6394	E1
Bronx Writing Academy, 270 E 167th St, BRNX, 10456	6613	A1
Brooklyn Academy High School, 832 Marcy Av, BKLN - 11216	6822	C7
Brooklyn Acad of Science & the Environment - 883 Classon Av, BKLN, 11225	6923	A3
Brooklyn Amity School, 1501 Hendrickson St, BKLN - 11234	7023	D3
Brooklyn Avenue School, 24 Brooklyn Av, VLYS, 11581	6928	D4
Brooklyn Charter School, 545 Willoughby Av, BKLN - 11206	6822	C6
Brooklyn College Academy, 2900 Bedford Av, BKLN - 11210	7023	B1
Brooklyn Collegiate School, 2021 Bergen St, BKLN - 11233	6924	B2
Brooklyn Comprehensive Night School - 6565 Flatlands Av, BKLN, 11236	7024	A1
Brooklyn Excelsior Charter School, 856 Quincy St, BKLN - 11221	6822	E7
Brooklyn Friends School, 375 Pearl St, BKLN, 11201	121	B5
Brooklyn Heights Montessori School, 185 Court St - BKLN, 11201	121	A7
Brooklyn High School of the Arts, 345 Dean St, BKLN - 11217	6922	D1
Brooklyn International High School, 49 Flatbush Av Ext - BKLN, 11201	121	C4
Brooklyn Preparatory High School, 300 Willoughby Av - BKLN, 11205	6822	B6
Brooklyn School for Global Studies, 284 Baltic St, BKLN - 11201	121	A7
Brooklyn School for Music & Theatre, 883 Classon Av - BKLN, 11225	6923	B3
Brooklyn Secnd Sch for Collaborative Studies - 610 Henry St, BKLN, 11231	6922	B1
Brooklyn Seventh Day Adventist Elem School - 1260 Ocean Av, BKLN, 11230	7023	B1
Brooklyn Studio Secondary School, 8310 21st Av, BKLN - 11214	7022	C5
Brooklyn Technical High School, 29 Fort Greene Pl, BKLN - 11217	121	D6
Browning School, 52 E 62nd St, MHTN, 10065	113	A6
Brownsville Academy High School, 1150 E New York Av - BKLN, 11212	6924	A3
Bruno M Ponterio Ridge Street School, 390 N Ridge St - RYEB, 10573	6170	A2
Brunswick Middle School, 1252 King St, GrwT, 06831	6051	D3
Bruriah High School for Girls, 35 North Av, ELIZ, 07208	6917	D1
Buckley Country Day School, 2 IU Willets Rd, NHLS - 11576	6724	A3
Buckley School, 113 E 73rd St, MHTN, 10021	113	B4
Building Blocks Montessori School, 55 Forest Av, STNL - 10301	7020	C1
Burnet Street School, 28 Burnet St, NWRK, 07102	6713	D6
Bushwick Community High School, 231 Palmetto St - BKLN, 11221	6823	A6
Bushwick High School, 400 Irving Av, BKLN, 11237	6823	B6
Bushwick Leaders High School, 271 Melrose St, BKLN - 11206	6822	E5
Bs Computer App & Entrepreneurship Sch - 207-01 116th Av, QENS, 11411	6826	D6
Business School-Entrepreneurial Studies, 977 Fox St - BRNX, 10459	6613	D3
Butler Elementary School 23, 501 Union Av, ELIZ, 07208	6917	E2
Caedmon School, 416 E 80th St, MHTN, 10075	113	E4
Calhoun School, 160 W 74th St, MHTN, 10023	112	D2
Calhoun School, 433 W End Av, MHTN, 10024	112	D1
Calvary Christian School, 17 Lyons Av, NWRK, 07112	6817	A4
Calvin Coolidge Elementary School, 614 Tillman St, HlsT - 07205	6816	B5
Cambria Center for Gifted Children, 23310 Linden Blvd - QENS, 11411	6827	A7
Camden Middle School, 321 Bergen St, NWRK, 07103	6817	B1
Camden Street Elementary School, 281 Camden St - NWRK, 07103	6713	B7
Canarsie High School, 1600 Rockaway Pkwy, BKLN - 11236	6924	C7
Cardinal Hayes High School, 650 Grand Concourse, BRNX - 10451	107	E5
Cardinal McCarrick High School, 310 Augusta St, SAMB - 08879	7205	B7
Cardinal Spellman High School, 1 Cardinal Spellman Pl - BRNX, 10466	6505	D1
Career Academy, 525 Montgomery St, JSYC, 07302	6820	A2
Career Education Center, 448 W 56th St, MHTN, 10019	112	B6
Caritas Academy, 2495 John F Kennedy Blvd, JSYC, 07304	6819	E2
Carl Dixson Primary School, 22 S Hillside Av, EMFD - 10523	6049	A6
Carlstadt Elementary School, 550 Washington St, CARL - 07072	6500	C7
Carmel Christian School, 126 Rogers Av, BKLN, 11216	6923	B2
Carson School of Coastal Studies, 501 West Av, BKLN - 11224	7120	E1
Carteret Elementary School, 158 Grove St, BlmT, 07003	6713	C2
Carteret High School, 199 Washington Av, CART, 07008	7115	C1
Carteret Middle School, 300 Carteret Av, CART, 07008	7115	C1
Cascades High School, 198 Forsyth St, MHTN, 10002	119	A4
Cathedral High School, 350 E 56th St, MHTN, 10022	117	A1
Cathedral School, 910 Union St, BKLN, 11215	6922	E2
Cathedral School, 319 E 74th St, MHTN, 10021	113	D5
Cathedral School, 1047 Amsterdam Av, MHTN, 10025	109	B3
Catherine E Doyle Elementary School - 250 Wood Ridge Av, WRDG, 07075	6500	C5
Catherine McAuley High School, 710 E 37th St, BKLN - 11203	6923	D7
Catholic Academy of Northern Valley, 300 High St, CLST - 07624	6278	A3
Catholic Academy of Northern Valley, 573 Piermont Rd - DMRT, 07627	6278	B5
CCB School of Douglaston, 4514 251st St, QENS, 11362	6722	E3
Cecil Parker Elementary School, 461 S 6th Av, MTVN - 10550	6394	E6
Cedar Place Elementary School, 20 Cedar Pl, YNKR - 10705	6393	C2
Celia Cruz Bronx High School of Music, 2780 Reservoir Av - BRNX, 10468	6504	C3
Center Avenue Elementary School, 55 Centre Av, ERKY - 11518	6929	C5
Center for Continuing Education, 75 Riverdale Av, YNKR - 10701	6393	C2
Center Street School, 240 Center St, NHmT, 11596	6724	C4
Central Elementary School, 33 Cleveland St, COrT - 07050	6712	C2
Central Elementary School, 1100 Palmer Av, MrnT - 10538	6282	C7
Central High School, 100 Summit St, NWRK, 07103	6713	D7
Central Park East Elementary School, 1573 Madison Av - MHTN, 10029	109	E5
Central Park East High School, 1573 Madison Av, MHTN - 10029	109	E5
Ceres Elementary School, 445 State St, PTHA, 08861	7205	E3
Chabad Academy, 80 Shore Rd, MHVN, 11050	6508	C7
Chaminade High School, 340 Jackson Av, MNLA, 11501	6724	D6
Chancellor Avenue Elementary Annex School - 255 Chancellor Av, NWRK, 07112	6816	E4
Chancellor Avenue Elementary School - 844 Chancellor Av, IrvT, 07111	6816	B3
Chancellor Avenue Elementary School - 321 Chancellor Av, NWRK, 07112	6816	D4
Chapel School, 172 White Plains Rd, BRXV, 10708	6281	A7
Chapin School, 100 E End Av, MHTN, 10028	114	A4
Chatsworth Avenue Elementary School - 34 Chatsworth Av, LRMT, 10538	6396	C2
Cheder School, The, 129 Elmwood Av, BKLN, 11230	7022	E1
Chelsea Career & Technical Education HS - 131 Avenue of the Americas, MHTN, 10013	118	D3
Chestnut Street School, 252 Chestnut St, HmpT, 11552	6828	D6
Childrens Center School, 2800 Victory Blvd, STNL, 10314	7019	A4
Childrens Storefront School, 70 E 129th St, MHTN - 10035	110	B2
Childrens Workshop School, 610 E 12th St, MHTN, 10009	119	D3
Child School, 587 Main St, MHTN, 10044	113	E7
Choir Academy of Harlem, 2005 Madison Av, MHTN - 10035	110	B2
Christ Crusader Academy, 302 W 124th St, MHTN, 10027	109	D1
Christian Heritage Academy, 1100 E 42nd St, BKLN - 11210	7023	D1
Christ Lutheran School, 24801 Francis Lewis Blvd, QENS - 11422	6928	A3
Christopher Columbus High School, 925 Astor Av, BRNX - 10469	6505	B4
Christ the King Regional High School - 6802 Metropolitan Av, QENS, 11379	6823	D4
Christ the King School, 1345 Grand Concourse, BRNX - 10452	105	B7
Christ the King School, 750 N Broadway, YNKR, 10703	6279	D4
Christ the Teacher School, 359 Whiteman St, FTLE, 07024	6502	E6
Christy J Cugini Port Richmond School, 161 Park Av - STNL, 10302	6919	D7
Churchill School & Center, 301 E 29th St, MHTN, 10016	116	D6
Church of God Christian Academy, 1332 Central Av - QENS, 11691	7027	C4
Church Street School, 295 Church St, WHPL, 10603	6050	A7
Cicely Tyson School, 161 Elmwood Av, EORG, 07018	6712	D5
City & Country School, 146 W 13th St, MHTN, 10011	115	E7
City College Academy of Arts, 4600 Broadway, MHTN - 10040	104	D1
Clara Barton High School, 901 Classon Av, BKLN, 11225	6923	B3
Clara H Carlson Elementary School, 235 Belmont Blvd - HmpT, 11003	6827	D5
Clara Muhammad School, 120 Madison St, BKLN, 11216	6923	B1
Claremont Preparatory School, 41 Broad St, MHTN - 10004	120	B2
Clarendon No 4 Elementary School, 685 5th St, SECS - 07094	6610	A7
Clearstream Avenue School, 60 Clearstream Av, VLYS - 11580	6928	B3
Cleveland Elementary School, 388 Bergen St, NWRK - 07103	6817	B1
Cleveland Middle School 70, 436 1st Av, ELIZ, 07206	6918	B5
Cleveland Street Elementary School, 355 Cleveland St - COrT, 07050	6712	D1
Cliffside Park Elementary School 3, 397 Palisade Av - CLFP, 07010	6611	D3
Cliffside Park Elementary School 4, 279 Columbia Av - CLFP, 07010	6611	D2
Cliffside Park Elementary School 5, 214 Day Av, CLFP - 07010	108	A1
Cliffside Park Elementary School 6, 440 Oakdene Av - CLFP, 07010	6611	C2
Clinton Avenue Early Childhood Center, 534 Clinton Av - NWRK, 07108	6817	A2
Clinton Elementary School, 27 Berkshire Rd, MplT - 07040	6816	A1
Coalition School for Social Change, 220 W 58th St - MHTN, 10019	112	C6
Cobble Hill School of American Studies, 347 Baltic St - BKLN, 11201	121	B7
Collaborative Academy of Science, 220 Henry Street - MHTN, 10002	119	C7
Collegiate Institute for Math & Science, 925 Astor Av - BRNX, 10469	6505	B4
Collegiate School, 260 W 78th St, MHTN, 10024	112	C1
Colonial Elementary School, 315 Highbrook Av, PLHM - 10803	6395	C5
Columbia Grammar & Preparatory School, 5 W 93rd St - MHTN, 10025	109	A6
Columbus Elementary School, 1 Carteret Av, CART - 07008	7115	D2
Columbus Elementary School, 370 Westervelt Pl, LODI - 07644	6500	C1
Columbus Elementary School, 640 Lake Av, LynT, 07071	6609	A4
Columbus Elementary School 8, 147 Cedar St, GRFD - 07026	6500	A2
Columbus Elementary School 15, 511 3rd Av, ELIZ - 07202	6918	A5
Columbus Magnet Elementary School - 275 Washington Av, NRCH, 10801	6395	D4
Commerce Middle School, 201 Palisade Av, YNKR, 10703	6279	D7
Community Health Academy of the Heights - 511 W 182nd St, MHTN, 10033	104	D4
Community Partnership Charter School, 241 Emerson Pl - BKLN, 11205	6822	B6
Community Preparatory High School, 40 E 29th St - MHTN, 10016	116	B5
Community Roots Charter School, 51 St. Edwards St - BKLN, 11205	121	D5
Community School, 228 Fisher Av, WHPL, 10606	6168	A3
Community School for Social Justice, 350 Gerard Av - BRNX, 10451	107	D6
Comprehensive Model School 327, 580 Crotona Park S - BRNX, 10456	6613	C1
Concord High School, 109 Rhine Av, STNL, 10304	7020	C4
Concord Road Elementary School, 2 Concord Rd, ARDY - 10502	6166	D4
Convent of Sacred Heart School, 1177 King St, GrwT - 06831	6051	D3
Convent of Sacred Heart School, 1 E 91st St, MHTN - 10128	113	C1
Conwell Elementary School 3, 70 Bright St, JSYC, 07302	6820	B3
Copernicus Public School No 25 - 3385 John F Kennedy Blvd, JSYC, 07032	6716	B6
Cordero Public School No 37, 158 Erie St, JSYC, 07302	6820	C2
Corlears School, 324 W 15th St, MHTN, 10011	115	D6
Cornwell Avenue School, 250 Cornwell Av, HmpT, 11552	6828	C7
Corpus Christi School, 215 Kipp Av, HSBH, 07604	6500	E4
Corpus Christi School, 535 W 121st St, MHTN, 10027	109	C1
Corpus Christi School, 135 S Regent St, PTCH, 10573	6170	A6
Corpus Christi School, 3129 60th St, QENS, 11377	6719	C5
County Preparatory High School, 525 Montgomery St - JSYC, 07302	6820	A2
County Road Elementary School, 130 County Rd, DMRT - 07627	6278	B6
Covert Avenue Elementary School, 144 Covert Av, HmpT - 11003	6827	E4
Create Charter School, 164 Lembeck Av, JSYC, 07305	6819	C6
Cresskill High School, 1 Lincoln Dr, CRSK, 07626	6278	A6
Cross Street Elementary School, 6 Cross St, WLPK - 11596	6724	E4
Crotona Academy High School, 639 St. Anns Av, BRNX - 10455	6613	B3
CS 173, 1871 Walton Av, BRNX, 10453	105	C4
Culbreth Public School 14, 153 Union St, JSYC, 07304	6819	D3
Curtis High School, 105 Hamilton Av, STNL, 10301	6920	D6
Cynthia Jenkins School, 17937 137th Av, QENS, 11434	6927	C2
D & G Koloidis Parochial School, 8502 Ridge Blvd, BKLN - 11209	7021	D2
Dalton School, 53 E 91st St, MHTN, 10128	113	D1
Daniel Warren Elementary School, 1310 Harrison Av - MRNK, 10543	6283	B5
Daniel Webster Elementary School, 95 Glenmore Dr - NRCH, 10801	6395	D3
Daniel Webster Elementary School, 2700 Palisade Av - WhkT, 07086	6716	E3
David Grayson Christian School, 1237 Eastern Pkwy - BKLN, 11213	6923	E3
Davison Avenue Elementary School, 49 Davison Av - LNBK, 11563	6929	B3
Dayton Street Elementary School, 226 Dayton St, NWRK - 07114	6817	A6
Defuccio Public School 39, 214 Plainfield Av, JSYC - 07306	6819	D1
De Gauiter Institute for Law, 1440 Story Av, BRNX - 10473	6613	E3
De la Salle Academy, 202 W 97th St, MHTN, 10025	109	A5
Demarest Middle School, 568 Piermont Rd, DMRT, 07627	6278	B5
Demarest Middle School, 158 4th St, HBKN, 07030	6716	D7
Democracy Preparatory Charter School, 222 W 134th St - MHTN, 10030	107	A7
Denton Avenue Elementary School, 1050 Denton Av - NHmT, 11040	6724	B5
DeWitt Clinton High School, 100 W Mosholu Pkwy S - BRNX, 10468	6504	D2
Dickinson High School, 2 Palisade Av, JSYC, 07306	6820	B1
Dionne Warwick Institute, 120 Central Av, EORG, 07018	6713	A5
Discovery High School, 2780 Reservoir Av, BRNX, 10468	6504	C3
Dobbs Ferry High School, 505 Broadway, DBSF, 10522	6166	A3
Dobbs Ferry Middle School, 505 Broadway, DBSF, 10522	6166	A3
Dominican Academy, 44 E 68th St, MHTN, 10065	113	A5
Donald A Quarles Elementary School, 186 Davison Pl - EGLD, 07631	6392	A5
Donohoe Elementary School 4, 25 E 5th St, BAYN - 07002	6919	D5
Dows Lane Elementary School, 6 Dows Ln, IRVN, 10533	6166	A1
Dr Albert Einstein Academy 29, 919 N Broad St, ELIZ - 07208	6816	E7
Dr E Alma Flagg Elementary School, 150 3rd St, NWRK - 07107	6713	C5
Dreamyard Preparatory School, 240 E 172nd St, BRNX - 10456	105	C7
Dr Herbert N Richardson 21st Century School - 318 Stockton St, PTHA, 08861	7205	C3
Dr Martin Luther King Junior School, 108 S 9th St - NWRK, 07107	6713	B6
Dr Sun Yat Sen Middle School 131, 100 Hester St, MHTN - 10002	119	A6
Drs Yeshiva High School, 700 Ibsen St, HmpT, 11598	6928	A7
Dr William H Horton Elementary School, 291 N 7th St - NWRK, 07107	6713	C4
Dutch Broadway Elementary School - 1880 Dutch Broadway, HmpT, 11003	6827	C7
Dwight-Englewood School, 315 E Palisade Av, EGLD - 07631	6392	A7
Dwight School, 291 Central Park W, MHTN, 10024	109	A7
Eagle Academy for Young Men, 244 E 164th St, BRNX - 10456	6613	A2
Eagle Avenue Middle School, 307 Eagle Av, HmpT - 11552	6828	D7
Eagle Hill School, 45 Glenville Rd, GrwT, 06831	6170	E2
Eames Place School No 307, 124 Eames Pl, BRNX, 10468	102	E6
Early Childhood Center, 144 Coe Av, HlsT, 07205	6816	D7
Earth School, 600 E 6th St, MHTN, 10009	119	C4
East Bronx Academy for the Future, 1716 Southern Blvd - BRNX, 10460	6613	D1
Eastchester Middle School, 550 White Plains Rd, EchT - 10709	6281	B4
Eastchester Senior High School, 2 Stewart Pl, EchT - 10709	6281	B4
East Elementary School, 456 Neptune Blvd, LBCH, 11561	7029	E6
East Flatbush Community Research School - 905 Winthrop St, BKLN, 11203	6923	E4
East Harlem Career Academy, 240 E 109th St, MHTN - 10029	110	A6
East Harlem Village Academy Charter School - 413 E 120th St, MHTN, 10035	110	D4
East Newark Elementary School, 501 N 3rd St, ENWK - 07029	6714	A5
East New York Family Academy, 2057 Linden Blvd, BKLN - 11207	6924	D4
East Orange Campus 9 School, 129 Renshaw Av, EORG - 07017	6713	A2
East Orange Campus High School, 344 Prospect St - EORG, 07017	6713	A2
East Orange Community Charter School, 682 Park Av - EORG, 07017	6712	D2
East Rockaway Junior-Senior High School, 443 Ocean Av - ERKY, 11518	6929	D6
East Side Community High School, 420 E 12th St, MHTN - 10009	119	C2
East Side High School, 238 Van Buren St, NWRK, 07105	6818	A2
East Side Middle School, 1458 York Av, MHTN, 10075	113	E5
East Village Community School, 610 E 12th St, MHTN - 10009	119	D3
East West School of International Studies - 4621 Colden St, QENS, 11355	6721	A5
Ebbetts Field Middle School, 46 McKeever Pl, BKLN - 11225	6923	B3
EBC-ENY High School for Public Safety & Law - 1495 Herkimer St, BKLN, 11233	6924	C1
EBC-High School for Public Service-Bush - 1155 DeKalb Av, BKLN, 11221	6822	E6
Ebenezer Preparatory School, 5464 Kings Hwy, BKLN - 11203	6923	E6
Ecole Toussaint Louverture Elementary School - 330 Central Av, EORG, 07018	6712	E5

INDEX 74

New York City/5 Borough Points of Interest Index

Schools

FEATURE NAME Address City ZIP Code	MAP#	GRID
Edgemont Junior-Senior High School, 200 White Oak Ln - GrbT, 10583	6167	C6
Edgewood Elementary School, 1 Roosevelt Pl, SCDL - 10583	6281	D1
Edison Elementary School, 132 Rectory St, PTCH, 10573	6170	C5
Edward A Reynolds West Side High School - 140 W 102nd St, MHTN, 10025	109	A4
Edward H Bryan Elementary School, 51 Brookside Av - CRSK, 07626	6278	A7
Edward J Patten Elementary School, 500 Charles St - PTHA, 08861	7205	D2
Edward R Murrow High School, 1600 Avenue L, BKLN - 11230	7023	B2
Edward T Bowser Unique School of Excellence - 180 Lincoln St, EORG, 07017	6712	E3
Edward Williams Elementary School, 9 Union Ln, MTVN - 10553	6394	E5
Eighteenth Avenue School of Science & Tech - 229 18th Av, NWRK, 07108	6817	B1
El Bethel Christian Academy, 910 Jewett Av, STNL - 10314	7019	D3
Eleanor Roosevelt High School, 411 E 76th St, MHTN - 10021	113	D5
Elementary School 02, 1 Donahue Av, HmpT, 11096	7027	D3
Elementary School 05, 305 Cedarhurst Av, CDHT, 11516	7028	A2
Elementary School 05, 118 Lockwood Av, EchT, 10708	6395	C1
Elementary School 06, 523 Church Av, HmpT, 11598	7028	A1
Elementary School 09, 53 Fairview St, YNKR, 10703	6279	D7
Elementary School 13, 195 McLean Av, YNKR, 10705	6393	D4
Elementary School 16, 759 N Broadway, YNKR, 10701	6279	D4
Elementary School 17, 745 Midland Av, YNKR, 10701	6394	A1
Elementary School 21, 100 Lee Av, YNKR, 10705	6393	E4
Elementary School 22, 1408 Nepperhan Av, YNKR, 10703	6280	A3
Elementary School 23, 56 Van Cortlandt Park Av, YNKR - 10701	6393	D2
Elementary School 30, 30 Nevada Pl, YNKR, 10708	6394	D2
Elijah Stroud Middle School, 750 Classon Av, BKLN - 11238	6923	B2
Elisabeth Morrow School, 435 Lydecker St, EGLD, 07631	6392	B5
Elite Academy, 190 Sylvan Av, EGLC, 07632	6503	B3
Elizabeth High School, 425 Grier Av, ELIZ, 07202	6917	E4
Elizabeth High School-Aboff House, 699 South St, ELIZ - 07202	6917	E4
Elizabeth High School-Dwyer House, 600 Pearl St, ELIZ - 07202	6917	E4
Elizabeth High School-Edison House, 625 Summer St - ELIZ, 07202	6917	E5
Elizabeth High School-Halsey House, 600 Pearl St, ELIZ - 07202	6917	E4
Elizabeth High School-Jefferson House - 27 Martin Luther King Plz, ELIZ, 07201	6917	E3
Elizabethport Catholic School, 227 Court St, ELIZ, 07206	6918	C5
Ella Baker School, 317 E 67th St, MHTN, 10065	113	C6
Elliott Street Elementary School, 243 Woodside Av - NWRK, 07104	6713	E2
Elmont Memorial High School, 555 Ridge Rd, HmpT - 11003	6827	B6
Elmora Elementary School 12, 638 Magie Av, ELIZ - 07208	6917	C3
El Puente Academy for Peace & Justice, 186 N 6th St - BKLN, 11211	6822	A3
Eltingville Lutheran School, 300 Genesee Av, STNL - 10312	7116	E5
EM Baker Elementary School, 69 Baker Hill Rd, GTNK - 11023	6617	A5
Emerson High School, 318 18th St, UNCT, 07087	6716	D4
Emerson Middle School, 160 Bolmer Av, YNKR, 10703	6279	E4
Emmanuel Childrens Mission School, 32 S 5th Av, MTVN - 10550	6394	D4
English Math Institute, 410 Broad Av, PALP, 07650	6502	C6
Enrico Fermi Performing Arts School, 27 Poplar St - YNKR, 10701	6393	D1
Epiphany Elementary School, 234 E 22nd St, MHTN - 10010	116	C7
Epiphany Lutheran School, 721 Lincoln Pl, BKLN, 11216	6923	C2
Erasmus Campus for Business-Technology - 911 Flatbush Av, BKLN, 11226	6923	B5
Erasmus Campus for Humanities, 911 Flatbush Av, BKLN - 11226	6923	B5
Essence School, 590 Sheffield Av, BKLN, 11207	6924	D4
Essex Street Academy, 350 Grand St, MHTN, 10002	119	B5
Ethical Culture Fieldston Lower School - 3901 Fieldston Rd, BRNX, 10471	6393	B7
Ethical Culture-Fieldston School, 3901 Fieldston Rd - BRNX, 10471	6393	B7
Euclid Elementary School, 1 Burton Av, HSBH, 07604	6500	D5
Eugenio Maria de Hostos School, 75 Morris St, YNKR - 10705	6393	C3
Evander Childs High School, 800 E Gun Hill Rd, BRNX - 10467	6505	B2
Evangel Christian School, 3921 Crescent St, QENS, 11101	6718	D5
Excellence Charter School of Bedford, 225 Patchen Av - BKLN, 11233	6923	E1
Excelsior Elementary School, 418 E 45th St, BKLN - 11203	6923	D5
Excelsior Preparatory High School, 14310 Springfield Blvd - QENS, 11413	6927	C3
Eximius College Preparatory Academy, 1363 Fulton Av - BRNX, 10456	6613	C1
Explorations Academy, 1595 Bathgate Av, BRNX, 10457	105	E7
Explore Charter School, 15 Snyder Av, BKLN, 11226	6923	B5
Ezra Academy, 11945 Union Tpk, QENS, 11375	6824	E3
Faith Christian Elementary School, 1401 Flatbush Av - BKLN, 11210	6923	C7
Family Life Academy Charter School, 14 W 170th St - BRNX, 10452	105	B7
Family School 32, 1 Montclair Pl, YNKR, 10710	6280	D4
Fannie Lou Hamer Freedom High School - 1021 Jennings St, BRNX, 10460	6613	D1
Fannie Lou Hamer Middle School, 1001 Jennings St - BRNX, 10460	6613	D1
Farragut Middle School, 27 Farragut Av, HAOH, 10706	6165	E7
FDNY High School for Fire & Life Safety - 400 Pennsylvania Av, BKLN, 11207	6924	C3
FE Bellows Elementary School, 200 Carroll Av, MRNK - 10543	6283	A5
Felician School for Exceptional Children, 260 S Main St - LODI, 07644	6500	B3
Ferris High School, 35 Colgate St, JSYC, 07302	6820	B2
Fifteenth Avenue Elementary School, 557 15th Av - NWRK, 07103	6713	A7
Fiorello H Laguardia High School, 100 Amsterdam Av - MHTN, 10023	112	B4
Fire Fighter Christopher A Santora School, 8615 37th Av - QENS, 11372	6719	E5
First Avenue Elementary School, 214 1st Av W, NWRK - 07107	6713	C3
Flatbush Catholic Academy, 2520 Church Av, BKLN - 11226	6923	B5
Flatbush Seventh Day Adventist Elem School - 5810 Snyder Av, BKLN, 11203	6924	A5
Floral Park-Bellrose Elementary School, 2 Larch Av - FLPK, 11001	6827	B2
Floral Park Memorial High School, 210 Locust St, FLPK - 11001	6827	C3
Florence A Smith Elementary School 2, 2745 Terrell Av - HmpT, 11572	6929	E6
Florence Avenue Elementary School, 1324 Springfield Av - IrvT, 07111	6816	B2
Flushing Christian School, 4154 Murray St, QENS, 11355	6721	B4
Flushing High School, 3501 Union St, QENS, 11354	6721	A3
Flushing International High School, 14480 Barclay Av - QENS, 11355	6721	B4
Fontbonne Hall Academy School, 9901 Shore Rd, BKLN - 11209	7021	C3
Food & Finance High School, 525 W 50th St, MHTN - 10019	112	A6
Fordham High School for the Arts, 500 E Fordham Rd - BRNX, 10458	6504	D4
Fordham Leadership Acad for Business & Tech - 500 E Fordham Rd, BRNX, 10458	6504	D5
Fordham Preparatory School, 441 E Fordham Rd, BRNX - 10458	6504	D4
Foreign Language Academy of Global Studies - 470 Jackson Av, BRNX, 10455	6613	B4
Forest Hills High School, 6701 110th St, QENS, 11375	6824	D1
Forest Hills Jewish Center, 106-06 Queens Blvd, QENS - 11375	6824	C2
Forest Hills Montessori School, 6704 Austin St, QENS - 11375	6824	C2
Forest Road School, 16 Forest Rd, HmpT, 11581	6928	B4
Forest Street Elementary School, 651 Forest St, COrT - 07050	6712	A3
Fort Hamilton High School, 8301 Shore Rd, BKLN, 11209	7021	C1
Fort Lee High School, 3000 Lemoine Av, FTLE, 07024	103	B2
Fort Lee Number 1 Elementary School, 250 Hoym St - FTLE, 07024	6502	E6
Fort Lee Number 2 Elementary School, 2047 Jones Rd - FTLE, 07024	6502	E4
Fort Lee Number 3 Elementary School, 2405 2nd St - FTLE, 07024	6503	A4
Fort Lee Number 4 Elementary School - 1193 Anderson Av, FTLE, 07024	6502	D7
Forward School, 3710 Barnes Av, BRNX, 10467	6505	B1
Foundations Academy, 70 Tompkins Av, BKLN, 11206	6822	C6
Fourteenth Avenue Elementary School, 186 14th Av - NWRK, 07103	6713	B7
Fourth Avenue Elementary School, 199 4th Av, EORG - 07017	6713	A3
Foxfire School, 1061 N Broadway, YNKR, 10701	6279	E3
Fox Meadow Elementary School, 59 Brewster Rd, SCDL - 10583	6167	D6
Francis School, 4240 Amboy Rd, STNL, 10308	7117	A6
Francis X Hegarty Elementary School, 100 Radcliffe Rd - ISPK, 11558	7029	C5
Frank Conwell Elementary School 3, 111 Bright St, JSYC - 07302	6820	B3
Franklin Delano Roosevelt High School, 5800 20th Av - BKLN, 11204	7022	D2
Franklin Early Childhood Center, 1180 Henrietta Pl - HmpT, 11557	6928	C7
Franklin Elementary School, 100 Davis Av, KRNY, 07032	6714	B5
Franklin Elementary School, 42 Park Av, NWRK, 07104	6713	D5
Franklin Elementary School, 1550 Lindy Ter, UnnT - 07083	6816	A5
Franklin Elementary School 3, 5211 Columbia Av, NBgT - 07047	6610	D7
Franklin Elementary School 13, 248 Ripley Pl, ELIZ - 07206	6918	C5
Franklin K Lane High School, 999 Jamaica Av, BKLN - 11208	6824	A7
Frank Sinatra School of the Arts High School - 3020 Thomson Av, QENS, 11101	6718	D6
Frederick Douglass Academy II, 215 W 114th St, MHTN - 10026	109	D3
Frederick Douglass Academy III, 3630 3rd Av, BRNX - 10456	6613	B1
Frederick Douglass Academy IV, 1010 Lafayette Av - BKLN, 11221	6822	D6
Frederick Douglass Academy VI, 821 Bay 25th St, QENS - 11691	7027	B5
Frederick Douglass Academy VII, 226 Bristol St, BKLN - 11212	6924	A3
Frederick Douglass Academy VIII, 1400 Pennsylvania Av - BKLN, 11239	6924	E6
Frederick Douglass Academy Vs Middle School - 2111 Crotona Av, BRNX, 10457	6504	D6
Freedom Academy High School, 116 Nassau St, BKLN - 11201	121	B4
French-American School, 111 Larchmont Av, LRMT - 10538	6396	D2
French-American School of New York, 145 New St - MRNK, 10543	6282	E5
Fulton Avenue Elementary School 8, 3252 Fulton Av - HmpT, 11572	7029	E1
Future Leaders Institute School, 134 W 122nd St, MHTN - 10027	109	E2
Gandhi Public School 23, 143 Romaine Av, JSYC, 07306	6819	E1
Gan Yisroel School, 3909 15th Av, BKLN, 11218	6922	D7
Garden City High School, 170 Rockaway Av, GDNC - 11530	6828	D1
Garden City Middle School, 98 Cherry Valley Av, GDNC - 11530	6828	E2
Garden City Park Elementary School, 51 Central Av - NHmT, 11040	6724	B7
Garden School, 3316 79th St, QENS, 11372	6719	D5
Garfield Catholic Academy, 200 MacArthur Av, GRFD - 07026	6500	B2
Garfield Elementary School, 360 Belgrove Dr, KRNY - 07032	6714	A3
Garfield High School, 500 Palisade Av, GRFD, 07026	6500	A1
Garfield Jackson Academy, 106 Prospect St, EORG - 07017	6712	E3
Gateway Academy, 200 Boscombe Av, STNL, 10309	7206	C2
Gateway Charter School, 119 Newkirk St, JSYC, 07306	6820	A1
Gateway Christian Academy, 257 Bay Ridge Av, BKLN - 11220	6921	E7
Gateway School, 60 High St, CART, 07008	7115	D2
Gateway Sch of Environmental Research & Tech - 1980 Lafayette Av, BRNX, 10473	6614	C3
Gelder Elementary School, 251 Undercliff Av, EDGW - 07020	6611	E3
Genesis Day School, 317 3rd St, JSYC, 07302	6820	B2
Geneva School of Manhattan, 123 W 57th St, MHTN - 10019	112	D6
George H Murray Academy, 760 DeKalb Av, BKLN - 11216	6822	C7
George M Davis Elementary School, 80 Iselin Dr, NRCH - 10583	6281	E3
George Washington Carver Elementary School - 333 Clinton Pl, NWRK, 07112	6816	E4
George Washington Carver High School - 14310 Springfield Blvd, QENS, 11413	6927	C3
George Washington Carver Institue, 410 N Grove St - EORG, 07017	6713	B3
George Washington Carver Institute, 135 Glenwood Av - EORG, 07017	6712	E2
George Washington Elementary School, 1530 Leslie St - HlsT, 07205	6816	D5
George Washington Elementary School, 100 Orchard St - WHPL, 10604	6050	B6
George Washington School, 347 William St, HmpT - 11552	6828	D4
German School of New York, 50 Partridge Rd, WHPL - 10605	6168	E4
Get Set Elementary School, 2301 Snyder Av, BKLN - 11226	6923	B5
Gilmore Elementary School, 815 17th St, UNCT, 07087	6716	C3
Girls Preparatory Charter School, 52 Chambers St - MHTN, 10007	118	C7
Global Enterprise High School, 925 Astor Av, BRNX - 10469	6505	B4
Globe School for Environmental Research - 3710 Barnes Av, BRNX, 10467	6505	B1
Goldie Maple Academy, 365 Beach 56th St, QENS, 11692	7026	E6
Good Counsel Lower Academy, 52 N Broadway, WHPL - 10603	6168	B1
Good Shepard Academy, 285 Nesbit Ter, IrvT, 07111	6816	B3
Good Shepherd School, 1943 Brown St, BKLN, 11229	7023	D5
Good Shepherd School, 620 Isham St, MHTN, 10034	102	A6
Gordon Parks Academy, 98 Greenwood Av, EORG, 07017	6713	B4
Gorton High School, 100 Shonnard Pl, YNKR, 10703	6279	D6
Gotham Avenue Elementary School, 181 Gotham Av - HmpT, 11003	6827	B5
Grace Church School, 86 4th Av, MHTN, 10003	119	A2
Grace Dodge Career & Technical Education HS - 2474 Crotona Av, BRNX, 10458	6504	E5
Grace Lutheran Day School, 10005 Springfield Blvd, QENS - 11429	6826	E3
Grace Lutheran School, 400 Hempstead Av, MLVN, 11565	6929	C1
Graham Elementary-Magnet School, 421 E 5th St - MTVN, 10553	6395	A5
Grand Concourse Charter Academy, 116 E 169th St - BRNX, 10452	6613	A1
Grant Elementary School, 104 Henry St, RDFP, 07660	6501	E6
Greater New York Academy, 4132 58th St, QENS, 11377	6719	B6
Great Neck North High School, 35 Polo Rd, GTNK - 11023	6616	E5
Great Neck North Middle School, 77 Polo Rd, GTNK - 11023	6616	E5
Great Neck South Middle School, 349 Lakeville Rd, LKSU - 11020	6723	D4
Greek American Institute-New York, 3573 Bruckner Blvd - BRNX, 10461	6505	E6
Greenacres Elementary School, 41 Huntington Rd, SCDL - 10583	6167	E4
Greenburg Academy, 108 Shonnard Pl, YNKR, 10703	6279	E6
Green Sch- An Acad for Environmental Careers - 223 Graham Av, BKLN, 11206	6822	C4
Greenvale Elementary School, 1 Gabriel Resicgno Dr - EchT, 10583	6281	C3
Greenville Elementary School, 100 Glendale Rd, GrbT - 10583	6167	A6
Greenwich Japanese Institute, 15 Ridge Pl, GrwT, 06831	6170	D3
Greenwich Village Middle School, 490 Hudson St, MHTN - 10014	118	C1
Gregorio Luperon High School Science Math - 516 W 181st St, MHTN, 10033	104	D4
Gretta R Ostrovsky Middle School, 540 Windsor Rd - WRDG, 07075	6500	D6
Grimes Performing Arts Magnet School, 58 S 10th Av - MTVN, 10550	6394	D5
Grove Street Elementary School, 602 Grove St, IrvT - 07111	6712	E7
Guardian Angel School, 193 10th Av, MHTN, 10011	115	C4
Guggenheim Elementary School, 38 Poplar Pl, NHmT - 11050	6508	D6
Guild Exceptional Child School, 1273 57th St, BKLN - 11219	7022	C1
Hackensack High School, 135 1st St, HKSK, 07601	6501	B1
Hackley School, 293 Benedict Av, TYTN, 10591	6048	C3
Haftr Lower School, 33 Washington Av, LWRN, 11559	7028	A3
Haftr Middle School, 44 Frost Lane, LWRN, 11559	7028	A3
Haftr Upper School, 635 Central Av, CDHT, 11516	7028	B2
Hallen School, 97 Centre Av, NRCH, 10801	6395	E5
Halloran Elementary School 22, 1014 S Elmora Av, ELIZ - 07202	6917	D5
Hamilton Avenue Elementary School - 1 Western Junior Hwy, GrwT, 06830	6170	D5
Hamilton Elementary School, 20 Oak St, MTVN, 10550	6394	D4
Hamilton Middle School 72, 310 Cherry St, ELIZ, 07208	6917	D3
Hampton Street Elementary School, 10 Hampton Rd - GDNC, 11530	6828	D2
Hannah Senesh Community Day School, 342 Smith St - BKLN, 11231	6922	C1
Hanson Place Seventh Day Adventist Elem Sch - 38 Lafayette Av, BKLN, 11217	121	D7
Harbor Morningside Children's Center, 311 W 120th St - MHTN, 10027	109	D2
Harbor Sciences-Arts Charter School, 1 E 104th St - MHTN, 10029	109	E6
Harlem Day Charter School, 240 E 123rd St, MHTN - 10035	110	C3
Harlem Link Charter School, 134 W 122nd St, MHTN - 10027	109	E2
Harlem Renaissance High School, 22 E 128th St, MHTN - 10035	110	B1
Harlem School at Exodus House, 340 E 104th St, MHTN - 10029	110	B7
Harlem School of the Arts, 645 St. Nicholas Av, MHTN - 10031	107	A5
Harma Religious Institute for Girls, 30 Lancaster Av - BKLN, 11223	7023	A6
Harold Wilson School, 190 Muhammad Ali Av, NWRK - 07108	6817	B2
Harriet Tubman Charter School, 3565 3rd Av, BRNX - 10456	6613	B1
Harris Elementary School 1, 135 Avenue C, BAYN, 07002	6919	D5
Harrison Avenue Elementary School, 480 Harrison Av - HRSN, 10528	6283	B2
Harrison Elementary School, 310 Harrison Av, ROSL - 07203	6917	A4
Harrison High School, 800 Hamilton St, HRSN, 07029	6714	B5
Harrison High School, 255 Union Av, HRSN, 10528	6282	E2
Harry L Bain Elementary School, 6200 Broadway, WNYK - 07093	6611	B7
Harry S Truman High School, 750 Baychester Av, BRNX - 10475	6505	E2
Harry Van Arsdale High School, 257 N 6th St, BKLN - 11211	6822	B3
Hasbrouck Heights High School, 365 Boulevard, HSBH - 07604	6500	D3
Hasbrouck Heights Middle School, 365 Boulevard, HSBH - 07604	6500	E3
Hastings High School, 1 Mt Hope Blvd, HAOH, 10706	6166	A7

Schools

New York City/5 Borough Points of Interest Index

Schools

FEATURE NAME Address City ZIP Code	MAP#	GRID
Hawkins Street Elementary School, 8 Hawkins St, NWRK - 07105	6818	C1
Hawthorne Avenue School, 428 Hawthorne Av, NWRK - 07112	6816	E3
Hawthorne Country Day, 5 Bradhurst Av, MtPT, 10532	6049	C1
Hawthorne Elementary School, 201 Fycke Ln, TnkT - 07666	6502	B2
Hazel Avenue Elementary School, 45 Hazel Av, WOrT - 07052	6712	A3
Health Opportunities High School, 350 Gerard Av, BRNX - 10451	107	D6
Heathcote Elementary School, 26 Palmer Av, SCDL - 10583	6282	A1
Hebrew Academy of Long Beach, 530 W Broadway - LBCH, 11561	7029	A7
Hebrew Academy of Nassau County, 609 Hempstead Av - HmpT, 11010	6828	C4
Hebrew Academy of West Queens, 7502 113th St, QENS - 11375	6824	E3
Hebrew Academy-Special Children, 555 Remsen Av - BKLN, 11236	6924	A5
Hebron Seventh Day Adventist Bilingual Sch - 920 Park Pl, BKLN, 11213	6923	C2
Heights Middle School 7, 222 Laidlaw Av, JSYC, 07306	6716	A7
Hellenic Classical Charter School, 646 5th Av, BKLN - 11232	6922	C3
Henry Street School International Studies, 220 Henry St - MHTN, 10002	119	B7
Henry Viscardi School, 201 IU Willets Rd, NHmT, 11577	6724	E2
Herber Middle School, 75 Ocean Av, MLVN, 11565	6929	C2
Herbert Lehman High School, 3000 E Tremont Av, BRNX - 10461	6505	E7
Heritage School, 1680 Lexington Av, MHTN, 10029	110	A6
Herricks Middle School, 7 Hilldale Dr, NHmT, 11507	6724	C2
Herricks Senior High School, 100 Shelter Rock Rd, NHmT - 11576	6724	C4
Hewitt Lower School, 3 E 76th St, MHTN, 10021	113	B4
Hewitt Upper School, 45 E 75th St, MHTN, 10021	113	B4
Hewlett Elementary School, 1570 Broadway, HmpT - 11557	6928	E6
Hewlett High School, 60 Everit Av, HBPK, 11557	6928	D7
Heywood Avenue Elementary School, 421 Heywood Av - COrT, 07050	6712	B4
H Frank Carey Junior-Senior High School, 230 Poppy Av - HmpT, 11010	6828	B3
Highland Elementary School, 19310 Peck Av, QENS - 11365	6721	E6
High School for Arts & Business - 105-25 Horace Harding Expwy N, QENS, 11368	6720	C7
High School for Civil Rights, 400 Pennsylvania Av, BKLN - 11207	6924	D3
HS for Construction Trades Engineer & Arch - 9406 104th St, QENS, 11416	6824	D7
High School for Contemporary Arts, 800 E Gun Hill Rd - BRNX, 10467	6505	B2
High School for Dual Language-Asian Studies - 350 Grand St, MHTN, 10002	119	B5
High School for Enterprise, Business & Tech - 850 Grand St, BKLN, 11206	6822	D4
High School for Environmental Studies, 444 W 56th St - MHTN, 10019	112	B6
High School for Global Citizenship, 883 Classon Av - BKLN, 11225	6923	B3
HS for Health Professions & Human Srvs Sch - 345 E 15th St, MHTN, 10003	119	C1
HS for International Business & Finance - 549 Audubon Av, MHTN, 10040	104	E2
HS for Law Advocacy & Community Justice - 122 Amsterdam Av, MHTN, 10023	112	B3
HS for Law Enforcement & Public Safety - 11625 Guy R Brewer Blvd, QENS, 11434	6825	E7
High School for Leadership & Public Service - 90 Trinity Pl, MHTN, 10006	120	B1
HS for Mathematics-Science-Engineering - 140 Convent Av, MHTN, 10031	106	E6
High School for Public Service, 600 Kingston Av, BKLN - 11203	6923	D4
High School for Service & Learning, 790 E New York Av - BKLN, 11203	6923	D4
High School for Teaching & Professions - 2780 Reservoir Av, BRNX, 10468	6504	C3
High School for Violin & Dance, 1110 Boston Rd, BRNX - 10456	6613	C2
HS for Youth & Comm Development at Erasmus - 911 Flatbush Av, BKLN, 11226	6923	B5
HS of Amer Studies at Lehman College, 2925 Goulden Av - BRNX, 10468	6504	C3
High School of Applied Communication - 3020 Thomson Av, QENS, 11101	6718	D6
High School of Computers & Technology - 800 E Gun Hill Rd, BRNX, 10467	6505	B2
High School of Economics & Finance, 100 Trinity Pl - MHTN, 10006	120	B1
High School of Fashion Industries, 225 W 24th St, MHTN - 10011	115	E5
High School of Graphic Communication Arts - 439 W 49th St, MHTN, 10019	112	B7
High School of Health Careers-Sciences, 549 Audubon Av - MHTN, 10040	104	E2
High School of Hospitality Management, 525 W 50th St - MHTN, 10019	112	A6
High School of Law & Public Service, 549 Audubon Av - MHTN, 10040	104	E2
High School of Media & Community, 549 Audubon Av - MHTN, 10040	104	E2
High School of Telecommunication Arts & Tech - 350 67th St, BKLN, 11220	6921	E7
High School of World Cultures, 1300 Boynton Av, BRNX - 10472	6613	E1
High Technology High School, 2000 85th St, NBgT - 07047	6611	A4
Highview Elementary School, 200 N Central Av, GrbT - 10530	6167	D3
Highway Christian Academy, 132 E 111th St, MHTN - 10029	110	A5
Hillcrest High School, 16005 Highland Av, QENS, 11432	6825	C4
Hillers Elementary School, 56 Longview Av, HKSK, 07601	6501	A1
Hillside Catholic Academy, 397 Columbia Av, HlsT, 07205	6816	C6
Hillside Elementary School, 340 Homans Av, CLST - 07624	6278	C4
Hillside Elementary School, 1 Lefurgy Av, HAOH, 10706	6166	A7
Hillside Grade School, 150 Maple Dr W, NHmT, 11040	6723	E7
Hillside High School, 1085 Liberty Av, HlsT, 07205	6816	C6
Hilltop Elementary School, 200 Woodside Av, LODI - 07644	6500	D3
Hoboken Catholic Academy-Hudson Campus - 410 Hudson St, HBKN, 07030	6716	D7
Hoboken Catholic Academy-Madison Campus - 555 7th St, HBKN, 07030	6716	D6
Hoboken Charter School, 158 4th St, HBKN, 07030	6716	D6
Hoboken High School, 900 Clinton St, HBKN, 07030	6716	D6
Holcombe L Rucker School of Comm Research - 965 Longwood Av, BRNX, 10459	6613	C3
Holmes Elementary School, 195 N Columbus Av, MTVN - 10553	6395	A3
Holmes Middle School 71, 436 1st Av, ELIZ, 07206	6918	B5
Holy Child Jesus School, 11102 86th Av, QENS, 11418	6824	E6
Holy Child Middle School, 220 E 4th St, MHTN, 10009	119	C4
Holy Cross High School, 2620 Francis Lewis Blvd, QENS - 11358	6721	D2
Holy Cross School, 1846 Randall Av, BRNX, 10473	6614	B3
Holy Cross School, 15 Frank E Rodgers Blvd S, HRSN - 07029	6714	A6
Holy Cross School, 332 W 43rd St, MHTN, 10036	116	B1
Holy Family Academy, 239 Avenue A, BAYN, 07002	6919	C4
Holy Family School, 2169 Blackrock Av, BRNX, 10472	6614	C2
Holy Family School, 200 Summit St, NRWD, 07648	6164	B7
Holy Family School, 7415 175th St, QENS, 11366	6825	D1
Holy Innocents School, 249 E 17th St, BKLN, 11226	6923	A6
Holy Name of Jesus School, 241 Prospect Park W, BKLN - 11215	6922	E4
Holy Name of Jesus School, 202 W 97th St, MHTN - 10025	109	A5
Holy Name of Jesus School, 2 Broadway, MtPT, 10595	6050	A3
Holy Name of Jesus School, 70 Petersville Rd, NRCH - 10801	6396	A3
Holy Name of Mary School, 90 S Grove St, VLYS, 11580	6928	D4
Holy Rosary Academy, 501 15th St, UNCT, 07087	6716	D4
Holy Rosary School, 1500 Arnow Av, BRNX, 10469	6505	D3
Holy Rosary School, 18 Central Av, PTCH, 10573	6170	C7
Holy Rosary School, 100 Jerome Av, STNL, 10305	7020	D6
Holy Spirit School, 1960 Dr Martin L King Junior Bl, BRNX - 10453	105	C3
Holy Spirit School, 970 Suburban Rd, UnnT, 07083	6816	A7
Holy Trinity Community School, 9020 191st St, QENS - 11423	6826	B4
Holy Trinity School, 1445 143rd St, QENS, 11357	6721	A1
Homestead School, 2 Homestead Av, GDNC, 11530	6828	B1
Hommocks Middle School, 130 Hommocks Rd, MRNK - 10538	6396	E1
Horace Mann Elementary School 09, 1215 83rd St, NBgT - 07047	6611	A5
Horace Mann-Lower School, 4440 Tibbett Av, BRNX - 10471	6393	C7
Horace Mann No 6 Elementary School, 25 W 38th St - BAYN, 07002	6920	A2
Horace Mann School, 231 W 246th St, BRNX, 10471	6393	C7
Horizons High School, 1515 Hazen St, BRNX, 11370	6613	E7
Hospital Schools, 3450 E Tremont Av, BRNX, 10465	6615	A1
Hostos-Lincoln Academy of Science - 475 Grand Concourse, BRNX, 10451	107	D6
Howell Road School, 1475 Howell Rd, HmpT, 11580	6928	D1
HS 560 M City As School, 16 Clarkson St, MHTN, 10014	118	C2
Huber Street Elementary School, 1520 Paterson Plank Rd - SECS, 07094	6610	A6
Hudson Catholic High School, 790 Bergen Av, JSYC - 07306	6819	E2
Hudson Country Montessori School, 340 Quaker Ridge Rd - NRCH, 10804	6281	E5
Hudson Elementary School, 167 19th St, UNCT, 07087	6716	D4
Hudson Elementary School 25, 525 1st Av, ELIZ, 07206	6918	B5
Hudson School, 601 Park Av, HBKN, 07030	6716	D6
Hudson View Christian Academy, 170 Hudson Ter, YNKR - 10701	6279	D5
Humanities & Arts Magnet High School, 207-01 116th Av - QENS, 11411	6826	D5
Humanities Preparatory Academy, 351 W 18th St, MHTN - 10011	115	D5
Hunter College Campus Schools, 71 E 94th St, MHTN - 10128	113	D1
Hurden-Looker Elementary School, 1261 Liberty Av - HlsT, 07205	6816	C6
Hutchinson Elementary School, 301 Third Av, PLHM - 10803	6395	B4
Hyde Leadership Charter School, 730 Bryant Av, BRNX - 10474	6613	E3
Icahn Charter School, 1525 Brook Av, BRNX, 10457	105	D7
Ichud School, 1604 Avenue R, BKLN, 11229	7023	B4
Ideal Islamic School, 3129 12th St, QENS, 11106	114	C5
Immaculate Conception High School, 258 S Main St - LODI, 07644	6500	B3
Immaculate Conception School, 378 E 151st St, BRNX - 10455	6613	A3
Immaculate Conception School, 760 E Gun Hill Rd, BRNX - 10467	6505	B2
Immaculate Conception School, 16 N Broadway, IRVN - 10533	6048	B7
Immaculate Conception School, 419 E 13th St, MHTN - 10009	119	C2
Immaculate Conception School, 2163 29th St, QENS - 11105	6719	B2
Immaculate Conception School, 17914 Dalny Rd, QENS - 11432	6825	E3
Immaculate Conception School, 760 Post Pl, SECS - 07094	6610	B7
Immaculate Conception School, 104 Gordon St, STNL - 10304	7020	D2
Immaculate Conception School, 53 Winter Hill Rd, TCKA - 10707	6281	A6
Immaculate Heart of Mary School - 3002 Fort Hamilton Pkwy, BKLN, 11218	6922	E6
Immaculate Heart of Mary School, 201 Boulevard, SCDL - 10583	6281	C2
Incarnation School, 570 W 175th St, MHTN, 10033	104	C5
Incarnation School, 8915 Francis Lewis Blvd, QENS, 11427	6826	C3
Independence High School, 16 Clarkson St, MHTN - 10014	118	C2
Independence High School, 850 10th Av, MHTN, 10019	112	B5
Information Technology High School, 2116 44th Rd - QENS, 11101	6718	C6
Institute for Collaborative Education, 345 E 15th St - MHTN, 10003	119	C1
In Technology Academy, 2975 Tibbett Av, BRNX, 10463	102	C3
International Arts Business School, 600 Kingston Av - BKLN, 11203	6923	C4
International Christian School, 312 Coney Island Av - BKLN, 11218	6922	E5
International Christian School of Brooklyn - 302 Vanderbilt St, BKLN, 11218	6922	E5
International Community High School, 968 Cauldwell Av - BRNX, 10456	6613	B2
International HS at Prospect Heights, 883 Classon Av - BKLN, 11225	6923	B3
International School of Liberal Arts, 2780 Reservoir Av - BRNX, 10468	6504	C3
Iona Grammar School, 173 Stratton Rd, NRCH, 10804	6281	E4
Iona Preparatory School, 255 Wilmot Rd, NRCH, 10804	6281	D4
Ironbound Catholic Academy, 366 E Kinney St, NWRK - 07105	6818	A2
Irvington High School, 40 N Broadway, IRVN, 10533	6048	A7
Irvington High School, 1253 Clinton Av, IrvT, 07111	6816	C1
Irvington Middle School, 40 N Broadway, IRVN, 10533	6048	B7
IS 02 George L Egbert School, 333 Midland Av, STNL - 10306	7118	B1
IS 005 The Walter Crowley Intermediate Sch - 50-40 Jacobus St, QENS, 11373	6719	D7
IS 007 Elias Bernstein School, 1270 Huguenot Av, STNL - 10312	7207	C2
IS 010 Horace Greeley School, 4511 31st Av, QENS - 11103	6719	B4
IS 024 Myra S Barnes School, 225 Cleveland Av, STNL - 10308	7117	B6
IS 25 Adrien Block School, 3465 192nd St, QENS, 11358	6721	E3
IS 027 Anning S Prall School, 11 Clove Lake Pl, STNL - 10310	7019	E1
IS 30 Mary White Ovington School, 415 Ovington Av - BKLN, 11209	7021	E1
IS 34 Totten Intermediate School, 528 Academy Av - STNL, 10307	7206	B4
IS 049 Bertha Dreyfus School, 101 Warren St, STNL - 10304	7020	D2
IS 051 Edwin Markham School, 20 Houston St, STNL - 10302	7019	B2
IS 53 Brian Piccolo School, 1045 Nameoke St, QENS - 11691	7027	D5
IS 055 Ocean Hill Brownsville School, 2021 Bergen St - BKLN, 11233	6924	B2
IS 061 Leonardo Da Vinci School, 9850 50th Av, QENS - 11368	6720	B7
IS 061 William A Morris School, 445 Castleton Av, STNL - 10301	6920	B7
IS 068 Isaac Bildersee School, 956 E 82nd St, BKLN - 11236	6924	B7
IS 072 Rocco Laurie School, 33 Ferndale Av, STNL, 10314	7019	A6
IS 073 The Frank Sansivieri Intermediate Sch - 7002 54th Av, QENS, 11378	6823	D1
IS 075 Frank Paulo School, 455 Huguenot Av, STNL - 10312	7116	B6
IS 077, 9-76 Seneca Av, QENS, 11385	6823	C5
IS 90 Mirabel Sisters School, 21 Jumel Pl, MHTN, 10032	104	C7
IS 093 Ridgewood School, 6656 Forest Av, QENS, 11385	6823	C5
IS 096 Seth Low School, 99 Avenue P, BKLN, 11204	7022	D4
IS 098 Bay Academy School, 1401 Emmons Av, BKLN - 11235	7023	B7
IS 98 Hermann Ridder, 1619 Boston Rd, BRNX, 10460	6613	D1
IS 117 Joseph H Wade School, 1865 Morris Av, BRNX - 10453	105	D4
IS 119 The Glendale School, 7401 78th Av, QENS, 11385	6824	A5
IS 125 Thom J McCann Woodside, 4602 47th Av, QENS - 11377	6719	A7
IS 136 Charles O'Dewey School, 4004 4th Av, BKLN - 11232	6922	B5
IS 141 Steinway School, 3711 21st Av, QENS, 11105	6719	B2
IS 145 Joseph Pulitzer School, 3334 80th St, QENS - 11372	6719	D5
IS 158 Theodore Gathings, 800 Home St, BRNX, 10456	6613	C2
IS 171 Abraham Lincoln School, 528 Ridgewood Av - BKLN, 11208	6824	A7
IS 174 Eugene T Maleska School, 456 White Plains Rd - BRNX, 10473	6614	C4
IS 180 Daniel Hale Williams School, 700 Baychester Av - BRNX, 10475	6505	E2
IS 181 Pablo Casals School, 800 Baychester Av, BRNX - 10475	6505	E2
IS 184 Rafael Cordero Y Molina School, 778 Forest Av - BRNX, 10456	6613	B3
IS 187, 1171 65th St, BKLN, 11219	7022	B1
IS 190, 1550 Crotona Park E, BRNX, 10460	6613	D1
IS 192 Linden School, 10989 204th St, QENS, 11412	6826	C5
IS 192 Piagentini Jones School, 650 Hollywood Av, BRNX - 10465	6615	B2
IS 195 Roberto Clemente School, 625 W 133rd St, MHTN - 10031	106	D5
IS 204 Oliver W Holmes School, 3641 28th St, QENS - 11106	6718	E5
IS 206 Ann Mersereau School, 2280 Aqueduct Av, BRNX - 10468	105	D1
IS 211 John Wilson School, 1001 E 100th St, BKLN, 11236	6924	C6
IS 217 Rafael Hernandez Intermediary School - 977 Fox St, BRNX, 10459	6613	D2
IS 218 Salome Ukena School, 4600 Broadway, MHTN - 10040	104	D1
IS 219 New Venture School, 3630 3rd Av, BRNX, 10456	6613	C1
IS 223 Mott Hall School, 71 Convent Av, MHTN, 10027	106	D6
IS 227 Louis Armstrong School, 3202 Junction Blvd - QENS, 11369	6720	A4
IS 228 David A Boody School, 228 Avenue S, BKLN - 11223	7022	E5
IS 229 Roland Patterson School - 275 Roberto Clemente State Park, BRNX, 10453	105	A3
IS 230, 7310 34th Av, QENS, 11372	6719	D5
IS 231 Magnetech 2000 School, 14500 Springfield Blvd - QENS, 11413	6927	C3
IS 232, 1700 Macombs Rd, BRNX, 10453	105	B4
IS 232 Winthrop School, 905 Winthrop St, BKLN, 11203	6923	E4
IS 237, 4621 Colden St, QENS, 11355	6721	A6
IS 238 Susan B Anthony School, 8815 182nd St, QENS - 11423	6826	A4
IS 239 Mark Twain Sch for Gifted & Talented - 2401 Neptune Av, BKLN, 11224	7120	C1
IS 246 Walt Whitman School, 72 Veronica Pl, BKLN - 11226	6923	B5
IS 252 Arthur S Somers School, 1084 Lenox Rd, BKLN - 11212	6924	A4
IS 254, 2452 Washington Av, BRNX, 10458	6504	D4
IS 271 John M Coleman School, 1137 Herkimer St, BKLN - 11233	6924	A1
IS 281 Joseph B Cavallaro School, 8787 24th Av, BKLN - 11214	7022	C6
IS 285 Meyer Levin School, 5909 Beverley Rd, BKLN - 11203	6924	A6
IS 286 Renaissance Military, 509 W 129th St, MHTN - 10027	106	D6
IS 289, 201 Warren St, MHTN, 10013	118	D6
IS 303 Herbert S Eisenberg School, 501 West Av, BKLN - 11224	7120	E1
IS 303 Leadership & Community Service - 1700 Macombs Rd, BRNX, 10453	105	B4
IS 313 School of Leadership Development - 1600 Webster Av, BRNX, 10457	105	E6
IS 318 Math, Science & Tech Through Arts - 1919 Prospect Av, BRNX, 10457	6504	D7
IS 339 School of Community Technology - 1600 Webster Av, BRNX, 10457	105	E6
IS 340, 227 Sterling Pl, BKLN, 11238	6923	A2
IS 347 School of Humanities, 35 Starr St, BKLN, 11221	6822	E5
IS 349 Math, Science & Technology School, 35 Starr St - BKLN, 11221	6822	E5
IS 364 Gateway School, 1426 Freeport Lp, BKLN, 11239	6924	E6
IS 381, 1599 E 22nd St, BKLN, 11210	7023	C3
IS 392 School, 104 Sutter Av, BKLN, 11212	6924	A3
IS 528 Bea Fuller Rodgers School, 180 Wadsworth Av - MHTN, 10033	104	C4

Schools

New York City/5 Borough Points of Interest Index

FEATURE NAME Address City ZIP Code	MAP#	GRID
Isaac E Young Middle School, 270 Centre Av, NRCH - 10805	6396	A5
Isaac Newton Junior High School Science-Math - 280 Pleasant Av, MHTN, 10029	110	D5
Islamic Day School, 215 N Oraton Pkwy, EORG, 07017	6713	A3
Islamic Elementary School, 13008 Rockaway Blvd, QENS - 11420	6926	C2
Island Academy, 1111 Hazen St, BRNX, 11370	6613	E6
Jackson Avenue Elementary School, 421 Jackson Av - HKSK, 07601	6501	C4
Jackson Avenue Elementary School, 300 Jackson Av - MNLA, 11501	6724	D6
Jackson Heights Seventh Day Adventist School - 7225 Woodside Av, QENS, 11377	6719	D6
Jacqueline Kennedy Onassis High School, 120 W 46th St - MHTN, 10036	116	C1
Jamaica Day School-St. Demetrios, 8435 152nd St - QENS, 11432	6825	C4
Jamaica High School, 16701 Gothic Dr, QENS, 11432	6825	D3
Jamas Children University, 86 Washington St, EORG - 07017	6712	D2
James A Dever School, 585 N Corona Av, HmpT, 11580	6928	E1
James Baldwin School, 351 W 18th St, MHTN, 10011	115	D5
James J Flynn Elementary School, 850 Chamberlain Av - PTHA, 08861	7114	B7
James Madison High School, 3787 Bedford Av, BKLN - 11229	7023	C4
James Madison School 10, 99 Marsellus Pl, GRFD, 07026	6500	B3
James Weldon Johnson School, 176 E 115th St, MHTN - 10029	110	B4
Jane Addams Vocational High School, 900 Tinton Av - BRNX, 10456	6613	B2
Jean Nuzzi Intermediate School, 21310 92nd Av, QENS - 11428	6826	D2
Jefferson Elementary School, 100 Prospect Av, NARL - 07031	6714	C1
Jefferson Elementary School, 131 Weyman Av, NRCH - 10805	6395	D6
Jefferson Elementary School, 3400 Palisade Av, UNCT - 07087	6716	E2
Jefferson Elementary School, 30 Pine St, WLTN, 07057	6500	B5
Jefferson Middle School, 75 1st St, LODI, 07644	6500	C2
Jersey City Golden Door School, 180 9th St, JSYC - 07302	6820	C1
Jewish Educational Center, 330 Elmora Av, ELIZ, 07208	6917	C3
Jewish Foundation School, 400 Caswell Av, STNL, 10314	7019	B3
Jewish Institute of Queens, 6005 Woodhaven Blvd, QENS - 11373	6824	A1
JHS 008 Richard S Grossley School, 10835 167th St - QENS, 11433	6825	E6
JHS 013 Jackie Robinson School, 1573 Madison Av - MHTN, 10029	109	E5
JHS 14 Shell Bank School, 2424 Batchelder St, BKLN - 11235	7023	D6
JHS 022 Jordan L Mott School, 270 E 167th St, BRNX - 10456	6613	A1
JHS 033 Mark Hopkins School, 70 Tompkins Av, BKLN - 11206	6822	C6
JHS 044 William J O'Shea School, 100 W 77th St, MHTN - 10024	112	D2
JHS 045 John S Roberts School, 2351 1st Av, MHTN - 10035	110	C4
JHS 045 Thomas C Giordano School, 2502 Lorillard Pl - BRNX, 10458	6504	D5
JHS 049 William J Gaynor School, 223 Graham Av, BKLN - 11206	6822	C4
JHS 050 John D Wells, 183 S 3rd St, BKLN, 11211	6822	B4
JHS 052 Inwood School, 650 Academy St, MHTN, 10034	101	E7
JHS 054 Booker T Washington, 103 W 107th St, MHTN - 10025	109	B4
JHS 57 Whitelaw Reid, 125 Stuyvesant Av, BKLN, 11221	6822	E7
JHS 062 The Ditmas School, 700 Cortelyou Rd, BKLN - 11218	6923	A7
JHS 078 Roy H Mann School, 1420 E 68th St, BKLN - 11234	7024	B2
JHS 080 The Mosholu Parkway School - 149 E Mosholu Pkwy N, BRNX, 10467	6504	E2
JHS 104 Simon Baruch School, 330 E 21st St, MHTN - 10010	116	C7
JHS 113-Old 294 Edmonds Center, 300 Adelphi St, BKLN - 11205	6822	A7
JHS 113 Richard R Green School, 3710 Barnes Av, BRNX - 10467	6505	B1
JHS 117 Francis Scott Key School, 300 Willoughby Av - BKLN, 11205	6822	B6
JHS 118 William W Niles School, 577 E 179th St, BRNX - 10457	6504	D6
JHS 123 James M Kiernan School, 1025 Morrison Av - BRNX, 10472	6614	A2
JHS 125 Henry Hudson School, 1111 Pugsley Av, BRNX - 10472	6614	B2
JHS 126 John Ericsson School, 424 Leonard St, BKLN - 11222	6822	C3
JHS 127 The Castle Hill School, 1560 Purdy St, BRNX - 10462	6505	C7
JHS 131 Albert Einstein School, 885 Bolton Av, BRNX - 10473	6614	B2
JHS 135 Frank D Whalen School, 2441 Wallace Av, BRNX - 10467	6505	B4
JHS 142 John Philip Sousa, 3750 Baychester Av, BRNX - 10466	6505	D1
JHS 143 Eleanor Roosevelt School, 515 W 182nd St - MHTN, 10033	104	D4
JHS 144 Michelangelo School, 2545 Gunther Av, BRNX - 10469	6505	E4
JHS 145 Arturo Toscaninni School, 1000 Teller Av, BRNX - 10456	6613	A2
JHS 151 Lou Gehrig Academy School - 250 Thurman Munson Wy, BRNX, 10451	6613	A2
JHS 157 Stephen A Halsey School, 6355 102nd St, QENS - 11375	6824	C1
JHS 162 Lola Rodriguez de Tio, 600 St. Anns Av, BRNX - 10455	6613	B3
JHS 162 Willoughby School, 1390 Willoughby Av, BKLN - 11237	6823	A4
JHS 166 George Gershwin School, 800 Van Siclen Av - BKLN, 11207	6924	E4
JHS 166 Roberto Clemente School, 250 E 164th St - BRNX, 10456	6613	A2
JHS 167 Robert F Wagner School, 220 E 76th St, MHTN - 10021	113	C4
JHS 185 Edward Bleeker School, 14726 25th Dr, QENS - 11354	6721	A2
JHS 189 Daniel Carter Beard, 14480 Barclay Av, QENS - 11355	6721	A4
JHS 190 Russell Sage School, 6817 Austin St, QENS - 11375	6824	C2
JHS 194 William Carr School, 15460 17th Av, QENS - 11357	6721	C1
JHS 201 The Dyker Heights School, 8010 12th Av, BKLN - 11228	7022	A3

FEATURE NAME Address City ZIP Code	MAP#	GRID
JHS 202 Robert H Goddard School, 13830 Lafayette St - QENS, 11417	6925	D2
JHS 210 Elizabeth Blackwell School, 9311 101st Av - QENS, 11416	6925	D1
JHS 217 Robert A Van Wyck School, 8505 144th St, QENS - 11435	6825	B4
JHS 218 James P Sinnott School, 370 Fountain Av, BKLN - 11208	6925	A2
JHS 220 John J Pershing School, 4812 9th Av, BKLN - 11220	6922	B7
JHS 223 The Montauk School, 4200 16th Av, BKLN - 11219	6922	D7
JHS 227 Edward B Shallow School, 6500 16th Av, BKLN - 11219	7022	C2
JHS 234 Arthur W Cunningham, 1875 E 17th St, BKLN - 11229	7023	B5
JHS 258 David Ruggles School, 141 Macon St, BKLN - 11216	6923	C1
JHS 259 William McKinley, 7301 Fort Hamilton Pkwy - BKLN, 11228	7022	A2
JHS 265 Susan S McKinney School, 101 Park Av, BKLN - 11205	121	E4
JHS 278 Marine Park School, 1925 Stuart St, BKLN - 11229	7023	D4
JHS 291 Roland Hayes School, 231 Palmetto St, BKLN - 11221	6823	A6
JHS 292 Margaret S Douglas School, 301 Vermont St - BKLN, 11207	6924	D2
JHS 296 Halsey School, 125 Covert St, BKLN, 11207	6823	B7
JHS 302 Rafael Cordero School, 350 Linwood St, BKLN - 11208	6924	E2
JHS 318 Eugenio Maria Dehostos, 101 Walton St, BKLN - 11206	6822	C5
JHS 383 Philippa Schuyler School, 1300 Greene Av, BKLN - 11237	6823	A6
J Levin High School, 240 E 172nd St, BRNX, 10456	105	C7
J M Rapport School-Career Development - 470 Jackson Av, BRNX, 10455	6613	B4
John Bowne High School, 6325 Main St, QENS, 11367	6721	A7
John Dewey High School, 50 Avenue X, BKLN, 11223	7022	E7
John F Kennedy Elementary School, 1210 11th St, NBgT - 07047	6716	C4
John F Kennedy High School, 99 Terrace View Av, MHTN - 10463	102	B3
John F Kennedy Magnet Elementary School, 40 Olivia St - PTCH, 10573	6170	B6
John F Kennedy School, 311 S 10th St, NWRK, 07103	6713	A6
John Hus Moravian School, 153 Ocean Av, BKLN, 11226	6923	B5
John J Daly Elementary School, 36 Rockwood Av, NHmT - 11050	6508	E6
John L Costley Middle School, 116 Hamilton St, EORG - 07017	6713	A2
John Lewis Childs Elementary School, 10 Elizabeth St - FLPK, 11001	6827	D2
John Marshall Elementary School 20, 521 Magnolia Av - ELIZ, 07206	6918	B4
Johnnie L Cochran Junior Academy, 190 Midland Av - EORG, 07017	6712	E1
Johnny Ray Youngblood Academy, 818 Schenck Av - BKLN, 11207	6924	E4
John Paulding School, 154 N Broadway, TYTN, 10591	6048	B2
John Philip Sousa Elementary School, 101 Sands Point Rd - SNPT, 11050	6508	B6
John Street Elementary School, 560 Nassau Blvd, HmpT - 11010	6828	C5
Jonas Bronck Academy, 4525 Manhattan College Pkwy - BRNX, 10471	6393	C7
Jose Marti Middle School, 1800 Summit Av, UNCT - 07087	6716	C3
Joseph F Brandt Middle School, 215 9th St, HBKN - 07030	6716	D6
Juan Morel Campos Secondary School, 215 Heyward St - BKLN, 11211	6822	B5
Julia A Barnes Public School No 12, 91 Astor Pl, JSYC - 07304	6819	E3
Kahlil Gibran School, 18 Rosedale Rd, YNKR, 10710	6280	D4
Kappa Academy, 3630 3rd Av, BRNX, 10456	6613	C1
Kappa III School, 2055 Mapes Av, BRNX, 10460	6504	D6
Kappa IV Scool, 6 Edgecombe Av, MHTN, 10030	107	A6
Kappa V School, 985 Rockaway Av, BKLN, 11212	6924	B5
Kearny Christian Academy, 172 Midland Av, KRNY - 07032	6714	C3
Kearny High School, 336 Devon St, KRNY, 07032	6714	B4
Keio Academy of New York, 3 College Rd, HRSN, 10577	6169	B2
Kennedy School No 9, 222 Mercer St, JSYC, 07302	6820	B2
Kew Forest School, 119-17 Union Tpk, QENS, 11375	6824	E3
King High Tech Computer Magnet School - 135 Locust Hill Av, YNKR, 10701	6279	C7
King Public School No 11, 886 Bergen Av, JSYC, 07306	6820	A1
Kings Academy, 2341 3rd Av, MHTN, 10035	110	C2
Kingsborough Early College School, 2001 Oriental Blvd - BKLN, 11235	7121	D1
Kingsbridge International High School - 2780 Reservoir Av, BRNX, 10468	6504	C3
King Street Elementary School, 697 King St, PTCH - 10573	6170	B3
Kinneret Day School, 2600 Netherland Av, BRNX, 10463	102	B3
KIPP Academy Charter School, 250 Thurman Munson Wy - BRNX, 10451	6613	A2
KIPP Star College Preparatory Charter School - 433 W 123rd St, MHTN, 10027	109	D1
Lafayette High School, 2630 Benson Av, BKLN, 11214	7022	D6
Lafayette Street Elementary School, 205 Lafayette St - NWRK, 07105	6817	E1
Lakeville Elementary School, 4727 Jayson Av, NHmT - 11020	6723	A2
Landing Elementary School, 60 McLoughlin St, GLCV - 11542	6509	E4
Landmark High School, 220 W 58th St, MHTN, 10019	112	D6
Langston Hughes School, 160 Rhode Island Av, EORG - 07018	6712	D5
La Salle Academy, 44 E 2nd St, MHTN, 10003	119	B3
Lavelle School for the Blind, 3830 Paulding Av, BRNX - 10469	6505	C1
Lawerence Woodmere Academy, 336 Woodmere Blvd - HmpT, 11598	6928	B7
Law Government & Community Service HS - 207-01 116th Av, QENS, 11411	6826	D6
Lawrence Middle School, 195 Broadway, LWRN, 11559	7027	E4
Lawrence Senior High School, 2 Reilly Rd, CDHT, 11516	7027	E1
Leadership Institute, 1701 Fulton Av, BRNX, 10457	6504	C7
Leadership Village Academy, 315 E 113th St, MHTN - 10029	110	B5
League School, 567 Kingston Av, BKLN, 11203	6923	D4
Learning Tree Multi-Cultural School, 801 Bartholdi St - BRNX, 10467	6505	B2
Learning Tree Multi-Cultural School, 10302 Northern Blvd - QENS, 11368	6720	B4
Lee F Jackson School, 2 Saratoga Rd, GrbT, 10607	6167	E1
Legacy School for Integrated Studies, 34 W 14th St - MHTN, 10011	116	A7
Leif Ericson Day School, 1037 72nd St, BKLN, 11228	7022	A2

FEATURE NAME Address City ZIP Code	MAP#	GRID
Leon Goldstein High School for the Sciences - 1830 Shore Blvd, BKLN, 11235	7121	D1
Leonia Middle School, 500 Broad Av, LEON, 07605	6502	D3
Lewis F Cole Middle School, 467 Stillwell Av, FTLE - 07024	6502	D6
Lexington School-Center for Deaf, 2626 75th St, QENS - 11370	6719	D4
Liberty Academy Charter School, 303 Warren St, JSYC - 07302	6820	C3
Liberty High School, 140 Sip Av, JSYC, 07306	6820	A1
Liberty High School Academy for Newcomers - 250 W 18th St, MHTN, 10011	115	D6
Liberty Montessori School, 631 W Boston Post Rd, MRNK - 10543	6282	E7
Lifeline Center for Child Development - 8009 Winchester Blvd, QENS, 11427	6722	E7
Life Sciences Secondary School, 320 E 96th St, MHTN - 10128	114	A1
Life-Skills School, 9730 Queens Blvd, QENS, 11374	6824	B2
Lincoln Avenue Elementary School, 216 Lincoln Av - COrT, 07050	6712	C3
Lincoln Community School, 208 Prospect Av, BAYN - 07002	6920	A3
Lincoln Elementary School, 140 Anderson Av, FRVW - 07022	6611	C4
Lincoln Elementary School, 302 Burton Av, HSBH, 07604	6500	E4
Lincoln Elementary School, 121 Beech St, KRNY, 07032	6714	B3
Lincoln Elementary School, 170 E Lincoln Av, MTVN - 10550	6394	E3
Lincoln Elementary School, 87 Richelieu Ter, NWRK - 07106	6712	C6
Lincoln Elementary School, 712 Lincoln Av, RDFP, 07660	6501	E4
Lincoln Elementary School 03, 221 Cross St, HRSN - 07029	6714	A6
Lincoln Elementary School 05, 1206 63rd St, NBgT - 07047	6610	E6
Lincoln Elementary School 6, 111 Palisade Av, GRFD - 07026	6500	A3
Lincoln Elementary School 14, 50 Grove St, ELIZ, 07202	6917	D4
Lincoln High School, 60 Crescent Av, JSYC, 07304	6819	E3
Lincoln High School, 375 Kneeland Av, YNKR, 10704	6394	A3
Lincoln Orens Middle School, 150 Trafalgar Blvd, HmpT - 11558	7029	E4
Lindbergh Elementary School, 401 Glen Av, PALP - 07650	6502	C6
Lindell Elementary School, 601 Lindell Blvd, LBCH - 11561	7029	A6
Linden Number 2 Elementary School, 1700 S Wood Av - LNDN, 07036	7017	C2
Linden Number 4 Elementary School, 1602 Dill Av - LNDN, 07036	6917	B6
Linden Number 5 Elementary School, 1014 Bower St - LNDN, 07036	6917	A6
Linden Number 6 Elementary School, 19 E Morris Av - LNDN, 07036	7017	A1
Linden Seventh Day Adventist School, 13701 228th St - QENS, 11413	6927	D2
Link Community School, 120 Livingston St, NWRK, 07103	6817	B1
Little Friends School, 43-42 47th St, QENS, 11104	6719	A6
Little Friends School, 85-03 Britton Av, QENS, 11373	6719	E6
Little Red School House Irwin High School - 272 Avenue of the Americas, MHTN, 10012	118	D2
Livingston Elementary School, 960 Midland Blvd, UnnT - 07083	6816	A7
L M Goldstein High School for Sciences - 20001 Oriental Blvd, BKLN, 11235	7121	D1
Lodi High School, 99 Putnam St, LODI, 07644	6500	C1
Long Beach Catholic Regional School, 735 W Broadway - LBCH, 11561	7029	A7
Longfellow Elementary School, 625 S 4th Av, MTVN - 10550	6394	E6
Longfellow Middle School, 624 S 3rd Av, MTVN, 10550	6394	E6
Long Island City High School, 1430 Broadway, QENS - 11106	114	C6
Lorge School, 353 W 17th St, MHTN, 10011	115	D6
Louis D Brandeis High School, 145 W 84th St, MHTN - 10024	112	E1
Louise A Spencer School, 66 Muhammad Ali Av, NWRK - 07108	6817	C2
Louis M Klein Middle School, 50 Union Av, HRSN, 10528	6283	B2
Lowell School, 2420 Parsons Blvd, QENS, 11357	6721	A2
Lowell School of Bayside, 20305 32nd Av, QENS, 11360	6721	E3
Lower East Side Preparatory High School - 145 Stanton St, MHTN, 10002	119	B5
Loyola School, 63 E 83rd St, MHTN, 10028	113	C3
Lubavitcher Yeshiva School, 570 Crown St, BKLN, 11213	6923	D3
Luis Munoz Marin Middle School, 663 Broadway, NWRK - 07104	6714	A2
Lutheran Elementary School of Bay Ridge - 440 Ovington Av, BKLN, 11209	7021	E1
Lutheran School of Flushing-Bayside, 36-01 Bell Blvd - QENS, 11361	6722	A3
Lycee Francais de New York School, 505 E 75th St - MHTN, 10021	113	E5
Lyceum Kennedy Francais School, 225 E 43rd St, MHTN - 10017	116	E3
Lynbrook North Middle School, 529 Merrick Rd, LNBK - 11563	6929	A4
Lynbrook Senior High School, 9 Union Av, LNBK, 11563	6929	B5
Lynbrook South Middle School, 333 Union Av, HmpT - 11563	6929	A6
Lyons Community School, 223 Graham Av, BKLN, 11206	6822	C4
Machon Bais Yaakov School, 1681 42nd St, BKLN, 11218	6922	E7
Madison Avenue Elementary School, 163 Madison Av - IrvT, 07111	6816	D1
Madison Avenue Elementary School, 823 S 16th St - NWRK, 07108	6816	E2
Madison-Monroe Elementary School 16, 1091 North Av - ELIZ, 07201	6918	A1
Magen David Yeshiva Elementary School - 2130 McDonald Av, BKLN, 11223	7022	E5
Magen David Yeshiva High School, 7801 Bay Pkwy - BKLN, 11214	7022	C4
Magnet School for Science & Technology, 1625 11th Av - BKLN, 11218	6922	E4
Magnet School of Math, Science & Design Tech - 511 7th Av, BKLN, 11215	6922	D4
Main Street School, 369 Main St, COrT, 07050	6712	C2
Main Street School, 101 Main St, IRVN, 10533	6166	A1
Malcolm X Shabazz High School, 80 Johnson Av, NWRK - 07108	6817	B3
Malverne Senior High School, 80 Ocean Av, MLVN - 11565	6929	C2
Mamaroneck Avenue Elementary School - 850 Mamaroneck Av, MRNK, 10543	6282	E5
Mamaroneck Avenue Elementary School, 7 Nosband Av - WHPL, 10605	6168	C3
Mamaroneck High School, 1000 W Boston Post Rd, MRNK - 10543	6282	D7
Manhasset High School, 200 Memorial Pl, NHmT, 11030	6617	D6
Manhasset Middle School, 200 Memorial Pl, NHmT - 11030	6617	D6

New York City/5 Borough Points of Interest Index

FEATURE NAME Address City ZIP Code	MAP#	GRID
Manhattan Bridges High School, 525 W 50th St, MHTN - 10019	112	A6
Manhattan Center for Science & Mathematics - 260 Pleasant Av, MHTN, 10029	110	C5
Manhattan Charter School, 100 Attorney St, MHTN - 10002	119	C5
Manhattan Christian Academy, 401 W 205th St, MHTN - 10034	102	B7
Manhattan Comp Night & Day High School, 240 2nd Av - MHTN, 10003	119	B1
Manhattan Country School, 7 E 96th St, MHTN, 10029	109	D7
Manhattan Day School, 310 W 75th St, MHTN, 10023	112	C2
Manhattan High School for Girls, 154 E 70th St, MHTN - 10021	113	B5
Manhattan Hunter Science High School - 122 Amsterdam Av, MHTN, 10023	112	A3
Manhattan International High School, 317 E 67th St - MHTN, 10065	113	C6
Manhattan Theatre Lab School, 122 Amsterdam Av - MHTN, 10023	112	C3
Manhattan Village Academy, 43 W 22nd St, MHTN - 10010	116	A6
Manorhaven Elementary School, 1 Morewood Oaks - NHmT, 11050	6508	C6
Manor Oaks-William Bowie School, 1950 Hillside Av - NHmT, 11040	6724	A5
Man School for Career Development, 113 E 4th St - MHTN, 10003	119	B3
Maple Avenue Elementary School, 33 Maple Av, NWRK - 07112	6816	E4
Marble Hill HS for International Studies - 99 Terrace View Av, MHTN, 10463	102	C3
Maria Regina High School, 500 W Hartsdale Av, GrbT - 10530	6167	B1
Marie Curie High School for Med & Nursing - 120 W 231st St, BRNX, 10463	102	E4
Marion Street School, 100 Marion St, ERKY, 11563	6929	B6
Marist High School, 1241 Kennedy Blvd, BAYN, 07002	6819	A7
Mark Twain Middle School, 160 Woodlawn Av, YNKR - 10704	6394	B5
Marquis de Lafayette School No 6, 1071 Julia St, ELIZ - 07201	6918	A2
Marshall Elementary School, 262 Grove Rd, SOrT, 07079	6712	B6
Marta Valle Secondary School, 145 Stanton St, MHTN - 10002	119	C5
Martin de Porres School, 13625 218th St, QENS, 11413	6927	C2
Martin Luther High School, 6002 Maspeth Av, QENS - 11378	6823	B2
Martin Luther King Junior High School, 1 S Broadway - HAOH, 10706	6279	E2
Martin Public School No 41, 59 Wilkinson Av, JSYC - 07305	6819	D5
Marylawn of the Oranges High School, 445 Scotland Rd - SOrT, 07079	6712	A5
Mary Louis Academy, 17621 Wexford Ter, QENS, 11432	6825	E3
Mary McDowell Center for Learning, 20 Bergen St - BKLN, 11201	121	A7
Marymount School of New York, 1026 5th Av, MHTN - 10028	113	B2
Mary Queen of Heaven School, 1326 E 57th St, BKLN - 11234	7024	A2
Marys Nativity School, 14628 Jasmine Av, QENS, 11355	6721	B5
Masores Bais Yaakov School, 1395 Ocean Av, BKLN - 11210	7023	B1
Masters School, 49 Clinton Av, DBSF, 10522	6166	A4
Math & Science Exploratory School K447, 345 Dean St - BKLN, 11217	6922	E1
Math Science Research Magnent High School - 207-01 116th Av, QENS, 11411	6826	D5
Matthew Jago Elementary School, 99 Glen Cove Av - WbgT, 07077	7114	E4
Maurice W Downing Elementary School, 55 Lindner Pl - MLVN, 11565	6929	B2
Mawbey Street Elementary School, 275 Mawbey St - WbgT, 07095	7114	B4
McAuliffe Middle School 77, 300 S Broad St, ELIZ, 07202	6917	E4
McAuliffe School No 28, 167 Hancock Av, JSYC, 07032	6716	C6
McKenzie Elementary School, 135 Carlton Av, ERTH - 07073	6500	A6
McKinley Elementary School, 1 Colonnade Pl, NWRK - 07104	6713	D5
McKinley Elementary School 10, 3110 Liberty Av, NBgT - 07047	6716	C2
McNair Academic High School, 123 Coles St, JSYC - 07302	6820	B2
Meadow Drive Elementary School, 25 Meadow Dr - NHmT, 11507	6724	E2
Medgar Evers Prep Sch at Medgar Evers Coll - 1186 Carroll St, BKLN, 11225	6923	B3
Mek Review School, 261 1st St, PALP, 07650	6502	B6
Melrose Community School, 838 Brook Av, BRNX, 10451	6613	B3
Memorial Elementary School, 130 Liberty St, LFRY - 07643	6501	C6
Memorial Elementary School, 1 Dyer Av, SHkT, 07606	6501	C3
Memorial High School, 5501 Park Av, WNYK, 07093	111	B1
Merrick Academy Queens Charter School - 207-01 Jamaica Av, QENS, 11428	6826	C3
Merritt Memorial Elementary School, 1 Dogwood Ln - CRSK, 07626	6278	B7
Mesivta Berlin School, 1585 Coney Island Av, BKLN - 11230	7023	A3
Mesivta Eitz Chaim of Bobav, 1577 48th St, BKLN - 11219	7022	D1
Mesivta Forest Hills School, 92-15 69th Av, QENS, 11375	6824	C3
Mesivta Mkor Chaim School, 1571 55th St, BKLN, 11219	7022	C1
Mesivta Nachlas Yakov School, 185 Wilson St, BKLN - 11211	6822	B4
Mesivta Rab Jacob Joseph School, 3495 Richmond Rd - STNL, 10306	7117	C2
Mesivta Sanz School, 3400 New York Av, UNCT, 07087	6716	E2
Mesivta Tifereth Jerusalem, 145 E Broadway, MHTN - 10002	119	A7
Mesivta Yesode Hatorah-Boys, 187 Hooper St, BKLN - 11211	6822	B5
Metropolitan Corporate Academy High School - 362 Schermerhorn St, BKLN, 11217	121	C7
Metropolitan High School, 1121 Intervale Av, BRNX - 10459	6613	C2
Metropolitan Montessori School, 325 W 85th St, MHTN - 10024	108	D7
Michael Conti Elementary School PS 5, 182 Merseles St - JSYC, 07302	6820	B2
Michael J Petrides High School, 715 Ocean Ter, STNL - 10301	7020	A4
Midd College Charter High School, 45-35 Van Dam St - QENS, 11101	6718	D6
Middle College HS at Laguardia Comm College - 3110 Thomson Av, QENS, 11101	6718	D6
Middle Sch for Academic & Social Excellence - 1224 Park Pl, BKLN, 11213	6923	D2
Middle School for the Arts, 790 E New York Av, BKLN - 11203	6923	D4
Middlesex Co Vo-Tech Perth Amboy, 457 High St, PTHA - 08861	7205	E3
Middlesex Co Vocational-Technical Woodbridge - 1 Convery Blvd, WbgT, 07095	7114	C6
Midland Elementary School, 324 Midland Av, RYE - 10580	6284	A2
Midtown Community School, 550 Avenue A, BAYN - 07002	6919	D3
Midtown Ethical Culture School, 33 Central Park W - MHTN, 10021	112	D5
Midwood High School, 2839 Bedford Av, BKLN, 11210	7023	B1
Mildred Barry-Garvin School, 276 Parker Av, MplT - 07040	6816	B1
Milestone School, 70 Broad St W, MTVN, 10552	6394	D2
Millenium Art Academy, 1980 Lafayette Av, BRNX, 10473	6614	C3
Millennium High School, 75 Broad St, MHTN, 10004	120	B2
Miller Street Elementary School, 47 Miller St, NWRK - 07114	6817	C3
Milton Elementary School, 12 Hewlett St, RYE, 10580	6283	E5
Mineola High School, 10 Armstrong Rd, NHmT, 11040	6724	C6
Mineola Middle School, 200 Emory Rd, MNLA, 11501	6724	D6
Minue School, 83 Post Blvd, CART, 07008	7017	C5
Miraj Islamic School, 307 Victory Blvd, STNL, 10301	6920	D7
Mirrer Yeshiva High School, 1791 Ocean Pkwy, BKLN - 11223	7023	A4
Mirrer Yeshiva K Tana School, 1791 Ocean Pkwy, BKLN - 11223	7023	A4
Modern Elementary School, 870 Riverside Dr, MHTN - 10032	104	A7
Mohawk Country Home School, 200 Old Tarrytown Rd - GrbT, 10603	6049	E6
Monroe Academy for Business-Law, 1300 Boynton Av - BRNX, 10472	6613	E1
Monroe Academy for Visual Arts & Design - 1300 Boynton Av, BRNX, 10472	6613	E1
Monsignor Farrell High School, 2900 Amboy Rd, STNL - 10306	7117	D3
Monsignor Joaos Antao School 31, 1014 S Elmora Av - ELIZ, 07202	6917	D5
Monsignor McClancy Memorial High School - 7106 31st Av, QENS, 11370	6719	D4
Monsignor Scanlan High School - 915 Hutchinson River Pkwy, BRNX, 10465	6614	D2
Montessori Family School, 323 E 47th St, MHTN, 10017	117	A3
Montessori School 11, 99 Wakefield Av, YNKR, 10704	6394	B5
Montessori School 27, 132 Valentine Ln, YNKR, 10705	6393	C4
Montessori School 31, 7 Ravenswood Rd, YNKR, 10710	6280	C5
Montessori School of New York, 347 E 55th St, MHTN - 10022	117	B1
Moore Catholic High School, 100 Merrill Av, STNL - 10314	7018	E4
Moriah School of Englewood, 53 S Woodland St, EGLD - 07631	6503	B1
Morris Academy for Collaborative Studies - 1110 Boston Rd, BRNX, 10456	6613	C2
Morris Elementary School 18, 860 Cross Av, ELIZ, 07208	6917	E1
Morton Street School, 75 Morton St, NWRK, 07103	6817	C1
Most Precious Blood School, 133 27th Av, BKLN, 11214	7022	D6
Most Precious Blood School, 3252 37th St, QENS, 11106	6719	A4
Mother Cabrini High School, 701 Fort Washington Av - MHTN, 10040	104	C2
Mother Seton Parochial School, 1501 New York Av - UNCT, 07087	6716	D4
Mott Hall 3 School, 450 St. Pauls Pl, BRNX, 10456	6613	B1
Mott Hall Bronx High School, 1595 Bathgate Av, BRNX - 10457	105	E7
Mott Hall High School, 6 Edgecombe Av, MHTN, 10030	107	A6
Mott Hall II School, 234 W 109th St, MHTN, 10025	109	B3
Mott Hall IV School, 1137 Herkimer St, BKLN, 11233	6924	A1
Mott Hall V School, 2055 Mapes Av, BRNX, 10460	6504	D6
Mott Haven Village Preparatory High School - 701 St. Anns Av, BRNX, 10455	6613	B3
Mt Carmel-Holy Rosary School, 371 Pleasant Av, MHTN - 10035	110	D4
Mt Moriah Christian Academy, 1149 Eastern Pkwy, BKLN - 11213	6923	E3
Mt Pisgah Elementary School, 577 Bergen Av, JSYC - 07304	6819	E3
Mt Pleasant-Blythedale School, 90 Woods Rd, MtPT - 10595	6049	C1
Mt St. Michael Academy, 4300 Murdock Av, BRNX - 10466	6394	D6
Mt Vernon Avenue School, 54 Mt Vernon Av, IrvT, 07111	6816	C3
Mt Vernon High School, 100 California Rd, MTVN, 10552	6395	B2
Mt Vernon School, 142 Mt Vernon Pl, NWRK, 07106	6712	B7
MS 002, 655 Parkside Av, BKLN, 11225	6923	C4
MS 51 William Alexander School, 350 5th Av, BKLN - 11215	6922	D2
MS 061 Gladstone H Atwell School, 400 Empire Blvd - BKLN, 11225	6923	C3
MS 072 Catherine & Count Basie Middle School - 13325 Guy R Brewer Blvd, QENS, 11434	6927	A2
MS 088 Peter Rouget Middle School, 544 7th St, BKLN - 11215	6922	E3
MS 088 Peter Rouget School, 544 7th Av, BKLN, 11215	6922	D4
MS 101 PO Edward R Byrne, 2750 Lafayette Av, BRNX - 10465	6614	E2
MS 143 Performing & Fine Arts School, 800 Gates Av - BKLN, 11221	6822	E7
MS 201X School Theatre Arts Research, 730 Bryant Av - BRNX, 10474	6613	D3
MS 203, 339 Morris Av, BRNX, 10451	107	E7
MS 222 Dr Mario Salvadori School, 468 E 140th St - BRNX, 10454	6613	A4
MS 223 Lab School of Finance & Technology - 360 E 145th St, BRNX, 10454	6613	A4
MS 226 Middle School, 212-10 Rockaway Blvd, QENS - 11420	6926	B2
MS 243 Center School, 270 W 70th St, MHTN, 10023	112	C3
MS 245 Computer School, 100 W 77th St, MHTN, 10024	112	D2
MS 246M Crossroads School, 234 W 109th St, MHTN - 10025	109	A3
MS 247M Dual Language Middle School, 32 W 92nd St - MHTN, 10025	109	A7
MS 250 West Side Collab School, 735 W End Av, MHTN - 10025	108	E5
MS 255 Salk School of Science, 320 E 20th St, MHTN - 10003	119	C1
MS 256 Academic & Athletic Excellence, 154 W 93rd St - MHTN, 10025	109	A6
MS 258 Community Action School, 154 W 93rd St - MHTN, 10025	109	A6
MS 260 Clinton School Writers, 320 W 21st St, MHTN - 10011	115	D5
MS 266 Park Place Community Middle School - 62 Park Pl, BKLN, 11217	6922	E1
MS 267 Math, Science & Technology, 800 Gates Av - BKLN, 11221	6822	E7
MS 301 Paul L Dunbar Middle School, 890 Cauldwell Av - BRNX, 10456	6613	B2
MS 302 Luisa Dessus Cruz Middle School, 681 Kelly St - BRNX, 10455	6613	C3
MS 319, 120 E 184th St, BRNX, 10468	105	E1
MS 319 Maria Teresa, 21 Jumel Pl, MHTN, 10032	104	C7
MS 321-Minerva School, 21 Jumel Pl, MHTN, 10032	104	C7
MS 322, 4600 Broadway, MHTN, 10040	104	D1
MS 324 Patria, 21 Jumel Pl, MHTN, 10032	104	C7
MS 326, 401 W 164th St, MHTN, 10032	104	B7
MS 327 Health Opportunities Middle School - 350 Gerard Av, BRNX, 10451	107	D6
MS 328 Manhattan School of Science & Inquiry - 401 W 164th St, MHTN, 10032	104	C7
MS 390, 1930 Andrews Av, BRNX, 10453	105	C3
MS 390 Maggie L Walker School, 1224 Park Pl, BKLN - 11213	6923	D2
MS 391, 2225 Webster Av, BRNX, 10457	6504	C5
MS 394K, 188 Rochester Av, BKLN, 11213	6923	E2
MS 571, 80 Underhill Av, BKLN, 11238	6923	A1
MS 577, 320 Manhattan Av, BKLN, 11211	6822	C3
MS 582, 207 Bushwick Av, BKLN, 11206	6822	D4
MS 584, 130 Rochester Av, BKLN, 11213	6923	E2
MS-HS 368 Middle School, 3333 Henry Hudson Pkwy W - BRNX, 10463	102	C1
Munsey Park Elementary School, 1 Hunt Ln, MNPK - 11030	6617	E6
Murray Avenue Elementary School, 250 Murray Av - MrnT, 10538	6282	B7
Murray Public School No 38, 339 Stegman Pkwy, JSYC - 07305	6819	C4
Murry Bergtraum High School, 411 Pearl St, MHTN - 10038	118	D7
Muscota Elementary School, 4862 Broadway, MHTN - 10034	102	A6
Museum School 25, 579 Warburton Av, YNKR, 10701	6279	C5
Muslim Center Elementary School, 13758 Geranium Av - QENS, 11355	6721	A5
Mustard Seed School, 422 Willow Av, HBKN, 07030	6716	D7
Nathan Hale Elementary School, 679 Roosevelt Av, CART - 07008	7017	D7
Nativity-Blessed Lady School, 3893 Dyre Av, BRNX - 10466	6394	E7
Nazareth Regional High School, 475 E 57th St, BKLN - 11203	6924	A6
Nefesh Academy, 2005 E 17th St, BKLN, 11229	7023	B5
Neighborhood School, 121 E 3rd St, MHTN, 10009	119	B4
Nelson R Mandela Community High School - 47 S 11th Av, MTVN, 10550	6394	D4
Newark Vocational School, 301 W Kinney St, NWRK - 07103	6817	B1
Newcomer Center, 350 Main St, WHPL, 10601	6168	C1
Newcomers High School, 2801 41st Av, QENS, 11101	6718	D5
New Covenant Christian School, 1497 Needham Av - BRNX, 10469	6505	C1
New Day Academy, 800 Home St, BRNX, 10456	6613	C2
New Design High School, 350 Grand St, MHTN, 10002	119	B6
New Dorp High School, 465 New Dorp Ln, STNL, 10306	7118	A2
New Explorations School, 111 Columbia St, MHTN - 10002	119	D5
New Explorers High School, 701 St. Anns Av, BRNX - 10455	6613	B3
New Heights Academy Charter School - 1818 Amsterdam Av, MHTN, 10031	107	A3
New Horizons School, 317 Hoyt St, BKLN, 11231	6922	C1
New Hyde Park Memorial High School, 500 Leonard Blvd - NHmT, 11040	6724	A6
New Hyde Park Road Elementary School - 300 New Hyde Park Rd, NHPK, 11040	6724	A7
New Jersey Regional Day School, 334 Lyons Av, NWRK - 07112	6816	D4
New Lebanon Elementary School, 25 Mead Av, GrwT - 06830	6170	C6
New Millennium Business Acad Middle School - 1000 Teller Av, BRNX, 10456	6613	A2
New Rochelle High School, 265 Clove Rd, NRCH, 10804	6395	D2
New School for Arts & Science, 965 Longwood Av, BRNX - 10459	6613	C3
New School for Leadership, 120 W 231st St, BRNX - 10463	102	E4
Newton Street School, 150 Newton St, NWRK, 07103	6713	C7
Newtown High School, 4801 90th St, QENS, 11373	6720	A7
New Utrecht High School, 1601 80th St, BKLN, 11214	7022	B3
New Vistas Academy, 3321 Glenwood Rd, BKLN, 11210	6923	C7
New Vistas Academy, 2261 Church Av, BKLN, 11226	6923	B5
New Voices Sch of Academic & Creative Arts - 330 18th St, BKLN, 11215	6922	D4
New York City Museum School, 333 W 17th St, MHTN - 10011	115	C5
New York English School, 3550 157th St, QENS, 11354	6721	C3
New York Film Academy, 100 E 17th St, MHTN, 10003	116	B7
New York Habor School, 400 Irving Av, BKLN, 11237	6823	B6
New York Institute of Special Education - 999 Pelham Pkwy N, BRNX, 10469	6505	B4
New York School for the Deaf, 555 Knollwood Rd, GrbT - 10603	6049	D6
Nicholas S Lacorte Peterstown Elem School 3 - 700 2nd Av, ELIZ, 07202	6918	A4
Nichols Public School 42, 700 Newark Av, JSYC, 07306	6820	A1
Nightingale Bamford School, 20 E 92nd St, MHTN - 10128	113	D1
Nolan Middle School 40, 88 Gates Av, JSYC, 07305	6819	B7
Norman Thomas High School, 111 E 33rd St, MHTN - 10016	116	D5
North 13th Street Center, 300 N 13th St, EORG, 07017	6713	C3
North Arlington Middle School, 45 Beech St, NARL - 07031	6714	C1
North Bergen High School, 7317 Kennedy Blvd, NBgT - 07047	6611	A5
North Cliff Elementary School, 642 Floyd St, EGLC - 07632	6392	C7
Northeastern Academy, 532 W 215th St, MHTN, 10034	102	B5
North Hudson Academy, 4411 Liberty Av, NBgT, 07047	6716	D1
North Shore Hebrew Elementary Academy, 16 Cherry Ln - KNGP, 11024	6616	D3
North Shore Hebrew High School, 175 Community Dr - NHmT, 11030	6723	C1
North Shore Hebrew Middle Academy, 26 Old Mill Rd - GTNK, 11023	6616	E6
Northside Catholic Academy-St. Vincent, 180 N 7th St - BKLN, 11211	6822	B3
Northside Montessori School, 26310 Union Tpk, QENS - 11004	6723	C6
North Star Academy Charter School, 10 Washington Pl - NWRK, 07102	6713	E7
Norwood Elementary School, 177 Summit St, NRWD - 07648	6164	A7
Notre Dame Academy, 78 Howard Av, STNL, 10301	7020	C1
Notre Dame Academy High School, 134 Howard Av - STNL, 10301	7020	C1
Notre Dame High School, 327 W 13th St, MHTN, 10014	115	C6
Notre Dame Interparochial Primary School - 555 Prospect Av, RDGF, 07657	6611	B1
Notre Dame Interparochial School, 312 1st St, PALP - 07650	6502	C6
Notre Dame School, 25 Mayfair Rd, NHmT, 11040	6723	E5

INDEX 78

New York City/5 Borough Points of Interest Index

Schools

FEATURE NAME Address City ZIP Code	MAP#	GRID
Number 3 Elementary School, 403 Cliff St, FRVW, 07022	6611	C3
Number 3 Elementary School Annex, 240 4th St, FRVW - 07022	6611	C3
Nunnery Public School 29, 123 Claremont Av, JSYC - 07305	6819	D4
NYC Lab School for Collaborative Studies, 333 W 17th St - MHTN, 10011	115	D5
NYC Vocational Training Center, 1150 E New York Av - BKLN, 11212	6924	A3
Oakdale Academy, 366 Oakdale St, STNL, 10312	7116	E6
Oakview Preparatory School, 29 Chestnut St, YNKR - 10701	6393	D1
Oakwood Avenue Elementary School, 135 Oakwood Av - COrT, 07050	6712	D3
Oasis Christian School, 100 E 22nd St, BAYN, 07002	6920	A4
Offsite Educational Services School, 9001 Sutphin Blvd - QENS, 11435	6825	B5
Ogden Elementary School, 875 Longview Av, HmpT - 11581	6928	B5
Oholei Torah Mesivta School, 667 Eastern Pkwy, BKLN - 11213	6923	C2
Oliver Street Elementary School, 104 Oliver St, NWRK - 07105	6817	E2
Opportunity Charter School, 240 W 113th St, MHTN - 10026	109	D3
Orange High School, 400 Lincoln Av, COrT, 07050	6712	B4
Orange Middle School, 400 Central Av, COrT, 07050	6712	B3
Orchard School, 1156 N Broadway, YNKR, 10701	6279	E3
Osborn Elementary School, 10 Osborn Rd, RYE, 10580	6283	D4
Our Lady-Blessed Sacrament School, 3445 202nd St - QENS, 11361	6721	E3
Our Lady Help of Christian School, 23 Summit St, STNL - 10307	7206	B4
Our Lady Help of Christians School, 23 N Clinton St - EORG, 07017	6712	E3
Our Lady-Miraculous Medal School, 6232 61st St, QENS - 11385	6823	C4
Our Lady of Angels School, 337 74th St, BKLN, 11209	7021	E1
Our Lady of Angels School, 2865 Claflin Av, BRNX - 10468	102	E4
Our Lady of Assumption School, 1617 Parkview Av - BRNX, 10461	6506	A6
Our Lady of Czestochowa School, 248 Marin Blvd, JSYC - 07302	6820	C3
Our Lady of Fatima School, 2538 80th St, QENS, 11370	6719	D4
Our Lady of Fatima School, 963 Scarsdale Rd, YNKR - 10583	6281	B1
Our Lady of Good Counsel High School - 243 Woodside Av, NWRK, 07104	6713	E2
Our Lady of Good Counsel School, 239 Woodside Av - NWRK, 07104	6713	E2
Our Lady of Good Counsel School, 42 Austin Pl, STNL - 10304	7020	C1
Our Lady of Grace Montessori, 29 Shelter Rock Rd, NHLS - 11030	6724	A1
Our Lady of Grace School, 385 Avenue W, BKLN, 11223	7023	A6
Our Lady of Grace School, 3981 Bronxwood Av, BRNX - 10466	6505	C1
Our Lady of Grace School, 400 Kamena St, FRVW, 07022	6611	C3
Our Lady of Grace School, 15820 101st St, QENS, 11414	6925	E4
Our Lady of Guadalupe School, 1518 73rd St, BKLN - 11228	7022	B3
Our Lady of Hope School, 6121 71st St, QENS, 11379	6823	D2
Our Lady of Libera School, 5800 Kennedy Blvd W, WNYK - 07093	6610	E7
Our Lady of Lourdes School, 468 W 143rd St, MHTN - 10031	106	E4
Our Lady of Lourdes School, 76 Park Blvd, MLVN, 11565	6929	B2
Our Lady of Lourdes School, 9280 220th St, QENS - 11428	6826	E2
Our Lady of Mercy School, 2512 Marion Av, BRNX - 10458	6504	D4
Our Lady of Mercy School, 254 Bartholdi Av, JSYC - 07305	6819	B5
Our Lady of Mercy School, 7025 Kessel St, QENS, 11375	6824	C3
Our Lady of Mt Carmel-Bronx, 2465 Bathgate Av, BRNX - 10458	6504	D5
Our Lady of Mt Carmel School, 23 E 22nd St, BAYN - 07002	6919	E4
Our Lady of Mt Carmel School, 59 E Main St, EMFD - 10523	6049	B5
Our Lady of Mt Carmel School, 285 Clove Rd, STNL - 10310	7019	D1
Our Lady of Mt Carmel School, 10 County Rd, TFLY - 07670	6392	A2
Our Lady of the Angelus School, 9805 63rd Dr, QENS - 11374	6824	B1
Our Lady of the Cenacle School, 8725 136th St, QENS - 11418	6825	B5
Our Lady of the Snows School, 7933 258th St, QENS - 11004	6723	C6
Our Lady of Trust at St. Jude Campus, 1696 Canarsie Rd - BKLN, 11236	7024	D1
Our Lady of Trust School, 744 E 87th St, BKLN, 11236	6924	B7
Our Lady of Trust Sch Holy Family Sch Campus - 9719 Flatlands Av, BKLN, 11236	6924	C6
Our Lady of Peace School, 21 Fowler Av, LNBK, 11563	6929	B4
Our Lady of Peace School, 656 Amboy Av, PTHA, 08861	7205	C2
Our Lady of Perpetual Help School, 5902 6th Av, BKLN - 11220	6922	A7
Our Lady of Perpetual Help School, 575 Fowler Av - PLMM, 10803	6395	C6
Our Lady of Perpetual Help School, 11110 115th St - QENS, 11420	6926	A1
Our Lady of Pompeii School, 240 Bleecker St, MHTN - 10014	118	D2
Our Lady of Refuge School, 2708 Briggs Av, BRNX - 10458	6504	D3
Our Lady of Sorrows School, 219 Stanton St, MHTN - 10002	119	C5
Our Lady of Sorrows School, 3534 105th St, QENS - 11368	6720	B5
Our Lady of Sorrows School, 888 Mamaroneck Av, WHPL - 10605	6168	C4
Our Lady of Victories School, 240 Ege Av, JSYC, 07304	6819	D3
Our Lady of Victory Academy, 565 Broadway, DBSF - 10522	6166	A3
Our Lady of Victory School, 2 Bellmore St, FLPK, 11001	6827	D2
Our Lady of Victory School, 38 N 5th Av, MTVN, 10550	6394	D4
Our Lady Queen of Angels School, 232 E 113th St - MHTN, 10029	110	B5
Our Lady Queen of Martyrs School, 71 Arden St, MHTN - 10040	101	E7
Our Lady Queen of Martyrs School, 7255 Austin St - QENS, 11375	6824	C2
Our Lady Queen of Peace School, 22 Steele Av, STNL - 10306	7117	E1
Our Lady Star of the Sea School, 5411 Amboy Rd, STNL - 10312	7116	C7
Our Saviour Lutheran School, 1734 Williamsbridge Rd - BRNX, 10461	6505	C6
Our Saviour Lutheran School, 6433 Woodhaven Blvd - QENS, 11374	6824	B2
Our World Neighborhood Charter School, 3612 35th Av - QENS, 11106	6718	E5
Pablo Neruda Acad for Arch & World Studies - 1980 Lafayette Av, BRNX, 10473	6614	B3
PACE High School, 100 Hester St, MHTN, 10002	119	A6
Pacific High School, 112 Schermerhorn St, BKLN, 11201	121	B6
Packer Collegiate Institute, 170 Joralemon St, BKLN - 11201	121	A5
PACS-St. Mary Middle School, 680 Catherine St, PTHA - 08861	7205	D2
Paideia School 15, 175 Westchester Av, YNKR, 10707	6281	A4
Paideia School 24, 50 Colin St, YNKR, 10701	6280	A6
Palisades Park Junior-Senior High School, 1 Veterans Plz - PALP, 07650	6502	C7
Park Avenue Elementary School, 268 Capuchin Wy, COrT - 07050	6712	C3
Park Avenue Elementary School, 75 Park Av, PTCH - 10573	6170	B4
Park East Day School, 164 E 68th St, MHTN, 10065	113	B6
Parkway School, 5566 Kings Hwy, BKLN, 11203	6923	E6
Parsons Memorial Elementary School, 200 Halstead Av - HRSN, 10528	6283	B3
Passages Academy, 17 Bristol St, BKLN, 11212	6924	B2
Pathways College Preparatory School, 10989 204th St - QENS, 11412	6826	C4
Patricia A Dichiaro School, 373 Bronxville Rd, YNKR - 10708	6280	D6
Patrick Francis Healy Middle School, 116 Hamilton St - EORG, 07017	6713	A2
Paul D Schreiber High School, 101 Campus Dr, NHmT - 11050	6618	A1
Paul Robeson High School, 150 Albany Av, BKLN, 11213	6923	D2
Peace & Diversity Academy, 3441 Steenwick Av, BRNX - 10475	6505	E1
PEARLS Hawthorne School, 350 Hawthorne Av, YNKR - 10705	6393	C3
Pelham Memorial High School, 575 Colonial Av, PLHM - 10803	6395	B6
Pelham Middle School, 28 Franklin Pl, PLHM, 10803	6395	B5
Pelham Preparatory Academy, 925 Astor Av, BRNX - 10469	6505	B4
Pennington Elementary School, 20 Fairway St, MTVN - 10552	6394	E2
Peoples Christian School, 9410 Flatlands Av, BKLN - 11236	6924	C6
Performing Arts & Technology High School - 400 Pennsylvania Av, BKLN, 11207	6924	D3
Perth Amboy Catholic School, 613 Carlock Av, PTHA - 08861	7205	B1
Perth Amboy Elementary School 7, 163 Patterson St - PTHA, 08861	7205	D4
Perth Amboy High School, 300 Eagle Av, PTHA, 08861	7205	D2
Peshine Avenue School, 433 Peshine Av, NWRK, 07112	6817	A4
Pierrepont Elementary School, 70 E Pierrepont Av, RTFD - 07070	6609	A3
Polk Elementary School, 1100 Warren St, ROSL, 07203	6917	A6
Polk Street Elementary School, 960 Polk Av, HmpT - 11010	6828	A6
Poly Preparatory Lower School, 50 Prospect Park W - BKLN, 11215	6922	E3
Polytech Preparatory Day School, 9216 7th Av, BKLN - 11228	7021	E3
Port Chester Middle School, 113 Bowman Av, RYEB - 10573	6169	E5
Port Chester Senior High School, 1 Tamarack Rd, RYEB - 10573	6170	A4
Port Reading Elementary School, 77 Turner St, WbgT - 07064	7115	B2
Port Richmond High School, 85 St. Josephs Av, STNL - 10302	6919	C7
Port Washington Child Center, 232 Main St, NHmT - 11050	6617	D1
Post Road Elementary School, 175 W Post Rd, WHPL - 10606	6168	A3
Powell Middle Sch for Law & Social Justice - 509 W 129th St, MHTN, 10027	106	D6
Prepatory Academy for Writers, 14310 Springfield Blvd - QENS, 11413	6927	C3
Presentation of the Blessed Virgin Mary Sch - 8813 Parsons Blvd, QENS, 11432	6825	C4
Preston High School, 2780 Schurz Av, BRNX, 10465	6615	A4
Primary Preparatory School, 41 Tuers Av, JSYC, 07306	6820	A2
Professional Children's School, 132 W 60th St, MHTN - 10023	112	B5
Professional Performing Arts High School - 328 W 48th St, MHTN, 10036	112	B7
Professor Juan Bosch Public School, 12 Elwood St - MHTN, 10040	104	D1
Progress HS for Professional Careers, 850 Grand St - BKLN, 11206	6822	D4
Promise Academy Charter School, 35 E 125th St, MHTN - 10035	110	B2
Prospect Hill School, 1000 Washington Av, PLMM, 10803	6395	C7
Prospect Park Bnos Leah High School, 1601 Avenue R - BKLN, 11229	7023	B4
Prospect Park Yeshiva, 1784 E 17th St, BKLN, 11229	7023	B4
Providing Urban Learners Success, 560 E 179th St, BRNX - 10457	6504	D6
PS 001 Courtlandt School, 335 E 152nd St, BRNX, 10451	6613	A3
PS 001 The Bergen School, 309 47th St, BKLN, 11220	6922	A5
PS 01, 128 Duncan Av, JSYC, 07306	6819	E2
PS 001 Alfred E Smith School, 8 Henry St, MHTN, 10038	118	E7
PS 001 Tottenville School, 58 Summit St, STNL, 10307	7206	B4
PS 01, 6129 Madison St, WNYK, 07093	6611	A7
PS 002 Alfred Zimberg School, 7510 21st Av, QENS - 11370	6719	D3
PS 002 Meyer London School, 122 Henry St, MHTN - 10002	119	A7
PS 002 Morrisania School, 1260 Franklin Av, BRNX - 10456	6613	C1
PS 02, 52nd St & Broadway, WNYK, 07093	111	B2
PS 003 Bedford Village School, 50 Jefferson Av, BKLN - 11216	6923	B1
PS 003 Charrette School, 490 Hudson St, MHTN, 10014	118	C1
PS 003 Margaret Gioiosa School, 80 S Goff Av, STNL - 10309	7206	E2
PS 003 Raul Julia Micro Society, 2100 La Fontaine Av - BRNX, 10457	6504	D6
PS 03, 5401 Polk St, WNYK, 07093	6610	E7
PS 4K, 530 Stanley Av, BKLN, 11207	6924	D4
PS 004 Duke Ellington School, 500 W 160th St, MHTN - 10032	107	B1
PS 4Q, 19625 Peck Av, QENS, 11365	6722	A7
PS 004 Maurice Wollin School, 200 Nedra Pl, STNL - 10312	7116	B5
PS 04, 6300 Palisade Av, WNYK, 07093	6611	A7
PS 005 Dr Ronald McNair School, 820 Hancock St, BKLN - 11233	6823	A7
PS 005 Ellen Lurie School, 3703 10th Av, MHTN, 10034	105	A1
PS 005 Huguenot School, 348 Deisius St, STNL, 10312	7207	C1
PS 005 Port Morris School, 564 Jackson Av, BRNX, 10455	6613	B4
PS 05, 5401 Hudson Av, WNYK, 07093	111	A1
PS 006, 43 Snyder Av, BKLN, 11226	6923	B5
PS 006 Lillie D Blake School, 45 E 81st St, MHTN, 10028	113	C3
PS 006 West Farms School, 1000 E Tremont Av, BRNX - 10460	6504	E7
PS 6 Corporal Allan F Kivlehan School, 555 Page Av - STNL, 10309	7206	C3
PS 007 Abraham Lincoln School, 858 Jamaica Av, BKLN - 11208	6824	A7
PS 007 Kingsbridge School, 3201 Kingsbridge Av, BRNX - 10463	102	D2
PS 007 Louise F Simeone School, 8055 Cornish Av, QENS - 11373	6719	E7
PS 007 Samuel Stern School, 160 E 120th St, MHTN - 10035	110	B3
PS 008 Isaac Varian School, 3010 Briggs Av, BRNX - 10458	6504	E3
PS 008 Luis Belliard School, 465 W 167th St, MHTN - 10032	104	C7
PS 008 Robert Fulton School, 37 Hicks St, BKLN, 11201	121	A3
PS 08, 96 Franklin St, JSYC, 07032	6716	B6
PS 8 Shirlee Solomon, 112 Lindenwood Rd, STNL, 10308	7117	B5
PS 009, 5874 57th St, QENS, 11378	6823	B3
PS 009 Sarah Anderson School, 100 W 84th St, MHTN - 10024	112	E1
PS 009 Teunis G Bergen School, 80 Underhill Av, BKLN - 11238	6923	A1
PS 010X, 2750 Lafayette Av, BRNX, 10465	6614	E2
PS 011 Highbridge School, 1257 Ogden Av, BRNX, 10452	104	E7
PS 011 Kathryn Phelan School, 5425 Skillman Av, QENS - 11377	6719	B6
PS 011 Purvis J Behan School, 419 Waverly Av, BKLN - 11238	6822	A7
PS 011 Thomas Dongan School, 50 Jefferson St, STNL - 10304	7020	B7
PS 011 William T Harris School, 320 W 21st St, MHTN - 10011	115	D5
PS 012, 430 Howard Av, BKLN, 11233	6924	A2
PS 012 James B Colgate School, 4200 72nd St, QENS - 11377	6719	D7
PS 012X Lewis & Clark School, 2555 Tratman Av, BRNX - 10461	6505	D7
PS 013 Clement C Moore School, 5501 94th St, QENS - 11373	6720	A7
PS 013 ML Lindemeyer School, 191 Vermont Av, STNL - 10305	7020	E3
PS 013 Roberto Clemente School, 557 Pennsylvania Av - BKLN, 11207	6924	D3
PS 014 Cornelius Vanderbilt, 100 Tompkins Av, STNL - 10304	7020	D2
PS 014 Fairview School, 10701 Otis Av, QENS, 11368	6720	C7
PS 014 Senator John Calandra School - 3041 Bruckner Blvd, BRNX, 10461	6615	A1
PS 015 Institute for Environmental Learning - 2195 Andrews Av, BRNX, 10453	105	D1
PS 015 Jackie Robinson Sch of Perf Arts, 12115 Lucas St - QENS, 11413	6826	C7
PS 015 Patrick F Daly School, 71 Sullivan St, BKLN - 11231	6922	A2
PS 015 Roberto Clemente School, 333 E 4th St, MHTN - 10009	119	D4
PS 016 Wakefield School, 4550 Carpenter Av, BRNX - 10470	6394	C5
PS 16Q, 41-15 104th St, QENS, 11368	6720	B6
PS 016 John J Driscoll School, 80 Monroe Av, STNL - 10301	6920	D7
PS 016 Leonard Dunkly School, 157 Wilson St, BKLN - 11211	6822	B5
PS 17X, 778 Forest Av, BRNX, 10456	6613	B3
PS 017 Henry Thoreau School, 2837 29th St, QENS - 11102	6719	A3
PS 017 Henry Woodworth School, 208 N 5th St, BKLN - 11211	6822	B3
PS 018 Edward Bush School, 101 Maujer St, BKLN, 11206	6822	C4
PS 018 John G Whittier School, 221 Broadway, STNL - 10310	6919	E7
PS 018 John Peter Zenger School, 502 Morris Av, BRNX - 10451	6613	A3
PS 018 Park Terrace, 4124 9th Av, MHTN, 10034	102	C5
PS 019 Asher Levy School, 185 1st Av, MHTN, 10003	119	C2
PS 019 Curtis School, 780 Post Av, STNL, 10310	7019	D1
PS 019 Judith K Weiss School, 4318 Katonah Av, BRNX - 10470	6394	A6
PS 019 Marino Jeantet, 9802 Roosevelt Av, QENS, 11368	6720	A6
PS 019 Roberto Clemente School, 325 S 3rd St, BKLN - 11211	6822	B4
PS 020 Anna Silver School, 166 Essex St, MHTN, 10002	119	B4
PS 020 Clinton Hill School, 225 Adelphi St, BKLN, 11205	6822	A7
PS 20, 160 Danforth Av, JSYC, 07305	6819	C6
PS 020 John Bowne Elementary School, 14230 Barclay Av - QENS, 11355	6721	A4
PS 020 PO George J Werdan III, 3050 Webster Av, BRNX - 10467	6504	E3
PS 021 Crispus Attucks School, 180 Chauncey St, BKLN - 11233	6923	E1
PS 021 Edward Hart School, 14736 26th Av, QENS - 11354	6721	A2
PS 021 Phillip H Sheridan School, 715 E 225th St, BRNX - 10466	6394	B7
PS 21 Elm Park Elementary School, 168 Hooker Pl, STNL - 10303	7019	B1
PS 022, 443 St. Marks Av, BKLN, 11238	6923	B2
PS 022 Graniteville School, 1860 Forest Av, STNL, 10303	7019	B2
PS 022 Thomas Jefferson School, 15333 Sanford Av - QENS, 11355	6721	B4
PS 023 Carter C Woodson School, 545 Willoughby Av - BKLN, 11206	6822	C6
PS 023 The New Children's School, 2151 Washington Av - BRNX, 10457	6504	C5
PS 23Q Hillside Campus School, 7559 263rd St, QENS - 11004	6723	C5
PS 023 Richmondtown School, 30 Natick St, STNL - 10306	7117	D2
PS 024, 427 38th St, BKLN, 11232	6922	B5
PS 024 Andrew Jackson School, 14111 Holly Av, QENS - 11355	6721	B5
PS 024 Spuyten Duyvil School, 660 W 236th St, BRNX - 10463	102	B1
PS 025 Bilingual School, 811 E 149th St, BRNX, 10455	6613	B4
PS 025 Eubie Blake School, 787 Lafayette Av, BKLN - 11221	6822	D7
PS 25 St. Joseph School Mt Lorto, 6581 Hylan Blvd, STNL - 10309	7206	D4
PS 26 Jesse Owens School, 1014 Lafayette Av, BKLN - 11221	6822	E7
PS 026 Carteret School, 4108 Victory Blvd, STNL, 10314	7018	C6
PS 027 Agnes Y Humphrey Sch for Leadership - 27 Huntington St, BKLN, 11231	6922	B2
PS 028 Mt Hope School, 1861 Anthony Av, BRNX, 10457	105	E4
PS 028 The Warren School, 1001 Herkimer St, BKLN - 11233	6924	A1

New York City/5 Borough Points of Interest Index

FEATURE NAME Address City ZIP Code	MAP#	GRID
PS 028 Wright Brothers School, 475 W 155th St, MHTN - 10032	107	B2
PS 28 Thomas Emmanuel, 10910 47th Av, QENS, 11368	6720	C6
PS 029 Bardwell School, 1581 Victory Blvd, STNL, 10314	7019	E3
PS 029 John M Harrigan School, 425 Henry St, BKLN - 11201	120	E7
PS 029 Queens School, 12510 23rd Av, QENS, 11356	6720	D2
PS 30 Wilton School, 510 E 141st St, BRNX, 10454	6613	A4
PS 030 Queens School, 12610 Bedell St, QENS, 11434	6927	A1
PS 030 Westerleigh School, 200 Wardwell Av, STNL - 10314	7019	D3
PS 31, 3055 John F Kennedy Blvd, JSYC, 07306	6716	A7
PS 031 Bayside School, 21145 46th Rd, QENS, 11361	6722	B4
PS 031 Samuel F Dupont School, 75 Meserole Av, BKLN - 11222	6822	B2
PS 031 William T Davis School, 55 Layton Av, STNL - 10301	6920	D6
PS 032 Belmont School, 690 E 183rd St, BRNX, 10457	6504	D5
PS 032 Gifford School, 32 Elverton Av, STNL, 10308	7117	A4
PS 032 Samuel Mills Sprole School, 317 Hoyt St, BKLN - 11231	6922	C1
PS 032 State Street School, 17111 35th Av, QENS, 11358	6721	D3
PS 033 Chelsea Preparatory School, 281 9th Av, MHTN - 10001	115	D4
PS 033 Edward M Funk School, 9137 222nd St, QENS - 11428	6826	E2
PS 033 Timothy Dwight School, 2424 Jerome Av, BRNX - 10468	105	E1
PS 33, 362 Union St, JSYC, 07304	6819	D3
PS 34, 1830 John F Kennedy Blvd, JSYC, 07305	6819	C5
PS 034 Franklin Roosevelt School, 730 E 12th St, MHTN - 10009	119	E3
PS 034 John Harvard School, 10412 Springfield Blvd - QENS, 11429	6826	E4
PS 034 Oliver H Perry School, 131 Norman Av, BKLN - 11222	6822	C2
PS 035, 317 W 52nd St, MHTN, 10019	112	B7
PS 035 Clove Valley School, 60 Foote Av, STNL, 10301	7020	B3
PS 035 Franz Sigel School, 261 E 163rd St, BRNX, 10456	6613	A2
PS 035 Nathaniel Woodhull School, 19102 90th Av - QENS, 11423	6826	B3
PS 035 Stephen Decatur School, 272 Macdonough St - BKLN, 11233	6923	D1
PS 36K, 2045 Linden Blvd, BKLN, 11207	6924	D4
PS 036 Drumgoole School, 255 Ionia Av, STNL, 10312	7116	C6
PS 036 Margaret Douglas School, 123 Morningside Dr - MHTN, 10027	109	D1
PS 036 St. Albans School, 18701 Foch Blvd, QENS, 11412	6826	B7
PS 036 Unionport School, 1070 Castle Hill Av, BRNX - 10472	6614	C2
PS 037 Multiple Intelligence School, 360 W 230th St - BRNX, 10463	102	C3
PS 37R, 15 Fairfield St, STNL, 10308	7117	B3
PS 038 George Cromwell School, 421 Lincoln Av, STNL - 10306	7118	B1
PS 038 Roberto Clemente School, 232 E 103rd St, MHTN - 10029	110	A7
PS 038 Rosedale School, 13521 241st St, QENS, 11422	6927	E2
PS 038 The Pacific School, 450 Pacific St, BKLN, 11217	121	C7
PS 039 Henry Bristow School, 417 6th Av, BKLN, 11215	6922	D3
PS 39 Francis J Murphy Junior School, 71 Sand Ln, STNL - 10305	7020	E5
PS 040 Augustus St. Gaudens, 319 E 19th St, MHTN - 10003	116	C7
PS 040 George W Carver School, 265 Ralph Av, BKLN - 11233	6924	A1
PS 040 Samuel Huntington School, 10920 Union Hall St - QENS, 11433	6825	D6
PS 041 Francis White School, 411 Thatford Av, BKLN - 11212	6924	B4
PS 041 Greenwich Village School, 116 W 11th St, MHTN - 10011	115	E7
PS 041 Gun Hill Road School, 3352 Olinville Av, BRNX - 10467	6505	A2
PS 041 New Dorp School, 216 Clawson St, STNL, 10306	7118	A2
PS 042 Benjamin Altman School, 71 Hester St, MHTN - 10002	119	A6
PS 042 Claremont Community School - 1537 Washington Av, BRNX, 10457	105	E7
PS 042 Eltingville School, 380 Genesee Av, STNL, 10312	7116	D5
PS 042 R Vernam School, 488 Beach 66th St, QENS - 11692	7026	D6
PS 043, 160 Beach 29th St, QENS, 11691	7027	C6
PS 043 Jonas Bronck School, 165 Brown Pl, BRNX, 10454	6613	A5
PS 044 David C Farragut School, 1825 Prospect Av, BRNX - 10457	6504	D7
PS 044 Marcus Garvey School, 432 Monroe St, BKLN - 11221	6822	D7
PS 044 Thomas C Brown School, 80 Maple Pkwy, STNL - 10303	7019	A1
PS 045 Horace E Greene School, 84 Schaefer St, BKLN - 11207	6823	B7
PS 045 John Tyler School, 58 Lawrence Av, STNL, 10310	7020	A1
PS 046 Albert V Maniscalco School, 41 Reid Av, STNL - 10305	7020	D6
PS 046 Arthur Tappan School - 2987 Frederick Douglass Blvd, MHTN, 10039	107	C2
PS 046 Edgar Allen Poe School, 279 E 196th St, BRNX - 10458	6504	D3
PS 046 Edward C Blum School, 100 Clermont Av, BKLN - 11205	121	E5
PS 047 Chris Galas School, 9 Power Rd, QENS, 11693	7026	A4
PS 047 John Randolph, 1794 E 172nd St, BRNX, 10472	6614	A1
PS 048 Joseph R Drake School, 1290 Spofford Av, BRNX - 10474	6613	D4
PS 048 Mapleton School, 6015 18th Av, BKLN, 11204	7022	D2
PS 048 Officer M J Buczek School, 4360 Broadway - MHTN, 10033	104	C3
PS 048 William C Wilcox School, 1055 Targee St, STNL - 10304	7020	C5
PS 048 William Wordsworth School, 15502 108th Av - QENS, 11433	6825	D6
PS 049 Dorothy Bonawit Kole, 7915 Penelope Av, QENS - 11379	6824	A3
PS 049 Willis Avenue School, 383 E 139th St, BRNX - 10454	6613	A4
PS 050 Clara Barton School, 1550 Vyse Av, BRNX, 10460	6613	D1
PS 050 Frank Hankinson School, 200 Adelaide Av, STNL - 10306	7117	D4
PS 050 Talfourd Lawn Elementary School - 14326 101st Av, QENS, 11435	6825	C6
PS 051 Bronx New School, 3200 Jerome Av, BRNX, 10468	6504	D2
PS 051 Elias Howe School, 520 W 45th St, MHTN, 10036	112	A7
PS 052 John C Thompson School, 450 Buel Av, STNL - 10305	7118	C1
PS 052 Queens School, 17837 146th Ter, QENS, 11434	6927	B4
PS 052 Sheepshead Bay School, 2675 E 29th St, BKLN - 11235	7023	D7
PS 53K, 720 Livonia Av, BKLN, 11207	6924	D3
PS 053 Basheer Quisim School, 360 E 168th St, BRNX - 10456	6613	B1
PS 053 Bay Terrace School, 330 Durant Av, STNL, 10308	7117	C5
PS 054 Charles W Leng School, 1060 Willowbrook Rd - STNL, 10314	7019	C5
PS 054 Hillside School, 8602 127th St, QENS, 11418	6825	A5
PS 055 Benjamin Franklin School, 450 St. Pauls Pl, BRNX - 10456	6613	B1
PS 055 Henry M Boehm School, 54 Osborne St, STNL - 10312	7116	E7
PS 055 Maure School, 13110 97th Av, QENS, 11419	6825	B6
PS 056 Lewis H Latimer School, 170 Gates Av, BKLN - 11238	6822	B7
PS 056 Louis Desario School, 250 Kramer Av, STNL - 10309	7115	E6
PS 056 Norwood Heights School, 341 E 207th St, BRNX - 10467	6505	A2
PS 057 Crescent School, 2111 Crotona Av, BRNX, 10457	6504	D6
PS 057 Hubert H Humphrey School, 140 Palma Dr, STNL - 10304	7020	D4
PS 058, 459 E 176th St, BRNX, 10457	6504	C6
PS 058 School of Heroes, 7250 Grand Av, QENS, 11378	6823	D1
PS 058 The Carroll School, 330 Smith St, BKLN, 11231	6922	C1
PS 059 Beekman Hill International School, 228 E 57th St - MHTN, 10022	117	A1
PS 059 Community School of Technology - 2185 Bathgate Av, BRNX, 10457	6504	D5
PS 059 William Floyd School, 211 Throop Av, BKLN - 11206	6822	C6
PS 060 Alice Austen School, 55 Merrill Av, STNL, 10314	7018	E4
PS 061 Francisco Oller School, 1550 Crotona Park E - BRNX, 10460	6613	D1
PS 062 Inocensio Casanova School, 660 Fox St, BRNX - 10455	6613	C4
PS 063 Authors Academy, 1261 Franklin Av, BRNX, 10456	6613	C1
PS 063 William McKinley School, 121 E 3rd St, MHTN - 10009	119	C4
PS 064 Pura Belpre School, 1425 Walton Av, BRNX - 10452	105	B7
PS 064 Robert Simon School, 600 E 6th St, MHTN, 10009	119	D4
PS 065 Mother Hale Academy, 677 E 141st St, BRNX - 10454	6613	B5
PS 66, 845 E 96th St, BKLN, 11236	6924	B5
PS 066 School of Higher Expectations, 1001 Jennings St - BRNX, 10460	6613	D1
PS 067 Charles A Dorsey School, 51 St. Edwards St, BKLN - 11205	121	D5
PS 067 Mohegan School, 2024 Mohegan Av, BRNX - 10460	6504	E7
PS 068 Bronx, 4011 Monticello Av, BRNX, 10466	6394	D7
PS 69 Vincent D Grippo School, 884 63rd St, BKLN - 11220	7022	A1
PS 069 Daniel D Tompkins School, 144 Keating Pl, STNL - 10314	7019	A6
PS 069 Jackson Heights School, 7702 37th Av, QENS - 11372	6719	D6
PS 069 Little Red School House, 158 Richmond St, BKLN - 11208	6924	E1
PS 069 New Vision School, 560 Thieriot Av, BRNX, 10473	6614	B3
PS 070 Max Schoenfeld School, 1691 Weeks Av, BRNX - 10457	105	D5
PS 070 Queens School, 3045 42nd St, QENS, 11103	6719	B4
PS 071 Forest School, 6285 Forest Av, QENS, 11385	6823	B4
PS 071 Rose E Scala School, 3040 Roberts Av, BRNX - 10461	6505	E6
PS 072, 131 E 104th St, MHTN, 10029	109	E6
PS 072 Annette Goldman School, 605 Shepherd Av - BKLN, 11208	6924	E3
PS 072 Dr William Dorney School, 2951 Dewey Av, BRNX - 10465	6615	B2
PS 073 Bronx School, 1020 Anderson Av, BRNX, 10452	107	E2
PS 073 Thomas S Boyland School, 251 MacDougal St - BKLN, 11233	6924	B1
PS 075, 984 Faile St, BRNX, 10459	6613	D2
PS 075 Emily Dickinson School, 735 W End Av, MHTN - 10025	108	E5
PS 075 Mayda Cortiella School, 95 Grove St, BKLN - 11221	6823	A6
PS 076 A Philip Randolph School, 220 W 121st St, MHTN - 10027	109	E2
PS 076 Bennington School, 900 Adee Av, BRNX, 10469	6505	B3
PS 076 William Hallett School, 3636 10th St, QENS - 11106	6718	D4
PS 77K, 62 Park Pl, BKLN, 11217	6922	E1
PS 77 Lower Lab School, 1700 3rd Av, MHTN, 10128	113	E1
PS 078 Anne Hutchinson School, 1400 Needham Av - BRNX, 10469	6505	C2
PS 079 Creston School, 125 E 181st St, BRNX, 10453	105	E2
PS 79M Horan School, 55 E 120th St, MHTN, 10035	110	A3
PS 079 Francis Lewis School, 14727 15th Dr, QENS - 11357	6615	B7
PS 080 Thurgood Marshall School, 17105 137th Av - QENS, 11434	6927	B2
PS 081 Jean Paul Richter School, 559 Cypress Av, QENS - 11385	6823	B5
PS 081 Robert J Christian School, 5550 Riverdale Av - BRNX, 10471	6393	B5
PS 081 Thaddeus Stevens School, 990 DeKalb Av, BKLN - 11221	6822	D6
PS 082 Hammond School, 8802 144th St, QENS, 11435	6825	B5
PS 083 Donald Hertz School, 950 Rhinelander Av, BRNX - 10462	6505	B6
PS 083 Luis Munoz Rivera School, 219 E 109th St, MHTN - 10029	110	B6
PS 084 Jose de Diego School, 250 Berry St, BKLN, 11211	6822	A3
PS 084 Lillian Weber School, 32 W 92nd St, MHTN - 10025	109	A7
PS 084 Steinway School, 2245 41st St, QENS, 11105	6719	B3
PS 085 Great Expectations School, 2400 Marion Av - BRNX, 10458	6504	D4
PS 085 Judge Charles Vallone, 2370 31st St, QENS - 11105	6719	A2
PS 086, 8741 Parsons Blvd, QENS, 11432	6825	C4
PS 086 Irvington School, 220 Irving Av, BKLN, 11237	6823	A5
PS 086 Kingsbridge Heights School, 2756 Reservoir Av - BRNX, 10468	6504	C3
PS 087 Bronx School, 1935 Bussing Av, BRNX, 10466	6394	D6
PS 087 Middle Village School, 6754 80th St, QENS - 11379	6824	A4
PS 087 William Sherman School, 160 W 78th St, MHTN - 10024	112	D2
PS 088 Seneca School, 6085 Catalpa Av, QENS, 11385	6823	C5
PS 088 S Silverstein Little School, 1340 Sheridan Av - BRNX, 10456	105	C7
PS 089 Bronx School, 980 Mace Av, BRNX, 10469	6505	B4
PS 089 Cypress Hills School, 350 Linwood St, BKLN - 11208	6924	E2
PS 089 Elmhurst School, 8528 Britton Av, QENS, 11373	6719	E6
PS 089 School, 201 Warren St, MHTN, 10282	118	A6
PS 90 Edna Cohen School, 2840 W 12th St, BKLN, 11224	7120	E1
PS 090 George Meany School, 1116 Sheridan Av, BRNX - 10456	6613	A1
PS 091 Albany Avenue School, 532 Albany Av, BKLN - 11203	6923	D4
PS 091 Bronx School, 2200 Aqueduct Av E, BRNX, 10453	105	D2
PS 091 Richard Arkwright School, 6810 Central Av - QENS, 11385	6823	E5
PS 092 Adrian Hegeman School, 601 Parkside Av, BKLN - 11225	6923	B4
PS 092 Bronx School, 700 E 179th St, BRNX, 10457	6504	D6
PS 092 Harry T Stewart Senior School, 9901 34th Av - QENS, 11368	6720	A5
PS 092 Mary McLeod Bethune School, 222 W 134th St - MHTN, 10030	107	A7
PS 093 Albert G Oliver School, 1535 Story Av, BRNX - 10473	6613	E3
PS 093 William H Prescott School, 31 New York Av, BKLN - 11216	6923	C1
PS 094 Henry Longfellow School, 5010 6th Av, BKLN - 11220	6922	B6
PS 094 Kings College School, 3530 Kings College Pl - BRNX, 10467	6505	A1
PS 94M, 442 E Houston St, MHTN, 10009	119	D5
PS 095 Eastwood School, 17901 90th Av, QENS, 11432	6825	E4
PS 095 Sheila Mencher School, 3961 Hillman Av, BRNX - 10463	6504	D1
PS 095 The Gravesend School, 345 Van Sicklen St, BKLN - 11223	7022	E6
PS 096 Joseph Lanzetta School, 216 E 120th St, MHTN - 10035	110	C4
PS 096 Richard Rodgers School, 650 Waring Av, BRNX - 10467	6505	A4
PS 097 Bronx School, 1375 Mace Av, BRNX, 10469	6505	D4
PS 097 Highlawn School, 1855 Stillwell Av, BKLN, 11223	7022	D5
PS 098 Shorac Kappock School, 512 W 212th St, MHTN - 10034	102	B6
PS 099 Isaac Asimov School, 1120 E 10th St, BKLN - 11230	7023	A2
PS 099 Kew Gardens School, 8237 Kew Gardens Rd - QENS, 11415	6825	A4
PS 100 Coney Island School, 2951 W 3rd St, BKLN, 11224	7121	A1
PS 100 Isaac Clason School, 800 Taylor Av, BRNX, 10473	6614	B3
PS 101 Andrew Draper School, 141 E 111th St, MHTN - 10029	110	A5
PS 101 School In the Gardens, 2 Russell Pl, QENS, 11375	6824	D3
PS 101 The Verrazano School, 2360 Benson Av, BKLN - 11214	7022	C6
PS 102 Bayview School, 55-24 Van Hom St, QENS, 11373	6823	E1
PS 102 Jacques Cartier School, 315 E 113th St, MHTN - 10029	110	B5
PS 102 Joseph O Loretan School, 1827 Archer St, BRNX - 10460	6505	B7
PS 102 The Bayview School, 211 72nd St, BKLN, 11209	6921	D7
PS 103 Hector Fontanez School, 4125 Carpenter Av - BRNX, 10466	6394	B7
PS 105 Bay School, 420 Beach 51st St, QENS, 11691	7027	A6
PS 105 Sen Abraham Bernstein, 725 Brady Av, BRNX - 10462	6505	A5
PS 105 The Blythebourne School, 1031 59th St, BKLN - 11219	7022	B1
PS 106, 180 Beach 35th St, QENS, 11691	7027	B6
PS 106 Edward Everett Hale School, 1314 Putnam Av - BKLN, 11221	6823	B6
PS 106 Parkchester School, 2120 St. Raymonds Av, BRNX - 10462	6505	C7
PS 107, 1695 Seward Av, BRNX, 10473	6614	A3
PS 107 John W Kimball School, 1301 8th Av, BKLN - 11215	6922	E4
PS 107 Thomas Dooley School, 16702 45th Av, QENS - 11358	6721	D5
PS 108 Assembly Angelo del Toro, 1615 Madison Av - MHTN, 10029	109	E5
PS 108 Philip J Abinanti School, 1166 Neill Av, BRNX - 10461	6505	C5
PS 108 Sal Abbracciamento School, 200 Linwood St - BKLN, 11208	6924	E1
PS 109, 1001 E 45th St, BKLN, 11203	6923	E7
PS 109 Sedgwick School, 1771 Popham Av, BRNX, 10453	105	A3
PS 110 Florence Nightingale School, 285 Delancey St - MHTN, 10002	119	D6
PS 110 The Monitor School, 124 Monitor St, BKLN, 11222	6822	D2
PS 110 Theodore Schoenfeld School, 580 Crotona Park S - BRNX, 10456	6613	C1
PS 111 Adolph S Ochs School, 440 W 53rd St, MHTN - 10019	112	B6
PS 111 Jacob Blackwell School, 3715 13th St, QENS - 11101	6718	D4
PS 111 Seton Falls School, 3740 Baychester Av, BRNX - 10466	6505	D1
PS 112 Bronxwood School, 1925 Schieffelin Av, BRNX - 10466	6505	D1
PS 112 Dutch Kills School, 2505 37th Av, QENS, 11106	6718	D5
PS 112 Jose Celso Barbosa School, 535 E 119th St - MHTN, 10035	110	D5
PS 112 Lefferts Park School, 7115 15th Av, BKLN, 11228	7022	B3
PS 113 Isaac Chauncey School, 8721 79th Av, QENS - 11385	6824	B5
PS 114 Luis Llorens Torres School, 1155 Cromwell Av - BRNX, 10452	6613	A1
PS 114 Ryder Elementary School, 1077 Remsen Av - BKLN, 11236	6924	B6
PS 115 Alexander Humboldt School, 586 W 177th St - MHTN, 10033	104	C5
PS 115 Daniel Mucatel School, 1500 E 92nd St, BKLN - 11236	7024	D1
PS 116 Elizabeth Farrell School, 515 Knickerbocker Av - BKLN, 11237	6823	A6
PS 116 Mary Lindley Murray School, 210 E 33rd St - MHTN, 10016	116	D5
PS 116 William Hughley School, 10725 Wren Pl, QENS - 11433	6825	E5
PS 117 J Keld-Briarwood School, 8515 143rd St, QENS - 11435	6825	B4
PS 118 Lorraine Hansberry School, 19020 109th Rd - QENS, 11412	6826	B5
PS 119, 1075 Pugsley Av, BRNX, 10472	6614	B2
PS 119 Amersfort School, 3829 Avenue K, BKLN, 11210	7023	D2
PS 120 Carlos Tapia School, 18 Beaver St, BKLN, 11206	6822	D5
PS 120 Queens School, 5801 136th St, QENS, 11355	6720	E6
PS 121 Nelson A Rockefeller School, 5301 20th Av - BKLN, 11204	7022	E2
PS 121 Queens School, 12610 109th Av, QENS, 11420	6926	B1
PS 121 Throop School, 2750 Throop Av, BRNX, 10469	6505	C3
PS 122 Mamie Fay School, 2121 Ditmars Blvd, QENS - 11105	6719	A1
PS 123 Mahalia Jackson School, 301 W 140th St, MHTN - 10030	107	A5
PS 123 Suydam School, 100 Irving Av, BKLN, 11237	6823	A5
PS 124 Silas B Dutcher School, 515 4th Av, BKLN, 11215	6922	D3
PS 124 Yung Wing School, 40 Division St, MHTN, 10002	118	E6
PS 125 Ralph Bunche School, 425 W 123rd St, MHTN - 10027	109	D1
PS 126 Dr Marjorie H Dunbar, 175 W 166th St, BRNX - 10452	107	E1
PS 126 Jacob August Riis School, 80 Catherine St, MHTN - 10038	118	E7

New York City/5 Borough Points of Interest Index

FEATURE NAME Address City ZIP Code	MAP#	GRID
PS 127 Aerospace Science Magnet School, 9801 25th Av - QENS, 11369	6720	A3
PS 127 McKinley Park School, 7805 7th Av, BKLN, 11228	7022	A2
PS 128 Audubon School, 560 W 169th St, MHTN, 10032	104	B6
PS 128 Juniper Valley School, 6926 65th Dr, QENS - 11379	6823	D3
PS 128 The Bensonhurst School, 2075 84th St, BKLN - 11214	7022	C4
PS 129 John H Finley School, 425 W 130th St, MHTN - 10027	106	E7
PS 129 Patricia Larkin School, 12802 7th Av, QENS - 11356	6614	D7
PS 129 Twin Parks Upper School, 2055 Mapes Av, BRNX - 10460	6504	D6
PS 130 Abram S Hewitt School, 750 Prospect Av, BRNX - 10455	6613	C3
PS 130 Hernando Desoto School, 143 Baxter St, MHTN - 10013	118	E5
PS 130 The Parkside School, 70 Ocean Pkwy, BKLN - 11218	6922	E5
PS 131 Abigail Adams School, 17045 84th Av, QENS - 11432	6825	D3
PS 131 Brooklyn School, 4305 Fort Hamilton Pkwy, BKLN - 11219	6922	C7
PS 132 Conselya School, 320 Manhattan Av, BKLN, 11211	6822	C3
PS 132 Garrett A Morgan School, 1245 Washington Av - BRNX, 10456	6613	B1
PS 132 Juan Pablo Duarte School, 185 Wadsworth Av - MHTN, 10033	104	C4
PS 132 Ralph Bunche School, 13215 218th St, QENS - 11413	6927	D1
PS 133 Fred R Moore School, 2121 5th Av, MHTN, 10037	110	B1
PS 133 William A Butler School, 375 Butler St, BKLN - 11217	6922	E1
PS 134, 4001 18th Av, BKLN, 11230	7022	E1
PS 134 George F Bristow School, 1330 Bristow St, BRNX - 10459	6613	D1
PS 134 Henrietta Szold School, 293 E Broadway, MHTN - 10002	119	C6
PS 134 The Hollis School, 20302 109th Av, QENS, 11412	6826	C4
PS 135 Sheldon A Brookner School, 684 Linden Blvd - BKLN, 11203	6923	E5
PS 136 Roy Wilkins School, 20115 115th Av, QENS - 11412	6826	C6
PS 137 John L Bernstein School, 327 Cherry St, MHTN - 10002	119	B7
PS 137 Rachel Jean Mitchell, 121 Saratoga Av, BKLN - 11233	6924	A1
PS 138 Brooklyn School, 760 Prospect Pl, BKLN, 11216	6923	C2
PS 138 Samuel Randall School, 2060 Lafayette Av, BRNX - 10473	6614	C2
PS 138 Sunrise School, 25111 Weller Av, QENS, 11422	6927	E4
PS 139 Alexine A Fenty School, 330 Rugby Rd, BKLN - 11226	6923	A6
PS 139 Rego Park School, 9306 63rd Dr, QENS, 11374	6824	B1
PS 140 Eagle School, 916 Eagle Av, BRNX, 10456	6613	B2
PS 140 Edward K Ellington School, 11600 166th St - QENS, 11434	6825	E7
PS 140 K, 985 Rockaway Av, BKLN, 11212	6924	B4
PS 140 Nathan Straus School, 123 Ridge St, MHTN - 10002	119	C5
PS 142 Amalia Castro School, 100 Attorney St, MHTN - 10002	119	C5
PS 142 Harbor Magnet Middle School, 610 Henry St - BKLN, 11231	6922	B1
PS 143 Louis Armstrong School, 3474 113th St, QENS - 11368	6720	C5
PS 144 Colonel Jeromus Remsen School, 9302 69th Av - QENS, 11375	6824	C3
PS 145 Andrew Jackson School, 100 Noll St, BKLN - 11206	6822	E5
PS 145 Bloomingdale School, 150 W 105th St, MHTN - 10025	109	B4
PS 146, 610 Henry St, BKLN, 11231	6922	B1
PS 146 Anna M Short School, 421 E 106th St, MHTN - 10029	110	B7
PS 146 Edward Collins School, 968 Cauldwell Av, BRNX - 10456	6613	B2
PS 147 Isaac Remsen School, 325 Bushwick Av, BKLN - 11206	6822	D5
PS 147 Ronald McNair School, 21801 116th Av, QENS - 11411	6826	E6
PS 148 Queens School, 8902 32nd Av, QENS, 11369	6719	E4
PS 149 Christa McAuliffe School, 9311 34th Av, QENS - 11372	6720	A5
PS 149 Danny Kaye School, 700 Sutter Av, BKLN, 11207	6924	D3
PS 149 Sojourner Truth School, 41 W 117th St, MHTN - 10026	110	A3
PS 150, 334 Greenwich St, MHTN, 10013	118	B5
PS 150 Charles James Fox School, 920 E 167th St, BRNX - 10459	6613	D2
PS 150 Christopher School, 364 Sackman St, BKLN - 11212	6924	B3
PS 150 Queens School, 4001 43rd Av, QENS, 11104	6719	A6
PS 151 Lyndon B Johnson School, 763 Knickerbocker Av - BKLN, 11237	6823	B6
PS 151 Mary D Carter School, 5005 31st Av, QENS - 11377	6719	B4
PS 152 Dyckman Valley School, 93 Nagle Av, MHTN - 10040	104	E1
PS 152 Evergreen School, 1007 Evergreen Av, BRNX - 10472	6613	E2
PS 152 Gwendoline Alleyne School, 3352 62nd St, QENS - 11377	6719	C5
PS 152 School of Science & Technology, 725 E 23rd St - BKLN, 11210	7023	B1
PS 153 Adam Clayton Powell School, 1750 Amsterdam Av - MHTN, 10031	107	A3
PS 153 Helen Keller School, 650 Baychester Av, BRNX - 10475	6505	E2
PS 153 Homecrest School, 1970 Homecrest Av, BKLN - 11229	7023	B5
PS 153 Maspeth Elementary School, 6002 60th Ln - QENS, 11378	6823	C3
PS 154 Jonathan D Hyatt School, 333 E 135th St, BRNX - 10454	110	E1
PS 154 Queens School, 7502 162nd St, QENS, 11366	6825	C2
PS 155 Nicholas Herkimer School, 1355 Herkimer St - BKLN, 11233	6924	B1
PS 155 William Paca School, 319 E 117th St, MHTN - 10035	110	C4
PS 156 Benjamin Banneker School, 750 Concourse Vl W - BRNX, 10451	6613	A2
PS 156 The Laurelton School, 22902 137th Av, QENS - 11413	6927	D2
PS 156 Waverly School, 104 Sutter Av, BKLN, 11212	6924	A3
PS 157 Benjamin Franklin School, 850 Kent Av, BKLN - 11205	6822	B6
PS 157 Grove Hill School, 757 Cauldwell Av, BRNX - 10456	6613	B3
PS 158 Bayard Taylor School, 1458 York Av, MHTN - 10075	113	E5
PS 158 Warwick School, 400 Ashford St, BKLN, 11207	6924	E2
PS 159 Isaac Pitkin School, 2781 Pitkin Av, BKLN, 11208	6925	A2
PS 159 Luis Munoz Marin Biling, 2315 Washington Av - BRNX, 10458	6504	D5
PS 160 Walt Disney School, 4140 Hutchinson River Pkwy E - BRNX, 10475	6506	A4
PS 160 Walter F Bishop School, 10959 Inwood St, QENS - 11435	6825	D7
PS 160 William T Sampson, 5105 Fort Hamilton Pkwy - BKLN, 11219	6922	C7
PS 161 Arthur Ashe School, 10133 124th St, QENS - 11419	6825	A7
PS 161 Pedro Albizu Campos School, 499 W 133rd St - MHTN, 10031	106	D6
PS 161 Ponce de Leon School, 628 Tinton Av, BRNX - 10455	6613	B4
PS 161 The Crown School, 330 Crown St, BKLN, 11225	6923	C3
PS 163 Alfred E Smith School, 163 W 97th St, MHTN - 10025	109	A5
PS 163 Arthur A Schomberg School, 2075 Webster Av - BRNX, 10457	6504	C5
PS 163 Bath Beach School, 1664 Benson Av, BKLN - 11214	7022	B4
PS 163 Flushing Heights School, 15901 59th Av, QENS - 11365	6721	C7
PS 164 Caesar Rodney School, 4211 14th Av, BKLN - 11219	6922	D7
PS 164 Queens Valley School, 13801 77th Av, QENS - 11367	6825	A2
PS 165 Edith K Bergtraum School, 7035 150th St, QENS - 11367	6825	B1
PS 165 Ida Posner School, 76 Lott Av, BKLN, 11212	6924	B4
PS 165 Robert E Simon School, 234 W 109th St, MHTN - 10025	109	B3
PS 166 Henry Gradstein School, 3309 35th Av, QENS - 11106	6718	E4
PS 166 Rogers School Arts Technology, 132 W 89th St - MHTN, 10024	108	E7
PS 167 The Parkway School, 1025 Eastern Pkwy, BKLN - 11213	6923	D3
PS 168, 3050 Webster Av, BRNX, 10467	6504	E3
PS 169 Bay Terrace School, 1825 212th St, QENS, 11360	6722	A1
PS 169M Robert F Kennedy School, 110 E 88th St, MHTN - 10128	113	D2
PS 169 Sunset Park School, 4305 7th Av, BKLN, 11232	6922	B6
PS 170, 1598 Townsend Av, BRNX, 10452	105	C5
PS 170 Lexington School, 7109 6th Av, BKLN, 11209	7022	A1
PS 171 Patrick Henry School, 19 E 103rd St, MHTN - 10029	109	E6
PS 171 Peter G Van Alst School, 1414 29th Av, QENS - 11102	114	D5
PS 172 Beacon School of Excellence, 825 4th Av, BKLN - 11232	6922	B4
PS 173, 306 Fort Washington Av, MHTN, 10033	104	B5
PS 174 Dumont School, 574 Dumont Av, BKLN, 11207	6924	C3
PS 174 William Sidney Mt School, 6510 Dieterle Cres - QENS, 11374	6824	B3
PS 175 City Island School, 200 City Island Av, BRNX - 10464	6506	E6
PS 175 Henry H Garnet School, 175 W 134th St, MHTN - 10030	107	A7
PS 175 Lynne Gross Discovery School, 6435 102nd St - QENS, 11375	6824	C1
PS 176 Cambria Heights School, 12045 235th St, QENS - 11411	6827	A7
PS 176X, 850 Baychester Av, BRNX, 10475	6505	E2
PS 177Q, 5637 188th St, QENS, 11365	6721	E6
PS 177 The Marlboro School, 346 Avenue P, BKLN - 11223	7022	E4
PS 178 Dr Selman Waxsman School, 850 Baychester Av - BRNX, 10475	6505	E2
PS 178 St. Clair McKelway School, 2163 Dean St, BKLN - 11233	6924	A2
PS 179 Kensington School, 202 Avenue C, BKLN, 11218	6922	E7
PS 179 Kensington School, 19625 188th st, QENS, 11365	6721	E6
PS 179 School of International Cultures, 468 E 140th St - BRNX, 10454	6613	A4
PS 180 Homewood School, 5601 16th Av, BKLN, 11204	7022	D2
PS 180 Hugo Newman College Prep School - 370 W 120th St, MHTN, 10026	109	D2
PS 181 Brookfield School, 14815 230th St, QENS, 11413	6927	C4
PS 181 Brooklyn School, 1023 New York Av, BKLN, 11203	6923	C6
PS 182, 601 Stickball Blvd, BRNX, 10473	6614	C3
PS 182 Samantha Smith School, 9036 150th St, QENS - 11435	6825	C5
PS 183 Daniel Chappie James School, 76 Riverdale Av - BKLN, 11212	6924	B4
PS 183 Robert L Stevenson School, 419 E 66th St, MHTN - 10065	113	C7
PS 184 Flushing Manor School, 16315 21st Rd, QENS - 11357	6721	C2
PS 184M Shuang Wen School, 327 Cherry St, MHTN - 10002	119	B7
PS 184 Newport School, 273 Newport St, BKLN, 11212	6924	C4
PS 185 John M Langston School, 20 W 112th St, MHTN - 10026	109	E4
PS 185 Walter Kassenbrock School, 8601 Ridge Blvd - BKLN, 11209	7021	D2
PS 186 Dr Irving A Gladstone, 7601 19th Av, BKLN - 11214	7022	C4
PS 186X Walter J Damrosch School, 750 Jennings St - BRNX, 10459	6613	C1
PS 187 Hudson Cliffs School, 349 Cabrini Blvd, MHTN - 10040	104	C2
PS 188, 760 Grote St, BRNX, 10460	6504	E6
PS 188 Island School, 442 E Houston St, MHTN, 10009	119	D5
PS 188 Michael E Berdy School, 3314 Neptune Av, BKLN - 11224	7120	B1
PS 189, 2580 Amsterdam Av, MHTN, 10040	104	E3
PS 189 Lincoln Terrace School, 1100 E New York Av - BKLN, 11212	6923	E3
PS 190 Sheffield School, 590 Sheffield Av, BKLN, 11207	6924	D4
PS 191 Amsterdam School, 210 W 61st St, MHTN, 10023	112	B5
PS 191 Paul Robeson School, 1600 Park Pl, BKLN, 11233	6923	E2
PS 192 Brooklyn School, 4715 18th Av, BKLN, 11204	7022	E1
PS 192 Jacob High Schiff School, 500 W 138th St, MHTN - 10031	106	E5
PS 193 Alfred J Kennedy School, 15220 11th Av, QENS - 11357	6615	B7
PS 193 Gil Hodges School, 2515 Avenue L, BKLN, 11210	7023	C2
PS 194 Countee Cullen School, 242 W 144th St, MHTN - 10030	107	B5
PS 194 Raoul Wallenberg School, 3117 Avenue W, BKLN - 11229	7023	D6
PS 195, 1250 Ward Av, BRNX, 10472	6613	E1
PS 195 Manhattan Beach School, 131 Irwin St, BKLN - 11235	7121	C1
PS 195 William Haberle School, 25350 149th Av, QENS - 11422	6927	E5
PS 196, 1240 Ward Av, BRNX, 10472	6613	E1
PS 196 Grand Central Parkway School, 7125 113th St - QENS, 11375	6824	E2
PS 196 Ten Eyck School, 207 Bushwick Av, BKLN, 11206	6822	D4
PS 197, 1250 Ward Av, BRNX, 10472	6613	D1
PS 197 Brooklyn School, 1599 E 22nd St, BKLN, 11210	7023	C4
PS 197 John B Russwurm School, 2230 5th Av, MHTN - 10037	107	C7
PS 198, 1180 Tinton Av, BRNX, 10456	6613	C2
PS 198 Brooklyn School, 4105 Farragut Rd, BKLN, 11203	6923	D7
PS 198 Isador E Ida Straus School, 1700 3rd Av, MHTN - 10128	113	E1
PS 199 Frederick Wachtel School, 1100 Elm Av, BKLN - 11230	7023	A3
PS 199 Jesse Isador Strauss, 270 W 70th St, MHTN - 10023	112	C3
PS 199 Maurice A Fitzgerald, 3920 48th Av, QENS - 11104	6718	E7
PS 199X Shakespeare School, 1449 Shakespeare Av - BRNX, 10452	105	A6
PS 200 Benson Elementary School, 1940 Benson Av - BKLN, 11214	7022	B5
PS 200 James Smith School - 2589 Adam Clayton Powell Junior, MHTN, 10039	107	C4
PS 200 Pomonok School, 7010 164th St, QENS, 11365	6825	C1
PS 201 Kissena School, 6511 155th St, QENS, 11367	6721	B7
PS 202 Ernest S Jenkyns School, 982 Hegeman Av, BKLN - 11208	6925	A3
PS 203 Floyd Bennett School, 5101 Avenue M, BKLN - 11234	7023	E2
PS 204 Morris Heights School, 108 W 174th St, BRNX - 10453	105	B5
PS 204 Vince Lombardi School, 8101 15th Av, BKLN - 11228	7022	B3
PS 205 Clarion School, 6701 20th Av, BKLN, 11204	7022	D3
PS 205 Fiorello Laguardia School, 2475 Southern Blvd - BRNX, 10458	6504	E5
PS 206 Horace Harding School, 6121 97th Pl, QENS - 11374	6824	B1
PS 206 Jose Celso Barbosa School, 508 E 120th St - MHTN, 10035	110	D4
PS 206 Joseph F Lamb School, 2200 Gravesend Neck Rd - BKLN, 11229	7023	C6
PS 207, 3030 Godwin Ter, BRNX, 10463	102	D3
PS 207 Elizabeth G Leary School, 4011 Fillmore Av, BKLN - 11234	7023	E3
PS 208 Alaine L Locke School, 21 W 111th St, MHTN - 10026	109	E4
PS 208 Elsa Ebeling School, 4801 Avenue D, BKLN - 11203	6923	E6
PS 209, 313 E 183rd St, BRNX, 10458	6504	C5
PS 209 Clearview Gardens School, 1610 Utopia Pkwy - QENS, 11357	6721	D1
PS 209 Margaret Mead School, 2609 E 7th St, BKLN - 11235	7023	B7
PS 211, 1919 Prospect Av, BRNX, 10457	6504	D7
PS 212, 800 Home St, BRNX, 10456	6613	C2
PS 212, 3425 82nd St, QENS, 11372	6719	E5
PS 212 Lady Deborah Moody School, 87 Bay 49th St - BKLN, 11214	7022	D7
PS 212 Midtown West School, 328 W 48th St, MHTN - 10036	112	B7
PS 213 New Lots School, 580 Hegeman Av, BKLN, 11207	6924	D4
PS 214, 1970 W Farms Rd, BRNX, 10460	6504	E7
PS 214 Cardwallader Colden, 3115 140th St, QENS - 11354	6721	A3
PS 214 Michael Friedsam School, 2944 Pitkin Av, BKLN - 11208	6925	B2
PS 215 Lucretta Mott School, 535 Briar Pl, QENS, 11691	7027	C5
PS 215 Morris H Weiss School, 415 Avenue S, BKLN - 11223	7023	A5
PS 216 Arturo Toscanini School, 350 Avenue X, BKLN - 11223	7023	A7
PS 217 Colonel David Marcus School, 1100 Newkirk Av - BKLN, 11230	7023	A1
PS 218 R Hernandez Dual Language, 1220 Gerard Av - BRNX, 10452	6613	A1
PS 219 Kennedy-King School, 1060 Clarkson Av, BKLN - 11212	6924	A4
PS 219 Paul Klapper School, 14439 Gravett Rd, QENS - 11367	6721	A7
PS 220 Edward Mandel School, 6110 108th St, QENS - 11368	6720	C7
PS 220 Mott Haven Village School, 468 E 140th St, BRNX - 10454	6613	A4
PS 221 Toussaint L Ouverture, 791 Empire Blvd, BKLN - 11213	6923	D3
PS 222 Katherine R Snyder School, 3301 Quentin Rd - BKLN, 11234	7023	D3
PS 224 Hale A Woodruff School, 755 Wortman Av, BKLN - 11208	6925	B3
PS 224Q, 25212 72nd Av, QENS, 11426	6723	B5
PS 226, 1950 Sedgwick Av, BRNX, 10453	105	B2
PS 226 Alfred de B Mason School, 6006 23rd Av, BKLN - 11204	7022	E3
PS 226M, 345 E 15th St, MHTN, 10003	119	C1
PS 228 Early Childcare Center School, 32-65 93rd St - QENS, 11369	6720	A4
PS 229 Dyker School, 1400 Benson Av, BKLN, 11228	7022	A4
PS 229 Emanuel Kaplan School, 6725 51st Rd, QENS - 11377	6823	C1
PS 230 Doris L Cohen School, 1 Albemarle Rd, BKLN - 11218	6922	E6
PS 231K, 5601 16th Av, BKLN, 11204	7022	D2
PS 233 Langston Hughes School, 9301 Avenue B, BKLN - 11236	6924	B5
PS 233Q, 20302 109th Av, QENS, 11412	6826	C4
PS 234, 3015 29th St, QENS, 11102	6719	A3
PS 234 Independence School, 292 Greenwich St, MHTN - 10007	118	B6
PS 235 Lennox School, 525 Lenox Rd, BKLN, 11203	6923	D5
PS 236 Langston Hughes School, 499 E 175th St, BRNX - 10457	6504	C6
PS 236 Mill Basin School, 6302 Avenue U, BKLN, 11234	7024	B3
PS 238 Anne Sullivan School, 1633 E 8th St, BKLN - 11223	7023	A4
PS 239, 1715 Weirfield St, QENS, 11385	6823	C5
PS 241 Emma L Johnston School, 976 President St, BKLN - 11225	6923	B3
PS 241 Family Academy, 240 W 113th St, MHTN, 10026	109	D3
PS 242 LP Stavisky Early Childhood Sch, 29-66 137th St - QENS, 11354	6720	E3
PS 242M G P Brown Computer School, 134 W 122nd St - MHTN, 10027	109	E2
PS 243 Weeksville School, 1580 Dean St, BKLN, 11213	6923	D2
PS 244 Richard R Green School, 5400 Tilden Av, BKLN - 11203	6923	E6
PS 245, 249 E 17th St, BKLN, 11226	6923	A6
PS 245 Elementary School, 2222 Church Av, BKLN - 11226	6923	B5
PS 246 Poe Center School, 2641 Grand Concourse, BRNX - 10468	6504	C3
PS 247 Brooklyn School, 7000 21st Av, BKLN, 11204	7022	D3
PS 249 The Caton School, 18 Marlborough Rd, BKLN - 11226	6923	A5

New York City/5 Borough Points of Interest Index

Schools

FEATURE NAME Address City ZIP Code	MAP#	GRID
PS 250 George H Lindsay School, 108 Montrose Av - BKLN, 11206	6822	C4
PS 251 Paedergat School, 1037 E 54th St, BKLN, 11234	7024	A1
PS 251 Queens School, 14451 Arthur St, QENS, 11413	6927	C3
PS 253, 601 Ocean View Av, BKLN, 11235	7121	B1
PS 253, 1307 Central Av, QENS, 11691	7027	D4
PS 254 Dag Hammarskjold School, 1801 Avenue Y, BKLN - 11235	7023	C6
PS 255 Barbara Reing School, 1866 E 17th St, BKLN - 11229	7023	B5
PS 255Q, 15840 76th Rd, QENS, 11366	6825	C2
PS 256 Benjamin Banneker Elementary School - 114 Kosciusko St, BKLN, 11216	6822	C7
PS 257 John F Hylan School, 60 Cook St, BKLN, 11206	6822	D5
PS 260 Breuckelen School, 875 Williams Av, BKLN, 11207	6924	D5
PS 261 Philip Livingston School, 314 Pacific St, BKLN - 11201	121	B7
PS 262 El Hajj Malik Shabazz School, 500 Macon St - BKLN, 11233	6923	E1
PS 268 Emma Lazarus School, 133 E 53rd St, BKLN - 11203	6923	E4
PS 268Q, 9207 175th St, QENS, 11433	6825	E4
PS 269 Nostrand School, 1957 Nostrand Av, BKLN, 11210	6923	C7
PS 270 Johann DeKalb School, 241 Emerson Pl, BKLN - 11205	6822	B6
PS 273 Wortman School, 923 Jerome St, BKLN, 11207	6924	E4
PS 274 Kosciusko School, 800 Bushwick Av, BKLN, 11221	6822	E6
PS 276 Louis Marshall School, 1070 E 83rd St, BKLN - 11236	6924	B7
PS 277, 519 St. Anns Av, BRNX, 10455	6613	B4
PS 277 Gerritsen Beach School, 2529 Gerritsen Av, BKLN - 11234	7023	E6
PS 279 Capt Manuel Rivera Junior, 2100 Walton Av - BRNX, 10453	105	D3
PS 279 Herman Schreiber School, 1070 E 104th St, BKLN - 11236	6924	D6
PS 280 Mosholu Parkway School, 3202 Steuben Av - BRNX, 10467	6504	E2
PS 282 Park Slope School, 180 6th Av, BKLN, 11217	6922	E2
PS 284 Lew Wallace School, 220 Watkins St, BKLN - 11212	6924	B3
PS 287 Bailey K Ashford School, 50 Navy St, BKLN - 11201	121	C4
PS 288 Shirley Tanyhill School, 2950 W 25th St, BKLN - 11224	7120	C2
PS 289 George V Brower School, 900 St. Marks Av, BKLN - 11213	6923	D2
PS 290 Juan Morel Campos School, 135 Schenck Av - BKLN, 11207	6924	D1
PS 290 Manhattan New School, 311 E 82nd St, MHTN - 10028	113	D3
PS 291, 2195 Andrews Av, BRNX, 10453	105	C1
PS 295, 330 18th St, BKLN, 11215	6922	D4
PS 297 Abraham Stockton School, 700 Park Av, BKLN - 11206	6822	C6
PS 298 Dr Betty Shabazz School, 85 Watkins St, BKLN - 11212	6924	B2
PS 299 Thomas Warren Field, 88 Woodbine St, BKLN - 11221	6823	A7
PS 304 Casimir Pulaski School, 280 Hart St, BKLN, 11206	6822	D6
PS 304 Early Childhood School, 2750 Lafayette Av, BRNX - 10465	6614	E2
PS 305 Dr Peter Ray School, 344 Monroe St, BKLN - 11216	6822	C7
PS 306, 40 W Tremont Av, BRNX, 10453	105	C3
PS 306 Ethan Allen School, 970 Vermont St, BKLN, 11207	6924	D4
PS 307 Daniel Hale Williams, 209 York St, BKLN, 11201	121	C3
PS 308 Clara Cardwell School, 616 Quincy St, BKLN - 11221	6822	D7
PS 309 George E Webican School, 794 Monroe St, BKLN - 11221	6822	E7
PS 310 Marble Hill School, 260 W Kingsbridge Rd, BRNX - 10463	102	D5
PS 312 Bergen Beach School, 7103 Avenue T, BKLN - 11234	7024	B2
PS 315, 2310 Glenwood Rd, BKLN, 11210	7023	B1
PS 315 Lab School, 2246 Jerome Av, BRNX, 10453	105	E2
PS 316 Elijah Stroud School, 750 Classon Av, BKLN - 11238	6923	B2
PS 319, 360 Keap St, BKLN, 11211	6822	B4
PS 321 William Penn School, 180 7th Av, BKLN, 11215	6922	E2
PS 326, 1800 Utica Av, BKLN, 11234	7023	E1
PS 327 Dr Rose B English School, 111 Bristol St, BKLN - 11212	6924	B3
PS 328 Phyllis Wheatley School, 330 Alabama Av, BKLN - 11207	6924	C3
PS 329 Surfside School, 2929 W 30th St, BKLN, 11224	7120	C2
PS 332 Charles H Houston School, 51 Christopher Av - BKLN, 11212	6924	B2
PS 333 Manhattan School for Child, 154 W 93rd St - MHTN, 10025	109	A6
PS 335 Granville T Woods School, 130 Rochester Av - BKLN, 11213	6923	E2
PS 340, 25 W 195th St, BRNX, 10468	6504	C3
PS 345 Patrolman Robert Bolden School - 111 Berriman St, BKLN, 11208	6924	E2
PS 346 ABE Stark School, 1400 Pennsylvania Av, BKLN - 11239	6924	E6
PS 360, 2880 Kingsbridge Ter, BRNX, 10463	102	E4
PS 361, 3109 Newkirk Av, BKLN, 11226	6923	C7
PS 368K, 70 Tompkins Av, BKLN, 11206	6822	C6
PS 369K Coy L Cox School, 383 State St, BKLN, 11217	121	C7
PS 370, 3000 W 1st St, BKLN, 11224	7121	A1
PS 371 Lillian L Rashkis School, 355 37th St, BKLN - 11232	6922	B5
PS 372 Children's School, 512 Carroll St, BKLN, 11215	6922	D2
PS 373 Brooklyn Transition Center, 185 Ellery St, BKLN - 11206	6822	C6
PS 373R, 91 Henderson Av, STNL, 10301	6920	B7
PS 375 Jackie Robinson School, 46 McKeever Pl, BKLN - 11225	6923	B3
PS 376, 194 Harman St, BKLN, 11237	6823	A6
PS 377 Alejandrina B Degautier, 200 Woodbine St, BKLN - 11221	6823	A6
PS 380 John Wayne Elementary School, 370 Marcy Av - BKLN, 11206	6822	B5
PS 396, 1930 Andrews Av, BRNX, 10453	105	C3
PS 396K, 110 Chester St, BKLN, 11212	6924	B3
PS 397 Foster Laurie School, 490 Fenimore St, BKLN - 11203	6923	C4
PS 398 Walter Weaver School, 60 E 94th St, BKLN, 11212	6923	E4
PS 399 Stanley Eugene Clark, 2707 Albemarle Rd, BKLN - 11226	6923	C6
PS 499 Queens Coll Sch for Math, Sci & Tech - 14820 Reeves Av, QENS, 11367	6721	A7
PS 505 Journ Technolgy, 330 59th St, BKLN, 11220	6921	E6
PS 721, 64 Avenue X, BKLN, 11223	7022	D7
PS 721 Man Occupational Training Center - 250 W Houston St, MHTN, 10014	118	C2
PS 721 Queens Occupational Training Center - 5712 94th St, QENS, 11373	6720	A7

FEATURE NAME Address City ZIP Code	MAP#	GRID
PS 721 Staten Island Occal Training Ctr, 155 Tompkins Av - STNL, 10304	7020	D2
PS 721X Stephen McSweeney School - 2697 Westchester Av, BRNX, 10461	6505	D6
PS 753K School for Career Development - 510 Clermont Av, BKLN, 11238	6923	A1
PS 811K Connie Lekas School, 2525 Haring St, BKLN - 11235	7023	D6
PS 811M Mickey Mantle School, 466 W End Av, MHTN - 10024	108	D7
PS 811Q, 6125 Marathon Pkwy, QENS, 11362	6723	A4
PS 811X, 1434 Longfellow Av, BRNX, 10459	6613	D1
PS 993Q, 8515 258th St, QENS, 11001	6827	C1
PS 210 21st Century Academy, 4111 Broadway, MHTN - 10033	104	B5
PS-IS 54, 2703 Webster Av, BRNX, 10458	6504	D4
PS-IS 104 The Fort Hamilton School, 9115 5th Av, BKLN - 11209	7021	E3
PS-IS 208, 7430 Commonwealth Blvd, QENS, 11426	6723	A6
PS-IS 217 Roosevelt Islands, 645 Main St, MHTN, 10044	113	E7
PS-IS 224, 345 Brook Av, BRNX, 10454	6613	A4
PS-IS 270Q, 23315 Merrick Blvd, QENS, 11422	6927	E2
PS-IS 323, 210 Chester St, BKLN, 11212	6924	B3
PS-IS 384 Frances E Carter School, 242 Cooper St, BKLN - 11207	6823	C7
PS K225 Eileen E Zaglin School, 1075 Ocean View Av - BKLN, 11235	7121	B1
PS K771, 1075 Ocean View Av, BKLN, 11235	7121	B1
PS-MS 004 Crotona Park West School, 1701 Fulton Av - BRNX, 10457	6504	C7
PS-MS 029 Melrose School, 758 Courtlandt Av, BRNX - 10451	6613	A3
PS-MS 031 William L Garrison School - 250 Thurman Munson Wy, BRNX, 10451	6613	A2
PS-MS 194, 1301 Zerega Av, BRNX, 10462	6614	D1
PS-MS 278, 421 W 219th St, MHTN, 10034	102	C5
Purchase Elementary School, 2995 Purchase St, HRSN - 10577	6051	B6
Quaker Ridge Elementary School, 125 Weaver St, SCDL - 10583	6282	A4
Queen of All Saints School, 300 Vanderbilt Av, BKLN - 11205	6822	A7
Queen of Angels School, 44 Irvine Turner Blvd, NWRK - 07103	6817	C1
Queens School of Inquiry, The, 15840 76th Rd, QENS - 11366	6825	B2
Queens Academy High School, 13811 35th Av, QENS - 11354	6720	E3
Queens Center for Progress, 8225 164th St, QENS - 11432	6825	C3
Queens Gateway to Health Sci Secondary Sch - 150-91 87th Rd, QENS, 11432	6825	B4
Queens HS for the Sciences at York College - 9450 159th St, QENS, 11433	6825	D5
Queens Lutheran School, 3120 21st Av, QENS, 11105	6719	B2
Queens Preparatory Academy, 14310 Springfield Blvd - QENS, 11413	6927	C3
Queens School Career Development, 142-10 Linden Blvd - QENS, 11436	6926	D1
Queens Vocational & Technical High School - 3702 47th Av, QENS, 11101	6718	E7
Quitman Avenue School, 21 Quitman St, NWRK, 07103	6817	C1
Rabbi Harry Halpern Day School, 1256 E 21st St, BKLN - 11210	7023	B2
Rabbi Jacob Joseph School, 400 Caswell Av, STNL - 10314	7019	B3
Rachel Carson HS for Coastal Studies, 521 West Av - BKLN, 11224	7120	E1
Rafael Cordero Bilingual Academy, 2351 1st Av, MHTN - 10035	110	C4
Rafael Hernandez School, 345 Broadway, NWRK, 07104	6713	E4
Ralph McKee Vocational High School, 290 St. Marks Pl - STNL, 10301	6920	D6
Ralph S Maugham Elementary School, 111 Magnolia Av - TFLY, 07670	6392	B2
Ramaz Lower School, 125 E 85th St, MHTN, 10028	113	D2
Ramez Middle School, 114 E 85th St, MHTN, 10028	113	C2
Rauch Chaim School, 2818 Avenue K, BKLN, 11210	7023	C2
Razi School, 5511 Queens Blvd, QENS, 11377	6719	B6
Redeemer Lutheran School, 6926 Cooper Av, QENS - 11385	6823	E5
Regent School, 719 E 216th St, BRNX, 10467	6505	B1
Regina Pacis School, 1201 66th St, BKLN, 11219	7022	B1
Regional Day School, 425 Johnston Av, JSYC, 07304	6820	A3
Regis High School, 55 E 84th St, MHTN, 10028	113	C2
Reisenbach Charter School, 257 W 117th St, MHTN - 10026	109	D2
Renaissance Charter School, 3559 81st St, QENS, 11372	6719	D5
Repertory Co High School for Theater Arts - 123 W 43rd St, MHTN, 10036	116	C2
Resurrection-Ascension School, 8525 61st Rd, QENS - 11374	6824	A2
Resurrection Grammar School, 116 Milton Rd, RYE - 10580	6283	E2
Resurrection School-Brunswick, 189 Brunswick St, JSYC - 07302	6820	B2
Resurrection School-St. Bridget, 372 Montgomery St - JSYC, 07302	6820	B3
Rhame Avenue Elementary School, 100 Rhame Av - ERKY, 11518	6929	C7
Rice High School, 74 W 124th St, MHTN, 10027	110	A2
Richard J Bailey Elementary School, 33 Hillside Av S - GrbT, 10607	6049	D7
Richard J Bailey Elementary School, 33 Hillside Ter - WHPL, 10601	6168	A1
Richard R Green High School of Teaching, 421 E 88th St - MHTN, 10128	114	A3
Rich Street Early Childhood School, 13 Arlington Av - NWRK, 07104	6713	E3
Ridgefield Memorial High School, 555 Walnut St, RDGF - 07657	6611	C1
Ridgefield Park Junior Senior High School - 1 Ozzie Nelson Dr, RDFP, 07660	6502	A4
Ridge Street Elementary School, 735 Ridge St, NWRK - 07104	6713	E2
Ridgeway Elementary School, 225 Ridgeway, WHPL - 10605	6168	C5
Rimbam High School, 15 Frost Ln, LWRN, 11559	7028	A3
Riverdale Country School, 5250 Fieldston Rd, BRNX - 10471	6393	C6
Riverdale Kingsbridge Academy, 660 W 237th St, BRNX - 10463	6393	B7
River East School, 508 E 120th St, MHTN, 10035	110	D4
Riverside Elementary School, 110 Riverside Dr, RKVC - 11570	6929	D5
Riverside High School, 565 Warburton Av, YNKR, 10701	6279	C5
Robert C Dodson School, 105 Avondale Rd, YNKR, 10710	6280	E4
Robert E Peary School, 1666 Hancock St, QENS, 11385	6823	C6
Robert F Kenndy Middle School, 15840 76th Rd, QENS - 11366	6825	C2
Robert F Kennedy Community High School - 7540 Parsons Blvd, QENS, 11367	6825	B2

Schools

FEATURE NAME Address City ZIP Code	MAP#	GRID
Robert Fulton Elementary School 02, 7407 Hudson Av - NBgT, 07047	6611	B6
Robert Fulton School Annex, 7111 Polk St, NBgT, 07047	6611	A6
RF Wagner Jr Secnd Sch for Arts & Tech, 4707 30th Pl - QENS, 11101	6718	D7
Robert L Craig Elementary School, 20 W Park St, MNCH - 07074	6501	B7
Robert N Wilentz School, 51 1st St, PTHA, 08861	7205	D5
Roberto Clemente Elementary School, 257 Summer Av - NWRK, 07104	6713	E4
Robert Treat Academy Charter School, 443 Clifton Av - NWRK, 07104	6713	D3
Robert Waters Elementary School, 2800 Summit Av - UNCT, 07087	6716	D2
Robert W Carbonaro School, 50 Hungry Harbor Rd, HmpT - 11581	6928	C5
Robinson Elementary School 3, 95 W 31st St, BAYN - 07002	6919	E2
Rodeph Sholom Day School, 10 W 84th St, MHTN - 10024	113	A1
Ronald Reagan School 30, 730 Pennsylvania Av, ELIZ - 07208	6918	A1
Roosevelt Elementary School, 43 Schuyler Av, KRNY - 07032	6714	D2
Roosevelt Elementary School, 435 Passaic Av, LODI - 07644	6500	C2
Roosevelt Elementary School, 508 Teaneck Rd, RDFP - 07660	6502	A4
Roosevelt Elementary School, 4507 Hudson Av, UNCT - 07087	6716	E2
Roosevelt Elementary School 7, 225 Lincoln Pl, GRFD - 07026	6500	B2
Roosevelt High School, 631 Tuckahoe Rd, YNKR, 10710	6280	D5
Roosevelt Middle School, 36 Gilbert Pl, WOrT, 07052	6712	A3
Roosevelt School 17, 650 Bayway Av, ELIZ, 07202	6917	E6
Rosemarie Ann Siragusa School 14, 60 Crescent Pl - YNKR, 10704	6394	C3
Roseville Avenue Elementary School, 70 Roseville Av - NWRK, 07107	6713	B5
Roslyn Heights Primary School, 240 Willow St, NHmT - 11577	6618	E7
Roslyn High School, 475 Round Hill Rd, EHLS, 11577	6618	E7
Ross Global Academy Charter School, 52 Chambers St - MHTN, 10007	118	C7
Ross Street Elementary School 11, 110 Ross St, WbgT - 07095	7114	C4
RT Hudson Elementary School, 1122 Forest Av, BRNX - 10456	6613	C2
Rudolf Steiner School, 15 E 79th St, MHTN, 10075	113	B3
Rutherford High School, 56 Elliott Pl, RTFD, 07070	6609	A2
Rye High School, 1 Parsons St, RYE, 10580	6283	E3
Rye Lake School Campus, 1606 Old Orchard St, HRSN - 10604	6050	D2
Rye Middle School, 3 Parsons St, RYE, 10580	6283	E3
Rye Neck High School, 300 Hornidge Rd, MRNK, 10543	6283	B5
Rye Neck Middle School, 300 Hornidge Rd, MRNK, 10543	6283	B5
Ryer Avenue Elementary School, 230 E 183rd St, BRNX - 10457	6504	C5
Sacred Heart High School, 34 Convent Av, YNKR, 10703	6279	D6
Sacred Heart Lower School, 34 Convent Av, YNKR - 10703	6279	D6
Sacred Heart Middle School, 1248 Nelson Av, BRNX - 10452	104	E7
Sacred Heart Primary School, 95 W 168th St, BRNX - 10452	104	E7
Sacred Heart Private School, 1651 Zerega Av, BRNX - 10462	6505	C7
Sacred Heart R C School, 11550 221st St, QENS, 11411	6826	E6
Sacred Heart School, 59 Wilson St, GrbT, 10530	6167	D3
Sacred Heart School, 183 Bayview Av, JSYC, 07305	6819	D4
Sacred Heart School, 22 Wilson Av, KRNY, 07032	6714	A4
Sacred Heart School, 71T Sharp Blvd, MTVN, 10550	6394	E4
Sacred Heart School, 24 Hazelwood Av, NWRK, 07106	6712	C6
Sacred Heart School, 21601 38th Av, QENS, 11361	6722	B3
Sacred Heart School, 8405 78th Av, QENS, 11385	6824	B5
Sacred Heart School, 301 N Burgher Av, STNL, 10310	7020	A1
Sacred Heart School of Jesus, 456 W 52nd St, MHTN - 10019	112	B6
Saddle Rock Elementary School, 10 Hawthorne Ln - NHmT, 11023	6616	D7
St. Adalbert School, 5217 83rd St, QENS, 11373	6823	E1
St. Adalbert School, 355 Morningstar Rd, STNL, 10303	7019	B1
St. Agatha School, 736 48th St, BKLN, 11220	6922	B6
St. Agnes Academic High School, 1320 124th St, QENS - 11356	6614	D7
St. Agnes Boys High School, 555 W End Av, MHTN - 10024	108	D6
St. Agnes Cathedral School, 70 Clinton Av, RKVC, 11570	6929	E4
St. Aidan School, 510 Willis Av, WLPK, 11596	6724	E4
St. Aloysius Elementary School, 721 W Side Av, JSYC - 07306	6819	D2
St. Aloysius High School, 721 W Side Av, JSYC, 07306	6819	D2
St. Aloysius School, 223 W 132nd St, MHTN, 10027	107	A7
St. Aloysius School, 3-60 Seneca Av, QENS, 11385	6823	A4
St. Anastasia School, 4511 245th St, QENS, 11362	6722	E3
St. Andrew Avellino School, 3550 158th St, QENS, 11354	6721	C3
St. Andrew School, 126 Broadway, BAYN, 07002	6919	D5
St. Angela Merici School, 266 E 163rd St, BRNX, 10451	6613	A2
St. Anne School, 255 Congress St, JSYC, 07032	6716	B5
St. Anne's School, 25 Dartmouth St, GDNC, 11530	6828	A3
St. Ann School, 3511 Bainbridge Av, BRNX, 10467	6504	E1
St. Ann School, 314 E 110th St, MHTN, 10029	110	B6
St. Ann School, 14245 58th Rd, QENS, 11355	6721	A6
St. Ann School, 125 Cromwell Av, STNL, 10304	7020	B6
St. Ann School, 40 Brewster Av, YNKR, 10701	6394	B1
St. Ann's School, 129 Pierrepont St, BKLN, 11201	121	A5
St. Anselm School, 365 83rd St, BKLN, 11209	7021	E2
St. Anselm School, 685 Tinton Av, BRNX, 10455	6613	B3
St. Anthony High School, 175 8th St, JSYC, 07302	6820	C2
St. Anthony of Padua School, 45 Gainsborg Av E, HRSN - 10604	6168	D1
St. Anthony of Padua School, 12518 Rockaway Blvd - QENS, 11420	6926	B2
St. Anthony-St. Alphonsus School, 725 Leonard St, BKLN - 11222	6822	B1
St. Anthony School, 1776 Mansion St, BRNX, 10460	6505	A7
St. Anthony School, 4520 Matilda Av, BRNX, 10470	6394	C6
St. Anthony School, 227 Center St, ELIZ, 07202	6918	A4
St. Anthony School, 1395 Nepperhan Av, YNKR, 10703	6280	A3
St. Athanasius School, 6120 Bay Pkwy, BKLN, 11204	7022	E3
St. Athanasius School, 830 Southern Blvd, BRNX, 10459	6613	C3
St. Augustine School, 1176 Franklin Av, BRNX, 10456	6613	C2
St. Augustine School, 3920 New York Av, UNCT, 07087	6716	E2
St. Barnabas High School, 425 E 240th St, BRNX, 10470	6394	B6
St. Barnabas School, 413 E 241st St, YNKR, 10704	6394	B5
St. Bartholomew School, 4415 Judge St, QENS, 11373	6719	E6
St. Bartholomew School, 278 Saw Mill River Rd, YNKR - 10701	6279	E6
St. Benedict Joseph Labre School, 94-25 117th St, QENS - 11419	6824	E6
St. Benedict Preparatory School - 520 Martin Luther King Junior B, NWRK, 07102	6713	D7

Schools

New York City/5 Borough Points of Interest Index

Schools

FEATURE NAME Address City ZIP Code	MAP#	GRID
St. Benedict School, 1016 Edison Av, BRNX, 10465	6615	A1
St. Bernadette School, 1313 83rd St, BKLN, 11228	7022	A3
St. Bernard School, 2030 E 69th St, BKLN, 11234	7024	B2
St. Bernards School, 4 E 98th St, MHTN, 10029	109	D7
St. Brendan School, 268 E 207th St, BRNX, 10467	6504	E2
St. Brigid School, 438 Grove St, BKLN, 11237	6823	B5
St. Brigid School, 185 E 7th St, MHTN, 10009	119	D3
St. Camillus School, 185 Beach 99th St, QENS, 11694	7026	A7
St. Casimir School, 259 Nepperhan Av, YNKR, 10701	6393	D1
St. Catharine Academy, 2250 Williamsbridge Rd, BRNX - 10469	6505	B4
St. Catherine of Genoa School, 870 Albany Av, BKLN - 11203	6923	D5
St. Catherine of Genoa School, 508 W 153rd St, MHTN - 10031	107	A2
St. Catherine of Sienna School, 990 Holzheimer St, HmpT - 11010	6828	A4
St. Catherine of Sienna School, 11834 Riverton St, QENS - 11412	6826	B7
St. Catherine-St. George School, 2230 33rd St, QENS - 11105	6719	B2
St. Cecilia School, 15 Monitor St, BKLN, 11222	6822	D3
St. Charles Borromeo School, 23 Sidney Pl, BKLN, 11201	121	A5
St. Charles Borromeo School, 214 W 142nd St, MHTN - 10030	107	B5
St. Charles School, 200 Penn Av, STNL, 10306	7117	E3
St. Christopher School, 15 Lisbon Pl, STNL, 10306	7118	A1
St. Clare School, 1911 Hone Av, BRNX, 10461	6505	B6
St. Clare School, 13725 Brookville Blvd, QENS, 11422	6927	E3
St. Clare School, 151 Lindenwood Rd, STNL, 10308	7117	B6
St. Davids School, 12 E 89th St, MHTN, 10128	113	C1
St. Demetrios School, 3003 30th Dr, QENS, 11102	6719	A3
St. Dominic Academy, 2572 John F Kennedy Blvd, JSYC - 07304	6819	E2
St. Edmund Preparatory High School, 2474 Ocean Av - BKLN, 11229	7023	C5
St. Edmund School, 1902 Avenue T, BKLN, 11229	7023	C5
St. Elizabeth School, 612 W 187th St, MHTN, 10033	104	D3
St. Elizabeth School, 9401 85th St, QENS, 11416	6824	C7
St. Elizabeth Seton School, 751 Knickerbocker Av, BKLN - 11237	6823	B6
St. Ephrem School, 7415 Fort Hamilton Pkwy, BKLN - 11228	7022	A2
St. Eugene School, 707 Tuckahoe Rd, YNKR, 10710	6280	D6
St. Fidelis School, 12406 14th Av, QENS, 11356	6720	D1
St. Finbar School, 1825 Bath Av, BKLN, 11214	7022	B5
St. Fortunata School, 2635 Linden Blvd, BKLN, 11208	6925	A3
St. Frances Cabrini School, 181 Suydam St, BKLN, 11221	6822	E5
St. Frances de Chantal School, 2962 Harding Av, BRNX - 10465	6615	B3
St. Frances of Rome School, 4321 Barnes Av, BRNX - 10466	6394	C6
St. Francis Academy, 1601 Central Av, UNCT, 07087	6716	C4
St. Francis de Sales-St. Lucy, 116 E 97th St, MHTN - 10029	109	E7
St. Francis de Sales School, 219 Beach 129th St, QENS - 11694	7123	C1
St. Francis de Sales School-Deaf, 260 Eastern Pkwy - BKLN, 11225	6923	B2
St. Francis of Assisi School, 400 Lincoln Rd, BKLN, 11225	6923	C4
St. Francis of Assisi School, 4300 Baychester Av, BRNX - 10466	6394	D6
St. Francis of Assisi School, 2118 46th St, QENS, 11105	6719	C2
St. Francis of Assisi School, 110 Mt Vernon St, RDFP - 07660	6501	E5
St. Francis Preparatory School, 6100 Francis Lewis Blvd - QENS, 11365	6722	A7
St. Francis School, 100 S Main St, HKSK, 07601	6501	C2
St. Francis Xavier School, 763 President St, BKLN, 11215	6922	E2
St. Francis Xavier School, 1711 Haight Av, BRNX, 10461	6505	C6
St. Francis Xavier School, 594 N 7th St, NWRK, 07107	6713	C3
St. Gabriel School, 590 W 235th St, BRNX, 10463	102	C1
St. Gabriel School, 97th St & Astoria Blvd, QENS, 11369	6720	A4
St. Gabriels High School, 24 Shea Pl, NRCH, 10801	6395	E5
St. Genevieve School, 209 Princeton Rd, ELIZ, 07208	6917	B3
St. George Academy High School, 215 E 6th St, MHTN - 10003	119	B2
St. Gerard Majella School, 18816 91st Av, QENS, 11423	6826	B4
St. Gregory the Great School, 991 St. Johns Pl, BKLN - 11213	6923	C2
St. Gregory the Great School, 138 W 90th St, MHTN - 10024	108	E7
St. Gregory the Great School, 24444 87th Av, QENS - 11426	6827	B1
St. Helena School, 2050 Benedict Av, BRNX, 10462	6614	C1
St. Helen School, 8309 157th Av, QENS, 11414	6925	C4
St. Ignatius Loyola School, 48 E 84th St, MHTN, 10028	113	C3
St. James Catholic School, 341 Amboy Av, WbgT, 07095	7114	C5
St. James School, 37 St. James Pl, MHTN, 10038	118	E7
St. Jean Baptiste High School, 173 E 75th St, MHTN - 10021	113	C4
St. Jerome School, 465 E 29th St, BKLN, 11226	6923	C7
St. Jerome School, 222 Alexander Av, BRNX, 10454	110	E1
St. Joan of Arc School, 3527 82nd St, QENS, 11372	6719	E5
St. John Chrysostom School, 1144 Hoe Av, BRNX, 10459	6613	D2
St. John Lutheran School, 12307 22nd Av, QENS, 11356	6720	D1
St. John Lutheran School, 8824 Myrtle Av, QENS, 11385	6824	B5
St. John School, 3143 Kingsbridge Av, BRNX, 10463	102	D2
St. John School, 455 White St, COrT, 07050	6712	C2
St. John School, 260 Harrison St, LEON, 07605	6502	D3
St. John's Lutheran School, 663 Manor Rd, STNL, 10314	7019	E4
St. Johns Preparatory School, 2121 Crescent St, QENS - 11105	6719	B1
St. John the Baptist School, 82 Lewis Av, BKLN, 11206	6822	D6
St. John the Baptist School, 670 Yonkers Av, YNKR - 10704	6394	A2
St. John Vianney School, 2141 Seward Av, BRNX, 10473	6614	C3
St. John Villa Academy, 57 Cleveland Pl, STNL, 10305	7020	E5
St. John Villa Academy High School, 26 Landis Av, STNL - 10305	7020	E5
St. Joseph & Dominic Academy, 140 Montrose Av, BKLN - 11206	6822	C4
St. Joseph By the Sea High School, 5150 Hylan Blvd - STNL, 10312	7207	D1
St. Joseph High School, 80 Willoughby St, BKLN, 11201	121	C6
St. Joseph Hill Academy High School, 850 Hylan Blvd - STNL, 10305	7020	E5
St. Joseph Hill Lower Academy, 850 Hylan Blvd, STNL - 10305	7020	E5
St. Joseph-Holy Family School, 168 Morningside Av - MHTN, 10027	106	D7
St. Joseph In Greenwich Village, 111 Washington Pl - MHTN, 10014	118	D1
St. Joseph of the Palisades Elem School - 6408 Palisade Av, WNYK, 07093	6611	A7
St. Joseph of the Palisades High School, 5400 Broadway - WNYK, 07093	111	B1
St. Joseph Parochial School, 139 St. Marys Av, STNL - 10305	7020	E3
St. Joseph-St. Thomas School, 50 Maguire Av, STNL - 10309	7206	E1
St. Joseph School, 131 E Fort Lee Rd, BGTA, 07603	6501	E2

FEATURE NAME Address City ZIP Code	MAP#	GRID
St. Joseph School, 1946 Bathgate Av, BRNX, 10457	6504	C6
St. Joseph School, 30 Meadow Av, BRXV, 10708	6280	E7
St. Joseph School, 865 Roosevelt Av, CART, 07008	7017	C6
St. Joseph School, 115 Telford St, EORG, 07018	6712	D5
St. Joseph School, 20 Hackensack St, ERTH, 07073	6609	C1
St. Joseph School, 509 Pavonia Av, JSYC, 07306	6820	A1
St. Joseph School, 1 Monroe St, MHTN, 10002	118	E7
St. Joseph School, 2846 44th St, QENS, 11103	6719	B4
St. Joseph School for the Deaf - 1000 Hutchinson River Pkwy, BRNX, 10465	6614	E2
St. Joseph's Parish Day School, 21755 100th Av, QENS - 11429	6826	E3
St. Joseph's School-Yorkville, 420 E 87th St, MHTN - 10028	113	E3
St. Jude School, 433 W 204th St, MHTN, 10034	102	A7
St. Kevin School, 4550 195th St, QENS, 11358	6721	E5
St. Leo-Sacred Heart School, 123 Myrtle Av, IrvT, 07111	6816	D1
St. Leo School, 10419 49th Av, QENS, 11368	6720	B6
St. Lucy School, 830 Mace Av, BRNX, 10467	6505	B4
St. Lucy School, 12 Amity Pl, NWRK, 07104	6713	D5
St. Luke School, 608 E 139th St, BRNX, 10454	6613	A5
St. Luke School, 1601 150th Pl, QENS, 11357	6615	B7
St. Lukes School, 487 Hudson St, MHTN, 10014	118	C1
St. Margaret Mary School, 121 E 177th St, BRNX, 10453	105	D4
St. Margaret Mary School, 556 Lincoln Av, STNL, 10306	7118	C2
St. Margaret of Cortona School, 452 W 260th St, BRNX - 10471	6393	C5
St. Margaret School, 6610 80th St, QENS, 11379	6824	A3
St. Mark School, 2602 E 19th St, BKLN, 11235	7023	C7
St. Mark's Day School, 1346 President St, BKLN, 11213	6923	C3
St. Mark's Lutheran School, 626 Bushwick Av, BKLN - 11206	6822	D6
St. Mark's Lutheran School, 7 St. Marks Pl, YNKR, 10704	6394	A5
St. Mark the Evangelist School, 55 W 138th St, MHTN - 10037	107	C6
St. Martin of Tours School, 695 E 182nd St, BRNX, 10457	6504	D6
St. Mary Assumption Elementary School, 237 S Broad St - ELIZ, 07202	6917	E4
St. Mary Elementary School, 1340 Northern Blvd, NHmT - 11030	6617	D7
St. Mary Gate of Heaven School, 10406 101st Av, QENS - 11416	6824	D7
St. Mary High School, 209 3rd St, JSYC, 07302	6820	C2
St. Mary High School, 64 Chestnut St, RTFD, 07070	6609	A1
St. Mary Mother of Jesus School, 8401 23rd Av, BKLN - 11214	7022	D5
St. Mary of the Assumption High School, 237 S Broad St - ELIZ, 07202	6917	D4
St. Mary School, 180 William St, BlvT, 07109	6714	A1
St. Mary School, 3956 Carpenter Av, BRNX, 10466	6394	B7
St. Mary School, 180 William St, NWRK, 07103	6817	C1
St. Mary School, 72 Chestnut St, RTFD, 07070	6609	A2
St. Mary School, 301 2nd St, SAMB, 08879	7205	C7
St. Mary School, 1124 Bay St, STNL, 10305	7020	E3
St. Mary School, 15 St. Marys St, YNKR, 10701	6393	C2
St. Mary's High School, 51 Clapham Av, NHmT, 11030	6617	D7
St. Mary's Park Institute, 2213 E Tremont Av, BRNX - 10462	6505	B7
St. Mary Star of the Sea School, 19 W 13th St, BAYN - 07002	6919	D4
St. Mary Star of the Sea School, 580 Minnieford Av - BRNX, 10464	6506	E5
St. Mary Star of the Sea School, 595 Beach 19th St - QENS, 11691	7027	D5
St. Matthew School, 16 Villard Av, HAOH, 10706	6165	E6
St. Matthias School, 5825 Catalpa Av, QENS, 11385	6823	C5
St. Mel School, 15424 26th Av, QENS, 11354	6721	C2
St. Michael Academy, 425 W 33rd St, MHTN, 10001	115	E3
St. Michael School, 237 Jerome St, BKLN, 11207	6924	D2
St. Michael School, 27 Crittenden St, NWRK, 07104	6713	D5
St. Michael's School, 13658 41st Av, QENS, 11355	6720	E4
St. Nicholas of Tolentine School, 2336 Andrews Av - BRNX, 10468	105	D1
St. Nicholas of Tolentine School, 8022 Parsons Blvd - QENS, 11432	6825	C3
St. Nicholas School, 287 Powers St, BKLN, 11211	6822	D4
St. Nicholas School, 118 Ferry St, JSYC, 07032	6716	B7
St. Pancras School, 6820 Myrtle Av, QENS, 11385	6823	E5
St. Patrick High School, 221 Court St, ELIZ, 07206	6918	C5
St. Patrick Old Cathedral School, 233 Mott St, MHTN - 10012	118	E4
St. Patrick School, 401 97th St, BKLN, 11209	7021	D3
St. Patrick School, 509 Bramhall Av, JSYC, 07304	6819	E3
St. Patrick School, 3560 Richmond Rd, STNL, 10306	7117	C2
St. Paul School, 114 E 118th St, MHTN, 10035	110	B4
St. Paul School, 129 Clinton Av, STNL, 10301	6920	B6
St. Paul the Apostle School, 77 Lee Av, YNKR, 10705	6393	E4
St. Peter Claver School, 14918 Jamaica Av, QENS, 11435	6825	C5
St. Peter Elementary School, 300 Richmond Ter, STNL - 10301	6920	D6
St. Peter High School for Girls, 300 Richmond Ter, STNL - 10301	6920	D5
St. Peter of Alcantara, 1321 Port Washington Blvd, NHmT - 11050	6508	E7
St. Peter School, 152 William St, BlvT, 07109	6714	A1
St. Peter School, 204 Hawthorne Av, YNKR, 10705	6393	C2
St. Peters High School for Boys, 200 Clinton Av, STNL - 10301	6920	B7
St. Peters Preparatory High School, 144 Grand St, JSYC - 07302	6820	C3
St. Philip Neri School, 3031 Grand Concourse, BRNX - 10468	6504	D2
St. Philips Academy, 342 Central Av, NWRK, 07103	6713	C6
St. Pius V High School, 500 Courtlandt Av, BRNX, 10451	6613	A3
St. Pius V School, 413 E 144th St, BRNX, 10454	6613	A4
St. Raphael School, 4825 37th St, QENS, 11101	6718	E7
St. Raymond Elementary School, 2380 E Tremont Av - BRNX, 10462	6505	C7
St. Raymond High School, 2151 St. Raymonds Av, BRNX - 10462	6505	C7
St. Raymond High School Academy, 2380 E Tremont Av - BRNX, 10462	6505	C7
St. Raymond School, 263 Atlantic Av, ERKY, 11518	6929	C5
St. Rita School, 260 Shepherd Av, BKLN, 11208	6924	E1
St. Rita School, 30 Wellbrook Av, STNL, 10314	7019	D5
St. Robert Bellarmine School, 5610 214th St, QENS - 11364	6722	B5
St. Rocco School, 21 Ashland St, NWRK, 07103	6713	A7
St. Roch School, 465 Villa Av, STNL, 10302	7019	B1
St. Rose of Lima School, 517 W 164th St, MHTN, 10032	104	B7
St. Rose of Lima School, 540 Orange St, NWRK, 07107	6713	B5
St. Rose of Lima School, 154 Beach 84th St, QENS, 11693	7026	C7
St. Saviour High School, 588 6th St, BKLN, 11215	6922	E3
St. Saviour School, 701 8th Av, BKLN, 11215	6922	E3
St. Sebastian School, 3976 58th St, QENS, 11377	6719	B6
Saints Hilda & Hugh School, 619 W 114th St, MHTN - 10025	109	B2
St. Simon Stock School, 2195 Valentine Av, BRNX, 10457	6504	C5
Saints Joachim & Anne School, 21819 105th Av, QENS - 11429	6826	E4
Saints John & Paul School, 280 Weaver St, MrnT, 10538	6282	C7

FEATURE NAME Address City ZIP Code	MAP#	GRID
Saints Mary & Elizabeth Academy, 170 Hussa St, LNDN - 07036	7017	A1
Saints Peter & Paul School, 838 Brook Av, BRNX, 10451	6613	B3
Saints Peter & Paul School, 125 E Birch St, MTVN, 10552	6394	E2
Saints Philip & James School, 1160 E 213th St, BRNX - 10469	6505	C2
St. Spyridon Parochial School, 120 Wadsworth Av, MHTN - 10033	104	C4
St. Stanislaus Bishop-Martyr School, 9001 101st Av - QENS, 11416	6925	C1
St. Stanislaus Kostka School, 12 Newell St, BKLN, 11222	6822	C2
St. Stanislaus Kostka School, 6117 Grand Av, QENS - 11378	6823	C2
St. Stephen of Hungary School, 408 E 82nd St, MHTN - 10028	113	E4
St. Stephen School, 131 Midland Av, KRNY, 07032	6714	B3
St. Stephens Lutheran School, 2806 Newkirk Av, BKLN - 11226	6923	C7
St. Sylvester School, 396 Grant Av, BKLN, 11208	6925	A1
St. Sylvester School, 884 Targee St, STNL, 10304	7020	C4
St. Teresa of Avila School, 10955 128th St, QENS, 11420	6926	B1
St. Teresa School, 1632 Victory Blvd, STNL, 10314	7019	E3
St. Theresa School, 2872 St. Theresa Av, BRNX, 10461	6505	E6
St. Theresa School, 705 Clinton St, LNDN, 07036	7017	B1
St. Therese of Lisieux School, 4410 Avenue D, BKLN - 11203	6923	D6
St. Therese School, 220 Jefferson Av, CRSK, 07626	6278	A7
St. Thomas Aquinas School, 211 8th St, BKLN, 11215	6922	D2
St. Thomas Aquinas School, 1909 Daly Av, BRNX, 10460	6504	E7
St. Thomas the Apostle School, 12 Westminster Rd - HmpT, 11552	6828	E5
St. Thomas the Apostle School, 8749 87th St, QENS - 11421	6824	C6
St. Vincent Academy, 228 W Market St, NWRK, 07103	6713	C7
St. Vincent de Paul School, 80 W 47th St, BAYN, 07002	6920	A1
St. Vincent Ferrer High School, 151 E 65th St, MHTN - 10065	113	B6
St. Vincent Ferrer School, 1603 Brooklyn Av, BKLN - 11210	7023	D1
Salesian High School, 148 E Main St, NRCH, 10801	6396	B4
Samuel E Shull School, 380 Hall Av, PTHA, 08861	7205	D2
Samuel Gompers Career & Technical Edu HS - 455 Southern Blvd, BRNX, 10455	6613	B4
Samuel J Preston Elementary School, 50 Taylor Av - HRSN, 10604	6168	D1
Samuel J Tilden High School, 5800 Tilden Av, BKLN - 11203	6924	A6
Santa Maria School, 1510 Zerega Av, BRNX, 10461	6505	C7
S A R Academy, 655 W 254th St, BRNX, 10471	6393	B5
Satellite Academy, 120 W 30th St, MHTN, 10001	116	A4
Satellite East Middle School, 344 Monroe St, BKLN - 11216	6822	C7
Satellite Three School, 170 Gates Av, BKLN, 11238	6822	B7
Satellite West Middle School, 209 York St, BKLN, 11201	121	C3
Saunders Trades-Technical High School, 183 Palmer Rd - YNKR, 10701	6280	A7
Scarsdale High School, 1057 Post Rd, SCDL, 10583	6167	D7
Scarsdale Middle School, 134 Mamaroneck Rd, SCDL - 10583	6168	A7
Scholars Academy High School, 320 Beach 104th St - QENS, 11694	7026	A7
Scholastic Academy, 77 Park Hill Av, YNKR, 10701	6393	D2
Schomburg Charter Elementary School, 508 Grand St - JSYC, 07302	6820	A3
School at Columbia University, 556 W 110th St, MHTN - 10025	109	B3
School for Community Research, 1980 Lafayette Av - BRNX, 10473	6614	B2
School for Excellence, 1110 Boston Rd, BRNX, 10456	6613	C2
School for Human Rights, 600 Kingston Av, BKLN, 11203	6923	C4
School for Inquiry & Social Justice, 1025 Morrison Av - BRNX, 10472	6614	A2
School for International Studies, 284 Baltic St, BKLN - 11201	121	A7
School for Legal Studies, 850 Grand St, BKLN, 11206	6822	D4
School for the Physical City High School, 55 E 25th St - MHTN, 10010	116	B5
School No 14, 101 W 23rd St, BAYN, 07002	6919	E3
Sch of Business Finance & Entrepreneurship - 125 Stuyvesant Av, BKLN, 11221	6822	E7
School of Democracy Leadership, 600 Kingston Av - BKLN, 11203	6923	D4
School of Integrated Learning, 1224 Park Pl, BKLN - 11213	6923	D2
School of the Future High School, 127 E 22nd St, MHTN - 10010	116	C7
School of the Holy Child, 2225 Westchester Av, HRSN - 10580	6169	C4
School of the Transfiguration, 98-07 38th Av, QENS - 11368	6720	A5
School of Performing Arts, 977 Fox St, BRNX, 10459	6613	D2
School of Science & Applied Learning, 2050 Prospect Av - BRNX, 10460	6504	D6
Schuyler Elementary School, 644 Forest St, KRNY, 07032	6714	C2
Science Park High School, 260 Norfolk St, NWRK, 07103	6713	C7
Science Skills Center High School, 49 Flatbush Av Ext - BKLN, 11201	121	C4
Science Tech & Res Early Coll HS at Erasmus - 911 Flatbush Av, BKLN, 11226	6923	B5
Scott Elementary School 02, 125 Madison Av, ELIZ - 07201	6917	E3
Sea Cliff Elementary School, 280 Carpenter Av, SCLF - 11579	6509	E6
Searingtown Elementary School, 106 Beverly Dr, NHmT - 11507	6724	D2
Secaucus High School, 11 Millridge Rd, SECS, 07094	6610	B5
Secaucus Middle School, 11 Millridge Rd, SECS, 07094	6610	B5
Secondary School for Journalism, 237 7th Av, BKLN - 11215	6922	D2
Secondary School for Law, 237 7th Av, BKLN, 11215	6922	E2
Secondary School for Research, 237 7th Av, BKLN - 11215	6922	E3
Seely Place Elementary School, 51 Seely Pl, GrbT, 10583	6167	B7
Seth Boyden Elementary School, 274 Boyden Av, MplT - 07040	6816	A2
Seton Hall Preparatory School, 120 Northfield Av, WOrT - 07052	6712	A2
Sewanhaka High School, 500 Tulip Av, HmpT, 11001	6827	E3
Shaarei Torah Elementary School, 222 Ocean Pkwy - BKLN, 11218	6922	E6
Shaarei Zion Ohel Bracha School - 7524 Grand Central Pkwy, QENS, 11375	6824	E3
Shaar Hatorah School, 1680 Coney Island Av, BKLN - 11230	7023	A3
Shaw Avenue School, 99 Shaw Av, VLYS, 11580	6928	B2
Sheepshead Bay High School, 3000 Avenue X, BKLN - 11235	7023	D6
Sherman Elementary School, 375 E Grant Av, ROSP - 07204	6917	A3
Shevach High School, 7509 Main St, QENS, 11367	6825	B2
Shield Institute- Develop Disabled, 1800 Andrews Av S - BRNX, 10453	105	B4

Schools

New York City/5 Borough Points of Interest Index

Schools

FEATURE NAME Address City ZIP Code	MAP#	GRID
Shulamith School for Girls, 1277 E 14th St, BKLN, 11230	7023	B2
Sinai Academic Center, 2025 79th St, BKLN, 11214	7022	C4
Sisulu Children S Charter School, 125 W 115th St, MHTN - 10026	109	E3
Skillman High School, 24-30 Skillman Av, QENS, 11101	6718	C7
Sleepy Hollow High School, 210 N Broadway, SYHW - 10591	6048	B1
Sleepy Hollow Middle School, 210 N Broadway, SYHW - 10591	6048	B1
Slocum-Skewes Elementary School, 650 Prospect Av - RDGF, 07657	6611	B1
Smith Elementary School, 101 Downey Dr, TFLY, 07670	6392	B4
Snyder High School, 239 Bergen Av, JSYC, 07305	6819	D4
Soehl Middle School, 300 E Henry St, LNDN, 07036	6917	A7
Sojourner Truth Middle School, 116 Hamilton St, EORG - 07017	6713	A2
Solomon Schechter Day School, 122 Gregory Av, WOrT - 07052	6712	A2
Solomon Schechter School, 30 Dellwood Rd, WHPL - 10605	6168	E6
Solomon Schechter School-Queens, 7616 Parsons Blvd - QENS, 11367	6825	B2
Solomon Schecter School-West Campus, 15 W 86th St - MHTN, 10024	109	A7
Soterios Ellenas Parochial School, 224 18th St, BKLN - 11232	6922	C3
South 17th Street Elementary School, 619 S 17th St - NWRK, 07103	6816	E1
South Bronx Academy for Applied Media, 778 Forest Av - BRNX, 10456	6613	B3
South Bronx Classical Charter School, 977 Fox St, BRNX - 10459	6613	D3
South Bronx Preparatory School, 360 E 145th St, BRNX - 10454	6613	A4
South Brooklyn Community High School, 173 Conover St - BKLN, 11231	6922	A1
Southern Westchester Boces, 65 Grasslands Rd, GrbT - 10603	6049	E3
South Salem Elementary School, 10 Newbury Rd, NHmT - 11050	6618	B3
South Shore High School, 6565 Flatlands Av, BKLN - 11236	7024	A1
South Side Middle School, 67 Hillside Av, RKVC, 11570	6929	E4
South Street Elementary School, 151 South St, NWRK - 07114	6817	D2
Space Shuttle Columbia School, 77 Marsh Av, STNL - 10314	7019	A7
Speedway Avenue Elementary School, 26 Speedway Av - NWRK, 07106	6712	E6
Spence School, 22 E 91st St, MHTN, 10128	113	D1
Sports Profession High School, 2545 Gunther Av, BRNX - 10469	6505	D4
Springfield Gardens High School, 14310 Springfield Blvd - QENS, 11413	6927	C2
Springhurst Elementary School, 175 Walgrove Av, DBSF - 10522	6166	A4
Staten Island Academy, 715 Todt Hill Rd, STNL, 10304	7020	A6
Staten Island Montessori School, 500 Butler Blvd, STNL - 10309	7206	D4
Staten Island Technical High School, 485 Clawson St - STNL, 10306	7117	E3
Steen Elementary School, 152 W Main St, BGTA, 07603	6501	D2
Stein Yeshiva of Lincoln Park, 287 Central Park Av, YNKR - 10704	6394	A4
Stephen Gaynor School, 148 W 90th St, MHTN, 10024	108	E7
Stevens Cooperative School, 301 Garden St, HBKN - 07030	6716	D7
Stewart Manor Elementary School, 38 Stewart Av - STMN, 11530	6828	A2
Stratford Avenue School, 97 Stratford Av, GDNC, 11530	6828	C1
Studio School, 117 W 95th St, MHTN, 10025	109	A6
Stuyvesant High School, 345 Chambers St, MHTN, 10013	118	A5
Sullivan Public School No 30, 171 Seaview Av, JSYC - 07305	6819	B6
Summit School, 18730 Grand Central Pkwy, QENS, 11432	6826	A2
Summitt School Annex, 18302 Union Tpk, QENS, 11432	6825	E2
Sunset Park Preparatory School MS 821, 4004 4th Av - BKLN, 11232	6922	B5
Susan E Wagner High School, 1200 Manor Rd, STNL - 10314	7019	D5
Sussex Avenue School, 307 Sussex Av, NWRK, 07107	6713	C5
Tag Elementary School, 240 E 109th St, MHTN, 10029	110	B6
Tag Young Scholars School, 240 E 109th St, MHTN - 10029	110	B6
Talent Unlimited High School, 300 E 68th St, MHTN - 10065	113	C6
Talmud Torah Bais Yechiel, 194 Division Av, BKLN, 11211	6822	B4
Talmud Torah of Kasho School, 324 Penn St, BKLN - 11211	6822	C5
Talmud Torait Toldois Yakov Yos, 1373 43rd St, BKLN - 11219	6922	D7
Tal Torah Toldos Yakov Yosef, 105 Heyward St, BKLN - 11211	6822	B5
Tappan Zee Elementary School, 561 Highland Av, PRMT - 10968	6164	E1
Teachers Preparatory High School, 226 Bristol St, BKLN - 11212	6924	B3
Technical Career Center, 91 W Market St, NWRK, 07103	6713	C7
Technology Arts Science Studio, 185 1st Av, MHTN - 10003	119	C2
Technology High School, 187 Broadway, NWRK, 07104	6713	E5
Tenafly High School, 19 Columbus Dr, TFLY, 07670	6392	A1
Tenafly Middle School, 36 Sunset Ln, TFLY, 07670	6392	A2
Tenakill Middle School, 275 High St, CLST, 07624	6278	A2
Terence C Reilly Middle School, 425 Grier Av, ELIZ - 07202	6917	E5
TG Connors Elementary School, 201 Monroe St, HBKN - 07030	6716	C7
Theatre Arts Production School, 2225 Webster Av, BRNX - 10457	6504	C5
Theodore Roosevelt Elementary School, 1 Louisa Pl - WhkT, 07086	111	A3
Thirteenth Avenue Elementary School, 359 13th Av - NWRK, 07103	6713	B6
Thomas A Edison School, 507 West St, UNCT, 07087	6716	C5
Thomas Edison Career High School, 16565 84th Av - QENS, 11432	6825	D3
Thomas Jefferson Elementary School, 441 Tappan Rd - NVLE, 07647	6164	B4
Thomas Jefferson Middle School, 655 Teaneck Rd, TnkT - 07666	6502	B1
Thornton-Donovan School, 100 Overlook Cir, NRCH - 10804	6395	E1
Thorton Elementary School, 121 S 6th Av, MTVN, 10550	6394	E5
Three Hierarchs Parochial School, 1724 Avenue P, BKLN - 11229	7023	B4
Thurgood Marshall Academy, 200 W 135th St, MHTN - 10030	107	A6
Tiferes Miriam School for Girls, 6510 17th Av, BKLN - 11204	7022	C2
TIMES School, 240 E 109th St, MHTN, 10029	110	A6
Tito Puente Education Complex, 240 E 109th St, MHTN - 10029	110	B6
Tomer Dvora High School-Girls, 5801 16th Av, BKLN - 11204	7022	C2
Tomer Dvora School, 4500 9th Av, BKLN, 11220	6922	C6
Tompkins Square Middle School Extension, 600 E 6th St - MHTN, 10009	119	D4
Torah Academy for Girls Elementary School - 444 Beach 6th St, QENS, 11691	7027	E5
Torah Academy for Girls High School, 444 Beach 6th St - QENS, 11691	7027	E5
Torah High School of Long Beach, 205 W Beech St, LBCH - 11561	7029	B7
Tottenville High School, 100 Luten Av, STNL, 10312	7207	B1
Town School, 540 E 76th St, MHTN, 10021	113	E5
Townsend Harris High School, 14911 Melbourne Av - QENS, 11367	6825	A1
Transfiguration School, 29 Mott St, MHTN, 10013	118	E6
Transfiguration School, 40 Prospect Av, TYTN, 10591	6048	B4
Transit Tech Career & Technical Education HS, 1 Wells St - BKLN, 11208	6925	A1
Traphagen Elementary School, 72 Lexington Av, MTVN - 10552	6395	A3
Trevor Day School Lower, 11 E 89th St, MHTN, 10128	113	C1
Trevor Day School Upper, 1 W 88th St, MHTN, 10024	109	A7
Trey Whitfield School, 17 Hinsdale St, BKLN, 11207	6924	C2
Trinity Christian Academy, 417 Pennington St, ELIZ - 07202	6917	C3
Trinity Elementary School, 180 Pelham Rd, NRCH, 10805	6396	A5
Trinity Lutheran School, 309 St. Pauls Av, STNL, 10304	7020	D1
Trinity School, 139 W 91st St, MHTN, 10025	109	A6
Trinity Temple Academy, 1500 Maple Av, HlsT, 07205	6816	D5
Tubman Elementary School, 504 S 10th St, NWRK - 07103	6817	A1
Tuckahoe High School, 65 Siwanoy Blvd, EchT, 10709	6281	B7
Tuckahoe Middle School, 65 Siwanoy Blvd, EchT, 10709	6281	B7
UFT Charter School, 300 Wyona St, BKLN, 11207	6924	D2
Union Avenue Middle School, 427 Union Av, IrvT, 07111	6816	B3
Union City Career Academy, 1901 West St, UNCT, 07087	6716	D3
Union Hill High School, 3808 Hudson Av, UNCT, 07087	6716	E2
United Academy Incorporated, 1177 Broad St, NWRK - 07114	6817	C2
United Lubavitcher Yeshivoth, 841 Ocean Pkwy, BKLN - 11230	7023	A1
United Talmudical Academy-Boys, 110 Throop Av, BKLN - 11206	6822	C5
United Talmudical Academy-Girls, 5301 14th Av, BKLN - 11219	7022	C1
Unity Center for Urban Technologies - 121 Avenue of the Americas, MHTN, 10013	118	C3
University 6 School, 1 University Pl, IrvT, 07111	6816	D1
University Academy Charter High School, 275 W Side Av - JSYC, 07305	6819	C4
University High School, 55 Clinton Pl, NWRK, 07108	6816	E2
University Middle School, 255 Myrtle Av, IrvT, 07111	6816	D1
University Neighborhood High School, 200 Monroe St - MHTN, 10002	119	A7
University Neighborhood Middle School, 220 Henry St - MHTN, 10002	119	B7
Upper School Elementary School, 143 Charlotte Pl, EGLC - 07632	6503	B2
Urban Academy Laboratory High School, 317 E 67th St - MHTN, 10065	113	C6
Urban Assembly Acad of Bs & Comm Development - 141 Macon St, BKLN, 11216	6923	C1
Urban Assembly of Music & Art, 49 Flatbush Av Ext - BKLN, 11201	121	C4
Urban Assembly Sch for Applied Math & Sci - 1595 Bathgate Av, BRNX, 10457	105	E7
Urban Assembly School for Careers In Sports - 701 St. Anns Av, BRNX, 10455	6613	B3
Urban Assembly School for Law & Justice, 50 Navy St - BKLN, 11201	121	D4
Urban Assembly Sch for the Performing Arts - 509 W 129th St, MHTN, 10027	106	D6
Urban Assembly Sch of Bus for Young Women - 420 E 12th St, MHTN, 10009	119	C2
Urban Assembly Sch of Design & Construction - 525 W 50th St, MHTN, 10019	112	A6
Urban Assembly School of Media, 122 Amsterdam Av - MHTN, 10023	112	C4
Urban Assembly Schoool, 1595 Bathgate Av, BRNX - 10457	105	E7
Urban Peace Academy, 2351 1st Av, MHTN, 10035	110	C4
Urban Science Academy, 1000 Teller Av, BRNX, 10456	6613	B2
Ursuline School, 1354 North Av, NRCH, 10804	6281	C6
Vailsburg Middle School, 107 Ivy St, NWRK, 07106	6712	C7
Valhalla Middle-High School, 300 Columbus Av, MtPT - 10595	6050	A1
Validus Prepatory Academy, 1595 Bathgate Av, BRNX - 10457	105	E7
Valley Stream Central High School, 135 Fletcher Av - VLYS, 11580	6928	D2
Valley Stream Christian School, 12 E Fairview Av, VLYS - 11580	6928	D3
Valley Stream Memorial Junior High School - 320 Fletcher Av, VLYS, 11580	6928	D2
Valley Stream North High School, 750 Herman Av, HmpT - 11010	6828	B7
Valley Stream South High School, 150 Jedwood Pl - HmpT, 11581	6928	B5
Vanguard High School, 317 E 67th St, MHTN, 10065	113	C6
Veteran Memorial School, 1401 Central Av, UNCT, 07087	6716	C4
Victory Christian School, 2301 Grier Av, LNDN, 07036	6917	D6
Vida Bogart School for All Children, 730 Bryant Av - BRNX, 10474	6613	E3
Village Community School, 272 W 10th St, MHTN, 10014	118	C1
Villa Maria Academy, 3335 Country Club Rd, BRNX - 10465	6506	B7
Virginia Road Elementary School, 86 Virginia Rd, GrbT - 10603	6050	A4
Visitation Academy, 8902 Ridge Blvd, BKLN, 11209	7021	D2
Visitation School, 171 W 239th St, BRNX, 10463	6504	C1
Visitation School, 3044 John F Kennedy Blvd, JSYC, 07306	6716	A7
Visual & Performing Arts High School - 2039 John F Kennedy Blvd, JSYC, 07305	6819	C4
Vroom Elementary School 2, 18 W 26th St, BAYN, 07002	6919	E3
Wadleigh Arts High School, 215 W 114th St, MHTN - 10026	109	D3
Wahlstorm Early Childhood Center, 340 Prospect St - EORG, 07017	6713	A2
Wakeman Public School Number 6, 100 St. Pauls Av - JSYC, 07306	6716	B7
Waldorf School of Garden City, The, 225 Cambridge Av - GDNC, 11530	6828	D3
Wallace Elementary School 6, 1100 Willow Av, HBKN - 07030	6716	D5
Wallington Junior Senior High School, 234 Main Av - WLTN, 07057	6500	A5
Walter O Krumbiegel Middle School, 145 Hillside Av - HlsT, 07205	6816	D6
Walton High School, 2780 Reservoir Av, BRNX, 10468	6504	C3
Warren Street School, 200 Warren St, NWRK, 07103	6713	C7
Washington Academy, 175 Sanford St, EORG, 07018	6712	D5
Washington Community School 9, 191 Avenue B, BAYN - 07002	6920	A1
Washington Elementary School, 80 Belgrove Dr, KRNY - 07032	6714	A5
Washington Elementary School, 123 Liberty St, LFRY - 07643	6501	C6
Washington Elementary School, 310 Main St, LODI - 07644	6500	D1
Washington Elementary School, 89 Wood St, RTFD - 07070	6609	A1
Washington Elementary School, 3905 New York Av - UNCT, 07087	6716	E2
Washington Elementary School 1, 250 Broadway, ELIZ - 07206	6918	C5
Washington Heights Expeditionary Lrn Sch - 511 W 182nd St, MHTN, 10033	104	D4
Washington Irving High School, 40 Irving Pl, MHTN - 10003	116	B7
Washington Irving Intermediate School, 103 S Broadway - TYTN, 10591	6048	B3
Washington Middle School, 1 N 5th St, HRSN, 07029	6714	A6
Washington Street Elementary School - 760 Washington St, HmpT, 11010	6828	B4
Waterfront Montessori School, 150 Warren St, JSYC - 07302	6820	C4
Watsessing Elementary School, 71 Prospect St, BlmT - 07003	6713	A1
Watters Public School No 24, 220 Virginia Av, JSYC - 07304	6819	D3
Waverly Park School, 320 Waverly Av, ERKY, 11518	6929	B7
Waverly School, 45 Hall Av, EchT, 10709	6281	B5
Webb Elementary Public School No 22, 264 Van Horne St - JSYC, 07304	6820	A4
W E B Dubois Academic High School, 402 Eastern Pkwy - BKLN, 11225	6923	B3
Weehawken High School, 53 Liberty Pl, WhkT, 07086	111	A4
Weequahic High School, 279 Chancellor Av, NWRK - 07112	6816	D4
West Bronx Academy for the Future, 500 E Fordham Rd - BRNX, 10458	6504	D4
West Brooklyn Community High School, 1053 41st St - BKLN, 11219	6922	C6
Westchester Area School, 456 Webster Av, NRCH, 10801	6395	D3
Westchester Day School, 856 Orienta Av, MRNK, 10543	6397	A1
Westchester Hills School 29, 47 Croydon Rd, YNKR - 10710	6280	E2
Westchester Special Education School, 45 Park Av - YNKR, 10703	6279	C7
West Elementary School, 91 Maryland Av, LBCH, 11561	7028	D7
West End Elementary School, 30 Clark Av, LNBK, 11563	6929	A3
Western Middle School, 1 Western Junior Hwy, GrwT - 06830	6170	D4
West Hempstead High School, 400 Nassau Blvd, HmpT - 11552	6828	C6
West Hempstead Middle School, 450 Nassau Blvd, HmpT - 11552	6828	C6
West New York Middle School, 201 57th St, WNYK - 07093	111	B1
West Side High School, 403 S Orange Av, NWRK, 07103	6713	A7
West Side Ninth Grade Academy, 301 W Kinney St - NWRK, 07103	6817	C1
Wheeler Avenue School, 1 Wheeler Av W, VLYS, 11580	6928	E2
White Plains Middle Highlands, 128 Grandview Av - WHPL, 10605	6168	B4
Whitestone Academy, 15034 12th Av, QENS, 11357	6615	B7
Whitney E Houston Academy, 215 Dodd St, EORG, 07017	6712	E1
W H Maxwell Career & Technical Education HS - 145 Pennsylvania Av, BKLN, 11207	6924	D2
Wildcat Academy Charter School, 17 Battery Pl, MHTN - 10004	120	A2
William A Shine Great Neck South High School - 341 Lakeville Rd, LKSU, 11020	6723	C3
William B Ward Elementary School, 311 Broadfield Rd - NRCH, 10804	6281	E5
William C McGinnis Middle School, 271 State St, PTHA - 08861	7205	D4
William Cottle Elementary School, 2 Siwanoy Blvd, EchT - 10708	6281	B7
William Cullen Bryant High School, 4810 31st Av, QENS - 11103	6719	B4
William E Grady Career & Technical Edu HS - 25 Brighton 4th Rd, BKLN, 11235	7121	A1
William H Brown Junior Academy, 695 Bergen St, NWRK - 07108	6817	A3
William L Buck School, 75 Horton Av, VLYS, 11581	6928	E5
William O Schaefer Elementary School, 140 Lester Dr - OrgT, 10983	6164	B2
Williamsburg Charter School, 424 Leonard St, BKLN - 11222	6822	C3
Williamsburg Preparatory School, 257 N 6th St, BKLN - 11211	6822	B3
William Spyropoulos School, 4315 196th St, QENS - 11358	6721	E4
Willow Road Elementary School, 880 Catalpa Dr, HmpT - 11010	6828	A7
Wilson Avenue Elementary School, 19 Wilson Av, NWRK - 07105	6818	A2
Wilson Elementary School, 80 Union St, LODI, 07644	6500	D2
Wilson Elementary School 19, 529 Edgar Rd, ELIZ, 07202	6917	D5
Windmill Montessori School, 1317 Avenue T, BKLN - 11229	7023	B5
Windsor School, 13623 Sanford Av, QENS, 11355	6720	E4
Windward School, 13 Windward Av, WHPL, 10605	6168	E7
Windward Upper School, 40 W Red Oak Ln, HRSN, 10604	6169	B4
Wings Academy, 1122 E 180th St, BRNX, 10460	6505	A7
Winston Preparatory School, 126 W 17th St, MHTN - 10011	115	E6
WL Morse Elementary School, 30 Pocantico St, SYHW - 10591	6048	B1
Woodbridge High School, 25 Samuel Lupo Pl, WbgT - 07095	7114	B3
Woodbridge Middle School, 525 Barron Av, WbgT - 07095	7114	C4
Woodlands Middle-High School, 475 W Hartsdale Av - GrbT, 10607	6167	C1
Woodmere Middle School, 1170 Peninsula Blvd, HmpT - 11557	6928	C6
Wood-Ridge High School, 258 Hackensack St, WRDG - 07075	6500	D6
Woodrow Wilson Elementary School, 101 W 56th St - BAYN, 07002	6819	B7
Woodrow Wilson Elementary School, 80 Hauxhurst Av - WhkT, 07086	6716	E3
Woodrow Wilson Elementary School 5, 205 Outwater Ln - GRFD, 07026	6500	A1
World Acad for Total Community Health HS - 400 Pennsylvania Av, BKLN, 11207	6924	D3
World Journalism Prep- A College Board Sch - 3465 192nd St, QENS, 11358	6721	E3
Xaverian High School, 7100 Shore Rd, BKLN, 11209	6921	D7

Schools

New York City/5 Borough Points of Interest Index

Transportation

FEATURE NAME Address City ZIP Code	MAP#	GRID
Xavier High School, 30 W 16th St, MHTN, 10011	116	A7
Xcel School, 261 1st St, PALP, 07650	6502	C6
Yesh Bais Yizchok School, 1413 45th St, BKLN, 11219	6922	D7
Yesheva Shaari Torah School, 1202 Avenue P, BKLN - 11229	7023	A4
Yeshira Ketana of Long Isle, 410 Hungry Harbor Rd, HmpT - 11581	6928	B6
Yeshiva Ahavas Israel School, 2 Lee Av, BKLN, 11211	6822	A4
Yeshiva Ahavas Torah School, 2961 Nostrand Av, BKLN - 11229	7023	C3
Yeshiva Ateres Yisorel School, 8101 Avenue K, BKLN - 11236	7024	B1
Yeshiva Bais Ephraim School, 2802 Avenue J, BKLN - 11210	7023	C2
Yeshiva Bais Hillez Dkrasna, 1364 42nd St, BKLN, 11219	6922	D7
Yeshiva Bais Yitzchok Dspinka, 575 Bedford Av, BKLN - 11211	6822	B5
Yeshiva Beth Hatalmud School, 2127 82nd St, BKLN - 11214	7022	C4
Yeshiva Boyan School, 1205 44th St, BKLN, 11219	6922	C7
Yeshiva Chsan Sofer School, 1876 50th St, BKLN, 11204	7022	E2
Yeshiva Darchei Torah School, 257 Beach 17th St, QENS - 11691	7027	D6
Yeshiva Derech Hatorah School, 2810 Nostrand Av, BKLN - 11229	7023	C3
Yeshiva Farm Settlement School, 194 Division Av, BKLN - 11211	6822	B4
Yeshiva Har Torah School, 25010 Grand Central Pkwy - QENS, 11426	6723	B5
Yeshivah School of Crown Heights, 6363 Avenue U - BKLN, 11234	7024	B3
Yeshiva Imrei Yosef Spinka School, 5801 15th Av, BKLN - 11219	7022	C2
Yeshiva Karlin Stolin School, 1818 54th St, BKLN, 11204	7022	D2
Yeshiva Kehilath Yakov-Girls, 62 Harrison Av, BKLN - 11211	6822	B5
Yeshiva Ketana of Manhattan, 346 W 89th St, MHTN - 10024	108	D6
Yeshiva Ketana of Queens School, 7815 Parsons Blvd - QENS, 11366	6825	C2
Yeshiva Machzikei Hadas School, 1601 42nd St, BKLN - 11218	6922	E7
Yeshiva Mesivta High School, 1544 Coney Island Av - BKLN, 11230	7023	A2
Yeshiva-Mesivta Torah Temimah, 555 Ocean Pkwy, BKLN - 11218	6922	E7
Yeshiva-Mesivta Toras Chaim, 1170 William St, HmpT - 11557	6928	C6
Yeshiva of Brooklyn Boys Division, 1200 Ocean Pkwy - BKLN, 11230	7023	A2
Yeshiva of Central Queens School, 14737 70th Rd, QENS - 11367	6825	A1
Yeshiva of Flatbush Elementary School, 919 E 10th St - BKLN, 11230	7023	A2
Yeshiva of Flatbush-JB High School, 1609 Avenue J - BKLN, 11230	7023	B2
Yeshiva of Kings Bay School, 2611 Avenue Z, BKLN - 11235	7023	C7
Yeshiva of Manhattan Beach, 60 W End Av, BKLN - 11235	7121	B1
Yeshiva Ohel Moshe School, 7914 Bay Pkwy, BKLN - 11214	7022	D4
Yeshiva Ohr Haiim School, 8606 135th St, QENS, 11418	6825	A5
Yeshiva Ohr Shraga, 1102 Avenue L, BKLN, 11230	7023	A2
Yeshiva Rabbi Chaimberlin, 1310 Avenue I, BKLN, 11230	7023	A1
Yeshiva R'tzahd School, 965 E 107th St, BKLN, 11236	6924	D6
Yeshiva School of Far Rockaway, 802 Hicksville Rd - QENS, 11691	7027	E5
Yeshiva Share Hayosher, 1334 Ocean Pkwy, BKLN, 11230	7023	A3
Yeshiva Sharre Torah Boys High School - 1680 Coney Island Av, BKLN, 11230	7023	A3
Yeshivat Ateret Torah School, 901 Quentin Rd, BKLN - 11223	7023	A4
Yeshiva Tiferes Yisroel, 1271 E 35th St, BKLN, 11210	7023	D2
Yeshiva Tifereth Elimelech School, 1650 56th St, BKLN - 11204	7022	D2
Yeshiva Tifereth Moshe Dov Rev, 7102 113th St, QENS - 11375	6824	D2
Yeshiva Tifereth Moshe School, 8306 Abingdon Rd, QENS - 11415	6824	E4
Yeshivat Ohel Torah, 1760 53rd St, BKLN, 11204	7022	D2
Yeshivat Ohr Haiim School, 24537 60th Av, QENS, 11362	6723	A4
Yeshiva Torah Vodaath School, 425 E 9th St, BKLN - 11218	6923	A7
Yeshiva University High School-Girls, 8686 Palo Alto St - QENS, 11423	6826	A3
Yeshiva Yagdil Torah School, 5110 18th Av, BKLN, 11204	7022	D1
Yeshiva Yesode Hatorah School, 131 Lee Av, BKLN - 11211	6822	B5
Yeshiva Yesode Hatorah School, 1350 50th St, BKLN - 11219	7022	C1
Yesh Mesivta Arugath Habosen, 40 Lynch St, BKLN - 11206	6822	B5
Yonkers Christian Academy, 229 N Broadway, YNKR - 10701	6279	C7
Yonkers Middle-High School, 150 Rockland Av, YNKR - 10705	6393	D2
York Preparatory School, 40 W 68th St, MHTN, 10023	112	D4
Young Primary School No 15, 135 Stegman St, JSYC - 07305	6819	D5
Young Scholars Academy, 3710 Barnes Av, BRNX, 10467	6505	B1
Young School, 1041 Maple Av, PALP, 07650	6502	B7
Young Womens Leadership Bronx, 2060 Lafayette Av - BRNX, 10473	6614	C2
Young Womens Leadership School, 105 E 106th St - MHTN, 10029	110	A6
Young Womens Leadership School, 10920 Union Hall St - QENS, 11433	6825	D6
Zero Tolerance Secondary School, 1 Canal St, JSYC - 07302	6820	C3
Ziccolella Elementary-Middle School, 1 S Broadway - YNKR, 10701	6279	E2
Zichron Yehuda Bais Simcha, 1051 59th St, BKLN, 11219	7022	B1
Zvi Dov Roth Acad of Yeshiva Rambam School - 3300 Kings Hwy, BKLN, 11234	7023	C2

Shopping Centers

FEATURE NAME Address City ZIP Code	MAP#	GRID
Bay Plaza Shopping Center, 2090 Bartow Av, BRNX - 10475	6506	A3
Bay Terrace Shopping Center, 212-45 26th Av, QENS - 11360	6722	A1
Charleston Retail Center, 409 Englewood Av, STNL - 10309	7206	D1
City Center at White Plains, Main St, WHPL, 10606	6168	A2
Cross County Shopping Center, North Dr, YNKR, 10704	6394	C2
Galleria at White Plains, 100 Main St, WHPL, 10601	6168	A2
Gateway Center, 409 Gateway Plz, BKLN, 11239	6925	A5
Gateway Center, E 149th St, BRNX, 10451	107	D5
Green Acres Mall, W Sunrise Hwy, HmpT, 11581	6928	B4
Jersey Gardens, 651 Kapkowski Rd, ELIZ, 07201	6918	D4
Kings Plaza Shopping Center, 5100 Flatbush Av, BKLN - 11234	7024	A4
Manhattan Mall, 100 W 33rd St, MHTN, 10001	116	B4
Metro Mall, 66-26 Metropolitan Av, QENS, 11379	6823	D4
Mill Creek Mall, 3 Mill Creek Dr, SECS, 07094	6610	B7
Newport Centre Mall, 30 Mall Dr W, JSYC, 07310	6820	D2
New Roc City, 33 Main St, NRCH, 10801	6396	A4
Queens Center Mall, 90-15 Queens Blvd, QENS, 11373	6824	A1
Shops at Columbus Circle, The, 10 Columbus Cir, MHTN - 10019	112	C6
Soundview Marketplace, 115 Shore Rd, PTWN, 11050	6508	C7
Staten Island Pergament Mall, 2655 Richmond Av, STNL - 10314	7116	E1
Vernon Hills Shopping Center, 700 White Plains Rd, EchT - 10583	6281	C3
Westchester Mall, 125 Westchester Av, WHPL, 10601	6168	B2
White Plains Mall, 200 Hamilton Av, WHPL, 10601	6168	A1
Woodbridge Center Mall, 250 Woodbridge Center Dr - WbgT, 07095	7114	A4

Subdivisions & Neighborhoods

FEATURE NAME Address City ZIP Code	MAP#	GRID
Adelphi, BKLN	6923	A1
Ampere, EORG	6713	B3
Annadale, STNL	7116	D6
Ardsley On Hudson, IRVN	6166	A2
Arlington, KRNY	6714	C2
Arlington, STNL	7018	E1
Arthur Manor, SCDL	6281	D2
Barber, PTHA	7205	E1
Battery Park City, MHTN	118	A7
Bayberry Park, NRCH	6282	A6
Baychester, BRNX	6505	D4
Bay Terrace, STNL	7117	C4
Bayway, LNDN	6917	E7
Bedford-Stuyvesant, BKLN	6923	C1
Beech Hill, YNKR	6281	A1
Beechhurst, QENS	6615	C7
Beechmont, NRCH	6395	E1
Beechmont Woods, NRCH	6396	A1
Bellaire, QENS	6826	C3
Belmont, BRNX	6504	D5
Bergen, JSYC	6820	A1
Bergenline, UNCT	6716	C3
Bergen Point, BAYN	6919	C6
Blissville, QENS	6822	C1
Bonnie Crest, NRCH	6281	E4
Brick Church, EORG	6712	D4
Brills, NWRK	6818	C2
Broad Channel, QENS	7026	A5
Broadway, QENS	6721	A3
Bronxdale, BRNX	6505	A5
Bronxville Heights, YNKR	6280	D6
Brooklyn Heights, BKLN	121	A4
Bryn Mawr Park, YNKR	6280	A6
Bulls Head, STNL	7018	E4
Cambria Heights, QENS	6826	E6
Carlton Hill, WLTN	6500	A6
Castle Point, HBKN	6716	E6
Caven Point, JSYC	6819	E7
Cecil Park, YNKR	6281	A2
Cedar Knolls, YNKR	6280	D6
Cedar Manor, QENS	6825	E7
Central, EORG	6712	D4
Chelsea, STNL	7018	B5
Chester Hill Park, MTVN	6395	A2
Chrome, CART	7115	E1
Clason Point, BRNX	6614	A3
Cliff Park, CLFP	6611	C1
Clinton Hill, NWRK	6816	E2
Colonial Heights, YNKR	6280	D4
Communipaw, JSYC	6820	A4
Concord, STNL	7020	D4
Constable Hook, BAYN	6920	B4
Country Ridge Estates, RYEB	6169	E2
Coytesville, FTLE	6503	A4
Crestwood, YNKR	6281	A4
Crestwood Gardens, YNKR	6281	A3
Crown Heights, BKLN	6923	D2
Croxton, JSYC	6716	A7
Cypress Hills, BKLN	6924	D2
Doddtown, EORG	6713	A1
Dongan Hills, STNL	7020	B7
Douglaston, QENS	6722	D3
Dunwoodie, YNKR	6394	B2
Dyker Heights, BKLN	7022	A2
Eastern Parkway, BKLN	6923	D3
East Flatbush, BKLN	6923	E5
East Tremont, BRNX	6504	D6
East White Plains, HRSN	6168	D1
Edenwald, BRNX	6505	D1
Edgewater Park, BRNX	6615	B2
Elizabethport, ELIZ	6918	C5
Elmora, ELIZ	6917	D4
Elm Park, STNL	7019	B1
Emerson Hill, STNL	7020	B4
Fieldston, BRNX	6393	B7
Fleetwood, MTVN	6394	E2
Forest Hills, QENS	6824	C3
Forest Knolls, NRCH	6282	A7
Fort Greene, BKLN	6822	A6
Fort Hamilton, BKLN	7021	D3
Forty-Fifth Street, UNCT	6716	E2
Fox Hills, STNL	7020	D3
Fresh Pond, QENS	6823	B4
Fresh Pond Junction, QENS	6823	D5
General Lafayette, JSYC	6820	A3
Gerritsen, BKLN	7023	E6
Glen Oaks, QENS	6723	C6
Glenwood, YNKR	6279	C6
Governors Island, MHTN	6922	A1
Graniteville, STNL	7019	A2
Grasmere, STNL	7020	C5
Grasselli, LNDN	7018	A3
Gray Oaks, YNKR	6280	A4
Greenhaven, RYE	6283	C6
Greenridge, STNL	7116	E3
Greenville, JSYC	6819	C5
Greystone, YNKR	6279	D3
Gulfport, STNL	7018	B1
Gunther Park, YNKR	6394	C1
Hamilton Beach, QENS	6926	A5
Hamilton Heights, MHTN	106	E5
Heartland Village, STNL	7019	A7
Heathcote, SCDL	6282	A1
Hillside, QENS	6825	E4
Hollis, QENS	6826	B3
Homecrest, BKLN	7023	B6
Homestead Park, NRCH	6396	A3
Huguenot, STNL	7116	B7
Huguenot Park, NRCH	6395	D3
Hunters Point, QENS	117	D5
Ironbound, NWRK	6818	B2
Isle of San Souci, NRCH	6396	B6
Jackson, BAYN	6920	C3
Jackson Heights, QENS	6719	D5
Journal Square, JSYC	6820	A1
Kings Bridge Heights, BRNX	102	E5
Kings Woods, ALPN	6278	E6
Lawrence Park, YNKR	6280	C7
Lincoln, YNKR	6393	E5
Linden Hill, QENS	6721	A2
Little Neck, QENS	6722	E4
Locust Point, BRNX	6615	C3
Ludlow, YNKR	6393	C2
Malba, QENS	6615	A7
Manhattanville, MHTN	106	D6
Maplewood, NRCH	6281	D4
Marion, JSYC	6819	E1
Mechanicsville, SRVL	7205	B7
Melrose, SRVL	7205	A6
Midtown, NWRK	6713	C7
Midwood, BKLN	7023	B2
Milton Point, RYE	6283	E4
Mohegan Heights, YNKR	6280	D5
Monitor, WNYK	6611	A7
Morningside Heights, MHTN	109	C2
Morsemere, RDGF	6502	B7
Mount Hope, HAOH	6166	A7
Mount Loretto, STNL	7206	D4
Mount Vincent, BRNX	6393	B4
Murray Hill, SCDL	6167	E6
Nepera Park, YNKR	6280	B2
Nepperhan, YNKR	6280	A5
New Dorp, STNL	7117	E2
New Dorp Beach, STNL	7118	B3
North, NWRK	6713	D4
North Beach, QENS	6720	A3
North Elizabeth, ELIZ	6918	A1
North Newark, NWRK	6714	A1
Oak Island, NWRK	6818	C4
Oak Island Junction, NWRK	6818	B4
Oakwood, STNL	7117	E3
Oakwood Heights, STNL	7117	C3
Old Town, STNL	7020	C6
Old Village, GTNK	6617	A6
Orienta, MRNK	6397	A1
Outwater, GRFD	6500	A1
Pamrapo, BAYN	6919	D5
Park Hill, YNKR	6393	D2
Parkside, MTVN	6395	A6
Parkside, QENS	6824	C4
Parkville, BKLN	7022	D1
Pinebrook, NRCH	6282	A4
Pinebrook Heights, NRCH	6282	A5
Pine Ridge Estates, RYEB	6170	A2
Port Ivory, STNL	6918	C7
Port Johnson, BAYN	6919	E5
Port Newark, NWRK	6818	B6
Port Richmond, STNL	7019	C1
Princes Bay, STNL	7207	A1
Prospect Park West, BKLN	6922	A2
Purchase, HRSN	6051	B7
Quaker Ridge, NRCH	6281	E3
Red Hook, BKLN	6922	B2
Residence Park, NRCH	6395	E5
Richmond, STNL	7117	C2
Richmondtown, STNL	7117	C2
Ridgeway, WHPL	6168	B6
Riverdale, BRNX	6393	B6
Rochdale Village, QENS	6927	A2
Rochelle Heights, NRCH	6395	E2
Rochelle Park, NRCH	6395	D3
Roseville, NWRK	6713	B5
Rossville, STNL	7115	E4
Roxbury, QENS	7122	D3
Rye Hills, RYEB	6170	A4
Sailors Snug Harbor, STNL	6920	B7
St. George, STNL	6920	D6
St. Mary's Park, BRNX	6613	A4
Scarsdale Downs, NRCH	6281	E1
Shore Acres, MRNK	6283	A6
Shore Acres, STNL	7020	E6
Silver Lake, STNL	7020	B2
Sommerville, QENS	7027	A5
South, NWRK	6817	B5
South Brooklyn, BKLN	6922	C1
South Flushing, QENS	6825	B1
South Jamaica, QENS	6825	D7
Spring Creek, BKLN	6925	A5
Spuyten Duyvil, BRNX	102	B2
Starrett City, BKLN	6925	A6
Stuyvesant, BKLN	6923	D1
Sun Haven, NRCH	6396	A2
Sunny Brae, MTVN	6395	A1
Sunnyside, STNL	7020	B3
Terrace Heights, QENS	6826	B2
Times Plaza, BKLN	6922	E1
Tremley, LNDN	7017	C3
Tremont, BRNX	105	D4
Union Square, ELIZ	6918	A4
University Heights, BRNX	105	D1
Uptown, HBKN	6716	D5
Vailsburg, NWRK	6712	D6
Van Cortlandt Lake, BRNX	6393	C7
Vernon Park, MTVN	6395	A4
Victory Park, NRCH	6281	D5
Washington Park, NWRK	6713	D6
Washington Street, HBKN	6716	D7
Wave Crest, QENS	7027	B5
West, NWRK	6713	A7
West Bergen, JSYC	6819	C4
West Carteret, CART	7017	A6
Westerleigh, STNL	7019	D2
West Hudson, KRNY	6714	A4
West Mount Vernon, MTVN	6394	C4
West New Brighton, STNL	6920	A7
West Side, JSYC	6819	C3
West View, RDFP	6501	D4
White Birches, NRCH	6281	E3
Willowbrook, STNL	7019	C5
Wilmot Woods, NRCH	6281	E2
Woodside, QENS	6719	B6
Wykagyl, NRCH	6281	C7
Wykagyl Park, NRCH	6281	E7

Transportation

FEATURE NAME Address City ZIP Code	MAP#	GRID
Amatrak-New Rochelle, NRCH	6395	E4
Amtrak-Bronxville, BRXV	6280	E7
Amtrak-Newark, NWRK	6713	E7
Amtrak-Penn Station-New York, MHTN	116	A3
Amtrak-Yonkers, YNKR	6393	B1
Grand Central Terminal, MHTN	116	D3

INDEX 85

New York City/5 Borough Points of Interest Index

Transportation

FEATURE NAME Address City ZIP Code	MAP#	GRID
Greyhound-Battery Park Station, MHTN	120	A3
Greyhound-Brooklyn, BKLN	6923	E2
Greyhound-Brooklyn, BKLN	121	C7
Greyhound-Brooklyn, BKLN	6923	C6
Greyhound-Mineola, MNLA	6724	E6
Greyhound-Newark Penn Station, NWRK	6817	D1
Greyhound-New Rochelle, NRCH	6396	A4
Greyhound-Port Authority, MHTN	116	A2
Greyhound-Queens Village, QENS	6826	D1
Greyhound-St. George Bus Terminal, STNL	6920	E6
Greyhound-White Plains, WHPL	6168	A1
Hart Island Ferry Terminal, BRNX	6507	A5
Hart Island Ferry Terminal-Fordham Dock, BRNX	6506	E6
Irvington Bus Terminal, IrvT	6816	C2
LIRR-Albertson, NHmT	6724	E2
LIRR-Auburndale, QENS	6721	E4
LIRR-Bayside, QENS	6722	A4
LIRR-Bellerose, FLPK	6827	B2
LIRR-Belmont Park, QENS	6827	A4
LIRR-Broadway, QENS	6721	C4
LIRR-Cedarhurst, CDHT	7028	A2
LIRR-Centre Av, ERKY	6929	C5
LIRR-Douglaston, QENS	6722	C3
LIRR-East New York, BKLN	6924	B2
LIRR-East Rockaway, ERKY	6929	C6
LIRR-East Williston, WLPK	6724	E4
LIRR-Far Rockaway, QENS	7027	D4
LIRR-Flatbush Av, BKLN	6922	E1
LIRR-Floral Park, FLPK	6827	C2
LIRR-Flushing Main St, QENS	6720	D4
LIRR-Forest Hills, QENS	6824	D3
LIRR-Garden City, GDNC	6828	E2
LIRR-Gibson, VLYS	6928	D5
LIRR-Great Neck, GTPZ	6617	A7
LIRR-Hempstead Gardens, HmpT	6828	E6
LIRR-Hewlett, HmpT	6928	C7
LIRR-Hollis, QENS	6826	B4
LIRR-Hunterspoint Av, QENS	6718	C7
LIRR-Inwood, HmpT	7027	D3
LIRR-Island Park, ISPK	7029	C5
LIRR-Jamaica, QENS	6825	B5
LIRR-Kew Gardens, QENS	6824	E4
LIRR-Lakeview, HmpT	6828	D7
LIRR-Laurelton, QENS	6927	D3
LIRR-Lawrence, HmpT	7027	E3
LIRR-Little Neck, QENS	6722	E2
LIRR-Locust Manor, QENS	6927	B2
LIRR-Long Beach, LBCH	7029	C7
LIRR-Long Island City, QENS	117	C6
LIRR-Lynbrook, LNBK	6929	A4
LIRR-Malverne, MLVN	6929	B2
LIRR-Manhasset, NHmT	6617	D6
LIRR-Merillon Av, NHmT	6724	C7
LIRR-Mineola, MNLA	6724	E7
LIRR-Murray Hill, QENS	6721	B4
LIRR-Nassau Blvd, GDNC	6828	C2
LIRR-New Hyde Park, NHPK	6828	A1
LIRR-Nostrand Av, BKLN	6923	C2
LIRR-Oceanside, HmpT	6929	D7
LIRR-Pennsylvania Station-New York, MHTN	116	A4
LIRR-Plandome, PLNM	6617	D4
LIRR-Port Washington, NHmT	6617	E1
LIRR-Queens Village, QENS	6826	C3
LIRR-Rockville Centre, RKVC	6929	D4
LIRR-Rosedale, QENS	6927	E3
LIRR-Roslyn, NHmT	6618	E7
LIRR-St. Albans, QENS	6826	B7
LIRR-Shea Stadium, QENS	6720	D5
LIRR-Stewart Manor, GDNC	6828	A2
LIRR-Valley Stream, VLYS	6928	C3
LIRR-West Hempstead, HmpT	6828	E5
LIRR-Westwood, MLVN	6929	A3
LIRR-Woodmere, HmpT	7028	C1
LIRR-Woodside, QENS	6719	C6
Metro-North-Ardsley-On-Hudson, IRVN	6165	E3
Metro-North-Botanical Garden, BRNX	6504	E3
Metro-North-Bronxville, BRXV	6280	E7
Metro-North-Crestwood, TCKA	6281	A5
Metro-North-Dobbs Ferry, DBSF	6165	D4
Metro-North-Fleetwood, MTVN	6394	D2
Metro-North-Fordham, BRNX	6504	D4
Metro-North-Glenwood, YNKR	6279	C6
Metro-North-Grand Central Terminal, MHTN	116	D3
Metro-North-Greystone, YNKR	6279	D3
Metro-North-Harlem 125th St, MHTN	110	C2
Metro-North-Harrison, HRSN	6283	B3
Metro-North-Hartsdale, GrbT	6167	D4
Metro-North-Hastings-On-Hudson, HAOH	6165	E7
Metro-North-Irvington, IRVN	6048	A7
Metro-North-Larchmont, LRMT	6396	B1
Metro-North-Ludlow, YNKR	6393	B3
Metro-North-Mamaroneck, MRNK	6282	E5
Metro-North-Marble Hill, MHTN	102	B4
Metro-North-Melrose, BRNX	6613	A2
Metro-North-Morris Heights, BRNX	105	A3
Metro-North-Mt Vernon East, MTVN	6394	E4
Metro-North-Mt Vernon West, MTVN	6394	C4
Metro-North-New Rochelle, NRCH	6395	E4
Metro-North-North White Plains, WHPL	6050	A6
Metro-North-Pelham, PLHM	6395	B4
Metro-North-Port Chester, PTCH	6170	C6
Metro-North-Riverdale, BRNX	6393	A5
Metro-North-Rye, RYE	6284	A1
Metro-North-Scarsdale, SCDL	6167	C7
Metro-North-Spuyten Duyvil, BRNX	102	A3
Metro-North-Tarrytown, TYTN	6048	A2
Metro-North-Tremont, BRNX	6504	B6
Metro-North-Tuckahoe, TCKA	6280	E6
Metro-North-University Heights, BRNX	102	B7
Metro-North-Valhalla, MtPT	6050	A3
Metro-North-Wakefield, BRNX	6394	B5
Metro-North-White Plains, WHPL	6168	A1
Metro-North-Williams Bridge, BRNX	6505	A2
Metro-North-Woodlawn, BRNX	6394	A6
Metro-North-Yonker, YNKR	6393	B1
New York City Passenger Ship Terminal, MHTN	111	E6
New York Waterway-E 34th St, MHTN	117	A5
New York Waterway-Hoboken, HBKN	6820	E1
New York Waterway-Weehawken, WhkT	111	B4
New York Waterway-Whitehall St, MHTN	120	A2
NJ Transit-Arlington, KRNY	6714	C3
NJ Transit-Avenel, WbgT	7114	C1
NJ Transit-Brick Church, EORG	6712	E3
NJ Transit Bus Terminal-Hoboken, HBKN	6820	D1
NJ Transit-East Orange, EORG	6712	E4
NJ Transit-Elizabeth, ELIZ	6917	C1
NJ Transit-Essex St, HKSK	6501	B2
NJ Transit-Garfield, GRFD	6500	B3
NJ Transit-HBLR-Danforth Av, JSYC	6819	C6
NJ Transit-HBLR-E 34th St, BAYN	6920	A2
NJ Transit-HBLR-E 45th St, BAYN	6920	B1
NJ Transit-HBLR-Essex St, JSYC	6820	D4
NJ Transit HBLR-Exchange Pl, JSYC	6820	D3
NJ Transit-HBLR-Garfield Av, JSYC	6819	E4
NJ Transit-HBLR-Harborside, JSYC	6820	D3
NJ Transit-HBLR-Harsimus Cove, JSYC	6820	D2
NJ Transit-HBLR-Jersey Av, JSYC	6820	B4
NJ Transit-HBLR-Lincoln Harbor, WhkT	6716	E4
NJ Transit-HBLR-Marin Blvd, JSYC	6820	C3
NJ Transit-HBLR-Pavonia-Newport, JSYC	6820	D2
NJ Transit-HBLR-Port Imperial, WhkT	111	B3
NJ Transit-HBLR-West Side Av, JSYC	6819	C3
NJ Transit-Highland Av, COrT	6712	B3
NJ Transit-Hoboken Terminal, HBKN	6820	D1
NJ Transit-Liberty State Park, JSYC	6820	A4
NJ Transit-Linden, LNDN	7017	A1
NJ Transit-Martin Luther King Dr, JSYC	6819	E4
NJ Transit-Mountain Station, SOrT	6712	A5
NJ Transit-Newark-Broad St Station, NWRK	6713	E6
NJ Transit-NLR-Atlantic St, NWRK	6713	E6
NJ Transit-NLR-Bloomfield Av, NWRK	6713	D3
NJ Transit-NLR-Branch Brook Park, NWRK	6713	D1
NJ Transit-NLR-Broad St, NWRK	6713	D6
NJ Transit-NLR-Davenport Av, NWRK	6713	D2
NJ Transit-NLR-Grove St, BlmT	6713	C1
NJ Transit-NLR-Norfolk, NWRK	6713	C6
NJ Transit-NLR-Park Av, NWRK	6713	C5
NJ Transit-NLR-Park Av, NWRK	6713	C4
NJ Transit-NLR-Riverfront Stadium, NWRK	6713	E6
NJ Transit-NLR-Silver Lake, BlvT	6713	C1
NJ Transit-NLR-Warren St, NWRK	6713	D7
NJ Transit-NLR-Washington Park, NWRK	6713	E6
NJ Transit-NLR-Washington St, NWRK	6713	D3
NJ Transit-North Elizabeth, ELIZ	6918	A1
NJ Transit-Orange, COrT	6712	C2
NJ Transit PATH-9th St, MHTN	118	E1
NJ Transit PATH-14th St, MHTN	115	E7
NJ Transit PATH-23rd St, MHTN	116	A5
NJ Transit PATH-33rd St, MHTN	116	B4
NJ Transit PATH-Christopher St, MHTN	118	C1
NJ Transit PATH-Exchange Pl, JSYC	6820	D3
NJ Transit PATH-Grove St, JSYC	6820	C3
NJ Transit PATH-Harrison, HRSN	6714	A7
NJ Transit PATH-Journal Square, JSYC	6820	A1
NJ Transit PATH-Newark-Penn Station, NWRK	6817	E1
NJ Transit PATH-Pavonia, JSYC	6820	D2
NJ Tran PATH-World Trade Ctr Temporary Sta, MHTN	118	B7
NJ Transit-Penn Station-New York, MHTN	116	A3
NJ Transit-Perth Amboy, PTHA	7205	D4
NJ Transit-Plauderville, GRFD	6500	B1
NJ Transit-Richard St, JSYC	6819	D6
NJ Transit-Rutherford, RTFD	6609	B2
NJ Transit-South Amboy, SAMB	7205	C7
NJ Transit-Teterboro, HSBH	6501	A4
NJ Transit-Union, UnnT	6917	C1
NJ Transit-Watsessing, BlmT	6713	B1
NJ Transit-Woodbridge, WbgT	7114	C4
NJ Transit-Wood-Ridge, WRDG	6500	D6
Pennsylvania Station-Newark, NWRK	6817	E1
Pennsylvania Station-New York, MHTN	116	A3
Secaucus Rail Station, SECS	6715	D4
Staten Island Ferry-St. George, STNL	6920	E6
Staten Island Ferry-South Ferry, MHTN	120	B3
Staten Island Railway-Annadale, STNL	7116	D6
Staten Island Railway-Atlantic, STNL	7206	B3
Staten Island Railway-Bay Terrace, STNL	7117	C4
Staten Island Railway-Clifton, STNL	7020	E2
Staten Island Railway-Dongan Hills, STNL	7020	B7
Staten Island Railway-Eltingville, STNL	7116	E6
Staten Island Railway-Grant City, STNL	7118	A1
Staten Island Railway-Grasmere, STNL	7020	C5
Staten Island Railway-Great Kills, STNL	7117	B5
Staten Island Railway-Huguenot, STNL	7116	B7
Staten Island Railway-Jefferson Av, STNL	7020	B7
Staten Island Railway-Nassau, STNL	7206	B2
Staten Island Railway-New Dorp, STNL	7117	E2
Staten Island Railway-Oakwood Heights, STNL	7117	D3
Staten Island Railway-Old Town, STNL	7020	C6
Staten Island Railway-Pleasant Plains, STNL	7206	E2
Staten Island Railway-Princes Bay, STNL	7207	A1
Staten Island Railway-Richmond Valley, STNL	7206	D2
Staten Island Railway-St. George, STNL	6920	E6
Staten Island Railway-Stapleton, STNL	7020	E2
Staten Island Railway-Tompkinsville, STNL	6920	E7
Staten Island Railway-Tottenville, STNL	7206	A3
Subway-1st Av-L, MHTN	119	C2
Subway-2nd Av/Houston St-F,V, MHTN	119	A4
Subway-3rd Av/138th St-6, BRNX	110	E1
Subway-3rd Av/149th St-2,5, BRNX	6613	A3
Subway-3rd Av-L, MHTN	119	B1
Subway-4th Av-D,F, BKLN	6922	C2
Subway-5th Av/Bryant Park-7, MHTN	116	C2
Subway-5th Av-E,V, MHTN	112	E7
Subway-5th Av-N,R,W, MHTN	112	E6
Subway-6th Av-L, MHTN	115	E7
Subway-7th Av-B,D,E, MHTN	112	C7
Subway-7th Av-B,Q, BKLN	6922	E1
Subway-7th Av/Park Slope-F, BKLN	6922	D3
Subway-8th Av-L, MHTN	115	D6
Subway-8th Av-N, BKLN	6922	A7
Subway-8th St/New York University-N,R,W, MHTN	119	A2
Subway-9th Av-D,M, BKLN	6922	C6
Subway-9th St-M,N,R, BKLN	6922	D2
Subway-14th St-1,2,3, MHTN	115	D7
Subway-14th St-A,C,E, MHTN	115	D6
Subway-14th St-F,V, MHTN	115	D7
Subway-14/Union Sq-L,N,Q,R,W,4,5,6, MHTN	116	A7
Subway-15th St/Prospect Park-F, BKLN	6922	D4
Subway-18th Av-D,M, BKLN	7022	B4
Subway-18th Av-F, BKLN	7022	E1
Subway-18th Av-N, BKLN	7022	D2
Subway-18th St-1, MHTN	115	D6
Subway-20th Av-D,M, BKLN	7022	B4
Subway-20th Av-N, BKLN	7022	D3
Subway-21st St/Queens Bridge-F, QENS	6718	C5
Subway-21st St/Van Alst-G, QENS	117	E5
Subway-23rd St-1, MHTN	115	E5
Subway-23rd St-4,6, MHTN	116	B6
Subway-23rd St-A,C,E, MHTN	115	E5
Subway-23rd St/Ely Av-E,V, QENS	6718	C6
Subway-23rd St-F,V, MHTN	116	A5
Subway-23rd St-N,R,W, MHTN	116	A6
Subway-25th Av-D, BKLN	7022	C5
Subway-25th St-D,M,N,R, BKLN	6922	C4
Subway-28th St-4,6, MHTN	116	B5
Subway-28th St-N,R,W, MHTN	116	B5
Subway-30th Av-N,W, QENS	6719	A3
Subway-33rd St-4,6, MHTN	116	C5
Subway-33rd St/Rawson St-7, QENS	6718	E6
Subway-34th St-B,D,F,N,Q,R,W,V, MHTN	116	B4
Subway-34th St/Penn Station-1,2,3, MHTN	116	A3
Subway-34th St/Penn Station-A,C,E, MHTN	116	A3
Subway-36th Av/Washington Av-N,W, QENS	6718	D5
Subway-36th St-D,M,N,R, BKLN	6922	B5
Subway-36th St-E,G,R,V, QENS	6718	E5
Subway-39th Av/Washington Av-N,W, QENS	6718	E5
Subway-40th St-7, QENS	6718	E6
Subway-42nd St-A,C,E, MHTN	116	A2
Subway-42nd St-B,D,F,V, MHTN	116	C2
Subway-42nd St/Grand Central-6,7, MHTN	116	E3
Subway-42nd St/Grand Central-S,4,5, MHTN	116	E3
Subway-42nd St/Time Square-1,2,3,7,N,Q,R,S,W, MHTN	116	B2
Subway-45th Rd/Court House Square-7, QENS	6718	C6
Subway-45th St-N,R, BKLN	6922	B5
Subway-46th St/Bliss St-7, QENS	6719	A7
Subway-46th St-E,G,R,V, QENS	6719	A4
Subway-47-50th St/Rockefeller Center-B,D,F,V, MHTN	116	D1
Subway-49th St-N,R,W, MHTN	116	C1
Subway-50th St-1, MHTN	112	C7
Subway-50th St-A,C,E, MHTN	112	B7
Subway-50th St-D,M, BKLN	6922	C7
Subway-51st St-E,F,4,6, MHTN	116	E2
Subway-52nd St-7, QENS	6719	A6
Subway-53rd St-N,R, BKLN	6922	A6
Subway-55th St-D,M, BKLN	7022	C1
Subway-57th St/6th Av-F, MHTN	112	D6
Subway-57th St-N,R,W,Q, MHTN	112	C6
Subway-59th St-4,5,6, MHTN	113	A7
Subway-59th St/Columbus Cir-1, MHTN	112	D6
Subway-59th St/Columbus Cir-A,B,C,D, MHTN	112	C6
Subway-59th St-N,R, BKLN	6922	A6
Subway-61st St/Woodside-7, QENS	6719	B6
Subway-62nd St-D,M, BKLN	7022	B2
Subway-63rd Rd/Rego Park-E,G,R,V, QENS	6824	B1
Subway-65th St-E,G,R,V, QENS	6719	C6
Subway-66th St/Lincoln Center-1, MHTN	112	C4
Subway-67th Av-E,G,R,V, QENS	6824	C2
Subway-68th St/Hunter College-4,6, MHTN	113	B6
Subway-69th St-7, QENS	6719	C6
Subway-71st St-D,M, BKLN	7022	C3
Subway-72nd St-1,2,3, MHTN	112	C3
Subway-72nd St-A,B,C, MHTN	112	D3
Subway-74th St/Broadway-7, QENS	6719	D6
Subway-75th Av-E,F, QENS	6824	D3
Subway-75th St/Elderts Lane-J,Z, QENS	6824	B7
Subway-77th St-4,6, MHTN	113	C4
Subway-77th St-R, BKLN	7021	D1
Subway-79th St-1, MHTN	112	D1
Subway-79th St-D,M, BKLN	7022	B4
Subway-80th St/Hudson St-A, QENS	6925	C1
Subway-82nd St/Jackson Heights-7, QENS	6719	E6
Subway-85th St/Forest Pkwy-J, QENS	6824	B6
Subway-86th St-1, MHTN	108	E7
Subway-86th St-4,5,6, MHTN	113	D2
Subway-86th St-A,B,C, MHTN	113	A1
Subway-86th St/Gravesend-N, BKLN	7022	D6
Subway-86th St-R, BKLN	7021	E2
Subway-88th St/Boyd Av-A, QENS	6925	C1
Subway-90th St/Elmhurst Av-7, QENS	6720	A6
Subway-95th St/Bay Ridge-R, BKLN	7021	D3
Subway-96th St-1,2,3, MHTN	108	E5
Subway-96th St-4,5,6, MHTN	113	E1
Subway-96th St-A,B,C, MHTN	109	B6
Subway-103rd St-1, MHTN	109	A4
Subway-103rd St-4,6, MHTN	110	A6
Subway-103rd St-A,B,C, MHTN	109	C5
Subway-103rd St/Corona Plaza-7, QENS	6720	A5
Subway-104th St/102nd St-J,Z, QENS	6925	D1
Subway-104th St-J,Z, QENS	6824	D6
Subway-104th St/Oxford Av-A, QENS	6925	E1
Subway-110th St-4,6, MHTN	110	A5
Subway-110th St/Central Park N-2,3, MHTN	109	E4
Subway-111th St-7, QENS	6720	C5
Subway-111th St/Greenwood Av-A, QENS	6824	E7
Subway-111th St-J, QENS	6824	E6
Subway-116th St-2,3, MHTN	109	E3
Subway-116th St-4,6, MHTN	110	B4
Subway-116th St-A,B,C, MHTN	109	D3
Subway-116th St/Columbia University-1, MHTN	109	B2
Subway-121st St-J,Z, QENS	6825	A5
Subway-125th St-1, MHTN	106	C6
Subway-125th St-2,3, MHTN	110	A2
Subway-125th St-4,5,6, MHTN	110	B3
Subway-125th St-A,B,C,D, MHTN	109	E1
Subway-135th St-2,3, MHTN	107	B6
Subway-135th St-A, MHTN	106	E5
Subway-135th St-B,C, MHTN	107	A6
Subway-137th St/City College-1, MHTN	106	D5
Subway-138th St/Grand Concourse-4,5, BRNX	107	D7
Subway-145th St-1, MHTN	106	E3
Subway-145th St-3, MHTN	107	B5
Subway-145th St-A,B,C,D, MHTN	107	A4
Subway-149th St/Grand Concourse-4,5, BRNX	107	E5
Subway-155th St-A,C, MHTN	107	B2
Subway-155th St-B,D, MHTN	107	C2
Subway-157th St-1, MHTN	107	A1
Subway-161st St/Yankee Stadium-4, BRNX	107	E2
Subway-161st St/Yankee Stadium-B,D, BRNX	107	E3
Subway-163rd St/Amsterdam Av-A,C, MHTN	107	B1
Subway-167th St-4, BRNX	6613	A1
Subway-167th St-B,D, BRNX	6613	A1
Subway-168th St/Broadway-A,B,C,1, MHTN	104	A6
Subway-169th St-F, QENS	6825	D4
Subway-170th St-4, BRNX	105	B6
Subway-170th St-B,D, BRNX	105	B7
Subway-174th St/175th St-B,D, BRNX	105	D5
Subway-174th St-2,5, BRNX	6504	D7
Subway-175th St-A, MHTN	104	B5
Subway-176th St-4, BRNX	105	C4
Subway-179th St/Jamaica-F, QENS	6825	E3
Subway-181st St-1, MHTN	104	C4
Subway-181st St-A, MHTN	104	B4
Subway-182nd St/183rd St-B,D, BRNX	105	E2
Subway-183rd St-4, BRNX	105	D1
Subway-190th St-A, MHTN	104	C2
Subway-191st St-1, MHTN	104	D2
Subway-205th St-D, BRNX	6504	E2
Subway-207th St-1, MHTN	102	A7
Subway-215th St-1, MHTN	102	B5
Subway-219th St-2,5, BRNX	6505	B1
Subway-225th St-1, MHTN	102	C4
Subway-225th St-2,5, BRNX	6505	B1
Subway-231st St-1, BRNX	102	D3
Subway-233rd St-2,5, BRNX	6394	C7
Subway-238th St-1, BRNX	102	E1
Subway-241st St-2,5, BRNX	6394	C5
Subway-242nd St/Van Cortlandt-1, BRNX	6393	C7
Subway-Alabama Av-J, BKLN	6924	C2
Subway-Allerton Av-2,5, BRNX	6505	A4
Subway-Aqueduct/N Conduit Av-A, QENS	6925	E3
Subway-Astoria Blvd-N,W, QENS	6719	A3
Subway-Astor Pl-4,6, MHTN	119	A2
Subway-Atlantic Av-B,Q,2,3,4,5, BKLN	6922	E1
Subway-Atlantic Av-L, BKLN	6924	C2
Subway-Avenue H-Q, BKLN	7023	A1
Subway-Avenue I-F, BKLN	7022	E2

New York City/5 Borough Points of Interest Index

Transportation

Visitor Information

FEATURE NAME Address City ZIP Code	MAP#	GRID
Subway-Avenue J-Q, BKLN	7023	A2
Subway-Avenue M-Q, BKLN	7023	B3
Subway-Avenue N-F, BKLN	7022	E3
Subway-Avenue P-F, BKLN	7022	E4
Subway-Avenue U-A, BKLN	7022	E5
Subway-Avenue U-N, BKLN	7022	E6
Subway-Avenue U-Q, BKLN	7023	B5
Subway-Avenue X-F, BKLN	7022	E6
Subway-Bay 50th St-B, BKLN	7022	D7
Subway-Baychester Av-5, BRNX	6505	D1
Subway-Bay Pkwy-D,M, BKLN	7022	C5
Subway-Bay Pkwy-F, BKLN	7022	E2
Subway-Bay Pkwy-N, BKLN	7022	D3
Subway-Bay Ridge Av-R, BKLN	7021	D1
Subway-Beach 25th St/Wavecrest-A, QENS	7027	B5
Subway-Beach 36th St/Edgemere-A, QENS	7027	B6
Subway-Beach 44th St/Frank Av-A, QENS	7027	A6
Subway-Beach 60th St-A, QENS	7026	E6
Subway-Beach 67th St/Gaston-A, QENS	7026	D6
Subway-Beach 90th St/Holland-A,S, QENS	7026	B7
Subway-Beach 98th St/Playground-A,S, QENS	7026	B7
Subway-Beach 105th St/Seaside-A,S, QENS	7026	A7
Subway-Bedford & Nostrand Av-G, BKLN	6822	C7
Subway-Bedford Av-L, BKLN	6822	B3
Subway-Bedford Park Blvd-B,D, BRNX	6504	D3
Subway-Bedford Pk/Lehman College-4, BRNX	6504	C2
Subway-Bergen St-2,3,4, BKLN	6922	E1
Subway-Bergen St-F,G, BKLN	121	A7
Subway-Beverley Rd-Q, BKLN	6923	A6
Subway-Beverly Rd-2,5, BKLN	6923	C6
Subway-Bleecker St-4,6, MHTN	118	E3
Subway-Bontanic Gardens-S, BKLN	6923	B2
Subway-Borough Hall-2,3,4,5, BKLN	121	B5
Subway-Bowery-J,M,Z, MHTN	119	A5
Subway-Bowling Green-4,5, MHTN	120	A2
Subway-Brdwy/Lafayette St-B,D,F,V, MHTN	118	E3
Subway-Brighton Beach-B,Q, BKLN	7121	A1
Subway-Broad Channel-A,S, QENS	7026	B4
Subway-Broad St-J,M,Z, MHTN	120	B1
Subway-Broadway/Eastern Pkwy-J,L,Z, BKLN	6924	B1
Subway-Broadway-G, BKLN	6822	C5
Subway-Broadway Junction-A,C, BKLN	6924	C1
Subway-Broadway Junction/E New York-A,C, BKLN	6924	C1
Subway-Broadway-N,W, QENS	114	D7
Subway-Broadway/Nassau St-A,C,J,M,Z, MHTN	118	C7
Subway-Bronx Park East-2,5, BRNX	6505	A6
Subway-Brook Av-6, BRNX	6613	A5
Subway-Brooklyn Brg/City Hall-4,5,6, MHTN	118	C7
Subway-Buhre Av-6, BRNX	6505	E6
Subway-Burke Av-2,5, BRNX	6505	A3
Subway-Burnside Av-4, BRNX	105	C3
Subway-Bushwick Av-Aberdeen St-L, BKLN	6924	B1
Subway-Canal St-1, MHTN	118	C4
Subway-Canal St-4,6, MHTN	118	D5
Subway-Canal St-A,C,E, MHTN	118	C4
Subway-Canal St-J,M,Z, MHTN	118	E5
Subway-Canal St-N,Q,R,W, MHTN	118	D5
Subway-Carroll St-F,G, BKLN	6922	C1
Subway-Castle Hill Av-6, BRNX	6614	C1
Subway-Cathedral Pkwy/110th St-B,C, MHTN	109	B2
Subway-Cathedral Pkwy-A,B,C, MHTN	109	C3
Subway-Central Av-M, BKLN	6822	E6
Subway-Chambers St-1,2,3, MHTN	118	C6
Subway-Chambers St-A,C,E, MHTN	118	C6
Subway-Chambers St-J,M,Z, MHTN	118	D7
Subway-Chauncey St-J,Z, BKLN	6924	B1
Subway-Christopher St/Sheridan Sq-1, MHTN	118	D1
Subway-Church Av-2,5, BKLN	6923	B5
Subway-Church Av-B,Q, BKLN	6923	A5
Subway-Church Av-F, BKLN	6922	E6
Subway-City Hall-N,R,W, MHTN	118	C7
Subway-Clark St-2,3, BKLN	121	A4
Subway-Classon Av-G, BKLN	6822	B7
Subway-Cleveland St-J, BKLN	6924	E1
Subway-Clinton Av/Washington Av-G, BKLN	6822	A7
Subway-Clinton/Washington Av-A, BKLN	6923	A1
Subway-Clinton/Washington Av-C, BKLN	6923	A1
Subway-Cortelyou Rd-Q, BKLN	6923	A6
Subway-Court Square-G, QENS	6718	D6
Subway-Court St-M,N,R, BKLN	121	A5
Subway-Crescent St-J,Z, BKLN	6925	A1
Subway-Crown Heights-Utica Av-3,4, BKLN	6923	D3
Subway-Cypress Av-6, BRNX	6613	A5
Subway-Cypress Hills-J, BKLN	6824	A7
Subway-DeKalb Av-B,D,M,N,Q,R, BKLN	121	C6
Subway-DeKalb Av-L, BKLN	6823	A5
Subway-Delancey St-F, MHTN	119	B5
Subway-Ditmars Blvd/Astoria-N,W, QENS	6719	A2
Subway-Ditmas Av-F, BKLN	6922	E7
Subway-Dyckman St-1, MHTN	104	E1
Subway-Dyckman St-A, MHTN	101	E7
Subway-Dyre Av-5, BRNX	6394	E7
Subway-E 143rd St/St Mary's St-6, BRNX	6613	B4
Subway-E 177th St/Parkchester-6, BRNX	6614	B1
Subway-East 105th St-L, BKLN	6924	C5
Subway-East 149th St-6, BRNX	6613	C4
Subway-East 180th St-2,5, BRNX	6505	A7
Subway-East Broadway-F, MHTN	119	B6
Subway-East Pkwy/Brooklyn Museum-2,3,4, BKLN	6923	A2
Subway-Elder Av-6, BRNX	6613	E2
Subway-Elmhurst Av-E,G,R,V, QENS	6719	B6
Subway-Essex St-J,M,Z, MHTN	119	B5
Subway-E Tremont Av/Westfarm Sq-2,5, BRNX	6504	E7
Subway-Euclid Av-A,C, BKLN	6925	A2
Subway-Far Rockaway/Mott Av-A, QENS	7027	B4
Subway-Flatbush Av/Brooklyn College-2,5, BKLN	7023	C1
Subway-Flushing Av-G, BKLN	6822	C5
Subway-Flushing Av-J,M, BKLN	6822	D5
Subway-Fordham Rd-4, BRNX	102	E7
Subway-Fordham Rd-B,D, BRNX	6504	C4
Subway-Forest Av-M, QENS	6823	C5
Subway-Forest Hills/71st Av-E,F,G,R,V, QENS	6824	D2
Subway-Fort Hamilton Pkwy-D,M, BKLN	6922	B7
Subway-Fort Hamilton Pkwy-F, BKLN	6922	E5
Subway-Fort Hamilton Pkwy-N, BKLN	7022	A1
Subway-Franklin Av-2,3,4,5, BKLN	6923	B2
Subway-Franklin Av-A,C,S, BKLN	6923	B1
Subway-Franklin St-1, MHTN	118	C5
Subway-Freeman St-2,5, BRNX	6613	D1
Subway-Fresh Pond Rd-M, QENS	6823	C4
Subway-Fulton St-2,3, MHTN	120	C1
Subway-Fulton St-4,5, MHTN	118	C7
Subway-Fulton St-G, BKLN	121	D7
Subway-Fulton St-J,M,Z, MHTN	118	C7
Subway-Gates Av-J,Z, BKLN	6823	A5
Subway-Graham Av-L, BKLN	6822	C3
Subway-Grand Army Plaza-2,3, BKLN	6923	A2
Subway-Grand Av/Newtown-E,G,R,V, QENS	6719	E7
Subway-Grand St-B,D, MHTN	119	A5
Subway-Grand St-L, BKLN	6822	C4
Subway-Grant Av-A, BKLN	6925	A1
Subway-Greenpoint Av-G, BKLN	6822	B1

FEATURE NAME Address City ZIP Code	MAP#	GRID
Subway-Gun Hill Rd-2,5, BRNX	6505	B2
Subway-Gun Hill Rd-5, BRNX	6505	C3
Subway-Halsey St-J, BKLN	6823	B7
Subway-Halsey St-L, BKLN	6823	B6
Subway-Harlem-148th St-3, MHTN	107	B4
Subway-Hewes St-J,M, BKLN	6822	C4
Subway-High St/Brooklyn Bridge-A,C, BKLN	121	B4
Subway-Houston St-1, MHTN	118	D3
Subway-Howard Beach/JFK Airport-A, QENS	6925	E4
Subway-Hoyt St-Fulton Mall-2,3, BKLN	121	B6
Subway-Hoyt St/Schermerhorn-A,C,G, BKLN	121	B6
Subway-Hunters Point Av-7, QENS	117	E5
Subway-Hunts Point Av-6, BRNX	6613	D3
Subway-Intervale Av-2,5, BRNX	6613	C2
Subway-Inwood/207th St-A, MHTN	102	A6
Subway-Jackson Av-2,5, BRNX	6613	B3
Subway-Jamaica Center-E,J,Z, QENS	6825	C5
Subway-Jamaica/Van Wyck-E, QENS	6825	A5
Subway-Jay St/Borough Hall-A,C,F, BKLN	121	B5
Subway-Jefferson St-L, BKLN	6822	E4
Subway-Junction Blvd-7, QENS	6720	A4
Subway-Junius St-3,4, BKLN	6924	B3
Subway-Kingsbridge Rd-4, BRNX	6504	C3
Subway-Kingsbridge Rd-B,D, BRNX	6504	D4
Subway-Kings Highway-B,Q, BKLN	7023	B4
Subway-Kings Highway-F, BKLN	7022	E5
Subway-Kings Highway-N, BKLN	7022	E5
Subway-Kingston Av-3,4, BKLN	6923	D3
Subway-Kingston Av/Throop Av-A,C, BKLN	6923	D1
Subway-Knickerbocker Av-M, BKLN	6823	A5
Subway-Kosciuszko St-J, BKLN	6822	E6
Subway-Lafayette Av-A,C, BKLN	121	E7
Subway-Lawrence St/Metrotech-M,N,R, BKLN	121	B5
Subway-Lefferts Blvd-A, QENS	6825	A7
Subway-Lexington Av/3rd Av-E,F, MHTN	117	A1
Subway-Lexington Av/63rd St-F, MHTN	113	A6
Subway-Lexington Av-N,R,W, MHTN	113	A7
Subway-Liberty Av-C, BKLN	6924	C2
Subway-Livonia Av-3, BKLN	6924	B3
Subway-Longwood Av-6, BRNX	6613	C3
Subway-Lorimer St-G,L, BKLN	6822	C3
Subway-Lorimer St-J,M, BKLN	6822	C5
Subway-Main St/Flushing-7, QENS	6720	E4
Subway-Marcy Av-J,M,Z, BKLN	6822	B4
Subway-McDonald Av-F, BKLN	7022	E1
Subway-Metropolitan Av/Grand St-G, BKLN	6822	C4
Subway-Metropolitan Av-M, QENS	6823	D4
Subway-Middletown Rd-6, BRNX	6505	E6
Subway-Montrose Av-L, BKLN	6822	D4
Subway-Morgan Av-L, BKLN	6822	D4
Subway-Morrison Av/Sound View Av-6, BRNX	6614	A1
Subway-Morris Park-5, BRNX	6505	B5
Subway-Mosholu Pkwy-4, BRNX	6504	D1
Subway-Mt Eden Av-4, BRNX	105	C5
Subway-Museum of Natural History-A,B,C, MHTN	112	E1
Subway-Myrtle Av-M,J,Z, BKLN	6822	D6
Subway-Myrtle Av/Willoughby Av-G, BKLN	6822	B6
Subway-Myrtle-Wyckoff Av-L, QENS	6823	A5
Subway-Nassau Av-G, BKLN	6822	C2
Subway-Neck Rd-Q, BKLN	7023	B6
Subway-Neptune Av/Van Sicklen-F, BKLN	7120	E1
Subway-Nereid Av/238th St-2,5, BRNX	6394	C6
Subway-Nevins St-2,3,4,5, BKLN	121	D6
Subway-Newkirk Av-2,5, BKLN	6923	C7
Subway-Newkirk Av-B,Q, BKLN	6923	A7
Subway-New Lots Av-3,4, BKLN	6924	E3
Subway-New Lots Av-L, BKLN	6924	C4
Subway-New Utrecht Av-N, BKLN	7022	C1
Subway-Northern Blvd-E,G,R,V, QENS	6719	B5
Subway-Norwood Av-J,Z, BKLN	6924	E1
Subway-Nostrand Av-3, BKLN	6923	C3
Subway-Nostrand Av-A,C, BKLN	6923	B1
Subway-Ocean Pkwy-Q, BKLN	7121	A2
Subway-Pacific St-D,M,N,R, BKLN	6922	D1
Subway-Park Place-2,3, MHTN	118	C7
Subway-Park Place-S, BKLN	6923	B2
Subway-Parkside Av-Q, BKLN	6923	A5
Subway-Parsons/Archer Av-E,J,Z, QENS	6825	D5
Subway-Parsons Blvd-F, QENS	6825	C4
Subway-Pelham Bay Park-6, BRNX	6506	A5
Subway-Pelham Pkwy-2,5, BRNX	6505	A5
Subway-Pelham Pkwy-5, BRNX	6505	C4
Subway-Pennsylvania Av-3, BKLN	6924	D3
Subway-President St-2,5, BKLN	6923	B3
Subway-Prospect Av-2,5, BRNX	6613	C3
Subway-Prospect Av-D,M,N,R, BKLN	6922	C3
Subway-Prospect Park-B,Q,S, BKLN	6923	A4
Subway-Queensboro Plaza-N,W,7, QENS	6718	D5
Subway-Queens Plaza-E,F,G,R, QENS	6718	D6
Subway-Ralph Av-A,C, BKLN	6924	A1
Subway-Rector St-1, MHTN	120	B1
Subway-Rector St-N,R,W, MHTN	120	B1
Subway-Rockaway Av-3, BKLN	6924	B4
Subway-Rockaway Av-A,C, BKLN	6924	B1
Subway-Rockaway Blvd-A, QENS	6925	D1
Subway-Rockaway Park/116th St-A,S, QENS	7123	E1
Subway-Rockaway Pkwy-L, BKLN	6924	C6
Subway-Roosevelt Av/Jackson Hts-E,F, QENS	6719	C6
Subway-Roosevelt Av/Jackson Hts-G,R, QENS	6719	D6
Subway-Roosevelt Av/Jackson Hts-V, QENS	6719	D6
Subway-Roosevelt Island-F, MHTN	117	D1
Subway-St. Lawrence Av, BRNX	6614	A1
Subway-Saratoga Av-3,4, BKLN	6924	A4
Subway-Seneca Av-M, BKLN	6823	B5
Subway-Sheepshead Bay-B,Q, BKLN	7023	B7
Subway-Shepherd Av-A,C, BKLN	6924	E2
Subway-Simpson St-2,5, BRNX	6613	C2
Subway-Smith St/9th St-F,G, BKLN	6922	C2
Subway-South Ferry-1, MHTN	120	B3
Subway-Spring St-4,6, MHTN	118	E4
Subway-Spring St-A,C,E, MHTN	118	D3
Subway-Steinway St-E,G,R,V, QENS	6719	A4
Subway-Sterling St-2,5, BKLN	6923	B4
Subway-Stillwell Av/Coney Island-F,N, BKLN	7120	D1
Subway-Sutphin Blvd/Archer Av-E,J,Z, QENS	6825	C5
Subway-Sutphin Blvd-F, QENS	6825	B5
Subway-Sutter Av-L, BKLN	6924	C3
Subway-Sutter Av/Rutland Rd-3,4, BKLN	6924	A3
Subway-Tremont Av-B,D, BRNX	105	D4
Subway-Union St-D,M,N,R, BKLN	6922	D1
Subway-Union Tpke/Kew Gardens-E,F, QENS	6824	E3
Subway-Utica Av-A,C, BKLN	6923	E1
Subway-Van Siclen Av-3,4, BKLN	6924	D3
Subway-Van Siclen Av-A,C, BKLN	6924	D2
Subway-Van Siclen Av-Z,J, BKLN	6924	D2
Subway-Vernon Blvd/Jackson Av-7, QENS	117	D5
Subway-W 4th St/Wash Sq-A,B,C,D,E,F, MHTN	118	D2
Subway-W 4th St/Wash Sq-V, MHTN	118	D2
Subway-W 8th St/Mu Aquarium-F,Q, BKLN	7120	D1
Subway-Wall St-2,3, MHTN	120	C2
Subway-Wall St-4,5, MHTN	120	B1

FEATURE NAME Address City ZIP Code	MAP#	GRID
Subway-Westchester Sq/Tremont Av-6, BRNX	6505	D7
Subway-Whitlock Av-6, BRNX	6613	D2
Subway-Willets Point/Shea Stadium-7, QENS	6720	D5
Subway-Wilson Av-L, BKLN	6823	C7
Subway-Winthrop St-2,5, BKLN	6923	C4
Subway-Woodhaven Blvd-J,Z, QENS	6824	C6
Subway-Woodhaven Blvd/Queens Mall-E,G,R,V, QENS	6824	A1
Subway-Woodlawn-4, BRNX	6504	E1
Subway-York St-F, BKLN	121	B3
Subway-Zerega Av-6, BRNX	6505	C7

Visitor Information

FEATURE NAME Address City ZIP Code	MAP#	GRID
34th Street Partnership Visitors Center, 250 W 34th St - MHTN, 10001	116	A3
Bloomingdale's International Visitors Center - Lexington Av, MHTN, 10022	113	A7
Fashion BID Visitors Center, 209 W 39th St, MHTN - 10018	116	B2
Grand Central Partnership Visitors Center, 6 E 42nd St - MHTN, 10017	116	D3
Harlem Visitors & Convention Association, 1 W 126th St - MHTN, 10027	110	B2
Lower Tenement Museum Visitors Center - 108 Orchard St, MHTN, 10002	119	B5
Manhattan Mall Info Booth, Avenue of the Americas - MHTN, 10001	116	B3
New York City Heritage Tourism Center, Broadway - MHTN, 10007	118	C7
New York University Information Center, 50 W 4th St - MHTN, 10012	118	E2
Saks Fifth Avenue Visitors Center, 611 5th Av, MHTN - 10022	116	D1
Travelers Aid At Times Square, 825 8th Av, MHTN - 10036	116	A1
Travelers Aid-Victims Services, Lafayette St, MHTN - 10007	118	D6
United Nations Volunteer Info Desk, United Nations Plz - MHTN, 10017	117	A3
Westchester County Office Of Tourism - 222 Mamaroneck Av, MRNK, 10543	6282	E6